"Light Fun," Watercolor primitive of Barnegat Inlet and Barnegat Lighthouse, on Long Beach Island, New Jersey.

Northeast

BOATERS ALMANAC

2004
EDITION

www.BoatersAlmanac.com

Welcome to the 2004 Edition of Northeast Boaters Almanac.

NEW in this edition is a section entitled **GATEWAY TO THE NORTHEAST** which covers the Chesapeake Bay (the Headwaters, the Eastern Shore to Cambridge, the Western Shore to Solomons), the C&D Canal, and the Delaware River to Trenton.

CRUISING THE NORTHEAST features from Cape May, New Jersey, the Hudson River to Canada, and all the way up the Atlantic coastline through the state of Maine – and into the navigable rivers and creeks along the way.

You'll find corresponding NOS chart numbers are placed in the Cruising Guide so you'll have the right chart at hand when using the Almanac. We've placed waypoint coordinates in the Cruising Guide next to important lights and marks, added bridge clearance information, highlights of things to do ashore, restaurants for docking and dining, and some editor notes, telling readers about our own experiences.

The purpose of a boaters cruising guide is primarily to point out destinations worth visiting in your boat and give boaters information about the area. This guide, or any other boaters guide, should never replace good navigating skills and equipment, and the current NOS charts, including Mariners Updates, for the areas where you plan to cruise.

We invite you to join other boaters and share information about your own cruising experiences on our website, www.BoatersAlmanac.com.

Carla and Bill Miners,
Publishers

Hudson

Saugerties

Connecticut

Kingston

Hartford

Hyde Park

HUDSON RIVER Poughkeepsie

New York

Newburgh

Connecticut River

West Point

Houstonic River

New Haven

Essex

Peekskill

Bridgeport

LONG ISLAND SOUND

Ossining

Westport

Greenport

Upper Nyack

S. Norwalk Stamford

Mattituck Inlet

Greenwich

Mamaroneck

Port Jefferson

Long Island

Southa...

Huntington

Hampton Bays

New Jersey

Port Washington

SHINNECC

Bay Shore

Newark

Brooklyn

Lindenhurst

GREAT SOUTH BAY

Elizabeth

FIRE ISLAND INLET

LOWER BAY

Perth Amboy

Raritan Bay

SANDY HOOK

Raritan River Navesink River

Red Bank Sea Bright

Pennsylvania

Shrewsbury River

Shark River

MANASQUAN INLET

PHILADELPHIA

CAMDEN

Toms River

Sea Girt

BARNEGAT INLET

Atlantic Ocean

Wilmington

Ship Bottom

Christina River

Long Beach Island

Upper Chesapeake Bay

Tuckerton

LITTLE EGG INLET

Havre de Grace

Maryland

C & D CANAL

ABSECON INLET

Atlantic City

Elk River

Delaware River

Great Egg Harbor Bay

GREAT EGG HARBOR INLET

Sassafras River

Ocean City

CORSON INLET

Sparrows Pt.

Chester River

DELAWARE BAY

HEREFORD INLET

Wildwood

CAPE MAY CANAL

ANNAPOLIS

Cape May CAPE MAY INLET

ST. MICHAELS EASTON

CAPE HENELOPEN

Delaware

Maine
Brunswick
Bath
MUSCONGUS BAY
Freeport
Boothbay Hbr.
Monhegan Isl.
Martinicus Rk.
Portland
Bailey I.
CASCO BAY
Saco
Cape Elizabeth
Kennebunkport
Cape Neddick Hbr.
New Hampshire
Portsmouth
Isles of Shoals
Exeter
Newburyport
Haverhill
CAPE ANN
Gloucester
Salem
Marblehead
Massachusetts
MASSACHUSETTS BAY
BOSTON
Provincetown
Plymouth
Manomet Pt.
CAPE COD BAY
CAPE COD CANAL
Cape Cod
Taunton
Providence
Chatham
Harwich Port
Rhode Island
New Bedford
Fall River
Woods Hole
Hyannis
Monomoy Pt.
BUZZARDS BAY
Falmouth
Norwich
NANTUCKET SOUND
Newport
Gay Head
Martha's Vineyard
New London
Pt. Judith
Nantucket Isl.
Fishers Isl.
BLOCK ISLAND SOUND
Plum Isl.
Block Isl.
Montauk Pt.
thampton
ays
North Atlantic Ocean
OCK INLET

Northeast BOATERS ALMANAC

2004

AREAS OF COVERAGE

12 REGIONAL SECTIONS

GATEWAY TO THE NORTHEAST

Delaware River and Delaware Bay

C&D Canal

Chesapeake Bay:
the Headwaters, and the Eastern
and Western Shores

CRUISING THE NORTHEAST

New Jersey Coast and ICW

New York & Hudson River

South Shore of Long Island

North Shore of Long Island

Connecticut

Rhode Island

Southern Massachusetts

Northern Massachusetts

New Hampshire & Maine

Our thanks to the National Oceanic and Atmospheric Administration (NOAA) ,
the U.S.Coast Guard,and the U.S. Army Corps of Engineers

The Northeast Boaters Almanac has made every effort to ensure the accuracy
of the information placed in this publication. However, we cannot guarantee accuracy
and we assume no liability for errors.

Harbor Locator Charts are reproductions of NOAA charts.
The Northeast Boaters Almanac Logo is the exclusive property of
Northeast Boaters Almanac and may not be reproduced without permission.

CHARTS & MAPS IN THIS BOOK ARE NOT FOR USE IN NAVIGATION
This guide, and any other guide to cruising on the water, is intended for use
in conjunction with good navigational skills and up-to-date NOAA marine charts.
Always check the chart "Updates for Mariners" before cruising.
Prudent mariners should always carry the appropriate printed charts
to back up their electronic navigation equipment.

ISBN 0-9659325-6-7

Copyright © 2004 Northeast Boaters Almanac

Library of Congress Card Number: 97-76462

FLYLEAF: "Light Fun," watercolor primitive of Barnegat Light, New Jersey.
Specifications:Size: 28" x 22" Printed on 100 lb. acid-free fine art paper
Limited edition of 1,000, signed and numbered by the artist.
AVAILABLE at Long Beach Island Art Studio and Gallery, 609-494-4232.

COVER PHOTO:
Slack Water at Dawn on the C&D Canal at the Chesapeake City Bridge
Photo by Dave Hawley
U.S. Army Corps of Engineeers, Philadelphia District

Published by Northeast Boaters Almanac™
P.O. Box 299, Chesapeake City, MD 21915
TEL: 866-6BOATER   FAX: 410-885-5172
EMAIL: Sales@BoatersAlmanac.com
www.BoatersAlmanac.com

Printed in Canada

RIGHTS OF PASSAGE

DID YOU KNOW?

Each operator of a self-propelled vessel 39.4 ft. (12 meters) or more in length must carry on board and maintain for ready reference, a copy of the U.S. Inland Navigational Rules. Should your boat be boarded by the U.S. Coast Guard for an inspection, this little booklet better be handy. "Navigational Rules, International and Inland" (Part No. 050-012-00287-8) is available free, from the U.S Government Printing Office (202) 512-1800, FAX: (202)512-2250.

Whether you're in control of a motor vehicle, an airplane, a bicycle, or a boat there are rules of the road that you must be aware of. While vehicle operators, airplane pilots, and commercial boat captains are required to be licensed, in most parts of the United States licensing for recreational boaters is still only under discussion.

Legal actions and highly publicized jury trials against careless boaters have made big headlines in the past few years, pointing out just where the responsibility lies for mishaps on the water.

Every year more and more vessels populate our coastal waterways - from personal watercraft to windsurfers to kayaks to runabouts, to fishing boats, motor cruisers and sailboats. In many places the waters are as crowded as rush hour traffic around Manhattan. Since our waterways are not like highways on land–no traffic lights, one way streets, or marked passing or no-passing lanes, it is important that every person in control of a vessel afloat know the maritime rules of the road, or navigational rules.

The most common boating accident is a collision between vessels, some resulting in personal injuries and even fatalities. Unlike our cars with anti-locking brakes, vessels afloat can't "stop on a dime."

The laws of the United States, Canada, and at least 30 other maritime countries make every vessel operator –including sailboarders, responsible for knowing the rules.

Learning the Navigation Rules and understanding their application is easy to do. Call your local Coast Guard station and find out when the **Coast Guard Auxiliary** is teaching their course, **"Safety at Sea."** The **United States Power Squadron** is another outstanding organization which is dedicated to teaching boating safety and other nautical skills. Find out more: **www.americasboatingcourse.com**

GOOD POLICY: Just because you know the rules of "right of way" doesn't necessarily mean the skipper of the vessel in your way knows them. Act accordingly to avoid collision at all times even if you are in the right. *–CCM*

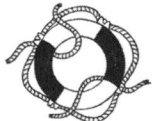

WE'D LIKE TO HEAR FROM YOU!

The most valuable information a cruising boater can have is
LOCAL KNOWLEDGE.

We invite you to share your cruising experiences with our *Northeast Boaters Almanac* readers and website visitors. Tell us about your favorite destinations, the best way to navigate to an out of the way cove, great anchorages and hurricane holes, navigational hazards you've encountered, waterfront dining spots, boat cleaning tips, good things to cook aboard and more... and, if you find information we need to change for future editions... you can do it all on

www.BoatersAlmanac.com

What happens when you dump?

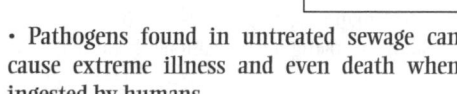

LOOK FOR THIS SYMBOL AT MARINAS FOR PUMPOUT SERVICE

Did you know that the amount of bacterial pollution from one weekend boater's discharge of untreated sewage is equal to the amount from the treated sewage of 10,000 people during the same time period?

SOURCE: EPA OFFICE OF WATER

• Pathogens found in untreated sewage can cause extreme illness and even death when ingested by humans.

• Raw or poorly treated sewage can spread disease, contaminate shellfish beds and lower oxygen levels in the water. Waterborne diseases including hepatitis, typhoid and cholera can be transmitted by shellfish. Organic matter in sewage is decomposed in the water by bacteria. During this process, the bacteria use oxygen. As a result, sewage in the water may deplete the water's oxygen level causing stress to fish and other aquatic animals. And, can you imagine going for a swim?

• Shellfish are filter feeders that eat tiny food particles filtered through their gills into their stomachs along with bacteria from sewage. Shellfish can convey nearly all waterborne pathogens to humans.

• Sewage contamination is measured in terms of fecal coliforms–bacteria produced in the intestines of all warm blooded animals.

• Areas most likely to be affected are sheltered waters with low flushing rates such as lakes, slow moving rivers, marinas, many of our bays, and areas set aside for shellfish harvesting, State and Federally designated significant habitats such as those in Coastal Zone programs, as well as waters designated by the Environmental Protection Agency as "No Discharge Zones." ⚓

Current designated NO DISCHARGE ZONES for vessel sewage from The Chesapeake Bay to Maine:

MARYLAND

Herring Bay; All NorthernCoastal Bays

MASSACHUSETTS

Wellfleet, Westport Harbor, Waquoit Bay, Nantucket Harbor, Wareham Harbor, Stage Harbor Complex, Harwich, Buzzards Bay

NEW JERSEY

Shark River, Manasquan River, Shrewsbury River, Navesink River, Barnegat Bay

NEW YORK

Peconic Estuary, Mamaroneck River Lake George, Hudson River, East Hampton (7 bodies of water), Greater Huntington and Northport

RHODE ISLAND

Great Salt Pond, Block island; All of Rhode Island's waters

VERMONT

All of Vermont and Lake Champlain

For information on pumpout and dump station locations call **1-800-ASK-FISH**

HOW TO USE the Northeast Boaters Almanac

ELEVEN REGIONAL SECTIONS: The Almanac is divided into 11 regional sections. These sections include Maine & New Hampshire, Northern Massachusetts, Southern Massachusetts, Rhode Island, Connecticut, North Shore of Long Island, South Shore of Long Island, New York & Hudson River area, the New Jersey Coast, Delware River in NJ, PA and DE, the C&D Canal, the Headwaters of the Chesapeake Bay, and the Eastern Shore to Cambridge, the Western Shore to Solomons, in the Chesapeake.

WHAT'S IN EACH SECTION: Each area contains a cruising narrative, chart details, advertising from local facilities, an Authorized Dealer & Repair Section and comprehensive tables listing just about every marine-oriented facility in the area –their amenities–and selected shoreside places to visit.

On the Title Page of each section you will find a listing of locations and the chart locator numbers they correspond to. If you are seeking a specific location, this would assist you in finding it. If you are interested in locating a specific marina, you can look it up in the alphabetical index then locate it by its corresponding locator number on the chart.

The detailed locator charts show waterfront facilities available to boaters. Each number corresponds to a number in the table section. Advertisements highlight additional information on marinas that can't be found elsewhere in this book. Advertisers often include additional information that is useful to transient boaters or boaters seeking repairs. Advertisers' facilities are noted with a number inside a ★.

The Table Section contains the telephone numbers and chart location or numbers of all the marinas contained in the book. Information on when marinas are open, the VHF station they monitor, what transient facilities are available, the location of boat launch ramps, and other important data are contained in these tables.

TIDE TABLES: The Tide Tables in this book cover the entire Northeast and Chesapeake Bay. The Northeast Boaters Almanac Tide Tables are divided into three Primary Harmonic Stations. In addition, there are many secondary reference stations. These Secondary Stations allow tides to be more accurately predicted at localized areas. To predict the tides, first access the Secondary Reference Station and find the High Water time difference. Then locate the Primary Harmonic Station and date & time. Add or subtract the Primary Stations and Secondary Stations time difference. Adjust for Daylight Saving Time when necessary. The High Water mean ranges given for all of the Secondary Reference Stations were formulated specifically for the Northeast Boaters Almanac and may not be reproduced in any form.

CURRENT TABLES: The Current Tables are located following the Tide Tables and should be adjusted in accordance with Table 2 Current Differences and other Constants.

CRUISE GUIDE: The Cruise Guide contains important information for boaters on specific harbors and waterways plus onshore tourism information. The Cruise Guide takes you from Maine to the lower Chesapeake Bay and to many tributaries in between. It's a great aid for the boater in unfamiliar areas. ⚓

COPY THIS PAGE AND FILL IT OUT COMPLETELY
to leave a Float Plan with a relative or friend
before leaving on a boating trip. This information is important
should assistance become necessary.

FLOAT PLAN

OPERATORS Name: _____ TEL No: _____

(BUSINESS)TEL No: _____ CELL or PAGE No: _____

DESCRIPTION OF BOAT

BOAT Name: _____

Type: _____ Color _____ REG.No: _____

Make/Model_____ Length: _____ Engine Type: _____

Type of Fuel: _____ Fuel Capacity: _____

Other: _____

PERSONS ABOARD

Name: _____ Age: _____ Address:_____

Name: _____ Age: _____ Address: _____

Name: _____ Age: _____ Address: _____

Name: _____ Age: _____ Address: _____

SURVIVAL EQUIPMENT (circle appropriate equipment)

PFD'S   FLARES   MIRROR   SMOKE SIGNALS   WATER

FLASHLIGHT   FOOD   ANCHOR   EPIRB No: _____

DINGHY/RAFT Other: _____

RADIO (Yes or No)_____ Type: (VHF OR CB) _____

Frequencies: _____

TRIP PLAN

Depart from: _____ Going to: _____

Departure Time & Date: _____ Expected Arrival Date: _____

Expected to return by: _____ Not later than: _____

Name & address of destination: _____

EMERGENCY NOTIFICATION

Call COAST GUARD if not returned by: _____

Other notification to: _____

AUTOMOBILE INFORMATION

Auto License No.: _____ Color/Make_____

Where parked: _____

CONTENTS

www.BoatersAlmanac.com
1-866-6BOATER

PUBLISHED BY:
Miner's Associates, Inc.

PUBLISHER:
William J. Miners

EDITOR
& ART DIRECTOR:
Carla Coutts-Miners

VICE PRESIDENT
MARKETING:
Gerard J. Bennett

VICE PRESIDENT
ADVERTISING & PROMOTION:
Daniel A. Bennett

VICE PRESIDENT
ADVERTISING & DISTRIBUTION
Richard Lull

WEBSITE CONSULTANT:
John Poole

ADVERTISING & DISTRIBUTION
INFORMATION:
1-866-6BOATER

Sales@BoatersAlmanac.com

RETAIL COPY SALES:
www.BoatersAlmanac.com

DEALER SALES:
1-866-6BOATER

NORTHEAST BOATERS ALMANAC
Box 299
Chesapeake City, MD 21915

PRINTING:
Manahawkin Printing Company
www.booksprintedhere.com
Indian Mills, NJ

CONTENTS:

C & D CANAL PASSAGE HEADING TO THE NORTHEAST

GATEWAY TO THE NORTHEAST

CONTENTS:

U.S. COAST GUARD STATION LOCATIONS & COMMUNICATIONS

Oil or HAZMAT Spill?
Call the National Response Center
800-424-8802

DELAWARE RIVER & BAY

REGION HEADQUARTERS
Philadelphia, PA 19102
Telephone215-271-4847
VHF-16

INDIAN RIVER INLET, DE
Telephone 302-227-2440
VHF-16

OCEAN CITY, MD
Telephone 410 289-7457
Telephone 410-289-7559
VHF-16

MARYLAND

COVE POINT LIGHT STATION
Solomons, MD 20688
Telephone 410-326-3254
VHF-16

U. S. Coast Guard Cutter
CHOKESBERRY
Crisfield, MD
Telephone 410-968-0962
VHF-16

U. S. COAST GUARD
SEARCH AND RESCUE
24 Hour Emergency Response
Telephone 410-576-2525
VHF-16

ST. INIGOES, MD 20684
Telephone 301-872-4344
VHF-16

CURTIS BAY, MD 21226
Telephone 410-789-1600
VHF-16

OXFORD, MD 21654
Telephone 410-226-0580
VHF-16

STILL POND, MD
Telephone 410-778-2201
VHF-16

ANNAPOLIS, MD
Telephone 410-267-8108
VHF-16

NEW JERSEY

ATLANTIC CITY
U.S.C.G Station Atlantic City
VHF-16
Telephone 609-344-6594

AVON BY THE SEA
U.S.C.G. Station Shark River
Avon By the Sea
VHF 16

BARNEGAT LIGHT
U.S.C.G. Station Barnegat Light
VHF 16
Telephone 609-494-2261

BEACH HAVEN (OPEN SUMMER)
U.S.C.G. Station Beach Haven
Beach Haven

CAPE MAY
U.S.C.G. Station Cape May
Trainng Center
VHF 16
Telephone 609-898-6695
Telephone 609-898-6997

FORTESCUE (OPEN SUMMER)
U.S.C.G. Station Fortescue
VHF 16
Telephone 856-447-4422

SANDY HOOK
U.S.C.G. Station Sandy Hook
Highlands
VHF 16

OCEAN CITY (OPEN SUMMER)
U.S.C.G. Station Great Egg
VHF 16
Telephone 609-399-0119

POINT PLEASANT BEACH
U.S.C.G. Station Manasquan Inlet
VHF 16

SEA ISLE CITY (SUMMER ONLY)
U.S.C.G. Station Townsend Inlet

NEW YORK

ATLANTIC BEACH
Ft. Tilden, NY 11695-0511
Telephone 718-634-2848

BABYLON
U.S.C.G. Station Fire Island
VHF-16
Babylon, NY 11702-4602
EMERGENCY 631-661-9100

EAST MORICHES
U.S.C.G. Station
Telephone 631-395-4421

FREEPORT
U.S.C.G. Station
VHF-16
Telephone 516-785-2988

HELP!
Don't forget to
file a copy
of your
Float Plan with
a friend or relative.

HAMPTON BAYS
VHF-16
Telephone 631-728-1171

MONTAUK
U.S.C.G. Station Montauk
VHF-16
Telephone 631-668-2773

NORTHPORT
U.S.C.G. Station Eatons Neck
VHF-16
Telephone 631-261-6868

SAUGERTIES
U.S.C.G. Station Saugerties
VHF 16
Telephone 914-246-7612

WILLETS POINT
U.S.C.G. Station Fort Totten
VHF-16
(BOAT ONLY AT LOCATION)

CONNECTICUT

LONG ISLAND SOUND
U.S.C.G. Group Long Island Sound
VHF-16 & SSB-2182
New Haven,
Telephone 203-468-4400

NEW HAVEN
U.S.C.G. Station New Haven
VHF-16
Telephone 203-468-4486
EMERGENCY 203-468-4400

NEW LONDON
U.S.C.G. Station New London
VHF-16
New London, CT 06320-5593

RHODE ISLAND

BLOCK ISLAND
U.S.C.G. Station Block Island
VHF-16
Telephone 401-466-2086

NARRAGANSETT
U.S.C.G. Station Point Judith
VHF-16
Telephone 401-789-0444
EMERGENCY 401-783-3021

FYI!
For GPS STATUS and FORECASTS
hear taped recordings 24/7
by calling **U.S.C.G. NAVIGATION INFORMATION SERVICE**
(703) 313-5907 or go to:
www.navcen.uscg.gov

NEWPORT
U.S.C.G. Station Castle Hill
VHF-16
Telephone 401-846-3675/6

MASSACHUSETTS

BOSTON
U.S.C.G. Group Boston
SSB-2182 & VHF-16
Telephone 617-565-9200
617-223-3224

CHATHAM
U.S.C.G. Station Chatham
VHF-16
Telephone 508-945-3830
EMERGENCY 508-945-0164

CHILMARK
U.S.C.G. Station Menemsha
VHF-16
Telephone 508-645-2661

GLOUCESTER
U.S.C.G. Station Gloucester
VHF-16 & SSB-2182
Telephone 508-283-0704

HULL
U.S.C.G. Station Point Allerton
VHF-16 & SSB-2182
Telephone 781-925-0165

NANTUCKET
U.S.C.G. Station Brant Point
VHF-16
Telephone 508-288-0398

NEWBURYPORT
U.S.C.G. Station Merrimac River
VHF-16 & SSB-2182
Telephone 978-465-0731/5921

PROVINCETOWN
U.S.C.G. Station Provincetown
VHF-16
EMERGENCY 508-487-0070

SANDWICH
U.S.C.G. Station Cape Cod Canal
VHF-13, 16
Telephone 508-888-0020

SCITUATE
U.S.C.G. Station Scituate
VHF-16
EMERGENCY 781-545-3800

WOODS HOLE
U.S.C.G. Group Woods Hole
EMERGENCY 508-548-5151

NEW HAMPSHIRE

NEW CASTLE
U.S.C.G. Station Portsmouth Hbr.
VHF-16 & SSB-2182
Telephone 603-436-4415

MAINE

BOOTHBAY HARBOR
U.S.C.G. Station Boothbay Harbor
VHF-16
Telephone 207-633-2644

EASTPORT
U.S.C.G. SAR Detach, Eastport
VHF-16
Telephone 207-853-2845

JONESPORT
U.S.C.G. Station Jonesport
VHF-16
Telephone 207-497-2200

ROCKLAND
U.S.C.G. Station Rockland
VHF-16 & SSB-2182
Telephone 207-596-6667

SOUTH PORTLAND
U.S.C.G. Group Portland
VHF-16 & SSB-2182
Telephone 207-799-1680

SOUTHWEST HARBOR
VHF-16 & SSB-2182
U.S.C.G. Group Southwest Harbor
Southwest Harbor, ME 04679
Telephone 207-244-5121/5517

Please take a few minutes to read the information below so that you can be aware of what is happening in terms of Homeland Security on the water while you are cruising to various ports of call.
A combination of being alert for the items you see listed, and good old-fashioned common sense, is the best approach.
And don't be caught out on the water without the same kind of I.D. you would take to the airport.

SEE PAGE 666 FOR HARBOR SECURITY INFORMATION.

Operation ON GUARD
800-424-8802

Operation "On-Guard" was created to help thwart terrorist attacks. Its basis is forming close lines of communication between federal and local law enforcement agencies and the general public.

Effectively, everyone plays a role in the operation, acting as each other's "eyes and ears" and reporting suspicious activities to appropriate authorities.

FOR EXAMPLE: marina operators, marine dealers, bridge tenders, commerical fishermen, or the general boating public, might see or hear a suspicious activity, after which they would alert the appropriate authorities. Authorities, in turn, would take measures to alert other agencies and, if deemed necessary, civilians. In this manner, terrorist activities and threats can be thwarted and the terrorists will realize that their activites will be dutifully seen and reported.

The Department of Homeland Security (DHS) encourages the maritime public to report information concerning suspicious activity to their local Federal Bureau of Information (FBI) Joint Terrorism Task Force (JTTF) Office, or to other appropriate authorities.

Individuals can contact the DHS Watch and Warning Unit at (202) 323-3205, toll free at 1-888-585-9078, or by E-Mail to nipc.watch@fbi.gov.

THE ITEMS TO REPORT ARE:

• Suspicious persons conducting unusual activities

• Suspicious persons photographing/making sketches

• Suspicious person loitering for extended periods

• Suspicious person renting watercraft

• Unknown vendors attempting to sell/deliver merchandise

• Unknown persons asking detailed questions

Urgent situations requiring an immediate response should still be reported to local authorities by dialing 911 or an alternative emergency telephone number. Operation On-Guard watch standers have been trained to ask specific questions for such reports and will immediately pass the information to the proper agencies for response.

Maritime Safety and Security Teams (MSSTs) are a new Coast Guard rapid response force assigned to vital ports and capable of nationwide deployment via air, ground or sea transportation to meet emerging threats. MSSTs were created in direct response to the terrorist attacks on Sept. 11, 2001, and are a part of the Department of Homeland Security's layered strategy directed at protecting our seaports and waterways. ⚓

Advection Fog: Produced by winds carrying warm, moist air over a colder surface.

Steam Fog: When cold air passes over warmer water.

Precipitation Fog: When rain falls from a layer of warmer air into a layer of colder air at the earth's surface.

Ground Fog: Forms at night in air moister and colder than surface air. It's the fog you see at dawn which soon evaporates over land.

SAIL
underway

1 long (4-6 second) 2 short (1 second) Blasts
in 2 minute intervals

USING POWER
underway-making way

1 prolonged (4-6 second) Blast
at intervals of not more than two minutes

POWER
not anchored-not making way

2 prolonged (4-6 second) Blasts -
two seconds apart
at intervals of not more than two minutes

POWER or SAIL
at anchor

Bell: Strike at 5 second intervals
for less than 5 minutes
Vessels under 39.4-ft (12 meters)
are not required to use a bell but are required
to make some sound at two minute intervals.

POWER or SAIL - AGROUND
3 Strikes on a Bell before
Rapid Bell Ringing

Cruising with Man's Best Friend

We've never cruised with a pet. In over 20 years of boating the closest we came to pets onboard was having our children and their friends on the boat when they were young.

We've been boat-free for a couple of years now and are looking to find another. Of course now we have a dog.

We've met a lot of pets on boats over the years. As we contemplate our next boat, we remember vividly the people we used to whisper about way back when, wondering what could they be thinking to bring an animal onboard.

Two Irish Setters would show up at our marina every weekend to go cruising on a 30 foot sailboat. The dogs wore big red biker bandanas around their necks. We never could figure out whether it was to keep them cool, collect the 'slobber,' or gag them to stop their incessant barking.

A couple we knew cruised with a Cocker Spaniel. At anchor the dog would jump off the stern, paddle around for a while then actually climb back up the boarding ladder.

Another family went everywhere on their boat with their miniature schnauzers. These are small, manageable dogs you can carry on like a bag of groceries. But out there in the anchorage on Sunday mornings, right about dawn, you could count on hearing the putt-putt of a small outboard breaking the early morning quiet as the Captain made way to shore with a pair of perky schnauzers perched like figureheads on the bow of his inflatable. Noses into the wind, and ears laid back, they were anticipating the first constitutional of the day.

When we brought our boat to the Chesapeake, we acquired a boat neighbor who had two huge talking birds on board. His foul language was often repeated by his pets at a much higher decibel.

We know a Labrador retriever who loves to go out fly fishing but gets mal-de-mer at anchor; an Australian cattle dog whose favorite summer pastime is herding jet skis; and a Sharpei who wears sunglasses while scooting about in a jet boat.

When long-term cruising to different countries, pets can be a serious problem.

First there's the various quarantine regulations to consider, and then there's the real fact that in some countries your pet could easily end up as someone's dinner.

Hank Schmitt, of Offshore Passage Opportunities, has single-handed his Cheoy Lee sailboat to most parts of the world. Today, he puts captains and crew together for offshore sailing ventures. He says, "Guns and pets – leave them home, you're just inviting trouble in other countries."

Yet, Tania Aebi, the 16 year old who set sail alone out of New York Harbor to circumnavigate the globe in the 80s, acquired a kitten companion along the way, and all worked out well.

Nowadays, pet owners seem to take their animals just about everywhere they go. Books have been written about pet-friendly motels and hotels. In Maryland, a new bill was introduced to the legislature this past winter approving pet-friendly sections in restaurants. New homes are being built with "Pet Playrooms!"

The popularity of people bringing their pets – and it's mostly dogs — to their boats has grown to the point where boating guides are classifying marinas as "pet friendly" or not.

Many marinas have created dog-walking areas along with boxes offering pooper-scooper bags to ensure the area is kept clean.

Boating with your favorite animal requires a lot of responsibility and work on your part, and often, some serious discomfort for your pet. If you're a daytripper, a pet on board is a lot easier to deal with than those on board and out of the marina for a weekend or longer.

INTRODUCING FIDO TO THE BOAT

First, get your cat or dog a PFD. Some animals can't swim and, even if he can swim, if your pet falls overboard, odds are he will tire or get hypothermia long before you figure out how to get him back on the boat.

Cats and dogs both like stable environments. How well they cope with boat motion is your first problem. Animals prone to carsickness will need a longer adjustment period than those who are not. You can buy motion sickness medicine in your favorite pet store to help things along, but keep in mind, these are usually tranquilizing.

Start out by bringing the dog to the boat on weekends early in the spring, long before you plan to leave the dock. Let the dog get used to the boat's motion. At the same time he should be wearing the PFD – that takes getting used to also.

Turn on the engine every once in while. See if the sound bothers the dog. Some will be very frightened and others will just howl or bark until the noise stops. Let him get used to your engine's particular sounds.

Find a place on board that can forever be his spot and place a mat, a pad, or pet bed there. This is a place he can always go to feel secure. After he gets used to the new environment and becomes comfortable, it's time for a few short trips…like a quickie to the fuel dock and back.

SUPPLIES

PLENTY OF WATER: Dogs can easily get dehydrated in the sun on a boat, and they lose a great deal of body fluid just panting in the heat.

PET BED or substitute. A 'castle' of cushions for kitty.

NON-SKID-BOTTOM WATER AND FOOD DISH or one of those non-skid rubbery type open-weave mats sold for galley storage, in marine stores.

AWNING OR BIMINI to create a shaded area on deck. Your pooch can get sunstroke, heat exhaustion and sunburned skin.

LITTER BOX for the cat. Keep it on the lowest and most level part of the boat. Expect to find litter pieces everywhere on the boat your cat walks including your berth, because these little pieces get stuck in the pads of their paws only to fall out later. Choose the litter type accordingly. Long-term cruisers can't take enough litter along for a cat's needs — imagine a boat laden down with sacks and sacks of kitty litter. There are alternatives.

POOPER SCOOPER BAGS and/or shovel and a deodorized container (like the ones sold in baby stores to hold soiled disposable diapers) to keep them in. Don't throw them overboard. On land, use the appropriate waste facility.

ON and OFF and UP and DOWN

When you set out to sea with a dog too heavy to carry, you've added the boarding problem. Any dog can jump off a boat but how do you get him back on? Want to take your big dog on your sailboat? It's hard enough for humans to scale some of the sailboat companionway ladders I've seen, much less a dog. And then there's in and out of the dinghy to think about. Orvis and L.L. Bean catalogs sell portable fold-up, lightweight ramps intended for ageing and arthritic dogs. These might work.

OTHER CONSIDERATIONS

Don't wax the non-skid or any places your dog will walk on deck where he can slip and fall overboard. Consider putting up safety netting sold in marine stores. Pet stores do sell a concoction you can rub on pet's footpads to alleviate sliding or skidding on slippery floors – try it.

Keep a bucket of water or shower bag handy to wet down the dog in the heat and wet down the decks. Oiled or varnished teak and fiberglass can get hot enough under foot to burn the pads of your pet's paws.

REMEMBER, dogs (and other pets) are like kids. Some are well behaved and some are not. Some are a pleasure to be around, and some are not. And, odds are some of your marina neighbors are not pet-friendly. Don't let your on-board pet drive other boaters to seek a new harbor.. ⚓ –CCM

FITTING FIDO TO A PFD

■ West Marine stores will allow you to bring in your pet for a try-on session. One size does not fit all in pet PFDs.

■ Make sure the straps go around the dog in the right place – if they are too tight or in the wrong spot he won't be able to walk which means he won't be able to swim either. The PFDs with the quick release straps are the only ones to buy.

■ Look for handles on the PFD of choice so you can easily pick your pooch up out of the drink.

■ Pick a bright color so you can spot the dog quickly. Don't buy cammo!

■ If your dog absolutely hates his PFD try the newer lightweight versions.

VHF RADIO TELEPHONE INFORMATION

CHANNEL	TRANSMIT	RECEIVE	CHANNEL APPLICATION
1 A	156.050	156.050	Port operations & Commercial
5 A	156.250	156.250	Port operations
6	156.300	156.300	**INTERSHIP SAFETY. USCG use at emergencies.**
7A	156.350	156.350	Commercial
8	156.400	156.400	Commercial - ship to ship only
9	156.450	156.450	Commercial
10	156.500	156.500	Commercial
11	156.550	156.550	Commercial
12	156.600	156.600	Ship to Shore & Ship to Ship. Harbormasters & Port Op.
13	156.650	156.650	Bridge & Lock tenders information
14	156.700	156.700	Port Operations Bridge & Lock tenders
16	156.800	156.800	**DISTRESS & SAFETY** (Calling to establish contact only)
18 A	156.900	156.900	Commercial
19 A	156.950	156.950	Commercial
20 A	157.000	157.000	Ship to Shore & Ship to Ship. Harbormasters & Port Op.
22 A	157.100	157.100	**USCG communication** after vessel makes contact on 16.
24	157.200	161.800	Marine Telephone Operator. Ship to Shore.
25	157.250	161.850	Marine Telephone Operator. Ship to Shore.
26	157.300	161.900	Marine Telephone Operator. Ship to Shore.
27	157.350	161.950	Marine Telephone Operator. Ship to Shore.
28	157.400	162.000	Marine Telephone Operator. Ship to Shore.
65 A	156.275	156.275	Ship to Shore & Ship to Ship. Harbormasters & Port Op.
66 A	156.325	156.325	Ship to Shore & Ship to Ship. Harbormasters & Port Op.
67	156.375	156.375	Commercial
68	156.425	156.425	Ship to Shore & Ship to Ship. Pleasure Craft Non-Comm.
69	156.475	156.475	Ship to Shore & Ship to Ship. Pleasure Craft Non-Comm.
71	156.575	156.575	Ship to Shore & Ship to Ship. Pleasure Craft Non-Comm.
72	156.625	156.625	Ship to Shore & Ship to Ship. Pleasure Craft Non-Comm.
73	156.675	156.675	Ship to Shore & Ship to Ship. Harbormasters & Port Op.
74	156.725	156.725	Ship to Shore & Ship to Ship. Harbormasters & Port Op.
77	156.875	156.875	Ship to Shore & Ship to Ship. Harbormasters & Port Op.
78 A	156.925	156.925	Ship to Shore & Ship to Ship. Pleasure Craft Non-Comm.
79 A	156.975	156.975	Commercial
80 A	157.025	157.025	Commercial
84	157.225	157.225	Marine Telephone Operator. Ship to Shore.
85	157.275	161.875	Marine Telephone Operator. Ship to Shore.
86	157.325	161.925	Marine Telephone Operator. Ship to Shore.
87	157.375	161.975	Marine Telephone Operator. Ship to Shore.
88A	157.425	157.425	Commercial , Intership only

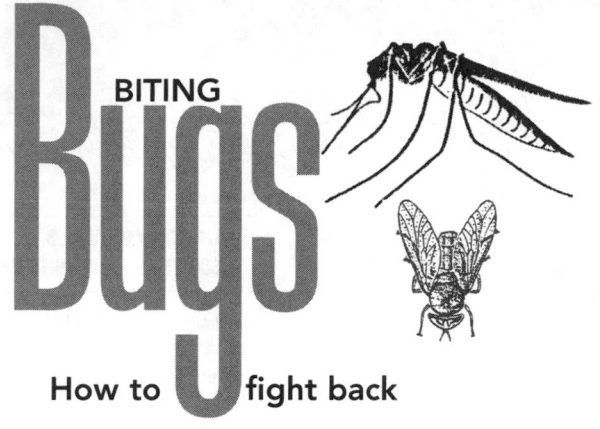

BITING Bugs

How to fight back

Eco-cruising on the scenic waterways in marshes and wetlands usually means you'll see more than exotic birds and wildlife. An army of biting flies and mosquitoes often await to take the joy out of your journey. Early morning and twilight are the worst times of day for these annoying predators.

The following clinical analysis of insect repellents was published in a recent issue of in the "New England Journal of Medicine." After reading below, you may want to try something new.

The study also says that the use of DEET is much less harmful than the risk of contracting West Nile Virus or other diseases from the mosquito's saliva ...which is what makes your bug bite itch.

Protection time listed below is MAXIMUM in ideal conditions. If you are perspiring or if you get wet... reapply the repellent right away.

Product	Ingredient	Max. Protection Time (hours)
Deep Woods OFF	DEET 23.8%	6
Sawyer Controlled Release	DEET 20%	5.4
Skintastik OFF	DEET 6.6%	3.8
Bite Blocker For Kids	Soybean Oil 2%	3.25
Skintastik OFF For Kids	DEET 4.7%	2
Skin-So-Soft Bug Guard Plus	JR3535* 7.5%	1
Herbal Armor	Citronella, Cedar Oil Peppermint Oil, Lemongrass Oil, Geranium Oil	1
Nurapel	Citronella 10%	1
Buzz Away	Citronella 5%	1/2
Skin-So-Soft Bug Guard	Citronella .1%	1/2
Skin-So-Soft Bath Oil	Uncertain	1/4
Gone Original Wristband	DEET 9.5%	1-1/2
Repello Wristband	DEET 9.5%	3/4
Gone Plus Repelling Wristband	Citronella 25%	3/4

* ethyl butylactylaminopropionate

The Beaufort Wind Scale

BEAUFORT NO.	MPH	KNOTS	INTERNATIONAL DESCRIPTION	WATER CONDITIONS
0	Less than 1	Less than 1	Calm	Sea like a mirror
1	1 – 3	1-3	Light air	Ripples with appearance of scales; no foam crests
2	3-7	4-6	Light breeze	Small wavelets; crests of glassy appearance, not breaking
3	8-12	7 10	Gentle breeze	Large wavelets; crests begin to break, scattered white ecaps
4	13-18	11-16	Moderate	Small waves becoming longer, numerous whitecaps
5	19-24	17-21	Fresh	Moderate waves taking longer form; many whitecaps; some spray
6	25-31	22-27	Strong	Larger waves forming; whitecaps everywhere, more spray
7	32-38	28-33	Near Gale	Sea heaps up, white foam from breaking waves blow in streaks.
8	39-46	34-40	Gale	Moderately high waves of greater length; edge of crests begin to break in spindrift; foam is blown in well-marked streaks
9	47-54	41-47	Strong Gale	High waves (6 meters); sea begins to roll; dense streaks of foam; spray may reduce visibiliby.
10	55-63	48-55	Storm	Very high waves with overhanging crests; sea takes on white appearance, foam blown in dense streaks; heavy rolling; reduced visibility
11	64-73	56-63	Violent Storm	Waves exceptionally high, sea covered with white foam patches; further reduced visibility.
12	74-82	64-71	Hurricane	Air filled with foam; waves over 14 meters; sea completely white; driving spray; visibility greatly reduced

STORM WATCH

This Storm Chart provides the necessary grids to accurately track the path of a storm. Simply record the latitude and longitude data from NOAA Radio weather broadcasts, locate that point where they intersect on the chart, and mark the spot. Follow the same procedure as the storm moves and new advisories are issued. Then connect the points to track the storm center. This will give you an accurate track of the storm's path. "Hurricane season" is officially June through November. The National Weather Service issues storm advisories at regularly scheduled intervals. NOAA Weather Radio broadcasts hurricane data, giving latitude and longitude positions at the center. Hurricanes have been known to quickly change their path.

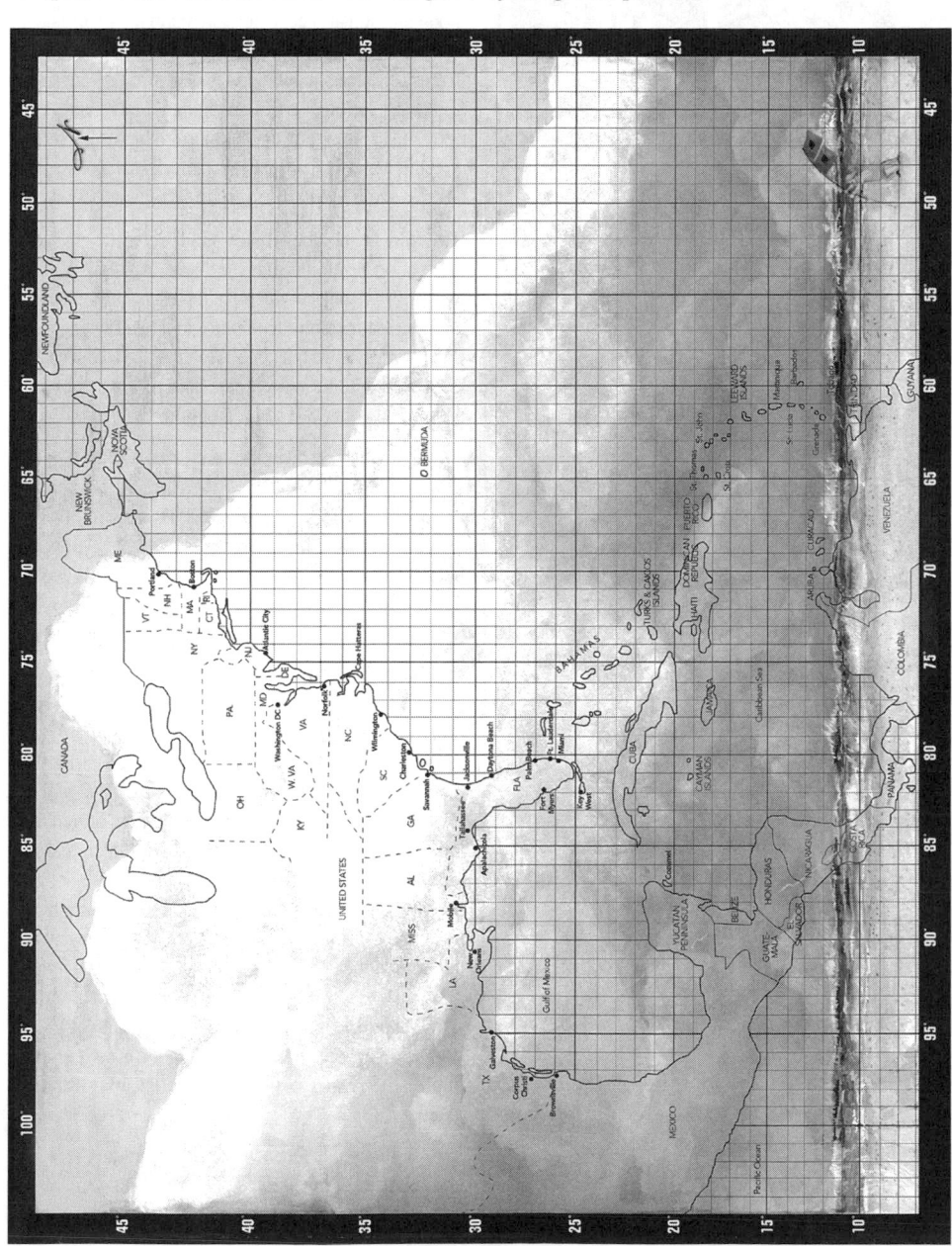

Phases of the Moon

New Moon

The NEW MOON lies between the earth and the sun. Because the sunlit side is away from the earth, we can't see it.

Waxing Crescent

As the moon moves along its orbit, it appears as a crescent on the right side. As the visible part grows - it is 'waxing.'

First Quarter

After the moon completes a quarter of its orbit...it appears as a half circle.

Waxing Gibbous

When more than half of the sunlit side is visible...the moon is 'gibbous.'

Full Moon

When the moon reaches the second quarter of its orbit, the entire daylight side is visible as a perfect circle.

Waning Gibbous

As the sunlit side turns away from us, the moon begins to 'wane.'

Last Quarter

The moon reaches the third quarter of its orbit and appears as a backwards 'd.'

Waning Crescent

The visible portion of the moon dwindles to a crescent and it starts all over again.

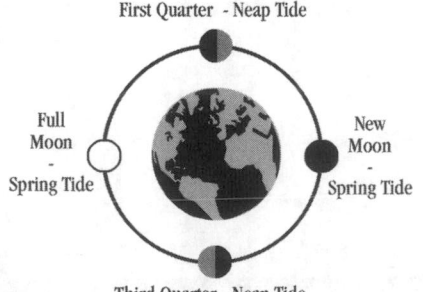

First Quarter - Neap Tide

Full Moon - Spring Tide

New Moon - Spring Tide

Third Quarter - Neap Tide

Astronomical Tide-Producing Forces:

At the surface of the earth, the earth's force of gravitational attraction acts in a direction inward toward its center of mass, and thus holds the ocean water confined to this surface. However, the gravitational forces of the moon and sun also act externally upon the earth's ocean waters. These external forces are exerted as tide-producing, or so-called "tractive" forces. Their effects are superimposed upon the earth's gravitational force and act to draw the ocean waters to positions on the earth's surface directly beneath these respective celestial bodies (i.e., towards the "sublunar" and "subsolar" points).

High tides are produced in the ocean waters by the "heaping" action resulting from the horizontal flow of water toward two regions of the earth representing positions of maximum attraction of combined lunar and solar gravitational forces. Low tides are created by a compensating maximum withdrawal of water from regions around the earth midway between these two humps.

The alternation of high and low tides is caused by the daily (or diurnal) rotation of the earth with respect to these two tidal humps and two tidal depressions. The changing arrival time of any two successive high or low tides at any one location is the result of numerous factors.

To all outward appearances, the moon revolves around the earth, but in actuality, the moon and earth revolve together around their common center of mass, or gravity. The two astronomical bodies are held together by gravitational attraction, but are simultaneously kept apart by an equal and opposite centrifugal force produced by their individual revolutions around the center-of-mass of the earth-moon system. This balance of forces in orbital revolution applies to the center-of-mass of the individual bodies only. At the earth's surface, an imbalance between these two forces results in the fact that there exists, on the hemisphere of the earth turned toward the moon, a net (or differential) tide-producing force which acts in the direction of the moon's gravitational attraction, or toward the center of the moon. On the side of the earth directly opposite the moon, the net tide-producing force is in the direction of the greater centrifugal force, or away from the moon.

Similar differential forces exist as the result of the revolution of the center-of-mass of the earth around the center-of-mass of the earth-sun system.

Courtesy: The Nautical Almanac Office, United States Naval Observatory.

NEW MOONS FOR 2004 (Universal Time)			
p	m	d	h : m
●	Jan	21	21:05
●	Feb	20	09:18
●	Mar	20	22:41
●	Apr	19	13:91
●	May	19	04:52
●	Jun	17	20:27
●	Jul	17	11:24
●	Aug	1	01:24
●	Sep	14	14:29
●	Oct	14	02:48
●	Nov	12	14:27
●	Dec	12	01:29

Moon in apogee

FULL MOONS FOR 2004 (Universal Time)			
p	m	d	h : m
○	Jan	7	15:40
○	Feb	6	08:47
○	Mar	6	23:14
○	Apr	5	11:03
○	May	4	20:33
○	Jun	3	04:20
○	Jul	2	11:09
○	Jul	31	18:05
○	Aug	30	02:22
○	Sep	28	13:09
○	Oct	28	03:07
○	Nov	26	20:07
○	Dec	26	15:06

Moon in perogee

FIRST QUARTER MOONS FOR 2004 (Universal Time)			
p	m	d	h : m
◑	Jan	29	06:03
◑	Feb	28	03:24
◑	Mar	28	23:48
◑	Apr	27	17:32
◑	May	27	07:57
◑	Jun	25	19:08
◑	Jul	25	03:37
◑	Aug	23	10:12
◑	Sep	21	15:54
◑	Oct	20	21:59
◑	Nov	19	05:50
◑	Dec	18	16:40

Moon farthest from the Equator

LAST QUARTER MOONS FOR 2004 (Universal Time)			
p	m	d	h : m
◐	Jan	15	04:46
◐	Feb	13	13:40
◐	Mar	13	21:01
◐	Apr	12	03:46
◐	May	11	11:04
◐	Jun	9	20:02
◐	Jul	9	07:34
◐	Aug	7	22:01
◐	Sep	6	15:11
◐	Oct	6	10:12
◐	Nov	5	05:53
◐	Dec	5	00:53

Moon on Equator

P - PHASE   M - MONTH   D - DAY   H : M - HOUR : MINUTE

Greenwich mean time (GMT) or universal time (UT) is the mean solar time on the Greenwich meridian reckoned in days of 24 mean solar hours written as 00h at midnight and 12h at noon. To convert the above times to those of the other standard time meridians, add 1 hour for each 15° of east longitude of the desired meridian and subtract 1 hour for each 15° of west longitude. *This table was compiled from data supplied by The Nautical Almanac Office, United States Naval Observatory.*

Sunrise 2004 Sunset

New York, New York · Location: WO73° 55, N40° 44

EASTERN STANDARD TIME · 0000 IS MIDNIGHT, 1200 IS NOON

ADD ONE HOUR FOR DAYLIGHT TIME.

Day	JANUARY Rise h m	Set h m	FEBRUARY Rise h m	Set h m	MARCH Rise h m	Set h m	APRIL Rise h m	Set h m	MAY Rise h m	Set h m	JUNE Rise h m	Set h m
01	0720	1639	0706	1713	0630	1747	0540	1820	0455	1852	0427	1920
02	0720	1640	0705	1714	0629	1748	0538	1821	0454	1853	0426	1921
03	0720	1640	0704	1715	0627	1749	0537	1822	0452	1854	0426	1922
04	0720	1641	0703	1717	0626	1750	0535	1823	0451	1855	0426	1923
05	0720	1642	0702	1718	0624	1751	0533	1824	0450	1856	0425	1923
06	0720	1643	0701	1719	0622	1752	0532	1825	0449	1857	0425	1924
07	0720	1644	0700	1720	0621	1753	0530	1826	0447	1858	0425	1924
08	0720	1645	0659	1722	0619	1754	0528	1827	0446	1859	0425	1925
09	0720	1646	0658	1723	0618	1756	0527	1828	0445	1900	0424	1926
10	0719	1647	0656	1724	0616	1757	0525	1830	0444	1901	0424	1926
11	0719	1648	0655	1725	0614	1758	0524	1831	0443	1902	0424	1927
12	0719	1649	0654	1726	0613	1759	0522	1832	0442	1903	0424	1927
13	0719	1650	0653	1728	0611	1800	0521	1833	0441	1904	0424	1928
14	0718	1652	0651	1729	0610	1801	0519	1834	0440	1905	0424	1928
15	0718	1653	0650	1730	0608	1802	0517	1835	0439	1906	0424	1928
16	0717	1654	0649	1731	0606	1803	0516	1836	0438	1907	0424	1929
17	0717	1655	0647	1733	0605	1804	0514	1837	0437	1908	0424	1929
18	0716	1656	0646	1734	0603	1805	0513	1838	0436	1909	0424	1930
19	0716	1657	0645	1735	0601	1806	0511	1839	0435	1909	0424	1930
20	0715	1658	0643	1736	0600	1807	0510	1840	0434	1910	0424	1930
21	0715	1700	0642	1737	0558	1808	0509	1841	0434	1911	0424	1930
22	0714	1701	0641	1738	0556	1810	0507	1842	0433	1912	0425	1930
23	0713	1702	0639	1740	0555	1811	0506	1843	0432	1913	0425	1931
24	0713	1703	0638	1741	0553	1812	0504	1844	0431	1914	0425	1931
25	0712	1704	0636	1742	0551	1813	0503	1845	0431	1915	0426	1931
26	0711	1706	0635	1743	0550	1814	0501	1846	0430	1916	0426	1931
27	0710	1707	0633	1744	0548	1815	0500	1847	0429	1917	0426	1931
28	0710	1708	0632	1745	0546	1816	0459	1848	0429	1917	0427	1931
29	0709	1709	-------	-------	0545	1817	0457	1849	0428	1918	0427	1931
30	0708	1710	-------	-------	0543	1818	0456	1850	0428	1919	0428	1931
31	0707	1712	-------	-------	0542	1819	-------	-------	0427	1920	-------	-------

Sunrise **2004** Sunset

New York, New York • Location: W073° 55, N40° 44

EASTERN STANDARD TIME • 0000 IS MIDNIGHT, 1200 IS NOON

ADD ONE HOUR FOR DAYLIGHT TIME.

Day	JULY Rise h m	JULY Set h m	AUGUST Rise h m	AUGUST Set h m	SEPTEMBER Rise h m	SEPTEMBER Set h m	OCTOBER Rise h m	OCTOBER Set h m	NOVEMBER Rise h m	NOVEMBER Set h m	DECEMBER Rise h m	DECEMBER Set h m
01	0428	1931	0452	1911	0522	1828	0552	1738	0626	1652	0700	1629
02	0429	1931	0453	1910	0523	1827	0553	1737	0627	1651	0701	1629
03	0429	1930	0454	1909	0524	1825	0554	1735	0628	1650	0702	1629
04	0430	1930	0455	1908	0525	1824	0555	1733	0629	1649	0703	1628
05	0430	1930	0456	1907	0526	1822	0556	1732	0630	1648	0704	1628
06	0431	1930	0457	1906	0527	1820	0557	1730	0632	1647	0705	1628
07	0431	1929	0458	1905	0528	1819	0558	1728	0633	1646	0706	1628
08	0432	1929	0459	1903	0529	1817	0559	1727	0634	1645	0707	1628
09	0433	1929	0500	1902	0530	1815	0600	1725	0635	1643	0708	1628
10	0433	1928	0501	1901	0531	1814	0601	1724	0636	1642	0708	1628
11	0434	1928	0502	1859	0532	1812	0602	1722	0637	1642	0709	1628
12	0435	1927	0503	1858	0533	1810	0603	1721	0639	1641	0710	1628
13	0436	1927	0504	1857	0534	1809	0604	1719	0640	1640	0711	1629
14	0436	1926	0505	1855	0535	1807	0605	1717	0641	1639	0712	1629
15	0437	1926	0506	1854	0536	1805	0606	1716	0642	1638	0712	1629
16	0438	1925	0507	1853	0537	1804	0608	1714	0643	1637	0713	1629
17	0439	1925	0508	1851	0538	1802	0609	1713	0644	1636	0714	1630
18	0439	1924	0509	1850	0539	1800	0610	1711	0646	1636	0714	1630
19	0440	1923	0510	1848	0540	1758	0611	1710	0647	1635	0715	1630
20	0441	1922	0511	1847	0541	1757	0612	1708	0648	1634	0716	1631
21	0442	1922	0511	1846	0542	1755	0613	1707	0649	1634	0716	1631
22	0443	1921	0512	1844	0543	1753	0614	1706	0650	1633	0717	1632
23	0444	1920	0513	1843	0544	1752	0615	1704	0651	1632	0717	1632
24	0445	1919	0514	1841	0545	1750	0616	1703	0653	1632	0718	1633
25	0445	1918	0515	1839	0546	1748	0618	1701	0654	1631	0718	1633
26	0446	1917	0516	1838	0547	1747	0619	1700	0655	1631	0718	1634
27	0447	1917	0517	1836	0548	1745	0620	1659	0656	1630	0719	1635
28	0448	1916	0518	1835	0549	1743	0621	1657	0657	1630	0719	1635
29	0449	1915	0519	1833	0550	1742	0622	1656	0658	1630	0719	1636
30	0450	1914	0520	1832	0551	1740	0623	1655	0659	1629	0719	1637
31	0451	1913	0521	1830	--------	--------	0624	1654	--------	--------	0720	1638

Moonrise **2004** Moonset

New York, New York • Location: W073° 55, N40° 44

EASTERN STANDARD TIME • 0000 IS MIDNIGHT, 1200 IS NOON

ADD ONE HOUR FOR DAYLIGHT TIME.

Day	JANUARY Rise h m	JANUARY Set h m	FEBRUARY Rise h m	FEBRUARY Set h m	MARCH Rise h m	MARCH Set h m	APRIL Rise h m	APRIL Set h m	MAY Rise h m	MAY Set h m	JUNE Rise h m	JUNE Set h m
01	1247	0147	1248	0342	1214	0326	1411	0404	1517	0322	1754	0304
02	1311	0248	1333	0440	1311	0415	1520	0432	1629	0346	1915	0341
03	1339	0350	1426	0534	1415	0458	1630	0458	1745	0410	2034	0426
04	1412	0451	1526	0621	1522	0534	1741	0522	1903	0438	2143	0524
05	1453	0552	1631	0702	1631	0605	1855	0546	2025	0511	2239	0634
06	1541	0649	1739	0736	1741	0632	2011	0612	2144	0551	2322	0750
07	1636	0740	1847	0805	1851	0657	2129	0641	2257	0642	2355	0907
08	1738	0825	1956	0831	2002	0721	2248	0716	2358	0744	1021	2333
09	1843	0902	2104	0854	2114	0745	0800	0854	0023	1131	2354	1235
10	1950	0934	2214	0918	2229	0812	0003	0853	0046	1009	0046	1237
11	2057	1002	2325	0942	2345	0842	0109	0956	0124	1122	0108	1341
12	2204	1027	1009	0919	0203	1107	0154	1233	0128	1444	0044	1544
13	2312	1050	0039	1041	0101	1004	0246	1219	0219	1340	0150	1546
14	--------	1113	0154	1120	0211	1100	0321	1331	0241	1444	0214	1649
15	0022	1139	0309	1208	0313	1205	0349	1441	0302	1548	0241	1752
16	0134	1207	0418	1308	0404	1316	0413	1547	0323	1650	0313	1853
17	0250	1242	0518	1417	0444	1430	0435	1652	0345	1753	0352	1950
18	0408	1325	0606	1532	0517	1542	0456	1756	0410	1856	0437	2042
19	0523	1420	0645	1647	0544	1652	0517	1859	0438	1959	0530	2127
20	0632	1525	0716	1759	0608	1759	0541	2003	0512	2100	0629	2204
21	0729	1639	0743	1909	0630	1904	0607	2106	0553	2156	0732	2236
22	0814	1756	0806	2015	0652	2008	0637	2208	0641	2245	0836	2303
23	0849	1911	0828	2120	0714	2112	0713	2308	0736	2328	0941	2327
24	0918	2021	0850	2223	0738	2215	0757	--------	0836	--------	1046	2349
25	0943	2129	0913	2326	0806	2318	0847	0002	0940	0003	1152	1310
26	1006	2233	0938	0839	0944	--------	--------	0049	1045	0034	1300	0012
27	1027	2335	1008	0029	0917	0019	1047	0129	1151	0100	1411	0035
28	1049	--------	1043	0131	1004	0117	1152	0203	1258	0124	1526	0101
29	1112	0037	1124	0230	1057	0208	1259	0232	1406	0147	1646	0133
30	1139	0139	--------	--------	1158	0253	1407	0258	1518	0210	1806	0213
31	1210	0241	--------	--------	1303	0332	--------	--------	1634	0235	--------	--------

Moonrise 2004 Moonset

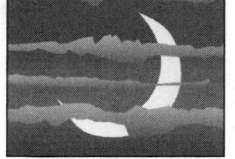

New York, New York • Location: WO73° 55, N40° 44

EASTERN STANDARD TIME • 0000 IS MIDNIGHT, 1200 IS NOON

ADD ONE HOUR FOR DAYLIGHT TIME.

Day	JULY Rise h m	JULY Set h m	AUGUST Rise h m	AUGUST Set h m	SEPTEMBER Rise h m	SEPTEMBER Set h m	OCTOBER Rise h m	OCTOBER Set h m	NOVEMBER Rise h m	NOVEMBER Set h m	DECEMBER Rise h m	DECEMBER Set h m
01	1920	0304	2019	0533	1958	0802	1911	0905	1943	1101	2028	1109
02	2023	0408	2048	0651	2020	0910	1942	1011	2037	1152	2131	1141
03	2113	0523	2112	0805	2045	1016	2018	1115	2137	1235	2234	1208
04	2152	0643	2135	0914	2113	1121	2101	1216	2240	1310	2338	1231
05	2223	0801	2157	1021	2145	1226	2152	1310	2344	1340	------	1253
06	2248	0915	2220	1127	2224	1328	2249	1358	------	1406	0042	1314
07	2311	1025	2245	1231	2310	1426	2351	1438	0049	1429	0149	1336
08	1131	2314	1335	1518	1512	0154	1451	0258	------	1401	------	------
09	2348	1438	0003	1602	------	0055	1540	0301	------	1513	0412	1430
10	1338	1538	0103	1640	0201	1605	0411	1537	0530	1506	------	------
11	0018	1441	0029	1633	0206	1712	0307	1628	0524	1604	0651	1553
12	0118	1723	0312	1739	0415	1650	0641	1636	0808	1653	------	------
13	0114	1646	0214	1805	0418	1803	0523	1713	0801	1717	0915	1805
14	0151	1745	0315	1840	0525	1825	0634	1738	0920	1810	1009	1924
15	0234	1838	0420	1910	0632	1847	0749	1806	1031	1914	1051	2044
16	0325	1925	0525	1936	0740	1910	0906	1841	1130	2027	1123	2200
17	0423	2005	0631	1959	0851	1936	1023	1925	1216	2144	1150	2311
18	0525	2039	0736	2021	1004	2006	1137	2020	1252	2259	1213	------
19	0629	2107	0843	2043	1119	2043	1241	2126	1321	1235	0020	------
20	0734	2132	0950	2106	1234	2129	1334	2239	1346	0011	1256	0126
21	0839	2154	1100	2133	1344	2227	1416	2354	1408	0120	1319	0231
22	0943	2216	1213	2204	1445	2335	1449	------	1429	0227	1345	0335
23	1050	2238	1328	2244	1535	1517	------	0108	1451	0333	1415	0440
24	1158	2302	1443	2334	1614	0050	1541	0220	1515	0438	1450	0544
25	2331	1552	1646	0206	1603	0329	1542	0543	1533	0645	------	------
26	------	1425	1650	0037	1713	0321	1624	0436	1613	0649	1623	0740
27	1542	0006	1738	0149	1737	0433	1647	0543	1651	0752	1719	0828
28	1658	0050	1815	0307	1759	0543	1712	0649	1736	0852	1820	0909
29	1805	0147	1846	0426	1821	0651	1741	0755	1829	0946	1922	0942
30	1901	0256	1912	0541	1845	0758	1814	0901	1926	1031	2025	1011
31	1945	0414	1935	0653	------	------	1855	1004	------	------	2128	1035

In 2004 Daylight Time begins April 4 and ends October 31.

Sunrise 2004 Sunset

Annapolis, Maryland · Location: W076 30, N38 58

EASTERN STANDARD TIME · 0000 IS MIDNIGHT, 1200 IS NOON

ADD ONE HOUR FOR DAYLIGHT TIME.

	JANUARY		FEBRUARY		MARCH		APRIL		MAY		JUNE	
Day	Rise h m	Set h m	Rise h m	Set h m	Rise h m	Set h m	Rise h m	Set h m	Rise h m	Set h m	Rise h m	Set h m
01	0725	1654	0713	1727	0638	1759	0550	1830	0508	1859	0442	1926
02	0725	1655	0712	1728	0636	1800	0548	1831	0506	1900	0442	1927
03	0725	1656	0711	1729	0635	1801	0547	1832	0505	1901	0441	1927
04	0725	1657	0710	1730	0634	1802	0545	1833	0504	1902	0441	1928
05	0725	1658	0709	1731	0632	1803	0544	1834	0503	1903	0441	1929
06	0725	1658	0708	1732	0631	1804	0542	1835	0502	1904	0441	1929
07	0725	1659	0707	1734	0629	1805	0541	1836	0501	1905	0440	1930
08	0725	1700	0706	1735	0627	1806	0539	1837	0500	1906	0440	1930
09	0725	1701	0705	1736	0626	1807	0538	1838	0459	1907	0440	1931
10	0725	1702	0704	1737	0624	1808	0536	1839	0458	1908	0440	1931
11	0725	1703	0703	1738	0623	1809	0535	1840	0457	1909	0440	1932
12	0724	1704	0702	1739	0621	1810	0533	1841	0456	1909	0440	1932
13	0724	1705	0700	1740	0620	1811	0532	1842	0455	1910	0440	1933
14	0724	1706	0659	1742	0618	1812	0530	1843	0454	1911	0440	1933
15	0723	1707	0658	1743	0617	1813	0529	1844	0453	1912	0440	1933
16	0723	1708	0657	1744	0615	1814	0527	1845	0452	1913	0440	1934
17	0723	1710	0656	1745	0614	1815	0526	1846	0451	1914	0440	1934
18	0722	1711	0654	1746	0612	1816	0525	1846	0450	1915	0440	1934
19	0722	1712	0653	1747	0610	1817	0523	1847	0450	1916	0440	1935
20	0721	1713	0652	1748	0609	1818	0522	1848	0449	1917	0441	1935
21	0721	1714	0650	1749	0607	1819	0520	1849	0448	1917	0441	1935
22	0720	1715	0649	1751	0606	1820	0519	1850	0448	1918	0441	1935
23	0720	1716	0648	1752	0604	1821	0518	1851	0447	1919	0441	1935
24	0719	1717	0646	1753	0603	1822	0516	1852	0446	1920	0442	1935
25	0718	1719	0645	1754	0601	1823	0515	1853	0446	1921	0442	1936
26	0718	1720	0644	1755	0559	1824	0514	1854	0445	1922	0442	1936
27	0717	1721	0642	1756	0558	1825	0513	1855	0444	1922	0443	1936
28	0716	1722	0641	1757	0556	1826	0511	1856	0444	1923	0443	1936
29	0715	1723	0639	1758	0555	1827	0510	1857	0443	1924	0443	1936
30	0715	1724	-------	-------	0553	1828	0509	1858	0443	1925	0444	1936
31	0714	1725	-------	-------	0552	1829	-------	-------	0443	1925	-------	-------

Sunrise 2004 Sunset

Annapolis, Maryland • Location: W076 30, N38 58

EASTERN STANDARD TIME • 0000 IS MIDNIGHT, 1200 IS NOON

ADD ONE HOUR FOR DAYLIGHT TIME.

Day	JULY Rise h m	JULY Set h m	AUGUST Rise h m	AUGUST Set h m	SEPTEMBER Rise h m	SEPTEMBER Set h m	OCTOBER Rise h m	OCTOBER Set h m	NOVEMBER Rise h m	NOVEMBER Set h m	DECEMBER Rise h m	DECEMBER Set h m
01	0444	1935	0507	1917	0535	1836	0602	1748	0634	1705	0706	1644
02	0445	1935	0508	1916	0536	1834	0603	1746	0635	1704	0707	1644
03	0445	1935	0509	1915	0537	1833	0604	1745	0636	1703	0708	1644
04	0446	1935	0510	1914	0538	1831	0605	1743	0637	1702	0709	1644
05	0446	1935	0511	1912	0539	1830	0606	1742	0638	1701	0710	164
06	0447	1934	0512	1911	0540	1828	0607	1740	0639	1700	0711	1644
07	0448	1934	0513	1910	0541	1826	0608	1739	0640	1659	0712	1644
08	0448	1934	0513	1909	0541	1825	0609	1737	0642	1658	0713	1644
09	0449	1933	0514	1908	0542	1823	0610	1736	0643	1657	0713	1644
10	0450	1933	0515	1907	0543	1822	0611	1734	0644	1656	0714	1644
11	0450	1933	0516	1905	0544	1820	0612	1733	0645	1655	0715	1644
12	0451	1932	0517	1904	0545	1818	0613	1731	0646	1654	0716	1644
13	0452	1932	0518	1903	0546	1817	0614	1730	0647	1653	0717	1644
14	0452	1931	0519	1902	0547	1815	0615	1728	0648	1653	0717	1645
15	0453	1931	0520	1900	0548	1814	0616	1727	0649	1652	0718	1645
16	0454	1930	0521	1859	0549	1812	0617	1725	0650	1651	0719	1645
17	0455	1929	0522	1858	0550	1810	0618	1724	0652	1650	0719	1646
18	0455	1929	0523	1856	0550	1809	0619	1723	0653	1650	0720	1646
19	0456	1928	0523	1855	0551	1807	0620	1721	0654	1649	0720	1646
20	0457	1927	0524	1853	0552	1806	0621	1720	0655	1648	0721	1647
21	0458	1927	0525	1852	0553	1804	0622	1719	0656	1648	0721	1647
22	0459	1926	0526	1851	0554	1802	0623	1717	0657	1647	0722	1648
23	0459	1925	0527	1849	0555	1801	0624	1716	0658	1647	0722	1648
24	0500	1924	0528	1848	0556	1759	0625	1715	0659	1646	0723	1649
25	0501	1923	0529	1846	0557	1758	0626	1713	0700	1646	0723	1650
26	0502	1923	0530	1845	0558	1756	0627	1712	0701	1646	0724	1650
27	0503	1922	0531	1843	0559	1754	0628	1711	0702	1645	0724	1651
28	0504	1921	0532	1842	0600	1753	0629	1710	0703	1645	0724	1652
29	0504	1920	0533	1840	0600	1751	0631	1708	0704	1645	0724	1652
30	0505	1919	0533	1839	0601	1750	0632	1707	0705	1644	0725	1653
31	0506	1918	0534	1837	-------	-------	0633	1706	-------	-------	0725	1654

In 2004 Daylight Time begins April 4 and ends October 31.

Moonrise 2004 Moonset

Annapolis, Maryland · Location: W076 30, N38 58

EASTERN STANDARD TIME · 0000 IS MIDNIGHT, 1200 IS NOON

ADD ONE HOUR FOR DAYLIGHT TIME.

Day	JANUARY Rise h m	Set h m	FEBRUARY Rise h m	Set h m	MARCH Rise h m	Set h m	APRIL Rise h m	Set h m	MAY Rise h m	Set h m	JUNE Rise h m	Set h m
01	1300	0156	1305	0347	1232	0329	1425	0410	1529	0332	1800	0319
02	1325	0256	1351	0444	1329	0419	1533	0440	1639	0356	1920	0356
03	1355	0356	1444	0538	1432	0502	1642	0506	1753	0423	2038	0444
04	1429	0456	1544	0625	1538	0540	1752	0532	1910	0452	2146	0543
05	1510	0556	1648	0706	1645	0612	1904	0557	2030	0526	2243	0652
06	1558	0653	1754	0742	1754	0640	2019	0625	2148	0608	2327	0807
07	1654	0744	1901	0812	1902	0706	2136	0656	2300	0700	--------	0923
08	1755	0829	2008	0839	2012	0732	2253	0732	--------	0802	0002	1035
09	1859	0908	2115	0904	2123	0757	--------	0817	0002	0912	0031	1144
10	2004	0941	2223	0929	2236	0825	0007	0911	0051	1025	0055	1248
11	2110	1009	2333	0955	2351	0857	0112	1014	0129	1137	0118	1351
12	2216	1035	--------	1023	--------	0935	0207	1124	0201	1246	0140	1452
13	2322	1100	0045	1056	0105	1021	0251	1236	0227	1352	0203	1554
14	--------	1125	0159	1136	0215	1118	0327	1346	0251	1455	0228	1655
15	0031	1151	0313	1226	0316	1223	0356	1454	0313	1557	0257	1757
16	0142	1221	0421	1326	0408	1333	0422	1559	0335	1659	0330	1857
17	0256	1257	0521	1435	0450	1445	0445	1702	0358	1800	0409	1954
18	0413	1342	0611	1548	0524	1556	0507	1805	0424	1902	0455	2046
19	0527	1437	0651	1702	0552	1704	0530	1907	0454	2004	0548	2131
20	0635	1543	0724	1813	0617	1810	0554	2009	0529	2104	0646	2209
21	0733	1657	0751	1921	0641	1914	0622	2112	0611	2159	0748	2242
22	0819	1812	0816	2026	0704	2017	0653	2213	0659	2249	0851	2310
23	0856	1925	0839	2129	0727	2119	0730	2311	0754	2332	0954	2335
24	0926	2034	0902	2231	0753	2221	0814	--------	0853	--------	1058	2359
25	0952	2140	0926	2333	0822	2323	0905	0005	0956	0008	1203	
26	1016	2243	0953	--------	0855		1002	0053	1059	0040	1309	0022
27	1039	2344	1024	0034	0935	0023	1103	0134	1204	0107	1419	0047
28	1102	--------	1059	0135	1021	0120	1208	0209	1310	0132	1533	0115
29	1126	0045	1142	0234	1115	0212	1313	0239	1417	0157	1651	0148
30	1154	0146	--------	--------	1215	0257	1420	0306	1527	0221	1810	0229
31	1227	0246	--------	--------	1319	0337	--------	--------	1641	0248	--------	--------

Day	JULY Rise h m	JULY Set h m	AUGUST Rise h m	AUGUST Set h m	SEPTEMBER Rise h m	SEPTEMBER Set h m	OCTOBER Rise h m	OCTOBER Set h m	NOVEMBER Rise h m	NOVEMBER Set h m	DECEMBER Rise h m	DECEMBER Set h m
01	1923	0322	2026	0549	2009	0813	1926	0912	2001	1105	2044	1114
02	2027	0427	2056	0705	2033	0919	1958	1016	2055	1155	2146	1147
03	2118	0541	2122	0817	2059	1023	2035	1119	2154	1239	2248	1215
04	2158	0659	2146	0926	2128	1128	2119	1219	2256	1315	2351	1239
05	2230	0816	2209	1031	2202	1231	2210	1314	2359	1346	-------	1302
06	2257	0928	2233	1135	2241	1332	2306	1401	-------	1413	0054	1325
07	2321	1036	2300	1238	2328	1429	-------	1442	0102	1438	0159	1348
08	2344	1141	2330	1341	-------	1521	0007	1517	0207	1501	0307	1414
09	-------	1244	-------	1442	0021	1606	0111	1547	0312	1524	0419	1444
10	0007	1346	0005	1542	0120	1645	0215	1613	0420	1549	0536	1522
11	0031	1448	0047	1637	0222	1718	0320	1637	0532	1618	0655	1611
12	0059	1550	0136	1726	0327	1746	0426	1700	0648	1652	0811	1711
13	0130	1650	0232	1809	0432	1811	0533	1725	0806	1734	0919	1823
14	0208	1749	0332	1846	0537	1835	0643	1751	0923	1828	1013	1941
15	0252	1842	0435	1917	0643	1858	0756	1821	1034	1932	1056	2059
16	0343	1929	0540	1944	0750	1923	0911	1858	1133	2045	1130	2213
17	0440	2010	0644	2008	0859	1950	1027	1943	1221	2200	1158	2324
18	0541	2044	0748	2031	1011	2021	1140	2039	1258	2314	1223	-------
19	0644	2114	0853	2054	1125	2059	1244	2144	1329	-------	1246	0030
20	0748	2140	0959	2119	1238	2147	1338	2256	1355	0025	1309	0135
21	0851	2203	1108	2147	1348	2245	1421	-------	1418	0132	1333	0239
22	0955	2226	1220	2220	1448	2353	1456	0010	1441	0238	1400	0342
23	1100	2250	1333	2301	1539	-------	1525	0123	1504	0342	1431	0446
24	1207	2316	1447	2352	1620	0106	1550	0233	1529	0446	1507	0549
25	1317	2345	1555	-------	1653	0221	1613	0340	1557	0550	1550	0649
26	1431	-------	1654	0055	1721	0335	1636	0446	1630	0654	1641	0744
27	1547	0022	1743	0207	1746	0446	1700	0551	1709	0757	1737	0832
28	1701	0107	1822	0324	1810	0554	1726	0656	1754	0856	1837	0913
29	1809	0205	1854	0440	1834	0701	1756	0801	1847	0949	1938	0948
30	1905	0314	1921	0554	1859	0806	1831	0906	1944	1035	2040	1017
31	1950	0431	1946	0705	-------	-------	1913	1007	-------	-------	2141	1042

CURRENT TERMS

CURRENT SET: The direction toward which the current is flowing. For example, if the current is flowing from the east toward the west it is referred to as "westerly". This example would result in a set of 180 degrees.

DRIFT: The speed of the current. This is generally specified in knots to the nearest tenth. For example: 1.4 knots.

SPEED: The rate the current is moving.

FLOOD TIDAL CURRENTS: Those currents flowing from the sea towards the shore.

EBB TIDAL CURRENTS: Those currents flowing from the shore towards the sea.

SLACK WATER: The time at which the current stops flowing just prior to reversing direction.

MAXIMUM CURRENT: The top speed of the current under normal conditions. This may be given in terms of maximum speed at ebb or at flood. Speed is generally given in knots under "normal" conditions. Weather conditions may have an effect on current speed. The more extreme the weather conditions the greater the possible effect on current speed.

DRIFT & SET: This term refers to the effect the movement of the current has on a vessel afloat. The navigator's course correction depends upon both the set (direction of the current) and the drift (speed of the current). ⚓

A Basic Primer on Tides and Currents

Understanding tides and currents is of great importance to the cruising mariner.

The differences between currents and tides are sometimes a point of confusion for boaters. To put it simply, currents flow horizontally as opposed to tides, which move vertically.

Currents have a significant affect on the mariner because they are both directional and variable. The direction and speed of the current at one single location may be quite different from that of a location only several thousand yards from that point.

On the other hand, an ebbing tide (outgoing tide) generally flows at a constant rate over a specific time period. More simply put, as the tide continues to fall the depth of the water under the keel recedes and as the tide rises the depth of the water under the keel increases.

Tide Tables are stated in terms of specific locations called Reference Stations. Typical examples of Reference Stations for this area are: Boston, Bridgeport, and Sandy Hook. Once the tide at a specific reference station is located you may use the appropriate published time difference tables to calculate the times of high and low water in a specific area.

The tide tables published in The Northeast Boaters Almanac are corrected to take into account the time change resulting in Daylight Savings Time unless otherwise noted. Tide tables published elsewhere may or may not include this feature, so be certain when calculating tidal information that corrections for Daylight Savings Time are considered.

In wider bays the current may have a minimal effect, while in more narrow areas the tidal currents may play a much more important role.

Then there is Tidal Current! This term is used to describe the horizontal flow of waters (current) from one place to another which results from different tidal heights at both places.

A perfect example of areas where both tides and currents are of prime concern are Hell Gate and The Bay of Fundy, where large tide differentials contribute to stronger currents and swift flowing tides.

The combination of wind, tide and current can also have an effect on the cruising mariner. As an example: when the tide is running directly opposite from the direction from which a strong wind is coming and the currents are swirling, the result can be a heavy chop causing uncomfortable, and sometimes even dangerous, conditions.

Both the sun and the moon dictate tidal heights. Each month when the moon is NEW (lined up as Sun, Moon, Earth), and when the moon is FULL (lined up as Sun, Earth, Moon), you can count on greater than average tidal ranges called "Spring Tides" – having nothing to do with the season of Spring! ⚓

WHY ARE TIDE MEASUREMENTS AVERAGED OVER A 19 YEAR PERIOD?

The tidal range at any given place varies from month to month and year to year depending on the gravitational effects of the sun. The positions of the sun in relation to the earth repeat in 19 year cycles.

TIDAL TERMS

DIURNAL TIDES: One single high water and one single low water each day.

SEMI-DIURNAL TIDES: Two high water and two low water marks each taking place in approximately a twenty-four hour period.

HIGH TIDE: (High Water) – The highest level reached by a rising tide on a given day.

LOW TIDE: (Low Water)- The lowest level reached by a falling tide on a given day.

TIDAL RANGE: The difference between the high water and low water marks.

MEAN LOW WATER: (MLW)-The average height of all low water marks over a 19 year period.

MEAN LOWER LOW WATER: (MLLW) – The average height of the lower low waters of a 19 year period.

MEAN HIGH WATER: (MHW) – The average height of all high water marks over a 19 year period. Measurement used for bridge clearances.

MEAN HIGHER HIGH WATER: (MHHW)– The average height of the higher high waters over a 19 year period.

TIDAL DATUM: Also known on the chart as Chart Datum, this information provides information to the mariner regarding water levels based upon a previous 19 year period. Height of Tide – Not to be confused with water depth, this is the vertical measurement between the surface of the water and the tidal datum.

MEAN SEA LEVEL: The average height of the sea surface for all tidal stages.

STAND: The point when vertical movement ceases, not to be confused with 'slack water.'

TIDE CHARTS: A series of maps showing the water levels through out a bay or estuary at a particular point in time. These maps normally show the water levels on an hourly basis after high tide and are generally available for only a limited number of locations around the United States.

LUNITIDAL INTERVAL: The average time difference between the time the moon passes over the local or Greenwich meridian and the following high or low tide. ⚓

Timeline for trash to decompose in the marine environment:

Glass bottles . . . . .1 million years

Monofiliment fishing line . . . . .600 years

Plastic beverage bottles . . . . .450 years

Disposable diapers . . . . .450 years

Aluminum cans . . . . .80 to 100 years

Foamed plastic buoy . . . . .80 years

Rubber boot sole . . . . .50 to 80 years

Leather . . . . .50 years

Nylon fabric . . . . .30 to 40 years

Plastic film canister . . . . .20 to 30 years

Plastic bag . . . . .10 to 20 years

Cigarette filter . . . . .1 to 5 years

Wool sock . . . . .1 to 3 years

Plywood . . . . .1 to 3 years

Waxed milk carton . . . . .3 months

Apple core . . . . .2 months

Newspaper . . . . .6 weeks

Orange or banana peel . . . . .2 to 5 weeks

Paper towel . . . . .2 to 4 weeks

Sea-borne trash and plastic is deadly to marine life.

Whales, dolphins, turtles and seabirds have died
from ingesting or getting tangled in all types of common plastic products:

Balloons • Six-pack holders
Strapping and packing materials • Fishing lines and nets

Debris eaten by marine life will clog the digestive tract, causing starvation.
Sea turtles mistake plastic bags for jellyfish, and birds eat bits of styrofoam.
When fish, turtles, and birds ingest plastic and other debris,
it blocks their intestines and they die a painful slow death.
Plastic debris is like a silent time bomb, waiting to kill marine life.
Plastic persists in the environment – when it does break down it only breaks down into is smaller
and smaller pieces, which are increasingly attractive to smaller and younger sea life,
as are cigarette butts carelessly thrown overboard!

Information source: National Park Service; Mote Marine Lab, Sarasota, FL

tides and currents

HIGH WATER TIME DIFFERENCES & MEAN RANGE OF TIDE

LOCATIION USE THIS CHART WITH DAILY TIDE TABLES IN THE FOLLOWING SECTION	HIGHWATER TIME DIFFERENCE	MEAN RANGE
Use Boston Tide Tables		
Us Atlantic Coast Maine (Based on Boston Tide Tables)		
Eastport	- 0 25	18.4
Gleason Cove, Western Passage	- 0 16	18.4
St Croix River (Based on Boston Tide Tables)		
Roberinson	- 0 17	19.2
St Croix Island	- 0 18	19.6
Cobscook Bay (Based on Boston Tide Tables)		
Deep Cove Moose Island	- 0 16	18.7
East Bay	- 0 10	19.1
Coffins Point	+0 09	18.3
Birch Islands	+0 41	17.6
Horand Head, South Bay	- 0 06	19.2
Lubec	- 0 27	17.5
West Quoddy Head	- 0 33	15.7
Moose Cove	- 0 34	14.8
Cutler , Little River	- 0 35	13.5
Cutler, Naval Radio Station	- 0 31	12.8
Stone Island, Machias Bay	- 0 36	12.4
Machiasport, Machias River	- 0 24	12.6
Shoppee Point, Englishman Bay	- 0 30	12.1
Steele Harbor Island	- 0 38	11.6
Jonesport, Moosabec Reach	- 0 33	11.5
Gibbs Island, Pleasant River	- 0 30	11.3
Addison, Pleasant River	- 0 10	11.8
Trafton Island, Narraquaqus Bay	- 0 33	11.1
Milbridge, Narraquaqus River	- 0 30	11.3
Pigon Hill	- 0 33	11.1
Green Island Petit Manan Bar	- 0 40	10.6
Pinkham Bay, Dyer Bay	- 0 35	10.9
Garden Point, Goulsboro Bay	- 0 35	10.8
Corea Harbor	- 0 37	10.5
Prospect Harbor	- 0 36	10.5
Frenchman Bay (Based on Boston Tide Tables)		
White Harbor	- 0 35	10.1
Eastern Point Harbor	- 0 32	10.5
Sullivan	- 0 22	10.5
Mount Desert Narrows	- 0 20	10.5
Mount Desert Island (Based on Boston Tide Tables)		
Salsbury Cove	- 0 27	10.6
Bar Harbor	- 0 34	10.6
Southwest Harbor	- 0 34	10.2
Bass Harbor	- 0 03	9.9
Pretty Marsh Harbor	- 0 25	10.2
Mount Desert	- 0 28	10.6
Blue Hill Bay (Based on Boston Tide Tables)		
Union River	- 0 21	10.4
Blue Hill Harbor	- 0 25	10.1
Allen Cove	- 0 24	10.3
Mackerel Cove	- 0 32	10.0
Burnt Coat Harbor, Swan Island	- 0 35	9.5
Penobscot Bay Eqqemoqqin Reach (Based on Boston Tide Tables)		
Naskeaq Harbor	- 0 28	10.2
Center Harbor	- 0 25	10.1
Sedqwick	- 0 23	10.2
Little Deer Isle	- 0 18	10.0
Isle Au Haut	- 0 18	10.0
Head Harbor, Isle Au Haut	- 0 32	9.1
Kimball Island	- 0 32	9.6

HIGH WATER TIME DIFFERENCES & MEAN RANGE OF TIDE

LOCATIION USE THIS CHART WITH DAILY TIDE TABLES IN THE FOLLOWING SECTION	HIGHWATER TIME DIFFERENCE	MEAN RANGE
Oceanville, Deer Isle	- 0 30	10.1
Stonington, Deer Isle	- 0 26	9.7
Northwest Harbor, Deer Isle	- 0 24	10.1
Matinicus Harbor	- 0 29	9.0
Vinalhaven,vinalhaven Isle	- 0 25	9.3
North Haven Island	- 0 20	9.9
Castine	- 0 19	10.1
Pumpkin Island, South Bay	- 0 01	10.3
Penobscot River (Based on Boston Tide Tables)		
Fort Point	- 0 18	10.3
Gross Pont, Eastern Channel	- 0 40	10.4
Bucksport	- 0 38	10.8
Winterport	- 0 37	11.7
South Orrington	- 0 11	12.3
Hampden	- 0 10	12.8
Bangor	- 0 42	13.5
Belfast	- 0 22	10.2
Camden	- 0 24	9.6
Rockland	- 0 20	9.3
Owls Head	- 0 28	9.4
Dyer Point, Weskeaq River	- 0 22	9.6
Maine Outer Coast (Based on Boston Tide Tables)		
Tenants Harbor	- 0 23	9.3
Monhegan Island	- 0 25	8.8
Burnt Island, Georges Island	- 0 25	8.9
St George River (Based on Boston Tide Tables)		
Port Clyde	- 0 23	8.9
New Harbor, Musconqus Bay	- 0 22	8.8
Musconqus Harbor, Musconqus Sound	- 0 21	9.0
Friendship Harbor	- 0 30	9.0
Medomak River (Based on Boston Tide Tables)		
Jones Neck	- 0 22	9.1
Waldoboro	- 0 28	9.5
Pemaquid Harbor, Johns Bay	- 0 17	8.8
Damariscotta River (Based on Boston Tide Tables)		
East Boothbay	- 0 14	8.9
Newcastle	+0 04	9.3
Damaiscove Harbor	- 0 21	8.8
Boothbay Harbor	- 0 18	8.8
Southport, Townsend Gut	- 0 11	8.9
Sheepscot River (Based on Boston Tide Tables)		
Isle of Springs	- 0 14	8.9
Cross River Entrance	- 0 05	9.1
Wiscasset	+0 04	9.4
Sheepscot	+0 08	9.6
Kennebec River (Based on Boston Tide Tables)		
Fort Propham	- 0 03	7.7
Phippsburg	+0 14	8.0
Bath	+0 49	6.4
Sturgen Island	+1 48	5.3
Richmond	+2 36	5.3
Nehumkeaq Island	+3 09	5.3
Gardiner	+3 31	5.0
Hallowell	+3 41	4.3
Augusta	+3 50	4.1
Casco Bay (Based on Boston Tide Tables)		
Small Point	- 0 24	8.8

HIGH WATER TIME DIFFERENCES & MEAN RANGE OF TIDE

LOCATIION USE THIS CHART WITH DAILY TIDE TABLES IN THE FOLLOWING SECTION	HIGHWATER TIME DIFFERENCE	MEAN RANGE
Cundy Harbor, New Meadows River	- 0 13	8.9
Harbor Point New Meadows River	- 0 17	9.0
Lowell Cove, Orrs Island	- 0 19	8.8
Harpswell Harbor	- 0 17	9.0
South Harpswell, Potts Harbor	- 0 10	8.9
Wilson Cove, Middle Bay	- 0 10	9.1
Little Flying Point, Maquoit Bay	- 0 13	9.0
South Freeport	0 00	9.0
Chebeaque Point	- 0 16	9.0
Prince Point	- 0 12	9.2
Doyle Point	- 0 14	9.2
Falmouth Foreside	- 0 11	9.1
Great Chebeaqe Island	- 0 09	9.1
Cliff Island Luckse Sound	- 0 14	9.1
Vaill Island	- 0 07	9.0
Lond Island	- 0 13	9.1
Cow Island	- 0 13	9.1
Presumpscot River Bridge	- 0 11	9.2
Back Cove	- 0 10	9.1
Great Diamond Island	- 0 13	9.0
Peaks Island	- 0 16	9.0
Cushing Island	- 0 11	9.0
Portland	- 0 12	9.1
Fore River	- 0 10	9.1
Portland Head Light	- 0 14	8.9
Maine Outer Coast *(Based on Boston Tide Tables)*		
Richmond Island	- 0 15	8.9
Old Orchard Beach	- 0 13	8.8
Wood Island Harbor	- 0 10	8.7
Cape Porpoise	0 00	8.7
Kennebunkport	+0 04	8.6
York Harbor	- 0 09	8.6
Seapoint, Cutts Island	- 0 11	8.8
Maine & New Hampshire Portsmouth Harbor *(Based on Boston Tide Tables)*		
Jaffrey Point	- 0 15	8.7
Gerrish Island	- 0 14	8.7
Fort Point	- 0 09	8.6
Kittery Point	- 0 19	8.1
Seavey Island	+0 08	8.1
Portsmouth	+0 10	7.8
Piscataqua River *(Based on Boston Tide Tables)*		
Atlantic Heights	+0 25	7.5
Dover Point	+1 21	6.4
Salmon Falls River	+1 23	6.8
Squamscott River Rr Bridge	+2 08	6.8
Gosport Harbor, Isles of Shoals	- 0 10	8.5
Hampton Harbor	+0 02	8.3
Massachusetts Outer Coast *(Based on Boston Tide Tables)*		
Merrimack River	+0 08	8.3
Newburyport Merrimack River	+0 19	7.8
Plum Island Sound	0 00	8.6
Annisquam	- 0 12	8.7
Rockport	- 0 08	8.6
Gloucester Harbor	- 0 01	8.7
Charles River *(Based on Boston Tide Tables)*		
Charlestown Bridge	+0 04	9.5
Charles River Dam	+0 07	9.5
Charlestown	0 00	9.5
Chelsea St. Bridge, Chelsea River	+0 01	9.6
Neponset River	- 0 02	9.4

HIGH WATER TIME DIFFERENCES & MEAN RANGE OF TIDE

LOCATIION USE THIS CHART WITH DAILY TIDE TABLES IN THE FOLLOWING SECTION	HIGHWATER TIME DIFFERENCE	MEAN RANGE
Moon Head	+0 01	9.6
Rainsford Island, Nantasket Roads	0 00	9.1
Hingham Bay *(Based on Boston Tide Tables)*		
Nut Island	+0 09	9.2
Sheep Island	+0 09	9.5
Weymouth Fore River Bridge	+0 09	9.5
Crow Point, Hingham Harbor	+0 02	9.4
Hingham	+0 09	9.5
Natasket Beach, Weir River	+0 06	9.4
Strawberry Hill	+0 07	9.5
Hull	+0 05	9.3
Cohasset Harbor to Davis Bank *(Based on Boston Tide Tables)*		
Cohasset Harbor, White Head	+0 04	8.8
Scituate	- 0 03	8.8
Damons Point, North River	+0 20	8.5
Cape Cod Bay *(Based on Boston Tide Tables)*		
Gurnet Point	+0 04	9.2
Plymoutth	+0 07	9.5
Cape Cod Canal East Entrance	- 0 05	8.7
Cape Cod Canal Sagamore	- 0 11	7.9
Cape Cod Canal Bourne	- 0 22	6.2
Barnstable Harbor, Beach Point	+0 11	9.5
Wellfleet	+0 14	10.0
Provincetown	+0 16	9.1
Race Point	- 0 01	9.0
Cape Cod *(Based on Boston Tide Tables)*		
Cape Cod Lighthouse	+0 12	7.6
Nauset Harbor	+0 32	6.0
Chatham Outer Coast	+0 32	6.0
Chatham (Inside)	+1 56	3.6
Pleasant Bay	+2 28	3.2
Monomoy Point	+0 42	3.7
Georges Shoal	- 0 47	4.2
Davis Bank, Nantucket Shoals	+0 06	1.3
Nantucket Sound North Side *(Based on Boston Tide Tables)*		
Stage Harbor	+0 57	3.9
Wychmere Harbor	+0 52	3.7
Dennis Port	+1 03	3.4
South Yarmouth, Bass River	+1 48	2.8
Hyannis Port	+1 03	3.1
Cotuit Highlands	+1 17	2.5
Poponesset Island & Bay	+2 03	2.3
Succonnesset Point	+0 54	2.3
Falmouth Heights	- 0 16	1.3
Nantucket Island *(Based on Boston Tide Tables)*		
Tom Nevers Head	- 0 55	1.2
Sasconset	+0 17	1.2
Wauwinet (Outer Shore)	+1 08	3.3
Great Point	+0 43	3.1
Nantucket, Nantucket Island	+1 11	3.6
Eel Point	+0 39	2.3
Tuckermuck Island East Pond	+0 46	2.6
Museqet Island (North Side)	+0 25	2.0
Miacomet Rid	- 3 20	1.7
Martha's Vineyard *(Based on Boston Tide Tables)*		
Wasque Point, Chappaquiddick	- 1 33	1.1
Off Jobs Neck Pond	- 3 34	2.7
Off Chilmark Pond	- 3 51	2.9

HIGH WATER TIME DIFFERENCES & MEAN RANGE OF TIDE

LOCATIION USE THIS CHART WITH DAILY TIDE TABLES IN THE FOLLOWING SECTION	HIGHWATER TIME DIFFERENCE	MEAN RANGE
Saquibnocket Point	- 4 20	2.9
Nomans Land	- 3 54	3.0
Gay Head	- 3 41	2.9
Menemsha Bight	- 3 33	2.7
Cedar Tree Neck	- 3 25	2.0
Off Lake Tashmoo	- 2 27	2.0
West Chop	+0 18	1.4
Vinyard Haven	+0 27	1.7
East Chop	+0 29	1.7
Oak Bluffs	+0 32	1.7
Edgartown	+0 57	1.9
Cape Porqe, Chappaquiddick	+0 46	2.2

Vineyard Sound   *(Based on Boston Tide Tables)*

Nobska Point	- 2 54	1.5

Woods Hole   *(Based on Boston Tide Tables)*

Little Harbor	- 3 03	1.4
Oceangraphic Institution	- 3 13	1.8
Uncatena Island	- 3 23	3.6
Trapaulin Cove	- 3 24	1.9

Quicks Hole   *(Based on Boston Tide Tables)*

South Side	- 3 45	2.5
Middle	- 3 35	3.0
Northside	- 3 47	3.5

Buzzards Bay   *(Based on Boston Tide Tables)*

Cuttyhunk Pond	- 3 34	3.4
Penikese Island	- 3 52	3.4
Kettle Cove	- 3 26	3.8
Chappaquoit Point, West Falmouth	- 3 25	3.9
West Falmouth Harbor	- 3 12	4.0
Barlows Landing, Pocasset Harbor	- 3 15	4.0
Abiels Ledge	- 3 24	3.9
Monument Beach	- 3 14	4.0
Cape Cod Canal, Rr Bridge	- 3 22	3.5
Great Hill	- 3 23	4.0
Wareham, Wareham River	- 3 13	4.1
Bird Island	- 3 30	4.2
Marion, Sippican Harbor	- 3 25	4.0
Mattapoisett, Mattapoisett Harbor	- 3 24	3.9
West Island	- 3 26	3.7
Clarks Point	- 3 21	3.6
New Bedford	- 3 28	3.7
Belleville, Acushnet River	- 3 28	3.7
South Dartmouth, Apponaqandsett Bay	- 3 14	3.7
Dumpling Rocks	- 3 34	3.7

Westport River   *(Based on Boston Tide Tables)*

Westport Harbor	- 3 26	3.0
Hixbrodge, East Branch	- 1 55	2.7

Use Bridgeport Connecticut Tide Tables

Rhode Island Narraqansett Bay   *(Based on Bridgeport Connecticut Tide Tables)*

Sakonnet	- 3 44	3.1
Anthony Point, Sakonnet River	- 3 33	3.8
Beavertail	- 3 36	3.5
Castle Hill	- 3 36	3.3
Newport Rhode Island	- 3 35	3.5
Cananicut Point	- 3 24	3.8
Prudence Island	- 3 33	3.8
Bristol Point	- 3 13	4.0
Bristol Highlands	- 3 23	4.2

HIGH WATER TIME DIFFERENCES & MEAN RANGE OF TIDE

LOCATIION USE THIS CHART WITH DAILY TIDE TABLES IN THE FOLLOWING SECTION	HIGHWATER TIME DIFFERENCE	MEAN RANGE
Bristol Ferry	- 3 11	4.1
Fall River State Pier	- 3 14	4.4

Rhode Island & Massachusetts   Narransett Bay
(Based on Bridgeport Connecticut Tide Tables)

Fall River Massachusetts	- 3 03	4.4
Tauton, Tauton River Ma	- 2 25	2.8
Bristol, Bristol Harbor	- 3 08	4.1
Warren	- 3 13	4.6
Nayatt Point	- 3 22	4.6
Providence State Pier	- 3 20	4.5

Rhode Island Outer Coast   *(Based on Bridgeport Connecticut Tide Tables)*

Point Judith Harbor of Refuge	- 3 41	3.1
Block Island Great South Pond	- 3 33	2.6
Block Island Old Harbor	- 3 57	2.9
Watch Hill Point	- 2 50	2.6
Westerly, Pawcatuck River	- 2 03	2.6

Connecticut, Long Island Sound
(Based on Bridgeport Connecticut Tide Tables)

Stonington, Fishers Island Sound	- 2 14	2.7
Noank, Mystic River	- 2 02	2.3
West Harbor Fisher Island NY	- 1 40	2.5
Silver Eel Pond, Fisher Island NY	- 1 56	2.3

Thames River   *(Based on Bridgeport Connecticut Tide Tables)*

New London State Pier	- 1 40	2.6
Smith Cove Entrance	- 1 40	2.5
Norwich	- 1 29	3.0
Millstone Point	- 1 33	2.7

Connecticut River   *(Based on Bridgeport Connecticut Tide Tables)*

Saybrook Jetty	- 0 31	3.5
Saybrook Point	- 0 31	3.2
Lyme, Highway Bridge	- 0 17	3.1
Essex	- 0 03	3.0
Hadlyme	+0 36	2.7
East Haddam	+1 00	2.9
Haddam	+1 06	2.5
Higganum Creek	+1 13	2.6
Portland	+2 09	2.2
Rocky Hill	+3 02	2.0
Hartford	+3 48	1.9
Westbrook, Duck Island Roads	- 0 24	4.1
Duck Island	- 0 26	4.5
Madison	- 0 21	4.9
Falkner Island	- 0 14	54.
Sachem Head	- 0 11	5.4
Money Island	- 0 12	5.6
Branford Harbor	- 0 08	5.9
New Haven Harbor	- 0 09	6.2
New Haven City Dock	- 0 01	6.0
Milford Harbor	- 0 08	6.6
Stratford, Houstonic River	+0 26	5.5
Shelton Houstonic River	+1 25	5.0
Saugatuck River Entrance	- 0 02	7.0
South Norwalk	+0 09	7.1
Greens Ledge	- 0 02	7.2
Stamford	+0 03	7.2
Cos Cob Harbor	+0 05	7.2
Greenwich	+0 01	7.4
Great Captain Island	0 00	7.3

HIGH WATER TIME DIFFERENCES & MEAN RANGE OF TIDE

LOCATIION USE THIS CHART WITH DAILY TIDE TABLES IN THE FOLLOWING SECTION	HIGHWATER TIME DIFFERENCE	MEAN RANGE
New York Long Island Sound Northside		
Based on Bridgeport Connecticut Tide Tables)		
Portchester	- 0 11	7.2
Rye Beach	- 0 30	7.2
Mamaroneck	- 0 10	7.3
New Rochelle	- 0 26	7.3
Davids Island	- 0 04	7.2
City Island	- 0 05	7.2
Throgs Neck	0 00	7.0
East River *(Based on Bridgeport Connecticut Tide Tables)*		
Whitestone	- 0 04	7.1
Old Ferry Point	+0 02	7.1
College Point Flushing Bay	+0 06	6.8
Norhtern Blvd Bridge	+0 21	6.8
Westchester, Westchester Creek	+0 08	7.0
Hunts Point	+0 03	6.9
Westchester Ave Bridge, Bronx River	+0 08	6.9
North Brother Island	+0 07	6.6
Port Morris Stony Point	- 0 04	6.3
Lawrence Point	- 0 05	6.4
Wollott Ave	- 0 05	6.4
Hell Gate Wards Island	- 0 04	6.0
Hell Gate Hallets Point	- 1 02	5.1
Horns Hook East 90th Street	- 1 10	4.7
Roosevelt Island North End	- 1 13	4.3
37th Ave L.i.c.	- 2 00	4.3
East 41st Street NYC	- 2 00	4.3
Hunters Point Newtown Creek	- 1 40	4.1
E27th Street Bellevue Hospital	- 1 50	4.2
E19th Street NYC	- 1 56	4.1
North 3rd Street Brooklyn	- 2 03	4.1
Williamsburg Bridge	- 2 06	4.1
Wallabout Bay	- 2 30	4.3
Brooklyn Bridge	- 2 45	4.3
Harlem River *(Based on Bridgeport Connecticut Tide Tables)*		
East 110th Street NYC	- 1 06	5.1
Randalls Island	- 1 20	5.1
Madison Ave Bridge	- 1 06	4.6
Central Bridge	- 1 06	4.7
Washington Bridge	- 1 06	4.4
University Heights Bridge	- 1 18	4.0
Broadway Bridge	- 1 38	3.8
Long Island Sound South Side *(Based on Bridgeport Connecticut Tide Tables)*		
Willets Point	- 0 08	7.1
Hewlett Point	- 0 05	7.1
Port Washington, Manhasset Bay	- 0 03	7.3
Execution Rocks	- 0 08	7.3
Glen Cove, Hempstead Harbor	- 0 13	7.3
Oyster Bay *(Based on Bridgeport Connecticut Tide Tables)*		
Oyster Bay Harbor	+0 07	7.3
Bayville Bridge	+0 12	7.4
Cold Spring Harbor	+0 07	7.4
Eatons Neck Point	+0 02	7.1
Lloyd Harbor, Huntington Bay	+0 07	7.4
Northport, Northport Bay	+0 02	7.3
Nissegodque River Entrance	- 0 04	7.0
Stony Brook, Smithtown Bay	+0 07	6.1
Stratford Shoal	- 0 06	6.6
Port Jefferson Harbor Entrance	+0 02	6.6
Port Jefferson	+0 06	6.6
Setauket Harbor	+0 03	6.7
Conscience Bay	+0 01	6.7

HIGH WATER TIME DIFFERENCES & MEAN RANGE OF TIDE

LOCATIION USE THIS CHART WITH DAILY TIDE TABLES IN THE FOLLOWING SECTION	HIGHWATER TIME DIFFERENCE	MEAN RANGE
Mount Sinai Harbor	+0 04	6.0
Herod Point	- 0 08	5.9
Northville	- 0 03	5.4
Mattituck Inlet	+0 04	5.2
Horton Point	- 0 21	4.0
Hashamomuck Beach	+0 03	4.2
Truman Beach	- 0 43	3.4
Plum Gulf Harbor, Plum Island	- 1 14	2.6
Little Gull Island	- 1 29	2.2
Shelter Island Sound *(Based on Bridgeport Connecticut Tide Tables)*		
Orient	- 1 05	2.5
Greenport	- 0 37	2.4
Southold	+0 02	2.3
Noyack Bay	+0 24	2.3
Sag Harbor	- 0 42	2.5
Cedar Point	+0 03	2.5
Peconic Bays *(Based on Bridgeport Connecticut Tide Tables)*		
New Suffolk	+0 45	2.6
South Jamesport	+0 51	2.7
Shinnecock Canal	+0 52	2.7
Three Mile Harobr	- 1 20	2.4
Promise Land	- 1 57	2.3
Montauk Harbor	- 2 06	1.9
Montauk Fort Pond Bay	- 2 12	2.1
Montauk Point North Side	- 3 47	2.5
Use Sandy Hook NJ Tide Tables		
Peconic Bays *(Based on Sandy Hook NJ Tide Tables)*		
Shinnecock Inlet Ocean	- 0 51	2.9
Ponquogue Bridge	+0 28	2.3
Pontunk Point, Moriches Bay	+3 34	0.5
Moriches Inlet	+0 57	2.9
Mastic Beach	+3 27	0.5
Fire Island Breakwater	- 0 40	4.1
Democrat Point Fire Isladn Inlet	- 0 39	2.6
Great South Bay *(Based on Sandy Hook NJ Tide Tables)*		
Fire Island Coast Guard Station	- 0 20	1.9
Fire Island Radiobeacon	+0 46	0.7
West Fire Island	+2 08	0.6
Point O'woods	+2 25	0.7
Bellport	+3 43	0.8
Patchogue	+3 22	0.7
Sayville Browns River	+3 38	0.6
Great River Connetquot River	+3 19	0.7
Bayshore Watchoque Creek	+2 07	1.0
Oakbeach	+2 23	0.7
Bablyon	+2 11	0.6
Gilgo	+2 22	1.1
Amityville	+2 20	1.2
Biltmore Shores, South Oyster Bay	+2 04	1.4
Jones Inlet Point Lookout	- 0 20	3.6
Hempstead Bay *(Based on Sandy Hook NJ Tide Tables)*		
Deep Creek Meadow	+1 00	2.4
Green Island	+1 21	1.9
Cuba Island	+1 07	2.3
Bellmore Creek	+1 28	2.0
Neds Creek	+1 49	2.7
Freeport Creek	+0 33	3.1
Freeport Baldwin Bay	+0 37	3.0
Long Beach	+0 10	3.9

HIGH WATER TIME DIFFERENCES & MEAN RANGE OF TIDE

LOCATIION USE THIS CHART WITH DAILY TIDE TABLES IN THE FOLLOWING SECTION	HIGHWATER TIME DIFFERENCE	MEAN RANGE
Long Beach Outer Coast	- 0 30	4.5
East Rockaway	+0 41	3.9
Woodmere, Brosenere Bay	+0 34	3.9
East Rockaway Inlet	- 0 07	4.1
Jamaica Bay *(Based on Sandy Hook NJ Tide Tables)*		
Plumb Beach Channel	+0 02	4.9
Barren Island, Rockaway Inlet	- 0 01	5.0
Beach Channel Bridge	+0 37	5.1
Motts Basin	+0 39	5.1
Norton Point	+0 38	5.4
Jfk International Airport	+0 25	5.3
Grassy Bay Bridge	+0 43	5.2
Canarsie	+0 27	5.2
Mill Basin	+0 28	5.2
New York & New Jersey		
New York Harbor *(Based on Sandy Hook NJ Tide Tables)*		
Coney Island	- 0 04	4.7
Norton Point	- 0 01	4.7
Fort Wadsworth	+0 06	4.8
Fort Hamilton	+0 02	4.7
Bay Ridge	+0 10	4.6
St George Island	+0 13	4.5
Gowanus Bay	+0 23	4.4
Governors Island	+0 23	4.4
New York the Battery	+0 30	4.6
Hudson River *(Based on Sandy Hook NJ Tide Tables)*		
Jersey City	+0 41	4.4
New York Desbrosses Street	+0 44	4.4
NY Chelsea Docks	+0 51	4.3
Hoboken, Castle Point NJ	+0 51	4.3
Weehawken NJ	+0 43	4.4
NY Union Stock Yards	+1 01	4.2
Edgewater NJ	+0 43	4.4
NY 130th Street	+1 11	4.0
George Washington Bridge	+1 20	3.9
Spuyten Duyvil Creek	+1 22	3.9
Riverdale NY	+1 18	3.9
Alpine NJ	+1 35	3.8
Dobbs Ferry	+2 03	3.4
Tarrytown	+2 19	3.2
Ossining	+2 27	3.1
Haverstraw	+2 33	2.9
Peekskill	+2 58	2.9
West Point	+2 50	2.7
Newburgh	+3 16	2.8
New Hamburg	+3 34	2.9
Poughkeepsie	+3 04	3.1
Hyde Park	+4 50	3.7
Kingston Point	+4 50	3.7
Tivoli	+5 20	3.9
Catskill	+6 11	4.1
Hudson	+6 28	4.0
Coxsackie	+7 25	3.9
New Baltimore	+7 52	4.1
Albany	+8 26	4.6
Troy	+8 34	4.7
The Kills & Newark Bay Kill Van Kull *(Based on Sandy Hook NJ Tide Tables)*		
Constable Hook	+0 12	4.6
Bayonne Bridge	+0 22	5.0
Port Elizabeth	+0 28	5.1
Port Newark Terminal	+0 33	5.1

HIGH WATER TIME DIFFERENCES & MEAN RANGE OF TIDE

LOCATIION USE THIS CHART WITH DAILY TIDE TABLES IN THE FOLLOWING SECTION	HIGHWATER TIME DIFFERENCE	MEAN RANGE
Passaic River *(Based on Sandy Hook NJ Tide Tables)*		
Kearny Point	+0 30	5.2
Bellville	+0 34	5.5
Passaic	+0 35	5.7
Hackensack River		
Kearny Point	+0 38	5.2
Amtrack Rr Bridge	+1 04	5.3
Fish Creek	+1 32	5.3
Ridgefield Park	+1 30	5.7
Hackensack	+1 35	5.9
New Millford	+1 49	4.7
Arthur Kill *(Based on Sandy Hook NJ Tide Tables)*		
Port Ivory	+0 27	5.1
Rahway River	+0 17	5.3
Chelsea	+0 23	5.0
Carteret	+0 22	5.1
Rossville	+0 14	5.2
Woodbridge Creek	+0 08	5.2
Tottenville	+0 02	5.3
Perth Amboy	+0 12	5.2
Lower NY Bay *(Based on Sandy Hook NJ Tide Tables)*		
New Drop Beach	- 0 05	4.9
Great Kills Harbor	+0 06	4.7
Princess Bay	.0 00	4.9
Atlantic Highland	- 0 10	4.7
Shrewsbury River		
Highlands	+0 16	4.7
Oceanic Bridge	+1 13	3.4
Sea Bright	+1 15	3.2
Gooseneck Point Bridge	+2 18	2.6
Outer Coast *(Based on Sandy Hook NJ Tide Tables)*		
Long Branch	- 0 26	4.4
Asbury Park	- 0 35	4.3
Shark River *(Based on Sandy Hook NJ Tide Tables)*		
Inlet Entrance	- 0 19	4.0
Shark River Island Rr Bridge	- 0 25	4.3
Shark River Hills	- 0 25	4.4
New Bedford	- 0 25	4.4
Belmar	- 0 35	4.4
Sea Girt	- 0 35	4.3
Manasquan Inlet	- 0 25	4.0
Barnegat Bay *(Based on Sandy Hook NJ Tide Tables)*		
Matoloking	+4 28	0.3
Kettle Creek, Green Island	+4 23	0.4
Ocean Beach	+4 17	0.4
Silver Bay	+4 26	0.4
Goose Creek Entrance	+4 06	0.4
Coates Point	+4 00	0.4
Toms River	+4 02	0.4
Seaside Park	+3 40	0.4
Barnegat Pier, Sloop Creek	+3 35	0.3
Forked River	+3 08	0.3
Oyster Creek	+3 30	0.3
Waretown	+2 43	0.3
Barnegat Inlet	- 0 11	2.4
High Bar	+1 04	0.5
Double Creek	+2 03	0.3
Loveladies Harbor	+2 02	0.5

45

HIGH WATER TIME DIFFERENCES & MEAN RANGE OF TIDE

LOCATIION USE THIS CHART WITH DAILY TIDE TABLES IN THE FOLLOWING SECTION	HIGHWATER TIME DIFFERENCE	MEAN RANGE
Manahawkin Bay *(Based on Sandy Hook NJ Tide Tables)*		
Flat Creek	+3 33	0.8
North Beach	+3 02	1.0
Manahawkin Creek	+2 50	1.3
Manahawkin Bridge	+2 47	1.3
Little Egg Harbor *(Based on Sandy Hook NJ Tide Tables)*		
Mill Creek	+2 32	1.6
Cedar Run	+2 10	1.9
Beach Haven Crest	+2 05	1.9
Westecunk Creek	+1 55	2.0
West Creek	+2 05	2.1
Beach Haven	+1 12	2.2
Great Bay *(Based on Sandy Hook NJ Tide Tables)*		
Little Egg Inlet	+0 16	3.4
Little Sheepshead Creek	+0 30	3.2
Seven Islands	+0 32	3.4
Graveling Point	+0 38	3.2
Mullica River *(Based on Sandy Hook NJ Tide Tables)*		
New Gretna, Bass River	+1 47	3.1
Wading River	+2 43	3.0
Green Bank	+2 59	3.0
Sweetwater	+3 23	2.4
Brigantine Channel	+0 31	3.7
Absecon Creek	+0 59	3.9
Atlantic City Ocean	- 0 27	4.0
Atlantic City Steel Pier	- 0 31	
Ventor City Ocean Pier	- 0 30	4.1
Longport Inside Great Egg Harbor Inlet	- 0 02	3.9
Pleasantville Great Egg Harbor Inlet	+0 32	4.0
Great Egg Harbor Bay *(Based on Sandy Hook NJ Tide Tables)*		
Beesley's Point	+0 28	3.6
Tuckahoe	+1 45	3.5
Cedar Swamp Creek	+2 49	3.0
May's Landing	+2 22	4.1
Corson Inlet *(Based on Sandy Hook NJ Tide Tables)*		
Strathmere Bay	+0 03	3.9
Middle Thorofare, Ocean Drive Bridge	+0 03	4.0
Ludlam Bay	+0 28	4.0
Townsend's Inlet *(Based on Sandy Hook NJ Tide Tables)*		
Ocean Drive Bridge	+0 07	3.9
Townsend Sound	+0 40	3.8
Stites Sound & Long Reach	+0 40	4.0
Ingram Thorofare	+0 17	4.0
Hereford Inlet *(Based on Sandy Hook NJ Tide Tables)*		
Stone Harbor, Great Channel	+0 34	4.0
Nummy Island	+0 05	4.0
West Wildwood	+0 30	4.3
Wildwood Crest Ocean Pier	- 0 24	4.4
Cape May Inlet *(Based on Sandy Hook NJ Tide Tables)*		
Swain Channel Taylor Sound	+0 28	4.5
Wildwood Crest Sunset Lake	+0 25	4.5
Cape May Harbor	+0 06	4.5
Cape Island Creek	+0 13	4.5
Cape May Atlantic Ocean	+0 07	4.6

HIGH WATER TIME DIFFERENCES & MEAN RANGE OF TIDE

LOCATIION USE THIS CHART WITH DAILY TIDE TABLES IN THE FOLLOWING SECTION	HIGHWATER TIME DIFFERENCE	MEAN RANGE
Use Breakwater Harbor, DE Tide Tables		
DELAWARE BAY & RIVER Eastern Shore *Based on Breakwater Harbor Tide Tables)*		
Brandywine Shoal Light	+0 00	6.0
Cape May Point, Sunset Light	-0 05	5.7
Cape May Ferry Terminal	-0 09	5.8
North Highlands Beach	+0 04	6.1
Dias Creek Rte. 47 Bridge	+1 09	2.2
Bidwell Creek entrance	+0 15	6.8
Bidwell Creek Rte. 47 Bridge	+0 36	6.7
Dennis Crek 2.5 nm above ent.	+0 55	6.2
Sluice Creek Rte. 47 Bridge	+1 49	6.0
Dennis Creek Rte. 47 Bridge	+2 01	5.9
East Creek Rte. 47 Bridge	+1 46	4.6
West Creek 0.7 nm above ent.	+0 20	5.3
West Creek Rte. 47 Bridge	+2 20	2.8
Riggins Ditch .05 nm above ent.	+0.29	6.0
Riggins Ditch, Heislerville	+1 36	5.5
East Point, Maurice River Cove	+0 40	6.8
MAURICE RIVER		
Bivalve	+0 39	6.6
Mauricetown	+2 17	5.1
Port Elizabeth Manumuskin River	+2 52	5.1
Manantico Creek entrance	+3 06	5.4
Millville	+3 33	6.8
DIVIDING CREEK		
Entrance	+0 29	6.6
Weir Creek Bridge	+1 38	3.5
Dividing Creek Town	+3 07	⸺
Use Reedy Point, DE Tide Tables		
Based on Reedy Point Tide Tables)		
Fishing Creek Entrance	-1 51	6.1
Fortescue	-1 51	
Hollywood Beach, The Glades	+1 45	1.3
Money Island , Nantunxent Creek ent.	-1 43	6.6
Newport Landing, Nantuxent Creek	-0 03	4.4
Cedar Creek Ent. Nantuxent Cove	-1 37	6.5
Husted Landing, Ogden Creek, Back Creek	-0 47	
Greenwich Pier, Cohansey River	-0 42	6.0
Tindalls Wharf, Cohansey River	+1 01	6.5
Use Breakwater Harbor, DE Tide Tables		
DELAWARE BAY Western Shore *Based on Breakwater Harbor Tide Tables)*		
Cape Henelopen	-0 10	4.9
BREAKWATER HARBOR use daily predictions tide tables		4.9
Roosevelt Inlet	+0 04	5.2
Use Reedy Point, DE Tide Tables		
DELAWARE RIVER, DE, NJ & PA *Based on Reedy Point Tide Tables)*		
Liston Point, DE	-0 55	6.4
Hope Creek 6 mi. above entr. NJ	-0 25	6.3
Hope Creek upper end NJ	+0 49	
Taylors Bridge Blackbird Creek, DE	+1 47	3.3
Artificial Island Salem Nuclear Plant, NJ	-0 35	6.5
Alloway Creek, NJ		
.08 nm above entrance	+0 21	5.9
Abbotts Meadow	+0 44	5.6
2.5 nm above entrance	+0 51	5.4
Coopers Creek Bridge	+1 51	4.7
Quinton	+2 24	4.1
Alloway	+3 37	

HIGH WATER TIME DIFFERENCES & MEAN RANGE OF TIDE

LOCATIION — USE THIS CHART WITH DAILY TIDE TABLES IN THE FOLLOWING SECTION	HIGHWATER TIME DIFFERENCE	MEAN RANGE
Use Reedy Point, DE Tide Tables		
Mill Creek, Elsenboro, NJ	-0 04	
SALEM RIVER, NJ		
Sinnickson Landing	+0 04	5.8
Salem	+0 49	4.6
Kates Creek Meadow	+1 54	——
Winslow Farms	+2 09	
Beaver Dam	+2 32	
REEDY POINT, DE ...... use daily predictions tide tables		6.0
CHESAPEAKE AND DELAWARE (C&D) CANAL		
St. Georges, DE	-0 13	4.8
Summit Bridge, DE	-0 34	3.9
Chesapeake City, MD	-0 40	3.0
Delaware City Branch Ch. Bridge, DE	+0 03	6.0
Pea Patch Island, blukhead Schl Ch, DE	+0 06	6.1
Mill Creek, Penns Neck, NJ	0 08	——
New Castle, DE	+0 32	5.7
Salem Canal Entrance, NJ	+0 36	6.0
CHRISTINA RIVER, DE		
Wilmington Marine Terminal	+0 53	5.7
Millside RR Bridge	+1 11	5.8
Edgemoor, DE	+0 55	6.0
Pedricktown, Oldmans Creek	+2 11	4.5
Auburn, Oldmans Creek	+4.24	2.5
Use Philadelphia, PA Tide Tables		
Marcus Hook, PA	-1 29	5.9
Bridgeport, Racoon Creek, NJ	-1 13	6.0
Swedesboro, Racoon Creek, NJ	+0 34	——
DARBY CREEK, PA		
Wanamaker Bridge	-1 47	5.9
Norwood City	-0 39	5.6
Tinicum National Wildlife Refuge	-0 28	5.8
Tinicum National Wildlife Refuge Center	-0 26	——
Billingsport, NJ	-0 4 1	5.9
Paulsboro, Mantua Creek, NJ	-0 25	5.9
Mantua, Mantua Creek	+1 28	4.4
Woodbury Creek, NJ	-0 19	6.1
SCHUYLKILL RIVER, PA		
Penrose Bridge	-0 28	6.1
Market Street Bridge	-0 26	6.3
Westville Big Timber Creek,Nj	-0 04	6.8
Sunset Beach Big Timber Creek, NJ	+1 26	
PHILADELPHIA Municipal Pier 11, PA ...... use daily predictions tide tables		6.5
Pavonia Cooper River Railroad Bridge, NJ	-0 08	6.6
Philadelphia Bridesburg, PA	+0 11	6.8
Palmyra Pennsauken Creek, Rte. 73, Nj	+0 49	5.5
Cinnaminson Pensauken Creek	+1 31	
Pompeston Creek	+0 19	6.7
Bridgesboro Rancocas Creek, NJ	+1 09	6.7
North Branch Rancocas Creek, NJ	+2 52	3.0
Hainesport South Branch Rancocas Creek, NJ	+2 52	3.9
Cornwells Heights, PA	+0 40	7.4
Burlington, NJ	+0 41	7.6
Assiscunk Creek, Rte. 30 Bridge, NJ	+1 04	7.1
Edgely, PA	+1 02	8.1
Fieldsboro, NJ	+1 01	8.3
Blacks Creek, Rte. 130 Bridge, NJ	+1 07	——
Crosswicks Creek, Rte. 130 Bridge, NJ	+3 01	——
Trenton, NJ	+1 12	8.5

HIGH WATER TIME DIFFERENCES & MEAN RANGE OF TIDE

LOCATIION USE THIS CHART WITH DAILY TIDE TABLES IN THE FOLLOWING SECTION	HIGHWATER TIME DIFFERENCE	MEAN RANGE

Use Baltimore Tide Tables

CHESAPEAKE BAY Eastern Shore, MD

LITTLE CHOPTANK RIVER

Location	Time Diff	Mean Range
Taylors Island, Slaughter Creek	-3 05	1.4
Woolford, Church Creek	-3 21	1.6
Cherry Island, Beckwith Creek	-3 17	1.5
Hudson Creek	3 45	1.6
Sharps Island Light	-3 47	1.5

CHOPTANK RIVER

Location	Time Diff	Mean Range
Choptank River Light	-3 13	1.6
Cambridge	-2 44	1.7
Choptank	-2 09	1.8
Dover Bridge	-0 34	1.9
Denton	+0 17	2.5
Greensboro	+1 22	2.9
Wayman Wharf, Tuckahoe Creek	+0 57	2.8

TRED AVON RIVER

Location	Time Diff	Mean Range
Oxford	-3 01	1.6
Easton Point	-2 55	1.7
Deep Neck Point, Broad Creek	-3 06	1.6
St. Michaels, San Domingo Creek	-3 04	1.6
Avalon, Dogwood Harbor	-3 04	1.5
Poplar Island	-3 08	1.3
Ferry Cove, Eastern Bay	-2 57	1.2
Claiborne, Eastern Bay	-2 36	1.3
St. Michaels, Miles River	-2 14	1.4
Wye Landing, Wye East River	-2 01	1.5
Kent Island Narrows	-1 40	1.1
Matapeake, Kent Island	-1 29	1.3
Bloody Point Bar Light	-2 42	1.3
Kent Point Marina	-2 32	1.2

CHESTER RIVER

Location	Time Diff	Mean Range
Love Point	-0 26	1.3
Queenstown	-0 04	1.5
Shipyard Landing, Langford Creek	+0 18	1.7
Centreville Landing, Corsica River	+0 10	1.8
Cliffs Point	+0 02	1.7
Chestertown	+0 47	2.1
Deep Landing, Swan Creek	-0 08	1.3
Tolchester	+0 28	1.4
Worton Creek Entrance	+1 11	1.5
Sassafras River Entrance, Betterton		

ELK RIVER

Location	Time Diff	Mean Range
Town Point Wharf	+3 17	2.4
Courthouse Point	+2 53	2.5
C&D Canal (see Delaware River)		
Old Frenchtown Wharf	+3 04	2.6
Charlestown, Northeast River	+3 42	2.2

CHESAPEAKE BAY Western Shore, MD

SUSQUEHANNA RIVER

Location	Time Diff	Mean Range
Havre de Grace	+3 11	1.9
Port Deposit	+4 04	2.4
Fishing Battery Light	+2 33	2.4
Pond Point	+1 37	1.6
Pooles Island	+0 55	1.4
Battery Point Gunpowder River	+1 04	1.4
Bowley Bar, Middle River	+0 51	1.4
Seven Foot Knoll Light	-0 06	1.1
Rocky Point Back River	+0 46	1.2

HIGH WATER TIME DIFFERENCES & MEAN RANGE OF TIDE

LOCATIION	USE THIS CHART WITH DAILY TIDE TABLES IN THE FOLLOWING SECTION	HIGHWATER TIME DIFFERENCE	MEAN RANGE
PATAPSCO RIVER			
North Point		+0 02	1.2
BALTIMORE Fort McHenry	use daily predictions tide tables		1.3
Fells Point		+0 09	1.3
Middle Branch		+0 26	1.2
	Use Annapolis Tide Tables		
Mountain Point, Magothy River		+1 24	1.0
Sandy Point		+0 17	0.9
Greenbury Point Shoal Light		-0 08	0.9
SEVERN RIVER			
Cedar Point		+0 51	0.8
Brewer Point		+0 38	0.9
Annapolis	use daily predictions tide tables		1.1
Thomas Point Shoal Light		-0 26	1.0
Edgewater, South River		-0 23	1.0
Rhode River County Wharf		-0 26	1.1
Galesville, West River		-0 10	1.0
Fairhaven, Herring Bay		-1 17	1.0
Rose Haven, Herrington Harbor		-1 09	1.0
Chesapeake Beach		-1 14	1.1
Long Beach		-2 32	1.2
Cove Point		-2 27	1.5
PATUXENT RIVER			
Drum Point		-3 13	1.4
Solomons island		-3 07	1.3

NOTES:

Boston, Massachusetts, 2004

Times and Heights of High and Low Waters

April

Day	Time	Height (ft)	Height (cm)
1 Th	0135	1.9	58
	0751	9.3	283
	1413	1.0	30
	2029	8.7	265
2 F	0227	1.3	40
	0842	9.7	296
	1459	0.6	18
	2114	9.3	283
3 Sa	0316	0.7	21
	0929	10.1	308
	1543	0.1	3
	2156	9.9	302
4 Su	0502	0.0	0
	1115	10.5	320
	1726	−0.3	−9
	2337	10.5	320
5 M ○	0548	−0.6	−18
	1200	10.7	326
	1808	−0.5	−15
6 Tu	0018	11.1	338
	0633	−1.1	−34
	1245	10.8	329
	1852	−0.6	−18
7 W	0101	11.4	347
	0720	−1.3	−40
	1332	10.7	326
	1937	−0.5	−15
8 Th	0145	11.5	351
	0809	−1.3	−40
	1421	10.4	317
	2024	−0.2	−6
9 F	0234	11.5	351
	0900	−1.1	−34
	1514	10.0	305
	2115	0.2	6
10 Sa	0326	11.2	341
	0955	−0.7	−21
	1611	9.5	290
	2210	0.7	21
11 Su	0424	10.7	326
	1055	−0.2	−6
	1713	9.1	277
	2311	1.1	34
12 M ○	0527	10.3	314
	1159	0.2	6
	1820	8.9	271
13 Tu	0017	1.3	40
	0636	10.0	305
	1306	0.4	12
	1929	8.9	271
14 W	0125	1.3	40
	0746	9.9	302
	1412	0.5	15
	2034	9.2	280
15 Th	0232	1.1	34
	0852	9.9	302
	1511	0.4	12
	2132	9.5	290
16 F	0332	0.7	21
	0951	10.0	305
	1604	0.3	9
	2222	9.9	302
17 Sa	0426	0.3	9
	1043	10.1	308
	1650	0.3	9
	2306	10.2	311
18 Su	0513	0.0	0
	1129	10.1	308
	1731	0.3	9
	2345	10.4	317
19 M ●	0556	−0.1	−3
	1211	10.0	305
	1810	0.5	15
20 Tu	0022	10.4	317
	0637	−0.2	−6
	1251	9.8	299
	1848	0.7	21
21 W	0059	10.4	317
	0716	−0.1	−3
	1330	9.5	290
	1926	1.0	30
22 Th	0135	10.2	311
	0756	0.1	3
	1410	9.2	280
	2005	1.3	40
23 F	0213	10.0	305
	0836	0.4	12
	1451	8.9	271
	2045	1.6	49
24 Sa	0254	9.7	296
	0919	0.8	24
	1534	8.6	262
	2129	1.9	58
25 Su	0338	9.4	287
	1005	1.1	34
	1622	8.3	253
	2216	2.2	67
26 M	0427	9.2	280
	1055	1.4	43
	1713	8.1	247
	2308	2.4	73
27 Tu ○	0520	9.0	274
	1148	1.5	46
	1807	8.1	247
28 W	0003	2.4	73
	0616	8.9	271
	1242	1.5	46
	1901	8.3	253
29 Th	0101	2.2	67
	0713	9.1	277
	1336	1.3	40
	1954	8.7	265
30 F	0157	1.7	52
	0809	9.3	283
	1428	1.0	30
	2043	9.2	280

May

Day	Time	Height (ft)	Height (cm)
1 Sa	0251	1.1	34
	0902	9.7	296
	1517	0.6	18
	2130	9.9	302
2 Su	0343	0.4	12
	0954	10.0	305
	1604	0.2	6
	2216	10.6	323
3 M	0433	−0.3	−9
	1043	10.4	317
	1651	−0.1	−3
	2301	11.2	341
4 Tu ○	0522	−1.0	−30
	1133	10.6	323
	1737	−0.3	−9
	2347	11.7	357
5 W	0611	−1.4	−43
	1223	10.7	326
	1825	−0.4	−12
6 Th	0034	12.0	366
	0700	−1.6	−49
	1313	10.6	323
	1914	−0.3	−9
7 F	0123	12.0	366
	0752	−1.6	−49
	1406	10.4	317
	2005	0.0	0
8 Sa	0216	11.8	360
	0845	−1.3	−40
	1501	10.0	305
	2059	0.3	9
9 Su	0311	11.4	347
	0941	−0.8	−24
	1600	9.7	296
	2156	0.7	21
10 M	0411	10.9	332
	1041	−0.3	−9
	1702	9.4	287
	2258	1.4	34
11 Tu ○	0515	10.4	317
	1143	0.1	3
	1807	9.3	283
12 W ○	0003	1.3	40
	0622	10.0	305
	1246	0.5	15
	1911	9.4	287
13 Th	0110	1.3	40
	0729	9.7	296
	1347	0.6	18
	2011	9.6	293
14 F	0215	1.1	34
	0833	9.6	293
	1444	0.7	21
	2105	9.8	299
15 Sa	0314	0.8	24
	0930	9.5	290
	1534	0.8	24
	2153	10.0	305
16 Su	0406	0.5	15
	1021	9.5	290
	1620	0.9	27
	2236	10.2	311
17 M	0452	0.3	9
	1107	9.4	287
	1701	1.0	30
	2316	10.3	314
18 Tu	0534	0.2	6
	1149	9.4	287
	1741	1.2	37
	2353	10.3	314
19 W ●	0614	0.1	3
	1229	9.2	280
	1819	1.3	40
20 Th	0030	10.3	314
	0653	0.2	6
	1308	9.1	277
	1858	1.5	46
21 F	0108	10.2	311
	0732	0.3	9
	1347	8.9	271
	1938	1.6	49
22 Sa	0147	10.0	305
	0812	0.5	15
	1427	8.8	268
	2018	1.8	55
23 Su	0228	9.8	299
	0854	0.7	21
	1510	8.6	262
	2102	2.0	61
24 M	0311	9.6	293
	0937	0.9	27
	1554	8.5	259
	2147	2.1	64
25 Tu	0357	9.4	287
	1023	1.1	34
	1641	8.5	259
	2237	2.1	64
26 W	0447	9.3	283
	1112	1.1	34
	1730	8.6	262
	2329	2.1	64
27 Th ○	0539	9.2	280
	1202	1.1	34
	1820	8.9	271
28 F	0025	1.8	55
	0634	9.2	280
	1253	1.0	30
	1910	9.3	283
29 Sa	0121	1.4	43
	0729	9.4	287
	1345	0.8	24
	2000	9.8	299
30 Su	0217	0.8	24
	0825	9.6	293
	1436	0.6	18
	2049	10.4	317
31 M	0311	0.1	3
	0920	9.8	299
	1528	0.3	9
	2139	11.1	338

June

Day	Time	Height (ft)	Height (cm)
1 Tu	0405	−0.6	−18
	1015	10.1	308
	1619	0.1	3
	2229	11.6	354
2 W	0457	−1.1	−34
	1109	10.2	311
	1710	−0.1	−3
	2320	12.0	366
3 Th ○	0550	−1.5	−46
	1202	10.4	317
	1801	−0.2	−6
4 F	0012	12.2	372
	0643	−1.7	−52
	1257	10.4	317
	1854	−0.1	−3
5 Sa	0106	12.1	369
	0736	−1.6	−49
	1352	10.3	314
	1948	0.0	0
6 Su	0201	11.9	363
	0830	−1.3	−40
	1448	10.1	308
	2043	0.2	6
7 M	0258	11.5	351
	0925	−0.9	−27
	1546	9.9	302
	2141	0.5	15
8 Tu	0357	11.0	335
	1022	−0.4	−12
	1645	9.8	299
	2242	0.8	24
9 W ●	0459	10.4	317
	1120	0.1	3
	1744	9.7	296
	2344	1.0	30
10 Th	0601	9.9	302
	1218	0.5	15
	1842	9.7	296
11 F	0048	1.1	34
	0704	9.5	290
	1314	0.9	27
	1938	9.8	299
12 Sa	0150	1.1	34
	0805	9.2	280
	1409	1.1	34
	2031	9.8	299
13 Su	0248	0.9	27
	0902	9.0	274
	1459	1.3	40
	2119	9.9	302
14 M	0341	0.6	18
	0954	8.9	271
	1546	1.5	46
	2204	10.0	305
15 Tu	0428	0.6	18
	1042	8.8	268
	1630	1.6	49
	2245	10.0	305
16 W	0511	0.5	15
	1125	8.8	268
	1712	1.6	49
	2326	10.1	308
17 Th	0551	0.4	12
	1207	8.8	268
	1752	1.6	49
18 F	0005	10.1	308
	0631	0.4	12
	1246	8.8	268
	1833	1.7	52
19 Sa	0044	10.1	308
	0710	0.4	12
	1326	8.8	268
	1913	1.7	52
20 Su	0124	10.0	305
	0749	0.5	15
	1405	8.7	265
	1954	1.7	52
21 M	0205	10.0	305
	0829	0.5	15
	1445	8.8	268
	2037	1.7	52
22 Tu	0246	9.9	302
	0910	0.6	18
	1526	8.8	268
	2121	1.7	52
23 W	0330	9.7	296
	0953	0.7	21
	1609	8.9	271
	2208	1.6	49
24 Th	0416	9.6	293
	1038	0.9	27
	1654	9.1	277
	2259	1.5	46
25 F ○	0506	9.4	287
	1125	0.8	24
	1741	9.5	290
	2352	1.3	40
26 Sa	0559	9.4	287
	1214	0.8	24
	1830	9.8	299
27 Su	0048	0.9	27
	0655	9.3	283
	1307	0.7	21
	1921	10.3	314
28 M	0146	0.5	15
	0753	9.4	287
	1401	0.6	18
	2014	10.8	329
29 Tu	0243	−0.1	−3
	0852	9.5	290
	1456	0.5	15
	2109	11.2	341
30 W	0341	−0.6	−18
	0950	9.7	296
	1552	0.3	9
	2204	11.6	354

Heights are referred to mean lower low water which is the chart datum of soundings.
All times are local time. Daylight Saving Time has been used when needed.

NOTES:

Boston, Massachusetts, 2004

Times and Heights of High and Low Waters

July

Day	Time (h m)	Height (ft)	Height (cm)		Day	Time (h m)	Height (ft)	Height (cm)
1 Th	0437	-1.1	-34		16 F	0527	0.7	21
	1048	9.9	302			1142	8.6	262
	1647	0.1	3			1727	1.7	52
	2300	11.9	363			2342	10.0	305
2 F ○	0532	-1.4	-43		17 Sa ●	0607	0.5	15
	1145	10.1	308			1222	8.7	265
	1742	-0.1	-3			1808	1.6	49
	2356	12.1	369					
3 Sa	0626	-1.5	-46		18 Su	0023	10.1	308
	1241	10.2	311			0646	0.4	12
	1837	-0.2	-6			1301	8.8	268
						1849	1.4	43
4 Su	0051	12.1	369		19 M	0102	10.2	311
	0720	-1.5	-46			0724	0.3	9
	1336	10.3	314			1339	9.0	274
	1932	-0.1	-3			1930	1.3	40
5 M	0147	11.8	360		20 Tu	0142	10.1	308
	0812	-1.3	-40			0802	0.3	9
	1430	10.3	314			1417	9.1	277
	2027	0.0	0			2012	1.2	37
6 Tu	0242	11.4	347		21 W	0222	10.1	308
	0905	-0.9	-27			0841	0.3	9
	1525	10.2	311			1456	9.3	283
	2122	0.3	9			2055	1.1	34
7 W	0338	10.9	332		22 Th	0304	10.0	305
	0957	-0.4	-12			0922	0.3	9
	1618	10.1	308			1536	9.5	290
	2219	0.6	18			2141	1.0	30
8 Th	0435	10.2	311		23 F	0349	9.8	299
	1050	0.1	3			1005	0.4	12
	1712	9.9	302			1619	9.7	296
	2318	0.8	24			2230	0.9	27
9 F ○	0533	9.6	293		24 Sa	0437	9.6	293
	1143	0.7	21			1051	0.6	18
	1806	9.8	299			1705	10.0	305
						2323	0.7	21
10 Sa	0017	1.0	30		25 Su ○	0530	9.3	283
	0631	9.1	277			1141	0.7	21
	1236	1.2	37			1756	10.2	311
	1859	9.7	296					
11 Su	0117	1.2	37		26 M	0020	0.5	15
	0730	8.7	265			0628	9.2	280
	1329	1.6	49			1236	0.8	24
	1951	9.6	293			1850	10.5	320
12 M	0216	1.2	37		27 Tu	0120	0.3	9
	0828	8.5	259			0728	9.1	277
	1422	1.8	55			1334	0.8	24
	2042	9.6	293			1948	10.8	329
13 Tu	0310	1.1	34		28 W	0221	-0.1	-3
	0923	8.4	256			0831	9.1	277
	1512	1.9	58			1433	0.7	21
	2130	9.7	296			2047	11.1	338
14 W	0400	1.0	30		29 Th	0322	-0.4	-12
	1013	8.4	256			0933	9.3	283
	1559	1.9	58			1532	0.5	15
	2216	9.8	299			2147	11.4	347
15 Th	0445	0.8	24		30 F	0420	-0.8	-24
	1100	8.5	259			1033	9.6	293
	1644	1.8	55			1631	0.2	6
	2300	9.9	302			2246	11.7	357
					31 Sa ○	0516	-1.1	-34
						1130	9.9	302
						1727	-0.1	-3
						2343	11.8	360

August

Day	Time (h m)	Height (ft)	Height (cm)		Day	Time (h m)	Height (ft)	Height (cm)
1 Su	0610	-1.3	-40		16 M ●	0616	0.3	9
	1225	10.2	311			1231	9.2	280
	1822	-0.3	-9			1824	1.0	30
2 M	0038	11.8	360		17 Tu	0037	10.3	314
	0701	-1.3	-40			0654	0.1	3
	1317	10.4	317			1307	9.5	290
	1915	-0.3	-9			1905	0.7	21
3 Tu	0131	11.6	354		18 W	0116	10.3	314
	0750	-1.1	-34			0732	0.0	0
	1407	10.5	320			1344	9.7	296
	2007	-0.2	-6			1947	0.5	15
4 W	0223	11.1	338		19 Th	0157	10.3	314
	0839	-0.7	-21			0811	0.0	0
	1456	10.4	317			1422	10.0	305
	2059	0.0	0			2030	0.4	12
5 Th	0314	10.6	323		20 F	0239	10.1	308
	0926	-0.2	-6			0851	0.1	3
	1545	10.2	311			1502	10.2	311
	2152	0.4	12			2116	0.3	9
6 F	0406	9.9	302		21 Sa	0324	9.9	302
	1015	0.4	12			0935	0.3	9
	1633	10.0	305			1546	10.3	314
	2246	0.7	21			2205	0.3	9
7 Sa ○	0500	9.3	283		22 Su	0414	9.6	293
	1104	1.1	34			1022	0.6	18
	1723	9.7	296			1634	10.4	317
	2341	1.1	34			2259	0.3	9
8 Su	0555	8.7	265		23 M ○	0508	9.2	280
	1155	1.6	49			1115	0.8	24
	1815	9.4	287			1728	10.4	317
						2358	0.3	9
9 M	0039	1.3	40		24 Tu	0608	9.0	274
	0653	8.3	253			1213	1.0	30
	1249	2.0	61			1827	10.5	320
	1909	9.3	283					
10 Tu	0137	1.4	43		25 W	0101	0.3	9
	0752	8.1	247			0712	8.9	271
	1344	2.2	67			1314	1.1	34
	2003	9.2	280			1930	10.6	323
11 W	0235	1.4	43		26 Th	0205	0.1	3
	0849	8.1	247			0818	9.0	274
	1438	2.2	67			1417	0.9	27
	2057	9.3	283			2034	10.8	329
12 Th	0328	1.3	40		27 F	0307	-0.2	-6
	0942	8.2	250			0921	9.2	280
	1529	2.1	64			1519	0.6	18
	2147	9.5	290			2137	11.1	338
13 F	0415	1.0	30		28 Sa	0406	-0.5	-15
	1030	8.4	256			1021	9.6	293
	1616	1.8	55			1618	0.2	6
	2234	9.8	299			2236	11.3	344
14 Sa	0458	0.8	24		29 Su	0501	-0.8	-24
	1113	8.6	262			1116	10.1	308
	1700	1.5	46			1714	-0.1	-3
	2317	10.0	305			2331	11.4	347
15 Su	0538	0.5	15		30 M ○	0551	-0.9	-27
	1153	8.9	271			1206	10.4	317
	1743	1.2	37			1806	-0.4	-12
	2358	10.2	311					
					31 Tu	0023	11.4	347
						0639	-0.9	-27
						1253	10.6	323
						1856	-0.5	-15

September

Day	Time (h m)	Height (ft)	Height (cm)		Day	Time (h m)	Height (ft)	Height (cm)
1 W	0112	11.1	338		16 Th	0049	10.5	320
	0724	-0.6	-18			0700	-0.1	-3
	1339	10.7	326			1309	10.5	320
	1945	-0.4	-12			1921	-0.2	-6
2 Th	0159	10.7	326		17 F	0131	10.4	317
	0808	-0.2	-6			0740	-0.1	-3
	1423	10.5	320			1349	10.7	326
	2033	-0.1	-3			2006	-0.4	-12
3 F	0247	10.2	311		18 Sa	0215	10.2	311
	0852	0.3	9			0822	0.1	3
	1507	10.3	314			1431	10.8	329
	2121	0.3	9			2053	-0.4	-12
4 Sa	0335	9.6	293		19 Su	0303	9.9	302
	0937	0.9	27			0908	0.4	12
	1552	9.9	302			1518	10.8	329
	2210	0.7	21			2144	-0.2	-6
5 Su	0425	9.0	274		20 M	0355	9.5	290
	1024	1.5	46			0959	0.7	21
	1639	9.6	293			1610	10.7	326
	2302	1.1	34			2240	0.0	0
6 M	0518	8.5	259		21 Tu ○	0453	9.1	277
	1115	2.0	61			1055	1.0	30
	1731	9.2	280			1708	10.5	320
	2358	1.5	46			2341	0.2	6
7 Tu	0614	8.1	247		22 W	0556	8.9	271
	1209	2.3	70			1156	1.3	40
	1826	9.0	274			1812	10.3	314
8 W	0056	1.7	52		23 Th	0046	0.3	9
	0713	7.9	241			0702	8.8	268
	1306	2.5	76			1301	1.3	40
	1924	9.0	274			1919	10.3	314
9 Th	0155	1.7	52		24 F	0151	0.3	9
	0812	8.0	244			0809	9.0	274
	1402	2.4	73			1407	1.1	34
	2021	9.1	277			2026	10.5	320
10 F	0250	1.5	46		25 Sa	0254	0.1	3
	0906	8.2	250			0912	9.4	287
	1456	2.1	64			1510	0.7	21
	2114	9.4	287			2128	10.7	326
11 Sa	0339	1.2	37		26 Su	0351	-0.2	-6
	0954	8.5	259			1008	9.9	302
	1546	1.7	52			1608	0.2	6
	2203	9.7	296			2226	10.8	329
12 Su	0423	0.8	24		27 M	0442	-0.4	-12
	1038	8.9	271			1058	10.3	314
	1631	1.3	40			1701	-0.2	-6
	2247	10.0	305			2318	10.9	332
13 M	0503	0.5	15		28 Tu ○	0529	-0.4	-12
	1117	9.3	283			1144	10.6	323
	1714	0.8	24			1750	-0.4	-12
	2328	10.3	314					
14 Tu ●	0542	0.2	6		29 W	0006	10.8	329
	1155	9.8	299			0613	-0.3	-9
	1756	0.4	12			1227	10.8	329
						1837	-0.5	-15
15 W	0009	10.4	317		30 Th	0051	10.5	320
	0621	0.0	0			0655	0.0	0
	1232	10.2	311			1308	10.7	326
	1838	0.0	0			1921	-0.4	-12

Heights are referred to mean lower low water which is the chart datum of soundings.
All times are local time. Daylight Saving Time has been used when needed.

NOTES:

Boston, Massachusetts, 2004
Times and Heights of High and Low Waters

October

Day	Time	ft	cm	Day	Time	ft	cm
1 F	0135	10.2	311	16 Sa	0108	10.4	317
	0737	0.4	12		0711	-0.1	-3
	1348	11.4	320		1319	11.4	347
	2005	-0.1	-3		1944	-1.0	-30
2 Sa	0219	9.7	296	17 Su	0155	10.2	311
	0819	0.8	24		0757	0.1	3
	1429	10.2	311		1406	11.4	347
	2050	0.3	9		2033	-0.9	-27
3 Su	0304	9.2	280	18 M	0246	9.9	302
	0901	1.4	43		0846	0.4	12
	1512	9.9	302		1456	11.2	341
	2136	0.7	21		2127	-0.6	-18
4 M	0351	8.7	265	19 Tu	0341	9.5	290
	0947	1.8	55		0940	0.8	24
	1559	9.5	290		1552	10.9	332
	2225	1.2	37		2224	-0.3	-9
5 Tu	0442	8.3	253	20 W	0441	9.2	280
	1036	2.2	67		1039	1.1	34
	1650	9.1	277		1654	10.5	320
	2318	1.5	46		2326	0.1	3
6 W ○	0536	8.0	244	21 Th	0546	9.0	274
	1130	2.5	76		1143	1.3	40
	1745	8.9	271		1801	10.2	311
7 Th	0015	1.7	52	22 F	0031	0.3	9
	0634	7.9	241		0653	9.0	274
	1227	2.6	79		1251	1.3	40
	1844	8.8	268		1909	10.1	308
8 F	0112	1.7	52	23 Sa	0136	0.3	9
	0732	8.0	244		0758	9.3	283
	1325	2.4	73		1357	1.0	30
	1942	9.0	274		2016	10.1	308
9 Sa	0207	1.6	49	24 Su	0236	0.3	9
	0825	8.3	253		0857	9.7	296
	1420	2.1	64		1500	0.6	18
	2036	9.2	280		2118	10.2	311
10 Su	0256	1.2	37	25 M	0331	0.1	3
	0913	8.8	268		0950	10.1	308
	1512	1.6	49		1556	0.2	6
	2126	9.6	293		2213	10.2	311
11 M	0342	0.8	24	26 Tu	0420	0.1	3
	0957	9.3	283		1037	10.5	320
	1559	1.0	30		1647	-0.1	-3
	2212	9.9	302		2302	10.2	311
12 Tu	0424	0.5	15	27 W	0505	0.2	6
	1037	9.9	302		1120	10.7	326
	1644	0.4	12		1733	-0.3	-9
	2256	10.2	311		2348	10.1	308
13 W	0505	0.1	3	28 Th ○	0547	0.3	9
	1116	10.4	317		1200	10.7	326
	1728	-0.2	-6		1817	-0.4	-12
	2339	10.4	317				
14 Th ●	0546	-0.1	-3	29 F	0031	9.9	302
	1156	10.9	332		0627	0.6	18
	1812	-0.6	-18		1239	10.6	323
					1858	-0.2	-6
15 F	0023	10.5	320	30 Sa	0112	9.6	293
	0628	-0.2	-6		0707	0.9	27
	1236	11.2	341		1317	10.4	317
	1857	-0.9	-27		1940	0.0	0
				31 Su	0153	9.2	280
					0648	1.2	37
					1257	10.1	308
					1921	0.3	9

November

Day	Time	ft	cm	Day	Time	ft	cm
1 M	0136	8.9	271	16 Tu	0131	9.9	302
	0729	1.6	49		0729	0.2	6
	1338	9.8	299		1340	11.5	351
	2005	0.7	21		2011	-1.0	-30
2 Tu	0221	8.5	259	17 W	0228	9.6	293
	0814	2.0	61		0825	0.5	15
	1424	9.5	290		1438	11.0	335
	2051	1.1	34		2109	-0.6	-18
3 W	0309	8.3	253	18 Th	0328	9.4	287
	0901	2.2	67		0925	0.9	27
	1513	9.2	280		1541	10.6	323
	2141	1.4	43		2209	-0.2	-6
4 Th	0400	8.1	247	19 F ○	0432	9.3	283
	0953	2.4	73		1030	1.1	34
	1606	8.9	271		1647	10.1	308
	2234	1.5	46		2312	0.2	6
5 F ○	0454	8.1	247	20 Sa	0536	9.4	287
	1049	2.5	76		1136	1.1	34
	1702	8.8	268		1755	9.8	299
	2327	1.6	49				
6 Sa	0548	8.2	250	21 Su	0013	0.4	12
	1146	2.3	70		0638	9.6	293
	1759	8.9	271		1243	0.9	27
					1900	9.6	293
7 Su	0020	1.4	43	22 M	0112	0.5	15
	0640	8.6	262		0735	9.9	302
	1242	1.9	58		1345	0.6	18
	1853	9.1	277		2001	9.5	290
8 M	0110	1.2	37	23 Tu	0206	0.6	18
	0728	9.1	277		0827	10.1	308
	1334	1.3	40		1441	0.3	9
	1945	9.3	283		2056	9.5	290
9 Tu	0158	0.8	24	24 W	0255	0.7	21
	0813	9.7	296		0913	10.3	314
	1425	0.7	21		1531	0.0	0
	2035	9.6	293		2145	9.4	287
10 W	0244	0.5	15	25 Th	0339	0.8	24
	0856	10.3	314		0955	10.4	317
	1513	0.0	0		1616	-0.1	-3
	2123	9.9	302		2230	9.3	283
11 Th	0328	0.2	6	26 F ○	0421	0.9	27
	0939	10.9	332		1035	10.4	317
	1600	-0.7	-21		1657	-0.1	-3
	2210	10.2	311		2312	9.2	280
12 F	0414	-0.1	-3	27 Sa	0502	1.1	34
	1023	11.4	347		1113	10.4	317
	1647	-1.2	-37		1737	-0.1	-3
	2258	10.3	314		2352	9.1	277
13 Sa	0459	-0.2	-6	28 Su	0541	1.2	37
	1108	11.7	357		1152	10.2	311
	1735	-1.4	-43		1817	0.1	3
	2347	10.3	314				
14 Su	0547	-0.2	-6	29 M	0031	8.9	271
	1156	11.9	363		0621	1.4	43
	1825	-1.5	-46		1231	10.0	305
					1857	0.3	9
15 M	0038	10.1	308	30 Tu	0112	8.7	265
	0636	0.0	0		0702	1.6	49
	1246	11.8	360		1312	9.8	299
	1917	-1.3	-40		1938	0.5	15

December

Day	Time	ft	cm	Day	Time	ft	cm
1 W	0154	8.5	259	16 Th	0212	9.9	302
	0745	1.8	55		0810	0.1	3
	1355	9.6	293		1424	11.1	338
	2021	0.8	24		2050	-0.9	-27
2 Th	0238	8.4	256	17 F	0310	9.8	299
	0831	2.0	61		0909	0.4	12
	1441	9.3	283		1525	10.5	320
	2107	1.0	30		2147	-0.4	-12
3 F	0324	8.3	253	18 Sa ○	0409	9.7	296
	0919	2.1	64		1011	0.7	21
	1530	9.1	277		1627	9.9	302
	2154	1.1	34		2245	0.1	3
4 Sa	0413	8.4	256	19 Su	0509	9.6	293
	1011	2.1	64		1115	0.8	24
	1621	8.9	271		1732	9.4	287
	2243	1.2	37		2343	0.5	15
5 Su ○	0502	8.6	262	20 M	0609	9.7	296
	1106	1.9	58		1221	0.8	24
	1715	8.9	271		1836	9.1	277
	2333	1.1	34				
6 M	0552	8.9	271	21 Tu	0041	0.9	27
	1201	1.6	49		0705	9.7	296
	1810	8.9	271		1324	0.7	21
					1938	8.8	268
7 Tu	0024	1.0	30	22 W	0136	1.1	34
	0641	9.4	287		0758	9.8	299
	1256	1.0	30		1421	0.5	15
	1905	9.0	274		2035	8.7	265
8 W	0115	0.8	24	23 Th	0227	1.2	37
	0729	10.0	305		0847	9.9	302
	1350	0.4	12		1512	0.3	9
	1959	9.3	283		2126	8.7	265
9 Th	0205	0.5	15	24 F	0314	1.3	40
	0818	10.6	323		0932	10.0	305
	1443	-0.3	-9		1557	0.2	6
	2052	9.6	293		2212	8.7	265
10 F	0255	0.2	6	25 Sa	0358	1.3	40
	0906	11.1	338		1013	10.0	305
	1534	-0.9	-27		1639	0.1	3
	2145	9.8	299		2254	8.7	265
11 Sa	0345	0.0	0	26 Su ○	0439	1.3	40
	0956	11.6	354		1053	10.1	308
	1625	-1.4	-43		1718	0.1	3
	2237	10.0	305		2333	8.7	265
12 Su ●	0435	-0.2	-6	27 M	0519	1.3	40
	1048	11.9	363		1132	10.1	308
	1717	-1.7	-52		1757	0.1	3
	2329	10.1	308				
13 M	0527	-0.3	-9	28 Tu	0011	8.7	265
	1138	12.1	369		0559	1.3	40
	1808	-1.8	-55		1211	10.0	305
					1835	0.2	6
14 Tu	0022	10.1	308	29 W	0049	8.7	265
	0619	-0.3	-9		0639	1.3	40
	1231	12.0	366		1250	9.9	302
	1901	-1.7	-52		1913	0.3	9
15 W	0116	10.0	305	30 Th	0128	8.7	265
	0713	-0.2	-6		0720	1.4	43
	1327	11.6	354		1330	9.7	296
	1955	-1.3	-40		1953	0.4	12
				31 F	0208	8.7	265
					0803	1.4	43
					1412	9.5	290
					2033	0.5	15

Heights are referred to mean lower low water which is the chart datum of soundings.
All times are local time. Daylight Saving Time has been used when needed.

NOTES:

Bridgeport, Connecticut, 2004
Times and Heights of High and Low Waters

April

Day	Time (h m)	Height (ft)	Height (cm)
1 Th	0149	1.0	30
	0759	6.4	195
	1420	0.5	15
	2030	6.5	198
2 F	0239	0.6	18
	0848	6.7	204
	1506	0.2	6
	2114	6.9	210
3 Sa	0327	0.2	6
	0934	7.0	213
	1548	-0.1	-3
	2156	7.3	223
4 Su	0512	-0.2	-6
	1118	7.2	219
	1730	-0.3	-9
	2337	7.7	235
5 M ○	0557	-0.6	-18
	1202	7.4	226
	1811	-0.4	-12
6 Tu	0018	8.0	244
	0642	-0.8	-24
	1247	7.4	226
	1854	-0.3	-9
7 W	0101	8.2	250
	0729	-0.8	-24
	1333	7.3	223
	1939	-0.2	-6
8 Th	0147	8.1	247
	0818	-0.7	-21
	1422	7.0	213
	2027	0.0	0
9 F	0237	7.9	241
	0911	-0.5	-15
	1516	6.8	207
	2122	0.3	9
10 Sa	0332	7.6	232
	1009	-0.1	-3
	1614	6.5	198
	2223	0.6	18
11 Su	0433	7.2	219
	1113	0.2	6
	1719	6.3	192
	2330	0.8	24
12 M ○	0542	6.9	210
	1220	0.4	12
	1827	6.3	192
13 Tu	0042	0.9	27
	0653	6.7	204
	1326	0.4	12
	1934	6.4	195
14 W	0151	0.7	21
	0801	6.8	207
	1428	0.3	9
	2036	6.7	204
15 Th	0255	0.5	15
	0902	6.9	210
	1522	0.2	6
	2130	7.0	213
16 F	0351	0.2	6
	0956	7.0	213
	1611	0.1	3
	2218	7.3	223
17 Sa	0440	-0.1	-3
	1044	7.0	213
	1654	0.1	3
	2302	7.5	229
18 Su	0525	-0.2	-6
	1128	7.0	213
	1734	0.1	3
	2341	7.6	232
19 M	0606	-0.3	-9
	1209	6.9	210
	1812	0.3	9
20 Tu	0019	7.6	232
	0645	-0.2	-6
	1249	6.8	207
	1848	0.5	15
21 W	0055	7.5	229
	0723	-0.1	-3
	1328	6.7	204
	1924	0.7	21
22 Th	0132	7.3	223
	0800	0.1	3
	1407	6.5	198
	2002	0.9	27
23 F	0210	7.1	216
	0839	0.3	9
	1448	6.3	192
	2043	1.1	34
24 Sa	0251	6.8	207
	0921	0.6	18
	1532	6.1	186
	2128	1.3	40
25 Su	0335	6.5	198
	1007	0.8	24
	1620	6.0	183
	2218	1.5	46
26 M	0426	6.3	192
	1059	1.0	30
	1712	5.9	180
	2314	1.5	46
27 Tu	0522	6.1	186
	1154	1.1	34
	1808	5.9	180
28 W	0014	1.5	46
	0621	6.1	186
	1250	1.0	30
	1904	6.1	186
29 Th	0113	1.3	40
	0720	6.2	189
	1344	0.8	24
	1957	6.4	195
30 F	0211	1.0	30
	0816	6.4	195
	1435	0.6	18
	2047	6.9	210

May

Day	Time (h m)	Height (ft)	Height (cm)
1 Sa	0304	0.5	15
	0909	6.7	204
	1523	0.3	9
	2134	7.3	223
2 Su	0355	0.1	3
	1000	6.9	210
	1610	0.1	3
	2219	7.8	238
3 M	0444	-0.4	-12
	1049	7.1	216
	1655	-0.1	-3
	2304	8.2	250
4 Tu ○	0533	-0.7	-21
	1137	7.3	223
	1741	-0.1	-3
	2350	8.4	256
5 W	0621	-0.9	-27
	1226	7.3	223
	1829	-0.1	-3
6 Th	0038	8.5	259
	0711	-0.9	-27
	1316	7.2	219
	1919	0.0	0
7 F	0128	8.4	256
	0803	-0.7	-21
	1408	7.1	216
	2012	0.1	3
8 Sa	0222	8.1	247
	0858	-0.4	-12
	1503	6.9	210
	2110	0.4	12
9 Su	0320	7.7	235
	0956	-0.1	-3
	1603	6.7	204
	2213	0.6	18
10 M	0422	7.3	223
	1058	0.2	6
	1706	6.7	204
	2320	0.8	24
11 Tu ○	0528	7.0	213
	1200	0.4	12
	1810	6.7	204
12 W	0029	0.8	24
	0635	6.7	204
	1302	0.4	12
	1913	6.8	207
13 Th	0135	0.7	21
	0739	6.6	201
	1359	0.5	15
	2011	7.0	213
14 F	0236	0.5	15
	0838	6.6	201
	1452	0.5	15
	2104	7.3	223
15 Sa	0330	0.3	9
	0932	6.6	201
	1540	0.5	15
	2150	7.4	226
16 Su	0418	0.1	3
	1020	6.7	204
	1623	0.5	15
	2233	7.5	229
17 M	0502	0.0	0
	1104	6.7	204
	1704	0.6	18
	2313	7.5	229
18 Tu	0543	0.0	0
	1146	6.6	201
	1742	0.7	21
	2351	7.5	229
19 W ●	0621	0.0	0
	1225	6.6	201
	1820	0.8	24
20 Th	0028	7.4	226
	0658	0.1	3
	1304	6.5	198
	1858	1.0	30
21 F	0106	7.2	219
	0735	0.2	6
	1344	6.4	195
	1937	1.1	34
22 Sa	0144	7.1	216
	0814	0.4	12
	1424	6.4	195
	2018	1.2	37
23 Su	0224	6.9	210
	0855	0.5	15
	1506	6.3	192
	2102	1.3	40
24 M	0308	6.7	204
	0938	0.7	21
	1550	6.2	189
	2150	1.4	43
25 Tu	0354	6.5	198
	1025	0.8	24
	1638	6.2	189
	2242	1.4	43
26 W	0445	6.4	195
	1114	0.8	24
	1729	6.3	192
	2337	1.3	40
27 Th ○	0540	6.4	195
	1206	0.8	24
	1820	6.5	198
28 F	0035	1.1	34
	0638	6.4	195
	1258	0.7	21
	1912	6.8	207
29 Sa	0133	0.8	24
	0735	6.4	195
	1350	0.6	18
	2004	7.2	219
30 Su	0230	0.4	12
	0832	6.6	201
	1442	0.4	12
	2055	7.6	232
31 M	0325	0.0	0
	0927	6.7	204
	1533	0.3	9
	2145	8.0	244

June

Day	Time (h m)	Height (ft)	Height (cm)
1 Tu	0418	-0.4	-12
	1021	6.9	210
	1624	0.2	6
	2236	8.3	253
2 W	0511	-0.7	-21
	1114	7.1	216
	1716	0.0	0
	2327	8.5	259
3 Th ○	0603	-0.8	-24
	1207	7.1	216
	1809	0.0	0
4 F	0020	8.5	259
	0655	-0.8	-24
	1300	7.2	219
	1903	0.0	0
5 Sa	0114	8.4	256
	0749	-0.7	-21
	1354	7.2	219
	2000	0.1	3
6 Su	0210	8.1	247
	0844	-0.5	-15
	1449	7.1	216
	2059	0.3	9
7 M	0307	7.7	235
	0939	-0.2	-6
	1547	7.1	216
	2200	0.5	15
8 Tu	0407	7.4	226
	1036	0.0	0
	1646	7.0	213
	2303	0.6	18
9 W ○	0508	7.0	213
	1133	0.3	9
	1745	7.0	213
10 Th	0007	0.7	21
	0610	6.7	204
	1230	0.5	15
	1843	7.1	216
11 F	0110	0.7	21
	0710	6.5	198
	1324	0.6	18
	1939	7.2	219
12 Sa	0209	0.6	18
	0808	6.3	192
	1416	0.7	21
	2030	7.2	219
13 Su	0302	0.5	15
	0902	6.3	192
	1505	0.8	24
	2118	7.3	223
14 M	0351	0.4	12
	0952	6.3	192
	1551	0.9	27
	2203	7.3	223
15 Tu	0436	0.3	9
	1038	6.3	192
	1634	1.0	30
	2245	7.3	223
16 W	0517	0.2	6
	1121	6.4	195
	1716	1.0	30
	2325	7.3	223
17 Th ●	0557	0.2	6
	1202	6.4	195
	1756	1.0	30
18 F	0005	7.2	219
	0635	0.3	9
	1242	6.5	198
	1836	1.0	30
19 Sa	0044	7.1	216
	0713	0.3	9
	1321	6.5	198
	1916	1.1	34
20 Su	0123	7.1	216
	0751	0.3	9
	1400	6.5	198
	1956	1.1	34
21 M	0202	7.0	213
	0830	0.4	12
	1440	6.5	198
	2039	1.1	34
22 Tu	0243	6.9	210
	0910	0.4	12
	1522	6.5	198
	2124	1.1	34
23 W	0326	6.8	207
	0953	0.5	15
	1605	6.6	201
	2212	1.1	34
24 Th	0414	6.7	204
	1038	0.5	15
	1651	6.8	207
	2305	1.0	30
25 F ○	0505	6.5	198
	1126	0.6	18
	1740	7.0	213
26 Sa	0001	0.9	27
	0601	6.4	195
	1217	0.6	18
	1832	7.2	219
27 Su	0100	0.6	18
	0700	6.4	195
	1311	0.6	18
	1926	7.5	229
28 M	0200	0.3	9
	0800	6.4	195
	1407	0.6	18
	2022	7.8	238
29 Tu	0259	0.0	0
	0900	6.5	198
	1504	0.5	15
	2118	8.0	244
30 W	0356	-0.3	-9
	0958	6.7	204
	1601	0.3	9
	2214	8.2	250

Heights are referred to mean lower low water which is the chart datum of soundings.
All times are local time. Daylight Saving Time has been used when needed.

NOTES:

Bridgeport, Connecticut, 2004

Times and Heights of High and Low Waters

July

Day	Time	ft	cm	Time	ft	cm	Time	ft	cm	Time	ft	cm
1 Th	0452	-0.5	-15	1055	6.9	210	1658	0.1	3	2310	8.4	256
2 F O	0547	-0.6	-18	1150	7.1	216	1754	0.0	0			
3 Sa	0006	8.4	256	0640	-0.7	-21	1243	7.2	219	1850	0.0	0
4 Su	0101	8.3	253	0733	-0.6	-18	1337	7.3	223	1946	0.0	0
5 M	0155	8.0	244	0824	-0.5	-15	1431	7.4	226	2043	0.1	3
6 Tu	0250	7.7	235	0916	-0.3	-9	1524	7.4	226	2140	0.3	9
7 W	0345	7.3	223	1007	0.0	0	1618	7.3	223	2239	0.5	15
8 Th	0441	6.9	210	1059	0.3	9	1713	7.2	219	2338	0.6	18
9 F O	0538	6.5	198	1152	0.6	18	1807	7.2	219			
10 Sa	0037	0.7	21	0636	6.2	189	1244	0.9	27	1901	7.1	216
11 Su	0135	0.8	24	0734	6.1	186	1337	1.1	34	1953	7.0	213
12 M	0229	0.7	21	0829	6.0	183	1429	1.2	37	2044	7.0	213
13 Tu	0320	0.7	21	0921	6.0	183	1519	1.2	37	2133	7.0	213
14 W	0407	0.6	18	1010	6.1	186	1606	1.2	37	2219	7.0	213
15 Th	0450	0.5	15	1055	6.3	192	1651	1.1	34	2302	7.1	216
16 F	0531	0.4	12	1137	6.4	195	1733	1.0	30	2343	7.1	216
17 Sa ●	0610	0.3	9	1217	6.5	198	1814	0.9	27			
18 Su	0023	7.1	216	0648	0.3	9	1256	6.6	201	1854	0.9	27
19 M	0101	7.1	216	0725	0.2	6	1334	6.7	204	1934	0.8	24
20 Tu	0139	7.1	216	0803	0.2	6	1412	6.8	207	2015	0.8	24
21 W	0218	7.1	216	0841	0.2	6	1451	6.9	210	2058	0.8	24
22 Th	0300	7.0	213	0921	0.3	9	1532	7.0	213	2145	0.7	21
23 F	0346	6.8	207	1004	0.4	12	1616	7.2	219	2237	0.7	21
24 Sa	0437	6.6	201	1051	0.5	15	1705	7.3	223	2333	0.6	18
25 Su O	0533	6.4	195	1143	0.7	21	1758	7.4	226			
26 M	0033	0.5	15	0633	6.3	192	1241	0.7	21	1857	7.5	229
27 Tu	0136	0.4	12	0737	6.3	192	1342	0.7	21	1958	7.7	235
28 W	0239	0.2	6	0840	6.4	195	1445	0.6	18	2100	7.9	241
29 Th	0340	0.0	0	0941	6.6	201	1546	0.4	12	2200	8.0	244
30 F	0437	-0.3	-9	1039	6.9	210	1645	0.2	6	2258	8.2	250
31 Sa O	0531	-0.4	-12	1134	7.2	219	1742	0.0	0	2353	8.2	250

August

Day	Time	ft	cm	Time	ft	cm	Time	ft	cm	Time	ft	cm
1 Su	0623	-0.5	-15	1226	7.4	226	1836	-0.1	-3			
2 M	0046	8.1	247	0712	-0.5	-15	1316	7.6	232	1930	-0.1	-3
3 Tu	0137	7.9	241	0759	-0.4	-12	1406	7.6	232	2022	0.0	0
4 W	0227	7.6	232	0846	-0.2	-6	1455	7.6	232	2115	0.2	6
5 Th	0317	7.2	219	0933	0.2	6	1544	7.5	229	2208	0.4	12
6 F	0409	6.7	204	1020	0.5	15	1634	7.3	223	2302	0.7	21
7 Sa	0503	6.3	192	1110	0.9	27	1725	7.1	216	2359	0.9	27
8 Su	0559	6.0	183	1203	1.2	37	1819	6.9	210			
9 M	0056	1.0	30	0657	5.9	180	1258	1.4	43	1914	6.7	204
10 Tu	0152	1.0	30	0754	5.9	180	1354	1.5	46	2010	6.7	204
11 W	0245	1.0	30	0849	5.9	180	1448	1.4	43	2103	6.7	204
12 Th	0335	0.9	27	0939	6.1	186	1538	1.3	40	2152	6.8	207
13 F	0420	0.7	21	1025	6.3	192	1625	1.1	34	2237	7.0	213
14 Sa	0502	0.5	15	1108	6.6	201	1708	0.9	27	2318	7.1	216
15 Su	0541	0.3	9	1148	6.8	207	1749	0.7	21	2357	7.2	219
16 M ●	0618	0.2	6	1226	7.0	213	1829	0.6	18			
17 Tu	0035	7.3	223	0655	0.1	3	1303	7.1	216	1909	0.5	15
18 W	0114	7.3	223	0732	0.1	3	1340	7.3	223	1950	0.4	12
19 Th	0153	7.2	219	0810	0.1	3	1418	7.4	226	2033	0.4	12
20 F	0236	7.1	216	0850	0.2	6	1459	7.5	229	2121	0.4	12
21 Sa	0322	6.9	210	0934	0.4	12	1545	7.5	229	2213	0.4	12
22 Su	0414	6.6	201	1023	0.6	18	1636	7.5	229	2311	0.5	15
23 M O	0512	6.4	195	1119	0.8	24	1734	7.4	226			
24 Tu	0014	0.5	15	0615	6.2	189	1222	0.9	27	1838	7.4	226
25 W	0120	0.5	15	0722	6.2	189	1329	0.9	27	1945	7.5	229
26 Th	0225	0.4	12	0827	6.4	195	1435	0.7	21	2050	7.6	232
27 F	0326	0.1	3	0928	6.7	204	1538	0.4	12	2151	7.8	238
28 Sa	0422	-0.1	-3	1025	7.1	216	1635	0.1	3	2247	8.0	244
29 Su	0513	-0.3	-9	1117	7.4	226	1729	-0.1	-3	2338	8.0	244
30 M O	0601	-0.4	-12	1205	7.7	235	1821	-0.2	-6			
31 Tu	0027	7.9	241	0646	-0.3	-9	1252	7.8	238	1909	-0.2	-6

September

Day	Time	ft	cm	Time	ft	cm	Time	ft	cm	Time	ft	cm
1 W	0114	7.7	235	0729	-0.2	-6	1337	7.8	238	1957	-0.1	-3
2 Th	0201	7.4	226	0812	0.1	3	1421	7.7	235	2045	0.2	6
3 F	0247	7.0	213	0855	0.5	15	1506	7.5	229	2133	0.5	15
4 Sa	0335	6.6	201	0940	0.9	27	1552	7.2	219	2223	0.8	24
5 Su	0426	6.2	189	1028	1.2	37	1642	6.9	210	2317	1.0	30
6 M O	0521	5.9	180	1121	1.5	46	1737	6.6	201			
7 Tu	0013	1.2	37	0618	5.8	177	1219	1.6	49	1835	6.4	195
8 W	0111	1.3	40	0717	5.8	177	1318	1.6	49	1934	6.4	195
9 Th	0207	1.2	37	0813	6.0	183	1416	1.5	46	2030	6.5	198
10 F	0258	1.0	30	0905	6.2	189	1508	1.3	40	2121	6.7	204
11 Sa	0344	0.8	24	0952	6.5	198	1556	1.0	30	2206	6.9	210
12 Su	0427	0.5	15	1034	6.8	207	1640	0.7	21	2248	7.1	216
13 M	0506	0.3	9	1114	7.1	216	1721	0.5	15	2328	7.3	223
14 Tu ●	0544	0.1	3	1152	7.4	226	1802	0.2	6			
15 W	0007	7.4	226	0621	0.0	0	1229	7.6	232	1843	0.1	3
16 Th	0047	7.4	226	0659	0.0	0	1307	7.8	238	1925	0.0	0
17 F	0129	7.3	223	0739	0.1	3	1347	7.8	238	2010	0.0	0
18 Sa	0213	7.1	216	0821	0.3	9	1430	7.8	238	2059	0.1	3
19 Su	0302	6.9	210	0909	0.5	15	1519	7.7	235	2154	0.2	6
20 M	0356	6.6	201	1003	0.8	24	1615	7.5	229	2254	0.5	15
21 Tu O	0457	6.3	192	1105	1.0	30	1719	7.3	223			
22 W	0001	0.6	18	0604	6.2	189	1213	1.0	30	1828	7.2	219
23 Th	0108	0.6	18	0712	6.3	192	1323	0.9	27	1937	7.2	219
24 F	0213	0.4	12	0817	6.6	201	1430	0.7	21	2042	7.4	226
25 Sa	0311	0.2	6	0916	7.0	213	1530	0.3	9	2140	7.6	232
26 Su	0404	0.0	0	1009	7.4	226	1625	0.0	0	2233	7.7	235
27 M	0452	-0.2	-6	1057	7.7	235	1715	-0.2	-6	2321	7.7	235
28 Tu O	0536	-0.2	-6	1142	7.9	241	1803	-0.3	-9			
29 W	0006	7.6	232	0618	-0.1	-3	1224	7.9	241	1847	-0.2	-6
30 Th	0050	7.3	223	0658	0.1	3	1305	7.8	238	1931	-0.1	-3

Heights are referred to mean lower low water which is the chart datum of soundings.
All times are local time. Daylight Saving Time has been used when needed.

NOTES:

Bridgeport, Connecticut, 2004
Times and Heights of High and Low Waters

October

Day	Time (h m)	Height (ft)	Height (cm)
1 F	0134	7.1	216
	0738	0.4	12
	1346	7.6	232
	2014	0.2	6
2 Sa	0217	6.7	204
	0818	0.8	24
	1428	7.3	223
	2058	0.5	15
3 Su	0303	6.4	195
	0901	1.1	34
	1512	7.0	213
	2144	0.8	24
4 M	0351	6.1	186
	0949	1.4	43
	1601	6.7	204
	2235	1.1	34
5 Tu	0443	5.9	180
	1042	1.6	49
	1655	6.4	195
	2330	1.3	40
6 W ○	0540	5.8	177
	1141	1.7	52
	1755	6.2	189
7 Th	0028	1.3	40
	0638	5.8	177
	1242	1.7	52
	1855	6.2	189
8 F	0124	1.2	37
	0734	6.0	183
	1340	1.5	46
	1952	6.3	192
9 Sa	0216	1.0	30
	0826	6.3	192
	1434	1.2	37
	2044	6.6	201
10 Su	0303	0.7	21
	0913	6.7	204
	1522	0.8	24
	2131	6.8	207
11 M	0347	0.5	15
	0956	7.1	216
	1608	0.5	15
	2214	7.0	213
12 Tu	0427	0.2	6
	1037	7.4	226
	1651	0.1	3
	2257	7.2	219
13 W	0507	0.0	0
	1116	7.7	235
	1734	-0.2	-6
	2339	7.3	223
14 Th ●	0547	0.0	0
	1155	8.0	244
	1818	-0.4	-12
15 F	0021	7.3	223
	0628	0.0	0
	1236	8.1	247
	1902	-0.4	-12
16 Sa	0106	7.2	219
	0711	0.1	3
	1320	8.1	247
	1950	-0.4	-12
17 Su	0154	7.0	213
	0758	0.3	9
	1408	8.0	244
	2042	-0.2	-6
18 M	0246	6.8	207
	0851	0.5	15
	1501	7.7	235
	2139	0.1	3
19 Tu	0343	6.5	198
	0950	0.7	21
	1602	7.4	226
	2241	0.3	9
20 W	0446	6.4	195
	1056	0.9	27
	1709	7.1	216
	2348	0.5	15
21 Th	0553	6.4	195
	1207	0.9	27
	1819	7.0	213
22 F	0054	0.5	15
	0700	6.5	198
	1317	0.8	24
	1927	7.0	213
23 Sa	0155	0.4	12
	0803	6.8	207
	1421	0.5	15
	2029	7.1	216
24 Su	0251	0.2	6
	0859	7.2	219
	1519	0.2	6
	2125	7.2	219
25 M	0341	0.1	3
	0950	7.5	229
	1611	-0.1	-3
	2215	7.2	219
26 Tu	0427	0.0	0
	1035	7.7	235
	1659	-0.2	-6
	2302	7.2	219
27 W	0509	0.1	3
	1117	7.8	238
	1743	-0.3	-9
	2345	7.1	216
28 Th ○	0549	0.2	6
	1157	7.8	238
	1825	-0.2	-6
29 F	0027	6.9	210
	0628	0.4	12
	1236	7.6	232
	1905	-0.1	-3
30 Sa	0108	6.7	204
	0707	0.7	21
	1315	7.4	226
	1945	0.1	3
31 Su	0150	6.5	198
	0646	0.9	27
	1255	7.1	216
	1926	0.4	12

November

Day	Time (h m)	Height (ft)	Height (cm)
1 M	0133	6.3	192
	0728	1.1	34
	1338	6.8	207
	2009	0.7	21
2 Tu	0218	6.1	186
	0815	1.3	40
	1425	6.5	198
	2057	0.9	27
3 W	0307	5.9	180
	0906	1.5	46
	1517	6.3	192
	2149	1.1	34
4 Th	0401	5.8	177
	1003	1.6	49
	1613	6.1	186
	2243	1.1	34
5 F ○	0456	5.9	180
	1102	1.5	46
	1711	6.1	186
	2337	1.1	34
6 Sa	0551	6.1	186
	1200	1.3	40
	1808	6.2	189
7 Su	0029	0.9	27
	0642	6.4	195
	1255	1.0	30
	1901	6.3	192
8 M	0118	0.6	18
	0730	6.8	207
	1346	0.6	18
	1951	6.5	198
9 Tu	0204	0.4	12
	0815	7.2	219
	1435	0.2	6
	2039	6.8	207
10 W	0248	0.2	6
	0858	7.6	232
	1522	-0.2	-6
	2125	6.9	210
11 Th	0332	0.0	0
	0941	7.9	241
	1608	-0.5	-15
	2212	7.1	216
12 F ●	0416	-0.1	-3
	1025	8.2	250
	1655	-0.7	-21
	2258	7.1	216
13 Sa	0501	-0.1	-3
	1111	8.3	253
	1743	-0.8	-24
	2346	7.1	216
14 Su	0549	-0.1	-3
	1159	8.2	250
	1834	-0.7	-21
15 M	0037	6.9	210
	0641	0.1	3
	1252	8.0	244
	1927	-0.5	-15
16 Tu	0131	6.8	207
	0738	0.3	9
	1349	7.7	235
	2025	-0.2	-6
17 W	0230	6.6	201
	0839	0.5	15
	1450	7.3	223
	2126	0.1	3
18 Th	0332	6.5	198
	0946	0.6	18
	1556	7.0	213
	2229	0.2	6
19 F ○	0438	6.6	201
	1055	0.6	18
	1703	6.8	207
	2332	0.3	9
20 Sa	0542	6.7	204
	1203	0.5	15
	1808	6.7	204
21 Su	0031	0.2	6
	0642	7.0	213
	1306	0.3	9
	1909	6.6	201
22 M	0125	0.2	6
	0737	7.2	219
	1403	0.1	3
	2005	6.6	201
23 Tu	0215	0.2	6
	0826	7.4	226
	1454	-0.1	-3
	2055	6.7	204
24 W	0301	0.2	6
	0911	7.5	229
	1540	-0.2	-6
	2141	6.6	201
25 Th	0343	0.3	9
	0953	7.5	229
	1623	-0.3	-9
	2225	6.6	201
26 F	0424	0.4	12
	1032	7.4	226
	1703	-0.2	-6
	2306	6.5	198
27 Sa	0503	0.6	18
	1111	7.3	223
	1741	-0.1	-3
	2346	6.4	195
28 Su	0542	0.7	21
	1150	7.1	216
	1820	0.1	3
29 M	0026	6.3	192
	0621	0.8	24
	1230	6.9	210
	1859	0.3	9
30 Tu	0106	6.2	189
	0702	0.9	27
	1311	6.7	204
	1940	0.4	12

December

Day	Time (h m)	Height (ft)	Height (cm)
1 W	0149	6.1	186
	0746	1.1	34
	1355	6.5	198
	2023	0.6	18
2 Th	0234	6.0	183
	0834	1.2	37
	1441	6.3	192
	2109	0.7	21
3 F	0322	6.0	183
	0926	1.2	37
	1532	6.1	186
	2158	0.7	21
4 Sa	0412	6.0	183
	1021	1.2	37
	1625	6.0	183
	2249	0.7	21
5 Su	0503	6.2	189
	1118	1.0	30
	1721	6.0	183
	2340	0.6	18
6 M	0555	6.5	198
	1214	0.8	24
	1817	6.1	186
7 Tu	0031	0.5	15
	0645	6.8	207
	1309	0.4	12
	1912	6.2	189
8 W	0121	0.4	12
	0734	7.2	219
	1402	0.0	0
	2005	6.4	195
9 Th	0211	0.2	6
	0822	7.6	232
	1454	-0.4	-12
	2057	6.6	201
10 F	0300	0.0	0
	0912	7.9	241
	1545	-0.7	-21
	2148	6.7	204
11 Sa	0350	-0.2	-6
	1001	8.1	247
	1635	-0.9	-27
	2238	6.9	210
12 Su ●	0441	-0.3	-9
	1052	8.2	250
	1727	-1.0	-30
	2330	6.9	210
13 M	0534	-0.3	-9
	1145	8.1	247
	1819	-0.9	-27
14 Tu	0022	6.9	210
	0628	-0.3	-9
	1240	7.9	241
	1913	-0.7	-21
15 W	0117	6.9	210
	0726	-0.1	-3
	1336	7.6	232
	2008	-0.5	-15
16 Th	0213	6.8	207
	0826	0.0	0
	1435	7.2	219
	2105	-0.3	-9
17 F	0313	6.8	207
	0930	0.2	6
	1536	6.9	210
	2203	-0.1	-3
18 Sa	0413	6.8	207
	1035	0.3	9
	1639	6.5	198
	2301	0.1	3
19 Su	0514	6.8	207
	1140	0.3	9
	1742	6.3	192
	2358	0.3	9
20 M	0612	6.9	210
	1243	0.3	9
	1843	6.1	186
21 Tu	0053	0.4	12
	0708	7.0	213
	1340	0.1	3
	1940	6.1	186
22 W	0145	0.4	12
	0759	7.0	213
	1432	0.0	0
	2033	6.1	186
23 Th	0234	0.5	15
	0846	7.0	213
	1519	-0.1	-3
	2120	6.1	186
24 F	0320	0.5	15
	0930	7.0	213
	1602	-0.1	-3
	2204	6.2	189
25 Sa	0402	0.5	15
	1012	7.0	213
	1642	0.0	0
	2246	6.2	189
26 Su ○	0443	0.5	15
	1052	6.9	210
	1720	-0.1	-3
	2325	6.2	189
27 M	0522	0.5	15
	1131	6.9	210
	1758	0.0	0
28 Tu	0004	6.2	189
	0601	0.6	18
	1210	6.8	207
	1835	0.0	0
29 W	0042	6.2	189
	0641	0.6	18
	1248	6.7	204
	1913	0.1	3
30 Th	0121	6.2	189
	0721	0.7	21
	1328	6.5	198
	1952	0.2	6
31 F	0202	6.2	189
	0804	0.7	21
	1409	6.4	195
	2032	0.2	6

Heights are referred to mean lower low water which is the chart datum of soundings.
All times are local time. Daylight Saving Time has been used when needed.

NOTES:

Sandy Hook, New Jersey, 2004
Times and Heights of High and Low Waters

April

Day	Time	ft	cm	Day	Time	ft	cm
1 Th	0423	4.5	137	16 F	0022	0.3	9
	1103	0.5	15		0625	5.1	155
	1706	4.3	131		1244	-0.1	-3
	2310	0.5	15		1856	5.2	158
2 F	0516	4.8	146	17 Sa	0112	0.1	3
	1147	0.2	6		0713	5.1	155
	1752	4.7	143		1327	-0.2	-6
	2359	0.2	6		1939	5.4	165
3 Sa	0602	5.1	155	18 Su	0158	0.0	0
	1229	-0.1	-3		0756	5.1	155
	1834	5.2	158		1408	-0.2	-6
					2018	5.6	171
4 Su	0048	-0.2	-6	19 M ●	0242	-0.1	-3
	0746	5.3	162		0837	5.1	155
	1411	-0.3	-9		1446	-0.1	-3
	2013	5.6	171		2054	5.6	171
5 M ○	0235	-0.4	-12	20 Tu	0323	-0.1	-3
	0828	5.3	162		0917	4.9	149
	1452	-0.5	-15		1523	0.0	0
	2054	5.8	177		2130	5.5	168
6 Tu	0322	-0.6	-18	21 W	0402	0.0	0
	0911	5.3	162		0956	4.7	143
	1534	-0.5	-15		1558	0.2	6
	2136	6.0	183		2205	5.3	162
7 W	0409	-0.6	-18	22 Th	0440	0.1	3
	0957	5.2	158		1038	4.4	134
	1616	-0.4	-12		1631	0.5	15
	2221	6.0	183		2240	5.1	155
8 Th	0456	-0.5	-15	23 F	0517	0.4	12
	1048	4.9	149		1121	4.1	128
	1659	-0.2	-6		1705	0.7	21
	2313	5.8	177		2317	4.9	149
9 F	0546	-0.3	-9	24 Sa	0555	0.7	21
	1146	4.6	140		1207	4.0	122
	1747	0.1	3		1739	1.0	30
					2358	4.7	143
10 Sa	0010	5.6	171	25 Su	0637	0.9	27
	0642	0.0	0		1256	3.8	116
	1247	4.4	134		1818	1.2	37
	1844	0.5	15				
11 Su	0111	5.3	162	26 M	0045	4.5	137
	0747	0.3	9		0729	1.1	34
	1351	4.3	131		1346	3.8	116
	1956	0.8	24		1911	1.4	43
12 M ○	0215	5.1	155	27 Tu ○	0136	4.4	134
	0900	0.4	12		0833	1.1	34
	1456	4.2	128		1438	3.8	116
	2116	0.8	24		2027	1.4	43
13 Tu	0320	5.0	152	28 W	0232	4.4	134
	1008	0.4	12		0937	1.0	30
	1603	4.3	131		1533	3.9	119
	2227	0.7	21		2142	1.3	40
14 W	0426	4.9	149	29 Th	0331	4.4	134
	1107	0.2	6		1031	0.8	24
	1708	4.5	137		1629	4.2	128
	2328	0.5	15		2244	1.0	30
15 Th	0529	5.0	152	30 F	0432	4.5	137
	1158	0.0	0		1119	0.5	15
	1806	4.8	146		1723	4.7	143
					2339	0.6	18

May

Day	Time	ft	cm	Day	Time	ft	cm
1 Sa	0531	4.7	143	16 Su	0049	0.3	9
	1204	0.2	6		0645	4.7	143
	1812	5.1	155		1252	0.2	6
					1910	5.5	168
2 Su	0031	0.2	6	17 M	0135	0.2	6
	0626	4.9	149		0730	4.7	143
	1248	0.0	0		1332	0.2	6
	1859	5.6	171		1948	5.6	171
3 M	0122	-0.1	-3	18 Tu	0218	0.1	3
	0716	5.1	155		0811	4.7	143
	1334	-0.2	-6		1412	0.3	9
	1943	6.0	183		2025	5.6	171
4 Tu ○	0213	-0.4	-12	19 W ●	0300	0.1	3
	0804	5.2	158		0852	4.6	140
	1420	-0.3	-9		1450	0.4	12
	2027	6.3	192		2100	5.5	168
5 W	0304	-0.6	-18	20 Th	0340	0.1	3
	0852	5.2	158		0932	4.5	137
	1508	-0.3	-9		1528	0.5	15
	2114	6.4	195		2134	5.4	165
6 Th	0354	-0.7	-21	21 F	0418	0.2	6
	0943	5.1	155		1013	4.3	131
	1556	-0.3	-9		1605	0.7	21
	2203	6.3	192		2209	5.2	158
7 F	0444	-0.6	-18	22 Sa	0455	0.4	12
	1038	4.9	149		1056	4.2	128
	1646	-0.1	-3		1641	0.8	24
	2258	6.1	186		2246	5.0	152
8 Sa	0536	-0.4	-12	23 Su	0533	0.5	15
	1139	4.7	143		1142	4.0	122
	1738	0.2	6		1717	1.0	30
	2358	5.8	177				
9 Su	0631	-0.1	-3	24 M	0611	0.7	21
	1242	4.6	140		1229	3.9	119
	1837	0.5	15		1756	1.2	37
10 M	0100	5.5	168	25 Tu	0011	4.7	143
	0733	0.1	3		0654	0.8	24
	1344	4.5	137		1316	4.0	122
	1947	0.8	24		1843	1.3	40
11 Tu ○	0201	5.2	158	26 W	0059	4.6	140
	0840	0.3	9		0745	0.9	27
	1444	4.5	137		1403	4.1	125
	2102	0.9	27		1946	1.4	43
12 W	0302	5.0	152	27 Th ○	0151	4.6	140
	0943	0.3	9		0843	0.8	24
	1545	4.6	140		1452	4.3	131
	2210	0.8	24		2101	1.3	40
13 Th	0402	4.8	146	28 F	0246	4.5	137
	1038	0.3	9		0940	0.7	21
	1644	4.8	146		1544	4.6	140
	2309	0.7	21		2209	1.0	30
14 F	0501	4.7	143	29 Sa	0345	4.5	137
	1127	0.2	6		1031	0.5	15
	1739	5.0	152		1638	5.0	152
					2308	0.6	18
15 Sa	0001	0.5	15	30 Su	0448	4.6	140
	0556	4.7	143		1121	0.2	6
	1211	0.2	6		1733	5.4	165
	1827	5.3	162				
				31 M	0004	0.2	6
					0550	4.7	143
					1210	0.0	0
					1825	5.9	180

June

Day	Time	ft	cm	Day	Time	ft	cm
1 Tu	0058	-0.1	-3	16 W	0153	0.3	9
	0648	4.9	149		0747	4.4	134
	1301	-0.1	-3		1340	0.5	15
	1916	6.2	189		1958	5.4	165
2 W	0153	-0.4	-12	17 Th	0236	0.2	6
	0742	5.0	152		0829	4.4	134
	1353	-0.2	-6		1422	0.5	15
	2006	6.5	198		2035	5.4	165 ●
3 Th ○	0247	-0.6	-18	18 F	0318	0.2	6
	0836	5.1	155		0910	4.3	131
	1447	-0.3	-9		1504	0.6	18
	2056	6.5	198		2111	5.4	165
4 F	0340	-0.7	-21	19 Sa	0357	0.2	6
	0930	5.0	152		0951	4.3	131
	1541	-0.2	-6		1543	0.7	21
	2149	6.4	195		2146	5.3	162
5 Sa	0431	-0.7	-21	20 Su	0435	0.3	9
	1027	4.9	149		1033	4.2	128
	1634	-0.1	-3		1622	0.7	21
	2246	6.2	189		2222	5.1	155
6 Su	0523	-0.6	-18	21 M	0511	0.4	12
	1128	4.9	149		1116	4.1	125
	1728	0.2	6		1659	0.8	24
	2345	5.9	180		2300	5.0	152
7 M	0616	-0.3	-9	22 Tu	0547	0.4	12
	1229	4.8	146		1200	4.1	125
	1826	0.4	12		1737	1.0	30
					2342	4.9	149
8 Tu	0045	5.5	168	23 W	0623	0.5	15
	0712	-0.1	-3		1243	4.2	128
	1328	4.8	146		1821	1.1	34
	1930	0.7	21				
9 W ○	0141	5.2	158	24 Th	0027	4.8	146
	0810	0.1	3		0703	0.6	18
	1424	4.8	146		1328	4.4	134
	2039	0.9	27		1915	1.1	34
10 Th	0236	4.9	149	25 F ○	0117	4.7	143
	0908	0.3	9		0751	0.6	18
	1518	4.9	149		1414	4.6	140
	2145	0.9	27		2024	1.1	34
11 F	0331	4.7	143	26 Sa	0210	4.6	140
	1002	0.3	9		0847	0.5	15
	1612	4.9	149		1504	4.9	149
	2244	0.8	24		2136	0.9	27
12 Sa	0426	4.4	134	27 Su	0309	4.5	137
	1050	0.4	12		0946	0.4	12
	1704	5.0	152		1559	5.2	158
	2336	0.7	21		2241	0.6	18
13 Su	0522	4.3	131	28 M	0413	4.4	134
	1134	0.4	12		1043	0.3	9
	1753	5.2	158		1658	5.6	171
					2340	0.3	9
14 M	0024	0.6	18	29 Tu	0521	4.5	137
	0614	4.3	131		1140	0.1	3
	1216	0.4	12		1757	5.9	180
	1838	5.3	162				
15 Tu	0109	0.4	12	30 W	0038	-0.1	-3
	0702	4.3	131		0626	4.6	140
	1258	0.5	15		1236	0.0	0
	1919	5.4	165		1855	6.2	189

Heights are referred to mean lower low water which is the chart datum of soundings.
All times are local time. Daylight Saving Time has been used when needed.

NOTES:

Sandy Hook, New Jersey, 2004
Times and Heights of High and Low Waters

July

Day	Time	Height (ft)	Height (cm)	Day	Time	Height (ft)	Height (cm)
1 Th	0135	−0.4	−12	**16** F	0211	0.3	9
	0726	4.8	146		0806	4.3	131
	1334	−0.1	−3		1357	0.6	18
	1949	6.4	195		2012	5.4	165
2 F ○	0231	−0.6	−18	**17** Sa ●	0253	0.2	6
	0822	5.0	152		0847	4.4	134
	1432	−0.2	−6		1441	0.6	18
	2043	6.4	195		2049	5.4	165
3 Sa	0324	−0.7	−21	**18** Su	0333	0.2	6
	0917	5.0	152		0927	4.4	134
	1528	−0.2	−6		1523	0.5	15
	2136	6.4	195		2125	5.3	162
4 Su	0416	−0.7	−21	**19** M	0410	0.1	3
	1013	5.1	155		1006	4.4	134
	1622	−0.2	−6		1603	0.6	18
	2231	6.1	186		2200	5.3	162
5 M	0505	−0.7	−21	**20** Tu	0445	0.1	3
	1110	5.0	152		1045	4.4	134
	1714	0.0	0		1641	0.6	18
	2327	5.8	177		2236	5.1	155
6 Tu	0553	−0.5	−15	**21** W	0518	0.2	6
	1208	5.0	152		1126	4.5	137
	1808	0.3	9		1720	0.7	21
					2315	5.0	152
7 W	0022	5.5	168	**22** Th	0551	0.2	6
	0642	−0.2	−6		1208	4.6	140
	1302	5.0	152		1802	0.8	24
	1905	0.6	18				
8 Th	0115	5.1	155	**23** F	0000	4.8	146
	0733	0.1	3		0626	0.3	9
	1354	5.0	152		1252	4.8	146
	2008	0.9	27		1851	0.9	27
9 F ○	0206	4.7	143	**24** Sa	0049	4.7	143
	0826	0.3	9		0708	0.4	12
	1444	4.9	149		1339	5.0	152
	2112	1.0	30		1955	0.9	27
10 Sa	0257	4.4	134	**25** Su ○	0144	4.5	137
	0918	0.5	15		0802	0.5	15
	1534	4.9	149		1431	5.1	155
	2213	1.0	30		2109	0.9	27
11 Su	0350	4.2	128	**26** M	0244	4.3	131
	1009	0.6	18		0909	0.5	15
	1625	4.9	149		1529	5.3	162
	2307	0.9	27		2219	0.6	18
12 M	0446	4.0	122	**27** Tu	0351	4.3	131
	1056	0.7	21		1017	0.4	12
	1716	5.0	152		1632	5.5	168
	2355	0.8	24		2322	0.3	9
13 Tu	0543	4.0	122	**28** W	0502	4.3	131
	1142	0.7	21		1121	0.3	9
	1805	5.1	155		1738	5.8	177
14 W	0042	0.6	18	**29** Th	0022	0.0	0
	0635	4.1	125		0611	4.5	137
	1227	0.7	21		1222	0.1	3
	1851	5.2	158		1840	6.0	183
15 Th	0127	0.5	15	**30** F	0119	−0.3	−9
	0722	4.2	128		0713	4.8	146
	1312	0.6	18		1321	−0.1	−3
	1933	5.3	162		1936	6.2	189
				31 Sa ○	0214	−0.5	−15
					0809	5.0	152
					1419	−0.2	−6
					2029	6.3	192

August

Day	Time	Height (ft)	Height (cm)	Day	Time	Height (ft)	Height (cm)
1 Su	0306	−0.7	−21	**16** M ●	0303	0.1	3
	0901	5.2	158		0858	4.7	143
	1514	−0.3	−9		1501	0.4	12
	2120	6.3	192		2100	5.4	165
2 M	0354	−0.7	−21	**17** Tu	0340	0.0	0
	0953	5.3	162		0935	4.8	146
	1606	−0.2	−6		1542	0.3	9
	2211	6.0	183		2135	5.4	165
3 Tu	0440	−0.7	−21	**18** W	0414	0.0	0
	1046	5.3	162		1012	4.9	149
	1655	−0.1	−3		1622	0.3	9
	2302	5.7	174		2211	5.3	162
4 W	0524	−0.5	−15	**19** Th	0447	0.0	0
	1138	5.2	158		1050	5.0	152
	1744	0.2	6		1702	0.4	12
	2353	5.3	162		2251	5.1	155
5 Th	0606	−0.2	−6	**20** F	0520	0.1	3
	1229	5.1	155		1132	5.1	155
	1835	0.6	18		1744	0.5	15
					2337	4.8	146
6 F	0043	4.9	149	**21** Sa	0555	0.2	6
	0650	0.2	6		1219	5.2	158
	1317	5.0	152		1834	0.6	18
	1931	0.9	27				
7 Sa ○	0133	4.5	137	**22** Su	0029	4.6	140
	0737	0.6	18		0637	0.4	12
	1405	4.9	149		1311	5.2	158
	2032	1.1	34		1935	0.8	24
8 Su	0223	4.2	128	**23** M ○	0127	4.4	134
	0829	0.8	24		0733	0.6	18
	1453	4.8	146		1407	5.3	162
	2136	1.2	37		2051	0.8	24
9 M	0315	4.0	122	**24** Tu	0231	4.2	128
	0925	1.0	30		0848	0.7	21
	1543	4.7	143		1509	5.3	162
	2234	1.1	34		2204	0.7	21
10 Tu	0412	3.8	116	**25** W	0340	4.2	128
	1020	1.0	30		1005	0.7	21
	1637	4.7	143		1617	5.4	165
	2325	1.0	30		2309	0.4	12
11 W	0511	3.9	119	**26** Th	0453	4.3	131
	1111	1.0	30		1112	0.5	15
	1732	4.8	146		1725	5.6	171
12 Th	0013	0.8	24	**27** F	0008	0.1	3
	0607	4.0	122		0602	4.6	140
	1200	0.9	27		1214	0.2	6
	1823	5.0	152		1828	5.9	180
13 F	0059	0.6	18	**28** Sa	0102	−0.2	−6
	0657	4.2	128		0701	4.9	149
	1247	0.7	21		1311	0.0	0
	1908	5.2	158		1923	6.1	186
14 Sa	0142	0.4	12	**29** Su	0154	−0.4	−12
	0741	4.4	134		0754	5.3	162
	1333	0.6	18		1406	−0.2	−6
	1948	5.3	162		2013	6.1	186
15 Su	0224	0.2	6	**30** M ○	0242	−0.6	−18
	0821	4.6	140		0842	5.5	168
	1418	0.5	15		1458	−0.3	−9
	2025	5.4	165		2100	6.1	186
				31 Tu	0328	−0.6	−18
					0929	5.6	171
					1547	−0.2	−6
					2146	5.8	177

September

Day	Time	Height (ft)	Height (cm)	Day	Time	Height (ft)	Height (cm)
1 W	0410	−0.5	−15	**16** Th	0340	−0.1	−3
	1015	5.5	168		0939	5.5	168
	1633	0.0	0		1602	0.0	0
	2233	5.5	168		2147	5.3	162
2 Th	0450	−0.3	−9	**17** F	0416	−0.1	−3
	1102	5.4	165		1018	5.6	171
	1718	0.2	6		1645	0.1	3
	2320	5.1	155		2230	5.0	152
3 F	0528	0.1	3	**18** Sa	0452	0.0	0
	1148	5.2	158		1102	5.6	171
	1803	0.5	15		1730	0.2	6
					2320	4.8	146
4 Sa	0009	4.7	143	**19** Su	0531	0.2	6
	0606	0.4	12		1153	5.5	168
	1235	5.0	152		1821	0.4	12
	1851	0.9	27				
5 Su	0059	4.3	131	**20** M	0018	4.5	137
	0647	0.8	24		0617	0.5	15
	1321	4.8	146		1251	5.4	165
	1948	1.2	37		1923	0.6	18
6 M	0150	4.1	125	**21** Tu ○	0121	4.3	131
	0736	1.1	34		0720	0.8	24
	1409	4.7	143		1353	5.3	162
	2053	1.3	40		2039	0.7	21
7 Tu	0242	3.9	119	**22** W	0227	4.2	128
	0838	1.3	40		0842	0.9	27
	1501	4.6	140		1458	5.3	162
	2157	1.3	40		2152	0.6	18
8 W	0339	3.8	116	**23** Th	0337	4.2	128
	0943	1.3	40		1000	0.8	24
	1556	4.6	140		1606	5.3	162
	2252	1.1	34		2256	0.4	12
9 Th	0439	3.8	116	**24** F	0447	4.4	134
	1041	1.2	37		1107	0.6	18
	1655	4.7	143		1713	5.4	165
	2341	0.9	27		2352	0.1	3
10 F	0536	4.0	122	**25** Sa	0551	4.8	146
	1133	1.0	30		1205	0.3	9
	1749	4.9	149		1814	5.6	171
11 Sa	0026	0.7	21	**26** Su	0042	−0.2	−6
	0627	4.3	131		0647	5.2	158
	1221	0.8	24		1259	0.0	0
	1837	5.1	155		1906	5.8	177
12 Su	0108	0.4	12	**27** M	0130	−0.3	−9
	0711	4.6	140		0736	5.5	168
	1308	0.5	15		1351	−0.1	−3
	1918	5.3	162		1954	5.8	177
13 M	0148	0.2	6	**28** Tu ○	0215	−0.4	−12
	0750	4.9	149		0820	5.7	174
	1353	0.3	9		1439	−0.2	−6
	1956	5.4	165		2038	5.7	174
14 Tu ●	0227	0.0	0	**29** W	0257	−0.4	−12
	0827	5.2	158		0902	5.8	177
	1437	0.2	6		1525	−0.2	−6
	2032	5.5	168		2120	5.5	168
15 W	0304	−0.1	−3	**30** Th	0336	−0.3	−9
	0902	5.4	165		0943	5.7	174
	1520	0.1	3		1609	0.0	0
	2109	5.4	165		2203	5.2	158

Heights are referred to mean lower low water which is the chart datum of soundings.
All times are local time. Daylight Saving Time has been used when needed.

NOTES:

Sandy Hook, New Jersey, 2004
Times and Heights of High and Low Waters

October

Day	Time (h m)	Height (ft)	Height (cm)	Day	Time (h m)	Height (ft)	Height (cm)
1 F	0414 / 1024 / 1650 / 2248	0.0 / 5.5 / 0.2 / 4.8	0 / 168 / 6 / 146	16 Sa	0348 / 0952 / 1630 / 2215	-0.2 / 6.0 / -0.3 / 4.9	-6 / 183 / -9 / 149
2 Sa	0450 / 1105 / 1732 / 2335	0.3 / 5.3 / 0.5 / 4.5	9 / 162 / 15 / 137	17 Su	0430 / 1040 / 1718 / 2309	0.0 / 5.9 / -0.1 / 4.7	0 / 180 / -3 / 143
3 Su	0525 / 1149 / 1815	0.6 / 5.0 / 0.8	18 / 152 / 24	18 M	0516 / 1136 / 1811	0.2 / 5.7 / 0.1	6 / 174 / 3
4 M	0025 / 0603 / 1236 / 1905	4.1 / 1.0 / 4.8 / 1.1	125 / 30 / 146 / 34	19 Tu	0012 / 0609 / 1238 / 1914	4.4 / 0.5 / 5.4 / 0.4	134 / 15 / 165 / 12
5 Tu	0117 / 0647 / 1325 / 2006	3.9 / 1.3 / 4.6 / 1.3	119 / 40 / 140 / 40	20 W	0118 / 0716 / 1343 / 2026	4.3 / 0.8 / 5.3 / 0.5	131 / 24 / 162 / 15
6 W ○	0211 / 0748 / 1418 / 2114	3.8 / 1.5 / 4.4 / 1.3	116 / 46 / 134 / 40	21 Th	0224 / 0837 / 1448 / 2137	4.3 / 0.9 / 5.1 / 0.4	131 / 27 / 155 / 12
7 Th	0306 / 0902 / 1514 / 2214	3.7 / 1.5 / 4.4 / 1.2	113 / 46 / 134 / 37	22 F	0330 / 0953 / 1553 / 2238	4.4 / 0.8 / 5.1 / 0.2	134 / 24 / 155 / 6
8 F	0403 / 1008 / 1611 / 2303	3.8 / 1.3 / 4.5 / 0.9	116 / 40 / 137 / 27	23 Sa	0435 / 1057 / 1656 / 2330	4.6 / 0.6 / 5.1 / 0.0	140 / 18 / 155 / 0
9 Sa	0459 / 1103 / 1707 / 2347	4.1 / 1.1 / 4.7 / 0.6	125 / 34 / 143 / 18	24 Su	0535 / 1154 / 1754	4.9 / 0.3 / 5.2	149 / 9 / 158
10 Su	0550 / 1153 / 1758	4.4 / 0.8 / 4.9	134 / 24 / 149	25 M	0018 / 0628 / 1245 / 1846	-0.2 / 5.3 / 0.1 / 5.3	-6 / 162 / 3 / 162
11 M	0028 / 0635 / 1240 / 1843	0.4 / 4.8 / 0.5 / 5.1	12 / 146 / 15 / 155	26 Tu	0102 / 0714 / 1333 / 1931	-0.3 / 5.5 / -0.1 / 5.3	-9 / 168 / -3 / 162
12 Tu	0108 / 0715 / 1326 / 1924	0.1 / 5.2 / 0.2 / 5.3	3 / 158 / 6 / 162	27 W	0144 / 0756 / 1420 / 2014	-0.3 / 5.7 / -0.1 / 5.2	-9 / 174 / -3 / 158
13 W	0148 / 0753 / 1412 / 2004	-0.1 / 5.6 / -0.1 / 5.3	-3 / 171 / -3 / 162	28 Th ○	0224 / 0834 / 1503 / 2055	-0.2 / 5.7 / -0.1 / 5.0	-6 / 174 / -3 / 152
14 Th ●	0227 / 0830 / 1458 / 2044	-0.2 / 5.8 / -0.2 / 5.3	-6 / 177 / -6 / 162	29 F	0303 / 0912 / 1545 / 2136	-0.1 / 5.6 / 0.0 / 4.8	-3 / 171 / 0 / 146
15 F	0307 / 0909 / 1543 / 2127	-0.2 / 6.0 / -0.3 / 5.2	-6 / 183 / -9 / 158	30 Sa	0341 / 0949 / 1625 / 2219	0.1 / 5.4 / 0.1 / 4.5	3 / 165 / 3 / 137
				31 Su	0317 / 0927 / 1604 / 2205	0.4 / 5.2 / 0.4 / 4.2	12 / 158 / 12 / 128

November

Day	Time (h m)	Height (ft)	Height (cm)	Day	Time (h m)	Height (ft)	Height (cm)
1 M	0352 / 1007 / 1645 / 2254	0.7 / 4.9 / 0.6 / 3.9	21 / 149 / 18 / 119	16 Tu	0407 / 1024 / 1701 / 2306	0.0 / 5.7 / -0.3 / 4.4	0 / 174 / -9 / 134
2 Tu	0429 / 1052 / 1729 / 2346	0.9 / 4.7 / 0.9 / 3.8	27 / 143 / 27 / 116	17 W	0504 / 1128 / 1801	0.3 / 5.4 / 0.0	9 / 165 / 0
3 W	0510 / 1142 / 1821	1.2 / 4.5 / 1.1	37 / 137 / 34	18 Th	0011 / 0610 / 1231 / 1906	4.3 / 0.5 / 5.2 / 0.1	131 / 15 / 158 / 3
4 Th	0038 / 0603 / 1234 / 1924	3.7 / 1.3 / 4.4 / 1.1	113 / 40 / 134 / 34	19 F ○	0113 / 0725 / 1332 / 2012	4.4 / 0.7 / 5.0 / 0.1	134 / 21 / 152 / 3
5 F	0130 / 0714 / 1327 / 2025	3.7 / 1.4 / 4.3 / 1.0	113 / 43 / 131 / 30	20 Sa	0215 / 0838 / 1432 / 2111	4.5 / 0.6 / 4.8 / 0.0	137 / 18 / 146 / 0
6 Sa	0223 / 0827 / 1421 / 2117	3.8 / 1.3 / 4.3 / 0.8	116 / 40 / 131 / 24	21 Su	0315 / 0942 / 1532 / 2202	4.7 / 0.5 / 4.7 / -0.1	143 / 15 / 143 / -3
7 Su	0315 / 0928 / 1517 / 2203	4.1 / 1.0 / 4.4 / 0.5	125 / 30 / 134 / 15	22 M	0412 / 1037 / 1629 / 2248	4.9 / 0.3 / 4.6 / -0.1	149 / 9 / 140 / -3
8 M	0406 / 1021 / 1612 / 2245	4.5 / 0.7 / 4.6 / 0.2	137 / 21 / 140 / 6	23 Tu	0503 / 1127 / 1721 / 2331	5.1 / 0.1 / 4.6 / -0.2	155 / 3 / 140 / -6
9 Tu	0454 / 1110 / 1703 / 2327	4.9 / 0.3 / 4.7 / 0.0	149 / 9 / 143 / 0	24 W	0549 / 1214 / 1808	5.3 / 0.0 / 4.6	162 / 0 / 140
10 W	0538 / 1159 / 1752	5.4 / 0.0 / 4.9	165 / 0 / 149	25 Th	0013 / 0630 / 1259 / 1852	-0.1 / 5.5 / -0.1 / 4.6	-3 / 168 / -3 / 140
11 Th	0009 / 0620 / 1248 / 1838	-0.2 / 5.8 / -0.3 / 5.0	-6 / 177 / -9 / 152	26 F ○	0054 / 0708 / 1342 / 1933	-0.1 / 5.5 / -0.1 / 4.5	-3 / 168 / -3 / 137
12 F ●	0053 / 0702 / 1337 / 1923	-0.3 / 6.0 / -0.5 / 5.0	-9 / 183 / -15 / 152	27 Sa	0134 / 0745 / 1423 / 2014	0.0 / 5.4 / -0.1 / 4.4	0 / 165 / -3 / 134
13 Sa	0139 / 0746 / 1427 / 2011	-0.4 / 6.2 / -0.6 / 4.9	-12 / 189 / -18 / 149	28 Su	0213 / 0821 / 1503 / 2055	0.2 / 5.2 / 0.0 / 4.2	6 / 158 / 0 / 128
14 Su	0227 / 0833 / 1516 / 2103	-0.4 / 6.1 / -0.6 / 4.8	-12 / 186 / -18 / 146	29 M	0251 / 0858 / 1541 / 2138	0.3 / 5.1 / 0.1 / 4.0	9 / 155 / 3 / 122
15 M	0316 / 0925 / 1607 / 2202	-0.4 / 6.0 / -0.5 / 4.6	-12 / 183 / -15 / 140	30 Tu	0328 / 0936 / 1620 / 2225	0.5 / 4.8 / 0.3 / 3.8	15 / 146 / 9 / 116

December

Day	Time (h m)	Height (ft)	Height (cm)	Day	Time (h m)	Height (ft)	Height (cm)
1 W	0405 / 1017 / 1659 / 2313	0.7 / 4.6 / 0.5 / 3.7	21 / 140 / 15 / 113	16 Th	0454 / 1113 / 1740 / 2354	-0.1 / 5.4 / -0.5 / 4.5	-3 / 165 / -15 / 137
2 Th	0443 / 1102 / 1741	0.9 / 4.4 / 0.6	27 / 134 / 18	17 F	0555 / 1212 / 1838	0.2 / 5.0 / -0.3	6 / 152 / -9
3 F	0002 / 0528 / 1149 / 1830	3.7 / 1.0 / 4.3 / 0.7	113 / 30 / 131 / 21	18 Sa	0053 / 0704 / 1309 / 1938	4.5 / 0.4 / 4.7 / -0.1	137 / 12 / 143 / -3
4 Sa	0049 / 0626 / 1239 / 1925	3.7 / 1.1 / 4.2 / 0.7	113 / 34 / 128 / 21	19 Su ○	0150 / 0815 / 1405 / 2036	4.5 / 0.5 / 4.4 / 0.0	137 / 15 / 134 / 0
5 Su	0137 / 0738 / 1330 / 2021	3.9 / 1.1 / 4.2 / 0.6	119 / 34 / 128 / 18	20 M	0245 / 0919 / 1502 / 2129	4.6 / 0.4 / 4.2 / 0.0	140 / 12 / 128 / 0
6 M	0226 / 0847 / 1425 / 2112	4.1 / 0.9 / 4.2 / 0.4	125 / 27 / 128 / 12	21 Tu	0341 / 1015 / 1600 / 2216	4.7 / 0.3 / 4.1 / 0.0	143 / 9 / 125 / 0
7 Tu	0317 / 0946 / 1524 / 2200	4.5 / 0.6 / 4.2 / 0.1	137 / 18 / 128 / 3	22 W	0433 / 1106 / 1655 / 2301	4.8 / 0.2 / 4.0 / 0.0	146 / 6 / 122 / 0
8 W	0410 / 1041 / 1624 / 2247	4.9 / 0.2 / 4.3 / -0.1	149 / 6 / 131 / -3	23 Th	0522 / 1153 / 1745 / 2344	4.9 / 0.1 / 4.1 / 0.0	149 / 3 / 125 / 0
9 Th	0501 / 1133 / 1722 / 2336	5.3 / -0.2 / 4.5 / -0.3	162 / -6 / 137 / -9	24 F	0605 / 1237 / 1831	5.0 / -0.1 / 4.1	152 / -3 / 125
10 F	0551 / 1226 / 1815	5.7 / -0.5 / 4.6	174 / -15 / 140	25 Sa	0027 / 0646 / 1321 / 1913	0.1 / 5.1 / -0.1 / 4.1	3 / 155 / -3 / 125
11 Sa	0026 / 0640 / 1319 / 1907	-0.5 / 6.0 / -0.8 / 4.7	-15 / 183 / -24 / 143	26 Su ○	0109 / 0724 / 1402 / 1954	0.1 / 5.1 / -0.2 / 4.1	3 / 155 / -6 / 125
12 Su ●	0119 / 0729 / 1411 / 1959	-0.6 / 6.1 / -0.9 / 4.7	-18 / 186 / -27 / 143	27 M	0151 / 0801 / 1442 / 2034	0.1 / 5.1 / -0.2 / 4.0	3 / 155 / -6 / 122
13 M	0212 / 0820 / 1503 / 2053	-0.6 / 6.1 / -0.9 / 4.7	-18 / 186 / -27 / 143	28 Tu	0230 / 0837 / 1520 / 2115	0.1 / 4.9 / -0.1 / 3.9	3 / 149 / -3 / 119
14 Tu	0305 / 0915 / 1554 / 2152	-0.5 / 5.9 / -0.9 / 4.6	-15 / 180 / -27 / 140	29 W	0309 / 0913 / 1556 / 2157	0.2 / 4.8 / 0.0 / 3.8	6 / 146 / 0 / 116
15 W	0358 / 1013 / 1646 / 2253	-0.4 / 5.7 / -0.7 / 4.5	-12 / 174 / -21 / 137	30 Th	0345 / 0949 / 1630 / 2239	0.3 / 4.6 / 0.1 / 3.8	9 / 140 / 3 / 116
				31 F	0422 / 1027 / 1705 / 2322	0.5 / 4.5 / 0.2 / 3.8	15 / 137 / 6 / 116

Heights are referred to mean lower low water which is the chart datum of soundings.
All times are local time. Daylight Saving Time has been used when needed.

NOTES:

Breakwater Harbor, Delaware, 2004

Times and Heights of High and Low Waters

April

Day	Time (h m)	Height (ft)	Height (cm)	Day	Time (h m)	Height (ft)	Height (cm)
1 Th	0521	4.2	128	16 F	0057	0.2	6
	1140	0.6	18		0724	4.6	140
	1748	3.7	113		1327	0.1	3
	2339	0.4	12		1949	4.4	134
2 F	0610	4.5	137	17 Sa	0148	0.1	3
	1222	0.3	9		0810	4.5	137
	1834	4.0	122		1408	0.0	0
					2030	4.6	140
3 Sa	0028	0.1	3	18 Su	0234	0.0	0
	0655	4.6	140		0851	4.4	134
	1301	0.0	0		1445	0.0	0
	1917	4.4	134		2107	4.8	146
4 Su	0115	-0.2	-6	19 M	0316	-0.1	-3
	0838	4.7	143		0928	4.3	131
	1440	-0.2	-6		1520	0.1	3
	2059	4.8	146		2142	4.8	146
5 M ○	0302	-0.4	-12	20 Tu	0356	0.0	0
	0921	4.7	143		1005	4.1	125
	1519	-0.3	-9		1554	0.1	3
	2142	5.1	155		2217	4.8	146
6 Tu	0349	-0.5	-15	21 W	0435	0.1	3
	1004	4.6	140		1041	3.9	119
	1600	-0.4	-12		1628	0.3	9
	2226	5.3	162		2252	4.8	146
7 W	0437	-0.5	-15	22 Th	0514	0.2	6
	1050	4.4	134		1117	3.7	113
	1643	-0.4	-12		1703	0.4	12
	2313	5.3	162		2328	4.7	143
8 Th	0528	-0.4	-12	23 F	0554	0.4	12
	1138	4.2	128		1156	3.5	107
	1729	-0.2	-6		1740	0.6	18
9 F	0002	5.3	162	24 Sa	0009	4.5	137
	0622	-0.2	-6		0636	0.6	18
	1230	3.9	119		1238	3.4	104
	1820	0.0	0		1821	0.8	24
10 Sa	0057	5.1	155	25 Su	0053	4.4	134
	0721	0.0	0		0723	0.8	24
	1329	3.7	113		1325	3.2	98
	1918	0.2	6		1908	0.9	27
11 Su	0159	4.9	149	26 M	0143	4.2	128
	0826	0.3	9		0814	0.9	27
	1435	3.5	107		1418	3.2	98
	2024	0.4	12		2001	1.0	30
12 M ○	0308	4.7	143	27 Tu ○	0238	4.1	125
	0936	0.4	12		0910	0.9	27
	1537	3.5	107		1517	3.2	98
	2137	0.5	15		2102	1.0	30
13 Tu	0421	4.5	137	28 W	0337	4.1	125
	1046	0.4	12		1007	0.9	27
	1703	3.6	110		1617	3.3	101
	2251	0.5	15		2205	0.9	27
14 W	0531	4.5	137	29 Th	0436	4.1	125
	1148	0.3	9		1100	0.7	21
	1808	3.9	119		1714	3.6	110
	2358	0.4	12		2307	0.7	21
15 Th	0632	4.5	137	30 F	0533	4.2	128
	1241	0.2	6		1148	0.5	15
	1902	4.1	125		1807	4.0	122

May

Day	Time (h m)	Height (ft)	Height (cm)	Day	Time (h m)	Height (ft)	Height (cm)
1 Sa	0005	0.4	12	16 Su	0130	0.3	9
	0626	4.3	131		0741	4.1	125
	1234	0.2	6		1332	0.2	6
	1856	4.4	134		2002	4.7	143
2 Su	0059	0.1	3	17 M	0216	0.2	6
	0716	4.4	134		0823	3.9	119
	1318	0.0	0		1410	0.2	6
	1943	4.9	149		2039	4.8	146
3 M	0151	-0.2	-6	18 Tu	0258	0.2	6
	0805	4.5	137		0902	3.8	116
	1401	-0.2	-6		1446	0.3	9
	2030	5.2	158		2115	4.9	149
4 Tu ○	0242	-0.4	-12	19 W	0337	0.2	6
	0853	4.4	134		0940	3.7	113
	1446	-0.4	-12		1521	0.3	9
	2117	5.5	168		2150	4.9	149
5 W	0332	-0.5	-15	20 Th	0416	0.2	6
	0942	4.4	134		1017	3.6	110
	1532	-0.4	-12		1557	0.4	12
	2205	5.7	174		2227	4.8	146
6 Th	0424	-0.5	-15	21 F	0454	0.3	9
	1032	4.2	128		1055	3.5	107
	1620	-0.3	-9		1634	0.5	15
	2255	5.7	174		2305	4.7	143
7 F	0517	-0.4	-12	22 Sa	0533	0.4	12
	1125	4.1	125		1134	3.4	104
	1711	-0.2	-6		1712	0.6	18
	2349	5.5	168		2345	4.6	140
8 Sa	0612	-0.3	-9	23 Su	0613	0.5	15
	1221	3.9	119		1216	3.4	104
	1806	0.0	0		1754	0.7	21
9 Su	0046	5.3	162	24 M	0028	4.5	137
	0711	0.0	0		0656	0.6	18
	1322	3.8	116		1301	3.3	101
	1907	0.3	9		1840	0.8	24
10 M	0148	5.0	152	25 Tu	0114	4.4	134
	0814	0.1	3		0741	0.7	21
	1428	3.7	113		1350	3.3	101
	2014	0.4	12		1931	0.9	27
11 Tu ○	0254	4.7	143	26 W	0203	4.3	131
	0919	0.3	9		0830	0.7	21
	1537	3.7	113		1442	3.4	104
	2126	0.6	18		2028	0.9	27
12 W	0401	4.5	137	27 Th	0256	4.2	128
	1021	0.3	9		0919	0.6	18
	1644	3.9	119		1538	3.6	110
	2237	0.6	18		2129	0.8	24
13 Th	0505	4.4	134	28 F	0350	4.1	125
	1118	0.3	9		1010	0.5	15
	1744	4.1	125		1633	3.9	119
	2342	0.5	15		2231	0.7	21
14 F	0603	4.3	131	29 Sa	0447	4.1	125
	1208	0.3	9		1059	0.3	9
	1836	4.3	131		1727	4.3	131
					2332	0.4	12
15 Sa	0039	0.4	12	30 Su	0543	4.1	125
	0655	4.2	128		1149	0.1	3
	1252	0.2	6		1820	4.7	143
	1922	4.5	137				
				31 M	0031	0.1	3
					0639	4.1	125
					1238	-0.1	-3
					1912	5.1	155

June

Day	Time (h m)	Height (ft)	Height (cm)	Day	Time (h m)	Height (ft)	Height (cm)
1 Tu	0128	-0.1	-3	16 W	0238	0.4	12
	0734	4.1	125		0836	3.5	107
	1327	-0.3	-9		1415	0.4	12
	2004	5.5	168		2050	4.8	146
2 W	0223	-0.3	-9	17 Th ●	0319	0.3	9
	0829	4.1	125		0916	3.5	107
	1418	-0.4	-12		1453	0.5	15
	2056	5.7	174		2128	4.8	146
3 Th ○	0317	-0.5	-15	18 F	0357	0.3	9
	0923	4.1	125		0955	3.5	107
	1509	-0.4	-12		1532	0.5	15
	2148	5.8	177		2207	4.8	146
4 F	0411	-0.5	-15	19 Sa	0435	0.4	12
	1018	4.1	125		1034	3.4	104
	1602	-0.4	-12		1611	0.5	15
	2242	5.8	177		2245	4.8	146
5 Sa	0505	-0.4	-12	20 Su	0512	0.4	12
	1113	4.0	122		1113	3.4	104
	1657	-0.2	-6		1650	0.5	15
	2337	5.6	171		2325	4.7	143
6 Su	0600	-0.3	-9	21 M	0549	0.4	12
	1211	4.0	122		1154	3.5	107
	1755	-0.1	-3		1732	0.6	18
7 M	0034	5.3	162	22 Tu	0005	4.6	140
	0657	-0.2	-6		0628	0.4	12
	1310	3.9	119		1236	3.5	107
	1855	0.2	6		1816	0.6	18
8 Tu	0132	5.0	152	23 W	0047	4.5	137
	0754	0.0	0		0709	0.4	12
	1411	3.9	119		1321	3.6	110
	1959	0.4	12		1905	0.7	21
9 W ○	0231	4.7	143	24 Th	0131	4.4	134
	0851	0.1	3		0751	0.4	12
	1513	4.0	122		1410	3.7	113
	2106	0.5	15		1959	0.7	21
10 Th	0331	4.4	134	25 F ○	0219	4.2	128
	0947	0.2	6		0837	0.3	9
	1614	4.1	125		1502	4.0	122
	2214	0.6	18		2058	0.7	21
11 F	0430	4.1	125	26 Sa	0311	4.1	125
	1039	0.3	9		0926	0.2	6
	1711	4.2	128		1556	4.3	131
	2317	0.6	18		2201	0.6	18
12 Sa	0527	3.9	119	27 Su	0407	3.9	119
	1128	0.3	9		1017	0.1	3
	1803	4.4	134		1652	4.6	140
					2305	0.4	12
13 Su	0016	0.6	18	28 M	0507	3.8	116
	0620	3.7	113		1111	0.0	0
	1213	0.4	12		1750	4.9	149
	1849	4.5	137				
14 M	0108	0.5	15	29 Tu	0008	0.2	6
	0709	3.6	110		0609	3.8	116
	1255	0.4	12		1206	-0.1	-3
	1932	4.7	143		1847	5.3	162
15 Tu	0155	0.4	12	30 W	0109	0.0	0
	0754	3.5	107		0710	3.8	116
	1336	0.4	12		1301	-0.2	-6
	2012	4.7	143		1944	5.5	168

Heights are referred to mean lower low water which is the chart datum of soundings.
All times are local time. Daylight Saving Time has been used when needed.

NOTES:

Breakwater Harbor, Delaware, 2004

Times and Heights of High and Low Waters

July

Day	Time (h m)	Height (ft)	Height (cm)	Day	Time (h m)	Height (ft)	Height (cm)
1 Th	0207	-0.2	-6	16 F	0257	0.5	15
	0810	3.9	119		0852	3.4	104
	1357	-0.3	-9		1430	0.5	15
	2040	5.7	174		2107	4.8	146
2 F ○	0303	-0.4	-12	17 Sa	0335	0.4	12
	0908	4.0	122		0932	3.5	107
	1453	-0.4	-12		1510	0.4	12
	2135	5.8	177		2146	4.8	146
3 Sa	0357	-0.4	-12	18 Su	0411	0.4	12
	1004	4.1	125		1011	3.6	110
	1548	-0.4	-12		1549	0.4	12
	2229	5.7	174		2225	4.9	149
4 Su	0450	-0.4	-12	19 M	0445	0.4	12
	1059	4.1	125		1049	3.7	113
	1644	-0.3	-9		1629	0.4	12
	2323	5.5	168		2302	4.8	146
5 M	0542	-0.3	-9	20 Tu	0520	0.3	9
	1153	4.2	128		1128	3.8	116
	1740	-0.1	-3		1711	0.4	12
					2340	4.7	143
6 Tu	0015	5.3	162	21 W	0556	0.3	9
	0633	-0.2	-6		1209	3.9	119
	1248	4.2	128		1755	0.4	12
	1838	0.1	3				
7 W	0108	4.9	149	22 Th	0019	4.6	140
	0724	-0.1	-3		0634	0.2	6
	1343	4.2	128		1252	4.0	122
	1937	0.3	9		1843	0.5	15
8 Th	0200	4.5	137	23 F	0102	4.4	134
	0815	0.1	3		0715	0.2	6
	1439	4.2	128		1339	4.2	128
	2039	0.5	15		1936	0.5	15
9 F ○	0254	4.2	128	24 Sa	0148	4.2	128
	0905	0.3	9		0800	0.2	6
	1534	4.2	128		1429	4.4	134
	2143	0.7	21		2034	0.6	18
10 Sa	0349	3.8	116	25 Su ○	0240	4.0	122
	0955	0.4	12		0849	0.2	6
	1630	4.3	131		1525	4.6	140
	2246	0.8	24		2138	0.6	18
11 Su	0445	3.6	110	26 M	0339	3.8	116
	1044	0.5	15		0944	0.2	6
	1723	4.3	131		1625	4.8	146
	2347	0.8	24		2245	0.5	15
12 M	0542	3.4	104	27 Tu	0443	3.7	113
	1133	0.6	18		1043	0.1	3
	1813	4.4	134		1727	5.0	152
					2351	0.3	9
13 Tu	0042	0.7	21	28 W	0550	3.6	110
	0636	3.3	101		1144	0.1	3
	1220	0.6	18		1830	5.3	162
	1900	4.5	137				
14 W	0132	0.6	18	29 Th	0054	0.1	3
	0725	3.3	101		0656	3.7	113
	1305	0.6	18		1245	-0.1	-3
	1945	4.6	140		1930	5.5	168
15 Th	0216	0.6	18	30 F	0153	0.0	0
	0810	3.4	104		0757	3.9	119
	1348	0.5	15		1344	-0.2	-6
	2027	4.7	143		2028	5.6	171
				31 Sa ○	0248	-0.2	-6
					0855	4.1	125
					1441	-0.3	-9
					2122	5.7	174

August

Day	Time (h m)	Height (ft)	Height (cm)	Day	Time (h m)	Height (ft)	Height (cm)
1 Su	0339	-0.3	-9	16 M ●	0338	0.4	12
	0948	4.3	131		0943	3.9	119
	1536	-0.3	-9		1527	0.3	9
	2214	5.6	171		2158	4.9	149
2 M	0428	-0.3	-9	17 Tu	0411	0.3	9
	1039	4.4	134		1021	4.1	125
	1630	-0.3	-9		1608	0.2	6
	2303	5.4	165		2235	4.9	149
3 Tu	0516	-0.3	-9	18 W	0445	0.2	6
	1129	4.5	137		1059	4.3	131
	1722	-0.1	-3		1650	0.2	6
	2350	5.1	155		2313	4.8	146
4 W	0602	-0.1	-3	19 Th	0521	0.2	6
	1218	4.5	137		1140	4.4	134
	1815	0.1	3		1735	0.3	9
					2353	4.6	140
5 Th	0037	4.8	146	20 F	0559	0.1	3
	0647	0.0	0		1223	4.6	140
	1307	4.4	134		1823	0.4	12
	1910	0.4	12				
6 F	0125	4.4	134	21 Sa	0036	4.4	134
	0732	0.3	9		0641	0.2	6
	1357	4.4	134		1310	4.7	143
	2006	0.6	18		1917	0.5	15
7 Sa ○	0214	4.0	122	22 Su	0124	4.1	125
	0819	0.5	15		0727	0.3	9
	1448	4.3	131		1402	4.7	143
	2107	0.8	24		2017	0.6	18
8 Su	0306	3.6	110	23 M	0219	3.8	116
	0907	0.7	21		0821	0.3	9
	1542	4.3	131		1501	4.8	146
	2210	1.0	30		2122 ○	0.6	18
9 M	0403	3.4	104	24 Tu	0322	3.6	110
	0959	0.8	24		0921	0.4	12
	1638	4.3	131		1606	4.9	149
	2313	1.0	30		2232	0.6	18
10 Tu	0503	3.3	101	25 W	0432	3.6	110
	1053	0.9	27		1026	0.4	12
	1735	4.4	134		1714	5.0	152
					2340	0.5	15
11 W	0012	0.9	27	26 Th	0543	3.7	113
	0602	3.2	98		1133	0.3	9
	1146	0.9	27		1820	5.2	158
	1828	4.5	137				
12 Th	0103	0.9	27	27 F	0043	0.3	9
	0655	3.3	101		0649	3.9	119
	1236	0.8	24		1237	0.1	3
	1917	4.6	140		1921	5.4	165
13 F	0148	0.7	21	28 Sa	0139	0.1	3
	0742	3.4	104		0748	4.1	125
	1323	0.6	18		1336	-0.1	-3
	2001	4.7	143		2016	5.5	168
14 Sa	0228	0.6	18	29 Su	0230	-0.1	-3
	0824	3.6	110		0841	4.4	134
	1406	0.5	15		1431	-0.2	-6
	2042	4.8	146		2106	5.5	168
15 Su	0304	0.5	15	30 M ○	0317	-0.2	-6
	0904	3.8	116		0930	4.6	140
	1447	0.4	12		1523	-0.2	-6
	2121	4.9	149		2153	5.4	165
				31 Tu	0401	-0.2	-6
					1016	4.7	143
					1613	-0.2	-6
					2238	5.2	158

September

Day	Time (h m)	Height (ft)	Height (cm)	Day	Time (h m)	Height (ft)	Height (cm)
1 W	0443	-0.1	-3	16 Th	0408	0.1	3
	1100	4.8	146		1030	4.9	149
	1701	0.0	0		1630	0.1	3
	2321	4.9	149		2246	4.7	143
2 Th	0524	0.0	0	17 F	0446	0.0	0
	1144	4.8	146		1111	5.0	152
	1750	0.2	6		1717	0.1	3
					2329	4.5	137
3 F	0004	4.5	137	18 Sa	0527	0.1	3
	0605	0.2	6		1156	5.1	155
	1227	4.7	143		1807	0.2	6
	1839	0.5	15				
4 Sa	0047	4.1	125	19 Su	0015	4.2	128
	0646	0.5	15		0612	0.2	6
	1312	4.6	140		1246	5.1	155
	1931	0.7	21		1903	0.4	12
5 Su	0134	3.8	116	20 M	0107	3.9	119
	0731	0.7	21		0702	0.3	9
	1400	4.4	134		1342	5.0	152
	2028	1.0	30		2004	0.5	15
6 M	0225	3.5	107	21 Tu	0207	3.7	113
	0819	1.0	30		0801	0.5	15
	1454	4.3	131		1445	4.9	149
	2130 ○	1.1	34		2112 ○	0.6	18
7 Tu	0323	3.3	101	22 W	0316	3.6	110
	0914	1.1	34		0907	0.6	18
	1553	4.3	131		1555	4.9	149
	2235	1.2	37		2223	0.6	18
8 W	0425	3.2	98	23 Th	0430	3.6	110
	1013	1.1	34		1018	0.6	18
	1654	4.3	131		1705	5.0	152
	2335	1.1	34		2330	0.5	15
9 Th	0527	3.3	101	24 F	0540	3.8	116
	1112	1.0	30		1128	0.4	12
	1752	4.4	134		1811	5.1	155
10 F	0027	1.0	30	25 Sa	0029	0.3	9
	0621	3.4	104		0642	4.1	125
	1206	0.9	27		1231	0.2	6
	1844	4.5	137		1909	5.1	155
11 Sa	0111	0.8	24	26 Su	0121	0.1	3
	0709	3.6	110		0736	4.4	134
	1255	0.7	21		1328	0.1	3
	1929	4.7	143		2000	5.2	158
12 Su	0149	0.7	21	27 M	0207	0.0	0
	0752	3.9	119		0824	4.7	143
	1340	0.5	15		1420	-0.1	-3
	2010	4.8	146		2047	5.1	155
13 M	0225	0.5	15	28 Tu	0249	-0.1	-3
	0832	4.2	128		0908	4.9	149
	1422	0.3	9		1509	-0.1	-3
	2049	4.9	149		2130 ○	5.0	152
14 Tu ●	0259	0.3	9	29 W	0329	-0.1	-3
	0911	4.4	134		0950	5.0	152
	1504	0.2	6		1555	0.0	0
	2128	4.9	149		2211	4.7	143
15 W	0333	0.2	6	30 Th	0408	0.0	0
	0950	4.7	143		1029	5.0	152
	1546	0.1	3		1639	0.1	3
	2206	4.8	146		2251	4.5	137

Heights are referred to mean lower low water which is the chart datum of soundings.
All times are local time. Daylight Saving Time has been used when needed.

NOTES:

Breakwater Harbor, Delaware, 2004

Times and Heights of High and Low Waters

October

Day	Time	ft	cm	Day	Time	ft	cm
1 F	0445	0.2	6	16 Sa	0415	-0.1	-3
	1108	5.0	152		1047	5.4	165
	1724	0.3	9		1702	-0.1	-3
	2331	4.2	128		2309	4.2	128
2 Sa	0523	0.4	12	17 Su	0500	0.0	0
	1148	4.8	146		1135	5.4	165
	1809	0.5	15		1754	0.0	0
3 Su	0012	3.9	119	18 M	0000	4.0	122
	0603	0.7	21		0550	0.1	3
	1230	4.7	143		1229	5.3	162
	1857	0.7	21		1851	0.2	6
4 M	0057	3.6	110	19 Tu	0057	3.8	116
	0646	0.9	27		0645	0.3	9
	1317	4.5	137		1328	5.1	155
	1950	1.0	30		1954	0.4	12
5 Tu	0147	3.4	104	20 W ●	0201	3.6	110
	0734	1.1	34		0749	0.5	15
	1410	4.3	131		1434	4.9	149
	2048	1.1	34		2102	0.5	15
6 W ○	0244	3.2	98	21 Th	0313	3.6	110
	0830	1.2	37		0859	0.6	18
	1509	4.2	128		1544	4.8	146
	2151	1.2	37		2210	0.5	15
7 Th	0346	3.2	98	22 F	0426	3.7	113
	0932	1.2	37		1013	0.6	18
	1610	4.2	128		1653	4.8	146
	2250	1.1	34		2313	0.4	12
8 F	0448	3.3	101	23 Sa	0532	4.0	122
	1034	1.1	34		1122	0.5	15
	1709	4.3	131		1756	4.8	146
	2342	1.0	30				
9 Sa	0543	3.5	107	24 Su	0008	0.2	6
	1131	0.9	27		0630	4.3	131
	1802	4.4	134		1224	0.3	9
					1851	4.7	143
10 Su	0025	0.8	24	25 M	0057	0.1	3
	0632	3.8	116		0720	4.6	140
	1223	0.7	21		1319	0.2	6
	1849	4.6	140		1940	4.7	143
11 M	0104	0.5	15	26 Tu	0140	0.0	0
	0716	4.2	128		0805	4.8	146
	1310	0.4	12		1408	0.1	3
	1933	4.7	143		2024	4.6	140
12 Tu	0140	0.3	9	27 W	0220	0.0	0
	0757	4.5	137		0845	5.0	152
	1355	0.2	6		1454	0.0	0
	2014	4.7	143		2105	4.4	134
13 W	0217	0.1	3	28 Th ○	0257	0.0	0
	0838	4.9	149		0924	5.0	152
	1440	0.0	0		1537	0.0	0
	2056	4.7	143		2145	4.2	128
14 ●	0255	0.0	0	29 F	0334	0.1	3
	0919	5.1	155		1000	5.0	152
	1526	-0.1	-3		1619	0.1	3
	2138	4.6	140		2223	4.0	122
15 F	0334	-0.1	-3	30 Sa	0410	0.3	9
	1002	5.3	162		1037	5.0	152
	1613	-0.1	-3		1700	0.3	9
	2222	4.4	134		2302	3.8	116
				31 Su	0347	0.4	12
					1016	4.8	146
					1642	0.5	15
					2242	3.6	110

November

Day	Time	ft	cm	Day	Time	ft	cm
1 M	0426	0.6	18	16 Tu	0434	-0.1	-3
	1057	4.6	140		1116	5.3	162
	1727	0.6	18		1740	-0.1	-3
	2325	3.4	104		2347	3.7	113
2 Tu	0508	0.8	24	17 W	0533	0.1	3
	1142	4.5	137		1216	5.1	155
	1815	0.8	24		1841	0.1	3
3 W	0013	3.2	98	18 Th	0052	3.6	110
	0555	1.0	30		0638	0.3	9
	1232	4.3	131		1320	4.8	146
	1907	0.9	27		1945	0.2	6
4 Th	0107	3.2	98	19 F ○	0201	3.7	113
	0649	1.1	34		0749	0.4	12
	1326	4.2	128		1426	4.6	140
	2002	1.0	30		2048	0.2	6
5 F ○	0205	3.2	98	20 Sa	0310	3.8	116
	0748	1.1	34		0901	0.5	15
	1423	4.1	125		1532	4.4	134
	2057	0.9	27		2147	0.2	6
6 Sa	0304	3.3	101	21 Su	0414	4.0	122
	0851	1.0	30		1010	0.4	12
	1520	4.1	125		1633	4.3	131
	2147	0.8	24		2240	0.1	3
7 Su	0400	3.6	110	22 M	0510	4.3	131
	0951	0.9	27		1112	0.3	9
	1614	4.2	128		1728	4.1	125
	2232	0.6	18		2327	0.0	0
8 M	0451	3.9	119	23 Tu	0559	4.5	137
	1047	0.6	18		1206	0.2	6
	1704	4.2	128		1817	4.0	122
	2315	0.3	9				
9 Tu	0538	4.3	131	24 W	0010	0.0	0
	1139	0.3	9		0643	4.7	143
	1753	4.3	131		1255	0.1	3
	2356	0.1	3		1902	3.9	119
10 W	0623	4.7	143	25 Th	0050	0.0	0
	1229	0.1	3		0723	4.8	146
	1839	4.3	131		1340	0.1	3
					1943	3.8	116
11 Th	0038	-0.1	-3	26 F ○	0128	0.1	3
	0707	5.1	155		0800	4.9	149
	1318	-0.2	-6		1421	0.1	3
	1926	4.3	131		2022	3.7	113
12 F ●	0120	-0.3	-9	27 Sa	0205	0.1	3
	0753	5.4	165		0837	4.9	149
	1407	-0.3	-9		1501	0.1	3
	2013	4.2	128		2100	3.6	110
13 Sa	0205	-0.4	-12	28 Su	0242	0.2	6
	0839	5.6	171		0913	4.8	146
	1457	-0.4	-12		1540	0.2	6
	2102	4.1	125		2138	3.4	104
14 Su	0251	-0.4	-12	29 M	0320	0.3	9
	0928	5.6	171		0951	4.7	143
	1548	-0.4	-12		1619	0.3	9
	2153	4.0	122		2217	3.3	101
15 M	0341	-0.3	-9	30 Tu	0358	0.4	12
	1020	5.5	168		1031	4.6	140
	1643	-0.2	-6		1700	0.4	12
	2248	3.8	116		2258	3.2	98

December

Day	Time	ft	cm	Day	Time	ft	cm
1 W	0439	0.5	15	16 Th	0521	-0.2	-6
	1113	4.4	134		1200	5.0	152
	1742	0.5	15		1820	-0.3	-9
	2343	3.2	98				
2 Th	0523	0.6	18	17 F	0034	3.8	116
	1158	4.3	131		0624	0.0	0
	1827	0.6	18		1258	4.6	140
					1918	-0.1	-3
3 F	0031	3.1	94	18 Sa ●	0137	3.8	116
	0612	0.7	21		0731	0.2	6
	1246	4.1	125		1359	4.3	131
	1914	0.6	18		2015	0.0	0
4 Sa	0123	3.2	98	19 Su	0242	3.9	119
	0707	0.8	24		0840	0.4	12
	1336	4.0	122		1501	4.0	122
	2002	0.6	18		2112	0.0	0
5 Su	0218	3.4	104	20 M	0344	4.0	122
	0807	0.8	24		0950	0.4	12
	1430	3.9	119		1602	3.7	113
	2051	0.5	15		2205	0.1	3
6 M	0314	3.6	110	21 Tu	0442	4.2	128
	0909	0.7	21		1054	0.4	12
	1524	3.8	116		1700	3.5	107
	2139	0.3	9		2254	0.1	3
7 Tu	0408	4.0	122	22 W	0534	4.3	131
	1010	0.5	15		1150	0.3	9
	1620	3.8	116		1753	3.4	104
	2227	0.1	3		2340	0.1	3
8 W	0500	4.4	134	23 Th	0620	4.5	137
	1109	0.2	6		1240	0.2	6
	1714	3.8	116		1841	3.4	104
	2315	-0.1	-3				
9 Th	0551	4.8	146	24 F	0023	0.1	3
	1205	-0.1	-3		0701	4.6	140
	1808	3.8	116		1325	0.1	3
					1924	3.3	101
10 F	0003	-0.3	-9	25 Sa	0104	0.1	3
	0641	5.2	158		0741	4.6	140
	1258	-0.3	-9		1406	0.1	3
	1902	3.9	119		2004	3.3	101
11 Sa	0053	-0.5	-15	26 Su	0143	0.1	3
	0731	5.4	165		0818	4.6	140
	1351	-0.5	-15		1444	0.1	3
	1954	3.9	119		2041	3.3	101
12 Su	0143	-0.6	-18	27 M	0221	0.1	3
	0822	5.6	171		0855	4.6	140
	1443	-0.6	-18		1521	0.1	3
	2047	3.9	119		2118	3.3	101
13 M	0234	-0.7	-21	28 Tu	0259	0.1	3
	0914	5.6	171		0933	4.6	140
	1536	-0.6	-18		1557	0.1	3
	2141	3.9	119		2155	3.3	101
14 Tu	0327	-0.6	-18	29 W	0336	0.1	3
	1008	5.5	168		1010	4.5	137
	1629	-0.5	-15		1633	0.2	6
	2236	3.8	116		2233	3.3	101
15 W	0423	-0.5	-15	30 Th	0415	0.2	6
	1103	5.3	162		1048	4.4	134
	1724	-0.4	-12		1710	0.2	6
	2333	3.8	116		2314	3.3	101
				31 F	0457	0.3	9
					1127	4.3	131
					1747	0.2	6
					2357	3.3	101

Heights are referred to mean lower low water which is the chart datum of soundings.
All times are local time. Daylight Saving Time has been used when needed.

NOTES:

Reedy Point, Delaware, 2004
Times and Heights of High and Low Waters

April

Day	Time	ft	cm	Day	Time	ft	cm
1 Th	0201	0.6	18	16 F	0408	0.3	9
	0759	5.6	171		0953	5.9	180
	1450	0.5	15		1640	0.1	3
	2033	5.3	162		2222	6.0	183
2 F	0258	0.4	12	17 Sa	0500	0.2	6
	0849	5.7	174		1042	5.9	180
	1538	0.3	9		1725	0.0	0
	2118	5.6	171		2307	6.1	186
3 Sa	0351	0.2	6	18 Su	0549	0.1	3
	0935	5.8	177		1127	5.9	180
	1623	0.2	6		1807	0.1	3
	2200	5.8	177		2349	6.2	189
4 Su	0543	0.0	0	19 M	0635	0.1	3
	1119	5.9	180		1211	5.8	177
	1807	0.1	3		1846	0.3	9
	2341	6.1	186		●		
5 M	0633	−0.1	−3	20 Tu	0028	6.2	189
	1202	5.9	180		0718	0.1	3
	1850	0.1	3		1253	5.7	174
	O				1923	0.5	15
6 Tu	0022	6.3	192	21 W	0105	6.2	189
	0722	−0.1	−3		0800	0.2	6
	1246	5.8	177		1333	5.5	168
	1933	0.1	3		1958	0.6	18
7 W	0104	6.4	195	22 Th	0141	6.1	186
	0812	0.0	0		0840	0.4	12
	1332	5.7	174		1414	5.3	162
	2016	0.2	6		2030	0.8	24
8 Th	0148	6.5	198	23 F	0216	6.0	183
	0903	0.1	3		0920	0.5	15
	1421	5.5	168		1454	5.2	158
	2103	0.3	9		2103	0.9	27
9 F	0236	6.4	195	24 Sa	0251	5.9	180
	0957	0.2	6		1000	0.7	21
	1515	5.3	162		1536	5.0	152
	2155	0.5	15		2138	0.9	27
10 Sa	0329	6.2	189	25 Su	0329	5.8	177
	1055	0.4	12		1044	0.9	27
	1616	5.1	155		1622	4.9	149
	2254	0.7	21		2222	1.0	30
11 Su	0432	5.9	180	26 M	0415	5.7	174
	1155	0.5	15		1132	1.0	30
	1723	4.9	149		1714	4.9	149
	2358	0.8	24		2315	1.0	30
12 M	0542	5.7	174	27 Tu	0510	5.6	171
	1258	0.5	15		1224	1.0	30
	1832	5.0	152		1810	4.9	149
	O				O		
13 Tu	0105	0.8	24	28 W	0016	1.0	30
	0653	5.6	171		0613	5.6	171
	1359	0.5	15		1319	0.9	27
	1939	5.2	158		1907	5.1	155
14 W	0210	0.7	21	29 Th	0121	1.0	30
	0800	5.7	174		0716	5.6	171
	1457	0.3	9		1413	0.8	24
	2039	5.4	165		2001	5.3	162
15 Th	0311	0.5	15	30 F	0225	0.8	24
	0859	5.8	177		0814	5.7	174
	1550	0.2	6		1505	0.6	18
	2133	5.7	174		2052	5.7	174

May

Day	Time	ft	cm	Day	Time	ft	cm
1 Sa	0325	0.6	18	16 Su	0437	0.3	9
	0908	5.7	174		1016	5.8	177
	1555	0.5	15		1651	0.3	9
	2139	6.0	183		2240	6.4	195
2 Su	0423	0.4	12	17 M	0526	0.3	9
	0959	5.8	177		1102	5.7	174
	1643	0.4	12		1733	0.4	12
	2225	6.3	192		2322	6.4	195
3 M	0519	0.2	6	18 Tu	0612	0.2	6
	1048	5.8	177		1146	5.6	171
	1731	0.3	9		1813	0.5	15
	2310	6.6	201				
4 Tu	0613	0.1	3	19 W	0001	6.4	195
	1137	5.8	177		0655	0.3	9
	1818	0.3	9		1228	5.5	168
	2355	6.7	204		1850	0.7	21
5 W	0706	0.0	0	20 Th	0038	6.3	192
	1226	5.7	174		0737	0.4	12
	1907	0.3	9		1309	5.4	165
					1926	0.8	24
6 Th	0042	6.8	207	21 F	0113	6.2	189
	0759	0.0	0		0817	0.5	15
	1317	5.6	171		1349	5.2	158
	1957	0.4	12		2001	0.9	27
7 F	0131	6.7	204	22 Sa	0147	6.2	189
	0852	0.1	3		0856	0.6	18
	1410	5.5	168		1427	5.1	155
	2049	0.5	15		2035	0.9	27
8 Sa	0223	6.6	201	23 Su	0221	6.1	186
	0946	0.2	6		0935	0.7	21
	1507	5.3	162		1506	5.0	152
	2144	0.6	18		2111	1.0	30
9 Su	0320	6.3	192	24 M	0256	6.0	183
	1042	0.3	9		1015	0.8	24
	1608	5.2	158		1547	5.0	152
	2243	0.8	24		2153	1.0	30
10 M	0422	6.1	186	25 Tu	0337	5.9	180
	1139	0.4	12		1057	0.9	27
	1713	5.2	158		1633	5.1	155
	2345	0.9	27		2242	1.0	30
11 Tu	0529	5.9	180	26 W	0427	5.8	177
	1236	0.4	12		1143	0.9	27
	1818	5.3	162		1724	5.2	158
	O				2340	1.0	30
12 W	0048	0.9	27	27 Th	0524	5.7	174
	0636	5.8	177		1232	0.8	24
	1333	0.4	12		1820	5.3	162
	1920	5.5	168		O		
13 Th	0150	0.8	24	28 F	0044	1.0	30
	0738	5.8	177		0627	5.7	174
	1427	0.3	9		1324	0.7	21
	2017	5.8	177		1915	5.6	171
14 F	0250	0.6	18	29 Sa	0150	0.9	27
	0835	5.8	177		0730	5.6	171
	1518	0.3	9		1417	0.6	18
	2109	6.0	183		2009	6.0	183
15 Sa	0345	0.5	15	30 Su	0255	0.8	24
	0928	5.8	177		0829	5.6	171
	1606	0.2	6		1510	0.5	15
	2156	6.2	189		2101	6.3	192
				31 M	0357	0.6	18
					0925	5.6	171
					1603	0.4	12
					2152	6.6	201

June

Day	Time	ft	cm	Day	Time	ft	cm
1 Tu	0456	0.4	12	16 W	0547	0.4	12
	1020	5.6	171		1121	5.4	165
	1657	0.4	12		1740	0.6	18
	2242	6.8	207		2335	6.3	192
2 W	0554	0.2	6	17 Th	0631	0.4	12
	1114	5.6	171		1204	5.3	162
	1751	0.3	9		1821	0.7	21
	2333	6.9	210		●		
3 Th	0650	0.1	3	18 F	0013	6.3	192
	1208	5.5	168		0714	0.4	12
	1846	0.3	9		1246	5.2	158
	O				1900	0.8	24
4 F	0025	6.9	210	19 Sa	0050	6.2	189
	0744	0.0	0		0755	0.5	15
	1302	5.5	168		1325	5.1	155
	1940	0.4	12		1938	0.8	24
5 Sa	0117	6.8	207	20 Su	0124	6.2	189
	0838	0.0	0		0833	0.6	18
	1358	5.4	165		1402	5.1	155
	2035	0.4	12		2014	0.8	24
6 Su	0212	6.6	201	21 M	0157	6.1	186
	0931	0.1	3		0911	0.6	18
	1455	5.4	165		1438	5.1	155
	2131	0.5	15		2052	0.9	27
7 M	0309	6.4	195	22 Tu	0231	6.1	186
	1023	0.1	3		0947	0.7	21
	1554	5.4	165		1514	5.2	158
	2228	0.7	21		2132	0.9	27
8 Tu	0408	6.1	186	23 W	0309	6.0	183
	1116	0.2	6		1024	0.7	21
	1654	5.4	165		1554	5.3	162
	2326	0.8	24		2218	0.9	27
9 W	0509	5.9	180	24 Th	0353	5.9	180
	1208	0.3	9		1103	0.6	18
	1755	5.5	168		1641	5.4	165
	O				2311	1.0	30
10 Th	0026	0.8	24	25 F	0446	5.8	177
	0611	5.8	177		1147	0.6	18
	1301	0.3	9		1734	5.6	171
	1853	5.7	174		O		
11 F	0125	0.8	24	26 Sa	0013	1.0	30
	0710	5.6	171		0546	5.6	171
	1352	0.3	9		1237	0.6	18
	1948	5.9	180		1832	5.9	180
12 Sa	0223	0.7	21	27 Su	0121	0.9	27
	0806	5.6	171		0651	5.5	168
	1441	0.4	12		1332	0.5	15
	2039	6.1	186		1930	6.1	186
13 Su	0318	0.6	18	28 M	0229	0.8	24
	0859	5.6	171		0756	5.4	165
	1529	0.4	12		1431	0.5	15
	2127	6.2	189		2028	6.4	195
14 M	0411	0.5	15	29 Tu	0335	0.7	21
	0948	5.5	168		0858	5.4	165
	1614	0.5	15		1531	0.4	12
	2211	6.3	192		2125	6.6	201
15 Tu	0500	0.4	12	30 W	0438	0.5	15
	1036	5.5	168		0958	5.4	165
	1658	0.5	15		1632	0.4	12
	2254	6.4	195		2220	6.7	204

Heights are referred to mean lower low water which is the chart datum of soundings.
All times are local time. Daylight Saving Time has been used when needed.

NOTES:

Reedy Point, Delaware, 2004

Times and Heights of High and Low Waters

July

Day	Time (h m)	ft	cm	Day	Time (h m)	ft	cm
1 Th	0537	0.3	9	**16** F	0605	0.4	12
	1056	5.4	165		1139	5.2	158
	1732	0.3	9		1754	0.6	18
	2316	6.8	207		2350	6.2	189
2 F ○	0634	0.1	3	**17** Sa ●	0648	0.4	12
	1152	5.4	165		1221	5.2	158
	1829	0.3	9		1836	0.6	18
3 Sa	0010	6.8	207	**18** Su	0028	6.2	189
	0728	0.0	0		0729	0.4	12
	1248	5.4	165		1300	5.2	158
	1926	0.3	9		1917	0.7	21
4 Su	0104	6.7	204	**19** M	0102	6.2	189
	0820	-0.1	-3		0807	0.5	15
	1343	5.5	168		1335	5.2	158
	2020	0.3	9		1956	0.7	21
5 M	0158	6.6	201	**20** Tu	0135	6.2	189
	0910	-0.1	-3		0844	0.5	15
	1438	5.5	168		1409	5.3	162
	2114	0.4	12		2035	0.7	21
6 Tu	0252	6.4	195	**21** W	0208	6.1	186
	0958	0.0	0		0918	0.5	15
	1533	5.6	171		1443	5.4	165
	2208	0.5	15		2115	0.8	24
7 W	0347	6.1	186	**22** Th	0245	6.1	186
	1046	0.1	3		0952	0.5	15
	1628	5.6	171		1521	5.6	171
	2302	0.7	21		2200	0.8	24
8 Th	0443	5.9	180	**23** F	0327	5.9	180
	1134	0.2	6		1028	0.5	15
	1723	5.7	174		1604	5.8	177
	2358	0.8	24		2251	0.9	27
9 F ○	0540	5.6	171	**24** Sa	0417	5.7	174
	1223	0.4	12		1109	0.5	15
	1818	5.8	177		1656	5.9	180
					2352	1.0	30
10 Sa	0055	0.8	24	**25** Su ○	0516	5.5	168
	0637	5.5	168		1158	0.5	15
	1311	0.5	15		1755	6.0	183
	1912	5.9	180				
11 Su	0152	0.8	24	**26** M	0101	1.0	30
	0733	5.4	165		0623	5.3	162
	1400	0.6	18		1258	0.6	18
	2004	6.0	183		1859	6.2	189
12 M	0247	0.7	21	**27** Tu	0211	0.9	27
	0828	5.3	162		0733	5.2	158
	1449	0.6	18		1404	0.6	18
	2054	6.1	186		2003	6.3	192
13 Tu	0341	0.6	18	**28** W	0318	0.8	24
	0919	5.3	162		0839	5.2	158
	1537	0.6	18		1512	0.5	15
	2141	6.2	189		2105	6.5	198
14 W	0431	0.5	15	**29** Th	0421	0.6	18
	1008	5.3	162		0942	5.2	158
	1624	0.6	18		1616	0.5	15
	2227	6.3	192		2205	6.6	201
15 Th	0520	0.5	15	**30** F	0520	0.3	9
	1055	5.3	162		1041	5.3	162
	1710	0.6	18		1717	0.3	9
	2309	6.3	192		2302	6.7	204
				31 Sa ○	0616	0.1	3
					1137	5.5	168
					1815	0.3	9
					2357	6.7	204

August

Day	Time (h m)	ft	cm	Day	Time (h m)	ft	cm
1 Su	0708	0.0	0	**16** M ●	0002	6.2	189
	1232	5.6	171		0659	0.4	12
	1910	0.2	6		1231	5.4	165
					1855	0.5	15
2 M	0049	6.6	201	**17** Tu	0038	6.2	189
	0757	-0.1	-3		0737	0.4	12
	1324	5.7	174		1306	5.5	168
	2003	0.2	6		1937	0.6	18
3 Tu	0140	6.5	198	**18** W	0112	6.2	189
	0843	-0.1	-3		0813	0.4	12
	1415	5.8	177		1339	5.7	174
	2054	0.3	9		2019	0.6	18
4 W	0230	6.3	192	**19** Th	0146	6.1	186
	0928	0.0	0		0847	0.4	12
	1505	5.8	177		1413	5.8	177
	2144	0.5	15		2101	0.7	21
5 Th	0320	6.0	183	**20** F	0223	6.0	183
	1012	0.2	6		0921	0.4	12
	1554	5.8	177		1451	6.0	183
	2235	0.6	18		2147	0.8	24
6 F	0412	5.8	177	**21** Sa	0306	5.8	177
	1056	0.4	12		0957	0.5	15
	1645	5.8	177		1535	6.1	186
	2327	0.8	24		2240	0.9	27
7 Sa ○	0505	5.5	168	**22** Su	0356	5.6	171
	1140	0.6	18		1041	0.5	15
	1737	5.8	177		1627	6.1	186
					2341	1.0	30
8 Su	0021	0.9	27	**23** M ○	0457	5.3	162
	0601	5.3	162		1135	0.7	21
	1227	0.7	21		1729	6.1	186
	1831	5.8	177				
9 M	0116	1.0	30	**24** Tu	0049	1.1	34
	0658	5.2	158		0607	5.1	155
	1317	0.8	24		1241	0.7	21
	1925	5.9	180		1830	6.1	186
10 Tu	0213	0.9	27	**25** W	0158	1.0	30
	0755	5.1	155		0719	5.0	152
	1408	0.8	24		1352	0.8	24
	2019	5.9	180		1947	6.2	189
11 W	0307	0.8	24	**26** Th	0304	0.8	24
	0849	5.1	155		0827	5.1	155
	1500	0.8	24		1501	0.7	21
	2110	6.1	186		2053	6.3	192
12 Th	0400	0.7	21	**27** F	0405	0.5	15
	0939	5.2	158		0930	5.3	162
	1551	0.7	21		1605	0.5	15
	2158	6.2	189		2153	6.5	198
13 F	0449	0.6	18	**28** Sa	0502	0.3	9
	1027	5.3	162		1028	5.5	168
	1640	0.6	18		1704	0.4	12
	2242	6.2	189		2249	6.6	201
14 Sa	0535	0.5	15	**29** Su	0555	0.1	3
	1111	5.3	162		1122	5.7	174
	1727	0.6	18		1800	0.2	6
	2324	6.3	192		2341	6.6	201
15 Su	0618	0.4	12	**30** M ○	0643	0.0	0
	1153	5.4	165		1213	5.9	180
	1812	0.5	15		1853	0.0	0
				31 Tu	0031	6.5	198
					0729	0.0	0
					1301	6.0	183
					1943	0.2	6

September

Day	Time (h m)	ft	cm	Day	Time (h m)	ft	cm
1 W	0118	6.4	195	**16** Th	0047	6.1	186
	0813	0.1	3		0740	0.3	9
	1347	6.0	183		1309	6.1	186
	2031	0.3	9		2002	0.5	15
2 Th	0205	6.2	189	**17** F	0125	6.0	183
	0854	0.2	6		0817	0.4	12
	1432	6.0	183		1346	6.3	192
	2118	0.5	15		2049	0.6	18
3 F	0251	5.9	180	**18** Sa	0205	5.9	180
	0934	0.4	12		0854	0.4	12
	1517	6.0	183		1426	6.3	192
	2205	0.7	21		2138	0.7	21
4 Sa	0339	5.6	171	**19** Su	0251	5.7	174
	1014	0.6	18		0936	0.5	15
	1603	5.9	180		1513	6.3	192
	2253	0.9	27		2227	0.9	27
5 Su	0430	5.4	165	**20** M	0344	5.4	165
	1055	0.8	24		1025	0.7	21
	1652	5.8	177		1608	6.2	189
	2345	1.0	30		2334	1.0	30
6 M ○	0524	5.1	155	**21** Tu ○	0447	5.2	158
	1140	0.9	27		1126	0.8	24
	1746	5.7	174		1713	6.1	186
7 Tu	0039	1.1	34	**22** W	0039	1.0	30
	0621	5.0	152		0559	5.0	152
	1231	1.0	30		1235	0.9	27
	1843	5.7	174		1826	6.0	183
8 W	0135	1.1	34	**23** Th	0145	0.9	27
	0719	5.0	152		0711	5.0	152
	1326	1.0	30		1345	0.9	27
	1940	5.8	177		1937	6.1	186
9 Th	0230	1.0	30	**24** F	0248	0.7	21
	0815	5.1	155		0818	5.2	158
	1422	0.9	27		1452	0.7	21
	2034	5.9	180		2042	6.2	189
10 F	0324	0.9	27	**25** Sa	0346	0.4	12
	0907	5.2	158		0918	5.5	168
	1517	0.8	24		1553	0.5	15
	2125	6.1	186		2140	6.3	192
11 Sa	0413	0.7	21	**26** Su	0440	0.2	6
	0955	5.4	165		1013	5.8	177
	1609	0.6	18		1650	0.3	9
	2211	6.2	189		2234	6.4	195
12 Su	0459	0.6	18	**27** M	0530	0.1	3
	1039	5.5	168		1104	6.0	183
	1659	0.5	15		1744	0.2	6
	2253	6.2	189		2323	6.4	195
13 M	0543	0.4	12	**28** Tu ○	0616	0.0	0
	1120	5.7	174		1151	6.1	186
	1746	0.4	12		1834	0.2	6
	2333	6.2	189				
14 Tu	0624	0.4	12	**29** W	0010	6.3	192
	1158	5.8	177		0659	0.1	3
	1833	0.4	12		1236	6.2	189
					1922	0.2	6
15 W	0010	6.2	189	**30** Th	0055	6.1	186
	0703	0.3	9		0740	0.2	6
	1234	6.0	183		1318	6.2	189
	1918	0.4	12		2007	0.4	12

Heights are referred to mean lower low water which is the chart datum of soundings.
All times are local time. Daylight Saving Time has been used when needed.

NOTES:

Reedy Point, Delaware, 2004
Times and Heights of High and Low Waters

October

Day	Time (h m)	Height (ft)	Height (cm)	Day	Time (h m)	Height (ft)	Height (cm)
1 F	0139	5.9	180	16 Sa	0105	5.8	177
	0819	0.4	12		0750	0.3	9
	1359	6.1	186		1323	6.5	198
	2052	0.5	15		2036	0.4	12
2 Sa	0223	5.7	174	17 Su	0150	5.6	171
	0855	0.6	18		0834	0.4	12
	1439	6.1	186		1407	6.5	198
	2136	0.7	21		2129	0.5	15
3 Su	0307	5.4	165	18 M	0240	5.4	165
	0932	0.8	24		0922	0.5	15
	1521	5.9	180		1458	6.3	192
	2221	0.9	27		2225	0.6	18
4 M	0355	5.2	158	19 Tu	0337	5.2	158
	1010	0.9	27		1018	0.6	18
	1606	5.8	177		1557	6.1	186
	2308	1.0	30		2324	0.7	21
5 Tu	0446	5.0	152	20 W	0442	5.0	152
	1054	1.0	30		1121	0.8	24
	1658	5.7	174		1704	5.9	180
6 W	0000	1.1	34	21 Th	0026	0.7	21
	0542	4.9	149		0552	4.9	149
	1145	1.1	34		1228	0.8	24
	1756	5.6	171		1816	5.8	177
7 Th	0054	1.2	37	22 F	0128	0.6	18
	0640	4.9	149		0701	5.1	155
	1243	1.0	30		1335	0.7	21
	1856	5.7	174		1925	5.9	180
8 F	0149	1.1	34	23 Sa	0227	0.5	15
	0736	5.0	152		0806	5.3	162
	1342	0.9	27		1439	0.6	18
	1953	5.8	177		2028	5.9	180
9 Sa	0242	0.9	27	24 Su	0323	0.2	6
	0829	5.2	158		0903	5.6	171
	1441	0.8	24		1538	0.4	12
	2046	5.9	180		2124	6.0	183
10 Su	0332	0.7	21	25 M	0414	0.1	3
	0918	5.4	165		0955	5.9	180
	1536	0.6	18		1634	0.2	6
	2133	6.0	183		2215	6.1	186
11 M	0419	0.5	15	26 Tu	0501	0.0	0
	1002	5.7	174		1043	6.1	186
	1629	0.5	15		1725	0.1	3
	2218	6.0	183		2303	6.0	183
12 Tu	0503	0.4	12	27 W	0546	0.0	0
	1044	5.9	180		1128	6.2	189
	1720	0.4	12		1814	0.1	3
	2300	6.1	186		2348	5.9	180
13 W	0546	0.3	9	28 Th	0628	0.1	3
	1124	6.1	186		1209	6.2	189
	1809	0.3	9		1900	0.1	3
	2341	6.0	183				
14 Th	0627	0.2	6	29 F	0032	5.7	174
	1202	6.3	192		0707	0.3	9
	1858	0.3	9		1249	6.2	189
					1944	0.3	9
15 F	0022	5.9	180	30 Sa	0114	5.5	168
	0708	0.2	6		0744	0.4	12
	1241	6.4	195		1328	6.1	186
	1947	0.3	9		2027	0.4	12
				31 Su	0156	5.3	162
					0720	0.6	18
					1306	6.0	183
					2008	0.6	18

November

Day	Time (h m)	Height (ft)	Height (cm)	Day	Time (h m)	Height (ft)	Height (cm)
1 M	0138	5.1	155	16 Tu	0131	5.1	155
	0755	0.7	21		0813	0.2	6
	1344	5.9	180		1349	6.2	189
	2050	0.7	21		2112	0.2	6
2 Tu	0222	5.0	152	17 W	0230	5.0	152
	0831	0.8	24		0910	0.3	9
	1425	5.7	174		1449	6.0	183
	2134	0.9	27		2209	0.3	9
3 W	0308	4.8	146	18 Th	0333	4.9	149
	0913	0.8	24		1011	0.5	15
	1512	5.6	171		1554	5.7	174
	2221	0.9	27		2307	0.3	9
4 Th	0359	4.7	143	19 F	0440	4.9	149
	1002	0.9	27		1115	0.5	15
	1606	5.5	168		1702	5.6	171
	2311	1.0	30				
5 F	0455	4.7	143	20 Sa	0004	0.2	6
	1100	0.9	27		0545	5.1	155
	1705	5.5	168		1219	0.5	15
					1807	5.5	168
6 Sa	0003	0.9	27	21 Su	0100	0.1	3
	0551	4.9	149		0646	5.3	162
	1201	0.8	24		1321	0.4	12
	1805	5.5	168		1907	5.5	168
7 Su	0055	0.7	21	22 M	0154	0.0	0
	0645	5.1	155		0742	5.6	171
	1303	0.7	21		1419	0.2	6
	1900	5.6	171		2002	5.6	171
8 M	0146	0.6	18	23 Tu	0244	−0.1	−3
	0735	5.4	165		0833	5.8	177
	1402	0.5	15		1514	0.1	3
	1952	5.6	171		2053	5.6	171
9 Tu	0234	0.4	12	24 W	0331	−0.1	−3
	0821	5.7	174		0920	5.9	180
	1459	0.4	12		1605	0.0	0
	2040	5.7	174		2141	5.5	168
10 W	0321	0.2	6	25 Th	0415	−0.1	−3
	0906	6.0	183		1003	6.0	183
	1554	0.2	6		1653	−0.1	−3
	2127	5.7	174		2226	5.4	165
11 Th	0407	0.1	3	26 F	0457	0.0	0
	0949	6.2	189		1045	6.0	183
	1647	0.1	3		1738	0.0	0
	2213	5.6	171		2310	5.3	162
12 F	0454	0.0	0	27 Sa	0537	0.2	6
	1033	6.4	195		1124	5.9	180
	1739	0.0	0		1822	0.1	3
	2300	5.5	168		2352	5.1	155
13 Sa	0540	0.0	0	28 Su	0615	0.3	9
	1118	6.5	198		1202	5.9	180
	1831	0.0	0		1903	0.2	6
	2348	5.4	165				
14 Su	0629	0.0	0	29 M	0032	5.0	152
	1204	6.5	198		0651	0.4	12
	1924	0.1	3		1239	5.8	177
					1943	0.3	9
15 M	0038	5.3	162	30 Tu	0112	4.8	146
	0719	0.1	3		0726	0.4	12
	1254	6.4	195		1315	5.7	174
	2017	0.1	3		2022	0.4	12

December

Day	Time (h m)	Height (ft)	Height (cm)	Day	Time (h m)	Height (ft)	Height (cm)
1 W	0151	4.7	143	16 Th	0217	4.9	149
	0801	0.4	12		0858	−0.1	−3
	1352	5.6	171		1437	5.8	177
	2101	0.5	15		2147	−0.2	−6
2 Th	0232	4.6	140	17 F	0317	4.9	149
	0841	0.5	15		0956	0.1	3
	1432	5.5	168		1538	5.5	168
	2142	0.6	18		2240	−0.1	−3
3 F	0315	4.6	140	18 Sa	0419	4.9	149
	0926	0.5	15		1056	0.2	6
	1518	5.4	165		1640	5.3	162
	2226	0.6	18		2334	−0.1	−3
4 Sa	0404	4.7	143	19 Su	0520	5.0	152
	1019	0.5	15		1157	0.2	6
	1612	5.3	162		1742	5.2	158
	2313	0.5	15				
5 Su	0457	4.8	146	20 M	0027	−0.1	−3
	1119	0.6	18		0619	5.2	158
	1711	5.2	158		1257	0.2	6
					1841	5.1	155
6 M	0003	0.4	12	21 Tu	0120	−0.1	−3
	0553	5.0	152		0715	5.4	165
	1224	0.5	15		1355	0.1	3
	1811	5.2	158		1937	5.1	155
7 Tu	0055	0.3	9	22 W	0210	−0.1	−3
	0647	5.3	162		0806	5.5	168
	1328	0.4	12		1450	−0.1	−3
	1909	5.2	158		2029	5.1	155
8 W	0147	0.2	6	23 Th	0259	−0.1	−3
	0739	5.6	171		0854	5.6	171
	1430	0.2	6		1542	−0.2	−6
	2004	5.2	158		2118	5.0	152
9 Th	0240	0.0	0	24 F	0344	−0.1	−3
	0829	5.8	177		0939	5.7	174
	1529	0.1	3		1630	−0.2	−6
	2057	5.2	158		2204	5.0	152
10 F	0333	−0.1	−3	25 Sa	0428	−0.1	−3
	0919	6.1	186		1021	5.7	174
	1626	−0.1	−3		1715	−0.2	−6
	2149	5.2	158		2248	4.9	149
11 Sa	0426	−0.2	−6	26 Su	0510	0.0	0
	1009	6.2	189		1102	5.7	174
	1722	−0.2	−6		1758	−0.1	−3
	2240	5.1	155		2330	4.8	146
12 Su	0519	−0.2	−6	27 M	0549	0.0	0
	1059	6.3	192		1141	5.6	171
	1816	−0.3	−9		1839	−0.1	−3
	2333	5.1	155				
13 M	0612	−0.1	−3	28 Tu	0010	4.7	143
	1151	6.3	192		0627	0.0	0
	1909	−0.3	−9		1217	5.6	171
					1918	0.0	0
14 Tu	0026	5.0	152	29 W	0047	4.7	143
	0707	−0.3	−9		0704	0.1	3
	1244	6.2	189		1252	5.5	168
	2002	−0.3	−9		1954	0.1	3
15 W	0120	5.0	152	30 Th	0123	4.6	140
	0801	−0.2	−6		0739	0.1	3
	1339	6.0	183		1325	5.5	168
	2054	−0.3	−9		2030	0.2	6
				31 F	0157	4.6	140
					0816	0.1	3
					1400	5.4	165
					2105	0.2	6

Heights are referred to mean lower low water which is the chart datum of soundings.
All times are local time. Daylight Saving Time has been used when needed.

NOTES:

65

Philadelphia, Pennsylvania, 2004

Times and Heights of High and Low Waters

April

Day	Time (h m)	Height (ft)	Height (cm)
1 Th	0459	0.7	21
	1046	6.2	189
	1744	0.8	24
	2317	5.8	177
2 F	0556	0.7	21
	1134	6.5	198
	1834	0.8	24
3 Sa	0002	6.2	189
	0650	0.6	18
	1219	6.7	204
	1922	0.7	21
4 Su	0044	6.6	201
	0842	0.5	15
	1402	6.8	207
	2107	0.7	21
5 M ○	0225	6.9	210
	0933	0.4	12
	1444	6.7	204
	2152	0.6	18
6 Tu	0305	7.1	216
	1022	0.3	9
	1527	6.6	201
	2237	0.5	15
7 W	0346	7.2	219
	1112	0.2	6
	1612	6.4	195
	2322	0.4	12
8 Th	0430	7.2	219
	1203	0.1	3
	1700	6.1	186
9 F	0010	0.3	9
	0519	7.1	216
	1255	0.2	6
	1754	5.8	177
10 Sa	0101	0.4	12
	0614	6.8	207
	1349	0.2	6
	1854	5.6	171
11 Su	0156	0.4	12
	0716	6.6	201
	1446	0.3	9
	1959	5.4	165
12 M ○	0254	0.5	15
	0822	6.4	195
	1545	0.5	15
	2105	5.5	168
13 Tu	0356	0.7	21
	0929	6.3	192
	1644	0.5	15
	2210	5.7	174
14 W	0458	0.7	21
	1032	6.4	195
	1742	0.6	18
	2310	6.0	183
15 Th	0558	0.8	24
	1131	6.6	201
	1837	0.6	18
16 F	0005	6.4	195
	0655	0.8	24
	1224	6.7	204
	1928	0.7	21
17 Sa	0055	6.8	207
	0749	0.7	21
	1313	6.8	207
	2015	0.8	24
18 Su	0141	7.1	216
	0839	0.7	21
	1359	6.8	207
	2059	0.8	24
19 M	0224	7.2	219
	0925	0.7	21
	1443	6.7	204
	2140	0.9	27
20 Tu	0304	7.2	219
	1009	0.7	21
	1525	6.5	198
	2219	1.0	30
21 W	0344	7.1	216
	1052	0.6	18
	1608	6.3	192
	2257	1.0	30
22 Th	0422	6.9	210
	1133	0.6	18
	1650	6.1	186
	2333	0.9	27
23 F	0501	6.7	204
	1214	0.6	18
	1734	5.7	174
24 Sa	0010	0.8	24
	0541	6.5	198
	1257	0.6	18
	1820	5.4	165
25 Su	0050	0.8	24
	0625	6.2	189
	1341	0.6	18
	1910	5.2	158
26 M	0134	0.8	24
	0715	6.1	186
	1430	0.7	21
	2004	5.2	158
27 Tu	0226	0.8	24
	0812	6.0	183
	1521	0.8	24
	2100	5.2	158
28 W	0324	0.9	27
	0912	6.0	183
	1616	0.9	27
	2156	5.5	168
29 Th	0426	1.0	30
	1010	6.1	186
	1710	1.0	30
	2249	5.8	177
30 F	0527	1.0	30
	1105	6.3	192
	1804	1.0	30
	2339	6.3	192

May

Day	Time (h m)	Height (ft)	Height (cm)
1 Sa	0627	0.9	27
	1156	6.5	198
	1856	0.9	27
2 Su	0026	6.7	204
	0724	0.8	24
	1244	6.6	201
	1945	0.8	24
3 M	0110	7.1	216
	0819	0.6	18
	1331	6.6	201
	2034	0.7	21
4 Tu ○	0154	7.4	226
	0911	0.4	12
	1417	6.6	201
	2122	0.6	18
5 W	0238	7.6	232
	1003	0.3	9
	1504	6.5	198
	2210	0.5	15
6 Th	0323	7.7	235
	1054	0.2	6
	1553	6.3	192
	2300	0.5	15
7 F	0411	7.6	232
	1146	0.1	3
	1645	6.1	186
	2350	0.5	15
8 Sa	0503	7.3	223
	1238	0.2	6
	1741	5.9	180
9 Su	0044	0.5	15
	0559	7.1	216
	1332	0.2	6
	1842	5.8	177
10 M	0139	0.6	18
	0701	6.8	207
	1427	0.4	12
	1946	5.7	174
11 Tu ○	0237	0.8	24
	0805	6.6	201
	1523	0.5	15
	2051	5.9	180
12 W	0337	0.9	27
	0910	6.5	198
	1619	0.6	18
	2153	6.1	186
13 Th	0437	1.0	30
	1011	6.5	198
	1714	0.7	21
	2251	6.5	198
14 F	0536	1.0	30
	1108	6.5	198
	1806	0.7	21
	2343	6.8	207
15 Sa	0632	0.9	27
	1200	6.6	201
	1856	0.8	24
16 Su	0031	7.1	216
	0725	0.8	24
	1249	6.6	201
	1942	0.8	24
17 M	0116	7.3	223
	0814	0.8	24
	1335	6.5	198
	2026	0.9	27
18 Tu	0158	7.3	223
	0901	0.7	21
	1419	6.4	195
	2107	1.0	30
19 W	0238	7.3	223
	0945	0.6	18
	1502	6.2	189
	2147	1.0	30
20 Th	0317	7.1	216
	1027	0.6	18
	1543	6.0	183
	2225	1.0	30
21 F	0354	7.0	213
	1108	0.6	18
	1625	5.7	174
	2303	1.0	30
22 Sa	0432	6.8	207
	1149	0.6	18
	1706	5.5	168
	2341	0.9	27
23 Su	0509	6.6	201
	1231	0.7	21
	1749	5.4	165
24 M	0022	0.9	27
	0548	6.4	195
	1314	0.7	21
	1834	5.3	162
25 Tu	0107	0.9	27
	0631	6.3	192
	1359	0.8	24
	1924	5.3	162
26 W	0158	1.0	30
	0723	6.2	189
	1447	0.9	27
	2018	5.5	168
27 Th	0254	1.1	34
	0823	6.1	186
	1537	0.9	27
	2114	5.7	174
28 F	0356	1.1	34
	0924	6.1	186
	1630	0.9	27
	2208	6.1	186
29 Sa	0458	1.1	34
	1022	6.2	189
	1723	0.9	27
	2300	6.5	198
30 Su	0600	1.0	30
	1118	6.2	189
	1817	0.8	24
	2350	7.0	213
31 M	0659	0.8	24
	1211	6.3	192
	1910	0.7	21

June

Day	Time (h m)	Height (ft)	Height (cm)
1 Tu	0038	7.3	223
	0756	0.6	18
	1302	6.3	192
	2003	0.6	18
2 W	0126	7.6	232
	0850	0.4	12
	1353	6.3	192
	2055	0.5	15
3 Th ○	0214	7.8	238
	0944	0.2	6
	1443	6.3	192
	2147	0.5	15
4 F	0303	7.8	238
	1036	0.1	3
	1535	6.2	189
	2239	0.4	12
5 Sa	0354	7.7	235
	1127	0.1	3
	1629	6.1	186
	2332	0.5	15
6 Su	0447	7.4	226
	1219	0.2	6
	1726	6.0	183
7 M	0026	0.6	18
	0543	7.2	219
	1311	0.2	6
	1826	6.0	183
8 Tu	0121	0.7	21
	0642	6.9	210
	1403	0.3	9
	1928	6.0	183
9 W ○	0217	0.9	27
	0744	6.6	201
	1456	0.4	12
	2030	6.1	186
10 Th	0314	1.0	30
	0845	6.5	198
	1548	0.5	15
	2129	6.4	195
11 F	0412	1.0	30
	0944	6.3	192
	1640	0.6	18
	2225	6.6	201
12 Sa	0510	1.0	30
	1040	6.3	192
	1731	0.7	21
	2316	6.8	207
13 Su	0605	0.9	27
	1133	6.2	189
	1820	0.7	21
14 M	0003	7.0	213
	0658	0.7	21
	1222	6.2	189
	1907	0.7	21
15 Tu	0048	7.1	216
	0747	0.6	18
	1309	6.1	186
	1952	0.8	24
16 W	0131	7.1	216
	0834	0.5	15
	1355	6.0	183
	2035	0.8	24
17 Th ●	0212	7.1	216
	0919	0.5	15
	1438	5.9	180
	2117	0.8	24
18 F	0252	7.0	213
	1002	0.5	15
	1520	5.7	174
	2158	0.8	24
19 Sa	0330	6.9	210
	1044	0.5	15
	1601	5.6	171
	2236	0.9	27
20 Su	0407	6.8	207
	1125	0.6	18
	1640	5.5	168
	2319	0.9	27
21 M	0442	6.7	204
	1206	0.7	21
	1719	5.4	165
22 Tu	0001	0.9	27
	0517	6.6	201
	1247	0.7	21
	1759	5.4	165
23 W	0046	1.0	30
	0555	6.4	195
	1329	0.8	24
	1843	5.5	168
24 Th	0136	1.0	30
	0641	6.3	192
	1413	0.8	24
	1933	5.7	174
25 F	0231	1.1	34
	0737	6.1	186
	1500	0.7	21
	2029	6.0	183
26 Sa	0330	1.1	34
	0841	6.0	183
	1551	0.7	21
	2127	6.3	192
27 Su	0433	1.0	30
	0944	5.9	180
	1645	0.7	21
	2223	6.6	201
28 M	0535	0.9	27
	1045	5.8	177
	1742	0.6	18
	2318	7.0	213
29 Tu	0636	0.7	21
	1142	5.9	180
	1840	0.5	15
30 W	0011	7.3	223
	0734	0.5	15
	1238	5.9	180
	1937	0.4	12

Heights are referred to mean lower low water which is the chart datum of soundings.
All times are local time. Daylight Saving Time has been used when needed.

NOTES:

Philadelphia, Pennsylvania, 2004
Times and Heights of High and Low Waters

July

Day	h m	ft	cm
1 Th	0103	7.5	229
	0830	0.3	9
	1332	6.0	183
	2032	0.4	12
2 F ○	0154	7.7	235
	0924	0.2	6
	1425	6.1	186
	2127	0.4	12
3 Sa	0245	7.7	235
	1016	0.1	3
	1518	6.2	189
	2220	0.4	12
4 Su	0337	7.6	232
	1107	0.2	6
	1612	6.2	189
	2313	0.5	15
5 M	0429	7.4	226
	1157	0.2	6
	1708	6.2	189
6 Tu	0006	0.7	21
	0524	7.2	219
	1247	0.3	9
	1804	6.2	189
7 W	0059	0.8	24
	0619	6.9	210
	1336	0.4	12
	1903	6.2	189
8 Th	0153	0.9	27
	0717	6.6	201
	1425	0.5	15
	2001	6.3	192
9 F ○	0248	1.0	30
	0815	6.3	192
	1514	0.5	15
	2057	6.4	195
10 Sa	0343	0.9	27
	0913	6.0	183
	1603	0.5	15
	2152	6.5	198
11 Su	0439	0.9	27
	1009	5.9	180
	1653	0.6	18
	2243	6.6	201
12 M	0534	0.7	21
	1103	5.8	177
	1742	0.6	18
	2332	6.7	204
13 Tu	0627	0.6	18
	1154	5.7	174
	1831	0.6	18
14 W	0019	6.8	207
	0717	0.5	15
	1243	5.7	174
	1918	0.6	18
15 Th	0104	6.9	210
	0806	0.4	12
	1330	5.7	174
	2004	0.6	18
16 F	0147	6.9	210
	0852	0.4	12
	1414	5.7	174
	2049	0.6	18
17 Sa ●	0228	6.9	210
	0936	0.5	15
	1457	5.7	174
	2132	0.7	21
18 Su	0307	6.9	210
	1018	0.5	15
	1536	5.6	171
	2215	0.8	24
19 M	0344	6.8	207
	1100	0.6	18
	1614	5.6	171
	2259	0.9	27
20 Tu	0418	6.8	207
	1140	0.7	21
	1650	5.7	174
	2343	0.9	27
21 W	0452	6.6	201
	1220	0.7	21
	1726	5.8	177
22 Th	0029	0.9	27
	0528	6.5	198
	1300	0.7	21
	1805	5.9	180
23 F	0118	1.0	30
	0610	6.3	192
	1343	0.6	18
	1853	6.0	183
24 Sa	0212	1.0	30
	0704	6.0	183
	1428	0.5	15
	1949	6.2	189
25 Su ○	0310	0.9	27
	0807	5.7	174
	1519	0.5	15
	2051	6.4	195
26 M	0411	0.9	27
	0915	5.5	168
	1615	0.6	18
	2152	6.6	201
27 Tu	0513	0.8	24
	1019	5.5	168
	1716	0.4	12
	2252	6.8	207
28 W	0615	0.6	18
	1120	5.6	171
	1817	0.4	12
	2349	7.1	216
29 Th	0714	0.5	15
	1218	5.8	177
	1916	0.4	12
30 F	0044	7.3	223
	0810	0.3	9
	1314	6.0	183
	2014	0.4	12
31 Sa ○	0137	7.5	229
	0904	0.3	9
	1408	6.2	189
	2109	0.4	12

August

Day	h m	ft	cm
1 Su	0229	7.6	232
	0955	0.3	9
	1501	6.4	195
	2202	0.5	15
2 M	0319	7.6	232
	1044	0.3	9
	1553	6.5	198
	2254	0.6	18
3 Tu	0410	7.4	226
	1132	0.4	12
	1645	6.5	198
	2345	0.8	24
4 W	0501	7.1	216
	1218	0.5	15
	1737	6.5	198
5 Th	0036	0.9	27
	0553	6.8	207
	1304	0.5	15
	1831	6.4	195
6 F	0127	0.9	27
	0647	6.4	195
	1349	0.6	18
	1925	6.4	195
7 Sa ○	0219	0.9	27
	0743	6.0	183
	1435	0.6	18
	2019	6.3	192
8 Su	0311	0.9	27
	0840	5.7	174
	1523	0.6	18
	2114	6.3	192
9 M	0405	0.8	24
	0937	5.5	168
	1612	0.5	15
	2207	6.3	192
10 Tu	0459	0.7	21
	1032	5.5	168
	1702	0.6	18
	2259	6.4	195
11 W	0553	0.5	15
	1125	5.5	168
	1753	0.5	15
	2349	6.6	201
12 Th	0645	0.5	15
	1216	5.6	171
	1844	0.5	15
13 F	0036	6.7	204
	0734	0.4	12
	1304	5.7	174
	1933	0.5	15
14 Sa	0121	6.9	210
	0822	0.3	9
	1348	5.8	177
	2021	0.6	18
15 Su	0203	6.9	210
	0907	0.5	15
	1430	5.9	180
	2108	0.7	21
16 M ●	0242	7.0	213
	0950	0.6	18
	1509	6.0	183
	2154	0.8	24
17 Tu	0319	6.9	210
	1031	0.7	21
	1546	6.0	183
	2239	0.8	24
18 W	0354	6.8	207
	1112	0.7	21
	1620	6.1	186
	2325	0.9	27
19 Th	0428	6.6	201
	1152	0.7	21
	1655	6.2	189
20 F	0012	0.9	27
	0505	6.4	195
	1232	0.6	18
	1734	6.3	192
21 Sa	0102	0.8	24
	0549	6.1	186
	1315	0.5	15
	1822	6.4	195
22 Su	0156	0.8	24
	0642	5.8	177
	1403	0.5	15
	1919	6.4	195
23 M ○	0253	0.8	24
	0747	5.5	168
	1456	0.4	12
	2023	6.4	195
24 Tu	0353	0.7	21
	0855	5.3	162
	1555	0.4	12
	2129	6.5	198
25 W	0454	0.7	21
	1002	5.3	162
	1657	0.4	12
	2232	6.7	204
26 Th	0555	0.6	18
	1105	5.5	168
	1759	0.5	15
	2332	7.0	213
27 F	0654	0.5	15
	1203	5.8	177
	1859	0.5	15
28 Sa	0028	7.2	219
	0749	0.5	15
	1259	6.2	189
	1957	0.5	15
29 Su	0121	7.4	226
	0842	0.4	12
	1352	6.5	198
	2051	0.6	18
30 M ○	0211	7.5	229
	0931	0.5	15
	1442	6.7	204
	2144	0.7	21
31 Tu	0300	7.4	226
	1018	0.5	15
	1531	6.8	207
	2234	0.8	24

September

Day	h m	ft	cm
1 W	0348	7.2	219
	1103	0.6	18
	1619	6.9	210
	2323	0.9	27
2 Th	0436	6.9	210
	1147	0.7	21
	1707	6.8	207
3 F	0011	0.9	27
	0524	6.5	198
	1229	0.7	21
	1755	6.6	201
4 Sa	0059	0.9	27
	0615	6.1	186
	1312	0.7	21
	1846	6.4	195
5 Su	0147	0.9	27
	0709	5.8	177
	1355	0.7	21
	1938	6.2	189
6 M ●	0237	0.8	24
	0805	5.5	168
	1441	0.6	18
	2033	6.1	186
7 Tu	0329	0.7	21
	0903	5.3	162
	1530	0.6	18
	2129	6.1	186
8 W	0422	0.7	21
	0959	5.3	162
	1622	0.6	18
	2223	6.2	189
9 Th	0516	0.6	18
	1054	5.4	165
	1716	0.6	18
	2316	6.4	195
10 F	0609	0.6	18
	1146	5.6	171
	1810	0.6	18
11 Sa	0005	6.6	201
	0700	0.6	18
	1234	5.8	177
	1903	0.6	18
12 Su	0051	6.8	207
	0748	0.6	18
	1319	6.0	183
	1954	0.7	21
13 M	0134	7.0	213
	0834	0.7	21
	1400	6.2	189
	2043	0.7	21
14 Tu	0214	7.0	213
	0918	0.7	21
	1439	6.4	195
	2117	0.7	21
15 W	0252	6.9	210
	1000	0.7	21
	1515	6.6	201
	2219	0.7	21
16 Th	0328	6.7	204
	1042	0.7	21
	1551	6.7	204
	2307	0.7	21
17 F	0406	6.5	198
	1123	0.6	18
	1628	6.7	204
	2356	0.7	21
18 Sa	0446	6.2	189
	1207	0.6	18
	1710	6.7	204
19 Su	0047	0.6	18
	0534	5.9	180
	1253	0.5	15
	1800	6.6	201
20 M	0140	0.6	18
	0630	5.6	171
	1343	0.4	12
	1859	6.5	198
21 Tu ○	0237	0.6	18
	0734	5.3	162
	1439	0.4	12
	2004	6.5	198
22 W	0335	0.6	18
	0843	5.3	162
	1539	0.5	15
	2112	6.5	198
23 Th	0435	0.6	18
	0949	5.4	165
	1641	0.5	15
	2216	6.6	201
24 F	0535	0.6	18
	1052	5.7	174
	1743	0.6	18
	2316	6.9	210
25 Sa	0632	0.5	15
	1150	6.1	186
	1843	0.6	18
26 Su	0012	7.1	216
	0726	0.5	15
	1244	6.5	198
	1940	0.7	21
27 M	0104	7.2	219
	0817	0.6	18
	1334	6.8	207
	2034	0.7	21
28 Tu ○	0153	7.3	223
	0905	0.6	18
	1422	7.0	213
	2124	0.8	24
29 W	0239	7.2	219
	0950	0.7	21
	1508	7.1	216
	2213	0.8	24
30 Th	0325	6.9	210
	1033	0.8	24
	1552	7.0	213
	2300	0.9	27

Heights are referred to mean lower low water which is the chart datum of soundings.
All times are local time. Daylight Saving Time has been used when needed.

NOTES:

Philadelphia, Pennsylvania, 2004
Times and Heights of High and Low Waters

October

Day	Time	ft	cm	Day	Time	ft	cm
1 F	0410	6.6	201	16 Sa	0345	6.2	189
	1114	0.8	24		1057	0.5	16
	1635	6.9	210		1605	7.0	213
	2345	0.9	27		2339	0.4	12
2 Sa	0457	6.2	189	17 Su	0430	6.0	183
	1154	0.8	24		1144	0.4	12
	1720	6.6	201		1651	7.0	213
3 Su	0030	0.8	24	18 M	0031	0.4	12
	0545	5.8	177		0522	5.7	174
	1234	0.8	24		1234	0.3	9
	1807	6.4	195		1744	6.8	207
4 M	0116	0.8	24	19 Tu	0124	0.4	12
	0636	5.5	168		0620	5.4	165
	1316	0.7	21		1327	0.3	9
	1857	6.2	189		1844	6.6	201
5 Tu	0203	0.7	21	20 W	0220	0.4	12
	0730	5.3	162		0725	5.3	162
	1400	0.7	21		1424	0.4	12
	1951	6.0	183		1950	6.5	198
6 W	0252	0.7	21	21 Th	0317	0.4	12
	0827	5.1	155		0831	5.3	162
	1449	0.6	18		1524	0.5	15
	2047	6.0	183		2056	6.5	198
7 Th	0344	0.7	21	22 F	0415	0.4	12
	0924	5.2	158		0937	5.6	171
	1543	0.6	18		1625	0.6	18
	2144	6.1	186		2200	6.5	198
8 F	0437	0.7	21	23 Sa	0512	0.5	15
	1019	5.3	162		1038	5.9	180
	1639	0.7	21		1726	0.6	18
	2238	6.3	192		2259	6.7	204
9 Sa	0530	0.7	21	24 Su	0607	0.5	15
	1112	5.6	171		1134	6.3	192
	1736	0.7	21		1825	0.7	21
	2329	6.5	198		2353	6.8	207
10 Su	0622	0.7	21	25 M	0700	0.5	15
	1200	5.9	180		1227	6.7	204
	1832	0.7	21		1921	0.7	21
11 M	0016	6.7	204	26 Tu	0044	6.8	207
	0711	0.7	21		0750	0.5	15
	1245	6.2	189		1315	6.9	210
	1926	0.7	21		2014	0.7	21
12 Tu	0100	6.8	207	27 W	0132	6.8	207
	0758	0.7	21		0836	0.6	18
	1327	6.5	198		1400	7.1	216
	2018	0.7	21		2104	0.7	21
13 W	0142	6.8	207	28 Th	0218	6.6	201
	0844	0.7	21		0920	0.7	21
	1406	6.8	207		1443	7.1	216
	2109	0.6	18		2151	0.7	21
14 Th	0223	6.7	204	29 F	0303	6.4	195
	0928	0.6	18		1002	0.8	24
	1444	6.9	210		1525	7.0	213
	2159	0.5	15		2236	0.7	21
15 F	0303	6.5	198	30 Sa	0347	6.1	186
	1012	0.6	18		1042	0.8	24
	1523	7.0	213		1606	6.8	207
	2249	0.5	15		2320	0.7	21
				31 Su	0331	5.8	177
					1021	0.8	24
					1548	6.5	198
					2303	0.6	18

November

Day	Time	ft	cm	Day	Time	ft	cm
1 M	0417	5.5	168	16 Tu	0410	5.5	168
	1100	0.7	21		1117	0.1	3
	1631	6.3	192		1631	6.8	207
	2346	0.6	18				
2 Tu	0505	5.2	158	17 W	0006	0.0	0
	1140	0.6	18		0509	5.4	165
	1718	6.1	186		1211	0.2	6
					1731	6.6	201
3 W	0030	0.6	18	18 Th	0100	0.1	3
	0556	5.1	155		0612	5.4	165
	1224	0.6	18		1308	0.3	9
	1809	6.0	183		1834	6.4	195
4 Th	0117	0.6	18	19 F	0155	0.1	3
	0650	5.0	152		0717	5.5	168
	1312	0.6	18		1407	0.4	12
	1904	5.9	180		1938	6.3	192
5 F	0206	0.6	18	20 Sa	0250	0.2	6
	0745	5.1	155		0820	5.7	174
	1406	0.6	18		1506	0.5	15
	2000	6.0	183		2039	6.3	192
6 Sa	0257	0.6	18	21 Su	0345	0.2	6
	0840	5.3	162		0919	6.0	183
	1503	0.7	21		1606	0.5	15
	2055	6.1	186		2137	6.3	192
7 Su	0348	0.6	18	22 M	0439	0.3	9
	0932	5.6	171		1014	6.3	192
	1602	0.7	21		1704	0.5	15
	2147	6.2	189		2231	6.3	192
8 M	0440	0.6	18	23 Tu	0530	0.3	9
	1021	5.9	180		1105	6.6	201
	1701	0.7	21		1800	0.5	15
	2237	6.2	189		2322	6.2	189
9 Tu	0531	0.6	18	24 W	0619	0.4	12
	1107	6.3	192		1152	6.7	204
	1758	0.6	18		1853	0.4	12
	2324	6.3	192				
10 W	0620	0.5	15	25 Th	0010	6.1	186
	1151	6.6	201		0706	0.4	12
	1853	0.5	15		1237	6.8	207
					1942	0.4	12
11 Th	0009	6.3	192	26 F	0056	6.0	183
	0709	0.5	15		0750	0.5	15
	1233	6.9	210		1319	6.8	207
	1947	0.4	12		2028	0.4	12
12 F	0054	6.2	189	27 Sa	0141	5.8	177
	0757	0.4	12		0832	0.5	15
	1316	7.1	216		1401	6.7	204
	2039	0.2	6		2112	0.4	12
13 Sa	0139	6.0	183	28 Su	0225	5.6	171
	0845	0.3	9		0912	0.5	15
	1400	7.1	216		1441	6.5	198
	2130	0.1	3		2155	0.4	12
14 Su	0226	5.9	180	29 M	0308	5.4	165
	0934	0.2	6		0952	0.5	15
	1446	7.1	216		1522	6.4	195
	2222	0.1	3		2237	0.4	12
15 M	0316	5.7	174	30 Tu	0351	5.2	158
	1025	0.1	3		1031	0.4	12
	1536	7.0	213		1602	6.2	189
	2313	0.0	0		2318	0.4	12

December

Day	Time	ft	cm	Day	Time	ft	cm
1 W	0436	5.0	152	16 Th	0455	5.5	168
	1111	0.4	12		1154	0.0	0
	1645	6.1	186		1715	6.6	201
2 Th	0000	0.4	12	17 F	0037	-0.2	-6
	0521	5.0	152		0555	5.6	171
	1154	0.4	12		1249	0.1	3
	1730	6.0	183		1814	6.4	195
3 F	0043	0.4	12	18 Sa	0129	-0.1	-3
	0610	5.0	152		0656	5.7	174
	1241	0.4	12		1346	0.2	6
	1819	5.9	180		1915	6.2	189
4 Sa	0128	0.4	12	19 Su	0221	-0.1	-3
	0701	5.0	152		0717	5.0	152
	1332	0.5	15		1444	0.3	9
	1912	5.8	177		2014	6.0	183
5 Su	0215	0.4	12	20 M	0314	0.0	0
	0754	5.2	158		0854	6.0	183
	1429	0.5	15		1542	0.4	12
	2007	5.7	174		2111	5.8	177
6 M	0305	0.4	12	21 Tu	0406	0.1	3
	0846	5.5	168		0948	6.1	186
	1529	0.6	18		1640	0.3	9
	2102	5.7	174		2206	5.7	174
7 Tu	0356	0.4	12	22 W	0458	0.1	3
	0937	5.8	177		1039	6.2	189
	1630	0.5	15		1735	0.3	9
	2155	5.7	174		2258	5.6	171
8 W	0449	0.3	9	23 Th	0547	0.2	6
	1026	6.2	189		1127	6.3	192
	1731	0.4	12		1828	0.2	6
	2247	5.7	174		2347	5.5	168
9 Th	0543	0.2	6	24 F	0635	0.2	6
	1115	6.5	198		1213	6.4	195
	1829	0.3	9		1917	0.1	3
	2337	5.6	171				
10 F	0636	0.1	3	25 Sa	0035	5.4	165
	1203	6.7	204		0720	0.2	6
	1925	0.1	3		1257	6.4	195
					2004	0.1	3
11 Sa	0027	5.6	171	26 Su	0120	5.3	162
	0729	0.0	0		0804	0.2	6
	1251	6.9	210		1339	6.3	192
	2019	0.0	0		2048	0.1	3
12 Su	0118	5.6	171	27 M	0204	5.2	158
	0822	-0.1	-3		0846	0.2	6
	1340	7.0	213		1420	6.3	192
	2111	-0.2	-6		2130	0.1	3
13 M	0209	5.6	171	28 Tu	0246	5.2	158
	0914	-0.1	-3		0926	0.2	6
	1430	7.0	213		1459	6.2	189
	2203	-0.2	-6		2211	0.2	6
14 Tu	0301	5.6	171	29 W	0328	5.1	155
	1007	-0.2	-6		1007	0.2	6
	1522	7.0	213		1538	6.2	189
	2254	-0.3	-9		2251	0.2	6
15 W	0357	5.6	171	30 Th	0408	5.0	152
	1100	-0.1	-3		1047	0.2	6
	1617	6.8	207		1616	6.1	186
	2346	-0.3	-9		2331	0.2	6
				31 F	0448	5.0	152
					1130	0.2	6
					1654	6.0	183

Heights are referred to mean lower low water which is the chart datum of soundings.
All times are local time. Daylight Saving Time has been used when needed.

NOTES:

Baltimore, Maryland, 2004

Times and Heights of High and Low Waters

April

Day	Time	ft	cm	Day	Time	ft	cm
1 Th	0306	1.1	34	**16** F	0503	1.4	43
	0926	0.2	6		1150	0.2	6
	1550	1.3	40		1749	1.4	43
	2232	0.4	12				
2 F	0356	1.2	37	**17** Sa	0010	0.4	12
	1024	0.2	6		0554	1.5	46
	1637	1.3	40		1245	0.2	6
	2308	0.3	9		1831	1.3	40
3 Sa	0443	1.3	40	**18** Su	0044	0.3	9
	1118	0.1	3		0642	1.6	49
	1719	1.3	40		1336	0.2	6
	2342	0.3	9		1909	1.3	40
4 Su	0628	1.4	43	**19** M	0113	0.3	9
	1311	0.1	3		0725	1.7	52
	1900	1.3	40		1424	0.3	9
					1945	1.2	37
5 M ○	0114	0.2	6	**20** Tu	0139	0.3	9
	0714	1.6	49		0806	1.7	52
	1404	0.1	3		1511	0.3	9
	1941	1.3	40		2021	1.1	34
6 Tu	0147	0.1	3	**21** W	0205	0.3	9
	0800	1.7	52		0845	1.7	52
	1500	0.1	3		1557	0.4	12
	2024	1.2	37		2059	1.1	34
7 W	0221	0.1	3	**22** Th	0233	0.3	9
	0847	1.8	55		0922	1.7	52
	1558	0.2	6		1641	0.4	12
	2109	1.1	34		2139	1.1	34
8 Th	0259	0.1	3	**23** F	0307	0.3	9
	0937	1.8	55		0959	1.7	52
	1658	0.2	6		1724	0.5	15
	2159	1.0	30		2222	1.0	30
9 F	0343	0.1	3	**24** Sa	0346	0.3	9
	1029	1.8	55		1038	1.6	49
	1800	0.3	9		1807	0.5	15
	2253	1.0	30		2308	1.0	30
10 Sa	0435	0.1	3	**25** Su	0433	0.4	12
	1125	1.8	55		1121	1.6	49
	1903	0.3	9		1852	0.5	15
	2352	1.0	30		2359	1.1	34
11 Su	0539	0.2	6	**26** M	0528	0.5	15
	1228	1.7	52		1209	1.5	46
	2005	0.3	9		1938	0.5	15
12 M ○	0056	1.0	30	**27** Tu	0052	1.1	34
	0656	0.2	6		0632	0.5	15
	1337	1.6	49		1304	1.4	43
	2104	0.4	12		2024	0.5	15
13 Tu	0202	1.1	34	**28** W	0147	1.2	37
	0820	0.2	6		0743	0.5	15
	1450	1.5	46		1402	1.4	43
	2158	0.4	12		2109	0.5	15
14 W	0306	1.2	37	**29** Th	0241	1.2	37
	0939	0.2	6		0854	0.5	15
	1600	1.4	43		1500	1.4	43
	2247	0.4	12		2152	0.5	15
15 Th	0407	1.3	40	**30** F	0334	1.4	43
	1049	0.2	6		1002	0.5	15
	1700	1.4	43		1554	1.4	43
	2332	0.4	12		2231	0.4	12

May

Day	Time	ft	cm	Day	Time	ft	cm
1 Sa	0425	1.5	46	**16** Su	0641	1.8	55
	1106	0.4	12		1242	0.4	12
	1645	1.4	43		1750	1.2	37
	2307	0.4	12		2352	0.4	12
2 Su	0515	1.6	49	**17** M	0626	1.9	58
	1207	0.4	12		1334	0.5	15
	1732	1.3	40		1830	1.2	37
	2343	0.3	9				
3 M	0603	1.8	55	**18** Tu	0020	0.3	9
	1306	0.3	9		0707	1.9	58
	1820	1.3	40		1422	0.5	15
					1910	1.1	34
4 Tu ○	0019	0.2	6	**19** W ●	0048	0.3	9
	0651	2.0	61		0744	1.9	58
	1404	0.3	9		1507	0.5	15
	1908	1.2	37		1951	1.1	34
5 W	0057	0.2	6	**20** Th	0118	0.4	12
	0739	2.1	64		0819	1.9	58
	1501	0.3	9		1547	0.5	15
	1957	1.1	34		2033	1.1	34
6 Th	0139	0.2	6	**21** F	0153	0.4	12
	0828	2.1	64		0853	1.9	58
	1558	0.3	9		1625	0.5	15
	2049	1.1	34		2116	1.1	34
7 F	0226	0.2	6	**22** Sa	0233	0.4	12
	0918	2.1	64		0928	1.8	55
	1654	0.3	9		1701	0.5	15
	2145	1.1	34		2201	1.1	34
8 Sa	0320	0.2	6	**23** Su	0318	0.5	15
	1012	2.0	61		1006	1.8	55
	1749	0.3	9		1737	0.5	15
	2243	1.1	34		2247	1.2	37
9 Su	0423	0.3	9	**24** M	0407	0.5	15
	1110	1.9	58		1048	1.7	52
	1845	0.4	12		1815	0.5	15
	2344	1.2	37		2334	1.2	37
10 M	0537	0.4	12	**25** Tu	0502	0.6	18
	1213	1.8	55		1134	1.6	49
	1939	0.4	12		1854	0.5	15
11 Tu ○	0048	1.3	40	**26** W	0024	1.3	40
	0659	0.4	12		0604	0.6	18
	1320	1.6	49		1223	1.6	49
	2031	0.5	15		1934	0.5	15
12 W	0152	1.4	43	**27** Th ○	0116	1.3	40
	0821	0.4	12		0713	0.7	21
	1426	1.5	46		1315	1.5	46
	2121	0.5	15		2014	0.5	15
13 Th	0256	1.5	46	**28** F	0209	1.4	43
	0936	0.4	12		0827	0.7	21
	1527	1.4	43		1408	1.5	46
	2206	0.4	12		2052	0.4	12
14 F	0356	1.6	49	**29** Sa	0303	1.6	49
	1044	0.4	12		0942	0.6	18
	1620	1.4	43		1502	1.4	43
	2246	0.4	12		2130	0.4	12
15 Sa	0451	1.7	52	**30** Su	0356	1.7	52
	1146	0.4	12		1054	0.6	18
	1707	1.3	40		1555	1.3	40
	2321	0.4	12		2209	0.3	9
				31 M	0448	1.9	58
					1201	0.5	15
					1649	1.2	37
					2249	0.2	6

June

Day	Time	ft	cm	Day	Time	ft	cm
1 Tu	0539	2.1	64	**16** W	0646	2.0	61
	1304	0.5	15		1413	0.6	18
	1744	1.2	37		1841	1.1	34
	2332	0.2	6				
2 W	0629	2.2	67	**17** Th	0009	0.4	12
	1402	0.4	12		0722	2.0	61
	1839	1.1	34		1452	0.5	15
				●	1927	1.1	34
3 Th ○	0019	0.2	6	**18** F	0048	0.4	12
	0720	2.3	70		0756	1.9	58
	1456	0.4	12		1527	0.5	15
	1936	1.1	34		2012	1.1	34
4 F	0111	0.2	6	**19** Sa	0130	0.5	15
	0811	2.3	70		0830	1.9	58
	1548	0.4	12		1600	0.5	15
	2033	1.1	34		2055	1.1	34
5 Sa	0208	0.2	6	**20** Su	0215	0.5	15
	0904	2.2	67		0905	1.9	58
	1638	0.4	12		1632	0.5	15
	2131	1.2	37		2138	1.2	37
6 Su	0312	0.3	9	**21** M	0301	0.5	15
	1000	2.1	64		0942	1.8	55
	1728	0.4	12		1704	0.5	15
	2229	1.3	40		2221	1.2	37
7 M	0421	0.4	12	**22** Tu	0350	0.6	18
	1057	1.9	58		1022	1.8	55
	1817	0.4	12		1737	0.5	15
	2330	1.4	43		2306	1.3	40
8 Tu	0535	0.5	15	**23** W	0442	0.6	18
	1155	1.8	55		1104	1.7	52
	1905	0.4	12		1811	0.5	15
					2354	1.4	43
9 W ○	0032	1.4	43	**24** Th	0541	0.7	21
	0652	0.5	15		1148	1.6	49
	1253	1.6	49		1846	0.4	12
	1952	0.4	12				
10 Th	0136	1.5	46	**25** F ○	0045	1.5	46
	0810	0.6	18		0650	0.7	21
	1349	1.5	46		1234	1.6	49
	2036	0.4	12		1921	0.4	12
11 F	0239	1.6	49	**26** Sa	0139	1.6	49
	0924	0.6	18		0809	0.8	24
	1442	1.4	43		1324	1.4	43
	2117	0.4	12		1957	0.3	9
12 Sa	0340	1.7	52	**27** Su	0234	1.8	55
	1035	0.6	18		0931	0.7	21
	1532	1.3	40		1418	1.3	40
	2153	0.4	12		2036	0.3	9
13 Su	0435	1.8	55	**28** M	0329	1.9	58
	1139	0.6	18		1049	0.7	21
	1620	1.2	37		1515	1.2	37
	2227	0.4	12		2119	0.2	6
14 M	0524	1.9	58	**29** Tu	0424	2.1	64
	1237	0.6	18		1157	0.6	18
	1707	1.1	34		1616	1.1	34
	2259	0.4	12		2208	0.2	6
15 Tu	0607	2.0	61	**30** W	0517	2.2	67
	1328	0.6	18		1257	0.5	15
	1754	1.1	34		1718	1.1	34
	2333	0.4	12		2301	0.2	6

Heights are referred to mean lower low water which is the chart datum of soundings.
All times are local time. Daylight Saving Time has been used when needed.

NOTES:

Baltimore, Maryland, 2004

Times and Heights of High and Low Waters

July

Day	Time	ft	cm	Day	Time	ft	cm
1 Th	0611	2.3	70	**16** F	0659	1.9	58
	1351	0.5	15		1424	0.6	18
	1819	1.1	34		1905	1.1	34
	2359	0.2	6				
2 F ○	0705	2.3	70	**17** Sa ●	0033	0.5	15
	1440	0.4	12		0735	1.9	58
	1919	1.2	37		1456	0.6	18
					1949	1.2	37
3 Sa	0101	0.2	6	**18** Su	0119	0.5	15
	0759	2.2	67		0809	1.9	58
	1527	0.4	12		1526	0.6	18
	2016	1.2	37		2031	1.2	37
4 Su	0205	0.3	9	**19** M	0204	0.5	15
	0853	2.1	64		0844	1.9	58
	1613	0.4	12		1556	0.5	15
	2113	1.3	40		2111	1.3	40
5 M	0310	0.3	9	**20** Tu	0250	0.6	18
	0946	2.0	61		0919	1.8	55
	1657	0.4	12		1626	0.5	15
	2211	1.4	43		2153	1.4	43
6 Tu	0417	0.4	12	**21** W	0337	0.6	18
	1038	1.9	58		0956	1.8	55
	1741	0.4	12		1655	0.5	15
	2309	1.5	46		2237	1.4	43
7 W	0525	0.5	15	**22** Th	0429	0.7	21
	1128	1.7	52		1034	1.7	52
	1823	0.4	12		1725	0.4	12
					2324	1.5	46
8 Th	0010	1.6	49	**23** F	0529	0.7	21
	0637	0.6	18		1115	1.6	49
	1216	1.6	49		1756	0.4	12
	1904	0.4	12				
9 F ○	0112	1.7	52	**24** Sa	0015	1.7	52
	0752	0.7	21		0643	0.8	24
	1304	1.4	43		1200	1.5	46
	1942	0.4	12		1830	0.3	9
10 Sa	0214	1.7	52	**25** Su ○	0109	1.8	55
	0909	0.7	21		0806	0.8	24
	1352	1.3	40		1249	1.4	43
	2019	0.4	12		1908	0.3	9
11 Su	0314	1.8	55	**26** M	0205	1.9	58
	1022	0.8	24		0930	0.8	24
	1442	1.2	37		1346	1.2	37
	2056	0.4	12		1953	0.2	6
12 M	0409	1.9	58	**27** Tu	0303	2.1	64
	1128	0.7	21		1044	0.7	21
	1535	1.1	34		1449	1.1	34
	2134	0.4	12		2045	0.2	6
13 Tu	0458	1.9	58	**28** W	0402	2.2	67
	1223	0.7	21		1148	0.6	18
	1630	1.1	34		1556	1.1	34
	2215	0.4	12		2146	0.2	6
14 W	0542	2.0	61	**29** Th	0501	2.2	67
	1310	0.6	18		1242	0.6	18
	1725	1.1	34		1702	1.1	34
	2259	0.4	12		2251	0.2	6
15 Th	0622	2.0	61	**30** F	0559	2.2	67
	1349	0.6	18		1330	0.5	15
	1817	1.1	34		1805	1.2	37
	2346	0.4	12		2358	0.3	9
				31 Sa ○	0655	2.2	67
					1415	0.5	15
					1903	1.3	40

August

Day	Time	ft	cm	Day	Time	ft	cm
1 Su	0103	0.3	9	**16** M ●	0110	0.5	15
	0748	2.1	64		0744	1.9	58
	1458	0.5	15		1443	0.6	18
	1959	1.4	43		2002	1.4	43
2 M	0206	0.3	9	**17** Tu	0155	0.6	18
	0839	2.0	61		0817	1.9	58
	1539	0.5	15		1511	0.5	15
	2054	1.5	46		2043	1.5	46
3 Tu	0307	0.4	12	**18** W	0241	0.6	18
	0926	1.9	58		0851	1.8	55
	1618	0.5	15		1539	0.5	15
	2149	1.6	49		2125	1.6	49
4 W	0408	0.5	15	**19** Th	0330	0.7	21
	1010	1.8	55		0927	1.8	55
	1656	0.4	12		1607	0.4	12
	2244	1.7	52		2209	1.7	52
5 Th	0511	0.6	18	**20** F	0426	0.7	21
	1052	1.7	52		1004	1.7	52
	1731	0.4	12		1636	0.4	12
	2341	1.7	52		2256	1.8	55
6 F	0619	0.7	21	**21** Sa	0532	0.8	24
	1134	1.5	46		1046	1.5	46
	1805	0.4	12		1707	0.3	9
					2347	1.9	58
7 Sa ○	0040	1.8	55	**22** Su	0647	0.8	24
	0733	0.8	24		1133	1.4	43
	1217	1.4	43		1745	0.3	9
	1840	0.4	12				
8 Su	0138	1.8	55	**23** M ○	0041	2.0	61
	0850	0.9	27		0809	0.8	24
	1305	1.2	37		1227	1.3	40
	1917	0.4	12		1830	0.3	9
9 M	0237	1.9	58	**24** Tu	0140	2.1	64
	1002	0.8	24		0925	0.8	24
	1358	1.1	34		1330	1.2	37
	2000	0.4	12		1925	0.3	9
10 Tu	0332	1.9	58	**25** W	0242	2.1	64
	1104	0.8	24		1032	0.7	21
	1458	1.1	34		1439	1.2	37
	2048	0.4	12		2032	0.3	9
11 W	0424	1.9	58	**26** Th	0347	2.1	64
	1154	0.8	24		1128	0.7	21
	1600	1.1	34		1548	1.2	37
	2143	0.5	15		2145	0.4	12
12 Th	0512	1.9	58	**27** F	0450	2.1	64
	1236	0.7	21		1217	0.6	18
	1659	1.1	34		1654	1.3	40
	2239	0.5	15		2258	0.3	9
13 F	0555	1.9	58	**28** Sa	0550	2.1	64
	1311	0.7	21		1302	0.6	18
	1752	1.2	37		1754	1.4	43
	2332	0.5	15				
14 Sa	0634	1.9	58	**29** Su	0005	0.3	9
	1344	0.6	18		0644	2.0	61
	1839	1.3	40		1344	0.5	15
					1850	1.5	46
15 Su	0023	0.5	15	**30** M ○	0107	0.3	9
	0710	1.9	58		0732	2.0	61
	1414	0.6	18		1422	0.5	15
	1922	1.3	40		1943	1.6	49
				31 Tu	0205	0.4	12
					0816	1.9	58
					1458	0.5	15
					2035	1.7	52

September

Day	Time	ft	cm	Day	Time	ft	cm
1 W	0301	0.5	15	**16** Th	0236	0.6	18
	0856	1.8	55		0819	1.7	52
	1531	0.4	12		1448	0.4	12
	2126	1.8	55		2058	1.8	55
2 Th	0358	0.6	18	**17** F	0331	0.7	21
	0935	1.7	52		0857	1.6	49
	1602	0.4	12		1516	0.3	9
	2217	1.8	55		2142	1.9	58
3 F	0458	0.7	21	**18** Sa	0432	0.7	21
	1013	1.5	46		0938	1.5	46
	1632	0.4	12		1548	0.3	9
	2308	1.9	58		2230	2.0	61
4 Sa	0603	0.8	24	**19** Su	0539	0.7	21
	1053	1.4	43		1024	1.4	43
	1703	0.4	12		1626	0.3	9
					2322	2.1	64
5 Su	0000	1.9	58	**20** M	0652	0.8	24
	0712	0.9	27		1117	1.2	37
	1136	1.3	40		1711	0.3	9
	1738	0.4	12				
6 M ○	0053	1.9	58	**21** Tu ○	0018	2.1	64
	0823	0.9	27		0804	0.7	21
	1226	1.2	37		1217	1.2	37
	1820	0.5	15		1808	0.3	9
7 Tu	0148	1.8	55	**22** W	0120	2.1	64
	0929	0.9	27		0910	0.7	21
	1324	1.1	34		1325	1.2	37
	1912	0.5	15		1918	0.4	12
8 W	0245	1.8	55	**23** Th	0228	2.0	61
	1024	0.8	24		1009	0.7	21
	1429	1.1	34		1436	1.2	37
	2013	0.6	18		2038	0.4	12
9 Th	0341	1.8	55	**24** F	0336	2.0	61
	1109	0.8	24		1100	0.6	18
	1533	1.2	37		1544	1.3	40
	2119	0.6	18		2157	0.4	12
10 F	0432	1.8	55	**25** Sa	0439	1.9	58
	1148	0.8	24		1147	0.6	18
	1631	1.2	37		1647	1.4	43
	2221	0.6	18		2308	0.4	12
11 Sa	0518	1.8	55	**26** Su	0535	1.9	58
	1222	0.7	21		1228	0.5	15
	1723	1.3	40		1744	1.5	46
	2318	0.6	18				
12 Su	0558	1.8	55	**27** M	0011	0.4	12
	1254	0.6	18		0623	1.8	55
	1809	1.4	43		1306	0.5	15
					1838	1.7	52
13 M	0009	0.6	18	**28** Tu ○	0109	0.4	12
	0634	1.8	55		0706	1.8	55
	1324	0.6	18		1341	0.4	12
	1852	1.5	46		1928	1.8	55
14 Tu ●	0057	0.6	18	**29** W	0204	0.5	15
	0709	1.8	55		0745	1.7	52
	1353	0.5	15		1411	0.4	12
	1934	1.6	49		2017	1.8	55
15 W	0146	0.6	18	**30** Th	0258	0.5	15
	0743	1.8	55		0822	1.6	49
	1420	0.4	12		1440	0.4	12
	2015	1.7	52		2103	1.9	58

Heights are referred to mean lower low water which is the chart datum of soundings.
All times are local time. Daylight Saving Time has been used when needed.

NOTES:

Baltimore, Maryland, 2004

Times and Heights of High and Low Waters

October

Day	Time (h m)	Height ft	cm	Day	Time (h m)	Height ft	cm
1 F	0352	0.6	18	16 Sa	0335	0.5	15
	0859	1.4	43		0830	1.3	40
	1507	0.3	9		1432	0.1	3
	2148	1.9	58		2119	2.0	61
2 Sa	0448	0.7	21	17 Su	0437	0.5	15
	0937	1.3	40		0917	1.2	37
	1535	0.3	9		1511	0.1	3
	2232	1.9	58		2208	2.1	64
3 Su	0546	0.8	24	18 M	0540	0.6	18
	1017	1.2	37		1010	1.1	34
	1608	0.4	12		1558	0.2	6
	2317	1.9	58		2302	2.0	61
4 M	0646	0.8	24	19 Tu	0644	0.6	18
	1103	1.2	37		1108	1.1	34
	1647	0.4	12		1654	0.2	6
5 Tu	0005	1.8	55	20 W	0001	2.0	61
	0745	0.8	24		0746	0.5	15
	1156	1.1	34		1213	1.1	34
	1736	0.5	15		1804	0.3	9
6 W	0056	1.7	52	21 Th	0106	1.9	58
	0841	0.8	24		0845	0.5	15
	1255	1.1	34		1321	1.1	34
	1835	0.5	15		1925	0.3	9
7 Th	0152	1.7	52	22 F	0215	1.8	55
	0930	0.8	24		0938	0.5	15
	1359	1.1	34		1431	1.2	37
	1943	0.6	18		2048	0.4	12
8 F	0249	1.7	52	23 Sa	0320	1.7	52
	1013	0.7	21		1027	0.5	15
	1501	1.2	37		1538	1.3	40
	2053	0.6	18		2204	0.3	9
9 Sa	0342	1.6	49	24 Su	0419	1.6	49
	1052	0.7	21		1111	0.4	12
	1559	1.3	40		1639	1.4	43
	2158	0.6	18		2311	0.3	9
10 Su	0429	1.6	49	25 M	0509	1.6	49
	1126	0.6	18		1150	0.3	9
	1651	1.3	40		1736	1.5	46
	2257	0.6	18				
11 M	0511	1.6	49	26 Tu	0012	0.4	12
	1158	0.5	15		0553	1.5	46
	1738	1.5	46		1225	0.3	9
	2352	0.5	15		1827	1.7	52
12 Tu	0550	1.6	49	27 W	0109	0.4	12
	1228	0.4	12		0633	1.4	43
	1822	1.6	49		1256	0.2	6
					1915	1.7	52
13 W	0046	0.5	15	28 Th	0204	0.4	12
	0628	1.6	49		0711	1.3	40
	1257	0.3	9		1323	0.2	6
	1905	1.7	52		1959	1.8	55
14 Th	0140	0.5	15	29 F	0256	0.5	15
	0706	1.5	46		0748	1.2	37
	1327	0.2	6		1350	0.1	3
	1948	1.8	55		2040	1.8	55
15 F	0237	0.5	15	30 Sa	0347	0.5	15
	0746	1.4	43		0827	1.1	34
	1357	0.2	6		1418	0.1	3
	2032	2.0	61		2119	1.8	55
				31 Su	0337	0.5	15
					0807	1.0	30
					1351	0.2	6
					2059	1.8	55

November

Day	Time (h m)	Height ft	cm	Day	Time (h m)	Height ft	cm
1 M	0425	0.6	18	16 Tu	0427	0.3	9
	0850	1.0	30		0859	0.9	27
	1429	0.2	6		1447	0.0	0
	2139	1.7	52		2149	1.8	55
2 Tu	0512	0.6	18	17 W	0523	0.3	9
	0937	1.0	30		0959	0.9	27
	1513	0.3	9		1553	0.0	0
	2223	1.6	49		2249	1.7	52
3 W	0559	0.6	18	18 Th	0618	0.3	9
	1029	1.0	30		1104	1.0	30
	1604	0.3	9		1709	0.1	3
	2311	1.5	46		2352	1.6	49
4 Th	0646	0.6	18	19 F	0712	0.3	9
	1125	1.0	30		1212	1.0	30
	1704	0.4	12		1829	0.2	6
5 F	0002	1.5	46	20 Sa	0054	1.5	46
	0730	0.5	15		0802	0.2	6
	1225	1.0	30		1321	1.1	34
	1810	0.4	12		1948	0.2	6
6 Sa	0055	1.4	43	21 Su	0153	1.4	43
	0812	0.5	15		0848	0.1	3
	1325	1.1	34		1428	1.2	37
	1908	0.4	12		2102	0.2	6
7 Su	0145	1.4	43	22 M	0245	1.3	40
	0850	0.4	12		0930	0.1	3
	1422	1.1	34		1530	1.3	40
	2028	0.5	15		2210	0.2	6
8 M	0233	1.4	43	23 Tu	0332	1.2	37
	0925	0.3	9		1007	0.0	0
	1516	1.3	40		1626	1.4	43
	2134	0.4	12		2312	0.3	9
9 Tu	0318	1.3	40	24 W	0416	1.1	34
	0958	0.2	6		1040	0.0	0
	1605	1.4	43		1716	1.5	46
	2237	0.4	12				
10 W	0401	1.3	40	25 Th	0010	0.3	9
	1030	0.1	3		0458	1.0	30
	1652	1.6	49		1111	-0.1	-3
	2338	0.4	12		1800	1.6	49
11 Th	0446	1.2	37	26 F	0103	0.3	9
	1103	0.0	0		0539	0.9	27
	1738	1.7	52		1146	-0.1	-3
					1840	1.6	49
12 F	0038	0.4	12	27 Sa	0152	0.3	9
	0531	1.1	34		0620	0.8	24
	1138	-0.1	-3		1211	-0.1	-3
	1823	1.8	55		1918	1.6	49
13 Sa	0136	0.3	9	28 Su	0236	0.3	9
	0618	1.0	30		0702	0.8	24
	1217	-0.1	-3		1246	-0.1	-3
	1910	1.9	58		1955	1.5	46
14 Su	0234	0.3	9	29 M	0317	0.3	9
	0709	1.0	30		0744	0.8	24
	1300	-0.1	-3		1324	-0.1	-3
	2000	1.9	58		2032	1.5	46
15 M	0331	0.3	9	30 Tu	0356	0.3	9
	0802	0.9	27		0828	0.8	24
	1350	-0.1	-3		1406	0.0	0
	2052	1.9	58		2110	1.4	43

December

Day	Time (h m)	Height ft	cm	Day	Time (h m)	Height ft	cm
1 W	0434	0.3	9	16 Th	0453	0.0	0
	0913	0.8	24		0945	0.8	24
	1451	0.0	0		1555	-0.2	-6
	2151	1.4	43		2234	1.4	43
2 Th	0512	0.3	9	17 F	0543	0.0	0
	1001	0.8	24		1048	0.9	27
	1541	0.1	3		1707	-0.1	-3
	2234	1.3	40		2329	1.2	37
3 F	0552	0.2	6	18 Sa	0632	0.0	0
	1053	0.8	24		1155	0.9	27
	1635	0.1	3		1822	0.0	0
	2318	1.3	40				
4 Sa	0631	0.2	6	19 Su	0023	1.1	34
	1148	0.8	24		0719	-0.1	-3
	1736	0.2	6		1304	1.0	30
					1939	0.0	0
5 Su	0004	1.2	37	20 M	0114	1.0	30
	0709	0.1	3		0803	-0.2	-6
	1246	0.9	27		1412	1.1	34
	1845	0.2	6		2054	0.1	3
6 M	0051	1.1	34	21 Tu	0204	0.9	27
	0746	0.0	0		0843	-0.2	-6
	1343	1.0	30		1515	1.2	37
	2000	0.3	9		2205	0.1	3
7 Tu	0138	1.1	34	22 W	0252	0.8	24
	0822	-0.1	-3		0921	-0.3	-9
	1439	1.1	34		1611	1.2	37
	2116	0.3	9		2308	0.1	3
8 W	0227	1.0	30	23 Th	0340	0.7	21
	0858	-0.2	-6		0957	-0.3	-9
	1532	1.3	40		1700	1.3	40
	2227	0.2	6				
9 Th	0317	0.9	27	24 F	0004	0.1	3
	0936	-0.2	-6		0427	0.6	18
	1622	1.5	46		1033	-0.3	-9
	2333	0.2	6		1743	1.3	40
10 F	0409	0.8	24	25 Sa	0053	0.1	3
	1017	-0.3	-9		0514	0.6	18
	1712	1.6	49		1110	-0.3	-9
					1823	1.3	40
11 Sa	0033	0.1	3	26 Su	0136	0.1	3
	0503	0.7	21		0559	0.6	18
	1102	-0.4	-12		1149	-0.3	-9
	1802	1.7	52		1900	1.3	40
12 Su	0129	0.1	3	27 M	0213	0.1	3
	0557	0.7	21		0642	0.6	18
	1152	-0.4	-12		1229	-0.3	-9
	1854	1.7	52		1940	1.3	40
13 M	0221	0.0	0	28 Tu	0248	0.1	3
	0652	0.7	21		0724	0.6	18
	1246	-0.4	-12		1311	-0.2	-6
	1947	1.7	52		2011	1.2	37
14 Tu	0312	0.0	0	29 W	0321	0.1	3
	0748	0.7	21		0806	0.6	18
	1344	-0.4	-12		1353	-0.2	-6
	2041	1.6	49		2047	1.2	37
15 W	0403	0.0	0	30 Th	0353	0.0	0
	0845	0.8	24		0848	0.6	18
	1448	-0.3	-9		1436	-0.2	-6
	2137	1.5	46		2123	1.2	37
				31 F	0426	0.0	0
					0932	0.6	18
					1521	-0.1	-3
					2200	1.1	34

Heights are referred to mean lower low water which is the chart datum of soundings.
All times are local time. Daylight Saving Time has been used when needed.

NOTES:

71

Annapolis (US Naval Academy), Maryland, 2004

Times and Heights of High and Low Waters

April

Day	h m	ft	cm	Day	h m	ft	cm
1 Th	0136	0.9	27	16 F	0333	1.2	37
	0742	0.2	6		1006	0.2	6
	1420	1.1	34		1619	1.2	37
	2048	0.4	12		2226	0.3	9
2 F	0226	1.0	30	17 Sa	0424	1.3	40
	0840	0.1	3		1101	0.2	6
	1507	1.1	34		1701	1.1	34
	2124	0.3	9		2300	0.3	9
3 Sa	0313	1.1	34	18 Su	0512	1.4	43
	0934	0.1	3		1152	0.2	6
	1549	1.1	34		1739	1.1	34
	2158	0.2	6		2329	0.3	9
4 Su	0458	1.2	37	19 M	0555	1.5	46
	1127	0.1	3		1240	0.2	6
	1730	1.1	34		1815	1.0	30
	2330	0.2	6		2355	0.3	9
5 M ○	0544	1.3	40	20 Tu	0636	1.5	46
	1220	0.1	3		1327	0.3	9
	1811	1.1	34		1851	1.0	30
6 Tu	0003	0.1	3	21 W	0021	0.2	6
	0630	1.5	46		0715	1.6	46
	1316	0.1	3		1413	0.4	12
	1854	1.0	30		1929	0.9	27
7 W	0037	0.1	3	22 Th	0049	0.2	6
	0717	1.6	49		0752	1.5	46
	1414	0.1	3		1457	0.4	12
	1939	1.0	30		2009	0.9	27
8 Th	0115	0.0	0	23 F	0123	0.3	9
	0807	1.6	49		0829	1.5	46
	1514	0.2	6		1540	0.4	12
	2029	0.9	27		2052	0.9	27
9 F	0159	0.0	0	24 Sa	0202	0.3	9
	0859	1.6	49		0908	1.4	43
	1616	0.2	6		1623	0.5	15
	2123	0.9	27		2138	0.9	27
10 Sa	0251	0.1	3	25 Su	0249	0.4	12
	0955	1.5	46		0951	1.4	43
	1719	0.3	9		1708	0.5	15
	2222	0.9	27		2229	0.9	27
11 Su	0355	0.2	6	26 M	0344	0.4	12
	1058	1.5	46		1039	1.3	40
	1821	0.3	9		1754	0.5	15
	2326	0.9	27		2322	1.0	30
12 M ○	0512	0.2	6	27 Tu	0448	0.5	15
	1207	1.4	43		1134	1.3	40
	1920	0.3	9		1840	0.5	15
13 Tu	0032	1.0	30	28 W	0017	1.0	30
	0636	0.2	6		0559	0.5	15
	1320	1.3	40		1232	1.2	37
	2014	0.4	12		1925	0.5	15
14 W	0136	1.0	30	29 Th	0111	1.1	34
	0755	0.2	6		0710	0.5	15
	1430	1.2	37		1330	1.2	37
	2103	0.4	12		2008	0.5	15
15 Th	0237	1.1	34	30 F	0204	1.2	37
	0905	0.2	6		0818	0.4	12
	1530	1.2	37		1424	1.2	37
	2148	0.4	12		2047	0.4	12

May

Day	h m	ft	cm	Day	h m	ft	cm
1 Sa	0255	1.3	40	16 Su	0411	1.5	46
	0922	0.4	12		1058	0.4	12
	1515	1.2	37		1620	1.1	34
	2123	0.3	9		2208	0.3	9
2 Su	0345	1.4	43	17 M	0456	1.6	49
	1023	0.4	12		1150	0.4	12
	1602	1.1	34		1700	1.0	30
	2159	0.3	9		2236	0.3	9
3 M	0433	1.6	49	18 Tu	0537	1.7	52
	1122	0.3	9		1238	0.4	12
	1650	1.1	34		1740	1.0	30
	2235	0.2	6		2304	0.3	9
4 Tu	0521	1.7	52	19 W	0614	1.7	52
	1220	0.3	9		1323	0.5	15
	1738	1.0	30		1821	0.9	27
	2313	0.2	6 ○		2334	0.3	9
5 W	0609	1.8	55	20 Th	0649	1.7	52
	1317	0.3	9		1403	0.5	15
	1827	1.0	30		1903	0.9	27
	2355	0.1	3				
6 Th	0658	1.9	58	21 F	0009	0.4	12
	1414	0.3	9		0723	1.6	49
	1919	1.0	30		1441	0.5	15
					1946	0.9	27
7 F	0042	0.2	6	22 Sa	0049	0.4	12
	0748	1.9	58		0758	1.6	49
	1510	0.3	9		1517	0.5	15
	2015	1.0	30		2031	1.0	30
8 Sa	0136	0.2	6	23 Su	0134	0.5	15
	0842	1.8	55		0836	1.5	46
	1605	0.3	9		1553	0.5	15
	2113	1.0	30		2117	1.0	30
9 Su	0239	0.3	9	24 M	0223	0.5	15
	0940	1.7	52		0918	1.5	46
	1701	0.4	12		1631	0.5	15
	2214	1.0	30		2204	1.0	30
10 M	0353	0.4	12	25 Tu	0318	0.6	18
	1043	1.5	46		1004	1.4	43
	1755	0.4	12		1710	0.5	15
	2318	1.1	34		2254	1.1	34
11 Tu ○	0515	0.4	12	26 W	0420	0.6	18
	1150	1.4	43		1053	1.4	43
	1847	0.4	12		1750	0.5	15
					2346	1.2	37
12 W	0022	1.2	37	27 Th ○	0529	0.6	18
	0637	0.4	12		1145	1.3	40
	1256	1.3	40		1830	0.5	15
	1937	0.4	12				
13 Th	0126	1.3	40	28 F	0039	1.2	37
	0752	0.4	12		0643	0.6	18
	1357	1.3	40		1238	1.3	40
	2022	0.4	12		1908	0.4	12
14 F	0226	1.4	43	29 Sa	0133	1.4	43
	0900	0.4	12		0758	0.6	18
	1450	1.2	37		1332	1.2	37
	2102	0.4	12		1946	0.4	12
15 Sa	0321	1.5	46	30 Su	0226	1.5	46
	1002	0.4	12		0910	0.6	18
	1537	1.1	34		1425	1.1	34
	2137	0.4	12		2025	0.3	9
				31 M	0318	1.7	52
					1017	0.5	15
					1519	1.1	34
					2105	0.2	6

June

Day	h m	ft	cm	Day	h m	ft	cm
1 Tu	0409	1.8	55	16 W	0516	1.7	52
	1120	0.5	15		1229	0.5	15
	1614	1.0	30		1711	0.9	27
	2148	0.2	6		2225	0.4	12
2 W	0459	1.9	58	17 Th	0552	1.7	52
	1218	0.4	12		1308	0.5	15
	1709	1.0	30		1757	0.9	27
	2235	0.2	6		● 2304	0.4	12
3 Th	0550	2.0	61	18 F	0626	1.7	52
	1312	0.4	12		1343	0.5	15
	1806	1.0	30		1842	0.9	27
	○ 2327	0.2	6		2346	0.4	12
4 F	0641	2.0	61	19 Sa	0700	1.7	52
	1404	0.3	9		1416	0.5	15
	1903	1.0	30		1925	1.0	30
5 Sa	0024	0.2	6	20 Su	0031	0.5	15
	0734	1.9	58		0735	1.6	49
	1454	0.3	9		1448	0.5	15
	2001	1.0	30		2008	1.0	30
6 Su	0128	0.3	9	21 M	0117	0.5	15
	0830	1.8	55		0812	1.6	49
	1544	0.4	12		1520	0.5	15
	2059	1.1	34		2051	1.1	34
7 M	0237	0.4	12	22 Tu	0206	0.6	18
	0927	1.7	52		0852	1.5	46
	1633	0.4	12		1553	0.5	15
	2200	1.2	37		2136	1.1	34
8 Tu	0351	0.4	12	23 W	0258	0.6	18
	1025	1.5	46		0934	1.5	46
	1721	0.4	12		1627	0.5	15
	2302	1.3	40		2224	1.2	37
9 W ○	0508	0.5	15	24 Th	0357	0.7	21
	1123	1.4	43		1018	1.4	43
	1808	0.4	12		1702	0.4	12
					2315	1.3	40
10 Th	0006	1.3	40	25 F ○	0506	0.7	21
	0626	0.6	18		1104	1.3	40
	1219	1.3	40		1737	0.4	12
	1852	0.4	12				
11 F	0109	1.4	43	26 Sa	0009	1.4	43
	0740	0.6	18		0625	0.7	21
	1312	1.2	37		1154	1.2	37
	1933	0.4	12		1813	0.3	9
12 Sa	0210	1.5	46	27 Su	0104	1.5	46
	0851	0.6	18		0747	0.7	21
	1402	1.1	34		1248	1.1	34
	2009	0.4	12		1852	0.2	6
13 Su	0305	1.6	49	28 M	0159	1.7	52
	0955	0.6	18		0905	0.7	21
	1450	1.0	30		1345	1.0	30
	2043	0.3	9		1935	0.2	6
14 M	0354	1.7	52	29 Tu	0253	1.8	55
	1053	0.6	18		1013	0.6	18
	1537	1.0	30		1446	1.0	30
	2115	0.3	9		2024	0.2	6
15 Tu	0437	1.7	52	30 W	0347	1.9	58
	1144	0.6	18		1113	0.5	15
	1624	0.9	27		1548	0.9	27
	2149	0.3	9		2117	0.2	6

Heights are referred to mean lower low water which is the chart datum of soundings.
All times are local time. Daylight Saving Time has been used when needed.

NOTES:

Annapolis (US Naval Academy), Maryland, 2004

Times and Heights of High and Low Waters

July

Day	Time	Height ft	Height cm	Day	Time	Height ft	Height cm
1 Th	0441	2.0	61	**16** F	0529	1.7	52
	1207	0.4	12		1240	0.6	18
	1649	0.9	27		1735	1.0	30
	2215	0.2	6		2249	0.4	12
2 F ○	0535	2.0	61	**17** Sa ●	0605	1.7	52
	1256	0.4	12		1312	0.5	15
	1749	1.0	30		1819	1.0	30
	2317	0.2	6		2335	0.5	15
3 Sa	0629	1.9	58	**18** Su	0639	1.6	49
	1343	0.4	12		1342	0.5	15
	1846	1.1	34		1901	1.1	34
4 Su	0021	0.2	6	**19** M	0020	0.5	15
	0723	1.9	58		0714	1.6	49
	1429	0.4	12		1412	0.5	15
	1943	1.2	37		1941	1.1	34
5 M	0126	0.3	9	**20** Tu	0106	0.5	15
	0816	1.7	52		0749	1.6	49
	1513	0.4	12		1442	0.5	15
	2041	1.2	37		2023	1.2	37
6 Tu	0233	0.4	12	**21** W	0153	0.6	18
	0908	1.6	49		0826	1.6	49
	1557	0.4	12		1511	0.4	12
	2139	1.3	40		2107	1.2	37
7 W	0341	0.5	15	**22** Th	0245	0.6	18
	0958	1.5	46		0904	1.5	46
	1639	0.4	12		1541	0.4	12
	2240	1.4	43		2154	1.3	40
8 Th	0453	0.6	18	**23** F	0345	0.7	21
	1046	1.4	43		0945	1.4	43
	1720	0.4	12		1612	0.3	9
	2342	1.4	43		2245	1.4	43
9 F ○	0608	0.7	21	**24** Sa	0459	0.8	24
	1134	1.2	37		1030	1.3	40
	1758	0.4	12		1646	0.3	9
					2339	1.6	49
10 Sa	0044	1.5	46	**25** Su ○	0622	0.8	24
	0725	0.7	21		1119	1.2	37
	1222	1.1	34		1724	0.2	6
	1835	0.3	9				
11 Su	0144	1.6	49	**26** M	0035	1.7	52
	0838	0.7	21		0746	0.8	24
	1312	1.0	30		1216	1.1	34
	1912	0.3	9		1809	0.2	6
12 M	0239	1.6	49	**27** Tu	0133	1.8	55
	0944	0.7	21		0900	0.7	21
	1405	1.0	30		1319	1.0	30
	1950	0.3	9		1901	0.2	6
13 Tu	0328	1.7	52	**28** W	0232	1.9	58
	1039	0.7	21		1004	0.6	18
	1500	0.9	27		1426	1.0	30
	2031	0.4	12		2002	0.2	6
14 W	0412	1.7	52	**29** Th	0331	1.9	58
	1126	0.6	18		1058	0.5	15
	1555	0.9	27		1532	1.0	30
	2115	0.4	12		2107	0.2	6
15 Th	0452	1.7	52	**30** F	0429	1.9	58
	1205	0.6	18		1146	0.5	15
	1647	0.9	27		1635	1.1	34
	2202	0.4	12		2214	0.2	6
				31 Sa ○	0525	1.9	58
					1231	0.5	15
					1733	1.1	34
					2319	0.3	9

August

Day	Time	Height ft	Height cm	Day	Time	Height ft	Height cm
1 Su ○	0618	1.8	55	**16** M ●	0614	1.6	49
	1314	0.5	15		1259	0.5	15
	1829	1.2	37		1832	1.2	37
2 M	0022	0.3	9	**17** Tu	0011	0.5	15
	0709	1.8	55		0647	1.6	49
	1355	0.4	12		1327	0.5	15
	1924	1.3	40		1913	1.3	40
3 Tu	0123	0.4	12	**18** W	0057	0.6	18
	0756	1.7	52		0721	1.6	49
	1434	0.4	12		1355	0.5	15
	2019	1.4	43		1955	1.4	43
4 W	0224	0.5	15	**19** Th	0146	0.6	18
	0840	1.6	49		0757	1.5	46
	1512	0.4	12		1423	0.4	12
	2114	1.4	43		2039	1.5	46
5 Th	0327	0.6	18	**20** F	0242	0.7	21
	0922	1.4	43		0834	1.4	43
	1547	0.4	12		1452	0.3	9
	2211	1.5	46		2126	1.6	49
6 F	0435	0.7	21	**21** Sa	0348	0.8	24
	1004	1.3	40		0916	1.3	40
	1621	0.4	12		1523	0.3	9
	2310	1.5	46		2217	1.7	52
7 Sa	0549	0.8	24	**22** Su	0503	0.8	24
	1047	1.2	37		1003	1.2	37
	1656	0.4	12		1601	0.3	9
					2311	1.7	52
8 Su ○	0008	1.6	49	**23** M ○	0625	0.8	24
	0706	0.8	24		1057	1.1	34
	1135	1.1	34		1646	0.3	9
	1733	0.4	12				
9 M	0107	1.6	49	**24** Tu	0010	1.8	55
	0818	0.8	24		0741	0.8	24
	1228	1.0	30		1200	1.0	30
	1816	0.4	12		1741	0.3	9
10 Tu	0202	1.6	49	**25** W	0112	1.8	55
	0920	0.8	24		0848	0.7	21
	1328	0.9	27		1309	1.0	30
	1904	0.4	12		1848	0.3	9
11 W	0254	1.6	49	**26** Th	0217	1.8	55
	1010	0.7	21		0944	0.6	18
	1430	0.9	27		1418	1.0	30
	1959	0.5	15		2001	0.3	9
12 Th	0342	1.6	49	**27** F	0320	1.8	55
	1052	0.7	21		1033	0.6	18
	1529	1.0	30		1524	1.1	34
	2055	0.5	15		2114	0.3	9
13 F	0425	1.6	49	**28** Sa	0420	1.8	55
	1127	0.7	21		1118	0.6	18
	1622	1.0	30		1624	1.2	37
	2148	0.5	15		2221	0.3	9
14 Sa	0504	1.6	49	**29** Su	0514	1.8	55
	1200	0.6	18		1159	0.5	15
	1709	1.1	34		1720	1.3	40
	2239	0.5	15		2323	0.3	9
15 Su	0540	1.6	49	**30** M ○	0602	1.7	52
	1230	0.6	18		1238	0.5	15
	1752	1.2	37		1813	1.4	43
	2326	0.5	15				
				31 Tu	0021	0.4	12
					0646	1.7	52
					1314	0.5	15
					1905	1.5	46

September

Day	Time	Height ft	Height cm	Day	Time	Height ft	Height cm
1 W	0117	0.5	15	**16** Th	0052	0.6	18
	0726	1.6	49		0649	1.5	46
	1347	0.4	12		1304	0.4	12
	1956	1.5	46		1928	1.6	49
2 Th	0214	0.6	18	**17** F	0147	0.6	18
	0805	1.5	46		0727	1.4	43
	1418	0.4	12		1332	0.3	9
	2047	1.6	49		2012	1.7	52
3 F	0314	0.7	21	**18** Sa	0248	0.7	21
	0843	1.3	40		0808	1.3	40
	1448	0.4	12		1404	0.3	9
	2138	1.6	49		2100	1.8	55
4 Sa	0419	0.8	24	**19** Su	0355	0.7	21
	0923	1.2	37		0854	1.2	37
	1519	0.4	12		1442	0.3	9
	2230	1.6	49		2152	1.8	55
5 Su	0528	0.8	24	**20** M	0508	0.7	21
	1006	1.1	34		0947	1.1	34
	1554	0.4	12		1527	0.3	9
	2323	1.6	49		2248	1.8	55
6 M ○	0639	0.9	27	**21** Tu ○	0620	0.7	21
	1056	1.0	30		1047	1.0	30
	1636	0.4	12		1624	0.3	9
					2350	1.8	55
7 Tu	0018	1.6	49	**22** W	0726	0.7	21
	0745	0.9	27		1155	1.0	30
	1154	1.0	30		1734	0.4	12
	1728	0.5	15				
8 W	0115	1.6	49	**23** Th	0058	1.7	52
	0840	0.8	24		0825	0.6	18
	1259	1.0	30		1306	1.0	30
	1829	0.5	15		1854	0.4	12
9 Th	0211	1.6	49	**24** F	0206	1.7	52
	0925	0.8	24		0916	0.6	18
	1403	1.0	30		1414	1.1	34
	1935	0.6	18		2013	0.4	12
10 F	0302	1.6	49	**25** Sa	0309	1.7	52
	1004	0.7	21		1003	0.6	18
	1501	1.1	34		1517	1.2	37
	2037	0.6	18		2124	0.4	12
11 Sa	0348	1.6	49	**26** Su	0405	1.6	49
	1038	0.7	21		1044	0.5	15
	1553	1.1	34		1614	1.3	40
	2134	0.5	15		2227	0.4	12
12 Su	0428	1.6	49	**27** M	0453	1.6	49
	1110	0.6	18		1122	0.5	15
	1639	1.2	37		1708	1.4	43
	2225	0.5	15		2325	0.4	12
13 M	0504	1.6	49	**28** Tu ○	0536	1.5	46
	1140	0.6	18		1157	0.4	12
	1722	1.3	40		1758	1.5	46
	2313	0.5	15				
14 Tu ●	0539	1.6	49	**29** W	0020	0.4	12
	1209	0.5	15		0615	1.4	43
	1804	1.4	43		1227	0.4	12
					1847	1.6	49
15 W	0002	0.6	18	**30** Th	0114	0.5	15
	0613	1.5	46		0652	1.4	43
	1236	0.4	12		1256	0.3	9
	1845	1.5	46		1933	1.6	49

Heights are referred to mean lower low water which is the chart datum of soundings.
All times are local time. Daylight Saving Time has been used when needed.

NOTES:

73

Annapolis (US Naval Academy), Maryland, 2004

Times and Heights of High and Low Waters

October

Day	Time (h m)	Height (ft)	Height (cm)	Day	Time (h m)	Height (ft)	Height (cm)
1 F	0208	0.6	18	16 Sa	0151	0.5	15
	0729	1.3	40		0700	1.1	34
	1323	0.3	9		1248	0.1	3
	2018	1.7	52		1949	1.8	55
2 Sa	0304	0.7	21	17 Su	0253	0.5	15
	0807	1.2	37		0747	1.0	30
	1351	0.3	9		1327	0.1	3
	2102	1.6	49		2038	1.8	55
3 Su	0402	0.7	21	18 M	0356	0.5	15
	0847	1.1	34		0840	1.0	30
	1424	0.3	9		1414	0.1	3
	2147	1.6	49		2132	1.8	55
4 M	0502	0.8	24	19 Tu	0500	0.5	15
	0933	1.0	30		0938	0.9	27
	1503	0.4	12		1510	0.2	6
	2235	1.6	49		2231	1.7	52
5 Tu	0601	0.8	24	20 W	0602	0.5	15
	1026	1.0	30		1043	0.9	27
	1552	0.4	12		1620	0.3	9
	2326	1.5	46	O	2336	1.6	49
6 W	0657	0.8	24	21 Th	0701	0.5	15
	1125	1.0	30		1151	1.0	30
O	1651	0.5	15		1741	0.3	9
7 Th	0022	1.5	46	22 F	0045	1.5	46
	0746	0.7	21		0754	0.5	15
	1229	1.0	30		1301	1.0	30
	1759	0.5	15		1904	0.3	9
8 F	0119	1.4	43	23 Sa	0150	1.5	46
	0829	0.7	21		0843	0.4	12
	1331	1.0	30		1408	1.1	34
	1909	0.6	18		2020	0.3	9
9 Sa	0212	1.4	43	24 Su	0249	1.4	43
	0908	0.6	18		0927	0.4	12
	1429	1.1	34		1509	1.2	37
	2014	0.5	15		2127	0.3	9
10 Su	0259	1.4	43	25 M	0339	1.4	43
	0942	0.6	18		1006	0.3	9
	1521	1.2	37		1606	1.3	40
	2113	0.5	15		2228	0.3	9
11 M	0341	1.4	43	26 Tu	0423	1.3	40
	1014	0.5	15		1041	0.2	6
	1608	1.3	40		1657	1.4	43
	2208	0.5	15		2325	0.4	12
12 Tu	0420	1.4	43	27 W	0503	1.2	37
	1044	0.4	12		1112	0.2	6
	1652	1.4	43		1745	1.5	46
	2302	0.5	15				
13 W	0458	1.4	43	28 Th	0020	0.4	12
	1113	0.3	9		0541	1.1	34
	1735	1.5	46		1139	0.2	6
	2356	0.5	15	O	1829	1.6	49
14 Th	0536	1.3	40	29 F	0112	0.5	15
	1143	0.2	6		0618	1.0	30
●	1818	1.6	49		1206	0.1	3
					1910	1.6	49
15 F	0053	0.5	15	30 Sa	0203	0.5	15
	0616	1.2	37		0657	1.0	30
	1213	0.2	6		1234	0.1	3
	1902	1.7	52		1949	1.8	49
				31 Su	0153	0.5	15
					0637	0.9	27
					1207	0.1	3
					1929	1.5	46

November

Day	Time (h m)	Height (ft)	Height (cm)	Day	Time (h m)	Height (ft)	Height (cm)
1 M	0241	0.5	15	16 Tu	0243	0.3	9
	0720	0.9	27		0729	0.8	24
	1245	0.2	6		1303	-0.1	-3
	2009	1.5	46		2019	1.6	49
2 Tu	0328	0.6	18	17 W	0339	0.3	9
	0807	0.8	24		0829	0.8	24
	1329	0.2	6		1409	0.0	0
	2053	1.4	43		2119	1.5	46
3 W	0415	0.6	18	18 Th	0434	0.3	9
	0859	0.8	24		0934	0.8	24
	1420	0.3	9		1525	0.1	3
	2141	1.3	40		2222	1.4	43
4 Th	0502	0.5	15	19 F	0528	0.2	6
	0955	0.8	24		1042	0.9	27
	1520	0.4	12		1645	0.1	3
	2232	1.3	40	O	2324	1.3	40
5 F	0546	0.5	15	20 Sa	0618	0.2	6
	1055	0.9	27		1151	1.0	30
	1626	0.4	12		1804	0.2	6
O	2325	1.2	37				
6 Sa	0628	0.4	12	21 Su	0023	1.2	37
	1155	0.9	27		0704	0.1	3
	1736	0.4	12		1258	1.0	30
					1918	0.2	6
7 Su	0015	1.2	37	22 M	0115	1.1	34
	0706	0.4	12		0746	0.1	3
	1252	1.0	30		1400	1.1	34
	1844	0.4	12		2026	0.2	6
8 M	0103	1.2	37	23 Tu	0202	1.0	30
	0741	0.3	9		0823	0.0	0
	1346	1.1	34		1456	1.2	37
	1950	0.4	12		2128	0.2	6
9 Tu	0148	1.2	37	24 W	0246	0.9	27
	0814	0.2	6		0856	-0.1	-3
	1435	1.2	37		1546	1.3	40
	2053	0.4	12		2226	0.2	6
10 W	0231	1.1	34	25 Th	0328	0.8	24
	0846	0.1	3		0927	-0.1	-3
	1522	1.4	43		1630	1.4	43
	2154	0.4	12		2319	0.2	6
11 Th	0316	1.0	30	26 F	0409	0.8	24
	0919	0.0	0		0956	-0.1	-3
	1608	1.5	46		1710	1.4	43
	2254	0.3	9	O			
12 F	0401	1.0	30	27 Sa	0008	0.3	9
	0954	-0.1	-3		0450	0.7	21
	1653	1.6	49		1027	-0.1	-3
●	2352	0.3	9		1748	1.4	43
13 Sa	0448	0.9	27	28 Su	0052	0.3	9
	1033	-0.1	-3		0532	0.7	21
	1740	1.7	52		1102	-0.1	-3
					1825	1.3	40
14 Su	0050	0.3	9	29 M	0133	0.3	9
	0539	0.8	24		0614	0.7	21
	1116	-0.1	-3		1140	-0.1	-3
	1830	1.7	52		1902	1.3	40
15 M	0147	0.3	9	30 Tu	0212	0.3	9
	0632	0.8	24		0658	0.6	18
	1206	-0.1	-3		1222	0.0	0
	1922	1.7	52		1940	1.2	37

December

Day	Time (h m)	Height (ft)	Height (cm)	Day	Time (h m)	Height (ft)	Height (cm)
1 W	0250	0.3	9	16 Th	0309	0.0	0
	0743	0.7	21		0815	0.7	21
	1307	0.0	0		1411	-0.2	-6
	2021	1.2	37		2104	1.2	37
2 Th	0328	0.3	9	17 F	0359	0.0	0
	0831	0.7	21		0918	0.7	21
	1357	0.1	3		1523	-0.2	-6
	2104	1.1	34		2159	1.1	34
3 F	0408	0.2	6	18 Sa	0448	-0.1	-3
	0923	0.7	21		1025	0.8	24
	1451	0.1	3		1638	-0.1	-3
	2148	1.1	34	O	2253	1.0	30
4 Sa	0447	0.2	6	19 Su	0535	-0.1	-3
	1018	0.7	21		1134	0.8	24
	1552	0.2	6		1755	0.0	0
	2234	1.0	30		2344	0.9	27
5 Su	0525	0.1	3	20 M	0619	-0.2	-6
	1116	0.8	24		1242	0.9	27
	1701	0.2	6		1910	0.1	3
O	2321	1.0	30				
6 M	0602	0.0	0	21 Tu	0034	0.7	21
	1213	0.9	27		0659	-0.2	-6
	1816	0.3	9		1345	1.0	30
					2021	0.1	3
7 Tu	0008	0.9	27	22 W	0122	0.6	18
	0638	-0.1	-3		0737	-0.3	-9
	1309	1.0	30		1441	1.1	34
	1932	0.3	9		2124	0.1	3
8 W	0057	0.8	24	23 Th	0210	0.6	18
	0714	-0.2	-6		0813	-0.3	-9
	1402	1.1	34		1530	1.1	34
	2043	0.2	6		2220	0.1	3
9 Th	0147	0.7	21	24 F	0257	0.5	15
	0752	-0.3	-9		0849	-0.3	-9
	1452	1.3	40		1613	1.2	37
	2149	0.2	6		2309	0.1	3
10 F	0239	0.7	21	25 Sa	0344	0.5	15
	0833	-0.3	-9		0926	-0.3	-9
	1542	1.4	43		1653	1.2	37
	2249	0.1	3		2352	0.1	3
11 Sa	0333	0.6	18	26 Su	0429	0.5	15
	0918	-0.4	-12		1005	-0.3	-9
	1632	1.5	46		1730	1.1	34
	2345	0.0	0	O			
12 Su	0427	0.6	18	27 M	0029	0.0	0
	1008	-0.4	-12		0512	0.5	15
	1724	1.5	46		1045	-0.3	-9
					1806	1.1	34
13 M	0037	0.0	0	28 Tu	0104	0.0	0
	0522	0.6	18		0554	0.5	15
	1102	-0.4	-12		1127	-0.3	-9
	1817	1.5	46		1841	1.1	34
14 Tu	0128	0.0	0	29 W	0137	0.0	0
	0618	0.6	18		0636	0.5	15
	1200	-0.4	-12		1209	-0.2	-6
	1911	1.4	43		1917	1.0	30
15 W	0219	0.0	0	30 Th	0209	0.0	0
	0715	0.7	21		0718	0.5	15
	1304	-0.3	-9		1252	-0.2	-6
	2007	1.3	40		1953	1.0	30
				31 F	0242	0.0	0
					0802	0.6	18
					1337	-0.1	-3
					2030	1.0	30

Heights are referred to mean lower low water which is the chart datum of soundings.
All times are local time. Daylight Saving Time has been used when needed.

NOTES:

TABLE 1. – DAILY CURRENT PREDICTIONS

EXPLANATION OF TABLE

This table gives the predicted times of slack water and the predicted times and speeds of maximum current-flood and ebb-for each day of the year at a number of stations on the Atlantic coast of North America. The times are given in hours and minutes and the speed in knots.

TIME.-The kind of time used for the predictions at each reference station is indicated by the time meridian at the bottom of each page. Daylight Saving Time is not used in this publication. If Daylight Saving Time is required, add one (1) hour to the predicted time.

SLACK WATER AND MAXIMUM CURRENT.-The columns headed "Slack" contain the predicted times at which there is no current; or, in other words, the times at which the current has stopped setting in a given direction and is about to begin to set in the opposite direction. Offshore, where the current is rotary, slack water denotes the time of minimum current. Beginning with the slack water before flood the current increases in speed until the strength or maximum speed of the flood current is reached; it then decreases until the following slack water or slack before ebb. The ebb current now begins, increases to a maximum speed, and then decreases to the next slack. The predicted times and speeds of maximum current are given in the columns headed "Maximum." Flood speeds are marked with an "F", the ebb speeds with an "E". An entry in the "Slack" column will be slack, flood begins if the maximum current which flows it is marked "F". Otherwise the entry will be slack, ebb begins.

DIRECTION OF SET.- The terms flood and ebb do not in all cases clearly indicate the direction of the current, the approximate direction toward which the currents flow are given at the top of each page to distinguish the two streams.

NUMBER OF SLACKS AND STRENGTHS. There are usually four slacks and four maximums each day. If one is missing in a given day, it will occur soon after midnight as the first slack or maximum of the following day. At some stations where the diurnal inequality is large, there may be on certain days a continuous flood or ebb current with varying speed throughout half the day giving only two slacks and two maximums on that particular day.

CURRENT AND TIDE. It is important to notice that the predicted slacks and strengths given in this table refer to the horizontal motion of the water and not to the vertical rise and fall of the tide. The relation of current to tide is not constant, but varies from place to place, and the time of slack water does not generally coincide with the time of high or low water, nor does the time of maximum speed of the current usually coincide with the time of most rapid change in the vertical height of the tide. At stations located on a tidal river or bay the time of slack water may differ from 1 to 3 hours from the time of high or low water. The times of high and low waters are given in the tide tables published by the National Ocean Service.

VARIATIONS FROM PREDICTIONS.-In using this table, bear in mind that actual times of slack or maximum occasionally differ from the predicted times by as much as half an hour and in rare instances the difference may be as much as an hour. Comparisons of predicted with observed times of slack water indicate that more than 90 percent of the slack waters occurred within half an hour of the predicted times. To make sure, therefore, of getting the full advantage of a favorable current or slack water, the navigator should reach the entrance or strait at least half an hour before the predicted time of the desired condition of current. Currents are frequently disturbed by wind or variations in river discharge. On days when the current is affected by such disturbing influences the times and speeds will differ from those given in the table, but local knowledge will enable one to make proper allowance for these effects.

TYPICAL CURRENT CURVES.-The variations in the tidal current from day to day and from place to place are illustrated on the opposite page by the current curves for representative ports along the Atlantic and Gulf Coasts of the United States. Flood current is represented by the solid line curve above the zero speed (slack water) line and the ebb current by the broken line curve below the slack water line. The curves show clearly that the currents along the Atlantic coast are semi-daily (two floods and two ebbs in a day) in character with their principal variations following changes in the Moon's distance and phase. In the Gulf of Mexico, however, the currents are daily in character. As the dominant factor is the change in the Moon's declination the currents in the Gulf tend to become semi-daily when the Moon is near the Equator. By reference to the curves it will be noted that with this daily type of current there are times when the current may be erratic (marked with an asterisk), or one flood or ebb current of the day may be quite weak. Therefore in using the predictions of the current it is essential to carefully note the speeds as well as the times.

TABLE 2.- CURRENT DIFFERENCES
AND OTHER CONSTANTS and ROTARY TIDAL CURRENTS

EXPLANATION OF TABLE

Reference stations are those for which daily predictions are listed in Table 1. Those stations appearing in Table 2 are called subordinate stations. The principal purpose of Table 2 is to present data that will enable one to determine the approximate times of minimum currents (slack waters) and the times and speeds of maximum currents at numerous subordinate stations on the Atlantic Coast of North America. By applying the specific corrections given in Table 2 to the predicted times and speeds of the current at the appropriate reference station, reasonable approximations of the current at the subordinate station may be compiled.

LOCATIONS AND DEPTHS

Because the latitude and longitude are listed according to the exactness recorded in the original survey records, the locations of the subordinate stations are presented in varying degrees of accuracy. Since a minute of latitude is nearly equivalent to a mile, a location given to the nearest minute may not indicate the exact position of the station. This should be remembered, especially in the case of a narrow stream, where the nearest minute of latitude or longitude may locate a station inland. In such cases, unless the description locates the station elsewhere, reference is made to the current in the center of the channel. In some instances, the charts may not present a convenient name for locating a station. In those cases, the position may be described by a bearing from some prominent place on the chart.

Although current measurements may have been recorded at various depths in the past, the data listed here for most of the subordinate stations are mean values determined to have been representative of the current at each location. For that reason, no specific current meter depths for those stations are given in Table 2. Beginning with the Boston Harbor tidal current survey in 1971, data for individual meter depths were published and subsequent new data may be presented in a similar manner.

Since most of the current data in Table 2 came from meters suspended from survey vessels or anchored buoys, the listed depths are those measured downward from the surface. Some later data have come from meters anchored at fixed depths from the bottom. Those meter positions were defined as depths below chart datum. Such defined depths, in this and subsequent editions will be accompanied by the small letter "d."

MINIMUM CURRENTS

The reader may note that at many locations the current may not diminish to a true slack water or zero stage. For that reason, the phrases, "minimum before flood" and "minimum before ebb" are used in Table 2 rather than "slack water" although either or both minimums may actually reach a zero speed value at some locations. Table 2 lists the average speeds and directions of the minimums.

MAXIMUM CURRENTS

Near the coast and in inland tidal waters, the current increases from minimum current (slack water) for a period of about 3 hours until the maximum speed or strength of the current is reached. The speed then decreases for another period of about 3 hours when minimum current is again reached and the current begins a similar cycle in the opposite direction. "The current that flows toward the coast or up a stream is known as the flood current; the opposite flow is known as the ebb current. Table 2 lists the average speeds and directions of the maximum floods and maximum ebbs. The directions are given in degrees, true, reading clockwise from 000° at north to 359° and are the directions toward which the current flow.

DIFFERENCES AND SPEED RATIOS

Table 2 contains mean time differences by which the reader can compile approximate times for the minimum and maximum current phases at the subordinate stations. Time differences for those phases should be applied to the corresponding phases at the reference station. It will be seen upon inspection that some subordinate stations exhibit either a double flood or a double ebb state, or both. Explanations of these states can be found in the glossary located elsewhere in this publication. In these cases, a separate time difference is listed for each of the three flood (or ebb) phases and these should be applied only to the daily maximum flood (or ebb) phase at the reference station. The results obtained by the application of the time differences will be based upon the time meridian shown above the name of the subordinate station. Differences of time meridians between a subordinate station and its reference station have been accounted for and no further adjustment by the reader is needed. Summer, or daylight saving time, is not used in this publication. Therefore, in the case of daylight saving time the reader should add one (1) hour to account for the time change.

The speed ratios are used to compile approximations of the daily current speeds at the subordinate stations and refer only to the maximum floods and ebbs. No attempt is made to predict the speeds of the minimum currents. Normally, these ratios should be applied to the corresponding maximum current phases at the reference station. As mentioned above, however, some subordinate stations may exhibit either a double flood or a double ebb or both. As with the time differences, separate ratios are listed for each of the three flood (or ebb) phases and should be applied only to the daily maximum flood (or ebb) speed at the reference station. It should be noted, that although the speed of a given current phase at a subordinate station is obtained by reference to the corresponding phase at the reference station, the directions of the current at the two places may differ considerably. Table 2 lists the average directions of the various current phases at the subordinate stations.

ROTARY CURRENTS

Briefly, a rotary current can be described as one which flows continually with the direction of flow changing through all points of the compass during the tidal period. The average speeds and directions are listed in half-hour increments as referred to the predicted times of a particular current phase at a reference station in Table 1. The Moon, at times of new, full, and perigee; may increase speeds 15 to 20 percent above average; or 30 to 40 percent if perigee occurs at or near the time of New or Full Moon. Conversely, the Moon at times of quadrature or apogee may decrease the speeds 15 to 20 percent, Or 30 to 40 percent if they occur together. Near average speeds may be expected when apogee occurs near or at the New or Full Moon, or when perigee occurs at or near quadrature. The directions of the currents are given in degrees true, reading clockwise from 000° at north to 359° and are the directions toward which the water is flowing.

EXAMPLE OF THE USE OF TABLE 2 (CURRENT DIFFERENCES AND OTHER CONSTANTS - PAGE 56)

Suppose we wish to calculate the times of the minimum currents and the times and speeds of the maximum currents on a particular morning at the location listed in Table 2 as Winthrop Head, 1.1 n. mi. east of. From Table 2 we learn that the reference station is Boston Harbor, whose morning currents are listed below. Currents for Winthrop Head can be approximated by using the Table 2 corrections as indicated.

	Minimum Before Flood	Maximum Flood		Minimum Before Ebb	Maxium Ebb	
	h.m.	h.m.	kn	h.m.	h.m.	kn
Boston Harbor 0052		0419	1.2	0645	1109	1.
Table 2 Corrections .... .0112		+0019	x0.4 ratio	+0031	-0146	x0.3 ratio
Winthrop Head .... .2340*		0438	0.5	0716	0923	0.4

*This minimum current phase is seen to occur just before midnight of the previous day.

Table 2 states that the average speeds and directions of the minimums before flood and ebb are 0.3 knots at 103° and 0.2 knots at 297°, respectively. The average directions of the maximum flood and maximum ebb are 205° and 019°, respectively.

TABLE 3.-SPEED OF CURRENT AT ANY TIME

EXPLANATION

Though the predictions in this publication give only the slacks and maximum currents, the speed of the current at any intermediate time can be obtained approximately by using this table. Directions for its use are given below the table.

Before using the table for a place listed in Table 2, the predictions for the day in question should be first obtained by means of the differences and ratios given in Table 2.

THE EXAMPLES BELOW FOLLOW THE NUMBERED STEPS IN THE DIRECTIONS.

EXAMPLE 1.-Find the speed of the current in The Race at 6:00 on a day when the predictions which immediately precede and follow 6:00 are as follows:

1. **Slack Water Time 4:18   Maximum(Flood) Time 7:36   Speed 3.2 knots**
   Directions under the table indicate TABLE A is to be used for this station.

2. Interval between slack and maximum flood is $7:36 - 4:18 = 3^h18^m$.
   Column heading nearest to 3h18m is 3^h20^m.

3. Interval between slack and time desired is $6:00-4:18=1^h42^m$.
   Line labeled 1^h40^m is nearest to 1^h42^m.

4. Factor in column 3^h20^m and on line 1^h40^m is 0.7.
   The above flood speed of 3.2 knots multiplied by 0.7 gives a flood speed of 2.24 knots (or 2.2 knots, since one decimal is sufficient) for the time desired.

EXAMPLE 2-Find the speed of the current in the Harlem River at Broadway Bridge at 16:30 on a day when the predictions (obtained using the difference and ratio in Table 2) which immediately precede and follow 16:30 are as follows:

1. **Maximum (Ebb)   Slack Water Time 13:49   Speed 2.5 knots Time 17:25**
   Directions under the table indicate Table B is to be used, since this station in Table 2 is referred to Hell Gate.

2. Interval between slack and maximum ebb is $17:25-13:49=3^h36^m$.
   Use column headed 3^h40^m.

3. Interval between slack and time desired is $17:25-16:30=0^h55^m$.
   Use line labeled 1^h00^m.

4. Factor in column 3^h40^m and on line 1^h00^m is 0.5. The above ebb speed of 2.5 knots multiplied by 0.5 gives and ebb speed of 1.2 knots for the desired time.

When the interval between slack and maximum current is greater than 5^h40^m, enter the table with and one-half the interval between slack and maximum current and one-half the interval between slack and the desired time use the factor thus found.

TABLE 3.-SPEED OF CURRENT AT ANY TIME

TABLE A

INTERVAL BETWEEN SLACK AND DESIRED TIME	INTERVAL BETWEEN SLACK AND MAXIMUM CURRENT														
	h. m. 1 20	h.m. 1 40	h.m 2 00	h.m 2 20	h.m 2 40	h.m. 3 00	h.m. 3 20	h.m 3 40	h.m 4 00	h.m 4 20	h.m 4 40	h.m 5 00	h.m. 5 20	h.m. 5 40	NOTES
h. m.	ft	ft	ft	ft	ft	ft	ft	ft	ft	ft	ft	ft	ft	ft	
0 20	0.4	0.3	0.3	0.2	0.2	0.2	0.2	0.1	0.1	0.1	0.1	0.1	0.1	0.1	
0 40	0.7	0.6	0.5	0.4	0.4	0.3	0.3	0.3	0.3	0.2	0.2	0.2	0.2	0.2	
1 00	0.9	0.8	0.7	0.6	0.6	0.5	0.5	0.4	0.4	0.4	0.3	0.3	0.3	0.3	
1 20	1.0	1.0	0.9	0.8	0.7	0.6	0.6	0.5	0.5	0.5	0.4	0.4	0.4	0.4	
1 40	—	1.0	1.0	0.9	0.8	0.8	0.7	0.7	0.6	0.6	0.5	0.5	0.5	0.4	
2 00	—	—	1.0	1.0	0.9	0.9	0.8	0.8	0.7	0.7	0.6	0.6	0.6	0.5	
2 20	—	—	—	1.0	1.0	0.9	0.9	0.8	0.8	0.7	0.7	0.7	0.6	0.6	
2 40	—	—	—	—	1.0	1.0	1.0	0.9	0.9	0.8	0.8	0.7	0.7	0.7	
3 00	—	—	—	—	—	1.0	1.0	1.0	0.9	0.9	0.8	0.8	0.8	0.7	
3 20	—	—	—	—	—	—	1.0	1.0	1.0	0.9	0.9	0.9	0.8	0.8	
3 40	—	—	—	—	—	—	—	1.0	1.0	1.0	0.9	0.9	0.9	0.9	
4 00	—	—	—	—	—	—	—	—	1.0	1.0	1.0	1.0	0.9	0.9	
4 20	—	—	—	—	—	—	—	—	—	1.0	1.0	1.0	1.0	0.9	
4 40	—	—	—	—	—	—	—	—	—	—	1.0	1.0	1.0	1.0	
5 00	—	—	—	—	—	—	—	—	—	—	—	1.0	1.0	1.0	
5 20	—	—	—	—	—	—	—	—	—	—	—	—	1.0	1.0	
5 40	—	—	—	—	—	—	—	—	—	—	—	—	—	1.0	

TABLE B

INTERVAL BETWEEN SLACK AND DESIRED TIME	INTERVAL BETWEEN SLACK AND MAXIMUM CURRENT														
	h. m 1 20	.h.m. 1 40	h.m. 2 00	h.m. 2 20	h.m. 2 40	h.m. 3 00	h.m. 3.20	h.m. 3 40	h.m. 4 00	h.m. 4 20	h.m. 4 40	h.m. 5 00	h.m. 5 20	h.m. 5 40	NOTES
h.m.	ft	ft	ft	ft	ft	ft	ft	ft	ft	ft	ft	ft	ft	ft	
0 20	0.5	0.4	0.4	0.3	0.3	0.3	0.3	0.3	0.2	0.2	0.2	0.2	0.2	0.2	
0 40	0.8	0.7	0.6	0.5	0.5	0.5	0.4	0.4	0.4	0.4	0.3	0.3	0.3	0.3	
1 00	0.9	0.8	0.8	0.7	0.7	0.6	0.6	0.5	0.5	0.5	0.4	0.4	0.4	0.4	
1 20	1.0	1.0	0.9	0.8	0.8	0.7	0.7	0.6	0.6	0.6	0.5	0.5	0.5	0.5	
1 40	—	1.0	1.0	0.9	0.9	0.8	0.8	0.7	0.7	0.7	0.6	0.6	0.6	0.6	
2 00	—	—	1.0	1.0	0.9	0.9	0.9	0.8	0.8	0.7	0.7	0.7	0.7	0.6	
2 20	—	—	—	1.0	1.0	1.0	0.9	0.9	0.8	0.8	0.8	0.7	0.7	0.7	
2 40	—	—	—	—	1.0	1.0	1.0	0.9	0.9	0.9	0.8	0.8	0.8	0.7	
3 00	—	—	—	—	—	1.0	1.0	1.0	0.9	0.9	0.9	0.9	0.8	0.8	
3 20	—	—	—	—	—	—	1.0	1.0	1.0	1.0	0.9	0.9	0.9	0.9	
3 40	—	—	—	—	—	—	—	1.0	1.0	1.0	1.0	0.9	0.9	0.9	
4 00	—	—	—	—	—	—	—	—	1.0	1.0	1.0	1.0	0.9	0.9	
4 20	—	—	—	—	—	—	—	—	—	1.0	1.0	1.0	1.0	0.9	
4 40	—	—	—	—	—	—	—	—	—	—	1.0	1.0	1.0	1.0	
5 00	—	—	—	—	—	—	—	—	—	—	—	1.0	1.0	1.0	
5 20	—	—	—	—	—	—	—	—	—	—	—	—	1.0	1.0	
5 40	—	—	—	—	—	—	—	—	—	—	—	—	—	1.0	

Use TABLE A for all places except: Cape Cod Canal, Hell Gate, Chesapeake & Delaware Canal, & all stations in Table 2 which are referred to them - then use TABLE B.

1. From predictions find the time of slack water and the time and velocity of maximum current (flood or ebb), one of that is immediately before and the other after the time for which the velocity is desired.
2. Find the interval of time between the above slack and maximum current. Enter the top of table A or B with the interval that most nearly agrees with this value.
3. Find the interval of time between the above slack and the time desired, enter the side of table A or B with the interval that most nearly agrees with this value.
4. Find, in the table, the factor corresponding to the above two intervals and multiply the maximum velocity by this factor.
   The result will be the approximate velocity at the time desired.

TABLE 2 – CURRENT DIFFERENCES AND OTHER CONSTANTS

No.	PLACE	Meter Depth (ft)	POSITION Latitude North	POSITION Longitude West	TIME DIFF. Min. before Flood (h m)	TIME DIFF. Flood (h m)	TIME DIFF. Min. before Ebb (h m)	TIME DIFF. Ebb (h m)	SPEED RATIOS Flood	SPEED RATIOS Ebb	Min. before Flood (knots)	Min. before Flood Dir.	Maximum Flood (knots)	Maximum Flood Dir.	Min. before Ebb (knots)	Min. before Ebb Dir.	Maximum Ebb (knots)	Maximum Ebb Dir.
	BAY OF FUNDY Time meridian, 60° W					on Bay of Fundy Entrance												
1	Brazil Rock, 6 miles east of		43° 22	66° 18′	−2 02	−2 00	−1 56	−2 00	0.4	0.4	0.0	– – –	1.2	275°	0.0	– – –	1.0	050°
6	Cape Sable, 3 miles south of		43° 20	65° 38′	−3 02	−2 00	−1 21	−2 10	1.0	0.8	0.0	– – –	2.2	275°	0.0	– – –	2.0	098°
11	Cape Sable, 12 miles south of		43° 11′	65° 37′	−1 12	−1 00	−0 46	−1 00	0.7	0.7	0.0	– – –	1.7	285°	0.0	– – –	1.6	090°
16	Blonde Rock, 5 miles south of		43° 16	65° 59′	−0 17	−0 50	−0 36	−0 50	0.9	0.7	0.0	– – –	2.0	310°	0.0	– – –	2.0	125°
21	Seal Island, 13 miles southwest of		43° 34′	66° 15	−0 38	+0 10	−0 39	+0 10	1.1	0.7	0.0	– – –	1.2	325°	0.0	– – –	1.6	140°
26	Cape Fourchu, 17 miles southwest of		43° 47	66° 24′	+0 45	+0 45	+0 44	+0 45	0.5	0.5	0.0	– – –	1.2	365°	0.0	– – –	1.7	145°
31	Cape Fourchu, 4 miles west of		43° 52	66° 15	0 08	0 00	−0 09	0 00	0.9	0.8	0.0	– – –	2.0	000°	0.0	– – –	1.7	175°
36	Lurcher Shoal, 8 miles east of		43° 46	66° 21′	−0 23	+0 30	−0 39	+0 30	0.6	0.5	0.0	– – –	1.4	000°	0.0	– – –	1.6	175°
41	Lurcher Shoal, 10 miles west of		44° 13′	66° 42′	−0 12	+0 30	−0 34	+0 30	0.8	0.5	0.0	– – –	1.8	008°	0.0	– – –	1.6	160°
46	Lurcher Shoal, 10 miles northwest of		44° 17	66° 30′	+0 43	+0 50	+0 54	+0 30	1.2	0.6	0.0	– – –	2.4	060°	0.0	– – –	2.2	189°
51	Brier Island, 6 miles west of		44° 29′	66° 44	−0 42	−0 15	+0 14	−0 15	1.6	1.0	0.0	– – –	2.6	040°	0.0	– – –	2.5	250°
56	Brier Island, 15 miles west of		44° 31′	66° 41′	−0 43	+0 35	+0 59	+0 90	0.8	0.8	0.0	– – –	1.6	020°	0.0	– – –	3.9	230°
61	Gannet Rock, 5 miles southeast of		44° 11.7	66° 23′	+0 38	+0 55	+0 54	+0 45	1.8	1.6	0.0	– – –	1.6	040°	0.0	– – –	2.0	205°
66	Boars Head, 10 miles northwest of		44° 58	66° 15	+0 51	+0 45	+0 57	+0 55	1.0	0.8	0.0	– – –	1.7	050°	0.0	– – –	1.6	245°
71	Prim Point, 20 miles west of		44° 45.2	65° 57					1.6	0.6	0.0	– – –	2.3	032°	0.1	302°	2.4	212°
76	Cape Spencer, 14 miles south of			66° 55.9′					0.7	0.7	0.0	– – –			0.0	– – –		
81	**BAY OF FUNDY ENTRANCE**						Daily predictions											
	East Penobscot Bay																	
111	Pond Point, 7.6 miles SSE of		44° 20.1′	67° 30.2	+0 13	−0 20	−1 33	−0 05	0.2	0.5	0.0		0.5	015°	0.0		1.2	215°
116	Moosabec Reach, east end		44° 31.7′	67° 34.36	−2 45	−3 08	−3 13	−3 39	0.4	0.5	0.0		1.0	110°	0.0		1.2	268°
121	Moosabec Reach, west end		44° 31.25′	67° 39.00	−1 43	−1 43	−2 00	−1 44	0.4	0.4	0.0		1.0	092°	0.0		1.0	263°
126	Bar Harbor, 1.2 miles east of <1>		44° 23.0′	68° 10.0	+0 13	+0 30			0.1	0.3	0.0		0.7	328°	0.0		0.7	148°
131	Casco Passage, east end, Blue Hill Bay		44° 11.7	68° 27.9	−1 49	−1 44	−1 02	−1 58	0.3	0.3	0.0		0.7	086°	0.0		0.7	284°
136	Hat Island, SE of, Jericho Bay		44° 08.0	68° 23.7	−1 02	−0 35	−0 50	−1 20	0.1	0.1	0.0		0.2	318°	0.0		0.3	124°
141	Clam I., NW of, Deer I. Thorofare	14	44° 09.87	68° 38.23	−2 14	−0 15	−0 57	−2 46	0.2	0.1	0.0		0.4	004°	0.0		0.2	199°
146	Rrog Island, E. of, Deer Island Thorofare	14	44° 09.72	68° 37.23	−2 16	−2 02	−2 27	−3 31	0.2	0.2	0.0		0.2	020°	0.1	302°	0.6	235°
151	Russ Island, N of, Deer Island Thorofare	14	44° 09.63	68° 37.18	−2 12	−2 02	−2 29	−3 16	0.2	0.2	0.0		0.4	074°	0.0		0.6	265°
156	Crotch Island, NW of, between <49>	14	44° 08.85	68° 30.58		Currents are unidirectional												
161	Isle au Haut, 0.8 mile E of Rich's Pt	11	44° 05	68° 35	−0 53	−1 07	−1 07	−1 19	0.6	0.6	0.0		1.4	336°	0.0		1.5	139°
	East Penobscot Bay																	
166	Mark Island, north of	14	44° 08.20	68° 42.17	−0 18	−1 01	−2 27	−0 22	0.1	0.2	0.0		0.3	013°	0.1	300°	0.4	164°
171	Widow Island-Stimpson Island, between	14	44° 07.95	68° 49.50	−0 18	−0 49	+0 04	−1 08	0.3	0.2	0.0	030°	0.6	302°	0.3		0.5	118°
176	Eagle Island, 0.4 nautical mile S of	14	44° 11.63	68° 46.93	−0 18	−0 55	−2 20	−1 46	0.4	0.5	0.1	347°	0.7	336°	0.3	050°	1.3	147°
181	Burnt Island-Oak Island, between	11	44° 11.47	68° 49.13	−0 18	−1 19	−2 22	−0 57	0.1	0.3	0.0		0.7	290°	0.0		1.0	098°
186	Butter I., 0.3 nautical mile SE of	11	44° 13.33	68° 46.67	−2 43	−2 14	−2 25	−1 36	0.2	0.1	0.0		0.2	050°	0.1	150°	0.6	194°
191	Bradbury Island, ESE of	14	44° 14.03	68° 44.07	+0 11	−0 17	−0 53	−0 56	0.2	0.1	0.2	306°	0.5	029°	0.1	304°	0.7	225°
196	Compass Island, 0.4 nmi. ENE of	14	44° 13.00	68° 51.33	−1 44	−1 22	−1 25	−1 01	0.2	0.1	0.0	092°	0.5	019°	0.1		0.3	175°
201	Scrag Island, 0.3 nautical mile SW of	14	44° 13.33	68° 50.62	−0 45	−0 27	−0 55	−0 55	0.2	0.1	0.0		0.4	010°	0.1	078°	0.3	197°
206	Great Spruce Head Island, west of	14	44° 14.30	68° 50.16	−1 14	−0 54	−0 26	−1 19	0.2	0.1	0.0		0.4	009°	0.0		0.3	174°
211	Horse Head Island, 0.2 nmi. ENE of	14	44° 15.07	68° 50.67														
216	Pickering Island, south of	14	44° 16.63	68° 46.38	−2 45	−1 37	−1 56	−2 37			0.2	209°	0.6	300°	0.3	201°	0.6	150°
221	Little Cash Island, NNE of	14	44° 16.48	68° 45.28	−0 43	+0 12	+0 02	−0 19	0.2	0.2	0.0		0.4	300°	0.2	224°	0.3	106°
226	Pickering Island, north of	14	44° 16.52	68° 46.87														
231	Hog Island, ESE of	14	44° 16.78	68° 46.87	−0 13	−0 02	−0 33	−0 51	0.1	0.2	0.0	231°	0.6	024°	0.2	108°	0.5	180°
236	Little Deer I.-Sheep I., between	14	44° 16.97	68° 43.43	−0 37	−0 37	+0 33	−0 52	0.2	0.2	0.0		0.6	310°	0.0		0.3	124°
241	Swains Ledge, WSW of	14	44° 17.13	68° 45.28	Current weak and variable													
246	Swains Ledge, 0.3 nautical mile SW of	14	44° 17.58	68° 49.00	−0 46	−0 22	−0 55	−1 07	0.2	0.2	0.0		0.5	358°	0.0		0.4	170°
251	Pond Island-Western Island, between	14	44° 18.17	68° 45.35	−0 46	−1 13	−1 56	−1 34	0.2	0.1	0.0		0.4	356°	0.0		0.6	172°
256	Birch Island, northwest of	14	44° 18.17	68° 48.60	−1 44	−1 31	−0 56	−1 30	0.2	0.1	0.0		0.3	022°	0.0		0.2	200°
261	Pond Island, north of	14	44° 18.28	68° 42.63	Current weak and variable													
266	Howard Ledges, ENE of, Eggemoggin Reach	14	44° 18.30	68° 42.08	Current weak and variable													
271	Howard Ledges, NE of, Eggemoggin Reach	14			Current weak and variable													
276	Spectacle Island, 0.2 nmi. NW of	14	44° 18.47	68° 47.33	Current weak and variable													

NOTES

SEE ENDNOTES ON PAGE 106

80

MAINE COAST—cont.
Time meridian, 75° W

No.	PLACE	Meter Depth (ft)	POSITION Latitude North	POSITION Longitude West	TIME DIFF. Min. before Flood (h m)	TIME DIFF. Flood (h m)	TIME DIFF. Min. before Ebb (h m)	TIME DIFF. Ebb (h m)	SPEED RATIOS Flood	SPEED RATIOS Ebb	Min. before Flood (knots)	Dir.	Maximum Flood (knots)	Dir.	Min. before Ebb (knots)	Dir.	Maximum Ebb (knots)	Dir.
	on Bay of Fundy Entrance				−3 14	−2 10	−1 54	−2 43	0.1	0.1	0.0	--	0.3	290°	0.1	340°	0.3	090°
	East Penobscot Bay—cont.																	
281	Pumpkin Island, north of	14	44°18.80	68°44.42	Current weak and variable													
286	Isleboro Harbor, Penobscot Bay	14	44°18.86	68°53.35	−1 00	−1 04	−0 36	−1 44	0.3	0.3	0.0	--	0.7	339°	0.0	--	0.8	171°
291	Thrum Cap I., E of, East Penobscot Bay	14	44°19.40	68°44.80	−1 19	−1 12	−1 31	−1 14	0.5	0.3	0.0	--	1.2	319°	0.0	--	0.8	165°
296	Turtle Head Pt., ESE of, Penobscot Bay	15	44°22.57	68°51.28	+0 11	−0 24	−0 25	−0 41	0.6	0.6	0.0	--	1.4	079°	0.0	--	1.4	262°
301	Castine Harbor <50>	40	44°22.57	68°51.28	−1 01	−0 47	−0 33	−1 09	0.7	0.5	0.0	--	1.4	087°	0.0	--	1.2	238°
	do.	15	44°22.76	68°48.62	−1 47	−0 38	−0 47	−1 30	0.8	0.4	0.0	--	1.5	017°	0.0	--	1.0	199°
	do.	40	44°22.76	68°48.62	−2 16	−1 17	−1 27	−1 00	0.2	0.2	0.0	--	0.5	029°	0.0	--	0.5	198°
306	Dice Head, west of, Penobscot Bay	60	44°22.75	68°50.72	−0 33	−0 33	−0 36	−0 18	0.2	0.2	0.0	--	0.6	334°	0.0	--	0.6	178°
	do.	58	44°22.77	68°50.72	+0 13	−0 26	−0 26	−0 57	0.2	0.2	0.0	--	0.4	312°	0.0	--	0.6	135°
311	Sears Island, S of, Penobscot Bay <53>	96	44°22.77	68°50.72	+0 10	+0 10	---	−1 57	1.8	1.8	0.0	--	4.2	012°	0.0	--	4.2	237°
	do.	15	44°25.12	68°53.25	−1 44	+0 04	---	−1 07	0.4	0.3	0.0	--	1.0	080°	0.0	--	1.0	270°
316	Jones Point, Bagaduce River <51>	40	44°25.12	68°53.25	−0 37	+0 03	−0 39	−0 48	0.5	0.5	0.0	--	1.0	053°	0.1	340°	1.0	237°
321	Fort Point, Cape Jellison, Penobscot Bay <51>	15	44°25.55	68°47.73	−0 08	+0 15	−0 30	−1 09	0.4	0.3	0.0	--	1.0	309°	0.0	--	0.8	166°
326	Verona Island, west of, Penobscot River <52>	40	44°27.95	68°47.80	−2 31	−0 43	−0 22	−0 23	0.8	0.8	0.0	--	0.8	008°	0.0	--	0.7	176°
	do.	15	44°27.83	68°48.30	+1 06	−0 01	−0 32	−0 16	0.8	0.8	0.0	--	1.9	339°	0.0	--	3.8	176°
	do.	35	44°31.73	68°48.30	+1 08	−0 20	−1 14	−3 47	0.6	0.6	0.0	--	1.3	327°	0.0	--	3.6	182°
	do.	60	44°31.73	68°48.30	−2 50	−1 17	+1 21	−2 28	0.4	0.4	0.0	--	2.0	319°	0.0	--	0.6	192°
331	Verona I., N of, Easter Ch, Penobscot R <52>	10	44°34.07	68°46.87	+1 54	+1 13	−1 54	−2 47	0.5	0.5	0.0	--	0.7	279°	0.0	--	0.6	179°
336	Bucksport, Penobscot River <52>	15	44°34.27	68°48.38	+0 42	+0 20	−1 26	−1 24	0.7	0.7	0.0	--	1.6	273°	0.0	--	1.6	176°
341	Winterport, Penobscot Bay <51>	45	44°34.27	68°48.38	−0 13	+0 00	−1 39	−1 19	0.8	0.8	0.0	--	2.0	281°	0.0	--	2.0	176°
		15	44°37.88	68°50.52	−1 05	+0 04	−0 56	−3 06	0.9	1.0	0.0	--	1.9	007°	0.0	--	2.0	182°
346	Oak Point, Penobscot River <51>	15	44°40.10	68°48.78	−0 19	−2 27	−0 39	−3 01	0.4	0.4	0.0	--	0.8	039°	0.0	--	0.7	192°
	do.	35	44°40.10	68°48.78	−1 17	+0 22	−0 59	−3 14	0.7	0.8	0.0	--	1.5	022°	0.0	--	0.6	206°
351	Snub Point, Penobscot River <51>	15	44°42.27	68°50.40	−0 11	−3 05	−0 50	−1 55	0.4	0.7	0.0	0.0	0.4	028°	0.0	--	3.6	176°
	West Penobscot Bay																	
356	Andrews Island, ESE of	15	43°59.65	69°00.78	−0 20	−0 44	−0 55	−1 14	0.7	0.3	0.0	--	0.4	011°	0.0	--	0.7	155°
361	Little Hurricane Island, southwest of	75	43°59.65	69°00.78	−1 15	−0 56	−0 20	−1 07	0.6	0.2	0.0	--	0.8	042°	0.0	--	0.6	188°
366	Heron Neck, Green Island	15	44°01.38	68°55.07	−1 05	−0 50	−0 18	−1 13	0.5	0.3	0.0	--	0.5	331°	0.0	--	0.8	157°
371	The Reach, Norton Point	40	44°01.38	68°56.07	−0 18	−0 35	−0 27	−0 36	0.4	0.3	0.0	--	0.5	300°	0.2	218°	0.7	125°
	Isle au Haut Bay — Current weak and variable																	
376	Triangle Ledge, SSE of	14	44°01.78	68°52.38	+1 47	−0 59	−0 68	−1 43	0.4	0.4	0.0	--	1.0	344°	0.0	--	0.6	165°
381	Moore Harbor, W of	15	44°02.47	68°45.48	+0 14	−0 17	−0 26	−0 17	0.3	0.3	0.0	--	0.7	354°	0.0	--	1.0	197°
	do.	75	44°02.53	68°41.55	−1 20	−0 39	−0 32	−1 16	0.2	0.2	0.0	--	0.6	317°	0.0	--	0.6	180°
	do.	15	44°02.53	68°41.55	0 00	−0 55	−0 16	−0 38	0.3	0.2	0.0	--	0.4	344°	0.1	063°	1.1	135°
	do.	120	44°02.53	68°41.55	−2 34	−0 43	−1 26	−1 19	0.3	0.1	0.0	--	0.7	345°	0.0	--	2.0	139°

SEE ENDNOTES ON PAGE 106

NOTES

81

TABLE 2 – CURRENT DIFFERENCES AND OTHER CONSTANTS

MAINE COAST—cont.
Time meridian, 75° W

Time differences referred to Bay of Fundy Entrance. West Penobscot Bay places (No. 491 and following) and Muscongus Sound places (No. 556 and following) as noted.

No.	PLACE	Meter Depth (ft)	Lat. North	Long. West	Min. before Flood	Flood	Min. before Ebb	Ebb	Flood	Ebb	Min. bef. Flood (kn)	Dir.	Max. Flood (kn)	Dir.	Min. bef. Ebb (kn)	Dir.	Max. Ebb (kn)	Dir.
	on Bay of Fundy Entrance																	
	West Penobscot Bay																	
386	The Reach, NNE of, Green Island	14	44° 02.57	68° 51.58	-3 23	-1 10	-1 55	-2 55	0.2	0.2	0.0	–	0.4	284°	0.1	150°	0.4	111°
391	White Islands, northeast of	14	44° 03.00	68° 54.40	-1 48	-2 18	-1 55	-2 08	0.2	0.2	0.0	262°	0.4	322°	0.3	258°	0.6	165°
396	Fisherman Island Passage	14	44° 03.12	68° 52.70	-2 44	-2 37	-2 26	-2 28	0.8	0.3	0.1	196°	0.6	053°	0.3	312°	0.7	240°
401	Crotch Island, east of	14	44° 03.62	68° 54.43	-0 49	-0 55	-1 21	-1 09	0.8	0.8	0.1	196°	1.9	343°	0.0	–	2.0	169°
406	Laireys Island, south of	14	44° 03.88	68° 53.78	-0 44	-0 18	-0 51	-1 51	0.2	0.4	0.1	073°	0.4	333°	0.0	–	0.8	155°
411	Sheep Island	14	44° 04.07	69° 03.47	-2 44	-1 19	-1 57	-2 16	0.2	0.5	0.0	–	0.5	320°	0.0	–	0.8	220°
416	Leadbetter I., SSW of southern tip	14	44° 04.16	68° 53.90	-0 18	-0 39	-0 28	-1 32	0.6	0.5	0.0	–	1.4	320°	0.0	–	1.3	126°
421	Leadbetter Island, E of southern tip	14	44° 04.07	68° 53.62	-0 18	-0 43	+0 37	-0 13	0.2	0.4	0.2	214°	0.4	360°	0.1	105°	0.6	175°
426	Leadbetter Island, northwest tip of	14	44° 05.03	68° 54.67	-0 48	-0 41	-0 53	-1 12	0.2	0.2	0.0	–	0.5	016°	0.1	135°	0.4	205°
431	Dodge Point–Monroe Island, between	14	44° 05.12	68° 02.62	-3 43	-1 43	-2 55	-3 07	0.2	0.2	0.2	267°	0.4	016°	0.1	092°	0.5	147°
436	Dogfish Island, NNE of	14	44° 05.52	68° 54.67	-2 14	-2 27	-2 55	-2 06	0.2	0.2	0.1	244°	0.5	016°	0.1	045°	0.4	205°
441	Rockland Harbor Breakwater	14	44° 06.13	68° 04.67	-1 18	-0 30	-1 04	-0 39	0.1	0.2	0.1	216°	0.3	319°	0.2	220°	0.2	197°
446	Browshead, Vinalhaven Island, NNW of	14	44° 06.78	68° 54.73	-1 43	-1 22	-0 55	-0 66	0.1	0.2	0.2	325°	0.3	319°	0.2	100°	0.2	229°
451	Crabtree Pt, North Haven I., NNE of	14	44° 09.60	68° 55.42	-3 13	-2 41	-0 55	-1 25	0.1	0.1	0.2	287°	0.2	009°	0.2	100°	0.2	228°
456	Fox Island Thorofare	14	44° 09.82	68° 53.68	-1 31	-1 31	-1 59	-1 28	0.2	0.2	0.0	–	0.2	070°	0.0	–	0.2	279°
461	Mark Island, 0.3 nmi., SSE of	14	44° 10.00	68° 57.97	-3 45	-2 31	-3 56	-2 13	0.1	0.2	0.0	331°	0.2	044°	0.1	169°	0.5	246°
466	Saddle Island, northwest of	14	44° 10.85	68° 57.30					0.1	0.2	0.2	272°	0.3	010°	0.1	101°	0.4	225°
471	Mark Island, 0.3 nautical mile, N of	14	44° 10.87	68° 58.92	-1 47	-1 31	-2 54	-1 46										
476	Lasell Island, SSW of	14	44° 11.20	68° 56.82	-1 37	-2 43	-3 57	-3 13	0.2	0.2	0.0	–	0.4	022°	0.0	–	0.4	217°
481	East Goose Rock, NNE of	14	44° 11.37	68° 58.08	-2 44	-4 06	-2 26	-1 56	0.1	0.1	0.0	–	0.4	000°	0.2	112°	0.4	210°
486	Camden Harbor Entrance	14	44° 12.17	69° 02.80		-3 10					0.0	–	0.2	354°	0.1	325°	0.3	190°
491	Ensign Island, SSE of	14	44° 13.40	68° 57.52	-1 30	-1 00	-1 19		0.2	0.1	0.0	–	0.3	022°	0.0	–	0.3	220°
496	Warren Island, northwest of	15	44° 16.65	68° 57.22	-2 17	-0 52	-1 23	-1 25	0.2	0.2	0.0	–	0.3	009°	0.0	–	0.4	248°
501	Ducktrap Harbor, northeast of	15	44° 18.00	68° 56.38	-1 07	-0 58	-1 23	-1 13	0.2	0.2	0.0	–	0.5	038°	0.0	–	0.4	285°
506	do.	40	44° 18.00	68° 56.37	-2 29	-1 28	-1 47	-1 41	0.2	0.2	0.0	–	0.5	354°	0.0	–	0.3	209°
	do.	90	44° 18.27	68° 57.55	-1 59	-1 29	-1 10	-1 33	0.2	0.1	0.0	–	0.4	012°	0.0	–	0.4	233°
511	Ducktrap Harbor, NNE of	160	44° 18.30	68° 57.55	+0 32	-0 29	-0 10	-0 27	0.2	0.1	0.0	–	0.5	038°	0.0	–	0.5	202°
	do.	15	44° 18.30	68° 57.55	-1 13	-0 13	-0 18	-0 36	0.3	0.2	0.0	–	0.4	058°	0.1	135°	0.5	230°
516	Flat Island, SSW of	130	44° 18.83	68° 55.45	-1 13	-0 52	-0 66	-0 11	0.3	0.3	0.0	–	0.6	013°	0.0	–	0.6	199°
521	Isleboro Harbor, NE of, Penobscot Bay	14	44° 18.97	68° 57.78	-1 04	-1 00	-1 36	-2 07	0.3	0.2	0.0	–	0.3	046°	0.3	248°	0.3	196°
526	Isleboro Harbor, NE of, Penobscot Bay	75	44° 19.03	68° 52.67	+0 24	-0 54	-1 24	-1 23	0.1	0.1	0.0	–	0.4	004°	0.0	–	0.4	154°
531	Head of the Cape, 0.8 nmi. W, of Penobscot Bay	15	44° 19.25	68° 50.80	-1 14	-0 14	-0 24	-0 28	0.2	0.1	0.0	–	0.4	334°	0.0	–	0.3	125°
536	Head of the Cape, NNW of, Penobscot Bay	125	44° 19.25	68° 50.80	-1 46	-0 39	-0 41	-0 51	0.3	0.2	0.0	–	0.1	354°	0.0	–	0.4	166°
	do.	15	44° 19.07	68° 50.17	-1 22	-0 47	-0 24	-0 59	0.3	0.3	0.0	–	0.6	015°	0.0	–	0.3	163°
	do.	15	44° 19.07	68° 50.17	-0 59	-1 20	-1 11	-0 59	0.6	0.3	0.0	–	0.5	366°	0.0	–	0.4	176°
541	Ram Island, west of, West Penobscot Bay	130	44° 21.28	68° 54.95	-0 43	-1 55	-2 63	-2 16	0.1	0.3	0.0	–	0.3	332°	0.0	–	0.4	172°
546	Temple Heights, NE of, W Penobscot Bay	14	44° 21.38	68° 55.33	-1 02	-1 23	-2 03	-0 18	0.2	0.2	0.0	–	0.4	004°	0.0	–	0.4	189°
	do.	15	44° 21.38	68° 55.33	-1 46	-0 21	-1 36	-1 33	0.3	0.3	0.0	–	0.4	004°	0.0	–	0.4	189°
551	Temple Heights, NNE of, W Penobscot Bay	65	44° 21.38	68° 56.33	-0 34	-0 21	-1 35	-1 05	0.3	0.3	0.0	–	0.4	354°	0.0	–	0.5	175°
	do.	15	44° 21.45	68° 56.62	-0 17	-0 26	-0 15	-0 43	0.3	0.3	0.0	–	0.6	005°	0.0	–	0.7	175°
	do.	30	44° 21.45	68° 56.62	-0 28	-0 30	-0 47	-0 39	0.3	0.2	0.0	–	0.6	344°	0.0	–	0.4	188°
	do.	50	44° 21.45	68° 46.3							0.0	–	0.5	339°			0.5	164°
	on Portsmouth Harbor Entrance																	
	Current weak and variable																	
	Muscongus Sound																	
556	Damariscotta River, off Cavis Point	14	44° 56.5	69° 26.9	-0 49	-0 44	-1 24	-1 18	0.5	0.6	0.0	–	0.6	350°	0.0	–	1.0	215°
561	Sheepscot River, off Barter Island	30	44° 52.5	69° 35.0	-0 48	-1 02	-1 16	-0 33	0.7	0.6	0.0	–	0.8	006°	0.0	–	1.1	200°
566	Lowe Point, NE of, Sasanoa River		44° 54.0	69° 41.6	-0 48	+0 09	-0 46	-0 27	1.4	1.0	0.0	–	1.7	327°	0.0	–	1.8	152°
571	Lower Hell Gate, Knubble Bay <2>		44° 51.1	69° 43.3	-0 23	+0 37	-0 46	+0 06	2.6	1.9	0.0	–	3.0	290°	0.0	–	3.5	155°
576	Lower Hell Gate, Sasanoa River		44° 52.6	69° 43.8	+3 31	+2 48	+1 20	+2 03	0.8	0.5	0.0	–	1.0	307°	0.0	–	0.8	142°
581	Upper Hell Gate, Sasanoa River		44° 53.7	69° 46.3														

NOTES · SEE ENDNOTES ON PAGE 106

TABLE 2 – CURRENT DIFFERENCES AND OTHER CONSTANTS

No.	PLACE	Meter Depth (ft)	POSITION Latitude North	POSITION Longitude West	TIME DIFFERENCES Min. before Flood (h m)	Flood (h m)	Min. before Ebb (h m)	Ebb (h m)	SPEED RATIOS Flood	Ebb	AVG Minimum before Flood (knots)	Dir.	Maximum Flood (knots)	Dir.	Minimum before Ebb (knots)	Dir.	Maximum Ebb (knots)	Dir.
	MAINE COAST—cont. Time meridian, 75° W **CASCO BAY**				on Portsmouth Harbor Entrance													
621	Broad Sound, west of Eagle Island	88	43° 42.7'	70° 03.8'	−1 16	−1 05	−1 27	−0 59	0.8	0.7	0.0	—	0.9	010°	0.0	—	1.3	168°
626	Ram Island, 1.8 nautical miles east of	81	43° 38.2'	70° 09.2'	−0 08	+0 10	−0 12	+0 39	0.2	0.4	0.1	241°	0.3	302°	0.0	209°	0.6	165°
631	Hussey Sound, northeast of Overset Island	15	43° 37'	70° 10.5'	−1 37	−1 18	−1 58	−1 12	0.9	0.6	0.0	—	1.1	311°	0.1	224°	1.2	159°
636	Hussey Sound, SW of Overset Island	25	43° 40.27'	70° 10.52'	−1 28	−1 18	−1 06	−1 30	0.9	0.6	0.1	—	1.1	318°	0.2	189°	1.1	159°
	do.	40	43° 40.27'	70° 10.52'	−1 58	−1 19	−1 05	−1 32	0.9	0.5	0.1	228°	1.1	314°	0.3	211°	1.1	155°
641	Hussey Sound, SE of Pumpkin Nob	40	43° 40.45'	70° 10.78'	−2 21	−1 29	−1 32	−1 14	1.0	0.6	0.1	068°	1.0	348°	0.1	200°	0.9	154°
646	Hussey Sound, east of Crow Island	71	43° 41.2'	70° 10.8'	−2 22	−0 35	−1 15	−1 27	0.8	0.4	0.0	—	0.3	004°	0.1	066°	0.8	168°
651	Hussey Sound, east of Crow Island	40	43° 41.33'	70° 10.79'	−2 18	−0 42	−1 12	−1 24	0.7	0.4	0.0	114°	0.3	016°	0.0	282°	0.8	193°
656	Long Island, 0.65 nautical mile NW of	41	43° 42.2'	70° 09.9'	−1 45	−1 39	−1 55	−1 30	0.2	0.5	0.0	—	0.3	015°	0.0	—	0.3	197°
661	Little Chebeague Island, southeast of	25	43° 42.4'	70° 08.7'	−2 40	−1 18	−1 53	−1 48	0.8	0.1	0.0	—	0.4	330°	0.0	—	0.3	176°
666	Long Island, 1.3 nautical miles NW of	20	43° 42.5'	70° 08.5'	−2 45	−0 18	−1 46	−1 36	0.3	0.1	0.0	—	0.1	218°	0.0	262°	0.9	051°
671	Waites Landing, northeast of	10	43° 43.5'	70° 12.5'	−2 34	−2 00	−3 28	−1 31	0.1	0.1	0.0	—	0.1	328°	0.0	—	0.2	168°
676	Clapboard Island, 0.5 nmi. northwest of	15	43° 44.2'	70° 12.0'	−2 12	−1 12	−2 12	−1 24	0.2	0.2	0.0	—	0.1	022°	0.0	—	0.2	232°
681	Sturdivant Island, southeast of	28	43° 44.3'	70° 10.5'	−1 34	−0 52	−1 23	−1 48	0.2	0.2	0.0	—	0.3	013°	0.0	—	0.3	216°
686	Sturdivant Island, west of	25	43° 44.3'	70° 11.5'	−1 42	−1 32	−1 28	−1 55	0.3	0.3	0.0	—	0.3	017°	0.0	—	0.3	213°
691	Cousin I. and Great Chebeague I., between	10	43° 37.3'	70° 08.3'	−1 47	−2 34	−1 29	−1 34	0.3	0.1	0.0	—	0.4	041°	0.1	200°	0.1	211°
696	Littlejohn Island, Town Landing	34	43° 38.7'	70° 07.5'	−1 43	−1 32	−1 29	−1 58	0.5	0.5	0.0	—	0.6	063°	0.0	—	1.0	252°
701	Cushing Island, 0.24 nautical mile SW of	53	43° 39.0'	70° 12.5'	−2 28	−1 28	−1 31	−1 30	0.6	0.3	0.0	—	0.4	397°	0.0	—	0.5	136°
706	Portland Harbor ent., SW of Cushing Island		43° 39.2'	70° 12.7'	−2 43	−1 43	−1 28	−1 18	0.7	0.5	0.1	319°	1.0	362°	0.1	—	0.7	044°
711	Portland Bridge, center of draw	19	43° 39.5'	70° 15.5'	−1 30	−1 36	−1 45	−1 06	0.5	0.4	0.0	—	0.6	352°	0.0	—	0.7	179°
716	Spring Point, 0.2 nautical mile east of	34	43° 39.6'	70° 13.1'		−1 09	−2 07	−1 06	0.3	0.3	0.0	—	0.6	012°	0.0	—	0.5	175°
721	House Island, east of	32		70° 12.3'		−1 47		−1 50	0.5	0.5	0.0	—		—	0.0	—		175°
726	Portland Breakwater Light, 0.3 mi. NM of <1><4>			70° 14.5'	−1 26	−1 12	−1 11	−1 06	0.8	0.5	0.1	—	0.6	260°	0.0	—	0.5	048°
731	Grand Trunk Wharves, off ends <1>			70° 14.7'							0.0	—	0.6	300°	0.0	—	0.4	040°
736	Diamond I. Ledge, midchannel SW of			70° 13.5'							0.6	—	0.9	—	0.0	—	0.9	150°
	MAINE COAST—cont.																	
761	Cape Elizabeth	15	43° 34'	70° 11'	−1 35	−1 35	−1 35	−1 35	0.2	0.2	0.0	—	0.3	349°	0.0	—	0.3	160°
766	Cape Porpoise	15	43° 22'	70° 24'	−0 55	−0 55	−0 55	−1 55	0.3	0.2	0.0	—	0.3	035°	0.0	—	0.3	216°
771	Cape Neddick		43° 10'	70° 35'	−0 15	−0 15	−0 15	−0 15	0.3	0.3	0.0	—	0.2	025°	0.0	—	0.2	205°
776	York Harbor entrance, 3 miles south of	15	43° 08'	70° 33'	+1 13	+1 46	+0 49	+2 16	0.4	0.5	0.0	—	0.4	—	0.0	—	0.4	205°
	PORTSMOUTH HARBOR																	
781	Odiorne Point, NNE of		43° 02.95'	70° 42.50'	−0 01	+0 05	+0 37	+1 05	0.5	0.5	0.0	—	0.6	339°	0.0	—	0.8	183°
786	Odiorne Point, northeast of	15	43° 03.00'	70° 42.80'	−1 00	+0 07	+0 38	+1 00	0.7	0.6	0.1	238°	0.6	320°	0.1	058°	1.0	168°
791	Kitts Rocks, WSW of <5>		43° 03.10'	70° 42'	−1 00	0 00	−1 00	0 00	0.7	0.9	0.2	191°	0.7	344°	0.0	—	1.6	173°
796	Kitts Rocks, 0.2 mile west of	15	43° 03'	70° 42'	−0 01	+0 18	+0 11	+0 12	0.6	0.6	0.1	—	0.7	328°	0.1	—	1.5	175°
801	Little Harbor entrance		43° 03.50'	70° 42.27'	+0 02	0.00	+0 31	−0 42	0.6	0.8	0.2	—	0.7	310°	0.1	—	1.0	130°
806	Whaleback Reef, west of		43° 03.8'	70° 42.3'	+0 05	+0 35	+0 05	+0 05	1.0	0.7	0.2	—	1.2	340°	0.0	—	1.5	144°
811	PORTSMOUTH HARBOR ENT. (off Wood I.)	15	43° 03.95'	70° 42.30'	+0 14	+0 10	+0 34	+0 10	1.2	1.1	0.2	291°	1.5	365°	0.1	278°	1.9	195°
816	Wood Island, northwest of		43° 04'	70° 43.02'	+0 10	+0 50	+0 10	+0 47	1.1	0.5	0.2	—	1.5	365°	0.2	—	2.0	199°
821	Fort Point		43° 04.68'	70° 43'	−0 35	−0 25	−0 35	−0 50	0.8	0.6	0.1	—	1.3	257°	0.0	—	0.8	130°
826	Salamander Point, north of		43° 05'	70° 43'	−0 25	−0 25	−0 25	−0 25	0.8	0.6	0.2	—	1.3	260°	0.1	167°	0.8	091°
831	Salamander Point		43° 05'	70° 43'	+0 15	+0 15	+0 15	+0 15	1.2	1.0	0.3	—	0.8	339°	0.0	—	0.8	086°
836	Hick Rocks and Clark Island, between		43° 05'	70° 43'	−1 10	−1 10	−1 10	−1 10	1.1	1.3	0.0	—	0.8	020°	0.0	—	1.0	195°
841	Kittery Point Bridge		43° 05'	70° 43'	−0 25	−0 25	−0 25	−0 25	1.5	0.5	0.0	—	1.4	316°	0.0	—	2.0	200°
846	Jamaica Island, northeast of		43° 05'	70° 44'	+0 15	+0 15	+0 15	+0 15	1.1	0.6	0.0	—	1.1	260°	0.0	—	1.8	135°
851	Seavey Island, north of		43° 05'	70° 44'						1.0	0.0	—	0.7	269°	0.0	—	0.8	080°
856	Clark I. and Seavey I., between <6>		43° 06'	70° 43.48'							0.0	—		209°	0.0	—		135°
861	Clark Island, southwest of	15	43° 06.43'	70° 43.67'	+0 23	+0 22	+0 36	+1 33	1.3	1.3	0.0	—	2.0	200°	0.0	—	2.3	089°
866	Clark Island, southwest of	15	43° 04.50'		+0 21	−0 14	+0 34	−0 04	1.5	0.5	0.0	—	0.7	269°	0.0	—	0.8	070°

NOTES   SEE ENDNOTES ON PAGE 106

TABLE 2 – CURRENT DIFFERENCES AND OTHER CONSTANTS

No.	PLACE	Meter Depth (ft)	POSITION Latitude North	POSITION Longitude West	TIME DIFFERENCES Min. before Flood (h m)	Flood (h m)	Min. before Ebb (h m)	Ebb (h m)	SPEED RATIOS Flood	Ebb	AVG SPEEDS Min. before Flood (knots)	Dir.	Maximum Flood (knots)	Dir.	Min. before Ebb (knots)	Dir.	Maximum Ebb (knots)	Dir.
	PORTSMOUTH HARBOR Time meridian, 75° W						on Portsmouth Harbor Entrance											
871	Seavey Island, south of		43° 04'	70° 44'	+0 15	+0 15	+0 15	+0 15	2.5	2.1	0.0	--	3.0	260°	0.0	--	3.8	090°
876	Marvin Island and Goat Island, between		43° 04.40'	70° 44'	-1 00	-1 00	-1 00	+1 00	1.3	1.0	0.0	--	1.2	160°	0.0	--	0.8	340°
881	Henderson Point, SSW of		43° 04.40'	70° 44.32	-0 04	+1 11	+0 16	+0 38	2.2	1.0	0.1	228°	1.6	306°	0.0	--	1.8	133°
886	Henderson Point, west of	15	43° 04.18'	70° 44.30	+0 30	+0 30	+0 30	+0 30	0.7	0.4	0.0	--	0.8	340°	0.0	--	2.3	170°
891	Shapleigh Island Bridge, south of		43° 04.55'	70° 44.55	-0 50	-0 27	-0 53	-0 35	2.4	0.7	0.1	249°	2.8	178°	0.0	--	0.7	348°
896	Pierces Island, northeast of		43° 05'	70° 45'	-0 18	+0 25	+0 39	-0 19	2.7	1.7	0.1	--	2.1	323°	0.0	--	1.3	114°
901	Off Gangway Rock		43° 05'	70° 45'	+0 30	+0 30	+0 30	+0 30	0.9	0.9	0.0	--	2.1	240°	0.0	--	3.4	110°
906	Badgers Island, east of	15	43° 05'	70° 45'	+0 30	+0 30	+0 26	+0 26	2.7	2.0	0.0	--	3.3	330°	0.0	--	3.7	050°
911	Badgers Island, southwest of		43° 05'	70° 45'	+0 30	+0 30	+0 30	+0 30										126°
	MASSACHUSETTS COAST																	
956	Gunboat Shoal		43° 01'	70° 42'	+0 05	+0 05	+0 05	+0 05	0.4	0.3	0.0	--	0.5	340°	0.0	--	0.5	160°
961	Isles of Shoals Light, White Island		42° 58'	70° 37'	0 00	0 00	0 00	0 00	0.2	0.2	0.0	--	0.3	020°	0.0	--	0.3	200°
							on Boston Harbor											
966	Merrimack River entrance	10	42° 49.1'	70° 48.6'	+1 04	+1 15	+1 04	-0 34	2.0	1.2	0.0	--	2.2	285°	0.0	--	1.4	105°
971	Newburyport, Merrimack River	45	42° 48.8'	70° 52.1'	+1 28	+1 48	+1 47	+0 35	1.4	1.2	0.0	--	1.5	288°	0.0	--	1.4	098°
976	Plum Island Sound entrance	80	42° 42.3'	70° 47.3'	+0 36	+0 50	+0 48	+0 07	1.5	1.1	0.0	--	1.6	316°	0.0	--	1.5	184°
981	Annisquam Harbor Light	15	42° 40.1'	70° 41.1'	+0 42	+0 49	+0 68	+0 03	0.3	0.1	0.0	--	0.3	200°	0.0	--	1.3	013°
986	Gloucester Harbor entrance	25	42° 34.9'	70° 40.5'	-0 28	+0 06	-0 16	-0 36	0.3	1.2	0.0	--	0.3	340°	0.0	--	0.3	195°
991	Blynman Canal ent., Gloucester Harbor	45	42° 36.6'	70° 40.4'	+1 09	+1 09	+1 09	+1 09	2.7	2.8	0.0	--	3.0	310°	0.0	--	3.3	130°
996	Marblehead Channel	15	42° 30'	70° 49'	-0 21	+0 49	+0 16	+1 00	0.4	0.3	0.0	--	0.7	285°	0.0	--	0.4	105°
1036	Nahant, 1.8 n.mi. NE of East Point	25	42° 26.00'	70° 52.02'	-0 25	+1 04	+1 14	+0 31	0.6	0.6	0.1	329°	0.7	252°	0.1	291°	0.7	144°
	....do.	65	42° 26.00'	70° 52.02'	-0 04	-0 41	+0 15	-0 31	0.3	0.1	0.0	118°	0.3	250°	0.0	--	0.2	070°
1041	Nahant, 0.4 n.mi. east of East Point	10	42° 25.23'	70° 53.63'	-0 03	-0 26	-0 08	+0 22	0.2	0.1	0.1	102°	0.2	238°	0.0	--	0.2	077°
	....do.	45	42° 25.23'	70° 53.63'	+0 04	-0 04	+1 13	+0 14	0.4	0.5	0.2	--	0.5	198°	0.0	282°	0.6	025°
1046	Nahant, 1 n.mi. SE of East Point	60	42° 23.83'	70° 53.67'	-0 53	-0 04	-0 42	-1 01	0.3	0.2	0.0	--	0.4	259°	0.0	--	0.5	074°
1051	Peal Island, 0.4 n.mi. southeast of	10	42° 24.83'	70° 54.13'	-0 22	+0 65	+0 57	+0 31	0.5	0.4	0.0	332°	0.5	261°	0.1	161°	0.5	090°
	....do.	10	42° 24.83'	70° 54.13'	-0 37	+0 34	+0 42	-0 14	0.5	0.3	0.0	351°	0.4	239°	0.0	--	0.3	069°
1056	Bass Point, 1.2 n.mi. southeast of	10	42° 24.12'	70° 55.07'	-0 22	+1 20	+0 68	-0 29	0.3	0.3	0.1	--	0.4	224°	0.0	--	0.3	048°
	....do.	10	42° 24.12'	70° 55.07'	-0 29	-0 10	+0 52	+1 59	0.4	0.6	0.1	--	0.4	271°	0.0	--	0.4	035°
	....do.	10	42° 24.12'	70° 55.07'	+0 04	-0 26	+0 31	-0 46	0.7	0.4	0.0	--	0.7	259°	0.0	--	0.7	066°
1071	Little Nahant Cupola, 0.6 n.mi. west of	8	42° 25.87'	70° 56.83'	+0 29	-0 17	+1 32	+0 27	0.4	0.4	0.0	--	0.4	251°	0.0	--	0.2	068°
1076	Sand Point, Black Marsh Channel	8	42° 26.58'	70° 56.52'	+0 05	-0 26	+1 00	+1 25	0.5	0.4	0.0	--	0.4	250°	0.1	137°	0.5	019°
1081	Lynn Harbor	6	42° 27.27'	70° 56.78'	+0 43	+0 19	+0 29	+0 41	0.5	0.2	0.0	--	0.4	039°	0.0	--	0.5	203°
1086	Point of Pines, 0.5 n.mi. south of	10	42° 25.97'	70° 57.53'	+0 01	+0 29	+1 00	+0 94	0.2	1.0	0.0	--	0.3	013°	0.0	--	0.5	090°
1091	Point of Pines, 0.1 n.mi. northeast of	10	42° 23.17'	70° 57.62'	-0 11	+1 05	+0 26	-0 28	0.8	0.6	0.0	--	0.5	274°	0.0	296°	1.2	131°
1096	Finn's Ledge Bell, 0.2 n.mi. west of	25	42° 22.17'	70° 55.42'	-1 12	+0 19	-0 38	+0 46	0.4	0.3	0.0	--	0.9	009°	0.0	--	0.5	033°
1101	Winthrop Head, 1.1 n.mi. east of	10	42° 21.30'	70° 55.63'	-1 52	-1 57	-0 14	-0 25	0.3	1.0	0.3	103°	0.9	298°	0.2	297°	0.4	019°
1106	Lowell Island, 1.3 n.mi. north of	10	42° 21.30'	70° 55.90'	-1 19	-0 59	-0 12	-0 13	0.8	0.6	0.2	112°	0.7	205°	0.2	300°	1.2	033°
	....do.	25	42° 21.30'	70° 55.90'					0.7	0.6	0.2	102°	0.7	197°	0.1	135°	0.7	033°

SEE ENDNOTES ON PAGE 106

NOTES

84

TABLE 2 – CURRENT DIFFERENCES AND OTHER CONSTANTS

No.	PLACE	Latitude North	Longitude West	Meter Depth (ft)	Min. before Flood (h m)	Flood (h m)	Min. before Ebb (h m)	Ebb (h m)	Speed Ratio Flood	Speed Ratio Ebb	Min. before Flood (knots)	Min. before Flood (Dir.)	Maximum Flood (knots)	Maximum Flood (Dir.)	Min. before Ebb (knots)	Min. before Ebb (Dir.)	Maximum Ebb (knots)	Maximum Ebb (Dir.)
	MASSACHUSETTS COAST Time meridian, 75° W						on Boston Harbor											
	BOSTON HARBOR APPROACHES																	
1111	The Graves, 0.3 n.mi. SSE of	42° 21.60	70° 52.00	10	+0 16	+1 08	+1 21	+0 19	0.5	0.5	0.1	171°	0.6	227°	0.1	135°	0.6	103°
	do.	42° 21.60	70° 52.00	45	+0 37	-0 52	+1 10	+0 58	0.3	0.4	0.1	186°	0.4	262°	--	--	0.5	085°
	do.	42° 21.60	70° 52.00	60	-0 49	-0 06	-0 16	-0 23	0.2	0.3	0.1	--	0.2	252°	--	--	0.3	070°
1116	Thieves Ledge	42° 19.28	70° 50.28	45	-0 15	+0 41	-0 40	-1 37	0.2	0.2	0.1	030°	0.2	304°	0.0	--	0.3	128°
1121	Little Brewster Island, 1.5 n.mi. E of	42° 19.68	70° 51.43	10	+2 19	-0 49	+0 05	-1 55	0.5	1.0	0.4	028°	0.3	289°	0.6	337°	0.5	080°
	do.	42° 19.68	70° 51.43	10	+0 63	-1 23	+1 31	+1 30	0.3	0.8	0.2	--	0.3	238°	0.6	212°	1.2	076°
	do.	42° 19.68	70° 51.43	35	-1 14	+0 19	+0 49	-0 45	0.8	0.8	0.1	265°	0.9	225°	0.1	--	1.0	047°
1126	Hypocrite Channel	42° 20.95	70° 53.63	60	+0 23	+0 19	-0 15	-0 31	0.8	0.6	0.2	345°	0.8	262°	0.1	351°	1.0	070°
1131	Little Calf Island, 0.4 n.mi. NW of	42° 21.05	70° 54.00	10	+0 14	+0 19	-0 41	-0 18	0.9	1.1	0.1	--	1.0	220°	0.1	290°	0.7	048°
1136	Boston Light, 0.2 n.mi. south of	42° 19.52	70° 53.40	10	-0 16	+0 04	+0 24	+0 40	0.5	0.5	0.1	203°	0.5	220°	0.1	--	0.4	100°
1171	Black Rock Channel	42° 19.73	70° 54.93	10	-0 15	-0 11	-4 11	-0 01	0.2	0.5	0.1	325°	0.2	247°	0.2	122°	0.9	046°
1176	Deer Island Light, 0.4 n.mi. NW of	42° 20.68	70° 55.70	10	-0 09	-2 10	-0 22	-1 46	1.1	1.0	0.0	330°	1.2	307°	0.1	--	0.8	116°
1181	Lovell Island, 0.4 n.mi. north of	42° 20.45	70° 55.80	35	-0 08	-0 14	-0 26	-0 29	1.1	1.1	0.0	--	1.2	259°	0.1	337°	1.2	064°
	do.	42° 20.65	70° 56.70	10	+0 27	+0 19	+0 38	-0 11	1.0	0.7	0.0	--	1.2	264°	--	--	0.9	074°
1186	Deer Island, 0.7 n.mi. ESE of	42° 20.65	70° 56.30	25	-0 01	-0 11	+0 41	+0 10	1.3	0.8	0.0	--	1.3	220°	0.0	--	1.4	048°
	do.	42° 20.65	70° 56.30	35	-0 04	-0 20	+0 20	-1 23	0.9	0.8	0.0	--	1.1	221°	0.2	138°	0.9	048°
1191	Deer Island Light, 0.8 n.mi. ESE of	42° 20.22	70° 56.28	10	+0 08	-1 13	+0 17	-0 16	0.7	--	0.3	138°	0.9	214°			1.0	066°
1196	Deer Island Light, 0.4 n.mi. east of	42° 20.45	70° 56.77	10		+1 02					0.3	319°	1.1	239°			1.0	057°
1201	Deer Island Light, 0.7 n.mi. ESE of	42° 20.45	70° 56.77	35	-0 32	+0 52	+0 44	+0 16	0.9	0.6	0.0	--	1.1	214°	0.0	--	0.8	053°
	do.	42° 20.25	70° 56.38	35	-0 23	-0 10	+0 25	-1 01	0.9	0.5	0.1	312°	1.0	239°	0.0	--	0.6	062°
	BOSTON HARBOR-PRESIDENT ROADS						*Daily predictions*											
1206	BOSTON HARBOR (Deer Island Light)	42° 20.27	70° 57.37	10	+0 02	+0 44	+0 15	+0 28	1.3	0.9	0.0	--	1.4	254°	0.3	184°	1.2	111°
1211	Deer Island Light, 0.3 n.mi. SSE of	42° 20.12	70° 57.42	10	-0 11	+0 46	-0 49	+0 28	1.3	0.8	0.0	--	1.4	265°	0.4	199°	1.0	082°
1216	Deer Island Light, 0.4 n.mi. SSE of	42° 20.12	70° 57.42	35	-0 08	+0 53	-0 43	+0 30	1.4	0.9	0.0	--	1.5	261°	0.2	--	1.0	090°
1221	Deer Island, southwest of	42° 19.97	70° 57.42	25	-0 02	+0 47	-0 62	+0 33	0.6	0.5	0.0	--	1.4	269°	0.3	178°	1.2	073°
1226	Long Island Head, 0.9 n.mi. NW of	42° 20.63	70° 58.43	10	-0 08	-0 36	-1 58	-1 08	0.4	0.3	0.3	--	0.4	352°	0.3	065°	0.6	061°
1231	Deer Island Flats	42° 20.40	70° 58.65	35	-0 01	+1 21	-0 50	-3 04	0.4	0.4	0.1	176°	0.4	304°	0.2	--	0.6	103°
1236	Deer Island Light, 1.3 n.mi. NW of	42° 20.83	70° 58.74	10	+0 27	+0 19	+0 31	+1 05	0.4	0.7	0.0	--	0.4	327°	0.4	--	0.5	107°
1241	Snake Island, southwest of	42° 21.12	70° 58.22	10	-0 05	+1 14	+2 10	+0 23	1.2	0.7	0.0	--	0.4	312°	0.0	049°	0.5	134°
1246	Deer Island Light, 1.0 n.mi. WSW of	42° 21.17	70° 58.43	10	+0 52	+1 33	+1 55	-2 46	1.1	0.4	0.1	--	0.4	254°			0.4	086°
1251	Spectacle I. and Long I., between	42° 19.97	70° 58.43	35	-0 04	-1 05	-0 34	+0 37	0.5	0.4	0.1	349°	1.2	273°	0.0	--	0.8	082°
1256	Spectacle Island, 0.2 n.mi. south of	42° 19.35	70° 58.45	10	-0 13	-1 05	-0 52	+0 31	0.8	0.5	0.2	--	1.1	217°	0.0	121°	0.4	038°
1261	Spectacle Island, 0.3 n.mi. north of	42° 18.98	70° 59.13	35	-0 37	+1 40	+1 42	+1 25	0.8	0.7	0.0	--	0.5	244°	0.1	180°	0.4	096°
1266	Spectacle Island, 0.7 n.mi. north of	42° 19.95	70° 59.13	25	-0 07	+1 32	+1 31	-0 52	0.2	0.5	0.0	--	0.2	271°	0.2	359°	0.8	081°
1271	Spectacle Island, 0.1 n.mi. north of	42° 20.10	70° 59.27	25	-0 03	+1 66	+1 26	-0 03	0.8	0.5	0.0	--	0.9	280°	0.0	--	0.8	088°
1276	Spectacle I. and Thompson I., between	42° 19.83	70° 59.27	10	-1 40	-3 54	-2 30	-2 56	0.2	0.3	0.2	227°	0.8	280°	0.2	007°	0.8	090°
1281	Thompson Island, 0.7 n.mi. NNE of	42° 19.25	70° 59.27	35	-0 28	+1 31	+1 10	-0 40	1.0	0.5	0.0	--	1.1	306°	0.0	--	0.4	127°
1286	Fort Independence, 0.3 n.mi. east of	42° 19.97	70° 59.90	10	-1 04	+1 31	+0 48	+1 12	0.2	0.5	0.0	--	0.2	281°	0.2	045°	0.4	086°
1291	Fort Independence, 0.4 n.mi. NW of	42° 20.33	71° 00.22	10	+0 36	+0 00 40	+1 30	+1 14	0.6	0.5	0.0	--	0.6	309°	0.1	061°	0.3	091°
1296	South Boston, Reserved Channel	42° 20.57	71° 01.97	10	+0 58	+1 19	+0 16	+1 13	0.6	0.3	0.0	--	0.5	299°	0.0	006°	0.3	118°
1301	South Boston, Pier 4, 0.2 n.mi. NNE of	42° 21.13	71° 01.85	25	-0 14	-0 25	+1 42	+1 15	0.3	0.1	0.0	--	0.4	030°	0.0	--	0.2	120°

Currents are unidirectional

SEE ENDNOTES ON PAGE 106

NOTES

TABLE 2 – CURRENT DIFFERENCES AND OTHER CONSTANTS

No.	PLACE	Meter Depth (ft)	POSITION Latitude North	POSITION Longitude West	TIME DIFFERENCES Min. before Flood (h m)	TIME DIFFERENCES Flood (h m)	TIME DIFFERENCES Min. before Ebb (h m)	TIME DIFFERENCES Ebb (h m)	SPEED RATIOS Flood	SPEED RATIOS Ebb	AVG SPEEDS Min. before Flood (knots)	Dir.	AVG SPEEDS Maximum Flood (knots)	Dir.	AVG SPEEDS Min. before Ebb (knots)	Dir.	AVG SPEEDS Maximum Ebb (knots)	Dir.
	BOSTON HARBOR–PRESIDENT ROADS—cont. Time meridian, 75° W					on Boston Harbor												
1306	Charles River	10	42° 22.18	71° 09.38		Current weak and variable												
1311	East Boston, Pier 10, southeast of	10	42° 22.55	71° 02.80	+1 35	+0 50	+0 28	+0 16	0.2	0.3	0.0	---	0.2	017°	0.0	---	0.4	194°
1316	Chelsea River, west of bascule bridge	25	42° 22.55	71° 02.80	+0 01	+1 05	+1 23	+0 51	0.2	0.2	0.0	---	0.3	030°	0.0	---	0.2	193°
1321	Chelsea River, below bascule bridge	10	42° 23.07	71° 02.53	+0 02	-0 26	+0 43	+0 46	0.2	0.2	0.0	---	0.2	048°	0.0	---	0.2	240°
1326	Mystic River Bridge, 0.1 n.mi. west of	10	42° 23.03	71° 01.70	+0 29	-0 15	+0 37	-0 04	0.1	0.1	0.0	---	0.2	088°	0.0	---	0.3	272°
1331	Mystic River Bridge, northwest of	10	42° 23.15	71° 03.02	-0 31	-0 10	-0 46	-0 16	0.1	0.1	0.0	---	0.1	287°	0.0	---	0.1	093°
1336	City Point, 0.8 n.mi. SSE of	10	42° 23.15	71° 02.95	-0 20	+1 04	+1 19	+1 03	0.5	0.5	0.0	---	0.1	300°	0.1	170°	0.1	096°
1341	Squantum Point, 0.8 n.mi. northeast of	10	42° 19.22	71° 00.88	+0 13	+0 34	+1 16	+1 44	0.4	0.4	0.0	---	0.4	248°	0.0	---	0.6	069°
1346	Squantum Point, 0.4 n.mi. NNE of	10	42° 18.63	71° 01.23	+0 18	+0 35	+1 16	+1 03	0.4	0.4	0.0	---	0.4	246°	0.0	---	0.5	091°
1351	Neponset River	10	42° 18.25	71° 02.58	-0 25	-0 32	+0 45	+0 35	0.4	0.4	0.0	---	0.4	218°	0.0	---	0.4	026°
	BOSTON HARBOR–NANTASKET ROADS																	
1356	Lowell Island, 0.1 n.mi. south of	10	42° 19.40	70° 55.48	+0 08	-1 54	-0 30	+0 17	0.6	0.9	0.2	206°	0.7	275°	0.2	169°	1.0	092°
	do.	24	42° 19.40	70° 55.48	-0 25	-0 43	-0 20	-0 01	0.4	—	0.0	---	0.6	263°	0.0	---	0.9	095°
1361	Georges Island, northeast of	10	42° 19.37	70° 55.53	-0 13	+1 08	-0 29	-0 01	0.5	—	0.2	191°	0.7	251°	0.0	---	0.8	100°
1366	Georges Island, north of	25	42° 19.42	70° 56.67	-1 25	-2 17	-0 29	-2 10	0.7	—	0.0	---	0.6	294°	0.2	183°	0.9	112°
	do.	10	42° 19.38	70° 55.93	+0 01	-1 05	-0 01	-1 46	0.5	0.6	0.0	---	0.6	282°	0.0	---	1.0	062°
1371	Gallops Island, 0.2 n.mi. SSE of	35	42° 19.45	70° 55.90	-0 07	-1 47	+0 21	+0 21	0.7	0.6	0.0	---	0.6	279°	0.0	---	0.9	069°
1376	Gallops Island, 0.1 n.mi. southeast of	20	42° 19.45	70° 55.97	-1 25	-0 53	+0 04	+0 27	0.6	—	0.0	---	0.7	279°	0.2	130°	1.0	052°
	do.	10	42° 19.62	70° 56.03	+0 49	+0 15	+0 17	+0 15	0.7	0.8	0.2	172°	0.7	274°	0.0	---	0.9	262°
1381	Gallops Island, The Narrows	24	42° 19.67	70° 56.03	+0 16	-1 45	+1 13	-0 46	0.8	0.8	0.2	252°	0.8	298°	0.0	---	0.5	293°
1386	Lowell Island, The Narrows	10	42° 19.72	70° 55.97	-0 04	+0 25	+0 49	-0 05	1.0	0.8	0.0	---	0.7	299°	0.0	---	1.2	299°
1391	Lowell Island, west of	10	42° 19.72	70° 55.97	+0 32	-0 16	+1 22	-0 29	0.9	0.9	0.0	---	0.8	305°	0.0	---	1.2	313°
	do.	25	42° 19.17	70° 54.97	-0 17	-0 38	+0 13	+0 02	0.8	0.7	0.3	165°	0.8	249°	0.2	161°	1.1	065°
1396	Georges Island, 0.5 n.mi. ESE of	35	42° 19.12	70° 54.97	-0 11	-0 38	+0 08	+0 13	0.4	0.4	0.3	180°	0.9	228°	0.0	---	1.0	057°
1401	Georges Island, 0.4 n.mi. east of	10	42° 18.62	70° 55.00	-0 21	-0 11	+0 03	+0 11	0.4	1.0	0.1	132°	0.9	265°	0.0	---	0.9	070°
1406	Georges Island, 0.5 n.mi. southeast of	35	42° 18.62	70° 55.00	+0 08	-0 34	+0 45	-0 03	0.9	1.0	0.1	169°	0.6	195°	0.0	---	1.1	078°
	do.	20	42° 18.78	70° 55.55	+0 16	-0 26	+0 47	-0 01	1.0	0.9	0.2	152°	0.4	128°	0.2	161°	1.4	079°
1411	Georges Island, 0.3 n.mi. SSE of	10	42° 18.78	70° 55.55	+0 14	-0 11	+0 34	+0 41	1.0	1.2	0.1	126°	0.4	134°	0.2	126°	0.9	048°
	do.	25	42° 18.67	70° 55.53	-0 12	-0 34	+0 58	-0 03	1.0	1.0	0.4	346°	0.4	136°	0.4	346°	0.9	074°
1416	Georges Island, 0.4 n.mi. SSE of	25	42° 18.67	70° 55.53	-0 10	+0 24	+0 32	+0 41	1.2	0.8	0.3	161°	1.0	244°	0.3	161°	1.0	070°
	do.	10	42° 18.87	70° 56.93	-0 09	+0 53	-1 40	-0 36	1.0	1.0	0.2	145°	1.1	247°	0.2	---	0.8	065°
1421	Nubble Channel	35	42° 19.78	70° 56.93	+0 07	+0 56	+0 56	+0 00	—	—	0.1	347°	1.2	240°	0.1	347°	1.0	008°
1426	Georges Island, 0.2 n.mi. WSW of	20	42° 19.02	70° 56.10	+0 51	+0 45	+0 45	+0 43	1.1	0.6	0.2	282°	0.8	187°	0.2	139°	1.8	360°
1431	Hull Gut	10	42° 18.20	70° 55.60	+0 14	+0 36	-0 01	+0 25	1.1	1.5	0.1	073°	1.2	163°	0.0	---	2.0	364°
1436	Peddocks Island, 0.2 n.mi. north of	25	42° 18.20	70° 56.00	+0 12	+0 40	+1 20	+0 29	1.2	1.6	0.0	079°	1.3	153°	0.0	---	0.7	257°
	do.	10	42° 18.32	70° 56.00	-0 10	+1 22	+1 30	-0 53	0.9	0.6	0.0	---	1.0	246°	0.1	178°	0.6	060°
1441	Peddocks Island, 0.3 n.mi. northwest of	25	42° 18.40	70° 56.13	+0 07	+1 04	+1 25	+0 56	0.9	0.5	0.1	337°	1.0	265°	0.0	---	1.0	060°
	do.	40	42° 18.40	70° 56.13	+0 51	+1 25	+1 32	+0 15	0.9	0.4	0.2	342°	0.8	248°	0.0	---	0.6	060°
1446	Rainsford I. and Windmill Pt., between	25	42° 18.40	70° 56.32	+0 37	+1 09	+1 45	+0 17	0.9	0.8	0.0	---	1.0	251°	0.3	168°	0.8	056°
	do.	25	42° 18.52	70° 56.32	+0 22	+1 19	+1 36	+0 05	0.7	0.4	0.0	---	0.8	256°	0.2	329°	0.5	059°

SEE ENDNOTES ON PAGE 106

TABLE 2 – CURRENT DIFFERENCES AND OTHER CONSTANTS

No.	PLACE	Meter Depth (ft)	Latitude N	Longitude W	Min. before Flood (h m)	Flood (h m)	Min. before Ebb (h m)	Ebb (h m)	Speed Ratio Flood	Speed Ratio Ebb	Min. before Flood (knots)	Dir.	Max. Flood (knots)	Dir.	Min. before Ebb (knots)	Dir.	Max. Ebb (knots)	Dir.
	CAPE COD BAY Time meridian, 75° W																	
	on Boston Harbor																	
1616	Race Point, 7 miles north of		42° 11'	70° 16'	-0 01	-0 01	-0 01	-0 01	1.4	1.2	0.0	—	1.5	290°	0.0	—	1.5	061°
1621	Race Point, 1 mile northwest of		42° 05'	70° 15'	-0 06	-0 06	-0 06	-0 06	0.9	0.8	0.0	—	1.0	228°	0.0	—	0.9	195°
1626	Provincetown Harbor		42° 03'	70° 10'	+0 04	+0 04	+0 04	+0 04	0.6	0.4	0.0	—	0.7	315°	0.0	—	0.4	200°
1631	Wellfleet Harbor		41° 54'	70° 03'	+0 04	+0 09	+0 09	+0 09	0.5	0.4	0.0	—	0.6	020°	0.0	—	0.5	004°
1636	Barnstable Harbor		41° 43.6'	70° 16.4'	+0 19	+0 58	+0 22	+0 29	1.1	1.2	0.0	—	1.2	192°	0.0	—	1.4	004°
1641	Sandwich Harbor		41° 46'	70° 29'	Current weak and variable				—	—	—	—	—	—	—	—	—	—
1646	Cape Cod Canal (see Index)		41° 48'	70° 31'	Current weak and variable				—	—	—	—	—	—	—	—	—	—
1651	Sagamore Beach		41° 51'	70° 30'														
1656	Ellisville Harbor, 1 mile east of		41° 56'	70° 32'	+0 14	+0 14	+0 14	+0 14	0.3	0.2	0.0	—	0.3	200°	0.0	—	0.3	020°
1661	Manomet Point		41° 56'	70° 35'	+0 04	+0 04	+0 04	+0 04	1.0	0.7	0.0	—	1.1	155°	0.0	—	1.0	010°
1666	Plymouth Harbor, 1 mile east of		41° 58'	70° 39'	-0 06	-0 06	-0 06	-0 06	1.3	0.8	0.0	—	1.4	250°	0.0	—	1.0	248°
1671	Farnham Rock, 1 mile east of		42° 06'	70° 35'	-0 04	-0 21	-0 21	-0 21	1.0	0.8	0.0	—	1.1	180°	0.0	—	0.9	010°
	MASSACHUSETTS COAST—cont.																	
1706	Old Man Shoal, Nantucket Shoals		41° 13.6'	69° 59.0'	+1 23	+1 03	+1 17	+1 14	0.9	0.9	0.0	—	1.9	080°	0.0	—	1.6	225°
1711	Miacomet Pond, 3.0 miles SSE of		41° 11.4'	70° 06.0'	+2 19	+2 03	+2 22	+2 16	0.6	0.8	0.0	—	1.3	080°	0.0	—	1.4	280°
1716	Tuckernuck Island, 4.2 miles SSW of		41° 13.57'	70° 16.90'	+4 08	-3 13	+2 17	-2 56	0.3	0.1	0.0	—	0.5	080°	0.0	—	0.3	090°
1721	Martha's Vineyard, 1.4 miles S of <1>		41° 19.50'	70° 39.90'	—	-2 53	—	-2 47	0.1	0.1	0.0	—	0.3	230°	0.0	—	0.3	098°
	NANTUCKET SOUND ENTRANCE																	
	on Pollock Rip Channel																	
1726	Pollock Rip Channel, east end		41° 33.9'	69° 55.4'	-0 14	-0 39	-0 23	-0 23	1.0	1.1	0.0	—	2.0	053°	0.0	—	1.8	212°
1731	POLLOCK RIP CHANNEL (Butler Hole)		41° 33'	69° 59'	Daily predictions						0.0	135°	2.0	037°	0.0	052°	1.8	228°
1736	Great Round Shoal Channel		— — —	— — —	Daily predictions						0.0	194°			0.0	256°		
	NANTUCKET SOUND																	
1741	Monomoy Pt., channel 0.2 mile west of		41° 33.0'	70° 01.3'	0 00	+0 39	+0 18	-0 23	0.8	1.2	0.0	—	1.7	170°	0.0	—	2.0	346°
1746	Chatham Roads		41° 38.6'	70° 01.7'	Current weak and variable				—	—	—	—	—	—	—	—	—	—
1751	Stage Harbor, 2 miles west of Morris Island		41° 40.7'	69° 58.5'	+3 07	+1 29	+1 29	+4 28	0.3	0.6	0.0	—	0.5	335°	0.0	—	1.0	144°
1756	Dennis Harbor, 2 miles south of		41° 33.5'	70° 04.0'	+1 22	+1 52	+1 27	+1 04	0.2	0.3	0.1	—	0.5	007°	0.1	—	0.3	269°
1761	Monomoy Point, 6 miles west of		41° 29.3'	70° 11.55'	+1 08	+1 10	+1 09	+1 22	0.6	0.3	0.0	—	0.5	080°	0.0	—	0.5	251°
1766	Handkerchief Lighted Whistle Buoy "H"		41° 29.05'	70° 04.0'	+1 42	+1 49	+1 49	+1 59	0.4	0.8	0.0	—	0.8	110°	0.0	—	0.6	265°
1771	Halfmoon Shoal, 1.9 miles northeast of		41° 28.1'	70° 03.7'	+1 13	+1 23	+1 06	+1 41	0.4	0.7	0.0	—	0.8	088°	0.0	—	0.9	265°
1776	Halfmoon Shoal, 3.5 miles east of		41° 23.6'	70° 03.7'	+1 25	+1 37	+1 13	+1 33	0.4	0.5	0.0	—	0.8	029°	0.0	—	0.6	195°
1781	Great Point, 5 mile west of		41° 24.3'	70° 10.4'	+1 22	+1 23	+1 09	+1 10	0.5	0.4	0.0	—	1.0	066°	0.0	—	1.0	248°
1786	Great Point, 3 miles west of		41° 24.25'	70° 06.30'	—	+1 34	—	+2 36	0.4	0.5	0.0	—	0.3	113°	0.3	186°	1.2	287°
1791	Tuckernuck Shoal, off east end		41° 18.4'	70° 06.0'	+3 22	+1 55	+2 44	+3 68	0.2	0.2	0.0	—	0.3	090°	0.0	—	0.9	275°
1796	Brant Point, 2 miles NNW of <1>		41° 21.0'	70° 06.0'	+1 19	+1 02	+1 02	-0 56	0.6	0.9	0.0	—	1.2	171°	0.3	186°	1.5	350°
1801	Nantucket Harbor entrance channel		41° 19.3'	70° 10.2'	+1 10	+1 43	+0 57	+0 18	0.3	0.2	0.1	000°	0.6	094°	0.0	—	1.5	284°
1806	Eel Pt., Nantucket 1.2.5 miles NE of		41° 21.0'	70° 17.1'	+1 40	-0 45	+1 29	+1 02	0.6	0.9	0.0	—	0.6	108°	0.0	—	1.5	295°
1811	Muskeget I., channel 1 mile northeast of		41° 20.9'	70° 23.6'	+1 30	+1 29	+1 11	+1 35	0.6	0.6	0.0	—	1.3	024°	0.0	—	1.3	192°
1816	Muskeget Rock, 1.3 miles southwest of		41° 20.9'	—	—	+1 04	—	+1 53	3.3	3.3	0.2	—	1.3	078°	0.1	224°	1.0	200°
1821	Muskeget Channel		41° 19.90'	70° 29.25'	—	—	—	—	1.9	1.6	0.2	000°	3.8	078°	0.1	—	3.3	200°
1826	Wasque Point, 2.0 miles southwest of										0.0	000°			0.0	—		
1831	Long Shoal–Norton Shoal, between		41° 24.50'	70° 20.0'	+1 31	+1 12	+1 26	+1 13	0.7	0.8	0.0	—	1.4	100°	0.0	—	1.3	260°
1836	Cape Poge Lt., 1.7 miles SSE of		41° 24.0'	70° 25.6'	+0 58	-0 07	+0 49	+1 49	0.8	0.5	0.0	—	1.6	025°	0.0	—	0.9	215°
1841	Cross Rip Channel		41° 26.9'	70° 24.0'	+0 48	+1 48	+1 55	+1 48	0.8	0.7	0.0	—	1.6	091°	0.0	—	1.3	300°
1846	Cape Poge Lt., 3.2 miles northeast of		41° 27.5'	70° 24.0'	+2 42	+2 03	+2 33	+2 37	0.6	0.5	0.0	—	1.6	095°	0.2	—	1.2	276°
1851	Broken Ground–Horseshoe Shoal, between		41° 35.3'	70° 17.1'	+1 46	+1 55	+1 55	+1 20	0.5	0.6	0.0	—	1.0	105°	0.1	—	1.0	260°
1856	Point Gammon, 1.2 miles south of		41° 37.4'	70° 15.4'	+1 15	+1 03	+1 06	+1 02	0.5	0.5	0.0	—	0.9	004°	0.0	—	1.3	184°
1861	Hyannis Harbor, entrance off breakwater		41° 37.9'	70° 16.4'	+2 46	+2 33	+2 44	+4 22	0.6	0.5	0.0	—	0.5	036°	0.0	224°	0.5	219°
1866	Lewis Bay entrance channel		41° 36.9'	70° 16.4'	+2 44	+2 33	+2 51	+1 20	0.5	0.3	0.0	—	1.7	062°	0.0	—	1.7	245°
1871	Cotuit Bay entrance (Bluff Point)		41° 32.0'	70° 25.7'	+2 47	+1 32	+1 44	+1 45	0.8	0.8	0.0	—	0.9	004°	0.0	—	1.3	184°
1876	Wreck Shoal–Eldridge Shoal, between				Current weak and variable				—	—	—	—	—	—	—	—	—	—

NOTES

SEE ENDNOTES ON PAGE 106

TABLE 2 – CURRENT DIFFERENCES AND OTHER CONSTANTS

No.	PLACE	POSITION Meter Depth (ft)	Latitude North	Longitude West	TIME DIFF. Min. before Flood (h m)	Flood (h m)	Min. before Ebb (h m)	Ebb (h m)	SPEED RATIOS Flood	Ebb	AVG SPEEDS Min. before Flood (knots)	Dir.	Maximum Flood (knots)	Dir.	Minimum before Ebb (knots)	Dir.	Maximum Ebb (knots)	Dir.
	NANTUCKET SOUND—cont. Time meridian, 75° W																	
	on Pollock Rip Channel																	
1881	Hedge Fence Lighted Gong Buoy 22		41°28.3'	70°29.0'	+2 48	+2 34	+2 38	+2 44	0.7	0.7	0.0	—	1.4	108°	0.0	—	1.2	268°
1886	Cape Poge Light, 1.4 miles west of		41°25.46	70°29.00	+2 13	+1 54	+1 26	+1 39	0.6	0.1	0.0	—	0.3	096°	0.0	—	0.2	250°
1891	Edgartown, Inner Harbor		41°23.4'	70°30.5'	+0 25	-1 04	+0 35	-0 20	0.3	0.6			1.1	075°			1.1	270°
1896	Katama Pt., 0.6 mi. NNW of, Katama Bay		41°21.9'	70°30.3'	+0 12		+0 20		0.3	0.4	0.0		0.6	070°	0.0		0.5	265°
	VINEYARD SOUND																	
1901	East Chop-Squash Meadow, between		41°27.9'	70°32.2'	+2 07	+1 55	+1 43	+2 04	0.3	0.3	0.0	—	0.4	325°	0.0	—	0.3	195°
1906	East Chop, 1 mile north of		41°29.1'	70°33.5'	+2 40	+1 52	+2 17	+2 11	0.2	0.1	0.0	—	0.4	328°	0.0	—	0.3	175°
1911	Vineyard Haven		41°28.1'	70°35.2'	Current weak and variable													
1916	West Chop, 0.8 mile north of		41°29.6'	70°35.7'	+2 29	+1 52	+1 58	+2 35	1.1	1.1	0.0	—	1.4	131°	0.0	—	1.8	329°
1921	Hedge Fence-L'Hommedieu Shoal, between		41°30.3'	70°32.2'	+3 27	+1 38	+2 01	+1 52	1.6	1.3	0.0	—	2.2	116°	0.0	—	2.2	297°
1926	Waquoit Bay entrance		41°32.9'	70°33.4'	+3 21	+2 14	+3 40	+4 01	1.0	1.8	0.0	—	3.1	096°	0.0	—	3.0	282°
1931	L'Hommedieu Shoal, north of west end		41°31.6'	70°34.6'	+2 30	+2 03	+2 12	+2 11	1.2	0.8	0.0	—	2.1	106°	0.0	—	2.2	276°
1936	Nobska Point, 1.8 miles east of		41°31.1'	70°37.1'	+2 13	+1 45	+1 55	+1 49	1.2	1.4	0.0	—	1.5	343°	0.0	—	1.4	209°
1941	West Chop, 0.2 mile west of		41°29.0'	70°36.6'	+1 19	+1 34	+1 50	+1 16	1.3	1.3	0.0	—	2.7	059°	0.0	—	1.4	241°
1946	Nobska Point, 0.5 mile southeast of		41°29.1'	70°38.6'	+2 33	+2 15	+2 25	+2 19	1.7	1.7	0.0	—	2.6	071°	0.0	—	2.4	259°
1951	Nobska Point, 0.5 mile north of		41°28.1'	70°39.9'	+1 55	+4 44	+2 12	+1 12	1.1	1.4	0.0	—	3.4	050°	0.0	—	2.4	240°
1956	Tarpaulin Cove, 1.5 miles east of		41°28.3'	70°43.5'	+2 49	+2 07	+2 11	+2 33	1.0	1.4	0.0	—	1.9	055°	0.0	—	2.3	235°
1961	Robinsons Hole, 1.2 miles southeast of		41°26.1'	70°46.8'	+2 30	+1 51	+2 11	+2 02	0.5	1.2	0.0	—	0.9	060°	0.0	—	2.1	240°
1966	Gay Head, 3 miles northeast of		41°21.3'	70°46.3'	+2 25	+1 50	+1 50	+2 11	0.6	0.8	0.0	—	0.9	081°	0.0	—	1.3	236°
1971	Menemsha Bight <6>		41°24.1'	70°51.8'		+1 24	+1 56	+1 17	1.0	0.7	0.0	—	1.1	074°	0.0	—	1.2	255°
1976	Gay Head, 3 miles north of		41°21.8'	70°51.8'	+2 13	+0 54	+1 42	+1 16	0.6	1.2	0.0	—	2.0	012°	0.0	—	2.0	249°
1981	Gay Head, 1.5 miles northwest of		41°23'	71°00'	+1 30	See table 5.	See table 5.											
1986	Cuttyhunk Island, 3.2 miles southwest of		41°21.8'	71°01.8'														
1991	Browns Ledge		41°19.8'	71°05.9'														
	on Cape Cod Canal																	
	VINEYARD SOUND-BUZZARDS BAY																	
	Woods Hole <59>																	
1996	South end		41°30.8'	70°40.2'	+0 29	+1 40	+1 17	+0 08	0.4	0.4	0.0	—	1.5	138°	0.0	—	1.1	318°
2001	0.1 mile SW of Devils Foot Island		41°31.2'	70°41.1'	+0 20	+1 41	+0 55	+0 31	0.9	0.8	0.0	—	3.5	094°	0.0	—	3.6	276°
2006	North end		41°31.5'	70°41.6'	-0 29	+1 25	+1 09	-0 04	0.2	0.2	0.0	—	0.8	160°	0.0	—	0.7	007°
	Robinsons Hole																	
2011	South end		41°26.7'	70°48.2'	+1 14	+1 42	+1 20	+1 01	0.2	0.2	0.0	—	0.8	162°	0.0	—	1.0	339°
2016	Middle		41°27.0'	70°48.4'	+1 30	+2 00	+1 02	+0 47	0.7	0.6	0.0	—	2.8	146°	0.0	—	2.9	316°
2021	North end		41°27.4'	70°48.7'	+1 54	+2 00	+0 52	+1 17	0.2	0.3	0.0	—	1.0	161°	0.0	—	1.2	339°
	Quicks Hole																	
2026	South end		41°26.3'	70°50.5'	+2 18	+1 42	+1 17	+0 63	0.6	0.4	0.0	—	1.9	140°	0.0	—	2.0	300°
2031	Middle		41°26.6'	70°50.9'	+2 21	+2 00	+1 26	+0 41	0.5	0.6	0.0	—	2.5	167°	0.0	—	2.2	339°
2036	North end		41°27.1'	70°51.0'	+2 42	+2 06	+1 44	+0 23	0.5	0.6	0.0	—	2.6	166°	0.0	—	2.6	002°
2041	Canapitsit Channel		41°25.4'	70°54.5'	+2 03	+2 27	+1 02	+0 26	0.6	0.4	0.0	—	2.6	156°	0.0	—	1.7	312°
	on Pollock Rip Channel																	
2046	Westport River entrance		41°30.5'	71°05.3'	+0 09	-0 05	-0 26	-1 13	1.1	1.5	0.0	—	2.2	290°	0.0	—	2.5	108°
	BUZZARDS BAY <7>																	
2056	Ribbon Reef-Sow & Pigs Reef, between		41°25.3'	70°58.2'	-0 19	-1 31	-2 44	-1 54	0.4	0.7	0.0	—	0.8	062°	0.0	—	1.2	237°
2061	Penikese Island, 0.8 mile northwest of		41°25.2'	70°56.2'	-1 37	-0 25	-0 55	-0 57	0.6	0.6	0.0	—	1.2	059°	0.0	—	1.1	254°
2066	Perikese Island, 0.2 mile south of		41°26.6'	70°55.5'	-1 43	-0 15	-1 30	-2 39	0.4	0.5	0.0	—	0.7	093°	0.0	—	0.9	287°

NOTES

SEE ENDNOTES ON PAGE 106

TABLE 2 – CURRENT DIFFERENCES AND OTHER CONSTANTS

No.	PLACE	Meter Depth (ft)	POSITION Latitude North	POSITION Longitude West	TIME DIFF. Min before Flood (h m)	TIME DIFF. Flood (h m)	TIME DIFF. Min before Ebb (h m)	TIME DIFF. Ebb (h m)	SPEED RATIOS Flood	SPEED RATIOS Ebb	Minimum before Flood knots	Minimum before Flood Dir	Maximum Flood knots	Maximum Flood Dir	Minimum before Ebb knots	Minimum before Ebb Dir	Maximum Ebb knots	Maximum Ebb Dir
	VINEYARD SOUND–BUZZARDS BAY–cont. Time meridian, 75° W				*on Cape Cod Canal*													
2071	Gull I. and Nashawena I., between		41°26.2'	70°54.2'	-2 15	-0 57	-2 01	-2 41	0.5	0.6	0.0	--	0.9	091°	0.0	--	1.1	247°
2076	Weepecket Island, south of		41°32.4'	70°44.3'	-3 16	-1 07	-1 28	-2 27	0.4	0.4	0.0	--	0.8	069°	0.0	--	0.6	255°
2081	Quamquissett Harbor entrance		41°32.4'	70°39.8'	Current weak and variable								0.4	--			0.3	--
2086	West Falmouth Harbor entrance		41°36.5'	70°39.3'	Current weak and variable													
2091	Megansett Harbor		41°38.8'	70°39.2'	Current weak and variable													
2096	Abiels Ledge, 0.4 mile south of		41°41.1'	70°40.4'	+0 26	-0 36	-0 06	-0 23	0.4	0.6	0.0	--	0.8	038°	0.0	--	1.0	216°
2101	Dumpling Rocks, 0.2 mile southeast of		41°32.0'	70°55.1'	-1 43	-1 03	-1 32	-2 09	0.4	0.6	0.0	--	0.8	068°	0.0	--	1.1	190°
2106	Apponagansett Bay		41°35'	70°57'	Current weak and variable													
2111	Clarks Cove		41°38'	70°55'	Current weak and variable													
2121	New Bedford Harbor and approaches	6	41°35.6'	70°50.4'	Current weak and variable				0.4		0.0	--	0.3	--	0.0	--	0.4	209°
2126	West Island and Long Island, between		41°34.0'	70°48.6'	-0 43	-0 43	-1 28	-1 42			0.0	--	0.7	079°	0.0	--	0.8	--
2131	West Island, 1 mile southeast of		41°37.1'	70°50.2'	Current weak and variable													
2136	Naskatucket Bay		41°38'	70°47'	Current weak and variable				0.3	0.4	0.0	--	0.3	022°	0.0	--	0.4	202°
2141	Sippican Harbor		41°41'	70°44'	-1 41	-0 31	-1 22	-1 23	0.4	0.4	0.0	--	0.7	010°	0.0	--	0.6	185°
2146	Mattapoisett Harbor		41°44.0'	70°43.0'	-1 49	-0 27	-1 22	-1 31									0.6	
2151	Wareham River, off Barneys Point		41°44.7'	70°42.4'														
	CAPE COD CANAL				*on Cape Cod Canal*													
2156	Onset Bay, south of Onset Island		41°43.9'	70°38.7'	Current weak and variable						0.0	--			0.0	--		
2161	Onset Bay, south of Wickets Island		41°44.1'	70°39.3'	Current weak and variable						0.0	--			0.0	--		
	CAPE COD CANAL				*on Pollock Rip Channel*													
2166	CAPE COD CANAL, railroad bridge		41°44.5'	70°36.8'	-0 03	-0 01	-0 03	-0 04	0.8	0.9	0.0	--	4.0	070°	0.0	--	4.5	250°
2171	Bourne Highway bridge		41°45'	70°35'	-0 07	-0 03	-0 09	-0 10	0.8	0.8	0.0	--	3.3	068°	0.0	--	4.0	245°
2176	Bournedale		41°46'	70°34'	*Daily predictions*	-0 03	-0 09	-0 13	0.7	0.6	0.0	--	2.9	030°	0.0	--	3.6	210°
2181	Sagamore Bridge		41°46'	70°33'	-0 09	-0 04	-0 11	-0 16	0.7	0.6	0.0	--	2.8	095°	0.0	--	2.5	275°
2186	Cape Cod Canal, east end	15	41°46.5'	70°30.0'	-0 13	-0 06	-0 17	-0 19	0.6	0.6	0.0	--	2.4	068°	0.0	--	2.6	245°
	NARRAGANSETT BAY <B>				*on Pollock Rip Channel*													
	Sakonnet River (except Narrows)				Current weak and variable													
2191	Black Point, SW of, Sakonnet River	15	41°30.4'	71°13.2'	-2 54	-1 55	-2 13	-2 26	0.2	0.2	0.0	--	0.4	012°	0.0	--	0.4	194°
2196	Almy Point Bridge, south of, Sakonnet River	15	41°37.3'	71°13.0'	-3 00	-2 10	-2 30	-3 13	0.2	0.8	0.0	--	0.4	034°	0.0	--	1.5	160°
2201	Tiverton, Stone bridge, Sakonnet R. <9>		41°37.5'	71°13.0'	-2 58	-2 52	-2 26	-3 06	1.3	1.6	0.0	--	2.6	010°	0.0	--	2.7	190°
2206					-3 04		-3 04				0.2		2.3	010°				
2211	Tiverton, RR. bridge, Sakonnet R. <10>	10	41°38.3'	71°12.9'	-3 26	-0 06	-2 48	-3 41	1.2	1.4	0.0		1.5	000°	0.0		2.4	180°
2216	Common Fence Point, northeast of	10	41°39.5'	71°12.5'	-2 38	-1 15	-2 32	-2 41	0.1	0.2	0.0		0.2	028°	0.0		0.3	210°
2221	Brenton Point, 1.4 n mi. southwest of	7	41°25.9'	71°22.6'	-1 03	-0 38	-1 20	-1 04	0.1	0.4	0.0	--	0.1	058°	0.0	--	0.6	170°
2226	Castle Hill, west of, East Passage	15	41°28.0'	71°22.1'	-0 06	-0 42	-1 07	-1 09	0.1	0.7	0.0	--	0.7	046°	0.0	--	1.2	237°
2231	Bull Point, east of	10	41°28.8'	71°21.0'	-1 10	-0 47	-1 10	-1 33	0.6	0.8	0.0	--	1.2	001°	0.0	--	1.5	206°
2236	Mackerel Cove		41°29'	71°20'	Current weak and variable													
2241	Newport Harbor, S and E of Goal Island	15	41°29'	71°28.5'	Current weak and variable				0.4	0.5	0.1	108°	0.8	310°	0.0	--	1.0	124°
2246	Rose Island, northeast of	15	41°30.2'	71°21.0'	-1 57	-1 17	-1 17	-1 08	0.4	0.5	0.0	--	0.8	310°	0.0	--	1.0	124°
2251	Rose Island, northwest of		41°30.4'	71°21.0'	-1 38	-1 18	-1 18	-1 39	0.4	0.4	0.1		0.7	317°	0.1	102°	1.0	160°
2256	Rose Island, west of		41°29.8'	71°21.0'	-0 42	-0 34	-1 14	-1 28	0.4	0.6	0.0		0.1	001°	0.1		1.0	172°
2261	Gould Island, southeast of	7	41°29.5'	71°20.2'	-0 16	-0 24	-1 14	-1 16	0.3	0.4	0.0		0.5	033°	0.0		0.7	217°
2266	Gould Island, west of	15	41°31.9'	71°21.5'	-0 16	-0 32	-1 13	-1 07	0.3	0.4	0.1	279°	0.6	351°	0.1	279°	0.8	199°

NOTES

SEE ENDNOTES ON PAGE 106

TABLE 2 – CURRENT DIFFERENCES AND OTHER CONSTANTS

No.	PLACE	Meter Depth (ft)	Position Lat. North	Position Long. West	Time Diff. Min. before Flood (h m)	Time Diff. Flood (h m)	Time Diff. Min. before Ebb (h m)	Time Diff. Ebb (h m)	Speed Ratio Flood	Speed Ratio Ebb	Min. before Flood knots	Min. before Flood Dir.	Max. Flood knots	Max. Flood Dir.	Min. before Ebb knots	Min. before Ebb Dir.	Max. Ebb knots	Max. Ebb Dir.
	VINEYARD SOUND–BUZZARDS BAY—cont. Time meridian, 75° W																	
2071	Gull I. and Nashawena I., between		41°26.2'	70°54.2'	−2 15	−0 57	−2 01	−2 41	0.5	0.6	0.0	—	0.9	091°	0.0	—	1.1	247°
2076	Weepecket Island, south of		41°30.4'	70°44.3'	−3 16	−1 07	−1 28	−2 27	0.4	0.4	0.0	—	0.8	069°	0.0	—	0.6	255°
2081	Quamquissett Harbor entrance		41°32.4'	70°39.8'	*on Cape Cod Canal*								0.4	—			0.3	—
2086	West Falmouth Harbor entrance		41°36.5'	70°39.3'	*Current weak and variable*													
2091	Megansett Harbor		41°38.8'	70°39.2'	*Current weak and variable*													
2096	Abiels Ledge, 0.4 mile south of		41°41.1'	70°40.4'	+0 26	−0 36	−0 06	−0 23	0.4	0.6	0.0	—	0.8	035°	0.0	—	1.0	216°
2101	Dumpling Rocks, 0.2 mile southeast of		41°32.0'	70°55.1'	−1 43	−1 03	−1 32	−2 09	0.4	0.6	0.0	—	0.8	066°	0.0	—	1.1	190°
2106	Apponagansett Bay		41°35'	70°57'	*Current weak and variable*													
2111	Clarks Cove		41°36'	70°55'	*Current weak and variable*													
2116	New Bedford Harbor approaches		41°35.6'	70°50.4'	*Current weak and variable*													
2121	West Island and Long Island, between		41°34.1'	70°48.6'	−0 43	−0 43	−1 28	−1 42	0.4	0.5	0.0	—	0.3	—	0.0	—	0.4	203°
2126	West Island, B mile southeast of	6	41°34'	70°55.2'	*Current weak and variable*								0.7	079°			0.8	—
2131	Naskeket Point		41°38'	70°47'	*Current weak and variable*												0.3	—
2136	Mattapoisett Harbor		41°41'	70°44'	*Current weak and variable*													
2141	Sippican Harbor		41°41.0'	70°43.0'	−1 41	−0 31	−1 22	−1 23	0.3	0.4	0.0	—	0.6	022°	0.0	—	0.6	202°
2146	Wareham River, off Long Beach Point		41°44.0'	70°42.4'													0.6	185°
2151	Wareham River, off Barneys Point		41°44.7'	70°42.4'	−1 49	−0 27	−1 22	−1 31	0.4	0.4	0.0	—	0.7	010°	0.0	—		
2156	Onset Bay, south of Onset Island		41°43.9'	70°38.7'	*on Cape Cod Canal*													
2161	Onset Bay, south of Wickets Island		41°44.1'	70°39.3'	*Current weak and variable*													
	CAPE COD CANAL																	
2166	CAPE COD CANAL, railroad bridge		41°44.5'	70°36.8'	−0 03	−0 01	−0 03	−0 04	0.8	0.9	0.0	—	4.0	070°	0.0	—	4.5	250°
2171	Bourne Highway bridge		41°45'	70°35'	−0 07	−0 03	−0 09	−0 10	0.8	0.8	0.0	—	3.3	068°	0.0	—	4.0	245°
2176	Bournedale		41°46'	70°34'	−0 09	−0 04	−0 11	−0 13	0.7	0.6	0.0	—	3.4	030°	0.0	—	3.6	210°
2181	Sagamore Bridge		41°46'	70°32'	−0 13	−0 06	−0 17	−0 19	0.6	0.6	0.0	—	2.8	098°	0.0	—	2.5	275°
2186	Cape Cod Canal, east end	15	41°46.5'	70°30.0'	*Daily predictions*								2.4	068°			2.8	245°
	NARRAGANSETT BAY <6>				*on Pollock Rip Channel*													
2191	Sakonnet River (except Narrows)		—	71°13.2'	*Current weak and variable*													
2196	Black Point, SW of, Sakonnet River	15	41°30.4'	71°13.2'	−2 54	−1 55	−2 13	−2 26	0.2	0.2	0.0	—	0.4	012°	0.0	—	0.4	194°
2201	Almy Point Bridge, south of, Sakonnet River	15	41°37.3'	71°13.0'	−3 00	−2 10	−2 30	−3 13	0.2	0.8	0.0	—	0.4	034°	0.0	—	1.5	180°
2206	Tiverton, Stone bridge, Sakonnet R. <9>		41°37.5'		−2 58	−2 02	−2 26	−3 06	1.4	1.6	0.0	—	2.7	010°	0.0	—	2.7	190°
2211	Tiverton, RR. bridge, Sakonnet R. <10>	10	41°38.3'	71°12.9'	−3 26	−3 26	−2 48	−3 41	1.2	1.4	0.0	—	2.6	010°	0.0	—	2.4	180°
2216	Common Fence Point, northeast of		41°39.5'	71°12.5'	−2 38	−2 32	−2 32	−2 41	0.1	0.2	0.0	—	0.3	000°	0.0	—	0.3	210°
2221	Brenton Point, 1.4 n.mi. southwest of	7	41°25.9'	71°22.6'	−1 03	−0 58	−1 20	−1 04	0.2	0.4	0.0	—	0.8	026°	0.0	—	0.6	170°
2226	Castle Hill, west of, East Passage	15	41°27.4'	71°22.7'	−0 06	−0 42	−1 07	−0 29	0.4	0.7	0.0	—	0.7	058°	0.0	—	1.2	237°
2231	Bull Point, east of	10	41°28.8'	71°21.0'	−1 10	−0 47	−1 10	−1 33	0.6	0.8	0.0	—	1.2	046°	0.0	—	1.5	208°
2236	Mackerel Cove		41°28.5'	71°22.8'	*Current weak and variable*								0.1	347°				
2241	Newport Harbor, S and E of Goat Island		41°29'	71°20'	*Current weak and variable*								0.2	013°				
2246	Rose Island, northeast of	15	41°30.2'	71°19.9'	−1 57	−0 26	−1 17	−2 08	0.4	0.5	0.1	106°	0.8	310°	0.0	—	1.0	124°
2251	Rose Island, northwest of	15	41°30.4'	71°21.1'	−1 38	−0 34	−1 38	−1 39	0.5	0.6	0.0	—	0.7	007°	0.1	102°	1.0	190°
2256	Rose Island, west of		41°29.8'	71°21.0'	−0 42	−1 28	−1 20	−1 28	0.6	0.6	0.0	—	0.7	001°	0.0	—	1.0	172°
2261	Gould Island, southeast of	7	41°29.8'	71°21.0'	−1 40	−1 28	−1 14	−1 16	0.4	0.4	0.0	—	0.7	035°	0.0	—	0.7	217°
2266	Gould Island, west of	15	41°31.9'	71°21.5'	−0 16	−0 52	−1 13	−1 07	0.3	0.4	0.0	—	0.6	351°	0.1	279°	0.8	193°

NOTES

SEE ENDNOTES ON PAGE 106

TABLE 2 – CURRENT DIFFERENCES AND OTHER CONSTANTS

No.	PLACE	Meter Depth (ft)	POSITION Latitude North	POSITION Longitude West	TIME DIFFERENCES Min. before Flood (h m)	TIME DIFFERENCES Flood (h m)	TIME DIFFERENCES Min. before Ebb (h m)	TIME DIFFERENCES Ebb (h m)	SPEED RATIOS Flood	SPEED RATIOS Ebb	AVG Minimum before Flood (knots)	Dir.	AVG Maximum Flood (knots)	Dir.	AVG Minimum before Ebb (knots)	Dir.	AVG Maximum Ebb (knots)	Dir.
	NARRAGANSETT BAY <B>—cont. Time meridian, 75° W																	
							on Pollock Rip Channel											
2271	Dyer Island–Carrs Point (between)	15	41° 34.5'	71° 17.8'	-1 58	-1 13	-0 50	-1 37	0.4	0.4	0.0	—	0.8	049°	0.0	—	0.6	296°
2276	Conanicut Point, ENE of	7	41° 34.5'	71° 20.5'	-2 05	-0 24	-1 18	-1 13	0.4	0.6	0.1	111°	0.8	048°	0.0	106°	0.4	189°
2281	Dyer Island, west of	18	41° 35.2'	71° 18.5'	-1 04	-0 46	-0 63	-1 34			0.0	—	0.3	023°	0.0	—	0.4	218°
						Daily Predictions												
2286	QUONSET POINT	17	41° 35.0'	71° 20.7'	-1 22	-1 34	-1 08	-0 58	0.6	0.8	0.1	262°	1.1	021°	0.0	—	1.4	200°
2291	Mount Hope Bridge	10	41° 38.4'	71° 15.6'	-2 16	-0 04	-0 30	-1 04	0.2	0.2	0.0	—	0.4	047°	0.0	—	0.4	239°
2296	Hog Island, northwest of	10	41° 38.8'	71° 17.7'	-2 16	+0 08	-1 00	-0 37	0.2	0.4	0.0	—	0.4	011°	0.0	—	0.4	199°
2301	Common Fence Point, west of	10	41° 39.0'	71° 14.7'	-1 13	-0 20	-1 03	-0 52	0.2	0.2	0.1	—	0.4	050°	0.1	133°	0.4	224°
2306	Mount Hope Point, northeast of	10	41° 40.8'	71° 14.7'	-2 01	-3 34	-1 19	-0 48	0.7	1.0	0.0	—	0.9	038°	0.1	121°	0.4	217°
2311	Kickamuit R. (Narrows), Mt. Hope Bay	10	41° 41.9'	71° 14.7'	-2 04	-1 40			0.9				1.4	000°	0.0	—	1.7	191°
2316	Warren River entrance		41° 42.7'	71° 17.8'	-0 14	+0 11	-0 22	-1 05	0.5	0.5	0.0	—	0.4	020°	0.0	—	0.3	200°
2321	Warren, Warren River		41° 43.7'	71° 17.3'	-0 11	-0 64	-1 31	-0 19	0.3	0.6	0.0	—	1.0	358°	0.0	—	0.9	171°
2326	Beavertail Point, 0.8 mile northwest of	15	41° 27.5'	71° 24.7'	Current weak and variable				0.2	0.5	0.0	—	0.5	003°	0.0	—	1.0	188°
2331	Dutch Island, east of, West Passage		41° 30.2'	71° 23.7'	-3 02	-5 10	-2 37	-2 46	0.2	0.5	0.1	103°	0.3	032°	0.2	126°	0.9	188°
2336	Dutch Island and Beaver Head, between	7	41° 29.8'	71° 24.2'	-1 56	-1 32	-1 58	-1 47	0.5	0.6	0.0	—	1.3	030°	0.0	—	1.0	233°
2341	Dutch Island, west of	15	41° 30.3'	71° 24.6'	-1 33	-1 49	-1 21	-1 16	0.2	0.7	0.0	—	0.5	012°	0.0	—	1.2	208°
2346	Jamestown–North Kingstown Bridge		41° 31.8'	71° 23.8'	-2 16	-4 10	-1 22	-1 33	0.2	0.7	0.1	112°	0.8	007°	0.1	097°	1.3	178°
2351	Wickford Harbor		41° 34'	71° 26'	Current weak and variable				0.4		0.0	—	0.3	—	0.0	—	0.3	—
2356	Greenwich Bay entrance		41° 40.0'	71° 23.6'	Current weak and variable				0.3		0.0	—	0.7	354°	0.0	—	0.3	157°
2361	Patience Island, narrows east of		41° 39.5'	71° 21.2'	-2 41	-2 29	-2 44	-2 37	0.7	0.5	0.0	—	0.6	040°	0.0	—	0.9	224°
2366	Patience I. and Warwick Neck, between		41° 39.8'	71° 22.4'	-1 40	-1 21	-1 18	-1 13	0.6	0.5	0.0	—	0.2	325°	0.0	—	0.8	128°
2371	Nayatt Point, WNW of	10	41° 43.7'	71° 23.7'	-2 24	+0 47	-1 00	-1 11	0.2	0.8	0.0	—	0.4	020°	0.0	—	0.2	180°
2376	India Point RR bridge, Seekonk River <3>		41° 49.0'	71° 23.3'	-1 48	-4 02	-1 31	-1 06	0.2		0.0	—	0.4	020°	0.0	—	1.4	—
2381	Fox Point, south of, Providence River		41° 48.8'	71° 24.0'	-3 02	+0 08	-0 27	-1 34	0.1	0.1	0.0	—	0.2	343°	0.0	—	0.1	166°
2386	Cold Spring Pt., Seekonk River <10>	10	41° 49.6'	71° 22.8'	-1 48	-2 24	-1 31	-1 02	0.1	0.8	0.0	—	0.8	030°	0.0	—	1.4	210°
	BLOCK ISLAND SOUND Time meridian, 75° W					on The Race												
2391	Harbor of Refuge, south entrance		41° 21.4'	71° 29.75'	-2 02	-2 31	-2 17	-1 10	0.2		0.0	—	0.6	329°	0.0	—	0.8	141°
	Point Judith																	
2396	Harbor of Refuge, west entrance		41° 22'	71° 31'	-3 02	-2 40	-3 07	-0 52	0.7	0.3	0.0	—	1.8	351°	0.0	—	0.4	141°
2401	Pond entrance		41° 23'	71° 31'	-0 27	+0 20	+0 27	-2 07	0.3	0.2	0.0	—	0.7	256°	0.0	—	0.7	141°
2406	2.4 miles southwest of		41° 19.87'	71° 30.65'	-0 19	+0 21	+0 30	+0 07	0.3	0.6	0.0	—	0.8	285°	0.0	—	1.5	188°
2411	4.5 miles southwest of		41° 18'	71° 33'	-0 30	-0 32	-0 21	-0 54	0.7	0.2	0.0	—	1.0	296°	0.0	—	0.6	090°
	Block Island																	
2416	four miles north of	15	41° 18'	71° 32'	-0 11	-0 12	-1 08	+0 06	0.7	0.7	0.0	—	0.8	285°	0.0	—	0.8	078°
2421	Sandy Point, 2.1 miles NNE of	7	41° 15.65'	71° 34.00'	-1 59	-1 19	+0 04	+0 54	0.3	0.2	0.0	—	1.9	315°	0.0	—	1.7	066°
2426	Sandy Pt., 1.5 miles north of	15	41° 14'	71° 34.85'	-0 01	-1 11	-0 06	+0 05	0.7	0.6	0.0	—	1.7	296°	0.0	—	2.1	063°
2431	Clay Head, 1.2 miles ENE of		41° 09.35'	71° 32.85'	-1 16	-0 47	-0 39	+0 24	0.6	0.2	0.0	220°	0.2	296°	0.0	—	1.8	144°
2436	Old Harbor Pt., 0.5 mile southeast of		41° 09'	71° 32.30'	-1 20	+0 57	-0 25	+0 11	0.5	0.2	0.0	—	1.9	336°	0.0	—	1.8	175°
2441	Lewis Pt., 1.0 mile southeast of		41° 08.20'	71° 38'	-3 57	-3 14	-0 49	+0 46	0.6	0.2	0.0	—	1.4	170°	0.0	—	1.7	139°
2446	Lewis Pt., 1.5 miles west of		41° 09'	71° 35.30'	-0 41	-0 40	-3 25	+0 11	0.3	0.1	0.0	—	0.3	166°	0.0	—	1.7	170°
2451	Great Salt Pond entrance		41° 11.97'	71° 36'	—	-1 03	-1 55	+0 46		0.2	0.0	—	0.4	166°	0.0	—	0.3	326°
2456	Great Salt Pond ent., 1 mile NW of		41° 12'	71° 35.13'	-0 45	-0 26	-0 25	-1 06	0.2	0.1	0.0	—	0.6	258°	0.0	—	0.6	035°
2461	Sandy Point, 0.4 mile west of <11>	7	41° 13.80'	71° 35.77'													0.7	035°
2466	Green Hill Point, 1.1 miles south of		41° 20.90'														0.4	070°

NOTES   SEE ENDNOTES ON PAGE 106

TABLE 2 – CURRENT DIFFERENCES AND OTHER CONSTANTS

No.	PLACE	POSITION Latitude North	POSITION Longitude West	Meter Depth (ft)	TIME DIFFERENCES Min. before Flood (h m)	TIME DIFFERENCES Flood (h m)	TIME DIFFERENCES Min. before Ebb (h m)	TIME DIFFERENCES Ebb (h m)	SPEED RATIOS Flood	SPEED RATIOS Ebb	Min. before Flood (knots)	Min. before Flood Dir.	Maximum Flood (knots)	Maximum Flood Dir.	Min. before Ebb (knots)	Min. before Ebb Dir.	Maximum Ebb (knots)	Maximum Ebb Dir.
	BLOCK ISLAND SOUND Time meridian, 75° W					on The Race												
2471	Sandy Point, 4.1 miles northwest of	41°17.10	71°38.00	15	+0 17	+0 32	+0 31	-0 07	0.3	0.2	0.0	--	0.7	270°	0.0	--	0.6	084°
2476	Grace Point, 2.0 miles northwest of	41°12'	71°38'		-0 30	See table 5.	+0 46	-0 31	0.4	0.1	0.0	--	1.1	249°	0.0	--	0.4	078°
2481	Quonochontaug Beach, 1.1 miles S of	41°18.80	71°42.82	15	+0 16	+0 27	+0 38	-0 03	0.3	0.2	0.0	--	0.7	249°	0.0	--	0.6	059°
2486	Quonochontaug Beach, 3.8 miles S of	41°16.35	71°43.00	15	+1 12	+1 01	-0 15	+0 22	0.6	0.4	0.0	--	0.6	289°	0.0	--	1.2	097°
2491	Lewis Point, 6.0 miles WNW of	41°11.60	71°43.20		-0 22	-0 15	-0 15	-0 52	0.5	0.6	0.0	--	1.5	321°	0.0	--	2.1	141°
2496	Southwest Ledge	41°07	71°42	15	+0 23	+0 31	+0 10	-0 32	0.5	0.7	0.0	--	1.5	354°	0.0	--	1.9	168°
2501	Southwest Ledge, 2.0 miles west of	41°06.80	71°43.00		-0 16	+0 13	+0 44	+0 01	0.4	0.4	0.0	--	1.2	260°	0.0	--	0.7	086°
2506	Watch Hill Point, 2.2 miles east of	41°18.16	71°48.60	15	+0 48	+0 39	+0 38	+0 01	0.3	0.3	0.0	--	0.7	269°	0.0	--	1.2	064°
2511	Watch Hill Point, 5.2 miles SSE of	41°13.20	71°49.00	15	+0 05	+0 15	-0 18	-0 02	0.3	0.5	0.1	176°	1.1	263°	0.0	--	0.9	092°
2516	Watch Hill Point, 5.3 n.mi. SE of	41°14.65	71°49.07	15d	+0 46	+0 18	-0 39	-0 03	1.0	0.9	0.0	--	2.8	346°	0.0	--	1.6	079°
2521	Montauk Point, 5.4 miles NNE of	41°04.50	71°46.43	15	-1 09	-0 48	-0 39	-0 03	0.9	0.9	0.0	--	1.1	346°	0.0	--	2.8	162°
2526	Montauk Point, 1.2 miles east of	41°09.55	71°49.48		-1 51	-1 11	-1 15	-1 55	0.6	0.6	0.0	--	2.4	358°	0.0	--	1.9	145°
2531	Montauk Point, 1 mile northeast of	41°04.50	71°49.80		-0 41	-0 11	+0 48	-0 18	0.3	0.3	0.0	--	1.5	250°	0.0	--	0.8	073°
2536	Wicopesset Island, 1.1 miles SSE of	41°18.50	71°51'	15	+1 03	+0 63	+0 48	+0 18	0.6	0.6	0.0	--	0.9	238°	0.0	--	1.8	079°
2541	East Pt., Fishers I., 1.1 miles east of	41°13.40	71°54.80	15	-0 02	-0 06	-0 24	-1 00	0.4	0.2	0.0	--	1.1	268°	0.0	--	1.8	092°
2546	Cerberus Shoal	41°07.40	71°55.17		-0 17	-0 26	-0 39	-0 49	0.7	0.6	0.0	--	1.9	090°	0.0	--	1.8	099°
2551	Stepping Stones Reef & Cerberus Shoal, between	41°07.05	71°55.17		-2 04	-2 26	-3 03	-1 10	0.4	0.2	0.0	--	1.2	228°	0.0	--	1.0	039°
2556	Montauk Harbor entrance	41°04.78	71°56.55	6							0.0	--			0.0	--	0.5	024°
2561	Mt. Prospect, 0.6 mile SSE of	41°14.75	71°59.80	15	-0 21	+0 15	+0 09	-0 40	0.6	0.3	0.0	--	1.7	279°	0.0	--	1.6	054°
2566	Cerberus Shoal and Fishers I., between	41°10.7'	72°02.1'	7	-0 46	+0 13	+0 06	-0 20	0.5	0.4	0.0	--	1.3	264°	0.0	--	1.3	096°
2571	Little Gull Island, 3.7 miles ESE of	41°07.9'	72°02.0'	10	-0 34	See table 5.	-0 26	-0 40	0.3	0.3	0.0	--	0.9	308°	0.0	--	1.0	138°
2576	Gardiners Island, 3 miles northeast of	41°07.12	72°04.85		-0 32	-1 30	-1 09	-2 34	0.4	0.3	0.0	--	1.0	290°	0.0	--	1.0	110°
2581	Eastern Plain Point, 1.2 miles N of	41°07.05	72°05.90		-0 48	-1 04	-0 24	-1 12	0.3	0.2	0.0	--	1.0	248°	0.0	--	1.0	096°
2586	Eastern Plain Pt., 3.9 miles ENE of	41°11.67	72°06.23		-1 57	-0 29	-0 24	-3 13	0.5	0.1	0.0	--	1.3	331°	0.0	--	0.1	252°
2591	Little Gull Island, 0.8 mile SSE of <3>			15	-1 09	-0 40	-0 50	-1 10	0.1	0.1	0.1	192°	0.3	259°	0.2	340°	0.3	174°
2596	Rocky Point, 2 miles WNW of	41°03.55	72°01.80			on The Race											0.6	066°
	GARDINERS BAY. etc.																	
2601	Goff Point, 0.4 mile northwest of	41°01.49	72°03.75		-1 33	-2 04	-1 26	-2 42	0.4	0.5	0.0	--	1.2	225°	0.0	--	1.6	010°
2606	Acabonack Hbr. ent., 0.6 mile ESE of	41°01.30	72°07.40		-1 21	-1 49	-1 06	-2 41	0.5	0.4	0.0	--	1.4	345°	0.0	--	1.2	140°
2611	Hog Creek Point, north of	41°04.10	72°09.70		-0 43	-0 28	-1 22	-2 03	0.1	0.1	0.0	--	0.3	281°	0.0	--	0.3	067°
2616	Orient Point, 2.2 miles east of	41°07.50	72°12.30		-0 32	-0 13	-0 15	-0 23	0.1	0.1	0.0	--	0.2	260°	0.0	--	0.3	099°
2621	Orient Point, 2.4 miles SSE of	41°09.50	72°08.83		+0 05	-0 04	+1 10	+0 42	0.2	0.1	0.0	--	0.4	270°	0.0	--	0.4	086°
2626	Gardiners Pt. Ruins, 1.1 miles N of	41°09.33	72°09.52	15	+0 14	-0 10	-0 33	+0 41	0.4	0.5	0.0	--	0.4	288°	0.0	--	0.6	100°
2631	Gardiners Point & Plum Island, between	41°05.8'	72°15.8'		+0 14	+0 19	+0 08	+1 06	0.5	0.6	0.0	--	0.4	270°	0.0	--	0.6	075°
2636	Ram Island, 1.4 miles NNE of	41°06.25	72°18.40	15	+0 46	+0 19	+0 43	+0 08	0.2	0.4	0.0	--	0.6	240°	0.0	--	1.8	101°
2641	Long Beach Pt., 0.7 mile southwest of	41°06.65	72°20.43		+0 33	+0 41	+1 00	+1 27	0.6	0.4	0.0	--	1.3	307°	0.0	--	1.2	025°
2646	Hay Beach Point, 0.3 mile NW of <44>							+1 08	0.6	0.3	0.0	--	1.5	210°	0.0	--	0.8	025°
2651	Jennings Point, 0.2 mile NNW of	41°04.48	72°22.95	13	+0 45	+0 30	+0 36	+1 08	0.7	0.5	0.0	--	1.6	290°	0.0	--	0.8	020°
2656	Cedar Point, 0.2 mile west of	41°02.38	72°16.07		+0 02	+0 05	+0 28	+0 52	0.8	0.5	0.0	--	1.8	300°	0.0	--	1.5	055°
2661	North Haven Peninsula, north of	41°02.47	72°19.25		+0 25	-0 09	+0 38	+0 05	0.9	0.7	0.0	--	2.4	230°	0.0	--	1.6	036°
2666	Paradise Point, 0.4 mile east of	41°02.88	72°22.67	13	+0 39	+0 24	+0 44	+0 05	0.8	0.6	0.0	--	2.1	145°	0.0	--	2.1	345°
2671	Little Peconic Bay entrance	41°01.58	72°23.08	19	+0 48	+0 22	+0 52	+0 10	0.6	0.7	0.0	--	1.6	240°	0.0	--	1.5	015°
2678	Robins Island, 0.5 mile south of	40°56.98	72°27.18		+0 45	+0 09	+0 55	+0 24	0.6	0.2	0.0	--	1.7	245°	0.0	--	0.6	065°

NOTES

SEE ENDNOTES ON PAGE 106

TABLE 2 – CURRENT DIFFERENCES AND OTHER CONSTANTS

No.	PLACE	POSITION Latitude North	POSITION Longitude West	Meter Depth (ft)	TIME DIFFERENCES Min. before Flood (h m)	Flood (h m)	Min. before Ebb (h m)	Ebb (h m)	SPEED RATIOS Flood	SPEED RATIOS Ebb	Min. before Flood (knots)	Dir.	Maximum Flood (knots)	Dir.	Min. before Ebb (knots)	Dir.	Maximum Ebb (knots)	Dir.
	FISHERS ISLAND SOUND Time meridian, 75° W																	
2681	Edwards Pt. and Sandy Pt., between	41° 19.90'	71° 53.88'	4	−2 13	−2 56 *on The Race*	−2 16	−3 52	0.4	0.3	0.0	--	1.1	035°	0.0	--	1.0	227°
2686	Napatree Point, 0.7 mile southwest of	41° 17.92'	71° 54.00'		−0 35	−0 46	−0 48	−1 42	0.6	0.7	0.0	--	1.7	284°	0.0	--	2.2	243°
2691	Little Narragansett Bay entrance	41° 20'	71° 53'	6	−1 45	−1 41	−2 14	−1 29	0.5	0.4	0.0	--	1.3	092°	0.0	--	1.3	234°
2696	Avondale, Pawcatuck River <43>	41° 19.90'	71° 50.73'		−1 35	−2 21	−2 08	−3 51	0.2	0.2	0.0	--	0.6	058°	0.0	--	0.5	113°
2701	Ram Island Reef, south of	41° 18.1'	71° 58.5'	7	−0 41	−0 29	−0 46	−1 04	0.5	0.5	0.0	--	1.3	255°	0.0	--	1.3	268°
2706	Noank <43>	41° 19.12'	71° 59.30'	4	−1 15	−2 55	−4 01	−4 41	0.2	0.2	0.0	--	0.5	340°	0.0	--	0.5	265°
2711	Mystic, Highway Bridge, Mystic River	41° 21.25'	71° 58.18'	6	−1 41	−2 29	−1 58	+0 08	0.2	0.1	0.0	--	0.5	039°	0.0	--	0.1	243°
	LONG ISLAND SOUND																	
2716	Clay Point, 1.3 miles NNE of	41° 17.88'	71° 58.53'		−0 21	−0 28	−0 31	−1 26	0.5	0.6	0.0	--	1.4	264°	0.0	--	1.6	035°
2721	North Hill Point, 1.1 miles NNW of	41° 17.57'	72° 01.68'	15	−0 44	−0 05	−0 09	−1 48	0.6	0.4	0.0	--	1.5	258°	0.0	--	1.8	082°
	The Race																	
2726	Race Point, 0.4 mile southwest of	41° 14.70'	72° 02.60'		−0 03	−0 14	−0 34	−0 56	1.0	1.2	0.0	--	2.6	288°	0.1	--	3.5	135°
2731	THE RACE, 0.6 n.mi. NW of Valiant Rock	41° 14.00'	72° 03.58'	38d	Daily predictions	Daily predictions			1.2	1.0	0.1	022°	2.7	302°	0.3	220°	3.0	143°
2736	0.5 mile NE of Little Gull Island	41° 13'	72° 06'	45d	−0 19	−0 16	−0 16	−0 40	1.2	1.5	0.1	011°	3.3	002°	0.5	036°	3.1	107°
2741	Little Gull Island, 1.4 n.mi NNE of	41° 13.53'	72° 05.52'		+0 15	+0 07	+0 07	−0 03	0.5	1.1	0.0	--	1.5	304°	0.0	--	1.6	100°
2746	Little Gull Island, 1.1 miles ENE of	41° 13.10'	72° 05.10'		+0 14	+0 10	+0 10	−0 06	1.5	1.1	0.0	--	4.0	301°	0.0	--	4.7	130°
2751	Little Gull Island, 0.8 mile ENE of	41° 11.67'	72° 06.99'	15	+0 38	−0 58	−0 22	−1 57	0.7	1.0	0.0	--	1.9	258°	0.0	--	2.9	043°
2756	Little Gull Island, 0.7 mile WSW of	41° 17.8'	72° 08.02'		−0 30	−0 12	−1 08	−1 53	1.0	0.1	0.0	--	2.6	299°	0.0	--	3.2	139°
2761	Great Gull Island, 1.5 miles south of	41° 19.08'	72° 04.4'		−1 46	−1 32	−2 03	−2 04	0.2	0.2	0.0	--	0.4	249°	0.0	--	0.4	055°
2766	Eastern Point, 1.5 miles south of; New London Harbor entrance	41° 21.63'	72° 05.02'		−1 01	−1 30		−1 26	0.1	0.7	0.0	--	0.1	348°	0.0	--	0.2	211°
	Thames River																	
2771	Winthrop Point		72° 05.30'		−0 56	−1 38	−0 45	−2 46	0.2	0.1	0.0	--	0.4	012°	0.0	--	0.4	180°
2776	Off Smith Cove	41° 23.98'	72° 06.18'	5	−0 57	−1 59	−1 20	−1 07	0.3	0.2	0.0	--	0.7	019°	0.0	--	0.2	186°
2781	Off Stoddard Hill	41° 27.65'	72° 04.12'	15	−0 56	−2 02	−0 31	−0 41	0.3	0.2	0.0	--	0.7	332°	0.0	--	0.4	185°
	Current weak and variable																	
2786	Lower Coal Dock	41° 30.88'	72° 04.72'	15	−0 44	−0 39	−0 54	−2 00	0.5	0.5	0.0	--	1.2	285°	0.0	--	1.6	062°
2791	Goshen Point, 1.9 miles SSE of	41° 16.00'	72° 06.30'	15	−0 50	−0 32	−0 32	−1 45	0.5	0.4	0.0	--	1.4	255°	0.0	--	1.3	090°
2796	Bartlett Reef, 0.2 mile south of	41° 16.2'	72° 07.7'		−0 45	−1 05	−1 04	−1 53	0.4	0.5	0.0	--	1.2	267°	0.0	--	1.6	267°
2801	Twotree Island Channel	41° 17.87'	72° 08.47'	11	−0 32	−1 06	−0 44	−1 51	0.6	0.5	0.0	--	1.6	352°	0.0	--	0.8	178°
2806	Niantic (Railroad Bridge)	41° 19.40'	72° 10.62'	5	−0 42	−0 44	−0 16	−1 21	0.6	0.5	0.0	--	2.1	260°	0.0	--	1.4	073°
2811	Black Point, 0.8 mile south of	41° 16.40'	72° 12.50'	15	−0 50	−0 50	+0 38	+0 15	0.8	0.8	0.0	--	1.7	236°	0.0	--	2.4	076°
2816	Black Point and Plum Island, between	41° 14.00'	72° 12.30'	15	+0 46	+0 25	−1 04	+0 52	0.8	0.8	0.0	--	1.9	247°	0.0	--	3.2	065°
2821	Plum Island, 0.8 mile NNW of	41° 11.87'	72° 11.92'		+0 05	−0 05	−1 12	−2 00	0.7	0.6	0.0	--	1.7	307°	0.0	--	1.9	119°
2826	Plum Gut	41° 09.91'	72° 12.75'		−1 22	−1 12	−0 28	−1 03	0.6	0.7	0.1	069°	1.7	258°	0.1	336°	3.2	058°
2831	Hatchett Point, 1.6 n.mi. S of	41° 15.40'	72° 15.37'	30d	−0 46	−0 28	−0 43	−0 48	0.5	0.6	0.1	160°	1.7	256°	0.0	--	1.9	065°
2836	Hatchett Point, 1.1 miles WSW of	41° 16.35'	72° 16.92'	15d	−0 41	−0 50	−0 24	−1 26	0.6	0.5	0.0	--	1.4	249°	0.0	--	1.4	070°
2841	Orient Point, 1 mile WNW of	41° 10.02'	72° 15.11'		−0 48	−1 41	−1 28	−1 28	0.5	1.0	0.0	--	3.1	249°	0.0	--	3.1	065°
2846	Saybrook Breakwater, 1.5 miles SE of	41° 14.78'	72° 19.06'		−1 09	−0 50	−0 46	−2 08	0.7	0.7	0.0	--	1.9	260°	0.0	--	2.0	070°

NOTES

SEE ENDNOTES ON PAGE 106

TABLE 2 – CURRENT DIFFERENCES AND OTHER CONSTANTS

No.	PLACE	Meter Depth (ft)	POSITION Latitude North	POSITION Longitude West	TIME DIFFERENCES Min. before Flood (h m)	Flood (h m)	Min. before Ebb (h m)	Ebb (h m)	SPEED RATIOS Flood	Ebb	Minimum before Flood knots	Dir.	Maximum Flood knots	Dir.	Minimum before Ebb knots	Dir.	Maximum Ebb knots	Dir.
	LONG ISLAND SOUND—cont. Time meridian, 75° W																	
	Connecticut River																	
2851	Lynde Point, channel east of		41°16'	72°20'	+0 53	+1 08	+0 13	+0 15	0.3	0.2	0.0	---	0.9	344°	0.0	---	0.7	161°
2856	Saybrook Point, 0.2 mile northeast of	15	41°17.02'	72°20.87'	+0 56	+1 12	+0 66	+0 19	0.6	0.5	0.0	---	1.0	355°	0.0	---	1.5	160°
2861	Railroad drawbridge		41°19.00'	72°20.77'	+0 48	-0 56	+1 03	+0 55	0.4	0.3	0.0	---	1.0	360°	0.0	---	1.0	198°
2866	Eustasia Island, 0.6 mile ESE of		41°23.30'	72°24.23'	+2 14	+1 59	+1 32	+1 15	0.2	0.5	0.0	---	0.6	359°	0.0	---	1.4	070°
2871	Eddy Rock Shoal, west of	15	41°26.57'	72°27.78'	+2 57	+2 37	+2 10	+1 09	0.4	0.3	0.0	---	0.9	358°	0.0	---	0.6	155°
2876	Higganum Creek, 0.5 mile ESE of		41°30.02'	72°32.62'	+3 27	+3 13	+2 44	+2 50	0.3	0.3	0.0	---	1.1	290°	0.0	---	1.0	080°
2881	Wilcox Island Park, east of		41°34.33'	72°38.88'	+4 02	+3 57	+3 16	+3 24	0.3	0.2	0.0	---	0.8	350°	0.0	---	1.0	160°
2886	Rocky Hill	9	41°39.82'	72°37.79'	+6 06	+5 00	+3 30	+3 19	0.2	0.2	0.0	---	0.9	270°	0.0	---	0.8	135°
2891	Hartford Jetty <35>	9	41°45.07'	72°39.02'	+6 15	-0 44	+3 31	+4 18	0.2	0.2	0.1	---	0.6	355°	0.0	---	0.7	095°
2896	Mulford Point, 3.1 miles northwest of	15	41°12.00'	72°19.08'	-0 06	-0 38	+0 04	-0 35	0.7	0.8	0.0	---	1.9	335°	0.0	---	2.3	066°
2901	Rocky Point, 0.3 mile north of	15	41°08.63'	72°21.42'	-1 14	-0 12	-0 53	-0 39	0.8	0.7	0.0	---	0.8	269°	0.0	---	2.1	041°
2906	Cornfield Point, 2.8 n.mi. SE of	15d	41°12.9'	72°23.33'	-0 45	-0 41	-0 08	-0 43	0.7	0.6	0.0	---	1.8	245°	0.0	---	1.4	085°
2911	Cornfield Point, 3 miles south of	7	41°12.9'	72°22.4'	-0 56	-0 46	-0 13	-0 34	0.7	0.7	0.0	---	1.8	279°	0.0	---	1.6	094°
2916	Cornfield Point, 1.1 miles south of	15	41°14.85'	72°23.40'	-0 14	-1 13	-1 26	-1 21	0.5	0.6	0.1	170°	1.3	249°	0.0	---	1.5	108°
2921	Cornfield Point, 1.9 n.mi. SW of	15d	41°14.48'	72°25.30'	-1 21	-1 14	-1 11	-1 11	0.5	0.5	0.1	174°	1.3	256°	0.0	358°	1.8	091°
2926	Kelsey Point, 2.1 miles southeast of		41°14.10'	72°27.93'	-0 14	-0 41	-1 25	-1 13	0.7	0.4	0.0	---	1.5	299°	0.0	---	1.5	070°
2931	Kelsey Point, 1 mile south of		41°14'	72°30'	+0 04	+0 09	-1 09	-2 05	0.7	0.4	0.0	---	2.0	272°	0.0	---	1.3	118°
2936	Six Mile Reef, 1.5 miles north of		41°12.66'	72°28.87'	-0 15	-0 09	-0 14	-0 52	0.6	0.7	0.0	---	1.0	260°	0.0	---	2.1	070°
2941	Six Mile Reef, 2 miles east of		41°10.83'	72°26.90'	+0 25	+0 29	+0 02	-0 46	0.5	0.7	0.0	---	1.4	235°	0.0	---	2.0	040°
2946	Horton Point, 1.4 miles NNW of		41°06.30'	72°27.40'	-0 38	-0 54	-0 35	-1 42	0.5	0.5	0.0	---	1.4	260°	0.0	---	1.4	040°
2951	Hammonasset Point, 1.2 miles SW of	15	41°14.22'	72°34.00'	-0 18	-0 18	-0 15	-1 13	0.5	0.5	0.0	---	1.4	287°	0.0	---	1.5	108°
2956	Hammonasset Point, 5 miles south of		41°09.80'	72°34.17'	-0 12	-0 12	-0 07	-1 14	0.4	0.4	0.0	---	1.2	253°	0.0	343°	0.9	090°
2961	Duck Pond Point, 3.2 n.mi. NW of	15d	41°04.73'	72°33.91'	0 00	-0 06	+0 01	-0 17	0.5	0.5	0.2	161°	1.2	241°	0.1	343°	1.0	071°
2966	Mattituck Inlet, 1 mile northwest of	15	41°01.68'	72°34.22'	-0 17	-0 15	-0 28	-1 13	0.5	0.4	0.0	---	0.9	255°	0.0	---	0.9	053°
2971	Sachem Head, 6.2 miles south of		41°08.65'	72°42.30'	-0 50	-0 15	-0 06	-1 04	0.3	0.3	0.0	---	0.6	255°	0.0	---	0.9	066°
2976	Roanoke Point, 5.6 miles north of	15	41°04.37'	72°42.83'	-0 19	-0 19	-0 01	-0 35	0.3	0.2	0.0	---	0.7	258°	0.0	---	0.7	065°
2981	Roanoke Point, 2.3 miles NNW of		41°00.92'	72°42.97'	-0 58	-0 01	-0 01	-0 40	0.5	0.2	0.0	---	0.9	270°	0.0	---	0.9	089°
2986	Roanoke Point	15d	41°12.57'	72°49.93'	-0 08	-0 07	0 00	-0 29	0.1	0.1	0.0	---	0.3	272°	0.0	---	0.7	070°
2991	Branford Reef, 1.5 miles southwest of	15	41°08.65'	72°49.87'	-0 20	-0 07	-0 05	-0 22	0.3	0.3	0.0	---	0.7	260°	0.0	---	0.8	068°
2996	Branford Reef, 5.0 miles east of	15	41°08.65'	72°49.80'	-0 08	-0 27	+0 21	+0 21	0.3	0.3	0.0	---	0.7	254°	0.0	---	0.8	074°
3001	Herod Point, 6.5 miles north of	15	41°00.97'	72°49.93'	+0 04	-0 04	-0 18	-0 17	0.2	0.2	0.1	020°	0.4	290°	0.1	020°	0.7	070°
3006	Herod Point, 2.8 miles north of	15	41°01.64'	72°54.75'	+0 18	+0 04	-0 28	+0 17	0.2	0.2	0.0	---	0.6	271°	0.0	---	0.6	090°
3011	Herod Point, 5.0 n.mi. NW of	15d	41°14'	72°55'	+0 32	+0 51	+0 42	0 00	0.5	0.1	0.1	179°	0.9	270°	0.0	---	0.9	089°
3016	New Haven Harbor entrance <12>		41°17.83'	72°58.00'		-1 16	-0 42	-1 29	0.1	0.1	0.0	---	0.4	319°	0.0	---	0.4	152°
3021	City Point, 1.3 miles northeast of		41°12.87'	72°58.00'	-1 01	-0 06	0 00	-0 68	0.5	0.1	0.0	---	0.3	015°	0.0	---	0.4	215°
3026	Oyster River Pl., 1.3 miles SSE of <1>		41°08.60'	72°58.08'	+0 22	-0 25	+0 05	-0 29	0.2	0.1	0.0	---	0.6	255°	0.0	---	0.3	060°
3031	Pond Point, 4.2 miles SSE of		41°04.52'	72°58.43'	+0 18	-0 19	+0 02	-0 20	0.2	0.2	0.0	---	0.6	254°	0.0	---	0.6	060°
3036	Stratford Shoal, 6 miles east of		41°00.93'	72°58.45'	+0 40	-0 15	-0 06	-0 36	0.4	0.3	0.0	---	0.9	265°	0.0	---	0.6	060°
3041	Sound Beach, 2.2 miles north of		41°10.77'	73°02.83'	+0 54	-0 34	-0 21	+1 05	0.4	0.3	0.0	---	1.2	270°	0.0	---	0.9	075°
3046	Charles Island, 0.8 mile SSE of																0.4	070°
	Housatonic River																	
3051	Milford Point, 0.2 mile west of	10	41°10.35'	73°08.67'	+0 15	+0 22	+0 24	+1 06	0.4	0.4	0.0	---	1.2	330°	0.0	---	1.2	135°
3056	Railroad drawbridge	5	41°11.40'	73°06.20'	+0 55	+0 31	+0 39	+1 08	0.4	0.4	0.0	---	1.1	350°	0.0	---	1.3	350°
3061	Fowler Island, 0.1 mile NNW of	5	41°14.67'	73°06.23'	+1 40	+0 64	+0 29	+0 11	0.2	0.1	0.0	---	0.6	020°	0.0	---	0.7	220°
3066	Wooster Island, 0.1 mile southwest of		41°16.73'	73°05.20'				+0 12			0.0	---		020°	0.0	---	0.4	095°
3071	Derby–Shelton Bridge, below <13>		41°18.73'	73°04.78'	-0 09	-0 15	+0 01	+0 03	0.5	0.4	0.0	---	1.3	251°	0.0	---	1.2	074°
3076	Point No Point, 2.1 miles south of	15	41°06.75'	73°07.13'	+0 33	+0 40	+0 14	+0 03	0.2	0.3	0.0	---	0.5	254°	0.0	---	1.0	075°
3081	Stratford Point, 4.3 miles south of	15	41°04.77'	73°06.67'	+0 15	+0 12	+0 25	+0 04	0.2	0.3	0.0	---	0.5	291°	0.0	---	0.8	079°
3086	do.	60, 15	41°02.97'	73°05.80'	+0 03	-0 10	-0 25	+0 19	0.4	0.3	0.0	---	1.0	267°	0.0	---	0.8	080°
3091	Stratford Point, 6.1 miles south of	51	41°02.97'	73°05.80'	+0 22	-0 10	-0 36	-0 23	0.2	0.2	0.0	---	0.5	273°	0.0	338°	0.8	087°
3091	Old Field Point, 2.9 n.mi. NNW of	16d	41°01.52'	73°08.57'	+0 40	-0 10	-0 02	-0 14	0.4	0.3	0.0	---	0.5	254°	0.1	338°	0.9	076°
3096	Old Field Point, 2 miles northeast of	15	41°00.23'	73°05.70'	+0 43	+0 34	-0 03	+0 30	0.4	0.4	0.0	---	0.6	266°	0.0	---	1.1	092°
3101	Old Field Point, 1 mile east of	40, 22	40°58.47'	73°05.80'	+3 47	+2 52	+2 34	+1 45	0.1	0.2	0.0	---	0.5	236°	0.0	---	0.6	308°
	do.		40°58.17'	73°05.80'	+2 61	+2 15	+2 26	+1 33	0.1	0.2	0.0	---	0.2	110°	0.0	---	0.5	297°

TABLE 2 – CURRENT DIFFERENCES AND OTHER CONSTANTS

No.	PLACE	Meter Depth (ft)	POSITION Latitude North	POSITION Longitude West	TIME DIFFERENCES Min. before Flood (h m)	Flood (h m)	Min. before Ebb (h m)	Ebb (h m)	SPEED RATIOS Flood	Ebb	AVG Min. before Flood (knots)	Dir.	Maximum Flood (knots)	Dir.	Minimum before Ebb (knots)	Dir.	Maximum Ebb (knots)	Dir.
	FISHERS ISLAND SOUND Time meridian, 75° W					on The Race												
2681	Edwards Pt. and Sandy Pt., between	4	41° 19.90'	71° 53.88'	-2 13	-2 56	-2 16	-3 52	0.4	0.3	0.0	—	1.1	036°	0.0	—	1.0	227°
2686	Napatree Point, 0.7 mile southwest of		41° 17.92'	71° 54.00'	-0 35	-0 46	-0 48	-1 42	0.6	0.1	0.0	—	1.7	284°	0.0	—	0.2	243°
2691	Little Narragansett Bay entrance	6	41° 20'	71° 53'	-1 45	-1 41	-2 14	-1 18	0.5	0.4	0.0	—	1.3	092°	0.0	—	1.3	234°
2696	Avondale, Pawcatuck River <43>		41° 19.90'	71° 50.73'	-1 35	-2 21	-2 08	-1 29	0.2	0.2	0.0	—	0.6	058°	0.0	—	0.5	268°
2701	Ram Island Reef, south of	7	41° 18.1'	71° 58.6'	-0 41	-0 29	-0 46	-1 04	0.5	0.5	0.0	—	1.3	255°	0.0	—	0.5	268°
2706	Noank <43>	4	41° 19.12'	71° 59.30'	-1 15	-2 55	-1 01	-1 41	0.2	0.2	0.0	—	0.5	340°	0.0	—	0.1	269°
2711	Mystic, Highway Bridge, Mystic River	6	41° 21.25'	71° 58.18'	-1 41	-2 29	-1 58	+0 08	0.2	0.1	0.0	—	0.5	039°	0.0	—	1.6	089°
2716	Clay Point, 1.3 miles NNE of	15	41° 17.88'	71° 58.53'	-0 21	-0 28	-0 31	-1 31	0.5	0.6	0.0	—	1.4	264°	0.0	—	0.3	179°
2721	North Hill Point, 1.1 miles NNW of		41° 17.57'	72° 01.68'	-0 44	-0 05	-0 09	-1 48	0.6	0.4	0.0	—	1.6	258°	0.0	—	0.5	162°
	LONG ISLAND SOUND *The Race*																	
2726	Race Point, 0.4 mile southwest of		41° 14.70'	72° 02.60'	-0 03	-0 14	-0 34	-0 56	1.0	1.2	0.1	—	2.6	288°	0.3	—	3.5	136°
2731	THE RACE, 0.6 n.mi. NW of Valiant Rock	38d	41° 14.00'	72° 03.58'	-0 19	Daily predictions	-0 16	-0 40	1.2	1.6	0.1	022°	2.7	302°	0.3	220°	3.0	112°
2736	0.5 mile NE of Little Gull Island	45d	41° 13.53'	72° 06.52'	-0 14	-0 38	+0 07	-0 33	1.5	1.5	0.1	011°	3.5	302°	0.5	036°	3.6	107°
2741	Little Gull Island, 1 n.mi. NNE of		41° 13.10'	72° 05.07'	+0 08	+0 38	+0 02	-0 56	1.0	1.1	0.1	—	4.0	301°	0.0	—	4.7	100°
2746	Little Gull Island, 1.1 miles ENE of	15	41° 13.07'	72° 06.93'	+0 30	-0 68	-0 22	-0 63	1.2	1.1	0.0	—	1.9	258°	0.0	—	2.9	130°
2751	Little Gull Island, 0.8 mile NNW of		41° 13.17'	72° 08.02'	+0 30	-0 12	-0 20	-0 53	1.0	1.0	0.0	—	2.6	299°	0.0	—	3.2	049°
2756	Great Gull Island, 0.7 mile WSW of		41° 11.67'	72° 04.47'	-1 46	-1 32	-1 08	-2 04	0.2	0.2	0.0	—	2.4	258°	0.0	—	0.4	133°
2761	Eastern Point, 1.5 miles south of		41° 19.08'	72° 05.02'	-1 01	-1 30	-2 03	-1 26	0.1	0.1	0.2	—	0.1	249°	0.0	—	0.2	055°
2766	New London Harbor entrance										0.4	—	0.4	348°	0.0	—		211°
	Thames River																	
2771	Winthrop Point		41° 21.63'	72° 05.30'	-0 56	-1 38	-0 45	-2 46	0.2	0.1	0.0	—	0.4	012°	0.0	—	0.4	180°
2776	Off Smith Cove	5	41° 23.98'	72° 06.18'	-0 57	-1 59	-1 20	-1 07	0.3	0.2	0.0	—	0.7	019°	0.0	—	0.2	186°
2781	Off Stoddard Hill	15	41° 27.65'	72° 04.12'	-0 56	-2 02	-0 31	-0 41	0.3	0.2	0.0	—	0.7	332°	0.0	—	0.3	185°
					Current weak and variable													
2786	Lower Coal Dock	15	41° 30.88'	72° 04.72'	-0 44	-0 39	-0 64	-2 00	0.5	0.5	0.0	—	1.2	286°	0.0	—	1.6	062°
2791	Goshen Point, 1.9 miles SSE of	15	41° 16.00'	72° 06.30'	-1 50	-0 32	-1 05	-0 45	0.4	0.4	0.0	—	1.4	255°	0.0	—	1.3	090°
2796	Bartlett Reef, 0.2 mile south of		41° 16.2'	72° 07.7'	-1 45	-1 06	-0 34	-0 51	0.4	0.5	0.0	—	1.2	267°	0.0	—	1.6	090°
2801	Niantic (Railroad Bridge)	11	41° 17.87'	72° 08.47'	-0 32	-0 42	-0 44	-1 00	0.6	0.5	0.0	—	1.6	352°	0.0	—	0.8	178°
2806	Twotree Island Channel	5	41° 19.40'	72° 10.62'	-0 29	-0 50	-0 16	-0 15	0.6	0.6	0.0	—	1.2	260°	0.0	—	1.4	070°
2811	Black Point, 0.8 mile south of	15	41° 16.40'	72° 12.50'	-0 46	+0 05	+0 38	-0 60	0.6	0.8	0.0	—	2.1	236°	0.0	—	2.4	065°
2821	Black Point and Plum Island, between	15	41° 14.00'	72° 12.30'	-0 25	-1 04	-0 16	-0 15	0.8	0.8	0.0	—	1.7	247°	0.0	—	3.2	066°
2826	Plum Island, 0.8 mile NNW of		41° 11.87'	72° 11.92'	-1 08	-1 22	-1 12	-0 60	0.6	0.6	0.0	—	1.7	207°	0.0	—	1.2	118°
2831	Plum Gut	30d	41° 09.91'	72° 12.75'	-0 16	-0 40	-0 23	-0 03	0.9	1.0	0.1	069°	1.7	240°	0.1	336°	3.1	075°
2836	Hatchett Point, 1.6 n.mi. S of		41° 15.40'	72° 12.75'	-0 16	-0 61	-0 28	-0 48	0.6	0.6	0.1	160°	1.4	240°	0.0	—	1.2	045°
2841	Hatchett Point, 1.1 miles WNW of	15d	41° 16.55'	72° 16.17'	-0 48	-1 41	-0 24	-0 26	0.5	1.0	0.0	—	1.9	249°	0.0	—	3.1	055°
2846	Orient Point, 1 mile WNW of		41° 14.78'	72° 19.05'	-1 09	-0 50	-0 46	-2 08	0.7	0.7	0.0	—	1.9	260°	0.0	—	2.0	070°
	Saybrook Breakwater, 1.5 miles SE of																	

TABLE 2 – CURRENT DIFFERENCES AND OTHER CONSTANTS

No.	PLACE	Meter Depth (ft)	Lat. North	Long. West	Min. before Flood h m	Flood h m	Min. before Ebb h m	Ebb h m	Speed Ratio Flood	Speed Ratio Ebb	Min. before Flood knots	Dir.	Max. Flood knots	Dir.	Min. before Ebb knots	Dir.	Max. Ebb knots	Dir.
	LONG ISLAND SOUND—cont. Time meridian, 75° W																	
	Connecticut River																	
2861	Lynde Point, channel east of		41° 16′	72° 20′	+0 53	+1 08	+0 13	+0 15	0.3	0.2	0.0	---	0.9	344°	0.0	---	0.7	161°
2856	Saybrook Point, 0.2 mile northeast of	15	41° 17.02	72° 20.87	+0 56	+1 12	+0 56	+0 19	0.4	0.5	0.0	---	1.5	355°	0.0	---	1.5	160°
2861	Railroad drawbridge		41° 19.00	72° 20.77	+0 48	-0 56	+1 03	+0 55	0.3	0.3	0.0	---	1.0	360°	0.0	---	1.0	198°
					on The Race													
2866	Eustasia Island, 0.6 mile ESE of	15	41° 23.30	72° 24.23	+2 14	+1 59	+1 32	+1 15	0.4	0.5	0.0	---	0.6	359°	0.0	---	1.4	070°
2871	Eddy Rock Shoal, west of		41° 26.67	72° 32.78	+2 02	+2 37	+2 10	+1 50	0.4	0.3	0.0	---	1.1	290°	0.0	---	0.6	065°
2876	Higganum Creek, 0.5 mile ESE of		41° 30.02	72° 36.62	+2 12	+3 57	+2 14	+1 60	0.3	0.3	0.0	---	0.8	350°	0.0	---	0.8	085°
2881	Wilcox Island Park, east of		41° 33.33	72° 37.88	+4 27	+3 58	+3 16	+2 24	0.2	0.3	0.0	---	0.9	359°	0.0	---	0.6	160°
2886	Rocky Hill	9	41° 39.82	72° 37.73	+5 02	+5 00	+3 30	+4 18	0.2	0.2	0.0	---	0.6	290°	0.0	---	0.8	135°
2891	Hartford Jetty <3b>	9	41° 46.07	72° 39.02	+6 06	-0 38	+3 31	+4 18	0.7	0.2	0.0	---	1.9	269°	0.0	---	0.7	095°
2896	Mulford Point, 3.1 miles northwest of	15	41° 12.00	72° 19.08	+6 16	+0 12	+0 04	+0 35	0.8	0.8	0.0	---	2.1	265°	0.0	---	2.3	066°
2901	Rocky Point, 0.3 mile north of	15d	41° 08.65	72° 21.42	-0 06	-0 41	-0 52	-0 39	0.8	0.7	0.0	---	1.8	279°	0.0	---	2.1	041°
2906	Cornfield Point, 2.8 n.mi. SE of	15d	41° 13.95	72° 20.53	-1 14	-0 36	-0 33	-1 43	0.7	0.5	0.1	170°	1.9	249°	0.0	---	1.4	085°
2911	Cornfield Point, 3 miles south of	7	41° 12.9	72° 22.4	-0 45	-0 40	-0 08	-0 34	0.7	0.6	0.0	---	2.4	256°	0.0	---	1.7	094°
2916	Cornfield Point, 1.1 miles SW of	15d	41° 14.85	72° 23.40	-0 06	-1 13	-0 25	-2 14	0.5	0.5	0.1	174°	1.5	272°	0.1	358°	1.6	08?°
2921	Cornfield Point, 1.3 miles SW of	15	41° 14.48	72° 23.07	-0 14	-0 41	-0 45	-1 22	0.5	0.6	0.0	---	1.5	260°	0.0	---	1.8	091°
2926	Kelsey Point, 2.1 miles southeast of	15d	41° 14.10	72° 22.93	-1 21	-0 42	-1 08	-1 11	0.6	0.6	0.0	---	1.0	249°	0.0	---	1.8	070°
2931	Kelsey Point, 1 mile south of		41° 14′	72° 30′	+0 04	+0 09	+0 02	+1 05	0.7	0.7	0.0	---	1.0	290°	0.0	---	1.5	096°
2936	Six Mile Reef, 1.5 miles north of		41° 10.83	72° 28.00	-0 15	+0 09	-0 14	-0 52	0.6	0.7	0.0	---	1.4	235°	0.0	---	1.3	095°
2941	Six Mile Reef, 2 miles east of		41° 06.30	72° 27.40	+0 04	-0 29	+0 02	+0 02	0.5	0.5	0.0	---	1.4	260°	0.0	---	2.1	040°
2946	Horton Point, 4 miles NNW of	15	41° 14.22	72° 34.00	+0 25	-0 54	-0 35	-0 29	0.6	0.6	0.0	---	1.0	287°	0.0	---	2.0	040°
2951	Hammonasset Point, 1.2 miles SW of	15d	41° 09.80	72° 34.17	-0 38	-0 38	-0 07	-1 42	0.5	0.5	0.0	---	1.4	284°	0.0	---	2.0	106°
2956	Hammonasset Point, 5 miles south of	15	41° 04.73	72° 34.22	-0 12	+0 12	-0 01	-0 17	0.5	0.4	0.2	161°	1.2	253°	0.1	343°	1.5	090°
2961	Duck Pond Point, 3.2 n.mi. NW of		41° 11.68	72° 34.22	+0 18	-0 06	-0 28	+0 37	0.4	0.3	0.2		0.9	241°	0.0	---	1.2	083°
2966	Mattituck Inlet, 1 mile northwest of		41° 03.68	72° 42.00	0 00	+0 01	-0 03	+0 00	0.3	0.3	0.0	---	1.0	265°	0.0	---	1.0	065°
2971	Sachem Head, 2 mile SSE of	15	41° 07.57	72° 42.00	-0 17	-0 16	-0 01	-0 15	0.3	0.3	0.0	---	1.6	065°	0.0	---	1.9	065°
2976	Falkner Island, 6.2 miles south of	15	41° 04.37	72° 42.53	-0 50	-0 50	-0 03	-1 15	0.2	0.2	0.0	---	0.7	260°	0.0	---	0.8	060°
2981	Roanoke Point, 5.6 miles north of		41° 00.92	72° 42.97	+0 19	+0 15	+0 01	-0 35	0.2	0.3	0.0	---	0.9	270°	0.0	---	0.7	070°
2986	Roanoke Point, 2.3 miles NNW of				-0 58	-0 01		-0 40	0.3	0.1	0.0	---	0.8	272°	0.0	---	0.7	070°
2991	Branford Reef, 1.5 miles southwest of	15d	41° 12.57	72° 49.83	+0 08	+0 07	0 00	-0 08	0.3	0.2	0.0	---	0.7	272°	0.0	---	0.7	068°
2996	Branford Reef, 5.0 miles south of	15d	41° 08.65	72° 49.87	+0 20	+0 30	+0 20	+0 18	0.3	0.2	0.0	---	0.9	260°	0.0	---	0.8	074°
3001	Herod Point, 6.5 miles north of	15d	41° 04.65	72° 49.80	-0 08	+0 24	-0 18	+0 03	0.2	0.2	0.0	---	0.4	254°	0.0	---	0.8	070°
3006	Herod Point, 2.8 miles north of	15	41° 00.97	72° 49.93	-0 08	+0 21	-0 18	-0 11	0.2	0.2	0.0	---	0.6	290°	0.0	---	0.6	090°
3011	Herod Point, 5.0 n.mi. NW of	15d	41° 01.84	72° 54.73	+0 04	+0 10	-0 28	-0 03	0.2	0.3	0.0	---	0.3	319°	0.0	---	0.7	089°
3016	New Haven Harbor entrance <12>		41° 14′	72° 55′	-0 32	-1 16	-0 42	+0 29	0.5	0.2	0.1	020°	0.3	015°	0.0	---	0.9	152°
3021	Oyster River Pt, 1.3 miles northeast of <1>		41° 17.83	72° 54.42	+0 55	+0 06	---	-0 68	0.3	0.1	0.1	179°	0.6	266°	0.1	020°	0.3	215°
3026	Pond Point, 4.2 miles SSE of		41° 12.87	72° 58.08	-0 01	-0 25	+0 05	-0 20	0.2	0.2	0.0	---	0.5	270°	0.0	---	0.6	069°
3031	Stratford Shoal, 6 miles east of		41° 06.60	72° 58.43	+0 22	+0 19	+0 02	-0 20	0.2	0.3	0.0	---	0.4	250°	0.0	---	0.6	060°
3036	Sound Beach, 2.2 miles north of		41° 04.52	72° 58.45	+0 22	+0 15	-0 06	-0 96	0.2	0.4	0.0	---			0.0	---	0.6	075°
3041	Charles Island, 0.8 mile SSE of	15d	41° 00.33	72° 58.45	+0 18	-0 07	-0 21	+1 05	0.2	0.2	0.1				0.0	---	0.9	075°
3046			41° 10.77	73° 02.83	-0 30	---			0.1	0.1	0.0	---			0.0	---	0.4	070°
	Housatonic River																	
3051	Milford Point, 0.2 mile west of	10	41° 10.56	73° 06.82	+0 15	+0 22	+0 24	-1 06	0.4	0.4	0.0	---	1.2	330°	0.0	---	1.2	135°
3056	Railroad drawbridge, above	5	41° 12.53	73° 06.67	+0 40	+0 34	+0 38	+0 37	0.4	0.4	0.0	---	1.1	360°	0.0	---	1.3	185°
3061	Fowler Island, 0.1 mile NNW of	5	41° 14.40	73° 06.23	+1 40	+0 54	+0 29	-0 17	0.2	0.1	0.0	---	0.6	040°	0.0	---	1.1	270°
3066	Wooster Island, 0.1 mile southwest of	5	41° 16.67	73° 05.20	-0 09	-0 15	+0 01	+0 11	0.2	0.2	0.0	---	---	020°	0.0	---	0.7	224°
3071	Derby-Shelton Bridge, below <13>	15	41° 18.73	73° 04.78	-0 33	+0 40	-0 12	-0 03	0.5	0.3	0.0	---	1.3	261°	0.0	---	0.4	095°
3076	Point No Point, 2.1 miles south of	15	41° 06.75	73° 07.13	-0 16	+0 12	-0 14	+0 04	0.2	0.3	0.0	---	0.6	294°	0.0	---	1.2	075°
3081	Stratford Point, 4.3 miles south of	60	41° 04.77	73° 06.67	+0 22	+0 24	+0 25	+0 19	0.3	0.2	0.0	---	0.6	26?°	0.0	---	1.0	075°
3086	do.	15	41° 02.97	73° 06.67	+0 40	+0 10	-0 36	-0 23	0.3	0.3	0.0	---	0.5	29?°	0.0	---	0.8	080°
	Stratford Point, 6.1 miles south of	51	41° 01.32	73° 06.57	+0 54	+0 34	-0 02	+0 14	0.3	0.4	0.0	---	0.5	254°	0.1	338°	0.9	080°
	do.	15d	41° 00.23	73° 05.70	+0 43	+0 03	+0 47	+0 47	0.3	0.4	0.0	---	0.5	238°	0.0	---	1.1	092°
3091	Old Field Point, 2.9 n.mi. NNW of	40	40° 58.47	73° 05.70	+3 47	+2 52	+2 34	+1 45	0.1	0.2	0.0	---	0.2	108°	0.0	---	0.6	308°
3096	Old Field Point, 2 miles northeast of	15	40° 58.47	73° 06.80	+2 51	+2 15	+2 26	+1 33	0.1	0.2	0.0	---	0.2	110°	0.0	---	0.5	297°
3101	do.	22		73° 06.80														

SEE ENDNOTES ON PAGE 106

TABLE 2 – CURRENT DIFFERENCES AND OTHER CONSTANTS

No.	PLACE	Meter Depth (ft)	POSITION Latitude North	POSITION Longitude West	TIME DIFFERENCES Min. before Flood (h m)	Flood (h m)	Min. before Ebb (h m)	Ebb (h m)	SPEED RATIOS Flood	Ebb	Minimum before Flood (knots)	Dir.	Maximum Flood (knots)	Dir.	Minimum before Ebb (knots)	Dir.	Maximum Ebb (knots)	Dir.
	LONG ISLAND SOUND—cont. Time meridian, 75° W																	
						on The Race												
3106	Port Jefferson Harbor entrance	4	40° 58′	73° 06′	+0 22	+0 58	+0 27	0 00	1.0	0.6	0.0	—	2.6	151°	0.0	—	1.9	323°
3111	Crane Neck Point, 0.5 mile northwest of		40° 58′	73° 10′	−0 34	−1 06	−1 43	−1 48	0.6	0.6	0.0	—	1.3	256°	0.0	—	1.5	016°
3116	Bridgeport Hbr. ent., btn. jetties <14>	15	41° 09′	73° 11′	−0 01	−0 04	0 00	−0 17	0.3	0.2	0.0	—	0.7	340°	0.0	—	0.6	176°
3121	Pine Creek Point, 2.5 miles SSE of	15	41° 05.06′	73° 14.40′	−0 01	+0 27	+0 30	+0 12	0.2	0.2	0.0	—	0.7	272°	0.0	—	0.6	084°
3128	Shoal Point, 6 miles south of	15	41° 01.70′	73° 14.03′	+0 43	+0 49	+0 51	+0 44	0.2	0.1	0.0	—	0.4	292°	0.0	—	0.4	047°
3131	Crane Neck Point, 3.4 miles WNW of	15	40° 59.00′	73° 13.87′	+0 09	+0 23	−0 16	−0 02	0.2	0.2	0.0	—	0.4	281°	0.0	—	0.6	079°
3136	Crane Neck Point, 3.7 miles WSW of	15	40° 56.30′	73° 13.87′	−1 11	−0 10	−0 15	−0 29	0.2	0.2	0.0	—	0.4	288°	0.0	—	0.6	232°
3141	Saugatuck River, 0.3 mi. NW of Bluff Pt	15	41° 06.27′	73° 21.92′	−0 09	−0 20	−0 29	−0 01	0.2	0.1	0.0	—	0.5	268°	0.0	—	0.4	080°
3146	Saugatuck R., 0.5 mile above Gregory Point		41° 05.20′	73° 25′	Current weak and variable													
3151	Norwalk River, off Gregory Point	15	41° 05.20′	73° 24.22′	+0 09	0 00	+0 38	+0 19	0.2	0.2	0.0	—	0.6	322°	0.0	—	0.5	156°
3156	Sheffield I. Hbr., 0.5 mile southeast of	12	41° 03.32′	73° 25.25′	−2 20	+1 00	+1 08	+0 22	0.3	0.2	0.0	—	0.9	229°	0.0	—	0.8	042°
3161	Sheffield I. Tower, 1.1 miles SE of	15	41° 01.97′	73° 24.33′	+0 54	+1 00	+1 08	+0 54	0.4	0.3	0.0	—	0.9	283°	0.0	—	0.8	081°
3166	Eatons Neck Pt., 3 miles north of	60	41° 00.38′	73° 23.80′	−0 06	+0 45	+0 45	+0 25	0.3	0.3	0.0	—	0.7	269°	0.0	—	0.9	046°
	do.	15	41° 00.38′	73° 24.33′	+1 01	+0 51	+0 35	+0 08	0.3	0.3	0.0	—	0.7	259°	0.0	—	0.9	078°
	do.	40	41° 00.38′	73° 23.80′	−0 17	+0 34	+0 34	+0 17	0.3	0.3	0.0	—	0.6	284°	0.1	341°	0.5	078°
	do.	170	41° 00.38′	73° 23.80′	−1 38	−1 33	−2 07	−2 20	0.6	0.5	0.0	—	0.6	188°	0.0	—	1.4	054°
	do.	15	40° 58.60′	73° 23.77′	−0 15	−0 43	−0 14	−0 43	0.2	0.2	0.1	164°	0.6	269°	0.0	—	0.5	073°
3171	Eatons Neck Point, 2.5 n.mi. NNW of	15	40° 59.73′	73° 25.05′	−0 68	−0 42	−0 33	−0 40	0.2	0.3	0.0	—	0.6	283°	0.0	—	0.3	069°
3176	Eatons Neck Pt., 1.3 miles north of	30	40° 55.60′	73° 25.05′	−0 33	−0 35	+0 14	−0 27	0.2	0.2	0.0	—	0.6	199°	0.0	—	0.3	069°
3181	Eatons Neck Pt., 1.8 miles west of	15	40° 55.60′	73° 24.46′	−0 10	+0 12	+0 21	−0 19	0.2	0.1	0.0	—	0.4	179°	0.0	—	0.3	014°
3186	Huntington Bay, off East Fort Point		40° 54.53′	73° 25.06′	+0 42	+0 16	+0 07	0 00	0.2	0.1	0.0	—	0.4	100°	0.0	—	0.3	007°
3191	Northport Bay entrance (in channel)	15	40° 55.60′	73° 28.68′	−0 59	+0 15	+1 23	+0 54	0.2	0.2	0.0	—	0.4	007°	0.0	—	0.4	267°
3196	Northport Bay, south of Duck I. Bluff	27	41° 01.58′	73° 28.68′	+0 44	+0 13	+1 29	+0 64	0.2	0.2	0.0	—	0.4	252°	0.0	—	0.5	286°
3201	Long Neck Point, 0.6 mile south of	40	41° 01.58′	73° 28.70′	+1 37	+0 15	+1 21	+1 21	0.2	0.3	0.0	—	0.4	257°	0.0	—	0.5	079°
	do.		40° 57.95′	73° 29.70′	+0 13	+0 34	+1 16	+0 26	0.4	0.4	0.0	—	1.0	256°	0.0	—	0.5	080°
3206	Lloyd Point, 1.3 miles NNW of	15	40° 59.90′	73° 31.00′	+0 49	+0 41	+0 22	+0 06	0.3	0.3	0.0	—	0.9	299°	0.0	—	0.7	055°
	do.	40	40° 59.98′	73° 31.03′	+0 31	+0 32	+0 55	+0 21	0.3	0.3	0.0	—	0.8	247°	0.0	—	0.8	071°
3211	Shippan Point, 1.3 miles SSE of	12	41° 00.88′	73° 32.20′	−1 09	−0 56	−1 58	−0 33	0.1	0.3	0.0	—	0.4	329°	0.0	—	0.8	134°
	do.		40° 55.15′	73° 30.03′	+0 32	+0 41	+0 23	+0 31	0.2	0.2	0.0	—	0.6	117°	0.0	—	0.5	306°
3216	Stamford Harbor entrance	15	40° 54′	73° 31′	+0 07	+0 26	−0 01	+0 10	0.3	0.3	0.0	—	0.6	244°	0.0	—	0.7	054°
	Oyster Bay		40° 53′	73° 32′	+0 37	+0 46	−0 04	+0 12	0.2	0.1	0.0	—	0.6	335°	0.0	—	0.4	140°
3221	Rocky Point, 1 mile east of		40° 53′	73° 29′	+1 34	+1 24	+1 48	+1 02	0.3	0.2	0.0	—	0.7	266°	0.0	—	0.8	073°
3226	Harbor ent., south of Plum Point	15	40° 59.02′	73° 34.02′	+1 37	+1 17	+1 50	+1 04	0.2	0.3	0.0	—	0.7	262°	0.0	—	0.4	062°
3231	Harbor, west of Soper Point	55	40° 59.02′	73° 34.68′	+1 07	+1 36	+2 24	+1 30	0.2	0.2	0.0	—	0.5	282°	0.0	—	0.6	065°
3236	Cold Spring Harbor	55	40° 57.60′	73° 33.68′	+1 45	+2 24	+2 24	+1 52	0.2	0.2	0.0	—	0.5	260°	0.0	—	0.5	072°
3241	Greenwich Harbor, 1.1 miles south of	15	40° 55.50′	73° 34.02′	+1 35	+2 10	+2 11	+1 54	0.2	0.3	0.0	—	0.6	300°	0.0	—	0.6	090°
	do.	30	40° 55.50′	73° 34.02′	+1 07	+1 40	−0 01	+2 01	0.2	0.3	0.0	—	0.6	013°	0.0	—	0.5	188°
3246	Greenwich Point, 2.5 miles south of		41° 01′	73° 36′	+1 45	+2 10	+1 48	+1 69	0.2	0.3	0.0	—	0.5	319°	0.0	—	0.5	118°
	do.		40° 59.65′	73° 35.67′	Current weak and variable													
3251	Oak Neck Point, 0.6 mile north of		40° 59.65′	73° 35.67′	+1 35	+1 40	+1 57	+1 69	0.3	0.4	0.0	—	0.6	312°	0.0	—	0.4	142°
	do.		40° 56.25′	73° 39.49′	+1 22	+0 49	+1 15	+1 01	0.3	0.3	0.0	—	0.5	319°	0.0	—	0.7	051°
3256	Cos Cob Harbor, off Goose Island	30	40° 56.32′	73° 40.50′	+1 33	+1 25	+1 06	+0 28	0.2	0.3	0.0	—	0.5	230°	0.0	—	0.7	035°
3261	Captain Hbr. Ent., 0.6 mile southwest of	15	40° 54.80′	73° 39.37′	+1 33	+1 25	+1 33	+1 03	0.2	0.3	0.0	—	0.4	226°	0.0	—	0.7	055°
	do.	40	40° 54.80′	73° 38.40′	+0 48	+0 33	+0 53	+0 21	0.2	0.3	0.0	—	0.4	234°	0.0	—	0.5	046°
3266	Parsonage Point, 1.3 n. mi. ESE of	15	40° 52.40′	73° 38.40′							0.0	—	0.5	233°	0.0	—	0.5	053°
3271	Peningo Neck, 0.6 mi. off Parsonage Pt.	15	40° 51.57′	73° 39.98′	−0 25	+0 26	Current weak and variable												
3276	Mallinecock Point, 1.7 miles northwest of	10	40° 49.66′	73° 39.00′	+0 02	−0 30	−0 68		0.1	0.2	0.0	—	0.9	157°	0.0	—	0.1	331°
3281	Mallinecock Point, 0.7 mile NNW of	15	40° 48.78′	73° 39.08′	−0 01	−0 01	−0 04		0.1	0.3	0.0	—	0.9	138°	0.0	—	0.7	320°
	do.		40° 55.00′	73° 42.73′	+0 58	+0 32	+1 13	+1 04	0.2	0.2	0.0	—	0.5	198°	0.0	—	—	—
3286	Hempstead Harbor, 0.3 mile north of	15	40° 54′	73° 46′		+0 35	+1 08	+0 38	0.2	0.1	0.0	—	0.4	244°	0.0	—	0.4	059°
3291	Hempstead Harbor, 0.5 mile east of	33				+0 32				0.1	0.0	—	0.4	299°	0.0	—	0.3	069°
3296	Hempstead Harbor, off Glenwood Landing				Current weak and variable													
3301	Old Town Wharf, 0.5 mile north of				Current weak and variable													
3306	Delancey Point, 1 mile southeast of				Current weak and variable													
3311	Mamaroneck Harbor				Current weak and variable													
3316	Echo Bay entrance				Current weak and variable													

SEE ENDNOTES ON PAGE 106

TABLE 2 – CURRENT DIFFERENCES AND OTHER CONSTANTS

No.	PLACE	Meter Depth (ft)	Latitude North	Longitude West	Time Diff. Min. before Flood (h m)	Time Diff. Flood (h m)	Time Diff. Min. before Ebb (h m)	Time Diff. Ebb (h m)	Speed Ratio Flood	Speed Ratio Ebb	Avg. Min. before Flood (knots)	Dir.	Avg. Max. Flood (knots)	Dir.	Avg. Min. before Ebb (knots)	Dir.	Avg. Max. Ebb (knots)	Dir.
	LONG ISLAND SOUND—cont. Time meridian, 75° W				**on Throgs Neck**													
3321	Davids Island, channel 0.1 mile east of	15	40° 53'	73° 46'	−2 54	−3 36	−2 29	−3 48	0.2	0.4	0.0	—	0.2	069°	0.0	—	0.2	234°
3326	Huckleberry Island, 0.2 mile NW of	15	40° 53.43'	73° 45.43'	−2 04	+0 07	−1 01	−2 32	0.3	0.4	0.0	—	0.4	025°	0.0	—	0.3	226°
3331	Huckleberry Island, 0.6 mile SE of	15	40° 52.80'	73° 44.75'	−2 17	−2 32	−1 35	−2 46	0.6	0.7	0.0	—	0.6	058°	0.0	—	0.4	246°
3336	Execution Rocks, 0.4 mile southwest of	15	40° 52.40'	73° 44.00'	+3 19	+2 58	+3 40	+2 56	0.4	0.5	0.0	—	0.4	115°	0.0	—	0.4	307°
3341	Manhasset Bay entrance	15	40° 49.75'	73° 43.78'	−2 02	−3 24	−3 04	−3 18	0.2	0.2	0.0	—	0.2	098°	0.0	—	0.3	264°
3346	Hart Island, 0.2 mile north of	15	40° 51.82'	73° 46.27'	*Current weak and variable*			−0 43									0.3	289°
3351	Hart Island, southeast of	15	40° 50.62'	73° 46.77'	−1 23	+0 24	−0 19	−0 31	0.6	0.6	0.1	—	0.6	032°	0.2	—	0.4	218°
3356	Hart Island, 0.3 n.mi. SSE of	15d	40° 50.43'	73° 46.94'	−1 05	−0 18	−0 54	−1 18	0.5	0.8	0.1	114°	0.5	040°	0.2	119°	0.4	216°
3361	Hart Island and City Island, between	15	40° 51.37'	73° 46.73'	−1 27	−2 20	−1 06	−1 10	0.2	0.3	0.0	—	0.2	349°	0.0	—	0.2	143°
3366	City Island Bridge	10	40° 51.47'	73° 47.60'	−2 38		−3 14				0.0	—	0.2	349°	0.0	—	0.3	150°
3371	Eastchester Bay, near Big Tom	5	40° 50.20'	73° 47.72'	−2 44	−3 20	−2 54	−3 35	0.1	0.3	0.0	—	0.1	327°	0.0	—	0.2	196°
3376	Hutchinson R., Pelham Highway Bridge	5	40° 51.70'	73° 49.00'	+3 02	+3 08	+3 04	+2 05	0.9	0.7	0.0	—	0.3	097°	0.0	—	0.4	294°
3381	City Island, 0.6 mile southeast of	15	40° 49.72'	73° 46.47'	−0 56	−0 14	−1 46	−2 14	0.5	0.7	0.0	—	0.5	038°	0.0	—	0.5	079°
	THROGS NECK																	
3391	THROGS NECK, 0.3 n.mi. NE of	15d	40° 48.64'	73° 47.13'	+0 57	+0 49	+1 33	+0 11	0.8	0.8	0.1	312°	1.0	015°	0.1	288°	0.6	199°
3396	Throgs Neck, 0.4 mile south of	15	40° 47.90'	73° 47.45'	*Daily predictions*													
3401	Throgs Neck, 0.2 mile S of (Willets Point)	15	40° 48.12'	73° 47.48'	+0 21	+0 31	+1 13	+0 05	0.7	1.0	0.0	—	0.8	090°	0.0	—	0.8	278°
3406	Throgs Neck Bridge	15	40° 48.1'	73° 47.6'	+0 24	+0 43	+0 50	+0 04	1.6	1.5	0.1	194°	1.5	122°	0.0	—	0.9	276°
	EAST RIVER				**on Hell Gate**													
3411	Cryders Point, 0.4 mile NNW of	14	40° 48.02'	73° 47.92'	−0 29	−0 43	−0 30	−1 00	0.4	0.2	0.0	—	1.3	110°	0.0	—	1.1	285°
3416	Bronx–Whitestone Bridge, East of	15d	40° 48.1'	73° 49.8'	−0 34	−0 46	−0 10	−1 27	0.5	0.4	0.0	—	1.7	076°	0.0	—	1.6	247°
3421	Clason Point, 0.3 n.mi. S of	15d	40° 48.06'	73° 50.81'	−0 25	−1 06	−0 32	−1 33	0.4	0.4	0.1	351°	1.5	089°	0.1	350°	1.4	269°
3426	College Point Reef, 0.25 n.mi. NW of		40° 45.9'	73° 51.28'	−0 27	−0 47		−1 00						074°				261°
3431	Flushing Creek entrance		40° 47'	73° 50.7'	*Current weak and variable*													
3436	Rikers I. chan., off La Guardia Field		40° 48.9'	73° 53'	+0 04	−0 04	+0 04	−0 08	0.3	0.3	0.0	—	1.1	088°	0.0	—	1.3	261°
3441	Bronx River (1 mile north of Hunts Pt.)	15	40° 48'	73° 52.5'	*Current weak and variable*													
3446	Hunts Point, southwest of		40° 47.8'	73° 53'	+0 01	−0 10	+0 01	−0 06	0.5	0.3	0.0	—	1.7	108°	0.0	—	1.3	280°
3451	South Brother Island, NW of		40° 47.2'	73° 58'	+0 07	+0 02	−0 01	−0 12	0.4	0.3	0.0	—	1.5	054°	0.0	—	1.2	252°
3456	Off Winthrop Ave., Astoria		40° 46.9'	73° 55.0'	+0 04	+0 05	−0 29	−0 11	1.0	0.5	0.0	—	3.4	040°	0.0	—	2.5	220°
3461	Mill Rock, northeast of		40° 46.7'	73° 56.5'	−0 23	+0 08	−0 02	−0 32	0.7	0.1	0.0	—	2.3	103°	0.0	—	0.4	209°
3466	Mill Rock, west of		40° 46.7'	73° 56.5'	−0 26	+0 08	−0 02	−0 17	0.4	0.2	0.0	—	3.4	000°	0.0	—	1.0	180°
3471	HELL GATE (off Mill Rock)		40° 46.7'	73° 56.3'	*Daily predictions*													4.6	230°
	Roosevelt Island																	
3476	west of, off 75th Street		40° 46'	73° 57'	−0 02	−0 04	−0 08	+0 07	1.1	1.0	0.0	—	3.8	037°	0.0	—	4.7	215°
3481	east of, off 96th Avenue		40° 45.74'	73° 57.24'	−0 08	−0 04	−0 08	+0 11	1.1	0.7	0.0	—	3.5	030°	0.0	—	3.4	210°
3486	west of, off 87th Street		40° 45.58'	73° 57.27'	+0 13	−0 08	+0 06	+0 13	1.1	0.9	0.0	—	3.6	011°	0.0	—	4.0	230°
3491	west of, off 63rd Street		40° 45.49'	73° 57.08'	+0 10	−0 06	0 00	+0 11	0.8	0.8	0.0	—	2.8	038°	0.1	—	2.9	229°
3496	east of		40° 44.38'	73° 58.17'	+0 09	−0 11	+0 02	+0 36	0.8	0.6	0.0	—	2.8	028°	0.0	—	2.6	229°
3501	Manhattan, off 31st Street		40° 44'	73° 57'	−0 08	−0 08	−0 08	+0 07	0.4	0.5	0.0	—	1.5	000°	0.0	—	2.1	175°
3506	Newtown Creek entrance		40° 44'	73° 58'	*Current weak and variable*													
3511	Pier 67, off 19th Street		40° 43.08'	73° 58.24'	−0 05	−0 01	−0 01	+0 10	0.5	0.4	0.0	—	1.8	355°	0.0	—	1.9	179°
3516	Williamsburg Bridge, 0.3 mile north of		40° 42.5'	73° 59.4'	−0 28	+0 12	−0 13	+0 03	0.8	0.6	0.0	—	2.7	020°	0.0	—	2.9	220°
3521	Manhattan Bridge, East of	15	40° 42.36'	73° 59.85'	+0 29	+0 19	+0 33	+0 09	0.7	0.8	0.0	—	2.5	083°	0.0	—	2.9	269°
3526	Brooklyn Bridge	15d	40° 42.2'	74° 00.2'	+0 18	+0 41	+0 04	−0 07	1.0	0.7	0.1	161°	2.7	063°	0.0	—	2.5	263°
3531	Brooklyn Bridge, 0.1 mile southwest of		40° 41.3'	74° 00.0'	−0 31	+0 08	+0 03	−0 18	0.9	0.8	0.1	324°	2.9	046°	0.0	—	3.5	222°
3536	Buttermilk Channel (SEE CAUTION NOTE)	15	40° 41.15'	74° 00.81'	−0 12	−0 18	+0 06	+0 18	0.5	0.5	0.0	—	1.8	050°	0.1	315°	2.4	220°
3541	Buttermilk Channel																	

NOTES   SEE ENDNOTES ON PAGE 106

TABLE 2 – CURRENT DIFFERENCES AND OTHER CONSTANTS

No.	PLACE	POSITION Latitude North	POSITION Longitude West	Meter Depth (ft)	TIME DIFFERENCES Min. before Flood (h m)	Flood (h m)	Min. before Ebb (h m)	Ebb (h m)	SPEED RATIOS Flood	SPEED RATIOS Ebb	AVG SPEEDS — Minimum before Flood (knots)	Dir.	Maximum Flood (knots)	Dir.	Minimum before Ebb (knots)	Dir.	Maximum Ebb (knots)	Dir.
	LONG ISLAND, South Coast Time meridian, 75° W				*on The Narrows*													
3586	Fire Island Lighted Whistle 2FI	40° 29'	73° 11'		+1 04	+0 34	+0 19	−0 42	—	0.8	—	—	1.8	—	—	—	1.5	180°
3591	Fire Island Inlet, 22 miles S of <15>	40° 16'	73° 16'		+0 04	−0 22	−0 38	−0 30	0.5	0.3	0.0	0.0	0.8	250°	0.0	—	0.6	090°
3596	Shinnecock Canal, railroad bridge <16>	40° 53.2'	72° 30.1'		+0 04	−0 50	−1 04	−1 02	1.6	1.1	0.0	0.0	2.5	350°	0.0	—	2.3	170°
3601	Ponquogue bridge, Shinnecock Bay	40° 50.6'	72° 28.7'		−0 07	−0 50	−1 04	−1 12	2.0	1.3	0.0	0.0	3.1	082°	0.0	—	2.4	244°
3606	Shinnecock Inlet	40° 37.78'	73° 18.40'		−0 44	+0 22	+0 24	−1 07	0.3	0.3	0.0	0.0	0.5	035°	0.0	—	3.1	217°
3616	Fire I. Inlet, 0.5 mi. S of Oak Beach	40° 37.5'	73° 34.0'											076°			0.6	277°
3621	Jones Inlet	40° 35.7'	73° 39.6'		−1 36	−1 36	−1 11	−1 45	1.4	1.2	0.0	0.0	2.2	042°	0.0	—	2.3	227°
	Long Beach, inside, between bridges	40° 35.4'	73° 45.3'															
3626	East Rockaway Inlet	40° 27'	73° 49'															
3631	Ambrose Light	40° 27'	73° 55															
3636	Sandy Hook App. Lighted Horn 2A																	
	JAMAICA BAY																	
3641	Rockaway Point	40° 32.18'	73° 56.48'	15	−2 28	−2 35	−1 46	−3 09	1.2	0.6	0.2	228°	1.9	301°	0.2	217°	1.1	149°
3646	Rockaway Inlet entrance	40° 33.7'	73° 56.1'		−1 45	−2 21	−1 41	−2 18	1.1	1.4	0.0	—	1.8	088°	0.0	—	2.7	244°
3651	Rockaway Inlet	40° 34.12'	73° 53.48'	14	−1 43	−2 01	−2 11	−2 36	1.0	0.9	0.0	—	1.6	088°	0.1	344°	1.5	261°
3656	Barren Island, east of	40° 35.0'	73° 53.0'		−1 49	−2 29	−1 59	−2 23	0.3	0.4	0.0	—	0.5	048°	0.0	—	0.7	192°
3661	Canarsie (midchannel, off pier)	40° 37.6'	73° 53.0'		−1 38	−1 14	−1 05	−2 32	1.2	1.1	0.0	—	1.0	062°	0.0	—	2.3	222°
3666	Beach Channel (bridge)	40° 36.0'	73° 49.0'		−1 11	−1 03	−1 05	−1 01	0.6	0.5	0.0	—	1.0	052°	0.0	—	2.0	228°
3671	Grass Hassock Channel		73° 47.1'															
	NEW YORK HARBOR ENTRANCE																	
3676	Ambrose Channel	40° 31.00'	73° 58.48'		−0 47	−1 11	−0 33	−0 14	1.0	0.9	0.1	025°	1.6	303°	0.0	—	1.7	129°
3681	Norton Point, WSW of	40° 33.30'	74° 01.30'		−0 03	−1 02	+0 18	+0 20	0.6	0.7	0.3	265°	1.0	341°	0.1	071°	1.9	126°
3686	THE NARROWS, midchannel	40° 36.56'	74° 02.77'					*Daily predictions*										
	do.	40° 36.56'	74° 02.77'		−0 23	−1 11	+0 13	+0 14	1.1	0.9	0.2	064°	1.6	336°	0.1	246°	1.9	164°
	do.	40° 36.56'	74° 02.77'		−0 44	−0 11	+0 17	+0 00	1.2	0.7	—	244°	1.3	332°	0.1	246°	1.6	156°
	do.	40° 36.56'	74° 02.77'		−1 10	−0 31	+0 10	−0 13	1.1	1.0	0.1	240°	1.7	331°	0.1	244°	1.7	147°
	NEW YORK HARBOR, Upper Bay																	
3691	Bay Ridge, west of	40° 37.54'	74° 03.24'	22	+0 59	+1 11	+0 34	+0 52	0.7	0.8	0.1	104°	1.4	354°	0.1	125°	1.5	185°
3698	Bay Ridge Channel	40° 39.18'	74° 01.54'	15	+1 14	−1 27	−0 58	+0 24	0.7	0.4	—	—	0.6	052°	0.0	—	0.7	212°
	do.	40° 39.18'	74° 01.54'	36	−1 27	−0 45	−0 06	+0 16	0.6	0.4	0.0	—	0.6	097°	0.0	—	0.4	225°
3701	Red Hook Channel	40° 39.45'	74° 03.50'		−0 53	−2 37	−0 58	−0 37	0.8	0.4	0.0	—	1.3	353°	0.1	—	1.6	170°
3706	Robbins Reef Light, east of	40° 40.0'	74° 01.2'		+0 51	+1 15	+0 39	+0 45	0.8	1.2	0.0	—	1.3	016°	0.0	—	2.3	204°
3711	Red Hook, 1 mile west of	40° 40.5'	74° 02.5'		+1 07	+0 57	+0 48	+0 52	0.9	1.0	0.1	292°	1.4	024°	0.0	—	1.9	206°
3716	Statue of Liberty, east of	40° 41.4'	74° 01.8'											031°				205°
	HUDSON RIVER, Midchannel <17>																	
3721	Hudson River entrance	40° 42.30'	74° 01.12'	14	+0 59	+1 11	+1 14	+2 11	0.9	0.7	0.1	—	1.6	009°	0.0	—	1.4	199°
3728	Grants Tomb	40° 48.48'	73° 58.06'	18	+1 14	+1 17	+1 50	+1 20	1.2	1.2	0.0	—	1.8	028°	0.0	—	1.8	200°
3731	George Washington Bridge	40° 51'	73° 57'		+1 51	+1 54	+1 42	+2 01	1.0	1.1	0.0	—	1.6	020°	0.0	—	2.2	200°
3736	Spuyten Duyvil	40° 53'	73° 56'		+2 21	+2 07	+1 49	+2 17	0.9	1.1	0.0	—	1.5	020°	0.0	—	2.1	—
3741	Riverdale	40° 54.42'	73° 54.48'	15	+1 36	+1 59	+1 54	+2 22	0.9	1.7	0.0	—	1.5	010°	0.0	—	1.7	—
3746	Mount St. Vincent College, SW of	41° 01'	73° 53'		+2 40	+2 32	+2 16	+2 42	0.8	1.0	0.0	—	1.5	007°	0.0	—	1.5	209°
3751	Dobbs Ferry	41° 05'	73° 53'		+2 47	+2 45	+2 32	+2 55	0.7	0.8	0.0	—	0.9	010°	0.0	—	1.3	206°
3756	Tarrytown	41° 12'	73° 54'		+3 00	+3 01	+2 57	+3 12	0.6	0.7	0.0	—	0.9	320°	0.0	—	1.3	205°
3761	Ossining	41° 17'	73° 57'		+3 05	+3 07	+3 05	+3 19	0.5	0.6	0.0	—	0.8	335°	0.0	—	1.3	—
3766	Haverstraw	41° 19'	73° 59'		+3 20	+3 23	+3 23	+3 35	0.5	0.6	0.0	—	0.8	000°	0.0	—	1.1	—
3771	Peekskill	41° 22'	73° 68'		+3 26	+3 30	+3 31	+3 41	0.6	0.6	0.0	—	1.0	000°	0.0	—	1.2	—
3776	Bear Mountain Bridge				+3 34	+3 36	+3 36	+3 55	0.6	0.6	0.0	—	1.0	008°	0.0	—		186°
3781	Highland Falls																	

NOTES

SEE ENDNOTES ON PAGE 106

TABLE 2 – CURRENT DIFFERENCES AND OTHER CONSTANTS

No.	PLACE	POSITION Meter Depth (ft)	POSITION Latitude North	POSITION Longitude West	TIME DIFFERENCES Min. before Flood (h m)	TIME DIFFERENCES Flood (h m)	TIME DIFFERENCES Min. before Ebb (h m)	TIME DIFFERENCES Ebb (h m)	SPEED RATIOS Flood	SPEED RATIOS Ebb	AVG Min. before Flood knots	Dir.	AVG Maximum Flood knots	Dir.	AVG Min. before Ebb knots	Dir.	AVG Maximum Ebb knots	Dir.
	HUDSON RIVER, Midchannel <17>—cont. Time meridian, 75° W																	
	on the Narrows																	
3786	West Point, off Duck Island		41°24'	73°57'	+3 42	+3 46	+3 43	+3 57	0.6	0.6	0.0	—	1.0	010°	0.0	—	1.1	—
3791	Newburgh		41°30'	74°00'	+4 00	+4 05	+3 55	+4 14	0.6	0.6	0.0	—	0.9	005°	0.0	—	1.1	—
3796	New Hamburg		41°35'	73°57'	+4 15	+4 19	+4 03	+4 26	0.6	0.6	0.0	—	1.0	005°	0.0	—	1.1	—
3801	Poughkeepsie		41°42'	73°57'	+4 36	+4 36	+4 13	+4 42	0.8	0.7	0.0	—	1.2	005°	0.0	—	1.2	—
3806	Hyde Park		41°47'	73°57'	+4 52	+4 47	+4 22	+4 53	0.8	0.9	0.0	—	1.3	005°	0.0	—	1.3	—
3811	Kingston Point <18>		41°56'	73°57'	+5 19	+5 08	+4 46	+5 12	0.9	0.9	0.0	—	1.4	005°	0.0	—	1.7	—
3816	Barrytown		42°00'	73°56'	+5 38	+5 20	+5 02	+5 29	0.9	0.9	0.0	—	1.5	010°	0.0	—	1.9	—
3821	Saugerties		42°04'	73°56'	+5 53	+5 41	+5 21	+5 39	1.0	1.0	0.0	—	1.6	000°	0.0	—	2.0	—
3826	Silver Point		42°09'	73°54'	+6 11	+6 13	+5 41	+5 43	1.0	1.0	0.0	—	1.6	090°	0.0	—	2.0	—
3831	Hatskill		42°15'	73°51'	+6 26	+6 36	+6 01	+5 59	1.0	1.1	0.0	—	1.6	355°	0.0	—	1.8	—
3836	Hudson		42°16'	73°48'	+6 33	+6 44	+6 12	+6 08	1.0	1.1	0.0	—	1.6	350°	0.0	—	1.6	—
3841	Coxsackie		42°21'	73°48'	+6 55	+6 56	+6 17	+6 37	1.0	1.1	0.0	—	1.6	030°	0.0	—	1.4	—
3846	New Baltimore		42°27'	73°47'	+7 05	+7 10	+6 45	+7 02	0.8	1.0	0.0	—	1.3	355°	0.0	—	1.1	—
3851	Castleton-on-Hudson		42°32'	73°46'	+7 45	+7 31	+7 04	+7 22	0.6	0.8	0.0	—	1.0	355°	0.0	—	0.8	—
3856	Albany		42°39'	73°45'	+8 39		+6 38	+7 40	0.2	0.4	0.0	—	0.3	020°	0.0	—	0.4	—
3861	Troy (below the locks) <19>		42°44'	73°42'	—	—	—	—	—	—	—	—	—	—	—	—	0.7	190°
	NEW YORK HARBOR, Lower Bay																	
3866	Sandy Hook Channel	15	40°29.06'	74°00.06'	-1 23	-2 04	-1 14	-1 30	1.0	0.5	0.0	—	1.6	288°	0.0	—	1.9	094°
3871	Sandy Hook Chan., 0.4 mi. W of N. Tip		40°28.79'	74°01.30'	-1 41	-1 56	-1 38	-1 57	1.3	0.9	0.0	—	2.0	235°	0.0	—	1.6	050°
3876	Sandy Hook Pt., 2 mi. W of (channel)		40°28.8'	74°03.6'	-1 35	-2 01	-1 58	-1 49	0.4	0.3	0.0	—	0.6	263°	0.0	—	0.6	088°
3881	Chapel Hill South Channel		40°29.90'	74°03.8'	-2 02	-2 31	-1 48	-1 23	0.4	0.3	0.0	—	0.7	255°	0.0	—	0.6	075°
3886	New Dorp Beach, 1.2 miles south of		40°30.24'	74°06.8'	-2 09	-3 37	-1 48	-2 09	0.3	0.2	0.0	—	0.5	225°	0.0	—	0.4	085°
3891	Old Orchard Shoal Lt., 1.2 mi. ENE of		40°31.1'	74°04.4'	-2 09	-2 08	-1 31	-2 09	0.3	0.2	0.0	—	0.5	270°	0.0	—	0.5	030°
3896	New Dorp Beach, 1.8 miles SE of <20>		40°32.9'	74°02.35'	—	+0 06	—	—	0.5	0.7	0.2	270°	0.8	335°	0.0	—	1.3	225°
3901	Midland Beach, 2.8 miles SE of <21>		40°32.8'	74°02.35'	-1 17	-1 57	-1 06	-1 00	0.7	0.7	0.0	—	0.6	046°	0.2	068°	0.8	160°
3906	Coney Island Lt., 1.5 miles SSE of		40°33.1'	74°00.3'	-1 33	-1 49	-0 25	-1 57	0.8	0.4	0.0	—	0.8	310°	0.0	—	1.3	210°
3911	Hoffman Island, 0.2 mile west of		40°35'	74°04'	-2 06	-2 13	-1 36	-1 50	0.9	0.8	0.0	—	0.9	020°	0.0	—	0.8	142°
3916	Rockaway Inlet Jetty, 1 mile SW of		40°31.8'	73°57.2'							0.0	—	1.2	287°	0.0	—	1.4	102°
3921	Coney Island Channel, west end		40°34.2'	74°00.5'	-1 14	-0 45	-0 32	-0 55	0.8	0.6	0.0	—	1.1	293°	0.0	—	1.2	—
	SANDY HOOK BAY <22>																	
3926	Highlands Bridge, Shrewsbury River		40°23.8'	73°58.8'	+0 31	+0 35	+0 25	+0 12	1.7	1.3	0.0	—	2.6	170°	0.0	—	2.5	147°
3931	Seabright Bridge, Shrewsbury River		40°21.9'	73°58.5'	+1 05	+1 05	+0 44	+0 44	0.9	0.9	0.0	—	1.4	188°	0.0	—	1.7	060°
	RARITAN BAY																	
3936	Raritan Bay Reach Channel	15	40°29.36'	74°07.06'	-1 55	-2 41	-0 46	-0 58	0.4	0.2	0.0	—	0.6	285°	0.0	—	0.4	094°
3941	Keyport Channel entrance		40°26.9'	74°11.9'	Current weak and variable													
3946	Red Bank, 1.4 miles south of	14	40°28.9'	74°12.6'	-1 35	-2 13	-1 30	-1 51	0.4	0.4	0.0	—	0.7	278°	0.0	—	0.5	079°
3951	Seguine Point	34	40°30.24'	74°11.12'	-1 52	-2 51	-0 56	-2 15	0.4	0.3	0.0	—	0.7	281°	0.1	008°	0.5	079°
3956	do.	14	40°30.24'	74°11.12'	-3 28	-2 52	-0 21	-2 31	0.3	0.2	0.0	—	0.5	285°	0.1	—	0.2	106°
3961	Ward Point, ESE		40°29.30'	74°13.48'	-1 45	-1 59	-0 19	-1 01	0.5	0.3	0.1	328°	0.7	244°	0.1	133°	0.5	048°
	RARITAN RIVER																	
3966	Railroad Bridge, Raritan River	15	40°29.54'	74°17.00'	-2 02	-2 26	-1 23	-2 08	0.6	0.4	0.0	—	0.9	328°	0.0	—	0.7	147°
3971	Washington Canal, north entrance		40°28.3'	74°22.1'	-1 02	-1 26	-1 38	-2 58	1.0	0.8	0.0	—	1.5	240°	0.0	—	1.5	060°
3976	South River entrance		40°28.7'	74°22.7'	-1 45	-2 15	-0 35	-1 51	0.7	0.5	0.0	—	1.1	180°	0.0	—	1.0	000°

NOTES

SEE ENDNOTES ON PAGE 106

TABLE 2 – CURRENT DIFFERENCES AND OTHER CONSTANTS

No.	PLACE	POSITION Meter Depth (ft)	POSITION Latitude North	POSITION Longitude West	TIME DIFF Min. before Flood (h m)	TIME DIFF Flood (h m)	TIME DIFF Min. before Ebb (h m)	TIME DIFF Ebb (h m)	SPEED RATIOS Flood	SPEED RATIOS Ebb	AVG Min. before Flood (knots)	AVG Min. before Flood (Dir)	AVG Max. Flood (knots)	AVG Max. Flood (Dir)	AVG Min. before Ebb (knots)	AVG Min. before Ebb (Dir)	AVG Max. Ebb (knots)	AVG Max. Ebb (Dir)
	ARTHUR KILL Time meridian, 75° W				*on The Narrows*													
3976	Tottenville, Arthur Kill River	15	40° 30.8'	74° 15.3'	−1 04	−1 28	−0 41	−1 30	0.7	0.6	0.0	---	1.0	029°	0.0	---	1.1	211°
	do.	32	40° 30.8'	74° 15.3'	−1 23	−1 06	−0 56	−1 10	0.4	0.3	0.0	---	0.6	026°	0.0	---	0.5	207°
3981	Tufts Point—Smoking Point		40° 33.4'	74° 19.4'	−0 38	−0 45	−0 32	−1 07	0.8	0.6	0.0	---	1.2	109°	0.0	---	1.0	287°
3986	Tremley Point Reach		40° 35.18'	74° 12.30'	−0 08	−0 55	+0 32	+0 15	0.6	0.4	0.0	---	1.5	015°	0.0	---	1.8	198°
3991	Elizabethport	21	40° 38.8'	74° 10.9'	+0 15	−0 10	+0 24	−0 03	0.9	0.6	0.0	---	1.4	090°	0.0	---	1.1	262°
	KILL VAN KULL																	
3996	BERGEN POINT REACH (BAYONNE BRIDGE)	16	40° 38.5'	74° 08.6'	*Daily predictions* −0 15	+0 02	+0 14	−0 04	0.8	0.9	0.1	346°	1.9	260°	0.0	---	1.4	078°
	do.	29	40° 38.5'	74° 08.6'							0.0	---	1.6	263°	0.0	---	1.3	079°
4001	Bergen Point, East Reach	15	40° 38.42'	74° 07.48'	*on The Narrows* −1 24	−2 14	−1 43	−1 51	0.7	0.6	0.0	---	1.1	274°	0.0	---	1.2	094°
4006	New Brighton	15	40° 39.00'	74° 05.06'	−1 34	−2 09	−1 32	−1 50	0.8	1.0	0.0	---	1.3	262°	0.0	---	1.9	072°
	NEWARK BAY																	
4011	South Reach, Newark Bay	15	40° 39.36'	74° 08.24'	−0 46	−1 46	−0 59	−1 13	0.4	0.4	0.0	---	0.7	031°	0.0	296°	0.7	218°
	HACKENSACK RIVER																	
4016	Lincoln Highway Bridge, north of		40° 44'	74° 06'	+0 04	+0 11	+0 39	−0 21	0.6	0.4	0.0	---	0.9	017°	0.0	---	0.8	181°
	PASSAIC RIVER																	
4021	Lincoln Highway Bridge		40° 44'	74° 07'	−0 21	−0 20	−0 20	−0 27	0.4	0.3	0.0	---	0.6	009°	0.0	---	0.5	180°
	NEW JERSEY COAST				*on Delaware Bay Entrance*													
4026	Shark River Entrance	5d	40° 11.24'	74° 00.76'	−2 05	−1 52	−2 06	−1 12	1.4	1.1	0.0	---	1.9	279°	0.0	---	1.5	098°
	do.	15d	40° 11.24'	74° 00.76'	−2 06	−1 51	−2 06	−1 14	0.9	0.9	0.0	---	1.5	278°	0.0	---	1.2	097°
4031	Manasquan Inlet		40° 06'	74° 02'	−0 43	−0 30	−1 12	−0 57	1.2	1.4	0.0	---	1.7	300°	0.0	---	1.8	120°
4036	Manasquan R., hwy. bridge, main chan.		40° 06'	74° 03'	−0 41	−0 50	−1 12	+2 10	1.6	1.5	0.0	---	2.2	230°	0.0	---	2.1	060°
4041	Point Pleasant Canal, north bridge <5<>		40° 05'	74° 04'	+1 46	+1 28	+0 48	+0 48	1.8	1.9	0.0	---	1.8	170°	0.0	---	2.0	350°
4046	Barnegat Inlet		39° 46'	74° 04'	+1 01	+1 12	+0 15	+4 21	2.1	2.5	0.1	---	2.1	270°	0.0	---	2.5	090°
4051	Manahawkin Drawbridge		39° 39'	74° 11'	+2 33	+2 43	+2 25	+4 18	1.1	0.9	0.1	055°	1.1	030°	0.0	---	0.9	210°
4056	Absecon Inlet	9d	39° 22.59'	74° 24.87'	−1 02	−1 06	−0 54	−1 18	1.3	1.3	0.1	239°	1.9	329°	0.0	---	1.8	147°
	do.	42d	39° 22.59'	74° 24.87'			−0 56	−1 08			0.1		1.9	327°	0.0	---	1.8	144°
4061	Cape May, 72 miles east of <29>		39° 04'	73° 25'	−1 50	−1 42	−1 02	−0 40	0.4	0.3	0.0	---	0.4	304°	0.0	---	0.4	121°
4066	Five-Fathom Bank NE, Buoy 2 FB		38° 58'	74° 32'	−2 34	−1 16	−1 21	−1 20	0.3	0.2	0.0	---	0.3	302°	0.0	---	0.3	128°
4071	Five-Fathom Bank Traffic Lane	35d	38° 47.30'	74° 42.68'	−0 34	−0 26	−1 43	−1 04	1.1	1.3	0.0	---	1.3	280°	0.0	---	1.3	100°
	do.	50d	38° 57.30'	74° 42.68'	−1 11	−1 23	−1 34	−1 07	1.1	1.3	0.0	---	1.6	329°	0.0	---	1.6	142°
4076	McCrie Shoal		38° 51'	74° 51'	−1 42	−1 23	−1 34	−1 05	0.9	1.3	0.0	---	1.2	322°	0.0	---	1.2	142°
4081	Cape May Harbor entrance	5d	38° 58.85'	74° 52.36'	−1 46	−1 22	−1 34	−1 05	1.1	1.5	0.0	---	1.9	322°	0.0	---	1.7	149°
	do.	15d	38° 58.85'	74° 52.36'	−1 47	−1 48	−1 53	−1 16	1.4	1.5	0.0	---	1.9	310°	0.0	---	1.9	130°
4086	Cape May Canal, east end	28d	38° 57'	74° 54'	−1 48	−1 48	−1 48	−1 16	0.6	0.7	0.0	---	0.9	264°	0.0	---	0.9	089°
4091	Cape May Canal, west end		38° 58'	74° 55'														

TABLE 2 – CURRENT DIFFERENCES AND OTHER CONSTANTS

No.	PLACE	Meter Depth (ft)	POSITION Latitude North	POSITION Longitude West	TIME DIFFERENCES Min before Flood (h m)	Flood (h m)	Min before Ebb (h m)	Ebb (h m)	SPEED RATIOS Flood	Ebb	AVG SPEEDS — Min before Flood knots	Dir	Max Flood knots	Dir	Min before Ebb knots	Dir	Max Ebb knots	Dir
	DELAWARE BAY and RIVER Time meridian, 75° W				*on Delaware Bay Entrance*													
4096	Cape May Channel	15d	38°54′	74°58′	−1 14	−1 30	−1 11	−0 45	1.1	1.8	0.0	---	1.5	306°	0.0	---	2.3	150°
4101	Cape May Point, 1.4 n.mi. SSW of	25d	38°54.37′	74°58.68′	−1 03	−1 18	−1 02	−0 41	1.0	1.3	0.1	030°	1.5	309°	0.1	214°	1.8	130°
	do.	15d	38°54.37′	74°58.68′	−0 56	−1 05	−1 00	−0 36	0.8	0.9	0.1	098°	1.2	306°	0.2	223°	1.2	139°
4106	Cape May Point, 2.7 n.mi. SSW of	15d	38°53.40′	74°59.13′	−1 08	−1 08	−0 47	−0 36	0.9	0.6	0.1	228°	1.2	299°	0.2	208°	0.9	148°
4111	DELAWARE BAY ENTRANCE	22	38°48.65′	75°02.58′	*Daily predictions*								1.2	327°			1.3	147°
4116	Cape Henlopen, 0.7 n.mi. ESE of	12d	38°47.97′	75°04.90′	−0 05	+0 04	−0 40	−0 03	1.3	1.8	0.0	---	1.2	331°	0.0	---	2.1	139°
	do.	70d	38°47.97′	75°04.90′	−1 26	−1 27	−0 24	+0 16	0.8	0.5	0.1	042°	1.2	317°	0.1	232°	2.3	150°
4121	Cape Henlopen, 2 miles northeast of	17d	38°49.2′	75°03.4′	−0 21	−0 21	−0 03	+0 59	1.4	1.8	0.2	---	1.7	315°	0.2	---	1.7	145°
4126	Cape Henlopen, 3.0 n.mi. NNE of	31d	38°51.22′	75°04.62′	−0 19	−0 38	+0 26	+0 55	1.3	1.3	0.1	252°	2.0	342°	0.2	062°	1.5	152°
	do.	57d	38°51.22′	75°04.62′	−0 11	−0 27	+0 31	+0 58	1.3	1.2	0.1	250°	1.9	338°	0.1	065°	1.3	152°
	do.	96d	38°51.22′	75°04.62′	−0 02	−0 12	+1 04	+1 04	1.3	1.0	0.0	---	1.9	334°	0.1	245°	1.3	154°
	do.	18d	38°51.22′	75°04.62′	−0 10	−0 11	+1 05	−0 57	0.7	0.9	0.2	053°	1.8	333°	0.2	229°	1.8	149°
4131	Cape Henlopen, 4.8 n.mi. northeast of	28d	38°51.55′	75°01.47′	−0 23	−1 00	+0 44	−0 03	0.7	1.4	0.2	241°	2.0	301°	0.2	220°	1.2	150°
	do.		38°51.55′	75°01.47′	−0 44	−0 59	+0 41	−0 05	0.7	1.5	0.2	228°	2.0	344°	0.2	229°	1.2	154°
4136	Cape Henlopen, 5 miles north of		38°53.0′	75°05.3′	−0 55	−0 50	−1 14	+1 08	1.6	1.7	0.1	---	0.8	268°	0.0	---	1.9	079°
4141	Breakwater Harbor		38°47.5′	75°06.5′	−1 38	−0 08	−1 03	−0 16	0.6	0.5	0.0	---	0.8	314°	0.1	229°	0.6	132°
4146	Roosevelt Inlet (between jetties) <24>	14d	38°56.8′	75°18.9′	−0 36	−2 29	+1 49	+0 01	1.1	0.5	0.0	---	1.5	028°	0.0	---	0.6	190°
4151	Broadkill Slough		38°54.68′	74°58.88′	−0 29	+0 05	−0 03	+0 52	0.6	0.5	0.1	098°	0.8	008°	0.1	275°	0.7	189°
4156	Mispillion River mouth	13d	38°59.08′	74°59.28′	−0 31	−0 51	−0 45	+0 35	0.7	0.7	---	---	0.8	008°	---	---	0.7	189°
4161	Bay Shore Channel (north)	15d	39°00.37′	75°08.35′	−0 09	+0 01	+0 02	+0 27	0.8	0.8	---	---	1.5	330°	0.1	241°	1.4	164°
4166	Bay Shore Channel (city of Town Bank)	15d	39°00.37′	75°08.35′	−0 36	0 00	−0 05	+0 24	0.5	0.4	---	---	0.6	339°	---	---	1.1	164°
4171	BRANDYWINE SHOAL LIGHT, 0.5mm west of	400	38°58.7′	75°16.6′	−0 44	−0 51	−0 41	−0 11	0.5	0.7	0.1	061°	0.7	334°	0.1	---	0.6	153°
4176	Brandywine Ra. (off Brandywine Shoal N)	15d	39°02.32′	75°17.05′	−0 07	−0 13	+0 04	+1 00	0.6	0.5	---	---	0.7	326°	0.1	233°	0.9	145°
4181	Big Stone Beach, 2.8 miles southeast of	120	39°02.32′	75°09.48′	−0 10	+0 13	+0 13	+1 06	0.9	0.5	---	---	0.6	319°	---	---	0.7	135°
4186	Big Stone Beach, 2.2 n.mi. ENE of	300	39°03.00′	75°09.48′	−0 20	+0 07	+0 10	+0 51	0.9	0.5	0.0	071°	1.2	344°	0.1	249°	1.2	160°
4191	Fourteen Ft. Bank Lt., 1.4 n.mi. SSE of	13d	39°03.00′	75°09.22′	−0 10	+0 07	+0 09	+0 01	0.7	0.5	0.0	069°	0.9	349°	0.1	---	0.7	179°
	do.		39°06.4′	75°09.22′	−0 53	−0 26	−0 08	−0 37	0.6	0.5	0.1	085°	0.9	352°	0.1	269°	1.6	174°
4196	Fourteen Ft. Bank Lt., 1.2 mi. east of		39°06.4′	75°11.28′	−0 30	−0 26	−0 31	−0 30	0.6	0.5	0.1	---	0.9	355°	---	---	0.9	159°
4201	Deadman Shoal, 3.1 n.mi. SW of	9d	39°04.97′	75°07.2′	−0 40	−0 03	−0 21	+1 40	0.7	0.6	0.1	067°	2.4	341°	1.0	---	1.0	159°
4206	Egg Island Flats		39°13.0′	74°59.6′	+0 51	+0 45	+1 04	+1 35	0.8	0.8	0.0	---	1.1	012°	1.0	---	1.0	192°
4211	Brandywine Range at Miah Mauli Range		39°17.2′	75°02.4′	+1 01	+1 27	+1 24	+1 29	1.7	1.2	---	---	0.2	000°	2.4	---	2.4	180°
4216	Maurice River entrance	16d	39°04′	76°23′	−0 01	−0 01	−0 04	+0 47	0.4	0.5	0.0	---	0.6	334°	0.0	---	0.7	122°
4221	Mauricetown Bridge, Maurice River		39°10.72′	75°16.40′	+0 19	+0 50	+0 11	+1 12	1.1	0.9	0.0	---	0.9	348°	0.0	---	1.2	164°
4226	Millville Drawbridge, Maurice River <25>	15d	39°11.4′	75°12	+1 19	+0 41	+1 27	+2 27	1.1	1.1	0.0	254°	0.9	338°	0.1	241°	1.3	160°
4231	St. Jones River ent., 1 mile east of	12d	39°14.87′	75°18.93′	+1 48	+1 30	+1 30	+2 37	1.4	1.7	0.2	047°	1.8	342°	0.2	047°	2.2	168°
4236	Kelly Island, 1.5 miles east of	43d	39°14.87′	75°20.88′	+2 06	+1 38	+1 17	+2 09	1.3	1.4	0.2	047°	1.9	321°	0.2	047°	2.2	147°
4241	Miah Mauli Range at Cross Ledge Range		39°16.3′	75°18.2′	+1 01	+1 17	+1 15	+1 21	0.6	0.9	0.1	---	1.2	328°	0.1	---	1.2	168°
4246	False Egg Island Point, 2 miles off		39°16.9′	75°18.2′	+0 57	+0 58	+1 31	+1 49	0.9	0.9	0.1	---	1.2	308°	0.1	---	0.3	122°
4251	Ben Davis Pt Shoal, southwest of	14d	39°20.9′	75°21.6′	+1 30	+1 20	+1 20	+1 31	1.1	1.1	0.1	---	1.2	074°	0.1	---	1.9	254°
4256	Ben Davis Point, 3.2 n.mi. SW of	29d	39°25.6′	75°14.2′	+2 27	+2 18	+2 27	+2 52	0.9	1.1	0.0	---	2.1	000°	0.0	---	0.3	180°
4261	Ben Davis Point, 0.8 mile southwest of		39°22.67′	75°28.07′	+1 50	+2 08	+2 16	+3 10	1.5	1.4	0.1	047°	2.1	324°	0.1	055°	1.9	140°
4266	Cohansey River, 0.5 mile above entrance		39°27.1′	75°28.07′	+1 49	+1 41	+2 18	+2 30	1.2	1.4	0.1	225°	1.2	327°	0.1	---	1.3	140°
4271	Bridgeton (Broad Street Bridge) <1>	14d	39°26.8′	75°30.8′	+3 24	+2 49	+2 16	+3 27	0.9	1.3	0.0	---	1.2	250°	0.0	---	1.5	070°
4276	Arnold Point, 2.2 n.mi WSW of		39°27.1′	75°33.8′	+3 02	+2 54	+2 38	+2 55	1.1	1.5	0.0	---	1.0	324°	0.0	---	1.9	151°
	do.	14d	39°28.20′	75°33.88′	+2 34	+2 38	+2 46	+4 06	1.1	0.9	0.0	267°	1.2	231°	0.0	---	1.2	048°
4281	Smyrna River entrance		39°30.7′	75°33.4′	+3 02	+3 00	+2 46	+3 44	1.7	2.0	0.0	---	2.1	346°	0.0	---	2.6	175°
4286	Stony Point, channel west of		39°31.6′	75°31.6′	+4 01	+4 18	+3 18	+4 27	1.5	1.6	0.0	---	2.4	027°	0.0	---	2.1	194°
4291	Appoquinimink River entrance		39°33.9′	75°31.7′	+3 57	+2 56	+3 28	+5 57	0.9	2.0	0.0	---	2.1	129°	0.0	---	2.1	325°
4296	Artificial Island (Baker Range)		39°27.1′	75°27.1′	+3 04	+3 04	+3 28	+4 21	1.4	1.6	0.0	---	1.1	000°	0.0	---	1.4	209°
4316	Chesapeake and Delaware Canal Entrance	15d	39°33.65′	75°34.20′	+6 05	+5 30	+6 31	+6 16	1.0	1.5	0.0	---	1.4	284°	0.0	---	2.0	067°

NOTES

SEE ENDNOTES ON PAGE 106

TABLE 2 – CURRENT DIFFERENCES AND OTHER CONSTANTS

NOTES

No.	PLACE	Meter Depth (ft)	POSITION Latitude North	POSITION Longitude West	TIME DIFF. Min. before Flood (h m)	TIME DIFF. Flood (h m)	TIME DIFF. Min. before Ebb (h m)	TIME DIFF. Ebb (h m)	SPEED RATIOS Flood	SPEED RATIOS Ebb	AVG Minimum before Flood (knots)	AVG Minimum before Flood (Dir.)	AVG Maximum Flood (knots)	AVG Maximum Flood (Dir.)	AVG Minimum before Ebb (knots)	AVG Minimum before Ebb (Dir.)	AVG Maximum Ebb (knots)	AVG Maximum Ebb (Dir.)
	CHESAPEAKE BAY—cont. Time meridian, 75° W						on Baltimore Harbor Approach, p.72											
4896	Cove Point, 1.1 n.mi. east of	17d	38°22.88	76°21.62	−2.57	−2.42	−2.40	−2.14	0.9	0.9	—	—	0.7	342°	—	—	0.7	165°
	do.	40d	38°22.88	76°21.62	−3.22	−3.19	−2.38	−3.26	0.8	0.7	—	—	0.6	343°	0.1	246°	0.6	165°
4901	Cove Point, 2.7 n.mi. east of	15d	38°22.80	76°19.52	−2.23	−2.39	−2.59	−2.40	0.5	0.9	—	—	0.4	344°	—	—	0.7	169°
	do.	40d	38°22.80	76°19.52	−3.15	−3.15	−1.53	−2.40	0.7	0.6	—	—	0.8	347°	—	—	0.5	170°
	do.	99d	38°22.80	76°19.52	−3.49	−4.02	−3.13	−3.36	0.7	0.5	—	—	0.6	341°	—	—	0.4	165°
4906	Cove Point, 3.9 n.mi. east of	11d	38°22.52	76°17.92	−2.29	−3.36	−4.08	−3.44	0.7	0.6	—	—	0.3	346°	—	—	0.6	171°
4911	Cove Point, 4.9 n.mi. NNE of	15d	38°22.60	76°22.60	−2.57	−2.29	−2.24	−2.26	0.4	0.7	—	—	0.8	333°	—	—	0.6	169°
	do.	40d	38°23.03	76°22.60	−3.23	−2.47	−1.58	−2.17	1.0	0.4	—	—	0.4	332°	—	—	0.3	149°
	do.	67d	38°28.9	76°28.9	−3.55	−3.38	−2.14	−2.58	0.6	0.4	0.0	—	0.4	321°	0.0	—	0.4	156°
4916	Kenwood Beach, 1.5 miles northeast of		38°31.1'	76°28.9	−2.16	−2.41	−2.46	−2.37	0.6	0.7	0.0	—	0.4	340°	0.0	—	0.4	175°
4921	James Island, 3.4 miles west of		38°31.5'	76°25.2	−2.31	−2.59	−3.01	−2.02	0.5	0.4	0.0	—	0.2	000°	0.0	—	0.3	175°
4926	James Island, 2.5 miles WNW of		38°32.5	76°23.6	−1.66	−2.31	−2.20	−2.36	0.2	0.7	0.0	—	0.2	000°	0.0	—	0.6	155°
4931	Plum Point, 1.4 miles ESE of		38°36.75	76°28.88	−2.31	−3.34	−2.20	−2.54	0.6	0.5	—	—	0.2	037°	—	—	0.6	209°
4936	Sharp Island Lt., 2.3 n.mi. SE of	20d	38°36.43	76°25.22	−3.15	−3.34	−1.33	−1.53	0.4	0.7	0.1	116°	0.4	357°	—	—	0.4	189°
4941	Sharp Island Lt., 2.5 n.mi. west of	18d	38°36.67	76°25.22	−1.49	−1.36	−1.57	−1.33	0.5	0.5	—	—	0.3	355°	—	—	0.3	186°
4946	Sharp Island Lt., 3.4 n.mi. west of	18d	38°38.63	76°26.88	−1.39	−1.41	−1.57	−2.04	0.4	0.4	—	—	0.3	353°	—	—	0.3	189°
4951	Plum Point, 2.1 n.mi. NNE of	35d	38°38.70	76°28.88	−2.34	−2.23	−2.23	−2.24	0.4	0.6	—	—	0.3	350°	0.1	272°	0.4	174°
4956	Poplar Island, 2.2 n.mi. WSW of	14d	38°45.37	76°25.77	−1.50	−1.51	−0.57	−0.49	0.4	0.5	—	—	0.5	359°	—	—	0.6	185°
4961	Poplar Island, 3.0 n.mi. WSW of	14d	38°44.98	76°26.73	−0.44	−1.26	−0.59	−1.08	0.6	0.8	0.0	095°	0.4	355°	0.0	—	0.3	189°
4966	Holland Point, 2.0 n.mi. east of	15d	38°44.98	76°26.73	−1.08	−1.22	+2.01	−1.00	0.5	0.4	—	—	0.5	350°	—	—	0.3	172°
4971	Kent Point, 4 miles southwest of		38°45.10	76°29.93	−0.68	−1.21	−1.11	+1.13	0.6	0.6	—	—	0.2	354°	—	—	0.5	180°
4976	Kent Point, 1.3 miles south of		38°49.00	76°26.00	−1.20	−1.24	−3.63	−3.32	0.6	0.6	—	—	0.4	026°	—	—	0.4	210°
4981	Horseshoe Point, 1.7 miles east of	19	38°50.30	76°27.27	−1.03	−1.04	−1.11	−1.05	0.9	0.5	0.0	—	0.5	05B°	0.0	—	0.3	200°
4986	Bloody Point Bar Light, 0.6 n.mi. NNW of		38°50.57	76°21.70	−3.52	−3.38	−0.49	−1.05	0.9	0.5	0.0	—	0.5	03B°	0.0	—	0.3	190°
4991	Thomas Pt. Shoal Lt., 1.8 n.mi. SW of	22d	38°53.75	76°23.21	−2.24	−2.27	+1.02	−1.05	0.6	0.4	—	—	0.5	340°	—	—	0.3	188°
4996	Thomas Pt., 2.0 n.mi. east of	16d	38°53.46	76°25.62	−1.05	−0.09	−2.22	−2.20	0.6	1.3	0.1	102°	0.8	007°	0.1	120°	1.0	191°
5001	Thomas Pt. Shoal Lt., 0.5 n.mi. SE of	33d	38°53.46	76°25.62	−0.25	−1.18	−1.43	−1.20	0.7	0.7	0.0	—	0.5	01B°	0.0	—	0.6	198°
5006	Tolly Point, 1.6 miles east of	15d	38°56.07	76°25.02	−0.64	−1.25	−1.25	−1.24	0.6	0.9	0.0	—	0.5	35B°	0.0	—	0.7	198°
5011	Chesapeake Bay Bridge, main channel	41d	38°59.57	76°23.10	−0.08	−0.03	−0.37	+0.27	0.6	0.6	—	—	0.7	020°	—	—	0.7	199°
5016	Sandy Point, 2.3 n.mi. east of	15d	39°00.16	76°20.93	+0.19	+0.13	+0.13	+0.29	1.1	0.9	—	—	0.8	021°	—	—	0.7	210°
5021	Sandy Point, 0.8 n.mi. ESE of	43d	39°00.16	76°20.93	−1.33	−1.14	−0.48	−0.39	0.8	0.6	0.0	276°	0.9	028°	0.1	276°	1.2	197°
5026	BALTIMORE HBR. APP. (off Sandy Point)		39°00.24	76°22.80	−0.11	+0.24	−0.15	+0.05	1.8	1.5	—	—	0.7	021°	—	—	0.9	197°
5031	Craighill Channel entrance, Buoy 2C	38d	39°00.24	76°22.80	−0.59	−1.10	−0.59	−1.02	1.0	1.0	0.0	116°	0.8	023°	—	—	0.7	189°
						Daily predictions											
5036	Love Point, 2.8 miles NNE of	5d	39°02.42	76°18.73	−0.04	−0.01	−0.06	+0.09	1.0	0.5	0.0	—	0.8	340°	—	—	0.8	189°
5041	Love Point, 2.5 miles north of	15d	39°02.67	76°18.19	0.00	+0.01	−1.08	+0.18	0.5	0.6	0.0	116°	0.4	325°	0.1	244°	0.4	147°
						Current weak and variable											
5046	Love Point, 2.0 n.mi. north of		39°04.78	76°18.19	−0.48	+0.19	+0.27	−0.07	0.8	0.6	0.0	—	0.6	05B°	0.0	—	0.4	240°
5051	Craighill Channel, NE of Mountain Pt.	18d	39°04.44	76°18.19	−1.33	−0.45	−0.49	−0.38	0.8	0.5	0.0	325°	0.6	067°	0.1	334°	0.5	238°
5056	Craighill Channel, Belvidere Shoal		39°04.44	76°18.32	−0.45	−0.05	−0.07	−0.35	0.8	0.6	0.0	—	0.6	05B°	0.0	—	0.6	240°
5061	Craighill Channel, right outside quarter		39°05.68	76°18.19	+0.28	+0.40	+0.25	+0.34	0.7	0.5	0.1	270°	0.6	350°	0.1	270°	0.7	175°
5066	Swan Point, 2.7 n.mi. SW of	14d	39°06.48	76°18.32	+0.10	+0.46	+0.33	+0.19	0.6	0.5	0.0	—	0.6	360°	0.1	—	0.5	188°
5071	Swan Point, 2.15 n.mi. west of	27d	39°06.48	76°19.48	+0.12	+0.27	+0.34	+0.25	0.7	0.4	0.0	078°	0.6	34B°	0.0	—	0.5	170°
5076	Swan Point, 1.6 miles northwest of	18d	39°08.85	76°19.48	+0.18	+0.42	+0.38	+1.17	0.6	0.4	—	—	0.4	006°	—	—	0.3	170°
5081	Brewerton Channel Eastern Ext., Buoy "7"	14d	39°08.85	76°17.98	−0.27	+0.30	+1.05	+1.26	0.6	0.6	0.0	090°	0.8	00B°	0.0	—	0.3	203°
5086	Tolchester Channel, SW of Buoy "58B"	17d	39°10.78	76°18.87	+0.16	−0.02	−0.14	+1.57	0.5	0.5	0.2	302°	0.9	013°	—	—	0.4	229°
5091	Tolchester Channel, Buoy "22"	25d	39°10.95	76°16.87	+0.44	+0.20	+0.48	+0.48	1.1	0.7	0.2	—	0.7	02B°	—	—	0.5	217°
5096	Tolchester Channel, south of Buoy "38B"	15d	39°11.47	76°15.95	−0.09	+1.10	+0.59	+1.23	0.9	0.8	0.2	—	0.7	061°	0.1	151°	0.6	231°
5101	North Point, 2.5 miles northeast of	7	39°12.87	76°23.72	+1.25	+1.00	+0.53	+1.06	0.4	0.5	0.0	—	0.3	03B°	0.0	—	0.4	225°

SEE ENDNOTES ON PAGE 106

TABLE 2 – CURRENT DIFFERENCES AND OTHER CONSTANTS

No.	PLACE	Meter Depth (ft)	POSITION Latitude North	POSITION Longitude West	TIME DIFF. Min. before Flood (h m)	TIME DIFF. Flood (h m)	TIME DIFF. Min. before Ebb (h m)	TIME DIFF. Ebb (h m)	SPEED RATIO Flood	SPEED RATIO Ebb	Min. before Flood knots	Min. before Flood Dir.	Maximum Flood knots	Maximum Flood Dir.	Min. before Ebb knots	Min. before Ebb Dir.	Maximum Ebb knots	Maximum Ebb Dir.
	CHESAPEAKE BAY—cont. Time meridian, 75° W																	
	on Baltimore Harbor Approach																	
5106	Tolchester Beach, 0.33 n.mi. west of	15d	39°13.03'	76°14.90'	+0 49	+1 20	+1 22	+1 24	1.2	1.1	0.1	285°	1.0	015°	—	—	0.8	201°
5111	Podies Island, 4 miles southwest of		39°13.60'	76°19.88'	+0 59	+0 48	+0 56	+1 12	0.6	0.8	0.0	—	0.5	025°	0.0	—	0.6	210°
5116	Podies Island, 2.0 n.mi. SSW of	15d	39°14.78'	76°17.80'	+1 01	+0 58	+1 03	+1 20	0.9	0.7	0.2	327°	0.7	038°	0.0	—	0.6	238°
5121	Podies Island, 0.8 mile south of	7	39°16.5'	76°16.4'	+1 29	+1 24	+1 12	+1 20	0.7	0.7	0.2	—	0.7	060°	0.0	—	1.0	266°
5126	Miller Island, 1.5 miles ENE of	16d	39°16.5'	76°19.9'	+0 11	+0 15	+0 37	+0 25	0.6	0.3	0.0	—	0.5	000°	0.1	289°	0.2	185°
5136	Robins Point, 0.7 mile E of	17d	39°16.47'	76°13.57'	+1 28	+1 34	+1 45	+1 03	1.1	1.0	0.1	—	0.6	014°	0.2	—	0.8	206°
5141	Worton Point, 1.5 n.mi. WSW of	17d	39°18.70'	76°13.03'	+0 03	+0 45	+1 27	+1 03	1.4	1.1	0.0	—	0.8	025°	0.2	298°	0.8	210°
5146	Worton Point, 1.1 miles northwest of		39°19.9'	76°12.0'	+0 04	+1 45	+1 38	+1 36	1.1	1.3	0.0	—	0.8	040°	0.0	—	1.0	245°
5151	Howell Point, 0.8 n.mi. west of	15d	39°22.23'	76°07.80'	+2 30	+1 48	+1 19	+1 32	1.1	1.5	0.1	—	0.6	051°	0.0	—	1.0	235°
5156	Howell Point, 0.4 mile NNW of		39°22.6'	76°06.9'	+1 28	+1 24	+1 20	+1 33	1.1	1.2	0.0	—	0.8	080°	—	—	0.9	245°
5161	Grove Point, 0.7 n.mi. NW of	14d	39°23.78'	76°03.02'	+2 40	+2 01	+1 31	+1 18	1.1	1.1	0.1	131°	0.5	034°	1.0	—	0.8	211°
5166	Turkey Point, 1.2 n.mi. SW of	9d	39°26.60'	76°02.03'	+2 39	+1 30	+0 58	+2 03	0.6	0.8	0.2	101°	0.5	021°	0.0	—	0.6	199°
5171	Spesutie Island, channel north of	7	39°28.83'	76°04.90'	+2 42	+1 20	+1 49	+1 40	0.6	0.6	0.0	—	0.5	288°	—	—	0.5	100°
5176	Rocky Pt. (Elk Neck), 0.25 n.mi. SW of	9d	39°29.30'	75°59.85'	+2 42	+1 28	+1 14	+0 45	0.6	0.7	0.0	—	0.7	009°	0.0	—	0.5	196°
5181	Red Point, 0.2 mile N of, Northeast River	7	39°31.75'	75°59.08'	+1 42	+1 28	+1 57	+1 47	0.9	0.6	0.0	—	—	—	—	—	—	—
5186	Havre de Grace, Susquehanna River		39°33.13'	76°05.08'	Current weak and variable													
	ELK RIVER																	
6241	Arnold Point, 0.4 mile west of	17d	39°27.83'	75°58.45'	+1 39	+1 45	+1 24	+1 32	1.0	1.0	0.0	—	0.8	040°	0.0	—	0.8	216°
6246	Old Town Point Wharf, northwest of	29d	39°30.23'	75°55.12'	+2 00	+1 53	+1 49	+1 45	1.3	1.6	—	—	1.1	054°	—	—	1.3	242°
6251	Hendersons Point		39°33.2'	75°51.6'	+2 07	+2 04	+2 05	+2 05	1.2	1.4	—	—	0.9	055°	—	—	1.1	237°
	CHESAPEAKE and DELAWARE CANAL																	
	on Chesapeake & Delaware Canal																	
6256	Back Creek, 0.3 n.mi. W of Sandy Pt.	14d	39°31.67'	75°51.97'	-0 08	-0 21	-0 02	-0 09	0.6	0.7	—	—	1.2	052°	—	—	1.4	244°
	do.	31d	39°31.67'	75°51.97'	-0 06	-0 34	+0 08	-0 07	0.6	0.6	0.0	—	1.2	062°	1.0	—	1.2	240°
6261	C&D CANAL, Chesapeake City bridge		39°31.7'	75°48.7'	Daily predictions													
6266	Chesapeake City Bridge, 0.45 n.mi. E of	26d	39°31.67'	75°48.43'	-0 29	-0 20	-0 16	-0 15	1.0	0.8	—	—	2.0	092°	—	—	1.9	290°
	do.	37d	39°31.67'	75°48.43'	-0 33	-0 25	+0 19	-0 22	0.7	0.5	—	—	1.5	110°	—	—	1.4	273°
6271	Conrail Bridge, east of	17d	39°32.55'	75°42.15'	-0 37	-0 34	+0 10	-0 16	0.8	0.5	—	—	1.6	083°	—	—	0.9	276°
	do.	34d	39°33.17'	75°39.00'	-0 42	-0 32	+0 07	-0 16	0.9	0.5	—	—	1.7	099°	—	—	1.3	281°
6276	St. George Bridge, 0.1 n.mi. ENE of	18d	39°33.62'	75°34.20'	-0 59	-1 17	-0 40	-1 16	1.0	0.7	—	—	1.7	064°	—	—	1.3	247°
6281	Reedy Point Radio Tower, south of	19d			-1 07	-1 04	-0 02	-0 24	1.0	0.7	—	—	1.9	078°	—	—	1.3	265°
	BACK, GUNPOWDER and BUSH RIVERS																	
	on Baltimore Harbor Approach																	
6211	Lynch Point, Back River		39°16.0'	76°26.3'	0 00	-0 10	0 00	-0 10	0.7	0.5	0.0	—	0.6	310°	0.0	—	0.4	190°
6216	Gunpowder River entrance		39°18.7'	76°18.5'	-0 24	-0 41	+0 25	+0 05	0.6	0.4	0.0	—	0.4	040°	0.0	—	0.3	205°
6221	Bush River, 0.4 mil. SW of Bush Point		39°21.4'	76°16.4'	+0 07	-0 24	+0 21	+0 20	0.8	0.6	0.0	—	0.6	328°	0.0	—	0.5	165°
	SEVERN and MAGOTHY RIVERS																	
6131	Greenbury Point, 1.8 miles east of	8	38°58.40'	76°25.00'	-0 57	-1 05	-0 51	-0 47	0.8	0.8	0.0	—	0.6	070°	0.0	—	0.6	245°
6136	Annapolis		38°58.95'	76°28.50'	—	-3 35	—	-2 26	0.5	0.4	0.0	—	0.4	320°	0.0	—	0.3	155°
6141	Brewer Point, Severn River		39°01.83'	76°31.23'	—	-1 22	—	-2 50	0.4	0.4	0.0	—	0.3	275°	0.0	—	0.3	105°
6146	Mountain Point, Magothy River entrance		39°03.47'	76°26.23'	-2 20	-2 00	-1 29	-2 04	0.8	0.4	0.0	—	0.6	315°	0.0	—	0.3	125°
	CHESTER RIVER																	
6151	Love Point, 1.6 n.mi. east of	16d	39°02.05'	76°16.07'	-1 42	-1 15	-0 47	-1 15	1.0	0.9	0.1	278°	0.4	202°	0.1	261°	0.4	341°
6156	Kent Island Narrows (highway bridge)	4	38°58.23'	76°14.83'	-2 07	-2 25	-2 11	-2 50	1.2	1.1	0.0	—	0.7	009°	0.0	—	0.9	190°
6161	Hall Point, 0.7 n.mi. east of	16d	39°00.63'	76°10.95'	-0 51	-1 08	-1 12	-1 37	0.6	0.9	0.0	—	0.4	002°	0.0	—	0.5	168°
6166	Deep Point		39°00.63'	76°07.23'	-0 31	-0 33	-0 32	-0 32	0.8	0.6	0.0	—	0.5	066°	0.0	—	0.7	260°
6171	Chestertown		39°12.43'	76°03.67'	-0 21	+0 05	-0 02	-0 17	0.8	0.6	0.0	—	0.5	023°	0.0	—	0.5	220°

NOTES

SEE ENDNOTES ON PAGE 106

TABLE 2 – CURRENT DIFFERENCES AND OTHER CONSTANTS

No.	PLACE	Meter Depth (ft)	POSITION Latitude North	POSITION Longitude West	TIME DIFF. Min. before Flood (h m)	TIME DIFF. Flood (h m)	TIME DIFF. Min. before Ebb (h m)	TIME DIFF. Ebb (h m)	SPEED RATIOS Flood	SPEED RATIOS Ebb	AVG Min. before Flood (knots)	Dir.	AVG Maximum Flood (knots)	Dir.	AVG Min. before Ebb (knots)	Dir.	AVG Maximum Ebb (knots)	Dir.
	EASTERN BAY Time meridian, 75° W				*on Baltimore Harbor Approach.													
6071	Poplar Island, east of south end		38° 44.9'	76° 21.2'	−2 20	−2 20	−2 20	−2 20			0.0	---	1.0	000°	0.0	---	0.6	170°
6076	Kent Point, 1.4 n.mi. east of	15d	38° 50.33'	76° 20.25'	−3 04	−3 18	−3 49	−3 12	1.2	0.8	---	---		043°	---	---	0.3	233°
6081	Long Point, 1 mile southeast of		38° 50.6'	76° 19.6'	−3 40	−3 40	−3 40	−3 40	0.6	0.4	0.0	---	0.6	040°	0.0	---	0.4	235°
6086	Turkey Point, 1.3 miles WSW of		38° 53.68'	76° 19.65'	Current weak, and variable													
6091	Parson Island, 1.4 miles west of		38° 54.83'	76° 16.77'	Current weak, and variable													
6096	Parson Island, 0.7 mile NNE of		38° 55.68'	76° 14.33'	---	−2 45	---	−2 50	0.2	0.2	0.0	---	0.2	305°	0.0	---	0.2	159°
6101	Tilghman Point, 1 mile north of		38° 52.78'	76° 15.18'	---	−3 15	−3 17	−3 00	0.8	0.9	0.0	---	0.6	090°	0.0	---	0.5	265°
6106	Wye River, west of Bruffs Island		38° 51.28'	76° 11.88'	−2 33	−3 18	−3 43	−3 00	0.6	0.6	0.0	---	0.6	030°	0.0	---	0.7	190°
6111	Deepwater Point, Miles River	9	38° 48.33'	76° 11.55'	−3 48	−3 52	---	−3 14	0.4	0.2	0.0	---	0.3	215°	0.0	---	0.5	025°
6116	Long Point, 0.8 mi. east of, Miles River		38° 46.43'	76° 09.92'	---	−3 24	---	−3 45						055°			0.2	245°
	WEST and SOUTH RIVERS																	
6121	Cheston Point, south of, West River		38° 51.33'	76° 31.43'	Current weak, and variable													
6126	South River entrance		38° 54.77'	76° 29.43'	Current weak, and variable													
	PATAPSCO RIVER																	
6176	North Point, Brewerton Channel	15d	39° 10.70'	76° 26.65'	Current weak, and variable													
6181	Brewerton Angle		39° 12.08'	76° 30.78'	Current weak, and variable													
6186	Fort McHenry Angle		39° 15.45'	76° 34.63'	Current weak, and variable													
6191	Bear Creek entrance		39° 13.8'	76° 29.9'	Current weak, and variable													
6196	Curtis Creek entrance		39° 13.1'	76° 34.6'	Current weak, and variable													
6201	Fort McHenry, NW Harbor entrance		39° 15.8'	76° 34.5'	Current weak, and variable													
6206	Middle Branch entrance		39° 15.4'	76° 37.0'	Current weak, and variable													
	SASSAFRAS RIVER																	
6226	Grove Point		39° 22.7'	76° 02.6'	+0 46	+0 46	+0 51	+0 44	0.5	0.4	0.0	---	0.4	099°	0.0	---	0.3	288°
6231	Ordinary Point, 0.4 mile west of		39° 22.45'	75° 59.25'	+0 50	+0 37	+1 17	+0 58	0.6	0.5	0.0	---	0.5	165°	0.0	---	0.4	345°
6236	Georgetown		39° 21.67'	75° 53.17'	+1 00	+0 25	+0 56	+1 25	0.4	0.5	0.0	---	0.3	090°	0.0	---	0.4	200°
	CHOPTANK RIVER																	
6006	Cook Point, 1.4 n.mi. NNW of	15d	38° 38.83'	76° 18.40'	−3 52	−4 06	−4 03	−4 24	0.8	0.7	0.0	---	0.5	049°	---	---	0.5	241°
6011	do. (Holland Point, 2.0 n.mi. SSW of)	45d	38° 38.83'	76° 18.40'	−4 09	−4 05	−4 03	−4 12	0.8	0.6	0.1	145°	0.6	068°	---	---	0.5	292°
6016	do. (Chlora Point, 0.5 n.mi. SSW of)	14d	38° 40.43'	76° 18.40'	−3 54	−4 21	−3 26	−3 58	0.3	0.5	---	---	0.5	089°	---	---	0.2	262°
6021	Martin Point, 0.6 n.mi. west of	17d	38° 37.70'	76° 09.10'	−3 48	−3 32	−3 13	−3 34	0.2	0.4	---	---	0.4	139°	---	---	0.4	332°
6026	Howell Point, 0.5 n.mi. south of	24d	38° 37.63'	76° 09.10'	−3 17	−3 42	−3 22	−3 42	0.4	0.4	---	---	0.4	143°	---	---	0.3	323°
6031	Cambridge hwy. bridge, W. of Swing Span	18d	38° 36.23'	76° 08.15'	−2 48	−4 04	−3 52	−3 34	0.3	0.5	---	---	0.3	155°	---	---	0.2	341°
6036	Off Jamaica Point		38° 34.72'	76° 03.67'	−2 05	−3 05	−1 07	−2 13	0.6	0.3	0.0	---	0.3	122°	---	---	0.6	274°
6041	Poplar Point, south of	7d	38° 36.52'	75° 59.98'	−1 52	−2 50	−1 44	−2 26	0.6	0.8	0.0	---	0.6	132°	---	---	0.6	316°
6046	Dover Bridge	18d	38° 40.07'	75° 59.92'	−1 19	−1 50	−1 56	−2 15	1.0	1.0	0.0	---	0.9	000°	---	---	0.8	205°
6051	Oxford, Tred Avon River		38° 41.72'	76° 10.67'	---	−4 06	−1 56	−1 47	1.1	1.0	0.0	---	0.9	308°	---	---	0.8	100°
6056	Easton Pt. 0.5 mi. below, Tred Avon River		38° 45.8'	76° 06.2'	Current weak, and variable													
6061	Mulberry Pt., 0.6 mi. S of, Broad Creek		38° 44.33'	76° 14.95'	−4 07	−4 10	---	−1 18	0.4	0.2	0.0	---	0.3	050°	0.0	---	0.2	170°
6066	Bald Eagle Pt., east of, Harris Creek		38° 43.75'	76° 18.30'	---	−4 27	−4 07	−1 14	0.5	0.5	0.0	---	0.4	040°	0.0	---	0.4	175°
	PATUXENT RIVER																	
5956	Hog Point, 0.6 n.mi. north of	13d	38° 19.08'	76° 24.07'	−4 45	−5 29	−5 59	−6 08	0.5	0.6	0.0	---	0.4	259°	0.1	358°	0.5	070°
5961	do.	41d	38° 19.08'	76° 24.07'	−6 24	−5 38	−5 56	−6 38	0.5	0.3	0.0	---	0.4	263°	0.0	---	0.2	061°
5966	Drum Point, 0.3 mile SSE of		38° 18.93'	76° 25.15'	−5 19	−5 20	−5 25	−5 16	0.5	0.5	0.0	---	0.4	246°	0.0	---	0.5	066°
5971	Sandy Point, 0.5 mile south of		38° 18.50'	76° 27.50'	−5 08	−5 49	−5 53	−6 01	0.5	0.9	0.0	---	0.4	300°	0.0	---	0.5	125°
5976	Point Patience, 0.1 mile southwest of	15	38° 19.70'	76° 29.20'	−5 07	−6 12	−0 46	−5 16	0.5	1.0	0.0	---	0.5	315°	0.0	---	0.8	145°
5981	Broomes Island, 0.4 mile south of <62>		38° 23.70'	76° 33.25'	−5 01	−5 16	−6 02	−5 02	0.5	0.8	0.0	---	0.4	290°	0.0	---	0.6	110°
5986	Sheridan Point, 0.1 mile southwest of		38° 22.97'	76° 38.88'	−4 33	−4 54	−4 38	−4 16	0.8	0.8	0.0	---	0.8	320°	0.0	---	0.5	155°
5991	Benedict, highway bridge		38° 30.70'	76° 40.33'	−4 45	−4 38	−4 09	−4 35	1.0	0.8	0.0	---	0.8	025°	0.0	---	0.5	190°
5991	Lyons Creek Wharf		38° 44.8'	76° 41.1'	−3 14	−3 24	−3 52	−3 29	1.4	1.1	0.0	---	1.1	318°	0.0	---	0.9	140°

NOTES

SEE ENDNOTES ON PAGE 106

END NOTES

< 1> The times of minimum before flood and minimum before ebb are indefinite.

< 2> Current speeds up to 9.0 knots have been observed in the vicinity of the Boilers.

< 3> Current turns westward, just before the end of the flood.

< 4> Current tends to rotate counterclockwise, flood direction swings from westward to southward.

< 5> Observations indicate that current floods about 11 hours and ebbs about 1 1/2 hours. Minimum before flood occurs about 4 1/2 hours earlier, maximum flood about 1 hour later, minimum before ebb about 1/2 hour later, and maximum ebb about 1 1/2 hours earlier than corresponding predictions at Portsmouth Harbor Entrance. Average ebb speed is less than 0.5 knot.

< 6> Current is variable; current speeds are usually less than 1 knot. Currents are strong in the entrance to Menemsha Pond.

< 7> In the open waters of Buzzards Bay, except in the entrance and off Penikese Island and West Island, the current is too weak and variable to be predicted.

< 8> The currents in Narragansett Bay have a pronounced irregularity which is evidenced at times during the month by a long period of approximate slack water preceding the flood, and at other times by a double flood of two distinct maximums of speed separated by a period of lesser speed. These peculiarities appear to be somewhat unstable, consequently, flood currents differing from those predicted should be expected. The ebb current is fairly regular and the predictions for maximum ebb will usually agree closely with the current encountered.

< 9> At minimum flood, current sometimes ebbs for a short period.

<10> At minimum flood, current frequently ebbs for a short period.

<11> Flood is too weak to be predicted. Time difference gives mid-point of 4 hour stand of weak and variable current and time of maximum ebb.

<12> Inside breakwaters, in channel, the current is only 0.4 knot.

<13> Current seldom floods.

<14> Near Tongue Point, Bridgeport Harbor, the current is weak and irregular.

<15> Tidal current is weak, averaging about 0.1 knot at maximum.

<16> For maximum southward current only, the gates of the lock being closed to prevent northward flow. Apply difference and ratio to maximum ebb at The Narrows.

<17> The values for the Hudson River are for the summer months, when the freshwater discharge is a minimum.

<18> In Roundout Creek entrance (between lights), eddies on the flood make navigation difficult. Little difficulty should be experienced on the ebb.

<19> Current does not flood.

<20> Current is rotary, turning clockwise. It flows northwest at times of "minimum before flood" at The Narrows; northeast 1 hour after maximum flood; southeast 1 1/2 hours after "minimum before ebb"; and southwest 2 hours after maximum ebb.

<21> Current is rotary, turning clockwise. Minimum current of 0.2 knot sets west about the time of "minimum before flood" at The Narrows. Minimum current of 0.2 knot sets ENE about the time of "minimum before ebb" at The Narrows.

<22> In Sandy Hook Bay (except in southern extremity) the current is weak.

<23> Tidal current is weak and rotary, averaging about 0.1 knot at maximum.

<24> The times of minimum before flood and ebb are variable.

<25> Current usually ebbs during the period 3 hours before to 3 hours after maximum ebb. Flood is weak and variable.

<26> To obtain speeds in midchannel use speed ratio 0.8.

<27> Flood is usually weak and of short duration. A weak ebb or flood current occurs about 6 hours after maximum flood at Delaware Bay Entrance.

<28> Tidal current is weak and rotary, averaging less than 0.1 knot. .

<29> Current tends to rotate clockwise. At times of "minimum before flood" there may be a weak current flowing WSW while at times of "minimum before ebb" there may be a weak current flowing ENE.

<30> Current tends to rotate clockwise. At times of "minimum before flood" there may be a weak current flowing southwest, while at times of "minimum before ebb" there may be a weak current flowing north.

<31> Flood usually flows northward, however, direction is variable.

<32> Flood is variable, current sometimes changes to ebb for a short time during the flood period.

<33> Due to changes in the waterway, average speed values given are probably too large.

<34> Flood usually occurs in a southerly direction and the ebb in a northeastwardly direction.

<35> Flood is weak and variable.

<36> Current tends to rotate clockwise. At times of "minimum before flood" there may be a weak current flowing northward while at times of "minimum before ebb" there may be a weak current flowing southeastward.

Continued on last page

Bay of Fundy Entrance (Grand Manan Channel), 2004

F—Flood, Dir. 032° True   E—Ebb, Dir. 212° True

April

Day	Slack h m	Maximum h m	knots
1 Th		0000	0.8E
	0235	0535	1.0F
	0850	1215	1.3E
	1505	1830	1.6F
	2205		
2 F		0100	1.4E
	0345	0650	1.5F
	0955	1310	1.8E
	1600	1915	2.2F
	2240		
3 Sa		0140	2.0E
	0435	0735	2.1F
	1040	1350	2.3E
	1645	1955	2.8F
	2315		
4 Su		0320	2.6E
	0615	0915	2.7F
	1220	1630	2.8E
	1825	2135	3.3F
5 M ○	0050	0355	3.1E
	0655	0955	3.1F
	1300	1605	3.1E
	1900	2210	3.7F
6 Tu	0120	0430	3.5E
	0730	1030	3.5F
	1340	1645	3.3E
	1940	2245	3.9F
7 W	0155	0505	3.7E
	0810	1110	3.6F
	1415	1720	3.3E
	2015	2320	3.9F
8 Th	0230	0545	3.7E
	0850	1145	3.6F
	1455	1800	3.1E
	2055		
9 F		0000	3.7F
	0310	0620	3.5E
	0930	1225	3.4F
	1540	1840	2.8E
	2135		
10 Sa		0040	3.3F
	0350	0650	3.1E
	1015	1310	3.0F
	1625	1925	2.3E
	2220		
11 Su ○		0125	2.8F
	0435	0750	2.6E
	1105	1400	2.5F
	1725	2025	1.8E
	2315		
12 M		0215	2.2F
	0525	0855	2.1E
	1205	1505	2.0F
	1840	2140	1.3E
13 Tu	0025	0325	1.6F
	0640	1015	1.7E
	1320	1630	1.7F
	2020	2320	1.2E
14 W	0200	0500	1.3F
	0820	1145	1.6E
	1445	1810	1.8F
	2150		
15 Th		0045	1.5E
	0335	0645	1.5F
	0950	1305	1.8E
	1600	1925	2.1F
	2250		
16 F		0150	1.9E
	0445	0750	1.9F
	1055	1405	2.2E
	1655	2020	2.5F
	2340		
17 Sa		0235	2.4E
	0535	0840	2.3F
	1145	1450	2.5E
	1745	2100	2.8F
18 Su	0015	0320	2.7E
	0620	0920	2.6F
	1230	1530	2.7E
	1820	2135	3.1F
19 M ●	0050	0355	3.0E
	0655	0955	2.8F
	1305	1605	2.7E
	1855	2205	3.1F
20 Tu	0120	0425	3.0E
	0730	1025	2.9F
	1335	1640	2.7E
	1925	2235	3.1F
21 W	0145	0455	3.0E
	0800	1055	2.9F
	1405	1710	2.5E
	1955	2300	3.0F
22 Th	0210	0525	2.9E
	0830	1125	2.8F
	1435	1735	2.3E
	2025	2320	2.8F
23 F	0235	0550	2.7E
	0900	1155	2.6F
	1505	1805	2.0E
	2055	2355	2.6F
24 Sa	0300	0620	2.4E
	0930	1225	2.3F
	1535	1830	1.7E
	2120		
25 Su		0025	2.2F
	0330	0650	2.1E
	1005	1300	2.1F
	1615	1905	1.3E
	2155		
26 M		0105	1.9F
	0405	0725	1.7E
	1045	1345	1.8F
	1700	1955	1.0E
	2245		
27 Tu		0150	1.5F
	0450	0815	1.4E
	1135	1440	1.5F
	1815	2110	0.8E
	2350		
28 W		0255	1.1F
	0555	0940	1.1E
	1240	1555	1.3F
	1955	2250	0.8E
29 Th	0130	0425	1.0F
	0740	1120	1.2E
	1410	1730	1.5F
	2115		
30 F		0020	1.2E
	0305	0600	1.2F
	0915	1235	1.5E
	1520	1840	1.9F
	2215		

May

Day	Slack h m	Maximum h m	knots
1 Sa		0115	1.7E
	0410	0710	1.7F
	1020	1330	1.9E
	1620	1935	2.4F
	2255		
2 Su		0205	2.3E
	0500	0800	2.3F
	1110	1415	2.4E
	1705	2020	2.9F
	2335		
3 M		0245	2.8E
	0545	0845	2.8F
	1155	1500	2.8E
	1750	2100	3.3F
4 Tu ○	0015	0325	3.2E
	0625	0925	3.2F
	1235	1540	3.0E
	1830	2140	3.6F
5 W	0050	0405	3.5E
	0705	1005	3.5F
	1315	1620	3.1E
	1910	2220	3.7F
6 Th	0130	0440	3.6E
	0745	1045	3.6F
	1400	1700	3.1E
	1955	2300	3.6F
7 F	0205	0520	3.5E
	0830	1125	3.5F
	1440	1740	2.9E
	2035	2340	3.4F
8 Sa	0245	0605	3.3E
	0910	1210	3.2F
	1525	1825	2.6E
	2120		
9 Su		0020	3.0F
	0330	0650	2.9E
	0955	1255	2.9F
	1620	1920	2.1E
	2210		
10 M		0110	2.5F
	0420	0740	2.5E
	1050	1350	2.5F
	1720	2020	1.7E
	2310		
11 Tu ○		0205	2.0F
	0520	0845	2.0E
	1150	1455	2.1F
	1835	2135	1.5E
12 W	0020	0315	1.6F
	0635	1000	1.7E
	1300	1610	1.8F
	2000	2255	1.4E
13 Th	0145	0445	1.4F
	0815	1120	1.6E
	1415	1735	1.9F
	2110		
14 F		0010	1.6E
	0305	0610	1.5F
	0925	1230	1.8E
	1520	1845	2.1F
	2210		
15 Sa		0110	2.0E
	0410	0715	2.0F
	1025	1330	2.0E
	1620	1935	2.3F
	2300		
16 Su		0200	2.3E
	0500	0805	2.1F
	1115	1415	2.1E
	1705	2020	2.5F
	2335		
17 M		0245	2.5E
	0545	0845	2.3F
	1200	1455	2.2E
	1745	2055	2.6F
18 Tu	0010	0320	2.7E
	0620	0925	2.5F
	1235	1535	2.3E
	1820	2130	2.7F
19 W ●	0040	0355	2.7E
	0655	0955	2.6F
	1310	1610	2.2E
	1855	2200	2.7F
20 Th	0110	0425	2.7E
	0730	1025	2.6F
	1340	1640	2.1E
	1925	2230	2.6F
21 F	0140	0455	2.6E
	0800	1055	2.6F
	1415	1710	2.0E
	2000	2300	2.5F
22 Sa	0205	0525	2.5E
	0830	1130	2.5F
	1445	1745	1.8E
	2030	2335	2.3F
23 Su	0235	0555	2.3E
	0905	1205	2.4F
	1520	1820	1.7E
	2110		
24 M		0010	2.1F
	0310	0635	2.1E
	0945	1245	2.2F
	1605	1900	1.5E
	2150		
25 Tu		0055	1.9F
	0355	0715	1.9E
	1030	1330	2.0F
	1655	1955	1.3E
	2245		
26 W		0145	1.7F
	0445	0810	1.6E
	1120	1425	1.9F
	1755	2100	1.2E
	2350		
27 Th		0245	1.5F
	0550	0920	1.5E
	1220	1530	1.8F
	1905	2215	1.3E
28 F	0105	0400	1.4F
	0710	1035	1.5E
	1330	1640	1.9F
	2015	2325	1.6E
29 Sa	0220	0515	1.5F
	0830	1145	1.7E
	1435	1750	2.1F
	2115		
30 Su		0025	2.0E
	0325	0620	1.9F
	0940	1245	1.9E
	1535	1850	2.4F
	2210		
31 M		0120	2.4E
	0420	0725	2.3F
	1035	1340	2.2E
	1630	1940	2.8F
	2255		

June

Day	Slack h m	Maximum h m	knots
1 Tu		0210	2.8E
	0510	0815	2.7F
	1125	1430	2.5E
	1720	2030	3.0F
	2340		
2 W		0255	3.1E
	0600	0900	3.0F
	1215	1515	2.7E
	1805	2115	3.2F
3 Th ○	0025	0340	3.3E
	0645	0945	3.2F
	1300	1600	2.8E
	1855	2200	3.3F
4 F	0105	0425	3.4E
	0730	1030	3.3F
	1345	1645	2.8E
	1940	2240	3.2F
5 Sa	0150	0510	3.3E
	0815	1115	3.3F
	1435	1735	2.7E
	2025	2320	3.0F
6 Su	0235	0555	3.1E
	0900	1200	3.1F
	1525	1825	2.5E
	2115		
7 M		0015	2.8F
	0325	0645	2.8E
	0945	1250	2.9F
	1615	1915	2.2E
	2210		
8 Tu		0105	2.4F
	0415	0735	2.5E
	1035	1340	2.6F
	1710	2015	2.0E
	2305		
9 W		0200	2.1F
	0510	0830	2.2E
	1130	1435	2.3F
	1810	2115	1.8E
10 Th	0005	0300	1.8F
	0620	0935	1.9E
	1230	1535	2.1F
	1915	2220	1.7E
11 F	0115	0410	1.6F
	0730	1040	1.7E
	1330	1640	2.0F
	2020	2325	1.7E
12 Sa	0230	0520	1.6F
	0840	1145	1.6E
	1430	1745	1.9F
	2115		
13 Su		0025	1.8E
	0325	0625	1.6F
	0945	1245	1.6E
	1525	1845	1.9F
	2205		
14 M		0115	2.0E
	0420	0725	1.6F
	1040	1335	1.6E
	1620	1935	2.0F
	2250		
15 Tu		0205	2.1E
	0505	0810	1.7F
	1130	1425	1.7E
	1705	2015	2.0F
	2330		
16 W		0245	2.2E
	0550	0850	2.1F
	1215	1505	1.7E
	1750	2055	2.1F
17 Th ●	0005	0325	2.3E
	0625	0930	2.2F
	1250	1545	1.8E
	1830	2130	2.2F
18 F	0040	0400	2.3E
	0705	1005	2.3F
	1325	1625	1.8E
	1905	2210	2.2F
19 Sa	0115	0435	2.3E
	0740	1040	2.4F
	1400	1700	1.8E
	1945	2245	2.2F
20 Su	0150	0510	2.3E
	0815	1115	2.5F
	1435	1735	1.9E
	2025	2320	2.1F
21 M	0225	0545	2.3E
	0850	1155	2.5F
	1515	1815	1.9E
	2105		
22 Tu		0005	2.2F
	0305	0625	2.3E
	0930	1235	2.5F
	1555	1900	1.9E
	2150		
23 W		0045	2.2F
	0415	0710	2.2E
	1015	1315	2.5F
	1640	1945	1.9E
	2240		
24 Th		0135	2.1F
	0440	0800	2.1E
	1100	1405	2.5F
	1730	2035	1.9E
	2335		
25 F		0230	2.0F
	0535	0850	2.0E
	1150	1455	2.4F
	1825	2135	1.9E
26 Sa	0035	0325	2.0F
	0635	0950	2.0E
	1245	1555	2.3F
	1920	2235	2.0E
27 Su	0135	0430	2.0F
	0745	1055	1.8E
	1345	1655	2.3F
	2020	2335	2.1E
28 M	0240	0540	2.0F
	0855	1200	1.8E
	1450	1800	2.3F
	2120		
29 Tu		0040	2.3E
	0345	0645	2.2F
	1005	1305	2.0E
	1550	1900	2.4F
	2315		
30 W		0135	2.5E
	0440	0745	2.5F
	1105	1405	2.1E
	1650	2000	2.6F
	2315		

All times are local time. Daylight Saving Time has been used when needed.

NOTES:

Bay of Fundy Entrance (Grand Manan Channel), 2004

F—Flood, Dir. 032° True   E—Ebb, Dir. 212° True

July

Date	Slack h m	Max h m	knots
1 Th		0230	2.8E
	0535	0840	2.7F
	1200	1500	2.3E
	1750	2055	2.7F
2 F ○		0325	3.0E
	0630	0935	3.0F
	1255	1555	2.5E
	1845	2145	2.9F
3 Sa	0055	0415	3.1E
	0715	1025	3.1F
	1345	1645	2.6E
	1935	2235	2.9F
4 Su	0145	0500	3.1E
	0805	1110	3.2F
	1430	1735	2.7E
	2025	2325	2.9F
5 M	0230	0550	3.1E
	0850	1155	3.2F
	1515	1820	2.7E
	2115		
6 Tu		0010	2.8F
	0320	0635	2.9E
	0935	1240	3.1F
	1605	1905	2.6E
	2200		
7 W		0055	2.6F
	0405	0720	2.7E
	1020	1325	2.9F
	1650	1955	2.4E
	2250		
8 Th		0145	2.4F
	0455	0810	2.4E
	1100	1405	2.6F
	1735	2045	2.2E
	2340		
9 F ○		0230	2.1F
	0545	0855	2.0E
	1150	1455	2.3F
	1825	2135	2.0E
10 Sa	0030	0320	1.8F
	0640	0950	1.7E
	1235	1540	2.0F
	1915	2225	1.8E
11 Su	0125	0420	1.6F
	0745	1045	1.3E
	1325	1635	1.7F
	2005	2325	1.6E
12 M	0225	0520	1.4F
	0855	1150	1.1E
	1425	1735	1.5F
	2105		
13 Tu		0025	1.5E
	0330	0630	1.4F
	1005	1255	1.0E
	1525	1840	1.4F
	2200		
14 W		0125	1.6E
	0425	0735	1.5F
	1110	1355	1.1E
	1630	1935	1.4F
	2255		
15 Th		0215	1.7E
	0520	0830	1.6F
	1200	1445	1.2E
	1725	2030	1.6F
	2340		
16 F		0305	1.8E
	0605	0915	1.9F
	1245	1535	1.4E
	1815	2115	1.7F
17 Sa ●	0025	0345	2.0E
	0645	0950	2.1F
	1320	1615	1.7E
	1855	2155	2.0F
18 Su	0100	0425	2.2E
	0720	1030	2.4F
	1355	1650	1.9E
	1940	2235	2.2F
19 M	0140	0500	2.4E
	0800	1105	2.7F
	1425	1730	2.2E
	2020	2315	2.4F
20 Tu	0220	0535	2.5E
	0835	1140	2.9F
	1500	1805	2.4E
	2100	2355	2.6F
21 W	0255	0615	2.6E
	0910	1215	3.0F
	1535	1840	2.6E
	2140		
22 Th		0035	2.7F
	0340	0650	2.6E
	0950	1255	3.1F
	1615	1920	2.6E
	2220		
23 F		0115	2.7F
	0420	0735	2.5E
	1030	1340	3.0F
	1655	2005	2.5E
	2305		
24 Sa ○		0200	2.6F
	0510	0820	2.3E
	1115	1420	2.8F
	1740	2055	2.5E
25 Su	0030	0250	2.4F
	0600	0910	2.1E
	1205	1510	2.6F
	1830	2145	2.3E
26 M	0055	0350	2.2F
	0705	1010	1.8E
	1300	1610	2.3F
	1930	2250	2.3E
27 Tu	0200	0455	2.0F
	0820	1120	1.6E
	1405	1715	2.1F
	2035		
28 W		0000	2.1E
	0310	0610	2.0F
	0940	1240	1.6E
	1520	1830	2.0F
	2150		
29 Th		0110	2.2E
	0420	0725	2.2F
	1055	1350	1.8E
	1640	1945	2.1F
	2300		
30 F		0220	2.4E
	0525	0830	2.5F
	1200	1455	2.1E
	1745	2045	2.4F
31 Sa ○		0315	2.7E
	0620	0930	2.8F
	1255	1550	2.4E
	1845	2145	2.6F

August

Date	Slack h m	Max h m	knots
1 Su		0410	3.0E
	0710	1020	3.2F
	1340	1640	2.7E
	1935	2235	2.9F
2 M	0140	0455	3.1E
	0755	1100	3.4F
	1420	1725	2.9E
	2020	2315	3.0F
3 Tu	0225	0535	3.2E
	0835	1140	3.4F
	1500	1805	3.0E
	2100		
4 W		0000	3.0F
	0305	0620	3.1E
	0915	1220	3.4F
	1540	1845	2.9E
	2145		
5 Th		0035	2.9F
	0345	0655	2.8E
	0950	1250	3.2F
	1615	1920	2.8E
	2220		
6 F		0115	2.7F
	0425	0735	2.5E
	1025	1330	2.9F
	1650	2005	2.5E
	2300		
7 Sa		0155	2.3F
	0505	0815	2.1E
	1105	1405	2.5F
	1725	2040	2.1E
	2345		
8 Su		0235	2.0F
	0550	0855	1.6E
	1140	1445	2.0F
	1805	2125	1.8E
9 M	0030	0320	1.6F
	0640	0940	1.1E
	1220	1535	1.6F
	1850	2215	1.4E
10 Tu	0125	0415	1.2F
	0750	1045	0.8E
	1310	1620	1.2F
	1945	2325	1.2E
11 W	0230	0530	1.0F
	0930	1210	0.6E
	1425	1735	1.0F
	2105		
12 Th		0045	1.1E
	0345	0700	1.1F
	1100	1335	0.7E
	1600	1905	1.0F
	2225		
13 F		0155	1.3E
	0455	0815	1.4F
	1155	1440	1.0E
	1715	2015	1.2F
	2325		
14 Sa		0245	1.6E
	0545	0900	1.8F
	1235	1525	1.4E
	1805	2105	1.6F
15 Su ●	0010	0330	2.0E
	0625	0940	2.2F
	1305	1600	1.8E
	1850	2145	2.0F
16 M		0410	2.3E
	0705	1010	2.6F
	1335	1635	2.3E
	1925	2225	2.4F
17 Tu	0130	0440	2.6E
	0740	1045	3.0F
	1405	1710	2.6E
	2005	2300	2.8F
18 W	0205	0515	2.9E
	0810	1120	3.3F
	1435	1740	3.0E
	2040	2335	3.0F
19 Th	0240	0550	3.0E
	0845	1155	3.5F
	1505	1815	3.1E
	2115		
20 F		0015	3.2F
	0320	0625	3.0E
	0925	1230	3.5F
	1540	1850	3.1E
	2155		
21 Sa		0050	3.1F
	0400	0705	2.8E
	1000	1305	3.4F
	1620	1930	3.0E
	2240		
22 Su		0135	3.0F
	0440	0745	2.5E
	1040	1350	3.1F
	1700	2015	2.8E
	2325		
23 M ○		0220	2.7F
	0530	0835	2.1E
	1130	1435	2.7F
	1750	2105	2.4E
24 Tu	0020	0315	2.3F
	0630	0935	1.7E
	1225	1530	2.2F
	1845	2210	2.1E
25 W	0125	0420	1.9F
	0755	1055	1.4E
	1335	1645	1.8F
	2005	2335	1.8E
26 Th	0240	0550	1.8F
	0930	1225	1.3E
	1510	1815	1.6F
	2135		
27 F		0100	1.9E
	0405	0720	2.0F
	1055	1350	1.6E
	1635	1945	1.8F
	2255		
28 Sa		0210	2.2E
	0510	0830	2.4F
	1155	1450	2.1E
	1740	2050	2.2F
	2355		
29 Su		0310	2.6E
	0605	0920	2.9F
	1245	1545	2.6E
	1840	2140	2.6F
30 M		0355	3.0E
	0655	1005	3.3F
	1325	1625	3.0E
	1925	2225	2.9F
31 Tu	0130	0440	3.2E
	0735	1045	3.5F
	1400	1705	3.2E
	2005	2300	3.1F

September

Date	Slack h m	Max h m	knots
1 W	0210	0515	3.2E
	0810	1120	3.6F
	1435	1740	3.3E
	2040	2335	3.2F
2 Th	0245	0550	3.1E
	0845	1150	3.5F
	1510	1815	3.2E
	2115		
3 F		0010	3.0F
	0320	0625	2.8E
	0920	1220	3.3F
	1540	1850	2.9E
	2150		
4 Sa		0045	2.8F
	0355	0700	2.4E
	0950	1250	2.9F
	1605	1920	2.6E
	2225		
5 Su		0115	2.5F
	0425	0730	2.0E
	1020	1320	2.5F
	1635	1950	2.2E
	2300		
6 M		0150	2.0F
	0505	0800	1.5E
	1050	1355	2.0F
	1705	2025	1.7E
	2335		
7 Tu		0225	1.6F
	0545	0840	1.0E
	1120	1430	1.5F
	1740	2110	1.3E
8 W	0025	0315	1.2F
	0650	0935	0.6E
	1205	1515	1.1F
	1830	2220	1.1E
9 Th	0135	0430	0.9F
	0900	1135	0.3E
	1335	1640	0.7F
	2005		
10 F		0010	0.9E
	0305	0630	0.9F
	1050	1320	0.6E
	1540	1845	0.7F
	2200		
11 Sa		0130	1.1E
	0425	0755	1.3F
	1135	1420	1.0E
	1700	2005	1.2F
	2310		
12 Su		0225	1.6E
	0520	0840	1.9F
	1205	1500	1.6E
	1750	2050	1.7F
13 M		0305	2.0E
	0600	0915	2.4F
	1235	1535	2.1E
	1830	2125	2.2F
14 Tu ○	0030	0340	2.5E
	0635	0945	2.9F
	1305	1610	2.6E
	1905	2200	2.7F
15 W	0105	0415	2.8E
	0710	1020	3.3F
	1335	1640	3.1E
	1940	2235	3.1F
16 Th	0140	0450	3.1E
	0745	1050	3.6F
	1405	1715	3.4E
	2015	2310	3.4F
17 F	0215	0525	3.2E
	0820	1125	3.8F
	1435	1745	3.5E
	2050	2345	3.5F
18 Sa	0255	0600	3.1E
	0855	1200	3.7F
	1510	1825	3.4E
	2130		
19 Su		0025	3.4F
	0335	0635	2.9E
	0935	1240	3.5F
	1550	1900	3.2E
	2210		
20 M		0105	3.1F
	0415	0720	2.5E
	1015	1320	3.1F
	1630	1940	2.8E
	2255		
21 Tu		0155	2.7F
	0505	0805	2.0E
	1100	1405	2.5F
	1715	2040	2.4E
	2350		
22 W		0250	2.2F
	0610	0910	1.5E
	1200	1510	2.0F
	1820	2150	1.9E
23 Th	0100	0400	1.8F
	0745	1025	1.2E
	1325	1625	1.5F
	1945	2320	1.7E
24 F	0225	0540	1.7F
	0925	1220	1.3E
	1505	1810	1.4F
	2125		
25 Sa		0050	1.8E
	0350	0710	2.0F
	1045	1340	1.7E
	1630	1940	1.8F
	2245		
26 Su		0200	2.5E
	0455	0820	2.5F
	1140	1435	2.3E
	1735	2040	2.3F
	2345		
27 M		0250	2.6E
	0545	0905	2.9F
	1215	1525	2.8E
	1820	2125	2.7F
28 Tu ○	0030	0335	2.9E
	0630	0940	3.3F
	1300	1600	3.1E
	1900	2200	3.0F
29 W	0110	0415	3.1E
	0710	1015	3.5F
	1330	1640	3.3E
	1940	2235	3.2F
30 Th	0145	0450	3.1E
	0740	1050	3.5F
	1405	1710	3.3E
	2010	2310	3.1F

All times are local time. Daylight Saving Time has been used when needed.

NOTES:

Bay of Fundy Entrance (Grand Manan Channel), 2004

F–Flood, Dir. 032° True   E–Ebb, Dir. 212° True

October

Day	Slack (h m)	Maximum (h m)	knots
1 F	0220	0520	2.9E
	0815	1120	3.3F
	1430	1745	3.2E
	2045	2340	3.0F
2 Sa	0250	0555	2.6E
	0845	1145	3.1F
	1500	1810	2.9E
	2115		
3 Su		0010	2.8F
	0320	0625	2.3E
	0910	1215	2.8F
	1525	1840	2.6E
	2145		
4 M		0040	2.4F
	0355	0650	1.8E
	0940	1245	2.4F
	1550	1910	2.2E
	2220		
5 Tu		0115	2.1F
	0425	0720	1.4E
	1010	1315	1.9F
	1620	1940	1.7E
	2255		
6 W ○		0150	1.6F
	0510	0755	0.9E
	1040	1350	1.5F
	1655	2020	1.3E
	2345		
7 Th		0240	1.3F
	0615	0900	0.5E
	1135	1445	1.0F
	1745	2135	0.9E
8 F	0055	0355	1.0F
	0820	1105	0.4E
	1315	1610	0.7F
	1930	2335	0.9E
9 Sa	0225	0545	1.0F
	1000	1245	0.7E
	1515	1815	0.8F
	2130		
10 Su		0055	1.2E
	0345	0710	1.5F
	1050	1340	1.3E
	1630	1930	1.3F
	2235		
11 M		0150	1.6E
	0440	0800	2.0F
	1125	1425	1.8E
	1715	2015	1.9F
	2325		
12 Tu		0230	2.1E
	0520	0835	2.6F
	1155	1500	2.4E
	1755	2055	2.4F
13 W ●	0005	0310	2.5E
	0600	0910	3.0F
	1235	1535	2.9E
	1835	2135	2.9F
14 Th	0040	0345	2.9E
	0640	0945	3.4F
	1310	1610	3.3E
	1910	2210	3.3F
15 F	0115	0420	3.1E
	0715	1020	3.7F
	1330	1645	3.5E
	1945	2245	3.5F
16 Sa	0155	0455	3.2E
	0750	1055	3.8F
	1405	1720	3.6E
	2025	2325	3.5F
17 Su	0235	0535	3.1E
	0830	1135	3.6F
	1445	1755	3.5E
	2105		
18 M		0005	3.4F
	0315	0615	2.8E
	0910	1215	3.3F
	1525	1840	3.2E
	2150		
19 Tu		0045	3.1F
	0400	0700	2.4E
	0955	1300	2.9F
	1605	1925	2.7E
	2235		
20 W ○		0135	2.7F
	0455	0755	1.9E
	1045	1350	2.3F
	1700	2025	2.2E
	2335		
21 Th		0235	2.2F
	0605	0905	1.5E
	1155	1455	1.8F
	1805	2140	1.8E
22 F	0045	0350	1.9F
	0735	1035	1.3E
	1320	1620	1.4F
	1940	2310	1.7E
23 Sa	0205	0525	1.8F
	0920	1205	1.5E
	1455	1800	1.5F
	2115		
24 Su		0030	1.8E
	0325	0645	2.1F
	1015	1315	1.9E
	1610	1920	1.9F
	2225		
25 M		0130	2.1E
	0425	0745	2.6F
	1105	1410	2.4E
	1710	2015	2.3F
	2320		
26 Tu		0225	2.4E
	0530	0830	2.9F
	1150	1455	2.7E
	1755	2055	2.6F
27 W ○	0005	0305	2.7E
	0600	0910	3.1F
	1230	1530	3.0E
	1835	2135	2.8F
28 Th	0045	0345	2.7E
	0635	0945	3.1F
	1300	1605	3.1E
	1910	2210	2.9F
29 F	0120	0420	2.7E
	0710	1015	3.1F
	1330	1640	3.1E
	1945	2240	2.9F
30 Sa	0155	0455	2.5E
	0740	1045	2.9F
	1355	1710	2.9E
	2015	2310	2.8F
31 Su	0125	0425	2.3E
	0715	1015	2.8F
	1325	1640	2.7E
	1945	2240	2.6F

November

Day	Slack (h m)	Maximum (h m)	knots
1 M	0155	0455	2.0E
	0740	1045	2.5F
	1350	1710	2.4E
	2020	2315	2.3F
2 Tu	0230	0525	1.7E
	0815	1115	2.2F
	1420	1740	2.1E
	2050	2350	2.1F
3 W	0305	0600	1.3E
	0850	1150	1.8F
	1455	1815	1.7E
	2130		
4 Th		0030	1.8F
	0355	0645	1.0E
	0930	1235	1.5F
	1535	1905	1.4E
	2220		
5 F ○		0120	1.5F
	0455	0755	0.8E
	1035	1335	1.1F
	1635	2020	1.1E
	2325		
6 Sa		0230	1.3F
	0625	0930	0.8E
	1205	1505	1.0F
	1805	2150	1.1E
7 Su	0040	0355	1.4F
	0750	1050	1.1E
	1335	1630	1.1F
	1945	2305	1.3E
8 M	0150	0510	1.7F
	0845	1150	1.5E
	1445	1750	1.5F
	2055		
9 Tu		0005	1.7E
	0250	0605	2.1F
	0930	1235	2.0E
	1535	1835	2.0F
	2145		
10 W		0050	2.1E
	0340	0650	2.6F
	1010	1320	2.5E
	1620	1920	2.5F
	2230		
11 Th		0135	2.4E
	0425	0735	3.0F
	1050	1400	3.0E
	1700	2000	2.9F
	2310		
12 F ●		0255	2.7E
	0505	0815	3.3F
	1125	1445	3.3E
	1740	2040	3.2F
	2355		
13 Sa		0255	2.9E
	0550	0855	3.5F
	1205	1520	3.4E
	1825	2125	3.4F
14 Su	0035	0335	2.9E
	0630	0935	3.5F
	1245	1600	3.5E
	1905	2205	3.4F
15 M	0120	0420	2.8E
	0715	1015	3.3F
	1325	1640	3.3E
	1950	2250	3.3F
16 Tu	0205	0505	2.6E
	0800	1100	3.1F
	1410	1725	3.0E
	2035	2335	3.0F
17 W	0255	0555	2.3E
	0850	1150	2.7F
	1455	1820	2.6E
	2125		
18 Th		0025	2.7F
	0350	0655	2.0E
	0945	1245	2.2F
	1555	1915	2.3E
	2220		
19 F ○		0125	2.3F
	0500	0805	1.7E
	1050	1345	1.9F
	1700	2025	1.9E
	2325		
20 Sa		0235	2.1F
	0615	0920	1.6E
	1210	1505	1.6F
	1825	2140	1.8E
21 Su	0035	0350	2.0F
	0730	1030	1.7E
	1325	1630	1.6F
	1945	2255	1.8E
22 M	0145	0505	2.1F
	0835	1135	2.0E
	1435	1740	1.8F
	2050		
23 Tu	0245	0605	2.3F
	0925	1230	2.3E
	1530	1835	2.1F
	2150		
24 W		0050	2.1E
	0335	0650	2.5F
	1010	1315	2.6E
	1620	1925	2.3F
	2235		
25 Th		0135	2.2E
	0420	0735	2.7F
	1050	1400	2.6E
	1700	2005	2.5F
	2320		
26 F ○		0215	2.2E
	0505	0815	2.8F
	1125	1435	2.7E
	1740	2040	2.6F
27 Sa	0000	0255	2.2E
	0540	0845	2.8F
	1155	1510	2.7E
	1815	2115	2.6F
28 Su	0035	0330	2.1E
	0615	0920	2.7F
	1230	1545	2.6E
	1850	2155	2.5F
29 M	0110	0405	1.9E
	0650	0950	2.4F
	1300	1620	2.4E
	1925	2220	2.4F
30 Tu	0140	0440	1.8E
	0725	1025	2.2F
	1330	1650	2.2E
	1955	2255	2.3F

December

Day	Slack (h m)	Maximum (h m)	knots
1 W	0220	0515	1.6E
	0800	1100	2.1F
	1405	1725	2.1E
	2035	2335	2.2F
2 Th	0255	0555	1.5E
	0845	1140	1.9F
	1445	1805	1.9E
	2115		
3 F		0015	2.0F
	0340	0645	1.7E
	0935	1230	1.7F
	1530	1855	1.7E
	2200		
4 Sa ○		0105	1.9F
	0435	0740	1.3E
	1030	1325	1.5F
	1630	1955	1.5E
	2255		
5 Su		0200	1.9F
	0535	0845	1.3E
	1135	1430	1.5F
	1740	2100	1.5E
	2355		
6 M		0305	1.8F
	0640	0950	1.5E
	1245	1540	1.5F
	1855	2210	1.6E
7 Tu	0055	0410	2.0F
	0740	1050	1.7E
	1350	1650	1.7F
	2005	2310	1.7E
8 W	0200	0510	2.2F
	0835	1150	2.1E
	1450	1750	2.1F
	2105		
9 Th		0010	1.9E
	0255	0605	2.5F
	0925	1240	2.5E
	1540	1845	2.4F
	2200		
10 F		0100	2.2E
	0350	0700	2.8F
	1010	1325	2.8E
	1630	1935	2.8F
	2250		
11 Sa ●		0150	2.4E
	0440	0745	3.0F
	1100	1415	3.0E
	1720	2020	3.0F
	2340		
12 Su		0240	2.5E
	0530	0835	3.1F
	1145	1500	3.2E
	1805	2110	3.2F
13 M	0025	0325	2.7E
	0615	0920	3.2F
	1230	1545	3.2E
	1855	2155	3.3F
14 Tu	0115	0415	2.7E
	0705	1005	3.0F
	1315	1635	3.2E
	1940	2240	3.2F
15 W	0210	0505	2.6E
	0755	1055	3.0F
	1405	1720	3.0E
	2025	2330	3.1F
16 Th	0250	0555	2.5E
	0850	1145	2.7F
	1455	1810	2.7E
	2115		
17 F		0020	2.9F
	0345	0650	2.3E
	0940	1235	2.4F
	1545	1905	2.4E
	2205		
18 Sa ○		0110	2.7F
	0440	0745	2.1E
	1040	1335	2.1F
	1645	2005	2.1E
	2300		
19 Su		0205	2.4F
	0540	0845	2.0E
	1140	1435	1.9F
	1750	2105	1.9E
	2355		
20 M		0305	2.2F
	0640	0945	1.9E
	1245	1540	1.7F
	1900	2205	1.7E
21 Tu	0055	0405	2.0F
	0735	1045	1.9E
	1350	1650	1.7F
	2010	2310	1.6E
22 W	0155	0505	1.9F
	0835	1145	2.0E
	1450	1750	1.8F
	2115		
23 Th		0010	1.6E
	0250	0605	1.9F
	0925	1240	2.0E
	1545	1850	1.9F
	2210		
24 F		0100	1.6E
	0345	0655	1.9F
	1010	1325	2.1E
	1630	1935	2.0F
	2300		
25 Sa		0150	1.6E
	0435	0740	2.0F
	1055	1410	2.2E
	1715	2020	2.1F
	2345		
26 Su ○		0235	1.7E
	0520	0820	2.1F
	1135	1450	2.2E
	1755	2100	2.2F
27 M	0025	0315	1.7E
	0600	0900	2.1F
	1210	1535	2.3E
	1830	2135	2.3F
28 Tu	0100	0355	1.8E
	0640	0940	2.1F
	1245	1605	2.3E
	1905	2210	2.5F
29 W	0135	0435	1.8E
	0720	1015	2.1F
	1320	1640	2.3E
	1940	2245	2.5F
30 Th	0210	0505	1.9E
	0800	1055	2.2F
	1355	1715	2.3E
	2020	2330	2.5F
31 F	0245	0545	1.9E
	0840	1135	2.2F
	1435	1755	2.2E
	2055		

All times are local time. Daylight Saving Time has been used when needed.

NOTES:

109

Portsmouth Harbor Entrance (off Wood I.), N.H., 2004

F–Flood, Dir. 355° True   E–Ebb, Dir. 195° True

April

Day	Slack (h m)	Maximum (h m)	knots
1 Th	0348	0535	0.8F
	0924	1218	1.6E
	1623	1810	0.9F
	2205		
2 F		0044	1.5E
	0437	0630	1.0F
	1014	1308	1.6E
	1705	1901	1.1F
	2250		
3 Sa		0134	1.7E
	0523	0721	1.1F
	1100	1355	1.9E
	1746	1949	1.3F
	2332		
4 Su		0320	1.9E
	0707	0910	1.3F
	1243	1540	2.1E
	1926	2135	1.6F
5 M ○	0112	0405	2.1E
	0751	0957	1.4F
	1326	1624	2.2E
	2006	2220	1.6F
6 Tu	0152	0450	2.3E
	0835	1044	1.5F
	1408	1709	2.2E
	2048	2306	1.7F
7 W	0233	0536	2.3E
	0921	1131	1.4F
	1452	1755	2.2E
	2132	2353	1.8F
8 Th	0316	0623	2.4E
	1010	1220	1.5F
	1540	1844	2.1E
	2220		
9 F		0041	1.7F
	0403	0713	2.3E
	1103	1310	1.4F
	1633	1935	2.0E
	2312		
10 Sa		0131	1.6F
	0455	0805	2.2E
	1201	1403	1.3F
	1734	2029	1.8E
11 Su ◑	0011	0224	1.4F
	0555	0902	2.1E
	1302	1459	1.2F
	1842	2128	1.7E
12 M	0116	0321	1.2F
	0701	1002	1.9E
	1407	1600	1.0F
	1953	2232	1.5E
13 Tu	0224	0421	1.0F
	0811	1108	1.8E
	1511	1704	0.9F
	2101	2344	1.5E
14 W	0331	0526	0.9F
	0917	1221	1.8E
	1612	1958	0.9F
	2204		
15 Th		0109	1.6E
	0434	0638	0.9F
	1019	1337	1.8E
	1708	2054	1.1F
	2300		
16 F		0224	1.7E
	0532	0910	1.0F
	1115	1438	1.9E
	1758	2141	1.2F
	2351		
17 Sa		0315	1.8E
	0624	0958	1.0F
	1206	1522	1.9E
	1844	2219	1.2F
18 Su	0037	0354	1.9E
	0712	1032	1.0F
	1253	1557	1.9E
	1927	2146	1.2F
19 M ●	0120	0424	1.9E
	0757	1003	1.0F
	1337	1629	1.8E
	2007	2215	1.2F
20 Tu	0159	0454	1.9E
	0840	1037	1.0F
	1418	1703	1.8E
	2046	2250	1.2F
21 W	0236	0528	1.9E
	0922	1115	1.0F
	1458	1739	1.7E
	2125	2328	1.2F
22 Th	0312	0605	1.9E
	1005	1155	1.0F
	1536	1819	1.6E
	2205		
23 F		0008	1.2F
	0345	0645	1.8E
	1049	1237	0.9F
	1615	1901	1.5E
	2247		
24 Sa		0051	1.1F
	0418	0728	1.8E
	1136	1321	0.9F
	1656	1946	1.4E
	2334		
25 Su		0136	1.0F
	0450	0814	1.7E
	1225	1409	0.8F
	1743	2035	1.3E
26 M	0025	0224	0.9F
	0528	0904	1.6E
	1317	1459	0.8F
	1839	2127	1.2E
27 Tu ◐	0122	0316	0.8F
	0620	0956	1.6E
	1410	1552	0.7F
	1941	2222	1.2E
28 W	0222	0410	0.8F
	0728	1050	1.5E
	1502	1646	0.8F
	2040	2319	1.3E
29 Th	0320	0506	0.8F
	0836	1145	1.6E
	1552	1741	0.9F
	2135		
30 F		0016	1.4E
	0414	0602	0.9F
	0937	1239	1.7E
	1638	1835	1.0F
	2225		

May

Day	Slack (h m)	Maximum (h m)	knots
1 Sa		0110	1.6E
	0505	0657	1.0F
	1032	1330	1.8E
	1723	1926	1.2F
	2312		
2 Su		0201	1.8E
	0553	0750	1.1F
	1122	1420	1.9E
	1806	2016	1.4F
	2356		
3 M		0250	2.1E
	0640	0842	1.3F
	1211	1508	2.1E
	1849	2105	1.4F
4 Tu ○	0040	0338	2.2E
	0727	0932	1.4F
	1259	1556	2.2E
	1933	2153	1.7F
5 W	0124	0425	2.4E
	0814	1021	1.5F
	1348	1644	2.2E
	2019	2241	1.8F
6 Th	0210	0514	2.5E
	0903	1111	1.6F
	1438	1733	2.2E
	2108	2329	1.8F
7 F	0257	0603	2.5E
	0954	1201	1.5F
	1531	1824	2.1E
	2200		
8 Sa		0019	1.7F
	0347	0655	2.4E
	1048	1253	1.4F
	1629	1917	1.9E
	2305		
9 Su		0111	1.6F
	0442	0748	2.3E
	1146	1348	1.3F
	1730	2014	1.8E
	2357		
10 M		0205	1.4F
	0542	0845	2.1E
	1245	1445	1.2F
	1835	2114	1.7E
11 Tu ◑	0102	0302	1.2F
	0645	0945	2.0E
	1347	1545	1.1F
	1940	2220	1.6E
12 W	0208	0403	1.0F
	0750	1050	1.9E
	1447	1650	1.0F
	2043	2336	1.5E
13 Th	0314	0507	0.9F
	0854	1200	1.8E
	1545	1934	1.0F
	2142		
14 F		0103	1.6E
	0416	0757	0.9F
	0954	1311	1.8E
	1638	2028	1.1F
	2235		
15 Sa		0208	1.7E
	0513	0854	0.9F
	1049	1408	1.8E
	1728	2115	1.1F
	2324		
16 Su		0256	1.8E
	0605	0944	0.9F
	1140	1451	1.7E
	1813	2153	1.1F
17 M	0009	0333	1.8E
	0652	1028	0.9F
	1227	1524	1.7E
	1856	2106	1.1F
18 Tu	0051	0359	1.9E
	0737	0935	0.9F
	1312	1556	1.6E
	1936	2140	1.1F
19 W ●	0130	0427	1.9E
	0820	1009	0.9F
	1354	1632	1.6E
	2016	2218	1.2F
20 Th	0206	0501	1.9E
	0901	1048	0.9F
	1434	1710	1.5E
	2056	2258	1.2F
21 F	0241	0538	1.9E
	0943	1129	0.9F
	1514	1751	1.5E
	2136	2339	1.1F
22 Sa	0314	0618	1.9E
	1026	1211	0.9F
	1554	1834	1.4E
	2219		
23 Su		0023	1.1F
	0345	0701	1.8E
	1110	1256	0.9F
	1635	1920	1.4E
	2305		
24 M		0109	1.0F
	0414	0746	1.8E
	1155	1343	0.9F
	1720	2008	1.3E
	2355		
25 Tu		0157	1.0F
	0448	0834	1.7E
	1242	1431	0.9F
	1809	2059	1.3E
26 W	0050	0247	0.9F
	0531	0924	1.7E
	1330	1522	0.9F
	1903	2152	1.3E
27 Th ◐	0147	0340	1.0F
	0628	1015	1.7E
	1419	1614	1.0F
	1958	2246	1.4E
28 F	0244	0434	0.9F
	0736	1108	1.7E
	1507	1707	1.1F
	2052	2341	1.6E
29 Sa	0339	0529	0.9F
	0844	1201	1.7E
	1554	1800	1.2F
30 Su		0035	1.7E
	0432	0625	1.0F
	0947	1254	1.8E
	1642	1853	1.4F
	2234		
31 M		0129	1.9E
	0524	0720	1.1F
	1046	1346	1.9E
	1729	1944	1.5F
	2323		

June

Day	Slack (h m)	Maximum (h m)	knots
1 Tu		0221	2.1E
	0614	0814	1.3F
	1142	1438	2.0E
	1817	2036	1.7F
2 W	0012	0312	2.3E
	0704	0907	1.4F
	1236	1530	2.1E
	1906	2127	1.8F
3 Th ○	0101	0403	2.4E
	0755	1000	1.5F
	1331	1622	2.1E
	1956	2218	1.8F
4 F	0151	0454	2.5E
	0846	1052	1.5F
	1426	1714	2.1E
	2049	2309	1.8F
5 Sa	0242	0546	2.5E
	0939	1145	1.5F
	1522	1807	2.0E
	2144		
6 Su		0001	1.7F
	0334	0638	2.4E
	1033	1238	1.4F
	1620	1902	1.9E
	2241		
7 M		0053	1.5F
	0429	0732	2.3E
	1128	1332	1.4F
	1719	1959	1.8E
	2341		
8 Tu		0147	1.3F
	0526	0827	2.2E
	1224	1428	1.2F
	1819	2058	1.7E
9 W ◑	0043	0243	1.1F
	0625	0924	2.0E
	1321	1525	1.1F
	1918	2201	1.6E
10 Th	0147	0340	1.0F
	0725	1024	1.9E
	1418	1624	1.1F
	2017	2311	1.6E
11 F	0250	0440	0.8F
	0825	1125	1.7E
	1513	1757	1.0F
	2112		
12 Sa		0030	1.6E
	0351	0543	0.7F
	0923	1226	1.6E
	1605	1957	1.0F
	2204		
13 Su		0137	1.6E
	0448	0832	0.7F
	1018	1321	1.6E
	1654	2045	1.0F
	2253		
14 M		0228	1.7E
	0541	0924	0.7F
	1111	1408	1.5E
	1741	2135	1.1F
	2338		
15 Tu		0306	1.7E
	0630	1012	0.7F
	1200	1447	1.5E
	1825	2228	1.0F
16 W	0021	0332	1.8E
	0715	0904	0.7F
	1001	1055	0.7F
	1246	1525†	1.4E
17 Th ●	0101	0401	1.8E
	0758	0943	0.7F
	1330	1605	1.4E
	1949	2149	1.1F
18 F	0140	0436	1.8E
	0840	1023	0.8F
	1413	1645	1.4E
	2030	2231	1.1F
19 Sa	0216	0514	1.9E
	0921	1105	0.9F
	1453	1727	1.4E
	2112	2314	1.1F
20 Su	0250	0554	1.9E
	1002	1148	0.9F
	1533	1811	1.4E
	2155	2358	1.1F
21 M	0321	0636	1.9E
	1043	1232	1.0F
	1613	1856	1.4E
	2239		
22 Tu		0044	1.1F
	0351	0720	1.9E
	1124	1317	1.0F
	1653	1942	1.4E
	2327		
23 W		0130	1.1F
	0422	0805	1.9E
	1206	1404	1.0F
	1735	2031	1.5E
24 Th	0017	0219	1.0F
	0500	0853	1.8E
	1250	1452	1.1F
	1822	2121	1.5E
25 F ◐	0110	0310	1.0F
	0548	0942	1.8E
	1336	1542	1.2F
	1913	2214	1.6E
26 Sa	0208	0403	1.0F
	0647	1034	1.8E
	1424	1634	1.2F
	2008	2308	1.7E
27 Su	0305	0458	1.0F
	0756	1127	1.8E
	1514	1727	1.3F
	2104		
28 M		0003	1.8E
	0402	0554	1.0F
	0908	1222	1.8E
	1606	1821	1.4F
	2200		
29 Tu		0059	2.0E
	0457	0652	1.1F
	1016	1317	1.9E
	1657	1916	1.5F
	2256		
30 W		0155	2.1E
	0552	0749	1.2F
	1120	1413	1.9E
	1752	2011	1.6F
	2350		

All times are local time. Daylight Saving Time has been used when needed.
If three consecutive entries are marked (F) the middle one is not a true maximum but an intermediate value to show the current pattern.
† See page 104 for the remaining currents on this day.

NOTES:

Portsmouth Harbor Entrance (off Wood I.), N.H., 2004

F—Flood, Dir. 355° True   E—Ebb, Dir. 195° True

July

Day	Slack (h m)	Maximum (h m)	knots
1 Th		0250	2.3E
	0645	0845	1.3F
	1220	1509	2.0E
	1846	2105	1.7F
2 F ○	0043	0344	2.4E
	0738	0941	1.4F
	1318	1604	2.0E
	1940	2158	1.7F
3 Sa	0136	0437	2.5E
	0830	1036	1.5F
	1414	1658	2.0E
	2034	2251	1.7F
4 Su	0228	0530	2.5E
	0922	1129	1.5F
	1509	1752	2.0E
	2129	2343	1.6F
5 M	0320	0622	2.4E
	1014	1222	1.5F
	1604	1846	2.0E
	2224		
6 Tu		0035	1.5F
	0412	0713	2.3E
	1106	1313	1.4F
	1659	1940	1.9E
	2321		
7 W		0127	1.3F
	0505	0805	2.2E
	1158	1404	1.3F
	1754	2035	1.8E
8 Th	0020	0219	1.1F
	0559	0857	2.0E
	1251	1455	1.2F
	1848	2131	1.7E
9 F ○	0120	0311	1.0F
	0655	0949	1.8E
	1344	1546	1.1F
	1943	2230	1.6E
10 Sa	0220	0405	0.8F
	0752	1043	1.7E
	1437	1637	1.0F
	2036	2333	1.6E
11 Su	0321	0500	0.7F
	0849	1137	1.5E
	1529	1728	0.9F
	2128		
12 M		0041	1.5E
	0419	0557	0.6F
		0700	1.5E
		0807	0.6F
	0945	1232	1.4E
13 Tu		0144	1.4E
	0514	0654	0.6F
		0759	1.4E
		0903	0.6F
	1040	1324†	1.3E
14 W		0229	1.6E
	0605	0953	0.6F
		1413	1.3E
	1756	1953	0.9F
	2351		
15 Th		0302	1.7E
	0651	1038	0.6F
	1221	1458	1.5E
	1841	2039	1.0F
16 F	0034	0336	1.8E
	0734	0918	0.7F
	1307	1540	1.4E
	1925	2123	1.0F
17 Sa ●	0115	0412	1.8E
	0815	1000	0.8F
	1349	1622	1.4E
	2007	2207	1.1F
18 Su	0153	0450	1.9E
	0855	1041	0.9F
	1430	1705	1.5E
	2049	2251	1.1F
19 M	0228	0530	1.9E
	0933	1124	1.0F
	1508	1747	1.5E
	2131	2335	1.2F
20 Tu	0301	0611	1.9E
	1011	1206	1.1F
	1545	1831	1.6E
	2214		
21 W		0019	1.2F
	0330	0653	1.9E
	1050	1250	1.2F
	1621	1916	1.6E
	2259		
22 Th		0105	1.2F
	0401	0737	1.9E
	1129	1335	1.2F
	1658	2002	1.7E
	2347		
23 F		0153	1.1F
	0437	0823	1.9E
	1211	1422	1.3F
	1740	2051	1.7E
24 Sa	0039	0242	1.1F
	0521	0911	1.8E
	1257	1511	1.3F
	1830	2143	1.7E
25 Su	0135	0335	1.1F
	0616	1003	1.8E
	1347	1603	1.3F
	1928	2238	1.8E
26 M	0235	0430	1.0F
	0725	1058	1.7E
	1442	1657	1.3F
	2030	2335	1.8E
27 Tu	0336	0528	1.0F
	0844	1155	1.7E
	1539	1754	1.4F
	2134		
28 W		0034	1.9E
	0436	0627	1.0F
	0959	1254	1.8E
	1638	1852	1.4F
	2235		
29 Th		0134	2.1E
	0533	0728	1.1F
	1107	1354	1.8E
	1736	1950	1.5F
30 F		0232	2.2E
	0629	0828	1.2F
	1208	1453	1.9E
	1832	2047	1.5F
31 Sa ○	0029	0329	2.3E
	0721	0926	1.3F
	1306	1550	2.0E
	1927	2142	1.6F

August

Day	Slack (h m)	Maximum (h m)	knots
1 Su	0122	0423	2.4E
	0812	1021	1.4F
	1400	1644	2.0E
	2020	2235	1.6F
2 M	0213	0514	2.4E
	0902	1113	1.5F
	1452	1736	2.0E
	2113	2326	1.5F
3 Tu	0303	0603	2.4E
	0951	1201	1.5F
	1542	1827	2.0E
	2206		
4 W		0014	1.4F
	0352	0650	2.3E
	1039	1248	1.4F
	1632	1916	1.9E
	2258		
5 Th		0102	1.3F
	0441	0736	2.1E
	1128	1333	1.3F
	1721	2005	1.8E
	2353		
6 F		0150	1.1F
	0530	0823	1.9E
	1217	1414	1.2F
	1811	2055	1.7E
7 Sa ○	0049	0238	0.9F
	0622	0911	1.7E
	1307	1505	1.1F
	1902	2146	1.6E
8 Su	0147	0328	0.8F
	0716	1001	1.5E
	1359	1554	1.0F
	1955	2241	1.5E
9 M	0247	0420	0.6F
	0813	1054	1.4E
	1453	1644	0.9F
	2048	2339	1.5E
10 Tu	0346	0515	0.5F
		0647	0.4F
		0742	0.4F
	0912	1149	1.5E
	1547	1736†	0.8F
11 W	0443	0612	0.5F
		0724	0.4F
		0835	0.5F
	1010	1246	1.2E
	1639	1829†	0.8F
12 Th		0139	1.5E
	0535	0808	0.5F
		0929	0.6F
	1104	1342†	1.2E
13 F		0226	1.6E
	0622	0903	0.6F
		1012	0.6F
	1154	1432†	1.3E
14 Sa		0317	1.7E
	0704	0850	0.7F
		1240	1.4E
	1902	2059	1.0F
15 Su ●	0049	0345	1.8E
	0744	0904	0.9F
	1322	1559	1.5E
	1944	2144	1.1F
16 M	0128	0424	1.9E
	0822	1015	1.0F
	1401	1641	1.6E
	2026	2228	1.2F
17 Tu	0204	0503	2.0E
	0859	1057	1.2F
	1438	1722	1.7E
	2107	2311	1.3F
18 W	0237	0543	2.0E
	0936	1139	1.3F
	1512	1805	1.8E
	2148	2355	1.3F
19 Th	0309	0625	2.0E
	1013	1222	1.4F
	1546	1848	1.9E
	2232		
20 F		0040	1.3F
	0341	0708	2.0E
	1052	1306	1.4F
	1622	1934	1.9E
	2319		
21 Sa		0127	1.3F
	0418	0754	1.9E
	1135	1353	1.4F
	1704	2023	1.9E
22 Su ○		0217	1.2F
	0503	0843	1.9E
	1223	1442	1.4F
	1754	2115	1.9E
23 M	0108	0309	1.1F
	0600	0936	1.8E
	1318	1535	1.3F
	1856	2211	1.8E
24 Tu	0211	0406	1.0F
	0715	1033	1.7E
	1419	1631	1.3F
	2005	2311	1.8E
25 W	0315	0505	1.0F
	0837	1134	1.6E
	1522	1731	1.3F
	2114		
26 Th		0013	1.9E
	0417	0608	1.0F
	0952	1237	1.7E
	1625	1832	1.3F
	2220		
27 F		0117	2.0E
	0517	0712	1.1F
	1058	1342	1.7E
	1725	1933	1.3F
	2320		
28 Sa		0219	2.1E
	0612	0811	1.2F
	1157	1443	1.8E
	1822	2033	1.4F
29 Su ○	0014	0313	2.2E
	0703	0915	1.3F
	1258	1540	2.0E
	1915	2129	1.4F
30 M	0107	0408	2.3E
	0752	1006	1.4F
	1342	1632	2.0E
	2006	2219	1.5F
31 Tu	0157	0455	2.3E
	0838	1052	1.4F
	1430	1719	2.1E
	2056	2306	1.4F

September

Day	Slack (h m)	Maximum (h m)	knots
1 W	0244	0539	2.3E
	0924	1135	1.4F
	1516	1803	2.1E
	2145	2351	1.4F
2 Th	0329	0622	2.1E
	1009	1216	1.4F
	1600	1847	2.0E
	2234		
3 F		0034	1.2F
	0414	0705	2.0E
	1054	1258	1.3F
	1645	1931	1.9E
	2324		
4 Sa		0119	1.1F
	0459	0748	1.8E
	1140	1341	1.2F
	1730	2017	1.7E
5 Su	0017	0204	0.9F
	0546	0834	1.6E
	1229	1426	1.0F
	1817	2105	1.6E
6 M ○	0113	0252	0.8F
	0639	0923	1.4E
	1321	1513	0.9F
	1908	2157	1.5E
7 Tu	0212	0344	0.6F
	0738	1015	1.3E
	1417	1604	0.8F
	2004	2253	1.4E
8 W	0311	0438	0.5F
	0839	1112	1.2E
	1514	1658	0.7F
	2101	2352	1.4E
9 Th	0408	0536	0.5F
		0708	0.4F
		0811	0.4F
	0940	1212	1.2E
	1610	1754†	0.7F
10 F	0500	0635	0.5F
		0753	0.5F
		0859	0.5F
	1035	1650†	0.7F
	1703	1850†	0.8F
11 Sa		0145	0.7F
	0546	0730	0.7F
	1125	1403	1.4E
	1752	1943	0.9F
12 Su		0231	1.7E
	0628	0818	0.9F
	1210	1449	1.5E
	1836	2032	1.0F
13 M	0019	0312	1.8E
	0708	0903	1.0F
	1250	1532	1.7E
	1919	2118	1.1F
14 Tu ●	0059	0353	1.9E
	0745	0945	1.2F
	1328	1614	1.8E
	2000	2203	1.3F
15 W	0136	0433	2.0E
	0819	1027	1.4F
	1404	1655	2.0E
	2041	2246	1.4F
16 Th	0211	0514	2.1E
	0859	1110	1.5F
	1439	1738	2.1E
	2123	2331	1.4F
17 F	0247	0557	2.1E
	0938	1153	1.6F
	1514	1822	2.1E
	2207		
18 Sa		0016	1.4F
	0324	0641	2.0E
	1019	1239	1.6F
	1552	1909	2.1E
	2255		
19 Su		0104	1.4F
	0406	0729	2.0E
	1105	1326	1.5F
	1637	1958	2.1E
	2349		
20 M		0154	1.3F
	0456	0820	1.8E
	1157	1417	1.4F
	1730	2051	2.0E
21 Tu	0048	0248	1.1F
	0601	0915	1.7E
	1257	1513	1.3F
	1835	2149	1.9E
22 W	0152	0346	1.0F
	0719	1015	1.6E
	1403	1609	1.2F
	1948	2251	1.8E
23 Th	0257	0447	1.0F
	0836	1119	1.6E
	1511	1711	1.1F
	2059	2357	1.9E
24 F	0400	0553	1.0F
	0945	1227	1.6E
	1615	1816	1.1F
	2205		
25 Sa		0105	1.9E
	0458	0700	1.0F
	1047	1337	1.7E
	1716	1921	1.1F
	2305		
26 Su		0209	2.0E
	0552	0809	1.2F
	1143	1444	1.8E
	1811	2023	1.2F
27 M		0305	2.1E
	0641	0906	1.3F
	1234	1533	2.0E
	1902	2117	1.3F
28 Tu ○	0050	0352	2.1E
	0728	0948	1.4F
	1321	1617	2.1E
	1951	2203	1.3F
29 W	0137	0433	2.1E
	0812	1026	1.4F
	1405	1658	2.1E
	2038	2244	1.2F
30 Th	0222	0513	2.1E
	0855	1104	1.4F
	1447	1737	2.1E
	2123	2325	1.2F

All times are local time. Daylight Saving Time has been used when needed.
If three consecutive entries are marked (F) the middle one is not a true maximum but an intermediate value to show the current pattern.
† See page 104 for the remaining currents on this day.

NOTES:

Portsmouth Harbor Entrance (off Wood I.), N.H., 2004

F–Flood, Dir. 355° True   E–Ebb, Dir. 195° True

October

Day	Slack (h m)	Maximum (h m, knots)
1 F	0305, 0937, 1527, 2210	0552 1.9E, 1143 1.3F, 1817 2.0E
2 Sa	0347, 1019, 1606, 2257	0006 1.1F, 0632 1.8E, 1223 1.3F, 1858 1.9E
3 Su	0429, 1104, 1646, 2347	0048 1.0F, 0714 1.6E, 1305 1.1F, 1942 1.8E
4 M	0515, 1152, 1728	0133 0.9F, 0759 1.5E, 1349 1.0F, 2029 1.7E
5 Tu	0040, 0606, 1244, 1816	0220 0.8F, 0848 1.3E, 1437 0.9F, 2119 1.5E
6 W ●	0136, 0704, 1342, 1913	0311 0.7F, 0941 1.2E, 1529 0.8F, 2213 1.5E
7 Th	0233, 0807, 1441, 2014	0405 0.6F, 1038 1.1E, 1623 0.7F, 2310 1.5E
8 F	0329, 0907, 1540, 2114	0502 0.6F, 1137 1.2E, 1720 0.7F
9 Sa	0419, 1001, 1633, 2209	0008 1.5E, 0558 0.7F, 1236 1.3E, 1817 0.8F
10 Su	0505, 1050, 1723, 2258	0102 1.6E, 0653 0.8F, 1329 1.4E, 1911 0.9F
11 M	0548, 1134, 1808, 2343	0151 1.7E, 0743 1.0F, 1417 1.6E, 2002 1.0F
12 Tu	0628, 1215, 1851	0236 1.8E, 0829 1.2F, 1502 1.8E, 2050 1.2F
13 W ●	0026, 0706, 1253, 1933	0319 2.0E, 0914 1.4F, 1545 2.0E, 2136 1.3F
14 Th	0106, 0745, 1331, 2016	0402 2.1E, 0957 1.5F, 1628 2.2E, 2221 1.4F
15 F	0145, 0824, 1408, 2100	0446 2.1E, 1042 1.7F, 1712 2.3E, 2307 1.5F
16 Sa	0226, 0906, 1447, 2146	0531 2.1E, 1127 1.7F, 1758 2.3E, 2354 1.5F
17 Su	0310, 0951, 1530, 2236	0617 2.1E, 1214 1.7F, 1846 2.3E
18 M	0400, 1042, 1619, 2331	0044 1.4F, 0707 2.0E, 1303 1.6F, 1937 2.2E
19 Tu	0458, 1139, 1715	0135 1.3F, 0800 1.8E, 1355 1.4F, 2032 2.1E
20 W ○	0031, 0606, 1243, 1821	0230 1.2F, 0857 1.7E, 1451 1.3F, 2130 2.0E
21 Th	0134, 0718, 1351, 1933	0329 1.1F, 1000 1.6E, 1551 1.1F, 2234 1.9E
22 F	0238, 0828, 1459, 2042	0432 1.0F, 1107 1.5E, 1654 1.0F, 2341 1.9E
23 Sa	0339, 0932, 1603, 2147	0540 1.0F, 1222 1.6E, 1801 1.0F
24 Su	0436, 1031, 1703, 2246	0051 1.9E, 0656 1.1F, 1338 1.7E, 1912 1.0F
25 M	0528, 1124, 1757, 2340	0156 1.9E, 0758 1.2F, 1439 1.9E, 2027 1.0F
26 Tu	0616, 1212, 1848	0248 2.0E, 0928 1.2F, 1525 2.0E, 2111 1.1F
27 W ○	0029, 0701, 1257, 1934	0331 1.9E, 0923 1.3F, 1602 2.0E, 2145 1.1F
28 Th	0115, 0744, 1338, 2019	0408 1.9E, 0956 1.3F, 1636 2.0E, 2221 1.1F
29 F	0159, 0825, 1418, 2103	0445 1.8E, 1032 1.3F, 1711 2.0E, 2258 1.1F
30 Sa	0241, 0906, 1455, 2147	0522 1.7E, 1110 1.3F, 1748 2.0E, 2338 1.0F
31 Su	0222, 0847, 1431, 2132	0502 1.6E, 1050 1.2F, 1728 1.9E, 2320 0.9F

November

Day	Slack (h m)	Maximum (h m, knots)
1 M	0304, 0931, 1506, 2219	0544 1.5E, 1133 1.1F, 1811 1.8E
2 Tu	0347, 1018, 1542, 2309	0004 0.9F, 0629 1.4E, 1217 1.0F, 1857 1.7E
3 W	0436, 1110, 1622	0051 0.8F, 0717 1.3E, 1305 0.9F, 1945 1.6E
4 Th ○	0001, 0531, 1207, 1714	0141 0.7F, 0809 1.2E, 1356 0.8F, 2037 1.5E
5 F	0053, 0630, 1306, 1817	0233 0.7F, 0905 1.2E, 1450 0.7F, 2131 1.5E
6 Sa	0145, 0728, 1405, 1922	0327 0.7F, 1002 1.2E, 1546 0.7F, 2226 1.5E
7 Su	0235, 0821, 1459, 2021	0422 0.8F, 1058 1.4E, 1642 0.8F, 2319 1.6E
8 M	0321, 0910, 1550, 2114	0515 1.0F, 1152 1.5E, 1737 0.9F
9 Tu	0404, 0955, 1637, 2204	0010 1.7E, 0606 1.2F, 1242 1.7E, 1829 1.0F
10 W	0447, 1038, 1723, 2251	0059 1.8E, 0654 1.3F, 1330 2.0E, 1920 1.2F
11 Th	0528, 1119, 1807, 2336	0146 1.9E, 0742 1.5F, 1416 2.2E, 2009 1.3F
12 F ●	0610, 1201, 1853	0232 2.0E, 0828 1.7F, 1502 2.3E, 2057 1.4F
13 Sa	0022, 0654, 1243, 1939	0319 2.1E, 0916 1.8F, 1549 2.4E, 2146 1.5F
14 Su	0110, 0740, 1328, 2028	0407 2.1E, 1003 1.8F, 1637 2.4E, 2235 1.5F
15 M	0201, 0830, 1415, 2120	0457 2.0E, 1052 1.7F, 1727 2.4E, 2326 1.5F
16 Tu	0256, 0925, 1508, 2215	0549 2.0E, 1143 1.6F, 1819 2.3E
17 W	0356, 1024, 1605, 2313	0019 1.4F, 0644 1.8E, 1237 1.4F, 1914 2.2E
18 Th	0501, 1128, 1709	0115 1.3F, 0742 1.7E, 1333 1.3F, 2013 2.1E
19 F	0014, 0607, 1235, 1815	0213 1.2F, 0845 1.6E, 1432 1.1F, 2115 1.9E
20 Sa	0120, 0711, 1342, 1921	0315 1.1F, 0954 1.6E, 1536 0.9F, 2220 1.8E
21 Su	0213, 0812, 1446, 2024	0421 1.1F, 1112 1.6E, 1642 0.9F, 2328 1.8E
22 M	0309, 0908, 1546, 2122	0653 1.1F, 1230 1.7E, 1922 0.9F
23 Tu	0401, 1000, 1641, 2216	0033 1.8E, 0744 1.1F, 1328 1.8E, 2017 0.9F
24 W	0449, 1047, 1731, 2307	0125 1.8E, 0826 1.2F, 1413 1.9E, 2105 0.9F
25 Th	0534, 1131, 1818	0206 1.7E, 0752 1.2F, 1447 1.9E, 2145 0.9F
26 F ○	0617, 1212, 1902	0242 1.7E, 0825 1.2F, 1516 1.9E, 2058 0.9F
27 Sa	0037, 0658, 1251, 1945	0318 1.6E, 0902 1.2F, 1548 1.9E, 2134 0.9F
28 Su	0120, 0739, 1328, 2027	0356 1.5E, 0941 1.2F, 1624 1.9E, 2214 0.9F
29 M	0201, 0820, 1403, 2110	0435 1.5E, 1022 1.1F, 1703 1.9E, 2255 0.9F
30 Tu	0242, 0903, 1436, 2153	0518 1.4E, 1105 1.1F, 1744 1.8E, 2339 0.9F

December

Day	Slack (h m)	Maximum (h m, knots)
1 W	0324, 0949, 1508, 2238	0602 1.4E, 1150 1.0F, 1828 1.8E
2 Th	0408, 1038, 1540, 2324	0024 0.9F, 0650 1.3E, 1237 1.0F, 1915 1.7E
3 F	0456, 1132, 1618	0112 0.9F, 0739 1.3E, 1326 0.9F, 2003 1.7E
4 Sa	0012, 0548, 1228, 1708	0201 0.9F, 0831 1.3E, 1418 0.8F, 2054 1.6E
5 Su	0100, 0641, 1325, 1812	0252 0.9F, 0925 1.4E, 1512 0.8F, 2146 1.6E
6 M	0147, 0734, 1421, 1920	0344 1.0F, 1020 1.5E, 1606 0.8F, 2239 1.6E
7 Tu	0235, 0825, 1514, 2023	0437 1.1F, 1114 1.6E, 1701 0.9F, 2331 1.7E
8 W	0321, 0914, 1605, 2122	0529 1.3F, 1207 1.8E, 1756 1.0F
9 Th	0408, 1002, 1655, 2217	0023 1.8E, 0621 1.4F, 1258 2.0E, 1850 1.1F
10 F	0454, 1049, 1743	0114 1.9E, 0712 1.6F, 1349 2.2E, 1943 1.3F
11 Sa ●	0542, 1136, 1832	0205 2.0E, 0802 1.7F, 1439 2.4E, 2035 1.4F
12 Su	0004, 0631, 1224, 1921	0256 2.0E, 0852 1.8F, 1529 2.5E, 2126 1.5F
13 M	0058, 0722, 1313, 2012	0348 2.1E, 0943 1.8F, 1619 2.5E, 2218 1.5F
14 Tu	0152, 0815, 1404, 2104	0440 2.1E, 1034 1.7F, 1710 2.5E, 2310 1.5F
15 W	0248, 0910, 1457, 2157	0533 2.0E, 1126 1.6F, 1803 2.4E
16 Th	0346, 1009, 1553, 2253	0004 1.5F, 0629 1.9E, 1219 1.5F, 1857 2.3E
17 F	0445, 1110, 1651, 2349	0058 1.4F, 0726 1.8E, 1314 1.3F, 1952 2.1E
18 Sa ○	0546, 1214, 1752	0153 1.3F, 0826 1.7E, 1411 1.1F, 2050 2.0E
19 Su	0046, 0645, 1318, 1854	0251 1.2F, 0931 1.7E, 1510 0.9F, 2151 1.8E
20 M	0143, 0744, 1422, 1956	0350 1.1F, 1044 1.6E, 1612 0.8F, 2253 1.7E
21 Tu	0238, 0839, 1523, 2055	0450 1.0F, 1154 1.7E, 1708 0.7F, 2356 1.6E
22 W	0331, 0931, 1620, 2150	0557 1.0F, 1308 1.7E, 1803 0.8F
23 Th	0421, 1020, 1712, 2242	0054 1.5E, 0657 1.0F, 1357 1.8E, 2005 0.8F
24 F	0508, 1105, 1800, 2331	0140 1.5E, 0716 1.0F, 1434 1.8E, 2142 0.8F
25 Sa	0552, 1147, 1844	0218 1.4E, 0755 1.0F, 1459 1.8E, 2057 0.7F
26 Su ○	0017, 0635, 1227, 1925	0255 1.4E, 0835 1.1F, 1528 1.9E, 2113 0.8F
27 M	0100, 0716, 1305, 2006	0333 1.4E, 0916 1.1F, 1602 1.9E, 2152 0.8F
28 Tu	0141, 0758, 1340, 2046	0413 1.4E, 0958 1.1F, 1640 1.9E, 2232 0.9F
29 W	0221, 0840, 1413, 2126	0455 1.4E, 1041 1.1F, 1720 1.9E, 2314 1.0F
30 Th	0300, 0923, 1444, 2206	0538 1.4E, 1125 1.1F, 1752 1.9E, 2358 1.0F
31 F	0339, 1009, 1512, 2247	0623 1.4E, 1211 1.1F, 1845 1.8E

All times are local time. Daylight Saving Time has been used when needed.
If three consecutive entries are marked (F) the middle one is not a true maximum but an intermediate value to show the current pattern.

NOTES:

Boston Harbor (Deer Island Light), Massachusetts, 2004

F–Flood, Dir. 254° True   E–Ebb, Dir. 111° True

April

Day	Slack h m	Max h m	knots
1 Th	0146	0504	1.0F
	0729	1158	1.2E
	1414	1734	1.1F
	2005		
2 F		0023	1.1E
	0236	0552	1.1F
	0820	1240	1.2E
	1500	1818	1.3F
	2053		
3 Sa		0103	1.2E
	0323	0636	1.3F
	0909	1315	1.3E
	1544	1858	1.4F
	2137		
4 Su		0136	1.3E
	0509	0815	1.4F
	1054	1440	1.3E
	1728	2033	1.5F
	2320		
5 M ○		0300	1.4E
	0553	0849	1.4F
	1139	1503	1.4E
	1810	2101	1.6F
6 Tu	0003	0326	1.4E
	0638	0920	1.5F
	1223	1535	1.4E
	1853	2132	1.6F
7 W	0045	0359	1.5E
	0723	0955	1.5F
	1307	1611	1.3E
	1938	2210	1.6F
8 Th	0129	0437	1.4E
	0810	1035	1.4F
	1353	1651	1.2E
	2026	2251	1.5F
9 F	0214	0520	1.3E
	0900	1120	1.3F
	1441	1737	1.1E
	2117	2337	1.4F
10 Sa	0302	0609	1.2E
	0955	1208	1.2F
	1533	1831	1.0E
	2211		
11 Su ○		0026	1.2F
	0355	0715	1.1E
	1052	1303	1.0F
	1631	2103	0.9E
	2312		
12 M		0122	1.2F
	0453	0936	1.1E
	1154	1432	0.9F
	1736	2211	0.9E
13 Tu	0018	0324	0.8F
	0557	1041	1.1E
	1259	1621	0.9F
	1843	2312	1.0E
14 W	0122	0447	0.8F
	0703	1141	1.2E
	1401	1726	0.9F
	1947		
15 Th		0010	1.2E
	0228	0551	0.9F
	0808	1237	1.3E
	1501	1823	1.1F
	2050		
16 F		0105	1.3E
	0328	0647	1.0F
	0910	1329	1.4E
	1554	1915	1.2F
	2148		
17 Sa		0156	1.4E
	0421	0739	1.1F
	1008	1418	1.4E
	1642	2003	1.3F
	2240		
18 Su		0244	1.5E
	0510	0826	1.2F
	1059	1505	1.4E
	1728	2048	1.3F
	2324		
19 M ●		0329	1.5E
	0556	0911	1.3F
	1145	1550	1.4E
	1810	2130	1.3F
20 Tu	0005	0414	1.5E
	0639	0954	1.3F
	1227	1634	1.3E
	1851	2210	1.3F
21 W	0044	0456	1.4E
	0721	1035	1.2F
	1308	1716	1.2E
	1932	2247	1.3F
22 Th	0123	0539	1.3E
	0803	1114	1.2F
	1348	1759	1.1E
	2014	2318	1.2F
23 F	0202	0621	1.2E
	0848	1149	1.1F
	1429	1844	1.0E
	2058	2333	1.1F
24 Sa	0242	0706	1.1E
	0931	1215	1.0F
	1511	1934	0.9E
	2143		
25 Su		0004	1.1F
	0326	0754	1.0E
	1019	1242	1.0F
	1558	2027	0.8E
	2232		
26 M		0048	1.0F
	0412	0848	1.0E
	1109	1328	0.9F
	1648	2121	0.8E
	2325		
27 Tu ○		0139	1.0F
	0503	0942	1.0E
	1200	1428	0.9F
	1741	2215	0.8E
28 W	0019	0238	1.0F
	0558	1035	1.0E
	1251	1551	1.0F
	1836	2305	0.9E
29 Th	0113	0354	1.0F
	0653	1124	1.0E
	1342	1651	1.1F
	1930	2353	1.0E
30 F	0208	0509	1.1F
	0749	1209	1.1E
	1432	1743	1.2F
	2023		

May

Day	Slack h m	Max h m	knots
1 Sa		0036	1.1E
	0259	0603	1.2F
	0842	1248	1.2E
	1521	1829	1.3F
	2113		
2 Su		0115	1.3E
	0349	0650	1.3F
	0934	1322	1.3E
	1609	1910	1.4F
	2201		
3 M		0148	1.4E
	0438	0734	1.4F
	1023	1354	1.3E
	1655	1948	1.5F
	2248		
4 Tu ○		0221	1.5E
	0525	0814	1.5F
	1111	1432	1.4E
	1740	2026	1.6F
	2333		
5 W		0259	1.5E
	0612	0854	1.5F
	1158	1512	1.4E
	1828	2105	1.6F
6 Th	0019	0340	1.5E
	0700	0935	1.5F
	1246	1556	1.3E
	1916	2148	1.5F
7 F	0106	0425	1.4E
	0750	1020	1.4F
	1335	1644	1.2E
	2007	2233	1.4F
8 Sa	0154	0516	1.3E
	0842	1108	1.3F
	1426	1741	1.1E
	2100	2322	1.3F
9 Su	0246	0623	1.2E
	0938	1204	1.1F
	1521	1936	1.0E
	2158		
10 M		0018	1.1F
	0341	0809	1.1E
	1036	1337	1.0F
	1621	2049	1.0E
	2259		
11 Tu ○		0158	0.9F
	0440	0919	1.1E
	1137	1456	1.0F
	1723	2152	1.0E
12 W ○	0002	0324	0.9F
	0544	1021	1.2E
	1239	1603	0.9F
	1827	2253	1.1E
13 Th	0108	0431	0.9F
	0649	1120	1.2E
	1340	1704	1.0F
	1930	2350	1.2E
14 F	0211	0531	1.1F
	0753	1216	1.3E
	1438	1800	1.1F
	2033		
15 Sa		0044	1.3E
	0310	0626	1.0F
	0856	1308	1.3E
	1530	1851	1.2F
	2130		
16 Su		0134	1.4E
	0402	0717	1.1F
	0954	1357	1.3E
	1619	1939	1.2F
	2219		
17 M		0222	1.4E
	0450	0804	1.2F
	1043	1444	1.3E
	1702	2023	1.2F
	2301		
18 Tu ●		0308	1.5E
	0534	0849	1.2F
	1126	1529	1.3E
	1745	2106	1.2F
	2340		
19 W		0352	1.4E
	0617	0931	1.2F
	1206	1613	1.2E
	1827	2146	1.2F
20 Th	0017	0435	1.4E
	0658	1012	1.1F
	1244	1656	1.1E
	1907	2223	1.2F
21 F	0055	0517	1.3E
	0739	1051	1.1F
	1322	1738	1.0E
	1949	2254	1.1F
22 Sa	0133	0556	1.2E
	0820	1125	1.1F
	1402	1818	1.0E
	2030	2303	1.1F
23 Su	0213	0632	1.1E
	0902	1144	1.0F
	1443	1857	0.9E
	2116	2335	1.1F
24 M	0256	0626	1.0E
	0948	1208	1.0F
	1527	1834	0.9E
	2202		
25 Tu		0018	1.1F
	0341	0653	1.0E
	1033	1251	1.1F
	1614	1914	0.9E
	2252		
26 W		0107	1.1F
	0430	0737	1.0E
	1121	1340	1.1F
	1704	2007	0.9E
	2344		
27 Th ○		0200	1.1F
	0522	0831	1.0E
	1211	1434	1.1F
	1757	2109	1.0E
28 F	0038	0256	1.1F
	0616	0931	1.1E
	1301	1530	1.2F
	1849	2215	1.1E
29 Sa	0130	0356	1.2F
	0711	1032	1.1E
	1352	1627	1.3F
	1942	2315	1.2E
30 Su	0223	0456	1.2F
	0805	1129	1.2E
	1442	1722	1.4F
	2034		
31 M		0009	1.3E
	0316	0554	1.1F
	0859	1223	1.2E
	1532	1814	1.4F
	2125		

June

Day	Slack h m	Max h m	knots
1 Tu		0059	1.4E
	0407	0648	1.4F
	0951	1315	1.3E
	1622	1903	1.5F
	2215		
2 W ○		0148	1.5E
	0458	0739	1.4F
	1043	1405	1.3E
	1712	1952	1.5F
	2305		
3 Th		0237	1.5E
	0549	0830	1.4F
	1134	1458	1.3E
	1803	2041	1.5F
	2354		
4 F		0329	1.5E
	0639	0921	1.4F
	1226	1554	1.3E
	1856	2131	1.4F
5 Sa	0045	0426	1.4E
	0731	1016	1.3F
	1319	1701	1.2E
	1949	2224	1.3F
6 Su	0137	0534	1.4E
	0825	1118	1.3F
	1412	1818	1.2E
	2045	2327	1.2F
7 M	0231	0647	1.3E
	0920	1227	1.2F
	1509	1925	1.1E
	2142		
8 Tu		0047	1.1F
	0327	0754	1.2E
	1018	1334	1.1F
	1607	2028	1.1E
	2242		
9 W ○		0200	1.0F
	0427	0857	1.2E
	1116	1438	1.2F
	1707	2129	1.1E
	2345		
10 Th		0306	1.0F
	0528	0957	1.2E
	1215	1538	1.2F
	1808	2228	1.2E
11 F	0048	0407	1.0F
	0631	1055	1.2E
	1312	1636	1.3F
	1909	2325	1.3E
12 Sa	0148	0505	1.0F
	0735	1151	1.2E
	1409	1731	1.4F
	2009		
13 Su		0019	1.3E
	0244	0559	1.0F
	0839	1243	1.2E
	1500	1822	1.4F
	2104		
14 M		0110	1.4E
	0337	0650	1.1F
	0938	1334	1.2E
	1550	1910	1.4F
	2152		
15 Tu		0159	1.4E
	0424	0739	1.1F
	1025	1422	1.2E
	1636	1956	1.4F
	2233		
16 W		0245	1.4E
	0510	0824	1.1F
	1106	1508	1.2E
	1719	2040	1.1F
	2312		
17 Th ●		0330	1.3E
	0551	0908	1.1F
	1143	1552	1.1E
	1800	2121	1.1F
	2350		
18 F		0413	1.3E
	0632	0949	1.1F
	1221	1635	1.1E
	1842	2200	1.1F
19 Sa	0028	0454	1.2E
	0713	1028	1.1F
	1258	1715	1.0E
	1923	2234	1.1F
20 Su	0106	0531	1.2E
	0753	1103	1.1F
	1336	1753	1.0E
	2007	2246	1.1F
21 M	0146	0559	1.1E
	0834	1122	1.1F
	1416	1816	1.0E
	2049	2311	1.1F
22 Tu	0229	0546	1.1E
	0917	1141	1.1F
	1549	1801	1.0E
	2135	2352	1.1F
23 W	0313	0616	1.1E
	1000	1221	1.2F
	1544	1839	1.0E
	2222		
24 Th		0039	1.2F
	0400	0658	1.1E
	1047	1307	1.2F
	1631	1926	1.1E
	2312		
25 F ○		0129	1.2F
	0450	0747	1.1E
	1135	1356	1.3F
	1721	2019	1.1E
26 Sa		0221	1.2F
	0542	0840	1.1E
	1225	1448	1.3F
	1812	2117	1.2E
27 Su		0316	1.2F
	0637	0938	1.1E
	1317	1541	1.4F
	1905	2217	1.2E
28 M		0412	1.3F
	0731	1039	1.2E
	1409	1636	1.4F
	1958	2320	1.3E
29 Tu		0511	1.3F
	0834	1142	1.2E
	1501	1732	1.4F
	2052		
30 W		0023	1.4E
	0339	0611	1.3F
	0923	1248	1.2E
	1556	1828	1.4F
	2146		

All times are local time. Daylight Saving Time has been used when needed.
At times of slack water before maximum ebb, the speed actually averages 0.3 knot in a direction of 184° true.

NOTES:

Boston Harbor (Deer Island Light), Massachusetts, 2004

F–Flood, Dir. 254° True   E–Ebb, Dir. 111° True

July

Day	Slack (h m)	Maximum (h m)	knots
1 Th		0127	1.4E
	0431	0713	1.3F
	1018	1357	1.3E
	1649	1926	1.4F
	2239		
2 F ○		0230	1.5E
	0526	0816	1.3F
	1113	1504	1.3E
	1743	2026	1.4F
	2332		
3 Sa		0331	1.5E
	0619	0916	1.3F
	1208	1606	1.3E
	1838	2128	1.4F
4 Su	0026	0431	1.5E
	0711	1016	1.3F
	1302	1706	1.3E
	1931	2232	1.3F
5 M	0120	0531	1.4E
	0805	1115	1.3F
	1357	1805	1.3E
	2029	2336	1.2F
6 Tu	0215	0631	1.4E
	0859	1214	1.3F
	1451	1905	1.3E
	2125		
7 W	0311	0039	1.2F
	0953	0731	1.3E
	1547	1313	1.2F
	2222	2004	1.2E
8 Th	0408	0140	1.1F
	1049	0831	1.2E
	1643	1411	1.2F
	2321	2103	1.2E
9 F ○	0507	0240	1.0F
	1146	0930	1.2E
	1741	1508	1.1F
		2200	1.2E
10 Sa	0020	0338	1.0F
	0608	1027	1.2E
	1241	1604	1.1F
	1839	2257	1.3E
11 Su	0119	0435	1.0F
	0711	1123	1.2E
	1336	1658	1.1F
	1936	2351	1.3E
12 M	0213	0529	1.0F
	0814	1217	1.1E
	1429	1750	1.1F
	2030		
13 Tu	0307	0043	1.3E
	0914	0621	1.0F
	1519	1308	1.1E
	2119	1840	1.1F
14 W	0356	0133	1.3E
	1002	0710	1.0F
	1607	1357	1.1E
	2203	1927	1.1F
15 Th	0441	0220	1.3E
	1042	0757	1.1F
	1651	1443	1.1E
	2244	2012	1.1F
16 F	0525	0305	1.3E
	1119	0841	1.1F
	1736	1528	1.1E
	2323	2055	1.1F
17 Sa ●	0606	0348	1.3E
	1155	0923	1.1F
	1818	1610	1.1E
		2135	1.1F
18 Su	0001	0427	1.2E
	0646	1002	1.1F
	1232	1649	1.0E
	1859	2210	1.1F
19 M	0041	0502	1.2E
	0725	1036	1.1F
	1310	1722	1.0E
	1940	2230	1.1F
20 Tu	0121	0515	1.1E
	0805	1053	1.2F
	1349	1718	1.0E
	2023	2249	1.2F
21 W	0202	0513	1.1E
	0846	1112	1.2F
	1430	1732	1.1E
	2108	2327	1.2F
22 Th	0246	0544	1.2E
	0928	1151	1.3F
	1514	1808	1.1E
	2154		
23 F	0332	0011	1.2F
	1012	0624	1.2E
	1600	1235	1.3F
	2242	1853	1.2E
24 Sa	0421	0100	1.2F
	1100	0711	1.2E
	1648	1323	1.4F
	2334	1943	1.2E
25 Su	0512	0150	1.2F
	1151	0803	1.1E
	1739	1413	1.4F
		2039	1.2E
26 M	0029	0243	1.2F
	0606	0902	1.1E
	1246	1506	1.3F
	1832	2142	1.2E
27 Tu	0123	0340	1.2F
	0703	1007	1.1E
	1340	1602	1.3F
	1928	2252	1.3E
28 W	0219	0441	1.2F
	0801	1124	1.1E
	1438	1702	1.3F
	2024		
29 Th	0316	0017	1.3E
	0900	0551	1.2F
	1533	1301	1.2E
	2121	1806	1.3F
30 F	0410	0130	1.4E
	0959	0707	1.2F
	1630	1405	1.2E
	2218	1919	1.3F
31 Sa ○	0506	0229	1.4E
	1055	0811	1.3F
	1726	1501	1.3E
	2314	2027	1.3F

August

Day	Slack (h m)	Maximum (h m)	knots
1 Su	0559	0325	1.5E
	1150	0909	1.3F
	1820	1556	1.4E
		2128	1.3F
2 M	0008	0419	1.5E
	0650	1004	1.3F
	1244	1650	1.4E
	1914	2225	1.3F
3 Tu	0102	0513	1.5E
	0742	1057	1.3F
	1336	1744	1.4E
	2009	2321	1.3F
4 W	0155	0608	1.4E
	0834	1151	1.3F
	1428	1839	1.4E
	2102		
5 Th	0249	0017	1.2F
	0926	0702	1.3E
	1520	1245	1.2F
	2158	1935	1.3E
6 F	0343	0113	1.1F
	1019	0802	1.2E
	1612	1339	1.2F
	2252	2033	1.3E
7 Sa ○	0439	0210	1.1F
	1111	0859	1.2E
	1706	1435	1.1F
	2349	2130	1.2E
8 Su	0538	0307	1.0F
	1207	0957	1.1E
	1801	1529	1.1F
		2226	1.2E
9 M	0046	0403	1.0F
	0638	1054	1.1E
	1300	1624	1.1F
	1857	2321	1.2E
10 Tu	0140	0458	1.0F
	0739	1148	1.1E
	1355	1717	1.1F
	1951		
11 W	0234	0014	1.2E
	0838	0550	1.0F
	1448	1240	1.1E
	2042	1808	1.0F
12 Th	0323	0113	1.3E
	0929	0640	1.0F
	1537	1329	1.1E
	2130	1857	1.0F
13 F	0410	0152	1.3E
	1011	0727	1.1F
	1622	1416	1.1E
	2213	1943	1.1F
14 Sa	0453	0236	1.3E
	1049	0811	1.1F
	1708	1459	1.1E
	2254	2026	1.1F
15 Su ●	0535	0318	1.2E
	1126	0853	1.2F
	1750	1540	1.1E
	2334	2106	1.1F
16 M	0614	0355	1.2E
	1203	0930	1.2F
	1831	1616	1.1E
		2140	1.2F
17 Tu	0014	0424	1.2E
	0653	1001	1.2F
	1241	1641	1.1E
	1913	2202	1.2F
18 W	0054	0422	1.2E
	0732	1015	1.3F
	1320	1637	1.2E
	1956	2223	1.2F
19 Th	0135	0440	1.2E
	0813	1042	1.3F
	1401	1702	1.2E
	2040	2300	1.3F
20 F	0219	0513	1.2E
	0857	1121	1.4F
	1444	1739	1.2E
	2127	2343	1.3F
21 Sa	0304	0554	1.2E
	0941	1204	1.4F
	1529	1823	1.2E
	2216		
22 Su	0353	0031	1.3F
	1031	0640	1.1E
	1618	1252	1.4F
	2309	1913	1.2E
23 M ○	0445	0121	1.2F
	1124	0733	1.1E
	1710	1343	1.4F
		2011	1.2E
24 Tu	0003	0215	1.1F
	0541	0835	1.0E
	1220	1437	1.2F
	1805	2121	1.2E
25 W	0101	0315	1.1F
	0641	0958	1.0E
	1319	1537	1.2F
	1904	2318	1.2E
26 Th	0200	0431	1.1F
	0742	1200	1.1E
	1419	1647	1.1F
	2004		
27 F	0258	0028	1.3E
	0844	0604	1.2F
	1518	1300	1.2E
	2104	1820	1.2F
28 Sa	0352	0125	1.4E
	0943	0707	1.2F
	1614	1355	1.3E
	2202	1926	1.2F
29 Su ○	0447	0219	1.4E
	1039	0802	1.3F
	1709	1448	1.3E
	2257	2023	1.3F
30 M	0539	0310	1.5E
	1132	0855	1.3F
	1802	1538	1.4E
	2350	2116	1.3F
31 Tu	0628	0401	1.5E
	1222	0945	1.4F
	1854	1629	1.5E
		2207	1.3F

September

Day	Slack (h m)	Maximum (h m)	knots
1 W	0042	0451	1.4E
	0718	1033	1.4F
	1311	1719	1.4E
	1945	2258	1.3F
2 Th	0132	0542	1.4E
	0806	1122	1.4F
	1400	1811	1.4E
	2037	2349	1.3F
3 F	0222	0636	1.3E
	0855	1211	1.4F
	1448	1905	1.3E
	2129		
4 Sa	0314	0042	1.1F
	0946	0731	1.2E
	1537	1303	1.3F
	2221	2001	1.3E
5 Su	0407	0136	1.0F
	1038	0828	1.1E
	1628	1357	1.1F
	2317	2058	1.2E
6 M ○	0502	0233	1.0F
	1130	0926	1.0E
	1721	1453	1.1F
		2155	1.2E
7 Tu	0011	0329	0.9F
	0559	1022	1.0E
	1227	1549	1.0F
	1815	2250	1.2E
8 W	0107	0425	0.9F
	0658	1117	1.0E
	1320	1644	1.0F
	1910	2343	1.2E
9 Th	0200	0518	1.0F
	0754	1209	1.0E
	1414	1736	1.0F
	2004		
10 F	0250	0033	1.2E
	0847	0608	1.0F
	1505	1258	1.1E
	2054	1825	1.0F
11 Sa	0336	0119	1.2E
	0933	0655	1.1F
	1551	1344	1.1E
	2140	1911	1.1F
12 Su	0419	0203	1.2E
	1014	0738	1.2F
	1637	1426	1.2E
	2223	1954	1.2F
13 M	0500	0242	1.2E
	1053	0818	1.3F
	1720	1504	1.2E
	2305	2032	1.2F
14 Tu ●	0540	0315	1.2E
	1132	0853	1.3F
	1801	1539	1.3E
	2345	2105	1.3F
15 W	0620	0329	1.2E
	1210	0919	1.4F
	1844	1544	1.3E
		2126	1.3F
16 Th	0026	0341	1.2E
	0700	0938	1.4F
	1250	1602	1.3E
	1928	2154	1.3F
17 F	0108	0410	1.2E
	0741	1011	1.4F
	1331	1633	1.3E
	2011	2233	1.3F
18 Sa	0152	0445	1.2E
	0827	1051	1.4F
	1415	1712	1.3E
	2100	2316	1.3F
19 Su	0238	0527	1.1E
	0914	1135	1.4F
	1501	1757	1.2E
	2150		
20 M	0328	0004	1.2F
	1007	0614	1.1E
	1551	1224	1.4F
	2247	1850	1.2E
21 Tu ○	0422	0055	1.1F
	1102	0712	1.0E
	1645	1316	1.3F
	2343	1954	1.1E
22 W	0521	0153	1.0F
	1202	0830	0.9E
	1744	1414	1.1F
		2215	1.1E
23 Th	0043	0310	1.0F
	0625	1053	1.0E
	1304	1529	1.0F
	1847	2321	1.2E
24 F	0143	0459	1.0F
	0729	1153	1.0E
	1407	1722	1.0F
	1950		
25 Sa	0241	0019	1.3E
	0831	0602	1.1F
	1506	1249	1.1E
	2050	1825	1.1F
26 Su	0337	0113	1.4E
	0929	0658	1.1F
	1601	1341	1.3E
	2148	1920	1.2F
27 M	0429	0204	1.4E
	1023	0749	1.3F
	1654	1431	1.3E
	2242	2011	1.3F
28 Tu ○	0518	0253	1.5E
	1113	0837	1.3F
	1744	1520	1.5E
	2332	2100	1.3F
29 W	0604	0341	1.5E
	1200	0923	1.4F
	1832	1607	1.5E
		2147	1.3F
30 Th	0021	0428	1.4E
	0650	1007	1.4F
	1245	1655	1.5E
	1920	2233	1.2F

All times are local time. Daylight Saving Time has been used when needed.
At times of slack water before maximum ebb, the speed actually averages 0.3 knot in a direction of 184° true.

NOTES:

Boston Harbor (Deer Island Light), Massachusetts, 2004

F–Flood, Dir. 254° True   E–Ebb, Dir. 111° True

October

Day	Slack h m	Maximum h m	knots
1 F	0108	0517	1.3E
	0738	1051	1.3F
	1329	1744	1.4E
	2009	2319	1.2F
2 Sa	0154	0607	1.2E
	0823	1135	1.2F
	1414	1835	1.3E
	2059		
3 Su		0008	1.1F
	0242	0701	1.0E
	0911	1221	1.1F
	1500	1929	1.2E
	2149		
4 M		0100	1.0F
	0331	0757	1.0E
	1002	1313	1.0F
	1549	2025	1.1E
	2241		
5 Tu		0156	0.9F
	0424	0853	0.9E
	1056	1411	0.9F
	1640	2121	1.1E
	2336		
6 W		0253	0.9F
	0519	0949	0.9E
	1150	1510	0.9F
	1734	2215	1.1E
7 Th	0029	0349	0.9F
	0615	1043	0.9E
	1247	1608	0.9F
	1829	2308	1.1E
8 F	0121	0442	1.0F
	0711	1135	1.0E
	1340	1701	1.0F
	1924	2357	1.1E
9 Sa	0211	0532	1.1F
	0803	1223	1.1E
	1430	1750	1.1F
	2016		
10 Su		0043	1.2E
	0258	0618	1.2F
	0852	1307	1.1E
	1519	1836	1.2F
	2105		
11 M		0124	1.2E
	0341	0700	1.3F
	0936	1347	1.2E
	1604	1918	1.3F
	2150		
12 Tu		0159	1.4E
	0424	0738	1.4F
	1017	1420	1.3E
	1648	1955	1.3F
	2233		
13 W		0223	1.3E
	0506	0811	1.5F
	1058	1441	1.4E
	1731	2026	1.4F
	2316		
14 Th		0240	1.3E
	0547	0835	1.5F
	1139	1501	1.4E
	1815	2053	1.4F
	2359		
15 F		0308	1.3E
	0629	0904	1.5F
	1220	1531	1.4E
	1859	2127	1.4F

Day	Slack h m	Maximum h m	knots
16 Sa	0042	0342	1.3E
	0712	0942	1.5F
	1303	1608	1.4E
	1947	2207	1.4F
17 Su	0127	0422	1.2E
	0800	1024	1.5F
	1348	1650	1.3E
	2037	2252	1.3F
18 M	0215	0506	1.1E
	0850	1110	1.3F
	1436	1738	1.2E
	2129	2341	1.2F
19 Tu	0307	0559	1.0E
	0946	1200	1.2F
	1528	1837	1.1E
	2227		
20 W		0035	1.0F
	0404	0710	0.9E
	1046	1255	1.0F
	1626	2059	1.1E
	2327		
21 Th		0144	0.9F
	0507	0939	0.9E
	1149	1404	0.9F
	1728	2209	1.1E
22 F	0028	0347	0.9F
	0612	1041	1.0E
	1252	1613	0.9F
	1833	2309	1.2E
23 Sa	0129	0453	1.0F
	0715	1139	1.1E
	1356	1718	1.0F
	1937		
24 Su		0006	1.3E
	0228	0551	1.1F
	0817	1224	1.3E
	1454	1815	1.1F
	2038		
25 M		0058	1.4E
	0321	0643	1.2F
	0914	1325	1.4E
	1549	1907	1.2F
	2135		
26 Tu		0148	1.4E
	0410	0731	1.3F
	1006	1414	1.6E
	1639	1955	1.2F
	2228		
27 W		0243	1.4E
	0457	0817	1.3F
	1053	1501	1.6E
	1726	2042	1.3F
	2315		
28 Th		0322	1.4E
	0541	0901	1.4F
	1137	1547	1.6E
	1811	2126	1.3F
29 F	0000	0408	1.3E
	0626	0943	1.3F
	1219	1633	1.6E
	1857	2209	1.2F
30 Sa	0044	0454	1.2E
	0709	1023	1.2F
	1300	1718	1.3E
	1941	2252	1.1F
31 Su	0127	0442	1.1F
	0654	1000	1.2E
	1242	1706	1.2E
	1929	2236	1.0F

November

Day	Slack h m	Maximum h m	knots
1 M	0111	0533	1.0E
	0740	1032	1.1F
	1325	1757	1.1E
	2017	2321	1.0F
2 Tu	0157	0625	0.9E
	0830	1059	1.0F
	1411	1850	1.1E
	2107		
3 W		0013	0.9F
	0246	0719	0.9E
	0921	1149	0.9F
	1500	1944	1.0E
	2158		
4 Th		0110	0.9F
	0338	0813	0.9E
	1015	1320	0.9F
	1553	2036	1.0E
	2249		
5 F		0207	0.9F
	0432	0905	0.9E
	1109	1424	0.9F
	1648	2128	1.0E
	2340		
6 Sa		0300	1.0F
	0526	0955	1.0E
	1202	1519	1.0F
	1743	2216	1.1E
7 Su	0030	0350	1.1F
	0619	1042	1.1E
	1254	1610	1.1F
	1837	2300	1.1E
8 M	0118	0436	1.2F
	0709	1125	1.2E
	1343	1656	1.2F
	1927	2338	1.2E
9 Tu	0203	0517	1.3F
	0756	1201	1.3E
	1430	1737	1.3F
	2016		
10 W		0007	1.3E
	0248	0554	1.4F
	0841	1246	1.4E
	1516	1815	1.4F
	2102		
11 Th		0032	1.3E
	0331	0626	1.5F
	0925	1255	1.4E
	1601	1849	1.5F
	2147		
12 F		0103	1.3E
	0416	0658	1.6F
	1008	1328	1.5E
	1648	1924	1.5F
	2232		
13 Sa		0141	1.3E
	0500	0735	1.6F
	1052	1407	1.5E
	1734	2003	1.5F
	2318		
14 Su		0221	1.3E
	0548	0817	1.5F
	1138	1449	1.4E
	1822	2046	1.4F
15 M	0006	0306	1.2E
	0638	0902	1.4F
	1225	1536	1.3E
	1914	2133	1.3F

Day	Slack h m	Maximum h m	knots
16 Tu	0056	0357	1.1E
	0731	0950	1.3F
	1315	1631	1.2E
	2009	2224	1.1F
17 W	0150	0503	1.0E
	0829	1042	1.1F
	1410	1827	1.1E
	2107	2326	1.0F
18 Th	0249	0717	1.0E
	0929	1145	1.0F
	1509	1947	1.1E
	2208		
19 F		0122	0.9F
	0352	0823	1.0E
	1033	1351	0.9F
	1613	2052	1.1E
	2310		
20 Sa		0234	0.9F
	0455	0924	1.1E
	1139	1502	0.9F
	1718	2151	1.2E
21 Su	0011	0336	1.0F
	0558	1022	1.2E
	1242	1603	1.0F
	1823	2248	1.3E
22 M	0109	0432	1.1F
	0700	1116	1.3E
	1341	1659	1.1F
	1925	2340	1.3E
23 Tu	0202	0524	1.2F
	0758	1207	1.4E
	1434	1750	1.2F
	2024		
24 W		0030	1.4E
	0251	0612	1.3F
	0849	1256	1.5E
	1522	1838	1.2F
	2115		
25 Th		0118	1.4E
	0337	0657	1.3F
	0934	1342	1.5E
	1609	1923	1.2F
	2201		
26 F		0204	1.3E
	0420	0740	1.3F
	1015	1427	1.5E
	1651	2007	1.2F
	2243		
27 Sa		0249	1.3E
	0502	0821	1.3F
	1055	1512	1.4E
	1735	2049	1.2F
	2323		
28 Su		0334	1.2E
	0546	0900	1.2F
	1134	1556	1.3E
	1818	2130	1.1F
29 M	0003	0419	1.1E
	0629	0935	1.1F
	1213	1640	1.2E
	1900	2208	1.0F
30 Tu	0044	0505	1.0E
	0712	0954	1.0F
	1254	1725	1.1E
	1946	2244	1.0F

December

Day	Slack h m	Maximum h m	knots
1 W	0126	0552	0.9E
	0759	1019	1.0F
	1338	1811	1.0E
	2031	2304	1.0F
2 Th	0211	0640	0.9E
	0849	1102	1.0F
	1424	1858	1.0E
	2119	2342	1.0F
3 F	0259	0729	0.9E
	0939	1152	0.9F
	1514	1946	1.0E
	2208		
4 Sa		0034	1.0F
	0350	0818	0.9E
	1030	1250	0.9F
	1607	2034	1.0E
	2258		
5 Su		0140	1.0F
	0442	0905	1.0E
	1123	1357	0.9F
	1701	2118	1.0E
	2347		
6 M		0242	1.1F
	0534	0949	1.1E
	1216	1507	1.1F
	1756	2156	1.1E
7 Tu	0037	0333	1.2F
	0626	1029	1.2E
	1307	1602	1.2F
	1849	2232	1.1E
8 W	0125	0419	1.3F
	0716	1104	1.3E
	1357	1650	1.3F
	1941	2311	1.2E
9 Th	0212	0502	1.4F
	0805	1141	1.4E
	1446	1734	1.4F
	2031	2353	1.3E
10 F	0300	0545	1.5F
	0853	1222	1.5E
	1534	1818	1.5F
	2120		
11 Sa		0037	1.3E
	0349	0628	1.6F
	0941	1305	1.5E
	1622	1901	1.5F
	2209		
12 Su		0123	1.3E
	0438	0712	1.6F
	1028	1351	1.5E
	1711	1946	1.5F
	2258		
13 M		0211	1.3E
	0528	0758	1.5F
	1117	1439	1.5E
	1801	2033	1.4F
	2348		
14 Tu		0303	1.2E
	0619	0846	1.4F
	1206	1533	1.4E
	1854	2124	1.3F
15 W	0040	0409	1.2E
	0713	0938	1.3F
	1259	1644	1.3E
	1949	2223	1.2F

Day	Slack h m	Maximum h m	knots
16 Th	0135	0546	1.1E
	0810	1037	1.1F
	1354	1816	1.2E
	2045	2347	1.1F
17 F	0232	0656	1.1E
	0911	1216	1.0F
	1453	1925	1.2E
	2144		
18 Sa		0103	1.0F
	0333	0800	1.1E
	1014	1334	0.9F
	1555	2028	1.1E
	2245		
19 Su		0209	1.0F
	0434	0901	1.2E
	1119	1440	0.9F
	1700	2128	1.2E
	2346		
20 M		0310	1.0F
	0536	0959	1.2E
	1221	1541	1.0F
	1804	2225	1.2E
21 Tu	0043	0407	1.1F
	0638	1054	1.3E
	1321	1637	1.0F
	1911	2319	1.2E
22 W	0139	0500	1.1F
	0738	1147	1.4E
	1416	1729	1.1F
	2015		
23 Th		0011	1.3E
	0229	0550	1.2F
	0831	1236	1.4E
	1505	1818	1.1F
	2108		
24 F		0100	1.3E
	0317	0636	1.2F
	0916	1323	1.4E
	1550	1905	1.2F
	2151		
25 Sa		0146	1.3E
	0400	0721	1.2F
	0956	1409	1.4E
	1631	1948	1.2F
	2229		
26 Su		0231	1.2E
	0442	0803	1.2F
	1034	1452	1.4E
	1714	2030	1.1F
27 M	0315		1.1E
	0524	0842	1.1F
	1112	1534	1.3E
	1755	2110	1.1F
	2342		
28 Tu		0357	1.1E
	0607	0918	1.1F
	1150	1614	1.2E
	1835	2146	1.1F
29 W	0020	0437	1.0E
	0648	0943	1.1F
	1229	1650	1.1E
	1916	2214	1.1F
30 Th	0058	0515	1.0E
	0730	0954	1.0F
	1309	1654	1.1E
	1958	2223	1.1F
31 F	0139	0500	0.9E
	0817	1032	1.1F
	1352	1700	1.0E
	2040	2259	1.1F

All times are local time. Daylight Saving Time has been used when needed.
At times of slack water before maximum ebb, the speed actually averages 0.3 knot in a direction of 184° true.

NOTES:

Pollock Rip Channel, Massachusetts, 2004

F–Flood, Dir. 035° True   E–Ebb, Dir. 225° True

April

Day	Slack h m	Max h m	knots
1 Th		0323	1.6F
	0616	0902	1.5E
	1207	1545	2.0F
	1851	2137	1.6E
2 F	0043	0407	1.8F
	0703	0949	1.7E
	1254	1627	2.1F
	1934	2219	1.7E
3 Sa	0125	0446	1.9F
	0746	1031	1.8E
	1337	1704	2.2F
	2014	2257	1.9E
4 Su	0304	0621	2.1F
	0927	1211	2.0E
	1518	1839	2.3F
	2153		
5 M ○		0034	2.0E
	0341	0655	2.2F
	1008	1251	2.1E
	1558	1913	2.3F
	2231		
6 Tu		0112	2.1E
	0418	0731	2.3F
	1049	1332	2.1E
	1639	1950	2.3F
	2310		
7 W		0152	2.1E
	0457	0810	2.4F
	1133	1415	2.1E
	1722	2030	2.2F
	2351		
8 Th		0235	2.1E
	0539	0853	2.3F
	1220	1501	2.1E
	1808	2114	2.1F
9 F	0036	0321	2.1E
	0625	0941	2.3F
	1312	1552	1.9E
	1859	2204	1.9F
10 Sa	0127	0411	1.9E
	0717	1036	2.1F
	1411	1647	1.7E
	1957	2303	1.7F
11 Su ○	0226	0508	1.7E
	0816	1141	1.9F
	1516	1751	1.5E
	2103		
12 M		0016	1.5F
	0332	0613	1.5E
	0924	1302	1.8F
	1627	1904	1.3E
	2219		
13 Tu		0145	1.4F
	0445	0728	1.4E
	1040	1429	1.8F
	1740	2027	1.3E
	2336		
14 W		0308	1.5F
	0557	0850	1.4E
	1155	1543	1.9F
	1847	2145	1.4E
15 Th	0046	0416	1.6F
	0705	1005	1.5E
	1304	1645	2.1F
	1947	2248	1.6E
16 F	0147	0514	1.9F
	0804	1107	1.6E
	1403	1739	2.2F
	2039	2340	1.7E
17 Sa	0238	0604	2.0F
	0857	1158	1.7E
	1455	1827	2.2F
	2125		
18 Su		0025	1.8E
	0323	0650	2.1F
	0944	1243	1.8E
	1541	1910	2.2F
	2207		
19 M ●		0104	1.8E
	0403	0731	2.2F
	1028	1323	1.8E
	1623	1950	2.1F
	2245		
20 Tu		0138	1.8E
	0440	0810	2.1F
	1109	1359	1.7E
	1701	2026	2.0F
	2323		
21 W		0211	1.8E
	0516	0848	2.1F
	1150	1434	1.7E
	1739	2101	1.9F
22 Th	0000	0245	1.7E
	0551	0921	2.0F
	1231	1510	1.6E
	1817	2136	1.7F
23 F	0039	0321	1.7E
	0629	0928	2.0F
	1314	1550	1.5E
	1858		
24 Sa	0121	0401	1.6E
	0710	1039	1.9F
	1400	1634	1.5E
	1944	2258	1.5F
25 Su	0208	0447	1.5E
	0755	1126	1.8F
	1450	1722	1.4E
	2034	2349	1.5F
26 M	0259	0537	1.5E
	0846	1219	1.8F
	1543	1817	1.4E
	2129		
27 Tu		0046	1.4F
	0354	0632	1.4E
	0940	1316	1.8F
	1637	1914	1.4E
	2226		
28 W		0147	1.5F
	0450	0729	1.4E
	1036	1414	1.8F
	1730	2010	1.4E
	2321		
29 Th		0244	1.5F
	0545	0825	1.5E
	1131	1507	1.9F
	1821	2103	1.5E
30 F	0013	0335	1.7F
	0637	0918	1.6E
	1224	1556	2.0F
	1908	2151	1.7E

May

Day	Slack h m	Max h m	knots
1 Sa	0100	0422	1.8F
	0726	1007	1.7E
	1313	1640	2.0F
	1953	2235	1.8E
2 Su	0144	0504	2.0F
	0812	1054	1.8E
	1400	1721	2.1F
	2035	2318	1.9E
3 M	0226	0543	2.1F
	0856	1138	1.9E
	1445	1801	2.2F
	2116	2359	2.0E
4 Tu ○	0306	0623	2.1F
	0941	1222	2.0E
	1529	1841	2.2F
	2157		
5 W		0041	2.1E
	0348	0704	2.3F
	1026	1307	2.1E
	1614	1923	2.1F
	2240		
6 Th		0125	2.1E
	0431	0748	2.4F
	1114	1354	2.0E
	1701	2008	2.1F
	2325		
7 F		0211	2.1E
	0517	0835	2.3F
	1205	1444	1.9E
	1752	2057	1.9F
8 Sa	0015	0300	2.0E
	0608	0928	2.3F
	1301	1538	1.8E
	1847	2153	1.8F
9 Su	0110	0355	1.8E
	0703	1024	2.1F
	1401	1637	1.6E
	1949	2259	1.6F
10 M	0212	0455	1.7E
	0805	1139	2.0F
	1506	1744	1.5E
	2057		
11 Tu ○		0016	1.5F
	0320	0603	1.5E
	0914	1258	1.9F
	1614	1858	1.4E
	2210		
12 W		0138	1.5F
	0431	0719	1.4E
	1026	1413	1.9F
	1720	2014	1.4E
	2320		
13 Th		0251	1.6F
	0541	0836	1.4E
	1137	1520	2.0F
	1822	2123	1.5E
14 F	0025	0354	1.8F
	0645	0945	1.5E
	1242	1619	2.1F
	1919	2222	1.6E
15 Sa	0121	0449	2.0F
	0743	1044	1.6E
	1340	1712	2.1F
	2009	2312	1.7E
16 Su	0211	0539	2.1F
	0835	1135	1.7E
	1431	1800	2.1F
	2055	2356	1.8E
17 M	0255	0625	2.2F
	0923	1220	1.7E
	1517	1844	2.0F
	2137		
18 Tu ●		0035	1.8E
	0335	0707	2.2F
	1007	1300	1.7E
	1559	1924	1.9F
	2216		
19 W		0110	1.7E
	0413	0746	2.1F
	1048	1337	1.6E
	1637	2001	1.8F
	2254		
20 Th		0143	1.7E
	0448	0822	2.1F
	1128	1412	1.6E
	1715	2036	1.7F
	2331		
21 F		0217	1.7E
	0524	0857	2.0F
	1209	1447	1.5E
	1754	2111	1.7F
22 Sa	0011	0253	1.7E
	0601	0933	2.0F
	1250	1526	1.5E
	1834	2147	1.6F
23 Su	0052	0333	1.6E
	0641	1011	2.0F
	1334	1608	1.5E
	1918	2229	1.6F
24 M	0137	0417	1.6E
	0724	1053	1.9F
	1420	1654	1.5E
	2005	2315	1.5F
25 Tu	0225	0505	1.6E
	0811	1140	1.9F
	1508	1743	1.5E
	2054		
26 W ○		0005	1.5F
	0317	0555	1.5E
	0902	1230	1.9F
	1557	1834	1.5E
	2146		
27 Th		0058	1.6F
	0410	0648	1.5E
	0954	1322	1.9F
	1647	1925	1.6E
	2237		
28 F		0152	1.6F
	0504	0742	1.6E
	1047	1414	2.0F
	1737	2016	1.6E
	2328		
29 Sa		0244	1.7F
	0545	0835	1.6E
	1141	1505	2.0F
	1825	2105	1.7E
30 Su	0016	0334	1.8F
	0648	0927	1.7E
	1233	1554	2.0F
	1911	2153	1.8E
31 M	0103	0422	2.0F
	0739	1017	1.8E
	1324	1641	2.0F
	1957	2240	1.9E

June

Day	Slack h m	Max h m	knots
1 Tu	0150	0509	2.1F
	0828	1107	1.8E
	1414	1727	2.0F
	2043	2327	2.0E
2 W ○	0236	0556	2.2F
	0918	1157	1.9E
	1504	1814	2.0F
	2129		
3 Th		0014	2.0E
	0323	0644	2.3F
	1009	1247	1.9E
	1554	1903	2.0F
	2217		
4 F		0103	2.0E
	0411	0734	2.3F
	1101	1338	1.9E
	1647	1954	1.9F
	2307		
5 Sa		0153	2.0E
	0502	0827	2.3F
	1155	1432	1.8E
	1741	2049	1.8F
6 Su	0000	0246	1.9E
	0556	0924	2.2F
	1251	1528	1.7E
	1839	2149	1.7F
7 M	0058	0343	1.8E
	0654	1026	2.2F
	1350	1629	1.6E
	1940	2256	1.7F
8 Tu	0159	0444	1.7E
	0755	1132	2.1F
	1451	1733	1.6E
	2044		
9 W ○		0007	1.6F
	0304	0550	1.6E
	0859	1241	2.0F
	1552	1840	1.5E
	2150		
10 Th		0118	1.7F
	0411	0700	1.5E
	1006	1348	2.0F
	1653	1948	1.5E
	2253		
11 F		0224	1.8F
	0516	0810	1.5E
	1111	1451	2.0F
	1751	2051	1.6E
	2353		
12 Sa		0324	1.9F
	0618	0916	1.5E
	1213	1549	2.0F
	1845	2148	1.6E
13 Su	0049	0420	2.0F
	0717	1015	1.5E
	1310	1642	2.0F
	1936	2239	1.7E
14 M	0139	0511	2.1F
	0810	1107	1.6E
	1402	1731	1.9F
	2023	2325	1.7E
15 Tu	0225	0558	2.1F
	0859	1154	1.6E
	1450	1817	1.9F
	2107		
16 W		0006	1.7E
	0307	0642	2.1F
	0944	1237	1.6E
	1534	1859	1.8F
	2148		
17 Th ●		0044	1.7E
	0346	0723	2.1F
	1026	1315	1.5E
	1614	1938	1.7F
	2227		
18 F		0118	1.7E
	0424	0800	2.1F
	1107	1351	1.5E
	1653	2014	1.7F
	2306		
19 Sa		0153	1.7E
	0500	0835	2.1F
	1146	1426	1.6E
	1731	2048	1.7F
	2345		
20 Su		0229	1.7E
	0537	0909	2.1F
	1225	1503	1.6E
	1810	2123	1.6F
21 M	0025	0308	1.7E
	0615	0944	2.1F
	1306	1542	1.6E
	1850	2200	1.7F
22 Tu	0108	0349	1.7E
	0656	1022	2.1F
	1348	1624	1.7E
	1933	2240	1.7F
23 W	0153	0434	1.7E
	0739	1103	2.1F
	1432	1708	1.7E
	2017	2324	1.7F
24 Th	0238	0521	1.7E
	0825	1147	2.0F
	1517	1754	1.7E
	2104		
25 F ○		0012	1.7F
	0331	0610	1.7E
	0914	1235	2.0F
	1604	1843	1.7E
	2153		
26 Sa		0103	1.7F
	0423	0702	1.7E
	1006	1325	2.0F
	1653	1933	1.7E
	2243		
27 Su		0156	1.8F
	0518	0755	1.6E
	1100	1418	2.0F
	1743	2024	1.7E
	2334		
28 M		0252	1.9F
	0614	0850	1.6E
	1156	1512	1.9F
	1834	2116	1.7E
29 Tu	0027	0346	1.9F
	0710	0946	1.6E
	1253	1608	1.8F
	1925	2209	1.8E
30 W	0119	0442	2.0F
	0806	1042	1.7E
	1350	1703	1.8F
	2017	2302	1.9E

All times are local time. Daylight Saving Time has been used when needed.

NOTES:

Pollock Rip Channel, Massachusetts, 2004

F—Flood, Dir. 035° True   E—Ebb, Dir. 225° True

July

July 1–15

Day	Slack (h m)	Maximum (h m)	knots
1 Th	0212	0538	2.1F
	0902	1138	1.7E
	1446	1759	1.8F
	2109	2355	1.9E
2 F	0306	0634	2.2F
	0956	1234	1.7E
	1542	1854	1.8F
	2201 ○		
3 Sa		0048	1.9E
	0359	0729	2.3F
	1051	1329	1.7E
	1637	1950	1.8F
	2255		
4 Su		0142	1.9E
	0453	0824	2.3F
	1145	1424	1.7E
	1733	2046	1.8F
	2349		
5 M		0237	1.9E
	0547	0920	2.3F
	1239	1519	1.7E
	1828	2144	1.8F
6 Tu	0045	0333	1.8E
	0643	1017	2.2F
	1333	1615	1.7E
	1924	2244	1.8F
7 W	0143	0430	1.7E
	0739	1115	2.1F
	1428	1712	1.6E
	2021	2345	1.8F
8 Th	0243	0530	1.6E
	0838	1215	2.0F
	1523	1811	1.6E
	2119		
9 F		0048	1.8F
	0344	0632	1.5E
	0938	1316	1.9F
	1619	1911	1.6E
	2218 ○		
10 Sa		0150	1.8F
	0446	0736	1.5E
	1038	1416	1.9F
	1714	2011	1.5E
	2316		
11 Su		0250	1.8F
	0547	0840	1.4E
	1139	1514	1.8F
	1809	2108	1.5E
12 M	0012	0347	1.9F
	0646	0941	1.4E
	1237	1610	1.8F
	1901	2203	1.6E
13 Tu	0105	0441	2.0F
	0742	1037	1.4E
	1332	1702	1.8F
	1951	2253	1.6E
14 W	0154	0531	2.0F
	0833	1127	1.5E
	1423	1750	1.8F
	2038	2337	1.6E
15 Th	0239	0616	2.1F
	0919	1212	1.5E
	1509	1834	1.8F
	2121		

July 16–31

Day	Slack (h m)	Maximum (h m)	knots
16 F		0018	1.7E
	0320	0658	2.1F
	1002	1252	1.5E
	1550	1914	1.8F
	2202		
17 Sa		0055	1.7E
	0359	0736	2.1F
	1042	1328	1.6E
	1629 ●	1950	1.7F
	2241		
18 Su		0130	1.7E
	0436	0810	2.2F
	1120	1402	1.6E
	1706	2023	1.8F
	2320		
19 M		0205	1.8E
	0512	0842	2.2F
	1157	1436	1.7E
	1743	2055	1.8F
	2358		
20 Tu		0242	1.8E
	0549	0914	2.2F
	1235	1517	1.8E
	1819	2128	1.8F
21 W	0038	0321	1.9E
	0627	0948	2.2F
	1314	1551	1.8E
	1858	2204	1.9F
22 Th	0120	0402	1.9E
	0707	1025	2.2F
	1354	1632	1.8E
	1939	2245	1.9F
23 F	0205	0447	1.9E
	0751	1107	2.1F
	1437	1716	1.8E
	2023	2330	1.9F
24 Sa	0254	0535	1.8E
	0838	1153	2.0F
	1523	1803	1.8E
	2110 ○		
25 Su		0020	1.9F
	0347	0626	1.7E
	0930	1243	1.9F
	1613	1854	1.7E
	2202		
26 M		0115	1.8F
	0445	0721	1.6E
	1026	1339	1.8F
	1707	1948	1.7E
	2258		
27 Tu		0216	1.8F
	0546	0820	1.5E
	1127	1441	1.7F
	1804	2046	1.7E
	2357		
28 W		0322	1.9F
	0649	0923	1.5E
	1231	1546	1.6F
	1902	2146	1.7E
29 Th	0058	0429	1.9F
	0751	1027	1.5E
	1335	1654	1.6F
	2000	2244	1.7E
30 F	0158	0533	2.0F
	0851	1130	1.6E
	1437	1756	1.7F
	2057	2345	1.8E
31 Sa	0256	0632	2.2F
	0947	1228	1.6E
	1535	1854	1.8F
	2152 ○		

August

August 1–15

Day	Slack (h m)	Maximum (h m)	knots
1 Su		0042	1.8E
	0351	0727	2.2F
	1040	1323	1.7E
	1629	1948	1.9F
	2245		
2 M		0135	1.9E
	0445	0819	2.3F
	1131	1415	1.8E
	1720	2040	1.9F
	2337		
3 Tu		0227	1.9E
	0536	0909	2.3F
	1220	1504	1.8E
	1810	2131	1.9F
4 W	0029	0318	1.9E
	0627	0958	2.2F
	1309	1553	1.7E
	1900	2222	1.9F
5 Th	0122	0409	1.8E
	0718	1049	2.1F
	1358	1643	1.7E
	1951	2316	1.9F
6 F	0217	0502	1.7E
	0810	1142	2.0F
	1449	1734	1.6E
	2043		
7 Sa		0012	1.8F
	0314	0558	1.5E
	0905	1238	1.8F
	1541	1828	1.5E
	2137 ○		
8 Su		0112	1.8F
	0413	0658	1.4E
	1003	1338	1.7F
	1636	1926	1.5E
	2234		
9 M		0213	1.8F
	0513	0801	1.3E
	1103	1438	1.6F
	1731	2026	1.4E
	2332		
10 Tu		0313	1.8F
	0614	0905	1.3E
	1203	1537	1.6F
	1827	2125	1.4E
11 W	0028	0409	1.9F
	0711	1005	1.3E
	1301	1632	1.7F
	1920	2219	1.5E
12 Th	0121	0501	2.0F
	0803	1057	1.4E
	1354	1722	1.7F
	2009	2308	1.6E
13 F	0208	0547	2.1F
	0850	1143	1.5E
	1441	1806	1.8F
	2054	2350	1.7E
14 Sa	0252	0629	2.1F
	0933	1223	1.6E
	1523	1846	1.8F
	2136		
15 Su		0028	1.7E
	0331	0707	2.2F
	1012	1258	1.7E
	1601 ●	1921	1.9F
	2215		

August 16–31

Day	Slack (h m)	Maximum (h m)	knots
16 M		0103	1.8E
	0408	0740	2.2F
	1049	1331	1.8E
	1636	1953	1.9F
	2252		
17 Tu		0138	1.9E
	0444	0810	2.3F
	1124	1404	1.8E
	1710	2022	2.0F
	2329		
18 W		0213	2.0E
	0520	0840	2.3F
	1200	1439	1.9E
	1745	2054	2.0F
19 Th	0008	0251	2.0E
	0557	0913	2.3F
	1237	1516	2.0E
	1821	2129	2.1F
20 F	0048	0331	2.0E
	0636	0949	2.2F
	1316	1556	2.0E
	1901	2209	2.1F
21 Sa	0133	0415	2.0E
	0719	1030	2.1F
	1359	1640	1.9E
	1944	2254	2.0F
22 Su	0222	0503	1.9E
	0807	1117	2.0F
	1446	1728	1.8E
	2033	2345	1.9F
23 M	0318	0556	1.7E
	0900	1210	1.8F
	1539	1821	1.7E
	2128 ○		
24 Tu		0044	1.9F
	0420	0654	1.5E
	1001	1312	1.6F
	1639	1920	1.6E
	2230		
25 W		0153	1.8F
	0527	0800	1.4E
	1109	1425	1.5F
	1743	2025	1.5E
	2337		
26 Th		0311	1.8F
	0636	0911	1.4E
	1221	1544	1.5F
	1848	2133	1.5E
27 F	0046	0427	1.9F
	0741	1022	1.4E
	1330	1656	1.6F
	1951	2241	1.6E
28 Sa	0140	0532	2.0F
	0841	1127	1.5E
	1432	1757	1.7F
	2050	2342	1.7E
29 Su	0250	0628	2.2F
	0931	1224	1.7E
	1527	1851	1.9F
	2144 ○		
30 M		0037	1.8E
	0344	0719	2.3F
	1025	1314	1.8E
	1617	1940	2.0F
	2234		
31 Tu		0127	1.9E
	0433	0806	2.3F
	1111	1400	1.8E
	1703	2026	2.0F
	2323		

September

September 1–15

Day	Slack (h m)	Maximum (h m)	knots
1 W		0214	1.9E
	0521	0851	2.2F
	1156	1443	1.8E
	1747	2111	2.0F
2 Th	0011	0259	1.9E
	0606	0934	2.1F
	1240	1525	1.8E
	1831	2156	2.0F
3 F	0059	0344	1.8E
	0652	1019	2.0F
	1325	1608	1.7E
	1916	2243	1.9F
4 Sa	0149	0432	1.6E
	0740	1106	1.8F
	1412	1654	1.6E
	2004	2334	1.8F
5 Su	0242	0522	1.5E
	0831	1159	1.7F
	1502	1745	1.5E
	2055		
6 M		0031	1.7F
	0339	0619	1.3E
	0927	1258	1.5F
	1557	1841	1.4E
	2151		
7 Tu		0133	1.7F
	0439	0721	1.3E
	1027	1401	1.5F
	1654	1942	1.3E
	2250		
8 W		0235	1.7F
	0539	0826	1.3E
	1129	1505	1.5F
	1752	2044	1.4E
	2349		
9 Th		0334	1.8F
	0636	0928	1.3E
	1228	1559	1.6F
	1847	2142	1.4E
10 F	0044	0427	1.9F
	0728	1022	1.4E
	1322	1651	1.7F
	1938	2233	1.5E
11 Sa	0134	0513	2.1F
	0815	1108	1.6E
	1409	1734	1.8F
	2024	2317	1.7E
12 Su	0219	0555	2.2F
	0858	1148	1.7E
	1450	1813	1.9F
	2106		
13 M		0001	1.8E
	0259	0631	2.2F
	0937	1223	1.8E
	1527	1847	2.0F
	2145		
14 Tu		0032	1.9E
	0337	0704	2.3F
	1013	1256	1.9E
	1602 ●	1921	2.1F
	2222		
15 W		0107	2.0E
	0413	0734	2.3F
	1048	1329	2.0E
	1635	1948	2.1F
	2300		

September 16–30

Day	Slack (h m)	Maximum (h m)	knots
16 Th		0143	2.1E
	0449	0805	2.3F
	1124	1404	2.0E
	1710	2020	2.2F
	2338		
17 F		0221	2.1E
	0527	0838	2.3F
	1201	1442	2.1E
	1746	2056	2.2F
18 Sa	0020	0302	2.1E
	0607	0916	2.2F
	1241	1523	2.0E
	1826	2137	2.2F
19 Su	0106	0347	2.0E
	0652	0959	2.1F
	1325	1608	1.9E
	1911	2224	2.1F
20 M	0158	0437	1.8E
	0742	1048	1.9F
	1415	1659	1.8E
	2003	2319	2.0F
21 Tu	0257	0533	1.6E
	0840	1146	1.7F
	1513	1755	1.6E
	2103 ○		
22 W		0025	1.8F
	0403	0636	1.4E
	0947	1257	1.5F
	1620	1900	1.5E
	2211		
23 Th		0145	1.8F
	0514	0748	1.3E
	1058	1424	1.4F
	1731	2013	1.4E
	2325		
24 F		0310	1.8F
	0625	0907	1.3E
	1217	1547	1.5F
	1840	2129	1.5E
25 Sa	0038	0423	1.9F
	0730	1020	1.5E
	1324	1654	1.7F
	1944	2239	1.7E
26 Su	0143	0524	2.1F
	0827	1122	1.6E
	1423	1750	1.8F
	2041	2338	1.7E
27 M	0240	0616	2.2F
	0918	1213	1.7E
	1514	1840	2.0F
	2133		
28 Tu		0029	1.8E
	0331	0704	2.3F
	1005	1258	1.8E
	1559 ○	1925	2.1F
	2221		
29 W		0115	1.9E
	0418	0747	2.2F
	1048	1339	1.8E
	1641	2008	2.1F
	2306		
30 Th		0157	1.8E
	0502	0829	2.1F
	1129	1417	1.8E
	1721	2049	2.1F
	2351		

All times are local time. Daylight Saving Time has been used when needed.

NOTES:

Pollock Rip Channel, Massachusetts, 2004

F–Flood, Dir. 035° True   E–Ebb, Dir. 225° True

October

Day	Slack (h m)	Max (h m)	knots
1 F		0238	1.8E
	0544	0908	2.0F
	1210	1455	1.7E
	1801	2129	2.0F
2 Sa	0036	0319	1.7E
	0626	0949	1.8F
	1252	1534	1.7E
	1842	2212	1.9F
3 Su	0123	0402	1.6E
	0710	1032	1.7F
	1336	1617	1.6E
	1926	2258	1.8F
4 M	0213	0449	1.4E
	0759	1121	1.5F
	1425	1705	1.5E
	2015	2351	1.8F
5 Tu	0307	0542	1.3E
	0853	1218	1.4F
	1519	1759	1.4E
	2109		
6 W ●		0051	1.7F
	0404	0642	1.3E
	0952	1321	1.4F
	1617	1858	1.3E
	2208		
7 Th		0153	1.7F
	0502	0745	1.3E
	1053	1424	1.4F
	1715	2000	1.3E
	2307		
8 F		0252	1.8F
	0557	0846	1.4E
	1151	1521	1.6F
	1811	2059	1.4E
9 Sa	0003	0346	1.9F
	0649	0939	1.5E
	1244	1612	1.7F
	1903	2152	1.5E
10 Su	0054	0433	2.0F
	0736	1026	1.6E
	1330	1656	1.8F
	1950	2238	1.7E
11 M	0141	0514	2.1F
	0818	1106	1.8E
	1412	1735	2.0F
	2032	2319	1.8E
12 Tu	0223	0551	2.2F
	0858	1143	1.9E
	1449	1809	2.1F
	2113	2357	1.9E
13 W ●	0302	0624	2.2F
	0935	1218	2.0E
	1525	1841	2.2F
	2152		
14 Th		0034	2.0E
	0341	0657	2.2F
	1012	1254	2.1E
	1600	1914	2.3F
	2231		
15 F		0113	2.1E
	0419	0730	2.2F
	1049	1331	2.1E
	1636	1949	2.3F
	2312		
16 Sa		0154	2.1E
	0500	0807	2.2F
	1127	1411	2.1E
	1716	2029	2.3F
	2357		
17 Su		0237	2.0E
	0543	0848	2.1F
	1210	1455	2.1E
	1759	2113	2.3F
18 M	0046	0325	1.9E
	0631	0935	1.9F
	1258	1543	1.9E
	1847	2204	2.2F
19 Tu	0141	0418	1.8E
	0725	1029	1.7F
	1352	1636	1.8E
	1942	2304	2.0F
20 W ○	0243	0517	1.6E
	0827	1134	1.5F
	1456	1737	1.6E
	2047		
21 Th		0016	1.9F
	0351	0625	1.4E
	0939	1255	1.4F
	1606	1847	1.4E
	2159		
22 F		0142	1.8F
	0502	0742	1.3E
	1055	1424	1.5F
	1719	2005	1.4E
	2315		
23 Sa		0302	1.9F
	0610	0901	1.4E
	1208	1539	1.6F
	1829	2123	1.5E
24 Su	0026	0409	2.0F
	0712	1009	1.5E
	1311	1641	1.8F
	1932	2230	1.6E
25 M	0129	0507	2.1F
	0807	1106	1.7E
	1406	1734	2.0F
	2027	2327	1.7E
26 Tu	0225	0558	2.2F
	0856	1155	1.8E
	1455	1823	2.1F
	2118		
27 W ●		0016	1.8E
	0315	0644	2.2F
	0941	1238	1.8E
	1538	1907	2.2F
	2205		
28 Th		0059	1.8E
	0400	0727	2.1F
	1022	1316	1.8E
	1618	1948	2.2F
	2249		
29 F		0139	1.7E
	0447	0807	2.0F
	1102	1352	1.8E
	1656	2028	2.1F
	2332		
30 Sa		0217	1.7E
	0522	0844	1.8F
	1141	1427	1.7E
	1734	2106	2.0F
31 Su	0015	0156	1.6E
	0502	0822	1.7F
	1121	1404	1.6E
	1713	2045	2.0F
	2359		

November

Day	Slack (h m)	Max (h m)	knots
1 M		0236	1.5E
	0544	0902	1.6F
	1204	1445	1.6E
	1754	2127	1.9F
2 Tu	0046	0321	1.4E
	0630	0947	1.5F
	1252	1531	1.5E
	1840	2215	1.8F
3 W	0135	0410	1.4E
	0721	1040	1.4F
	1343	1622	1.4E
	1931	2309	1.7F
4 Th	0228	0504	1.3E
	0816	1138	1.4F
	1439	1717	1.4E
	2026		
5 F		0006	1.8F
	0322	0601	1.4E
	0913	1237	1.5F
	1535	1815	1.4E
	2122		
6 Sa		0103	1.8F
	0415	0657	1.4E
	1008	1334	1.6F
	1630	1912	1.4E
	2217		
7 Su		0156	1.9F
	0505	0750	1.5E
	1100	1425	1.7F
	1723	2005	1.4E
	2309		
8 M		0244	2.0F
	0552	0857	1.7E
	1146	1510	1.8F
	1811	2053	1.7E
	2358		
9 Tu		0327	2.0F
	0636	0921	1.8E
	1229	1551	2.0F
	1857	2138	1.6E
10 W	0044	0407	2.1F
	0717	1001	1.9E
	1310	1629	2.1F
	1940	2221	1.9E
11 Th	0127	0445	2.1F
	0757	1041	2.0E
	1348	1706	2.2F
	2023	2303	2.0E
12 F ●	0209	0522	2.1F
	0837	1120	2.1E
	1428	1744	2.3F
	2106	2346	2.0E
13 Sa	0252	0601	2.1F
	0917	1202	2.1E
	1508	1825	2.4F
	2151		
14 Su		0030	2.0E
	0337	0643	2.1F
	1000	1246	2.1E
	1552	1909	2.4F
	2239		
15 M		0118	2.0E
	0424	0729	2.0F
	1047	1333	2.0E
	1639	1958	2.3F
	2332		
16 Tu		0209	1.9E
	0516	0820	1.8F
	1139	1424	1.9E
	1731	2053	2.2F
17 W	0029	0304	1.7E
	0614	0919	1.7F
	1237	1521	1.8E
	1830	2157	2.1F
18 Th	0131	0406	1.6E
	0719	1030	1.6F
	1342	1624	1.6E
	1935	2311	1.9F
19 F ○	0236	0515	1.5E
	0829	1151	1.5F
	1452	1736	1.5E
	2046		
20 Sa		0030	1.9F
	0343	0630	1.4E
	0940	1310	1.6F
	1603	1852	1.4E
	2158		
21 Su		0143	1.9F
	0448	0743	1.5E
	1048	1419	1.7F
	1711	2007	1.5E
	2307		
22 M		0247	2.0F
	0547	0847	1.6E
	1149	1519	1.9F
	1813	2112	1.6E
23 Tu	0009	0344	2.1F
	0641	0943	1.7E
	1243	1613	2.1F
	1910	2209	1.6E
24 W	0105	0435	2.1F
	0730	1032	1.7E
	1332	1702	2.1F
	2001	2258	1.7E
25 Th	0155	0523	2.0F
	0815	1115	1.8E
	1415	1748	2.2F
	2048	2343	1.7E
26 F ●	0241	0606	1.9F
	0857	1154	1.7E
	1455	1830	2.2F
	2132		
27 Sa		0023	1.6E
	0322	0646	1.8F
	0937	1230	1.7E
	1533	1909	2.1F
	2214		
28 Su		0100	1.6E
	0402	0724	1.7F
	1016	1304	1.7E
	1610	1946	2.1F
	2255		
29 M		0137	1.5E
	0441	0801	1.7F
	1056	1340	1.6E
	1648	2023	2.0F
	2336		
30 Tu		0215	1.5E
	0521	0838	1.6F
	1137	1420	1.6E
	1728	2101	2.0F

December

Day	Slack (h m)	Max (h m)	knots
1 W	0019	0255	1.5E
	0604	0918	1.5F
	1222	1502	1.6E
	1810	2143	1.9F
2 Th	0104	0340	1.5E
	0650	1003	1.5F
	1309	1549	1.5E
	1856	2228	1.9F
3 F	0151	0427	1.5E
	0739	1052	1.5F
	1400	1639	1.5E
	1945	2317	1.9F
4 Sa ○	0240	0517	1.5E
	0829	1145	1.6F
	1453	1731	1.5E
	2037		
5 Su		0008	1.9F
	0329	0608	1.6E
	0920	1237	1.6F
	1546	1824	1.5E
	2130		
6 M		0059	1.9F
	0418	0658	1.6E
	1010	1329	1.7F
	1639	1917	1.6E
	2222		
7 Tu		0149	1.9F
	0506	0747	1.7E
	1059	1419	1.8F
	1731	2008	1.6E
	2314		
8 W		0237	1.9F
	0552	0835	1.8E
	1145	1506	1.9F
	1820	2058	1.7E
9 Th	0004	0323	1.9F
	0638	0921	1.9E
	1231	1551	2.1F
	1909	2147	1.8E
10 F	0053	0408	2.0F
	0722	1006	1.9E
	1315	1636	2.2F
	1958	2235	1.9E
11 Sa ●	0142	0453	2.0F
	0807	1052	2.0E
	1401	1721	2.3F
	2046	2324	1.9E
12 Su	0231	0539	2.0F
	0852	1139	2.0E
	1447	1809	2.3F
	2136		
13 M		0013	1.9F
	0320	0627	1.9F
	0940	1227	2.1E
	1536	1858	2.3F
	2227		
14 Tu		0104	1.9E
	0412	0718	1.9F
	1031	1318	2.0E
	1627	1951	2.3F
	2320		
15 W		0157	1.8E
	0507	0813	1.8F
	1126	1412	1.9E
	1721	2048	2.2F
16 Th	0017	0254	1.7E
	0604	0914	1.7F
	1224	1509	1.8E
	1820	2150	2.1F
17 F	0115	0354	1.6E
	0706	1022	1.7F
	1327	1611	1.7E
	1922	2258	2.0F
18 Sa ○	0216	0458	1.6E
	0810	1134	1.7F
	1433	1718	1.6E
	2027		
19 Su		0008	2.0F
	0317	0606	1.7E
	0915	1245	1.7F
	1541	1830	1.5E
	2135		
20 M		0116	1.9F
	0418	0709	1.8E
	1019	1352	1.8F
	1647	1941	1.5E
	2241		
21 Tu		0219	1.9F
	0517	0817	1.6E
	1120	1453	1.9F
	1750	2047	1.5E
	2344		
22 W		0318	1.9F
	0612	0915	1.6E
	1215	1549	2.0F
	1848	2146	1.5E
23 Th	0042	0411	1.9F
	0703	1006	1.7E
	1306	1640	2.1F
	1941	2239	1.5E
24 F	0134	0500	1.9F
	0750	1052	1.7E
	1352	1727	2.1F
	2030	2325	1.5E
25 Sa	0221	0546	1.8F
	0834	1133	1.7E
	1434	1811	2.2F
	2114		
26 Su ●		0007	1.5E
	0304	0627	1.7F
	0915	1210	1.7E
	1513	1850	2.1F
	2155		
27 M		0044	1.5E
	0343	0706	1.7F
	0954	1245	1.7E
	1550	1927	2.1F
	2234		
28 Tu		0118	1.6E
	0421	0741	1.7F
	1033	1320	1.7E
	1626	2001	2.1F
	2313		
29 W		0153	1.6E
	0459	0815	1.7F
	1112	1356	1.7E
	1703	2035	2.1F
	2352		
30 Th		0229	1.6E
	0537	0850	1.7F
	1153	1435	1.7E
	1742	2110	2.1F
31 F	0032	0308	1.7E
	0617	0927	1.7F
	1236	1517	1.7E
	1823	2148	2.1F

All times are local time. Daylight Saving Time has been used when needed.

NOTES:

Cape Cod Canal (RR. Bridge), Massachusetts, 2004

F–Flood, Dir. 070° True   E–Ebb, Dir. 250° True

April

Day	Slack h m	Max h m	knots
1 Th	0005	0305	3.3F
	0619	0914	3.9E
	1228	1543	3.8F
	1907	2148	3.8E
2 F	0056	0357	3.6F
	0709	1005	4.2E
	1316	1628	4.1F
	1951	2234	4.1E
3 Sa	0141	0441	3.9F
	0755	1051	4.5E
	1401	1708	4.3F
	2031	2317	4.4E
4 Su	0322	0622	4.2F
	0937	1235	4.7E
	1543	1847	4.5F
	2208		
5 M		0059	4.6E
	0402	0702	4.5F
	1019	1318	4.8E
	1624	1925	4.6F
	2246		
6 Tu		0140	4.8E
	0442	0743	4.6F
	1102	1401	4.9E
	1705	2005	4.7F
	2324		
7 W		0223	4.8E
	0523	0825	4.7F
	1146	1446	4.9E
	1748	2046	4.6F
8 Th	0004	0307	4.9E
	0607	0910	4.7F
	1234	1533	4.7E
	1833	2130	4.5F
9 F	0046	0353	4.8E
	0655	0959	4.6F
	1327	1623	4.6E
	1923	2219	4.3F
10 Sa	0134	0444	4.7E
	0747	1052	4.5F
	1426	1718	4.3E
	2018	2313	4.0F
11 Su	0229	0540	4.5E
	0846	1153	4.2F
	1532	1819	4.1E
	2121		
12 M		0015	3.7F
	0333	0641	4.2E
	0953	1304	4.1F
	1644	1925	3.9E
	2232		
13 Tu		0128	3.6F
	0445	0748	4.2E
	1104	1423	4.0F
	1754	2034	3.9E
	2346		
14 W		0249	3.6F
	0557	0856	4.2E
	1215	1541	4.1F
	1859	2140	4.0E
15 Th	0054	0405	3.7F
	0704	1000	4.3E
	1319	1646	4.2F
	1955	2239	4.1E
16 F	0153	0506	4.0F
	0803	1058	4.4E
	1415	1738	4.4F
	2044	2330	4.3E
17 Sa	0243	0557	4.2F
	0855	1149	4.5E
	1505	1823	4.4F
	2128		
18 Su		0015	4.5E
	0328	0640	4.3F
	0943	1234	4.6E
	1549	1901	4.4F
	2208		
19 M		0056	4.5E
	0408	0718	4.4F
	1027	1316	4.6E
	1628	1935	4.3F
	2246		
20 Tu		0135	4.6E
	0445	0753	4.4F
	1108	1356	4.6E
	1706	2007	4.2F
	2321		
21 W		0213	4.5E
	0522	0827	4.3F
	1148	1435	4.4E
	1741	2039	4.1F
	2355		
22 Th		0251	4.5E
	0558	0901	4.2F
	1228	1515	4.2E
	1817	2112	3.9F
23 F	0030	0330	4.3E
	0635	0938	4.1F
	1310	1556	4.0E
	1855	2148	3.8F
24 Sa	0107	0412	4.2E
	0715	1017	3.9F
	1354	1641	3.8E
	1937	2229	3.5F
25 Su	0147	0458	4.0E
	0800	1102	3.8F
	1444	1729	3.6E
	2024	2315	3.3F
26 M	0235	0548	3.8E
	0850	1154	3.6F
	1540	1824	3.5E
	2119		
27 Tu		0009	3.2F
	0331	0643	3.7E
	0946	1252	3.5F
	1641	1921	3.4E
	2221		
28 W		0111	3.1F
	0435	0741	3.7E
	1047	1356	3.5F
	1741	2020	3.5E
	2324		
29 Th		0216	3.2F
	0539	0839	3.8E
	1147	1458	3.6F
	1835	2117	3.7E
30 F	0023	0319	3.4F
	0638	0935	4.0E
	1244	1554	3.9F
	1924	2209	3.9E

May

Day	Slack h m	Max h m	knots
1 Sa	0115	0414	3.7F
	0731	1028	4.2E
	1335	1643	4.1F
	2009	2257	4.2E
2 Su	0202	0503	4.0F
	0820	1117	4.4E
	1423	1728	4.3F
	2051	2343	4.5E
3 M	0247	0549	4.3F
	0908	1204	4.6E
	1509	1811	4.5F
	2131		
4 Tu		0027	4.7E
	0331	0634	4.6F
	0954	1250	4.8E
	1554	1854	4.6F
	2212		
5 W		0112	4.9E
	0416	0719	4.7F
	1042	1337	4.8E
	1639	1938	4.6F
	2254		
6 Th		0157	5.0E
	0501	0806	4.8F
	1131	1425	4.8E
	1726	2024	4.6F
	2338		
7 F		0244	5.0E
	0549	0854	4.8F
	1223	1515	4.7E
	1815	2112	4.4F
8 Sa	0025	0334	4.9E
	0640	0946	4.7F
	1318	1608	4.5E
	1908	2203	4.2F
9 Su	0117	0427	4.8E
	0735	1042	4.6F
	1418	1704	4.3E
	2006	2300	4.0F
10 M	0215	0524	4.6E
	0834	1145	4.4F
	1522	1804	4.1E
	2110		
11 Tu		0004	3.8F
	0320	0625	4.4E
	0939	1253	4.2F
	1628	1908	4.0E
	2219		
12 W		0117	3.6F
	0429	0729	4.3E
	1046	1407	4.0F
	1733	2013	4.0E
	2328		
13 Th		0233	3.7F
	0538	0834	4.2E
	1152	1517	4.1F
	1832	2115	4.0E
14 F	0031	0344	3.8F
	0642	0936	4.2E
	1254	1618	4.2F
	1926	2212	4.1E
15 Sa	0128	0443	4.0F
	0741	1032	4.3E
	1348	1710	4.2F
	2014	2301	4.3E
16 Su	0217	0533	4.1F
	0833	1122	4.3E
	1437	1754	4.2F
	2057	2346	4.4E
17 M	0301	0617	4.2F
	0921	1208	4.3E
	1521	1832	4.3F
	2137		
18 Tu		0027	4.4E
	0342	0655	4.2F
	1006	1250	4.3E
	1601	1906	4.1F
	2215		
19 W		0107	4.5E
	0420	0730	4.2F
	1048	1330	4.2E
	1638	1938	4.0F
	2251		
20 Th		0145	4.4E
	0457	0804	4.2F
	1129	1410	4.2E
	1715	2011	3.9F
	2326		
21 F		0224	4.4E
	0534	0839	4.1F
	1209	1451	4.1E
	1752	2046	3.8F
22 Sa	0002	0305	4.3E
	0612	0916	4.1F
	1250	1533	3.9E
	1831	2123	3.7F
23 Su	0039	0347	4.2E
	0652	0955	4.0F
	1334	1617	3.8E
	1912	2204	3.6F
24 M	0119	0431	4.1E
	0735	1038	3.9F
	1420	1704	3.7E
	1958	2249	3.4F
25 Tu	0204	0520	4.0E
	0821	1126	3.8F
	1510	1755	3.6E
	2049	2359	3.3F
26 W	0256	0611	3.9E
	0912	1218	3.7F
	1603	1848	3.6E
	2144		
27 Th		0035	3.3F
	0353	0705	3.9E
	1007	1314	3.7F
	1656	1942	3.7E
	2241		
28 F		0134	3.4F
	0454	0801	3.9E
	1103	1410	3.8F
	1749	2036	3.8E
	2338		
29 Sa		0233	3.5F
	0555	0856	4.0E
	1200	1506	3.9F
	1838	2129	4.0E
30 Su	0033	0331	3.8F
	0652	0951	4.2E
	1254	1559	4.1F
	1926	2220	4.3E
31 M	0125	0425	4.1F
	0748	1043	4.4E
	1346	1649	4.2F
	2012	2309	4.5E

June

Day	Slack h m	Max h m	knots
1 Tu	0215	0518	4.3F
	0841	1135	4.5E
	1437	1739	4.4F
	2057	2358	4.7E
2 W	0304	0609	4.6F
	0933	1225	4.6E
	1527	1827	4.5F
	2143		
3 Th		0047	4.9E
	0354	0659	4.7F
	1025	1316	4.7E
	1618	1916	4.5F
	2230		
4 F		0136	5.0E
	0444	0750	4.8F
	1118	1407	4.7E
	1708	2006	4.5F
	2318		
5 Sa		0226	5.0E
	0535	0842	4.8F
	1212	1459	4.6E
	1801	2057	4.4F
6 Su	0009	0317	5.0E
	0628	0936	4.8F
	1308	1553	4.5E
	1855	2151	4.3F
7 M	0103	0411	4.9E
	0723	1032	4.6F
	1405	1648	4.4E
	1953	2248	4.1F
8 Tu	0201	0506	4.7E
	0820	1131	4.5F
	1504	1746	4.2E
	2053	2349	3.9F
9 W	0303	0605	4.5E
	0920	1234	4.3F
	1604	1845	4.1E
	2156		
10 Th		0055	3.8F
	0407	0705	4.3E
	1021	1338	4.2F
	1702	1944	4.1E
	2259		
11 F		0204	3.7F
	0512	0805	4.2E
	1122	1442	4.1F
	1758	2042	4.1E
	2359		
12 Sa		0311	3.8F
	0615	0904	4.1E
	1221	1542	4.1F
	1850	2137	4.1E
13 Su	0055	0412	3.9F
	0714	1000	4.1E
	1316	1635	3.9F
	1939	2228	4.2E
14 M	0146	0505	3.9F
	0808	1052	4.0E
	1406	1721	3.9F
	2024	2315	4.2E
15 Tu	0233	0551	4.0F
	0858	1140	4.0E
	1451	1802	3.9F
	2106	2359	4.3E
16 W	0316	0632	4.1F
	0944	1224	4.0E
	1534	1839	3.8F
	2146		
17 Th		0040	4.3E
	0357	0710	4.1F
	1028	1307	4.0E
	1613	1914	3.8F
18 F		0121	4.4E
	0435	0745	4.1F
	1110	1348	4.0E
	1652	1949	3.8F
	2302		
19 Sa		0201	4.4E
	0514	0821	4.1F
	1150	1429	4.0E
	1730	2025	3.8F
	2339		
20 Su		0242	4.3E
	0552	0857	4.1F
	1231	1511	3.9E
	1809	2102	3.7F
21 M	0017	0324	4.3E
	0631	0935	4.1F
	1312	1554	3.9E
	1850	2142	3.7F
22 Tu	0056	0407	4.2E
	0711	1015	4.0F
	1353	1638	3.8E
	1932	2224	3.6F
23 W	0138	0452	4.2E
	0754	1058	4.0F
	1437	1725	3.8E
	2018	2310	3.6F
24 Th	0225	0540	4.1E
	0840	1145	3.9F
	1523	1813	3.8E
	2107		
25 F		0000	3.6F
	0317	0631	4.1E
	0930	1234	3.9F
	1611	1904	3.9E
	2200		
26 Sa		0055	3.6F
	0414	0724	4.1E
	1023	1327	3.9F
	1703	1957	4.0E
	2256		
27 Su		0153	3.7F
	0514	0820	4.1E
	1119	1423	3.9F
	1753	2051	4.1E
	2354		
28 M		0253	3.9F
	0619	0917	4.1E
	1217	1520	4.0F
	1846	2146	4.3E
29 Tu	0051	0354	4.1F
	0721	1014	4.2E
	1315	1617	4.1F
	1940	2240	4.5E
30 W	0148	0453	4.4F
	0820	1110	4.4E
	1412	1712	4.2F
	2029	2333	4.7E

All times are local time. Daylight Saving Time has been used when needed.

NOTES:

Cape Cod Canal (RR. Bridge), Massachusetts, 2004

F—Flood, Dir. 070° True   E—Ebb, Dir. 250° True

July

Day	Slack (h m)	Maximum (h m, knots)
1 Th	0243, 0918, 1507, 2121	0550 4.5F, 1205 4.5E, 1807 4.3F
2 F ○	0337, 1013, 1601, 2212	0026 4.9E, 0645 4.7F, 1259 4.6E, 1900 4.4F
3 Sa	0430, 1107, 1654, 2303	0118 5.0E, 0739 4.8F, 1352 4.6E, 1953 4.4F
4 Su	0522, 1200, 1747, 2355	0210 5.1E, 0832 4.8F, 1444 4.6E, 2045 4.4F
5 M	0614, 1252, 1840	0301 5.0E, 0924 4.8F, 1536 4.6E, 2137 4.3F
6 Tu	0049, 0707, 1345, 1933	0353 4.9E, 1016 4.7F, 1628 4.5E, 2231 4.2F
7 W	0143, 0759, 1437, 2027	0446 4.8E, 1109 4.5F, 1720 4.3E, 2326 4.1F
8 Th	0240, 0853, 1530, 2123	0539 4.6E, 1203 4.3F, 1814 4.2E
9 F ○	0340, 0949, 1624, 2221	0024 3.9F, 0634 4.3E, 1300 4.1F, 1908 4.1E
10 Sa	0441, 1045, 1718, 2320	0125 3.8F, 0731 4.1E, 1358 3.9F, 2003 4.0E
11 Su	0543, 1143, 1811	0230 3.7F, 0828 3.9E, 1457 3.7F, 2058 4.0E
12 M	0018, 0644, 1239, 1902	0334 3.7F, 0926 3.8E, 1554 3.6F, 2152 4.0E
13 Tu	0113, 0741, 1333, 1951	0433 3.7F, 1021 3.8E, 1647 3.6F, 2243 4.0E
14 W	0204, 0834, 1423, 2038	0525 3.8F, 1112 3.8E, 1734 3.6F, 2331 4.1E
15 Th	0251, 0922, 1509, 2121	0611 3.9F, 1200 3.8E, 1816 3.7F
16 F	0334, 1007, 1551, 2202	0016 4.2E, 0651 4.0F, 1244 3.9E, 1854 3.7F
17 Sa ●	0414, 1049, 1631, 2241	0058 4.3E, 0727 4.1F, 1327 4.0E, 1930 3.8F
18 Su	0453, 1128, 1709, 2319	0140 4.4E, 0802 4.2F, 1407 4.0E, 2005 3.8F
19 M	0531, 1207, 1747, 2356	0220 4.4E, 0836 4.2F, 1448 4.1E, 2042 3.9F
20 Tu	0608, 1244, 1825	0301 4.5E, 0912 4.2F, 1528 4.1E, 2119 3.9F
21 W	0033, 0646, 1322, 1904	0342 4.4E, 0949 4.2F, 1610 4.1E, 2159 3.9F
22 Th	0113, 0726, 1400, 1946	0425 4.4E, 1029 4.2F, 1653 4.1E, 2241 3.9F
23 F	0156, 0809, 1442, 2032	0510 4.3E, 1111 4.1F, 1739 4.1E, 2328 3.9F
24 Sa ○	0245, 0856, 1527, 2123	0559 4.2E, 1158 4.0F, 1828 4.0E
25 Su	0342, 0949, 1618	0021 3.9F, 0652 4.1E, 1250 4.0F, 1922 4.1E
26 M	0446, 1046, 1714, 2321	0119 3.9F, 0749 4.0E, 1347 3.9F, 2019 4.1E
27 Tu	0555, 1148, 1813	0223 3.9F, 0850 4.0E, 1449 3.9F, 2118 4.3E
28 W	0025, 0703, 1252, 1912	0330 4.0F, 0951 4.1E, 1553 3.9F, 2217 4.5E
29 Th	0128, 0807, 1355, 2010	0437 4.2F, 1052 4.2E, 1655 4.1F, 2315 4.7E
30 F	0228, 0906, 1454, 2106	0539 4.5F, 1150 4.4E, 1755 4.2F
31 Sa ○	0324, 1001, 1549, 2159	0010 4.9E, 0636 4.7F, 1245 4.5E, 1850 4.4F

August

Day	Slack (h m)	Maximum (h m, knots)
1 Su	0418, 1053, 1641, 2251	0103 5.0E, 0729 4.8F, 1336 4.6E, 1942 4.5F
2 M	0508, 1142, 1731, 2341	0154 5.1E, 0819 4.8F, 1426 4.7E, 2031 4.5F
3 Tu	0557, 1230, 1819	0243 5.0E, 0906 4.8F, 1514 4.6E, 2119 4.5F
4 W	0031, 0645, 1316, 1907	0332 4.9E, 0953 4.7F, 1602 4.6E, 2207 4.3F
5 Th	0122, 0733, 1403, 1955	0420 4.8E, 1039 4.5F, 1649 4.4E, 2256 4.2F
6 F	0214, 0821, 1451, 2046	0510 4.5E, 1125 4.2F, 1738 4.2E, 2346 4.0F
7 Sa ○	0308, 0911, 1540, 2139	0600 4.2E, 1214 3.9F, 1828 4.1E
8 Su	0407, 1004, 1633, 2236	0041 3.8F, 0654 3.9E, 1308 3.6F, 1922 3.9E
9 M	0509, 1102, 1728, 2336	0143 3.6F, 0751 3.7E, 1407 3.4F, 2018 3.8E
10 Tu	0612, 1202, 1825	0250 3.5F, 0850 3.6E, 1513 3.3F, 2115 3.8E
11 W	0036, 0713, 1301, 1919	0359 3.5F, 0949 3.5E, 1613 3.3F, 2211 3.9E
12 Th	0133, 0808, 1356, 2010	0458 3.7F, 1044 3.6E, 1707 3.4F, 2303 4.0E
13 F	0223, 0858, 1445, 2056	0547 3.8F, 1135 3.8E, 1753 3.6F, 2351 4.2E
14 Sa	0309, 0942, 1528, 2139	0627 4.0F, 1220 3.9E, 1832 3.8F
15 Su ●	0350, 1022, 1607, 2218	0034 4.3E, 0703 4.1F, 1302 4.1E, 1908 3.9F
16 M	0428, 1100, 1644, 2256	0116 4.5E, 0737 4.2F, 1342 4.2E, 1942 4.0F
17 Tu	0505, 1136, 1720, 2332	0156 4.6E, 0810 4.3F, 1421 4.3E, 2017 4.1F
18 W	0542, 1211, 1757	0235 4.6E, 0844 4.4F, 1500 4.3E, 2054 4.2F
19 Th	0009, 0619, 1246, 1834	0315 4.6E, 0920 4.4F, 1539 4.3E, 2132 4.2F
20 F	0048, 0658, 1323, 1915	0357 4.6E, 0958 4.3F, 1621 4.3E, 2214 4.2F
21 Sa	0132, 0740, 1403, 2001	0442 4.4E, 1039 4.2F, 1707 4.3E, 2300 4.1F
22 Su	0221, 0827, 1448, 2052	0530 4.3E, 1126 4.1F, 1756 4.2E, 2353 4.0F
23 M ○	0320, 0920, 1541, 2151	0625 4.1E, 1219 3.9F, 1852 4.2E
24 Tu	0427, 1022, 1643, 2258	0054 4.0F, 0725 4.0E, 1320 3.8F, 1952 4.1E
25 W	0541, 1130, 1750	0203 3.9F, 0829 3.9E, 1428 3.7F, 2056 4.2E
26 Th	0007, 0713, 1240, 1901	0317 4.0F, 0935 3.9E, 1540 3.8F, 2200 4.4E
27 F	0115, 0757, 1346, 1958	0429 4.2F, 1039 4.1E, 1648 3.9F, 2300 4.6E
28 Sa	0216, 0855, 1444, 2055	0533 4.4F, 1137 4.3E, 1748 4.2F, 2356 4.8E
29 Su ○	0312, 0946, 1537, 2148	0627 4.6F, 1230 4.5E, 1841 4.4F
30 M	0403, 1034, 1625, 2237	0048 4.9E, 0716 4.8F, 1319 4.6E, 1929 4.5F
31 Tu	0451, 1119, 1711, 2325	0136 5.0E, 0801 4.8F, 1404 4.7E, 2014 4.6F

September

Day	Slack (h m)	Maximum (h m, knots)
1 W	0536, 1202, 1754	0222 5.0E, 0843 4.7F, 1448 4.7E, 2057 4.5F
2 Th	0011, 0619, 1243, 1837	0307 4.9E, 0923 4.6F, 1531 4.6E, 2139 4.4F
3 F	0058, 0702, 1325, 1921	0352 4.7E, 1003 4.3F, 1615 4.5E, 2222 4.2F
4 Sa	0146, 0746, 1408, 2006	0438 4.4E, 1044 4.1F, 1700 4.3E, 2308 4.0F
5 Su	0236, 0831, 1454, 2056	0525 4.1E, 1128 3.8F, 1748 4.0E, 2358 3.7F
6 M	0332, 0922, 1545, 2151	0617 3.8E, 1218 3.4F, 1841 3.8E
7 Tu	0434, 1020, 1644, 2253	0056 3.5F, 0713 3.5E, 1316 3.2F, 1938 3.7E
8 W	0539, 1124, 1746	0204 3.4F, 0814 3.4E, 1425 3.1F, 2039 3.7E
9 Th	0642, 1229, 1846	0319 3.4F, 0916 3.4E, 1536 3.1F, 2138 3.8E
10 F	0058, 0738, 1327, 1940	0424 3.6F, 1015 3.5E, 1637 3.3F, 2233 3.9E
11 Sa	0151, 0827, 1417, 2028	0514 3.8F, 1106 3.8E, 1724 3.6F, 2322 4.2E
12 Su	0238, 0911, 1500, 2111	0555 4.0F, 1151 4.0E, 1804 3.8F
13 M	0319, 0950, 1538, 2151	0006 4.4E, 0631 4.2F, 1233 4.2E, 1840 4.0F
14 Tu ●	0358, 1026, 1615, 2229	0048 4.5E, 0705 4.3F, 1312 4.4E, 1915 4.2F
15 W	0435, 1101, 1651, 2307	0128 4.7E, 0738 4.4F, 1350 4.5E, 1950 4.4F
16 Th	0512, 1135, 1727, 2345	0207 4.7E, 0813 4.5F, 1429 4.6E, 2027 4.4F
17 F	0550, 1210, 1806	0248 4.7E, 0849 4.5F, 1509 4.6E, 2107 4.5F
18 Sa	0027, 0630, 1248, 1848	0331 4.6E, 0929 4.4F, 1552 4.6E, 2150 4.4F
19 Su	0112, 0714, 1329, 1936	0417 4.5E, 1011 4.3F, 1639 4.5E, 2238 4.3F
20 M	0205, 0803, 1417, 2029	0507 4.3E, 1100 4.1F, 1730 4.3E, 2333 4.2F
21 Tu ○	0307, 0900, 1514, 2132	0604 4.1E, 1156 3.8F, 1828 4.2E
22 W	0418, 1006, 1622, 2241	0037 4.0F, 0707 3.9E, 1253 3.6F, 1932 4.2E
23 Th	0532, 1120, 1735, 2354	0151 4.0F, 0815 3.8E, 1417 3.6F, 2039 4.3E
24 F	0643, 1232, 1845	0311 4.0F, 0923 3.9E, 1534 3.7F, 2145 4.4E
25 Sa	0102, 0744, 1337, 1947	0424 4.2F, 1026 4.1E, 1643 3.9F, 2246 4.6E
26 Su	0203, 0838, 1432, 2043	0523 4.4F, 1122 4.4E, 1740 4.2F, 2341 4.7E
27 M	0257, 0926, 1522, 2134	0614 4.6F, 1212 4.5E, 1829 4.4F
28 Tu ○	0345, 1011, 1606, 2222	0030 4.8E, 0658 4.7F, 1257 4.7E, 1913 4.5F
29 W	0430, 1052, 1648, 2307	0116 4.9E, 0738 4.6F, 1340 4.7E, 1954 4.6F
30 Th	0511, 1131, 1728, 2350	0159 4.8E, 0816 4.5F, 1420 4.7E, 2033 4.5F

All times are local time. Daylight Saving Time has been used when needed.

NOTES:

Cape Cod Canal (RR. Bridge), Massachusetts, 2004

F–Flood, Dir. 070° True   E–Ebb, Dir. 250° True

October

Day	Slack h m	Max h m	knots
1 F		0242	4.7E
	0551	0852	4.4F
	1209	1501	4.6E
	1808	2111	4.4F
2 Sa	0034	0324	4.5E
	0630	0928	4.2F
	1247	1542	4.4E
	1848	2150	4.2F
3 Su	0119	0407	4.2E
	0710	1005	3.9F
	1326	1625	4.2E
	1930	2232	4.0F
4 M	0206	0453	3.9E
	0754	1047	3.6F
	1409	1711	4.0E
	2017	2319	3.7F
5 Tu	0300	0543	3.6E
	0843	1134	3.3F
	1459	1803	3.8E
	2110		
6 W		0014	3.5F
	0400	0639	3.4E
	0940	1232	3.1F
	1559	1900	3.6E
	2211		
7 Th		0119	3.4F
	0504	0739	3.3E
	1046	1339	3.0F
	1705	2001	3.6E
	2315		
8 F		0231	3.4F
	0607	0841	3.4E
	1152	1452	3.1F
	1808	2102	3.7E
9 Sa	0017	0338	3.5F
	0702	0939	3.6E
	1252	1555	3.3F
	1905	2158	3.9E
10 Su	0112	0431	3.8F
	0751	1031	3.8E
	1342	1646	3.6F
	1955	2248	4.1E
11 M	0200	0514	4.0F
	0834	1117	4.1E
	1425	1728	3.9F
	2039	2333	4.4E
12 Tu	0244	0552	4.2F
	0913	1159	4.3E
	1505	1806	4.1F
	2121		
13 W		0016	4.6E
	0324	0628	4.4F
	0949	1231	4.4E
	1543	1844	4.4F
	2201		
14 Th		0058	4.7E
	0403	0705	4.5F
	1025	1319	4.7E
	1621	1922	4.5F
	2242		
15 F		0140	4.8E
	0443	0742	4.5F
	1101	1400	4.8E
	1700	2002	4.6F
	2324		
16 Sa		0223	4.8E
	0523	0821	4.5F
	1138	1442	4.8E
	1742	2045	4.7F
17 Su	0009	0308	4.7E
	0607	0903	4.4F
	1218	1527	4.7E
	1827	2131	4.6F
18 M	0059	0356	4.5E
	0654	0949	4.3F
	1303	1616	4.6E
	1917	2222	4.5F
19 Tu	0155	0449	4.3E
	0746	1041	4.0F
	1355	1710	4.5E
	2014	2320	4.3F
20 W	0259	0548	4.1E
	0847	1140	3.8F
	1457	1810	4.3E
	2118		
21 Th		0027	4.1F
	0409	0652	3.9E
	0956	1250	3.6F
	1608	1915	4.2E
	2228		
22 F		0143	4.0F
	0520	0800	3.9E
	1110	1408	3.6F
	1722	2023	4.2E
	2339		
23 Sa		0301	4.1F
	0626	0907	4.0E
	1220	1526	3.7F
	1831	2128	4.3E
24 Su	0046	0410	4.3F
	0724	1008	4.2E
	1322	1632	4.0F
	1933	2228	4.5E
25 M	0145	0506	4.4F
	0816	1102	4.4E
	1415	1717	4.2F
	2028	2322	4.6E
26 Tu	0237	0554	4.5F
	0902	1150	4.5E
	1502	1814	4.4F
	2118		
27 W		0010	4.6E
	0324	0636	4.5F
	0944	1233	4.6E
	1545	1855	4.5F
	2205		
28 Th		0016	4.6E
	0406	0713	4.4F
	1023	1314	4.7E
	1625	1934	4.5F
	2249		
29 F		0058	4.6E
	0446	0756	4.3F
	1100	1353	4.6E
	1704	2010	4.4F
	2331		
30 Sa		0136	4.4E
	0524	0822	4.2F
	1137	1432	4.5E
	1741	2046	4.6F
31 Su	0013	0157	4.3E
	0501	0756	4.0F
	1113	1412	4.4E
	1720	2023	4.2F
	2356		

November

Day	Slack h m	Max h m	knots
1 M		0240	4.0E
	0540	0833	3.8F
	1150	1455	4.2E
	1801	2104	4.0F
2 Tu	0041	0324	3.8E
	0622	0913	3.5F
	1232	1540	4.1E
	1845	2148	3.8F
3 W	0131	0413	3.6E
	0709	1000	3.3F
	1320	1630	3.9E
	1935	2239	3.6F
4 Th	0226	0506	3.5E
	0804	1054	3.1F
	1416	1725	3.7E
	2031	2337	3.5F
5 F	0326	0604	3.4E
	0906	1156	3.0F
	1520	1823	3.7E
	2131		
6 Sa		0041	3.5F
	0425	0702	3.4E
	1009	1302	3.1F
	1624	1921	3.7E
	2231		
7 Su		0143	3.6F
	0519	0759	3.6E
	1107	1404	3.3F
	1723	2017	3.9E
	2327		
8 M		0238	3.8F
	0607	0851	3.9E
	1159	1459	3.6F
	1815	2109	4.1E
9 Tu	0017	0326	4.0F
	0651	0938	4.1E
	1246	1547	3.9F
	1904	2158	4.3E
10 W	0104	0410	4.2F
	0732	1023	4.4E
	1329	1631	4.2F
	1950	2244	4.5E
11 Th	0149	0451	4.3F
	0811	1107	4.6E
	1411	1714	4.4F
	2035	2329	4.6E
12 F	0232	0532	4.7F
	0850	1150	4.8E
	1454	1757	4.6F
	2120		
13 Sa		0014	4.7E
	0315	0614	4.5F
	0930	1234	4.9E
	1537	1841	4.7F
	2207		
14 Su		0101	4.7E
	0358	0658	4.5F
	1011	1319	4.9E
	1623	1928	4.8F
	2256		
15 M		0149	4.7E
	0448	0744	4.4F
	1056	1407	4.9E
	1712	2018	4.7F
	2349		
16 Tu		0240	4.5E
	0538	0833	4.3F
	1146	1458	4.8E
	1805	2111	4.6F
17 W	0047	0334	4.3E
	0634	0928	4.1F
	1241	1553	4.7E
	1902	2210	4.4F
18 Th	0149	0433	4.2E
	0735	1029	3.9F
	1343	1653	4.5E
	2004	2316	4.0F
19 F	0254	0535	4.0E
	0842	1137	3.7F
	1453	1756	4.4E
	2111		
20 Sa		0027	4.2F
	0359	0640	4.0E
	0952	1253	3.7F
	1603	1901	4.3E
	2218		
21 Su		0139	4.1F
	0501	0744	4.1E
	1059	1407	3.8F
	1711	2005	4.3E
	2322		
22 M		0245	4.2F
	0557	0843	4.2E
	1159	1512	4.0F
	1813	2105	4.3E
23 Tu		0341	4.2F
	0648	0936	4.3E
	1252	1608	4.1F
	1909	2158	4.4E
24 W	0113	0430	4.2F
	0734	1024	4.4E
	1340	1655	4.3F
	2000	2247	4.4E
25 Th	0200	0512	4.2F
	0816	1108	4.5E
	1423	1738	4.3F
	2047	2332	4.3E
26 F	0248	0550	4.1F
	0856	1149	4.5E
	1504	1816	4.3F
	2131		
27 Sa		0014	4.3E
	0322	0624	4.1F
	0934	1229	4.5E
	1542	1852	4.3F
	2214		
28 Su		0054	4.2E
	0400	0658	4.0F
	1010	1308	4.5E
	1620	1927	4.2F
	2255		
29 M		0135	4.1E
	0437	0732	3.8F
	1047	1348	4.4E
	1658	2003	4.1F
	2336		
30 Tu		0217	4.0E
	0516	0809	3.7F
	1124	1430	4.3E
	1737	2042	4.0F

December

Day	Slack h m	Max h m	knots
1 W	0019	0300	3.8E
	0557	0848	3.6F
	1204	1514	4.2E
	1819	2123	3.9F
2 Th	0104	0346	3.7E
	0641	0932	3.5F
	1248	1601	4.0E
	1904	2209	3.8F
3 F	0152	0435	3.6E
	0730	1021	3.3F
	1338	1651	3.9E
	1954	2259	3.7F
4 Sa	0243	0527	3.6E
	0824	1114	3.3F
	1434	1744	3.8E
	2047	2353	3.7F
5 Su	0336	0621	3.6E
	0920	1212	3.3F
	1534	1839	3.8E
	2142		
6 M		0048	3.7F
	0428	0715	3.7E
	1017	1312	3.4F
	1635	1935	3.9E
	2238		
7 Tu		0144	3.8F
	0518	0808	3.9E
	1112	1410	3.6F
	1733	2029	4.0E
	2332		
8 W		0237	3.9F
	0606	0859	4.1E
	1204	1505	3.9F
	1828	2122	4.2E
9 Th	0025	0328	4.1F
	0651	0948	4.3E
	1254	1557	4.2F
	1921	2214	4.4E
10 F	0115	0416	4.2F
	0736	1036	4.6E
	1343	1647	4.4F
	2012	2303	4.5E
11 Sa	0204	0504	4.4F
	0820	1124	4.8E
	1431	1736	4.6F
	2103	2353	4.6E
12 Su	0253	0552	4.4F
	0905	1212	5.0E
	1519	1824	4.8F
	2154		
13 M		0043	4.6E
	0343	0640	4.5F
	0952	1301	5.0E
	1609	1916	4.8F
	2246		
14 Tu		0133	4.6E
	0433	0730	4.4F
	1041	1351	5.0E
	1700	2007	4.8F
	2339		
15 W		0225	4.6E
	0526	0821	4.4F
	1133	1443	5.0E
	1753	2101	4.7F
16 Th	0034	0319	4.5E
	0620	0916	4.2F
	1228	1537	4.8E
	1848	2157	4.6F
17 F	0131	0415	4.3E
	0719	1014	4.1F
	1328	1633	4.6E
	1946	2257	4.4F
18 Sa	0230	0512	4.2E
	0820	1118	3.9F
	1432	1733	4.4E
	2047		
19 Su		0000	4.2F
	0329	0612	4.1E
	0924	1226	3.8F
	1539	1834	4.3E
	2150		
20 M		0106	4.1F
	0427	0712	4.1E
	1027	1336	3.8F
	1646	1936	4.1E
	2252		
21 Tu		0211	4.0F
	0523	0810	4.1E
	1128	1444	3.9F
	1749	2036	4.1E
	2351		
22 W		0310	4.2F
	0616	0905	4.2E
	1224	1544	4.0F
	1847	2132	4.0E
23 Th		0403	3.9F
	0704	0956	4.2E
	1315	1636	4.0F
	1941	2223	3.9E
24 F	0135	0449	3.9F
	0749	1042	4.3E
	1401	1721	4.1F
	2030	2310	4.0E
25 Sa	0220	0529	3.9F
	0832	1126	4.4E
	1444	1801	4.2F
	2115	2353	4.0E
26 Su	0302	0605	3.8F
	0911	1207	4.4E
	1524	1838	4.2F
	2157		
27 M		0035	4.0E
	0341	0640	3.8F
	0950	1248	4.4E
	1602	1912	4.2F
	2237		
28 Tu		0115	4.0E
	0418	0714	3.8F
	1027	1328	4.4E
	1640	1946	4.2F
	2317		
29 W		0156	4.0E
	0456	0750	3.8F
	1104	1408	4.4E
	1717	2022	4.1F
	2356		
30 Th		0237	4.0E
	0534	0827	3.7F
	1142	1450	4.3E
	1756	2059	4.1F
31 F	0035	0319	3.9E
	0614	0907	3.7F
	1222	1533	4.2E
	1836	2139	4.0F

All times are local time. Daylight Saving Time has been used when needed.

NOTES:

The Race, Long Island Sound, 2004

F–Flood, Dir. 302° True   E–Ebb, Dir. 112° True

April

Day	Slack (h m)	Maximum (h m)	knots
1 Th	0213	0502	2.1F
	0820	1125	2.7E
	1445	1733	2.3F
	2052	2349	2.6E
2 F	0301	0551	2.5F
	0907	1211	3.0E
	1526	1816	2.7F
	2133		
3 Sa	0346	0034	3.0E
	0951	0636	2.8F
	1605	1254	3.2E
	2212	1857	3.0F
4 Su	0529	0116	3.4E
	1133	0819	3.1F
	1743	1436	3.4E
	2351	2038	3.3F
5 M	0611	0258	3.7E
	1215	0902	3.3F
	1822	1518	3.5E
		2119	3.5F
6 Tu	0031	0341	3.9E
	0654	0946	3.4F
	1258	1601	3.5E
	1903	2202	3.6F
7 W	0113	0426	4.0E
	0740	1031	3.4F
	1344	1646	3.4E
	1947	2247	3.5F
8 Th	0158	0513	3.9E
	0828	1120	3.2F
	1432	1735	3.2E
	2035	2336	3.3F
9 F	0248	0604	3.7E
	0922	1212	3.0F
	1526	1828	3.0E
	2129		
10 Sa	0344	0030	3.0F
	1021	0700	3.4E
	1627	1309	2.7F
	2231	1927	2.7E
11 Su	0448	0129	2.7F
	1127	0802	3.1E
	1736	1413	2.4F
	2342	2033	2.5E
12 M	0559	0237	2.4F
	1236	0909	2.9E
	1848	1524	2.3F
		2143	2.4E
13 Tu	0057	0351	2.3F
	0711	1018	2.8E
	1344	1639	2.3F
	1957	2253	2.6E
14 W	0209	0506	2.4F
	0819	1129	2.9E
	1446	1747	2.5F
	2057	2356	2.8E
15 Th	0312	0613	2.6F
	0920	1222	3.0E
	1540	1843	2.7F
	2151		
16 F	0407	0050	3.1E
	1013	0708	2.7F
	1627	1312	3.1E
	2237	1929	2.9F
17 Sa	0456	0138	3.3E
	1100	0754	2.8F
	1710	1357	3.2E
	2319	2009	3.0F
18 Su	0540	0221	3.4E
	1144	0834	2.9F
	1750	1438	3.2E
	2358	2045	3.0F
19 M	0620	0300	3.4E
	1224	0910	2.9F
	1827	1517	3.1E
		2119	2.9F
20 Tu	0034	0338	3.4E
	0658	0945	2.8F
	1302	1555	2.9E
	1902	2154	2.8F
21 W	0109	0415	3.3E
	0735	1020	2.6F
	1339	1633	2.7E
	1937	2229	2.7F
22 Th	0144	0454	3.1E
	0813	1058	2.5F
	1416	1712	2.5E
	2014	2307	2.5F
23 F	0220	0534	2.9E
	0853	1138	2.3F
	1456	1754	2.3E
	2053	2349	2.2F
24 Sa	0300	0618	2.6E
	0937	1222	2.0F
	1540	1840	2.0E
	2138		
25 Su	0345	0706	2.4E
	1027	1311	1.9F
	1631	1932	1.9E
	2231		
26 M	0438	0127	1.8F
	1122	0800	2.3E
	1730	1406	1.7F
	2332	2029	1.8E
27 Tu	0538	0224	1.7F
	1220	0858	2.2E
	1831	1504	1.7F
		2129	1.9E
28 W	0037	0325	1.7F
	0642	0956	2.2E
	1317	1603	1.9F
	1929	2228	2.1E
29 Th	0140	0426	1.9F
	0744	1052	2.4E
	1410	1658	2.1F
	2021	2322	2.4E
30 F	0237	0523	2.6F
	0840	1144	2.6E
	1457	1749	2.5F
	2108		

May

Day	Slack (h m)	Maximum (h m)	knots
1 Sa	0328	0012	2.8E
	0931	0615	2.5F
	1542	1233	2.9E
	2153	1836	2.8F
2 Su	0415	0100	3.3E
	1019	0704	2.8F
	1625	1320	3.1E
	2236	1921	3.0F
3 M	0501	0145	3.7E
	1105	0751	3.1F
	1708	1405	3.3E
	2319	2006	3.4F
4 Tu	0547	0231	4.0E
	1152	0838	3.4F
	1752	1451	3.5E
		2052	3.6F
5 W	0004	0317	4.1E
	0634	0925	3.5F
	1239	1538	3.5E
	1838	2139	3.6F
6 Th	0050	0405	4.2E
	0723	1013	3.4F
	1328	1627	3.4E
	1927	2228	3.6F
7 F	0140	0455	4.0E
	0814	1104	3.3F
	1420	1719	3.2E
	2020	2320	3.3F
8 Sa	0233	0548	3.8E
	0909	1158	3.0F
	1516	1815	3.0E
	2118		
9 Su	0332	0016	3.0F
	1008	0645	3.5E
	1618	1256	2.8F
	2223	1915	2.8E
10 M	0436	0117	2.7F
	1110	0746	3.2E
	1724	1400	2.6F
	2333	2020	2.7E
11 Tu	0544	0224	2.4F
	1215	0851	3.0E
	1831	1508	2.5F
		2127	2.6E
12 W	0045	0336	2.3F
	0652	0956	2.8E
	1318	1617	2.5F
	1934	2232	2.7E
13 Th	0153	0448	2.3F
	0757	1058	2.8E
	1416	1720	2.6F
	2032	2332	2.9E
14 F	0253	0552	2.4F
	0856	1154	2.8E
	1509	1814	2.7F
	2123		
15 Sa	0347	0025	3.1E
	0949	0646	2.5F
	1556	1244	2.8E
	2209	1859	2.7F
16 Su	0434	0112	3.2E
	1037	0731	2.6F
	1640	1330	2.8E
	2250	1939	2.8F
17 M	0517	0154	3.3E
	1120	0810	2.7F
	1720	1411	2.8E
	2329	2015	2.7F
18 Tu	0557	0233	3.3E
	1200	0846	2.7F
	1757	1450	2.7E
		2050	2.7F
19 W	0005	0311	3.2E
	0635	0921	2.5F
	1239	1528	2.6E
	1834	2125	2.6F
20 Th	0041	0349	3.1E
	0712	0956	2.5F
	1316	1607	2.5E
	1910	2202	2.5F
21 F	0116	0428	3.0E
	0750	1034	2.4F
	1354	1647	2.4E
	1947	2241	2.4F
22 Sa	0153	0509	2.9E
	0829	1114	2.2F
	1434	1729	2.2E
	2028	2323	2.2F
23 Su	0232	0551	2.7E
	0911	1157	2.1F
	1516	1814	2.1E
	2112		
24 M	0315	0008	2.1F
	0956	0638	2.6E
	1603	1244	2.0F
	2203	1904	2.0E
25 Tu	0404	0058	2.0F
	1044	0727	2.4E
	1655	1334	2.0F
	2259	1957	2.0E
26 W	0459	0151	1.9F
	1135	0820	2.4E
	1748	1426	2.0F
		2052	2.1E
27 Th	0000	0248	1.9F
	0558	0915	2.4E
	1227	1521	2.2F
	1842	2148	2.3E
28 F	0101	0347	2.0F
	0659	1010	2.4E
	1319	1614	2.4F
	1938	2243	2.6E
29 Sa	0159	0444	2.2F
	0758	1104	2.6E
	1409	1707	2.6F
	2025	2335	3.0E
30 Su	0254	0540	2.5F
	0854	1156	2.8E
	1459	1758	2.9F
	2115		
31 M	0346	0027	3.4E
	0948	0633	2.8F
	1548	1247	3.0E
	2203	1849	3.2F

June

Day	Slack (h m)	Maximum (h m)	knots
1 Tu	0437	0117	3.8E
	1040	0725	3.1F
	1638	1338	3.2E
	2253	1939	3.4F
2 W	0527	0206	4.0E
	1131	0815	3.3F
	1728	1428	3.3E
	2342	2029	3.6F
3 Th	0617	0256	4.2E
	1222	0906	3.4F
	1819	1519	3.4E
		2120	3.7F
4 F	0034	0347	4.2E
	0708	0958	3.4F
	1314	1611	3.4E
	1913	2212	3.7F
5 Sa	0126	0439	4.1E
	0800	1050	3.3F
	1408	1705	3.3E
	2009	2306	3.7F
6 Su	0221	0533	3.9E
	0855	1145	3.1F
	1505	1801	3.1E
	2108		
7 M	0319	0003	3.1F
	0950	0629	3.6E
	1603	1241	3.0F
	2211	1859	3.0E
8 Tu	0419	0102	2.8F
	1048	0727	3.3E
	1704	1341	2.8F
	2317	2000	2.9E
9 W	0522	0205	2.5F
	1146	0826	3.0E
	1805	1442	2.6F
		2102	2.8E
10 Th	0023	0312	2.3F
	0626	0926	2.8E
	1245	1544	2.6F
	1904	2203	2.8E
11 F	0127	0418	2.2F
	0728	1025	2.6E
	1341	1643	2.5F
	1959	2301	2.8E
12 Sa	0226	0521	2.2F
	0827	1121	2.5E
	1434	1736	2.5F
	2050	2354	2.9E
13 Su	0320	0616	2.2F
	0921	1212	2.5E
	1523	1824	2.5F
	2137		
14 M	0409	0042	3.0E
	1010	0704	2.3F
	1608	1300	2.5E
	2221	1907	2.5F
15 Tu	0453	0126	3.0E
	1055	0745	2.3F
	1651	1343	2.4E
	2301	1946	2.5F
16 W	0535	0208	3.1E
	1137	0823	2.3F
	1731	1425	2.4E
	2340	2024	2.5F
17 Th	0614	0247	3.1E
	1217	0859	2.3F
	1809	1505	2.4E
		2101	2.5F
18 F	0018	0327	3.1E
	0652	0935	2.3F
	1255	1545	2.4E
	1848	2139	2.4F
19 Sa	0054	0406	3.0E
	0729	1013	2.4F
	1334	1625	2.4E
	1926	2219	2.4F
20 Su	0131	0446	2.9E
	0807	1052	2.3F
	1412	1707	2.3E
	2006	2306	2.3F
21 M	0210	0527	2.9E
	0845	1133	2.3F
	1452	1750	2.3E
	2049	2344	2.3F
22 Tu	0250	0610	2.8E
	0925	1216	2.3F
	1534	1836	2.3E
	2136		
23 W	0334	0030	2.2F
	1007	0655	2.7E
	1618	1301	2.3F
	2228	1924	2.3E
24 Th	0424	0120	2.1F
	1052	0744	2.6E
	1706	1350	2.4F
	2324	2016	2.4E
25 F	0519	0213	2.1F
	1141	0836	2.5E
	1758	1441	2.4F
		2110	2.6E
26 Sa	0023	0310	2.2F
	0619	0930	2.5E
	1233	1535	2.6F
	1852	2206	2.8E
27 Su	0124	0409	2.3F
	0721	1027	2.5E
	1327	1630	2.7F
	1947	2302	3.1E
28 M	0223	0508	2.5F
	0822	1124	2.7E
	1424	1726	2.9F
	2043	2358	3.4E
29 Tu	0321	0606	2.7F
	0922	1220	2.9E
	1520	1822	3.1F
	2139		
30 W	0416	0053	3.7E
	1019	0703	2.8F
	1616	1315	3.1E
	2233	1917	3.3F

All times are local time. Daylight Saving Time has been used when needed.

NOTES:

The Race, Long Island Sound, 2004

F–Flood, Dir. 302° True   E–Ebb, Dir. 112° True

July

Day	Slack h m	Max h m	knots
1 Th	0510	0147	3.9E
	1114	0758	3.1F
	1711	1410	3.2E
	2327	2012	3.5F
2 F (O)	0602	0240	4.1E
	1208	0851	3.3F
	1806	1503	3.4E
		2105	3.6F
3 Sa	0021	0332	4.1E
	0654	0944	3.4F
	1301	1556	3.4E
	1901	2159	3.5F
4 Su	0114	0424	4.1E
	0745	1036	3.4F
	1354	1650	3.4E
	1957	2252	3.4F
5 M	0207	0516	3.9E
	0836	1127	3.3F
	1447	1743	3.3E
	2053	2346	3.1F
6 Tu	0301	0608	3.6E
	0927	1219	3.1F
	1540	1838	3.2E
	2151		
7 W	0356	0041	2.8F
	1019	0701	3.3E
	1635	1312	2.9F
	2251	1933	3.0E
8 Th	0453	0138	2.5F
	1112	0755	2.9E
	1730	1406	2.7F
	2352	2029	2.9E
9 F (O)	0552	0237	2.2F
	1206	0850	2.6E
	1826	1502	2.5F
		2127	2.7E
10 Sa	0053	0336	2.0F
	0653	0947	2.4E
	1301	1556	2.3F
	1921	2223	2.7E
11 Su	0153	0441	1.9F
	0752	1044	2.2E
	1356	1654	2.2F
	2014	2319	2.7E
12 M	0249	0540	1.9F
	0849	1138	2.2E
	1448	1747	2.2F
	2105		
13 Tu	0341	0010	2.7E
	0941	0633	2.0F
	1538	1229	2.2E
	2152	1836	2.2F
14 W	0428	0058	2.8E
	1029	0720	2.1F
	1624	1317	2.2E
	2236	1917	2.3F
15 Th	0511	0143	2.9E
	1113	0800	2.2F
	1708	1401	2.3E
	2318	2001	2.4F
16 F	0552	0225	3.0E
	1154	0838	2.3F
	1748	1443	2.4E
	2357	2040	2.4F
17 Sa (●)	0630	0305	3.0E
	1233	0914	2.4F
	1827	1523	2.5E
		2119	2.5F
18 Su	0034	0344	3.1E
	0706	0950	2.5F
	1310	1603	2.5E
	1906	2158	2.5F
19 M	0111	0422	3.1E
	0741	1028	2.5F
	1346	1643	2.6E
	1945	2238	2.5F
20 Tu	0147	0501	3.0E
	0816	1106	2.6F
	1423	1724	2.6E
	2026	2319	2.5F
21 W	0226	0542	3.0E
	0852	1146	2.6F
	1500	1806	2.7E
	2110		
22 Th	0307	0003	2.5F
	0931	0624	2.9E
	1541	1229	2.6F
	2158	1852	2.7E
23 F	0354	0051	2.4F
	1013	0711	2.7E
	1627	1315	2.6F
	2252	1942	2.8E
24 Sa (O)	0446	0142	2.3F
	1101	0801	2.6E
	1719	1406	2.6F
	2351	2036	2.8E
25 Su	0546	0239	2.3F
	1156	0857	2.5E
	1816	1501	2.6F
		2134	2.9E
26 M	0054	0339	2.3F
	0650	0957	2.5E
	1255	1600	2.7F
	1918	2235	3.1E
27 Tu	0159	0442	2.3F
	0758	1059	2.5E
	1359	1702	2.8F
	2021	2336	3.3E
28 W	0302	0546	2.5F
	0903	1200	2.7E
	1502	1803	3.0F
	2123		
29 Th	0401	0035	3.5E
	1004	0647	2.8F
	1603	1300	3.0E
	2221	1903	3.2F
30 F	0456	0132	3.8E
	1101	0745	3.0F
	1701	1356	3.2E
	2316	2000	3.4F
31 Sa (O)	0548	0226	4.0E
	1154	0838	3.3F
	1756	1450	3.4E
		2054	3.5F

August

Day	Slack h m	Max h m	knots
1 Su	0009	0317	4.0E
	0637	0929	3.4F
	1245	1541	3.6E
	1850	2145	3.5F
2 M	0100	0406	4.0E
	0725	1017	3.4F
	1334	1631	3.6E
	1942	2235	3.4F
3 Tu	0149	0454	3.8E
	0811	1104	3.3F
	1422	1720	3.5E
	2033	2324	3.1F
4 W	0239	0542	3.5E
	0857	1150	3.2F
	1510	1809	3.3E
	2125		
5 Th	0328	0013	2.8F
	0944	0630	3.2E
	1559	1237	2.9F
	2219	1859	3.1E
6 F	0420	0103	2.5F
	1032	0719	2.8E
	1649	1325	2.6F
	2315	1951	2.8E
7 Sa (O)	0515	0156	2.2F
	1124	0811	2.4E
	1742	1416	2.3F
		2045	2.6E
8 Su	0014	0253	1.9F
	0613	0907	2.1E
	1219	1511	2.1F
	1838	2143	2.4E
9 M	0115	0355	1.7F
	0705	1005	2.0E
	1317	1610	1.9F
	1936	2241	2.4E
10 Tu	0214	0500	1.7F
	0815	1103	1.9E
	1415	1710	1.9F
	2032	2338	2.4E
11 W	0310	0600	1.8F
	0911	1159	2.0E
	1510	1806	2.0F
	2124		
12 Th	0400	0030	2.6E
	1002	0652	1.9F
	1600	1250	2.1E
	2211	1855	2.2F
13 F	0444	0117	2.8E
	1047	0734	2.1F
	1645	1336	2.3E
	2254	1938	2.3F
14 Sa	0525	0200	2.9E
	1128	0812	2.3F
	1726	1419	2.5E
	2334	2018	2.5F
15 Su (●)	0601	0240	3.1E
	1205	0848	2.5F
	1805	1458	2.7E
		2056	2.6F
16 M	0011	0318	3.2E
	0636	0923	2.7F
	1240	1537	2.9E
	1843	2135	2.8F
17 Tu	0047	0355	3.2E
	0709	0959	2.8F
	1315	1616	3.0E
	1922	2214	2.8F
18 W	0124	0433	3.2E
	0743	1036	2.9F
	1349	1655	3.1E
	2001	2254	2.8F
19 Th	0202	0513	3.1E
	0818	1115	2.9F
	1426	1737	3.1E
	2044	2337	2.8F
20 F	0243	0555	3.0E
	0857	1158	2.9F
	1507	1822	3.1E
	2131		
21 Sa	0329	0024	2.6F
	0940	0641	2.8E
	1553	1244	2.8F
	2224	1912	3.0E
22 Su	0421	0115	2.5F
	1031	0733	2.6E
	1647	1336	2.7F
	2325	2007	3.0E
23 M	0523	0213	2.3F
	1129	0831	2.4E
	1750	1434	2.6F
		2109	2.9E
24 Tu (O)	0032	0316	2.2F
	0632	0935	2.4E
	1236	1539	2.5F
	1858	2215	3.0E
25 W	0141	0424	2.2F
	0744	1042	2.4E
	1346	1646	2.6F
	2008	2320	3.1E
26 Th	0247	0533	2.4F
	0852	1147	2.7E
	1454	1753	2.8F
	2113		
27 F	0347	0022	3.4E
	0953	0637	2.7F
	1557	1248	3.0E
	2212	1855	3.0F
28 Sa	0441	0119	3.6E
	1047	0733	3.0F
	1653	1344	3.3E
	2306	1951	3.3F
29 Su	0530	0211	3.8E
	1138	0824	3.3F
	1746	1435	3.5E
	2356	2042	3.4F
30 M	0616	0259	3.9E
	1224	0910	3.4F
	1835	1523	3.7E
		2129	3.4F
31 Tu	0043	0345	3.8E
	0700	0954	3.4F
	1309	1608	3.7E
	1923	2214	3.3F

September

Day	Slack h m	Max h m	knots
1 W	0128	0429	3.6E
	0742	1035	3.3F
	1352	1653	3.6E
	2009	2258	3.1F
2 Th	0213	0513	3.3E
	0824	1117	3.1F
	1435	1737	3.3E
	2055	2341	2.8F
3 F	0258	0557	3.0E
	0907	1159	2.8F
	1519	1823	3.1E
	2143		
4 Sa	0345	0027	2.4F
	0951	0643	2.6E
	1605	1244	2.5F
	2234	1911	2.7E
5 Su	0436	0115	2.1F
	1040	0732	2.2E
	1656	1332	2.1F
	2331	2003	2.5E
6 M (O)	0533	0209	1.8F
	1136	0827	1.9E
	1753	1426	1.9F
		2101	2.2E
7 Tu	0033	0309	1.6F
	0636	0927	1.8E
	1238	1527	1.7F
	1855	2202	2.2E
8 W	0136	0416	1.5F
	0740	1029	1.8E
	1342	1632	1.7F
	1956	2303	2.3E
9 Th	0235	0522	1.7F
	0839	1128	1.9E
	1441	1733	1.9F
	2052	2358	2.4E
10 F	0326	0616	1.9F
	0930	1221	2.2E
	1533	1826	2.1F
	2142		
11 Sa	0411	0046	2.7E
	1015	0701	2.2F
	1619	1308	2.4E
	2226	1911	2.4F
12 Su	0450	0130	2.9E
	1055	0739	2.5F
	1701	1350	2.7E
	2306	1951	2.6F
13 M	0526	0210	3.1E
	1131	0815	2.7F
	1740	1429	3.0E
	2344	2030	2.8F
14 Tu (●)	0600	0248	3.3E
	1206	0851	2.9F
	1818	1508	3.3E
		2109	3.0F
15 W	0022	0326	3.3E
	0634	0927	3.1F
	1240	1547	3.4E
	1856	2148	3.1F
16 Th	0059	0405	3.3E
	0709	1006	3.2F
	1316	1627	3.5E
	1937	2229	3.1F
17 F	0139	0445	3.2E
	0746	1046	3.2F
	1355	1709	3.5E
	2020	2313	3.0F
18 Sa	0221	0529	3.1E
	0828	1130	3.1F
	1438	1756	3.4E
	2109		
19 Su	0309	0001	2.8F
	0914	0617	2.9E
	1528	1219	2.9F
	2203	1847	3.2E
20 M	0404	0054	2.6F
	1009	0711	2.6E
	1626	1313	2.7F
	2306	1946	3.0E
21 Tu (O)	0509	0154	2.3F
	1113	0813	2.4E
	1733	1416	2.5F
		2051	2.9E
22 W	0016	0300	2.2F
	0622	0921	2.3E
	1227	1524	2.4F
	1847	2159	2.9E
23 Th	0127	0412	2.3F
	0735	1031	2.5E
	1341	1637	2.5F
	2007	2307	3.0E
24 F	0232	0523	2.5F
	0841	1137	2.7E
	1450	1747	2.7F
	2103		
25 Sa	0330	0008	3.2E
	0939	0626	2.8F
	1550	1237	3.1E
	2200	1848	2.9F
26 Su	0421	0103	3.4E
	1031	0719	3.1F
	1644	1330	3.4E
	2252	1941	3.1F
27 M	0509	0153	3.6E
	1117	0806	3.3F
	1733	1417	3.6E
	2339	2028	3.2F
28 Tu (O)	0552	0238	3.6E
	1201	0847	3.5F
	1820	1501	3.7E
		2110	3.2F
29 W	0023	0321	3.5E
	0633	0927	3.5F
	1241	1543	3.7E
	1901	2151	3.1F
30 Th	0106	0402	3.3E
	0712	1005	3.5F
	1321	1624	3.5E
	1943	2230	2.9F

All times are local time. Daylight Saving Time has been used when needed.

NOTES:

The Race, Long Island Sound, 2004

F–Flood, Dir. 302° True   E–Ebb, Dir. 112° True

October

Day	Slack (h m)	Maximum (h m, knots)
1 F	0147, 0751, 1359, 2025	0443 3.1E, 1043 2.9F, 1705 3.3E, 2310 2.7F
2 Sa	0228, 0830, 1439, 2109	0524 2.7E, 1123 2.6F, 1748 3.0E, 2352 2.3F
3 Su	0311, 0912, 1522, 2156	0608 2.4E, 1205 2.3F, 1834 2.7E
4 M	0359, 1000, 1610, 2250	0038 2.0F, 0656 2.1E, 1252 2.0F, 1924 2.4E
5 Tu	0454, 1055, 1707, 2350	0129 1.8F, 0750 1.8E, 1346 1.8F, 2021 2.2E
6 W	0557, 1159, 1811	0228 1.6F, 0850 1.7E, 1446 1.6F, 2122 2.1E
7 Th	0053, 0702, 1306, 1916	0332 1.6F, 0952 1.7E, 1551 1.6F, 2223 2.2E
8 F	0152, 0801, 1407, 2014	0436 1.7F, 1053 1.9E, 1654 1.8F, 2319 2.3E
9 Sa	0244, 0852, 1501, 2106	0532 1.9F, 1146 2.2E, 1749 2.1F
10 Su	0329, 0936, 1548, 2152	0009 2.6E, 0618 2.3F, 1234 2.6E, 1837 2.4F
11 M	0409, 1016, 1631, 2235	0054 2.8E, 0659 2.6F, 1317 3.0E, 1920 2.7F
12 Tu	0446, 1054, 1711, 2315	0135 3.1E, 0738 2.9F, 1357 3.3E, 2001 2.9F
13 W	0523, 1130, 1751, 2355	0216 3.2E, 0817 3.2F, 1438 3.6E, 2041 3.1F
14 Th	0559, 1207, 1832	0256 3.3E, 0856 3.3F, 1517 3.8E, 2123 3.3F
15 F	0035, 0638, 1247, 1915	0337 3.4E, 0937 3.4F, 1601 3.9E, 2206 3.3F
16 Sa	0118, 0719, 1329, 2001	0420 3.3E, 1021 3.4F, 1646 3.8E, 2252 3.1F
17 Su	0204, 0805, 1417, 2052	0507 3.1E, 1108 3.2F, 1735 3.6E, 2342 2.9F
18 M	0255, 0857, 1510, 2148	0558 2.9E, 1159 3.0F, 1829 3.4E
19 Tu	0354, 0956, 1612, 2252	0038 2.7F, 0656 2.7E, 1257 2.7F, 1929 3.1E
20 W	0501, 1106, 1721	0139 2.5F, 0800 2.5E, 1402 2.5F, 2035 2.9E
21 Th	0000, 0612, 1221, 1835	0248 2.3F, 0909 2.5E, 1514 2.4F, 2144 2.9E
22 F	0109, 0722, 1335, 1945	0400 2.4F, 1019 2.6E, 1628 2.4F, 2250 2.9E
23 Sa	0212, 0825, 1441, 2048	0509 2.6F, 1123 2.9E, 1738 2.6F, 2350 3.1E
24 Su	0308, 0920, 1539, 2144	0609 2.8F, 1221 3.2E, 1837 2.8F
25 M	0358, 1010, 1630, 2235	0009 3.2E, 0659 3.0F, 1311 3.4E, 1907 2.9F
26 Tu	0444, 1054, 1716, 2320	0131 3.3E, 0743 3.1F, 1357 3.6E, 2011 3.0F
27 W	0526, 1135, 1759	0215 3.3E, 0822 3.1F, 1438 3.6E, 2050 3.0F
28 Th	0003, 0605, 1214, 1839	0256 3.2E, 0900 3.1F, 1518 3.6E, 2128 2.9F
29 F	0043, 0643, 1251, 1919	0336 3.0E, 0936 2.9F, 1557 3.4E, 2204 2.7F
30 Sa	0123, 0720, 1328, 1958	0415 2.8E, 1012 2.7F, 1637 3.2E, 2242 2.5F
31 Su	0102, 0658, 1305, 1939	0355 2.5E, 0951 2.5F, 1618 2.9E, 2223 2.3F

November

Day	Slack (h m)	Maximum (h m, knots)
1 M	0143, 0739, 1346, 2023	0438 2.3E, 1033 2.3F, 1702 2.7E, 2307 2.1F
2 Tu	0228, 0825, 1432, 2113	0525 2.0E, 1119 2.0F, 1750 2.4E, 2356 1.9F
3 W	0320, 0919, 1524, 2207	0616 1.9E, 1211 1.8F, 1844 2.2E
4 Th	0418, 1020, 1625, 2305	0050 1.7F, 0714 1.8E, 1308 1.7F, 1941 2.2E
5 F	0518, 1126, 1728	0148 1.7F, 0813 1.8E, 1409 1.7F, 2039 2.2E
6 Sa	0001, 0615, 1228, 1829	0247 1.8F, 0912 2.0E, 1510 1.8F, 2135 2.3E
7 Su	0053, 0706, 1323, 1924	0342 2.1F, 1006 2.3E, 1607 2.0F, 2227 2.5E
8 M	0140, 0752, 1413, 2014	0431 2.4F, 1055 2.7E, 1658 2.3F, 2314 2.7E
9 Tu	0223, 0835, 1458, 2100	0517 2.7F, 1141 3.1E, 1745 2.7F
10 W	0305, 0916, 1542, 2145	0000 3.0F, 0601 3.0E, 1225 3.5E, 1830 2.9F
11 Th	0406, 0957, 1626, 2229	0044 3.2E, 0644 3.3F, 1309 3.8E, 1915 3.2F
12 F	0428, 1039, 1710, 2314	0128 3.3E, 0728 3.5F, 1353 4.0E, 2000 3.3F
13 Sa	0512, 1124, 1757	0213 3.3E, 0813 3.5F, 1439 4.1E, 2047 3.3F
14 Su	0001, 0559, 1211, 1846	0300 3.3E, 0900 3.5F, 1527 4.0E, 2136 3.2F
15 M	0051, 0649, 1302, 1938	0350 3.2E, 0951 3.5F, 1619 3.8E, 2228 3.1F
16 Tu	0145, 0745, 1358, 2035	0444 3.0E, 1045 3.1F, 1714 3.6E, 2324 2.9F
17 W	0244, 0848, 1500, 2136	0543 2.9E, 1144 2.8F, 1814 3.3E
18 Th	0349, 0957, 1607, 2240	0025 2.7F, 0646 2.7E, 1249 2.5F, 1917 3.0E
19 F	0456, 1110, 1717, 2343	0131 2.6F, 0753 2.7E, 1359 2.4F, 2022 2.9E
20 Sa	0601, 1220, 1825	0239 2.6F, 0900 2.8E, 1512 2.4F, 2126 2.8E
21 Su	0044, 0701, 1324, 1927	0345 2.6F, 1002 2.9E, 1620 2.4F, 2225 2.9E
22 M	0140, 0756, 1421, 2023	0443 2.8F, 1059 3.1E, 1719 2.6F, 2319 2.9E
23 Tu	0231, 0845, 1512, 2114	0534 2.8F, 1149 3.3E, 1809 2.7F
24 W	0317, 0929, 1557, 2200	0007 2.9E, 0618 2.9F, 1234 3.4E, 1852 2.7F
25 Th	0400, 1010, 1640, 2243	0052 2.9E, 0657 2.8F, 1315 3.4E, 1931 2.7F
26 F	0440, 1049, 1720, 2323	0133 2.8E, 0734 2.8F, 1355 3.3E, 2007 2.6F
27 Sa	0518, 1126, 1758	0212 2.7E, 0811 2.7F, 1434 3.2E, 2043 2.5F
28 Su	0002, 0556, 1203, 1836	0252 2.6E, 0847 2.6F, 1513 3.1E, 2120 2.4F
29 M	0040, 0634, 1240, 1915	0332 2.4E, 0926 2.4F, 1553 2.9E, 2159 2.3F
30 Tu	0120, 0714, 1319, 1956	0413 2.3E, 1007 2.3F, 1635 2.8E, 2241 2.2F

December

Day	Slack (h m)	Maximum (h m, knots)
1 W	0202, 0758, 1401, 2040	0458 2.1E, 1051 2.1F, 1720 2.6E, 2326 2.1F
2 Th	0248, 0847, 1448, 2126	0546 2.0E, 1140 1.9F, 1809 2.4E
3 F	0338, 0942, 1540, 2215	0015 2.0F, 0638 2.0E, 1232 1.8F, 1900 2.3E
4 Sa	0430, 1042, 1638, 2306	0106 2.0F, 0732 2.1E, 1328 1.8F, 1954 2.3E
5 Su	0523, 1142, 1738, 2358	0159 2.1F, 0828 2.2E, 1425 1.9F, 2048 2.3E
6 M	0615, 1240, 1837	0253 2.2F, 0922 2.5E, 1523 2.0F, 2142 2.4E
7 Tu	0048, 0705, 1334, 1933	0345 2.4F, 1015 2.8E, 1618 2.3F, 2234 2.6E
8 W	0137, 0753, 1426, 2026	0436 2.7F, 1105 3.2E, 1711 2.6F, 2326 2.8E
9 Th	0226, 0841, 1515, 2117	0526 3.0F, 1154 3.5E, 1802 2.8F
10 F	0314, 0929, 1604, 2207	0015 3.0E, 0615 3.3F, 1243 3.8E, 1852 3.1F
11 Sa	0403, 1017, 1653, 2256	0104 3.2E, 0704 3.7F, 1332 4.0E, 1941 3.3F
12 Su	0453, 1107, 1742, 2347	0153 3.3E, 0754 3.6F, 1422 4.1E, 2031 3.4F
13 M	0544, 1158, 1832	0244 3.4E, 0845 3.6F, 1512 4.1E, 2122 3.4F
14 Tu	0039, 0639, 1251, 1924	0336 3.4E, 0937 3.5F, 1604 4.0E, 2215 3.3F
15 W	0133, 0736, 1347, 2018	0431 3.3E, 1032 3.2F, 1658 3.7E, 2309 3.1F
16 Th	0230, 0837, 1445, 2114	0528 3.1E, 1130 3.0F, 1755 3.4E
17 F	0330, 0942, 1547, 2212	0007 3.0F, 0628 3.0E, 1231 2.7F, 1853 3.1E
18 Sa	0431, 1049, 1652, 2312	0107 2.8F, 0729 2.9E, 1336 2.4F, 1954 2.9E
19 Su	0532, 1156, 1757	0208 2.7F, 0832 2.9E, 1444 2.3F, 2055 2.7E
20 M	0010, 0630, 1259, 1900	0311 2.6F, 0933 2.9E, 1552 2.2F, 2154 2.6E
21 Tu	0107, 0726, 1357, 1958	0410 2.5F, 1030 2.9E, 1654 2.2F, 2250 2.5E
22 W	0201, 0817, 1450, 2051	0504 2.5F, 1123 3.0E, 1747 2.3F, 2342 2.5E
23 Th	0250, 0904, 1537, 2140	0552 2.5F, 1210 3.1E, 1833 2.3F
24 F	0336, 0947, 1621, 2224	0028 2.5E, 0634 2.5F, 1254 3.1E, 1913 2.4F
25 Sa	0418, 1028, 1701, 2305	0111 2.5E, 0713 2.5F, 1335 3.1E, 1950 2.4F
26 Su	0458, 1107, 1740, 2343	0152 2.5E, 0751 2.5F, 1414 3.1E, 2025 2.4F
27 M	0537, 1144, 1817	0232 2.5E, 0828 2.5F, 1453 3.1E, 2101 2.4F
28 Tu	0021, 0615, 1220, 1853	0311 2.4E, 0906 2.5F, 1531 3.0E, 2138 2.4F
29 W	0059, 0656, 1257, 1930	0352 2.4E, 0945 2.4F, 1611 2.9E, 2216 2.4F
30 Th	0136, 0734, 1335, 2007	0433 2.4E, 1027 2.3F, 1652 2.8E, 2257 2.3F
31 F	0216, 0819, 1416, 2046	0516 2.4E, 1111 2.2F, 1735 2.7E, 2340 2.3F

All times are local time. Daylight Saving Time has been used when needed.

NOTES:

Throgs Neck, Long Island Sound, New York, 2004

F–Flood, Dir. 015° True   E–Ebb, Dir. 193° True

April

Day	Slack (h m)	Maximum (h m / knots)
1 Th	0538, 1155, 1746	0226 0.9F, 0845 0.6E, 1451 0.8F, 2106 0.6E
2 F	0003, 0625, 1235, 1830	0316 0.9F, 0933 0.7E, 1540 0.9F, 2153 0.7E
3 Sa	0045, 0706, 1313, 1911	0405 1.0F, 1019 0.7E, 1629 1.0F, 2238 0.8E
4 Su	0126, 0846, 1451, 2053	0553 1.0F, 1204 0.8E, 1816 1.0F
5 M ○	0308, 0926, 1531, 2135	0023 0.8E, 0641 1.1F, 1248 0.8E, 1904 1.0F
6 Tu	0350, 1008, 1613, 2220	0108 0.8E, 0729 1.1F, 1333 0.8E, 1952 1.0F
7 W	0435, 1052, 1659, 2307	0154 0.8E, 0816 1.1F, 1420 0.8E, 2042 1.0F
8 Th	0522, 1138, 1747, 2358	0242 0.8E, 0907 1.0F, 1509 0.8E, 2132 1.0F
9 F	0613, 1229, 1840	0334 0.8E, 0959 1.0F, 1602 0.7E, 2225 1.0F
10 Sa	0053, 0708, 1325, 1939	0429 0.7F, 1052 0.9E, 1659 0.7F, 2319 0.9E
11 Su ○	0156, 0812, 1429, 2049	0528 0.7E, 1146 0.9F, 1758 0.6E
12 M	0310, 0930, 1543, 2213	0013 0.9F, 0626 0.6E, 1241 0.9F, 1859 0.6E
13 Tu	0431, 1059, 1659, 2330	0108 0.9F, 0731 0.6E, 1335 0.9F, 1959 0.6E
14 W	0541, 1207, 1805	0203 0.9F, 0830 0.6E, 1430 0.9F, 2056 0.7E
15 Th	0031, 0642, 1305, 1901	0257 0.9F, 0926 0.7E, 1522 0.9F, 2149 0.7E
16 F	0124, 0734, 1355, 1951	0348 1.0F, 1017 0.7E, 1613 0.9F, 2239 0.7E
17 Sa	0212, 0821, 1441, 2035	0438 1.0F, 1106 0.7E, 1703 1.0F, 2327 0.7E
18 Su	0255, 0903, 1523, 2115	0527 1.0F, 1152 0.7E, 1751 1.0F
19 M ●	0333, 0942, 1559, 2150	0011 0.7E, 0615 1.0F, 1236 0.7E, 1838 1.0F
20 Tu	0405, 1017, 1629, 2222	0055 0.7E, 0702 1.0F, 1319 0.7E, 1925 0.9F
21 W	0434, 1050, 1657, 2255	0138 0.7E, 0749 0.9F, 1402 0.7E, 2012 0.9F
22 Th	0506, 1123, 1728, 2331	0221 0.7E, 0836 0.9F, 1446 0.6E, 2100 0.9F
23 F	0543, 1159, 1806	0306 0.6E, 0924 0.8F, 1531 0.6E, 2149 0.8F
24 Sa	0013, 0625, 1240, 1849	0353 0.6E, 1014 0.8F, 1619 0.5E, 2239 0.8F
25 Su	0100, 0712, 1325, 1938	0443 0.5E, 1104 0.8F, 1709 0.5E, 2330 0.8F
26 M	0153, 0805, 1416, 2031	0537 0.5E, 1156 0.7F, 1802 0.5E
27 Tu ◑	0252, 0903, 1510, 2128	0022 0.8F, 0632 0.5E, 1248 0.8F, 1856 0.5E
28 W	0356, 1006, 1608, 2227	0114 0.8F, 0727 0.5E, 1339 0.8F, 1950 0.5E
29 Th	0459, 1108, 1705, 2324	0206 0.8F, 0820 0.5E, 1431 0.8F, 2042 0.6E
30 F	0555, 1203, 1758	0257 0.8F, 0911 0.6E, 1521 0.8F, 2132 0.7E

May

Day	Slack (h m)	Maximum (h m / knots)
1 Sa	0017, 0644, 1251, 1848	0347 0.9F, 1000 0.7E, 1611 0.9F, 2220 0.7E
2 Su	0106, 0730, 1336, 1936	0436 1.0F, 1048 0.7E, 1700 1.0F, 2307 0.8E
3 M	0153, 0814, 1420, 2023	0525 1.1F, 1134 0.8E, 1749 1.0F, 2354 0.8E
4 Tu ○	0239, 0858, 1505, 2111	0614 1.1F, 1221 0.8E, 1838 1.0F
5 W	0326, 0943, 1552, 2200	0042 0.8E, 0703 1.1F, 1309 0.8E, 1927 1.1F
6 Th	0414, 1030, 1641, 2251	0131 0.8E, 0752 1.1F, 1358 0.8E, 2018 1.0F
7 F	0504, 1120, 1733, 2346	0222 0.8E, 0843 1.1F, 1449 0.8E, 2109 1.0F
8 Sa	0558, 1213, 1829	0315 0.8E, 0935 1.0F, 1543 0.8E, 2202 1.0F
9 Su	0045, 0657, 1311, 1932	0411 0.7E, 1028 1.0F, 1640 0.7E, 2256 1.0F
10 M	0152, 0806, 1416, 2044	0510 0.7E, 1122 0.9F, 1738 0.7E, 2350 0.9F
11 Tu ○	0306, 0928, 1528, 2201	0610 0.6E, 1216 0.9F, 1837 0.7E
12 W	0417, 1043, 1638, 2308	0044 0.9F, 0709 0.6E, 1310 0.9F, 1935 0.7E
13 Th	0522, 1146, 1740	0138 0.9F, 0806 0.6E, 1404 0.9F, 2030 0.7E
14 F	0006, 0619, 1241, 1835	0230 0.9F, 0900 0.7E, 1456 0.9F, 2123 0.8E
15 Sa	0059, 0710, 1331, 1924	0321 0.9F, 0951 0.7E, 1546 0.9F, 2212 0.7E
16 Su	0146, 0756, 1417, 2008	0411 1.0F, 1039 0.7E, 1635 0.9F, 2259 0.7E
17 M	0229, 0838, 1459, 2048	0500 1.0F, 1125 0.7E, 1724 0.9F, 2344 0.7E
18 Tu ●	0306, 0916, 1535, 2123	0547 1.0F, 1209 0.7E, 1811 0.9F
19 W	0338, 0951, 1606, 2156	0028 0.7E, 0635 1.0F, 1253 0.7E, 1858 0.9F
20 Th	0407, 1023, 1632, 2230	0112 0.7E, 0722 0.9F, 1336 0.7E, 1946 0.9F
21 F	0439, 1054, 1703, 2308	0156 0.6E, 0809 0.9F, 1420 0.6E, 2034 0.9F
22 Sa	0516, 1130, 1740, 2350	0240 0.6E, 0858 0.9F, 1504 0.6E, 2122 0.8F
23 Su	0558, 1209, 1822	0327 0.6E, 0946 0.8F, 1551 0.6E, 2212 0.8F
24 M	0037, 0644, 1253, 1908	0416 0.5E, 1036 0.8F, 1639 0.5E, 2302 0.8F
25 Tu	0127, 0734, 1341, 1958	0507 0.5E, 1127 0.8F, 1729 0.5E, 2353 0.8F
26 W ○	0221, 0827, 1432, 2051	0559 0.5E, 1218 0.7F, 1821 0.5E
27 Th ◑	0318, 0923, 1525, 2146	0044 0.8F, 0653 0.5E, 1309 0.8F, 1913 0.6E
28 F	0415, 1020, 1621, 2242	0136 0.9F, 0745 0.6E, 1400 0.8F, 2006 0.6E
29 Sa	0511, 1116, 1716, 2337	0227 0.9F, 0837 0.6E, 1451 0.8F, 2057 0.7E
30 Su	0604, 1209, 1811	0317 1.0F, 0928 0.7E, 1542 0.9F, 2148 0.7E
31 M	0031, 0655, 1301, 1905	0407 1.0F, 1018 0.7E, 1632 1.0F, 2239 0.8E

June

Day	Slack (h m)	Maximum (h m / knots)
1 Tu	0123, 0745, 1353, 1958	0458 1.0F, 1107 0.8E, 1722 1.0F, 2329 0.8E
2 W ○	0214, 0834, 1444, 2051	0548 1.1F, 1157 0.8E, 1813 1.0F
3 Th	0306, 0923, 1535, 2145	0020 0.8E, 0638 1.1F, 1247 0.8E, 1903 1.1F
4 F	0358, 1013, 1628, 2240	0111 0.8E, 0729 1.1F, 1338 0.8E, 1955 1.1F
5 Sa	0451, 1105, 1723, 2338	0204 0.8E, 0820 1.1F, 1430 0.8E, 2046 1.1F
6 Su	0548, 1159, 1820	0257 0.8E, 0912 1.0F, 1524 0.8E, 2139 1.0F
7 M	0038, 0648, 1257, 1922	0353 0.7E, 1004 1.0F, 1619 0.7E, 2232 1.0F
8 Tu	0142, 0756, 1359, 2028	0449 0.7E, 1057 0.9F, 1715 0.7E, 2325 1.0F
9 W ○	0248, 0907, 1504, 2135	0546 0.7E, 1150 0.9F, 1811 0.7E
10 Th	0352, 1016, 1608, 2239	0018 0.9F, 0642 0.6E, 1243 0.9F, 1906 0.7E
11 F	0453, 1116, 1708, 2336	0110 0.9F, 0737 0.6E, 1336 0.8F, 2001 0.6E
12 Sa	0548, 1212, 1803	0202 0.9F, 0831 0.6E, 1427 0.8F, 2053 0.6E
13 Su	0029, 0641, 1306, 1853	0253 0.9F, 0922 0.6E, 1518 0.8F, 2143 0.6E
14 M	0117, 0731, 1350, 1939	0343 0.9F, 1011 0.6E, 1607 0.8F, 2231 0.6E
15 Tu	0201, 0812, 1434, 2021	0432 0.9F, 1058 0.6E, 1656 0.9F, 2317 0.7E
16 W	0241, 0851, 1513, 2100	0521 0.9F, 1143 0.7E, 1745 0.9F
17 Th ●	0315, 0927, 1545, 2136	0003 0.6E, 0608 0.9F, 1228 0.7E, 1832 0.9F
18 F	0346, 0959, 1612, 2212	0047 0.6E, 0656 0.9F, 1311 0.6E, 1920 0.9F
19 Sa	0418, 1030, 1642, 2250	0132 0.6E, 0744 0.9F, 1355 0.6E, 2008 0.9F
20 Su	0455, 1104, 1717, 2330	0217 0.6E, 0831 0.9F, 1438 0.6E, 2056 0.9F
21 M	0535, 1142, 1820	0302 0.6E, 0920 0.8F, 1523 0.6E, 2145 0.9F
22 Tu	0014, 0618, 1224, 1840	0349 0.6E, 1008 0.8F, 1609 0.6E, 2234 0.9F
23 W	0104, 0704, 1309, 1927	0437 0.6E, 1058 0.8F, 1656 0.6E, 2324 0.9F
24 Th	0149, 0753, 1358, 2017	0527 0.5E, 1148 0.9F, 1746 0.6E
25 F ○	0241, 0845, 1450, 2110	0018 0.9F, 0618 0.6E, 1239 0.9F, 1838 0.6E
26 Sa	0336, 0940, 1544, 2206	0106 0.9F, 0710 0.6E, 1330 0.9F, 1932 0.6E
27 Su	0432, 1037, 1642, 2303	0157 0.9F, 0804 0.6E, 1422 0.8F, 2026 0.7E
28 M	0529, 1135, 1741	0249 0.9F, 0857 0.6E, 1514 0.9F, 2120 0.7E
29 Tu	0001, 0626, 1234, 1841	0340 1.0F, 0950 0.7E, 1606 0.9F, 2214 0.7E
30 W	0059, 0721, 1332, 1940	0432 1.0F, 1043 0.7E, 1657 1.0F, 2307 0.8E

All times are local time. Daylight Saving Time has been used when needed.

NOTES:

Throgs Neck, Long Island Sound, New York, 2004

F–Flood, Dir. 015° True   E–Ebb, Dir. 193° True

July

Day	Slack (h m)	Maximum (h m / knots)
1 Th	0156, 0815, 1429, 2039	0523 1.1F, 1135 0.8E, 1749 1.0F
2 F ○	0252, 0908, 1524, 2136	0614 1.1F, 1227 0.8E, 1840 1.1F
3 Sa	0347, 1000, 1618, 2232	0053 0.8E, 0705 1.1F, 1319 0.8E, 1932 1.1F
4 Su	0442, 1052, 1712, 2328	0145 0.8E, 0756 1.1F, 1411 0.8E, 2023 1.1F
5 M	0537, 1144, 1807	0238 0.8E, 0848 1.0F, 1502 0.8E, 2114 1.1F
6 Tu	0024, 0634, 1238, 1902	0331 0.8E, 0939 1.0F, 1555 0.8E, 2206
7 W	0121, 0733, 1333, 2000	0424 0.7E, 1031 0.9F, 1648 0.7E, 2258 1.0F
8 Th	0219, 0835, 1430, 2100	0517 0.7E, 1122 0.9F, 1741 0.7E, 2349 0.9F
9 F ○	0318, 0939, 1529, 2202	0611 0.6E, 1214 0.9F, 1835 0.6E
10 Sa	0417, 1040, 1629, 2301	0041 0.9F, 0705 0.6E, 1306 0.8F, 1928 0.6E
11 Su	0515, 1138, 1726, 2356	0133 0.9F, 0759 0.6E, 1358 0.8F, 2021 0.6E
12 M	0609, 1232, 1820	0224 0.9F, 0851 0.6E, 1449 0.8F, 2113 0.6E
13 Tu	0047, 0659, 1322, 1910	0315 0.9F, 0942 0.6E, 1540 0.8F, 2203 0.6E
14 W	0135, 0744, 1408, 1956	0405 0.9F, 1030 0.6E, 1629 0.8F, 2251 0.6E
15 Th	0218, 0825, 1449, 2039	0454 0.9F, 1117 0.6E, 1718 0.9F, 2338 0.6E
16 F	0256, 0902, 1523, 2118	0542 0.9F, 1202 0.6E, 1807 0.9F
17 Sa	0329, 0934, 1550, 2155	0023 0.6E, 0630 0.9F, 1246 0.7E, 1854 0.9F
18 Su	0400, 1005, 1618, 2231	0108 0.6E, 0718 0.9F, 1329 0.7E, 1942 0.9F
19 M	0434, 1038, 1652, 2308	0152 0.6E, 0805 0.9F, 1412 0.7E, 2030 0.9F
20 Tu	0511, 1115, 1730, 2348	0236 0.6E, 0852 0.9F, 1455 0.7E, 2117 0.9F
21 W	0551, 1156, 1812	0320 0.6E, 0940 0.9F, 1539 0.7E, 2206 0.9F
22 Th	0032, 0634, 1240, 1857	0406 0.6E, 1029 0.8F, 1625 0.6E, 2255 0.9F
23 F	0118, 0721, 1327, 1946	0454 0.6E, 1119 0.8F, 1714 0.6E, 2346 0.9F
24 Sa ●	0208, 0811, 1419, 2039	0545 0.6E, 1210 0.8F, 1806 0.6E
25 Su	0301, 0906, 1514, 2136	0037 0.9F, 0638 0.6E, 1302 0.8F, 1902 0.6E
26 M	0359, 1006, 1615, 2236	0129 0.9F, 0734 0.6E, 1355 0.8F, 1959 0.6E
27 Tu	0501, 1110, 1719, 2340	0222 0.9F, 0831 0.6E, 1448 0.9F, 2057 0.7E
28 W	0604, 1216, 1827	0315 0.9F, 0928 0.7E, 1541 0.9F, 2153 0.7E
29 Th	0045, 0705, 1321, 1932	0408 1.0F, 1023 0.7E, 1634 1.0F, 2249 0.8E
30 F	0148, 0802, 1421, 2032	0500 1.0F, 1116 0.8E, 1726 1.0F, 2342 0.8E
31 Sa ○	0246, 0856, 1516, 2128	0551 1.1F, 1208 0.8E, 1817 1.1F

August

Day	Slack (h m)	Maximum (h m / knots)
1 Su	0341, 0947, 1608, 2221	0035 0.8E, 0642 1.1F, 1259 0.8E, 1908 1.1F
2 M	0432, 1036, 1657, 2311	0125 0.8E, 0733 1.1F, 1349 0.8E, 1958 1.1F
3 Tu	0522, 1124, 1745	0215 0.8E, 0823 1.0F, 1438 0.8E, 2048 1.1F
4 W	0001, 0611, 1212, 1834	0305 0.8E, 0913 1.0F, 1528 0.8E, 2139 1.0F
5 Th	0051, 0700, 1300, 1923	0355 0.7E, 1001 0.9F, 1618 0.7E, 2229 1.0F
6 F	0142, 0752, 1350, 2016	0446 0.7E, 1053 0.9F, 1709 0.7E, 2320 0.9F
7 Sa ●	0236, 0850, 1444, 2114	0538 0.6E, 1145 0.8F, 1801 0.6E
8 Su	0334, 0955, 1542, 2217	0011 0.9F, 0631 0.6E, 1236 0.8F, 1855 0.6E
9 M	0434, 1100, 1645, 2320	0103 0.8F, 0726 0.5E, 1328 0.8F, 1949 0.5E
10 Tu	0532, 1159, 1746	0155 0.8F, 0819 0.5E, 1420 0.8F, 2043 0.5E
11 W	0017, 0626, 1252, 1842	0246 0.8F, 0912 0.6E, 1512 0.8F, 2135 0.6E
12 Th	0109, 0714, 1339, 1932	0337 0.8F, 1002 0.6E, 1602 0.6E, 2225 0.6E
13 F	0155, 0756, 1419, 2016	0427 0.9F, 1050 0.6E, 1652 0.9F, 2313 0.6E
14 Sa	0235, 0833, 1453, 2056	0516 0.9F, 1135 0.7E, 1740 0.9F, 2358 0.7E
15 Su ●	0308, 0906, 1521, 2132	0604 0.9F, 1219 0.7E, 1828 0.9F
16 M	0337, 0937, 1550, 2206	0042 0.7E, 0651 0.9F, 1302 0.7E, 1915 1.0F
17 Tu	0409, 1011, 1625, 2242	0125 0.7E, 0738 0.9F, 1343 0.7E, 2002 1.0F
18 W	0445, 1048, 1703, 2320	0208 0.7E, 0825 0.9F, 1426 0.7E, 2049 1.0F
19 Th	0523, 1128, 1744	0251 0.7E, 0912 0.9F, 1509 0.7E, 2137 1.0F
20 F	0002, 0606, 1213, 1829	0336 0.7E, 1001 0.9F, 1555 0.7E, 2227 1.0F
21 Sa	0048, 0652, 1301, 1918	0423 0.6E, 1051 0.9F, 1645 0.7E, 2318 0.9F
22 Su	0138, 0743, 1353, 2012	0515 0.6E, 1142 0.8F, 1739 0.6E
23 M ●	0233, 0840, 1451, 2112	0010 0.9F, 0611 0.6E, 1236 0.8F, 1837 0.6E
24 Tu	0333, 0944, 1557, 2218	0103 0.9F, 0710 0.6E, 1330 0.8F, 1938 0.6E
25 W	0441, 1055, 1710, 2331	0157 0.9F, 0809 0.6E, 1424 0.9F, 2038 0.7E
26 Th	0551, 1210, 1824	0251 0.9F, 0908 0.7E, 1518 0.9F, 2136 0.7E
27 F	0045, 0655, 1318, 1929	0345 1.0F, 1004 0.7E, 1611 0.9F, 2232 0.7E
28 Sa	0148, 0752, 1415, 2025	0437 1.0F, 1057 0.8E, 1703 1.0F, 2324 0.8E
29 Su ○	0243, 0844, 1506, 2116	0528 1.0F, 1148 0.8E, 1754 1.1F
30 M	0332, 0932, 1552, 2204	0015 0.8E, 0618 1.1F, 1237 0.8E, 1844 1.1F
31 Tu	0418, 1017, 1636, 2249	0103 0.8E, 0708 1.1F, 1325 0.8E, 1933 1.1F

September

Day	Slack (h m)	Maximum (h m / knots)
1 W	0500, 1100, 1718, 2332	0151 0.8E, 0756 1.0F, 1412 0.8E, 2021 1.1F
2 Th	0541, 1142, 1759	0238 0.8E, 0845 1.0F, 1459 0.8E, 2110 1.0F
3 F	0016, 0622, 1224, 1842	0325 0.7E, 0934 0.9F, 1547 0.7E, 2200 0.9F
4 Sa	0100, 0705, 1308, 1927	0413 0.6E, 1024 0.9F, 1636 0.6E, 2250 0.9F
5 Su	0148, 0754, 1357, 2018	0504 0.6E, 1115 0.8F, 1728 0.6E, 2341 0.9F
6 M ●	0243, 0852, 1453, 2120	0557 0.5E, 1206 0.8F, 1822 0.5E
7 Tu	0344, 1007, 1601, 2237	0033 0.8F, 0652 0.5E, 1259 0.7F, 1917 0.5E
8 W	0448, 1118, 1711, 2345	0126 0.8F, 0747 0.5E, 1351 0.7F, 2013 0.5E
9 Th	0546, 1215, 1812	0218 0.8F, 0840 0.5E, 1443 0.7F, 2106 0.5E
10 F	0040, 0637, 1302, 1904	0309 0.8F, 0932 0.6E, 1534 0.8F, 2157 0.6E
11 Sa	0127, 0720, 1342, 1942	0359 0.8F, 1020 0.6E, 1624 0.9F, 2245 0.6E
12 Su	0206, 0758, 1415, 2027	0448 0.9F, 1106 0.7E, 1713 0.9F, 2330 0.7E
13 M	0238, 0832, 1445, 2102	0536 0.9F, 1149 0.7E, 1800 1.0F
14 Tu ●	0307, 0906, 1519, 2137	0014 0.7E, 0623 1.0F, 1232 0.7E, 1847 1.0F
15 W	0340, 0942, 1556, 2213	0056 0.7E, 0710 1.0F, 1314 0.8E, 1934 1.0F
16 Th	0416, 1021, 1635, 2252	0139 0.7E, 0757 1.0F, 1357 0.8E, 2021 1.0F
17 F	0456, 1103, 1718, 2335	0222 0.7E, 0845 0.9F, 1441 0.8E, 2110 1.0F
18 Sa	0540, 1149, 1804	0308 0.7E, 0934 0.9F, 1529 0.7E, 2200 0.9F
19 Su	0021, 0628, 1239, 1855	0357 0.7E, 1025 0.9F, 1621 0.7E, 2251 0.9F
20 M	0112, 0721, 1334, 1951	0450 0.6E, 1117 0.8F, 1717 0.6E, 2344 0.9F
21 Tu ○	0209, 0822, 1437, 2055	0548 0.6E, 1211 0.8F, 1818 0.6E
22 W	0314, 0931, 1551, 2211	0039 0.9F, 0649 0.6E, 1306 0.8F, 1920 0.6E
23 Th	0428, 1052, 1711, 2337	0134 0.9F, 0750 0.6E, 1401 0.9F, 2021 0.6E
24 F	0542, 1209, 1822	0228 0.9F, 0849 0.7E, 1455 0.9F, 2119 0.7E
25 Sa	0046, 0645, 1310, 1921	0322 0.9F, 0944 0.7E, 1548 1.0F, 2213 0.7E
26 Su	0142, 0740, 1402, 2012	0414 0.9F, 1037 0.8E, 1640 1.0F, 2304 0.8E
27 M	0232, 0829, 1449, 2059	0504 1.0F, 1127 0.8E, 1730 1.1F, 2353 0.8E
28 Tu ●	0317, 0913, 1532, 2143	0554 1.0F, 1214 0.8E, 1818 1.1F
29 W	0358, 0954, 1612, 2223	0039 0.8E, 0642 1.0F, 1300 0.8E, 1906 1.1F
30 Th	0436, 1033, 1648, 2302	0124 0.8E, 0730 1.0F, 1345 0.8E, 1954 1.0F

All times are local time. Daylight Saving Time has been used when needed.

NOTES:

Throgs Neck, Long Island Sound, New York, 2004

F–Flood, Dir. 015° True   E–Ebb, Dir. 193° True

October

Date	Slack (h m)	Maximum (h m)	knots
1 F		0209	0.7E
	0511	0818	1.0F
	1110	1430	0.7E
	1724	2042	1.0F
	2340		
2 Sa		0255	0.7E
	0546	0906	0.9F
	1148	1516	0.7E
	1802	2131	0.9F
3 Su	0020	0342	0.6E
	0625	0955	0.8F
	1230	1604	0.6E
	1844	2221	0.8F
4 M	0103	0431	0.6E
	0710	1046	0.8F
	1317	1655	0.5E
	1933	2312	0.8F
5 Tu	0151	0523	0.5E
	0801	1137	0.8F
	1413	1749	0.5E
	2029		
6 W		0004	0.7F
	0247	0618	0.5E
	0902	1230	0.7F
	1519	1846	0.5E
	2139		
7 Th		0056	0.7F
	0351	0713	0.5E
	1013	1322	0.8F
	1632	1942	0.5E
	2302		
8 F		0148	0.7F
	0454	0807	0.5E
	1121	1415	0.8F
	1735	2036	0.5E
9 Sa	0002	0240	0.8F
	0548	0858	0.6E
	1212	1506	0.9F
	1828	2126	0.6E
10 Su	0049	0330	0.8F
	0634	0947	0.6E
	1253	1555	0.9F
	1912	2214	0.6E
11 M	0127	0419	0.9F
	0715	1034	0.7E
	1331	1644	1.0F
	1951	2300	0.7E
12 Tu	0159	0507	0.9F
	0754	1118	0.7E
	1408	1732	1.0F
	2028	2344	0.7E
13 W	0233	0555	1.0F
	0832	1202	0.8E
	1446	1819	1.0F
	2105		
14 Th		0027	0.8E
	0310	0703	1.0F
	0913	1245	0.8E
	1527	1927	1.1F
	2144		
15 F		0111	0.8E
	0350	0730	1.0F
	0955	1330	0.8E
	1609	1954	1.0F
	2226		
16 Sa		0156	0.8E
	0433	0818	1.0F
	1041	1417	0.8E
	1655	2044	1.0F
	2311		
17 Su		0243	0.7E
	0519	0908	1.0F
	1129	1507	0.7E
	1743	2134	1.0F
	2359		
18 M		0334	0.7E
	0610	1000	0.9F
	1223	1601	0.7E
	1837	2227	0.9F
19 Tu	0052	0430	0.7E
	0706	1053	0.9F
	1322	1659	0.6E
	1936	2320	0.9F
20 W	0152	0529	0.6E
	0810	1148	0.9F
	1431	1800	0.6E
	2047		
21 Th		0015	0.9F
	0301	0629	0.6E
	0926	1243	0.9F
	1551	1902	0.6E
	2214		
22 F		0110	0.9F
	0418	0730	0.6E
	1049	1338	0.9F
	1706	2002	0.6E
	2332		
23 Sa		0204	0.9F
	0528	0828	0.7E
	1157	1432	0.9F
	1810	2058	0.7E
24 Su	0034	0258	0.9F
	0629	0923	0.7E
	1254	1524	1.0F
	1905	2152	0.7E
25 M	0127	0349	0.9F
	0722	1014	0.7E
	1344	1615	1.0F
	1954	2242	0.8E
26 Tu	0215	0439	1.0F
	0809	1103	0.8E
	1430	1704	1.0F
	2039	2329	0.8E
27 W	0259	0528	1.0F
	0852	1149	0.8E
	1511	1752	1.0F
	2120		
28 Th		0014	0.8E
	0338	0616	1.0F
	0931	1234	0.8E
	1547	1840	1.0F
	2159		
29 F		0059	0.7E
	0413	0703	1.0F
	1007	1318	0.7E
	1620	1927	1.0F
	2234		
30 Sa		0143	0.7E
	0444	0751	0.9F
	1042	1402	0.7E
	1653	2015	0.9F
	2309		
31 Su		0127	0.7E
	0416	0739	0.9F
	1018	1348	0.6E
	1629	2003	0.9F
	2245		

November

Date	Slack (h m)	Maximum (h m)	knots
1 M		0213	0.6E
	0453	0828	0.8F
	1100	1435	0.6E
	1710	2053	0.8F
	2325		
2 Tu		0301	0.6E
	0536	0918	0.8F
	1147	1525	0.5E
	1757	2143	0.7F
3 W	0010	0351	0.5E
	0623	1009	0.8F
	1240	1618	0.5E
	1850	2234	0.7F
4 Th	0100	0444	0.5E
	0717	1101	0.8F
	1340	1713	0.5E
	1950	2326	0.7F
5 F	0155	0537	0.5E
	0815	1153	0.8F
	1446	1808	0.5E
	2056		
6 Sa		0018	0.7F
	0253	0631	0.5E
	0914	1244	0.8F
	1548	1901	0.5E
	2200		
7 Su		0109	0.8F
	0350	0722	0.6E
	1010	1335	0.9F
	1642	1952	0.6E
	2252		
8 M		0200	0.8F
	0442	0812	0.6E
	1101	1425	0.9F
	1729	2041	0.6E
	2336		
9 Tu		0249	0.9F
	0530	0900	0.7E
	1147	1514	1.0F
	1812	2128	0.7E
10 W	0017	0338	0.9F
	0616	0946	0.7E
	1232	1603	1.0F
	1854	2213	0.7E
11 Th	0059	0427	1.0F
	0701	1032	0.8E
	1316	1651	1.1F
	1935	2259	0.8E
12 F	0142	0515	1.0F
	0747	1119	0.8E
	1401	1740	1.1F
	2018	2345	0.8E
13 Sa	0227	0604	1.0F
	0834	1206	0.8E
	1447	1829	1.1F
	2103		
14 Su		0033	0.8E
	0314	0654	1.0F
	0923	1256	0.8E
	1536	1919	1.0F
	2151		
15 M		0123	0.8E
	0404	0745	1.0F
	1016	1348	0.8E
	1627	2010	1.0F
	2242		
16 Tu		0215	0.8E
	0457	0837	1.0F
	1113	1443	0.7E
	1723	2103	1.0F
	2337		
17 W		0311	0.7E
	0556	0930	1.0F
	1216	1541	0.7E
	1826	2156	0.9F
18 Th	0038	0408	0.7E
	0702	1024	0.9F
	1327	1640	0.7E
	1941	2251	0.9F
19 F	0147	0507	0.7E
	0817	1119	0.9F
	1441	1740	0.6E
	2104	2345	0.9F
20 Sa	0259	0606	0.7E
	0932	1213	0.9F
	1549	1838	0.6E
	2213		
21 Su		0039	0.9F
	0407	0703	0.7E
	1035	1306	0.9F
	1649	1934	0.7E
	2312		
22 M		0132	0.9F
	0506	0757	0.7E
	1131	1358	1.0F
	1744	2027	0.7E
23 Tu	0005	0223	0.9F
	0559	0849	0.7E
	1222	1448	1.0F
	1833	2117	0.7E
24 W	0054	0313	0.9F
	0646	0937	0.7E
	1308	1538	1.0F
	1918	2204	0.7E
25 Th	0138	0402	0.9F
	0730	1024	0.7E
	1349	1626	1.0F
	1959	2250	0.7E
26 F	0219	0450	0.9F
	0809	1109	0.7E
	1426	1714	1.0F
	2037	2334	0.7E
27 Sa	0255	0537	0.9F
	0845	1153	0.7E
	1457	1801	0.9F
	2111		
28 Su		0018	0.7E
	0324	0625	0.9F
	0920	1238	0.7E
	1528	1849	0.9F
	2143		
29 M		0102	0.6E
	0353	0713	0.9F
	0957	1323	0.6E
	1604	1937	0.9F
	2217		
30 Tu		0146	0.6E
	0428	0801	0.8F
	1037	1409	0.6E
	1644	2025	0.8F
	2254		

December

Date	Slack (h m)	Maximum (h m)	knots
1 W		0232	0.6E
	0508	0851	0.8F
	1122	1457	0.5E
	1728	2115	0.8F
	2336		
2 Th		0320	0.6E
	0552	0941	0.8F
	1211	1548	0.5E
	1817	2205	0.8F
3 F	0022	0409	0.5E
	0640	1031	0.8F
	1304	1639	0.5E
	1909	2256	0.7F
4 Sa	0112	0501	0.5E
	0731	1123	0.8F
	1359	1732	0.6E
	2003	2347	0.7F
5 Su	0204	0553	0.6E
	0825	1214	0.8F
	1456	1824	0.5E
	2059		
6 M		0038	0.8F
	0259	0645	0.6E
	0920	1305	0.8F
	1551	1916	0.6E
	2154		
7 Tu		0129	0.8F
	0354	0736	0.6E
	1015	1355	0.9F
	1643	2006	0.6E
	2247		
8 W		0219	0.9F
	0448	0826	0.7E
	1108	1445	1.0F
	1733	2056	0.7E
	2339		
9 Th		0310	0.9F
	0541	0916	0.7E
	1159	1535	1.0F
	1822	2145	0.7E
10 F	0029	0400	1.0F
	0633	1006	0.8E
	1249	1625	1.0F
	1909	2233	0.8E
11 Sa	0118	0450	1.0F
	0726	1056	0.8E
	1339	1715	1.1F
	1957	2323	0.8E
12 Su	0209	0540	1.0F
	0818	1146	0.8E
	1430	1805	1.1F
	2046		
13 M		0013	0.8E
	0300	0631	1.1F
	0912	1238	0.8E
	1522	1855	1.0F
	2136		
14 Tu		0104	0.8E
	0352	0722	1.1F
	1007	1330	0.8E
	1616	1947	1.0F
	2228		
15 W		0156	0.8E
	0447	0814	1.0F
	1105	1425	0.8E
	1713	2039	1.0F
	2323		
16 Th		0250	0.8E
	0545	0906	1.0F
	1207	1520	0.7E
	1815	2132	1.0F
17 F	0022	0346	0.7E
	0648	0959	1.0F
	1311	1617	0.7E
	1925	2225	0.9F
18 Sa	0126	0442	0.7E
	0756	1052	1.0F
	1417	1714	0.7E
	2038	2318	0.9F
19 Su	0232	0539	0.7E
	0904	1146	0.9F
	1521	1811	0.6E
	2145		
20 M		0011	0.9F
	0337	0635	0.7E
	1007	1238	0.9F
	1622	1906	0.6E
	2245		
21 Tu		0104	0.9F
	0437	0729	0.7E
	1105	1330	0.9F
	1718	1959	0.6E
	2340		
22 W		0155	0.9F
	0532	0821	0.7E
	1157	1421	0.9F
	1809	2050	0.6E
23 Th	0031	0246	0.9F
	0622	0911	0.7E
	1245	1511	0.9F
	1855	2139	0.6E
24 F	0118	0335	0.9F
	0708	0959	0.7E
	1329	1600	0.9F
	1938	2225	0.7E
25 Sa	0200	0424	0.9F
	0750	1045	0.7E
	1408	1648	0.9F
	2016	2310	0.7E
26 Su	0238	0512	0.9F
	0828	1130	0.7E
	1442	1736	0.9F
	2050	2354	0.7E
27 M	0309	0600	0.9F
	0905	1215	0.7E
	1513	1823	0.9F
	2121		
28 Tu		0038	0.7E
	0335	0648	0.9F
	0941	1259	0.7E
	1545	1911	0.9F
	2152		
29 W		0121	0.6E
	0405	0735	0.9F
	1018	1344	0.6E
	1622	1959	0.9F
	2227		
30 Th		0204	0.6E
	0442	0824	0.9F
	1058	1430	0.6E
	1702	2047	0.9F
	2306		
31 F		0249	0.6E
	0522	0912	0.8F
	1142	1516	0.6E
	1745	2136	0.8F
	2349		

All times are local time. Daylight Saving Time has been used when needed.

NOTES:

Hell Gate (off Mill Rock), East River, New York, 2004

F–Flood, Dir. 050° True   E–Ebb, Dir. 230° True

April

Day	Slack (h m)	Maximum (h m / knots)
1 Th	0031, 0642, 1304, 1906	0335 3.1F, 0929 4.2E, 1602 3.1F, 2152 4.3E
2 F	0120, 0731, 1349, 1951	0423 3.3F, 1019 4.5E, 1647 3.4F, 2240 4.6E
3 Sa	0206, 0817, 1431, 2034	0508 3.6F, 1105 4.7E, 1729 3.6F, 2325 4.9E
4 Su	0350, 1002, 1612, 2217	0652 3.8F, 1249 4.9E, 1911 3.8F
5 M ○	0434, 1046, 1653, 2300	0109 5.1E, 0735 3.9F, 1333 5.0E, 1953 3.9F
6 Tu	0518, 1130, 1735, 2345	0154 5.2E, 0819 4.1F, 1417 5.0E, 2036 3.9F
7 W	0604, 1215, 1819	0239 5.2E, 0904 3.9F, 1502 5.0E, 2122 3.9F
8 Th	0031, 0652, 1304, 1907	0326 5.2E, 0952 3.8F, 1549 4.9E, 2210 3.8F
9 F	0122, 0745, 1356, 2000	0416 5.0E, 1043 3.6F, 1640 4.6E, 2304 3.5F
10 Sa	0217, 0843, 1454, 2101	0509 4.8E, 1140 3.3F, 1736 4.4E
11 Su ○	0319, 0950, 1559, 2211	0004 3.3F, 0609 4.5E, 1246 3.1F, 1839 4.1E
12 M	0428, 1102, 1709, 2327	0115 3.1F, 0718 4.2E, 1402 3.0F, 1953 4.0E
13 Tu	0541, 1214, 1818	0236 3.0F, 0840 4.1E, 1521 3.0F, 2119 4.0E
14 W	0040, 0651, 1320, 1921	0353 3.1F, 1004 4.2E, 1629 3.2F, 2236 4.2E
15 Th	0145, 0752, 1417, 2017	0458 3.3F, 1110 4.4E, 1726 3.3F, 2335 4.5E
16 F	0240, 0846, 1506, 2106	0552 3.5F, 1202 4.5E, 1814 3.5F
17 Sa	0329, 0934, 1550, 2150	0021 4.6E, 0638 3.6F, 1244 4.6E, 1857 3.6F
18 Su	0413, 1017, 1631, 2231	0101 4.8E, 0720 3.7F, 1321 4.7E, 1936 3.7F
19 M ●	0454, 1057, 1710, 2311	0137 4.8E, 0758 3.7F, 1355 4.7E, 2012 3.7F
20 Tu	0533, 1136, 1747, 2349	0210 4.8E, 0834 3.7F, 1427 4.7E, 2047 3.6F
21 W	0611, 1215, 1824	0243 4.8E, 0910 3.6F, 1501 4.6E, 2122 3.5F
22 Th	0028, 0649, 1254, 1902	0316 4.7E, 0946 3.5F, 1536 4.5E, 2159 3.4F
23 F	0107, 0729, 1334, 1941	0355 4.6E, 1024 3.3F, 1614 4.3E, 2238 3.2F
24 Sa	0147, 0810, 1416, 2023	0435 4.4E, 1105 3.1F, 1656 4.2E, 2321 3.0F
25 Su	0231, 0856, 1502, 2109	0519 4.3E, 1150 2.9F, 1741 4.0E
26 M	0320, 0946, 1552, 2201	0008 2.9F, 0607 4.1E, 1240 2.8F, 1831 3.9E
27 Tu ○	0413, 1041, 1646, 2259	0101 2.8F, 0700 4.1E, 1334 2.7F, 1926 3.9E
28 W	0510, 1137, 1741, 2357	0158 2.8F, 0756 4.0E, 1431 2.8F, 2022 4.0E
29 Th	0607, 1231, 1834	0256 2.9F, 0853 4.1E, 1527 2.9F, 2119 4.2E
30 F	0052, 0702, 1322, 1925	0352 3.1F, 0948 4.3E, 1619 3.1F, 2213 4.4E

May

Day	Slack (h m)	Maximum (h m / knots)
1 Sa	0145, 0754, 1410, 2013	0445 3.3F, 1041 4.6E, 1707 3.4F, 2305 4.7E
2 Su	0234, 0843, 1455, 2100	0534 3.6F, 1131 4.7E, 1754 3.6F, 2354 5.0E
3 M	0323, 0931, 1541, 2147	0622 3.7F, 1219 4.9E, 1841 3.8F
4 Tu ○	0411, 1018, 1626, 2235	0042 5.1E, 0709 3.9F, 1306 5.0E, 1927 3.9F
5 W	0459, 1106, 1713, 2323	0131 5.2E, 0757 3.9F, 1354 5.0E, 2015 3.9F
6 Th	0549, 1156, 1803	0219 5.3E, 0846 3.9F, 1443 5.0E, 2105 3.9F
7 F	0014, 0642, 1247, 1856	0310 5.2E, 0938 3.7F, 1534 4.8E, 2158 3.7F
8 Sa	0108, 0738, 1343, 1954	0403 5.0E, 1033 3.5F, 1628 4.6E, 2255 3.5F
9 Su	0206, 0839, 1442, 2058	0500 4.7E, 1134 3.3F, 1727 4.4E, 2359 3.3F
10 M	0310, 0945, 1547, 2209	0602 4.5E, 1241 3.1F, 1834 4.2E
11 Tu	0417, 1053, 1653, 2320	0112 3.1F, 0714 4.3E, 1355 3.0F, 1951 4.1E
12 W ○	0525, 1200, 1758	0228 3.1F, 0835 4.2E, 1506 3.0F, 2112 4.2E
13 Th	0027, 0630, 1300, 1857	0337 3.1F, 0949 4.2E, 1608 3.1F, 2219 4.3E
14 F	0127, 0727, 1353, 1949	0437 3.2F, 1048 4.3E, 1701 3.3F, 2312 4.5E
15 Sa	0220, 0818, 1440, 2037	0527 3.4F, 1135 4.4E, 1747 3.4F, 2355 4.6E
16 Su	0306, 0904, 1523, 2120	0612 3.5F, 1215 4.5E, 1828 3.5F
17 M	0348, 0946, 1603, 2200	0032 4.7E, 0652 3.5F, 1249 4.6E, 1906 3.5F
18 Tu ●	0428, 1025, 1641, 2239	0106 4.7E, 0729 3.5F, 1322 4.6E, 1941 3.5F
19 W	0507, 1104, 1718, 2317	0139 4.8E, 0805 3.5F, 1355 4.6E, 2016 3.5F
20 Th	0545, 1143, 1755, 2356	0213 4.8E, 0840 3.4F, 1429 4.6E, 2052 3.4F
21 F	0623, 1221, 1833	0249 4.7E, 0916 3.4F, 1506 4.5E, 2129 3.3F
22 Sa	0035, 0703, 1301, 1912	0327 4.7E, 0954 3.2F, 1545 4.4E, 2208 3.2F
23 Su	0115, 0744, 1342, 1953	0407 4.6E, 1035 3.1F, 1626 4.3E, 2250 3.1F
24 M	0158, 0828, 1426, 2038	0450 4.5E, 1118 3.0F, 1711 4.2E, 2336 3.0F
25 Tu	0244, 0914, 1513, 2127	0537 4.4E, 1205 2.9F, 1759 4.2E
26 W	0334, 1004, 1603, 2221	0026 2.9F, 0626 4.3E, 1255 2.8F, 1850 4.2E
27 Th ○	0428, 1056, 1655, 2317	0119 2.9F, 0719 4.3E, 1348 2.9F, 1945 4.3E
28 F	0524, 1148, 1749	0215 3.0F, 0813 4.3E, 1443 3.0F, 2040 4.4E
29 Sa	0015, 0620, 1241, 1843	0311 3.1F, 0909 4.4E, 1537 3.2F, 2136 4.6E
30 Su	0111, 0715, 1332, 1936	0407 3.3F, 1004 4.6E, 1630 3.4F, 2231 4.8E
31 M	0205, 0808, 1423, 2028	0501 3.5F, 1057 4.7E, 1722 3.6F, 2325 5.0E

June

Day	Slack (h m)	Maximum (h m / knots)
1 Tu	0259, 0901, 1514, 2120	0554 3.6F, 1150 4.9E, 1814 3.7F
2 W ○	0351, 0953, 1605, 2213	0018 5.1E, 0647 3.7F, 1242 4.9E, 1906 3.8F
3 Th	0445, 1045, 1657, 2306	0111 5.2E, 0739 3.8F, 1335 5.0E, 1959 3.9F
4 F	0539, 1138, 1752	0204 5.2E, 0833 3.7F, 1428 4.9E, 2053 3.8F
5 Sa	0001, 0634, 1233, 1849	0258 5.1E, 0928 3.6F, 1522 4.8E, 2149 3.7F
6 Su	0057, 0731, 1330, 1949	0354 5.0E, 1025 3.5F, 1619 4.7E, 2249 3.5F
7 M	0156, 0831, 1428, 2052	0452 4.8E, 1126 3.3F, 1720 4.5E, 2352 3.5F
8 Tu	0257, 0933, 1529, 2157	0555 4.5E, 1230 3.2F, 1825 4.4E
9 W ○	0359, 1035, 1630, 2302	0100 3.2F, 0702 4.4E, 1336 3.1F, 1936 4.3E
10 Th	0501, 1135, 1729	0207 3.1F, 0812 4.3E, 1439 3.1F, 2045 4.3E
11 F	0004, 0600, 1231, 1825	0310 3.1F, 0918 4.2E, 1537 3.1F, 2147 4.3E
12 Sa	0101, 0655, 1323, 1917	0406 3.1F, 1013 4.2E, 1629 3.1F, 2239 4.4E
13 Su	0152, 0745, 1410, 2004	0457 3.2F, 1100 4.3E, 1715 3.2F, 2322 4.5E
14 M	0239, 0831, 1453, 2048	0541 3.2F, 1140 4.5E, 1757 3.3F
15 Tu	0321, 0913, 1533, 2129	0622 4.5E, 1216 3.3F, 1835 4.4E
16 W	0402, 0954, 1612, 2209	0035 4.6E, 0700 3.3F, 1250 4.4E, 1912 3.4F
17 Th ●	0441, 1034, 1651, 2249	0110 4.7E, 0736 3.3F, 1325 4.5E, 1948 3.4F
18 F	0520, 1113, 1729, 2329	0145 4.7E, 0813 3.3F, 1401 4.5E, 2025 3.4F
19 Sa	0559, 1153, 1807	0222 4.7E, 0850 3.3F, 1439 4.5E, 2103 3.4F
20 Su	0008, 0636, 1232, 1845	0301 4.7E, 0928 3.3F, 1518 4.5E, 2142 3.3F
21 M	0049, 0717, 1312, 1925	0341 4.6E, 1007 3.2F, 1559 4.3E, 2223 3.3F
22 Tu	0130, 0758, 1353, 2008	0423 4.6E, 1048 3.1F, 1643 4.4E, 2306 3.2F
23 W	0214, 0840, 1437, 2053	0508 4.6E, 1132 3.1F, 1728 4.4E, 2353 3.1F
24 Th ○	0301, 0925, 1524, 2144	0554 4.5E, 1219 3.1F, 1817 4.5E
25 F	0351, 1013, 1615, 2239	0043 3.1F, 0644 4.5E, 1309 3.1F, 1910 4.5E
26 Sa	0445, 1105, 1709, 2338	0137 3.1F, 0737 4.5E, 1403 3.1F, 2005 4.6E
27 Su	0542, 1200, 1807	0234 3.2F, 0833 4.5E, 1459 3.2F, 2103 4.7E
28 M	0038, 0641, 1257, 1905	0333 3.3F, 0930 4.5E, 1557 3.4F, 2202 4.8E
29 Tu	0139, 0740, 1354, 2004	0433 3.4F, 1028 4.6E, 1656 3.5F, 2301 4.9E
30 W	0238, 0837, 1452, 2101	0532 3.5F, 1126 4.7E, 1754 3.7F, 2359 5.0E

All times are local time. Daylight Saving Time has been used when needed.

NOTES:

Hell Gate (off Mill Rock), East River, New York, 2004

F—Flood, Dir. 050° True   E—Ebb, Dir. 230° True

July

Day	Slack	Maximum	knots		Day	Slack	Maximum	knots
1 Th	0335	0630	3.6F		16 F		0042	4.5E
	0934	1224	4.8E			0413	0710	3.3F
	1549	1851	3.8F			1008	1257	4.4E
	2158					1622	1923	3.4F
						2226		
2 F ○	0432	0726	5.1E		17 Sa ●		0120	4.6E
	1030	1321	4.9E			0452	0747	3.3F
	1645	1948	3.8F			1048	1335	4.5E
	2255					1701	2000	3.5F
						2306		
3 Sa	0153	0822	5.1E		18 Su		0158	4.7E
	1125	1417	4.9E			0531	0824	3.4F
	1742	2044	3.8F			1128	1413	4.6E
	2351					1739	2038	3.5F
						2346		
4 Su		0249	5.1E		19 M		0236	4.7E
	0622	0918	3.7F			0608	0901	3.4F
	1315	1609	4.7E			1206	1452	4.6E
	1839	2141	3.7F			1816	2116	3.5F
5 M	0047	0345	4.9E		20 Tu	0026	0316	4.7E
	0717	1014	3.6F			0646	0939	3.4F
	1315	1609	4.7E			1245	1533	4.7E
	1936	2238	3.6F			1855	2156	3.5F
6 Tu	0142	0441	4.8E		21 W	0106	0356	4.7E
	0812	1110	3.5F			0723	1018	3.4F
	1410	1706	4.6E			1324	1615	4.7E
	2034	2336	3.5F			1935	2238	3.5F
7 W	0239	0537	4.6E		22 Th	0148	0439	4.7E
	0908	1207	3.3F			0802	1100	3.3F
	1505	1804	4.5E			1406	1659	4.7E
	2133					2019	2322	3.4F
8 Th		0035	3.3F		23 F	0233	0524	4.6E
	0335	0635	4.4E			0844	1145	3.3F
	1004	1305	3.2F			1452	1746	4.6E
	1601	1903	4.3E			2108		
	2232							
9 F ○		0135	3.1F		24 Sa		0011	3.3F
	0431	0734	4.2E			0322	0612	4.5E
	1059	1402	3.1F			0931	1234	3.3F
	1656	2004	4.2E			1543	1838	4.6E
	2329					2203		
10 Sa		0234	3.0F		25 Su ○		0104	3.3F
	0527	0833	4.1E			0415	0704	4.4E
	1153	1459	3.0F			1024	1329	3.3F
	1750	2103	4.2E			1639	1934	4.6E
						2304		
11 Su	0025	0329	3.0F		26 M		0203	3.2F
	0620	0928	4.0E			0515	0801	4.4E
	1245	1551	3.0F			1123	1429	3.5F
	1842	2156	4.2E			1741	2034	4.6E
12 M	0117	0421	3.0F		27 Tu	0009	0306	3.2F
	0711	1018	4.0E			0618	0903	4.4E
	1334	1640	3.0F			1227	1533	3.7F
	1931	2244	4.2E			1845	2138	4.6E
13 Tu	0205	0508	3.0F		28 W	0116	0412	3.3F
	0759	1102	4.1E			0722	1007	4.4E
	1419	1725	3.1F			1332	1638	3.5F
	2018	2326	4.3E			1949	2243	4.7E
14 W	0250	0551	3.1F		29 Th	0220	0517	3.4F
	0844	1142	4.2E			0824	1111	4.6E
	1502	1806	3.2F			1436	1742	4.5E
	2102					2051	2347	4.8E
15 Th		0005	4.4E		30 F	0320	0619	3.6F
	0332	0632	3.2F			0923	1213	4.7E
	0927	1220	4.3E			1536	1843	3.8F
	1543	1845	3.3F			2151		
	2144							
					31 Sa ○		0048	4.9E
						0417	0717	3.7F
						1020	1312	4.8E
						1633	1940	3.9F
						2247		

August

Day	Slack	Maximum	knots		Day	Slack	Maximum	knots
1 Su		0145	5.0E		16 M		0131	4.7E
	0511	0812	3.8F			0458	0756	3.5F
	1113	1408	4.9E			1102	1347	4.6E
	1728	2035	3.9F			1708	2012	3.7F
	2341					2323		
2 M		0239	5.0E		17 Tu		0210	4.8E
	0603	0904	3.8F			0534	0832	3.6F
	1206	1501	4.9E			1140	1426	4.8E
	1822	2128	3.9F			1745	2049	3.8F
3 Tu	0033	0330	4.9E		18 W	0003	0248	4.8E
	0654	0955	3.7F			0610	0909	3.6F
	1256	1552	4.8E			1218	1505	4.8E
	1914	2219	3.8F			1824	2129	3.8F
4 W	0125	0420	4.7E		19 Th	0042	0328	4.8E
	0743	1045	3.6F			0646	0948	3.5F
	1347	1641	4.7E			1257	1547	4.8E
	2006	2310	3.6F			1904	2210	3.7F
5 Th	0216	0508	4.6E		20 F	0124	0410	4.7E
	0833	1135	3.4F			0725	1029	3.6F
	1437	1731	4.5E			1339	1631	4.8E
	2058					1948	2256	3.6F
6 F		0002	3.4F		21 Sa	0209	0455	4.6E
	0307	0557	4.3E			0807	1114	3.6F
	0923	1226	3.2F			1426	1718	4.7E
	1528	1821	4.3E			2037	2343	3.5F
	2151							
7 Sa		0055	3.2F		22 Su	0258	0543	4.5E
	0359	0647	4.1E			0654	1205	3.4F
	1015	1319	3.1F			1518	1811	4.6E
	1621	1913	4.1E			2133		
	2245							
8 Su		0150	3.0F		23 M		0038	3.3F
	0452	0740	3.9E			0354	0637	4.3E
	1107	1413	2.9F			0950	1302	3.3F
	1714	2008	4.0E			1618	1909	4.5E
	2340					2237		
9 M		0246	2.9F		24 Tu		0140	3.2F
	0545	0835	3.8E			0457	0737	4.2E
	1201	1509	2.9F			1105	1407	3.4F
	1808	2105	3.9E			1726	2013	4.4E
						2344		
10 Tu	0035	0342	2.9F		25 W		0249	3.1F
	0638	0930	3.8E			0605	0843	4.1E
	1253	1603	2.9F			1208	1518	3.3F
	1901	2200	3.9E			1835	2123	4.3E
11 W	0127	0434	2.9F		26 Th	0100	0402	3.2F
	0729	1022	3.8E			0713	0954	4.2E
	1342	1652	3.0F			1319	1631	3.4F
	1951	2250	4.1E			1943	2235	4.4E
12 Th	0215	0520	3.0F		27 F	0206	0511	3.4F
	0817	1108	4.0E			0816	1105	4.4E
	1428	1737	3.2F			1425	1738	3.6F
	2037	2334	4.2E			2046	2343	4.6E
13 F	0259	0603	3.2F		28 Sa	0306	0612	3.6F
	0902	1151	4.2E			0915	1209	4.6E
	1511	1818	3.3F			1525	1837	3.8F
	2121					2144		
14 Sa		0015	4.4E		29 Su		0043	4.8E
	0341	0642	3.3F			0401	0707	3.7F
	0944	1230	4.3E			1008	1305	4.8E
	1551	1857	3.5F			1620	1931	3.9F
	2203					2237		
15 Su		0053	4.5E		30 M		0135	4.9E
	0420	0719	3.4F			0451	0757	3.8F
	1024	1309	4.5E			1059	1356	4.9E
	1630	1934	3.6F			1711	2021	3.9F
	2244					2327		
					31 Tu		0223	4.9E
						0538	0844	3.9F
						1146	1443	4.9E
						1759	2108	4.0F

September

Day	Slack	Maximum	knots		Day	Slack	Maximum	knots
1 W		0015	4.8E		16 Th		0220	4.9E
	0624	0929	3.8F			0536	0839	3.8F
	1233	1527	4.8E			1150	1439	5.0E
	1846	2153	3.8F			1756	2102	3.9F
2 Th	0101	0351	4.7E		17 F	0017	0301	4.9E
	0709	1013	3.7F			0613	0919	3.8F
	1319	1610	4.7E			1231	1521	5.0E
	1932	2238	3.7F			1838	2144	3.8F
3 F	0147	0433	4.5E		18 Sa	0100	0344	4.8E
	0753	1057	3.5F			0653	1002	3.8F
	1405	1653	4.5E			1315	1606	4.9E
	2019	2323	3.4F			1924	2230	3.7F
4 Sa	0234	0515	4.2E		19 Su	0147	0428	4.6E
	0839	1143	3.3F			0738	1049	3.6F
	1453	1737	4.2E			1404	1655	4.8E
	2107					2015	2321	3.5F
5 Su		0011	3.2F		20 M	0238	0520	4.4E
	0323	0600	4.0E			0829	1142	3.5F
	0927	1231	3.1F			1500	1749	4.5E
	1543	1824	4.0E			2114		
	2158							
6 M		0102	3.0F		21 Tu		0018	3.3F
	0414	0648	3.8E			0338	0616	4.2E
	1018	1324	2.9F			0930	1244	3.3F
	1636	1916	3.8E			1605	1850	4.3E
	2253					2222		
7 Tu		0159	2.8F		22 W		0125	3.1F
	0509	0742	3.6E			0445	0720	4.0E
	1113	1422	2.8F			1043	1355	3.2F
	1732	2013	3.7E			1716	2000	4.2E
	2350					2337		
8 W		0258	2.8F		23 Th		0241	3.1F
	0605	0841	3.6E			0557	0834	4.0E
	1210	1524	2.8F			1201	1514	3.2F
	1828	2113	3.7E			1829	2117	4.2E
9 Th	0045	0355	2.8F		24 F	0050	0358	3.2F
	0658	0939	3.7E			0705	0952	4.1E
	1303	1616	2.9F			1313	1627	3.4F
	1921	2210	3.9E			1937	2235	4.3E
10 F	0144	0446	3.0F		25 Sa	0155	0505	3.4F
	0748	1032	3.9E			0807	1105	4.3E
	1352	1704	3.1F			1417	1733	3.6F
	2010	2259	4.1E			2037	2344	4.5E
11 Sa	0224	0530	3.4F		26 Su	0251	0602	3.6F
	0833	1118	4.1E			0902	1204	4.6E
	1437	1747	3.4F			1514	1827	3.8F
	2055	2343	4.3E			2131		
12 Su	0306	0610	3.4F		27 M		0033	4.7E
	0915	1159	4.3E			0342	0652	3.8F
	1519	1827	3.6F			0951	1252	4.8E
	2137					1604	1916	3.9F
						2220		
13 M		0023	4.5E		28 Tu		0119	4.8E
	0345	0647	3.5F			0429	0737	3.9F
	0954	1239	4.6E			1038	1338	4.9E
	1558	1905	3.7F			1651	2001	4.0F
	2217					2306		
14 Tu		0102	4.7E		29 W		0201	4.8E
	0423	0724	3.7F			0512	0819	3.9F
	1033	1318	4.8E			1122	1419	4.9E
	1637	1943	3.9F			1735	2043	3.9F
	2257					2349		
15 W		0140	4.8E		30 Th		0240	4.7E
	0459	0801	3.8F			0554	0900	3.8F
	1111	1358	4.9E			1204	1458	4.8E
	1716	2022	3.9F			1818	2124	3.8F
	2337							

All times are local time. Daylight Saving Time has been used when needed.

NOTES:

129

Hell Gate (off Mill Rock), East River, New York, 2004

F–Flood, Dir. 050° True   E–Ebb, Dir. 230° True

October

Day	Slack (h m)	Maximum (h m)	knots
1 F	0032 0635 1247 1900	0318 0939 1536 2204	4.6E 3.7F 4.7E 3.6F
2 Sa	0115 0716 1330 1943	0356 1019 1615 2245	4.4E 3.5F 4.5E 3.4F
3 Su	0158 0758 1414 2028	0435 1101 1656 2329	4.2E 3.3F 4.3E 3.2F
4 M	0244 0844 1502 2116	0518 1147 1741	4.0E 3.1F 4.0E
5 Tu	0334 0934 1554 2210	0017 0605 1238 1831	2.9F 3.8E 2.9F 3.9E
6 W ○	0428 1029 1650 2308	0112 0657 1335 1927	2.8F 3.6E 2.8F 3.7E
7 Th	0524 1128 1747	0211 0755 1435 2027	2.7F 3.6E 2.8F 3.7E
8 F	0005 0619 1224 1842	0310 0846 1533 2125	2.8F 3.7E 2.9F 3.9E
9 Sa	0058 0710 1316 1933	0404 0950 1625 2218	2.9F 3.9E 3.1F 4.1E
10 Su	0146 0756 1403 2020	0450 1039 1710 2305	3.1F 4.2E 3.3F 4.3E
11 M	0229 0838 1447 2103	0532 1124 1753 2348	3.4F 4.5E 3.6F 4.6E
12 Tu	0310 0919 1529 2145	0612 1206 1833	3.6F 4.7E 3.8F
13 W ●	0349 0959 1610 2226	0029 0651 1248 1910	4.7E 3.8F 4.9E 3.9F
14 Th	0427 1040 1652 2308	0110 0730 1330 1955	4.9E 3.9F 5.1E 4.0F
15 F	0507 1122 1735 2351	0152 0811 1414 2038	4.9E 3.9F 5.1E 3.9F
16 Sa	0548 1206 1821	0235 0854 1459 2123	4.9E 3.9F 5.1E 3.8F
17 Su	0037 0633 1253 1910	0321 0941 1546 2212	4.8E 3.8F 5.0E 3.7F
18 M	0126 0722 1346 2005	0409 1031 1638 2306	4.6E 3.6F 4.8E 3.4F
19 Tu	0222 0819 1445 2108	0503 1128 1734	4.4E 3.4F 4.5E
20 W ○	0324 0927 1553 2219	0007 0603 1235 1839	3.2F 4.2E 3.2F 4.3E
21 Th	0433 1043 1706 2333	0119 0712 1351 1954	3.0F 4.0E 3.1F 4.1E
22 F	0544 1200 1817	0238 0831 1512 2117	3.0F 4.0E 3.2F 4.1E
23 Sa	0042 0650 1309 1922	0351 0953 1623 2231	3.2F 4.2E 3.3F 4.3E
24 Su	0142 0748 1408 2019	0453 1059 1721 2329	3.4F 4.4E 3.5F 4.5E
25 M	0235 0840 1501 2110	0546 1152 1812	3.6F 4.6E 3.7F
26 Tu	0323 0927 1548 2156	0017 0631 1237 1857	4.6E 3.7F 4.8E 3.8F
27 W ○	0406 1011 1632 2238	0058 0713 1316 1938	4.7E 3.8F 4.9E 3.8F
28 Th	0448 1053 1713 2319	0135 0753 1353 2017	4.7E 3.8F 4.9E 3.8F
29 F	0527 1133 1754 2359	0211 0830 1428 2055	4.9E 3.7F 4.8E 3.6F
30 Sa	0606 1213 1834	0248 0908 1504 2132	4.6E 3.6F 4.7E 3.5F
31 Su	0040 0546 1154 1815	0222 0846 1442 2111	4.5E 3.4F 4.6E 3.3F

November

Day	Slack (h m)	Maximum (h m)	knots
1 M	0021 0627 1236 1858	0301 0926 1522 2153	4.3E 3.2F 4.4E 3.1F
2 Tu	0104 0710 1321 1944	0342 1009 1606 2239	4.1E 3.0F 4.2E 2.9F
3 W	0151 0758 1410 2035	0428 1057 1654 2329	3.8E 2.9F 4.1E 2.8F
4 Th ○	0242 0851 1503 2130	0518 1150 1746	3.6E 2.8F 4.0E
5 F ○	0335 0948 1559 2225	0024 0612 1247 1842	2.7F 3.6E 2.7F 3.9E
6 Sa	0429 1045 1654 2318	0120 0709 1345 1938	2.7F 3.6E 2.8F 4.0E
7 Su	0521 1139 1747	0214 0804 1439 2032	2.9F 4.1E 3.0F 4.2E
8 M	0007 0609 1229 1836	0304 0857 1529 2123	3.1F 4.3E 3.2F 4.4E
9 Tu	0052 0655 1316 1923	0350 0946 1615 2210	3.3F 4.6E 3.5F 4.6E
10 W	0135 0740 1402 2009	0434 1033 1700 2256	3.5F 4.9E 3.7F 4.8E
11 Th	0218 0824 1447 2054	0518 1119 1745 2341	3.7F 5.1E 3.8F 4.9E
12 F ○	0301 0910 1533 2140	0602 1205 1831	3.9F 5.2E 3.9F
13 Sa	0346 0956 1621 2227	0027 0648 1252 1918	5.0E 3.9F 5.2E 3.8F
14 Su	0432 1044 1711 2316	0114 0735 1341 2007	5.0E 3.9F 5.2E 3.7F
15 M	0523 1136 1805	0203 0826 1432 2059	4.9E 3.8F 5.1E 3.6F
16 Tu	0009 0618 1232 1903	0255 0920 1526 2157	4.7E 3.6F 4.8E 3.4F
17 W	0106 0720 1333 2007	0352 1021 1625 2301	4.5E 3.4F 4.6E 3.2F
18 Th	0209 0829 1439 2115	0454 1129 1732	4.3E 3.2F 4.4E
19 F ○	0315 0942 1548 2224	0012 0605 1245 1847	3.0F 4.2E 3.1F 4.2E
20 Sa	0422 1053 1656 2328	0126 0725 1400 2007	3.0F 4.2E 3.1F 4.2E
21 Su	0525 1158 1757	0234 0841 1506 2115	3.1F 4.3E 3.2F 4.3E
22 M	0025 0622 1255 1852	0332 0943 1602 2209	3.3F 4.5E 3.3F 4.4E
23 Tu	0116 0713 1345 1942	0423 1033 1650 2254	3.4F 4.6E 3.4F 4.5E
24 W	0202 0759 1431 2026	0508 1115 1734 2334	3.5F 4.7E 3.5F 4.6E
25 Th	0245 0842 1513 2108	0549 1153 1814	3.5F 4.8E 3.5F
26 F ●	0325 0923 1553 2148	0009 0627 1227 1851	4.6E 3.5F 4.8E 3.5F
27 Sa	0404 1002 1633 2227	0043 0703 1302 1928	4.6E 3.5F 4.8E 3.4F
28 Su	0443 1041 1712 2306	0117 0740 1337 2005	4.6E 3.4F 4.8E 3.4F
29 M	0522 1121 1752 2346	0153 0817 1414 2043	4.5E 3.4F 4.7E 3.2F
30 Tu	0602 1202 1834	0232 0856 1454 2122	4.3E 3.2F 4.6E 3.1F

December

Day	Slack (h m)	Maximum (h m)	knots
1 W	0027 0644 1244 1917	0312 0938 1536 2205	4.4E 3.1F 4.5E 3.0F
2 Th	0110 0728 1329 2003	0356 1022 1621 2251	4.3E 3.0F 4.4E 2.8F
3 F	0156 0816 1417 2051	0443 1110 1709 2339	4.2E 2.9F 4.3E 2.8F
4 Sa ○	0244 0908 1509 2142	0532 1202 1800	4.2E 2.8F 4.2E
5 Su	0335 1003 1603 2233	0031 0625 1256 1853	2.8F 4.2E 2.9F 4.3E
6 M	0427 1058 1657 2323	0123 0719 1351 1947	2.9F 4.3E 3.0F 4.3E
7 Tu	0520 1152 1750	0216 0814 1445 2040	3.0F 4.5E 3.1F 4.5E
8 W	0013 0611 1245 1843	0308 0908 1538 2133	3.2F 4.7E 3.3F 4.6E
9 Th	0102 0703 1337 1934	0358 1001 1630 2225	3.4F 4.9E 3.5F 4.6E
10 F	0151 0753 1428 2025	0449 1053 1721 2316	3.6F 5.1E 3.6F 4.6E
11 Sa ●	0240 0845 1519 2116	0539 1144 1812	3.8F 5.2E 3.7F
12 Su	0331 0936 1611 2207	0007 0630 1236 1903	5.0E 3.8F 5.3E 3.7F
13 M	0423 1029 1702 2300	0059 0723 1328 1956	5.0E 3.8F 5.2E 3.7F
14 Tu	0516 1124 1800 2354	0151 0817 1422 2051	5.0E 3.7F 5.1E 3.5F
15 W	0616 1220 1858	0246 0914 1518 2149	4.8E 3.6F 4.9E 3.4F
16 Th	0051 0717 1320 1958	0343 1014 1617 2250	4.7E 3.4F 4.7E 3.2F
17 F	0151 0822 1421 2101	0445 1119 1720 2355	4.5E 3.2F 4.5E 3.1F
18 Sa ○	0252 0929 1524 2203	0552 1228 1829	4.4E 3.1F 4.4E
19 Su	0354 1035 1627 2304	0102 0704 1336 1940	3.0F 4.3E 3.0F 4.3E
20 M	0454 1137 1726	0206 0814 1439 2046	3.0F 4.3E 3.0F 4.3E
21 Tu	0001 0550 1233 1821	0304 0916 1535 2141	3.1F 4.4E 3.0F 4.3E
22 W	0052 0642 1324 1911	0356 1007 1625 2228	3.1F 4.5E 3.1F 4.4E
23 Th	0139 0729 1410 1956	0442 1051 1709 2308	3.2F 4.6E 3.3F 4.4E
24 F	0223 0813 1453 2039	0524 1129 1750 2344	3.3F 4.6E 3.3F 4.5E
25 Sa	0303 0855 1533 2119	0603 1204 1828	3.3F 4.7E 3.3F
26 Su	0343 0935 1612 2159	0018 0640 1238 1904	4.5E 3.4F 4.7E 3.3F
27 M	0421 1015 1651 2238	0053 0716 1314 1940	4.6E 3.4F 4.6E 3.3F
28 Tu	0459 1054 1729 2317	0129 0753 1350 2017	4.6E 3.4F 4.6E 3.2F
29 W	0538 1134 1808 2355	0206 0831 1428 2054	4.6E 3.3F 4.7E 3.2F
30 Th	0617 1214 1847	0245 0910 1508 2134	4.6E 3.3F 4.7E 3.1F
31 F	0035 0657 1255 1927	0326 0950 1550 2215	4.5E 3.2F 4.6E 3.0F

All times are local time. Daylight Saving Time has been used when needed.

NOTES:

130

The Narrows, New York Harbor, New York, 2004

F–Flood, Dir. 336° True   E–Ebb, Dir. 164° True

April

April 1–15

Day	Slack h:m	Max h:m	knots
1 Th	0056	0348	1.5F
	0654	1025	2.0E
	1339	1638	1.6F
	1924	2239	2.0E
2 F	0143	0437	1.8F
	0739	1102	2.2E
	1418	1712	1.8F
	2006	2319	2.2E
3 Sa	0228	0518	1.9F
	0821	1139	2.3E
	1455	1744	2.0F
	2045	2358	2.4E
4 Su	0411	0657	2.1F
	1001	1315	2.4E
	1630	1917	2.1F
	2223		
5 M ○		0136	2.4E
	0453	0735	2.1F
	1041	1352	2.4E
	1706	1953	2.2F
	2302		
6 Tu		0216	2.4E
	0535	0816	2.0F
	1121	1431	2.3E
	1742	2033	2.2F
	2344		
7 W		0257	2.4E
	0619	0901	1.8F
	1203	1510	2.2E
	1821	2117	2.1F
8 Th	0028	0339	2.2E
	0709	0948	1.6F
	1248	1551	2.0E
	1904	2204	1.9F
9 F	0117	0421	2.0E
	0805	1041	1.3F
	1338	1633	1.7E
	1954	2257	1.7F
10 Sa	0208	0507	1.8E
	0910	1141	1.1F
	1432	1722	1.5E
	2055	2356	1.5F
11 Su ○	0303	0605	1.5E
	1021	1249	0.9F
	1532	1832	1.2E
	2209		
12 M		0101	1.3F
	0403	0732	1.3E
	1132	1400	0.9F
	1642	2015	1.1E
	2329		
13 Tu		0208	1.3F
	0512	0903	1.3E
	1238	1518	0.9F
	1802	2141	1.2E
14 W	0045	0326	1.1F
	0628	1016	1.4E
	1337	1643	1.0F
	1917	2250	1.4E
15 Th	0151	0455	1.2F
	0736	1112	1.5E
	1431	1745	1.2F
	2019	2343	1.6E

April 16–30

Day	Slack h:m	Max h:m	knots
16 F	0250	0557	1.3F
	0833	1157	1.7E
	1519	1832	1.4F
	2109		
17 Sa		0028	1.8E
	0341	0644	1.5F
	0921	1237	1.8E
	1601	1912	1.5F
	2152		
18 Su		0110	1.8E
	0426	0725	1.6F
	1003	1316	1.9E
	1639	1945	1.5F
	2231		
19 M ●		0151	1.9E
	0508	0803	1.5F
	1043	1353	1.8E
	1712	2012	1.5F
	2308		
20 Tu		0231	1.8E
	0548	0839	1.4F
	1121	1431	1.8E
	1745	2036	1.5F
	2345		
21 W		0310	1.8E
	0631	0917	1.3F
	1201	1509	1.7E
	1817	2106	1.4F
22 Th	0023	0348	1.7E
	0717	0959	1.1F
	1244	1547	1.6E
	1853	2144	1.4F
23 F	0105	0426	1.6E
	0808	1047	1.0F
	1331	1627	1.4E
	1936	2228	1.3F
24 Sa	0150	0508	1.6E
	0903	1143	1.0F
	1421	1712	1.3E
	2027	2321	1.3F
25 Su	0237	0555	1.5E
	0957	1239	1.0F
	1513	1808	1.3E
	2126		
26 M		0018	1.3F
	0327	0701	1.5E
	1049	1329	1.1F
	1607	1917	1.3E
	2229		
27 Tu ○		0115	1.3F
	0420	0805	1.4E
	1138	1414	1.2F
	1705	2024	1.4E
28 W		0209	1.4F
	0518	0902	1.7E
	1224	1501	1.4F
	1802	2123	1.6E
29 Th	0027	0303	1.5F
	0617	0953	1.9E
	1309	1551	1.5F
	1856	2216	1.9E
30 F	0120	0401	1.7F
	0712	1040	2.1E
	1352	1641	1.8F
	1945	2304	2.2E

May

May 1–15

Day	Slack h:m	Max h:m	knots
1 Sa	0210	0457	1.9F
	0802	1123	2.3E
	1434	1727	2.0F
	2030	2347	2.4E
2 Su	0258	0546	2.0F
	0847	1203	2.4E
	1514	1807	2.2F
	2113		
3 M		0028	2.6E
	0345	0630	2.1F
	0931	1242	2.5E
	1554	1846	2.4F
	2155		
4 Tu ●		0109	2.6E
	0430	0711	2.1F
	1013	1321	2.4E
	1633	1925	2.4F
	2237		
5 W		0151	2.6E
	0516	0754	2.0F
	1056	1403	2.3E
	1712	2007	2.4F
	2321		
6 Th		0236	2.5E
	0604	0841	1.8F
	1141	1447	2.2E
	1755	2053	2.2F
7 F	0008	0322	2.3E
	0656	0932	1.5F
	1230	1535	1.9E
	1843	2144	1.9F
8 Sa	0059	0409	2.1E
	0755	1030	1.3F
	1326	1625	1.6E
	1941	2242	1.6F
9 Su	0154	0501	1.8E
	0902	1139	1.1F
	1428	1725	1.4E
	2053	2350	1.4F
10 M	0254	0607	1.5E
	1014	1301	1.0F
	1535	1851	1.2E
	2215		
11 Tu		0107	1.2F
	0357	0737	1.4E
	1123	1413	1.0F
	1647	2026	1.2E
	2335		
12 W ○		0222	1.1F
	0507	0859	1.4E
	1226	1522	1.1F
	1805	2144	1.3E
13 Th	0046	0337	1.1F
	0621	1007	1.5E
	1322	1631	1.2F
	1916	2247	1.5E
14 F	0148	0449	1.2F
	0726	1100	1.6E
	1414	1731	1.3F
	2013	2337	1.7E
15 Sa	0244	0547	1.3F
	0820	1143	1.7E
	1501	1819	1.4F
	2101		

May 16–31

Day	Slack h:m	Max h:m	knots
16 Su		0021	1.8E
	0334	0634	1.4F
	0906	1221	1.7E
	1541	1858	1.5F
	2140		
17 M		0100	1.8E
	0419	0715	1.4F
	0945	1255	1.7E
	1615	1929	1.4F
	2215		
18 Tu		0137	1.8E
	0459	0752	1.3F
	1021	1329	1.6E
	1644	1948	1.4F
	2246		
19 W		0213	1.7E
	0537	0825	1.2F
	1056	1402	1.6E
	1711	2000	1.4F
	2316		
20 Th		0247	1.7E
	0615	0855	1.0F
	1132	1437	1.5E
	1738	2025	1.4F
	2349		
21 F		0320	1.6E
	0654	0926	1.0F
	1211	1513	1.4E
	1811	2102	1.4F
22 Sa	0025	0353	1.6E
	0736	1005	0.9F
	1255	1553	1.4E
	1852	2147	1.3F
23 Su	0107	0428	1.6E
	0821	1052	0.9F
	1344	1636	1.4E
	1943	2239	1.3F
24 M	0155	0509	1.6E
	0908	1145	1.0F
	1436	1726	1.4E
	2043	2337	1.4F
25 Tu	0245	0601	1.7E
	0957	1237	1.2F
	1527	1828	1.4E
	2147		
26 W		0036	1.4F
	0338	0703	1.7E
	1045	1325	1.4F
	1620	1935	1.6E
	2249		
27 Th ○		0132	1.6F
	0433	0805	1.8E
	1133	1412	1.6F
	1715	2036	1.8E
	2347		
28 F		0225	1.7F
	0530	0901	2.0E
	1220	1459	1.8F
	1810	2132	2.0E
29 Sa	0042	0319	1.8F
	0627	0953	2.1E
	1305	1550	1.9F
	1903	2225	2.2E
30 Su	0135	0415	1.8F
	0721	1042	2.3E
	1350	1641	2.1F
	1953	2313	2.4E
31 M	0227	0510	1.9F
	0811	1127	2.4E
	1434	1730	2.3F
	2041	2358	2.6E

June

June 1–15

Day	Slack h:m	Max h:m	knots
1 Tu	0318	0601	2.0F
	0859	1209	2.4E
	1518	1815	2.5F
	2127		
2 W ○		0042	2.6E
	0409	0647	2.0F
	0945	1252	2.4E
	1602	1859	2.5F
	2212		
3 Th		0127	2.6E
	0458	0734	1.9F
	1032	1339	2.3E
	1647	1944	2.4F
	2259		
4 F		0216	2.5E
	0548	0823	1.7F
	1122	1429	2.1E
	1736	2034	2.2F
	2349		
5 Sa		0307	2.3E
	0641	0918	1.5F
	1216	1524	1.9E
	1831	2130	1.9F
6 Su	0043	0359	2.1E
	0740	1021	1.3F
	1317	1622	1.7E
	1936	2234	1.6F
7 M	0143	0455	1.9E
	0846	1138	1.2F
	1422	1727	1.5E
	2052	2350	1.4F
8 Tu	0244	0601	1.7E
	0955	1257	1.2F
	1529	1850	1.4E
	2211		
9 W ○		0109	1.3F
	0348	0722	1.5E
	1101	1404	1.3F
	1638	2015	1.4E
	2324		
10 Th		0217	1.3F
	0454	0838	1.5E
	1202	1503	1.5F
	1751	2128	1.5E
11 F	0031	0321	1.3F
	0602	0942	1.6E
	1258	1606	1.6F
	1859	2231	1.6E
12 Sa	0132	0428	1.3F
	0705	1037	1.6E
	1349	1707	1.7F
	1957	2323	1.7E
13 Su	0229	0528	1.3F
	0800	1122	1.6E
	1435	1758	1.7F
	2046		
14 M		0008	1.7E
	0323	0619	1.3F
	0847	1201	1.6E
	1516	1840	1.6F
	2125		
15 Tu		0048	1.7E
	0411	0703	1.2F
	0928	1235	1.5E
	1550	1912	1.4F
	2158		

June 16–30

Day	Slack h:m	Max h:m	knots
16 W		0124	1.7E
	0452	0742	1.1F
	1004	1308	1.4E
	1618	1929	1.3F
	2226		
17 Th		0157	1.7E
	0528	0816	1.0F
	1037	1340	1.4E
	1644	1934	1.3F
	2252		
18 F		0227	1.6E
	0600	0841	0.9F
	1110	1413	1.3E
	1711	1957	1.3F
	2321		
19 Sa		0255	1.6E
	0630	0900	0.9F
	1145	1449	1.3E
	1744	2033	1.4F
	2354		
20 Su		0325	1.7E
	0702	0930	1.0F
	1226	1528	1.4E
	1825	2118	1.4F
21 M	0035	0357	1.7E
	0739	1011	1.0F
	1311	1609	1.5E
	1914	2208	1.4F
22 Tu	0121	0434	1.8E
	0821	1059	1.2F
	1400	1654	1.5E
	2010	2304	1.5F
23 W	0210	0518	1.8E
	0907	1150	1.4F
	1449	1745	1.4E
	2109		
24 Th		0001	1.6F
	0301	0610	1.9E
	0955	1241	1.5F
	1539	1843	1.4E
	2209		
25 F ○		0056	1.6F
	0353	0709	1.9E
	1043	1329	1.7F
	1631	1946	1.4E
	2308		
26 Sa		0148	1.7F
	0446	0808	2.0E
	1132	1417	2.0F
	1720	2046	2.0E
27 Su	0006	0241	1.7F
	0543	0904	2.1E
	1221	1506	2.0F
	1822	2144	2.1E
28 M	0102	0336	1.7F
	0640	0959	2.1E
	1308	1559	2.1F
	1917	2238	2.3E
29 Tu	0159	0435	1.7F
	0735	1051	2.2E
	1357	1654	2.3F
	2009	2329	2.4E
30 W	0254	0533	1.7F
	0828	1140	2.2E
	1446	1746	2.4F
	2100		

All times are local time. Daylight Saving Time has been used when needed.

NOTES:

The Narrows, New York Harbor, New York, 2004

F–Flood, Dir. 336° True   E–Ebb, Dir. 164° True

July

Day	Slack (h m)	Maximum (h m)	knots
1 Th		0017	2.5E
	0348	0625	1.8F
	0920	1229	2.2E
	1537	1836	2.4F
	2150		
2 F ○		0106	2.5E
	0439	0716	1.8F
	1012	1320	2.2E
	1629	1926	2.3F
	2240		
3 Sa		0157	2.4E
	0530	0808	1.7F
	1106	1416	2.1E
	1724	2020	2.2F
	2333		
4 Su		0251	2.3E
	0622	0905	1.6F
	1202	1515	2.0E
	1822	2119	1.9F
5 M	0028	0346	2.2E
	0719	1009	1.5F
	1303	1614	1.9E
	1928	2226	1.7F
6 Tu	0128	0441	2.0E
	0821	1121	1.4F
	1407	1716	1.7E
	2039	2340	1.6F
7 W	0228	0542	1.8E
	0926	1233	1.4F
	1510	1828	1.6E
	2151		
8 Th		0052	1.5F
	0328	0652	1.7E
	1029	1336	1.4F
	1614	1947	1.6E
	2300		
9 F ○		0155	1.4F
	0429	0803	1.7E
	1129	1433	1.4F
	1721	2100	1.6E
10 Sa	0006	0255	1.3F
	0532	0907	1.6E
	1225	1532	1.4F
	1829	2204	1.6E
11 Su	0108	0358	1.2F
	0635	1005	1.6E
	1316	1634	1.4F
	1930	2301	1.7E
12 M	0209	0503	1.2F
	0734	1055	1.5E
	1403	1730	1.4F
	2021	2350	1.7E
13 Tu	0307	0559	1.2F
	0826	1138	1.5E
	1446	1816	1.4F
	2103		
14 W		0031	1.8E
	0357	0647	1.2F
	0911	1216	1.4E
	1524	1851	1.3F
	2136		
15 Th		0107	1.7E
	0438	0727	1.1F
	0948	1250	1.4E
	1556	1913	1.3F
	2205		
16 F		0137	1.7E
	0510	0801	1.1F
	1021	1323	1.4E
	1626	1920	1.3F
	2231		
17 Sa		0205	1.7E
	0537	0823	1.0F
	1052	1357	1.4E
	1657	1941	1.4F
	2300		
18 Su		0232	1.7E
	0602	0835	1.0F
	1124	1432	1.5E
	1730	2015	1.4F
	2332		
19 M		0300	1.7E
	0629	0901	1.1F
	1200	1508	1.6E
	1809	2057	1.5F
20 Tu	0010	0332	1.8E
	0701	0938	1.3F
	1241	1546	1.7E
	1852	2144	1.6F
21 W	0054	0407	1.9E
	0739	1021	1.4F
	1326	1626	1.8E
	1942	2234	1.6F
22 Th	0140	0446	2.0E
	0822	1109	1.5F
	1413	1709	1.8E
	2036	2327	1.6F
23 F	0228	0529	2.0E
	0908	1159	1.7F
	1501	1758	1.9E
	2133		
24 Sa ○		0021	1.6F
	0316	0620	2.0E
	0956	1251	1.8F
	1551	1856	1.9E
	2232		
25 Su		0115	1.6F
	0406	0716	1.9E
	1046	1339	1.9F
	1644	1959	1.9E
	2333		
26 M		0207	1.5F
	0501	0817	1.9E
	1138	1429	2.0F
	1742	2103	2.0E
27 Tu	0034	0302	1.5F
	0601	0919	1.9E
	1232	1523	2.0F
	1842	2206	2.1E
28 W	0134	0403	1.4F
	0703	1020	1.9E
	1326	1622	2.0F
	1941	2304	2.2E
29 Th	0233	0508	1.5F
	0804	1119	2.0E
	1423	1723	2.1F
	2037	2357	2.3E
30 F	0328	0608	1.6F
	0901	1213	2.0E
	1521	1820	2.2F
	2131		
31 Sa ○		0047	2.3E
	0421	0701	1.7F
	0956	1308	2.1E
	1618	1914	2.2F
	2223		

August

Day	Slack (h m)	Maximum (h m)	knots
1 Su		0139	2.3E
	0510	0753	1.7F
	1050	1404	2.1E
	1715	2009	2.1F
	2316		
2 M		0233	2.3E
	0600	0848	1.7F
	1145	1502	2.1E
	1811	2107	2.0F
3 Tu	0011	0327	2.2E
	0653	0947	1.6F
	1243	1558	2.0E
	1911	2210	1.8F
4 W	0107	0419	2.1E
	0750	1051	1.6F
	1342	1654	1.9E
	2016	2316	1.7F
5 Th	0204	0513	2.0E
	0850	1158	1.5F
	1442	1756	1.7E
	2122		
6 F		0024	1.6F
	0300	0613	1.8E
	0950	1301	1.5F
	1541	1909	1.6E
	2230		
7 Sa ○		0126	1.4F
	0357	0720	1.7E
	1049	1357	1.4F
	1642	2023	1.6E
	2336		
8 Su		0225	1.3F
	0456	0825	1.6E
	1145	1452	1.4F
	1747	2131	1.6E
9 M		0041	1.3F
	0600	0927	1.5E
	1237	1551	1.5F
	1849	2231	1.7E
10 Tu	0142	0433	1.1F
	0715	1023	1.4E
	1326	1652	1.3F
	1922	2322	1.7E
11 W	0240	0533	1.1F
	0801	1112	1.4E
	1413	1744	1.3F
	2030		
12 Th		0004	1.8E
	0329	0622	1.2F
	0848	1153	1.4E
	1456	1823	1.3F
	2107		
13 F		0039	1.8E
	0408	0702	1.2F
	0927	1230	1.5E
	1514	1851	1.4F
	2139		
14 Sa		0108	1.8E
	0438	0733	1.2F
	1000	1305	1.5E
	1610	1907	1.4F
	2209		
15 Su ●		0136	1.8E
	0503	0753	1.3F
	1030	1339	1.6E
	1643	1928	1.5F
	2239		
16 M		0205	1.8E
	0528	0807	1.3F
	1102	1413	1.7E
	1717	2000	1.6F
	2312		
17 Tu		0234	1.9E
	0555	0832	1.4F
	1136	1448	1.8E
	1754	2038	1.7F
	2349		
18 W		0306	2.0E
	0626	0907	1.6F
	1213	1523	1.9E
	1833	2121	1.7F
19 Th	0029	0340	2.0E
	0701	0949	1.6F
	1255	1600	2.0E
	1918	2208	1.7F
20 F	0112	0417	2.1E
	0742	1034	1.7F
	1340	1639	2.0E
	2008	2257	1.6F
21 Sa	0157	0456	2.0E
	0826	1122	1.8F
	1428	1723	1.9E
	2104	2350	1.5F
22 Su	0243	0540	1.9E
	0913	1214	1.8F
	1517	1814	1.9E
	2204		
23 M ○		0045	1.4F
	0332	0632	1.8E
	1005	1306	1.8F
	1609	1916	1.8E
	2309		
24 Tu		0139	1.3F
	0427	0736	1.6E
	1103	1358	1.7F
	1708	2028	1.7E
25 W	0014	0235	1.2F
	0530	0848	1.5E
	1205	1455	1.7F
	1812	2140	1.8E
26 Th	0116	0339	1.2F
	0641	1003	1.6E
	1309	1558	1.7F
	1917	2246	1.9E
27 F	0216	0452	1.2F
	0748	1108	1.7E
	1413	1708	1.8F
	2019	2342	2.0E
28 Sa	0311	0559	1.4F
	0848	1205	1.9E
	1514	1811	1.9F
	2115		
29 Su ○		0033	2.1E
	0350	0651	1.7F
	0943	1258	2.0E
	1611	1906	2.0F
	2208		
30 M		0122	2.2E
	0450	0740	1.7F
	1035	1351	2.1E
	1705	1958	1.9F
	2258		
31 Tu		0213	2.2E
	0536	0828	1.7F
	1125	1444	2.1E
	1757	2051	1.9F
	2349		

September

Day	Slack (h m)	Maximum (h m)	knots
1 W		0303	2.2E
	0624	0920	1.7F
	1218	1536	2.1E
	1850	2147	1.8F
2 Th	0040	0352	2.1E
	0715	1014	1.6F
	1312	1627	2.0E
	1948	2246	1.6F
3 F	0134	0440	2.0E
	0809	1112	1.5F
	1407	1721	1.8E
	2051	2350	1.5F
4 Sa	0227	0532	1.8E
	0905	1214	1.4F
	1502	1825	1.6E
	2158		
5 Su		0055	1.3F
	0322	0632	1.6E
	1001	1313	1.3F
	1558	1939	1.6E
	2305		
6 M ○		0155	1.2F
	0419	0739	1.4E
	1058	1405	1.3F
	1656	2049	1.6E
7 Tu	0009	0253	1.1F
	0522	0845	1.3E
	1154	1512	1.2F
	1757	2151	1.6E
8 W	0107	0355	1.1F
	0627	0946	1.3E
	1247	1558	1.2F
	1855	2243	1.7E
9 Th	0159	0456	1.1F
	0726	1039	1.4E
	1337	1658	1.2F
	1946	2325	1.8E
10 F	0244	0546	1.2F
	0815	1124	1.5E
	1424	1744	1.3F
	2029		
11 Sa		0001	1.8E
	0322	0639	1.3F
	0855	1203	1.7E
	1508	1811	1.5F
	2107		
12 Su		0032	1.9E
	0354	0654	1.4F
	0930	1239	1.8E
	1547	1843	1.6F
	2141		
13 M		0103	2.0E
	0423	0714	1.6F
	1003	1314	2.0E
	1624	1910	1.7F
	2215		
14 Tu ●		0133	2.1E
	0452	0735	1.7F
	1036	1348	2.1E
	1659	1941	1.8F
	2249		
15 W		0205	2.1E
	0521	0803	1.8F
	1110	1424	2.1E
	1736	2018	1.8F
	2325		
16 Th		0239	2.2E
	0553	0839	1.9F
	1147	1500	2.2E
	1815	2059	1.8F
17 F	0004	0314	2.1E
	0627	0919	1.9F
	1228	1537	2.1E
	1859	2143	1.7F
18 Sa	0045	0350	2.1E
	0706	1003	1.9F
	1312	1615	2.1E
	1948	2232	1.5F
19 Su	0130	0428	1.9E
	0749	1051	1.8F
	1359	1656	2.0E
	2045	2325	1.3F
20 M	0217	0510	1.8E
	0839	1143	1.7F
	1449	1744	1.8E
	2147		
21 Tu		0022	1.2F
	0309	0601	1.5E
	0936	1240	1.6F
	1542	1845	1.6E
	2255		
22 W		0121	1.0F
	0406	0710	1.3E
	1043	1337	1.5F
	1643	2006	1.5E
23 Th	0002	0221	1.0F
	0515	0840	1.3E
	1156	1438	1.4F
	1752	2128	1.5E
24 F	0105	0328	1.0F
	0631	1002	1.4E
	1307	1548	1.4F
	1902	2237	1.6E
25 Sa		0209	1.1F
	0740	1107	1.6E
	1412	1708	1.5F
	2002	2332	1.8E
26 Su	0255	0557	1.3F
	0840	1201	1.7E
	1512	1811	1.6F
	2102		
27 M		0020	1.9E
	0344	0645	1.5F
	0931	1250	2.0E
	1605	1901	1.8F
	2152		
28 Tu		0105	2.1E
	0429	0726	1.7F
	1019	1337	2.1E
	1653	1947	2.1F
	2238		
29 W		0150	2.1E
	0512	0807	1.7F
	1105	1425	2.1E
	1740	2033	1.8F
	2324		
30 Th		0236	2.1E
	0554	0849	1.7F
	1151	1512	2.0E
	1829	2122	1.6F

All times are local time. Daylight Saving Time has been used when needed.

NOTES:

The Narrows, New York Harbor, New York, 2004

F—Flood, Dir. 336° True   E—Ebb, Dir. 164° True

October

Day	Slack	Maximum	Knots
1 F	0011	0321	2.0E
	0637	0933	1.6F
	1239	1559	1.9E
	1922	2215	1.5F
2 Sa	0101	0406	1.8E
	0723	1021	1.5F
	1329	1647	1.8E
	2022	2315	1.3F
3 Su	0153	0452	1.6E
	0814	1113	1.3F
	1420	1741	1.6E
	2126		
4 M		0021	1.1F
	0247	0544	1.4E
	0909	1212	1.3F
	1511	1846	1.5E
	2230		
5 Tu		0122	1.1F
	0342	0649	1.3E
	1007	1309	1.2F
	1604	1956	1.5E
	2330		
6 W ○		0216	1.1F
	0441	0759	1.2E
	1107	1401	1.2F
	1701	2058	1.6E
7 Th	0022	0309	1.1F
	0543	0903	1.3E
	1205	1453	1.2F
	1800	2151	1.6E
8 F	0109	0403	1.4E
	0641	0959	1.4E
	1258	1551	1.3F
	1855	2236	1.8E
9 Sa	0150	0453	1.3F
	0731	1047	1.7E
	1348	1648	1.4F
	1944	2316	1.9E
10 Su	0229	0534	1.5F
	0814	1129	1.9E
	1434	1733	1.6F
	2028	2351	2.1E
11 M	0305	0605	1.7F
	0853	1208	2.1E
	1517	1809	1.8F
	2107		
12 Tu		0025	2.2E
	0340	0632	1.9F
	0930	1244	2.3E
	1557	1843	1.9F
	2145		
13 W ●		0059	2.3E
	0413	0701	2.0F
	1007	1320	2.4E
	1637	1918	2.0F
	2222		
14 Th		0134	2.3E
	0447	0734	2.1F
	1044	1358	2.4E
	1716	1956	1.9F
	2300		
15 F		0210	2.3E
	0521	0811	2.2F
	1122	1436	2.4E
	1758	2037	1.8F
	2339		
16 Sa		0247	2.2E
	0557	0852	2.1F
	1204	1516	2.3E
	1844	2122	1.6F
17 Su	0022	0327	2.0E
	0637	0937	2.0F
	1249	1557	2.1E
	1935	2212	1.4F
18 M	0110	0408	1.8E
	0722	1026	1.8F
	1338	1639	2.0E
	2034	2308	1.2F
19 Tu	0202	0453	1.6E
	0818	1122	1.6F
	1431	1728	1.7E
	2140		
20 W ○		0010	1.0F
	0259	0549	1.3E
	0926	1225	1.4F
	1527	1834	1.5E
	2249		
21 Th		0117	0.9F
	0403	0716	1.1E
	1044	1330	1.3F
	1630	2005	1.4E
	2355		
22 F		0222	0.9F
	0515	0852	1.2E
	1203	1437	1.2F
	1742	2126	1.4E
23 Sa	0055	0337	1.0F
	0631	1008	1.3E
	1312	1555	1.2F
	1855	2231	1.5E
24 Su	0150	0458	1.1F
	0738	1108	1.6E
	1414	1715	1.3F
	1956	2322	1.7E
25 M	0241	0555	1.3F
	0833	1157	1.9E
	1509	1811	1.5F
	2048		
26 Tu		0006	1.8E
	0327	0638	1.5F
	0921	1242	1.9E
	1558	1856	1.6F
	2135		
27 W ○		0047	1.9E
	0409	0715	1.6F
	1005	1325	1.9E
	1644	1937	1.6F
	2148		
28 Th		0128	1.9E
	0447	0747	1.6F
	1045	1407	1.9E
	1728	2018	1.5F
	2300		
29 F		0209	1.9E
	0524	0818	1.6F
	1126	1451	1.9E
	1812	2100	1.4F
	2343		
30 Sa		0251	1.7E
	0600	0852	1.5F
	1207	1533	1.8E
	1901	2147	1.2F
31 Su	0029	0233	1.6E
	0539	0832	1.4F
	1151	1515	1.7E
	1855	2141	1.1F

November

Day	Slack	Maximum	Knots
1 M	0018	0316	1.5E
	0624	0918	1.3F
	1237	1600	1.6E
	1952	2241	1.0F
2 Tu	0111	0403	1.3E
	0717	1011	1.2F
	1326	1651	1.5E
	2049	2341	1.0F
3 W	0205	0500	1.2E
	0817	1111	1.2F
	1416	1754	1.5E
	2141		
4 Th		0031	1.1F
	0259	0608	1.2E
	0920	1209	1.2F
	1509	1856	1.6E
	2229		
5 F ○		0114	1.2F
	0354	0714	1.4E
	1020	1301	1.3F
	1605	1951	1.5E
	2314		
6 Sa		0156	1.3F
	0449	0812	1.6E
	1116	1353	1.4F
	1702	2041	1.8E
	2356		
7 Su		0241	1.5F
	0542	0903	1.8E
	1207	1447	1.5F
	1756	2126	2.0E
8 M	0036	0327	1.7F
	0630	0950	2.0E
	1256	1541	1.7F
	1844	2208	2.2E
9 Tu	0117	0411	1.9F
	0714	1032	2.3E
	1342	1630	1.9F
	1929	2247	2.3E
10 W	0156	0450	2.1F
	0756	1112	2.4E
	1428	1712	2.0F
	2012	2324	2.4E
11 Th	0234	0527	2.3F
	0837	1151	2.5E
	1512	1753	2.0F
	2053		
12 F ●		0002	2.4E
	0312	0605	2.4F
	0917	1232	2.6E
	1557	1834	1.9F
	2134		
13 Sa		0041	2.3E
	0351	0645	2.4F
	0959	1314	2.5E
	1642	1917	1.8F
	2217		
14 Su		0124	2.1E
	0431	0728	2.2F
	1043	1358	2.4E
	1730	2005	1.6F
	2304		
15 M		0210	1.9E
	0516	0816	2.0F
	1131	1443	2.2E
	1824	2058	1.3F
	2357		
16 Tu		0258	1.7E
	0608	0910	1.8F
	1223	1531	1.9E
	1925	2159	1.1F
17 W	0056	0351	1.5E
	0713	1012	1.5F
	1320	1624	1.7E
	2031	2310	1.0F
18 Th	0158	0458	1.3E
	0831	1123	1.3F
	1420	1738	1.5E
	2139		
19 F ○		0024	1.0F
	0303	0632	1.2E
	0951	1236	1.2F
	1524	1904	1.4E
	2243		
20 Sa		0130	1.1F
	0415	0757	1.3E
	1105	1346	1.1F
	1634	2018	1.4E
	2341		
21 Su		0239	1.1F
	0528	0907	1.4E
	1210	1500	1.1F
	1742	2119	1.5E
22 M	0035	0348	1.2F
	0633	1004	1.6E
	1309	1601	1.2F
	1842	2209	1.6E
23 Tu	0124	0444	1.3F
	0727	1052	1.7E
	1404	1704	1.3F
	1934	2252	1.7E
24 W	0209	0529	1.4F
	0813	1135	1.8E
	1453	1750	1.4F
	2019	2331	1.7E
25 Th	0249	0605	1.5F
	0853	1215	1.8E
	1539	1832	1.3F
	2100		
26 F ○		0008	1.7E
	0325	0633	1.5F
	0929	1255	1.8E
	1621	1911	1.2F
	2140		
27 Sa		0046	1.6E
	0357	0652	1.4F
	1003	1333	1.7E
	1702	1949	1.1F
	2219		
28 Su		0124	1.5E
	0428	0717	1.4F
	1038	1410	1.7E
	1744	2027	1.0F
	2301		
29 M		0205	1.4E
	0503	0753	1.3F
	1115	1447	1.6E
	1828	2107	0.9F
	2347		
30 Tu		0246	1.3E
	0543	0836	1.3F
	1158	1524	1.6E
	1914	2153	0.9F

December

Day	Slack	Maximum	Knots
1 W	0036	0329	1.3E
	0634	0927	1.2F
	1245	1604	1.6E
	2000	2243	1.0F
2 Th	0126	0418	1.3E
	0733	1024	1.3F
	1334	1653	1.6E
	2046	2331	1.1F
3 F	0215	0516	1.4E
	0835	1123	1.3F
	1424	1750	1.7E
	2132		
4 Sa ○		0015	1.3F
	0306	0619	1.5E
	0934	1217	1.4F
	1517	1849	1.8E
	2217		
5 Su		0058	1.5F
	0358	0719	1.7E
	1031	1308	1.6F
	1611	1943	1.9E
	2302		
6 M		0142	1.7F
	0451	0814	1.9E
	1125	1359	1.6F
	1706	2034	2.0E
	2346		
7 Tu		0229	1.8F
	0544	0906	2.1E
	1217	1453	1.7F
	1759	2122	2.0E
8 W	0030	0319	2.0F
	0633	0955	2.3E
	1308	1549	1.8F
	1850	2207	2.3E
9 Th	0113	0408	2.2F
	0721	1040	2.5E
	1359	1640	1.9F
	1938	2250	2.4E
10 F	0157	0454	2.4F
	0806	1123	2.6E
	1448	1727	1.9F
	2024	2333	2.5E
11 Sa ●	0240	0538	2.6F
	0851	1207	2.6E
	1537	1813	1.9F
	2111		
12 Su		0017	2.3E
	0325	0622	2.4F
	0937	1253	2.6E
	1625	1859	1.8F
13 M		0105	2.1E
	0412	0709	2.3F
	1024	1342	2.4E
	1715	1950	1.6F
14 Tu		0158	2.0E
	0504	0802	2.0F
	1116	1432	2.2E
	1809	2047	1.4F
15 W		0253	1.8E
	0603	0901	1.8F
	1212	1524	2.0E
	1909	2152	1.3F
16 Th	0048	0352	1.6E
	0713	1008	1.5F
	1311	1621	1.8E
	2013	2307	1.2F
17 F	0151	0501	1.5E
	0829	1124	1.4F
	1412	1730	1.6E
	2118		
18 Sa ○		0019	1.2F
	0255	0626	1.4E
	0944	1236	1.3F
	1513	1848	1.5E
	2221		
19 Su		0120	1.3F
	0404	0745	1.4E
	1053	1340	1.2F
	1618	1958	1.5E
	2319		
20 M		0222	1.3F
	0515	0854	1.5E
	1157	1446	1.2F
	1729	2059	1.5E
21 Tu	0013	0328	1.3F
	0621	0954	1.6E
	1258	1554	1.2F
	1825	2152	1.6E
22 W	0104	0428	1.4F
	0716	1044	1.7E
	1357	1653	1.2F
	1919	2237	1.6E
23 Th	0150	0516	1.4F
	0803	1129	1.7E
	1450	1743	1.2F
	2007	2317	1.5E
24 F	0231	0556	1.4F
	0841	1209	1.7E
	1537	1827	1.2F
	2049	2354	1.4E
25 Sa	0306	0625	1.3F
	0914	1246	1.7E
	1617	1907	1.1F
	2127		
26 Su		0030	1.4E
	0337	0650	1.3F
	0944	1319	1.6E
	1652	1942	1.0F
	2203		
27 M		0106	1.3E
	0407	0655	1.3F
	1014	1350	1.6E
	1725	2010	0.9F
	2239		
28 Tu		0144	1.3E
	0440	0726	1.3F
	1047	1421	1.6E
	1757	2033	0.9F
	2318		
29 W		0222	1.3E
	0518	0807	1.3F
	1126	1452	1.7E
	1831	2105	1.0F
30 Th	0000	0210	1.4E
	0604	0855	1.3F
	1209	1527	1.7E
	1909	2146	1.1F
31 F	0046	0343	1.5E
	0656	0947	1.4F
	1256	1606	1.8E
	1951	2233	1.3F

All times are local time. Daylight Saving Time has been used when needed.

NOTES:

Delaware Bay Entrance, 2004

F—Flood, Dir. 327° True   E—Ebb, Dir. 147° True

April

Day	Slack (h m)	Maximum (h m)	knots	Day	Slack (h m)	Maximum (h m)	knots
1 Th		0311	1.2F	16 F	0227	0523	1.5F
	0633	1006	1.2F		0846	1205	1.5E
	1303	1555	1.0F		1509	1753	1.4F
	1854	2215	1.1E		2110		
2 F	0049	0404	1.3F	17 Sa		0024	1.4E
	0726	1054	1.3E		0320	0612	1.5F
	1348	1640	1.2F		0930	1248	1.5E
	1946	2306	1.3E		1550	1837	1.5F
					2152		
3 Sa	0147	0453	1.4F	18 Su		0110	1.5E
	0813	1139	1.4E		0408	0658	1.6F
	1429	1724	1.4F		1010	1328	1.5E
	2033	2357	1.5E		1626	1918	1.5F
					2231		
4 Su	0342	0642	1.6F	19 M		0153	1.5E
	0959	1324	1.5E		0452	0742	1.6F
	1649	1907	1.6F		1047	1405	1.4E
	2219			●	1658	1957	1.6F
5 M		0146	1.6E	20 Tu		0233	1.5E
O	0434	0731	1.6F		0533	0824	1.4F
	1042	1408	1.6E		1123	1440	1.3E
	1731	1952	1.8F		1728	2033	1.5F
	2303				2342		
6 Tu		0234	1.7E	21 W		0309	1.4E
	0526	0819	1.7F		0613	0903	1.3F
	1126	1451	1.6E		1200	1512	1.2E
	1731	2036	1.9F		1756	2107	1.5F
	2349						
7 W		0321	1.8E	22 Th	0017	0345	1.4E
	0618	0907	1.6F		0652	0942	1.2F
	1212	1535	1.5E		1238	1543	1.1E
	1816	2121	1.9F		1826	2141	1.4F
8 Th	0037	0411	1.7E	23 F	0052	0419	1.3E
	0711	0957	1.5F		0730	1021	1.1F
	1301	1622	1.4E		1316	1613	1.0E
	1902	2210	1.9F		1858	2217	1.3F
9 F	0128	0505	1.7E	24 Sa	0130	0457	1.2E
	0807	1050	1.4F		0810	1103	0.9F
	1353	1717	1.3E		1356	1648	0.9E
	1955	2304	1.7F		1935	2255	1.2F
10 Sa	0222	0605	1.5E	25 Su	0211	0542	1.1E
	0907	1149	1.3F		0853	1149	0.8F
	1450	1820	1.2E		1438	1733	0.8E
	2053				2018	2341	1.1F
11 Su		0004	1.6F	26 M	0258	0635	1.0E
	0324	0709	1.4E		0942	1238	0.7F
O	1012	1252	1.2F		1528	1830	0.8E
	1556	1926	1.1E		2109		
	2159						
12 M		0108	1.5F	27 Tu		0033	1.1F
	0434	0815	1.3E		0353	0731	1.0E
	1121	1357	1.1F	O	1037	1330	0.7F
	1708	2033	1.1E		1625	1934	0.8E
	2311				2208		
13 Tu		0215	1.4F	28 W		0130	1.0F
	0546	0921	1.3E		0453	0831	1.0E
	1228	1505	1.1F		1132	1424	0.8F
	1819	2140	1.1E		1725	2042	0.8E
					2313		
14 W	0022	0324	1.4F	29 Th		0230	1.1F
	0654	1023	1.4E		0552	0931	1.1E
	1328	1610	1.2F		1224	1520	0.9F
	1924	2241	1.2E		1823	2146	1.0E
15 Th	0128	0428	1.5F	30 F	0019	0332	1.2F
	0754	1117	1.5E		0649	1025	1.2E
	1421	1705	1.3F		1312	1612	1.1F
	2021	2335	1.3E		1918	2244	1.2E

May

Day	Slack (h m)	Maximum (h m)	knots	Day	Slack (h m)	Maximum (h m)	knots
1 Sa	0122	0430	1.3F	16 Su		0001	1.4E
	0743	1114	1.4E		0304	0549	1.3F
	1358	1701	1.4F		0858	1213	1.3E
	2010	2338	1.4E		1510	1806	1.5F
					2125		
2 Su	0224	0523	1.4F	17 M		0045	1.4E
	0835	1201	1.4E		0351	0634	1.3F
	1444	1747	1.6F		0938	1252	1.3E
	2101				1544	1846	1.5F
					2202		
3 M		0030	1.6E	18 Tu		0127	1.4E
	0323	0615	1.5F		0434	0718	1.3F
	0925	1249	1.5E		1017	1330	1.2E
	1529	1834	1.8F	●	1616	1924	1.5F
	2150				2238		
4 Tu		0122	1.8E	19 W		0207	1.5E
	0418	0707	1.6F		0515	0800	1.3F
O	1014	1337	1.5E		1055	1407	1.2E
	1615	1922	2.0F		1647	2001	1.5F
	2238				2313		
5 W		0213	1.9E	20 Th		0244	1.4E
	0512	0759	1.6F		0553	0840	1.2F
	1103	1426	1.5E		1133	1442	1.1E
	1702	2011	2.0F		1719	2037	1.5F
	2327				2349		
6 Th		0304	1.9E	21 F		0320	1.4E
	0606	0850	1.6F		0631	0918	1.1F
	1154	1516	1.5E		1212	1516	1.0E
	1751	2101	2.0F		1752	2112	1.4F
7 F	0018	0356	1.9E	22 Sa	0025	0357	1.3E
	0700	0942	1.5F		0708	0956	1.0F
	1247	1608	1.4E		1252	1550	1.0E
	1845	2153	1.9F		1829	2148	1.3F
8 Sa	0112	0452	1.7E	23 Su	0103	0435	1.2E
	0757	1037	1.4F		0746	1035	0.9F
	1343	1706	1.3E		1331	1627	0.9E
	1941	2249	1.7F		1909	2226	1.2F
9 Su	0210	0552	1.6E	24 M	0144	0518	1.2E
	0856	1136	1.3F		0826	1117	0.9F
	1442	1809	1.2E		1413	1712	0.8E
	2042	2350	1.6F		1952	2310	1.2F
10 M	0312	0655	1.5E	25 Tu	0228	0603	1.1E
	0959	1240	1.2F		0909	1204	0.8F
	1547	1913	1.1E		1500	1807	0.8E
	2150				2043		
11 Tu		0055	1.4F	26 W		0001	1.1F
	0421	0757	1.4E		0317	0657	1.1E
O	1105	1343	1.1F		0956	1254	0.9F
	1659	2017	1.1E		1553	1907	0.8E
	2301				2141		
12 W		0201	1.3F	27 Th		0056	1.1F
	0529	0859	1.3E		0411	0749	1.1E
	1206	1447	1.2F	O	1046	1344	1.0F
	1807	2121	1.1E		1651	2009	0.9E
					2247		
13 Th	0011	0307	1.3F	28 F		0154	1.1F
	0631	0956	1.3E		0508	0844	1.1E
	1300	1548	1.2F		1135	1436	1.1F
	1906	2221	1.2E		1748	2113	1.1E
					2353		
14 F	0114	0408	1.3F	29 Sa		0255	1.2F
	0726	1047	1.3E		0605	0940	1.2E
	1349	1640	1.3F		1224	1530	1.3F
	1959	2313	1.3E		1842	2214	1.3E
15 Sa	0212	0501	1.3F	30 Su	0100	0357	1.3F
	0814	1132	1.3E		0701	1034	1.3E
	1432	1725	1.4F		1313	1621	1.6F
	2044				1937	2310	1.5E
				31 M	0203	0455	1.4F
					0759	1125	1.3E
					1403	1714	1.8F
					2031		

June

Day	Slack (h m)	Maximum (h m)	knots	Day	Slack (h m)	Maximum (h m)	knots
1 Tu		0005	1.7E	16 W		0100	1.4E
	0305	0550	1.5F		0415	0653	1.1F
	0855	1218	1.4E		0947	1256	1.1E
	1456	1805	1.9F		1537	1853	1.4F
	2124				2211		
2 W		0100	1.8E	17 Th		0141	1.4E
	0402	0645	1.5F		0455	0736	1.1F
O	0950	1312	1.5E		1029	1337	1.1E
	1548	1857	2.0F		1613	1933	1.4F
	2216				2249		
3 Th		0155	1.9E	18 F		0222	1.4E
	0459	0741	1.6F		0533	0818	1.1F
	1045	1407	1.5E		1110	1418	1.1E
	1640	1951	2.0F		1650	2012	1.4F
	2309				2327		
4 F		0249	1.9E	19 Sa		0300	1.4E
	0553	0835	1.6F		0610	0856	1.1F
	1139	1501	1.5E		1151	1457	1.0E
	1736	2045	2.0F		1729	2049	1.4F
5 Sa	0004	0343	1.9E	20 Su	0005	0338	1.4E
	0649	0928	1.5F		0646	0933	1.1F
	1234	1555	1.4E		1231	1535	1.0E
	1831	2139	1.9F		1808	2126	1.4F
6 Su	0100	0438	1.8E	21 M	0043	0416	1.3E
	0744	1023	1.4F		0722	1010	1.0F
	1331	1652	1.3E		1310	1613	1.0E
	1930	2235	1.8F		1849	2204	1.3F
7 M	0158	0536	1.6E	22 Tu	0122	0456	1.3E
	0841	1121	1.3F		0759	1049	1.0F
	1429	1753	1.2E		1351	1657	0.9E
	2030	2335	1.6F		1934	2246	1.3F
8 Tu	0257	0634	1.5E	23 W	0202	0538	1.2E
	0939	1221	1.2F		0837	1132	1.0F
	1531	1854	1.2E		1434	1747	0.9E
	2134				2024	2334	1.2F
9 W		0037	1.4F	24 Th	0245	0622	1.2E
	0357	0731	1.4E		0918	1218	1.1F
O	1038	1320	1.2F		1523	1842	1.0E
	1637	1954	1.1E		2121		
	2242						
10 Th		0139	1.3F	25 F		0028	1.2F
	0458	0825	1.3E		0334	0709	1.2E
	1132	1418	1.2F	O	1003	1307	1.2F
	1740	2054	1.1E		1617	1939	1.1E
	2350				2224		
11 F		0240	1.2F	26 Sa		0125	1.2F
	0554	0919	1.2E		0428	0800	1.2E
	1222	1514	1.2F		1051	1358	1.3F
	1836	2153	1.1E		1714	2042	1.2E
					2332		
12 Sa	0053	0339	1.1F	27 Su		0225	1.2F
	0646	1008	1.2E		0527	0857	1.2E
	1306	1605	1.3F		1142	1453	1.5F
	1926	2246	1.2E		1810	2146	1.3E
13 Su	0151	0434	1.1F	28 M	0039	0328	1.2F
	0733	1053	1.1E		0627	0956	1.2E
	1346	1650	1.4F		1237	1550	1.7F
	2011	2333	1.3E		1907	2247	1.5E
14 M	0244	0522	1.1F	29 Tu	0145	0431	1.3F
	0816	1134	1.1E		0729	1057	1.3E
	1424	1732	1.4F		1332	1647	1.8F
	2052				2006	2345	1.7E
15 Tu		0017	1.3E	30 W	0249	0529	1.4F
	0332	0608	1.1F		0831	1155	1.3E
	0904	1215	1.1E		1430	1742	1.9F
	1501	1812	1.4F		2104		
	2132						

All times are local time. Daylight Saving Time has been used when needed.

NOTES:

134

Delaware Bay Entrance, 2004

F—Flood, Dir. 327° True   E—Ebb, Dir. 147° True

July

Day	Slack (h m)	Maximum (h m)	knots
1 Th		0043	1.8E
	0349	0627	1.5F
	0932	1254	1.4E
	1529	1839	2.0F
	2201		
2 F ○		0140	1.9E
	0445	0724	1.5F
	1029	1352	1.5E
	1627	1936	2.0F
	2257		
3 Sa		0236	1.9E
	0540	0820	1.6F
	1125	1447	1.5E
	1723	2031	2.0F
	2353		
4 Su		0329	1.9E
	0634	0914	1.6F
	1220	1541	1.5E
	1820	2125	1.9F
5 M	0048	0421	1.8E
	0727	1006	1.5F
	1315	1635	1.4E
	1917	2219	1.8F
6 Tu	0141	0513	1.7E
	0819	1059	1.4F
	1409	1731	1.3E
	2013	2315	1.6F
7 W	0232	0605	1.5E
	0909	1154	1.3F
	1504	1827	1.2E
	2112		
8 Th		0012	1.4F
	0324	0655	1.4E
	0958	1248	1.3F
	1602	1923	1.1E
	2215		
9 F ○		0108	1.2F
	0416	0744	1.2E
	1046	1339	1.2F
	1659	2019	1.1E
	2321		
10 Sa		0205	1.1F
	0508	0832	1.1E
	1130	1430	1.2F
	1753	2116	1.1E
11 Su	0024	0303	1.0F
	0559	0921	1.0E
	1212	1521	1.2F
	1843	2211	1.1E
12 M	0123	0400	0.9F
	0648	1009	0.9E
	1252	1610	1.2F
	1931	2301	1.1E
13 Tu	0218	0453	0.9F
	0739	1055	0.9E
	1335	1656	1.3F
	2018	2347	1.2E
14 W	0308	0541	1.0F
	0830	1140	0.9E
	1419	1741	1.3F
	2103		
15 Th		0032	1.3E
	0352	0627	1.0F
	0919	1226	1.0E
	1503	1824	1.4F
	2147		
16 F		0116	1.3E
	0432	0711	1.0F
	1004	1311	1.0E
	1547	1907	1.4F
	2228		
17 Sa ●		0159	1.4E
	0510	0754	1.1F
	1048	1356	1.1E
	1629	1949	1.4F
	2308		
18 Su		0239	1.4E
	0546	0832	1.1F
	1129	1438	1.1E
	1709	2028	1.4F
	2346		
19 M		0317	1.4E
	0620	0908	1.1F
	1209	1519	1.1E
	1750	2106	1.4F
20 Tu	0023	0354	1.4E
	0653	0943	1.2F
	1248	1558	1.1E
	1833	2144	1.4F
21 W	0100	0431	1.4E
	0728	1020	1.2F
	1327	1640	1.1E
	1920	2225	1.4F
22 Th	0137	0508	1.3E
	0803	1100	1.3F
	1409	1726	1.1E
	2009	2311	1.3F
23 F	0217	0549	1.3E
	0842	1145	1.1F
	1455	1818	1.1E
	2105		
24 Sa ○		0004	1.2F
	0304	0634	1.2E
	0926	1234	1.4F
	1546	1915	1.2E
	2207		
25 Su		0101	1.2F
	0356	0725	1.2E
	1015	1327	1.5F
	1644	2016	1.3E
	2314		
26 M		0201	1.1F
	0458	0825	1.1E
	1110	1423	1.6F
	1744	2123	1.4E
27 Tu	0023	0306	1.1F
	0602	0933	1.1E
	1209	1525	1.7F
	1845	2229	1.5E
28 W	0130	0411	1.2F
	0709	1039	1.2E
	1311	1627	1.7F
	1948	2347	1.6E
29 Th	0235	0513	1.3F
	0815	1141	1.3E
	1416	1727	1.8F
	2051		
30 F		0030	1.7E
	0336	0612	1.4F
	0918	1241	1.4E
	1518	1825	1.9F
	2151		
31 Sa ○		0127	1.8E
	0431	0710	1.5F
	1017	1339	1.5E
	1617	1923	2.0F
	2247		

August

Day	Slack (h m)	Maximum (h m)	knots
1 Su		0221	1.9E
	0524	0805	1.6F
	1111	1433	1.5E
	1712	2018	2.0F
	2340		
2 M		0311	1.9E
	0615	0856	1.6F
	1203	1524	1.5E
	1807	2110	1.9F
3 Tu	0030	0358	1.8E
	0702	0944	1.6F
	1253	1613	1.5E
	1900	2159	1.8F
4 W	0117	0444	1.7E
	0747	1031	1.5F
	1342	1703	1.4E
	1952	2249	1.6F
5 Th	0201	0529	1.5E
	0829	1119	1.4F
	1430	1754	1.2E
	2045	2341	1.3F
6 F	0245	0613	1.3E
	0908	1207	1.3F
	1518	1846	1.1E
	2141		
7 Sa ○		0034	1.1F
	0330	0657	1.1E
	0947	1254	1.2F
	1609	1937	1.0E
	2243		
8 Su		0127	1.0F
	0418	0741	0.9E
	1027	1342	1.1F
	1701	2031	1.0E
	2347		
9 M		0223	0.8F
	0510	0829	0.8E
	1110	1433	1.1F
	1755	2128	1.0E
10 Tu	0047	0322	0.8F
	0605	0922	0.8E
	1158	1526	1.1F
	1848	2224	1.0E
11 W	0144	0419	0.8F
	0700	1016	0.8E
	1248	1620	1.2F
	1941	2315	1.1E
12 Th	0236	0511	0.8F
	0755	1108	0.9E
	1340	1710	1.2F
	2033		
13 F		0002	1.2E
	0322	0558	0.9F
	0849	1157	0.9E
	1433	1756	1.3F
	2121		
14 Sa		0048	1.3E
	0402	0642	1.0F
	0938	1246	1.0E
	1522	1841	1.4F
	2204		
15 Su		0132	1.4E
	0439	0724	1.1F
	1021	1333	1.1E
	1608	1924	1.4F
	2245		
16 M		0213	1.4E
	0513	0803	1.2F
	1103	1417	1.2E
	1651	2005	1.5F
	2322		
17 Tu		0251	1.5E
	0546	0839	1.3F
	1142	1459	1.3E
	1736	2044	1.5F
	2359		
18 W		0327	1.5E
	0619	0914	1.4F
	1221	1539	1.3E
	1820	2124	1.5F
19 Th	0035	0403	1.4E
	0652	0950	1.5F
	1301	1621	1.3E
	1908	2205	1.4F
20 F	0113	0439	1.4E
	0729	1030	1.5F
	1342	1706	1.3E
	1958	2252	1.3F
21 Sa	0154	0519	1.3E
	0809	1115	1.5F
	1428	1758	1.3E
	2052	2344	1.2F
22 Su	0240	0607	1.2E
	0855	1206	1.6F
	1520	1856	1.3E
	2153		
23 M ○		0042	1.2F
	0335	0703	1.1E
	0948	1302	1.5F
	1619	1959	1.3E
	2300		
24 Tu		0144	1.1F
	0440	0808	1.1E
	1048	1402	1.5F
	1724	2108	1.3E
25 W	0010	0249	1.1F
	0549	0921	1.1E
	1155	1507	1.6F
	1831	2217	1.4E
26 Th	0118	0357	1.2F
	0658	1030	1.2E
	1302	1614	1.6F
	1939	2319	1.6E
27 F	0223	0500	1.3F
	0806	1132	1.3E
	1409	1716	1.7F
	2043		
28 Sa		0017	1.7E
	0322	0559	1.4F
	0908	1230	1.4E
	1511	1814	1.8F
	2141		
29 Su ○		0111	1.8E
	0415	0654	1.5F
	1004	1325	1.5E
	1609	1910	1.9F
	2233		
30 M		0202	1.8E
	0503	0746	1.6F
	1055	1416	1.6E
	1701	2002	1.9F
	2321		
31 Tu		0248	1.8E
	0549	0834	1.6F
	1142	1504	1.6E
	1752	2051	1.8F

September

Day	Slack (h m)	Maximum (h m)	knots
1 W	0006	0330	1.7E
	0630	0917	1.6F
	1227	1549	1.5E
	1841	2136	1.7F
2 Th	0048	0410	1.6E
	0709	0959	1.6F
	1310	1633	1.4E
	1929	2222	1.5F
3 F	0128	0448	1.4E
	0743	1040	1.4F
	1351	1718	1.3E
	2017	2308	1.3F
4 Sa	0207	0527	1.3E
	0815	1123	1.3F
	1433	1804	1.1E
	2106	2357	1.1F
5 Su	0248	0606	1.0E
	0848	1207	1.2F
	1518	1852	1.0E
	2200		
6 M		0049	0.9F
	0333	0648	0.8E
	0926	1254	1.1F
	1609	1944	0.9E
	2300		
7 Tu		0142	0.7F
	0426	0736	0.7E
	1012	1344	1.0F
	1705	2041	0.9E
8 W	0002	0239	0.7F
	0523	0834	0.7E
	1108	1440	1.0F
	1804	2142	0.9E
9 Th	0100	0340	0.7F
	0622	0937	0.7E
	1207	1540	1.1F
	1903	2238	1.0E
10 F	0153	0436	0.8F
	0720	1036	0.8E
	1306	1636	1.1F
	1958	2328	1.1E
11 Sa	0240	0523	0.9F
	0816	1129	1.0E
	1403	1726	1.3F
	2049		
12 Su		0014	1.2E
	0321	0606	1.0F
	0906	1218	1.1E
	1457	1812	1.4F
	2134		
13 M		0058	1.4E
	0358	0647	1.2F
	0951	1306	1.2E
	1547	1856	1.4F
	2215		
14 Tu		0140	1.4E
	0432	0726	1.3F
	1032	1352	1.3E
	1633	1939	1.5F
	2253		
15 W		0219	1.5E
	0506	0804	1.5F
	1112	1436	1.5E
	1720	2021	1.5F
	2331		
16 Th		0257	1.5E
	0541	0842	1.6F
	1153	1518	1.5E
	1807	2103	1.5F
17 F	0010	0334	1.5E
	0618	0921	1.7F
	1234	1601	1.6E
	1856	2147	1.5F
18 Sa	0051	0413	1.4E
	0658	1003	1.7F
	1318	1648	1.5E
	1947	2235	1.4F
19 Su	0136	0457	1.3E
	0742	1050	1.7F
	1406	1742	1.5E
	2041	2329	1.3F
20 M	0226	0551	1.2E
	0832	1144	1.6F
	1500	1843	1.4E
	2142		
21 Tu		0028	1.2F
	0324	0654	1.1E
	0930	1244	1.5F
	1603	1948	1.3E
	2251		
22 W		0131	1.1F
	0432	0803	1.0E
	1038	1348	1.5F
	1713	2057	1.3E
23 Th	0000	0238	1.1F
	0544	0914	0.9E
	1149	1457	1.5F
	1824	2205	1.4E
24 F	0107	0346	1.2F
	0653	1022	1.0E
	1259	1605	1.5F
	1931	2306	1.5E
25 Sa	0208	0449	1.3F
	0759	1122	1.1E
	1405	1707	1.6F
	2033		
26 Su		0303	1.4F
	0858	1217	1.2E
	1505	1802	1.7F
	2127		
27 M		0000	1.6E
	0352	0635	1.5F
	0949	1308	1.3E
	1559	1854	1.8F
	2214		
28 Tu		0050	1.7E
	0437	0723	1.6F
	1035	1357	1.4E
	1649	1943	1.7F
	2257		
29 W		0137	1.7E
	0516	0807	1.6F
	1117	1441	1.6E
	1736	2029	1.7F
	2337		
30 Th		0258	1.6E
	0552	0847	1.6F
	1157	1523	1.5E
	1821	2112	1.5F

All times are local time. Daylight Saving Time has been used when needed.

NOTES:

Delaware Bay Entrance, 2004

F–Flood, Dir. 327° True   E–Ebb, Dir. 147° True

October

Day	Slack h m	Max h m	knots
1 F	0016	0354	1.4E
	0625	0925	1.6F
	1235	1602	1.4E
	1906	2154	1.4F
2 Sa	0054	0408	1.2E
	0656	1002	1.5F
	1313	1642	1.3E
	1949	2237	1.2F
3 Su	0133	0441	1.1E
	0727	1041	1.3F
	1352	1723	1.2E
	2032	2322	1.0F
4 M	0213	0516	0.9E
	0800	1122	1.2F
	1434	1808	1.0E
	2119		
5 Tu		0011	0.8F
	0257	0558	0.8E
	0839	1209	1.1F
	1522	1859	0.9E
	2211		
6 W ○		0103	0.7F
	0347	0650	0.7E
	0927	1300	1.0F
	1619	1956	0.9E
	2311		
7 Th		0157	0.7F
	0445	0751	0.7E
	1025	1356	1.0F
	1720	2057	0.9E
8 F	0008	0255	0.7F
	0546	0859	0.7E
	1129	1457	1.0F
	1820	2156	1.0E
9 Sa	0100	0352	0.8F
	0644	1002	0.9E
	1231	1557	1.1F
	1916	2248	1.1E
10 Su	0146	0442	0.9F
	0739	1057	1.0E
	1332	1650	1.2F
	2008	2334	1.2E
11 M	0229	0525	1.1F
	0830	1148	1.2E
	1430	1738	1.3F
	2055		
12 Tu		0019	1.3E
	0308	0606	1.3F
	0916	1237	1.4E
	1523	1824	1.4F
	2139		
13 W ●		0102	1.4E
	0347	0647	1.5F
	1000	1325	1.5E
	1614	1910	1.5F
	2221		
14 Th		0144	1.5E
	0425	0729	1.7F
	1042	1412	1.7E
	1704	1957	1.5F
	2303		
15 F		0226	1.5E
	0504	0811	1.8F
	1125	1457	1.7E
	1753	2043	1.5F
	2347		
16 Sa		0309	1.4E
	0547	0855	1.9F
	1210	1544	1.7E
	1844	2130	1.5F
17 Su	0033	0353	1.4E
	0632	0941	1.9F
	1258	1634	1.7E
	1937	2220	1.4F
18 M	0122	0443	1.3E
	0722	1032	1.8F
	1350	1731	1.6E
	2032	2316	1.3F
19 Tu	0217	0543	1.2E
	0819	1129	1.6F
	1448	1833	1.4E
	2134		
20 W		0017	1.2F
	0318	0649	1.1E
	0921	1232	1.5F
	1553	1938	1.4E
	2241		
21 Th		0121	1.1F
	0428	0751	1.1E
	1032	1338	1.4F
	1705	2044	1.3E
	2349		
22 F		0227	1.1F
	0540	0905	1.1E
	1146	1447	1.4F
	1815	2149	1.4E
23 Sa	0051	0333	1.2F
	0648	1010	1.2E
	1254	1554	1.4F
	1918	2244	1.5E
24 Su	0147	0433	1.3F
	0749	1108	1.3E
	1357	1653	1.5F
	2015	2337	1.5E
25 M	0238	0525	1.5F
	0843	1200	1.5E
	1455	1746	1.6F
	2105		
26 Tu		0023	1.5E
	0323	0612	1.6F
	0930	1249	1.5E
	1547	1835	1.6F
	2149		
27 W		0107	1.5E
	0403	0655	1.6F
	1011	1335	1.6E
	1635	1922	1.5F
	2229		
28 Th		0147	1.4E
	0439	0737	1.6F
	1050	1418	1.6E
	1720	2007	1.5F
	2308		
29 F		0225	1.4E
	0512	0816	1.6F
	1127	1457	1.6E
	1802	2049	1.4F
	2347		
30 Sa		0300	1.2E
	0543	0853	1.5F
	1203	1534	1.4E
	1843	2129	1.3F
31 Su	0025	0233	1.1E
	0514	0829	1.4F
	1140	1511	1.3E
	1823	2109	1.1F

November

Day	Slack h m	Max h m	knots
1 M	0004	0305	1.0E
	0547	0906	1.3F
	1218	1549	1.2E
	1902	2151	1.0F
2 Tu	0044	0339	0.9E
	0623	0945	1.2F
	1259	1632	1.1E
	1944	2237	0.8F
3 W	0127	0421	0.8E
	0705	1030	1.1F
	1345	1722	1.0E
	2030	2326	0.8F
4 Th	0214	0516	0.7E
	0753	1121	1.0F
	1438	1816	1.0E
	2121		
5 F ○		0017	0.7F
	0310	0617	0.7E
	0850	1216	1.0F
	1536	1911	1.0E
	2214		
6 Sa		0109	0.8F
	0409	0721	0.8E
	0953	1313	1.0F
	1633	2008	1.0E
	2304		
7 Su		0202	0.9F
	0506	0825	0.9E
	1059	1413	1.1F
	1728	2101	1.1E
	2349		
8 M		0253	1.1F
	0559	0923	1.1E
	1201	1510	1.2F
	1820	2156	1.2E
9 Tu	0033	0340	1.3F
	0650	1016	1.3E
	1302	1602	1.3F
	1912	2237	1.3E
10 W	0118	0425	1.5F
	0739	1107	1.5E
	1400	1653	1.4F
	2001	2323	1.4E
11 Th	0202	0509	1.7F
	0827	1158	1.7E
	1455	1743	1.5F
	2050		
12 F ●		0010	1.4E
	0248	0556	1.9F
	0913	1248	1.8E
	1548	1834	1.5F
	2138		
13 Sa		0059	1.4E
	0333	0644	2.0F
	1000	1338	1.9E
	1640	1924	1.5F
	2227		
14 Su		0148	1.4E
	0422	0733	2.0F
	1050	1429	1.8E
	1732	2015	1.5F
	2318		
15 M		0239	1.4E
	0514	0824	1.9F
	1142	1522	1.8E
	1827	2107	1.4F
16 Tu	0012	0334	1.3E
	0610	0918	1.8F
	1239	1620	1.6E
	1923	2204	1.3F
17 W	0110	0436	1.2E
	0710	1017	1.6F
	1338	1721	1.5E
	2023	2305	1.3F
18 Th	0212	0540	1.2E
	0814	1121	1.5F
	1443	1823	1.4E
	2126		
19 F		0008	1.2F
	0321	0645	1.1E
	0925	1226	1.4F
	1551	1924	1.4E
	2229		
20 Sa		0111	1.2F
	0431	0749	1.2E
	1037	1332	1.4F
	1655	2024	1.4E
	2326		
21 Su		0213	1.3F
	0534	0852	1.2E
	1143	1436	1.3F
	1753	2119	1.4E
22 M	0018	0310	1.4F
	0631	0949	1.3E
	1245	1534	1.3F
	1847	2207	1.4E
23 Tu	0105	0359	1.5F
	0721	1040	1.4E
	1342	1626	1.4F
	1935	2252	1.3E
24 W	0147	0444	1.5F
	0806	1127	1.5E
	1433	1713	1.3F
	2020	2334	1.3E
25 Th	0226	0525	1.6F
	0846	1211	1.5E
	1520	1800	1.3F
	2101		
26 F ○		0014	1.2E
	0301	0606	1.6F
	0923	1253	1.5E
	1603	1844	1.3F
	2141		
27 Sa		0053	1.2E
	0335	0646	1.6F
	1000	1333	1.5E
	1643	1926	1.2F
	2220		
28 Su		0131	1.1E
	0408	0724	1.5F
	1037	1410	1.4E
	1722	2006	1.2F
	2300		
29 M		0206	1.1E
	0441	0801	1.4F
	1114	1447	1.3E
	1800	2045	1.1F
	2340		
30 Tu		0241	1.0E
	0518	0838	1.3F
	1152	1525	1.3E
	1837	2124	1.0F

December

Day	Slack h m	Max h m	knots
1 W	0020	0317	0.9E
	0557	0917	1.3F
	1233	1605	1.2E
	1915	2206	0.9F
2 Th	0101	0359	0.9E
	0639	0959	1.2F
	1316	1651	1.1E
	1955	2251	0.9F
3 F	0146	0451	0.8E
	0727	1046	1.1F
	1401	1738	1.1E
	2038	2338	0.9F
4 Sa ○	0236	0547	0.8E
	0821	1139	1.1F
	1451	1826	1.1E
	2123		
5 Su		0025	0.9F
	0331	0646	0.8E
	0922	1233	1.1F
	1545	1917	1.1E
	2210		
6 M		0114	1.1F
	0426	0746	1.0E
	1028	1330	1.1F
	1639	2011	1.1E
	2257		
7 Tu		0205	1.2F
	0519	0847	1.2E
	1133	1431	1.2F
	1734	2105	1.2E
	2343		
8 W		0256	1.4F
	0611	0944	1.4E
	1237	1529	1.2F
	1830	2157	1.2E
9 Th	0032	0347	1.6F
	0704	1039	1.6E
	1338	1624	1.3F
	1926	2248	1.3E
10 F	0124	0437	1.8F
	0757	1133	1.7E
	1437	1718	1.4F
	2022	2342	1.4E
11 Sa ●	0218	0529	1.9F
	0849	1228	1.8E
	1531	1813	1.5F
	2116		
12 Su		0037	1.4E
	0311	0622	2.0F
	0942	1322	1.9E
	1626	1907	1.5F
	2210		
13 M		0133	1.4E
	0406	0717	2.0F
	1036	1416	1.9E
	1720	2001	1.5F
	2305		
14 Tu		0227	1.4E
	0501	0811	2.0F
	1132	1510	1.8E
	1814	2054	1.5F
15 W	0001	0323	1.4E
	0600	0906	1.9F
	1229	1606	1.7E
	1909	2149	1.4F
16 Th	0059	0423	1.3E
	0700	1004	1.7F
	1326	1703	1.6E
	2005	2248	1.4F
17 F	0159	0524	1.3E
	0803	1106	1.5F
	1425	1800	1.5E
	2102	2348	1.3F
18 Sa	0303	0625	1.2E
	0910	1208	1.4F
	1525	1855	1.4E
	2159		
19 Su ○		0046	1.3F
	0409	0726	1.2E
	1020	1309	1.3F
	1624	1950	1.3E
	2251		
20 M		0143	1.3F
	0509	0827	1.2E
	1126	1411	1.2F
	1719	2043	1.2E
	2339		
21 Tu		0238	1.3F
	0603	0924	1.2E
	1228	1509	1.1F
	1811	2132	1.2E
22 W	0024	0328	1.4F
	0652	1015	1.3E
	1325	1602	1.1F
	1901	2217	1.1E
23 Th	0106	0413	1.4F
	0737	1102	1.3E
	1416	1650	1.1F
	1948	2300	1.1E
24 F	0147	0456	1.4F
	0818	1146	1.4E
	1502	1736	1.1F
	2033	2342	1.1E
25 Sa	0225	0538	1.4F
	0858	1229	1.4E
	1544	1822	1.1F
	2115		
26 Su		0024	1.1E
	0303	0620	1.4F
	0937	1310	1.4E
	1623	1904	1.1F
	2157		
27 M		0106	1.1E
	0340	0700	1.4F
	1016	1349	1.4E
	1701	1945	1.1F
	2238		
28 Tu		0145	1.0E
	0418	0739	1.4F
	1054	1426	1.4E
	1737	2022	1.1F
	2318		
29 W		0223	1.0E
	0457	0816	1.4F
	1132	1503	1.3E
	1811	2059	1.1F
	2358		
30 Th		0301	1.0E
	0537	0854	1.3F
	1210	1541	1.3E
	1845	2136	1.0F
31 F	0038	0342	1.0E
	0619	0933	1.3F
	1248	1620	1.2E
	1920	2216	1.0F

All times are local time. Daylight Saving Time has been used when needed.

NOTES:

Chesapeake and Delaware Canal (Chesapeake City), 2004

F—Flood, Dir. 110° True   E—Ebb, Dir. 290° True

April

Day	Slack h m	Max h m	knots
1 Th		0326	1.8F
	0549	0920	2.0E
	1302	1609	2.0F
	1913	2156	1.6E
2 F	0055	0421	1.9F
	0652	1014	2.0E
	1350	1657	2.0F
	1952	2245	1.8E
3 Sa	0152	0514	2.0F
	0754	1107	2.0E
	1434	1742	2.0F
	2027	2331	1.9E
4 Su	0344	0705	2.1F
	0954	1257	2.0E
	1615	1926	2.0F
	2200		
5 M		0115	2.1E
	0432	0755	2.2F
	1053	1346	1.9E
	1653	2009	2.0F
	2235		
6 Tu		0158	2.2E
	0520	0845	2.2F
	1152	1435	1.8E
	1729	2052	1.9F
	2311		
7 W		0242	2.3E
	0609	0936	2.3F
	1250	1524	1.7E
	1806	2137	1.9F
	2351		
8 Th		0328	2.4E
	0700	1028	2.3F
	1350	1614	1.6E
	1845	2225	1.8F
9 F	0035	0417	2.4E
	0756	1121	2.3F
	1452	1707	1.4E
	1929	2317	1.7F
10 Sa	0124	0511	2.3E
	0857	1218	2.2F
	1557	1804	1.3E
	2023		
11 Su		0014	1.7F
	0221	0610	2.2E
	1006	1316	2.1F
	1704	1906	1.2E
	2141		
12 M		0116	1.6F
	0327	0715	2.1E
	1118	1416	2.1F
	1807	2013	1.3E
	2326		
13 Tu		0221	1.7F
	0443	0824	2.0E
	1227	1515	2.0F
	1903	2120	1.4E
14 W	0050	0326	1.7F
	0606	0933	2.0E
	1329	1612	2.1F
	1950	2224	1.6E
15 Th	0156	0429	1.9F
	0729	1038	1.9E
	1425	1704	2.1F
	2032	2319	1.8E
16 F	0253	0527	2.0F
	0841	1138	1.9E
	1516	1753	2.1F
	2109		
17 Sa		0006	2.0E
	0343	0621	2.1F
	0944	1231	1.9E
	1602	1838	2.1F
	2143		
18 Su		0048	2.1E
	0428	0710	2.2F
	1039	1318	1.8E
	1646	1921	2.0F
	2214		
19 M		0127	2.2E
	0509	0757	2.3F
	1129	1401	1.8E
	1726	2003	2.0F
	2243		
20 Tu		0204	2.2E
	0547	0840	2.3F
	1214	1441	1.7E
	1802	2043	1.9F
	2312		
21 W		0240	2.2E
	0622	0923	2.3F
	1256	1519	1.6E
	1834	2124	1.8F
	2342		
22 Th		0316	2.2E
	0655	1005	2.3F
	1336	1557	1.5E
	1858	2204	1.7F
23 F	0014	0352	2.2E
	0727	1048	2.2F
	1414	1635	1.5E
	1919	2246	1.6F
24 Sa	0051	0430	2.1E
	0802	1132	2.1F
	1452	1715	1.4E
	1946	2329	1.6F
25 Su	0132	0511	2.1E
	0841	1218	2.1F
	1533	1759	1.4E
	2022		
26 M		0017	1.5F
	0218	0556	2.1E
	0925	1306	2.0F
	1616	1846	1.4E
	2110		
27 Tu		0108	1.5F
	0310	0647	2.0E
	1015	1357	2.0F
	1702	1938	1.4E
	2210		
28 W		0204	1.6F
	0409	0743	2.0E
	1108	1448	2.0F
	1748	2032	1.5E
	2320		
29 Th		0301	1.7F
	0514	0843	1.9E
	1203	1538	2.0F
	1831	2126	1.7E
30 F	0032	0359	1.8F
	0624	0942	1.9E
	1257	1628	2.0F
	1913	2219	1.9E

May

Day	Slack h m	Max h m	knots
1 Sa	0136	0455	1.9F
	0736	1041	1.8E
	1350	1716	2.0F
	1952	2309	2.0E
2 Su	0233	0550	2.1F
	0847	1138	1.8E
	1440	1803	2.0F
	2031	2357	2.2E
3 M	0326	0644	2.3F
	0954	1233	1.7E
	1527	1849	1.9F
	2110		
4 Tu		0044	2.3E
	0417	0736	2.4F
	1058	1326	1.7E
	1613	1936	1.9F
	2151		
5 W		0131	2.4E
	0508	0828	2.4F
	1200	1419	1.6E
	1657	2023	1.9F
	2234		
6 Th		0219	2.5E
	0600	0920	2.4F
	1259	1511	1.5E
	1743	2113	1.8F
	2321		
7 F		0309	2.5E
	0654	1013	2.4F
	1358	1604	1.4E
	1832	2205	1.7F
8 Sa	0012	0402	2.4E
	0751	1107	2.3F
	1457	1659	1.3E
	1932	2301	1.7F
9 Su	0108	0458	2.3E
	0851	1202	2.2F
	1553	1757	1.3E
	2051		
10 M		0001	1.6F
	0211	0558	2.2E
	0954	1258	2.2F
	1647	1859	1.4E
	2222		
11 Tu		0104	1.6F
	0323	0702	2.0E
	1057	1353	2.1F
	1736	2002	1.5E
	2341		
12 W		0208	1.7F
	0444	0807	1.9E
	1157	1447	2.1F
	1821	2103	1.7E
13 Th	0047	0312	1.8F
	0611	0912	1.8E
	1253	1539	2.0F
	1902	2158	1.8E
14 F	0144	0412	1.9F
	0731	1015	1.7E
	1346	1629	2.0F
	1939	2247	2.0E
15 Sa	0235	0508	2.0F
	0839	1112	1.6E
	1436	1716	2.0F
	2015	2331	2.1E
16 Su	0320	0559	2.2F
	0939	1204	1.6E
	1523	1801	2.0F
	2048		
17 M		0012	2.2E
	0402	0647	2.2F
	1031	1250	1.6E
	1607	1845	1.9F
	2121		
18 Tu		0051	2.3E
	0442	0731	2.3F
	1118	1333	1.5E
	1648	1928	1.9F
	2153		
19 W		0129	2.3E
	0518	0814	2.3F
	1201	1413	1.5E
	1724	2009	1.8F
	2226		
20 Th		0206	2.3E
	0553	0857	2.3F
	1241	1452	1.5E
	1754	2051	1.7F
	2300		
21 F		0243	2.2E
	0626	0938	2.3F
	1319	1530	1.4E
	1817	2132	1.6F
	2336		
22 Sa		0320	2.2E
	0658	1021	2.2F
	1354	1608	1.4E
	1840	2215	1.6F
23 Su	0014	0358	2.2E
	0730	1104	2.2F
	1429	1648	1.4E
	1912	2259	1.5F
24 M	0057	0438	2.1E
	0805	1148	2.1F
	1504	1730	1.4E
	1955	2346	1.5F
25 Tu	0144	0521	2.1E
	0844	1234	2.1F
	1540	1816	1.4E
	2049		
26 W		0038	1.5F
	0238	0610	2.0E
	0926	1321	2.0F
	1618	1905	1.6E
	2153		
27 Th		0135	1.6F
	0340	0705	1.9E
	1012	1409	2.0F
	1657	1957	1.7E
	2303		
28 F		0233	1.7F
	0450	0804	1.8E
	1101	1457	2.0F
	1737	2049	1.9E
29 Sa	0011	0332	1.8F
	0606	0907	1.7E
	1153	1546	2.0F
	1818	2142	2.1E
30 Su	0114	0431	2.0F
	0725	1009	1.6E
	1247	1636	1.9F
	1900	2234	2.3E
31 M	0213	0528	2.2F
	0843	1111	1.6E
	1343	1726	1.9F
	1944	2325	2.4E

June

Day	Slack h m	Max h m	knots
1 Tu	0308	0623	2.3F
	0955	1210	1.5E
	1438	1816	1.9F
	2030		
2 W		0017	2.5E
	0403	0718	2.4F
	1102	1307	1.4E
	1534	1907	1.8F
	2118		
3 Th		0109	2.5E
	0458	0811	2.5F
	1203	1403	1.4E
	1630	2000	1.8F
	2209		
4 F		0202	2.5E
	0553	0905	2.5F
	1301	1458	1.4E
	1729	2054	1.8F
	2303		
5 Sa		0255	2.5E
	0648	0958	2.4F
	1355	1554	1.4E
	1836	2150	1.8F
	2347		
6 Su	0000	0350	2.4E
	0744	1050	2.4F
	1445	1650	1.4E
	1952	2248	1.7F
7 M	0101	0447	2.3E
	0839	1143	2.3F
	1531	1746	1.5E
	2110	2348	1.7F
8 Tu	0120	0544	2.1E
	0933	1234	2.2F
	1614	1843	1.6E
	2223		
9 W		0049	1.7F
	0322	0644	1.9E
	1026	1325	2.1F
	1654	1939	1.7E
	2328		
10 Th		0151	1.8F
	0444	0744	1.7E
	1118	1414	2.1F
	1732	2032	1.9E
11 F	0027	0251	1.8F
	0606	0844	1.6E
	1209	1503	2.0F
	1808	2122	2.0E
12 Sa	0119	0348	1.9F
	0721	0943	1.5E
	1259	1551	2.0F
	1845	2208	2.1E
13 Su	0207	0441	2.1F
	0827	1038	1.4E
	1349	1638	1.9F
	1921	2252	2.2E
14 M	0251	0531	2.2F
	0924	1130	1.4E
	1437	1724	1.9F
	1958	2335	2.3E
15 Tu	0333	0619	2.3F
	1014	1217	1.4E
	1523	1810	1.8F
	2035		
16 W		0016	2.3E
	0413	0704	2.3F
	1100	1302	1.4E
	1605	1854	1.8F
	2113		
17 Th		0057	2.3E
	0452	0748	2.3F
	1142	1343	1.4E
	1642	1938	1.7F
18 F		0136	2.3E
	0528	0831	2.3F
	1222	1423	1.3E
	1712	2021	1.7F
	2228		
19 Sa		0215	2.3E
	0602	0913	2.2F
	1258	1503	1.3E
	1740	2104	1.6F
	2307		
20 Su		0253	2.2E
	0634	0955	2.2F
	1330	1542	1.3E
	1810	2147	1.6F
	2347		
21 M		0331	2.2E
	0703	1037	2.2F
	1400	1621	1.4E
	1849	2232	1.5F
22 Tu	0031	0410	2.1E
	0733	1119	2.1F
	1429	1702	1.5E
	1937	2320	1.5F
23 W	0120	0452	2.1E
	0806	1201	2.1F
	1459	1746	1.6E
	2033		
24 Th		0012	1.6F
	0216	0539	2.0E
	0843	1244	2.1F
	1532	1832	1.8E
	2135		
25 F		0109	1.7F
	0321	0632	1.8E
	0924	1325	2.0F
	1608	1921	1.9E
	2241		
26 Sa		0207	1.8F
	0433	0731	1.7E
	1009	1417	2.0F
	1647	2013	2.1E
	2347		
27 Su		0307	1.9F
	0554	0835	1.5E
	1059	1507	1.9F
	1731	2107	2.3E
28 M	0051	0407	2.1F
	0719	0941	1.4E
	1153	1600	1.9F
	1817	2203	2.4E
29 Tu	0154	0506	2.2F
	0842	1046	1.3E
	1253	1654	1.8F
	1908	2259	2.5E
30 W	0254	0604	2.3F
	0955	1149	1.3E
	1358	1750	1.8F
	2002	2356	2.5E

All times are local time. Daylight Saving Time has been used when needed.

NOTES:

Chesapeake and Delaware Canal (Chesapeake City), 2004

F—Flood, Dir. 110° True   E—Ebb, Dir. 290° True

July

Date	Slack (h m)	Maximum (h m)	knots
1 Th	0353	0700	2.4F
	1100	1250	1.3E
	1507	1846	1.8F
	2058		
2 F ○		0053	2.6E
	0451	0755	2.4F
	1157	1349	1.3E
	1619	1942	1.8F
	2156		
3 Sa		0149	2.5E
	0546	0848	2.4F
	1248	1446	1.4E
	1733	2039	1.8F
	2256		
4 Su		0244	2.5E
	0639	0940	2.4F
	1333	1540	1.5E
	1845	2136	1.8F
	2357		
5 M		0339	2.3E
	0730	1029	2.3F
	1415	1634	1.6E
	1954	2234	1.8F
6 Tu	0101	0432	2.2E
	0818	1118	2.3F
	1453	1726	1.7E
	2100	2332	1.8F
7 W	0208	0526	2.0E
	0904	1205	2.2F
	1529	1816	1.8E
	2203		
8 Th		0029	1.8F
	0319	0620	1.8E
	0948	1251	2.1F
	1603	1905	1.9E
	2300		
9 F		0127	1.8F
	0434	0714	1.6E
	1032	1337	2.0F
	1638	1952	2.0E
	2354		
10 Sa		0223	1.9F
	0549	0809	1.4E
	1117	1424	2.0F
	1713	2039	2.1E
11 Su	0044	0317	2.0F
	0659	0905	1.3E
	1204	1512	1.9F
	1751	2126	2.2E
12 M	0132	0409	2.0F
	0802	0959	1.2E
	1254	1600	1.8F
	1832	2212	2.2E
13 Tu	0218	0459	2.1F
	0858	1052	1.2E
	1345	1649	1.8F
	1915	2258	2.3E
14 W	0302	0548	2.2F
	0948	1141	1.2E
	1434	1737	1.8F
	1958	2343	2.3E
15 Th	0345	0635	2.2F
	1033	1228	1.3E
	1519	1824	1.8F
	2041		
16 F		0027	2.3E
	0426	0720	2.2F
	1115	1312	1.3E
	1600	1910	1.7F
	2124		
17 Sa		0110	2.3E
	0504	0804	2.2F
	1153	1354	1.3E
	1638 ●	1955	1.7F
	2205		
18 Su		0150	2.3E
	0539	0846	2.2F
	1226	1435	1.4E
	1714	2039	1.7F
	2247		
19 M		0229	2.2E
	0608	0927	2.2F
	1254	1514	1.5E
	1753	2124	1.7F
	2330		
20 Tu		0308	2.2E
	0635	1007	2.2F
	1319	1553	1.6E
	1835	2210	1.7F
21 W	0016	0347	2.1E
	0702	1047	2.1F
	1344	1632	1.7E
	1923	2258	1.7F
22 Th	0108	0428	2.0E
	0731	1127	2.1F
	1412	1713	1.8E
	2016	2350	1.7F
23 F	0206	0514	1.8E
	0805	1208	2.0F
	1444	1758	2.0E
	2114		
24 Sa ○		0045	1.8F
	0311	0606	1.7E
	0843	1252	1.9F
	1521	1846	2.1E
	2217		
25 Su		0143	1.9F
	0425	0705	1.5E
	0925	1340	1.9F
	1604	1940	2.2E
	2324		
26 M		0244	2.0F
	0548	0810	1.3E
	1014	1434	1.8F
	1652	2038	2.3E
27 Tu	0032	0345	2.1F
	0717	0918	1.2E
	1111	1531	1.8F
	1746	2138	2.4E
28 W	0140	0446	2.2F
	0840	1026	1.1E
	1219	1631	1.8F
	1844	2240	2.5E
29 Th	0245	0546	2.3F
	0949	1133	1.1E
	1339	1731	1.8F
	1946	2342	2.5E
30 F	0345	0643	2.3F
	1046	1236	1.3E
	1507	1831	1.9F
	2050		
31 Sa ○		0041	2.5E
	0442	0737	2.4F
	1135	1435	1.4E
	1628	1929	1.9F
	2154		

August

Date	Slack (h m)	Maximum (h m)	knots
1 Su		0138	2.4E
	0534	0828	2.4F
	1218	1430	1.6E
	1737	2026	1.9F
	2257		
2 M		0232	2.4E
	0623	0916	2.4F
	1257	1521	1.7E
	1840	2122	2.0F
3 Tu	0000	0324	2.2E
	0708	1002	2.3F
	1332	1609	1.8E
	1940	2217	2.0F
4 W	0102	0414	2.1E
	0750	1047	2.2F
	1405	1655	1.9E
	2036	2311	2.0F
5 Th	0205	0503	1.9E
	0829	1131	2.1F
	1436	1739	2.0E
	2129		
6 F		0004	1.9F
	0309	0551	1.7E
	0906	1215	2.0F
	1508	1823	2.1E
7 Sa		0056	1.9F
	0414	0641	1.6E
	0942	1300	1.9F
	1541	1908	2.1E
	2312		
8 Su		0149	2.1F
	0520	0732	1.3E
	1019	1346	1.9F
	1619	1955	2.1E
9 M	0002	0241	2.0F
	0625	0825	1.2E
	1102	1435	1.8F
	1702	2043	2.1E
10 Tu	0052	0333	2.0F
	0726	0918	1.2E
	1153	1525	1.8F
	1748	2133	2.2E
11 W	0141	0425	2.0F
	0821	1012	1.2E
	1249	1615	1.8F
	1837	2223	2.2E
12 Th	0229	0515	2.1F
	0911	1104	1.2E
	1346	1706	1.8F
	1927	2312	2.2E
13 F	0315	0604	2.1F
	0956	1154	1.3E
	1440	1755	1.8F
	2015	2359	2.2E
14 Sa	0357	0650	2.2F
	1036	1240	1.3E
	1530	1844	1.8F
	2102		
15 Su		0043	2.2E
	0435	0734	2.2F
	1110	1324	1.4E
	1615 ●	1931	1.8F
	2148		
16 M		0125	2.2E
	0509	0816	2.2F
	1139	1405	1.6E
	1658	2017	1.8F
	2234		
17 Tu		0206	2.2E
	0537	0856	2.2F
	1204	1444	1.7E
	1739	2103	1.8F
	2322		
18 W		0246	2.1E
	0603	0935	2.1F
	1228	1522	1.8E
	1822	2149	1.9F
19 Th	0011	0326	2.0E
	0629	1013	2.1F
	1254	1600	1.9E
	1907	2238	1.9F
20 F	0105	0409	1.9E
	0657	1052	2.0F
	1324	1641	2.1E
	1957	2329	1.9F
21 Sa	0204	0455	1.7E
	0730	1133	1.9F
	1359	1725	2.2E
	2053		
22 Su		0024	2.0F
	0310	0547	1.5E
	0807	1219	1.8F
	1440	1815	2.2E
	2156		
23 M		0122	2.0F
	0424	0646	1.3E
	0850	1311	1.8F
	1528 ○	1912	2.3E
	2306		
24 Tu		0224	2.0F
	0550	0752	1.1E
	0941	1410	1.7F
	1623	2015	2.3E
25 W	0020	0326	2.1F
	0718	0902	1.0E
	1047	1513	1.7F
	1725	2121	2.3E
26 Th	0131	0428	2.1F
	0831	1013	1.1E
	1215	1617	1.8F
	1833	2227	2.3E
27 F	0235	0527	2.2F
	0929	1121	1.2E
	1402	1719	1.8F
	1944	2331	2.4E
28 Sa	0333	0623	2.3F
	1017	1223	1.4E
	1526	1820	1.9F
	2054		
29 Su		0031	2.3E
	0426	0715	2.3F
	1058	1319	1.6E
	1633 ○	1918	2.0F
	2201		
30 M		0126	2.3E
	0514	0800	2.3F
	1135	1409	1.8E
	1731	2013	2.1F
	2304		
31 Tu		0218	2.2E
	0559	0848	2.3F
	1209	1454	1.9E
	1825	2105	2.1F

September

Date	Slack (h m)	Maximum (h m)	knots
1 W		0004	2.1E
	0640	0931	2.2F
	1241	1537	2.0E
	1915	2156	2.1F
2 Th	0101	0352	1.9E
	0718	1013	2.1F
	1311	1618	2.1E
	2002	2245	2.1F
3 F	0157	0436	1.7E
	0752	1055	2.0F
	1340	1658	2.1E
	2049	2334	2.1F
4 Sa	0252	0521	1.6E
	0822	1137	1.9F
	1412	1739	2.1E
	2135		
5 Su		0023	2.0F
	0347	0606	1.4E
	0851	1222	1.8F
	1448	1823	2.1E
	2223		
6 M		0113	2.0F
	0444	0654	1.3E
	0923	1309	1.7F
	1529 ○	1910	2.1E
	2313		
7 Tu		0204	2.0F
	0543	0744	1.2E
	1004	1358	1.7F
	1615	2000	2.1E
8 W	0006	0256	2.0F
	0641	0838	1.1E
	1057	1450	1.7F
	1707	2053	2.1E
9 Th	0059	0349	2.0F
	0735	0933	1.2E
	1202	1544	1.7F
	1801	2146	2.1E
10 F	0150	0440	2.0F
	0824	1027	1.2E
	1310	1637	1.7F
	1857	2238	2.1E
11 Sa	0237	0529	2.1F
	0906	1119	1.4E
	1413	1728	1.7F
	1952	2328	2.1E
12 Su	0319	0616	2.1F
	0943	1206	1.5E
	1508	1819	1.9F
	2045		
13 M		0015	2.1E
	0357	0700	2.2F
	1014	1250	1.7E
	1556	1907	1.9F
	2137		
14 Tu		0100	2.1E
	0431	0741	2.2F
	1041	1331	1.8E
	1640 ○	1955	2.0F
	2228		
15 W		0143	2.0E
	0500	0821	2.1F
	1108	1411	2.0E
	1722	2042	2.0F
	2320		
16 Th		0225	2.0E
	0528	0900	2.1F
	1136	1449	2.1E
	1805	2130	2.1F
17 F	0013	0309	1.8E
	0555	0939	2.0F
	1206	1529	2.3E
	1850	2219	2.1F
18 Sa	0109	0353	1.7E
	0626	1020	1.9F
	1241	1611	2.3E
	1941	2311	2.1F
19 Su	0209	0441	1.5E
	0700	1104	1.8F
	1321	1658	2.3E
	2037		
20 M		0006	2.1F
	0315	0534	1.3E
	0739	1154	1.7F
	1408	1752	2.3E
	2142		
21 Tu		0104	2.1F
	0431	0635	1.1E
	0826	1251	1.7F
	1502 ○	1853	2.3E
	2255		
22 W		0206	2.0F
	0553	0742	1.0E
	0928	1355	1.7F
	1605	2000	2.2E
23 Th	0006	0308	2.1F
	0708	0853	1.1E
	1101	1501	1.7F
	1716	2109	2.2E
24 F	0118	0409	2.1F
	0807	1004	1.2E
	1307	1607	1.8F
	1834	2217	2.2E
25 Sa	0219	0506	2.2F
	0854	1109	1.5E
	1426	1710	1.9F
	1951	2320	2.2F
26 Su	0313	0558	2.2F
	0936	1207	1.7E
	1531	1809	2.0F
	2104		
27 M		0019	2.1E
	0403	0647	2.2F
	1013	1257	1.9E
	1626	1905	2.1F
	2209		
28 Tu		0111	2.1E
	0448	0732	2.2F
	1047	1341	2.0E
	1716 ○	1957	2.2F
	2309		
29 W		0200	2.0E
	0530	0815	2.2F
	1118	1422	2.1E
	1802	2046	2.2F
30 Th	0004	0245	1.9E
	0609	0857	2.1F
	1148	1501	2.2E
	1845	2132	2.2F

All times are local time. Daylight Saving Time has been used when needed.

NOTES:

138

Chesapeake and Delaware Canal (Chesapeake City), 2004

F—Flood, Dir. 110° True   E—Ebb, Dir. 290° True

October

Days 1–15

Day	Slack (h m)	Maximum (h m)	knots
1 F	0055	0327	1.7E
	0643	0938	2.0F
	1217	1539	2.2E
	1926	2218	2.2F
2 Sa	0143	0408	1.6E
	0713	1019	1.9F
	1248	1618	2.2E
	2007	2303	2.1F
3 Su	0230	0450	1.5E
	0738	1101	1.8F
	1321	1657	2.2E
	2048	2349	2.1F
4 M	0317	0532	1.3E
	0802	1145	1.7F
	1359	1740	2.1E
	2132		
5 Tu		0038	2.0F
	0406	0617	1.2E
	0835	1233	1.7F
	1443	1826	2.1E
	2221		
6 W		0128	2.0F
	0458	0706	1.2E
	0919	1323	1.6F
	1533	1917	2.1E
	○ 2314		
7 Th		0220	2.0F
	0551	0800	1.2E
	1017	1417	1.6F
	1627	2011	2.0E
8 F	0008	0312	2.0F
	0642	0855	1.3E
	1129	1512	1.7F
	1726	2107	2.0E
9 Sa	0059	0402	2.0F
	0727	0950	1.4E
	1244	1607	1.7F
	1828	2201	2.0E
10 Su	0147	0451	2.0F
	0806	1042	1.6E
	1350	1701	1.8F
	1929	2304	2.0E
11 M	0230	0537	2.1F
	0840	1129	1.8E
	1445	1754	1.9F
	2030	2344	2.0E
12 Tu	0309	0621	2.1F
	0912	1214	1.9E
	1534	1844	2.0F
	2129		
13 W		0033	1.9E
	0345	0704	2.1F
	0944	1256	2.1E
	1619	1933	2.1F
	2226		
14 Th		0119	1.9E
	0418	0745	2.0F
	1015	1338	2.2E
	1703	2022	2.2F
	2322		
15 F		0206	1.8E
	0451	0826	2.0F
	1049	1419	2.3E
	1749	2111	2.2F

Days 16–31

Day	Slack (h m)	Maximum (h m)	knots
16 Sa	0019	0252	1.6E
	0623	0908	1.9F
	1126	1502	2.4E
	1837	2202	2.2F
17 Su	0117	0340	1.5E
	0558	0953	1.8F
	1207	1549	2.4E
	1930	2255	2.2F
18 M	0218	0431	1.3E
	0636	1042	1.8F
	1253	1640	2.4E
	2029	2350	2.2F
19 Tu	0324	0526	1.2E
	0723	1137	1.7F
	1346	1737	2.3E
	2135		
20 W		0048	2.1F
	0435	0628	1.1E
	0824	1239	1.6F
	1447	1840	2.2E
	○ 2245		
21 Th		0148	2.1F
	0542	0735	1.1E
	0958	1345	1.6F
	1558	1948	2.1E
	2354		
22 F		0248	2.1F
	0640	0845	1.3E
	1201	1452	1.7F
	1718	2057	2.0E
23 Sa	0057	0345	2.1F
	0728	0952	1.5E
	1323	1557	1.8F
	1843	2203	2.0E
24 Su	0154	0438	2.1F
	0810	1052	1.7E
	1427	1659	1.9F
	2003	2306	1.9E
25 M	0245	0528	2.1F
	0848	1143	1.9E
	1521	1756	2.1F
	2112		
26 Tu		0002	1.9E
	0332	0615	2.1F
	0924	1229	2.1E
	1610	1848	2.2F
	2213		
27 W		0053	1.8E
	0417	0659	2.1F
	0957	1310	2.2E
	1655	1937	2.2F
	○ 2308		
28 Th		0138	1.8E
	0458	0742	2.1F
	1029	1349	2.3E
	1736	2023	2.3F
	2357		
29 F		0221	1.7E
	0535	0823	2.0F
	1100	1427	2.3E
	1816	2107	2.3F
30 Sa	0043	0301	1.6E
	0608	0905	1.9F
	1131	1504	2.3E
	1853	2150	2.2F
31 Su	0126	0240	1.5E
	0533	0846	1.8F
	1104	1442	2.2E
	1830	2134	2.2F

November

Days 1–15

Day	Slack (h m)	Maximum (h m)	knots
1 M	0107	0319	1.4E
	0555	0928	1.7F
	1139	1521	2.2E
	1908	2219	2.1F
2 Tu	0149	0400	1.3E
	0620	1012	1.6F
	1219	1602	2.1E
	1948	2305	2.0F
3 W	0231	0444	1.2E
	0656	1059	1.6F
	1304	1647	2.1E
	2031	2353	2.0F
4 Th	0315	0531	1.2E
	0745	1150	1.6F
	1354	1736	2.0E
	2117		
5 F		0043	2.0F
	0359	0623	1.3E
	0848	1244	1.6F
	1450	1829	2.0E
	○ 2205		
6 Sa		0132	2.0F
	0442	0717	1.4E
	1002	1341	1.6F
	1553	1925	1.9E
	2254		
7 Su		0221	2.0F
	0523	0810	1.6E
	1117	1438	1.7F
	1700	2022	1.9E
	2342		
8 M		0309	2.0F
	0601	0902	1.8E
	1222	1534	1.9F
	1809	2118	1.9E
9 Tu	0028	0356	2.0F
	0638	0950	2.0E
	1317	1628	2.0F
	1917	2212	1.8E
10 W	0112	0441	2.0F
	0715	1037	2.2E
	1408	1720	2.2F
	2022	2305	1.7E
11 Th	0154	0526	2.0F
	0752	1122	2.3E
	1457	1812	2.3F
	2125	2356	1.7E
12 F	0235	0611	2.0F
	0831	1208	2.4E
	1546	1903	2.3F
	2225		
13 Sa		0047	1.6E
	0314	0656	1.9F
	0912	1255	2.5E
	1637	1954	2.4F
	2324		
14 Su		0137	1.5E
	0354	0743	1.9F
	0957	1343	2.5E
	1729	2046	2.3F
15 M	0023	0228	1.4E
	0437	0833	1.8F
	1045	1434	2.5E
	1825	2140	2.3F

Days 16–30

Day	Slack (h m)	Maximum (h m)	knots
16 Tu	0123	0322	1.3E
	0527	0927	1.8F
	1136	1528	2.4E
	1924	2234	2.2F
17 W	0222	0419	1.2E
	0631	1026	1.7F
	1237	1627	2.3E
	2026	2330	2.1F
18 Th	0319	0521	1.3E
	0802	1129	1.7F
	1343	1729	2.1E
	2128		
19 F		0026	2.1F
	0411	0626	1.4E
	0949	1234	1.7F
	1500	1834	2.0E
	○ 2229		
20 Sa		0122	2.1F
	0458	0730	1.6E
	1110	1340	1.8F
	1626	1940	1.9E
	2326		
21 Su		0215	2.1F
	0541	0830	1.8E
	1215	1443	1.9F
	1751	2044	1.8E
22 M	0019	0306	2.1F
	0621	0924	2.0E
	1312	1542	2.0F
	1907	2145	1.7E
23 Tu	0110	0354	2.0F
	0659	1012	2.1E
	1402	1637	2.1F
	2012	2239	1.6E
24 W	0158	0441	2.0F
	0735	1056	2.2E
	1447	1727	2.2F
	2108	2329	1.6E
25 Th	0242	0526	2.0F
	0813	1138	2.3E
	1530	1814	2.2F
	2159		
26 F		0013	1.5E
	0322	0609	1.9F
	0846	1217	2.3E
	1611	1858	2.3F
	○ 2244		
27 Sa		0055	1.5E
	0401	0652	1.9F
	0920	1256	2.3E
	1649	1941	2.3F
	2326		
28 Su		0134	1.4E
	0432	0734	1.8F
	0954	1334	2.3E
	1726	2024	2.2F
29 M	0006	0213	1.4E
	0456	0816	1.7F
	1030	1412	2.2E
	1802	2107	2.2F
30 Tu	0051	0251	1.3E
	0518	0858	1.7F
	1107	1450	2.2E
	1836	2150	2.1F

December

Days 1–15

Day	Slack (h m)	Maximum (h m)	knots
1 W	0119	0331	1.3E
	0549	0942	1.6F
	1148	1530	2.2E
	1910	2234	2.1F
2 Th	0154	0413	1.3E
	0630	1028	1.6F
	1232	1612	2.1E
	1945	2319	2.0F
3 F	0229	0458	1.4E
	0722	1118	1.6F
	1322	1658	2.0E
	2022		
4 Sa		0005	2.0F
	0305	0546	1.5E
	0824	1213	1.6F
	1420	1748	1.9E
	○ 2103		
5 Su		0051	2.0F
	0342	0636	1.6E
	0933	1310	1.7F
	1524	1844	1.8E
	2147		
6 M		0138	2.0F
	0421	0728	1.8E
	1043	1407	1.8F
	1635	1942	1.8E
	2234		
7 Tu		0226	2.0F
	0501	0820	2.0E
	1148	1505	1.9F
	1750	2042	1.7E
	2323		
8 W		0314	1.9F
	0542	0911	2.2E
	1247	1601	2.1F
	1904	2141	1.6E
9 Th	0014	0403	1.9F
	0625	1002	2.3E
	1344	1652	2.2F
	2016	2239	1.5E
10 F	0104	0452	1.9F
	0710	1053	2.4E
	1439	1751	2.3F
	2123	2334	1.5E
11 Sa	0154	0542	1.9F
	0758	1145	2.5E
	1534	1845	2.4F
	● 2225		
12 Su		0029	1.4E
	0244	0632	1.9F
	0848	1237	2.5E
	1629	1938	2.4F
	2324		
13 M		0123	1.4E
	0337	0725	1.9F
	0940	1330	2.5E
	1725	2031	2.4F
14 Tu	0019	0217	1.3E
	0434	0819	1.9F
	1035	1424	2.5E
	1820	2123	2.3F
15 W	0111	0312	1.4E
	0542	0916	1.8F
	1133	1519	2.3E
	1915	2216	2.2F

Days 16–31

Day	Slack (h m)	Maximum (h m)	knots
16 Th	0159	0409	1.4E
	0703	1015	1.8F
	1237	1616	2.2E
	2009	2308	2.2F
17 F	0244	0507	1.5E
	0829	1117	1.8F
	1347	1715	2.0E
	2103	2359	2.1F
18 Sa	0327	0605	1.7E
	0946	1219	1.8F
	1505	1815	1.8E
	○ 2155		
19 Su		0050	2.1F
	0408	0702	1.8E
	1053	1321	1.9F
	1628	1916	1.7E
	2247		
20 M		0140	2.0F
	0449	0757	2.0E
	1152	1421	1.9F
	1748	2017	1.5E
	2339		
21 Tu		0230	2.0F
	0529	0848	2.1E
	1246	1518	2.0F
	1858	2116	1.5E
22 W	0031	0319	1.9F
	0610	0936	2.2E
	1335	1611	2.1F
	1959	2210	1.4E
23 Th	0120	0407	1.9F
	0650	1022	2.2E
	1421	1700	2.2F
	2052	2259	1.4E
24 F	0206	0453	1.9F
	0731	1106	2.3E
	1504	1747	2.2F
	2140	2345	1.4E
25 Sa	0249	0539	1.9F
	0808	1148	2.3E
	1546	1832	2.2F
	2223		
26 Su		0027	1.4E
	0327	0623	1.9F
	0849	1229	2.3E
	1626	1916	2.2F
	○ 2304		
27 M		0107	1.4E
	0359	0707	1.9F
	0927	1308	2.3E
	1703	1958	2.2F
	2341		
28 Tu		0146	1.4E
	0426	0750	1.8F
	1005	1347	2.2E
	1737	2040	2.2F
29 W	0014	0224	1.4E
	0450	0832	1.7F
	1044	1425	2.2E
	1808	2122	2.1F
30 Th	0044	0303	1.6E
	0529	0916	1.7F
	1125	1503	2.1E
	1835	2203	2.1F
31 F	0111	0343	1.5E
	0612	1002	1.8F
	1210	1542	2.1E
	1904	2244	2.0F

All times are local time. Daylight Saving Time has been used when needed.

NOTES:

Baltimore Harbor Approach (off Sandy Pt.), Maryland, 2004

F–Flood, Dir. 025° True   E–Ebb, Dir. 190° True

April

Day	Slack	Maximum
1 Th	—	0227 0.5F
	0519	0811 0.5E
	1054	1422 0.8F
	1738	2054 0.8E
2 F	0016	0307 0.6F
	0604	0902 0.6E
	1155	1511 0.8F
	1822	2132 0.8E
3 Sa	0045	0344 0.8F
	0647	0950 0.8E
	1251	1558 0.8F
	1902	2208 0.8E
4 Su	0112	0521 0.9F
	0829	1136 0.9E
	1446	1742 0.8F
	2041	2343 0.8E
5 M (O)	0239	0557 1.0F
	0912	1221 1.0E
	1540	1827 0.7F
	2118	
6 Tu	—	0018 0.8E
	0309	0635 1.1F
	0956	1307 1.0E
	1635	1911 0.6F
	2155	
7 W	—	0054 0.7E
	0341	0715 1.2F
	1042	1355 1.0E
	1731	1958 0.5F
	2233	
8 Th	—	0133 0.7E
	0418	0759 1.2F
	1130	1446 1.0E
	1828	2048 0.5F
	2316	
9 F	—	0217 0.6E
	0500	0847 1.2F
	1222	1539 1.0E
	1929	2143 0.4F
10 Sa	0007	0308 0.6E
	0549	0940 1.1F
	1317	1637 1.0E
	2030	2244 0.4F
11 Su (O)	0109	0408 0.5E
	0647	1039 1.0F
	1416	1737 0.9E
	2129	2350 0.4F
12 M	0223	0518 0.5E
	0756	1145 0.9F
	1517	1839 0.9E
	2223	
13 Tu	—	0056 0.5E
	0342	0635 0.5E
	0916	1255 0.9F
	1618	1939 0.9E
	2311	
14 W	—	0158 0.6F
	0455	0750 0.6E
	1038	1403 0.6F
	1717	2034 0.9E
	2355	
15 Th	—	0254 0.7F
	0559	0858 0.7E
	1155	1506 0.8F
	1812	2124 0.9E
16 F	0035	0343 0.8F
	0654	0957 0.8E
	1304	1603 0.8F
	1902	2210 0.8E
17 Sa	0113	0429 1.0F
	0744	1050 0.9E
	1405	1655 0.7F
	1948	2253 0.8E
18 Su	0149	0511 1.0F
	0830	1139 1.0E
	1501	1744 0.7F
	2032	2333 0.8E
19 M (●)	0224	0552 1.1F
	0914	1225 1.0E
	1553	1829 0.6F
	2113	
20 Tu	—	0012 0.7E
	0258	0631 1.1F
	0955	1309 1.0E
	1643	1914 0.6F
	2154	
21 W	—	0050 0.6E
	0332	0709 1.1F
	1036	1352 1.0E
	1732	1958 0.5F
	2235	
22 Th	—	0128 0.6E
	0406	0748 1.0F
	1117	1436 0.9E
	1822	2044 0.4F
	2319	
23 F	—	0208 0.5E
	0442	0829 1.0F
	1200	1522 0.9E
	1914	2133 0.4F
24 Sa	0008	0252 0.4E
	0521	0913 0.9F
	1244	1610 0.9E
	2007	2226 0.3F
25 Su	0103	0342 0.4E
	0606	1001 0.8F
	1332	1701 0.8E
	2059	2323 0.3F
26 M	0206	0439 0.3E
	0700	1055 0.8F
	1423	1754 0.8E
	2148	
27 Tu (O)	—	0020 0.4F
	0312	0544 0.3E
	0805	1154 0.7F
	1515	1846 0.8E
	2231	
28 W	—	0113 0.4F
	0413	0650 0.4E
	0920	1253 0.7F
	1609	1935 0.8E
	2308	
29 Th	—	0201 0.5F
	0507	0752 0.5E
	1035	1354 0.6F
	1700	2021 0.8E
	2341	
30 F	—	0244 0.7F
	0555	0849 0.6E
	1146	1450 0.6F
	1749	2103 0.8E

May

Day	Slack	Maximum
1 Sa	0011	0324 0.8F
	0639	0941 0.7E
	1250	1542 0.6F
	1834	2142 0.7E
2 Su	0040	0403 0.9F
	0722	1030 0.9E
	1351	1632 0.6F
	1917	2220 0.7E
3 M	0110	0441 1.1F
	0805	1117 1.0E
	1447	1719 0.6F
	1958	2258 0.7E
4 Tu	0142	0521 1.2F
	0848	1204 1.1E
	1542	1806 0.5F
	2039	2337 0.7E
5 W (O)	0218	0602 1.3F
	0933	1250 1.1E
	1635	1854 0.5F
	2121	
6 Th	—	0019 0.7E
	0257	0646 1.3F
	1019	1338 1.2E
	1728	1943 0.5F
	2208	
7 F	—	0105 0.6E
	0341	0732 1.3F
	1108	1428 1.1E
	1821	2035 0.4F
	2302	
8 Sa	—	0156 0.6E
	0431	0823 1.2F
	1158	1520 1.1E
	1913	2132 0.5F
9 Su	0004	0254 0.5E
	0528	0918 1.1F
	1250	1614 1.0E
	2004	2231 0.5F
10 M	0115	0401 0.5E
	0634	1019 1.0F
	1345	1710 1.0E
	2053	2333 0.6F
11 Tu (O)	0230	0514 0.5E
	0752	1125 0.8F
	1442	1807 0.9E
	2140	
12 W	—	0035 0.7F
	0344	0631 0.6E
	0917	1234 0.7F
	1540	1903 0.9E
	2224	
13 Th	—	0132 0.8F
	0450	0743 0.6E
	1041	1342 0.6F
	1637	1956 0.8E
	2307	
14 F	—	0225 0.9F
	0548	0848 0.7E
	1159	1446 0.6F
	1732	2046 0.8E
	2347	
15 Sa	—	0314 1.0F
	0640	0945 0.8E
	1307	1544 0.6F
	1824	2132 0.7E
16 Su	0026	0359 1.1F
	0727	1037 0.9E
	1408	1637 0.5F
	1913	2216 0.7E
17 M	0103	0442 1.1F
	0811	1124 1.0E
	1502	1726 0.5F
	1959	2258 0.6E
18 Tu (●)	0139	0522 1.1F
	0852	1209 1.0E
	1553	1813 0.5F
	2044	2338 0.6E
19 W	0214	0601 1.1F
	0931	1251 1.0E
	1640	1858 0.4F
	2129	
20 Th	—	0017 0.5E
	0249	0639 1.1F
	1010	1333 1.0E
	1727	1943 0.4F
	2214	
21 F	—	0058 0.5E
	0324	0718 1.1F
	1049	1415 1.0E
	1812	2029 0.4F
	2302	
22 Sa	—	0140 0.4E
	0402	0758 1.0F
	1129	1457 1.0E
	1857	2116 0.4F
	2354	
23 Su	—	0226 0.4E
	0443	0841 0.9F
	1210	1541 0.9E
	1940	2205 0.4F
24 M	0051	0317 0.3E
	0532	0928 0.8F
	1254	1626 0.9E
	2021	2254 0.5F
25 Tu	0151	0401 0.3E
	0631	1019 0.7F
	1339	1712 0.8E
	2059	2344 0.5F
26 W	0250	0518 0.3E
	0741	1116 0.6F
	1427	1758 0.8E
	2134	
27 Th (O)	—	0031 0.6F
	0347	0623 0.4E
	0900	1216 0.6F
	1515	1843 0.8E
	2206	
28 F	—	0116 0.7F
	0438	0726 0.5E
	1021	1316 0.5F
	1604	1927 0.7E
	2237	
29 Sa	—	0159 0.8F
	0526	0823 0.6E
	1137	1415 0.5F
	1652	2023 0.7E
	2308	
30 Su	—	0242 1.0F
	0613	0919 0.8E
	1247	1512 0.4F
	1739	2051 0.7E
	2342	
31 M	—	0324 1.1F
	0658	1010 0.9E
	1350	1605 0.4F
	1826	2134 0.7E

June

Day	Slack	Maximum
1 Tu	0018	0407 1.2F
	0743	1059 1.0E
	1448	1657 0.4F
	1913	2218 0.7E
2 W (O)	0057	0451 1.3F
	0828	1147 1.1E
	1540	1747 0.4F
	2003	2304 0.7E
3 Th	0141	0536 1.4F
	0914	1234 1.2E
	1630	1837 0.4F
	2055	2353 0.6E
4 F	0228	0624 1.4F
	1000	1322 1.2E
	1716	1929 0.5F
	2153	
5 Sa	—	0046 0.6E
	0320	0713 1.3F
	1047	1410 1.2E
	1801	2021 0.5F
	2255	
6 Su	—	0144 0.6E
	0416	0805 1.2F
	1135	1459 1.1E
	1845	2116 0.6F
7 M	0001	0246 0.6E
	0519	0901 1.1F
	1224	1549 1.1E
	1929	2212 0.6F
8 Tu	0111	0353 0.5E
	0630	1000 0.9F
	1314	1640 1.0E
	2012	2309 0.7F
9 W (O)	0222	0505 0.5E
	0749	1103 0.7F
	1406	1732 0.9E
	2055	
10 Th	—	0006 0.8F
	0329	0617 0.6E
	0913	1209 0.6F
	1459	1824 0.8E
	2138	
11 F	—	0101 0.9F
	0431	0726 0.7E
	1036	1316 0.5F
	1553	1916 0.8E
	2221	
12 Sa	—	0153 1.0F
	0527	0830 0.8E
	1154	1420 0.4F
	1648	2006 0.7E
	2302	
13 Su	—	0242 1.1F
	0618	0927 0.8E
	1303	1521 0.4F
	1743	2054 0.7E
	2343	
14 M	—	0329 1.1F
	0705	1019 0.9E
	1404	1616 0.4F
	1836	2141 0.6E
15 Tu	0022	0412 1.1F
	0748	1106 1.0E
	1457	1708 0.4F
	1927	2225 0.6E
16 W	0101	0454 1.2F
	0829	1150 1.0E
	1546	1756 0.4F
	2017	2309 0.5E
17 Th	0139	0534 1.1F
	0908	1232 1.1E
	1630	1841 0.4F
	2107	2351 0.5E
18 F	0217	0614 1.1F
	0946	1312 1.1E
	1712	1926 0.4F
	2156	
19 Sa	—	0034 0.4E
	0256	0653 1.1F
	1024	1352 1.0E
	1751	2009 0.4F
	2245	
20 Su	—	0119 0.4E
	0337	0734 1.0F
	1102	1431 1.0E
	1828	2052 0.4F
	2335	
21 M	—	0205 0.4E
	0424	0816 0.9F
	1141	1511 1.0E
	1902	2134 0.5F
22 Tu	0028	0256 0.4E
	0516	0901 0.8F
	1220	1550 0.9E
	1935	2217 0.5F
23 W	0121	0351 0.4E
	0617	0949 0.7F
	1301	1630 0.9E
	2005	2301 0.6F
24 Th	0216	0451 0.5E
	0727	1042 0.6F
	1341	1710 0.8E
	2035	2345 0.7F
25 F	0310	0553 0.5E
	0845	1139 0.5F
	1423	1751 0.7E
	2105	
26 Sa (O)	—	0030 0.8F
	0404	0657 0.6E
	1008	1239 0.4F
	1507	1834 0.7E
	2138	
27 Su	—	0116 0.9F
	0455	0758 0.7E
	1130	1341 0.3F
	1554	1919 0.6E
	2214	
28 M	—	0203 1.1F
	0546	0856 0.8E
	1244	1443 0.3F
	1645	2007 0.6E
	2254	
29 Tu	—	0251 1.2F
	0635	0950 0.9E
	1348	1541 0.3F
	1740	2057 0.5E
	2339	
30 W	—	0339 1.3F
	0723	1043 1.0E
	1442	1637 0.3F
	1839	2149 0.6E

All times are local time. Daylight Saving Time has been used when needed.

NOTES:

Baltimore Harbor Approach (off Sandy Pt.), Maryland, 2004

F—Flood, Dir. 025° True   E—Ebb, Dir. 190° True

July

Day	Slack h m	Maximum h m	knots
1 Th	0028	0428	1.4F
	0810	1130	1.1E
	1529	1730	0.4F
	1940	2244	0.6E
2 F ○	0120	0518	1.4F
	0856	1217	1.2E
	1611	1821	0.4F
	2041	2340	0.7E
3 Sa	0215	0608	1.3F
	0942	1303	1.2E
	1651	1912	0.5F
	2144		
4 Su		0037	0.7E
	0313	0659	1.3F
	1028	1348	1.2E
	1730	2002	0.6F
	2247		
5 M		0136	0.7E
	0414	0751	1.1F
	1113	1434	1.1E
	1809	2053	0.7F
	2351		
6 Tu		0238	0.6E
	0519	0845	1.0F
	1159	1520	1.1E
	1849	2145	0.8F
7 W	0055	0341	0.6E
	0628	0941	0.8F
	1244	1607	1.0E
	1929	2237	0.9F
8 Th	0159	0447	0.6E
	0742	1040	0.7F
	1331	1655	0.9E
	2011	2331	0.9F
9 F ○	0302	0553	0.6E
	0901	1142	0.5F
	1419	1744	0.8E
	2053		
10 Sa		0024	1.0F
	0402	0700	0.6E
	1022	1246	0.4F
	1511	1835	0.7E
	2136		
11 Su		0117	1.0F
	0458	0803	0.7E
	1140	1352	0.3F
	1606	1927	0.6E
	2220		
12 M		0209	1.1F
	0550	0902	0.8E
	1250	1455	0.3F
	1705	2019	0.6E
	2304		
13 Tu		0258	1.1F
	0638	0955	0.9E
	1350	1553	0.3F
	1804	2110	0.5E
	2348		
14 W		0344	1.1F
	0723	1043	0.9E
	1441	1646	0.3F
	1902	2159	0.5E
15 Th	0031	0428	1.1F
	0804	1127	1.0E
	1525	1734	0.4F
	1956	2246	0.5E
16 F	0114	0511	1.1F
	0844	1208	1.0E
	1604	1819	0.4F
	2047	2331	0.5E
17 Sa ●	0157	0552	1.1F
	0923	1247	1.0E
	1640	1900	0.4F
	2135		
18 Su		0016	0.5E
	0242	0633	1.1F
	1000	1325	1.0E
	1714	1940	0.5F
	2221		
19 M		0101	0.5E
	0328	0713	1.0F
	1037	1401	1.0E
	1744	2018	0.5F
	2307		
20 Tu		0147	0.5E
	0418	0755	0.9F
	1114	1436	1.0E
	1813	2056	0.6F
	2354		
21 W		0236	0.5E
	0512	0838	0.8F
	1150	1511	0.9E
	1840	2134	0.7F
22 Th	0044	0327	0.5E
	0612	0924	0.7F
	1225	1547	0.8E
	1907	2215	0.8F
23 F	0136	0423	0.5E
	0719	1013	0.5F
	1301	1624	0.8E
	1936	2258	0.8F
24 Sa ○	0230	0523	0.6E
	0835	1107	0.4F
	1338	1703	0.7E
	2008	2345	0.9F
25 Su	0326	0627	0.6E
	0958	1208	0.3F
	1419	1748	0.6E
	2046		
26 M		0036	1.0F
	0423	0730	0.7E
		1313	*
	1606		0.6E
	2130		
27 Tu		0129	1.1F
	0518	0832	0.8E
		1419	*
		1934	0.6E
	2221		
28 W		0223	1.2F
	0611	0929	0.9E
		1511	*
		2034	0.6E
	2316		
29 Th		0318	1.2F
	0702	1021	1.0E
	1419	1619	0.3F
	1826	2135	0.6E
30 F	0015	0412	1.3F
	0751	1110	1.1E
	1459	1712	0.4F
	1933	2236	0.7E
31 Sa ○	0116	0505	1.3F
	0838	1155	1.1E
	1537	1802	0.6F
	2036	2335	0.7E

August

Day	Slack h m	Maximum h m	knots
1 Su	0217	0557	1.2F
	0924	1240	1.1E
	1613	1850	0.7F
	2136		
2 M		0032	0.7E
	0317	0648	1.1F
	1007	1323	1.1E
	1649	1937	0.8F
	2234		
3 Tu		0129	0.8E
	0418	0738	1.0F
	1050	1406	1.1E
	1726	2024	0.9F
	2332		
4 W		0225	0.8E
	0520	0829	0.9F
	1133	1448	1.0E
	1804	2112	0.9F
5 Th	0029	0323	0.7E
	0624	0921	0.7F
	1215	1532	0.9E
	1844	2201	1.0F
6 F	0127	0422	0.7E
	0732	1015	0.6F
	1258	1617	0.8E
	1924	2252	1.0F
7 Sa ○	0225	0524	0.7E
	0844	1114	0.4F
	1345	1705	0.7E
	2007	2344	1.0F
8 Su	0324	0627	0.7E
	1001	1217	0.3F
	1436	1757	0.6E
	2052		
9 M		0038	1.0F
	0421	0731	0.7E
	1117	1323	0.3F
	1534	1851	0.5E
	2140		
10 Tu		0132	1.0F
	0515	0830	0.8E
	1224	1428	0.3F
	1639	1948	0.5E
	2229		
11 W		0225	1.0F
	0605	0925	0.8E
	1321	1528	0.3F
	1744	2044	0.5E
	2320		
12 Th		0316	1.0F
	0652	1014	0.9E
	1407	1620	0.3F
	1844	2138	0.5E
13 F	0010	0403	1.0F
	0735	1057	0.9E
	1447	1706	0.4F
	1938	2227	0.5E
14 Sa	0100	0448	1.0F
	0816	1138	1.0E
	1522	1748	0.5F
	2026	2314	0.5E
15 Su ●	0149	0531	1.1F
	0856	1215	1.0E
	1553	1826	0.6F
	2110	2359	0.6E
16 M	0237	0612	1.0F
	0933	1250	1.0E
	1622	1902	0.6F
	2153		
17 Tu		0044	0.6E
	0327	0654	0.9F
	1009	1324	0.9E
	1648	1937	0.7F
	2235		
18 W		0129	0.7E
	0418	0735	0.9F
	1044	1357	0.9E
	1714	2013	0.8F
	2320		
19 Th		0215	0.7E
	0512	0817	0.7F
	1118	1430	0.8E
	1740	2050	0.8F
20 F	0007	0304	0.7E
	0611	0901	0.6F
	1151	1504	0.8E
	1808	2131	0.9F
21 Sa	0057	0357	0.7E
	0715	0950	0.5F
	1226	1541	0.7E
	1840	2215	1.0F
22 Su	0152	0455	0.7E
	0828	1044	0.3F
	1303	1623	0.6E
	1919	2305	1.0F
23 M ○	0249	0558	0.7E
		1145	*
	1713		0.6E
	2005		
24 Tu		0001	1.0F
	0349	0703	0.8E
		1253	*
		1812	0.5E
	2100		
25 W		0101	1.1F
	0449	0806	0.8E
		1401	*
		1919	0.5E
	2202		
26 Th		0202	1.1F
	0546	0904	0.9E
	1257	1504	0.3F
	1718	2027	0.6E
	2310		
27 F		0303	1.1F
	0640	0956	1.0E
	1339	1600	0.4F
	1829	2133	0.6E
28 Sa	0018	0400	1.1F
	0730	1044	1.0E
	1417	1651	0.6F
	1933	2235	0.7E
29 Su ○	0123	0455	1.1F
	0817	1129	1.0E
	1453	1739	0.7F
	2030	2332	0.8E
30 M	0225	0547	1.1F
	0902	1212	1.0E
	1528	1824	0.9F
	2125		
31 Tu		0026	0.9E
	0325	0636	1.0F
	0944	1253	1.0E
	1604	1908	0.9F
	2217		

September

Day	Slack h m	Maximum h m	knots
1 W		0118	0.9E
	0423	0724	0.9F
	1026	1334	0.9E
	1640	1952	1.0F
	2308		
2 Th		0210	0.9E
	0520	0812	0.7F
	1106	1415	0.9E
	1717	2037	1.0F
	2359		
3 F		0302	0.9E
	0619	0901	0.6F
	1147	1457	0.8E
	1756	2123	1.0F
4 Sa	0051	0356	0.8E
	0720	0953	0.5F
	1231	1540	0.7E
	1836	2211	1.0F
5 Su	0144	0452	0.8E
	0826	1049	0.4F
	1318	1628	0.6E
	1920	2302	0.9F
6 M ○	0239	0552	0.7E
	0936	1151	0.3F
	1413	1721	0.5E
	2007	2357	0.8F
7 Tu	0335	0653	0.7E
	1044	1256	0.3F
	1518	1820	0.4E
	2100		
8 W		0054	0.9F
	0431	0752	0.8E
	1145	1401	0.3F
	1627	1923	0.4E
	2158		
9 Th		0151	0.9F
	0524	0847	0.8E
	1236	1458	0.4F
	1732	2023	0.4E
	2257		
10 F		0245	0.9F
	0614	0936	0.8E
	1318	1548	0.4F
	1828	2119	0.5E
	2355		
11 Sa		0336	0.9F
	0700	1019	0.9E
	1354	1631	0.5F
	1917	2210	0.6E
12 Su	0051	0423	0.9F
	0743	1059	0.9E
	1426	1709	0.6F
	2001	2257	0.6E
13 M	0144	0508	0.9F
	0823	1135	0.9E
	1454	1745	0.7F
	2042	2341	0.7E
14 Tu	0236	0551	0.9F
	0901	1209	0.9E
	1521	1820	0.8F
	2123		
15 W		0025	0.8E
	0328	0633	0.8F
	0937	1242	0.9E
	1547	1855	0.9F
	2205		
16 Th		0109	0.8E
	0420	0715	0.7F
	1012	1315	0.8E
	1613	1931	1.0F
	2248		
17 F		0155	0.9E
	0514	0757	0.6F
	1045	1348	0.7E
	1642	2010	1.0F
	2334		
18 Sa		0243	0.9E
	0611	0843	0.5F
	1120	1425	0.7E
	1714	2052	1.1F
19 Su	0024	0335	0.9E
	0713	0932	0.4F
	1158	1506	0.6E
	1753	2139	1.1F
20 M	0117	0431	0.9E
	0820	1028	0.3F
	1244	1554	0.5E
	1839	2232	1.0F
21 Tu	0215	0532	0.8E
	0928	1131	0.3F
	1342	1653	0.5E
	1936	2333	1.0F
22 W	0315	0635	0.8E
	1031	1239	0.3F
	1455	1802	0.5E
	2043		
23 Th		0038	1.0F
	0417	0736	0.8E
	1124	1345	0.4F
	1615	1917	0.5E
	2159		
24 F		0145	0.9F
	0516	0834	0.9E
	1210	1445	0.5F
	1728	2029	0.6E
	2316		
25 Sa		0249	0.9F
	0612	0926	0.9E
	1250	1538	0.6F
	1832	2134	0.7E
26 Su		0349	0.9F
	0703	1014	0.9E
	1328	1627	0.7F
	1929	2233	0.8E
27 M	0134	0444	0.9F
	0751	1058	0.9E
	1405	1712	0.8F
	2021	2326	0.9E
28 Tu	0235	0535	0.8F
	0836	1140	0.9E
	1441	1756	1.0F
	2109		
29 W		0017	1.0E
	0332	0623	0.8F
	0918	1221	0.9E
	1517	1838	1.1F
	2156		
30 Th		0105	1.0E
	0426	0711	0.7F
	0959	1301	0.8E
	1553	1920	1.1F
	2242		

All times are local time. Daylight Saving Time has been used when needed.
* Current weak and variable.

NOTES:

Baltimore Harbor Approach (off Sandy Pt.), Maryland, 2004

F–Flood, Dir. 025° True   E–Ebb, Dir. 190° True

October

Day	Slack h m	Maximum h m	knots
1 F		0153	1.0E
	0520	0756	0.6F
	1041	1341	0.7E
	1630	2002	1.1F
	2328		
2 Sa		0240	0.9E
	0614	0844	0.5F
	1123	1422	0.6E
	1707	2045	1.0F
3 Su	0015	0329	0.9E
	0710	0934	0.4F
	1209	1506	0.5E
	1748	2131	0.9F
4 M	0103	0421	0.8E
	0808	1029	0.4F
	1302	1555	0.5E
	1832	2220	0.9F
5 Tu	0153	0516	0.8E
	0908	1128	0.3F
	1403	1651	0.4E
	1923	2315	0.8F
6 W ○	0247	0612	0.8E
	1006	1231	0.3F
	1511	1754	0.3E
	2022		
7 Th		0013	0.8F
	0341	0709	0.8E
	1058	1330	0.4F
	1618	1900	0.4E
	2129		
8 F		0113	0.7F
	0436	0802	0.8E
	1142	1423	0.5F
	1718	2002	0.4E
	2238		
9 Sa		0211	0.7F
	0527	0850	0.8E
	1220	1509	0.6F
	1808	2059	0.5E
	2343		
10 Su		0305	0.7F
	0616	0933	0.8E
	1253	1550	0.7F
	1853	2150	0.6E
11 M	0044	0355	0.8F
	0701	1012	0.8E
	1323	1632	0.8F
	1935	2237	0.7E
12 Tu	0141	0442	0.7F
	0743	1049	0.8E
	1350	1703	0.9F
	2015	2322	0.9E
13 W ●	0235	0527	0.7F
	0822	1123	0.8E
	1418	1739	1.0F
	2056		
14 Th		0051	0.9E
	0328	0611	0.7F
	0859	1158	0.7E
	1446	1816	1.1F
	2137		
15 F		0051	1.0E
	0421	0657	0.6F
	0935	1233	0.7E
	1517	1854	1.2F
	2221		
16 Sa	0515	0136	1.0E
		0739	0.5F
	1013	1310	0.7E
	1551	1935	1.2F
	2307		
17 Su		0224	1.0E
	0610	0827	0.4F
	1054	1352	0.6E
	1631	2020	1.2F
	2356		
18 M		0315	1.0E
	0707	0919	0.4F
	1142	1440	0.6E
	1717	2110	1.1F
19 Tu	0048	0409	1.0E
	0804	1017	0.4F
	1241	1537	0.5E
	1813	2207	1.0F
20 W ○	0143	0506	0.9E
	0859	1119	0.4F
	1352	1644	0.5E
	1920	2310	0.9F
21 Th	0242	0605	0.9E
	0950	1223	0.5F
	1509	1800	0.5E
	2039		
22 F		0018	0.9F
	0342	0704	0.9E
	1037	1325	0.5F
	1624	1917	0.5E
	2204		
23 Sa		0128	0.8F
	0441	0759	0.8E
	1120	1422	0.7F
	1729	2027	0.7E
	2325		
24 Su		0234	0.7F
	0537	0851	0.8E
	1201	1513	0.9F
	1827	2130	0.8E
25 M	0038	0335	0.7F
	0630	0939	0.8E
	1240	1600	1.0F
	1919	2226	0.9E
26 Tu	0144	0430	0.7F
	0719	1024	0.8E
	1318	1645	1.1F
	2007	2317	1.0E
27 W ○	0243	0521	0.6F
	0805	1107	0.8E
	1355	1727	1.1F
	2052		
28 Th		0005	1.0E
	0337	0609	0.6F
	0850	1148	0.7E
	1432	1809	1.2F
	2135		
29 F		0051	1.0E
	0429	0656	0.5F
	0933	1228	0.6E
	1508	1849	1.1F
30 Sa		0135	1.0E
	0519	0742	0.5F
	1017	1309	0.6E
	1545	1930	1.1F
	2259		
31 Su		0120	1.0E
	0508	0729	0.4F
	1004	1251	0.5E
	1523	1911	1.0F
	2242		

November

Day	Slack h m	Maximum h m	knots
1 M		0205	1.0E
	0558	0818	0.4F
	1055	1336	0.4E
	1603	1955	0.9F
	2325		
2 Tu		0252	0.9E
	0648	0911	0.4F
	1152	1427	0.4E
	1649	2043	0.8F
3 W	0011	0341	0.9E
	0737	1005	0.4F
	1255	1524	0.3E
	1743	2135	0.8F
4 Th ○	0100	0432	0.8E
	0823	1101	0.4F
	1400	1628	0.3E
	1849	2233	0.7F
5 F	0151	0523	0.8E
	0906	1154	0.5F
	1501	1734	0.3E
	2003	2333	0.6F
6 Sa	0243	0612	0.8E
	0944	1242	0.6F
	1555	1837	0.4E
	2119		
7 Su		0033	0.6F
	0335	0658	0.8E
	1018	1326	0.7F
	1642	1934	0.6E
	2231		
8 M		0130	0.6F
	0424	0741	0.7E
	1049	1406	0.8F
	1725	2026	0.7E
	2337		
9 Tu		0224	0.6F
	0511	0821	0.7E
	1119	1445	0.9F
	1807	2115	0.8E
10 W	0038	0314	0.5F
	0554	0859	0.7E
	1149	1523	1.1F
	1849	2201	0.9E
11 Th	0135	0402	0.5F
	0636	0937	0.7E
	1220	1601	1.2F
	1931	2247	1.0E
12 F ●	0229	0448	0.5F
	0717	1015	0.7E
	1254	1642	1.3F
	2014	2332	1.1E
13 Sa	0321	0535	0.5F
	0759	1056	0.6E
	1332	1724	1.3F
	2058		
14 Su		0018	1.1E
	0412	0623	0.4F
	0845	1140	0.6E
	1414	1808	1.3F
	2144		
15 M		0106	1.1E
	0501	0713	0.4F
	0936	1229	0.6E
	1502	1857	1.2F
	2232		
16 Tu		0155	1.1E
	0550	0806	0.4F
	1036	1325	0.5E
	1557	1949	1.1F
	2322		
17 W		0246	1.1E
	0637	0903	0.5F
	1144	1429	0.5E
	1701	2047	1.0F
18 Th	0014	0339	1.0E
	0723	1002	0.6F
	1257	1540	0.5E
	1816	2151	0.9F
19 F ○	0108	0433	0.9E
	0807	1101	0.7F
	1410	1656	0.5E
	1940	2258	0.7F
20 Sa	0204	0528	0.9E
	0851	1159	0.8F
	1518	1810	0.6E
	2107		
21 Su		0007	0.6F
	0301	0622	0.8E
	0933	1254	0.9F
	1619	1918	0.7E
	2230		
22 M		0114	0.6F
	0357	0713	0.8E
	1015	1345	1.0F
	1713	2019	0.8E
	2343		
23 Tu		0216	0.5F
	0452	0802	0.7E
	1056	1433	1.1F
	1803	2114	0.9E
24 W	0048	0313	0.5F
	0544	0849	0.7E
	1136	1518	1.2F
	1850	2204	1.0E
25 Th	0146	0405	0.5F
	0634	0934	0.6E
	1214	1601	1.2F
	1933	2251	1.1E
26 F ○	0238	0455	0.4F
	0722	1017	0.6E
	1245	1642	1.2F
	2015	2335	1.1E
27 Sa	0327	0542	0.4F
	0810	1059	0.5E
	1330	1722	1.2F
	2054		
28 Su		0018	1.1E
	0413	0628	0.4F
	0858	1142	0.5E
	1408	1802	1.1F
	2134		
29 M		0059	1.0E
	0457	0714	0.4F
	0949	1226	0.4E
	1448	1843	1.0F
	2213		
30 Tu		0141	1.0E
	0539	0801	0.4F
	1042	1313	0.4E
	1530	1926	0.9F
	2253		

December

Day	Slack h m	Maximum h m	knots
1 W		0224	1.0E
	0620	0848	0.4F
	1138	1404	0.3E
	1619	2011	0.8F
	2335		
2 Th		0307	0.9E
	0659	0936	0.5F
	1237	1500	0.3E
	1716	2101	0.7F
3 F	0018	0351	0.8E
	0736	1024	0.5F
	1335	1601	0.3E
	1824	2155	0.6F
4 Sa	0103	0436	0.8E
	0811	1111	0.6F
	1430	1704	0.4E
	1940	2253	0.5F
5 Su ○	0150	0520	0.8E
	0844	1156	0.7F
	1522	1807	0.5E
	2101		
6 M	0238	0604	0.7E
	0915	1239	0.8F
	1610	1906	0.6E
	2218		
7 Tu		0053	0.6F
	0326	0646	0.7E
	0947	1322	0.9F
	1656	2001	0.7E
	2330		
8 W		0150	0.4F
	0413	0728	0.6E
	1020	1404	1.1F
	1740	2052	0.9E
9 Th	0035	0245	0.4F
	0500	0811	0.6E
	1055	1447	1.1F
	1825	2141	1.0E
10 F	0133	0337	0.3F
	0548	0855	0.6E
	1134	1530	1.3F
	1909	2228	1.1E
11 Sa ●	0225	0427	0.4F
	0637	0941	0.6E
	1216	1613	1.3F
	1954	2314	1.2E
12 Su	0313	0516	0.4F
	0730	1029	0.6E
	1303	1701	1.4F
	2039		
13 M		0000	1.2E
	0357	0606	0.4F
	0826	1121	0.6E
	1354	1749	1.3F
	2124		
14 Tu		0046	1.2E
	0439	0656	0.5F
	0926	1221	0.6E
	1450	1840	1.2F
	2211		
15 W		0133	1.2E
	0520	0741	0.6F
	1031	1317	0.6E
	1551	1933	1.1F
	2258		
16 Th		0221	1.1E
	0601	0842	0.6F
	1138	1422	0.6E
	1700	2030	0.9F
	2346		
17 F		0310	1.0E
	0642	0937	0.7F
	1247	1531	0.6E
	1815	2131	0.8F
18 Sa ○	0035	0400	1.0E
	0724	1032	0.8F
	1355	1643	0.6E
	1938	2236	0.6F
19 Su	0127	0451	0.9E
	0806	1128	0.9F
	1459	1753	0.7E
	2103	2343	0.5F
20 M	0220	0543	0.8E
	0849	1222	1.0F
	1558	1900	0.8E
	2226		
21 Tu		0050	0.4F
	0316	0636	0.7E
	0933	1315	1.1F
	1653	2001	0.8E
	2340		
22 W		0154	0.4F
	0412	0727	0.7E
	1016	1404	1.1F
	1743	2057	0.9E
23 Th	0045	0253	0.4F
	0509	0817	0.6E
	1059	1451	1.2F
	1829	2147	1.0E
24 F	0141	0348	0.4F
	0605	0905	0.6E
	1141	1536	1.2F
	1912	2233	1.0E
25 Sa	0230	0439	0.4F
	0659	0951	0.5E
	1222	1618	1.2F
	1953	2316	1.1E
26 Su ○	0314	0526	0.4F
	0751	1037	0.5E
	1303	1659	1.1F
	2032	2357	1.1E
27 M	0354	0610	0.4F
	0842	1121	0.5E
	1345	1740	1.1F
	2110		
28 Tu		0037	1.1E
	0432	0653	0.4F
	0932	1207	0.5E
	1428	1820	1.0F
	2147		
29 W		0115	1.0E
	0508	0735	0.5F
	1022	1253	0.4E
	1514	1902	0.9F
	2225		
30 Th		0153	1.0E
	0541	0816	0.5F
	1112	1342	0.4E
	1605	1945	0.8F
	2303		
31 F		0231	0.9E
	0613	0858	0.6F
	1204	1435	0.4E
	1702	2032	0.7F
	2341		

NOTES:

Choking

If conscous but choking, give abdominal thrusts until object comes out.

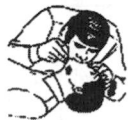

If a person becomes unconsclous: Step 1. Clear object from mouth.

Step 2. Give 2 slow breaths.

If air won't go in, give up to 5 abdominal thrusts.

Other Emergencies

BURNS

FIRST DEGREE: Signs/Symptoms - reddened skin. **Treatment**- Immerse quickly in cold water or apply ice until pain stops.

SECOND DEGREE: Signs/Symptoms - reddened skin. blisters. **Treatment**- (l) Cut away loose clothing. (2) Cover with several layers of cold moist dressings or, if limb is involved, immerse in cold water for relief of pain. (3) Treat for shock.

THIRD DEGREE: Signs/Symptoms -skin destroyed, tissues damaged, charring. **Treatment** -(1) Cut away loose clothing (do not remove clothing adhered to skin). (2) Cover with several layers of sterile, cold, moist dressings for relief of pain and to stop burning action. (3) Treat for shock.

POISONS

Treatment - (1) Dilute by drinking large quantities of water. (2) Induce vomiting except when poison is corrosive or a petroleum product. (3) Call the poison-control center or a doctor.

SHOCK

Shock may accompany any serious injury: blood loss, breathing impairment, heart failure, burns. Shock can kill-treat as soon as possible and continue until medical aid is available.

Signs/symptoms-(1) Shallow breathing. (2) Rapid and weak pulse. (3) Nausea, collapse, vomiting. (4) Shivering. (5) Pale, moist skin. (6) Mental confusion. (7) Drooping eyelids, dilated pupils. **Treatment**- (1) Establish and maintain an open airway. (2) Control bleeding. (3) Keep victim lying down. Exception: Head and chest injuries, heart attack, stroke, sun stroke. If no spine injury, victim may be more comfortable and breathe better in a semi-reclining position. If in doubt, keep the victim flat. Elevate the feet unless injury would be aggravated. Maintain normal body temperature. Place blankets under and over victim.

FROSTBITE

Most frequently frostbitten: toes, fingers, and ears. It is caused by exposure to cold. **Signs/Symptoms**-(1) Skin becomes pale or a grayish-yellow color. (2) Parts feel cold and numb. (3) Frozen parts feel doughy. **Treatment**- (1) Victim should be wrapped in woolen cloth and kept dry. (2) Do not rub, chafe, or manipulate frostbitten parts. (3) Bring victim indoors. (4) Warm the whole body first before warming extremities. Failure to do this may result in heart failure. (5) Place affected parts in warm water - never hot water and make sure water remains warm. Never thaw if the victim has to go back out into the cold, which may cause the affected area to be refrozen. (6) Do not use hot water bottles or a heat lamp, and do not place victim near a hot stove. (7) Do not give victim alchohol, hot coffee or food - use warm broth only. (8) For serious frostbite, seek medical aid for thawing because pain will be intense and tissue damage extensive.

HEAT EXHAUSTION

Signs/Symptoms - (1) Pale and clammy skin. (2) Profuse perspiration. (3) Rapid and shallow breathing. (4) Weakness, dizziness, and headache. **Treatment** - (1) Care for victim as if he or she were in shock. (2) Remove victim to a cool area, do not allow chilling. (3) If body gets too cold, cover victim.

HEAT CRAMPS

Affects people who work or do strenuous exercises in a hot environment. To prevent it, such people should drink large amounts of cool water and add a pinch of salt to each glass of water. **Signs/Symptoms** - (1) Painful muscle cramps in legs and abdomen. (2) Faintness. (3) Profuse perspiration. **Treatment** - (1) Move victim to a cool place. (2) Give victim sips of salted drinking water (one teaspoon of salt to one quart of water). (3) Apply manual pressure to the cramped muscle.

HEAT STROKE

Signs/Symptoms-(1) Face is red and flushed. (2) Victim becomes rapidly unconscious. (3) Skin is hot and dry with no perspiration. **Treatment** -(1) Lay victim down-head and shoulders raised. (2) Reduce the high body temperature as quickly as possible. (3) Appiy cold applications to the body and head. (4) Use ice and fan if available. (5) Watch for signs of shock and treat accordingly. (6) Get medical aid as soon as possible.

NOTE: The almanac is not responsible for actions undertaken by anyone using these first-aid procedures. This Information cannot substitute for a CPR or first-aid course. Contact your local Red Cross to find out about a variety of community programs that teach life-saving skills and safety Information. Sources: "Life-Saving Skills Summary" table and graphics from First Aid First© 1995 by the American Red Cross. "Other Emergencles" courtesy of First Aid, Mining Enforcement and Safety Administration, U.S. Dept. of the Interior.

Life-Saving Skills Summary

SKILL	ADULT (9 years or older	CHILD 1 to 8 years	INFANT birth to 1 year
Rescue breathing (used when victim is not breathing)	Give 1 slow breath about every 5 seconds; about 1½ seconds per breath; 1 minute = about 10 to 12 breaths	Give 1 slow breath about every 3 seconds; about 1½ seconds per breath; 1 minute = about 20 breaths	Give 1 slow breath about every 3 seconds; about 1½ seconds per breath; 1 minute=about 20 breaths
CPR (used if victim is not breathing and does not have a heartbeat)	Depth of compression is about 2 inches; compressions are performed with both hands; complete 15 compressions in about 10 seconds; do cycles of 15 compressions and 2 breaths	Depth of compression is about 1½ inches; compressions are performed with 1 hand; complete 5 compressions in about 3 seconds; do cycles of 5 compressions and 1 breath	Depth of compression is about 1 inch; compressions are performed with 2 fingers; complete 5 compressions in about 3 seconds; do cycles of 5 compressions and 1 breath
Choking (conscious)	Determine if person is choking; stand behind person and deliver abdominal thrusts; repeat until object is expelled or victim loses consciousness	Determine if child is choking; stand or kneel behind child and deliver abdominal thrusts; repeat until object is expelled or child loses consciousness	Determine if infant is choking; give 5 back blows; give 5 chest thrusts; repeat until object is expelled or infant loses consciousness
Choking (unconscious)	Give 2 slow breaths; retilt head and give 2 slow breaths; give up to 5 abdominal thrusts; do finger sweep; give 2 slow breaths; repeat abdominal thrusts, finger sweep, and 2 slow breaths	Give 2 slow breaths; retilt head and give 2 slow breaths; give up to 5 abdominal thrusts; check for object in throat; do finger sweep if object is visible; give 2 slow breaths; repeat abdominal thrusts, foreign-body check/finger sweep, and 2 slow breaths	Give 2 slow breaths; retilt heat and give 2 slow breaths; give 5 back blows; give 5 chest thrusts; check for object in throat; do finger sweep if object is visible; repeat back blows, chest thrusts, foreign-body check/finger sweep and 2 slow breaths

RESCUE BREATHING

1. With head tilted back, pinch nose shut.

2. ADULT: Give 1 slow breath about every 5 seconds

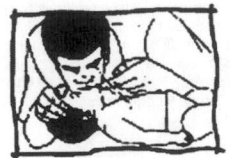

CHILD/INFANT: Give 1 slow breath about every 3 seconds.

CPR (Adult)

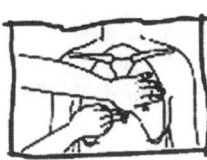

1. Find hand position.

2. Position shoulders over hands. Compress chest 15 times.

3. Give 2 slow breaths. Recheck pulse and breathing. If no pulse, continue sets of 15 compressions and 2 breaths.

cruising guide

LIBERTY LANDING MARINA IN JERSEY CITY. SEE NEW YORK HARBOR SECTION.

The Gateway to the Northeast

USE NOAA CHARTS:

DELAWARE BAY AND RIVER:
(from Cape May to Trenton)
12214, 12304, 12311, 12313, 12314

C & D CANAL:
12311

CHESAPEAKE BAY:
(Headwaters, Eastern Shore to Cambridge, Western Shore to Solomons)
12311, 12274, 12278, 12272, 12270, 12266, 12263, 12264, 12282, 12281

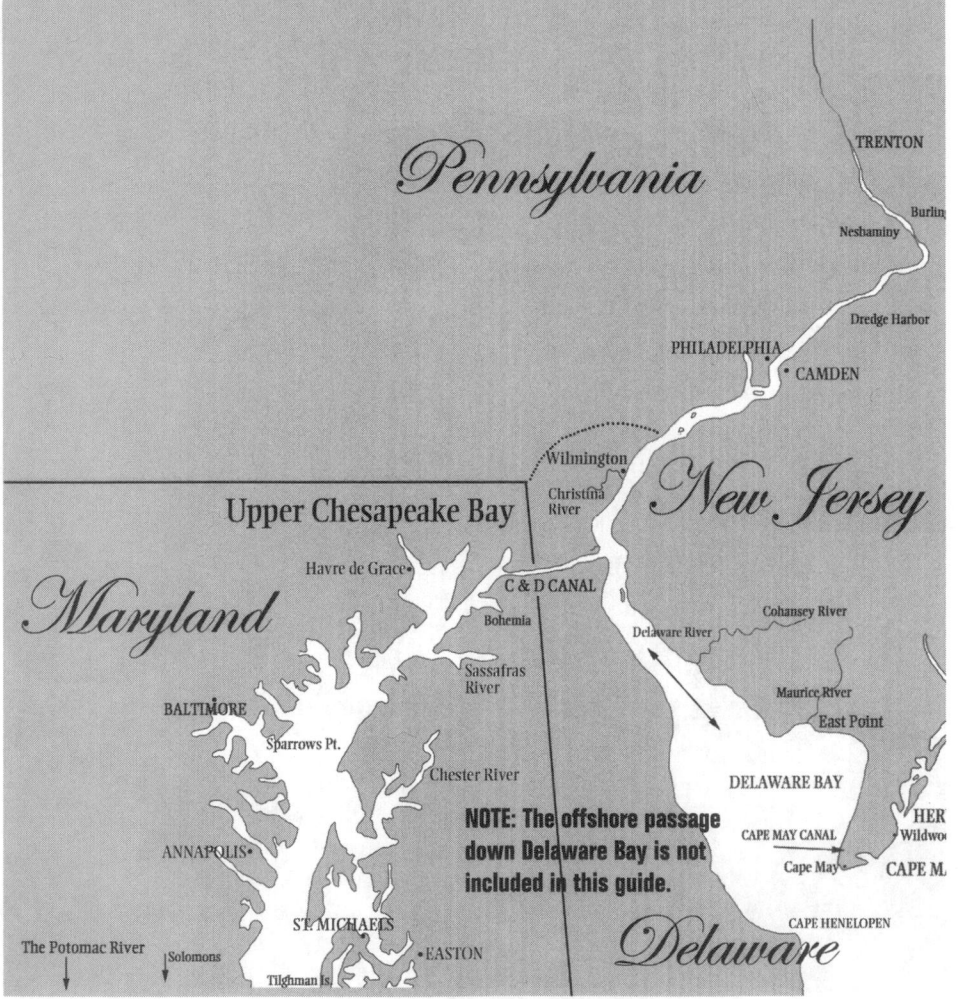

Pennsylvania

TRENTON

Burlin

Neshaminy

Dredge Harbor

PHILADELPHIA

CAMDEN

Wilmington

Christina River

New Jersey

Upper Chesapeake Bay

Havre de Grace

C & D CANAL

Bohemia

Cohansey River

Maryland

Delaware River

Sassafras River

Maurice River

BALTIMORE

East Point

Sparrows Pt.

Chester River

DELAWARE BAY

NOTE: The offshore passage down Delaware Bay is not included in this guide.

CAPE MAY CANAL

HER

Wildwo

ANNAPOLIS

Cape May

CAPE M.

ST. MICHAELS

CAPE HENELOPEN

The Potomac River

Solomons

EASTON

Delaware

Tilghman Is.

Map is not intended for navigational purposes.

The Gateway to the Northeast

MID TO UPPER CHESAPEAKE BAY
THE C & D CANAL
THE DELAWARE RIVER AND BAY
(in MARYLAND, DELAWARE, PENNSYLVANIA and NEW JERSEY)

CHESAPEAKE CITY BRIDGE ON THE C & D CANAL, LOOKING TOWARD THE ENTRANCE TO THE CHESAPEAKE BAY.
Photo by Dave Hawley, U.S. Army Corps of Engineers, Philadelphia District.

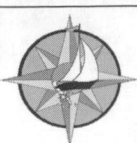

THE FOLLOWING AREAS ARE COVERED IN CHARTS IN THIS SECTION:

STERN OF DELAWARE'S TALL SHIP, BERTHED IN CHRISTINA RIVER

Exploring the Delaware Bay and Delaware River

Cruising the Delaware is as much about discovery today as it was in the 16th century when Henry Hudson dropped anchor at the mouth of the river in 1609. Instinct told him to avoid what he thought to be shoally waters and an estuary unprotected from strong easterlies. Consequently he sailed up the coastline and took his sailing ship to the protected inner harbor of New York. Hudson named the Delaware "South River," and the river coming into New York, the "North River," when laying claim to both bodies of water for his Dutch employers, the Dutch East India Company.

The next explorer to be tempted by the mighty Delaware was Dutchman, Cornelius Mey, who, in the 1620s put his name on the Jersey Cape but went no further. In 1638, Peter Minuit led a discovery expedition up the Delaware, sailing under the Swedish flag, bringing settlers and fancy things to trade with the native Americans. His group landed in a branch river he named "Christina," after the daughter of King Gustavus Adolphus. In exchange for his bounty of trading goods, he acquired title to lands all the way to the Schuylkill River (the name meaning "Hidden Creek") for settlements of both Swedish and Finnish colonists in what is now Wilmington and New Castle.

William Penn, the son of an admiral who served the British Crown, was given a grant of land bordering the Delaware, in payment of a debt owed his father by the reigning royal family. Penn arrived to explore the river aboard his ship "Welcome," in 1682, bringing a group of the religiously persecuted Quakers to build his settlement of "Pennsylvania." He chose a deep water spot along the river banks, just above the Schuylkill River. Within a year, twenty-three shiploads of settlers arrived to help Penn create the new community of 'Philadelphia.'

Starting with the Dutch in the late 1650s, scuffles for home rule took place among the different nationalities. Forts were built that you can visit now, battles were waged, and settlements grew and flourished up and down the river...except for those places where 'wicked mosquitoes' attacked, keeping their territory to themselves to this day.

Ed. Note: When cruising the Delaware Bay and River you'll need your tide and current charts and tables, and every bit of navigational tools you have, ready and waiting. Rivers and creeks are best entered in the first hour of the rising tide. Keep in mind, river entrances tend to shoaling. Docking is best done at slack water. Time everything right and the currents are your friend. You'll also deal with a great deal of commercial shipping, from car carriers to freighters and cargo ships, tugs and barges, and even cruise ships.

The scenery will vary from colorless oil refineries and smokestacks, old shipyards, broken down piers and rusting hulks, to the awesome natural beauty of a tidal estuary with all its glorious wildlife.

FYI
DELAWARE RIVER BRIDGES
in order of appearance heading upriver:

. . . .	MHW
Delaware Memorial	175'
Commodore Barry	181'
Walt Whitman	139'
Ben Franklin	129'
Conrail Lift Bridge	40'
Betsy Ross	129'
Tacony-Palmyra Bascule VHF 13	.53'
Burlington/Bristol DB VHF13	. . .62'

The Delaware is the last free-flowing river in the eastern U.S. It flows without any dams for 330 miles, from Hancock, New York all the way to the Atlantic, touching four states. For birdwatchers, it's one of the four major waterfowl routes in North America. For fishermen it's the place to catch shad,

THE DELAWARE

HOT TIP

Heading North?
Leave the Cape May
Canal at low tide for
favorable currents
going up-river.

striped bass, and river herring. For boaters, it's a challenge worth meeting.

Outstanding eco-touring abounds along the tributaries, just bring along enough weaponry to hold the bugs at bay while cruising in wetlands and marshy areas. Destinations such as **DELAWARE CITY, WILMINGTON, BIVALVE, SALEM**, charming **BURLINGTON CITY**...and the city of **PHILADELPHIA** are among the worthy ports of call.

Scenic rivers such as **the MAURICE,** and the **COHANSEY** offer uncrowded cruising in virtually unspoiled areas, coupled with an exciting sense of discovery. A wealth of America's history sits waiting for you to 'sail' your ship up the Delaware this season. Your seafaring tales will be much more interesting next winter. ⚓

CHARTS 12214 , 2304. ROUNDING THE CAPE: For mariners heading for **DELAWARE BAY,** the **C&D CANAL** or up the **DELAWARE RIVER,** whose vessels can't make the shortcut through the Cape May Canal because of the height (55 ft. clearance) of the fixed bridges in the Canal (See New Jersey Cruising Section), you'll have to go around the Cape. Note two long bars off the Cape, on the chart: Eph Shoal and Prissy Wicks Shoal. The shoals are mixed clay and sand and have the consistency of hardpan. These ridges run in approximately the same direction as the currents. Do not attempt to run the Cape May Channel (one mile southwest of the Cape) between the shoals unless you are armed with local knowledge. Stay well off the shoals to round the Cape. Prissy Wicks Shoal is about 2 miles south of **CAPE MAY LIGHT,** at Cape May Point (38° 55' 59" N, 74° 57' 37" W, 165 ft. above water.)

Heading into Delaware Bay and up the river requires attention at the helm and sharp navigational skills. You're sharing these shoally waters with large commercial shipping. Be prepared to get out of harm's way. Pre-preparing a compass course for your Delaware River/Bay destinations is also a good idea. Your next buoy may not be in sight so setting compass courses from specific waypoints will keep you off the shoals. Nighttime navigation is especially tricky when dealing with commercial shipping, so know your light signals. Is that tug towing or pushing an unlit barge , or is it steaming all alone? Between the tug and what you may not see is an iron-fast towline.

THE JERSEY SIDE SOUTH TO NORTH

If your goal is to run the Delaware Bay to the C&D Canal, you want to skip using the big ship channels, which not only add considerable distance to your route but also takes you through some of the bay's most turbulent waters.

BEST BET: Run a rhumb line between the Cape May Canal entrance and Ship John Shoal Lighthouse, avoiding the Cross-Ledge Lighthouse ruins which are tough to see, and the rip-rap at Brandywine Shoals. Keep a watch for crab pots and oyster stakes.

Oystering and boat building were once the main industries on the Jersey side of the Delaware Bay, and it's said that there were more millionaires per capita in this part of New Jersey than any other part of the U.S at one time.

GIT-ALONG LITTLE CRABBIES...

Want to be a part of a fishy roundup? Forget the Dude Ranch and head on down to King's Crab Ranch on the Maurice River for the annual Crab Herding. It's a hardy wintertime happening for those who want to be on the water no matter what the weather.

From mid-November to mid-April the folks at King's herd the crabs that bed down in winter on the crab ranch bottoms. Learn the art of using the long teeth oyster dredge and scallop dredge as you work alongside the pros. Call King's Crab Ranch and let them know you want to join in the roundup...not a job for city slickers!

King's Crab Ranch wholesales it's harvest to purveyors in Philadelphia, New York, Washington D.C., Chicago and Detroit, but they also have a marina facility with 80 slips and can take vessels up to 40-feet LOA. 856-785-2424. ⚓

If you plan just one stop in the Delaware Bay make it the **MAURICE RIVER** (locals say "Morris"). Boaters who like to bad-mouth New Jersey waters take it all back after discovering the Maurice. Settled by the Swedes in the 1600s, the Maurice River area and its tributaries are now nationally designated as a "Wild and Scenic River." In fact, nesting Bald Eagles hunt the river area from early spring through summer.

CHART12304. MAURICE RIVER COVE is bounded on the northwest by **EGG ISLAND** (approximately 15 NM from the Cape May Canal entrance), and **EAST POINT** Breakwater Harbor (approximately 13 NM from the Cape May Canal entrance). Coming from Cape May, set a course for **DEADMAN SHOAL** (G "105") then straight to RN "2") at the cove's entrance.

A well-marked channel takes you into the river and all the way up to Millville–it's best to do this on a rising tide due to currents and obstructions that may be covered at high tide. **Ed. Note:** A sandbar has reportedly built up southwest of East Point to RN "2."

The **East Point Lighthouse** (C: 1849; operational) at the eastern entrance to the river is easy to see from a distance during the daytime. This landmark is nearing the end of a restoration project and is open certain weekends, in season, for public touring. Do not confuse the lighthouse, which looks like a home with a similar structure nearby that is a private home.

The A.J. Meerwald

Big do-in's in Bivalve:

JUNE 5th & 6th, 2004

DELAWARE BAY DAY FESTIVAL

Fun family festival celebrating the rich history, culture and natural resources of the Delaware Bay. Festival includes Saturday morning parade, followed by multi-ethnic entertainment and food, artisans and craftsman, oyster shucking contest, Blue crab races, free deck tours on A.J. Meerwald and lots more.

JUNE 5th:

LIGHTED BOAT PARADE CRUISE

See the magnificently lighted Meerwald as she parades up and back on the Maurice River. Spectacular fireworks follow the parade.

CHECK OUT THE MEERWALD:

April 9 -24: Philadelphia, PA

April 24 - May 2: Burlington City, NJ

June 23: Washington D.C.

July 29 - Aug. 12: Liberty State Park, Jersey City, NJ

Aug. 15 - 22: Lewes DE

August 24 - Sept. 4 Cape May, NJ

info: 856-785-2060
www.ajmeeerwald.org

Several marinas serve the river in the waterfront towns of **HEISLERVILLE, MATT'S LANDING, BIVALVE, PORT NORRIS, SHELL PILE, LEESBURG, PORT ELIZABETH, AND DORCHESTER,** a shipbuilding mecca for over 200 years. Dorchester has a large working boatyard with slips and a marine railway as does Port Elizabeth, on the **MANUMUSKIN RIVER**, a tributary of the Maurice above Mauricetown..

A fixed bridge (25 ft. cl.) stops larger boats from transiting up to **MILLVILLE** where there is a municipal dock facility. Although the waters up to Millville are not charted, the passage is well-marked and has a controlling MLW depth of 7-ft.

A stop in **PORT NORRIS** is the thing to do. It's a stone's throw from **BIVALVE,** the home port to the **"A.J. Meerwald,"** (C: 1928; LOA: 85ft.) a restored Delaware Bay oyster schooner and officially, New Jersey's tall ship. A mini-museum salutes the oyster industry, and the heritage of the Delaware Bay and its resources. Under the umbrella of the "Bayshore Discovery Project," the Meerwald's mission is both environmental education and the teaching of seamanship skills. Port Norris Marina offers transient slips in this area.

The Maurice has 20 miles of navigable waters up to **MILLVILLE** where 2004 will see a new marina with transient space, and a new **River Walk** leading to the town's art district and restaurants and shops. A cruise up the tributary, **MANUMUSKIN RIVER,** takes you into fresh water.

> **FYI** From Ben Davis Shoal to Ship John Shoal Light, and on up to Reedy Island, the tides are stronger in the main channel but the seas are rougher on the flats.

THE DELAWARE

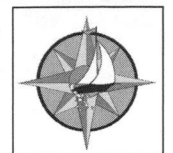

From **MAURICE COVE**, heading up the Delaware, **EGG ISLAND POINT** is marked by a light (39°10.8'N, 75°08.2'W). southwest of the point is **EGG ISLAND FLATS** with depths as low as 3-ft., and oyster bed stakes.

FORTESCUE, lies on the bay, above the Maurice, and is known for crabbing and fishing, with a generous size fleet of party boats, seafood restaurants, and launch ramps for itinerant crabbers. SAILBOATERS BEWARE: there is a 40-ft.

AM I IN THE BAY OR IN THE RIVER?

Q: Where does the Delaware Bay become the Delaware River?

A: 42 NM above the Delaware Capes... or draw a line from Liston Point, DE to the south side of the entrance to Hope Creek, NJ. Above the line? You're in the river.

power cable that crosses the Fortescue Creek about a quarter of a mile in from the entrance. The entrance can be tricky so take it slow. Once inside, the channel is well-marked. Depths range from 4-to 5-ft MLW at the entrance. In season, a Coast Guard Search and Rescue station is berthed here. Fuel and supplies are available in facilities near the bridge. **Ed. Note:** Here's a Fish Tale: Locals in Fortescue say it's the weakfish capital of the world. Believe it or not.

NANTUXENT CREEK, on the north side of Nantuxent Point, can be navigated for about 5 NM at high water to a small craft facility at **MONEY ISLAND.**

Next stop: **COHANSEY RIVER** and the quaint 18th c. village of **GREENWICH.** Take a straight 2.2 NM run north from **SHIP JOHN SHOAL LIGHT** to the Cohansey. The octagonal reddish-brown screwpile lighthouse, named "Ship John," was first lit in 1879 and is still operational in automated mode. It was named for a Massachusetts-built vessel, "Ship John," bringing household cargo and passengers from Hamburg, Germany to Philadelphia in 1797. The ship grounded in a winter storm and there it remained, icebound and accumulating drifting sand, creating a much larger shoal. The lighthouse is surrounded by rip-rap for protection. The light flashes white on the channel side and red on the shoal side. Fog horns emit a blast every 20 seconds when in use. Ship John Light looks like a floating Victorian cottage with its copper Mansard roof and multi-paned windows. It was a charming cast iron and concrete home for the lighthouse keeper!

There are two entrances to the **COHANSEY**. Choose the dredged cut to the north instead of the natural entrance through **COHANSEY COVE**. The preferred entrance has a 42-ft. tower with a white daymark (39°22.8'N, 75°24.2'W) on the island at the entrance. The river's controlling depth is 10-ft. all the way to Greenwich. When approaching Cohansey Cove from, or heading up river, take particular care. **DUNKS BAR SHOAL** has been slowly creeping in on the bay so stay well off RN "10."

Emergency anchorage is available behind the island made by the cut. Holding ground is iffy and currents are strong during the ebb and flood so use plenty of anchor rode. Well-protected anchorage can be found upstream around the first bend in the river. The river is unspoiled and pristine in its natural beauty. Look for bald eagles and other raptors flying overhead. Three miles upriver from the entrance is the historic town of Greenwich.

Approaching town you'll see Hancock's Harbor Marina to port or choose to continue ahead to Greenwich Boat Works. Docking is difficult here due to rapid currents at ebb and flood, (help will appear from the docks) but it's a piece of cake in slack water. You'll need to call ahead to make a reservation since space is at a premium. You can walk to town from either marina. Greenwich Boat Works is closest. Walking about the village is for admiring quaint, well-kept, 18th and 19th century homes, but no shopping. Some provisions and supplies are available at Greenwich Boat Works, and the Bait Box Restaurant (near Hancock's) serves up hearty fare.

DUCK-IN STORM SHELTERS: CEDAR CREEK is as thick with crab pots as a New England style chowder and only navigable at high tide. Skip it. **BACK CREEK** offers anchorage and is a good storm haven for cruisers. The entrance is well marked and easy, and it's navigable upstream for several miles. Also, **MAD HORSE CREEK** and **STOW CREEK** will look good to you if a storm blows up. Check your charts for shoals at the entrances. Avoid **ALLOWAY CREEK**.

THE DELAWARE

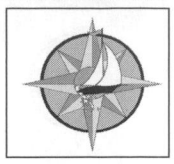

TO FIND MARINA LOCATIONS - SEE THE TABLES AND LOCATOR CHARTS AT THE END OF THIS SECTION.

CHART 12311. ARTIFICIAL ISLAND is an area of fill covering most of Baker Shoal. At the south end of the island you will see the landmark (three) domes of the Salem Nuclear Power Plant. **LOCAL MAGNETIC DISTURBANCE:** *From here to Marcus Hook, differences of about 2° to 5° from normal compass variation have been observed.*

Don't be tempted to take a shortcut to or from the main channel to or from the Artificial Island area. Steel mooring buoys for large ocean-going ships dot the commercial anchorage just northwest of the island, and you may not see one until too late. In fact, it's prudent to check your charts and avoid all commercial anchorage areas in the bay and river.

> **FYI** Call for the area's ultimate guide to birding, **"BIRDING GUIDE TO CUMBERLAND COUNTY, NJ"** From raptors to neotropical songbirds, you'll know what you're seeing when cruising the Maurice and nearby shores. **800-445-4935.**

When you first see the **BATTLESHIP NEW JERSEY,** you are amazed at its sheer size. Nearly three football fields long and over 11 stories high, the Battleship New Jersey was the longest battleship ever built. You will also marvel at its three turrets of three 16-inch guns each, which used to fire a six-foot long projectile with the weight of a Volkswagen Bug 23 miles. Once you enter the Quarterdeck and step on to its teak deck, you realize that this is one incredible vessel.

Built in the Philadelphia Naval Yard and launched on Dec. 7, 1942, you will find it difficult to believe that this ship is over 60-years old. It's Battle Stars, however, tell the well-versed naval aficionado that the "Big J" has seen action – from World War II through the Mid-East conflicts of the mid-1980s.

You don't have to be a Navy Admiral to view the New Jersey, the most decorated ship in US history. Knowledgeable, trained docents, take you through guided tours of the ship.

See the Battleship's newest exhibit, "Keepers of the Sea," a detailed look at the history and design of battleships. This exhibit, co-sponsored by the Battleship New Jersey Historical Society and Lockheed Martin, even features a "Build Your Own Battleship" area for kids!

ADMISSION: Adults - $12.50, Seniors & Veterans w/ID - $8, Children (6 to 11) - $8. Active Military & BB62 Veterans: Free ⚓

CHART 12277, 12311. The **SALEM RIVER** entrance is across the Delaware from the **C&D CANAL** entrance. Enter the river through the marked channel in **SALEM COVE.** No shortcuts please...rocks and dredge spoils fill the waters outside the marker buoys. Again, plan to enter the river on a rising tide. Current velocity here is 1.6 knots...in the land cut it's 3 knots maximum. There are lighted buoys in the channel to the southeast, from the Delaware River all the way to the Salem River marinas. Commercial shipping uses this channel also...barges and freighters. The approach channel follows the southeast side of Salem Cove for about 2 NM to the mouth of the river. Several marinas and boatyards are along the north bend of the river and at Salem itself. Slips, fuel and hull and engine repairs plus supplies are available. Depth is not a problem here and the mean range of tide is 5.6 feet. A walk about this historic village will take you to the town square where you'll see the "Treaty Oak," the spot where 18th C. Dutch and Swedish colonists sealed pacts with the local indian tribes. Stores for shopping and provisioning are easy to reach.

Traveling up-river and just southeast of the **DELAWARE MEMORIAL BRIDGE, PENNSVILLE** has a small marina with a lift and offers minor repairs.

Heading north after passing under the **COMMODORE BARRY BRIDGE**, check your charts for the sandbar moving in on the channel on its southern edge.

CHART 12312. WOODBURY CREEK, directly across from Philadelphia International Airport has the Whitebridge Tavern Marina. Enter the creek from the west-southwest due to a 2 foot shoal at the mouth of the creek. The controlling depth afterward is 6 feet up to the first bridge. Follow local boats if you can.

Commercial shipping ports and designated commercial anchorages line the Jersey side until you reach Camden. Touring the waterfront attractions at Camden will surprise you. **Wiggins Park Marina** is a pretty, park-

THE DELAWARE

like, secure facility for both power and sail – the marina is unusual in its circular-shape. The marina staff monitors VHF 16 and 68 in season.

Ed. Note: The **Riverlink Ferry** to Philadelphia is on site along with the **Thomas Kean Aquarium, the Tweeter Center** where you can see cool, big name concerts like the annual gathering of parrotheads – the Jimmy Buffet concert, and the **Camden Children's Garden**, a four acre creative, interactive garden of different themes, plus a carousel and a train ride. **The USS New Jersey Battleship**, the most decorated battleship in the U.S. Navy, is now a floating museum (856-966-1652). For Camden attractions, marina info and reservations: 856-541-7222.

Don't be tempted to transit or anchor behind **PETTY ISLAND**, to starboard, shoaling from both shores is extensive.

CHART 12314 Heading north about 10 NM from Camden is **DREDGE HARBOR**, a protected 'hurricane hole' with four major marinas. Entry into Dredge Harbor is a challenge so enter on a rising tide at least an hour after low tide, or at high tide. The channel is clearly marked. **Ed. Note:** Riverside Marina is full service and was once the place where Cherubini Yachts were built and commissioned. Today, Independence Trawlers are built here. Dredge Harbor Marina, the largest marina in the area, and very resort-like, has a restaurant, store and pool. You'll also find Clark's Landing Marina and the Winter Sailing Center in the area. A private Yacht Club is available for travelling Yacht Club members at **RIVERSIDE**.

Upriver from Dredge Harbor is **RANCOCAS CREEK** with decent anchorage. Take care not to drop the hook within swinging room of the channel.

BURLINGTON CITY is approximately 7 NM above Dredge Harbor. Curtin's Marina is tucked in behind Burlington Island, with a full service boatyard and a waterfront restaurant. Arriving at slack water is advised. **Ed. Note:** This town has resurrected itself back into 'charming.' The city dates back to 1677 and the historic district offers over 40 sites to visit with or without the audiocassette tour. See the homes of James Fennimore Cooper and 1812 war naval hero, James Lawrence. Free waterfront concerts at Riverfront Promenade Park happen every Thursday evening at 7:30pm in July and August. Also in the park is a 'Jersey Fresh' Farm Market and an authentic period ice cream parlor and outdoor cafe. There's always something going on in Burlington City, call (609) 386-0200 for dates and times of major doings.

TRENTON is the end of the Delaware's navigable waters. Hazardous rocks, covered at high tide, are just past green can "111." Trenton Marine Center offers an in and out rack service for powerboats up to 38 feet but no transient facilities.

Ed Note: BE PREPARED: Above Philadelphia, rapid currents and 8 foot tides combine with freshets that raise the river's water levels even higher. Also, heavy summer rainstorms can play instant havoc with tide heights, raising the levels up to 9 feet above MLW. Check bridge boards and abutments for actual tide heights as you pass.

THE PENNSYLVANIA/DELAWARE SIDE: NORTH TO SOUTH

CHART 12314. Heading downriver from Trenton, at the **Florence Bend** is **TULLYTOWN COVE** , A.K.A. **Warner Cove or PPI Cove**. Locals says it's nice and big, and easy to enter. You can anchor in this protected cove or contact Baum's Cove Marina..

NESHAMINY CREEK has depths of about 7 feet up to the fixed highway bridge (cl. 9 feet) There are several marinas and boatyards with repair services and fuel for small craft. **NESHAMINY STATE PARK** has a small boat basin with a controlling depth of 4 feet. A flashing light on the north side of the basin marks the entrance from the Delaware.

MUD ISLAND, just above Poquessing Creek is partially covered at high water. The channel between the island and the PA mainland has a controlling depth of 7 feet. Anchorage is available in the lower part of the channel. West of Mud Island is **POQUESSING CREEK** with a depth of 10 feet and a pleasant rural anchorage.

THE DELAWARE

Cruising downriver you'll notice the once beautiful riverfront mansions on the west bank, that sit regally on rolling lawns as aging witnesses to another time. **CHART 12313: PHILADELPHIA** is one of the major oil ports in the U.S. in addition to being a landing for for general cargo, sugar and ore. Cruising along the city's waterfront is alternately scenic and heavily industrial. Up until the late 70s, city fathers adhered to the directive that no building could be erected higher than the hat on William Penn's statue above City Hall. Today, skyscrapers of some elegance add to the city's waterfront beauty.

A stop in **PHILADELPHIA** will end up marked as one of your favorites in the ship's log. It's a great destination for a family-oriented cruise. Even the kids will have fun.

Two upscale marinas are available for transients above **PENN'S LANDING**, a city-owned waterfront park. The marinas were created out of old shipping piers and are located on either side of the **BEN FRANKLIN BRIDGE** within an easy walk to both the city's historic district and the up and coming artsy area of **Olde City**, with its boutique restaurants, sidewalk cafés and coffee houses, trendy shops, and avant-garde art galleries.

On the south side of the Ben Franklin Bridge is **Philadelphia Marine Center**, which can be easily accessed at every stage of tide. Red and green traffic lights warn slipholders of approaching traffic in the shipping channel. You'll receive a nice cloth carry bag filled with touring info and facts about the marina's facilities. Sunday mornings are a treat here with complementary coffee and donuts. Other amenities are free pump-out services, and free Satellite TV, along with 24-hour security, telephone hook-up, excellent shower facilities, and a ship's store. Staying for more than three days? You're eligible for the weekly rate! Right on premises is Dave & Buster's, a huge entertainment complex for kids of all ages. Enjoy the various dining areas or play game after game after game–from the most high-tech to those that bring back memories.

On the north side of the Ben Franklin, you'll find **Piers 3 & 5,** two marina locations within the same complex. This is the quieter side of the bridge but equally as convenient to attractions and sight-seeing. On premise is the elegant Ristorante La Veranda, one of the city's notable Italian restaurants.

Both of the Piers marina areas are sandwiched in between pier-built condos whose residents decorate their decks with colorful flowers, which adds a decidedly European ambience to the marina. Personal facilities are quite nice and there are comfortable patios available for relaxing and having get-togethers.

Making reservations well in advance is recommended. Until dredging is completed this year, both of these Philadelphia marinas are limited to the amount of slips available for deeper draft boats.

The Penn's Landing waterfront area itself is the place to go for summer weekends filled with international-style festivals and live musical entertainment, the **Independence Seaport Museum** (don't miss it), several hot nightclubs, and the **"Moshulu,"** the last of the American square-rigged, mercantile sailing vessels. It has been elegantly refurbished to create a fine luxury-liner dining experience. History buffs will want to read the book, "The Last Grain Race," by Eric Newby to discover the past life of this extraordinary ship.

From your slip you can walk to America's historic sites: **Independence Hall**, the new **Liberty Bell** pavilion, the **Betsy Ross House**, **Old Christ Church** (Sit in George Washington's pew!) and **Elfreth's Alley**.

Also, it's a quick walk to three good movie theaters, and the **Independence Visitors' Center**, where free tickets to many local historic sites are given out, and bus excursions to more distant sites are available.

Cruisers who want to visit the renowned **Philadelphia Art Museum** (remember the Rocky movies?), the **Franklin Institute, Museum of Natural History, Chinatown**, or go to **Rittenhouse Square**, the city's elegant shopping and dining area, can just hop on the **Philly Phlash**, a vividly-colored purple tourist jitney that offers an on-off all day pass for $4 (rides are free to over 65 folks). Or take a slow narrated ride about the historic area in a horse-drawn carriage.

THE DELAWARE

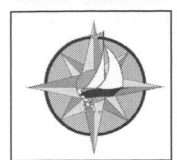

Boaters who want to provision in style can ride the Phlash downtown to the **Reading Terminal Market** which is wall to wall stalls and booths featuring everything from Amish foods like Shoofly Pie, and Scrapple, to Italian specialties like fresh made cannoli. Trendy bakeries offer unusual just-baked breads, and you can bring *real* bagels (and some Philadelphia Cream Cheese) back to the boat! Tables for eating are set up in the middle of the market and most days there's a live piano concert to enjoy while you munch.

A short taxi ride will take you from your marina to the **Italian Market** in South Philly, about a six block square area of fresh produce stalls, butcher shops, cheese shops, bakeries, and homemade pasta shops. Take a couple of 'boat bags' with you to fill up with provisions at rock bottom prices.

Just across the river from Penn's Landing is the **Thomas Kean Aquarium, The Camden Children's Garden, The USS Battleship New Jersey,** and **Wiggins Park** with the **Tweeter Concert Center** – all reachable by the **Riverlink Ferry**. *(See Delaware River New Jersey Side earlier in this section)* Additional in-town docking is located in the municipal marina at Penn's Landing itself, in front of the new Hyatt Hotel.

Heading downriver, you'll pass a pier holding the sadly rusting "**S.S. United States.**" With its canted twin stacks and sleek lines, it still gives off that unmistakeable air of old elegance. Believe it or not, this former luxury liner still holds the transatlantic crossing time record.

Further downriver, the former **Philadelphia Naval Shipyard** can be seen at the junction of the Delaware and Schuylkill Rivers. The yard officially closed in 1955 but a mothball fleet still sits waiting. A major Norwegian shipbuilder now operates a state-of-the-art ship building facility on the upper bank of the mouth of the Schuylkill, and, in season, luxury cruise ships now come and go from the former Navy Yard.

Twelve NM south of Philadelphia's waterfront is **ESSINGTON,** with several marinas for transients. Essington lies below the Philadelphia International Airport runways and is sheltered behind **Little Tinicum Island**. There is anchorage here between the seaplane base and the island. Holding ground is sand in 15 feet of water. Make sure the anchor is is hooked on sand and not snagged on the bottom debris. **Ed. Note:** Monitor VHF 13 and 16 for commercial traffic, as you travel south into the Marcus Hook area where tankers are busy loading and unloading.

PHILADELPHIA MARINE CENTER
We are the finest boating facility on the Delaware River

Three Award Wining waterfront Restaurants on site:
Dave & Buster's
Hibachi of Penn's Landing
Rock Lobster

- We can accommodate vessels up to 150' on a transient or seasonal basis
- We are the only 24/7 self-serve marine fueling facility in the region!
- We give all our seasonl customer free parking, fuel discounts, and more.

WHAT'S TO CONSIDER?
Come join the "PMC Family"
...call us at 215-931-1000,
or visit our website at
www.philamarinecenter.com
The choice is yours. Make it the best!
Make it The Philadelphia Marine Center!

CHART LOCATOR NO. 44

Philadelphia Marine Center
A PROPERTY OF
BRANDYWINE REALTY TRUST

PIER 12 NORTH AT THE BENJAMIN FRANKLIN BRIDGE

THE DELAWARE

CHART 12311: The **CHRISTINA RIVER** is essentially commercial/industrial but it also holds a few surprises. **Ed. Note:** At **BRANDYWINE CREEK**, on the north side of the river, 1.6 miles from the mouth, Up The Creek Marina, Restaurant and Nightclub, can take boats up to 34 feet in length. The marina has a delightful waterfront restaurant and outside dining deck. From here you can hop the River Taxi to **WILMINGTON'S** newest attraction, **The Riverfront, Arts Center, Shipyard Shops** and **BlueRocks Stadium.**

This waterfront complex uses old warehouse buildings blending with new to form a multi-acre attraction housing everything from museums, galleries, theatre, a farm market, restaurants, and upscale outlet shopping. It's all connected by a beautifully designed and landscaped river walk.

CRUISING and BASEBALL?

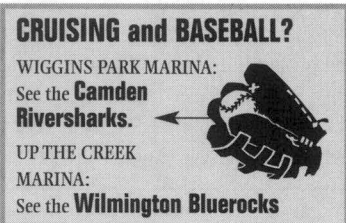

WIGGINS PARK MARINA:
See the **Camden Riversharks.**

UP THE CREEK MARINA:
See the **Wilmington Bluerocks**

Ed. Note: Don't even think of going into **OLD NEW CASTLE**. There are no facilities for boaters and attempting to drop anchor and dinghy ashore is a mistake. Submerged obstructions will cause any mariner serious damage. It is worth a trip by car when boating season's over! ⚓

DELAWARE CITY and the **C&D CANAL** are described in the **C&D Canal Gateway Section**, immediately after the Delaware River section in this guide. Areas below the entrance to the canal are considered part of the outside passage to the Chesapeake Bay and points south, and are currently not covered in this guide.

There are over 35 yacht clubs in the **Delaware River Yachtsman's League,** 29 of them are on the Delaware River and Bay! If your yacht club has reciprocal arrangements with other clubs it's likely you'll be welcome in the clubs of the DRYL. **www.dryl.org**
Members of the Chesapeake Bay Yacht Club Association exchange rights with the DRYL and others. **http://cbyca.org**

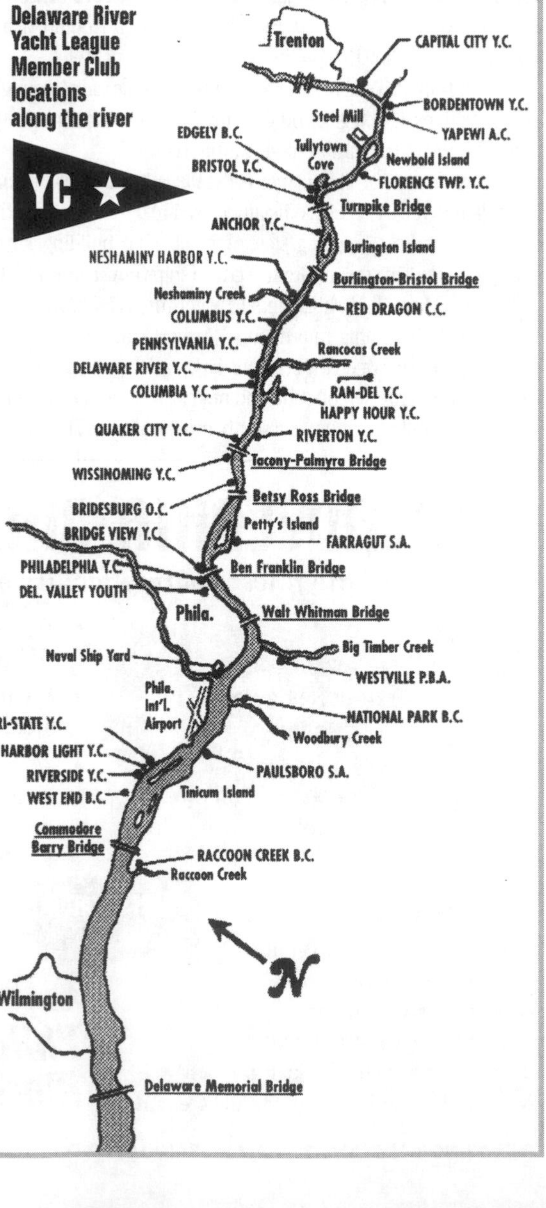

Delaware River Yacht League Member Club locations along the river

YC ★

Trenton — CAPITAL CITY Y.C.
BORDENTOWN Y.C.
Steel Mill
YAPEWI A.C.
EDGELY B.C.
Tullytown
BRISTOL Y.C.   Cove   Newbold Island
FLORENCE TWP. Y.C.
Turnpike Bridge
ANCHOR Y.C.
Burlington Island
NESHAMINY HARBOR Y.C.
Burlington-Bristol Bridge
Neshaminy Creek
COLUMBUS Y.C. — RED DRAGON C.C.
PENNSYLVANIA Y.C.
Rancocas Creek
DELAWARE RIVER Y.C.
COLUMBIA Y.C. — RAN-DEL Y.C.
HAPPY HOUR Y.C.
QUAKER CITY Y.C. — RIVERTON Y.C.
Tacony-Palmyra Bridge
WISSINOMING Y.C.
Betsy Ross Bridge
BRIDESBURG O.C.
Petty's Island
BRIDGE VIEW Y.C.
FARRAGUT S.A.
PHILADELPHIA Y.C.
DEL. VALLEY YOUTH
Ben Franklin Bridge
Phila.
Walt Whitman Bridge
Naval Ship Yard
Big Timber Creek
WESTVILLE P.B.A.
Phila.
Int'l.
TRI-STATE Y.C.   Airport
NATIONAL PARK B.C.
Woodbury Creek
HARBOR LIGHT Y.C.
RIVERSIDE Y.C. — PAULSBORO S.A.
WEST END B.C.
Tinicum Island
Commodore
Barry Bridge
RACCOON CREEK B.C.
Raccoon Creek

Wilmington

Delaware Memorial Bridge

N

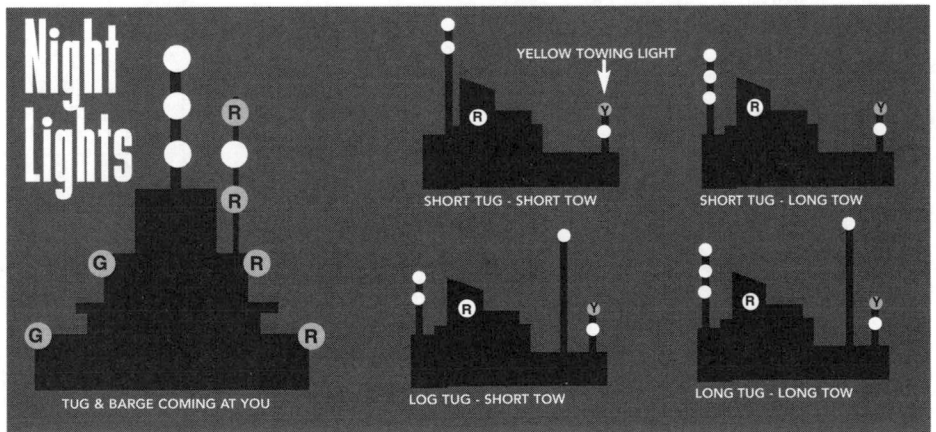

Night Lights

YELLOW TOWING LIGHT

TUG & BARGE COMING AT YOU

SHORT TUG - SHORT TOW

SHORT TUG - LONG TOW

LOG TUG - SHORT TOW

LONG TUG - LONG TOW

Delaware Bay

MARINA'S NAME & PHONE NUMBER

Column categories (diagonal headers, left to right):

- CHART LOCATER NUMBER
- MONITORS VHF CHANNEL
- TRANSIENT Electricity • Moorings • Berths
- Hull repairs • Engine repairs • Ramp
- WINTER STORAGE: Wet • Dry
- RAILWAY CAPACITY IN TONS
- LIFT CAPACITY IN FEET
- BOAT RENTAL: Canoe • Row • Motor
- BOAT RENTAL: Charter • House • Sail
- Restaurant • Lodging • Camping
- Pool • Showers • Laundry
- Bait • Tackle • Water • Ice
- Pumpout • Toilets
- Groceries • Hardware
- Diesel fuel • Gasoline

New Jersey Side

MAURICE RIVER

#	Marina's Name & Phone Number	VHF	Transient (Elec•Moor•Berth)	Repairs (Hull•Eng•Ramp)	Winter (Wet•Dry)	Railway (Tons)	Lift (Feet)	Rental (Canoe•Row•Motor)	Rental (Charter•House•Sail)	Restaurant•Lodging•Camping	Pool•Showers•Laundry	Bait•Tackle•Water•Ice	Pumpout•Toilets	Groceries•Hardware	Diesel•Gas
1	ANCHOR MARINA 856-785-9899			R						R		I W B T	T		G
2	KINGS CRAB RANCH 856-785-2424	70									S	I	T		
3	KINGS WHARF MARINA 856-785-2359														
4	EBB TIDE MARINA 856-785-1273	17 19		R					C			I B	T		G
5	PORT NORRIS MARINA 856-785-1205		E B								S	I	T	G	G D
6	ANDY'S MARINA 856-785-0101			R								I B T	T	H	G
7	COX'S PENNY HILL MARINE 856-785-0100	70	E B	H	D					R	S	I	P T	G	G D
8	DORCHESTER SHIPYARD 856-785-1242	70		H E		150	99+								
9	FOUR STAR MARINA 856-785-1273		E B	R							S	I W B T	T	H	G
10	LONGREACH MARINA 856-785-1818	10	E B	R	D		20			L	S	I W B T	P T	H	G
11	DRIFTWOOD MARINA 856-785-2293									R		I B T	T	H	G D
12	BOATWORLD MARINA 856-785-9875			H E	D		20					B T	T	H	G

COHANSEY RIVER

#	Marina's Name & Phone Number	VHF	Transient (Elec•Moor•Berth)	Repairs (Hull•Eng•Ramp)	Winter (Wet•Dry)	Railway (Tons)	Lift (Feet)	Rental (Canoe•Row•Motor)	Rental (Charter•House•Sail)	Restaurant•Lodging•Camping	Pool•Showers•Laundry	Bait•Tackle•Water•Ice	Pumpout•Toilets	Groceries•Hardware	Diesel•Gas
13	HANCOCKS HARBOR/BAIT BOX RESTAURANT 856-455-2610	16 68	E B	H						R	S	I	T	G	G D
14	GREENWICH MARINE 856-451-7777	16	E B	H E R	D		99+	R		R	S L	I W B T	T	G H	G D
15	SUN DOG MARINA 856-447-3992	16	E B	H	D					R		I	P T	H	G D

SALEM RIVER

#	Marina's Name & Phone Number	VHF	Transient (Elec•Moor•Berth)	Repairs (Hull•Eng•Ramp)	Winter (Wet•Dry)	Railway (Tons)	Lift (Feet)	Rental (Canoe•Row•Motor)	Rental (Charter•House•Sail)	Restaurant•Lodging•Camping	Pool•Showers•Laundry	Bait•Tackle•Water•Ice	Pumpout•Toilets	Groceries•Hardware	Diesel•Gas
16	PENN-SALEM MARINA 856-935-2628	16	E B	H							S L		P T		G D

Delaware River

CHART LOCATER NUMBER	MARINA'S NAME & PHONE NUMBER	MONITORS VHF CHANNEL	TRANSIENT Electricity • Moorings • Berths	Hull repairs • Engine repairs • Ramp	WINTER STORAGE: Wet • Dry	RAILWAY CAPACITY IN FEET	LIFT CAPACITY IN TONS	BOAT RENTAL: Canoe • Row • Motor	BOAT RENTAL: Charter • House • Sail	Restaurant • Lodging • Camping	Pool • Showers • Laundry	Pumpout • Toilets	Bait • Tackle • Water • Ice	Groceries • Hardware	Diesel fuel • Gasoline
17	BARBER'S BASIN 856-935-1261	16	E B	H E			40				S	T			G
	RACCOON CREEK														
18	BRIDGEPORT BOAT YARD 856-467-1976	16	E B	R H			12				S	T			
19	RICHARDS BUTTONWOOD MARINA 856-467-9173	16	E B	R								T			
	WOODBURY CREEK														
20	WHITEBRIDGE TAVERN & MARINA 856-853-9609	16	E B							R	S	T	I		
21	NATIONAL PARK MARINA 856-848-8656	16	B	R											
	BIG TIMBER CREEK														
22	WESTVILLE POWER BOAT ASSN. 856-456-9479			R											
23	WEST CREEK MARINA 856-456-4771														
24	HARGROVE'S MARINA 856-931-4004	16	E B	R H							S	T	I		G D
25	GROMLEY'S GLENVIEW MARINA 856-456-1644	16	E B	H E			20					T	I		
	CAMDEN														
26	WIGGINS PARK MARINA 856-541-7222	16 68	E B							R	S	T	I		
27	PYNE POYNT MARINE 856-966-1352	16		R								T			G D
	DREDGE HARBOR														
28	WINTER'S SAILING CENTER 800-753-4593		E B								S	P T			
29	CLARKS LANDING MARINA 856-461-2700														
30	DREDGE HARBOR MARINA 856-461-1194		E B	H						R	P S	P T	I	G H	G D
31	CASTLE HARBOR MARINA 856-461-1108														

Delaware River

MARINA'S NAME & PHONE NUMBER

Chart Locater Number	Marina's Name & Phone Number	Monitors VHF Channel	Transient: Electricity • Moorings • Berths	Hull repairs • Engine repairs • Ramp	Winter Storage: Wet • Dry	Railway Capacity in Tons	Lift Capacity in Feet	Boat Rental: Canoe • Row • Motor	Boat Rental: Charter • House • Sail	Restaurant • Lodging • Camping	Pool • Showers • Laundry	Pumpout • Toilets	Bait • Tackle • Water • Ice	Groceries • Hardware	Diesel fuel • Gasoline
32	RIVERSIDE MARINA 856-461-1077	16	E B	H E			40			R	S	P T		H G	G D
	RANCOCAS CREEK														
33	LIGHTNING JACKS'S MARINA 856-461-0086			R											G
35	EBLE'S MARINA 856-461-3835			R											
	BURLINGTON CITY														
36	CURTIN MARINA 609-386-4657	16	E B	R			7					T			
	Pennsylvania Side														
	NESHAMINY CREEK														
37	ECKERT'S MARINE 215-788-1757			R								T			
38	SNUG HARBOR MARINA 215-78809155														
39	JACK'S MARINE CENTER 215-785-5213		B	H						R	S	T	I B	G H	G D
40	THREE SEASONS MARINA 215-781-9877	16	B	H							S	T		H	G D
41	ED'S BOAT YARD 215-639-8546		B	R								T			
42	NESHAMINY STATE MARINA 215-639-3548		E B	R							S	T			
	PHILADELPHIA														
43	PENN'S LANDING MARINA 215-452-7524	16	E B									T			
44	**PHILADELPHIA MARINE CENTER 215-931-1000**	16	E B		W					R L	L S	P T	I W	H G	G D
45	**PIERS 3 AND 5 MARINA 215-351-4101**	16 68	E B		W					R L	L S	T	I	G	
	ESSINGTON														
46	ANCHORAGE MARINA 610-521-0660	16	E B								L S	P T	I		G

Chart Locater Number	Marina's Name & Phone Number	Monitors VHF Channel	Transient Electricity • Moorings • Berths	Hull repairs • Engine repairs • Ramp	Winter Storage: Wet • Dry	Railway Capacity in Feet	Boat Rental: Canoe • Row • Motor	Lift Capacity in Tons	Restaurant • Charter • Lodging • House • Sail	Pool • Showers • Camping	Bait • Tackle • Laundry	Pumpout • Toilets	Groceries • Water • Ice	Diesel fuel • Hardware • Gasoline
47	CORINTHIAN YACHT CLUB 610-521-4705		B						R	P S	T			
48	PHILADELPHIA MARINE SERVICE 610-731-1000							20						
49	HARBOR LIGHT MARINA 610-521-9919	16	E B	R				10			T			
50	ISLAND MARINE SERVICE 610-521-9522	16	E B	H					R L	S	T	I		
51	FOX'S GROVE MARINA 610-521-8808	16	E B	R				14			T			
52	ROSSE BOAT YARD 610-521-3155			H		RW								
53	DRIFTWOOD MARINA 610-521-2160	16	E B	R				20						
54	LAGOON MOTEL & MARINA 610-521-1400	16	E B					20	L	S	T			
	WILMINGTON													
55	BRANDYWINE MARINA 302-655-1984		E B								T			
56	UP THE CREEK MARINA & RESTAURANT 302-655-1984	16	E B						R		T			
	DELAWARE CITY MARINA/C&D CANAL SEE NEXT SECTION													

Delaware River & Bay

CAMDEN WATERFRONT, RIVER FERRY AND FERRY DOCK SEEN FROM PENN'S LANDNG ON PHILADELPHIA'S RIVERFRONT.

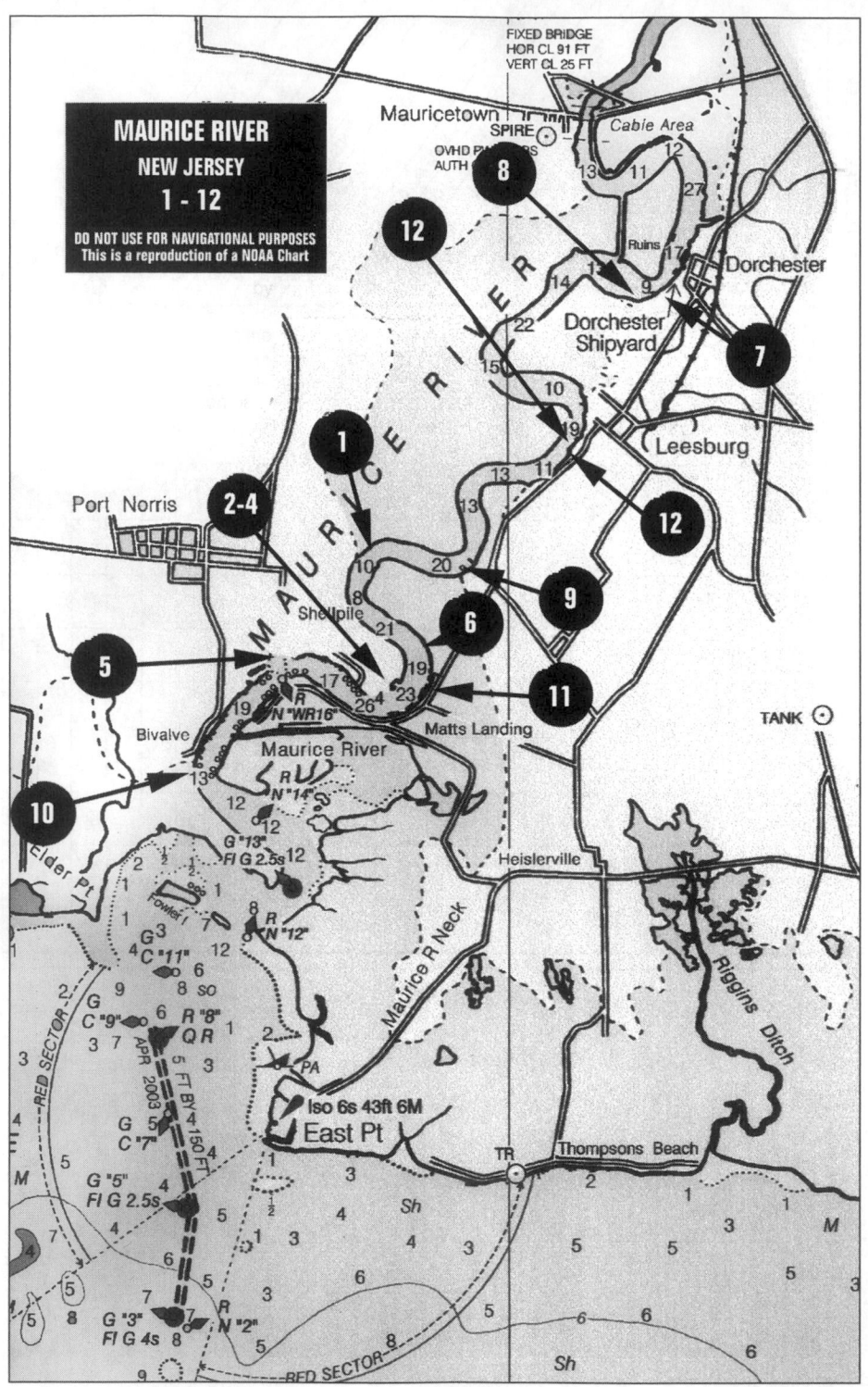

MAURICE RIVER
NEW JERSEY
1 - 12

DO NOT USE FOR NAVIGATIONAL PURPOSES
This is a reproduction of a NOAA Chart

164

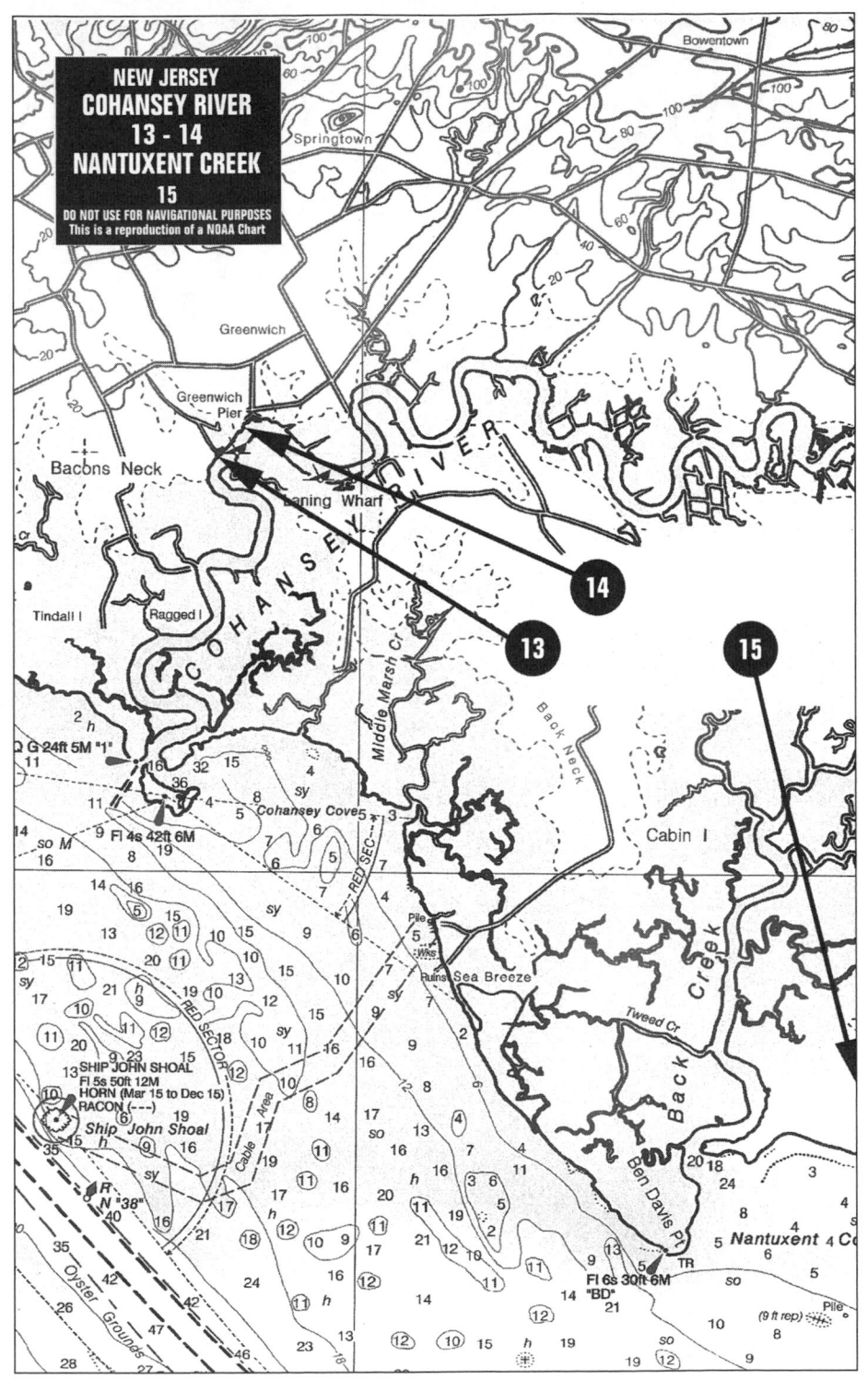

NEW JERSEY
COHANSEY RIVER
13 - 14
NANTUXENT CREEK
15
DO NOT USE FOR NAVIGATIONAL PURPOSES
This is a reproduction of a NOAA Chart

165

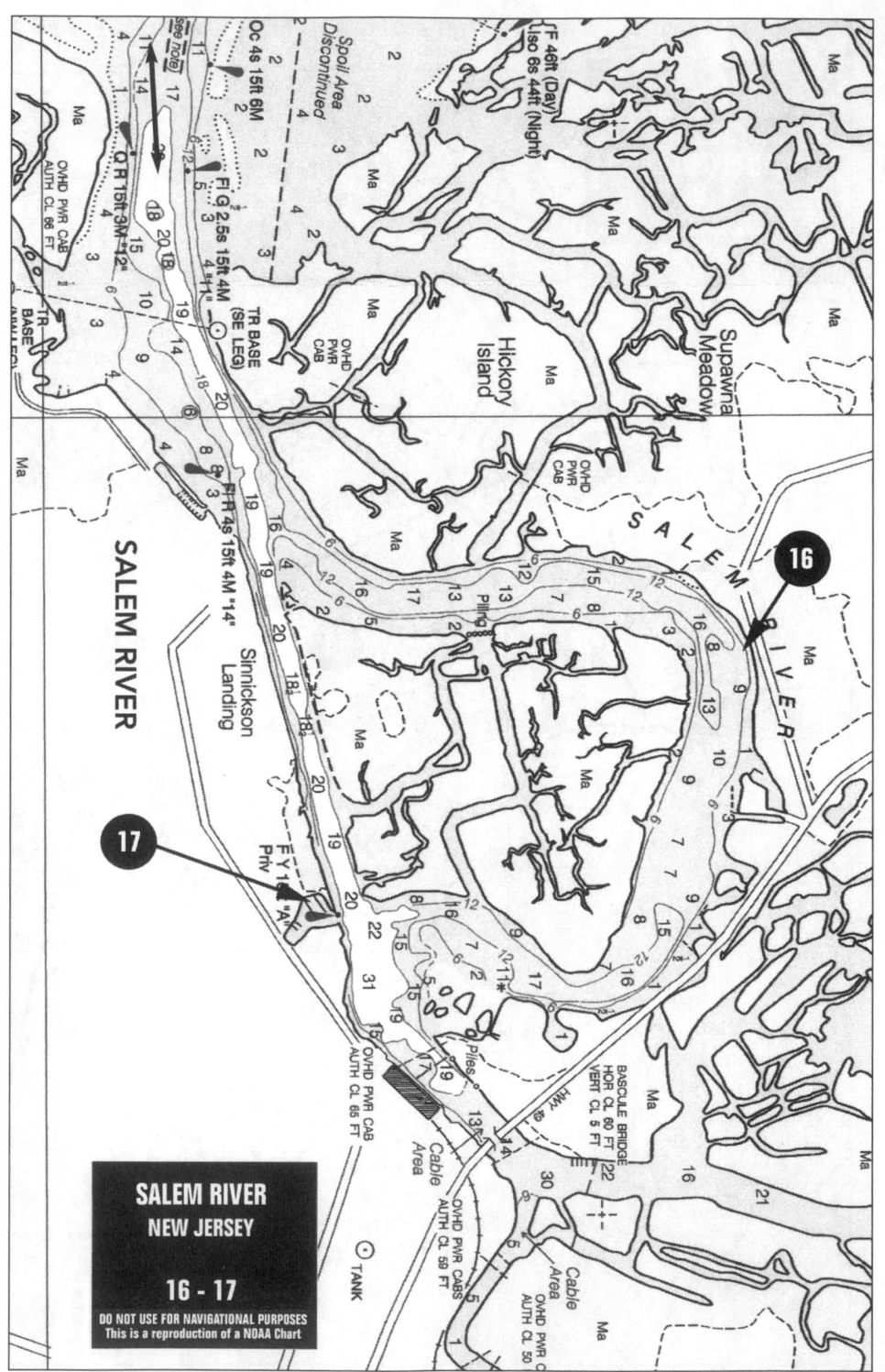

SALEM RIVER
NEW JERSEY
16 - 17

DO NOT USE FOR NAVIGATIONAL PURPOSES
This is a reproduction of a NOAA Chart

166

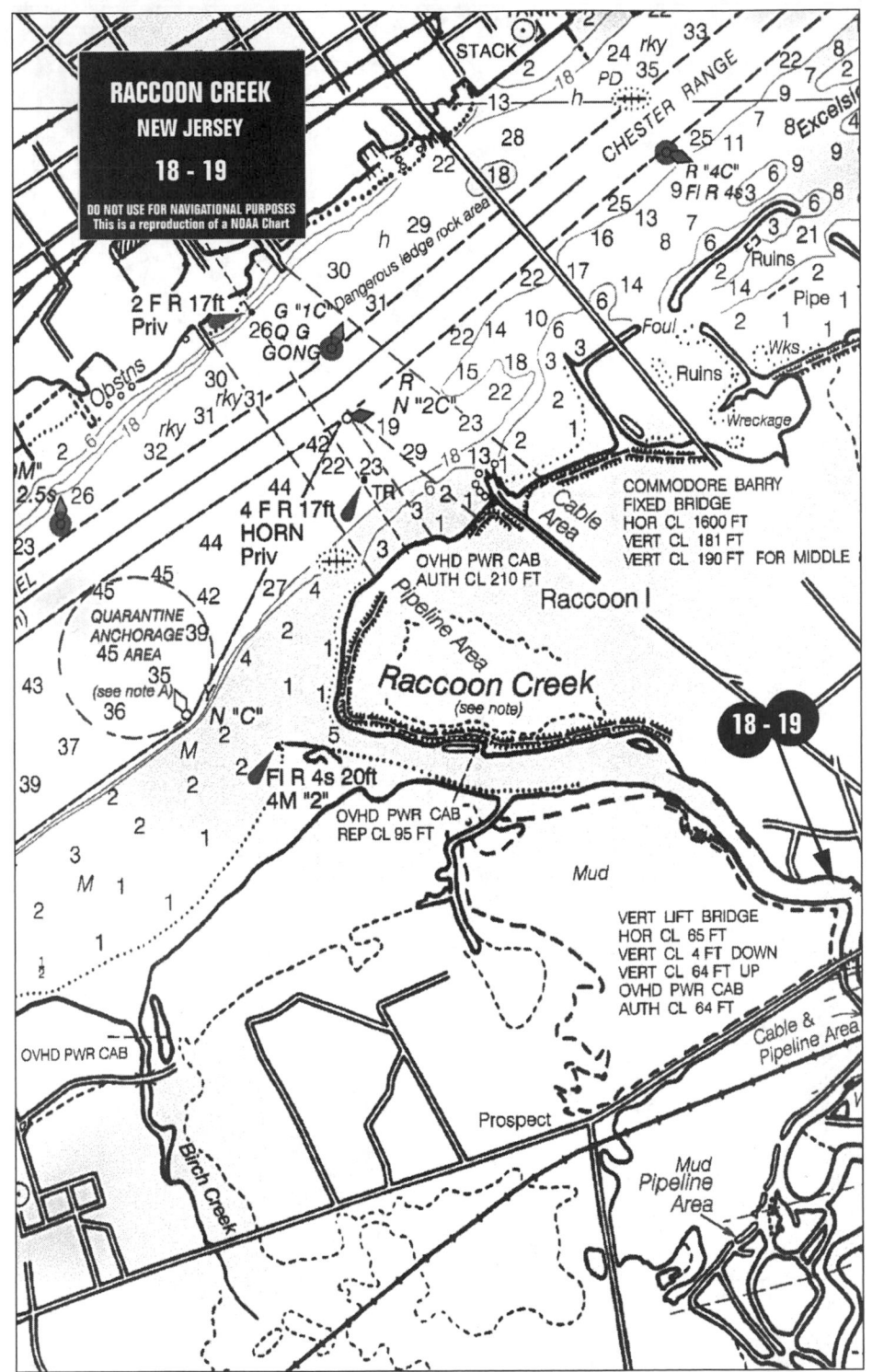

RACCOON CREEK
NEW JERSEY

18 - 19

DO NOT USE FOR NAVIGATIONAL PURPOSES
This is a reproduction of a NOAA Chart

167

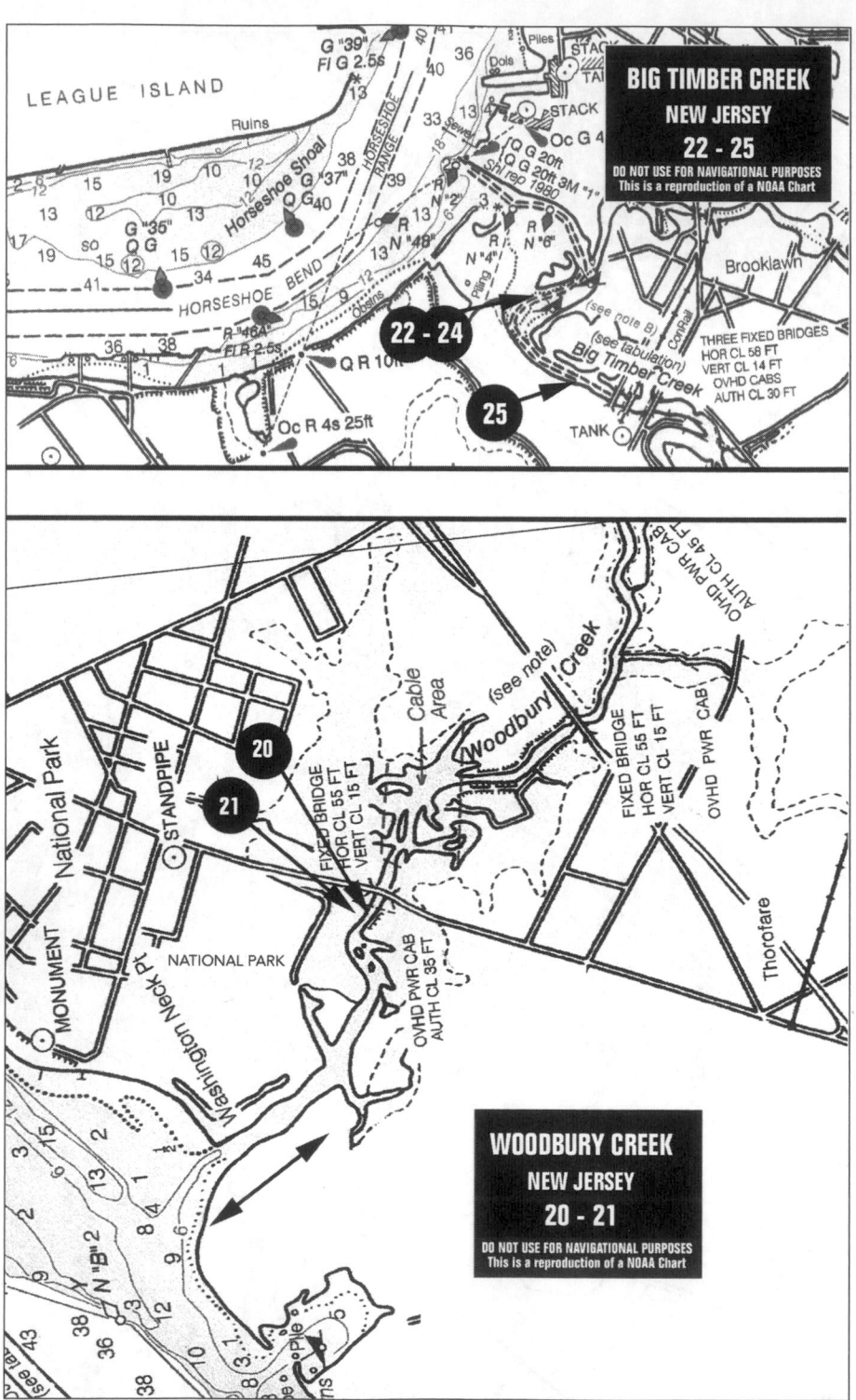

LEAGUE ISLAND

BIG TIMBER CREEK
NEW JERSEY
22 - 25
DO NOT USE FOR NAVIGATIONAL PURPOSES
This is a reproduction of a NOAA Chart

Horseshoe Shoal

HORSESHOE RANGE

HORSESHOE BEND

Brooklawn

Big Timber Creek

THREE FIXED BRIDGES
HOR CL 58 FT
VERT CL 14 FT
OVHD CABS
AUTH CL 30 FT

TANK

22 - 24

25

Woodbury Creek

National Park

STANDPIPE

MONUMENT

Washington Neck Pt.

NATIONAL PARK

FIXED BRIDGE
HOR CL 55 FT
VERT CL 15 FT

OVHD PWR CAB
AUTH CL 35 FT

Cable Area

(see note)

FIXED BRIDGE
HOR CL 55 FT
VERT CL 15 FT

OVHD PWR CAB

OVHD PWR CAB
AUTH CL 45 FT

Thorofare

20

21

WOODBURY CREEK
NEW JERSEY
20 - 21
DO NOT USE FOR NAVIGATIONAL PURPOSES
This is a reproduction of a NOAA Chart

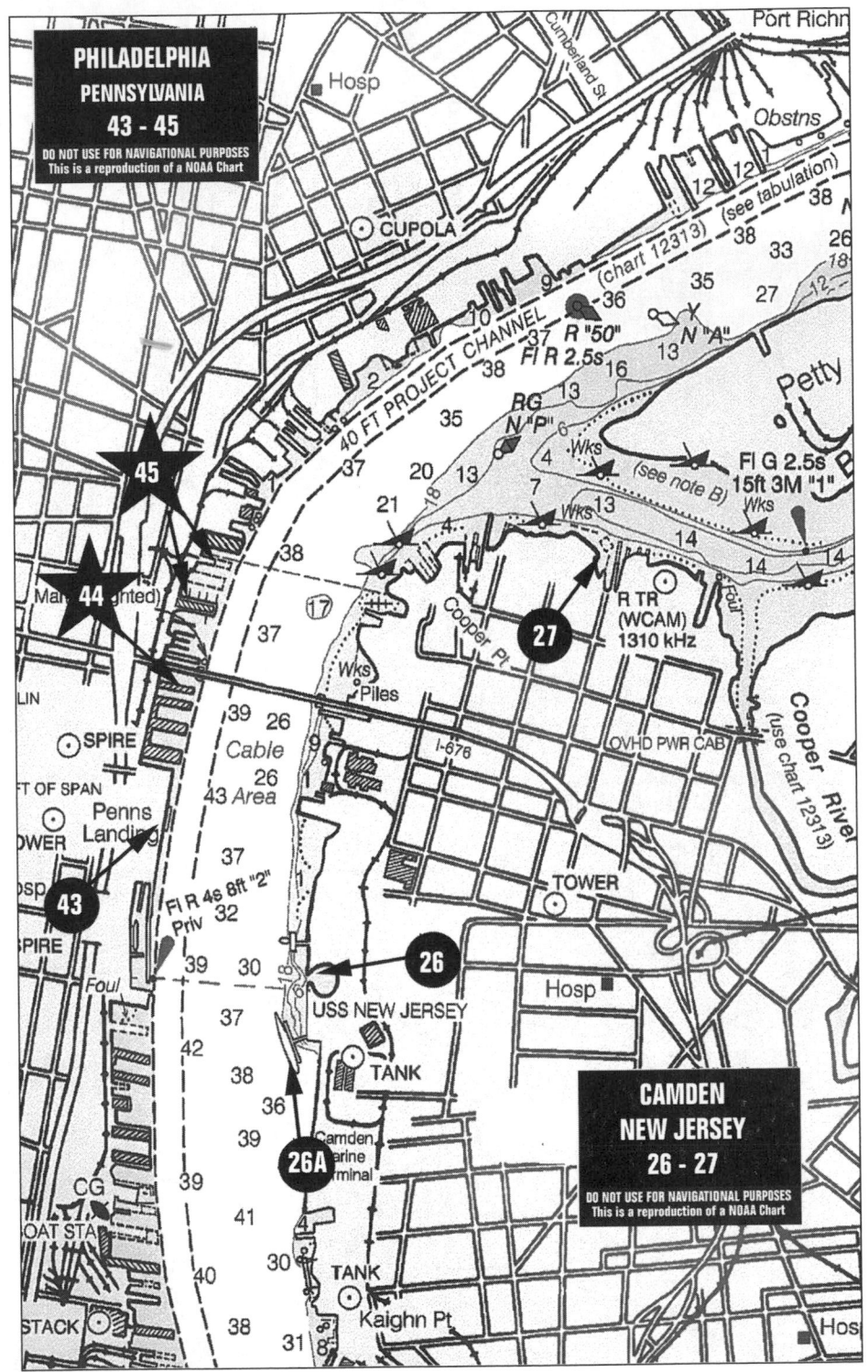

PHILADELPHIA
PENNSYLVANIA
43 - 45
DO NOT USE FOR NAVIGATIONAL PURPOSES
This is a reproduction of a NOAA Chart

CAMDEN
NEW JERSEY
26 - 27
DO NOT USE FOR NAVIGATIONAL PURPOSES
This is a reproduction of a NOAA Chart

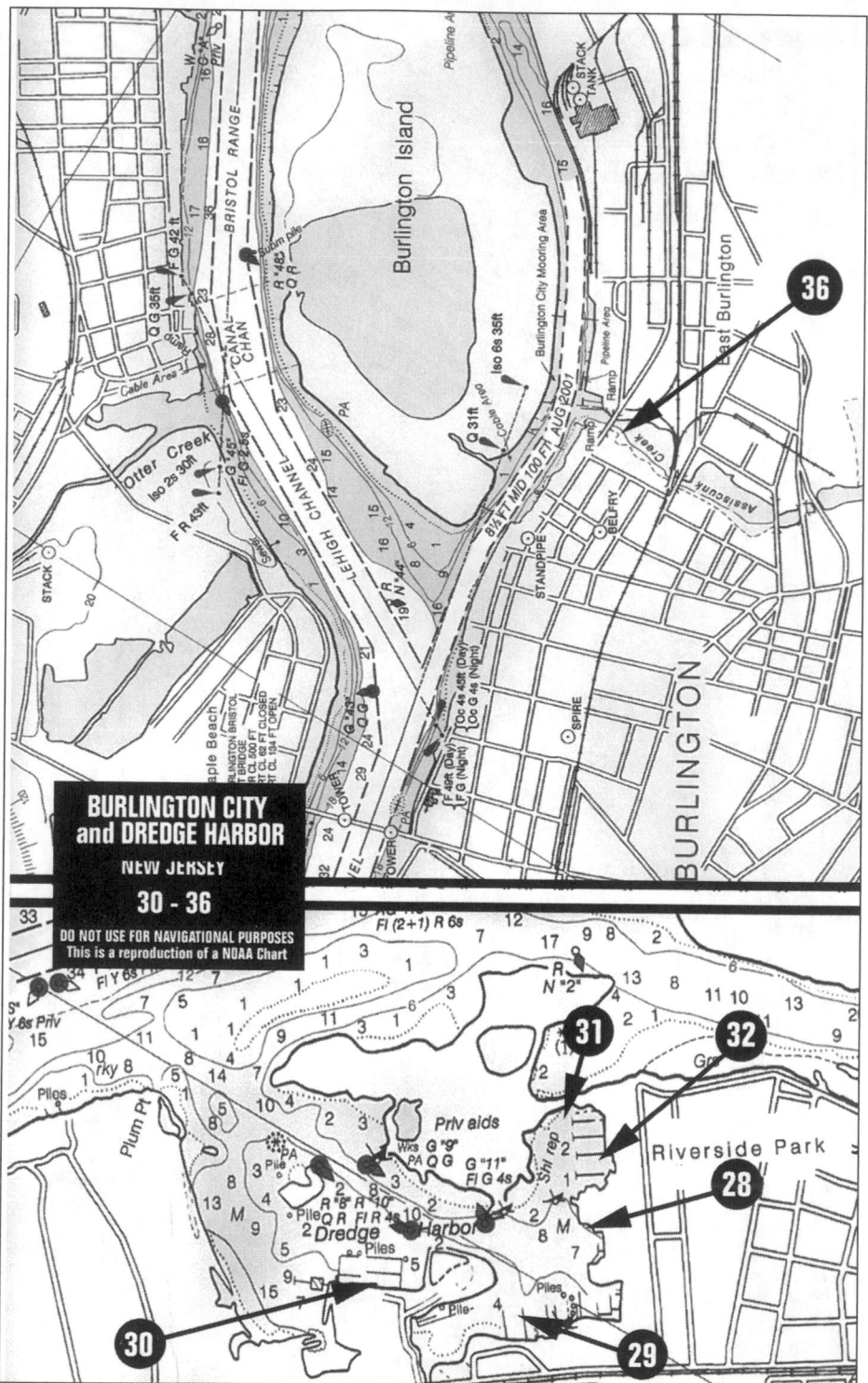

**BURLINGTON CITY
and DREDGE HARBOR**

NEW JERSEY

30 - 36

DO NOT USE FOR NAVIGATIONAL PURPOSES
This is a reproduction of a NOAA Chart

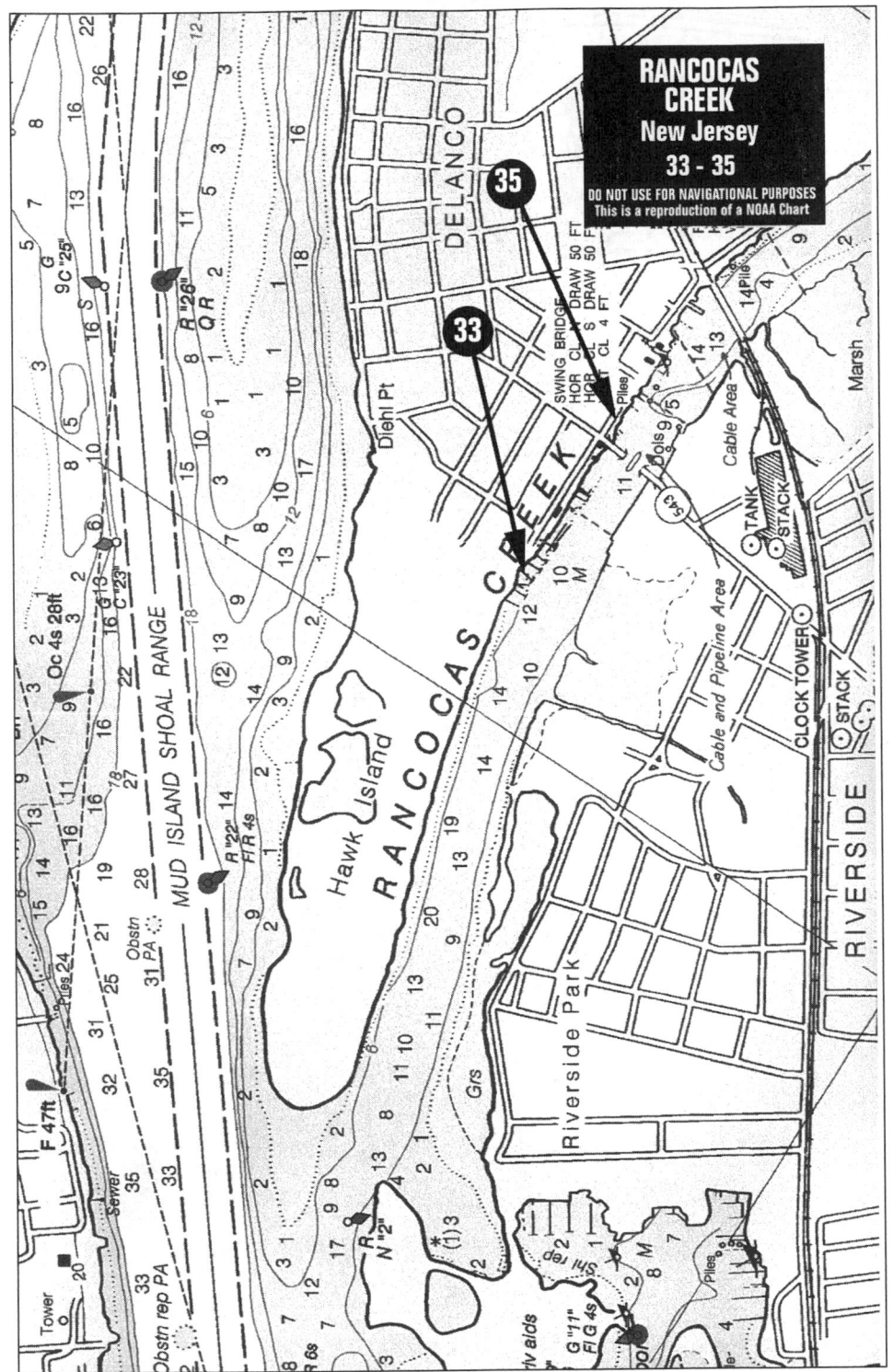

RANCOCAS
CREEK
New Jersey
33 - 35

DO NOT USE FOR NAVIGATIONAL PURPOSES
This is a reproduction of a NOAA Chart

171

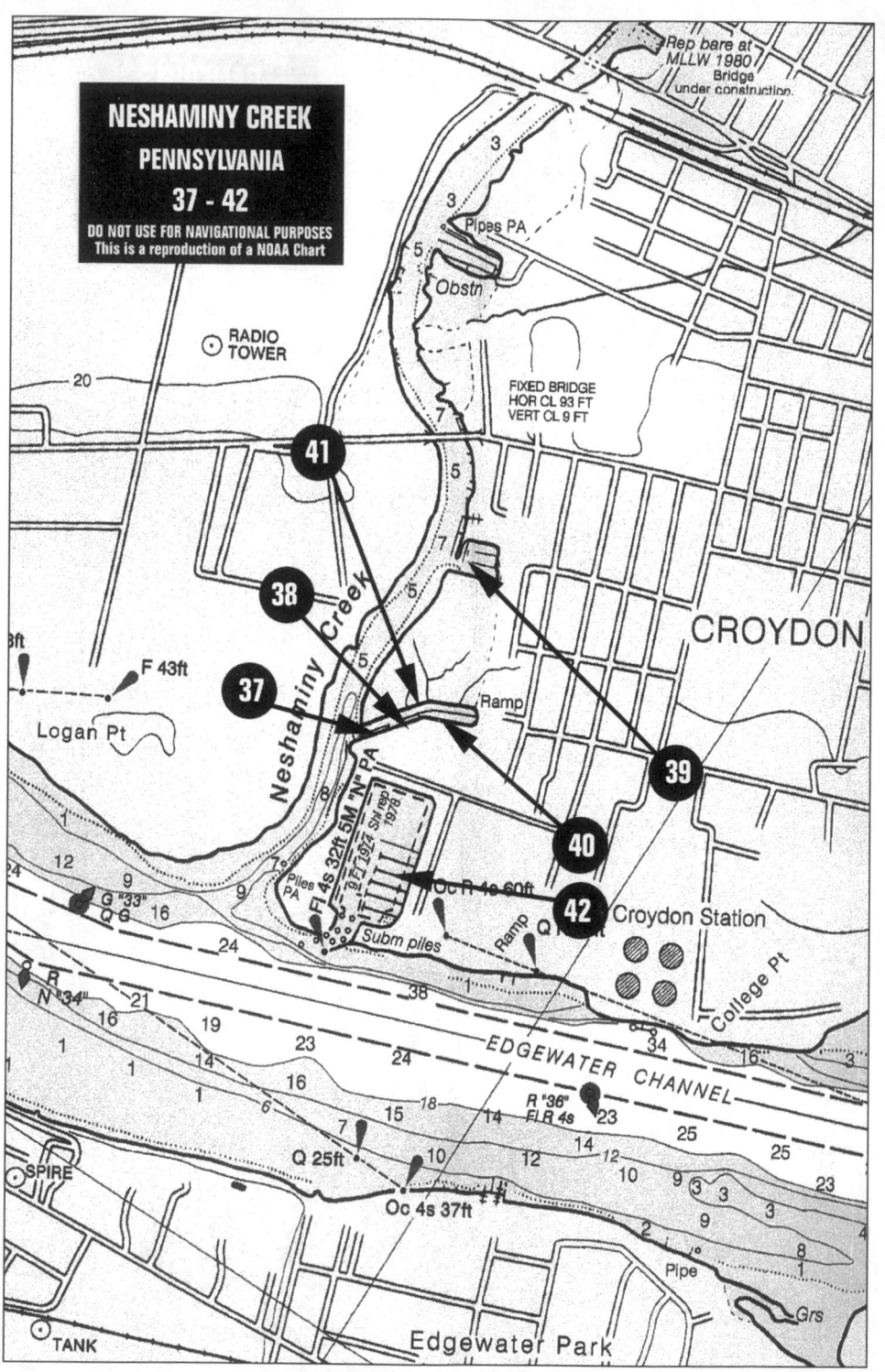

NESHAMINY CREEK
PENNSYLVANIA
37 - 42
DO NOT USE FOR NAVIGATIONAL PURPOSES
This is a reproduction of a NOAA Chart

172

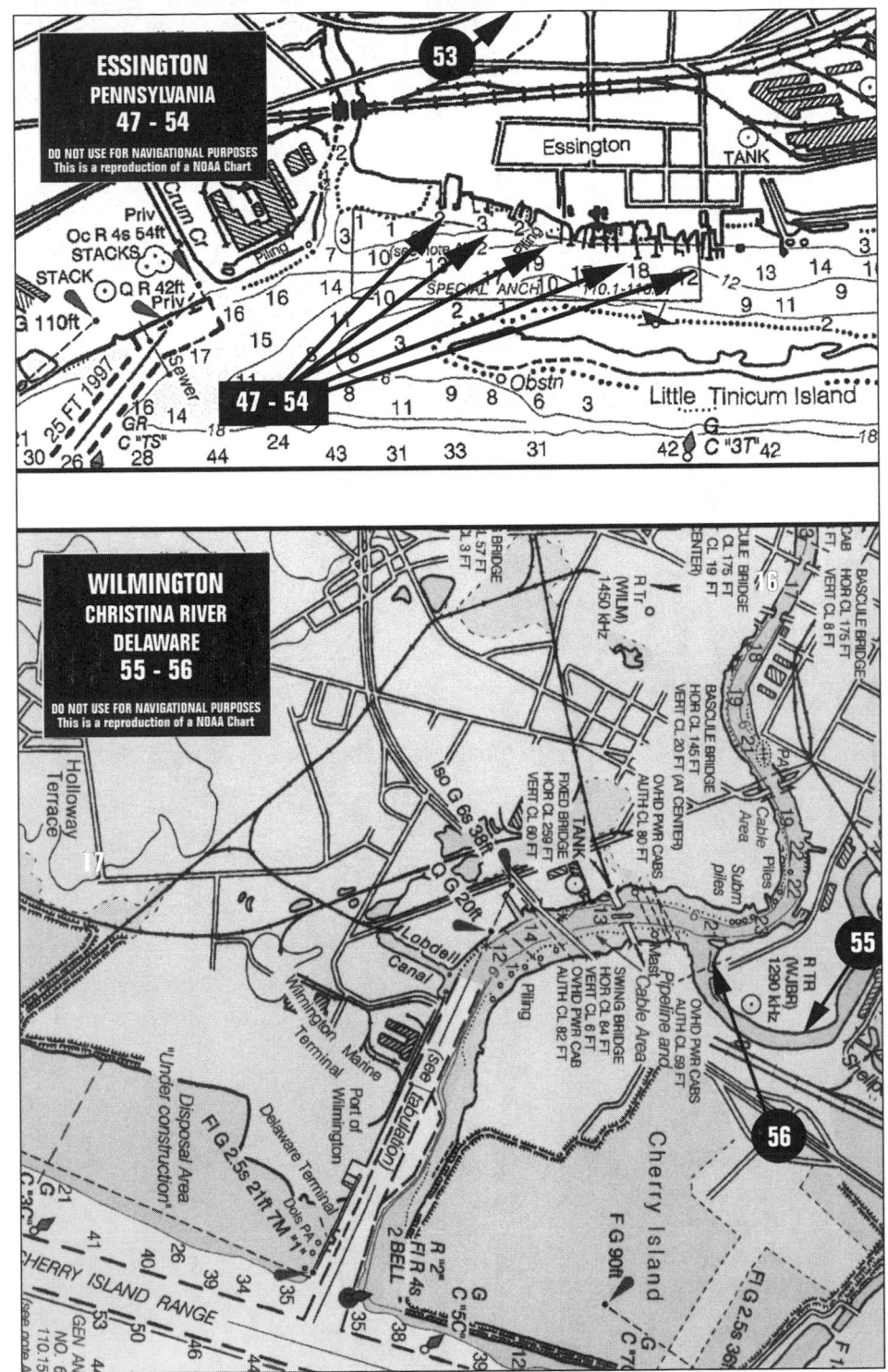

ESSINGTON
PENNSYLVANIA
47 - 54

DO NOT USE FOR NAVIGATIONAL PURPOSES
This is a reproduction of a NOAA Chart

WILMINGTON
CHRISTINA RIVER
DELAWARE
55 - 56

DO NOT USE FOR NAVIGATIONAL PURPOSES
This is a reproduction of a NOAA Chart

173

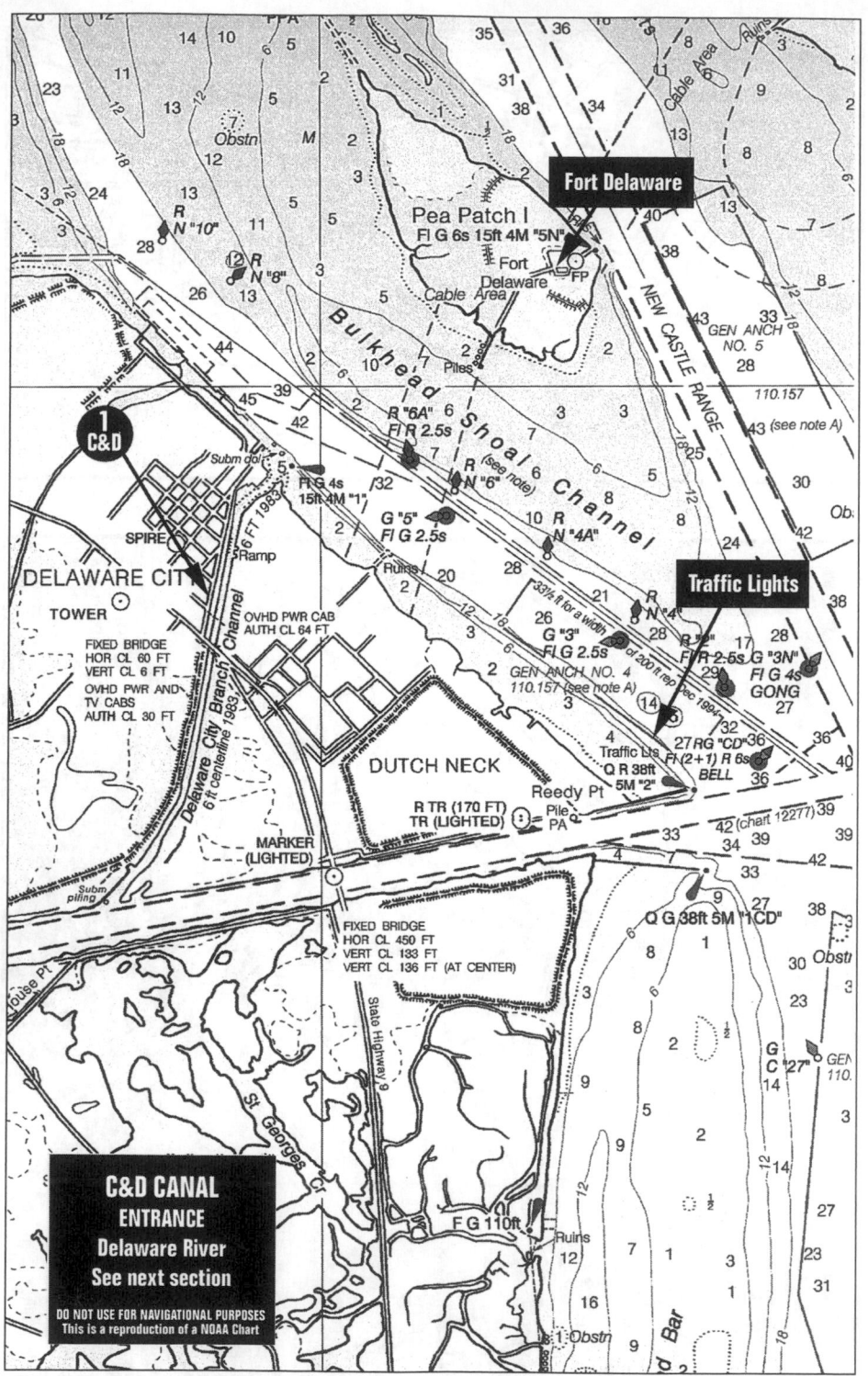

Fort Delaware

Traffic Lights

Pea Patch I
Fl G 6s 15ft 4M "5N"

Fort
Delaware
FP

Cable Area

Piles

NEW CASTLE RANGE

GEN ANCH
NO. 5

110.157

(see note A)

R N "10"

R N "8"

1
C&D

Subm pil

Fl G 4s
15ft 4M "1"

SPIRE

Ramp

DELAWARE CITY

TOWER

FIXED BRIDGE
HOR CL 60 FT
VERT CL 6 FT

OVHD PWR AND
TV CABS
AUTH CL 30 FT

OVHD PWR CAB
AUTH CL 64 FT

R "6A"
Fl R 2.5s

R N "6"
(see note)

G "5"
Fl G 2.5s

R N "4A"

G "3"
Fl R 2.5s

GEN ANCH NO. 4
110.157 (see note A)

R N "4"

R "2"
Fl R 2.5s   G "3N"
Fl G 4s
GONG

RG "CD"
Fl (2+1) R 6s
BELL

Bulkhead Shoal Channel

Delaware City Branch Channel

Ruins

DUTCH NECK

R TR (170 FT)
TR (LIGHTED)

Pile
PA

Reedy Pt

Traffic Lts
Q R 38ft
5M "2"

(chart 12277)

MARKER
(LIGHTED)

Subm
piling

Q G 38ft 5M "1CD"

Obstn

FIXED BRIDGE
HOR CL 450 FT
VERT CL 133 FT
VERT CL 136 FT (AT CENTER)

G
C "27"

GEN
110.

State Highway 9

St Georges Ct

F G 110ft

Ruins

Obstn

d Bar

The C & D Canal DELAWARE and MARYLAND

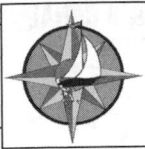

YOU HAVE YOUR CHOICE...take the long, arduous outside route around Cape Charles, Virginia to head up the Chesapeake Bay, or hop a ride on the fast-moving currents of the C&D to the headwaters of the bay.

The 19.1 official miles of the man-made C&D Canal were governed by locks from the early 1800s until the 1920s when the Army Corps of Engineers took over from the canal's private ownership. They improved upon the hand-dug ditch by 1927 and again in the 1940s, creating a 450-foot-wide, 35-foot deep and easy passage to and from industrial ports north and south.

The idea of a shortcut between Baltimore and ports east became a reality in 1802 when the private C&D Canal Company was formed, and over 2,000 men were hired to dig the ditch with picks and shovels. Giant waterwheels, powered by steam engines, filled the 100-foot long locks that gave mule drawn barges and early commercial shipping enough depth to proceed up or down the canal. Today, at the **C&D Canal Museum,** you can see the original wheel that fed the Chesapeake City locks, with all its operating paraphernalia – including one of the largest and oldest steam engines in captivity!

While the C&D is currently the busiest canal in the United States, and the third most-used canal in the world, it remains one of the best kept secrets to the general population. Tugs and barges, freighters, cargo ships, tankers, cruise ships, tall ships, and recreational boaters from around the globe all travel together to ride the 2 to sometimes 5 knot currents that carry traffic to and from the Chesapeake Bay.

Commercial shipping, cruise ships and tall ships come from Baltimore to head for the ports of Wilmington and Philadelphia, or down the Delaware Bay to New York, the Hudson, and the Northeast Atlantic coast. But ask a non-boater about the C & D, and they will mostly say, "Never heard of it."

FYI Seafaring tales tend to grow in magnitude as they are told and retold in boaters' watering holes. And teeth-clenching stories about transiting the C&D can get to be good as any.
If you plan ahead, and approach the canal armed with navigational research and good seamanship skills, your trip should be a pleasure. Remember, you're sharing the water with humongous vessels which have neither the stopping power or the maneuverability of your small craft. Anchoring is only allowed at the basin in Chesapeake City.

IMPORTANT: GO ONLINE TO
http://chartmaker.ncd.noaa.gov/nsd/coastpilot.htm
and download **Chapter 7** which explains all the regulations that govern both you and the big guys while traveling through the canal.

Quaint harbor villages, seemingly untouched by time, inhabit each end of the canal: **DELAWARE CITY,** which fronts on the Delaware Bay, and **CHESAPEAKE CITY,** which sits on both sides of the canal, in Maryland. Each was a major center of commerce and stopping place along the first rendition of the canal, and both suffered economically as the canal was improved and boats became bigger and faster. Today, these pocket-sized towns have come back to life welcoming visitors to artsy boutiques, galleries, antique shops, restaurants, Victorian B&Bs and a wealth of history to discover.

CURRENT FACTS coming from the Delaware:
- The current flows WEST during the first half of an ebbing current in the Delaware River. The current flows EAST during the last half of the ebbing current in the Delaware.
- The current flows EAST in the first half of the flood and it flows WEST in the last half of the flood.
- Current changes time and direction at times of high and low tides at Chesapeake City:
  from low to high tide, the current flows EAST from Chesapeake City, and from high to low tide, the current flows WEST from Chesapeake City.

Navigating the C & D

CHART 12277. Timing your departure just right, you can count on six hours of favorable current when leaving the Cape May Canal on route to the C&D. For sailboaters, that's not near enough, so sooner or later you'll have to buck the current. Ideally, you'll want to start off heading west in the C&D at the beginning of the first half of an ebbing current in the Delaware.

> Transitting the canal under sail between Reedy Point and Welch Point is prohibited, however, motorsailing is allowed.

CURRENT VELOCITY:

2.1 knots on the ebb and 2.6 knots on the flood at Reedy Point.

2 knots in Chesapeake City.

Storms, wind and moon can increase the currents up to 5 knots.

RED AND GREEN TRAFFIC LIGHTS are located at each end of the canal. One set on the north bank at **REEDY POINT** and another at **OLD TOWN POINT WHARF** on Town Point Neck at the Chesapeake Bay entrance. Don't make the mistake of thinking these lights are just for the big ships. Red means "stay out until traffic passes."

Getting ready to enter the canal, make sure your radio is on and monitoring both VHF 16 and 13. The canal is not straight so you need to know what's going on around the bend. Only transmit on VHF 13 if there is a serious problem.

Pay close attention at the helm when entering the canal and passing between the jetties on the Delaware Bay side. Currents can cause you to side-slip off course.

Commercial shipping *always* has the right of way. Big ships heading west are escorted by a Delaware River Pilot up to a point just before Chesapeake City where the transfer of pilot services is turned over to one of the Chesapeake pilots who are headquartered next to Schaefer's Canal House on the north side.

Concerning right of way between recreational vessels: "all vessels proceeding with the current shall have right of way over those proceeding against the current." Yelling "STARBOARD" doesn't work here.

The actual length of the canal itself is approximately 12 miles. It's maintained, and closely monitored and managed by a dispatcher at the Army Corps of Engineers (ACOE) canal headquarters in Chesapeake City. Traffic through the entire canal is visually monitored on a bank of large screens in a glass enclosed room at ACOE headquarters. In fact, the ACOE has a website where you can watch commercial traffic transit the canal in real time. Here, you can also see the canal's log book and find out which ships have recently come through, along with their country of origin, and personal measurements – some of which may totally astound you!

Buoys read " red right" from either entrance and reverse at Chesapeake City. Each bend in the canal is marked with a blinking amber light. Both banks of the canal have poles spaced 250 feet apart with every other pole having a mercury vapor luminary, at a height of 25 feet above mean high water, lighting the banks at night, as another aid to navigation for large shipping.

FYI TIDES:

The mean range of tide is 6 feet at Reedy Point and 2.9 feet at Chesapeake City.

High and low waters in the Delaware River are approximately 2 hours than in the Elk River.

You'll deal with **SIX BRIDGES** in the canal and all but one are fixed bridges with clearances high enough for the cargo ships and car carriers. The bridge clearances listed on the chart are for the center of the canal and that's where the big ships will be. At mile 7.5, is a railroad bridge which is a vertical lift bridge with a vertical clearance of 45 feet MHW when down, and 138 feet MHW when up. This bridge is mostly open.

Cruising the C & D

Chart 12311. DELAWARE CITY is 2 miles northwest of the eastern entrance to the canal. Head up **Bulkhead Shoal Channel** and turn to port on the green turning mark at the mouth of the **Delaware City Branch Channel**. The entrance depth is 7 feet which increases to 10 - 11 feet in the narrow passage. Delaware City was once named Newbold's Landing until 1826 when the new canal

C & D CANAL

brought new business. The Olde Canal Inn, still in operation, was then home to many of the area canal diggers. Today it's a cozy waterfront inn with rooms and suites, a boatman's tavern and a restaurant you might want to try.

The Delaware City Marina is the sole marina, and it sits uniquely on the only remaining portion of the original C&D Canal. This is a perfect place to refuel, provision and start exploring. It's a full service marina with floating docks, and the friendly natives will happily point out sights to see, places to go, and places to shop within walking distance.

Walking the city's streets takes you past restored Federal style homes from the 20s, Italianate 'Peach Houses' from the 1850s and 20th century homes purchased from mail-order catalogs – primarily Sears and Roebuck.

Upon entering the channel into Delaware City, you will have noticed a ferry dock to starboard. From here, the Delaware River Basin Authority runs the **Three Forts Ferry Service** — round trip excursions to **Fort Delaware State Park, Fort Mott State Park (NJ) and Fort DuPont State Park.** You can't visit these places in your own boat, so hop on one of theirs. Fort Delaware, a Union Civil War fortress, on **PEA PATCH ISLAND,** is a treat for Civil War buffs. The site once housed over 30,000 Confederate POWs, and was built to protect the ports of Wilmington and Philadelphia. Authentically-clad interpreters and re-enactors take you back to the summer of 1863.

But that's not all you'll see on **PEA PATCH.** The 3/4 mile nature trail starts at the fort and meanders through the largest nesting colony of herons, egrets and ibis on the East Coast.

Fort Mott was built at **FINN'S POINT** for defense during the Spanish-American War, but before it was built, a cemetery was created there for the graves of over 2,000 Confederate soldiers. Also interred are men who died in the Spanish-American War, WWI, and 13 German POWs. For more info: www.threeforts.com.

Departing **DELAWARE CITY** means you have to go back the way you came. While it looks on the chart as though you can take a shortcut through the old canal to the new, a fixed bridge holds everything at bay except perhaps a dinghy.

When you enter the **C&D,** you'll leave the river's industrial looking scenery behind you as well as the any saltwater ambience of the Atlantic. All of a sudden you're in a rural countryside. The canal itself has three marinas. The first, heading east to west, is Summit North Marina, in Delaware, on the north side. There is also a waterfront restaurant in this protected harbor which was once part of the original canal.

Crossing over into Maryland waters happens just east of **CHESAPEAKE CITY.** Chesapeake City's **SOUTH SIDE** has a blinking amber light indicating a bend in the canal in front of the town's protected anchorage and basin. This is a no-wake area continuing past the bridge.

PELL GARDENS PARK SUMMER CONCERT BANDSTAND, CHESAPEAKE CITY

Time your comings and goings to either side of Chesapeake City with the currents or at slack water. Entering or leaving the **SOUTH SIDE, BACK CREEK BASIN:** be aware there is a shoal in the center of the entrance but plenty of depth if you hug the eastern shore . Currents at the basin entrance can be faster than the reported 2 knots in the canal itself.

The best depths for anchoring are near the eastern and northern banks of the basin in the vicinity of the launch ramp and Army Corps of Engineers canal headquarters . This is the best place for a dinghy landing and not too far from everything.

The Chesapeake Inn, Restaurant and Marina, (410-885-2040) is a fun stop for party people to play on the outside decks with jumping live entertainment and outdoor dining, in season. The formal indoor dining room, and the Veranda, are elegantly nautical, with plenty of waterfront window tables to watch shipping go by in the canal while you dine. Cocktail piano music happens on weekends at the upstairs small bar. Boaters and locals alike have recognized this restaurant as one of the "Best of the Bay."

C & D CANAL

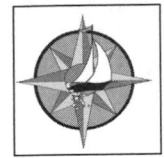

Reserve your slip for the night and take some time to discover the charming historic village of **CHESAPEAKE CITY**. Follow the printed, self-guided Walking Tour Map up and down quaint streets with brick sidewalks, restored homes and public buildings, unique boutiques, art galleries, antique shops and a lovely little park, called **Pell Gardens**. It has an ice cream parlor, picnic tables, and a music pavilion where you can enjoy a free concert on Sundays at twilight in the summertime. Free 24-hour dockage is available at the floating town docks by the park and rafting is permitted. **The C&D Canal Museum** is within an easy walk and worth the visit.

Canal Tour Boats sit at the town docks at the base of the park and will happily take you across the canal to the **CHESAPEAKE CITY'S NORTH SIDE** and **Schaefer's Canal House** (410-885-2200) where they pick up tour passengers also. Schaefer's has long been known as the primary stopping point in the canal for larger yachts and is also the base for the canal pilots who guide commercial shipping through the canal. The restaurant and marina has a fun outdoor canal-front Tiki Bar and Terrace with live entertainment, a sports bar, and a large dining room and lounge with a spectacular view of the canal and the city's other side. The shipping channel runs close to Schaefer's and big ships loom seemingly larger than life right in front your table as you dine. The North Side is completely residential with the exception of Schaefer's Canal House.

There is no fuel available on the South Side but, on the North Side, Schaefer's offers the service starting at 8 a.m. To find out more about Chesapeake City: www.chesapeakecity.com.

Rumor has it that a ferry dock is planned for the 2004 season, near Schaefer's, on the North Side of Chesapeake City, to shuttle folks back and forth across the canal to the South Side.

Leaving Chesapeake City and heading west, you're in **BACK CREEK** headed to the **ELK RIVER** and the headwaters of the **CHESAPEAKE BAY**. ⚓

CHART LOCATOR NO. 5

179

C & D Canal

MARINA'S NAME & PHONE NUMBER

CHART LOCATER NUMBER	MARINA'S NAME & PHONE NUMBER	MONITORS VHF CHANNEL	TRANSIENT Electricity • Moorings • Berths	Hull repairs • Engine repairs • Ramp	WINTER STORAGE: Wet • Dry	RAILWAY CAPACITY: Ramp	BOAT RENTAL: Canoe • Row • Motor	LIFT CAPACITY IN FEET	BOAT RENTAL: Charter • House • Sail	RAILWAY CAPACITY IN TONS	Restaurant • Lodging • Camping	Showers • Laundry • Pool	Bait • Tackle • Water • Ice	Pumpout • Toilets	Groceries • Hardware	Diesel fuel • Gasoline
	C&D CANAL															
1	DELAWARE CITY MARINA 302-834-4172	16	E B	H E	W D			20			R	S L	PT	WI BT	G H	G D
2	SUMMIT NORTH MARINA 302-836-1800	16	E B		W D			50			R	S L P	PT	WI		G D
3	**CHESAPEAKE INN RESTAURANT & MARINA 410-885-2040**	16	E B								R	S	PT	W I		
4 4A	PUBLIC BOAT RAMP & PICNIC AREA, AND C&D CANAL MUSEUM / 4A: PUBLIC DOCKS		E B	R												
5	**THE NEW SCHAEFER'S CANAL HOUSE & MARINA 410-885-2204**	16 9	E B								R L	S	P T	W I	G	G D
6	HARBOR NORTH MARINA / BOAT WAREHOUSE	16	E B	H E									PT	I		G

ROUTE 213 "RAINBOW BRIDGE" LAST BRIDGE BEFORE TOWN POINT

CHESAPEAKE CITY NORTH SIDE

5. SCHAEFFER'S CANAL HOUSE & MARINA

CANAL PILOTS

HISTORIC DISTRICT WALKING TOUR

4A. PUBLIC DOCKS

3. CHESAPEAKE INN RESTAURANT & MARINA

4. CANAL MUSEUM

CHESAPEAKE CITY SOUTH SIDE

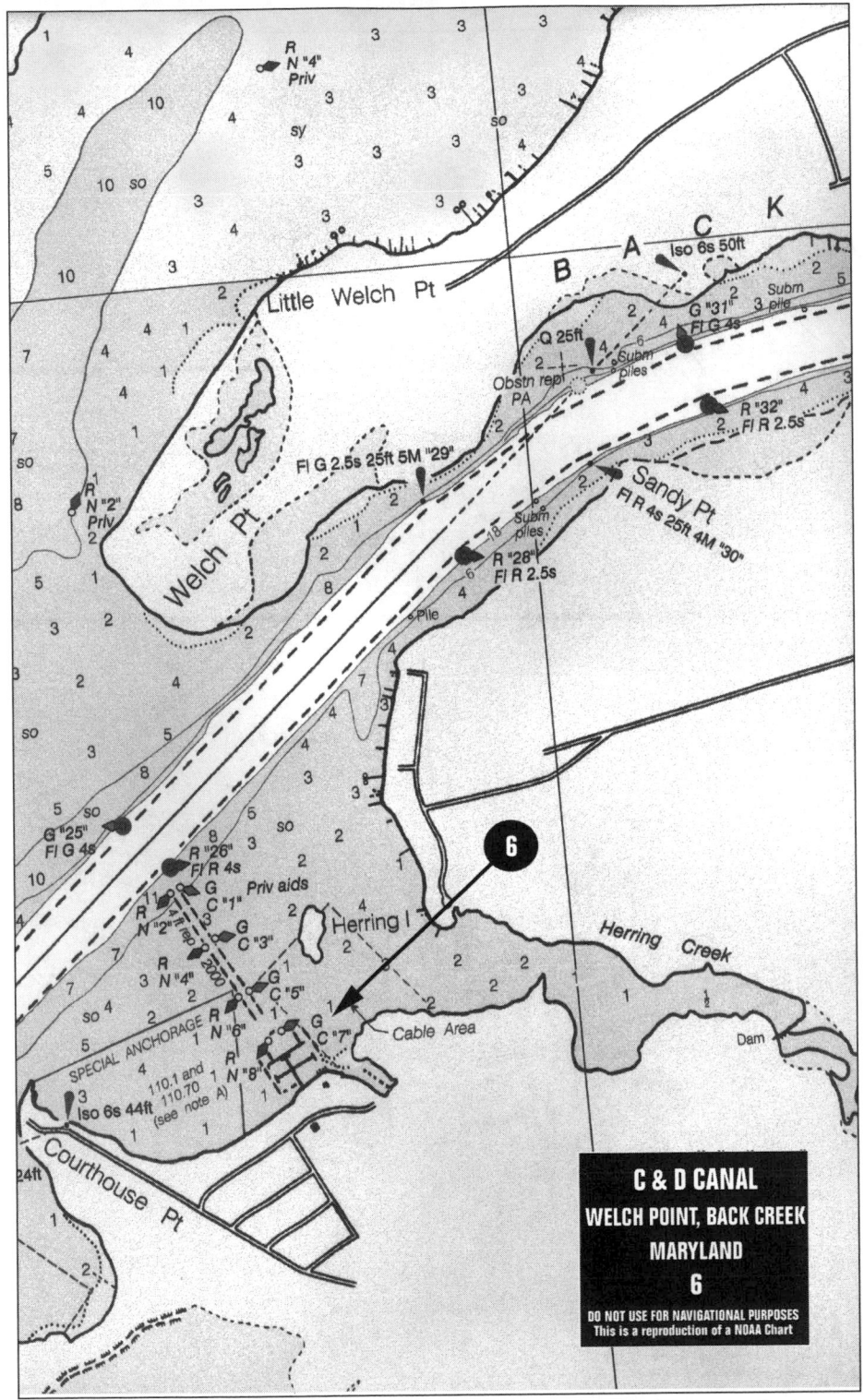

BACK

Little Welch Pt

Iso 6s 50ft

G "31"
Fl G 4s

Subm
pile

Q 25ft

Obstn rept
PA

Subm
piles

R "32"
Fl R 2.5s

Fl G 2.5s 25ft 5M "29"

Welch Pt

Sandy Pt

Fl R 4s 25ft 4M "30"

Subm
piles

R "28"
Fl R 2.5s

Pile

R N "4"
Priv

sy

R N "2"
Priv

G "25"
Fl G 4s

R "26"
Fl R 4s

Priv aids

Herring I

Herring Creek

G
C "1"

R
N "2"

G
C "3"

R
N "4"

G
C "5"

Dam

SPECIAL ANCHORAGE

R
N "6"

G
C "7"

Cable Area

Iso 6s 44ft

110.1 and
110.70
(see note A)

R
N "8"

Courthouse Pt

24ft

C & D CANAL

WELCH POINT, BACK CREEK

MARYLAND

6

DO NOT USE FOR NAVIGATIONAL PURPOSES
This is a reproduction of a NOAA Chart

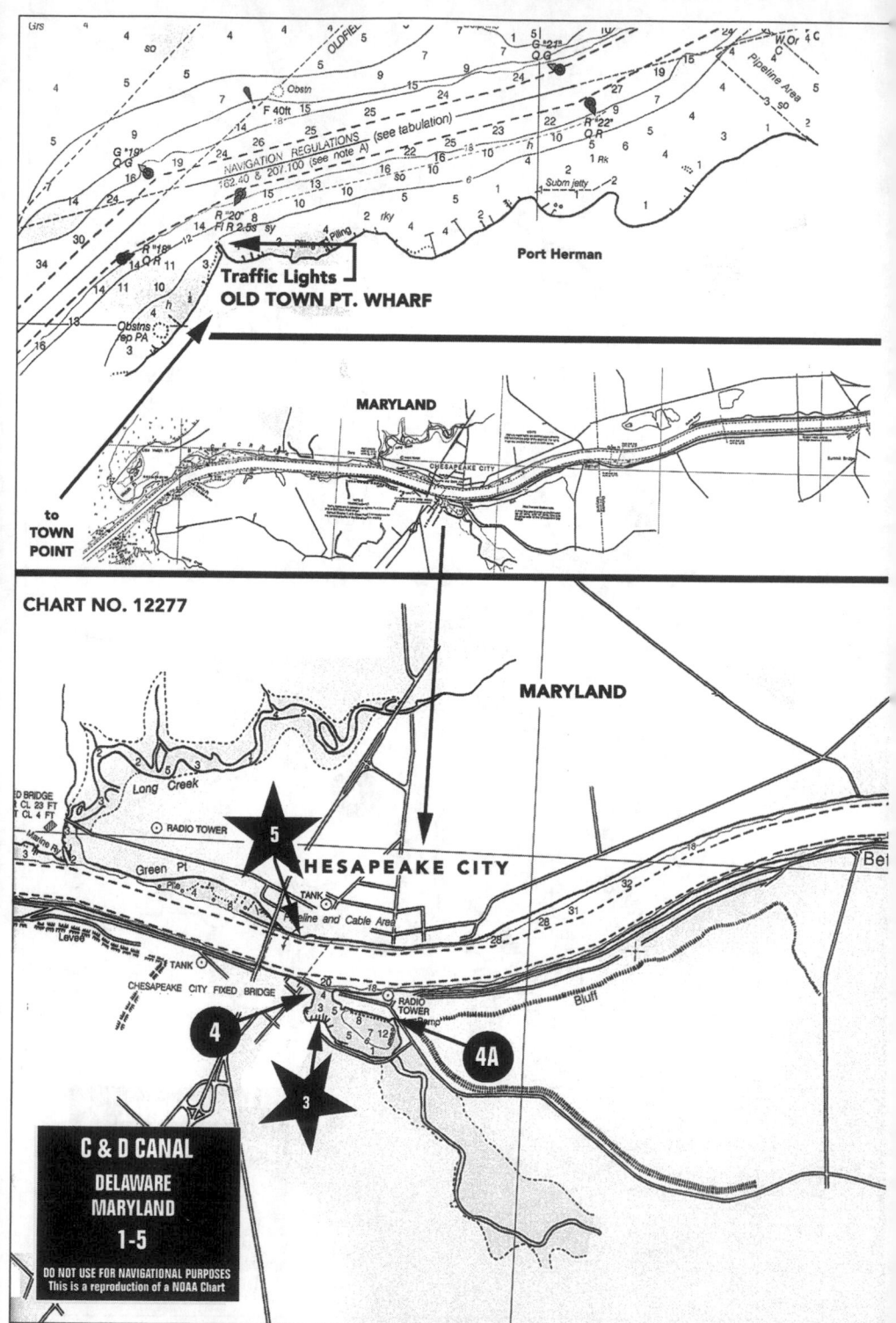

Traffic Lights
OLD TOWN PT. WHARF

Port Herman

MARYLAND

CHESAPEAKE CITY

to
TOWN POINT

CHART NO. 12277

MARYLAND

Long Creek

⊙ RADIO TOWER

Green Pt.

5

CHESAPEAKE CITY

TANK

Pipeline and Cable Area

Levee

TANK

CHESAPEAKE CITY FIXED BRIDGE

4

RADIO
TOWER

Bluff

Bet

4A

3

C & D CANAL
DELAWARE
MARYLAND
1-5

DO NOT USE FOR NAVIGATIONAL PURPOSES
This is a reproduction of a NOAA Chart

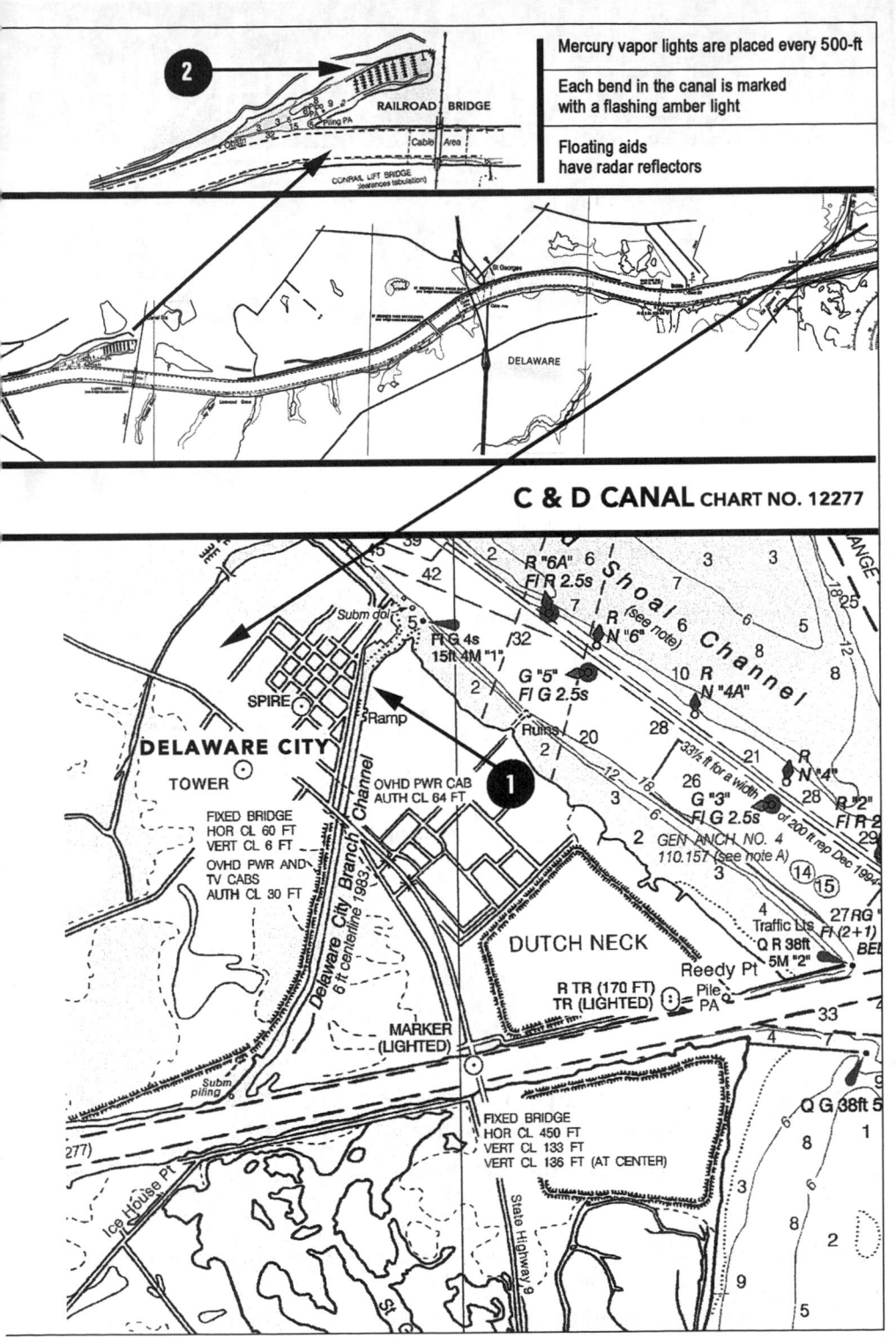

Mercury vapor lights are placed every 500-ft

Each bend in the canal is marked with a flashing amber light

Floating aids have radar reflectors

RAILROAD BRIDGE

CONRAIL LIFT BRIDGE (clearances tabulation)

Cable Area

DELAWARE

C & D CANAL CHART NO. 12277

R "6A" 6
Fl R 2.5s

Shoal Channel

R "6" (see note)
N "6"

Fl G 4s
15ft 4M "1"

G "5"
Fl G 2.5s

R N "4A"

Ruins

33¾ ft for a width

R N "4"

SPIRE

26
G "3"
Fl G 2.5s

of 200 ft rep Dec 1994

R "2"
Fl R 2

DELAWARE CITY

TOWER ⊙

FIXED BRIDGE
HOR CL 60 FT
VERT CL 6 FT

OVHD PWR AND
TV CABS
AUTH CL 30 FT

OVHD PWR CAB
AUTH CL 64 FT

Ramp

GEN ANCH NO. 4
110.157 (see note A)

(14)(15)

27 RG

Traffic Lts
Q R 38ft Fl (2+1)
5M "2"   BE

DUTCH NECK

Reedy Pt

Pile PA

R TR (170 FT)
TR (LIGHTED) ⊙

MARKER
(LIGHTED)

Subm piling

Ice House Pt

FIXED BRIDGE
HOR CL 450 FT
VERT CL 133 FT
VERT CL 136 FT (AT CENTER)

Q G 38ft 5

State Highway 9

Delaware City Branch Channel
6 ft centerline 1983

COASTAL PROPERTIES

MANAGEMENT, INC.

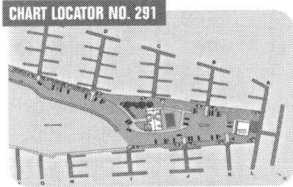

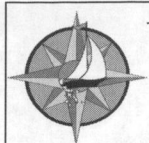

Chesapeake Bay

THE HEADWATERS and EASTERN and WESTERN SHORES OF THE UPPER and CENTRAL BAY

THE FOLLOWING AREAS ARE COVERED IN CHARTS IN THIS SECTION:

CHART LOCATOR NO. 29

Cruising Chesapeake Bay

From top to bottom, the Chesapeake Bay has a look and culture all its own, and a history that has made its mark around the world. Discovering the Chesapeake, its ecology, its wildlife, its tributaries and unspoiled hidden coves, its towns and cities, its cuisine, and the traditions of its watermen, is an enviable adventure available only to people on boats.

BAY FACTS: The Chesapeake Bay is an estuary having both fresh and salt water. It is the largest estuary in the United States as it stretches for 200 miles from Havre de Grace and the Susquehanna River all the way to Norfolk, Virginia. The Susquehanna is "the Mother of the Bay," flowing 450 miles from Otsego Lake, in upstate New York, carrying 19 million gallons of fresh water into the bay per minute. All in all, the bay holds more than 18 trillion gallons of fresh and salt water combined.

At its narrowest point (Aberdeen, Maryland), the bay is 3.4 miles wide and at its widest, the bay reaches across 35 miles near the mouth of the Potomac River.

Navigating in the Chesapeake's waters, you'll want to stay well off points of land, due to shoaling, and stay mid-channel. Keep a constant watch for the ubiquitous Chesapeake crab pot. ⚓

The Headwaters

Chart 12311. ELK RIVER

Around the **CHESAPEAKE CITY BRIDGE**, the canal merges into **BACK CREEK** which in turn merges into the **ELK RIVER**. Recent dredging between **WELCH POINT** and **LOCUST POINT** reportedly has waters to a new depth of 5 feet MLW. Deep draft boats should seek local knowledge before anchoring or heading into marinas in this area. Deeper draft boats heading south on the bay should seek anchorage or dockage on the **SASSAFRAS RIVER**.

OLD TOWN POINT WHARF, on the southeast side of the **ELK RIVER,** has depths of 10 feet at the outer end. Traffic lights governing the comings and goings at this official canal entrance are located here.

A local magnetic disturbance with differences of 3° to 8° from normal variation have been observed from Grove Point to Courthouse Point.

Chart 12274. THE NORTH EAST RIVER

You're heading where? North East. Where? North East! But, where exactly? North East!! And so it goes. The town and river at the head of the Chesapeake Bay has a continuing identity crisis. Not only is it a compass heading, **NORTH EAST** (the river and the place) is a destination worth exploring. The four-mile-long river is mostly wide and open, but relatively shallow in places. Boats drawing more than 4 feet should be wary. Much of what looks to be a vast expanse of water is in reality, **"THE SUSQUEHANNA FLATS,"** with MLW depths of 1 foot to bare.

Approach the **NORTH EAST RIVER** in a well-marked channel from **TURKEY POINT** and the western shore of **ELK NECK,** ultimately the eastern shore of the river. (Elk Neck State Park and beaches will be to port). The Flats shoal out from the west, so watch your depth finder, following the marks carefully. As you progress into the river, the marked course will take you more toward the middle. Several marinas dot the shoreline but none are really within an easy walking distance to the town itself.

The town of North East is on the eastern shore of the river and offers several marina facilities and restaurants. The most notable for docking and dining is The NautiGoose, a casual, fun restaurant with transient floating slips, and outdoor and indoor dining. From here it's a quick and pleasant walk through

the town's riverfront park to **The Upper Bay Decoy Museum**. This is as close to the quaint little village of North East as you are able to dock your boat. If you're up to the more than half mile trek each way, there are many upscale shops, boutiques and antique dealers to find along with Woody's Crab House where you can continue studying the many ways to chow down on the Chesapeake Bay Blues. Basket collectors will want to stop at the well-known Day Basket Factory where they've been making white oak baskets since 1876. The only provisions available in town are coffees, teas, spirits, and restaurant take-out. You'll be surprised to find out that North East is only 5 minutes from the bustle of civilization and I-95.

McDaniel Yacht Basin, a full service marina with good depths for both sail and power, is on the entrance of **FORD RUN**. This marina and brokerage has been in continuous operation for well over 50 years. A beautiful, new main building was completed at the end of the 2003 season. From McDaniel you can launch your dinghy to explore the shallow areas close to town.

On the western shore of the river are condominiums with a private marina facility and, further south, **CHARLESTOWN**. The town has a public landing and a full service marina. You should be able to find restaurants and bait and tackle within walking distance. This historic village was hit hard by Hurricane Isabel's tidal surge in the fall of 2003. Lastly, a small boat marina with fuel and supplies is tucked in the bend behind **CARPENTER POINT**.

THE SUSQUEHANNA RIVER

The shortcut approach to the Susquehanna River from North East is only a possibility for small cruisers of a draft under 3 feet. The natural channel of the Chesapeake turns northward off the mouth of the **ELK RIVER** and splits into two branches between **TURKEY POINT** and **SPESUTIE ISLAND**, 2.3 miles westward to the **SUSQUEHANNA**, and the sailing town of **HAVRE de GRACE**. Watch for the restricted areas around **ABERDEEN PROVING GROUNDS** and the shallow, sometimes non-existent waters of the **SUSQUEHANNA FLATS**. Between **TURKEY POINT** and **GROVE POINT** plot a course for RG"A" (midchannel buoy betwwen Turkey Point and Spesutie Island) to pick up the well-marked channel off **SPESUTIE ISLAND**, and then to north toward **FISHING BATTERY LIGHT** (39°29.7'N - 76°05.0'W), a black skeleton tower, 38 feet high. Stay mid-channel and keep a watch for commercial traffic, tugs with tows, and crab pots. (**FISHING BATTERY** is an island with a small white lighthouse, among other little wooded islands. It was once a commercial fishing center serving the flats and northern bay.) Follow the channel right into Havre de Grace.

HAVRE de GRACE (pronounce it have-er-deh-gray-se with a long 'a'), "harbor of mercy," was named by the Marquis de Lafayette in the 1780s. Using the true French pronunciation of the name will immediately label you as a 'first-timer.' This is both an historic town and a boaters town. Sailboaters in particular make up most of the boating population thanks to a sailing school, yacht clubs and myriad races. There are several marinas and walking around town is easy from most of them. Sights to see include **St. John's Street** and **Union Avenue** for shopping for everything from homemade chocolates to antique clocks, the famous **Havre De Grace Decoy Museum**, and several fine restaurants and eateries.

As you will see on the chart, depths here are not a problem. The first marina you'll see is the Havre de Grace Municipal Boat Basin to port. Call on VHF 68 for transient space. Next is a small boat and fishing boat marina, followed by a bullkheaded marina belonging to a condominium complex. Shortly thereafter is Tidewater Marina, a full service large marina and brokerage with a super friendly staff and a fantastic marine store.

Further up the river is the **SUSQUEHANNA RAILROAD BRIDGE** with a published vertical clearance of 52 feet. Another marina with slips, moorings, fuel and repair services is to port just under the bridge. This bridge will open for you if you call 24 hours in advance.

PERRYVILLE lies across the river from Havre de Grace. There is a condominium complex with private slips before the railroad bridge, and after the bridge there is another condominium complex with a

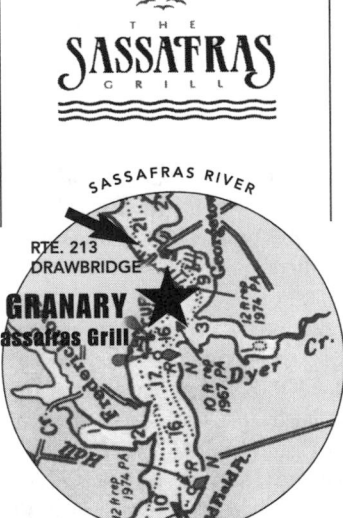

marina and transient facilities. The Perryville Yacht Club will also take transients if space is available. From this location you can hop the train to Philadelphia or Baltimore or points in between and beyond. You can also hail a cab and go to the **Perryville Outlet complex** which is near enough but much too far to walk.

Even further upriver, tucked in at the base of high cliffs, is **PORT DEPOSIT**, a small village with an historic past. Today, it's an up and coming river town, with yet another waterfront condo complex and marina which will take transients. Back in its glory days, Port Deposit was a major shipping and ferry port.

> ### NETTLE FREE SWIMMING
> in the Chesapeake and its tributaries is delightful above the salt line in summer. The infamous stinging nettles prefer more salty waters.

The Eastern Shore

PROVISIONING: Head down the Eastern Shore with all your provisions on board. Easy access to grocery stores is not an option until Rock Hall Harbor where a shuttle will take you for provisions, or St. Michaels where you can walk.

Chart 12274. THE BOHEMIA RIVER

Heading down bay from the **ELK RIVER** is the **BOHEMIA RIVER** which joins the Elk 4 miles below **BACK CREEK** or 5 miles before the mouth of the Elk, on the east side. A fixed highway bridge, 4 miles above the mouth of the Bohemia, has a clearance of 30 feet, keeping sailboaters out of **GREAT and LITTLE BOHEMIA CREEKS.**

Mostly freshwater, **THE BOHEMIA** introduces the cruiser to the beginning of the Eastern Shore's beautiful pastoral scenery – lush farmlands and rolling lawns of plantation-style estates that gracefully tumble down to meet the shoreline – a seascape that northeast cruisers aren't used to seeing.

Several marinas and boat yards dot the Bohemia, with the transient-friendly being on the north shore. Call ahead for docking space and entry depths. Shoals are charted and the river has a controlling depth of 7 feet but some facilities may have shoaling at their entries.

A pretty anchorage, for those who can get under the bridge, is in **GREAT and LITTLE BOHEMIA CREEKS** where depths range from 6 to 10 feet except on the north shore near the bridge. There is no marked channel so watch the depth sounder.

THE SASSAFRAS RIVER

Many cruisers just make a straight shot from the C&D to **THE SASSAFRAS**, one of the Eastern Shore's most beautiful rivers, rewarding cruisers with full service and resort style marinas located well upriver. Enter the river between **GROVE POINT and HOWELL POINT**. Depths are generally not a problem here although navigating a mine field of crab pots makes the entrance to the river seem like tackling a slalom course in the winter olympics.

To starboard, on the south side of the river, is the once lively resort town of **BETTERTON**. Condominiums and a swimming beach and park, mark the area. Vacationers from the western shores used to come here by ferry until the 1950s. Free dockage is available at the town pier with a one-night limit. You can also anchor off and dinghy in to use the waterfront park, beach, and picnic facilities.

Further upriver, at a bend in the channel, is **ORDINARY POINT** where boaters gather to anchor, raft up, swim and generally carouse. Make sure to stay well off the point and follow the buoys.

BACK CREEK comes out of the northern shore of the river, behind **KNIGHT ISLAND**, and is a quiet anchorage. Mount Harmon Plantation(410-275-8819), a tobacco plantation opposite the island, is open for touring in season. Call for dinghy landing instructions and hours.

FREEMAN CREEK and WOODLAND CREEK offer anchorage for shallow draft boats (under 4 feet) but are best explored in your dinghy.

You have a choice of seven marinas once you round **OLD FIELD POINT** and head into **GEORGETOWN HARBOR**. And the selection is greatly diversified. From any point here you can enjoy sunsets that rival any you've seen before, anywhere.

Georgetown Yacht Basin, on the south side of the drawbridge, offers a watertaxi service which is available to all the marinas in the area, with the exception of Gregg Neck Boatyard, upriver, past the drawbridge. **"Two Toots"** is the name of the taxi. Time was when two toots on the horn would get the taxi to you. Now a call on VHF 9 will do the trick. The taxi serves the restaurants and the marinas and the moorings.

The first marina to port calls itself a resort marina but in actuality that word applies to others in the area as well. Also on the northern side of the river, **The Granary Restaurant and Marina** offers dock and dine, and overnight dockage. **Sailing Associates,** a full service marina, just up from The Granary, is dedicated to sailboaters...although a few powerboaters hold seasonal slips here too. Amenities include a lovely pool, shaded lawns, barbecues, and air-conditioned shower facilities – a luxury that matters.

The Kitty Knight House, a local historic landmark, sits high on the hill, above Georgetown Yacht Basin, with a magnificent view of the harbor, the river and sunsets. Nighttime turns into magic from here with the twinkle of lights from boats below and anchor lights bobbing to and fro from sailboats' mast-tops.

If you wish to dine indoors in one of the formal dining rooms, a reservation is a must. Otherwise, take your chances and join the swinging crowd on the outside deck for lighter fare. Here you can take a break from sleeping on board and stay in one of the inn's charming guest rooms, or a staff member can happily transport you to their B&B, **The Anchorage**, just down the road apiece.

ED. NOTE: Above the Route 213 Georgetown drawbridge is a lovely cruising area and anchorage. Beautiful homes, many with docks, line the shores. We've often explored this area by dinghy since waters here are mostly unmarked. A large working boatyard, with a New England flavor, is up river on the starboard side, where you'll see classic old wooden boats in various stages of repair.

A local magnetic disturbance with differences of as much as 5° from normal variation have been observed from the mouth of the Sassafras to Pooles Island.

STILL POND

Two NM south of Howell Point is a small bay named, "**STILL POND**." While the majority of boats seem to anchor en-mass on the south side of the basin, anchoring can be good on the north side also. The trade-off is...on the north side you may feel wake from the shipping channel but you have more swinging room and privacy and the holding ground is equally as good. Anchor west of the channel marker leading into **STILL POND CREEK**. Swimming here is nettle-free until the last dog days of summer when the salt line may move this far up the bay due to lack of rain.

STILL POND is not the place to be in a westerly or northwesterly storm. Many boats have ended up on the rocks here during quickly-rising summer storms, due to poorly set anchors. It is possible to anchor inside **STILL POND CREEK,** where the local Coast Guard Station is located, but entering behind the sand spit can be a challenge with currents and the sharp dog-leg bend in the channel. On the opposite side of the basin, behind the anchorage area, is **CHURN CREEK**, an exciting dinghy excursion. **ED. NOTE:** If you time it right, you can get a dinghy or tubing thrill, riding through the creek's entrance, that rivals any waterpark. With the rush of rapid currents exiting the creek; you can repeat the ride over and over until the current subsides. Plan to play this game during the week when the anchorage is relatively empty.

Chart 12278. WORTON and FAIRLEE CREEKS

Both locations have good facilities, are very protected, yet very close to the bay and shipping channel, making them convenient spots for boaters to get a fast start to their day on the bay.

Entering **WORTON CREEK** heading southward, follow a compass bearing to the entrance markers from

JELLYFISH JOELS
ISLAND BAR
IN FAIRLEE CREEK

R "40." The channel is well marked but shoals to either side, with the larger shoal coming out from **HANDYS POINT.** Three marina facilities, welcoming transients, are tucked in this picturesque creek along with an excellent hilltop restaurant.

The entrance marker to **FAIRLEE CREEK** has changed from a floating red marker to a fixed marker, flashing R "2." **Ed. Note:** Entering and departing Fairlee Creek for the first time can give any helmsperson the heebie-jeebies. There is a very narrow dogleg plus strong currents to contend with, not to mention lots of weekend traffic. Following the marked channel in, you're heading right for the beach with all sorts of people lolling around in the water or sitting in beach chairs in the water. As you traverse the channel, be aware of the markers to port off the beach and off the starboard spit. Take your boat almost right up to the beach with your hand on the throttle ready to quickly gun the engine to make the sharp starboard turn into the dogleg, staying closer to the starboard sand spit and avoiding the people in the water. Depths here run 6 to 8 feet with a 4 foot shoal on the spit that holds Jellyfish Joel's jumping island-style bar. After doing this a few times, it's more like fun than terrifying.

Once inside you'll find both anchorage, and a large resort marina complete with guest rooms, pool, golf course (9 holes), a restaurant, a brokerage, and a fleet of charter sailboats.

POOLES ISLAND , in the middle of the bay and across from Fairlee Creek, is part of the **ABERDEEN PROVING GROUND** complex. Landing is prohibited since the island contains hazardous unexploded ordnance.

TOLCHESTER BEACH
You can't beat this location for easy access to the bay. The full service marina here offers a pool, ten-

nis, a beach and a mini-boardwalk along the bay plus a tiny restaurant making and serving some of the best homemade crab cakes you'll eat on the Eastern Shore. The approach here is straight into the marina from R "30," with depths of 6 feet at MLW.

ROCK HALL HARBOR, GRATITUDE, THE HAVEN and SWAN CREEK

Follow the main shipping channel past the point where the channel turns toward the western shore. Shallow draft boats and those with local knowledge can take the shortcut to **GRATITUDE, SWAN CREEK and THE HAVEN**, across **SWAN POINT BAR.**

The prudent mariner should take the marked route from Can "1" to the channel leading into **SWAN CREEK** or between the rock jetties and into **ROCK HALL HARBOR** itself. Water is shallow both east and west of the channel. Four marinas – one exclusively for sailors – plus the marina at Waterman's Crab House accept transients. If you're going to Waterman's specifically, call first. This restaurant and marina was severely damaged in Hurricane Isabel and may or may not be open for this season. Condominiums in the harbor have private slips.

SUMMER STORM APPROACHES SWAN CREEK

Finding slip space at one of the three marinas right in Rock Hall Harbor puts you in a fair walking distance to Rock Hall's shops, a replicated old-fashioned ice cream parlor, restaurants and a grocery store.

GRATITUDE and SWAN CREEK have excellent marina facilities including one resort-style facility. **THE HAVEN** has a large marina with a good marine store, swimming, and retail gift and apparel shop. It is also a resort-style facility. Anchorage is available in Swan Creek past the bend and to the north.

All of the marinas that are not within walking distance to town offer bikes, and shuttle buses to restaurants and shopping.

Sailboaters far outnumber both the powerboaters and the native watermen in this community. Rock Hall was once primarily a fishing village and home port to many of the bay's working watermen. Now its economics are more dictated by waterborne tourism.

How did the town get its name? There's speculation: some say its from the watermen's word for oyster reefs – "rocks;" and some say its from the days when large hauls of rockfish (a "rock haul") were more than plentiful. Either one is a good guess. The hot time here is the town's **Fourth of July Celebration** with parades, fireworks and lots of hoopla.

Chart 12272. THE CHESTER RIVER

The Chester River is one of the most scenic cruises of the bay. All the way up the river are small coves, creeks and anchorages to explore. Keep a watch for small buoys marking shoaled clamming areas. The river channel is north and east of **LOVE POINT LIGHT** – a 35 foot high skeleton tower with a red and white diamond-shaped daymark.

Head south and to round **EASTERN NECK** into the **CHESTER RIVER** (approximately six NM past Rock Hall). **KENT ISLAND NARROWS** will be to starboard. **EASTERN NECK ISLAND**, a 2,285 acre national wildlife refuge for waterfowl, is an interesting destination for boaters who carry bikes aboard or like hiking. There is a boat ramp on the east side of the island for eco-adventurers. Marked mileage trails are perfect for exploring. Note the hand-built wooden bridge connecting the island to the mainland – it's a work of art.

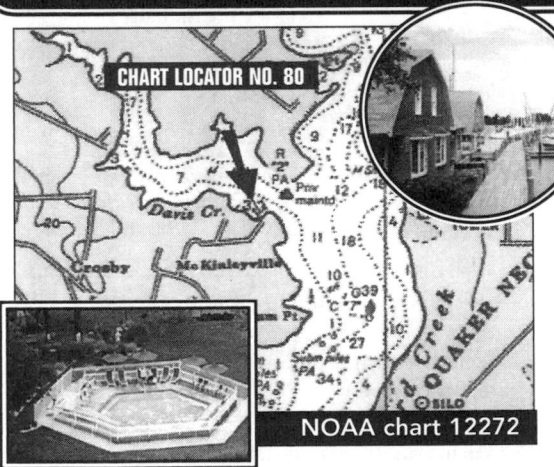

LANGFORD CREEK, ON THE CHESTER RIVER

This is one of the largest tributaries off the Chester River and has plenty of eco-touring opportunities. Enter **LANGFORD CREEK** between **GRAYS INN POINT** and **NICHOLS POINT** at **QUAKER NECK**. The creek divides into the western and the eastern forks with plenty of deep water in either fork.

Two marinas and the Rock Hall Yacht Club are nestled in protected waters off **LANGFORD CREEK**.

One marina is located in **LONG COVE** along with a public landing ramp , and the other is at the head of **DAVIS CREEK**, a tributary off the western side of **LANGFORD CREEK**. Picturesque buildings and the beautiful landscape of lush greenery and brightly colored summer flowers at **Lankford Bay Marina** combine to give the facility the tranquil look of an old-fashioned seaside English village. This marina is a welcoming destination for transients who want to relax and dinghy or bike about in a scenic natural area. Shuttle buses will take you to civilization.

CHESTERTOWN, ON THE CHESTER RIVER

The river travels upstream for 26 miles from **LOVE POINT LIGHT** to historic **CHESTERTOWN** where you'll find the peaceful campus of well-known **Washington College**, gaily-painted Victorian houses, gracious Georgian-style brick mansions, a turn-of-the-century hotel, a classic old movie theater, wonderful restaurants, coffee houses and a tea room, antique shops, small boutiques, and...no grocery store. There is an outdoor farm market in the town park on summer Saturdays. The two marinas in Chestertown proper welcome transients. If you don't mind crowds and crowded waters, time your visit for the end of May when townspeople re-enact the **Chestertown Tea Party and even** invite you to join in the fun. More info: www.chestertown.com.

The bridge at Chestertown opens on signal in season. There is ample depth for most boats to explore areas above the bridge still unspoiled by developers.

Chart 12272, 12270. KENT NARROWS and KENT ISLAND

AT THE CHESAPEAKE BAY BRIDGE

On the southern shore of the river, heading westerly is Rolph's Wharf, a combination marina, restaurant and B&B directly opposite **FRYINGPAN POINT,** on the north shore, (which of course is around the bend from **SKILLET POINT**).

Before entering the Narrows, note the red and white striped watertower on **KENT ISLAND**. This marks the entrance to Castle Harbor, a resort-style marina and popular cruising club destination.

BRIDGES & BUOYS ON THE NARROWS
MHW
Rt. 50/301
FIXED BRIDGE   65'
Local traffic
BASCULE BRIDGE   18'
May-Nov.: opens on signal every half hour from 6 a.m. to 9 p.m. Contact: VHF 13
Buoys are RED-RIGHT RETURNING at both the north and south entrances to the Narrows.

KENT ISLAND NARROWS connects the **CHESTER RIVER** to **PROSPECT BAY**, the **EASTERN BAY** and the **MILES RIVER**.

Choose a route to Eastern Bay: You can either take the shortcut passage through the Narrows or transit under the Bay Bridge, following the channel markers to round **BLOODY POINT BAR LIGHT** (38°50.0'N, 76°23.5'W) on **KENT POINT**. A shoal extends a mile out from Kent Point, so set a course for G "1" to begin transiting **EASTERN BAY**. This may be a longer, less challenging route, but you will miss all the good times to be had on **KENT ISLAND.**

(If you choose the route heading south from **LOVE POINT,** passing **Kent Island's western shoreline**, give the shoaling shore a wide berth. There are four marinas available to transients on this stretch before **BLOODY POINT BAR LIGHT**, the first, Bay Bridge Marina, is a 45-acre state-of-the-art facility, almost at the southern foot of the Bay Bridge.)

The **NEW CHANNEL** into **KENT NARROWS** from the **CHESTER RIVER** is shown on the most current chart. Approach the new northern entrance from the west, between daymarks "1" and "2." (The only signifi-

CHESAPEAKE

TO FIND MARINA LOCATIONS - SEE THE TABLES AND LOCATOR CHARTS AT THE END OF THIS SECTION.

cant shoaling in this new channel occurs around these daymarks; look for temporary buoys if shoaling begins to get significant. Otherwise, the new 75-foot-wide channel is reportedly 8 feet deep at MLW.) It's always wise to call the bridge tender or a local marina to confirm published depths in this area.

The mean tidal range in the Narrows is 1.5 feet and the flood current runs from 1 to 2 knots on an average. Flood current runs northward toward the Chester River, but there are strong currents all throughout the area, especially near the bridges.

Ed. Note: We've heard tales of boaters with drafts of around 4 feet, bumping bottom at low tide, right in the middle of the channel, just north of the fixed bridge. These stories continue to be passed around since the 90s when we were first warned.

KENT ISLAND has evolved into a boaters resort area destination. A plethora of marinas, and dock and dine restaurants, including those dedicated to crab eating afficionados, and the infamous Red Eye's Dock Bar are all here. A seasonal bus service and a taxi service will take you anywhere you want to go on Kent Island, and local pizza places deliver to marinas. **Piney Narrows Yacht Haven**, a **Coastal Properties** marina is located on the west side of the channel, north of the fixed bridge. The primarily condominium marina offers low fuel prices at a 400 foot fuel pier, and a free pump-out with your fuel purchase. Not a bad deal.

Commercial docks, and the Kent Island watermen and their workboats can be found on the west side of the island, south of the Bay Bridge.

Chart 12270. EASTERN BAY

EASTERN BAY is the approach to **ST. MICHAELS**, and the cruising grounds of the **WYE RIVER** and the **MILES RIVER**.

Coming through Kent Narrows, puts you in **PROSPECT BAY**, the northeastern part of Eastern Bay between **PARSON ISLAND and PINEY NECK POINT**, 9 miles from the mouth of Eastern Bay.

Ed. Note: A good place to anchor while waiting for favorable currents to head north through Kent Narrows is in **KIRWAN CREEK**, off **PROSPECT BAY and HOG ISLAND**.

Sailors will rejoice when hitting Eastern Bay...there is usually good wind all the way to St. Michaels in these waters. Turn off the engine and raise the sails!

The **WYE RIVER** is an integral part of the Chesapeake's crab mystique. It's a perfect habitat for the blue crab itself and the place where the popular Wye River Crab Spices originated.

There is a charted shoal at the mouth of the Wye. Follow the buoyed channel to the south of the river's mouth. Cruising the Wye River is an experience in appreciating the natural beauty of the Chesapeake and seeing magnificent homes along the way.

The river splits into two branches around **WYE ISLAND**. Anchoring off the channel, in the main stem of the river is possible in depths of 8 feet or more. Pretty anchorages available from the **WYE EAST** are behind **DRUM POINT**, at **SHAW BAY**–east of **BRUFFS ISLAND, LLOYD CREEK, DIVIDING CREEK,** and **GRANARY CREEK**.

The **MILES RIVER** is the route to **ST. MICHAELS**, a don't-

miss-it destination for every Chesapeake Bay cruiser.

There is an anchorage just outside on the east side of the small harbor and a water taxi to call for transportation to town. If you choose to anchor, outside the harbor, in **FOGG COVE**, or inside the harbor, make sure your boat stays within the specified anchorage area and will not swing into the channel with a wind shift. Marine Police will not hesitate to ticket you.

Reserving space in one of the five transient-friendly marinas is your best bet here where you'd rather be land cruising than on the boat.

St. Michaels Harbour Inn, Marina & Spa offers a resort experience for boaters which now includes a new spa facility. Boaters who spend a lot of time on the water will want to try the treatments offered to correct skin damage from overdoses of sun and wind...and the helmsperson could probably use a good massage. The dockside swimming pool and outdoor bar is a great place to meet fellow cruisers, and the inn has two exceptional restaurants that offer waterfront dining. You can walk, bike, ride in the inn's van, or take the water taxi to the opposite side of the harbor where all the action is. The marina has 10 feet at MLW.

Ed. Note: Dock staff here is exceptional in their attention to boaters. On one of our many cruises to the inn, our departure date coincided with a serious foul weather report. The Dockmaster insisted we stay at the slip much longer than our dock fee allowed, at no extra charge, in order to avoid the predicted storm.

Other places to tie up are tucked in this tiny harbor on the town side: St. Michaels Marina; the dock and dine Crab Claw restaurant, which attracts tour buses loaded with passengers craving Chesapeake blues; and the must-see **Chesapeake Bay Maritime Museum** displaying the relocated Hooper Island screwpile Lighthouse, formerly active in Hooper Straits.

ST. MICHAELS is an excellent place to re-stock your provisions with grocery and gourmet stores in walking distance on **Talbot Street**. The town offers many dining options from gourmet to casual, and shopping in the boutiques and small stores up and down the main street can take most of the day. Marine supplies are available in town and in St. Michaels Harbour Inn Marina ships store. Getting a slip at The Inn at Perry Cabin means staying off the beaten path, in **FOGG COVE,** but definitely in the lap of luxury.

Chart 12266. KNAPPS NARROWS: TILGHMAN ISLAND

The Island of Tilghman (till-man) still stands as a tribute to the way things were along the Chesapeake Bay in days gone by. Catch the ambience of a true watermen's village while you can because it too has been discovered.

Approach **TILGHMAN ISLAND** through the well-marked channel in **POPLAR ISLAND NARROWS,** south of the entrance to Eastern Bay, and east of **POPLAR ISLAND**, to **KNAPPS NARROWS**. (There is a marina and inn for boats with less than a 5 foot draft, off Ferry Cove at Lowes Wharf, mid-way through Poplar Island Narrows.)

Both entrances to Knapps Narrows are dredged on

Partners in Protection~
Maryland Clean Marinas, Boatyards, Yacht Clubs, and You!

Certified Clean Marinas voluntarily prevent pollution in all aspects of their operations. **Please support Maryland Clean Marinas!**

To locate a certified Clean Marina look for the Clean Marina logo in this guide, or call
410-260-8770
or visit
www.
dnr.state.md.us/boating/cleanmarina

a regular basis to a MLW depth of 8 to 9 feet. Between dredgings, however, the 2 knot currents constantly deposit silt at either end. Follow the marks carefully as the deepest part of the channel is narrow. At the opposite end of the channel you are in The Choptank River.

Again, as in the C&D Canal and Kent Narrows, red-right-returning works at either end of Knapps Narrows passage, and vessels traveling with the current have the right of way.

Several opportunities to tie up and enjoy the island are in the Narrows, including two inns, each with waterfront dining, and the not-to-be-missed Bay Hundred Restaurant–not so much for views but known for excellent seafood and gourmet vegetarian-style cuisine. The restaurant has no docking facility but can be walked to from any of the other marinas in the Narrows.

The bascule bridge at the center of the Narrows has a vertical clearance of 13 feet. Bridge tenders here are on the ball so you probably won't even have to toot the *one-long and one-short* horn signal to open the bridge. The island begins on the southern end of the bridge. There is an interesting maritime book store housed in an old bank building within easy walking distance from the bridge.

To the **SOUTH OF KNAPPS NARROWS**, on the **CHOPTANK**, is **DOGWOOD HARBOR** with an anchorage, a yacht club-marina and private home development, and an inn-marina popular with fishermen.

Chart 12263, 12266. CHOPTANK RIVER

The river and its tributaries deliver miles of beautiful scenery, plenty of peaceful anchorages, and a wealth of history to discover. If you haven't read James Michener's "Chesapeake," you'll want to have it along for the cruise since the novel is set on the Choptank.

BOATERS NOT USING KNAPPS NARROWS PASSAGE to the **CHOPTANK** should approach the mouth of the river by setting a course from **SHARPS ISLAND LIGHT** (38°38.3'N, 76°22.5'W, 54 feet above water)) and pass Tilghman Island to port at **BLACK WALNUT POINT** but staying well of the point due to shoals. Two well-marked channels head both north and south in the river. The north channel takes you back behind **TILGHMAN ISLAND**, and to **HARRIS CREEK** and **BROAD CREEK** for anchorages. Deep into **BROAD CREEK**, at **SAN DOMINGO CREEK**, you can anchor and dinghy into the public landing then walk right down **ST. MICHAELS'** Talbot Street.

Visible from the mouth of the Choptank, the **CHOPTANK RIVER LIGHT** (38°39.4'N, 76°11.1'W, 35 feet), is six miles upriver at the entrance to the **TRED AVON RIVER**.

MEARS YACHT HAVEN IN OXFORD

OXFORD ON THE TRED AVON RIVER

Two or so miles from the **CHOPTANK RIVER LIGHT**, on the **TRED AVON RIVER**, is the charming sailor's town of **OXFORD**. (Note on your chart that G "1" marks an expanding shoal from **BENONI POINT**.) Located on a peninsula at **OXFORD NECK**, Oxford borders the Tred Avon and **TOWN CREEK**. A watertank painted with the town name will let you know you're almost there.

Oxford is steeped in Chesapeake history...from boatbuilding, to tobacco shipping, to oystering. Some of the homes date back as far as the 1600s! Today, this quiet hamlet is almost tranquilizing in nature.

TOWN CREEK holds all but two of the nine marinas in Oxford, and you can walk to shops, a grocery store and restaurants, from any one of them.

Mears Yacht Haven, a **Coastal Properties** marina, is the first facililty to starboard as you enter the creek. Home of the Oxford Yacht Club, Mears offers dockage for vessels up to 130 feet with all the possible amenities any boater could want, including bike and car rentals.

Oxford Boatyard, also a **Coastal Properties** marina, offers deepwater slips and dockage for vessels up to

CHESAPEAKE

120 feet. This is a real New England type boatyard where serious work can be done on your boat. The craftsmen there can happily resurrect your old Trumpy and bring it back to life.

Also in Town Creek is the well-known Crockett Bros. Boatyard which has been purchased by Hinckley Yachts

Nearby to both Mears Yacht Haven and Oxford Boatyard is Schooner's Landing Restaurant, a former marine warehouse, where you can opt to dock and dine on steamed crabs.

Ed. Note: As you head for **TOWN CREEK**, you'll see a park and swimming beach to starboard. This is an area in Oxford known as "**The Strand.**" Taking a stroll along The Strand will make you envy those who live along this picturesque street which overlooks the river and a grassy, shade-treed park and a swimming beach. You might find yourself looking for ladies with parasols and humming the theme from "Somewhere in Time."

Boaters can anchor in front of The Strand in calm weather, dinghy in to the park, enjoy a picnic, read Michener's "Chesapeake" under a shade tree, swim in the river, and walk up to the historic Robert Morris Inn for spirited refreshment. Do not consider anchoring overnight here.

Keep a watch for the **Bellevue-Oxford Ferry**, a small passenger and car ferry coming from just east of St. Michaels area. The ferry wharf and town dock are located at the southern edge of The Strand, next to the Tred Avon Yacht Club. Reportedly, this is the oldest continuously operating ferry route in the United States, having begun in 1683.

Seven miles upriver on the Tred Avon, lies **EASTON POINT**.and a marina. The sophisticated city of **EASTON** is a taxi ride away.

Chart 12263, 12266, 12668. CAMBRIDGE ON THE CHOPTANK RIVER

A well-marked channel takes you seven miles up the **CHOPTANK RIVER** from the **CHOPTANK RIVER LIGHT** to **CAMBRIDGE,** Maryland's second largest commercial harbor! Keep an eye out for tugs and barges transiting up and down the channel, and honor all the red markers to avoid shoals from the opposite shore.

The Municipal Yacht Basin and Cambridge Yacht Club are located before the bridge to starboard. Head into the basin from G "1." If you want to enter **CAMBRIDGE HARBOR**, take a heading to a point on the bridge – about one third of the way across from the Cambridge side – and head directly for the entry markers into **CAMBRIDGE CREEK** and the town's harbor area.

The new, highly touted Cambridge Hyatt Regency Resort and Marina lies under the fixed Choptank River Bridge (cl. 50 feet) just north of **HURST CREEK**. ⚓

ABOUT THE CLEAN MARINA INITIATIVE

**Look for the
CLEAN MARINA LOGO
in the
Maryland Marina Tables.**

Certified "Maryland Clean Marinas" meet the rigorous pollution prevention standards established by the Maryland Clean Marina Committee and the Department of Natural Resources. These marina operators have voluntarily adopted measures to control pollution associated with marina operations, and stand as a notable example of the conservation ethic: individual responsibility for healthy land and water.

The Clean Marina Award is given in recognition of the operators' leadership and commitment to environmental stewardship.

**For a complete listing of all Maryland marinas awarded the "Clean Marina" classification:
www.dnr.state.md.us/boating/cleanmarina**

202

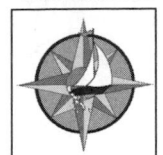

The Western Shore

Cruising the Western Shore could start off with a bang if you're not careful!

Chart 12272, 12273, 12274.

ABERDEEN PROVING GROUND:

THE BUSH RIVER, GUNPOWDER RIVER, portions of SENECA CREEK

Cruisers should avoid both of these tributaries as their lower areas, where they marge into the bay, lie in the restricted areas of the **U.S. ARMY'S ABERDEEN PROVING GROUNDS**.

Anchoring, swimming and going ashore are prohibited at all times and punishable as a Federal offense. The areas are clearly outlined on all navigational charts both printed and digital. They start at **SPESUTIE ISLAND** and **NARROWS** to the mouth of the **GUNPOWDER RIVER**, and are also northwest of **POOLES ISLAND**.

Some of these restricted areas are closed all the time and others are closed Mondays through Friday from 7 a.m. until 5 p.m. Get too close and you'll meet with a patrol boat marked with an orange stripe.

Additional information is available in the government pamphlet entitled, "Boaters Guide to Restricted Water Zones," which you can find at most local marinas. Concerns are two-fold: The area is filled with unexploded ordnance; when testing and firing is taking place, you and your boat could unwittingly cruise into the cross-hairs.

If weaponry fascinates you, The **U.S. Army Ordnance Museum,** shows the most complete collection of weapons in the world and is worth a visit. Dock in **HAVRE DE GRACE** and either rent a car or take a taxi to **ABERDEEN PROVING GROUNDS (APG)**. There is an open house every year, celebrating Armed Forces Day, when you can see awesome firepower demonstrations. The museum itself is open to the public, Tuesdays through Sundays, year 'round.

There are marine facilities on the upper reaches of the **BUSH** and **GUNPOWDER RIVERS** and **SENECA CREEK**, mostly for small power boats. See them listed in the marina tables.

Chart 12273, 12278. MIDDLE RIVER MIAMI BEACH, GALLOWAY CREEK, FROG MORTAR CREEK, STANSBURY CREEK, DARK HEAD CREEK, HOPKINS CREEK, SUE CREEK, HOG PEN CREEK, and NORMAN CREEK

BOWLEY'S MARINA, BEHIND BOWLEY BAR

Welcome to civilization. **MIDDLE RIVER,** with its many creeks, is populated with a gazillion pleasure boats, homes, docks, waterfront restaurants, and marinas. Resort marinas here are the destination...if they have available transient space.

Approach the river through two fixed marks at the mouth of the river: G "5" at **BOOBY POINT,** and R "6" at **BOWLEY BAR.** Look for the speed limit sign at the entrance to the river; it's strictly enforced. It's wise just to keep to a speed of 6 knots or less in the entire body of water. Good depths are throughout the area and the channels are well-marked, but be wary of shoals coming out from all points of land. Both Booby and Bowley send extensive shoaling out into the river 's mouth , so mind the marks.

Bowley's Marina, a **Coastal Properties** marina, is a well-designed resort marina located right on the point at **BOWLEY BAR**, at the edge of **GALLOWAY CREEK**, giving boaters a fast, almost traffic-free, access to the bay. Although the marina is totally member-owned, there can be transient spaces available on new floating

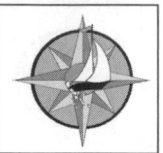

docks. The property is park-like with pretty covered pavilions, a picnic area, play-grounds, and a pool.

Five facilities are located in **FROG MORTAR CREEK**, entered past **GALLOWAY POINT**. Everyone wonders about the origination of the name. Ask around. There's no real answer...just choose the one you like the best. Explanations go from "frog drop-pings," to excessive frog croaking, to the convolution of a family name back in the 1800s. There are other answers too, but none are printable here and have anything to do with mortars or animal cruelty by Aberdeen Proving Grounds.

All together, nineteen facilities accept transient boaters in the Middle River area and a new watertaxi (410-375-1131) will take you to any of the many waterfront restaurants in the river and its tributaries.

Chart 12278. HART-MILLER ISLAND

HART-MILLER ISLAND lies south of Middle River at the southeast side of **HAWK COVE**, at the mouths of **MIDDLE RIVER** and **BACK RIVER**. The island will eventually become a state park consisting of over a thousand acres of fill. Anchoring off the island is possible in good weather, when wind is from south or east. It's also buggy at night. Dinghy in and join the other boaters enjoying the public beach. A wooden walkway on the island offers exploring possibilities and a three story observation tower can be climbed for fan-tastic bay views. Campsites are also available on a first come basis. There is a narrow channel with a reported depth of 6 feet between **HART MILLER** and **PLEASURE ISLAND**.

BACK RIVER

With depths of 4 to 7 feet, and an inside width of almost a mile, **BACK RIVER** (not to be confused with **BACK CREEK**) makes a nice cruising ground for shoal draft boats. Hidden behind **HAWK COVE** and a narrow entry channel, the river opens wide for 6 NM to a fixed bridge (16 feet cl.). There is a marina to starboard just past **WITCHCOAT POINT.**

Chart 12272, 12273, 12281. PATAPSCO RIVER

With all the rural scenery that comes with a Chesapeake Bay cruise, some folks may get a hankering for a 'city fix,' and set a course for **BALTIMORE HARBOR**, where the action is.

NAVIGATING TO THE PATAPSCO.

From the Eastern Shore: pick up the **Brewertown Channel** at the turning buoy, R "2BE" (39°08.9'N, 76°20.0'W) in Tolchester Channel. (The channel splits between G "11" and R "12.")

From the lower Western Shore: pick up the **Craighill Channel** off the Magothy River between R "8" and G "9" and head northwesterly to R "2B" in Brewerton Channel, northwest of **Seven Foot Knoll,**(39°09.3'N, 76°24.5'W). **From Middle River area:** follow the marked small boat channel from R "2A" off Middle River, to R "2B" in Brewerton Channel. Enter the river between **BODKIN POINT**, on the south side of the river and **NORTH POINT,** 2 miles northwest from Seven Foot Knoll.

Chart 12281. BODKIN CREEK ON THE PATAPSCO RIVER

Steer a course wide off G "BC" on the way toward **BODKIN CREEK** due to a nasty shoal. Shoals and rock also border the entrance channel to Bodkin Creek, so don't wander off course.

Enter the creek between **CEDAR POINT**, on Bodkin Neck, and **FRANKIE POINT** at Bayside Beach. Anchorage with good holding ground is in **BACK CREEK,** east of **HICKORY POINT;** across from **SPIT POINT** in a **COVE;** and in **JUBB COVE.** Housing and private docks encroach on all the shores so you may want to try a marina in this area, or head on down the river to the city.

Pleasure Cove, a lovely resort marina with a dock and dine waterfront restaurant, pool, gym and golf course, lies at the end of **MAIN CREEK,** the largest branch of **BODKIN CREEK.** Enter on the eastern side of **THE SPIT**.

ROCK CREEK ON THE PATAPSCO RIVER

Four miles up the Potapsco is **ROCK CREEK**, identifiable by a large formation of partially submerged rocks, known as **"White Rocks."** A yacht club and 5 marinas populate Rock Creek.

STONEY CREEK ON THE PATAPSCO RIVER

You can spot the entrance to **STONEY CREEK** by the red cliffs, a mile west of **"White Rocks."** Enter from R "2" and keep the reddish brown rocks to port. Stay in the middle of the channel. From R "6" head for R "8" to get into deep water. The **Route 173 bascule bridge,** a half mile from the entrance, opens on demand except during weekday rush hours. Bridge tender monitors VHF 13 and honors the traditional horn blast. Anchorage is in **NABBS CREEK** and **BIG BURLEY COVE**. A combination inn and marina can be found on the eastern side of Nabbs Creek.

BEAR CREEK ON THE PATAPSCO RIVER

On the north side of the Patapsco, just above **SPARROWS POINT,** and beyond **OLD ROAD BAY**, is **BEAR CREEK**. In the **LYNCH COVE** area there are two marinas with only a few available slips for transients.

CURTIS BAY ON THE PATAPSCO RIVER

One of the largest U.S. Coast Guard station bases on the East Coast is located here in Curtis Creek and Bay. This is where they build the service's steel and fiberglass vessels and conduct buoy maintenance. The facility is not open to the public with the exception of Armed Forces Day celebrations.

BALTIMORE HARBOR ON THE PATAPSCO RIVER

Maryland's largest and busiest commercial harbor sees the comings and goings of more than 4,000 ships in a year's time...not counting mega-yachts, tall ships, and all manner of pleasure boats! That means you should keep a sharp watch and give right of way all along the river in the shipping channels.

PRIDE OF BALTIMORE II, a top-sail schooner and a Baltimore Clipper

THE GREAT CHESAPEAKE BAY SCHOONER RACE

In mid-October, a gathering of schooners makes Baltimore its home port. Starting on a Sunday, there's a week filled with related activites for the public, in the harbor.

Historic schooners, from all points of the compass, dock in Fells Point awaiting a Thursday afternoon start at the Chesapeake Bay Bridge ending in a Friday finish in Norfolk. This annual event is held to benefit the Chesapeake Bay Foundation.

THE PATAPSCO RIVER splits at **FORT MCHENRY,** 8 NM from the mouth of the river. The portside fork takes you to **MIDDLE BRANCH,** past commercial shipping terminals to the Baltimore Yacht Basin. The starboard fork is **NORTHWEST HARBOR,** leading into the **INNER HARBOR.** Ten transient-friendly facilities surround the perimeter, and in-advance reservations are a must. Space may be available at the City Docks which are straight ahead at the head of the harbor. They do not accept reservations so call on VHF 68 or 410-396-3174. The mean range of tide here is 1.1 feet. with a 0.8 knot current on the flood and ebb. Speed limit is 6 mph.

There is an anchorage marked by white buoys near the **World Trade Center,** with a free dinghy dock nearby and restroom facilities by the aquarium. Make sure your anchor is set well here.

ED. NOTE: As you near the **FRANCIS SCOTT KEY BRIDGE** you will see a buoy decorated as an American Flag. This marks the spot where Key wrote the words to the Star Spangled Banner. Key was imprisoned aboard a British ship in this location during the War of 1812, at the time of the siege at **Fort McHenry.** After a frightening night of shelling, he woke to see the flag still flying over the shore "in the dawn's early light," and penned the words to our National Anthem. The **Star Spangled buoy** is in place in season.

BALTIMORE ASHORE

It has been decades now that the downtown has been revitalized into a seafaring destination for sight-seers, shoppers, nightclubbers, and connoisseurs of fine food. As it is with Philadelphia, this is a super stopover for the entire family, beginning with a visit to the **National Aquarium** (410-576-3800).

Right on the harbor, the **Maryland Science Center** offers interesting exhibits and the latest thrills to be seen in IMAX theater technology. The **Baltimore Marine Museum,** with the **Chesapeake Bay Lightship,** and **Russian submarine, "Torsk,"** is next to the aquarium, while a block or so away is the new **Port Discovery,** an interactive museum the kids will love. The **"U.S.S. Constellation,"** the last all-sail Navy warship, is also open for touring.

You can catch a baseball game at Oriole Park at **Camden Yards** – it's an easy walk from the harbor. Stadium tours are available when no games are scheduled. Well-known stores, specialty boutiques, restaurants, cafés, gourmet foods and a farm market all line the harbor.

Known as Baltimore's "original" port, **"HARBOR EAST,"** is bordered by the trendy neighborhoods of **FELL'S POINT,** and **CANTON.** More shopping and eating can be done with gusto here. Fell's Point once prospered as a hub for shipbuilding, in particular, the designing and the building of the famous Baltimore Clippers – hence another must-see is the **Fell's Point Maritime Museum.** Fell's Point is alive with B&Bs, little shops, antique stores, restored houses, casual eateries and waterfront restaurants. Canton offers yet more places to dine on

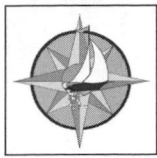

outstanding seafood. Five marinas are in this vicinity.

To cover the entire waterfront from your slip, no matter where you are tied up, a water taxi and a harbor shuttle are available with economical one-day passes and discount coupons. Plan in advance, save some money, and call 877-BALTIMORE, or go to www.Baltimore.org ,and purchase a "Harbor Pass," good for a three day admission to the top sites to see on land.

When you arrive, walk straight to the city docks and Science Center area – this is where you'll find the **Baltimore Visitors Center** for information about all that's available to you on your cruise to this fun city.

Harborview Resort Marina and Yacht Club, a **Coastal Properties** luxury facility, is located in the **FEDERAL HILL** section on the south side of the Inner Harbor. A new town-home community is also on the property. Swim indoors or out, and enjoy the health club and restaurant. From here you can walk to many Inner Harbor attractions, a nearby **Antique Warehouse** and the **Baltimore Museum of Industry**. A water taxi service is on site for trips across the harbor.

HARBORVIEW RESORT MARINA AND YACHT CLUB

Four blocks west of Harborview Marina, or five blocks south of the Science Center is **Cross Street Market** filled with stalls of food purveyors, including fresh produce vendors and butcher shops, mini-restaurants, and a lively bar. Locals rave about the sushi.

BALTIMORE LIGHT

NORWAY'S THREE-MASTED TALL SHIP, CHRISTIAN RADICH OFF BALTIMORE LIGHT

Chart 12278. THE MAGOTHY RIVER

DEEP CREEK, DIVIDING CREEK, MILL CREEK, CYPRESS CREEK, GRAYS CREEK, SILLERY BAY and GIBSON ISLAND

This pretty river is a sharp contrast to the industrial Patapsco and it offers nice cruising grounds, well-marked channels, some wind for sailors, comfortable anchorages, and lots of places to explore. Depths are good in the river with the exception being around points of land and **DOBBINS ISLAND.**

The entrance to the river is narrow between **MOUNTAIN POINT/PAVILION PEAK** and **PERSIMMON POINT**, off the **CRIAGHILL ENTRANCE CHANNEL**. Crab pots line the edges but the channel into the river is usually clear. **BALTIMORE LIGHT**, (39°03.5'N, 76°24.0, 52 feet) a cassion-style lighthouse, is just 1-1/2 miles east of the entrance.

Four of the five marinas, tucked into the river's rural creeks, offer space for transients. A popular anchorage with summer breezes is behind **DOBBINS ISLAND** in **SILLERY BAY**. Do not enter this anchorage from the west. The island is uninhabited and has a nice sandy beach, in the northwest corner, which you may use. Provisions are available from a marina off **GRAY'S CREEK**.

Ed. Note: If you're a card-carrying yacht club member whose club has reciprocal rights with other clubs, you'll want to cruise through **SILLERY BAY** and head into the channel at **MAGOTHY NARROWS,** marked with

two flashing lights, behind **GIBSON ISLAND** in an area called **"INNER HARBOR."** Beware of shoals off **HICKORY POINT** and **TAR COVE**. Follow the channel and private markers carefully to the private **Gibson Island Yacht Squadron**. In fact, the entire island is private with a guard house blocking the entrance road from land cruisers into this community. Calling the club's harbormaster and making reservations is a must (410-255-7632). He'll check to see if your club is on the list. The club offers moorings only and a lovely clubhouse with excellent shower facilities. Stff will hop on a tender to shuttle you back and forth from the mooring. The clubhouse sits on a narrow spit of land as wide as the two lane road that leads to the island, and that's all that separates the moorings from the bay. The shipping channel runs close to the road bed and bay watching from here is both delightful and protected.

SANDY POINT STATE PARK on BROAD NECK

On the way to busy Annapolis and the Severn River, **SANDY POINT** is a good place to hunker down in a storm. A 7 foot-plus dredged channel leads into a secure basin where you can anchor. It's also good for swimming from the sandy beach when the nettles aren't around and the crowds are gone. There are launch ramps and gas fuel here. On a pretty weekend this place is buzzing with boats and picnickers. Enter Sandy Point Park just northwest of the Bay Bridge piers.

You needn't pick the center (shipping channel) span to go under the **BAY BRIDGES**. If you're sailing, be ready for flukey winds under the bridges. As you look ahead toward the mouth of the Severn River, you'll see bulk cargo ships at anchor waiting to head into Baltimore and one or two U.S. Navy ships, also at anchor. And, on the weekends, a parade of boats coming and going from Annapolis.

Chart 12270, 12282. WHITEHALL BAY

Just north of the **SEVERN RIVER** entrance is **WHITEHALL BAY** with plenty of depth (9 to 15 feet) and anchorages in **WHITEHALL CREEK** and **MILL CREEK**. Look for flashing R "2W" off the **HACKETT POINT** shoal – take a wide berth of this point of land then round up on the flashing light in Whitehall Bay heading northward. Entering **MILL CREEK,** avoid the shoals off **POSSUM POINT**. Cantler's Riverside Inn, on Mill Creek, has dockage for 10 transients who want to chow down on crabs and other fresh bay seafood. Staying the night is possible with the promise of an early departure.

HORNPOINT HARBOR MARINA

Chart 12282. ANNAPOLIS SEVERN RIVER, SPA CREEK, BACK CREEK

Concerns regarding depth are not a problem as you approach the **SEVERN.** Coming from the Bay Bridges you could use GC "1" to set your course for R "6" and the channel into the river, avoiding the shoaling off **GREENBURY POINT**. G "3" - N "4" will duck you right into the entrance channel to Chesapeake Harbor, a condo marina with a few transient spaces available, and a fun bar and restaurant overlooking the boat basin.

The entrance to **BACK CREEK** and the boaters mecca of **EASTPORT** is marked with entrance lights 1 "E" and 2 "E." There are seven marinas here, several notable restaurants, marine supplies and chandleries, boat brokers, rigging services and repair yards.

FYI

Today, Annapolis is the Capital of Maryland but way back in 1783 Annapolis was the Capital of the United States for one year until the Treaty of Paris was ratified, ending the American Revolution.

Just past **BEMBE BEACH**, is **HORN POINT** and the **Horn Point Harbor Marina**, a **Coastal Properties** marina, is to starboard as you enter **BACK CREEK**. They welcome transients and the easy access in and out to the bay is a real plus in this generally crowded destination. The channel to the marina has 9 feet MLW and 7 feet MLW at the docks. **Horn Point Harbor** is actually in the **EASTPORT** section of Annapolis but is

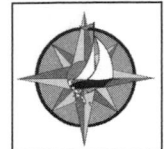

CHESAPEAKE

within walking distance, or a water taxi ride to everything Annapolis has to offer.

Anchorage in **BACK CREEK** is just off **Back Creek Nature Park,** near the water tower. The park offers restroom amenities, nature trails, barbecues and a place to catch your own crabs.

The large shoal off **HORN POINT** is marked by flashing white "HP." Stay in the channel, heading toward the Naval Academy seawall until "HP" is well behind you.

A popular anchorage in the Severn lies in front of the **U.S. Naval Academy**. This spot is often crowded. The holding ground is dense mud, and you are subject to the wakes of those boats coming and going from the harbor. Boats left with no one aboard have been known to drag anchor here and the rocky seawall bordering the Academy is not where anyone wants to be. Check with the Annapolis Harbormaster before dropping the hook here or anywhere else in the harbor area due to new Homeland Security restrictions.

A SUDDEN SUMMER SQUALL AS SEEN FROM THE MOORING FIELD.

Ed. Note: We often set the Loran/GPS alarm in tight coordinates, especially at night, to alert us of any unusual movement of the boat at anchor.

If you arrive in **ANNAPOLIS HARBOR** early enough in the day, you'll be one of the lucky ones to get a mooring or a city dock assignment, from the **Annapolis Harbormaster**. Call on VHF 9. A roving pump-out boat (for boats at anchor or on the moorings), the "Gerald W.," can also be reached on VHF 9. (Additional city moorings are available under the bascule bridge in **SPA CREEK**.)

You'll find, to your frustration, that some mooring transients leave their dinghy tied to a mooring, reserving their space while they take advantage of fair winds out on the bay.

Ed. Note: We've been hooked to one of these behemouth 400-lb mushroom moorings, in our 41-foot sailboat, in a storm with gusts clocking up to 90 mph, and experienced no drift or drag.

The **city moorings,** and the **city docks** (first come-first serve), have restroom and shower facilities available to boaters through the Harbormasters office. From the moorings, you can call the water taxi service or use your dinghy to head up **EGO ALLEY** to the **public dinghy dock**. At times there are so many dinghies tied up here that you may have to dinghy-hop from one to the other to get to dry land. It's all part of the fun.

EGO ALLEY is a narrow canal that leads to the city docks, dinghy dock and public landing. Boaters parade up and down Ego Alley, passing the crowds of boat watchers and revelers seated at the outside tables and bars of the Annapolis Waterfront Marriott and Pusser's Landing. Fawcett Marine Supplies, just past the hotel, also offers brief docking for customers.

Transient slips are also available at the marina next to the Marriott if there's space, and at the prestigious Annapolis Yacht Club if you're a club member with reciprocity. Marinas on the Eastport side of the harbor also may have transient space.

209

CHESAPEAKE

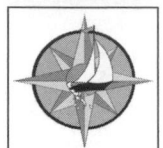

Anchorage can be had beyond the **SPA CREEK BASCULE BRIDGE**. It opens on the hour and half hour except for weekday rush hours (7:30 - 9 a.m. and 4:30 - 6 p.m.). Going upstream, in the channel, 10 feet or more MLW is reported. Any street ending at the water is a public dinghy landing in **SPA CREEK**. If you are able to find a spot, it is advisable to use two anchors.

For those who want to avoid the crowds in Annapolis, a cruise past the U.S. Naval Academy, to the head of the **SEVERN RIVER** will remind northeast boaters of the scenery found along the Hudson River. Two fixed bridges (75 foot cl. and 80 foot cl.) lead the way to scenic creeks and quiet anchorages.

ANCHORAGE IN FRONT OF U.S. NAVAL ACADEMY ON A WEEKDAY!

ANNAPOLIS ASHORE

With so much to see and do within walking distance to the City Dock, a pre-trip visit to www.visit-annapolis.org will help you plan your attack on shopping, dining, and sightseeing in this small historic area devoted to welcoming boaters. (Annapolis itself has several different districts encompassing outlying suburban areas and several zip codes.) A manned **Visitors Center** booth with all the information you need is also located near the Harbormasters office and restrooms. At the booth, you can also purchase tickets for theatre shows, walking tours, and events.

At the dinghy dock area, you'll see a life-sized statue of Alex Haley, author of "Roots." It marks the spot where Haley believed that his ancestor, Kunta Kinte, was originally sold into slavery. (The statue was almost totally under water after Hurricane Isabel's tidal surge in September, 2003.)

Steps away from the dinghy dock are so many places to eat, if you visit them all your life jacket won't fit. An Italian restaurant near the Harbormasters office offers more yummy flavors of authentic gelati than you can count and they're all on display at the Gelati Bar just inside the door. A bookstore/café combo has sidewalk tables, great coffee, delicious pastries and a god selection of books of interest to boaters. Pusser's Rum Shop, the British store popular in the Virgin Islands is in the Marriott Hotel. Crabmeat in every conceivable recipe can be easily found by browsing window-posted menus as you walk the blocks around the docks. Dining on various ethnic cuisines is an option too. Pub crawling is fun here if you have a designated dinghy driver.

A small marketplace with vendor stalls offers limited provisioning opportunities and quick bites, just opposite the dinghy dock. Upscale boutiques and shops and art galleries are all geared to the maritime theme. An independent, old-fashioned hardware stores –a rarity nowadays–is also near the dinghy dock. No prepackaged-shrink-wrapped stuff here. Go there for a good selection of brass oil lamps for your boat, a can of top grade marine varnish, or a couple of brass screws.

The U.S. Naval Academy has a museum and a fantastic gift shop worth visiting. You can also opt for a guided tour of the Academy. Be prepared to show plenty of good I.D. material to get past the Academy's guard gate, even if you're on foot.

Across the **Spa Creek bridge** are more fine restaurants, and marine supplies. Notable in Eastport, is Weems and Plath's headquarters and store, showing quality nautical instruments and shipboard lighting.

CHESAPEAKE

Chart 12270. SOUTH RIVER

THOMAS POINT LIGHT (38°53.9'N, 76°26.2W, 43ft.), a screwpile lighthouse and probably the most recognizable lighthouse on the Chesapeake, marks the shoals off Thomas Point, 5 miles south of the Severn River. **Ed. Note: THOMAS POINT SHOAL LIGHTHOUSE** (circa 1875) is a National Historic Landmark that was automated in the 1980s. The city of Annapolis is taking title to the lighthouse structure this year although the coast guard will maintain its light and horn. By the time boating season hits, the lighthouse may be open for tours. Check www.tpslh.org.

The entrance channel to **SOUTH RIVER** is just south of the lighthouse, between **THOMAS POINT** and **SAUNDERS POINT**. There are extensive shoals off all sides of both points, including **TURKEY POINT ISLAND**, inside the river, and behind Saunders Point. This entire area sees many waterskiers, PWCs and racers.

Four marinas, with minimal transient space, are located in **SELBY BAY**, behind Turkey Point Island. Be mindful of the long shoal coming off Long Point where depths can change from 7 foot to 1 foot.

LONDONTOWNE, an historic seaport-tobacco town (c: 1700), is bordered by **GLEBE BAY** and **ALMSHOUSE CREEK** and provisioning can be done from the dock provided for visiting the London Town Publick House and Gardens, a restored brick mansion and national historic landmark.

The Pier 7 marina on **LEES WHARF,** at the southwestern point of land beyond **WAREHOUSE CREEK,** advertises 20 transient slips while **EDGEWATER** (the northern side of the bridge) has plenty of deep water, marine facilities, including Liberty Marina which offers 25 transient spaces. Dock and dine waterfront restaurants are also located in the Edgewater area. The fixed bridge that lies up the river has a vertical clearance of 53 feet.

The nicest anchorages are reportedly available in **CHURCH CREEK, CRAB CREEK, GLEBE CREEK,** and **ABERDEEN CREEK.**

RHODE RIVER and WEST RIVER

These two rivers share a common entrance. From the north, **THOMAS POINT LIGHT** (38°53.9'N, 76°26.2W, 43ft.) is, once more, the mark to use when heading for the entrance to this popular two-river cruising grounds. Set a course for G "1A" being mindful of the long and extensive shoals off **CURTIS POINT**.

Enter the **RHODE RIVER** between **DUTCHMAN** and **CHESTON POINT**, passing G "3" on your way into the river. The Rhode is where the **Smithsonian Environmental Research Center** (SERC, actually headquartered in Edgewater) has placed many marks locating both submerged and visible scientific equipment in the waters. Take care not to damage any of these.

Marine facilities are on the north side but offer little or no transient space. Cadle Creek Marina does sell both gas and diesel fuel.

The **WEST RIVER** is much more transient-friendly with the rustic waterfront town of **GALESVILLE** as an attraction for provisioning and waterfront restaurants, plus several marine facilities and services are available. Enter the West River's Galesville area between R "4" and G "3" in depths of about 11 feet MLW. Then head for G "5" and R "6." Stay clear of both marks due to encroaching shoals. The West River Fuel Dock offers slips and moorings for transients, as does The Hartge Yacht Yard. (See the marine facilities tables and locator charts at the end of this section.)

HERRING BAY

HERRING BAY is the only natural harbor between the West River and the **PATUXENT RIVER,** and it is a worthy destination if only to spend time at the Herrington Harbor South Marina and Resort. This is a favorite long-term destination of cruising groups due to the endless amenities available to boaters and the large amount of allotted transient space. In fact, the actual place, "Herrington Harbor," a.k.a "Rose Haven," has become synonymous with the marina resort.

211

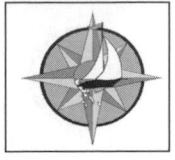

The south shore of Herring Bay is dotted with homes and rolling lawns that tumble down the hillside to the beach. The entire Herring Bay area offers several marine facilities and repair yards geared toward power boats, plus the charming watermen's village of **DEALE** with waterfront restaurants, provisioning and chandleries. There is also a large sportfishing charter fleet based in Deale, that fishes the plentiful grounds off the opposite Eastern Shore. Deale is on the western end of Herring Bay in **ROCKHOLD CREEK.**

HERRING BAY, between **HOLLAND POINT** and the marsh, 3 miles northward, has depths from 15- to 7 feet. A large shoal area, **LONG BAR**, (2- to 5 feet) extends 2 miles from the north side of the bay to within one mile of Holland Point on the south side of the bay.

Departing West River by way of the marked channel– take no shortcuts please, due to shoals off **CURTIS POINT** – pick up G "1" and set a course for YN "10B" off **FRANKLIN POINT** to YN "8B" to between flashing G "1" and flashing R "2" to pick up the channel into Herrington Harbor.

Herrington Harbor North, the sister marina to Herrington Harbor South, has a complete repair and service yard for both power and sail with several on-site vendors. It also has 650 slips – 50 allotted to visiting yachts. Herrington Harbor South is the only one of the two marinas actually located in **HERRINGTON HARBOR.** The marina's "Caribbean" ambience sets the mood for your stay by the bay complete with pool and beaches, and saunas, an inn and restaurant, and more. This facility has 600 slips, with 80 allotted for visitors. Both marinas also offer a courtesy car. Call either south or north on VHF 9.

Chart 12264. HEADING FOR THE PATUXENT

The 30 miles of cliff-lined shores between Herring Bay and The Patuxent River can remind a northeast cruiser of the upper north shore of Long Island, with no apparent port for a storm in sight except on the opposite shores. There are, however, two places to duck into on your way to **SOLOMONS**.

CHESAPEAKE BEACH and LONG BEACH

A well-marked channel and two jetties, guide you through the shoals, south of **HOLLAND POINT**, to **CHESAPEAKE BEACH**, a man-made fishing harbor with reported depths of 7 feet. Rod ' n Reel has 10 transient slips for vessels up to 65 feet, plus a restaurant and fuel. Depths at the docks are 4 feet MLW. Fishing Creek Landing can take 20 transients with dock depths at 6 feet MLW.

Further south, is **FLAG HARBOR** (below Calvert Beach, at **LONG BEACH**) with a large condo marine facility. Look for the 20-foot white pylon on the beach, just north of the entrance, which has extending stone jetties marked with a red and a green light. The **Calvert Cliffs Nuclear Power Plant** is another landmark to use, approximately 2 miles south of the entrance. Transients are welcome.

THE PATUXENT

This 110 mile long scenic river has almost lost its identity to **SOLOMONS**, one of the bay's most talked about cruising destinations. Nowadays cruisers say they're "heading for Solomons Island," not the Patuxent, which is where Solomons (not really an island anymore) sits...jutting out of the north side of the river's mouth.

The Chesapeake's Western Shore makes a gradual curve to the east coming from Herring Bay – the furthest point of land on the bay being **COVE POINT**. The Point is marked by **COVE POINT LIGHTHOUSE** (38° 23.2'N, 76°22.9'W, FL W 10s, 45ft.) and **COVE POINT PLATFORM LIGHT A** (38°24.1N, 76°23.2'W, FL Y 2.5S, 40ft.). Expect choppy waters as this is one of the narrowest parts of the bay and water is deep fairly close to the shorelines. Also be mindful of a restricted area near the point with research buoys. **LITTLE COVE POINT** has a shoal, reportedly 6 feet MLW, that extends out a half-mile.

You have a choice of two passages to enter the Solomons: one channel from the north and one from the east. They both skirt a heart-shaped patch of shoal marked by flashing R "6." The passage from the north is close to shore but has depths of 9- to 20 feet. If using the outer channel, stay well off R "6."

Sailboats seem to outnumber powerboats here. Most mariners' facilities are located on **BACK CREEK**. Eight marinas welcome transients. The Lighthouse Restaurant, Bowen's Inn and Restaurant, Catamaran's Restaurant, and the Back Creek Inn B&B have minimal dockage for patrons. Zahniser's Yachting Center has 50 transient spaces, Spring Cove Marina offers 30, as do Hospitality Harbor (Holiday Inn), and Calvert Marina. Solomons Island Yacht Club welcomes other yacht club cruisers with the appropriate membership card.

Town Center Marina, a **Coastal Properties** marina, has undergone extensive renovations and a name change. It is now called **Solomons Yachting Center** (410-326-2401) taking transients, up to 170 feet in length, on state-of-the-art, floating docks, with 40-foot finger piers. The marina is located on the point of **BACK CREEK**.

A dinghy dock and a free pumpout service is next to Catamaran's Restaurant. Good but crowded anchorage can be found up Back Creek near the **Calvert Marine Museum**, or in **MILL CREEK**, north beyond **MOLLY'S LEG,** near the condos.

Solomons Island is known for boat building and oystering and the area's history is well-presented at **The Calvert Marine Museum and Aquarium**, next to Zahnisers. The relocated screwpile **Drum Point Lighthouse** sits at its waterfront entrance. It has been authentically restored and is the museum's main attraction. Exhibits in the 30,000 square foot building include locally built vessels, a log oyster boat, fine art from the region, extraordinary fossils, artifacts from the War of 1812, and a look at the estuarine life of the Patuxent.

On-foot provisioning is available from the dinghy dock at the Holiday Inn's Hospitality Harbor Marina. Other marinas do rent bikes for exploring.

Heading upriver, 18th- century manor homes and tobacco plantations, designed and built in the Chesapeake style, line the river's shores making for a sightseeing trip back in time. Sailboaters can transit under the **Thomas Jefferson Memorial Bridge** (cl. 140 feet) at **TOWN POINT**, but it's extension, the **TOWN CREEK BRIDGE**, is fixed at 30 feet cl. Several creeks offer anchorage. Notable is **ST. LEONARD CREEK** on the north side of the river. St. Leonard is wide and exceptionally deep. Enter the creek on the starboard side of G "1," ignoring R "14" which is a river mark, not a creek mark. Pick an anchorage to suit your desires or head on up to Vera's White Sands Marina and Restaurant where dockside depths range from 12- to 15 feet MLW. As Vera says, "This is not a restaurant, it's a happening!" Vera's place offers 40 transient slips, gas and diesel, and a really good time. ⚓

Charts 12285, 12254. THE POTOMAC RIVER and LOWER BAY

This guide does not currently take cruisers past Solomons on the Western Shore or Cambridge on the Eastern Shore. If you're planning to explore the cruising grounds on the Potomac River– all the way to the nation's capital, the Virginia shorelines, and the Lower Chesapeake Bay you may want to consider the following marine facilities operated under the auspices of Coastal properties.

CHART 12285. On the Potomac: **Belmont Bay Harbor,** (703-490-5088) on Occoquan Bay; **Fort Washington Marina** 301-292-7700 on Piscataway Creek; and the **Gangplank Marina,** 202-554-5000, in Washington D.C. right off the Washington Channel behind Potomac Park.

CHART 12254. Lynnhaven Bay area, Cape Henry: **Long Bay Pointe Marina**, 757-321-4550.

CHESAPEAKE BAY FACILITIES alphabetical index

CHESAPEAKE BAY FACILITIES alphabetical index

CHESAPEAKE BAY FACILITIES alphabetical index

ABOUT OUR CHESAPEAKE BAY MARINA TABLES: SEE NOTE PAGE 232.

HEADWATERS

Chesapeake Bay

	MARINA'S NAME & PHONE NUMBER	MONITORS VHF CHANNEL	TRANSIENT Electricity • Moorings • Berths	Hull repairs • Engine repairs • Ramp	WINTER STORAGE: Wet • Dry	RAILWAY CAPACITY IN FEET	LIFT CAPACITY IN TONS	BOAT RENTAL: Canoe • Row • Motor	BOAT RENTAL: Charter • House • Sail	Restaurant • Lodging • Camping	Showers • Laundry • Pool	Pumpout • Toilets	Bait • Tackle • Water • Ice	Groceries • Hardware	Diesel fuel • Gasoline
	C&D CANAL														
1	DELAWARE CITY MARINA 302-834-4172	16	E B	H E	W D		20			R	S L	P T	WI BT	G H	G D
2	SUMMIT NORTH MARINA 302-836-1800	16	E B		W D		50			R	S L P	P T	W I		G D
3	**CHESAPEAKE INN RESTAURANT & MARINA 410-885-2040**	**16**	**E B**							**R**	**S**	**P T**	**W I**		
4	PUBLIC BOAT RAMP & PICNIC AREA, AND CHESAPEAKE CITY CANAL MUSEUM			R											
5	**THE NEW SCHAEFER'S CANAL HOUSE & MARINA 410-885-2204**	**16 9**	**E B**							**R L**	**S**	**P T**	**W I**	**G**	**G D**
5A	HARBOR NORTH MARINA 410-885-5656	16 9	EB	HE								PT	I		G
	SUSQUEHANNA RIVER														
6	HAVRE DE GRACE CITY YACHT BASIN 410-939-9448	68	E B								S	P T	I		G D
7	HAVRE DE GRACE MARINA, LONG POND 410-939-2161	16	E B	H E								P T	W I		
8	DECOY MUSEUM PUBLIC RAMP			R								T			
10	HAVRE DE GRACE MARINA/WATER ST. 410-939-2161	16 72	E B	H E	W D		L			R	S	P T		G H	G D
11	JEAN S. ROBERTS MEMORIAL PARK			R											
12	TYDINGS PARK PUBLIC RAMP			R								T			
13	PENN'S BEACH MARINA 410-939-2060	16	E B								S	P T	W I		G
14	TIDEWATER MARINA 410-939-0950	16 9	E B	R	W D		35			R	S	P T	W I B T		G D
15	OWEN'S MARINA 410-642-6646		E B								S	T			
16	PERRYVILLE YACHT CLUB 410-642-6364		E B	E											G
17	PERRYVILLE BOAT RAMP			R											
18	SUSQUEHANNA STATE PARK LAPIDUM BOAT RAMP			R								T			

CHART LOCATER NUMBER	MARINA'S NAME & PHONE NUMBER	MONITORS VHF CHANNEL	TRANSIENT: Electricity • Moorings • Berths	Hull repairs • Engine repairs • Ramp	WINTER STORAGE: Wet • Dry	RAILWAY CAPACITY IN TONS	LIFT CAPACITY IN FEET	BOAT RENTAL: Canoe • Row • Motor • Sail	BOAT RENTAL: Charter • House	Restaurant • Lodging • Camping	Showers • Laundry • Pool	Pumpout • Toilets	Bait • Tackle • Water • Ice	Groceries • Hardware	Diesel fuel • Gasoline
19	PORT DEPOSIT MARINA PARK			R								T			
	NORTHEAST RIVER														
20	CHARLESTOWN MARINA 410-287-8125	16	E B	H E R			50				S L	P T	W I	G H	G
21	CRAFT HAVEN 410-642-2515	16	E B								S	T	W I		
22	LEE'S MARINA 410-287-5100	16		H E											
23	WATER STREET BOAT RAMP			R											
24	WELLWOOD YACHT CLUB 410-287-6666		E B	H E R						R	S	T	W I	H	G D
25	ANCHOR MARINA 410-287-6000		E B	H E R			L			R	S	P T			G D
26	AVALON YACHT BASIN 410-287-6722		E B	H E			L			R	S	T	W I	H	
27	BAY BOAT WORKS, INC 410-287-8113		E B	H E R			35				S	P T			G D
28	JACKSON MARINE 410-287-9400		E B	H E			50			R	S	P T	W I	G H	G D
29	**MCDANIEL YACHT BASIN 410-287-8121**	**16**	**E B**	**H E**	**W D**	**60**	**50**				**S L P**	**P T**	**W I**	**H**	**G D**
30	NORTH EAST YACHT 410-287-6660	16	E B	H E	W D		40				S	P T	W I	H	
31	PAT'S MARINA 410-287-5298		E B	H E R	W D		L				S	P T	W I	H	
32	SHELTER COVE MARINA 410-287-9400	16	E B	H E	W D		25			R	S L	P T	W I / B T	G / H	G D
	ELK RIVER														
33	ROGUES HARBOR ELK POINT MARINA 410-398-6600		E B	H E R	W D						S	T	W I		
34	TRITON MARINA 410-398-7515		E B	H E R	W D		15			R	S	P T	W I	H	G
35	THE COVE MARINA 410-398-8163		E B	H E R	W D						S L	P T	W I	H	
36	LOCUST POINT MARINA 410-392-3588		E B R	H E	D		15				S	P T	W I	H	

EASTERN SHORE
Chesapeake Bay

Chart Locater Number	Marina's Name & Phone Number	Monitors VHF Channel	Transient: Electricity • Moorings • Berths	Hull repairs • Engine repairs • Ramp	Winter Storage: Wet • Dry	Railway Capacity in Feet	Lift Capacity in Tons	Boat Rental: Canoe • Row • Motor	Boat Rental: Charter • House • Sail	Restaurant • Lodging • Camping	Showers • Laundry • Pool	Pumpout • Toilets	Groceries • Water • Ice	Bait • Tackle	Diesel fuel • Gasoline • Hardware
37	HARBOUR NORTH MARINA 410-392-4994 SEE 5A ON C&D CANAL	16 9	EB R	HE	WD							PT	WI	BT	G H / G
38	TAYLOR'S MARINE 410-392-3588		EB	HE R	D		15				S P	PT	WI		H
39	STEMMERS RUN BOAT RAMP			R											

BOHEMIA RIVER

Chart Locater Number	Marina's Name & Phone Number	Monitors VHF Channel	Transient	Hull/Engine/Ramp	Winter Storage	Railway Capacity	Lift Capacity	Boat Rental C/R/M	Boat Rental Ch/H/S	Restaurant/Lodging/Camping	Showers/Laundry/Pool	Pumpout/Toilets	Groceries/Water/Ice	Bait/Tackle	Diesel/Gasoline/Hardware
40	BOHEMIA ANCHORAGE 410-275-8148	16	EB	HE	WD		20				S	PT	WI		
41	BOHEMIA MARINE SERVICES AT BOHEMIA BAY 410-885-2601	16 9	EB	HE	WD		40				SL P	PT	WI	G	G D
42	BOHEMIA VISTA YACHT BASIN 410-885-5402	16	EB R	HE	WD		20					PT	WI		H
43	HACK'S POINT MARINA 410-275-9151		EB	HE R	WD		15			R	S	PT	WI		
44	**TWO RIVERS YACHT BASIN 410-885-2257**	16	EB R	HE	WD		30			R	S P	PT	WI		G
45	RICHMOND'S MARINA 410-275-2061		EB	HE R	WD					R	S L P	PT	WI BT		G H / G D

SASSAFRAS RIVER

Chart Locater Number	Marina's Name & Phone Number	Monitors VHF Channel	Transient	Hull/Engine/Ramp	Winter Storage	Railway Capacity	Lift Capacity	Boat Rental C/R/M	Boat Rental Ch/H/S	Restaurant/Lodging/Camping	Showers/Laundry/Pool	Pumpout/Toilets	Groceries/Water/Ice	Bait/Tackle	Diesel/Gasoline/Hardware
46	BETTERTON BEACH WATERFRONT PARK			R								T			
47	SKIPJACK COVE YACHTING RESORT 410-275-2122	16	EB	HE R	WD		50				SL P	PT	WI BT		G H / G D
48	DUFFY CREEK MARINA 410-275-2141	16	EB	HE R	WD		50				SL	PT	WI BT		G H / G D
49	FREDERICKTOWN BOAT RAMP			R											
50	**SAILING ASSOCIATES 410-275-8171**	16 68	EB M	HE R	WD		L			R	S P L	PT	WI		
51	GEORGETOWN YACHT BASIN, INC. 410-648-5112	16 71	E B M	H E R	WD		110			R	S L P	PT	WI BT		G H / G D
52	**GRANARY RESTAURANT & MARINA 410-648-5112**	16 9	E B								S L P	T	W I		
53	**KITTY KNIGHT HOUSE 410-275-8600**									R					
54	SASSAFRAS HARBOR MARINA 410-275-1144	16	EB	HE	WD		70			R	SL P	PT	WI		H

Chesapeake Bay

CHART LOCATER NUMBER — **MARINA'S NAME & PHONE NUMBER**

#	Marina Name & Phone	Monitors VHF Channel	Transient Electricity•Moorings•Berths	Hull repairs•Engine repairs•Ramp	Winter Storage: Wet•Dry	Railway Capacity in Feet	Lift Capacity in Tons	Boat Rental: Canoe•Row•Motor	Boat Rental: Charter•House•Sail	Restaurant•Lodging•Camping	Showers•Laundry•Pool	Bait•Tackle•Water•Ice	Pumpout•Toilets	Groceries•Hardware	Diesel fuel•Gasoline
55	GREGG NECK BOAT YARD 410-648-5360		EB	HE R	WD		L				S	WI	PT	H	G D
	WORTON CREEK														
56	GREEN POINT MARINA 410-778-1615	16 79	EB	HE	WD		15				S	WI	PT	H	G D
57	WHARF AT HANDY'S POINT 410-778-4363	16	EB	HE	WD		L				SL	WI	T	H	
58	GREEN POINT BOAT RAMP			R											
59	BUCK NECK LANDING			R									T		
60	WORTON CREEK MARINA 410-778-3282	16 9	EB	HE	WD		70			R	SL P	WI	PT	G H	G D
	FAIRLEE CREEK AREA														
61	FAIRLEE PUBLIC LANDING														
62	MEARS GREAT OAK LANDING 410-778-5007	16 9	EB	HE R	WD		50		CS	R	SL P	WI	PT	G H	G D
63	TOLCHESTER MARINA, INC. BUOY #30 410-778-1400	16	EB	HE	WD		L			R	SL P	WI	PT	G H	G D
	SWAN CREEK/ROCK HALL														
64	SPRING COVE PUBLIC LANDING			R											
65	GRATITUDE MARINA 410-639-7011	16	EB	HE	WD		35				SP	WI	PT	G H	G D
66	OSPREY POINT MARINA AND INN 410-639-2663	16	EB	HE	WD					R L	SL P	WI	PT		
67	HAVEN HARBOUR MARINA 410-778-6697	16	EB	HE	WD		35				SL P	WI	PT	G H	G D
68	SWAN CREEK MARINA 410-639-7813	16 9	EB	HE	WD		L					WI	PT		
69	SPRING COVE MARINA		EB		WD						SP	WI	PT		
70	NORTH POINT MARINA, INC 410-639-2907	16 9	EB		W						SL P	WI	PT	H	G D
71	PELORUS YACHTING CENTER 410-639-2151	16	EB		WD		L				SL	WI	PT		

EASTERN SHORE
Chesapeake Bay

Chart Locater Number	Marina's Name & Phone Number	Monitors VHF Channel	Transient: Electricity • Moorings • Berths	Hull repairs • Engine repairs • Ramp	Winter Storage: Wet • Dry	Railway Capacity in Feet	Boat Rental: Canoe • Row • Motor	Lift Capacity in Tons	Boat Rental: Charter • House • Sail	Restaurant • Lodging • Camping	Showers • Laundry • Pool	Bait • Tackle • Toilets • Pumpout	Groceries • Water • Ice	Groceries • Hardware	Diesel fuel • Gasoline
72	ROCK HALL LANDING MARINA 410-639-2224	16	EB								SL P	P T	W I		
73	ROCK HALL MARINE RAILWAY 410-639-2263		EB	HE R	WD	25					S	T		H	
74	SAILING EMPORIUM 410-778-1342	16 9	EB	HE R	WD	35		CS			SL P	P T	W I	G H	G D
75	WATERMAN'S CRABHOUSE & RESTAURANT 410-639-2261 Check for opening - currently closed at publication time due to hurricane damage														
76	GREEN LANE PUBLIC LANDING			R											
	CHESTER RIVER AREA														
77	SKINNER'S NECK PUBLIC LANDING			R											
78	LONG COVE PUBLIC LANDING			R								T			
79	LONG COVE MARINA 410-778-6777	16	EB	HE		75					S	P T	W I	G H	G D
80	**LANKFORD BAY MARINA 410-778-6777**	**16**	**EB**	**HE R**	**WD**	**40**		**CS**			**SL P**	**P T**	**W I**	**G H**	**G D**
81	SHIPYARD LANDING RAMP			R								T			
82	KENNERSLEY POINT MARINA, INC. 410-758-2394	16	EB	HE	WD	L					SL P	P T	W I	H	
83	ROLPH'S WHARF MARINA Buoy 35 Chester River 410-778-6347	16	EB M	H R	D	30	CM			R L	SL P	P T	W I BT	H G	G D
84	SOUTHEAST CREEK PUBLIC LANDING			R											
85	SCOTTS POINT MARINA 410-778-2959	16	EB								S	T	W I		
86	CHESTERTOWN MARINA, INC. 410-778-3616	16	EB		WD	25					S L	P T	W I	H	G D
87	QUAKER NECK PUBLIC LANDING			R											
88	CLIFF CITY PUBLIC LANDING			R								T			
89	CENTREVILLE PUBLIC LANDING			R								T			
	KENT ISLAND/NEXT PAGE														

EASTERN SHORE

CHART LOCATER NUMBER	MARINA'S NAME & PHONE NUMBER	MONITORS VHF CHANNEL	TRANSIENT Electricity • Moorings • Berths	Hull repairs • Engine repairs • Ramp	WINTER STORAGE: Wet • Dry	RAILWAY CAPACITY IN FEET	LIFT CAPACITY IN TONS	BOAT RENTAL: Canoe • Row • Motor	BOAT RENTAL: Charter • House • Sail	Restaurant • Lodging • Camping	Showers • Laundry • Pool	Pumpout • Toilets	Bait • Tackle • Water • Ice	Groceries • Hardware	Diesel fuel • Gasoline
	KENT ISLAND SHORE & NARROWS														
90	ANGLER'S MARINA AND RESTAURANT 410-827-6717	16	E B	E			10			R	SL	PT	IW	G	
91	HARRIS CRAB HOUSE 410-827-9500									R					
92	MEARS POINT MARINA 410-827-8888	9	EB	HE			35			R	SLP				
93	**PINEY NARROWS YACHT HAVEN** **410-643-6600**	16	EB		W						SLP	PT	WI	G	G D
94	PINEY NARROWS PUBLIC LANDING			R											
95	KENT NARROWS YACHT YARD 410-643-4400		EB								SLP	P			
96	LIPPINCOTT MARINE 410-827-9300		EB	HE							SLP	PT	IW	H	
97	FISHERMAN'S INN & CRAB DECK RESTAURANT 401-827-8807									R			I		
98	SCOTT MARINE SERVICE 410-827-9053	16		H E			L				S L	PT	I	H	
99	CASTLE HARBOR MARINA 410-643-5599	9	EB								SLP	PT	IW	H	G D
100	BAY BRIDGE MARINA 410-643-3162	9 68	EB	HE		70	25				SLP	PT	IW	H	G D
101	KENTMORR HARBOUR MARINA 410-643-0029	9	EB	HE			35				SP	PT	I		G D
102	A & M MARINE SERVICES 410-827-7409			HE			35								
103	QUEEN ANNE MARINA. 410-643-5065	16 7	EB	HE			20					PT	WI	GH	G D
104	MATAPEAKE STATE PARK			R								T			
105	SHIIPPING CREEK LANDING			R											
106	SKIPJACK LANDING MARINA 410-643-2694		EB	HE			25				S	PT	WI	GH	G
	ST. MICHAELS/MILES RIVER														
112	MILES RIVER YACHT CLUB 410-745-9511	16 68	EB								SP	T	W I		G

#	MARINA'S NAME & PHONE NUMBER	MONITORS VHF CHANNEL	TRANSIENT Electricity • Moorings • Berths	Hull repairs • Engine repairs • Ramp	WINTER STORAGE: Wet • Dry	RAILWAY CAPACITY IN FEET	LIFT CAPACITY IN TONS	BOAT RENTAL: Canoe • Row • Motor	BOAT RENTAL: Charter • House • Sail	Restaurant • Lodging • Camping	Showers • Laundry • Pool	Pumpout • Toilets	Bait • Tackle • Water • Ice	Groceries • Hardware	Diesel fuel • Gasoline
114	INN AT PERRY CABIN 410-745-2200		EB							R L					
116	CHESAPEAKE BAY MARITIME MUSEUM 410-745-2916	16 9	EB							R	S	T	W I		
117	CRAB CLAW RESTAURANT 410-745-2900		B							R					
118	HIGGINS YACHT YARD 410-745-9303	16	EB	H E	WD	30					S	PT	WI		
119	ST. MICHAELS MARINA 410-745-2400	16 9	EB		W					R	S L P	PT	WI		G D
120	ST. MICHAELS HARBOUR INN, SPA & MARINA 410-745-9001	16 9	EB						C R	R L	S L P	PT	WI		G
121	OAK CREEK LANDING			R								T			
	TILGHMAN ISLAND/KNAPPS NARROWS														
122	LOWES WHARF MARINA INN 410-745-6684	16	EB							R L		PT	I W	H	G D
123	TILGHMAN ISLAND MARINA 410-886-2979	16	EB								SP	PT	WI	GH	
124	TILGHMAN ISLAND INN 410-886-2141	16	EB							R L	SP L	PT	WI		
125	KNAPPS NARROWS MARINA 410-886-2720	16	EB	H	WD	35				R	SP	T	WI	H	G D
126	SEVERN MARINE SERVICES 410-886-2159		EB	HE	WD		L			R	S	TP	WI	H	
127	HARRISON'S COUNTRY INN 410-886-2121	16	EB							L R	SP	T	WI		
128	TILGHMAN-ON-CHESAPEAKE 800-735-2933	16	EB								S L P	T P	WI		
	OXFORD/CAMBRIDGE AREAS, Tred Avon, the Choptank														
129	BELLEVUE PARK PUBLIC LANDING			R								T			
130	HORN POINT RAMP UNIVERSITY OF MARYLAND			R								T			
131	CAMPBELL'S BACHELOR POINT 410-226-5592	16	EB				L				S L P	PT	WI	H	
132	PIER STREET MARINA & RESTAURANT, INC. 410-226-5171	16	EB							R	S	T	WI		G D

Chesapeake Bay

MARINA'S NAME & PHONE NUMBER

Chart Locater Number	Marina's Name & Phone Number	Monitors VHF Channel	Transient: Electricity • Moorings • Berths	Hull repairs • Engine repairs • Ramp	Winter Storage: Wet • Dry	Railway Capacity in Feet	Lift Capacity in Tons	Boat Rental: Canoe • Row • Motor	Boat Rental: Charter • House • Sail	Restaurant • Lodging • Camping	Showers • Laundry • Pool	Pumpout • Toilets	Bait • Tackle • Water • Ice	Groceries • Hardware	Diesel fuel • Gasoline
133	OXFORD POINT LANDING			R											
134	**OXFORD BOAT YARD** 410-226-5101	16	EB	HE	WD		75				S L	P T	W I	H	
135	**MEARS YACHT HAVEN** 410-226-5450	16 9	EB		W					R	S L P	P T	W I	G	G D
136	SCHOONERS LANDING 410-226-0160		EB							R		T			
137	CUTTS & CASE INC 410-226-5416			HE				R		L	S	T	W I		
138	HINCKLEY YACHTS, (Was Crockett Bros. Boatyard) 410-226-5113	16	EB	HE			30				S L P	P T	W I	H	
139	BATES MARINE BASIN 410-226-5105	16	EB	HE						L	S	P T	W I	H	G D
140	CAMPBELL'S TOWN CREEK BOATYARD 410-226-0213	16	EB	HE						L	S L	T	W I	H	
141	OXFORD YACHT AGENCY 410-226-5454		EB	HE						L	S L	T	W I	H	D
143	GREAT MARSH PUBLIC LANDING			R								T			
144	GATEWAY MARINA 410-476-3304	16	EB	HE			20				S	P T	W I	H	G D
145	CAMBRIDGE MUNICIPAL YACHT BASIN 410-228-4031	16	EB								S L	P T	W I		
146	LONE WHARF LANDING			R								T			
147	FRANKLIN STREET RAMP			R											
148	CHOPTANK RIVER BOAT RAMP			R								T			
149	TRENTON STREET BOAT RAMP			R											
150	CAMBRIDGE MARINE LTD. 410-228-4820	72	EB	HE						L	S	P T	W I	H	
151	GENERATION III MARINA 410-228-2520	16	EB	HE				R		L	S P	P T		H	
152	YACHT MAINTENANCE CO. 410-228-8878	16		HE	WD		60				S	P T		H	
153	HYATT REGENCY CHESAPEAKE BAY GOLF RESORT, SPA & MARINA 410-901-1234		EB							L R	S P	P T	W I		G D

WESTERN SHORE — Chesapeake Bay

No.	Marina's Name & Phone Number	Monitors VHF Channel	Transient: Electricity • Moorings • Berths	Hull repairs • Engine repairs • Ramp	Winter Storage: Wet • Dry	Railway Capacity in Tons	Lift Capacity in Feet	Boat Rental: Canoe • Row • Motor	Boat Rental: Charter • House • Sail	Restaurant • Lodging • Camping	Showers • Laundry • Pool	Bait • Tackle • Ice	Pumpout • Toilets	Groceries • Water • Ice	Diesel fuel • Gasoline • Hardware	Diesel fuel • Gasoline
	WESTERN SHORE															
	BUSH RIVER & GUNPOWDER RIVER															
160	LEIGHT PARK			R						C			T			
161	FLYING POINT PARK PUBLIC LANDING			R									T			
162	FLYING POINT MARINA 410-676-7311		EB	HE R	D		L				S P		P T	WI	HG	G D
163	BUSH RIVER BOAT WORKS, INC. 410-272-1882	16	EB	HE R	D	R	L				S		P T		H	G
164	OTTER POINT PUBLIC LANDING			R									T			
165	GUNPOWDER COVE MARINA 410-679-5454	16	EB	HE	WD		15				S		P T	WI	H	G
166	MARINER POINT PARK			R									T			
167	GUNPOWDER FALLS STATE PARK			R									T			
	MIDDLE RIVER AREA															
168	PORTERS SENECA MARINA 410-335-6563		EB	HE	D		30				S P		P T	WI	H	G
169	GOOSE HARBOR MARINA 410-335-7474		EB	HE	D		L			R	S L P		P T	WI	H	G
170	GALLOWAY CREEK MARINA 410-335-3575		EB	HE			L				S		P T	WI		
171	❖ BOWLEY'S MARINA 410-335-3577	16 9	EB	HE R	WD		30			R	S L P		P T	WI		G D
172	BOATING CENTER OF BALTIMORE 410-687-2000			HE			24				S		P			
173	LONG BEACH MARINA 410-335-8602		EB	HE			L				S P		T	WI	GH	
174	MARYLAND MARINA 410-335-9343		EB	HE			L				S L		P T	WI		
175	EDWARD'S BOAT YARD 410-335-2311		EB	HE		R	L				S		P T	WI	H	G D
176	TRADEWINDS MARINA 410-335-7000		EB	HE			15				S		P T	WI	H	

WESTERN SHORE
Chesapeake Bay

Chart Locater Number	Marina's Name & Phone Number	Monitors VHF Channel	Transient: Electricity • Moorings • Berths	Hull repairs • Engine repairs • Ramp	Winter Storage: Wet • Dry	Railway Capacity in Feet	Lift Capacity in Tons	Boat Rental: Canoe • Row • Motor	Boat Rental: Charter • House • Sail	Restaurant • Lodging • Camping	Showers • Laundry • Pool	Pumpout • Toilets	Bait • Tackle • Water • Ice	Groceries • Hardware	Diesel fuel • Gasoline
177	CHESAPEAKE YACHTING CENTER 410-335-4900		EB	HE			25				S LP	PT	W I		G D
178	PARKSIDE MARINA 410-344-1187		EB							R	S P	PT	W I		
179	STANSBURY YACHT BASIN, INC 410-686-3909	16	EB	HE			L				S	PT	W I	H	G
180	MARKLEY'S MARINA 410-687-5575		EB	HE			L				S	PT	W I	H	
181	RIVER WATCH RESTAURANT & MARINA 410-687-1422		EB							R	S	PT	W I		G D
182	ANCHOR BAY MARINA 410-574-0777	16	EB								S L	PT	W I		
183	SUNSET HARBOR MARINA 410-687-7290		EB	HE			25				S	PT	W I	HG	
184	DECKLEMAN'S BOAT YARD, INC. 410-391-6482	16	EB	HE			L				S	PT	W I	HG	
185	ESSEX MARINA & BOAT SALES 410-686-3455		EB	HE	WD		25				S	PT	W I	HG	
186	CUTTER MARINE YACHT BASIN 410-391-7245		EB	HE			25				S P	PT	W I		
187	RILEY'S MARINA 410-686-0771		EB	HE			15				S	PT	W I	H	G
188	BUEDEL'S MARINA & BOATYARD INC. 410-687-3577		EB	HE							S	PT		HG	
189	NORMAN CREEK MARINA 410-686-9343		EB							R	S	PT	W I	HG	G D
190	SUE ISLAND YACHT BASIN 410-574-7915		EB	HE R							S	PT	W I	HG	
	BACK RIVER														
191	WEST SHORE YACHT CENTER 410-686-6998		EB	HE	D		30				S L	PT	W I	H	G
192	COX'S POINT PARK			R								T			
	PATAPSCO RIVER														
193	YOUNG'S BOAT YARD 410-477-8607		EB				15				S	PT	W I	HG	
194	ANCHOR BAY EAST MARINA 410-284-1044	16	EB	HE			L			R	S L	PT	W I	HG	G D

WESTERN SHORE
Chesapeake Bay

MARINA'S NAME & PHONE NUMBER

Chart Locater Number	Marina's Name & Phone Number	Monitors VHF Channel	Transient • Electricity	Hull repairs • Engine repairs	Moorings • Berths • Ramp	Winter Storage: Wet • Dry	Railway Capacity in Tons	Lift Capacity in Feet	Boat Rental: Canoe • Row • Motor	Boat Rental: Charter • House • Sail	Restaurant • Lodging • Camping	Showers • Laundry • Pool	Bait • Tackle • Water • Ice	Pumpout • Toilets	Groceries • Hardware	Diesel fuel • Gasoline
195	SHELTERED HARBOR MARINA 410-288-4100		EB	HE							L	S	W I	T	H	G
196	MARYLAND YACHT CLUB 410-255-4444	16 9	EB									S LP	W I	PT	H	G D
197	FAIRVIEW MARINA 410-437-3400		EB	HE	R						L	S LP	W I	PT	H	
198	PLEASURE COVE MARINA 410-686-9343	69	EB	HE	R			77			R	S LP	W I	PT	H	G D
200	OAK HARBOR MARINA 410-255-4070	16 72	EB	HE	R						L	S L	W I	PT	H	
201	PASADENA YACHT YARD, INC 410-255-1771		EB	HE	R						L	S	W I	PT	H	G D
202	WHITE ROCKS MARINA & YACHTING CENTER 410-255-3800		EB	HE	R						L R	S LP	W I	PT	HG	
203	MAURGALE INN & MARINA 410-437-0402		EB	HE	R			20			R	S	W I	PT		
	BALTIMORE															
205	BALTIMORE MARINE CENTER AT LIGHTHOUSE POINT 410-675-8888	16	EB	HE							L R	S LP	W I	PT	HG	G D
206	ANCHORAGE MARINA 410-477-8868	16	EB	E							R	S LP	W I	PT	HG	
207	HENDERSON'S WHARF MARINA & INN FELL'S POINT 410-732-1049	9	EB	HE								S L	W I	PT		
208	CENTER DOCK MARINA 410-685-9055 EXT. 223	16 71	EB	HE								S	W I	T		
209	INNER HARBOR EAST MARINA 410-625-1700	16/9 68	EB	HE							R	S L	W I	PT	G	G D
210	BALTIMORE CITY PUBLIC DOCKS 410-396-3174	68	EB	HE								S	W I	PT		
211	INNER HARBOR MARINA OF BALTIMORE 410-837-5339	16 69	EB	HE							R	S L	W I	PT	HG	G D
212	HARBORVIEW MARINA 410-752-1122	16	EB			W					R	S L P	W I	PT		
213	TIDEWATER YACHT SERVICE CENTER 410-625-4992	16	EB	HE				77				S		PT	H	G D
	MAGOTHY RIVER / BAY BRIDGE AREA															
214	SANDY POINT STATE PARK				R									T		

Chesapeake Bay

MARINA'S NAME & PHONE NUMBER

Chart Locater Number	Marina's Name & Phone Number	Monitors VHF Channel	Transient: Electricity • Moorings • Berths	Hull repairs • Engine repairs • Ramp	Winter Storage: Wet • Dry	Railway Capacity in Tons / Lift Capacity in Feet	Boat Rental: Canoe • Row • Motor	Boat Rental: Charter • House • Sail	Restaurant • Lodging • Camping	Showers • Laundry • Pool	Bait • Tackle • Water • Ice / Pumpout • Toilets	Groceries • Water • Hardware	Diesel fuel • Gasoline
215	PODICKORY POINT YACHT & BEACH CLUB 410-757-8000		EB						R	S LP	P T		
215A	WHITEHALL MARINA 410-757-4819		EB	HE							T		
216	GIBSON ISLAND YACHT CLUB 410-255-7632		M							S	P T	W I	G D
217	GIBSON ISLAND MARINA 410-360-2500		EB	HE		L			R	S LP	P T		
218	MAGOTHY MARINA 410-647-2356		EB R	E					R	S LP	P T	W I HG D	G
219	FERRY POINT MARINA & YACHT YARD 410-544-6368		EB	HE R		L			R	S	P T	W I H	
220	CYPRESS MARINE, INC. 410-647-7940		EB	HE		L				S	P T	W I H	
221	DEEP CREEK RESTAURANT & MARINA 410-757-4045		EB	HE		L			R	S L	P T		G D

ANNAPOLIS
SEVERN RIVER/SPA CREEK/EASTPORT

Chart Locater Number	Marina's Name & Phone Number	Monitors VHF Channel	Transient	Repairs	Winter Storage	Railway/Lift	Rental 1	Rental 2	Restaurant	Showers	Bait/Pumpout	Groceries	Fuel
224	CHESAPEAKE HARBOR MARINA 410-268-1969	16	EB						R	S P	P T		
225	MEARS MARINA 410-268-8282	16 9	EB	HE		L				S LP	P T		
226	ANNAPOLIS LANDING MARINA 410-263-0090	9 72	EB							S LP	P T	H	G
227	PORT ANNAPOLIS MARINA 410-269-1990	16	EB	HE		L			R	S LP	P T		
228	BERT JABIN'S YACHT YARD 410-268-9667	16	EB	HE		35			R	S L	P T	HG	
229	CHESAPEAKE RIGGING, LTD. 410-268-0956		EB	HE		L				S L	T	HG	
230	EASTPORT YACHT YARD 410-280-9988		EB	HE		L			R	S L	P T		
231	**HORN POINT HARBOR 410-269-0933**		EB		W				R	S	P T	W	
232	ANNAPOLIS MD. CAPITAL YACHT CLUB 410-269-5219	16	EB	H					R	S P	P T		
233	EASTPORT YACHT CLUB 410-267-9549	8	EB			L			R	S	T		G
234	ANNAPOLIS HARBOR BOAT YARD 410-267-9050	16	EB			L			R	S	P T		G

WESTERN SHORE
Chesapeake Bay

Chart Locater Number	Marina's Name & Phone Number	Monitors VHF Channel	Transient: Electricity • Moorings • Berths	Hull/Engine Repairs	Winter Storage: Wet • Dry	Railway Capacity (ft)	Lift Capacity (tons)	Boat Rental: Canoe • Row • Motor	Boat Rental: Charter • House • Sail	Restaurant • Lodging • Camping	Showers • Laundry • Pool	Bait • Tackle	Pumpout • Toilets	Water • Ice	Groceries • Hardware	Diesel • Gasoline
235	PIER FOUR MARINA 410-990-9515		EB							R	SL		PT		G	
236	ANNAPOLIS CITY MARINA 410-268-0660	9	EB							R	SL		T		HG	G D
237	PETRINI, INC. 410-263-4278	16	EB	H			50			R	S		T		HG	
238	SARLES BOAT & ENGINE SHOP, INC. 410-263-3661		EB	HE				R	L		S		T		HG	
239	CHESAPEAKE CATAMARAN CENTER 410-280-2288		EB	HE					L	R	S		T			
240	OLDE TOWNE MARINA LTD 410-263-9277		EB	HE						R	S		T		G	
241	ANNAPOLIS YACHT CLUB (RECIPROCAL ONLY) 410-263-9279	7	EB	HE						R	S		T			
242	THE YACHT BASIN COMPANY 410-263-3544	9	EB	HE						R	SL		PT		HG	
243	ANNAPOLIS MARRIOTT / PUSSER'S LANDING 410-263-7837	16 9	EB	HE						R			T			G D
244	FAWCETT BOAT SUPPLIES 410-267-8681 CUSTOMERS ONLY BULKHEAD		B										T			
245	ANNAPOLIS CITY DOCK 410-263-7973	9 17	EB	HE						R	SL		PT	WI	HG	

SOUTH RIVER/SELBY BAY

Chart Locater Number	Marina's Name & Phone Number	Monitors VHF Channel	Transient: Electricity • Moorings • Berths	Hull/Engine Repairs	Winter Storage: Wet • Dry	Railway Capacity (ft)	Lift Capacity (tons)	Boat Rental: Canoe • Row • Motor	Boat Rental: Charter • House • Sail	Restaurant • Lodging • Camping	Showers • Laundry • Pool	Bait • Tackle	Pumpout • Toilets	Water • Ice	Groceries • Hardware	Diesel • Gasoline
246	SELBY BAY YACHT BASIN 410-798-0232		EB	E						R	S		PT	WI	G	G D
247	HOLIDAY POINT MARINA 410-269-6674	16	EB	HE			35			R	S		PT	WI		
248	ANCHOR YACHT BASIN 410-269-6679		EB	HE			35				S		PT		H	G D
249	SOUTH RIVER MARINA 410-798-1717		EB	HE					L		S		PT		H	
250	TURKEY POINT MARINA 410-798-1369	16	EB	HE					L		S		PT		H	G
251	LONDONTOWNE MARINA 410-956-5077		EB	HE						R	S LP		PT		G	G
252	LIBERTY YACHT CLUB & MARINA 410-266-5633		EB	HE					L	R	S		PT		G	G D
253	OAK GROVE MARINE CENTER 410-266-6696		EB	HE					L		S		PT			G D

WESTERN SHORE
Chesapeake Bay

CHART LOCATER NUMBER	MARINA'S NAME & PHONE NUMBER	MONITORS VHF CHANNEL	TRANSIENT: Electricity • Engine repairs • Moorings • Berths	Hull repairs • Engine repairs • Moorings • Berths	WINTER STORAGE: Wet • Dry	RAILWAY CAPACITY IN FEET	BOAT RENTAL: Canoe • Row • Motor	LIFT CAPACITY IN TONS	BOAT RENTAL: Charter • House • Sail	Restaurant • Lodging • Camping	Showers • Laundry • Pool	Bait • Tackle • Water • Ice	Pumpout • Toilets	Groceries • Hardware	Diesel fuel • Gasoline
254	PIER 7 — 410-956-2288		EB								S		P T		G D
RHODE RIVER															
255	CADLE CREEK MARINA — 410-798-1915		EB	HE			R	L		R			P T	H	G D
256	CASA RIO MARINA — 410-261-7111	16	EB	HE				15					T		
257	RHODE RIVER MARINA — 410-798-1658		EB	HE			R	L					P T		
WEST RIVER															
258	WEST RIVER YACHT HARBOR — 410-867-4065	16	EB	HE				40			S P	W I	P T	HG	G D
259	WEST RIVER FUEL DOCK — 410-867-1444	16	EB								SP	W I	P T	HG	G D
260	PIRATE'S COVE — 410-867-2300	16	EB								S L		P T		
261	HARTGE YACHT YARD — 410-867-2188	16	EB	HE			R	30		R	S		P T	H	G D
262	STEAMBOAT LANDING — 410-867-7200	83	B							R			T		G
HERRING BAY															
263	HERRINGTON HARBOUR NORTH — 410-867-4343	16, 9	EB	HE				70		R	S LP		P T		G
264	SKIPPERS PIER — 410-867-7110		EB							R			T	HG	G D
265	HERRINGTON HARBOUR RESORT SOUTH — 410-741-5100	9	EB	HE						R	S LP		P T	HG	G D
266	SHIPWRIGHT HARBOR — 410-867-7686		EB	HE				15			S LP		P T		
267	BAY HARBOR BOAT YARD — 410-867-2392							15		R	S LP		T		G
268	ROCKHOLD CREEK MARINA — 410-867-7919		EB	HE				20		R	S LP		P T	HG	G D
269	HARBOR COVE — 301-261-9500	16	EB	HE				L		R	S LP		P T	HG	G
270	GATES MARINA — 410-867-2157		EB	HE				L		R	S P		P T	HG	G

WESTERN SHORE
Chesapeake Bay

MARINA'S NAME & PHONE NUMBER

CHART LOCATER NUMBER	MARINA'S NAME & PHONE NUMBER	MONITORS VHF CHANNEL	TRANSIENT: Electricity • Moorings • Berths	Hull repairs • Engine repairs • Ramp	WINTER STORAGE: Wet • Dry	RAILWAY CAPACITY IN FEET	LIFT CAPACITY IN TONS	BOAT RENTAL: Canoe • Row • Motor	BOAT RENTAL: Charter • House • Sail	Restaurant • Lodging • Camping	Showers • Laundry • Pool	Pumpout • Toilets	Bait • Tackle • Water • Ice	Groceries • Hardware	Diesel fuel • Gasoline
271	SHERMAN'S MARINA 301-261-5013		EB							R	S L	PT		H	G D
	CHESAPEAKE BEACH AREA														
272	WATERFRONT PARK			R											
273	ROD 'N REEL 301-855-8450	88A	EB						L		S	PT	WI BT	HG	G
274	FISHING CREEK LANDING 301-855-3572	16	EB	HE					L	R	S	T	WI	HG	G D
275	BREEZY POINT MARINA. 301-855-3572	16	EB	HE					L	R	S	T	WI	HG	G
	PATUXENT RIVER/SOLOMONS														
276	SOLOMONS BOAT RAMP			R											
277	HARBOR ISLAND MARINA 410-326-3441	16	EB	HE			25				S	PT	WI	GH	G D
278	LIGHTHOUSE INN 410-326-2444		B							R					
279	SOLOMON'S PIER RESTAURANT 410-326-2424		B							R					
280	DIGIOVANNI'S DOCK OF THE BAY 410-394-6400		B							R					
291	SOLOMONS YACHTING CENTER (formerly Town Center Marina) 410-326-2401	16	EB	HE	WD		50				S L	PT	WI BT		G D
292	BACK CREEK BED & BREAKFAST 410-326-2022		B							R L					
293	ZAHNISER'S YACHTING CENTER 410-326-2166	16 9	EB	HE		R	30			R	S LP	PT	WI	HG	
294	COMFORT INN BEACON MARINA 410-326-6303	16	EB							R L	S LP	PT		G	
295	SPRING COVE MARINA 410-326-2161	16	EB	HE					L	R	S LP	PT	WI	HG	G D
296	CALVERT MARINA 410-326-4251	16	EB	HE		R			L	R	S LP	PT	WI	HG	G D
297	HOSPITALITY HARBOR MARINA 410-326-1052	16	EB	HE					L	R	S LP	PT		HG	G
298	BOATEL CALIFORNA 301-737-1400	16 68	EB							R	S P	PT			

CHART LOCATER NUMBER	MARINA'S NAME & PHONE NUMBER	MONITORS VHF CHANNEL	TRANSIENT Electricity • Moorings • Berths	Hull repairs • Engine repairs • Ramp	WINTER STORAGE: Wet • Dry	RAILWAY CAPACITY IN FEET	LIFT CAPACITY IN TONS	BOAT RENTAL: Canoe • Row • Motor	BOAT RENTAL: Charter • House • Sail	Restaurant • Lodging • Camping	Showers • Laundry • Pool	Bait • Tackle • Pumpout • Toilets	Groceries • Water • Ice	Diesel fuel • Gasoline • Hardware
299	CLARK'S LANDING			R										
300	FOREST LANDING RECREATION AREA			R								T		
301	BLACKSTONE MARINA 301-373-2015	16	EB	HE			L				R	S LP	P T	HG	G
302	WINPISENGER EDUCATIONAL CENTER OF PLACID HARBOR 301-373-3300		EB									S	T		
302A	VERA'S WHITE SANDS RESTAURANT AND MARINA 410-586-1182		EB								R		P T	I	G D

Charts for the following marinas are not included in this guide.
Please call COASTAL PROPERTIES 410-269-0933,
or the numbers listed below each marina, for more information about these locations.

POTOMAC RIVER AREA														
⊕ FORT WASHINGTON MARINA 301-292-7700		16	EB M	HE R	WD	35	R		R	R	S L	P T	WI	G D
GANGPLANK MARINA 202-554-5000		16	EB	W			R		R	R	SL	PT	WI	

VIRGINIA														
BELMONT BAY HARBOR / POTOMAC RIVER 703-490-5088		16	EB	W							SL	PT	WI	G D
LONG BAY POINTE MARINA / VIRGINIA BEACH 757-321-4550		16	EB	W						R	SL	PT	WI BT	GH	G D

ABOUT OUR CHESAPEAKE BAY MARINE FACILITY TABLES

The checkpoints in the Chesapeake Bay Marina Tables differ slightly from the marina tables in the other cruising areas of this guide.

1. Most Chesapeake Bay marinas are open for office staff contact all year, so we eliminated the **seasonal checkpoint** from these tables.

2. We added the **swimming pool checkpoint** to the Chesapeake Bay tables because boaters consider this amenity important while cruising the bay and its tributaries, for two reasons:

ONE: the warmer weather and waters in this area;

TWO: the bay's ubiquitous jellyfish/stinging nettles which appear in the bay's saltwater areas from mid to late summer.

Ship's Bells Made Easy

Duties aboard a ship are called "watches," and each watch consists of a 4-hour period. A traditional 24-hour period is divided into six 4-hour periods. Time is kept and recorded by the ringing of the ship's clock every 30 minutes. The chiming of the clock is of significance because it identifies the time when a specific duty is to be performed, and recorded, by those on watch. The ringing of the 8 bells signifies the end of the watch and the beginning of the next watch. The process then repeats itself. The one exception to the 4-hour watch schedule is on the "Dog Watch," the watch running from 4:00 PM to 8:00 PM (1600 to 2000 hours). This watch is divided in two 2-hour periods: the "First Dog Watch" and the "Second Dog Watch." This is done to rotate the watch crew schedule, making certain that no member of the crew will always have the same watch time each day.

	TIME	NUMBER OF CHIMES	TIME	NUMBER OF CHIMES
	AM ....24-Hour Clock		PM............24-Hour Clock	
	Midnight 2400	**8 CHIMES**	Noon 1200	**8 CHIMES**
MIDDLE WATCH	12:30.......0030	1 CHIME	12.30 1230	1 CHIME
	1:00.........0100	2 CHIMES	1:00.........1300	2 CHIMES
	1:30.........0130	3 CHIMES	1:30.........1330	3 CHIMES
	2:00.........0200	4 CHIMES	2:00.........1400	4 CHIMES
	2:30.........0230	5 CHIMES	2:30.........1430	5 CHIMES
	3:00.........0300	6 CHIMES	3:00.........1500	6 CHIMES
	3:30.........0330	7 CHIMES	3:30.........1530	7 CHIMES
	4:00.........0400	8 CHIMES	4:00.........1600	8 CHIMES
MORNING WATCH	4:30.........0430	1 CHIME	4:30.........1630	1 CHIME
	5:00.........0500	2 CHIMES	5:00.........1700	2 CHIMES
	5:30.........0530	3 CHIMES	5:30.........1730	3 CHIMES
	6:00.........0600	4 CHIMES	6:00.........1800	4 CHIMES
	6:30.........0630	5 CHIMES	6:30.........1830	5 CHIMES
	7:00.........0700	6 CHIMES	7:00.........1900	6 CHIMES
	7:30.........0730	7 CHIMES	7:30.........1930	7 CHIMES
	8:00.........0800	8 CHIMES	8:00.........2000	8 CHIMES
FORENOON WATCH	8:30.........0830	1 CHIME	8:30.........2030	1 CHIME
	9:00.........0900	2 CHIMES	9:00.........2100	2 CHIMES
	9:30.........0930	3 CHIMES	9:30.........2130	3 CHIMES
	10:00.......1000	4 CHIMES	10:00.......2200	4 CHIMES
	10:30.......1030	5 CHIMES	10:30.......2230	5 CHIMES
	11:00.......1100	6 CHIMES	11:00.......2300	6 CHIMES
	11:30.......1130	7 CHIMES	11:30.......2330	7 CHIMES
	Noon 1200	8 CHIMES	Midnight ..2400	8 CHIMES

Right column watch labels: AFTERNOON WATCH (1230–1600), 1ST DOG WATCH / DOG WATCH (1630–1800), 2ND DOG WATCH (1830–2000), FIRST WATCH (2030–2400).

PLEASE TURN TO PAGE 14 FOR INFORMATION ABOUT HOMELAND SECURITY ON THE WATER

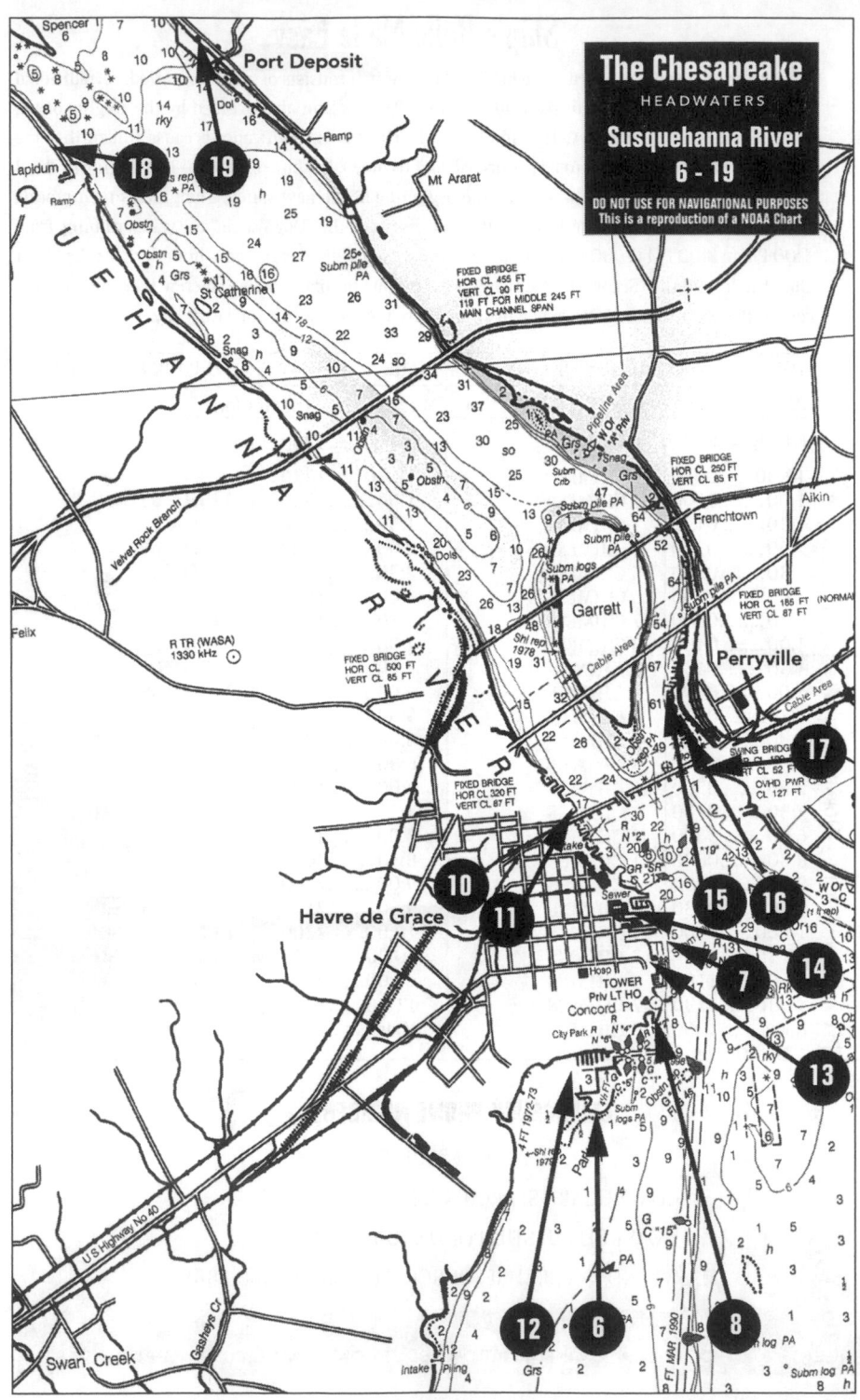

The Chesapeake

HEADWATERS

Susquehanna River
6 - 19

DO NOT USE FOR NAVIGATIONAL PURPOSES
This is a reproduction of a NOAA Chart

234

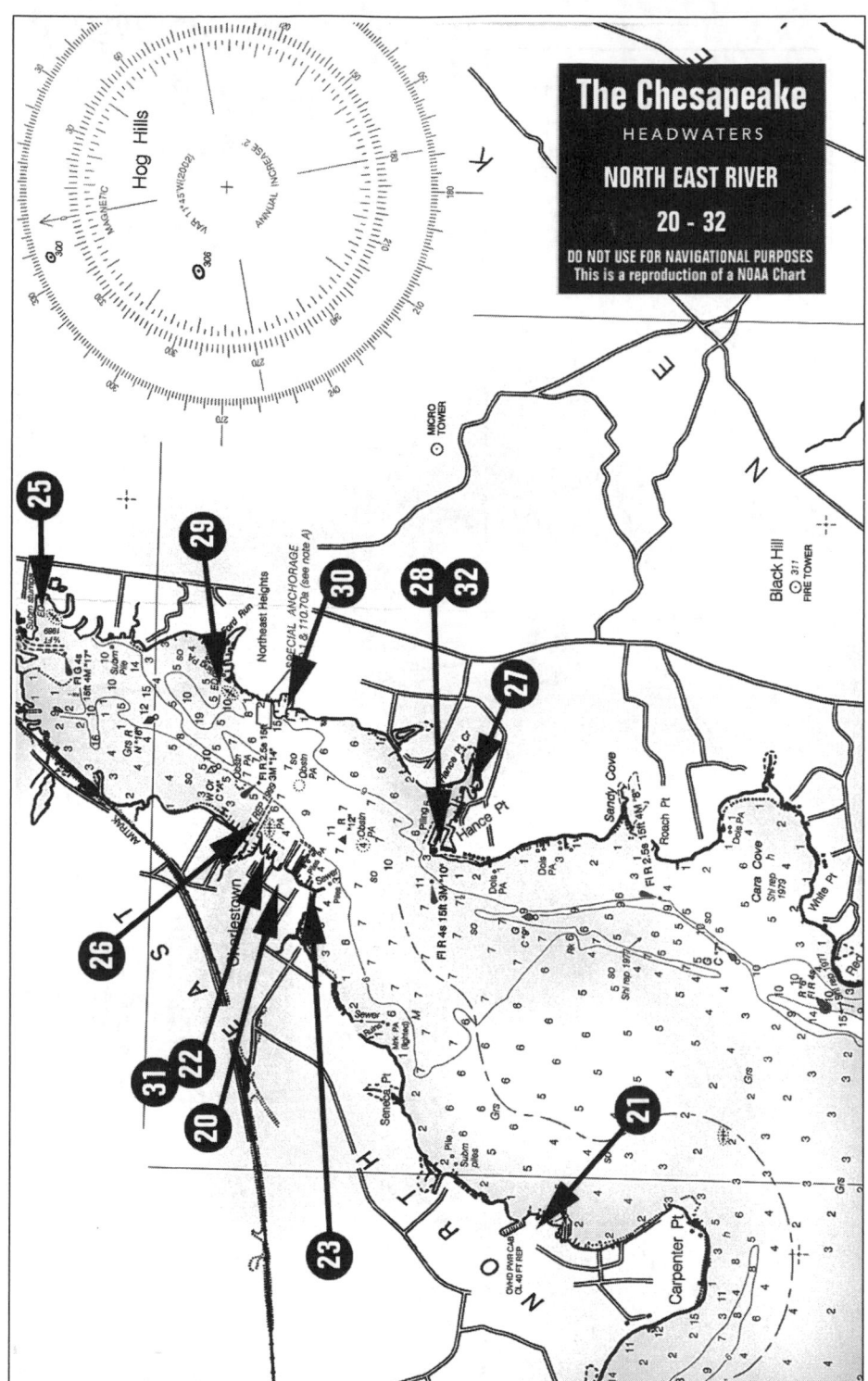

The Chesapeake

HEADWATERS

NORTH EAST RIVER

20 - 32

DO NOT USE FOR NAVIGATIONAL PURPOSES
This is a reproduction of a NOAA Chart

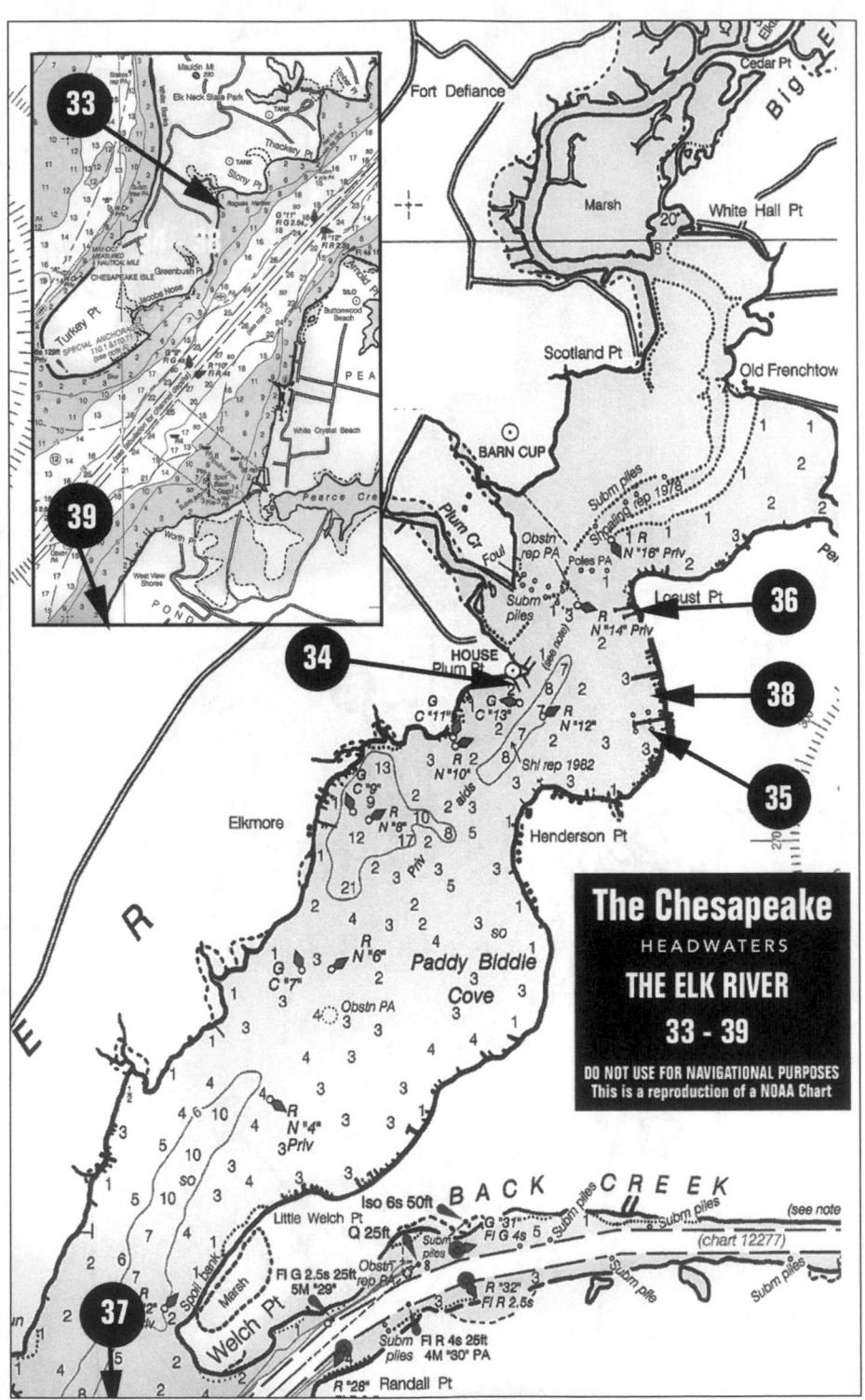

The Chesapeake

HEADWATERS

THE ELK RIVER

33 - 39

DO NOT USE FOR NAVIGATIONAL PURPOSES
This is a reproduction of a NOAA Chart

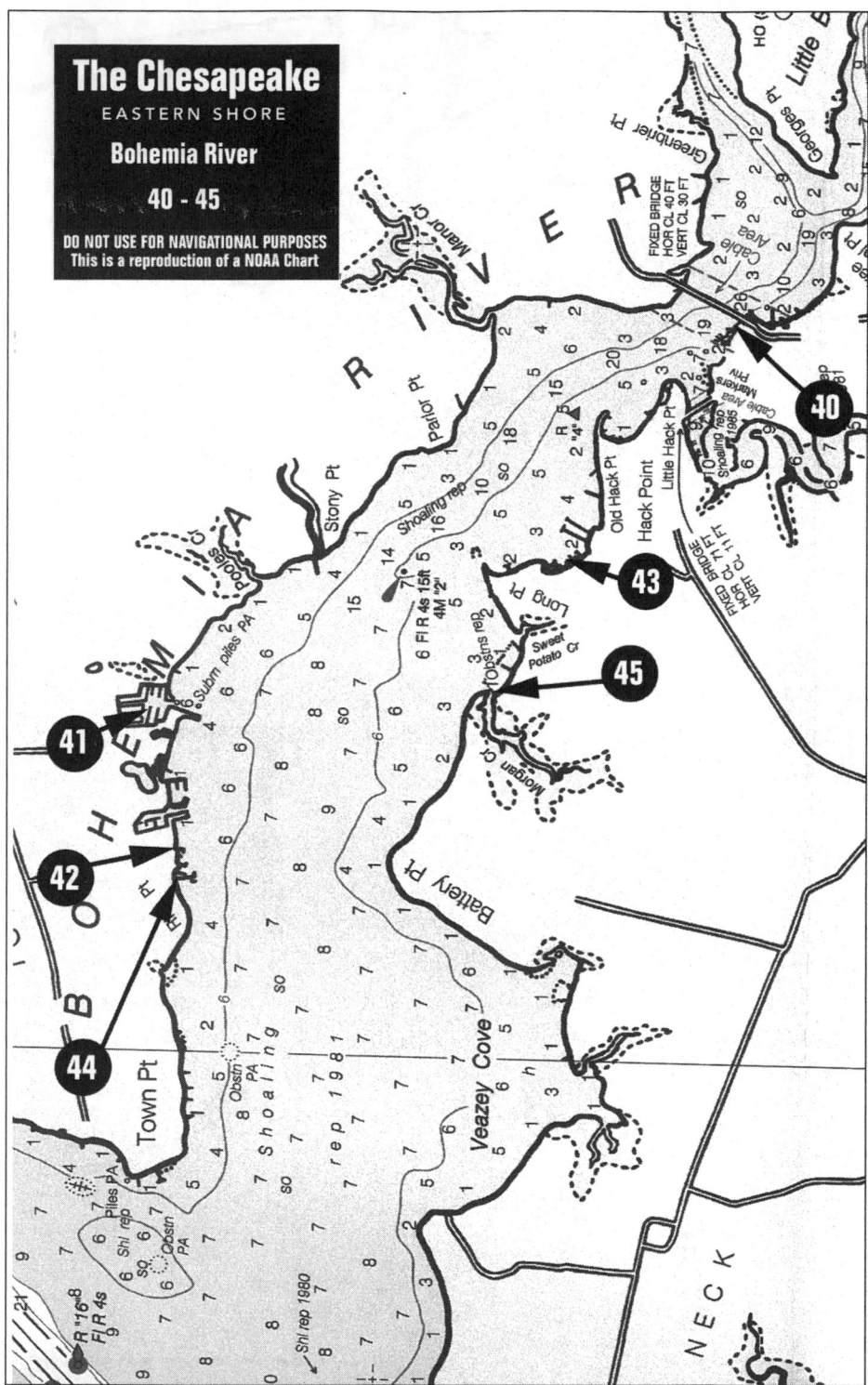

The Chesapeake
EASTERN SHORE
Bohemia River
40 - 45

DO NOT USE FOR NAVIGATIONAL PURPOSES
This is a reproduction of a NOAA Chart

237

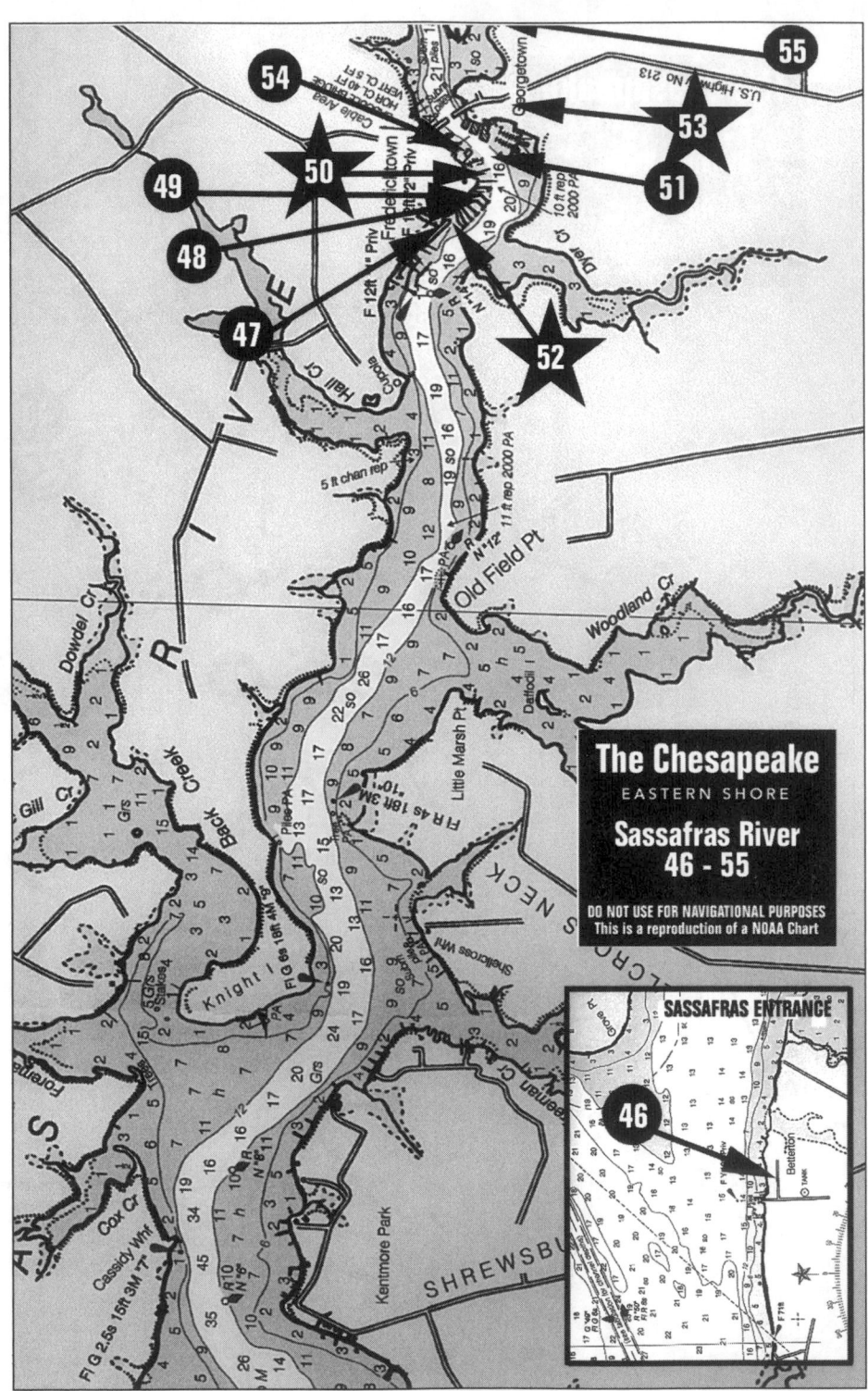

The Chesapeake
EASTERN SHORE
Sassafras River
46 - 55

DO NOT USE FOR NAVIGATIONAL PURPOSES
This is a reproduction of a NOAA Chart

SASSAFRAS ENTRANCE

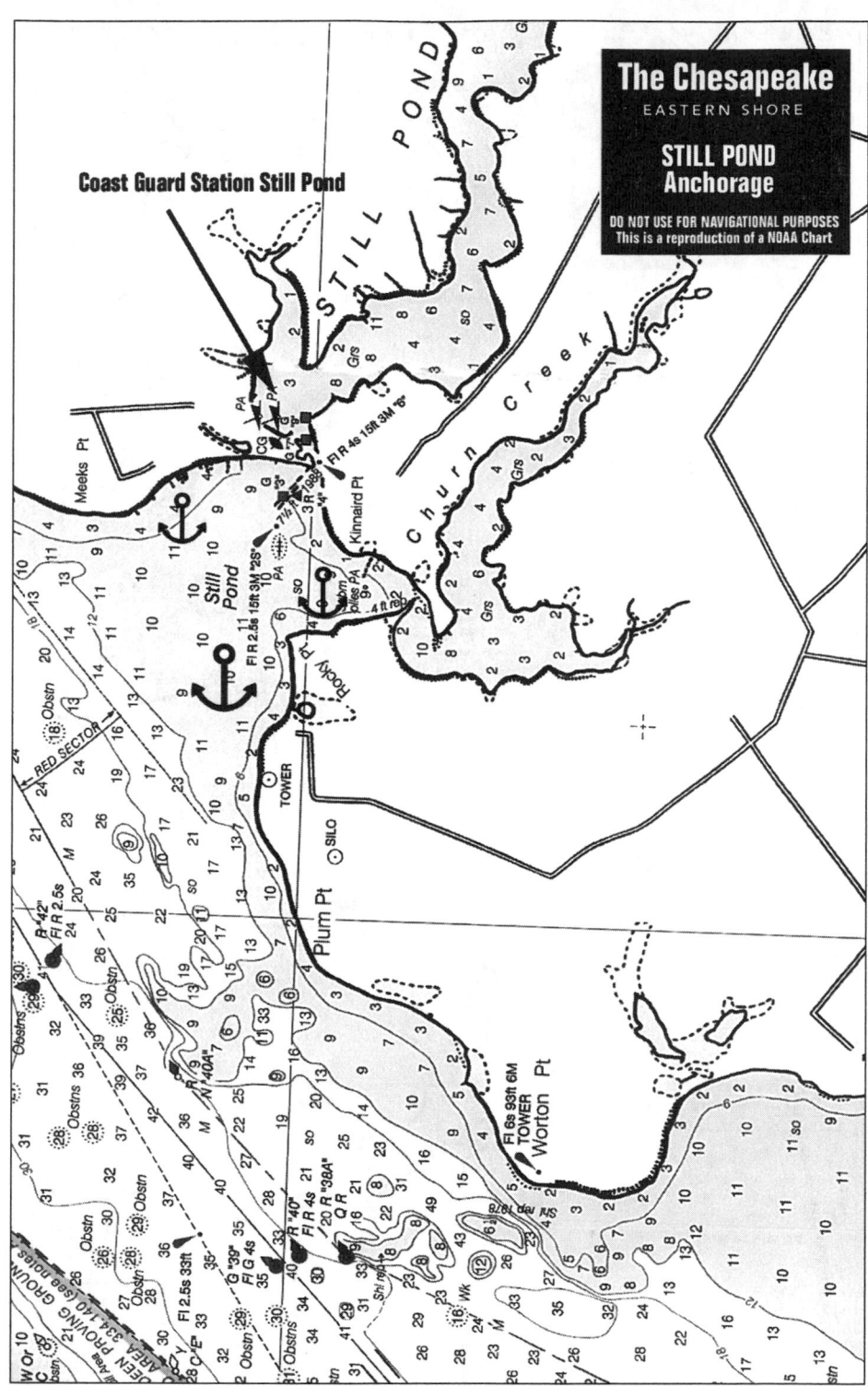

Coast Guard Station Still Pond

The Chesapeake
EASTERN SHORE

STILL POND
Anchorage

DO NOT USE FOR NAVIGATIONAL PURPOSES
This is a reproduction of a NOAA Chart

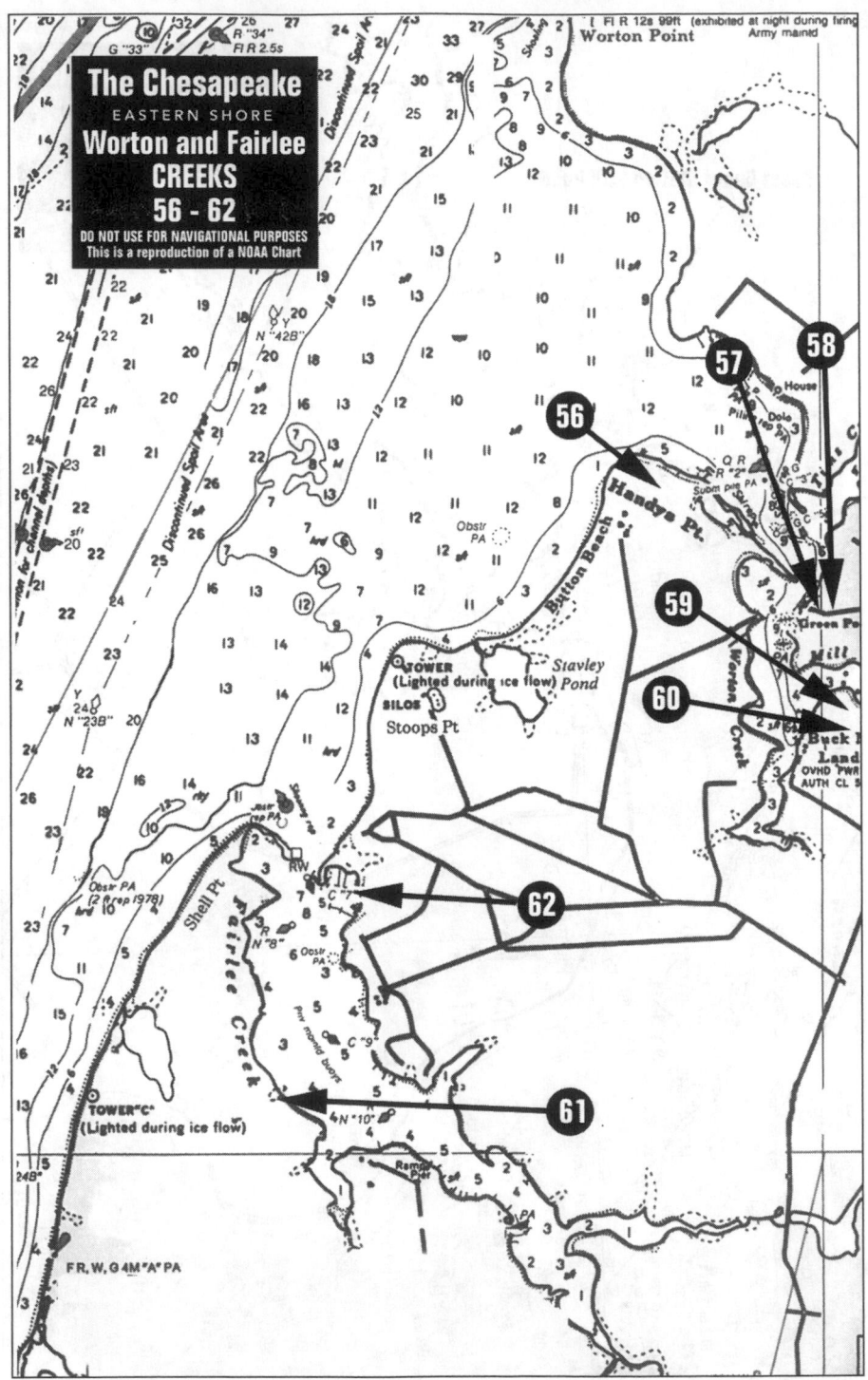

The Chesapeake
EASTERN SHORE
Worton and Fairlee
CREEKS
56 - 62

DO NOT USE FOR NAVIGATIONAL PURPOSES
This is a reproduction of a NOAA Chart

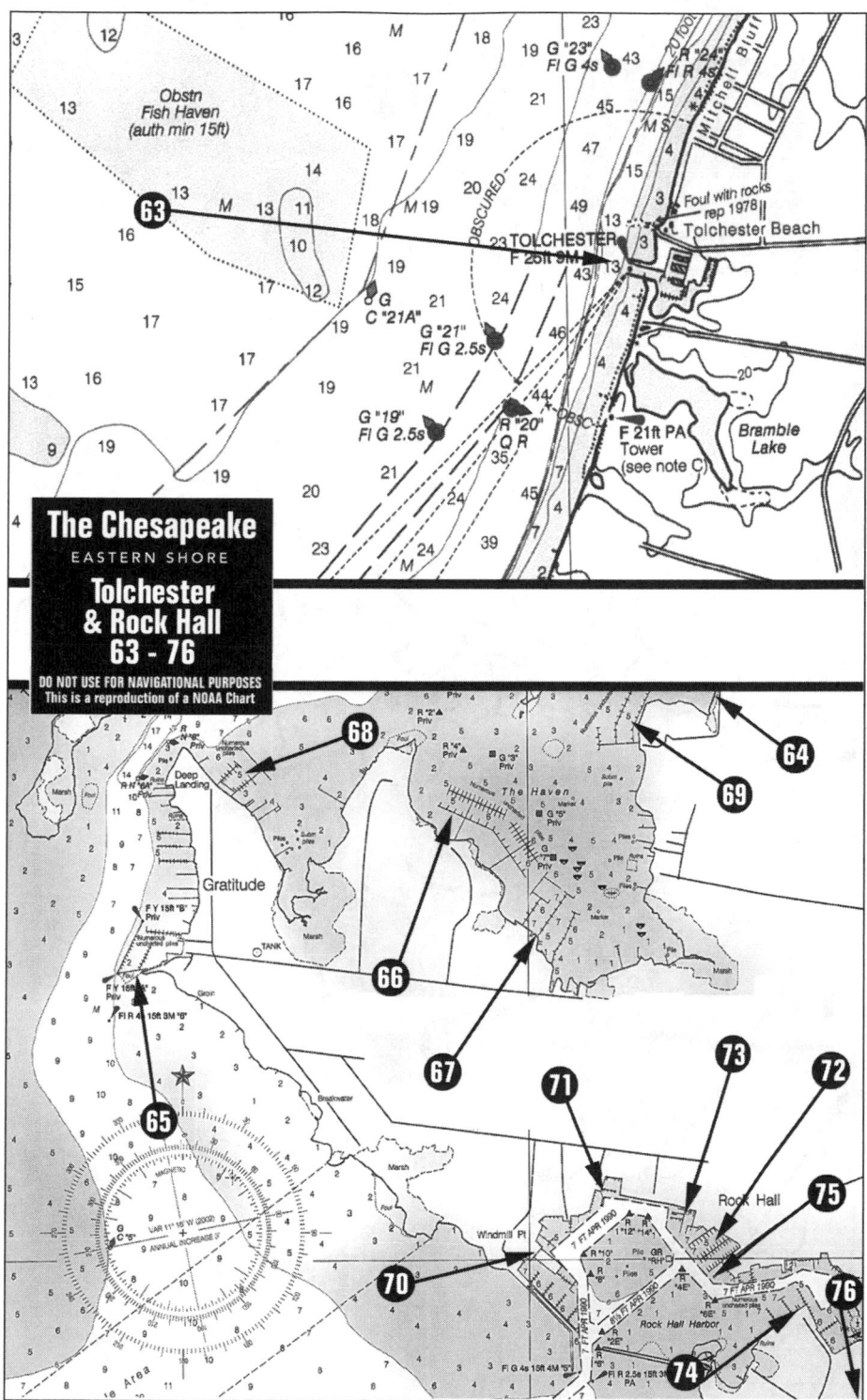

The Chesapeake
EASTERN SHORE

Tolchester
& Rock Hall
63 - 76

DO NOT USE FOR NAVIGATIONAL PURPOSES
This is a reproduction of a NOAA Chart

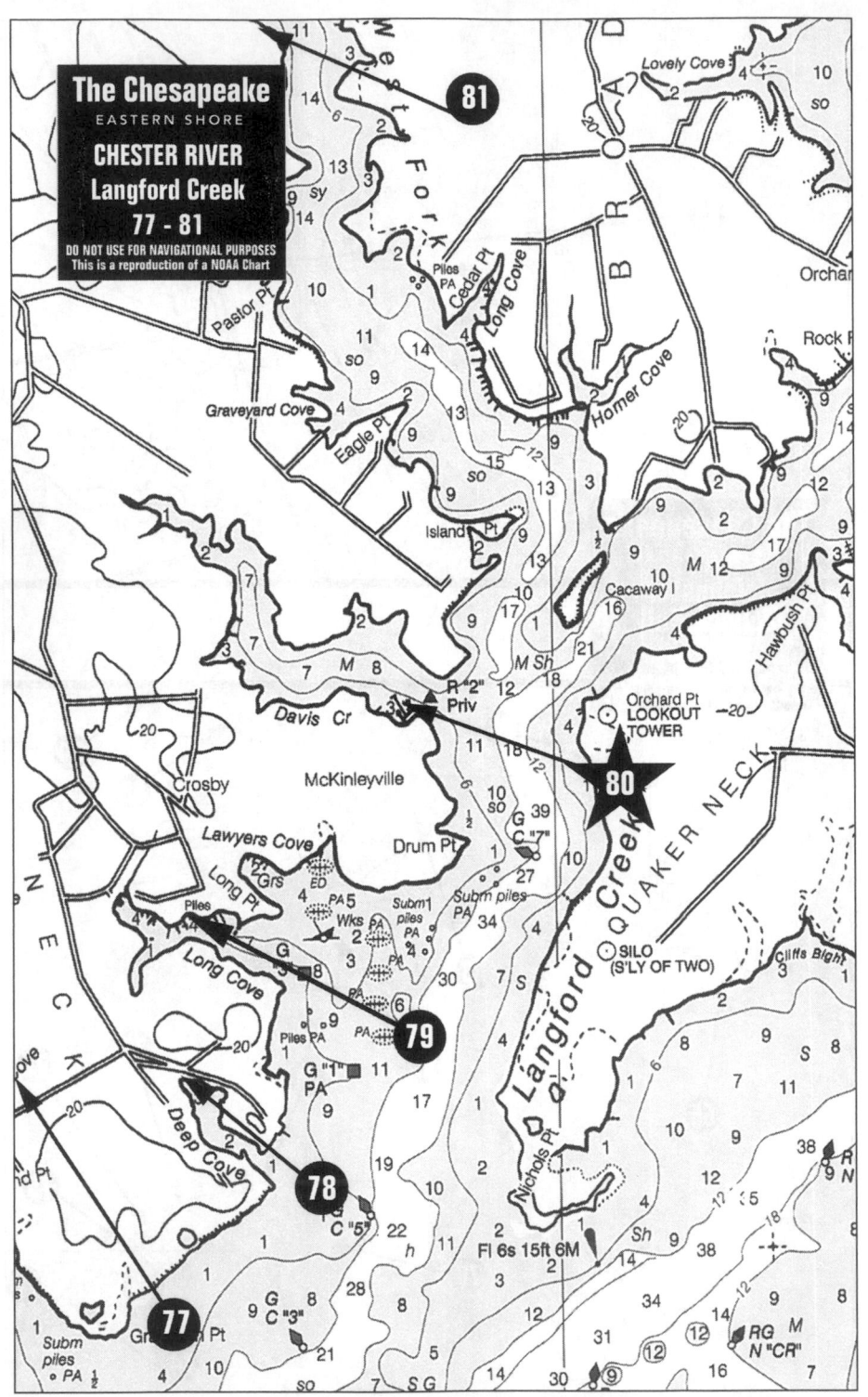

The Chesapeake
EASTERN SHORE
CHESTER RIVER
Langford Creek
77 - 81
DO NOT USE FOR NAVIGATIONAL PURPOSES
This is a reproduction of a NOAA Chart

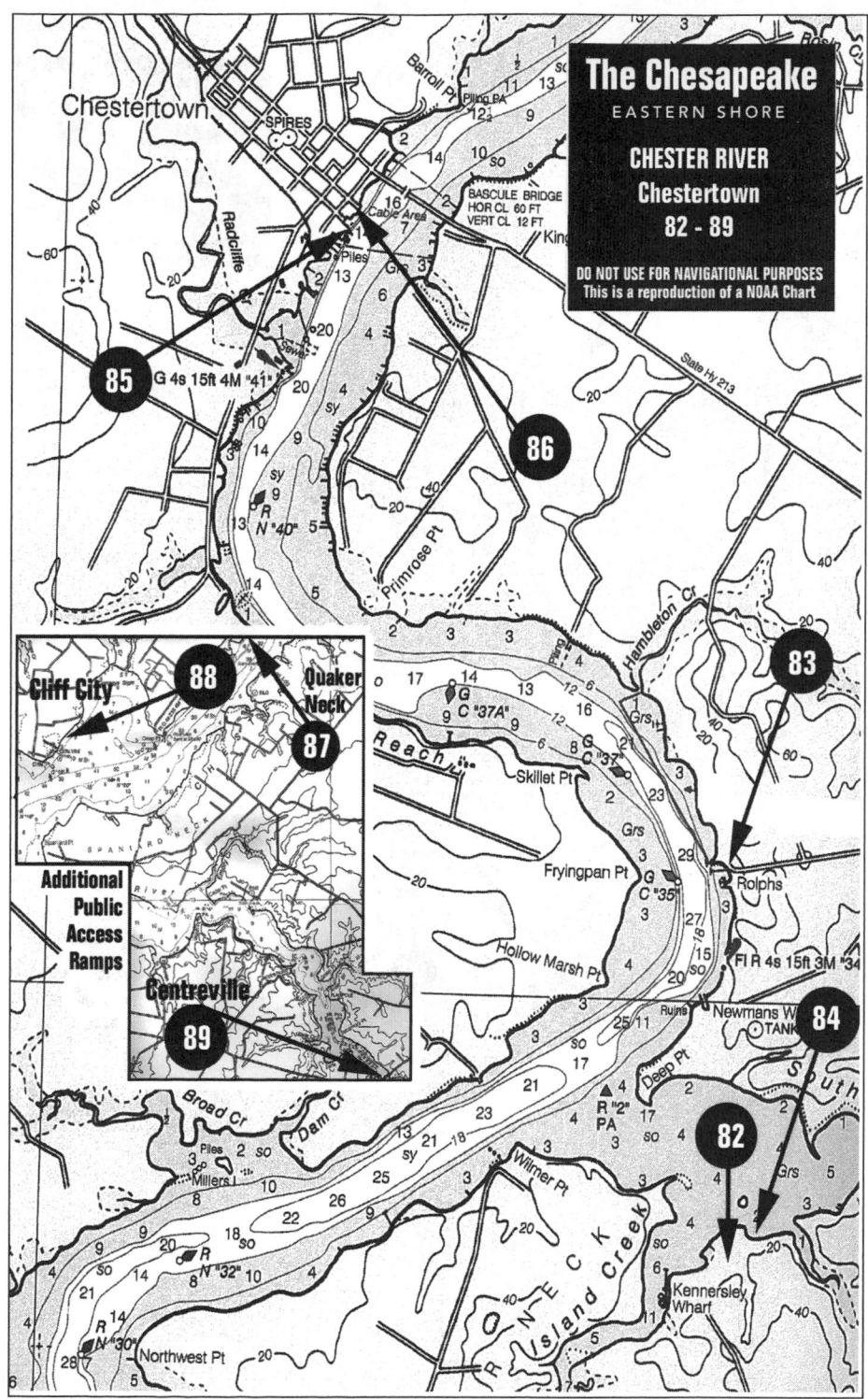

The Chesapeake
EASTERN SHORE

CHESTER RIVER
Chestertown
82 - 89

DO NOT USE FOR NAVIGATIONAL PURPOSES
This is a reproduction of a NOAA Chart

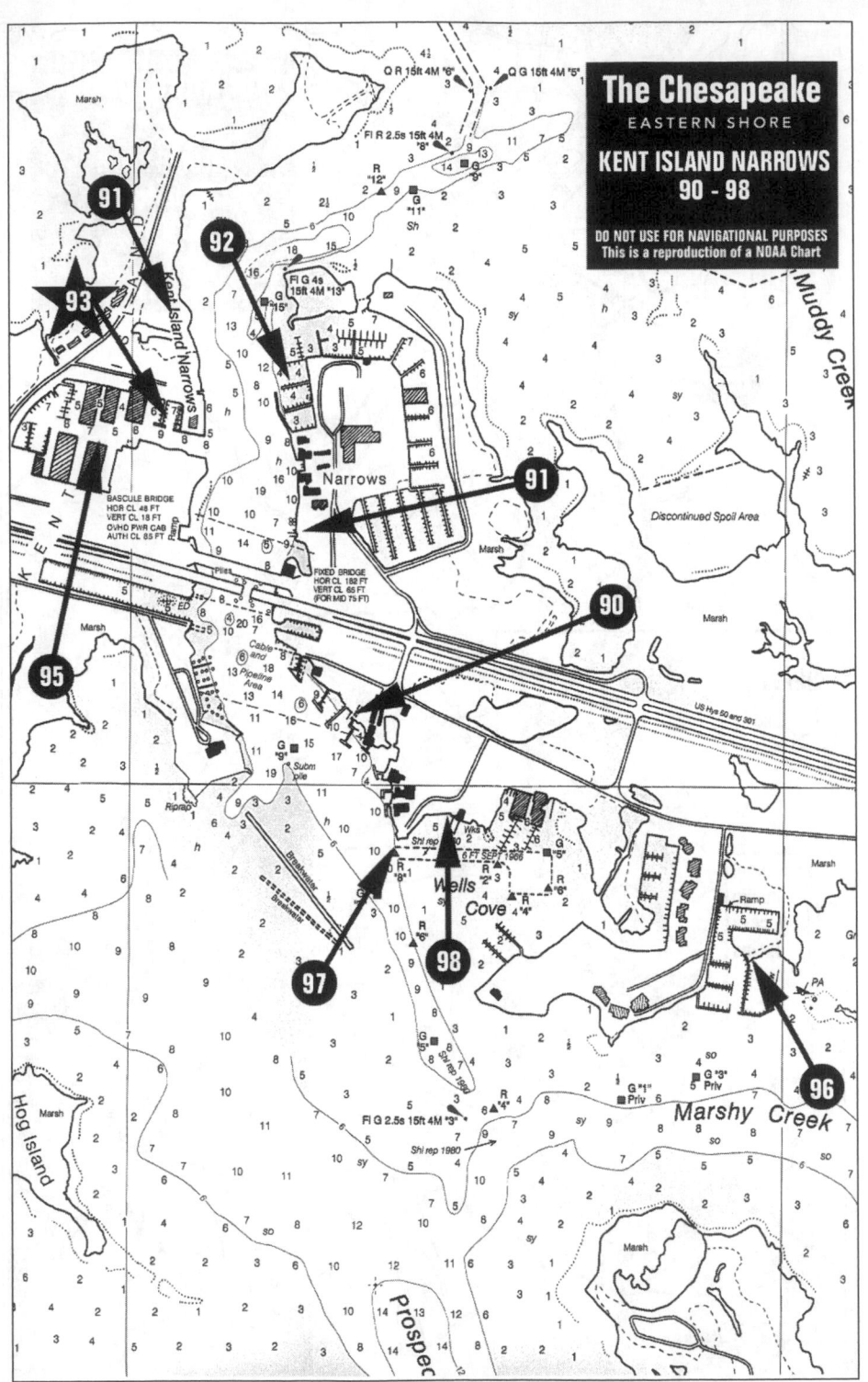

The Chesapeake
EASTERN SHORE

KENT ISLAND NARROWS
90 - 98

DO NOT USE FOR NAVIGATIONAL PURPOSES
This is a reproduction of a NOAA Chart

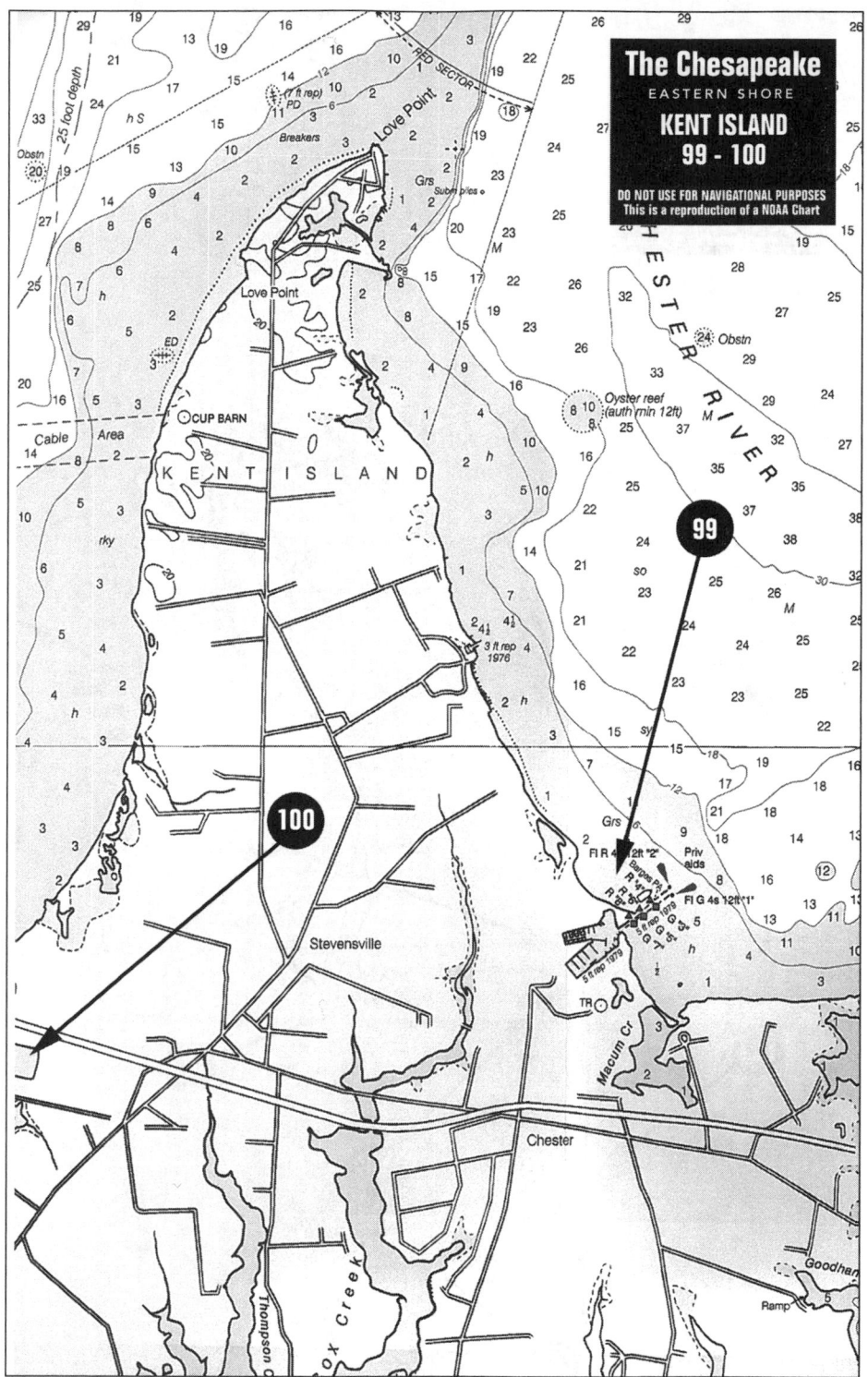

The Chesapeake
EASTERN SHORE
KENT ISLAND
99 - 100

DO NOT USE FOR NAVIGATIONAL PURPOSES
This is a reproduction of a NOAA Chart

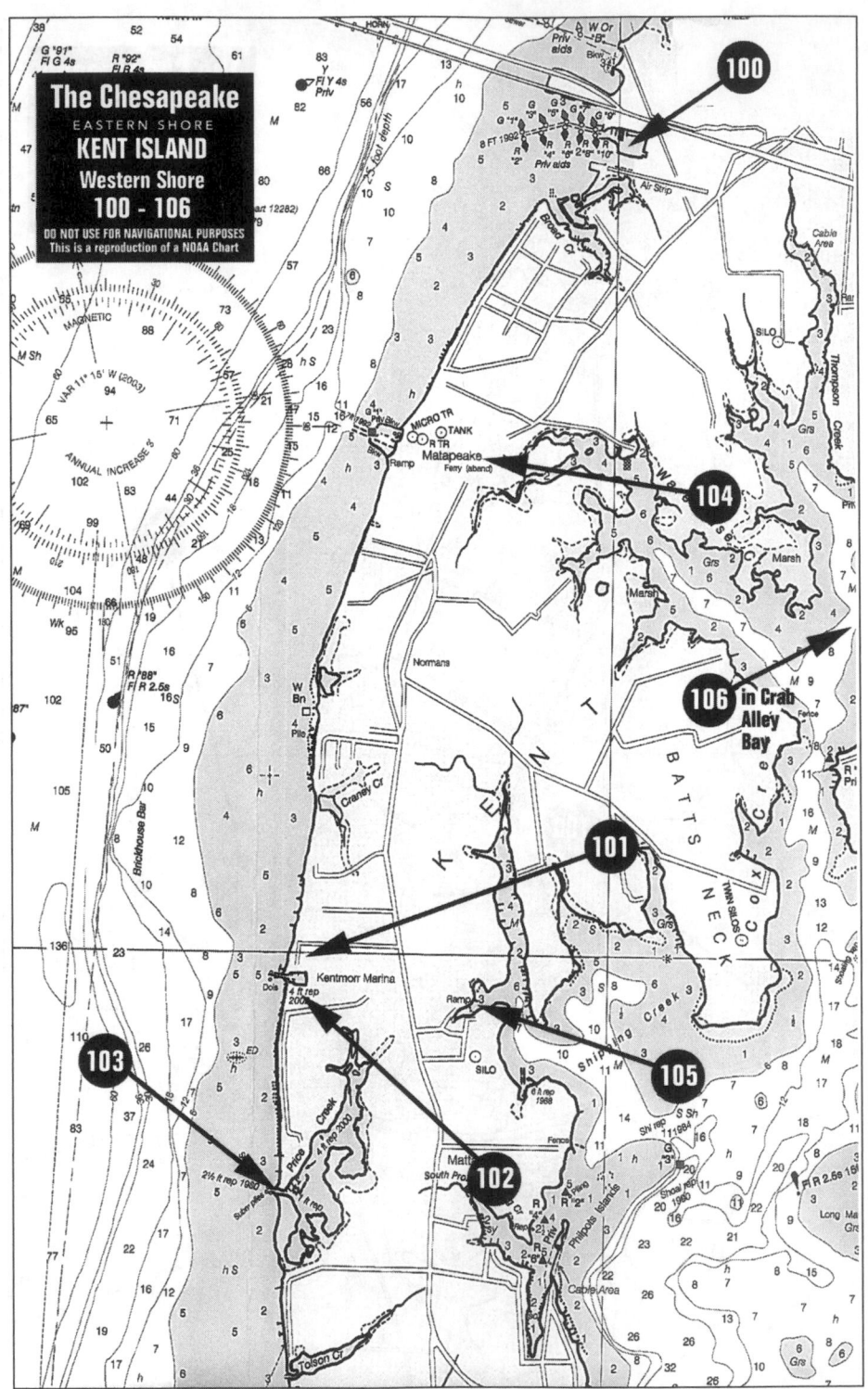

The Chesapeake
EASTERN SHORE
KENT ISLAND
Western Shore
100 - 106
DO NOT USE FOR NAVIGATIONAL PURPOSES
This is a reproduction of a NOAA Chart

106 in Crab Alley Bay

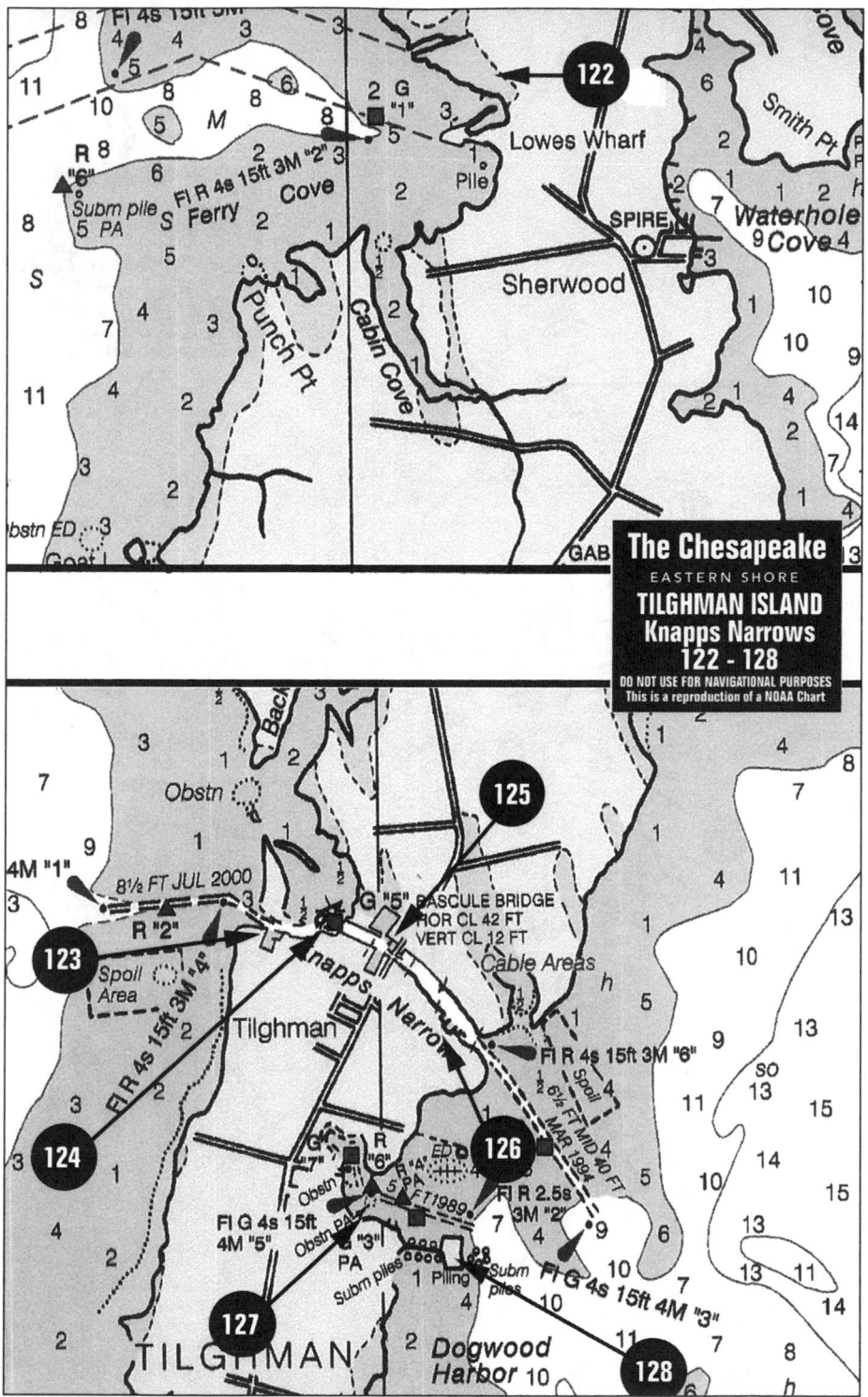

The Chesapeake

EASTERN SHORE

TILGHMAN ISLAND
Knapps Narrows
122 - 128

DO NOT USE FOR NAVIGATIONAL PURPOSES
This is a reproduction of a NOAA Chart

122
123
124
125
126
127
128

Fl 4s 15ft 3M
Lowes Wharf
Pile
SPIRE
Sherwood
Smith Pt
Waterhole Cove
R "6"
Subm pile PA
S Ferry Cove
Punch Pt
Cabin Cove
Fl R 4s 15ft 3M "2"
G "1"
M
S
Obstn ED
Goat I
GAB

Back
Obstn
4M "1"
8½ FT JUL 2000
R "2"
Spoil Area
Fl R 4s 15ft 3M "4"
Tilghman
Knapps Narrows
G "5" BASCULE BRIDGE
HOR CL 42 FT
VERT CL 12 FT
Cable Areas
Fl R 4s 15ft 3M "6"
Spoil
6½ FT MID 40 FT
MAR 1989
Fl R 2.5s 3M "2"
G "7"
R "6"
R "4"
Obstn
ED
PA
Fl 1989
Fl G 4s 15ft 4M "5"
Obstn PA
G "3"
PA
Subm piles
Piling
Subm piles
Fl G 4s 15ft 4M "3"
so
Dogwood Harbor
TILGHMAN

247

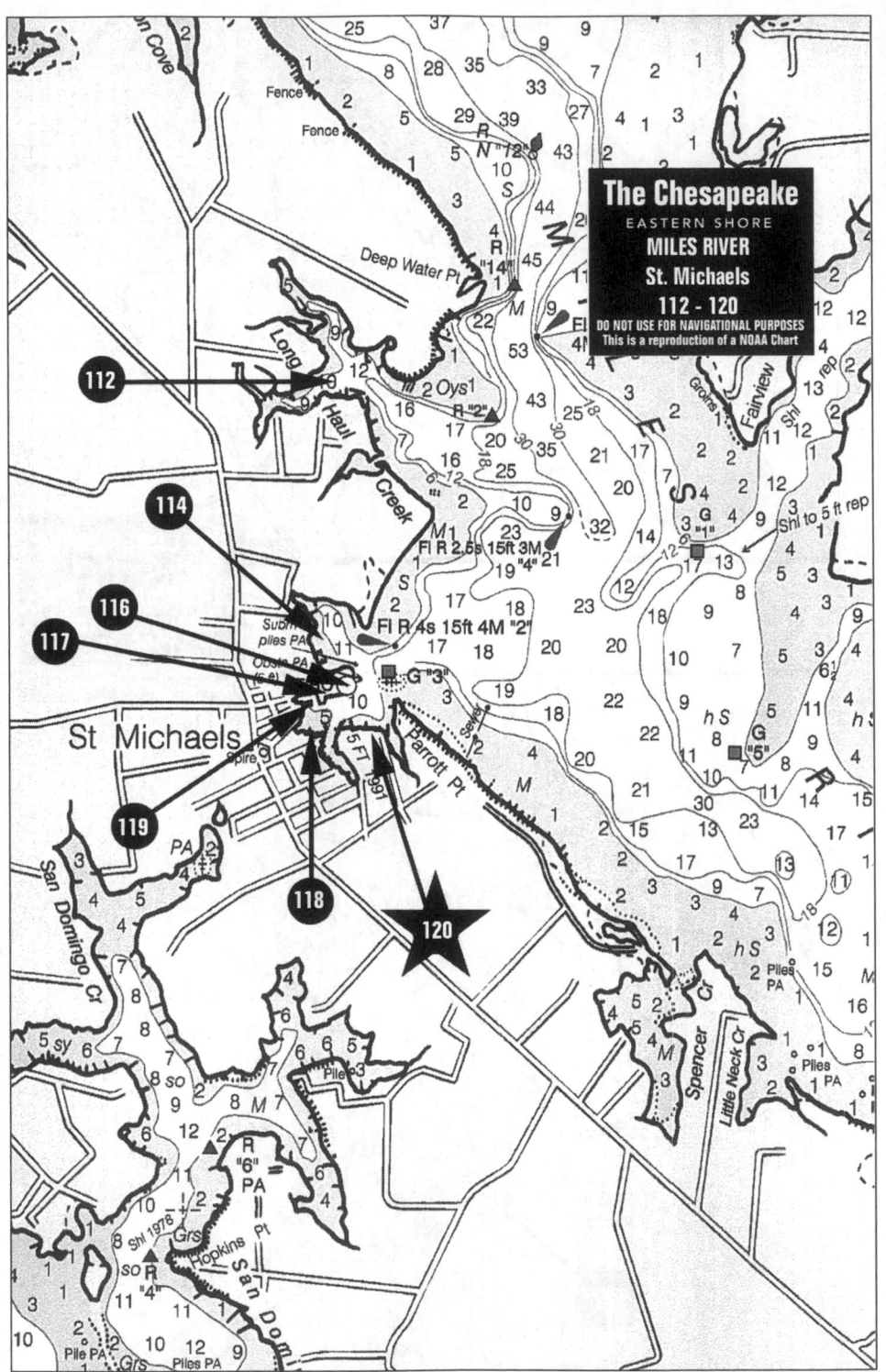

The Chesapeake
EASTERN SHORE
MILES RIVER
St. Michaels
112 - 120
DO NOT USE FOR NAVIGATIONAL PURPOSES
This is a reproduction of a NOAA Chart

248

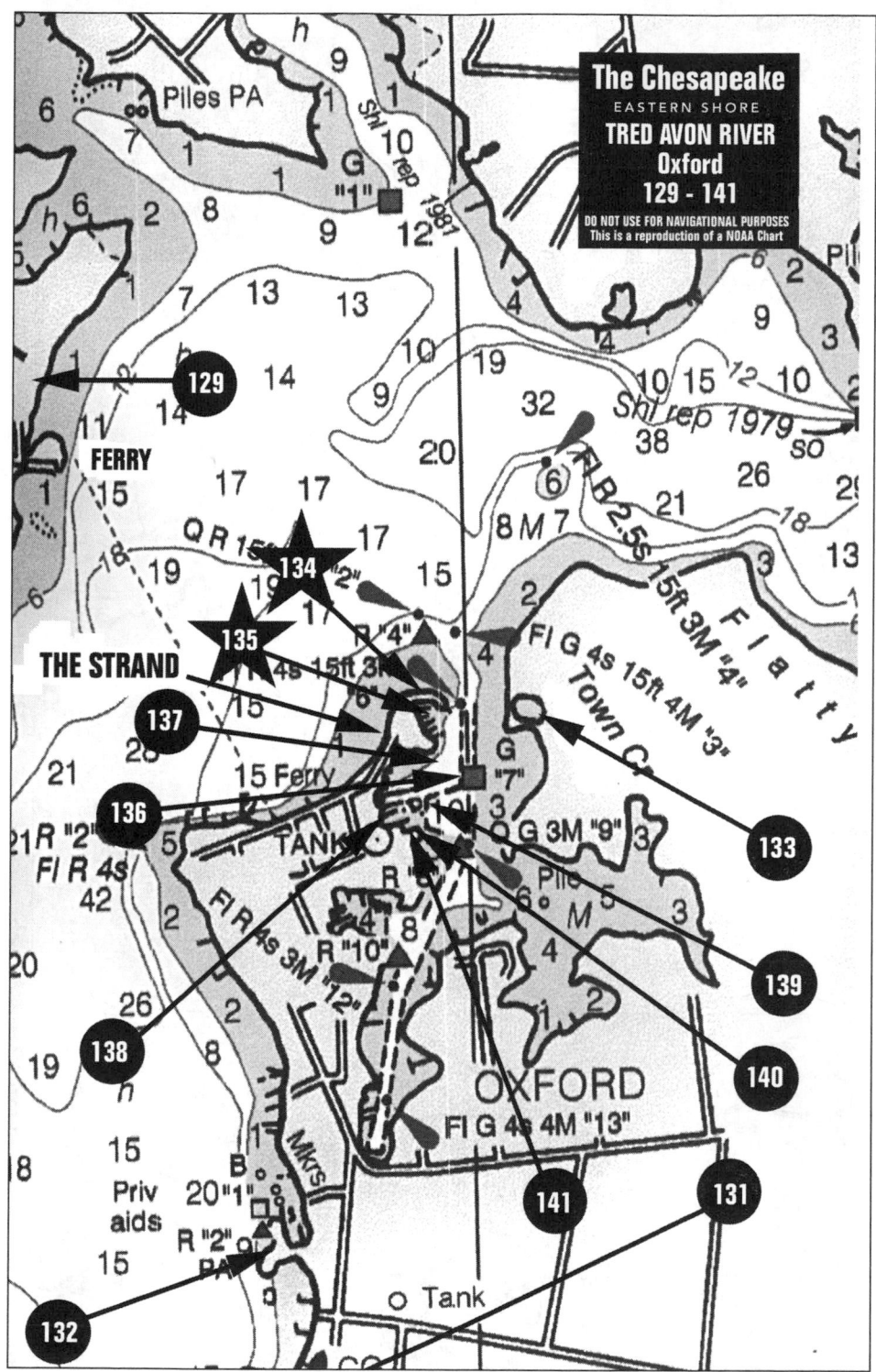

The Chesapeake
EASTERN SHORE
TRED AVON RIVER
Oxford
129 - 141

DO NOT USE FOR NAVIGATIONAL PURPOSES
This is a reproduction of a NOAA Chart

249

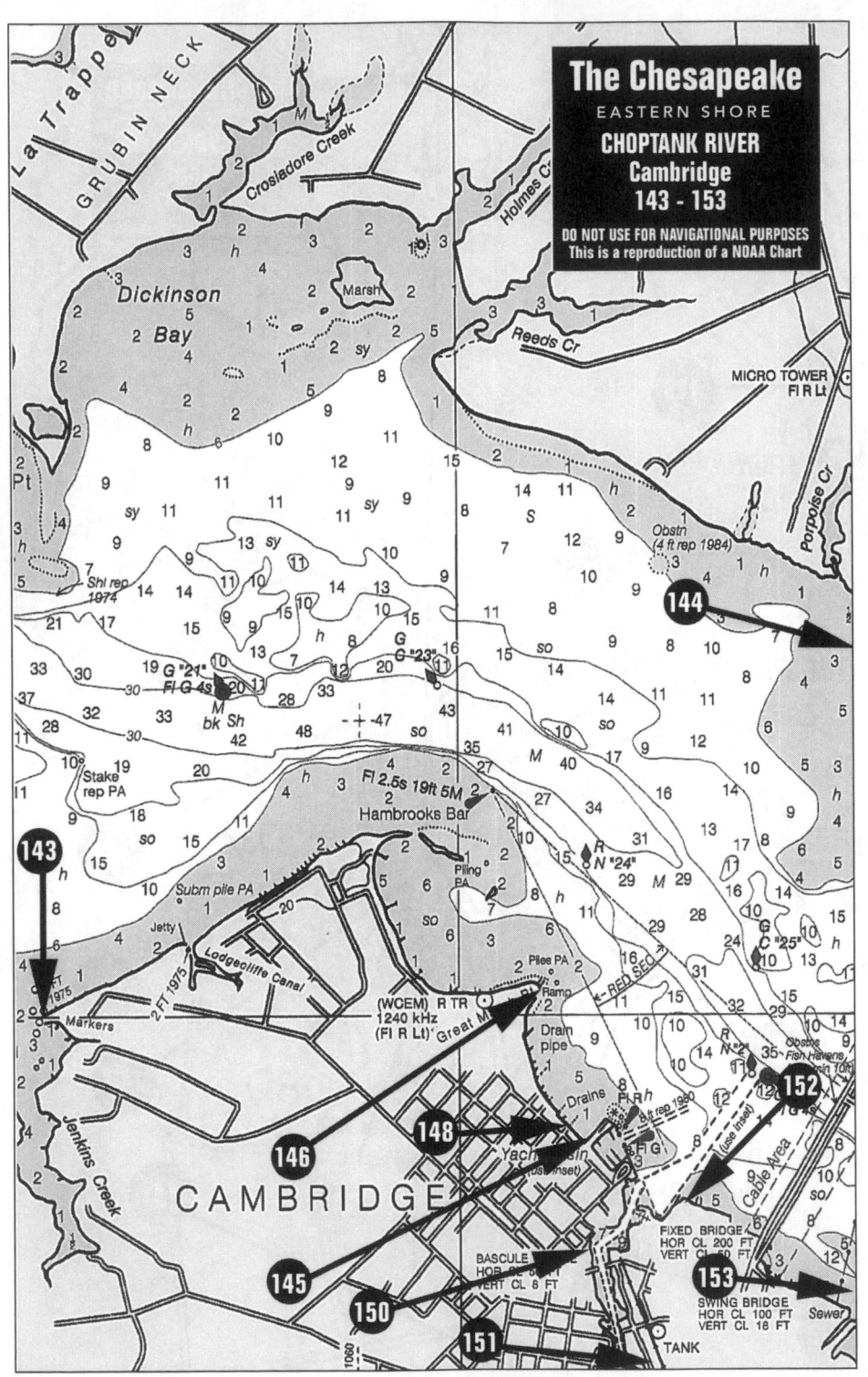

The Chesapeake

EASTERN SHORE

**CHOPTANK RIVER
Cambridge
143 - 153**

DO NOT USE FOR NAVIGATIONAL PURPOSES
This is a reproduction of a NOAA Chart

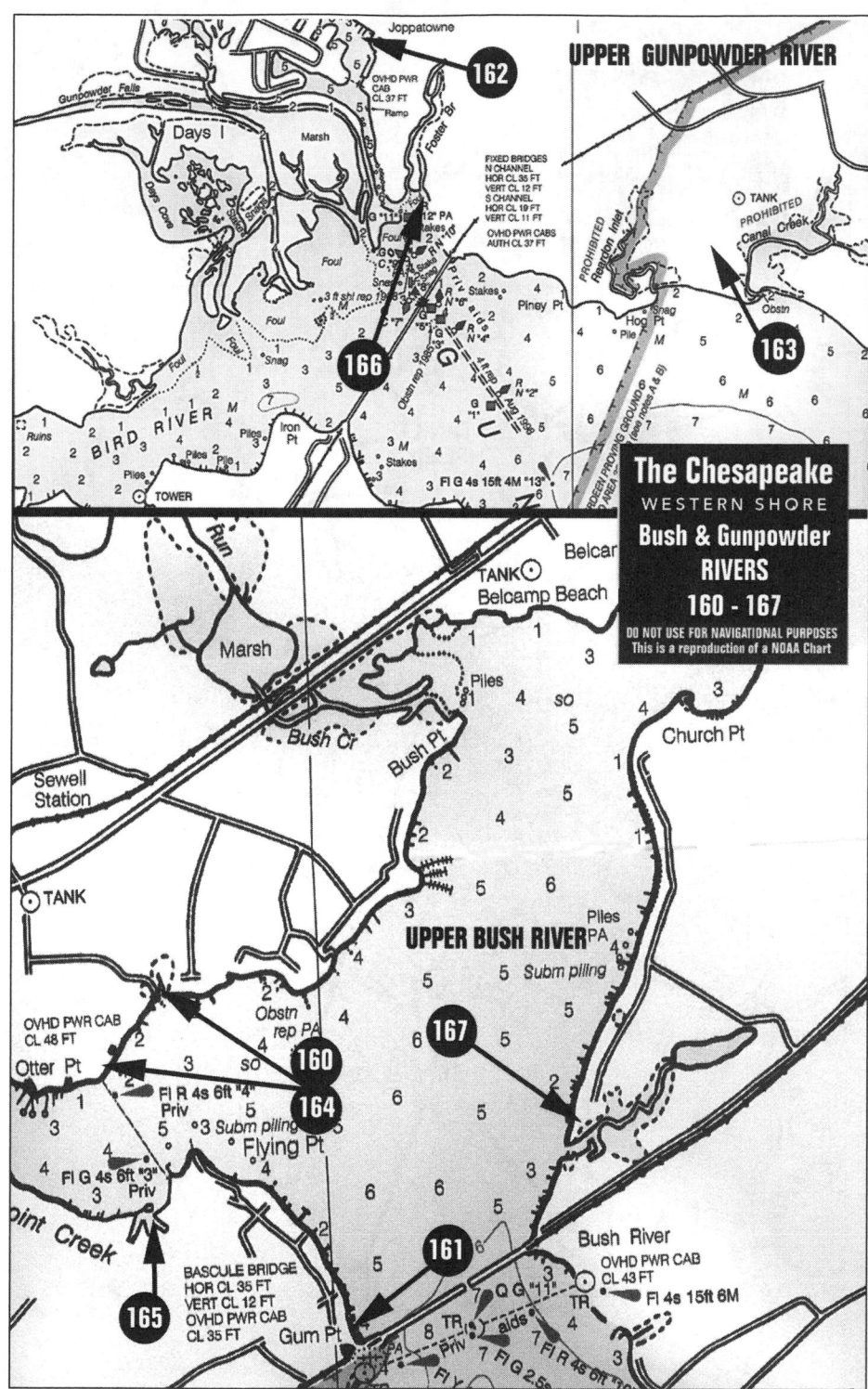

UPPER GUNPOWDER RIVER

Joppatowne

162

OVHD PWR CAB CL 37 FT

Ramp

Gunpowder Falls

Foster Br

Days I

Marsh

FIXED BRIDGES
N CHANNEL
HOR CL 35 FT
VERT CL 12 FT
S CHANNEL
HOR CL 19 FT
VERT CL 11 FT
OVHD PWR CABS
AUTH CL 37 FT

TANK

PROHIBITED
Canal Creek

Reardon Inlet

PROHIBITED

Piney Pt

Hog Pt

Pile

Snag

166

Foul

Foul

Snag

Obstn

163

BIRD RIVER

Ruins

Iron Pt

Piles

Pile

Stakes

Piles

TOWER

Fl G 4s 15ft 4M "13"

AREA

The Chesapeake

WESTERN SHORE

Bush & Gunpowder

RIVERS

160 - 167

DO NOT USE FOR NAVIGATIONAL PURPOSES
This is a reproduction of a NOAA Chart

Run

Belcamp

TANK
Belcamp Beach

Marsh

Piles

Church Pt

Bush Cr

Bush Pt

Sewell
Station

TANK

Piles

UPPER BUSH RIVER PA

Subm piling

167

OVHD PWR CAB
CL 48 FT

Otter Pt

Obstn
rep PA

160

164

Fl R 4s 6ft "4"
Priv

Subm piling

Flying Pt

Fl G 4s 6ft "3"
Priv

int Creek

BASCULE BRIDGE
HOR CL 35 FT
VERT CL 12 FT
OVHD PWR CAB
CL 35 FT

161

Bush River

OVHD PWR CAB
CL 43 FT

Fl 4s 15ft 6M

Q G "1"

TR

165

Gum Pt

TR

Fl R 4s 6ft

Fl G 2.5s

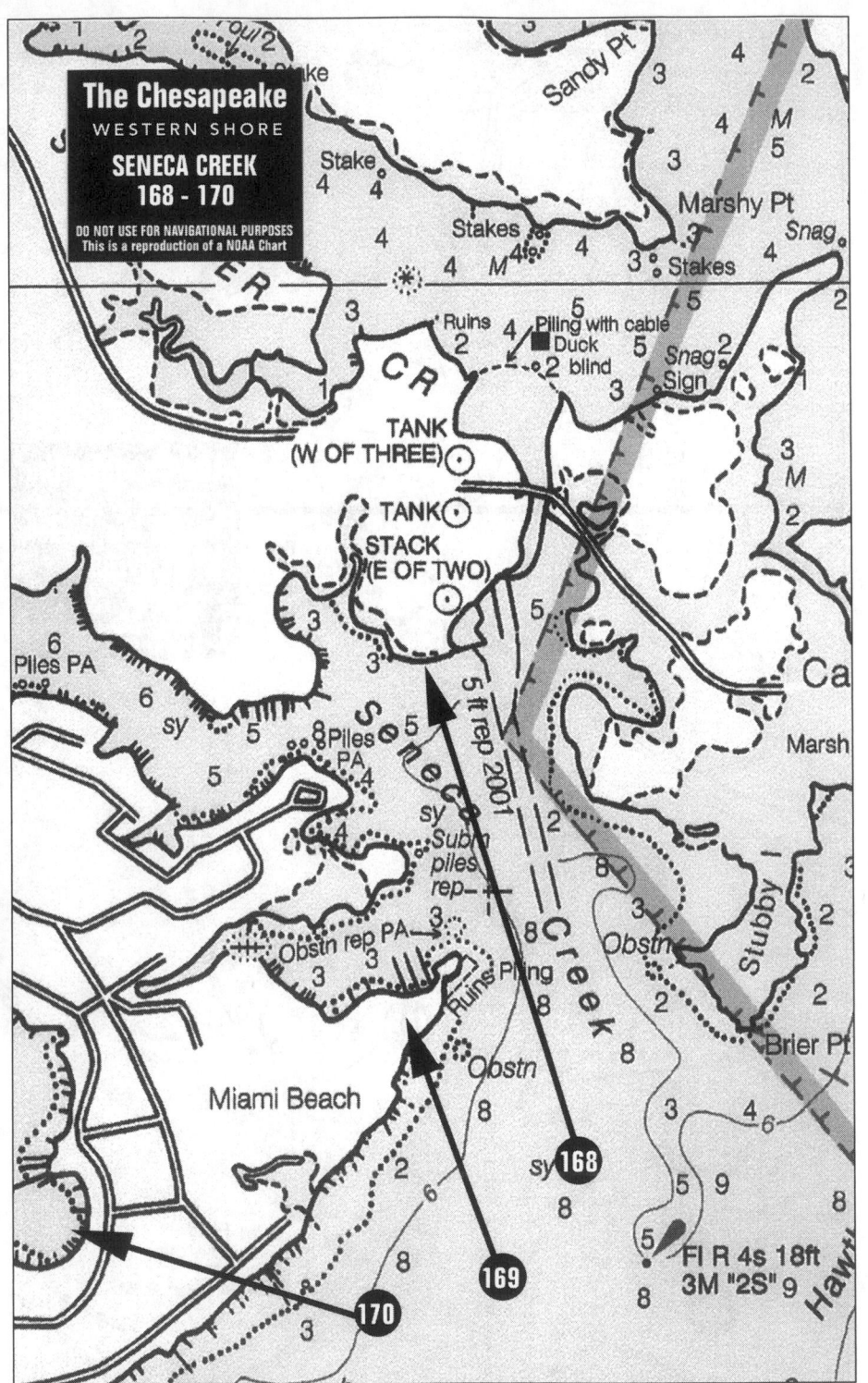

The Chesapeake
WESTERN SHORE
SENECA CREEK
168 - 170
DO NOT USE FOR NAVIGATIONAL PURPOSES
This is a reproduction of a NOAA Chart

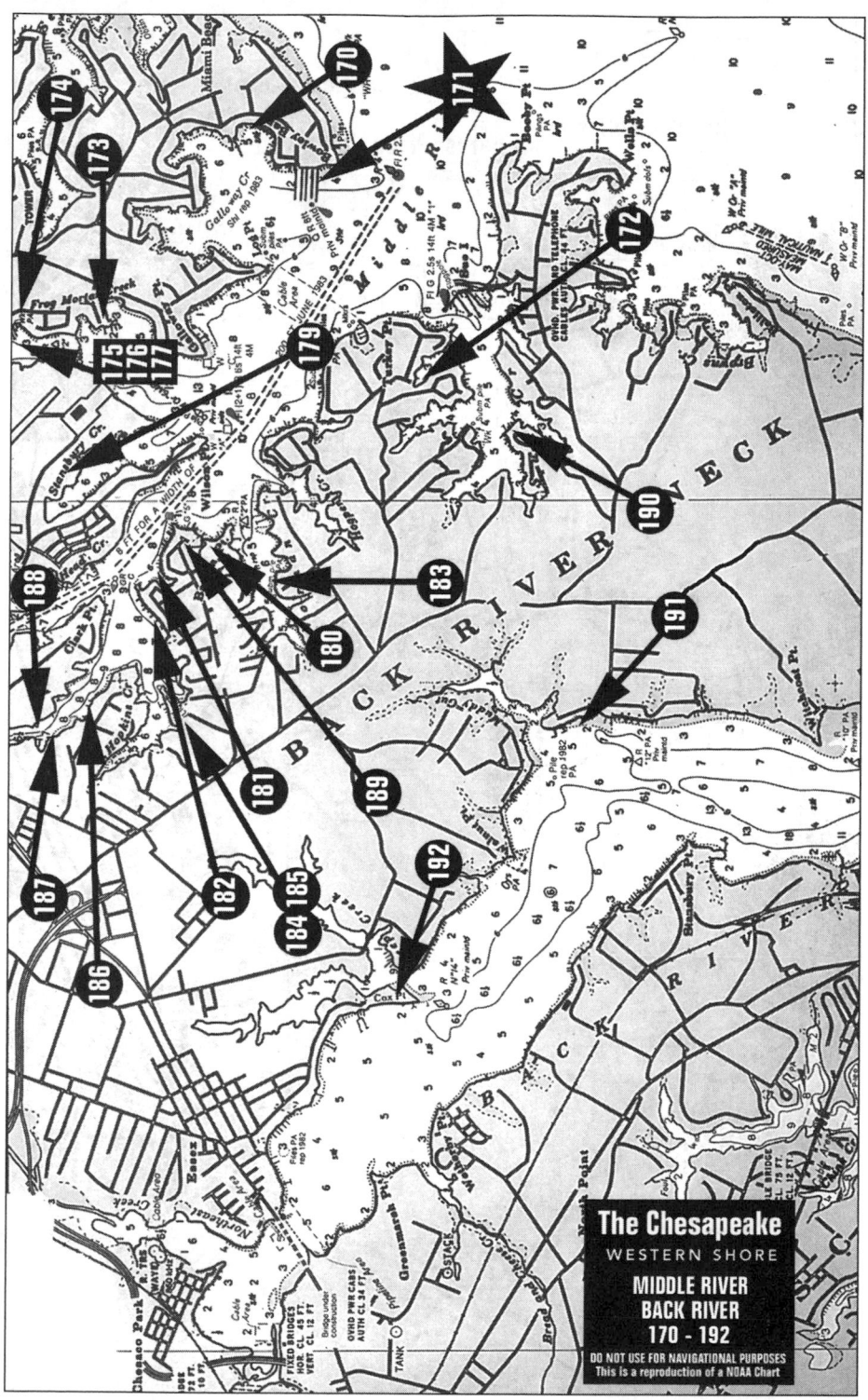

The Chesapeake
WESTERN SHORE

MIDDLE RIVER
BACK RIVER
170 - 192

DO NOT USE FOR NAVIGATIONAL PURPOSES
This is a reproduction of a NOAA Chart

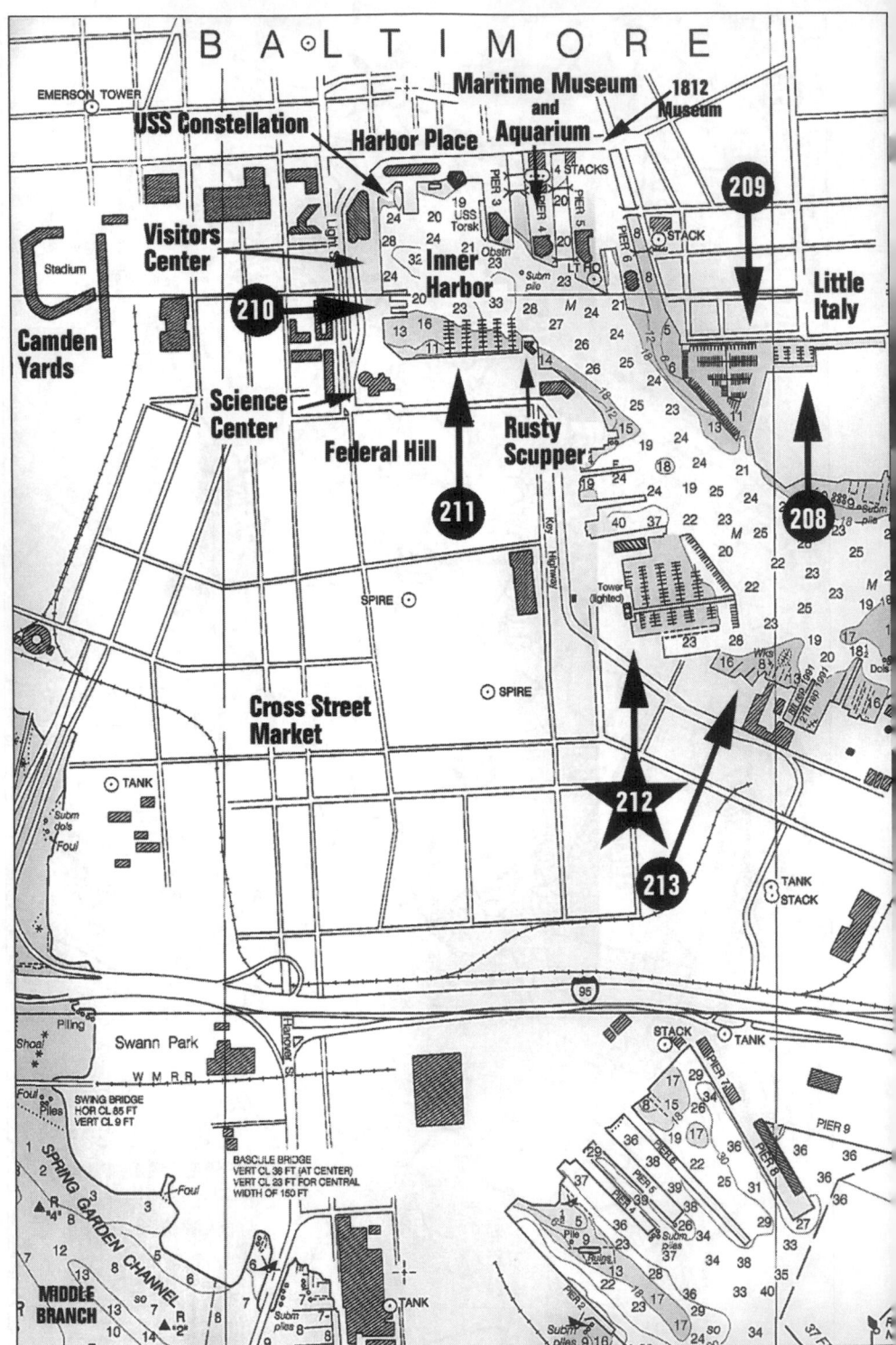

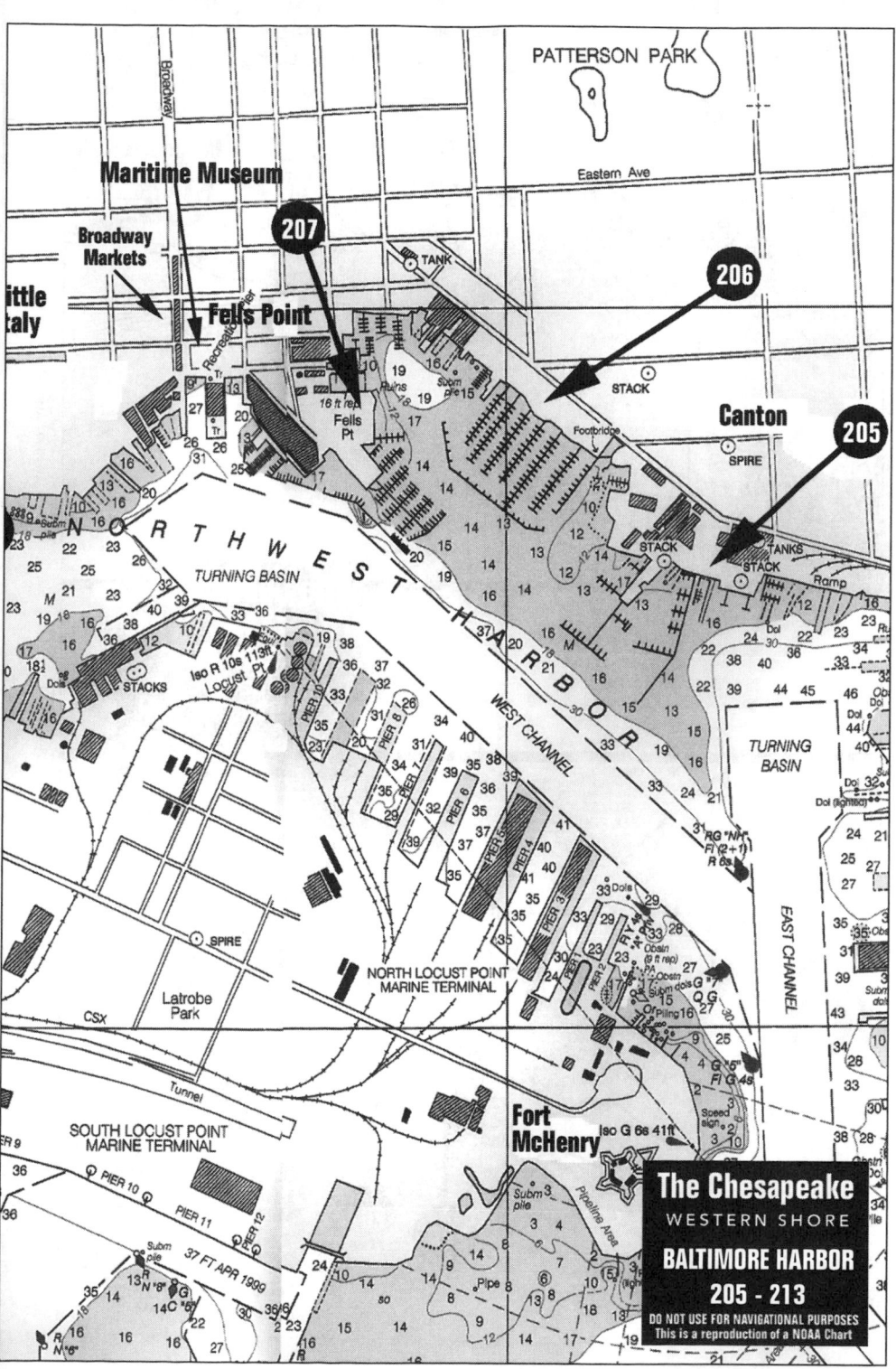

The Chesapeake
WESTERN SHORE

BALTIMORE HARBOR
205 - 213

DO NOT USE FOR NAVIGATIONAL PURPOSES
This is a reproduction of a NOAA Chart

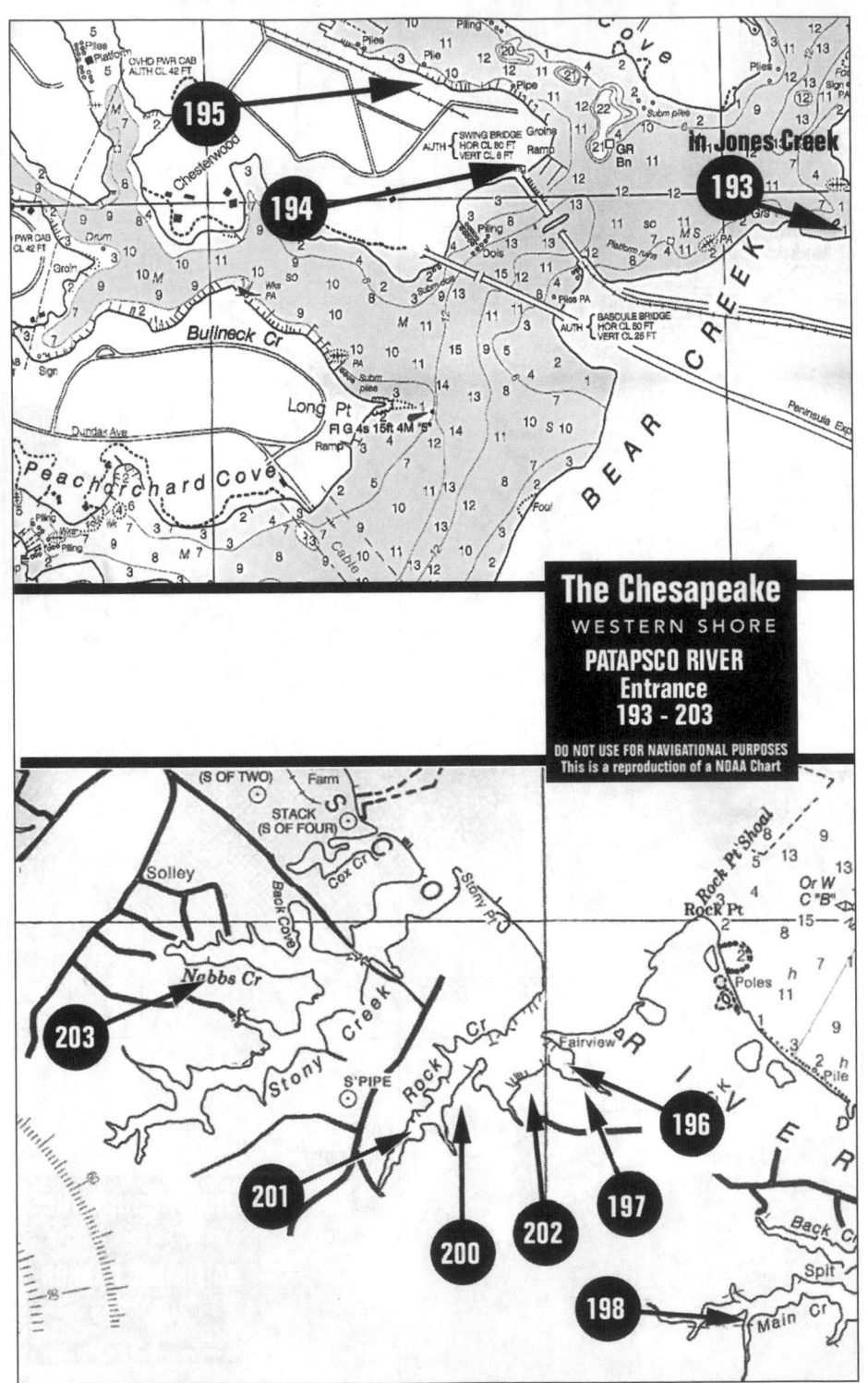

The Chesapeake
WESTERN SHORE

PATAPSCO RIVER
Entrance
193 - 203

DO NOT USE FOR NAVIGATIONAL PURPOSES
This is a reproduction of a NOAA Chart

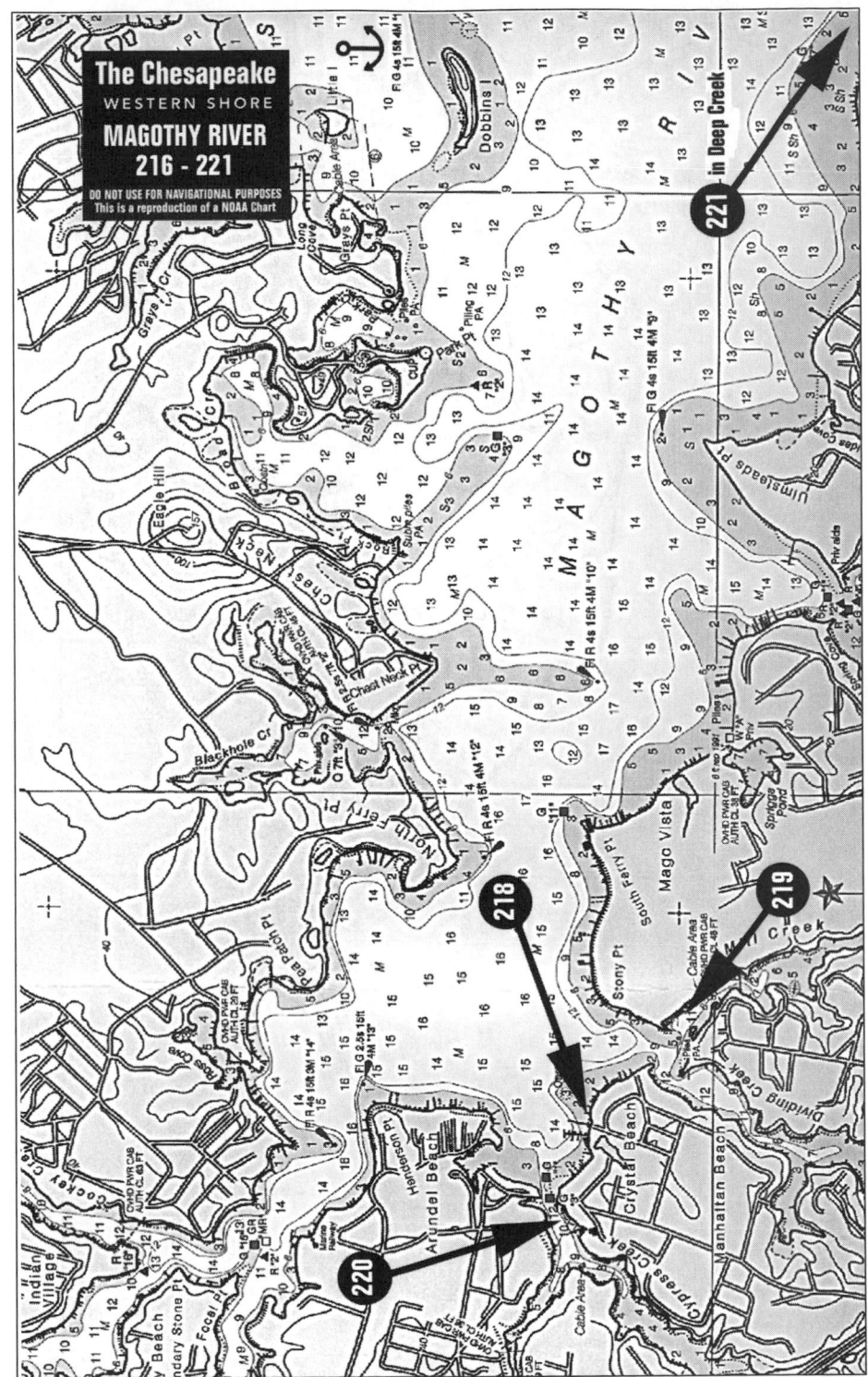

The Chesapeake
WESTERN SHORE
MAGOTHY RIVER
216 - 221
DO NOT USE FOR NAVIGATIONAL PURPOSES
This is a reproduction of a NOAA Chart

257

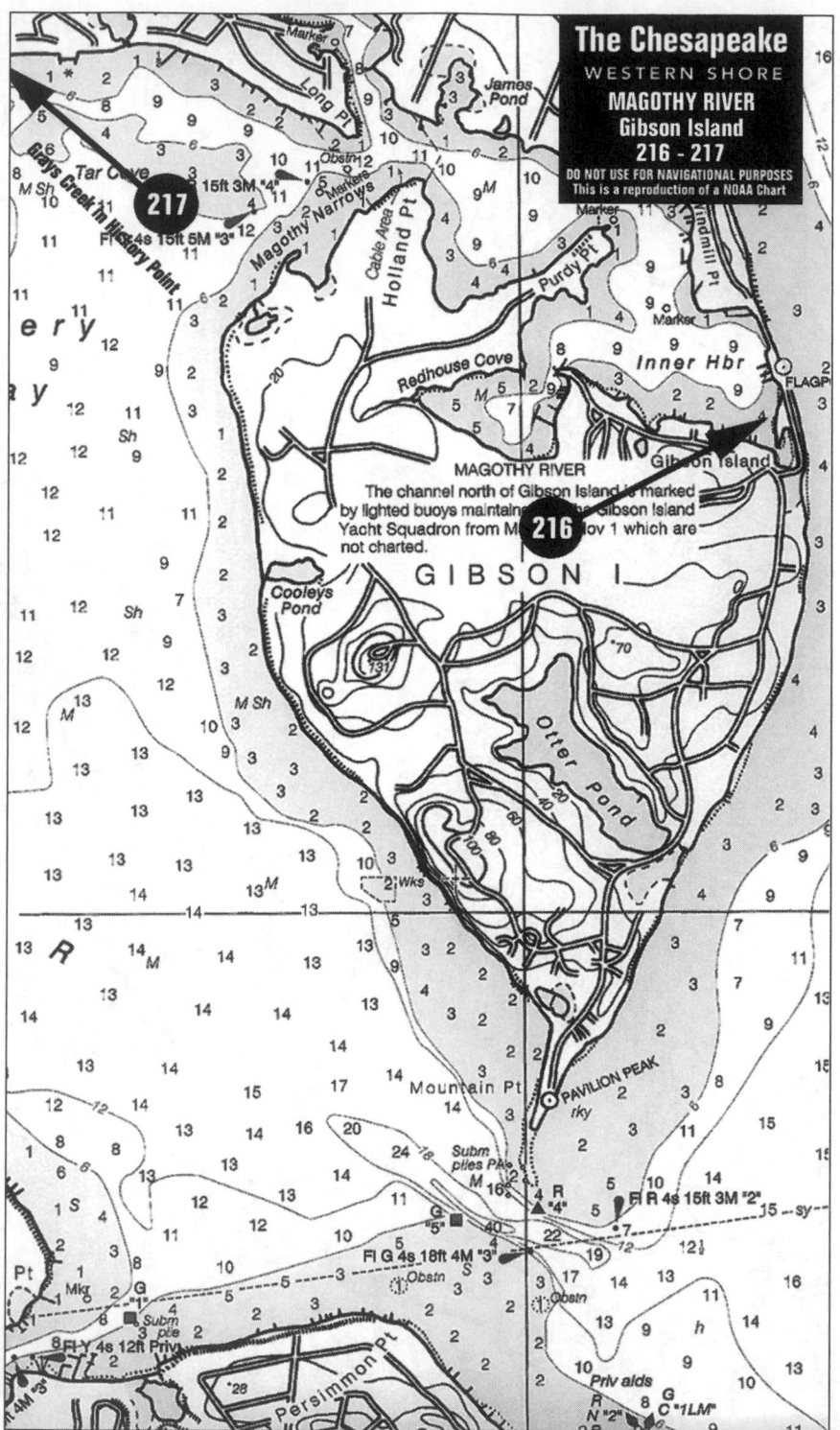

The Chesapeake
WESTERN SHORE
MAGOTHY RIVER
Gibson Island
216 - 217
DO NOT USE FOR NAVIGATIONAL PURPOSES
This is a reproduction of a NOAA Chart

MAGOTHY RIVER
The channel north of Gibson Island is marked by lighted buoys maintained by the Gibson Island Yacht Squadron from May to Nov 1 which are not charted.

GIBSON I.

The Chesapeake
WESTERN SHORE
BAY BRIDGE
213 - 215A

DO NOT USE FOR NAVIGATIONAL PURPOSES
This is a reproduction of a NOAA Chart

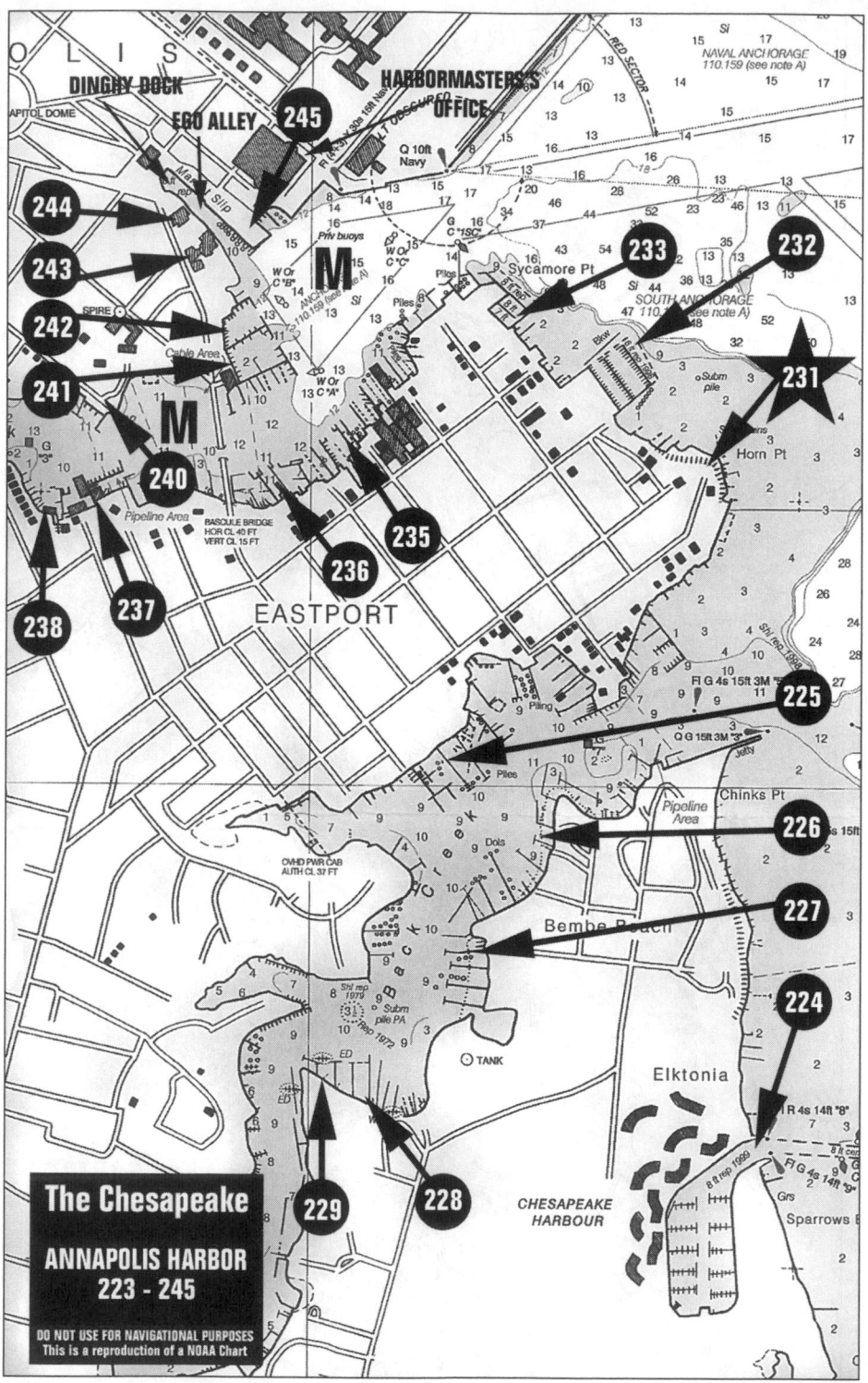

The Chesapeake

ANNAPOLIS HARBOR
223 - 245

DO NOT USE FOR NAVIGATIONAL PURPOSES
This is a reproduction of a NOAA Chart

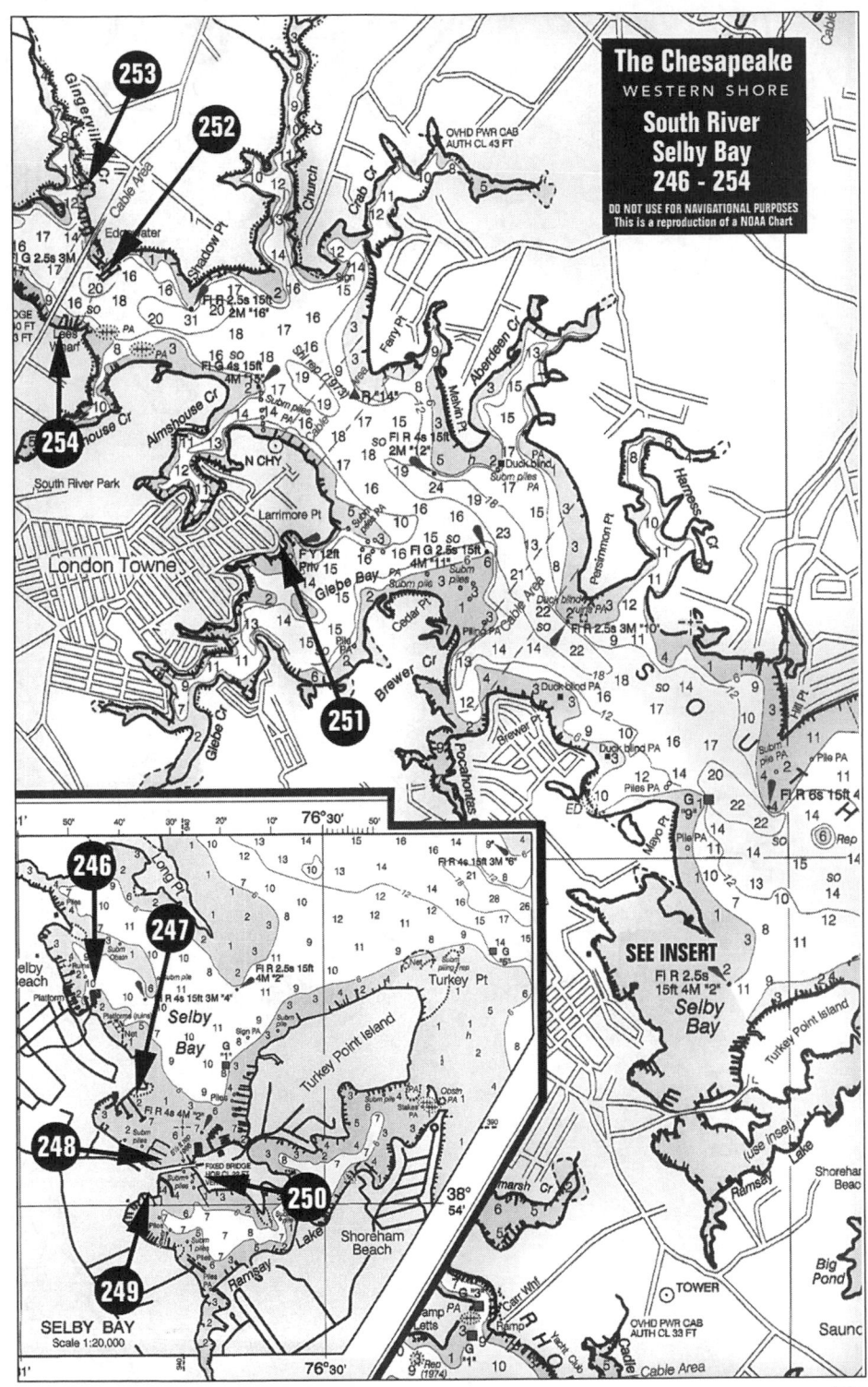

The Chesapeake
WESTERN SHORE
South River
Selby Bay
246 - 254

DO NOT USE FOR NAVIGATIONAL PURPOSES
This is a reproduction of a NOAA Chart

SELBY BAY
Scale 1:20,000

SEE INSERT
Fl R 2.5s
15ft 4M "2"
Selby
Bay

London Towne

Shoreham
Beach

TOWER

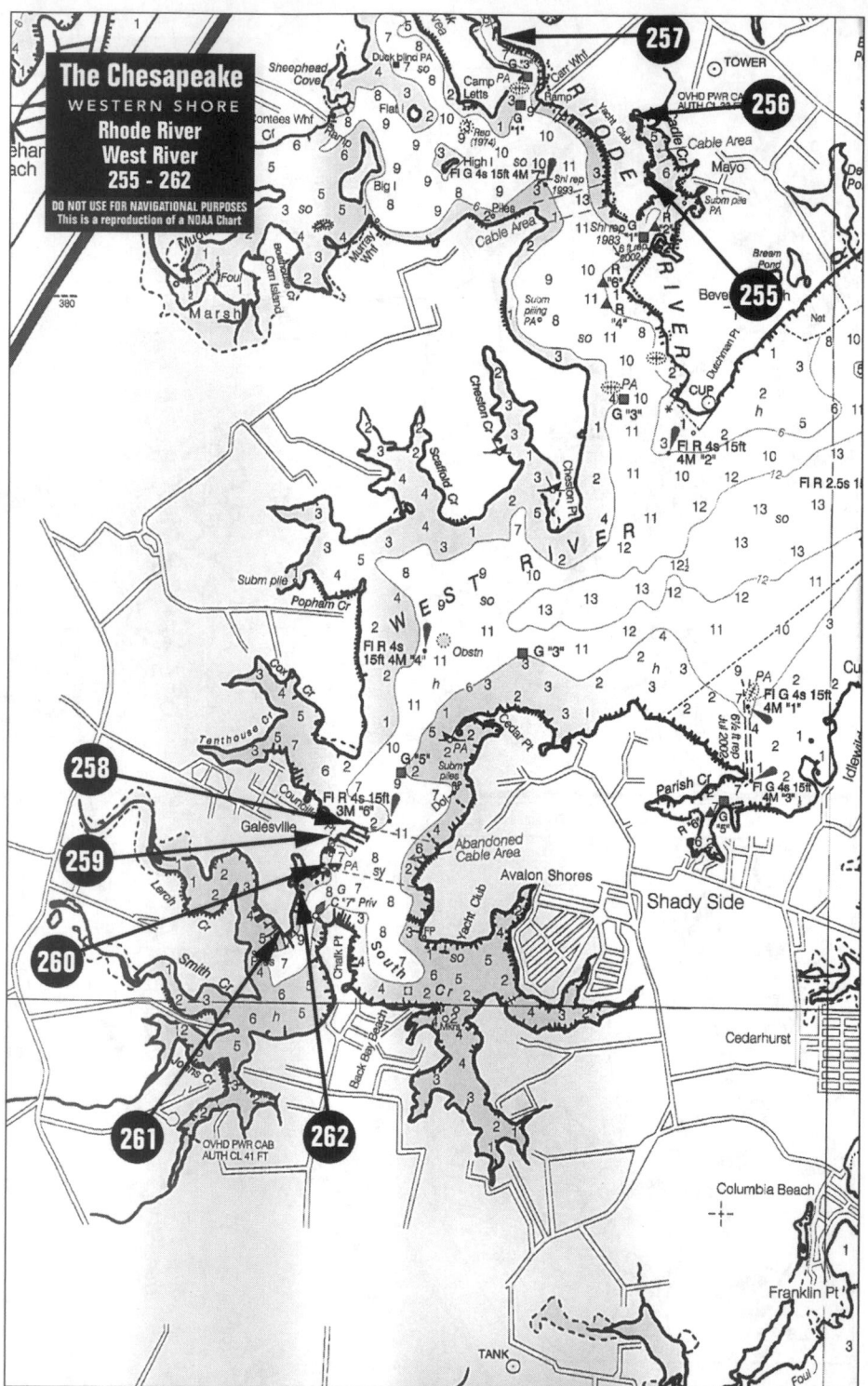

The Chesapeake
WESTERN SHORE
Rhode River
West River
255 - 262
DO NOT USE FOR NAVIGATIONAL PURPOSES
This is a reproduction of a NOAA Chart

257

256

255

258

259

260

261

262

Shady Side

Cedarhurst

Columbia Beach

Franklin Pt

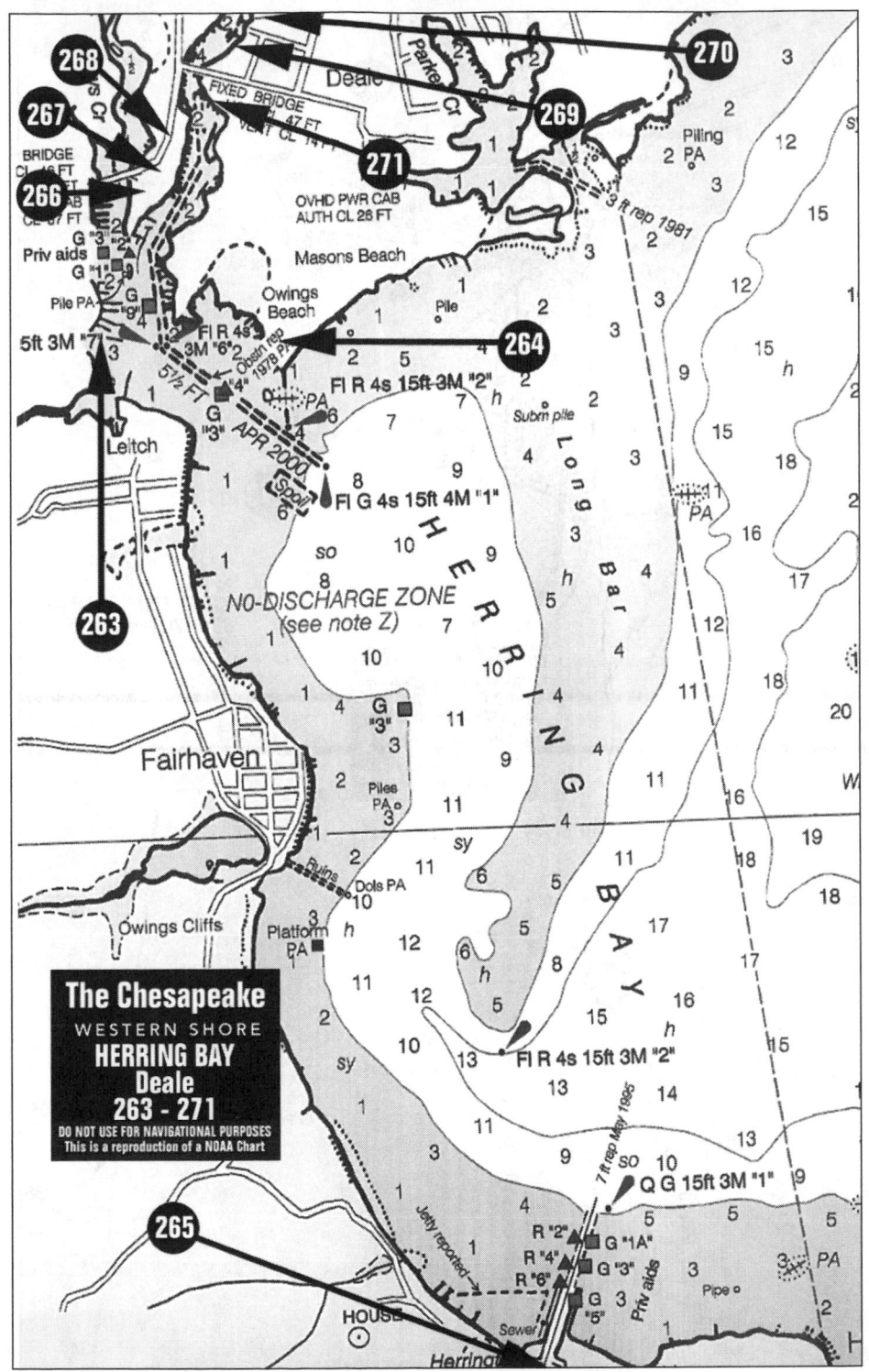

The Chesapeake
WESTERN SHORE
HERRING BAY
Deale
263 - 271
DO NOT USE FOR NAVIGATIONAL PURPOSES
This is a reproduction of a NOAA Chart

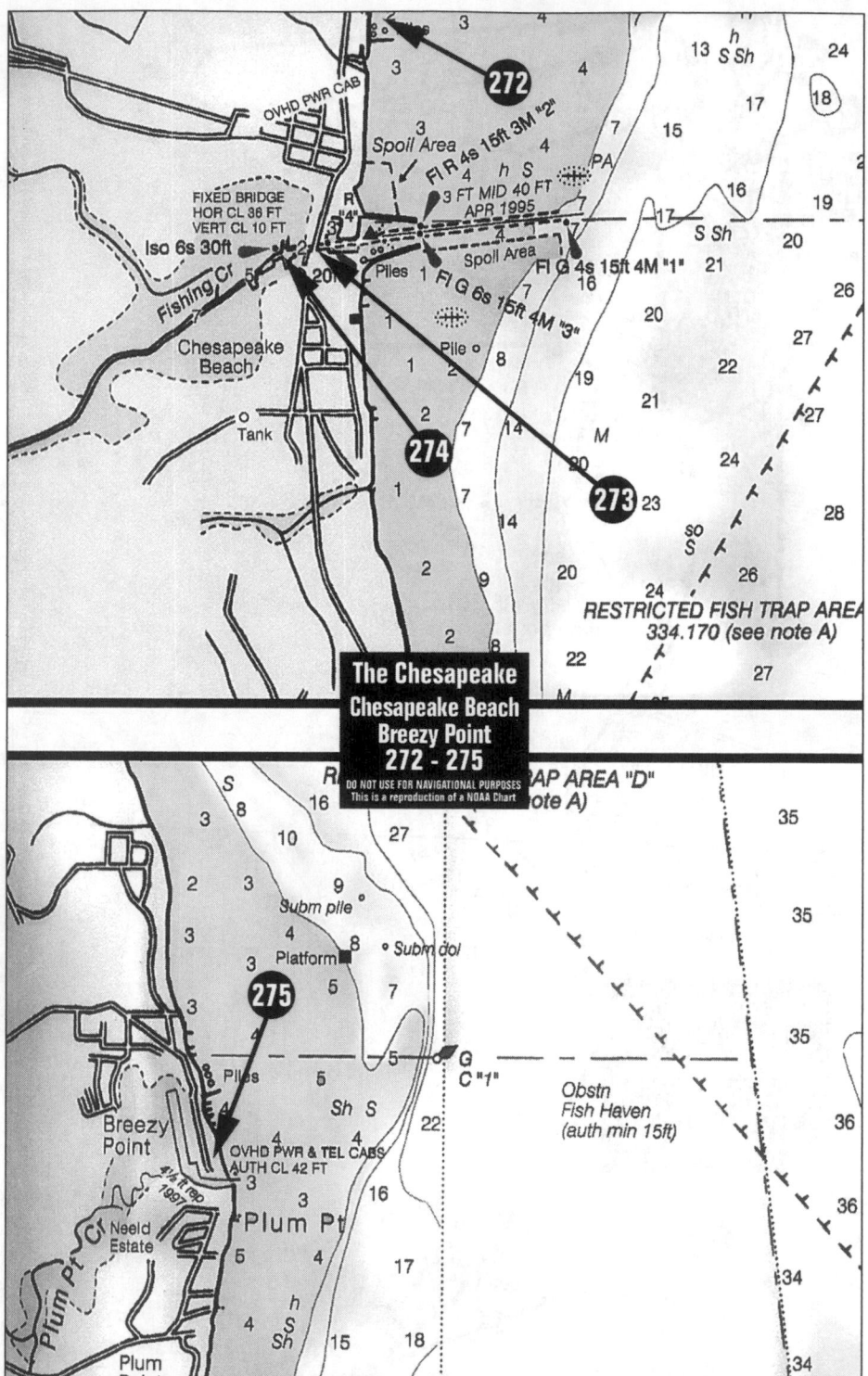

The Chesapeake
Chesapeake Beach
Breezy Point
272 - 275

DO NOT USE FOR NAVIGATIONAL PURPOSES
This is a reproduction of a NOAA Chart

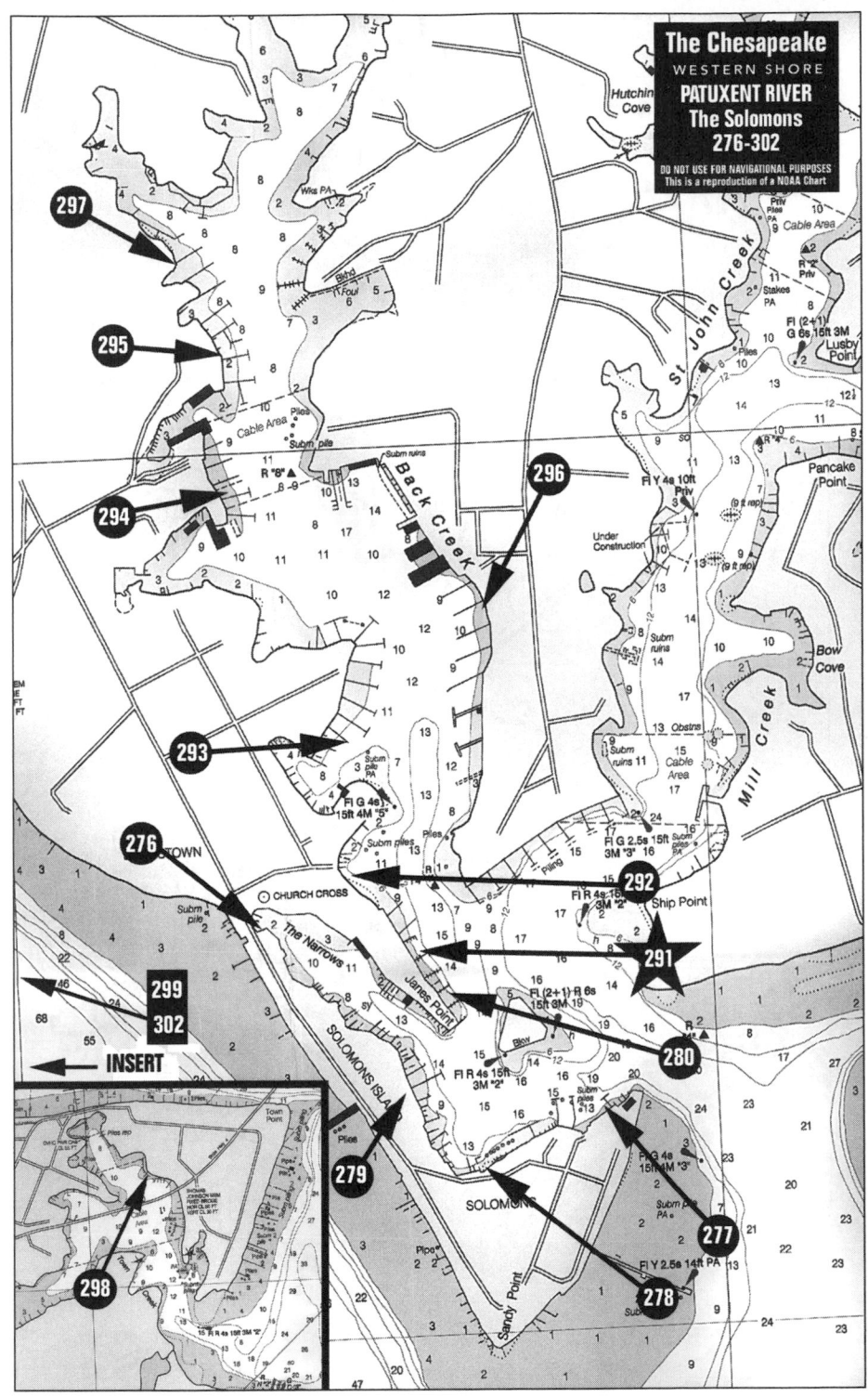

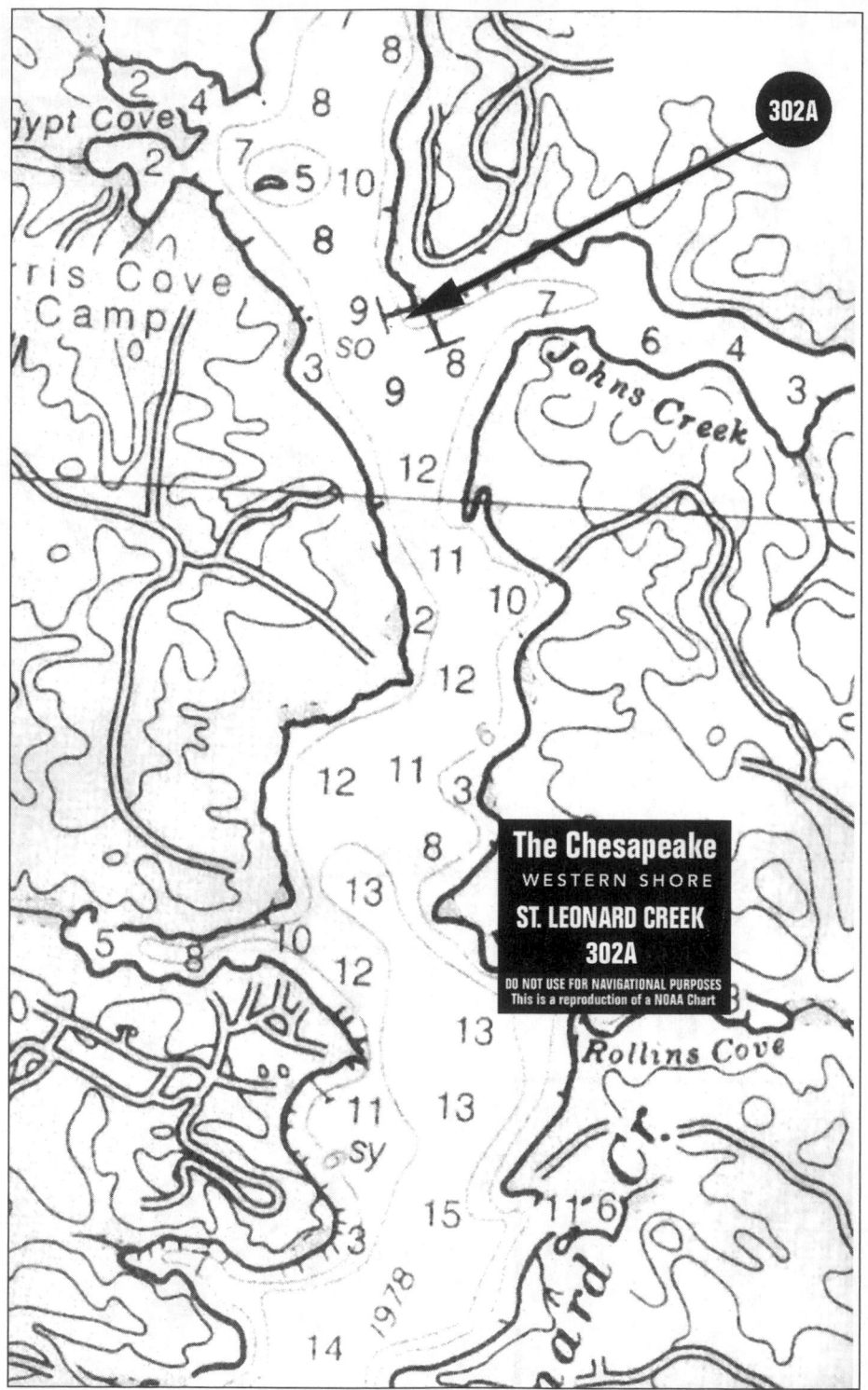

302A

The Chesapeake
WESTERN SHORE
ST. LEONARD CREEK
302A
DO NOT USE FOR NAVIGATIONAL PURPOSES
This is a reproduction of a NOAA Chart

Cruising
The Northeast

NEW JERSEY COASTLINE & ICW,
NEW YORK HARBOR, THE EAST RIVER, THE HUDSON RIVER,
LONG ISLAND COASTLINE, LONG ISLAND NORTH SHORE,
CONNECTICUT, RHODE ISLAND, BLOCK ISLAND, NANTUCKET, MARTHA'S VINEYARD
MASSACHUSETTS, NEW HAMPSHIRE & MAINE

BARNEGAT LIGHTHOUSE STATE PARK ON BARNEGAT INLET, IN THE TOWN OF BARNEGAT LIGHT
Photo by C. Miners.

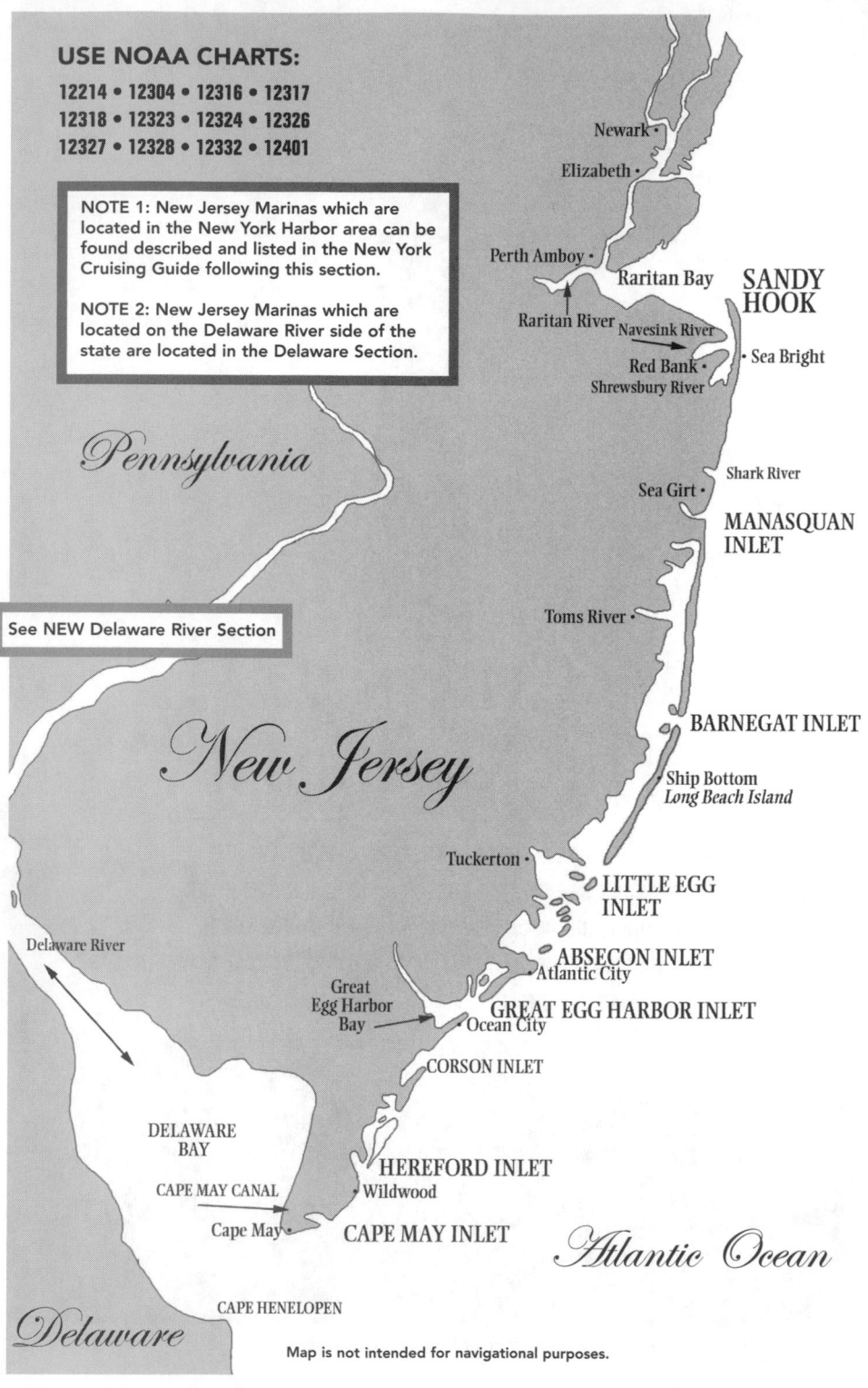

USE NOAA CHARTS:
12214 • 12304 • 12316 • 12317
12318 • 12323 • 12324 • 12326
12327 • 12328 • 12332 • 12401

NOTE 1: New Jersey Marinas which are located in the New York Harbor area can be found described and listed in the New York Cruising Guide following this section.

NOTE 2: New Jersey Marinas which are located on the Delaware River side of the state are located in the Delaware Section.

Pennsylvania

See NEW Delaware River Section

New Jersey

Newark •
Elizabeth •

Perth Amboy •

Raritan Bay

SANDY HOOK

Raritan River
Navesink River

Red Bank •
Shrewsbury River

• Sea Bright

Sea Girt •

Shark River

MANASQUAN INLET

Toms River •

BARNEGAT INLET

Ship Bottom
Long Beach Island

Tuckerton •

LITTLE EGG INLET

ABSECON INLET
Atlantic City

Great Egg Harbor Bay

GREAT EGG HARBOR INLET
Ocean City

CORSON INLET

Delaware River

DELAWARE BAY

CAPE MAY CANAL

Wildwood

HEREFORD INLET

Cape May •

CAPE MAY INLET

Atlantic Ocean

CAPE HENELOPEN

Delaware

Map is not intended for navigational purposes.

New Jersey Shoreline

THE FOLLOWING REGIONS ARE COVERED IN CHARTS IN THIS SECTION:

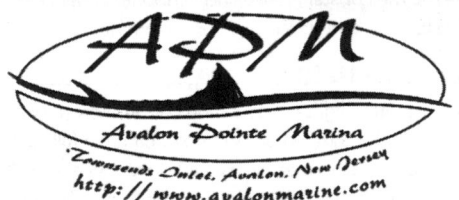

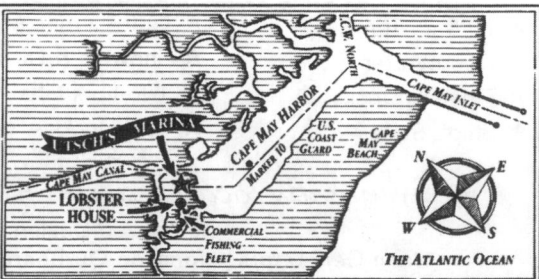

Cruising New Jersey

Between New York and the Delaware Bay is the New Jersey coast with its many resorts, inlets, and the Intracoastal Waterway. The Delaware Bay is the approach to the cities of Wilmington, Chester, Philadelphia, Camden and Trenton. Below Wilmington is the C & D Canal - the Delaware River entrance to the Chesapeake and Delaware. **SEE NEW SECTIONS ON THE DELAWARE RIVER, C&D CANAL AND UPPER CHESAPEAKE BAY.**

The coast of New Jersey extends in a general southerly direction for 44 miles from Sandy Hook to Barnegat Inlet, then southwesterly for 66 miles to Cape May Point. From Sandy Hook to Atlantic City the 60- foot curve is 5 to 10 miles for shore. Off Delaware Bay, the distance has increased to 17 miles.

The general tendency along this mostly sandy coast is for the ocean beaches and the points on the north sides of the inlets to wash away, and for the points on the south sides of the entrances to build out.

Light draft vessels can follow the shore if they pay strict attention to the charts for shoals, wrecks, and other obstructions. Small craft should wait for favorable weather before attempting an outside run along this coast. The principal entrances are **SHARK RIVER INLET, MANASQUAN INLET, BARNEGAT INLET, ABSECON INLET AND CAPE MAY INLET.** There are several others that are unimproved. The inlets are or may be obstructed by shifting bars, and most require local knowledge. The best time to enter is on a rising tide with a smooth sea. Passage is hazardous during easterly gales and heavy seas. In most cases the aids marking the various inlets are not charted due to the changing conditions. In fact, cruising sailboats would be wise to consider only Manasquan Inlet, Barnegat Inlet, Absecon Inlet and Cape May Inlet. The greater part of the New Jersey coast is a summer-resort area, and numerous standpipes and elevated water tanks are prominent from seaward. **THE NEW JERSEY INTRACOASTAL WATERWAY** is an inside passage from Manasquan Inlet to Delaware Bay. Sailboaters and larger power vessels will need to use the ocean passage south of the Absecon Inlet.

CHART 12332. The Raritan River is entered from the east by way of Great Beds Reach, and from the north by way of Arthur Kill and the Raritan River Channel Cut-Off. Consult the latest chart for the many fixed bridges that cross the river. South Amboy is a city on the south side of the river entrance. Provisioning can be easily done here from **Lockwood Boat Works.** Vessels transiting the coast looking for professional repair services should consider Lockwood as a destination. Certified mechanics are on location and they even work on wood in case you're cruising in a classic! Call Lockwood Boat Works (732-721-1605) in advance for information about repairs and transient slip reservations.

CHART 12326. Vessels awaiting favorable weather for an outside run, or favorable tides for transiting New York's East River, can anchor in **SANDY HOOK.**

SANDY HOOK on the south side of the entrance to New York Harbor, is the most northerly part of the New Jersey coast. **SANDY HOOK LIGHT** (40°27'7" N., 74°00'01" W FL W.), 88 feet above the water, is shown from an 85 foot stone tower 1.2 miles from the north end of the point. The light, established in 1764, is the oldest in continuous use in the United States.

Sandy Hook Coast Guard Station, a standpipe, several towers and two marine lights are prominent on the northern tip of the hook. There is a good anchorage in Sandy Hook Bay (in easterly winds) with plenty of depth behind the Coast Guard Station. A mile and a half south is **HORSESHOE COVE** — a pretty anchorage which is quite popular on summer weekends. Transit the area with care to avoid shoals. **Ed. Note:** When entering behind the hook at night, stay west of the shore to avoid giant fish traps which loomed out of the dark to our great surprise just south of the Coast Guard Station.

NEW JERSEY

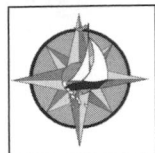

CHART 12327, 12401, 12324. An alternative to anchoring at the hook is **ATLANTIC HIGHLANDS,** located on the western shore opposite the hook and north of the entrance to the Navesink River. The Highlands makes a good storm haven and is an excellent place to stop for provisioning and shoreside amenities. **Atlantic Highlands Municipal Harbor** offers quick access to the ocean with no bridges to worry about. The marina monitors VHF Channel 9. Atlantic Highlands Yacht Club is also on site (732-291-1118 or VHF 9) with moorings and a launch service. As you get close to the harbor, you'll see a stone breakwater to use as a landmark to enter the harbor.

CHART 12325, 12324. The **TWIN LIGHTS OF NAVESINK,** built in 1862, tower 250 feet above Sandy Hook Bay and this unusual structure is now a museum and open to the public. An occulting white light can be seen during boating season emanating from the north tower. **THE NAVESINK RIVER AND SHREWSBURY RIVER** (a.k.a **THE TWIN RIVERS**) empty through a common entrance into the southern extremity of Sandy Hook Bay – eastward of the Highlands of Navesink. A red flashing bell buoy marks the entrance. Check the tides before entering as depths can be different than charted. Try not to enter on an ebb tide. Your reward for navigating these rivers is lovely scenery along the way, waterfront restaurants, marinas and boatyards, and scenic anchorages with relatively easy on-foot access to ocean beaches across the barrier strip. Just after entering the Shrewsbury River you will encounter **HIGHLANDS** and **HIGHLANDS BEACH.**

CHART 12324. SHARK RIVER INLET is protected by jetties, each marked by a light near its outer end. A fog signal is at the north side of the river about .3 mile above the jetties. A dredged channel leads through the inlet and river to Belmar. **SHARK INLET** and **SHARK RIVER**, the only small craft harbor between Sandy Hook and Manasquan Inlet are 17 miles south of Sandy Hook Light. The town of **AVON** fronts the ocean on the north side of the river, and **BELMAR** is on the south side, with restaurants, lodging and a NJ Transit station convenient for crew changes. Three bascule drawbridges cross the main or south channel of the Shark River and a fixed bridge (Route 35) with a reported 50-ft clearance. The Shark River Inlet is a good emergency storm haven on the stretch of coastline between Manasquan and Sandy Hook.

MANASQUAN INLET, 22 miles southward of Sandy Hook Light, and five miles south of Shark River, is the Atlantic entrance to **MANASQUAN RIVER** and the northern terminus of the New Jersey Intracoastal Waterway. A light near the outer end marks the north jetty. A fog signal is at the south jetty light, and a radiobeacon is close inshore of the light. A marked dredged channel leads through Manasquan Inlet and extends about 5 miles up Manasquan River. **Ed. Note:** On any given summer's day, this inlet is crowded with both commercial and recreational boating traffic causing enough chop to gain your attention. Entering Manasquan Inlet puts you in position to access the ICW through the **POINT PLEASANT CANAL.**

Ed. Note: About a mile from the inlet is the locally dreaded railroad bridge. The bridge remains open unless a train approaches. The current is swift here but the true hazards are other boaters, both coming and going,

squeezing through a horizontal clearance of 48 feet. On a summer weekend this can be a challenge. (Think of it as everyone heading for the one and only toll booth on the turnpike.) Anchorages are not the best in the Manasquan River due to crowds and wake. Several restaurants in the area offer transient docking but call ahead to see if you can reserve space.

TRAVELING 'INSIDE' ALONG THE INTRACOASTAL WATERWAY, PART I:

The ICW extends 118 statute miles from Manasquan Inlet to Delaware Bay. Mile 0 is calculated at 40° 06' 03" N and 74° 01' 55" W. Dredged channels are maintained at 6-ft minimum depth and is supervised by The Army Corps of Engineers - Philadelphia District.

CHARTS 12316, 12324. At the beginning of the ICW, in the Manasquan River, you'll find the towns of **BRIELLE** and **POINT PLEASANT**, each at opposite sides of the river. Commercial and charter fishing docks, marinas, and repair facilities are abundant. Provisioning is walkable from marinas in Brielle. Point Pleasant offers beaches, boardwalk and amusements.

Enter the two-mile-long **POINT PLEASANT CANAL** from the **MANASQUAN RIVER.** There are three bridges and its best to contact the bridge tenders (VHF 13) ahead of time to check for opening times depending on the season. The canal is narrow and bulkheaded, and has swift currents so time your transit well with the tides (Enter the canal no more than an hour before or after slack water – see Tide & Current Tables – slack high water is best.) so you can enjoy the scenery and handle the bridges easily.

BARNEGAT BAY. Prevailing summer winds are from the south and come up like clockwork around noon to one o'clock. It's not unusual to record winds from 15 to 20 knots on any given afternoon in boating season. The bay itself is extremely shallow with the exception of marked channels. A prolonged period of west or northwest winds tends to 'blow water out of the bay,' meaning depths are shallower than usual. Twigs stick up out of the water here and there all over the bay to mark private clam beds.

PUT YOURSELF IN THE DRIVER'S SEAT OF A VINTAGE SPEED BOAT AT THE NEW JERSEY MUSEUM OF BOATING, IN POINT PLEASANT.

CHARTS 12323, 12324. At the southern end of the canal —or the northern entrance — is the quaint seaside resort town of **BAY HEAD.** Victorian-style seaside cottages of yesteryear, surrounded by brightly colored summer gardens, bring to mind more of a New England feel than you expect to see at the New Jersey shore. This was once one of New Jersey's boatbuilding meccas and custom boatbuilders can still be found in the area. Johnson Brothers Boat Works, next to the Bay Head Yacht Club, offers transient slips plus the opportunity to visit **The New Jersey Museum of Boating** (732-859-4767) housed in Building 12 of Johnson Brothers Boat Yard. The museum celebrates vintage NJ built boats such as the famous NJ speed skiffs, sneakboxes, cat boats, Egg Harbors, Vikings, and more. Note the display of antique motors and boat building tools, plus a library of nautical books, publications, newspaper clippings and photographs from another time. Admission is free 365 days a year from 10 to 4. A classic wooden boat show is a major annual event held at the museum in September. Once inside, you'll sail back in time to boating life of yesteryear featuring NJ built boats such as the skiffs, sneakboxes, catboats, Egg Harbors, and Vikings, and more. Among the collections you'll see are your Grandpa's outboard motors, old nautical advertising, antique maps, ship models, vintage photographs, cross-section hull plans, samples of classic and famous Jersey-built boats – both life-sized and in model form, and exhibits relating to maritime commerce, defense, and recreation – including sportfishing, bay and river racing, and duck hunting.

This maritime museum is like a "please touch" experience for grown-ups. Odds are when you go you won't find museum staff on premises. That's okay. The founders wanted people to be able to experience the

NEW JERSEY

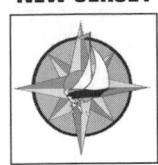

ever-growing collections in an informal, non-intimidating manner. So, on any given day, the public may wander the museum aisles, unescorted, taking their time to check out old photos, boatbuilding tools, antique motors and the boats themselves. A sizeable lending library is filled with vintage boating books, periodicals and literature.

Traveling down the ICW from Bay Head takes you past the scenic **METEDECONK RIVER**, on the western shore, easily navigable with good anchorages and marina facilities.

On the eastern shore, the barrier coast is dotted with seaside resort towns with their names boldly painted on towering water tanks. Marina facilities can be found in **MANTALOKING, NORMANDY BEACH, LAVALLETTE AND SEASIDE HEIGHTS.**

SILVER BAY offers a good anchorage along the southern marsh and swimming is good. A dinghy ride to the shore puts you in Cattus Island Park, with public facilities and ecotouring. The anchorage becomes crowded on summer weekends and local PWC operators can cause some rock and roll.

TOMS RIVER is a beautiful cruising area offering three stopping places to visit. **ISLAND HEIGHTS** on the northern shore has a small town pier, swimming beach and ramp. The town is full of steep hills — unexpected in New Jersey's shore area —and some of the most extraordinary Victorian homes you'll see anywhere. There are marinas with fuel and supplies. And there is a marina in **DILLON'S CREEK** which is entered before rounding **LONG POINT**. Consult your chart for the locations of shoals off Long Point. On the opposite side of the river there are facilities at Goodluck Point and in Ocean Gate. At the head of the river is the Tom's River Yacht Club, the Toms River Seaport Society and Museum, and other marina facilities.

Cruising south, Berkeley Island Park and Cedar Beach are on the northern point of **CEDAR CREEK.** Anchorage is available just north of the park's breakwater. Public facilities, swimming and clamming are available in the park. Entering Cedar Creek, follow the day markers carefully, hugging the southern shore to several marina facilities with fuel, including a sailing center.

Opposite Cedar Creek, to the southeast, is **TICES SHOAL,** a favorite summertime anchorage, protected from east, northeast and southeast winds, for locals and transients both. Depending on your 'spot' you can walk or dinghy to **ISLAND BEACH STATE PARK,** a beautiful barrier beach with excellent public facilities ocean swimming, ecotouring and surf fishing. This is a regular stop for the pumpout boat.

FORKED (FOR-KED) RIVER is known as one of the best Hurricane Holes on the Atlantic coast. It's also a scenic river, easy to navigate, with resort-style marina facilities and restaurants with transient slips on the North Fork. Provisioning is walkable from marinas at the head of the river's north fork.

TRAVELING 'OUTSIDE' FROM MANASQUAN TO BARNEGAT LIGHT:

Boats with drafts 6-ft. and over would be wise to avoid the winding ICW and transit from Manasquan south on the ocean side of New Jersey's coast. You can mark your passage by sighting the elevated water tanks in each resort beach town along the way.

BARNEGAT INLET, 21 miles southward of Manasquan Inlet, forms a passage from the Atlantic Ocean through Oyster Creek Channel up into the Barnegat Bay, meeting with the New Jersey ICW at mile 25.9.

A lighted whistle buoy about 1.7 miles SE of the North Jetty (39° 44' 62" N, 74° 03' 48" W) marks the approach to the inlet. Two jetties marked by lights protect the inlet — the north breakwater light 6: 39° 45' 60", 74° 05' 50" W; south breakwater light 7: 39° 45' 50" N, 74° 05' 60" W. A fog signal is at the south jetty light, and a radiobeacon is at the Barnegat Light Coast Guard Station inshore.

HELP! There's NO EXCUSE to to empty your holding tanks in NJ's inland waters! **3 FREE PUMP-OUT BOATS** transit the inland waters from Manasquan to Great Bay: one is based in the Manasquan area; another in the Seaside Heights area. and another covers from Manahawkin Bay to Great Bay. Reach them on VHF Channel 9, in season.

NOTE: Barnegat Bay is now designated as an official NO DISCHARGE ZONE.

NEW JERSEY

Barnegat Lighthouse is non-functioning and stands to the south side of the inlet. It is a 161 ft. high tower — red on top and white on the bottom. The buoys are maintained by the local Coast Guard and are frequently moved due to shifting bottom depths. Once known as one of the most dangerous inlets on the east coast, Barnegat Inlet has been improved by the construction of new jetties in the late '80s - early '90s. Be sure to follow the marks carefully in the winding channel as shoaling is prolific on the bay side of the inlet.

The channel to the small craft and fishing boat facilities, on the bay side of the town, is marked by privately maintained seasonal buoys or markers; these aids are not charted. A good anchorage is **MEYER'S HOLE** (locally known as 'behind the light') — follow the markers to this anchorage west of the town, on the eastern shore of High Bar Harbor, which is marked on charts as " The Dike."

LONG BEACH ISLAND: This 18-mile long barrier island is historically known for privateers, shipwrecks, and the beginnings of the U.S. Livesaving Service.

BARNEGAT LIGHT, at the northern end of Long Beach Island, is a quaint commercial fishing village located on the south side of Barnegat Inlet. The town is relatively untouched by time and the march of progress. Provisioning is easy here and several marinas offer transient slips and fuel. Barnegat Light State Park, borders the south side of the inlet and the state of New Jersey maintains the lighthouse there which is open for climbing. A few blocks away from the park, a restored schoolhouse sits as home to the town's museum, with a secret seaside garden maintained by LBI Master Gardeners, vintage photos and artifacts on exhibit, and the lighthouse's original Fresnel lens. Everything from restaurants to groceries, bait and tackle shops, charming boutiques and a lifeguarded beach is within walking distance from Barnegat Light marinas.

TRAVELING 'INSIDE' ALONG THE INTRACOASTAL WATERWAY, Part II:

OYSTER CREEK CHANNEL zig zags its way out of Barnegat Light in narrow widths, through serious shoals, to connect with the ICW at N "40." Don't cut any corners here and make sure to stay in the channel from start to finish. This can be difficult at times when coping with wakes from other boats. Buoys are not charted since they are moved by the Coast Guard as needed. **Ed. Note:** Take care not to confuse Oyster Creek Channel marks with those intended for Double Creek channel, you could end up hard aground .

Several large marina facilities are close to the top of Oyster Creek channel and just off the ICW. Most tell us they have no transient space available. Following the ICW southward, a fixed bridge in **MANAHAWKIN BAY** connects the barrier island with the mainland. Clearance is 60-ft. in the main channel. There are many small craft facilities along the bay side of Long Beach Island — once more marking your passage of towns through elevated watertanks.

LITTLE EGG HARBOR: Rounding Egg Island, on the way to Beach Haven, puts you in Little Egg Harbor bay. The ICW hugs the bay side of Long Beach Island. LBI, as the locals call it, is a better bet for boaters looking for transient space and beachtime.

BEACH HAVEN is the island's major resort area with amusement parks, mini-golf, arcades, shopping, restaurants and a summer theatre. **HOLGATE** marks the end of the island with a designated wildlife refuge.

From **Beach Haven (or Little Egg Inlet)**, consult the chart for a side trip to historic **TUCKERTON CREEK**. Crossing the flats in the dredged channel is not recommended for drafts of 5 ft. and over. Marinas line the creek and an overhead cable midway along the creek allows a clearance of 50-ft. **Ed. Note:** The walkable small

PHOTO COURTESY TUCKERTON SEAPORT

town of **Tuckerton** is at the top of the creek, as is **Tuckerton Seaport,** (609-294-8868) a museum featuring re-created historic buildings, decoy carvers, local seafaring history, a small restaurant, and a super gift shop. Daytime dockage is available, with admission fee. Stewarts Root Beer stand, just above the Seaport, also has a marina welcoming transients, right on the town's main street. Be sure to visit the Tuckerton Emporium, a collection of small boutiques and a charming luncheon spot.

ATTENTION BIRDERS! From here on through Brigantine, the birdwatching is amazing. Rutgers University Marine Station, that sits on a point in **GREAT BAY,** has catalogued over 163 species along this flyway.

The ICW continues past Little Egg Inlet turning southwestward. At G "139," you have entered **GREAT BAY,** with good fishing, and entrance to the truly scenic, deep and winding **MULLICA RIVER.** Only vessels that can handle the fixed highway bridge with a clearance of 30-ft. should consider touring the Mullica. The river is marked by lights and stake daybeacons as far as the bridge which is 6.5 miles from the mouth of the river. Stake daybeacons mark the reaches above the bridge. Sixteen and 17 miles, respectively, from the mouth of the Mullica, you will find the hidden towns of **GREEN BANK** and **SWEETWATER** — worth the visit. This is New Jersey of yesteryear with clean, cedar waters tinged with pine.

A little over 3 miles up the Mullica is the entrance to the deep **BASS RIVER** which leads north to a good hurricane hole and the town of **NEW GRETNA,** home of Viking Yachts.

The ICW leaves **GREAT BAY** at R "144" and makes a sharp turn to starboard to wind its way through marshlands and the **BRIGANTINE WILDLIFE REFUGE.** Try to transit this area on a rising tide. In summer months, proven insect repellent is required for this leg of the journey. And even more so in a west wind. As the channel turns eastward you can leave the ICW at G "181" and head into **ATLANTIC CITY.** A fixed bridge crossing from Atlantic City to Brigantine has a clearance of 60-ft. Currents are strong here. Even docking at one of the marinas can be a challenge.

From Atlantic City southward, the ICW is navigable through to Cape May by small craft only due to fixed bridges with clearances as low as 25 feet.

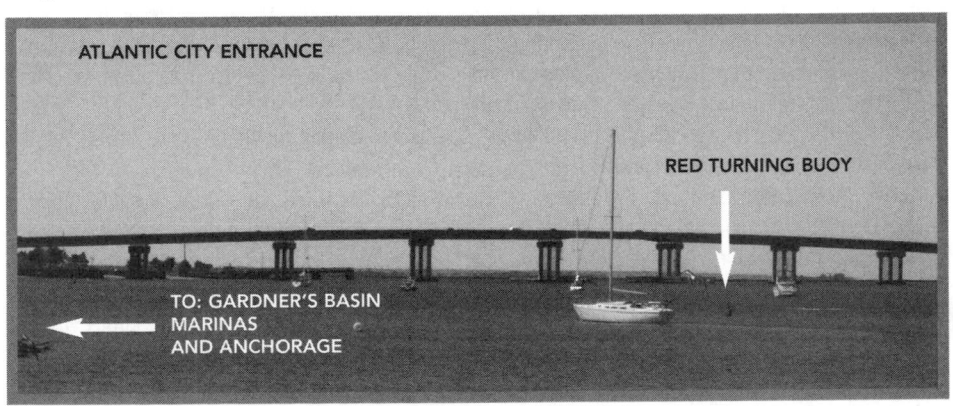

ATLANTIC CITY ENTRANCE

RED TURNING BUOY

TO: GARDNER'S BASIN
MARINAS
AND ANCHORAGE

TRAVELING 'OUTSIDE' FROM BARNEGAT LIGHT TO CAPE MAY:

CHARTS 12316, 12323. BEACH HAVEN INLET, 17 miles south southwestward of Barnegat Inlet, is unmarked. Numerous wrecks and shoals are at the entrance. Boaters are advised to use Little Egg Inlet.

CHARTS 12316, 12318. LITTLE EGG INLET, 19 miles south-southwestward of Barnegat Inlet, and close southward of Beach Haven Inlet, is used considerably by local pleasure and fishing boats. Depth over the bar is ample for any vessel that can navigate the inside waters, but in very heavy weather breakers form all the way across the bar. The inlet channels and shoreline are constantly changing; the entrance is well marked, but the buoys are not charted because they are frequently shifted in position.

NEW JERSEY

BRIGANTINE INLET, 2.6 miles south southwestward of Little Egg Inlet has shoaled to such and extent that it is unsafe for even the shallowest drafts. Brigantine Shoal, 3 miles south of the inlet, has at least a depth of 17 feet and is marked by a buoy.

ABSECON INLET, 8.7 miles southwestward of Little Egg Inlet, is on the northeast side of **ATLANTIC CITY,** The inlet is protected at the entrance by jetties.

ATLANTIC CITY LIGHT (39° 21' 80" N, 74° 24' 40" W, 29 feet above the water), is shown from a skeleton tower on the south side of Absecon Inlet; a radiobeacon is at the light. A light is on the outer end of the south jetty. The channel through the inlet is well marked to the entrance to **CLAM CREEK** and to a junction with the New Jersey ICW, 1 mile and 1.9 miles respectively, above the south jetty light.

CLAM CREEK, on the south side of **ABSECON INLET,** has a marked entrance one mile north of the south jetty light. Clam Creek will take you to **GARDNERS BASIN** where you can tour the new **Ocean Life Museum** or enjoy waterfront dining at **The Flying Cloud.** Across from the Coast Guard Station, and in the basin, is a protected anchorage. If you dinghy to shore from here, you'll need a taxi to get to **the Boardwalk** and shopping for provisions. Call the taxi service from Brigantine (opposite side of the inlet) for a less costly ride rather than Atlantic City cab services.

ATLANTIC CITY, the largest resort on the Jersey coast, and home to many Las Vegas style casinos, also offers great restaurants – both in and out of the gambling meccas, clean beaches, and the famous boardwalk where you can still catch a ride on the antique rolling chairs, shoot some Skee Ball, and buy fresh-made salt water taffy. Rail and air connections are available for crew changes. A new, 'upscale, outlet-style' shopping area on the Boardwalk, **"The Walk,"** is now open and ready for the summer season.

Going to Atlantic City need not be an adventure in roughing it. This is where you can 'slip in style.' Be prepared to eat up a storm, shop till you drop, see the sights, take in a show, and just have fun–it's a great family place to play even though you might think gambling is the only reason to go.

Trump Marina Resort and Casino is really the **Frank S. Farley NJ State Marina** with 640 slips on floating docks and a genuinely friendly and helpful staff. If you make your weekend reservation sooner, rather than later, you will most likely get a spot in one of their 140 transient slips. This floating resort brings visiting boaters all the amenities available to Trump Resort guests. Want to gad about town? A jitney bus runs 24/7 from the marina, on a five to ten minute schedule, to take you to other casinos and attractions such as the Boardwalk, and Gardners Basin. The cost is a mere buck-fifty.

Ed. Note: Boaters who remember going to **Harrah's Casino and Marina** should be aware that the marina facility has been closed for some time with no re-opening date available.

GREAT EGG HARBOR INLET, 7 miles southwest of Absecon Inlet, is subject to continual change due to severe shoaling. The buoys marking the inlet are not charted because they are shifted frequently to mark the best water. Many local fishing and pleasure boats use the inlet. Breakers extend along the bar even in moderate weather and are hazardous to small boats. Local knowledge is advised at all times.

CORSON INLET, 14 miles southwest of Absecon Inlet, is subject to constant change in depth and shouldn't be used by non-locals.

TOWNSENDS INLET, 20 miles southwest of Absecon Inlet, is subject to considerable changes in position and depth. Channel buoys are not charted, because they are shifted frequently to mark the best water. The depth over the bar is about 4 feet. Townsends Inlet is a small resort on the northeast side of the inlet. A seasonal Coast Guard station is on the Northeast side of the resort. The highway bridge over Townsends Inlet has a bascule span with a clearance of 23 feet. The route of the New Jersey ICW is just west of the bridge. **Avalon Pointe Marina** on ICW marker number 7, is located across from Townsends inlet and is recommended as a full service marina with excellent transient facilities in plenty of deep water. Golfing is nearby for those who stowed their clubs aboard. Reach Avalon Pointe Marina on VHF channel 16.

FYI: Bottle Nose Dolphins calve in the lower Delaware Bay in June, making Cape May Point an ideal place for dolphin watching. And, also keep a WATCH OUT for **Right Whales** and report sightings to the Cape May Coast Guard station.

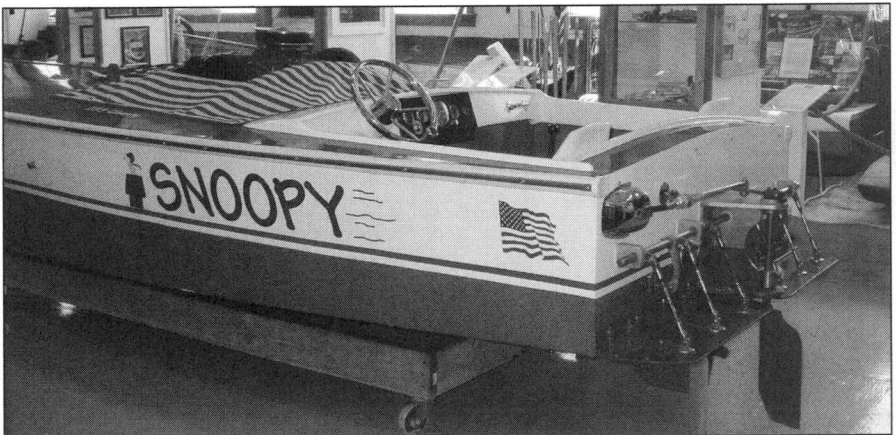

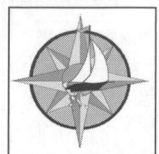

HEREFORD INLET, 28 miles southwest of Absecon Inlet is also subject to rapid change. Breakers form at all times on the shoals and, in moderate weather, on the sandbar. The approach to the inlet is extremely dangerous with a following sea.

CHARTS 12317, 12316, 12304. CAPE MAY INLET, 34 miles southwest of Absecon Inlet, is protected by jetties whose lights are inshore of the submerged ends. A fog signal is at the west jetty light, and a radiobeacon is at the inshore end. A lighted range marks the channel between the jetties. Buoys mark the channel inside the harbor. At night the lights on the towers on the East Side of the inlet are visible from well offshore. This is reportedly one of the safest and best marked inlets on the East Coast.

CAPE MAY is the pivotal stopping point for vessels traveling up and down the Atlantic Coast. It also lays claim to being New Jersey's first seaside resort. This Victorian resort town fronts the ocean 2 miles west of Cape May Inlet. **CAPE MAY HARBOR** is used by commercial fishing fleets, pleasure craft, and the Coast Guard. The fishing vessels operate from wharfs, both below and above the bridge, at the northeast end of the harbor, and from wharfs in Schellenger Creek, at the West End of the harbor. Pleasure craft facilities are on the north and west sides of the harbor. **Ed. Note: Utsch's Marina**, owned by the same family for over 52 years, is located between the Canal and Shellenger's Landing. This is a full service marina, complete marine state-of-the-art travel lifts and excellent transient facilities. **Utsch's Marina** has completely revamped its shoreside amenities to include an internet center for you web-browsing/e-mailing boaters, and their new restroom facilities rival those of a top hotel. Stockpile your saltspray-covered laundry...**Utsch's** has an outstanding commercial-style laundromat for boaters use only. In the same complex is **The Lobster House,** where you can dine inside, or out on the docks, and shop in their fresh seafood market. All fish here are right off the workboats. Call before you arrive – the marina monitors VHF Channel 16.

Ed. Note: CAPE MAY is tourism oriented and it fills every season with myriad events from fabulous Jazz Weekends to Walking Tours through selected Victorian seaside mansions. Any time of the year, you can stroll or bike the town to admire the amazing architecture and intricate gingerbread detailing on its famous "painted ladies."

Cape May beaches are among the best on the Jersey Shore and a few beachgoers can be lucky enough to find a **"Cape May Diamond"** in the sand off Sunset Boulevard. A Cape May Diamond is clear, nearly pure quartz crystal that has its source in the upper Delaware River where the water breaks up the quartz into pebbles. If you find one, have it polished and it truly will resemble a diamond.

CAPE MAY CANAL is the 3-1/2 mile 'short cut' between Cape May Inlet and the Delaware Bay. The canal is crossed by two bridges with a fixed vertical clearance of 55 feet. Keep an eye out for low cables to the side of the railroad swing bridge. Their vertical clearance is only 15 feet and they are hard to see from dusk on. The canal is 110- to 150-feet wide with a controlling depth of six feet. There is no dockage along the canal. At the western entrance to the canal, be aware that the Cape May/Lewes Ferry Terminals regularly dispatch ferries (crossing the Delaware Bay to Lewes, Delaware) large enough to block the entire channel.

ROUNDING THE CAPE: For mariners heading up **DELAWARE BAY** to the **C&D CANAL** or to **PHILADELPHIA**, whose vessels can't clear the fixed bridges in the Cape May Canal, note two long bars on the chart: Eph Shoal and Prissy Wicks Shoal. The shoals are mixed clay and sand and have the consistency of hardpan. These ridges run in approximately the same direction as the currents. Do not attempt to run the Cape May Channel (one mile southwest of the cape) between the shoals unless you are armed with local knowledge. Stay well off the shoals to round the Cape. Prissy Wicks Shoal is about 2 miles south of **CAPE MAY LIGHT,** at Cape May Point (38° 55' 59" N, 74° 57' 37" W, 165 ft. above water.) ⚓

Find more New Jersey cruising in the Delaware River Section.

NEW JERSEY SHORE FACILITIES alphabetical index

New Jersey

MARINA'S NAME & PHONE NUMBER

No.	Marina's Name & Phone Number	When Open	Monitors VHF Channel	Transient (Electricity/Moorings/Berths)	Repairs (Hull/Engine/Ramp)	Winter Storage (Wet/Dry)	Railway Capacity (ft)	Lift Capacity (tons)	Boat Rental (Canoe/Row/Motor)	Boat Rental (Charter/House/Sail)	Restaurant/Lodging/Camping	Showers/Laundry	Pumpout/Toilets	Bait/Tackle/Water/Ice	Groceries/Hardware	Diesel/Gasoline
1	**LIBERTY LANDING MARINA** 201-985-8000 **see NY Harbor Section**	ALL YR	16	EB	HE	WD			C	C	RL	SL	T	WI	GH	GD
3	PORT IMPERIAL MARINA 201-902-8787	ALL YR.	88A	EB	HE	W D		35		CS	RC	SL	PT	IW BT	GH	GD
4	LINCOLN HARBOR Y.C. 201-319-5100	ALL YR.	9	EB	HE	W D						S	PT	IW BT	GH	D
5	NEWPORT MARINA 201-626-5550	ALL YR.	16 72	EB		W					RL	SL	PT	IW	GH	
6	LIBERTY HARBOR MARINA 201-451-1000	ALL YR	68	EB	HE	D W		60				SL	T	IW		GD
7	OLSEN BOAT WORKS 732-264-4198	ALL YR.			HR	D	32	8					T		H	
8	HANS PEDERSEN 732-264-0971	ALL YR.		EB	HE	D	30				RL	S	T	IW	H	GD
9	SEABOARD MARINE INC 732-264-8910	ALL YR				D							T	I	H	
10	KEYPORT MARINE BASIN 732-264-9421	ALL YR.		EB	E	D		10			R	S	T P	IW BT	H G	G
12	BROWN'S POINT MARINA 732-264-7176	ALL YR.		EB	ER	D					R		T	W		
13	ZUBACK'S MARINE 732-727-3953	ALL YR.		EB	HE	D	40						T	IW BT	H	
14	VIKINGS MARINA 732-566-5961	ALL YR		EB M	HE	WD		25			R	S	T P	W BT	H	G
15	MORGAN MARINA 732-727-2289	ALL YR.		EB	HE	W D		25				S	T	IW	H	G
16	BARRONS BOAT YARD 732-721-3655	ALL YR.				D	34						T			
17	**LOCKWOOD BOAT WORKS** **732-721-1605**	ALL YR	72	EB	HE	wD		35				SL	PT	IW T	H	GD
18	ZUBACKS BOAT AND MOTOR 732-727-566-1035	ALL YR.			HE	D	25	15				S	T		H	G
19	LENTZ MARINA 732-787-213															
21	HARBORSIDE MARINE 732-291-4440	ALL YR.				D							T		H	
22	BAHRS LANDING 732-291-9554	ALL YR.		B	R								T	IW BT		GD
26	MARINA ON THE BAY 732-872-9300	ALL YR.		EB	E	W D		12				S	T	IW		

New Jersey

MARINA'S NAME & PHONE NUMBER

Chart Locater Number	Marina's Name & Phone Number	When Open	Monitors VHF Channel	Transient: Electricity•Moorings•Berths	Hull repairs•Engine repairs•Ramp	Winter Storage: Wet•Dry	Railway Capacity in Tons	Lift Capacity in Feet	Boat Rental: Canoe•Charter•Row•Motor•House•Sail	Restaurant•Lodging•Camping	Showers•Laundry	Pumpout•Toilets	Bait•Tackle•Water•Ice	Groceries•Hardware	Diesel fuel•Gasoline
28	SANDY HOOK BAY MARINA 732-872-1450	ALL YR.	16	E B	H E	D		30	C	R	S	T	I W		
29	ATLANTIC HIGHLANDS MUNICIPAL HARBOR 732-291-1670	ALL YR.	16	E M B	R	D		50	C	R	S	PT	I W B T		G D
30	SKIPPERS SHOP 732-872-0367	ALL YR.			H E	D				R L	L		I W B T	H	G
31	ATLANTIC HIGHLANDS BAIT & TACKLE 732-291-4500	MAR NOV							M	R		T	I B T		
32	WAGNER BOAT WORKS 732-291-1441	ALL YR.			H E	D		10							
33	LEONARDO NJ STATE MARINA 732-291-1333	ALL YR.	9 16	B E	R	W			C	R		PT	B T I W		
34	BELFORD MARINE RAILWAY 732-787-9023	ALL YR.	69 71		H E	D	110	99 +						H	
35	MONMOUTH COVE MARINA 732-495-9440	MAY OCT		E B	E	D		15			S	PT	I W		G
38	RUMSON RAMP				R										
39	BARNACLE BILLS MARINA 732-842-4963	MAY NOV		E B						R	S	T			
40	OCEANIC MARINA 732-842-1194	ALL YR.	16	E B M	H E	D		15	M	R L	S	PT	I B B T	H	
41	FAIR HAVEN YACHT WORKS 732-747-3010	ALL YR.	9	E M B	H E	D		15			S	PT	I W	H	
42	RED BANK TOWN MARINA											P			
43	IRWIN MARINA 732-741-0003	ALL YR.		E B	H E	W D		40		R L	S	PT	I W	G H	
44	WASHINGTON TOWN RAMP				R										
45	SEA LAND MARINA 732-741-5753	APR NOV	68 69							R		T	I W B T		
46	OYSTER POINT REST. & MARINA 732-530-8200	MAY NOV		E B						R L		T	I W		
47	MOLLY PITCHER INN 732-747-2500	APR OCT		E B						R L	S	PT	I W		
48	CHRIS RIVER PLAZA MARINA 732-741-9676	APR NOV			E R	D				R		T	I W B T		G
49	COVESAIL MARINA 732-842-5319	ALL YR.		E B	H E	W D		45	R		S L	PT	I W		

New Jersey

MARINA'S NAME & PHONE NUMBER

No.	Marina's Name & Phone Number	TRANSIENT / WHEN OPEN	MONITORS VHF CHANNEL	Hull repairs • Electricity	Engine repairs • Moorings • Berths	WINTER STORAGE: Wet • Dry	RAILWAY CAPACITY IN FEET • Ramp	LIFT CAPACITY IN TONS	BOAT RENTAL: Canoe • Row • Motor • Sail	BOAT RENTAL: Charter • House	Restaurant • Lodging • Camping	Showers • Laundry	Bait • Tackle • Pumpout • Toilets	Groceries • Water • Ice	Diesel fuel • Gasoline • Hardware
49A	ATLANTIS YACHT CLUB 732-222-9693														
49B	PATTEN POINT YACHT CLUB 732-229-2882														
50	CARRIAGE HOUSE MARINA 732-741-8113	ALL YR.		E B	H E	W D		35				S	P T	W	
51	SURFSIDE MARINA 732-842-0844	ALL YR.		E B	H E	D		10				S	T	W	H
52	ANGLERS MARINA 732-842-0204	ALL YR.			H E	D		7					T		
53	NAVESINK YACHT SALES & MARINA 732-842-3700	ALL YR.		E B	H E	D					R	S L	T	I W	
54	MONMOUTH BEACH RAMP						R								
55	FAIRBANKS MARINA 732-842-8450														
55A	GATEWAY MARINA 732-291-4440														
56	MONMOUTH MARINA 732-222-3492	ALL YR.			H	D		5					T		
57	CHANNEL CLUB MARINA 732-222-7717	ALL YR.		E B	H E	W D		60			R	S	T	I W H	G D
58	MARINERS EMPORIUM 732-870-2542	ALL YR.		E B	H E	D		30				S	T	I W H	
59	LONG BRANCH RAMP						R								
60	OCEANPORT RAMP						R								
61	PLEASURE BAY YACHT BASIN 732-222-8563	ALL YR.	16	E B / M	H E	W D		30				S L	T	I W B	H
62	OCEANPORT LANDING 732-229-4466	ALL YR.		E B	H E	W D		30			R L	S L	T	W	H
63	SHARK RIVER HILLS MARINA 732-775-7400	ALL YR.		E B	H / ER	D		15			R L	S	T	I W H	G
65	BRYS MARINA 732-775-7364	ALL YR.		E	H / R			15							
66	MAIN ONE MARINA INC 732-776-5992	MAR DEC	16 9	E B	H E	D		15				S	P T	I W B	G
67	SHARK ISLAND YACHT CLUB 732-502-0094	ALL YR.		E B	H E	W D		12			R L	S	T	I W	

New Jersey

CHART LOCATER NUMBER — MARINA'S NAME & PHONE NUMBER

Column key (diagonal headers, left to right):
When Open (Monitors VHF Channel) · Transient · Electricity • Moorings • Berths · Hull repairs • Engine repairs · Railway Capacity (Ramp) · Winter Storage: Wet • Dry · Lift Capacity in Tons · Boat Rental: Canoe • Row • Motor · Boat Rental: Charter • House • Sail · Restaurant • Lodging • Camping · Showers • Laundry · Pumpout • Toilets · Bait • Tackle • Water • Ice · Groceries • Hardware · Diesel fuel • Gasoline

No.	Marina Name & Phone	When Open	Trans.	E/M/B	Hull/Eng	Railway	Winter W/D	Lift (tons)	Rent C/R/M	Rent Ch/H/S	Rest/Lodg/Camp	Show/Laun	Pump/Toil	Bait/Tack/Wat/Ice	Groc/Hdw	Diesel/Gas
68	TOTAL MARINE AT SEAVIEW 732-775-7842	FEB/DEC					W D					S	PT			
69	BELMAR MARINE BASIN 732-681-2266	ALL YR.	16	EB		R	W		M R	C	RL	S	PT	IW BT	G H	G D
70	APS INLET MARINA 732-681-3303	APR/DEC		EB	E		W D	20					T	IW BT	H	G D
71	MANASQUAN RIVER CLUB 732-840-0300	ALL YR.	9	EB	HE		D W				RL	SL	PT	IW		G
72	PETERSONS RIVERA INN 732-840-1110	ALL YR.		EB							RL		T	IW		
73	McCARTHYS MARINE SALES 732-528-8200	ALL YR.			E		D						T		H	
73A	CRYSTAL POINT YACHT CLUB 732-892-2300															
74	CLARKS LANDING MARINA 732-899-5559	ALL YR.	5	EB	HE		D	30		C	RL	S	T	IW BT	H	G D
75	KENS LANDING 732-892-9787	ALL YR.	16				W			C		S	T	IB T		G D
76	JACK BAKERS WHARFSIDE 732-892-9100	ALL YR.									R					
78	SOUTH SIDE MARINA INC 732-892-0388	ALL YR.		EB	HE			15		C	RL	S	PT	IW BT	H	D
82	CARDINAL GARDEN STATE MARINA INC 732-892-4222	ALL YR.		EB			W	25			RL	S	T	IW		
83	SHRIMP BOX RESTAURANT 732-899-1637	ALL YR.		B							R					
84	ROBINSONS ANCHORAGE 732-223-2589	APR/NOV	68	EB							R	S	T	IW		G D
85	STRICTLY MARINE 732-223-4277	APR/DEC	5		HE	R	D					S	T	IW	HG	
86	DRAW BRIDGE STEAK HOUSE 732-223-8434	ALL YR.		EB			W				RL	S	T	IW BT		
87	JIM'S ROW BOATS 732-223-0188	APR/DEC							R				T	IB T	H	
88	UNION LANDING RESTAURANT 732-528-6665	MAR/NOV									R		T			
89	BRIELLE Y. C. & MARINA 732-528-6250	ALL YR.		EB						C	R	S	T	IW		G D
90	HOFFMANS MARINA 732-528-6160	ALL YR.	11 65	EB	HE		D	35		C		S	T	IW	H	G

New Jersey

Chart Locater No.	Marina's Name & Phone Number	When Open	Monitors VHF Channel	Transient (Elec./Moorings/Berths)	Hull/Engine/Ramp	Winter Storage (Wet/Dry)	Railway Cap. (ft)	Lift Cap. (tons)	Boat Rental	Restaurant/Lodging/Camping	Showers/Laundry	Pumpout/Toilets	Groceries/Water/Ice	Bait/Tackle/Hardware	Diesel/Gasoline
91	BRIELLE MARINE BASIN 732-528-6200	ALL YR.	16 9	EB	HE	W D		70	C	R	S	PT	IW BT	H	G D
92	**NEW JERSEY MUSEUM OF BOATING 732-681-1165**	**ALL YR.**		B								T			
92A	JOHNSON BROTHERS BOAT WORKS 732-892-9000	ALL YR.	16 9	EB	E					RL	SL	PT			G
93	BRENNAN BOAT WORKS 732-840-1100	ALL YR			HE	W D		25		R	S	PT	IW	H	
94	JOHNSON BOAT BASIN 732-840-9530	ALL YR.		EB	HE	W D	40	15		RL	S	PT	IW	H	G
95	GREEN COVE MARINA 732-840-9090	ALL YR.	16	EB	H ER					R	SL	PT	W	H	G
96	WEHRLEN BROTHERS 732-899-3505	ALL YR.		B	HE	W D		40		R	S	PT	IW		
97	MENTOR MARINE 732-295-4036	ALL YR.			HE	W D					S	T	IW	H	
98	SAILS AWEIGH INC 732-477-3252	ALL YR.		EB	HE	W D		10		RL	S	T	W		
99	CASSIDYS BRETON WOODS MARINA 732-477-1111	MAR DEC				D		20			S	T	IW		
100	SHERMANS BOAT BASIN 732-295-0103	ALL YR.	9	EB	H ER			20			S	T	IW BT		
101	COMSTOCK BOAT WORKS 732-899-3161	ALL YR.		EB	HE	D		40			S	T	IW	H	G D
102	STARCK'S LANDING 732-892-7558	ALL YR.		EB	R				R	M R		T T	IB		
103	FORSBERG'S BOAT WORKS 732-892-4246	ALL YR.			HE	W D		20			S	T	W	H	G
104	ARNOLD'S YACHT BASIN 732-892-3000	ALL YR.			HE	W		30		RL	S	T	IW	H	G
105	POINT PLEASANT FISHING YC 732-295-8543	ALL YR.		EB		D				R	S	T	IW		
106	CARVER BOAT SALES INC 732-892-0328	ALL YR.			HE	D		50							
107	TRADERS COVE INC 732-295-2500	ALL YR.				D		25							
108	WINTER YACHT BASIN INC 732-477-6700	ALL YR.	16	E B	H E	W D	75	75			S L	PT	IW	H	G D
156	SILVER CLOUD HAR. MARINA 609-693-2145	ALL YR.	16 68	EB	HE	W D	48	15		RL	SL	P T	IW BT	H	G D

New Jersey

MARINA'S NAME & PHONE NUMBER

Chart #	Marina Name & Phone	When Open	Monitors VHF	Transient (Elec•Moor•Berth)	Hull/Engine Repairs•Ramp	Winter Storage (Wet•Dry)	Railway Cap. (tons)	Lift Cap. (feet)	Boat Rental (Canoe•Row•Motor)	Boat Rental (Charter•House•Sail)	Restaurant•Lodging•Camping	Showers•Laundry	Pumpout•Toilets	Bait•Tackle•Water•Ice	Groceries•Hardware	Diesel•Gasoline
109	BEATON'S BOAT YARD 732-477-0259	ALL YR.			HE	D							T		H	
110	BAYWOOD MARINA 732-477-3322	ALL YR		E B	ER H	W D						S L	P T	B W I	H	G D
111	HARBOUR YACHT CLUB & REPAIRS 732-793-7975															
112	WINDOWS ON THE BAY RESTAURANT 732-269-6161	ALL YR									R					
113	DICKS LANDING 732-269-0867	MAY OCT			E	D				M R			T	IB T		
114	FULLERS MARINE 732-269-9494				ER							S	T	IB	H	G
115	BECKERS BOAT BASIN 732-269-3723	MAR OCT			R	D			7	R			T	IB T		G
116	WATERS EDGE RESTAURANT 732-269-3700	ALL YR.									R					
117	GOOD LUCK POINT MARINA 732-269-300	ALL YR.			H ER	D			25	M R				P T	I W BT	H	G D
118	OCEAN GATE YACHT BASIN 732-260-2565	ALL YR.		EB	H ER	D			35				S	T	IW	H	G D
119	SANTO MARINA 732-269-2730	ALL YR.														
121	RIVERBANK MARINE 732-244-2106	ALL YR.		EB	HE	W D			12				S	P T	IW	H	G
123	TOMS RIVER RAMP 732-349-1121				R											
125	TOMS RIVER TOWN RAMP				R											
127	TOMS RIVER RAILWAY CO 732-349-9484	ALL YR.			HE	D	60	20					S	T		H	
128	JACK BAKERS LOBSTER SHANTY RESTAURANT 732-349-8669										R		T			
129	ISLAND HEIGHTS TOWN RAMP				R											
130	NELSON MARINE BASIN 732-270-0022	ALL YR.		E B	H E	W D		25					S	T			
131	COZY COVE MARINA 732-929-1171	ALL YR.		E B	H E	W D		15					S	T	B T I W	H	G
132	DILLONS CREEK MARINA 732-270-8541	ALL YR.			E	D		20					S L	T	I W	H	

New Jersey

MARINA'S NAME & PHONE NUMBER

Chart #	Marina Name & Phone	When Open	VHF	Transient (Elec•Moor•Berth)	Repairs (Hull•Eng•Ramp)	Winter Storage (Wet•Dry)	Railway/Lift Capacity	Boat Rental (Canoe•Row•Motor)	Boat Rental (Charter•House•Sail)	Restaurant•Lodging	Showers•Laundry•Pumpout•Toilets	Groceries•Bait•Tackle•Water•Ice	Hardware	Diesel•Gasoline
133	BARNEGAT BAY BOAT SALES 732-929-1700	ALL YR.		E B		D	15				S T	W		G
134	EAST DOVER MARINA 732-270-1104	ALL YR.			HE R	D	20				T	W	H	G
135	**PIER ONE RESTAURANT 732-270-0914 SEE YELLOW PAGES**	ALL YR.		E B						R L	T	I W		
136	HOBBY LOBBY MARINE 732-929-1711	ALL YR.			H E		15				S T		H	
137	COTY MARINA 732-288-1000	ALL YR.			HE R	D	25			R L	S T	W	H	G
138	OCEAN BEACH MARINA 732-793-7227	ALL YR.		E B	E R	D	15			R	SL T	I W	H	G
139	OCEAN BEACH MARINA NORTH 732-793-7460	ALL YR.			H ER		20				S T	I W		
141	CRANBERRY INLET MARINA 732-793-8554	ALL YR.			H ER	D					S T		H	
142	SEA BREEZE BOATS 732-830-1882	JUN OCT						M R			T	B T		
143	SEASIDE HEIGHTS RAMP				R									
144	OCEAN BEACH MARINA CENTRAL 732-793-1700	ALL YR.		B		D	6				S T	W	H	G
145	SUNNYSIDE BOATS 732-793-0857	JUL SEP		M B	R									
146	DALE YACHT BOAT BASIN EAST 732-892-1569	ALL YR.									S T			
147	SEASIDE PARK RAMP				R									
148	RED TOP BOATS 732-793-0507	MAR DEC		B	E						T		H	
149	WHEELHOUSE MARINA 732-793-3296	MAY NOV			H ER	D			R	R	T	IB T		
150	OCEAN BEACH MARINA SO. 732-793-2347	ALL YR.		E B	HE	WD	25				S PT	I W	H	G
151	LANOKA HARBOR MARINA 609-693-2674	ALL YR.		E B	EH	WD	30				S T	IW BT	H	G D
153	TRIXIES LANDING 732-269-5838	APR OCT		E B	ER	D		M R			S T	IW BT	H	G
154	DOWNES FISHING CAMP 732-269-0137	ALL YR.	70	B	R	D					T	B T		G

CHART LOCATER NUMBER	MARINA'S NAME & PHONE NUMBER	WHEN OPEN	MONITORS VHF CHANNEL	TRANSIENT Electricity • Moorings • Berths	Hull repairs • Engine repairs • Ramp	WINTER STORAGE: Wet • Dry	RAILWAY CAPACITY IN FEET	LIFT CAPACITY IN TONS	BOAT RENTAL: Cance • Row • Motor	BOAT RENTAL: Charter • House • Sail	Restaurant • Lodging • Camping	Showers • Laundry	Pumpout • Toilets	Bait • Tackle • Water • Ice	Groceries • Hardware	Diesel fuel • Gasoline
157	RIVER'S EDGE MARINA 609-971-8777															
158	MARINA AT TALL OAKS 609-693-2145	ALL YR.	16 68	E B	H E	W D	45	15			RL	SL	P T	BT IW	H	G D
159	TED & SONS FORKED RIVER MARINA 609-693-2185				H E	D		12				S	T		H	G
160	TOWNSENDS MARINA 609-693-6100	ALL YR.		E B	HE R	D		15			RL	S	T	IW	H	
161	WILBERT'S MARINA 609-693-2145	ALL	16 68	EB	HE	D W		50			R L	S L	P T	IW	H	G
162	CAPTAINS INN RESTAURANT 609-693-3351	ALL YR.		E B							R	S	T			
163	SOUTHWINDS MARINA 609-693-6288	ALL YR.	68	E B	H ER	D		25			R	S	T I	IW BT	H	G D
164	GRANT BOAT WORKS /WOOD BOAT SPECIALIST 609-971-1075	ALL YR.			H	D	60	50					S	T		H	
165	TIDES END MARINA 609-693-9423	ALL YR.	9 16	E B	H E	D		50					S L	T	W	H	
166	RICKS MARINA 609-693-2134	ALL YR	9 16		HE R	D		30					S	T	IW B	H	G D
167	HOLIDAY HARBOR MARINA INC 609-693-2217	ALL YR.		EB	HE	W D		25			C		S L	PT	IW BT		G D
170	LONG KEY Y.C. 609-693-9444	ALL YR.			HE	W D		15					S L	PT	IW		G
171	KEY HARBOR MARINA 609-693-9355	ALL YR.		EB	HE	W D		20			R		S L	PT	IW		G D
172	LEAMINGS MARINA INC 609-971-1514	APR DEC	9 16	B	H E	D		7					S	T	IW BT	H	G
173	EDS BOAT RENTALS 609-494-2447	MAR OCT	16 72	B	R				M R				T	IB T		G
174	BARNEGAT LIGHT RAMP				R									T		
175	BAYVIEW ASSOCIATES 609-494-7450	ALL YR.				D		40			C			T	IW B	H	G D
176	LIGHTHOUSE MARINA 609-494-2305	ALL YR.		EB		D		10					S	T	IW BT		G D
177	MARINA AT BARNEGAT LIGHT															
178	KELLYS BOAT & MOTOR RENTALS 609-494-1520	APR NOV							M					B T		

New Jersey

MARINA'S NAME & PHONE NUMBER

Column key (left to right): Chart Locater Number · When Open · Monitors VHF Channel · Hull/Engine repairs • Transient Electricity • Moorings • Berths · Winter Storage (Wet•Dry) / Railway Capacity (Wet•Dry) · Lift Capacity (Tons) · Restaurant • Charter • Lodging / Boat Rental (Canoe•Row•Motor) · Showers • Laundry · Pumpout • Toilets · Bait • Tackle • Water • Ice · Groceries • Hardware · Diesel fuel • Gasoline

Chart #	Marina & Phone	When Open	VHF	Repairs / Transient	Storage / Railway	Lift (tons)	Rest. / Rental	Showers • Laundry	Pumpout • Toilets	Bait•Tackle•Water•Ice	Groceries•Hardware	Diesel•Gas
179	BOBBIES BOAT MOTOR RENTALS 609-494-1345	APR NOV					M R		T	I / BT		G
180	HIGH BAR HARBOR YACHT CLUB 609-494-8801	ALL		E B	R / W D			S L	T P			
181	MARGO'S INN & MARINA 609-597-8909	ALL YR.		E B / ER	D	10		S	T	IW / BT		G
182	HANCE & SMYTHE INC. 609-597-7813	ALL YR.		ER / H	D	4					H	
183	CAUSEWAY BOAT RENTALS 609-494-1371	MAR OCT			R		M		T	IB / T		G
184	DUCK INN MARINA 609-494-9010	MAY OCT		B	R / D							
185	SURF CITY MARINA 609-494-2200	ALL YR.	68	E B / H E	D	6		R L / S	T	I W	H	G
187	HOCHSTRASSER'S MARINA 609-494-5340	JAN DEC		E B / H E	D	10		R L	T	W	H	G
188	JIMS BOAT BASIN & TACKLE 609-494-1212	APR NOV		H			M R	S	T	IB / T	H	
189	WATER SPORTS 609-494-2727	APR NOV		H E			M		T			
190	ISLAND COVE MARINE 609-494-8100	ALL YR.		E B / H E	D	25		S	T	I W	H	
191	BARNEGAT TOWN RAMP				R				T			
192	SUN HARBOR MARINA 609-698-2116	ALL YR.	9	E B / H E	D	9		R / S	T	IW / BT	H	G
193	BOBS BAY MARINA 609-698-7264	APR NOV	68	E B / H E	W D	12		R / S	T	IW / BT	H	G
194	MARINER MARINA & YACHT SALES 609-698-1222	MAR DEC		E B / H E	D	20	S	R L / S L	P T	I W	H	G
195	CAPT BROWNIES SEAFOOD 609-698-7464	ALL YR.		E MB / H E	D							
196	SHERER'S BOAT BASIN 201-698-0463	ALL YR.			D	15			T	I		G
197	TOTAL MARINE 609-698-2220	ALL YR.		E	D	12			T		H	
198	BARNEGAT BOAT BASIN 609-698-8581	ALL YR.		E	D				T	IB / T	H	G
199	JIMS MOBILE MARINE 609-698-2248	ALL YR.		HE	R / D		R		T	IB / T		

New Jersey

CHART LOCATER NUMBER	MARINA'S NAME & PHONE NUMBER	WHEN OPEN	MONITORS VHF CHANNEL	TRANSIENT Electricity•Moorings•Berths	Hull•Engine repairs	RAILWAY Ramp	WINTER STORAGE Wet•Dry	LIFT CAPACITY IN TONS	BOAT RENTAL Canoe•Row•Motor	Restaurant•Lodging	Showers•Laundry	Pumpout•Toilets	Bait•Tackle•Water•Ice	Groceries•Hardware	Diesel fuel•Gasoline
202	LOVELADIES MARINA 609-494-9090	ALL YR.		E			D				S	T	I	H	
203	HARVEY CEDAR'S MARINA 609-494-0111														
205	CAPTAIN MIKES 609-296-4406	APR NOV		B					M			T	I / BT		G
207	CAPE HORN MARINA INC 609-296-4456	MAR NOV			H E				M	R		T	I / BT		G
208	MYSTIC ISLAND MARINA 609-296-2567	ALL YR.		E			D	10			S	T	IW / BT	H	G
209	MUNROS MARINA INC 609-296-8202	ALL YR.			HE	R	D					T		H	
210	FIRST BRIDGE MARINA 609-296-1888	APR OCT				R			M	R			I / BT		G
211	TOTAL MARINE 609-294-0480	ALL YR.		E B	HE	R	D	20			S	T	IW / BT	H	G
212	SCHIMPFS MARINA 609-296-6227	APR OCT					D	7			S	T	T / IB	H	G
213	SKINNERS MARINA 609-296-3051	ALL YR.		E B		R	D	7			S	T	IW / BT		G
214	GEB MARINA 609-294-1859	APR NOV		E			D	8			S	T	T / IB		
215	CEDAR COVE MARINA 609-296-2066	APR NOV	9 / 16	E B	HE		D	10		R L	S	T	IW / BT	H	G
216	TUCKERTON MARINE SERVICE CENTER 609-296-1820	ALL YR.	16 / 68	EB	H / ER		D	10			S	PT	I / BT	H	G / D
217	TUCKERTON SEAPORT 609-296-8868	ALL YR	88A	EB						R		T			
217 A	STEWART'S ROOT BEER 609-296-7895	APR NOV		EB						R		T	W		
218	SHELTERED COVE MARINA 609-296-9400														
219	MARITIME MARINA 609-294-9090														
222	ERNIE'S MARINA 609-296-4441	ALL YR.													
223	EAGLESWOOD MARINA 609-296-2177	ALL YR.			H E		D	10					B		
224	WEST CREEK MARINA 609-296-2715	MAR NOV		E B	HE		D	10				T	IW / BT	H	G

New Jersey

CHART LOCATER NUMBER	MARINA'S NAME & PHONE NUMBER	WHEN OPEN	MONITORS VHF CHANNEL	Elec / Hull / Engine	Moorings • Berths / Winter Storage	Railway / Ramp	Lift Cap. (ft)	Boat Rental	Restaurant / Lodging	Showers / Laundry	Pumpout / Toilets	Bait / Tackle	Groceries / Water / Ice	Diesel / Gas
225	NOTTES LANDING 609-296-8112	ALL YR.				D	8				T			
228	BAY HAVEN MARINA 609-492-3518	MAR NOV		B	HE				M	S		T	IW BT	G
229	MORRISON'S SEAFOOD RESTAURANT & MARINA 609-492-2150	APR NOV	68	EB		D				R	SL	P T	I W GH	D G
230	SHELTER HARBOR MARINA 609-492-8645	APR OCT	16	E B		W				R L	S L	PT	IW HG	
231	GEORGES BOAT RENTAL 609-492-7931	APR OCT		E B	H E	D	8	R M			S	T	I W BT	G
233	BEACH HAVEN Y. C. & MARINA 609-492-9101	APR DEC	16	E B	E				C	R L	S L	PT	IW BT	H G	G D
234	POLLYS ROW BOAT 609-492-2194	APR OCT						M				T	B T		
235	BLACK WHALE 609-492-0333	MAY OCT							C	R			T		
238	MORDECAI BOAT BASIN 609-492-5201	ALL YR.	16	E B	H E	D	14					T	I W BT	H	G
239	BUOY 77 MARINA 609-492-0011	ALL YR.		E B	H E		12			R L	S	T	I W BT	H	
240	PENNAS MARINA INC 609-492-0191	ALL YR.	68	E B	H E	D	20		C		S	T	I W BT	H	G D
241	JOLLY ROGER'S MARINA 609-266-3131	ALL YR.		E B	H E R	D				R L	S	T	I W BT	H	G
242	BRIGANTINE TOWN RAMP					R									
243	JERSEY STATE MARINE 609-266-7011	ALL YR.	16 68	E B	E R	D				R L		T	I W BT	H	G
244	DEEBOLD BOAT YARD 609-266-3214	ALL YR.	16	B	H E	D	4						B	H	G
245	BOBS OUTBOARD MARINE 609-266-7764				E							T	IB T	H	G
247	OYSTER CREEK INN INC. 609-652-8565	ALL YR.							R		T	I		
248	BAYSIDE MARINA 609-266-2819	ALL YR.	68	E B	H E	D	2	R M	C		S	T	IW BT	H	G
249	GARDNERS BASIN 609-348-2880				R										
251	ALBERT WESTCOAT 609-345-1974	ALL YR.	16		H E	D	60								

New Jersey

Chart #	Marina's Name & Phone Number	When Open	Monitors VHF Channel	Transient: Electricity • Moorings • Berths	Hull • Engine repairs • Ramp	Winter Storage: Wet • Dry	Railway Capacity (ft)	Lift Capacity (tons)	Boat Rental: Canoe • Row • Motor	Boat Rental: Charter • House • Sail	Restaurant • Lodging • Camping	Showers • Laundry	Pumpout • Toilets	Bait • Tackle • Water • Ice	Groceries • Hardware	Diesel fuel • Gasoline
252	KAMMERMANS MARINE 609-348-8418	ALL YR.	9 16	E B	H E					C	R L		PT	IW BT	HG	G D
253	ATLANTIC CITY FISH CENTER 609-344-4778	MAR NOV	B								C		T	I B T		
254	GILCHRIST REST. & MARINA 609-345-8278	ALL YR.									R		T	I		G
255	FRANKS BOATYARD 609-344-9185	ALL YR.			H E	D		40								
256	OLD WATERWAY INN 609-347-1793										R		T			
257	ATLANTIC CITY TOWN RAMP				R											
257A	TRUMP MARINA, HOTEL & CASINO 609-876-4386 (A.K.A Farley State Marina)	ALL YR	65	E B		W				C	R L	S L	PT	WI BT	GH H	G D
258	GD SUNRISE MARINA 609-344-6703	APR SEP		E B												G
259	DAFFY DUCK MARINA 609-645-6955															
260	ABSECON BAY SPORTSMEN CTR. 609-484-0409	ALL YR.			H E	D	35	9						I B T	H	G
261	ABSECON TOWN RAMP				R											
262	ABSECON MARINE 609-641-2260	ALL YR.		E B		D								T I B	H	
263	SCHUPPS LANDING 732-872-1479	APR NOV							M R				T	I B T		G D
264	CAPTAIN ANDYS 609-822-0916	APR OCT	68							C	R		T	BT	H	G D
265	HOLIDAY MARINA 609-823-5575												T			
270	ROSSELLS DOCK 609-823-1161		19						M R		R			BT		
271	SCOTTS DOCK 609-822-6819	MAR NOV	68					1	M R		R		T	I B T		G
272	CAMPBELL MARINE INC 609-641-0489	ALL YR.			H E	D		10				S	T	I B T	H	G
273	SEA VILLAGE MARINA 609-641-2699	ALL YR.		E B	H E	W D		30				S L	PT	BT W		
274	GRAEF BOAT YARD INC 609-927-2205	ALL YR.			H E	D		25					T		H	

New Jersey

CHART LOCATER NUMBER	MARINA'S NAME & PHONE NUMBER	WHEN OPEN	MONITORS VHF CHANNEL	TRANSIENT Electricity•Moorings•Berths	Hull repairs•Engine repairs•Ramp	WINTER STORAGE: Wet•Dry	RAILWAY CAPACITY IN FEET	LIFT CAPACITY IN TONS	BOAT RENTAL: Canoe•Row•Motor	BOAT RENTAL: Charter•House•Sail	Restaurant•Lodging•Camping	Showers•Laundry	Pumpout•Toilets	Bait•Tackle•Water•Ice	Groceries•Hardware	Diesel fuel•Gasoline
275	HARBOR COVE MARINE SERV. 609-926-9244	MAR DEC	16		H E	D		25				S	T	I		
276	MAYERS MARINE 609-927-5954	JAN DEC			H E	D		3					T	I	H	G
277	SMITHS MARINA 609-653-0190				R	D					R		T			
278	BAYVIEW MARINA 609-926-1700	ALL YR.	16		H E	D		6				S	T		H	G D
279	GREAT EGG BAY SAILING MARINA 609-653-1198	ALL YR.				D		5				S	T		H	
280	PATCONG HARBOR MARINA 609-927-8354	ALL YR.		E B	H E	D		20				L	T		H	
281	SOMERSET COVE MARINA 609-927-9393	ALL YR.			H E							S	T	I W B		
282	WOODS GATEWAY MARINA 609-927-3002				H E	D							T	I W B T	H	G
284	DOLFIN DOCK INC. 609-927-1730	APR NOV							M R				T	I B T	H	
285	BAYSHORE II REST. & MARINE 609-653-6772	ALL YR.			R						R					
286	CORLETO MARINA 609-927-3100	MAR NOV						3					T	I B T	H	G
287	KEY HARBOR 609-927-8886	ALL YR.		B	H E	D		60				S	T			G D
288	HOME PORT MARINA 609-398-8400	ALL YR.		E B							R L		T			
289	CHALLENGER FISHING FLEET 609-399-5011	APR OCT									C		T	I B T		G D
290	HARBOR HOUSE MARINA 609-399-8585	MAY OCT		E B							C	R L	S	T	I W B T	G D
291	BUCCANEER MARINA 609-398-0424	MAY NOV						4	R	C S	R	S	I T	B T	H	G D
292	DANS SEAFOOD MARKET 609-399-2279	ALL YR.												I B T		D G
293	MENTZER MARINE 609-390-3763	APR NOV		E B	D								T	I W B T		G
294	ALL SEASONS MARINA 609-390-1850	ALL YR.	16	E B	H E	D		12			R	S	P T	I W	H	G
295	BEESLEYS POINT RAMP				R								T			

New Jersey

MARINA'S NAME & PHONE NUMBER

No.	Marina's Name & Phone Number	When Open	Monitors VHF Channel	Transient Elec•Moor•Berth	Hull•Engine•Ramp	Winter Wet•Dry	Railway Cap. Tons	Lift Cap. Feet	Rental Canoe•Row•Motor	Rental Charter•House•Sail	Rest•Lodge•Camp	Showers•Laundry	Pumpout•Toilets	Bait•Tackle•Water•Ice	Groc•Hdwe	Diesel•Gas
296	MINMAR MARINE BASIN SALES 609-263-2201	ALL YR.	16	E B	H E	D W		35				S	T		H	
297	LARSENS MARINA 609-263-1554	APR NOV			R				M R				T	I B T		G D
299	STARFISH DEEP SEA FISHING 609-263-3800	APR OCT								C			T	I B T		
301	GIBSON TACKLE 609-263-6540	APR OCT												B T		
302	VITIELLOS BOAT RENTALS 609-263-7444	MAY OCT							M R				T	I B T		
303	WHALE CREEK MARINA 609-263-6093	APR OCT			H E				M R				T	I B T	H	G
305	FRANKS BOAT RENTALS 609-263-6913	MAY OCT							M R					I B T		
306	DEAUVILLE INN 609-263-2080	ALL YR.		E B	E						R		T	I W	H	G
315	PIER 88 MARINA 609-263-8888	MAY OCT		E B								S	T	I W B T		G D
316	AVALON ANCHORAGE MARINA 609-967-3592	APR DEC			R H E	D		5	M R	C		R	T	I B T	H	G D
317	**AVALON POINTE MARINA 609-967-4100**	**ALL YR.**	**16**	**E B**	**H E**	**D**		**70**				**S**	**P T**	**I W B T**	**H**	**G D**
318	AVALON TOWN RAMP 609-967-8200				R								T			
319	CAMP MARINE 609-368-1777	ALL YR.		E B	H E	D W		24					P T		H	
320	SMUGGLERS COVE 609-368-1700	ALL YR.	68						M R		R L		T	I B T		G D
321	GRASSY SOUND MARINA 609-523-0144	APR NOV	16	E B				3	M R			S	T	I W B T	H	G
322	DADS PLACE MARINA 609-522-3911	ALL YR.		E		D			M				T	I B T		
323	HEREFORD INLET MARINA 609-522-7396	APR NOV		E B	H E	D		12			R L	S	T	I W B T	H	G D
324	WILDWOOD RAMP				R											
325	BAY FRONT BOAT BASIN 609-522-0282	ALL YR.	68	E B	H E	D		15				S	T	W		G
326	REUTERS MARINA 609-522-0900	ALL YR.			H E	D						S	T	I W B T	H	G

Chart Locater Number	Marina's Name & Phone Number	When Open	Monitors VHF Channel	Transient: Electricity • Moorings • Berths	Hull repairs • Engine repairs • Ramp	Winter Storage: Wet • Dry	Railway Capacity in Feet	Lift Capacity in Tons	Boat Rental: Canoe • Row • Motor / Charter • House • Sail	Restaurant • Lodging • Camping	Showers • Laundry	Pumpout • Toilets	Bait • Tackle • Water • Ice	Groceries • Hardware	Diesel fuel • Gasoline
328	SCHOONER ISLAND MARINA 609-729-8900														
329	HARBOR VIEW MARINA 609-884-0808														
330	CEDAR CREEK BOAT WORKS 609-884-4217	ALL YR.										T			
331	YACHT LODGE MARINA 609-884-5224	ALL YR.		E B	H E	W			C	R L	S L	T	I W B T	H	G D
332	ROSEMANS BOATYARD 609-884-3370	ALL YR.			H E	W D		50	C	R L	L		I W B T	G H	G D
333	CAPE MAY MARINE 609-884-0262	ALL YR.	68	E B	R H E	D		25	C	R L	S L	T	I W B T		G D
334	SOUTH JERSEY MARINA 856-884-2400	ALL YR.	9 16	E B	H E				C	C I R L	S L	T	I W B T	G H	G D
335	TONYS MARINE RAILWAY INC 609-884-8781	ALL YR.			R H E	D	99 +					T	I W B T	H	
336	**THE LOBSTER HOUSE 609-884-8296**	**ALL YR.**			R							T	I		
337	**UTSCHS MARINA 609-884-2051**	**ALL YR>**	16	E B	H E	D		35	C	R C	S L	P T	I W B T	G H	G D
338	CANYON CLUB MARINA 609-884-0199	ALL YR.	9 16	E B	H E	W D		60		C R L	S	P T	I W	H	G D
339	CEDAR CREEK MARINA 609-884—4217	ALL YR.	23	E	D								I		
340	MILL CREEK MARINA 609-884-4391	MAR DEC				D						T	I B T		G D
341	McNEILS MARINA 609-884-7211	ALL YR.			R H E		27					T	I		
342	BREE-ZEE-LEE YACHT BASIN 609-884-4849	ALL YR.		E B	E R	D		35			S L	T	I W B T		G
343	HINCH MARINA 609-884-7289	MAR DEC		E B	R H E	D		7		R	S L	T	I W B T	G H	G
344	TWO MILE LANDING 609-522-1341	APR OCT	16	E B						R L	S	T	I W		
345	LIGHTHOUSE PT. CONDO ASSOC. 609-729-2229	ALL YR.	9 16	E B						R L	S L	P T	I W		G
346	PIER 47 MARINA 609-729-4774	ALL YR.	16	E B	E	D		6	M R			P T	I T W B	H	G
352	HAYES WATERWAY MARINA 609-522-0263	APR NOV		E B	H E	D		5	M R		S	T	I B T	H	G D

New Jersey

MARINA'S NAME & PHONE NUMBER

#	Marina Name & Phone	When Open	Monitors VHF	Elec/Moor/Berths	Hull/Engine/Ramp	Winter Storage (Wet/Dry)	Railway Tons	Lift Feet	Boat Rental (Canoe/Row/Motor/Sail)	Boat Rental (Charter/House)	Restaurant/Lodging/Camping	Showers/Laundry	Bait/Tackle/Water/Ice	Pumpout/Toilets	Groceries/Hardware	Diesel/Gas
353	URIES RESTAURANT 609-522-3345	APR OCT			R								I	T		
354	ADVENTURES DEEP SEA FISHING 609-729-7777	MAR NOV									C					
355	KURTZS WATERFRONT RESTAURANT 609-522-8329	CALL		E B					M R	C	R		I B	T		
356	ROYAL FLUSH FLEET 609-522-1395	APR NOV	66							C			I B	T		D
357	CAPTAIN JACK BLAKE 609-522-3587									C	R		I B	T		
358	SUNSET LAKE MARINA 609-522-3309	APR NOV		B			1							T		G
359	LAKEVIEW DOCKS 609-522-0471	JUN OCT		E B			2		M R				I W B T	T		G

YACHT CLUBS IN NJ

The Yacht Clubs listed below offer reciprocity and courtesy dockage or moorings. Only Yacht Clubs with space for 2 or more traveling Yacht Club members are listed.

ABOVE MANASQUAN INLET

ATLANTIC HIGHLANDS YC
732-291-1118

KEYPORT YACHT CLUB
732-739-0727

MANASQUAN RIVER Y.C.
732-528-6792

MONMOUTH BOAT CLUB
732-741-9858

RAHWAY YACHT CLUB
732-574-8594

RARITAN YACHT CLUB
732-826-2277

RARITAN RIVER BOAT CLUB
732-572-9856

RIVERTON YACHT CLUB
609-829-9894

RUMSON YACHT CLUB
732-842-3333

SHARK RIVER BEACH & YC
732-774-9819

SHREWSBURY RIVER YC
732-747-9873

SHREWSBURY SAILING & YC
732-229-9818

BARNEGAT BAY and LONG BEACH ISLAND

BARNEGAT BAY SAIL CLUB
609-693-0468

BARNEGAT LIGHT Y. C.
609-494-9868

BEACH HAVEN YACHT CLUB
609-492-9101

BRANT BEACH YACHT CLUB
609-494-4485

GILFORD PARK YACHT CLUB
732-929-9838

ISLAND HEIGHTS Y.C.
732-929-9813

LITTLE EGG HARBOR Y.C.
609-492-2529

METEDECONK YACHT CLUB
732-477-9781

SEASIDE PARK YACHT CLUB
732-793-9611

SPRAY BEACH YACHT CLUB
609-492-6845

TOMS RIVER YACHT CLUB
732-929-9809

ATLANTIC CITY AREA

GREATER ATLANTIC CITY Y.C.
609-348-3378

BRIGANTINE YACHT CLUB
609-266-9859

BELOW ATLANTIC CITY

AVALON YACHT CLUB
609-967-4444

OCEAN CITY YACHT CLUB
609-399-0549

SOMERS POINT YACHT CLUB
609-927-9600

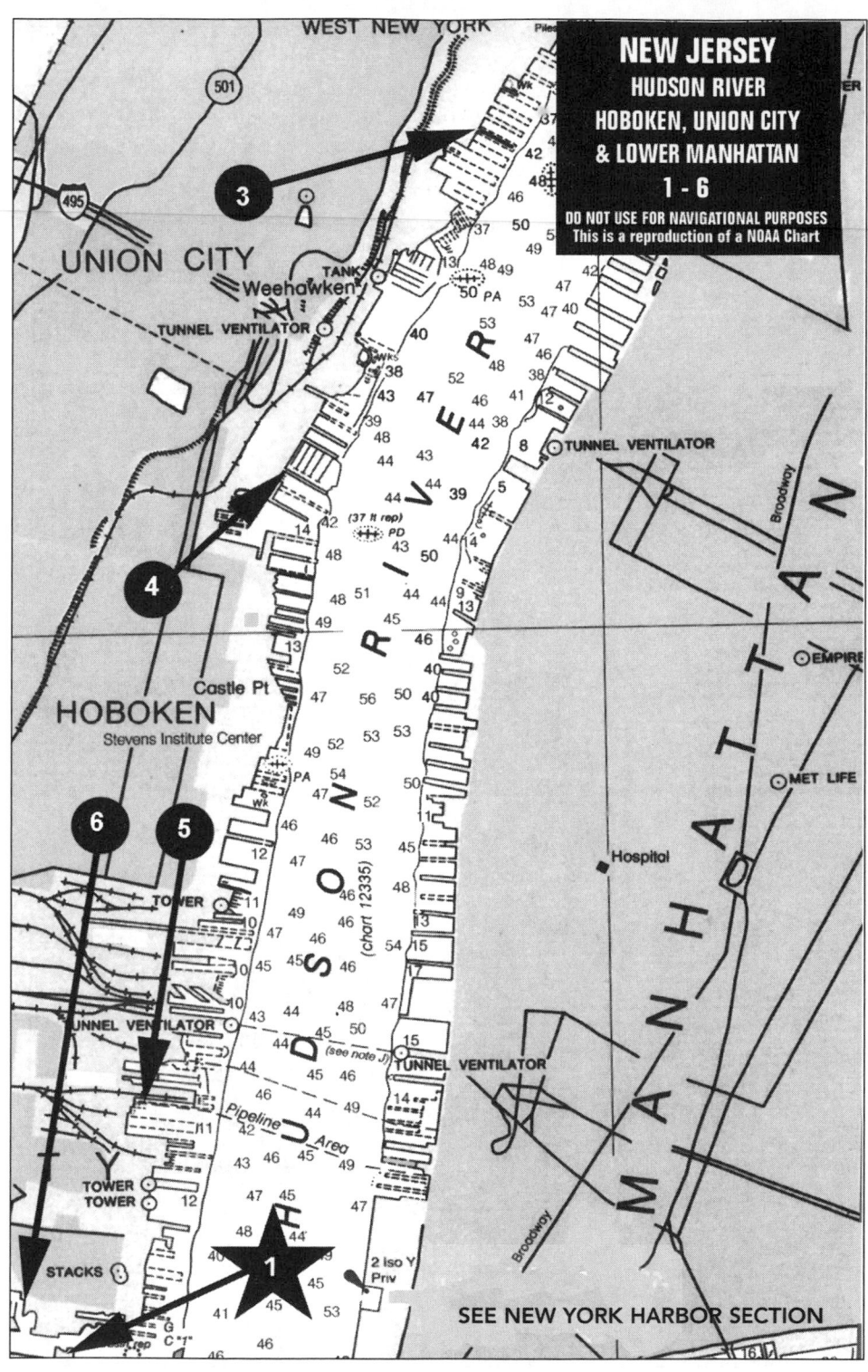

NEW JERSEY
HUDSON RIVER
HOBOKEN, UNION CITY
& LOWER MANHATTAN
1 - 6
DO NOT USE FOR NAVIGATIONAL PURPOSES
This is a reproduction of a NOAA Chart

WEST NEW YORK

UNION CITY

Weehawken

TUNNEL VENTILATOR

TANK

HOBOKEN

Castle Pt

Stevens Institute Center

TUNNEL VENTILATOR

TOWER

TUNNEL VENTILATOR

Pipeline Area

TOWER
TOWER

STACKS

TUNNEL VENTILATOR

TUNNEL VENTILATOR

Hospital

Broadway

EMPIRE

MET LIFE

MANHATTAN

Broadway

HUDSON RIVER

(chart 12335)

SEE NEW YORK HARBOR SECTION

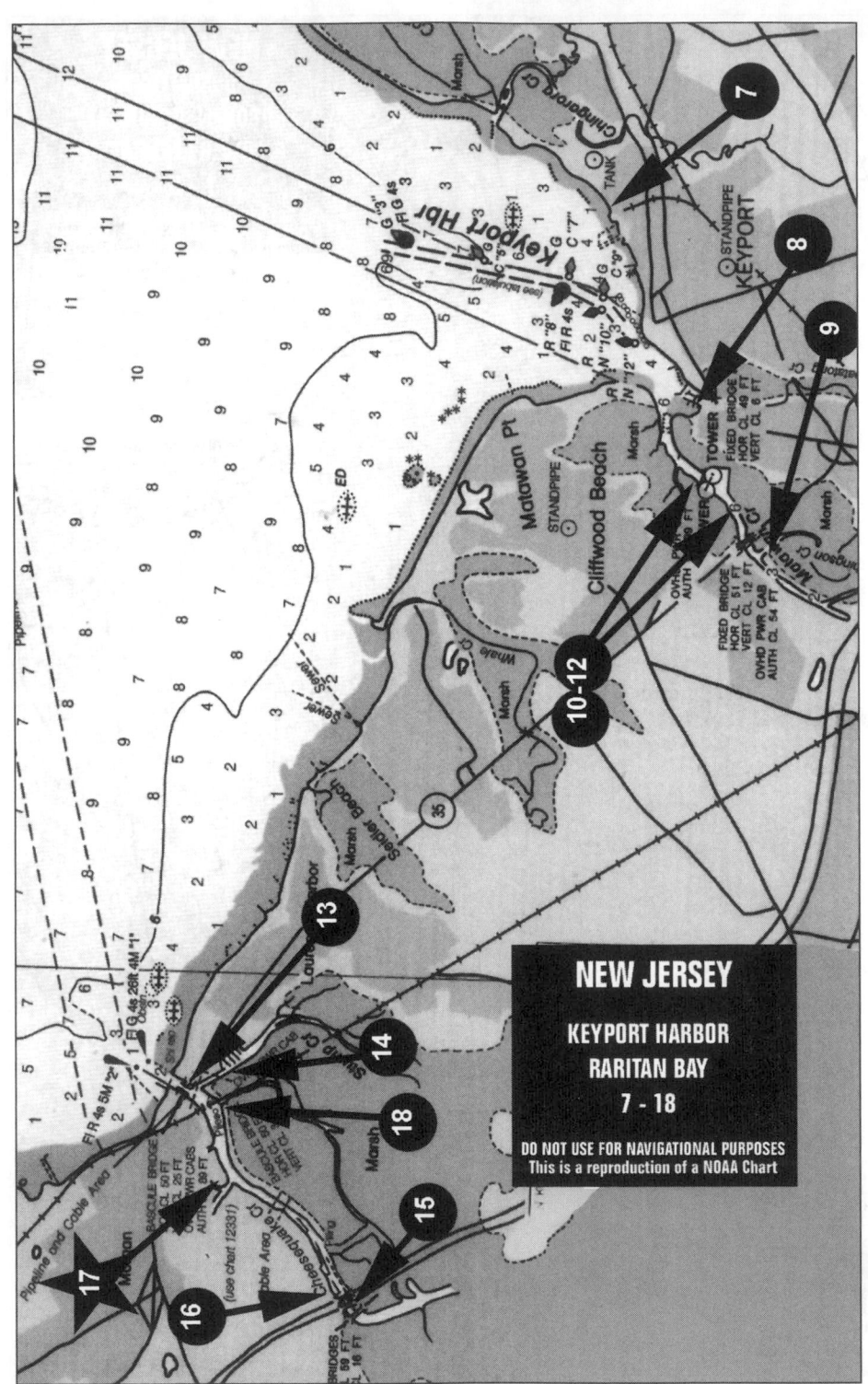

NEW JERSEY

KEYPORT HARBOR
RARITAN BAY
7 - 18

DO NOT USE FOR NAVIGATIONAL PURPOSES
This is a reproduction of a NOAA Chart

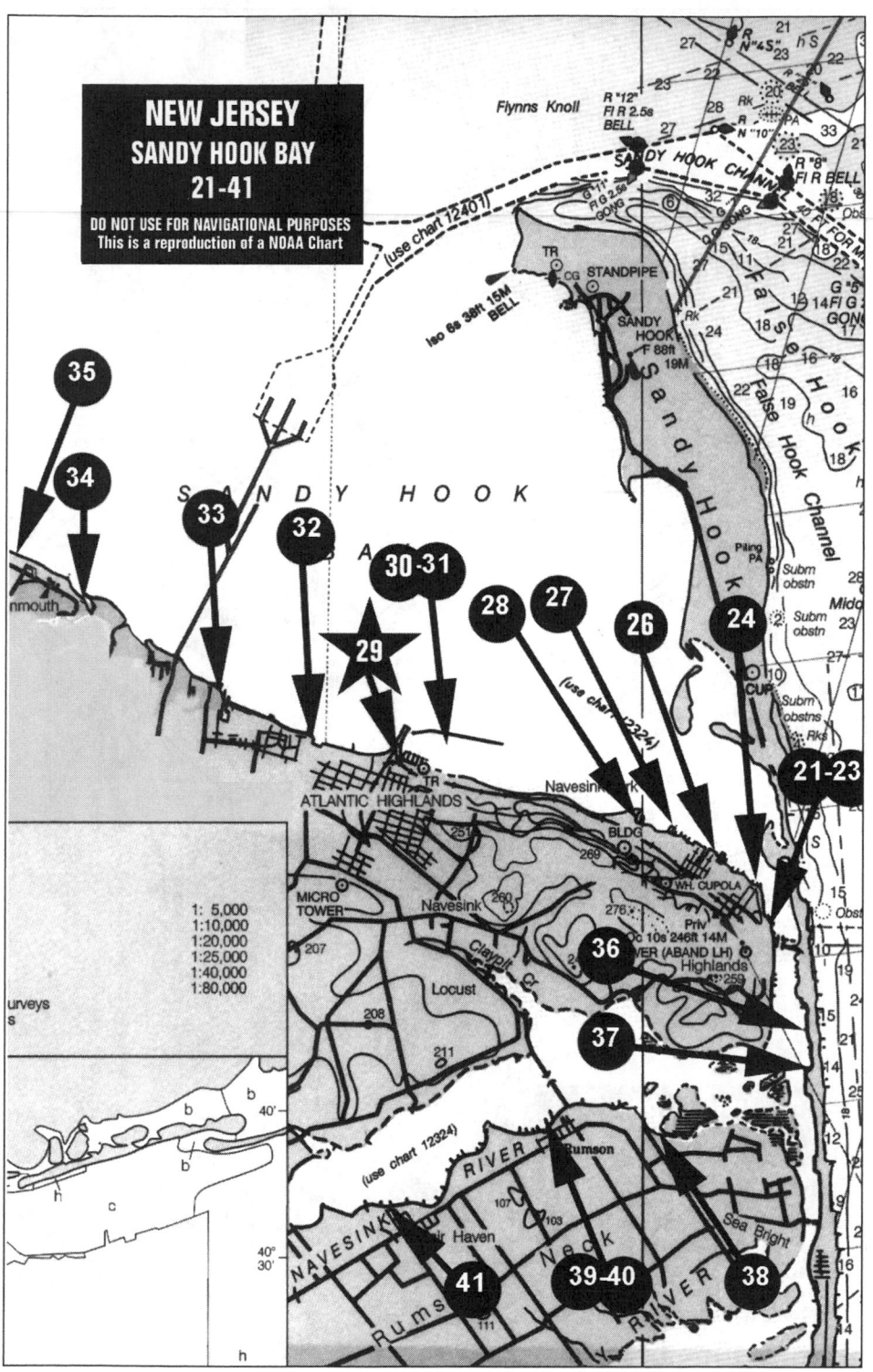

NEW JERSEY
SANDY HOOK BAY
21-41

DO NOT USE FOR NAVIGATIONAL PURPOSES
This is a reproduction of a NOAA Chart

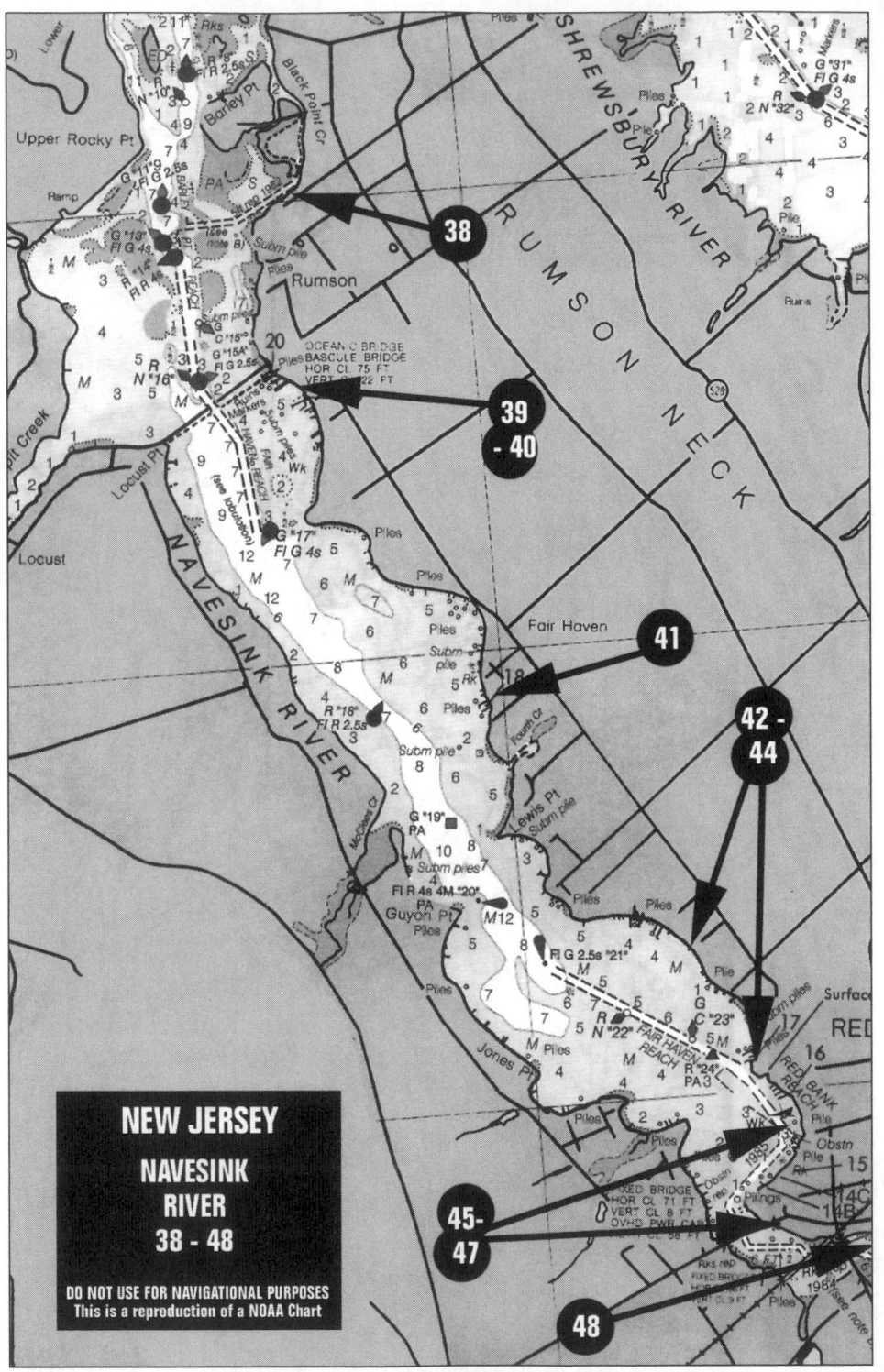

NEW JERSEY

NAVESINK
RIVER
38 - 48

DO NOT USE FOR NAVIGATIONAL PURPOSES
This is a reproduction of a NOAA Chart

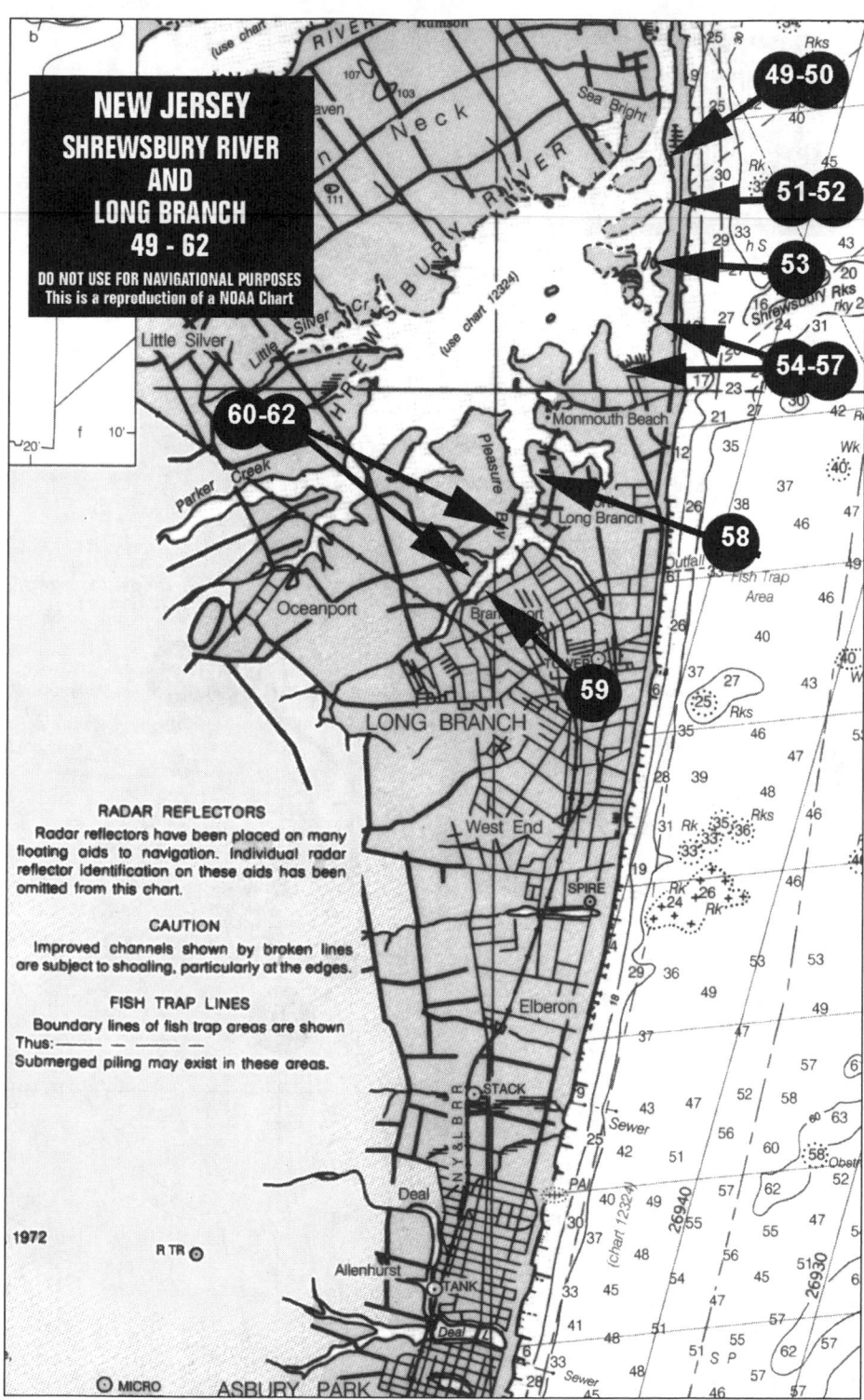

NEW JERSEY
SHREWSBURY RIVER
AND
LONG BRANCH
49 - 62

DO NOT USE FOR NAVIGATIONAL PURPOSES
This is a reproduction of a NOAA Chart

RADAR REFLECTORS

Radar reflectors have been placed on many
floating aids to navigation. Individual radar
reflector identification on these aids has been
omitted from this chart.

CAUTION

Improved channels shown by broken lines
are subject to shoaling, particularly at the edges.

FISH TRAP LINES

Boundary lines of fish trap areas are shown
Thus: ——— — ——— —
Submerged piling may exist in these areas.

1972

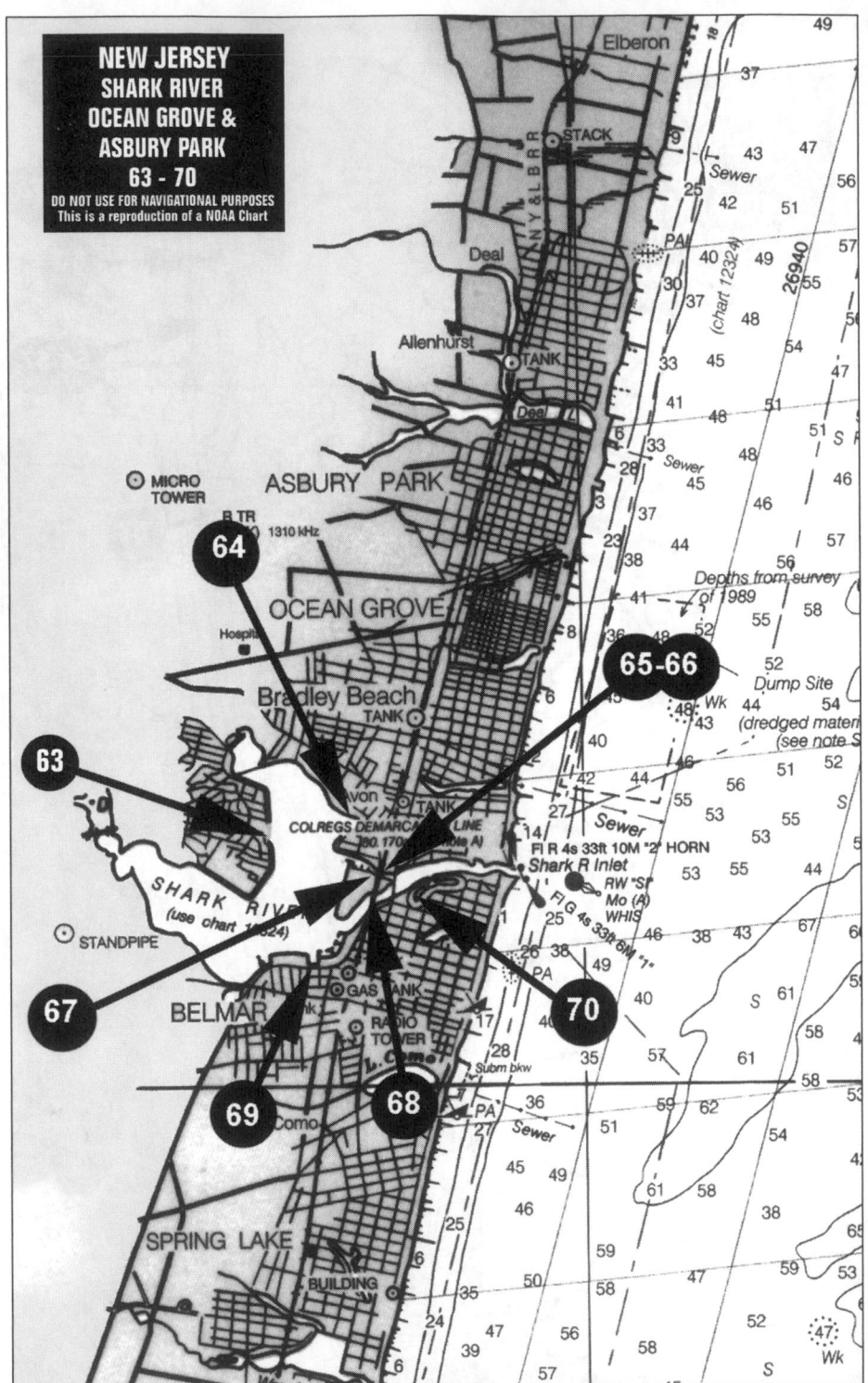

Elberon

STACK

Deal

Allenhurst

TANK

Deal

⊙ MICRO
   TOWER

ASBURY PARK

R TR
1310 kHz

OCEAN GROVE

Hospital

Bradley Beach

TANK

63

64

65-66

Sewer

Depths from survey
of 1989

Dump Site

52
Wk

(dredged material
(see note S

TANK

COLREGS DEMARCATION LINE
30.170

SHARK RIVER
(use chart 12324)

⊙ STANDPIPE

67

BELMAR

GAS TANK

RADIO
TOWER

69

Como

68

SPRING LAKE

BUILDING

Fl R 4s 33ft 10M "2" HORN
Shark R Inlet
RW "S"
Mo (A)
WHIS
Fl G 4s 33ft 6M "1"

PA

70

Subm bkw

PA

Sewer

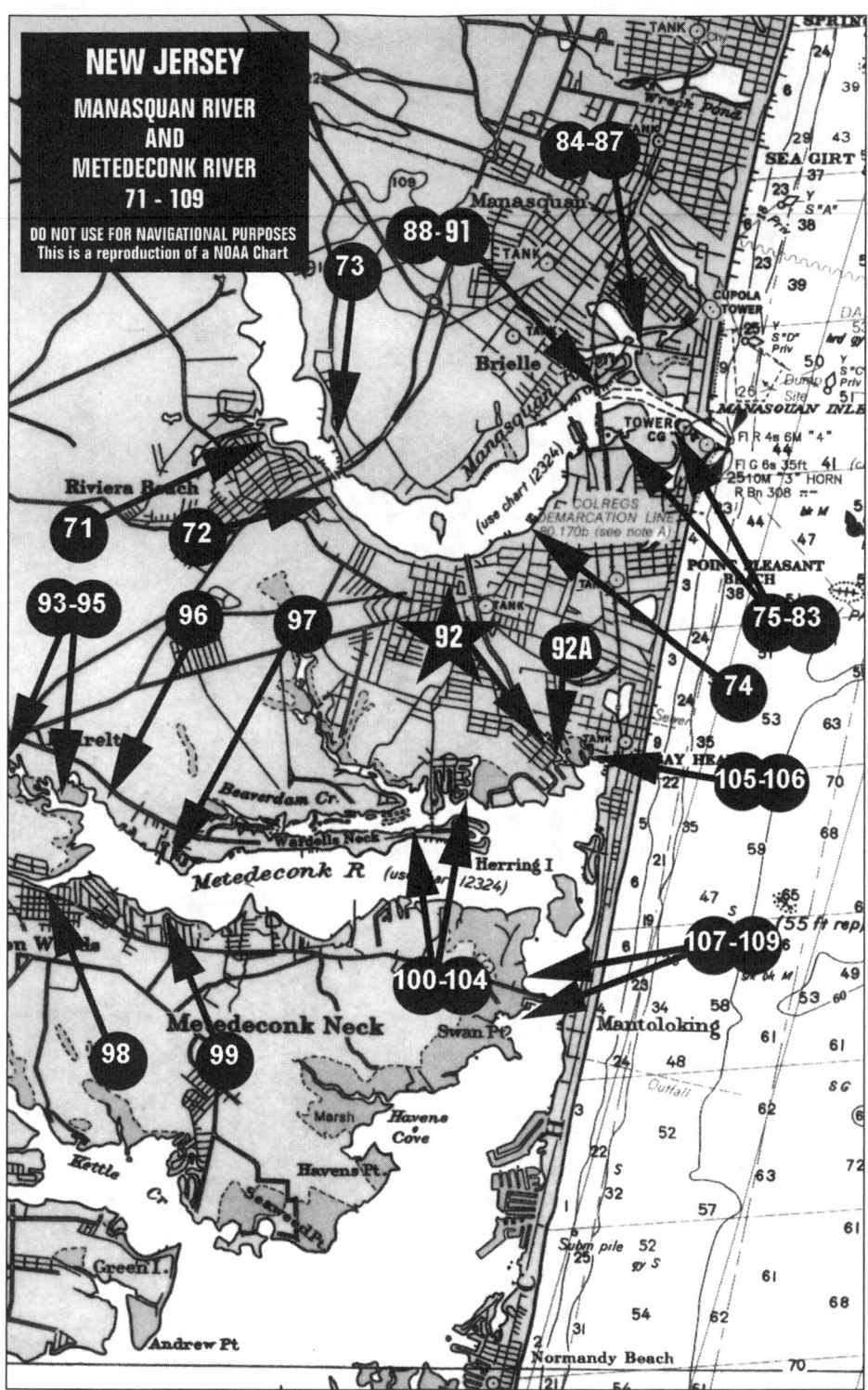

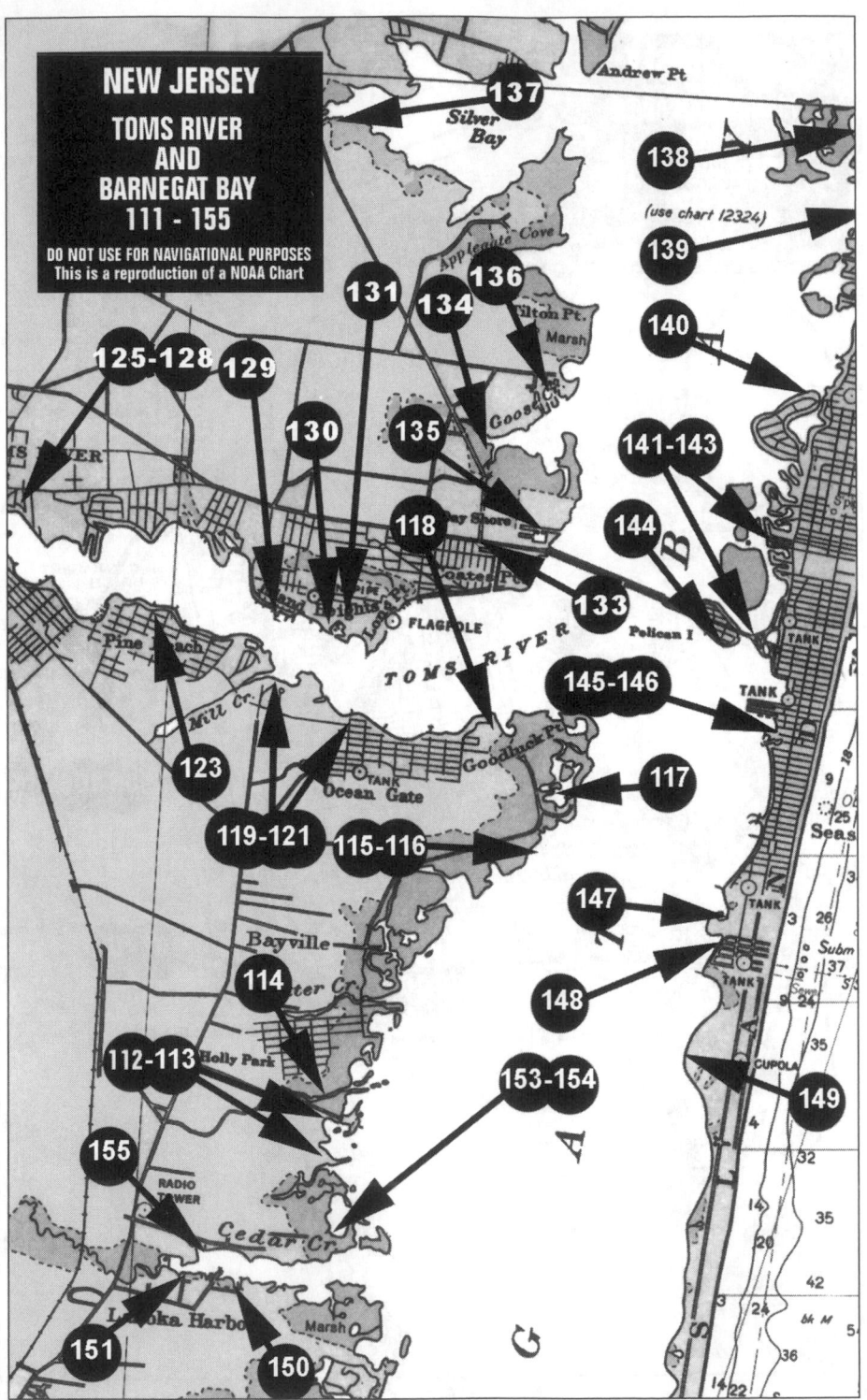

NEW JERSEY
TOMS RIVER
AND
BARNEGAT BAY
111 - 155

DO NOT USE FOR NAVIGATIONAL PURPOSES
This is a reproduction of a NOAA Chart

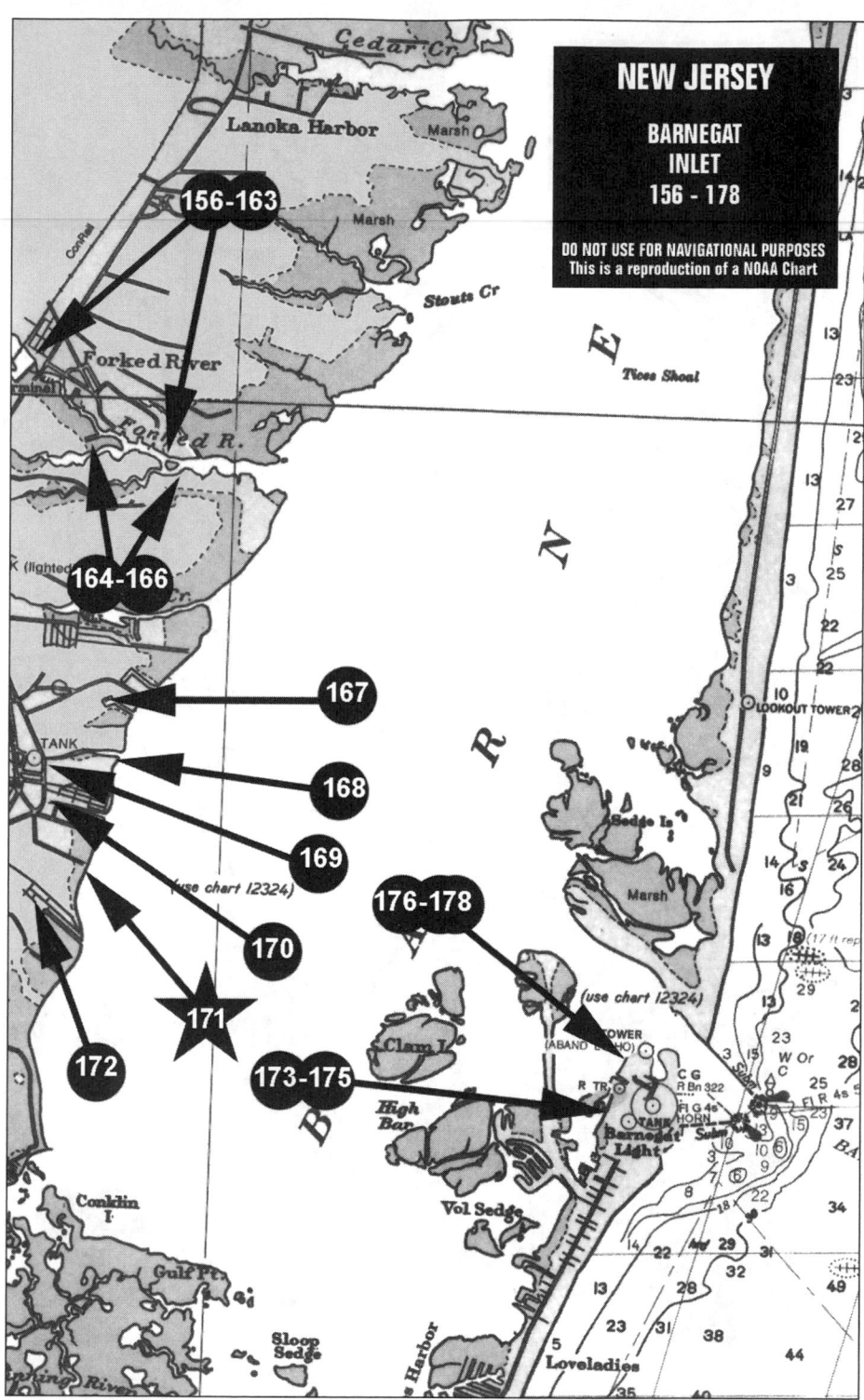

NEW JERSEY

BARNEGAT
INLET
156 - 178

Cedar Cr.

Lanoka Harbor   Marsh

Marsh

156-163

Stouts Cr

Coffee

Forked River

Forked R.

Tices Shoal

E

N

R

B

(lighted)

164-166

TANK

167

168

169

176-178

170

171

172

173-175

(use chart 12324)

(use chart 12324)

Clam I.

High
Bar

TOWER
(ABAND LT HO)

C G
R Bn 322

R TR

TANK
HORN

Barnegat
Light

Vol Sedge

Conklin
I.

Gulf Pt.

Sloop
Sedge

Harbor

Loveladies

LOOKOUT TOWER

Sedge Is.

Marsh

(17 ft rep)

W Or
C

Fl G 4s

FI R 4s

Sub

B4

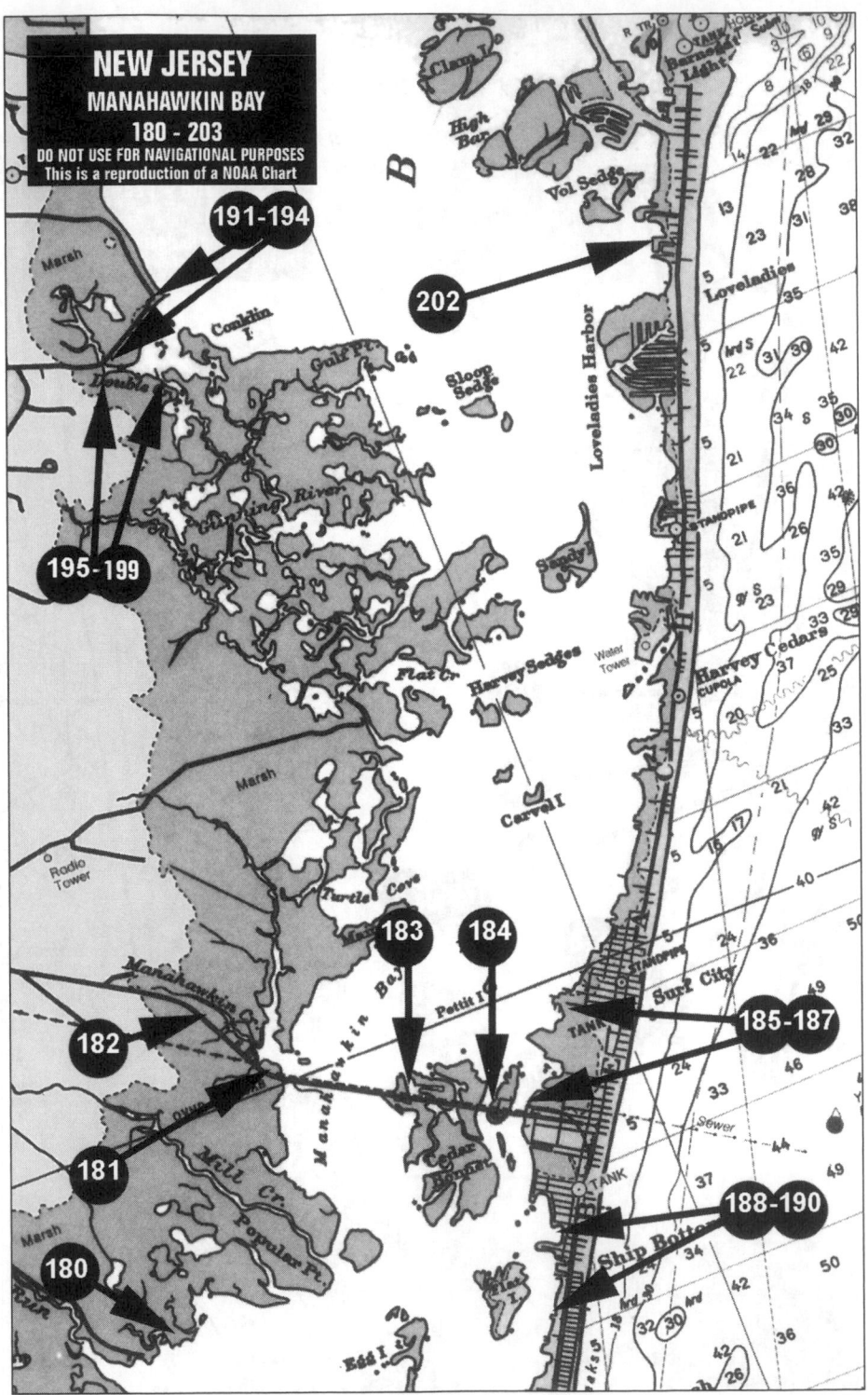

NEW JERSEY
MANAHAWKIN BAY
180 - 203
DO NOT USE FOR NAVIGATIONAL PURPOSES
This is a reproduction of a NOAA Chart

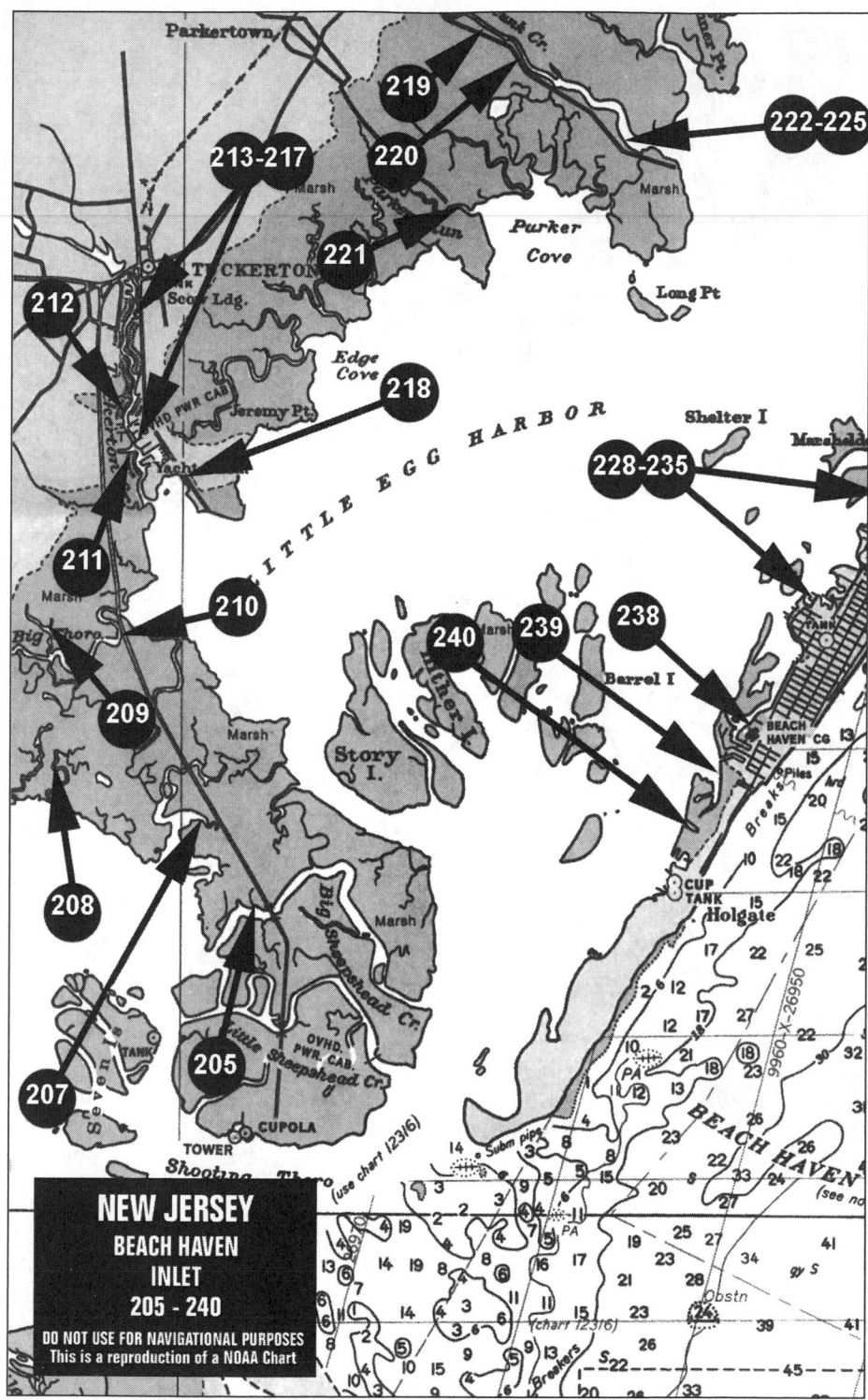

NEW JERSEY
BEACH HAVEN
INLET
205 - 240

DO NOT USE FOR NAVIGATIONAL PURPOSES
This is a reproduction of a NOAA Chart

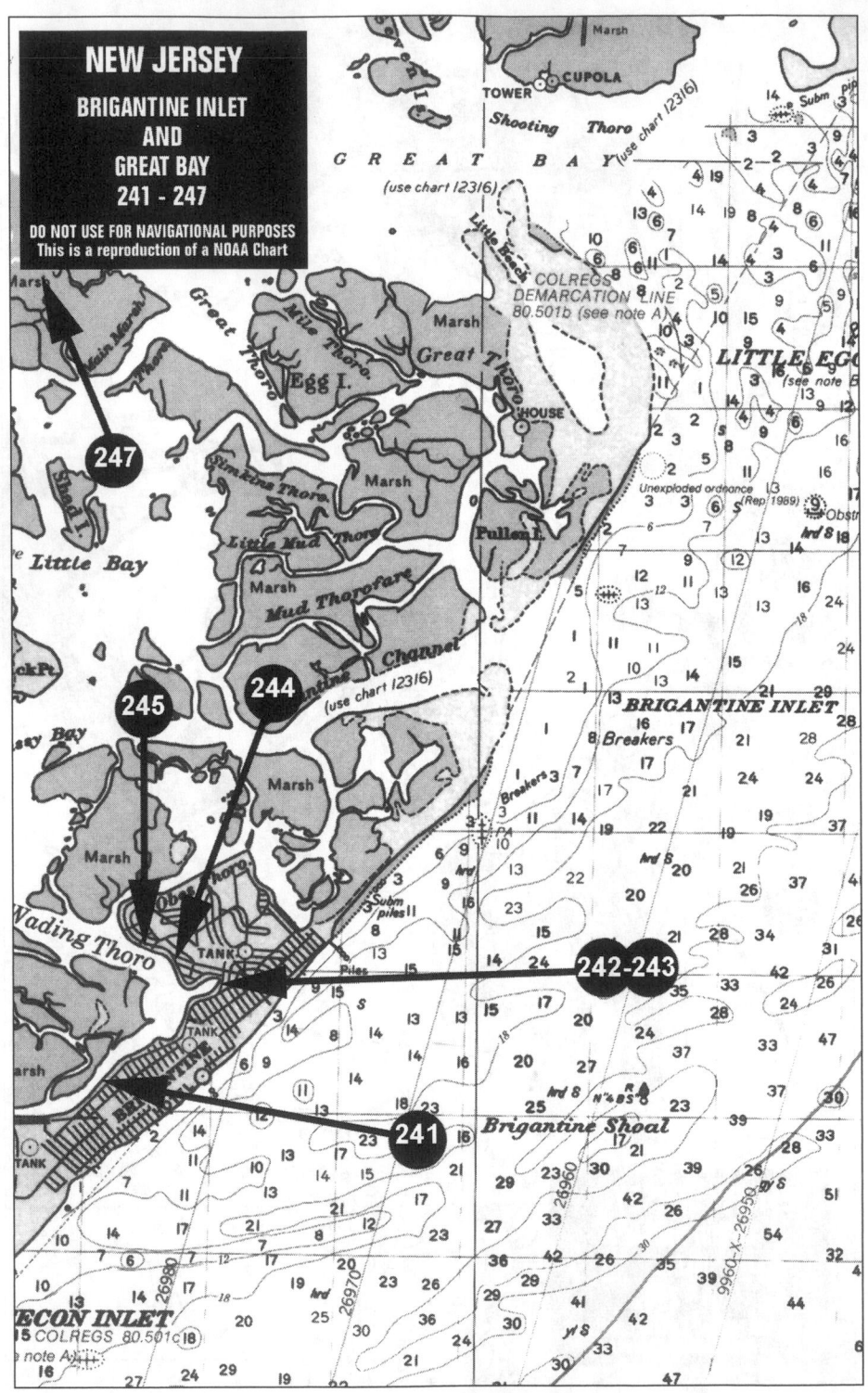

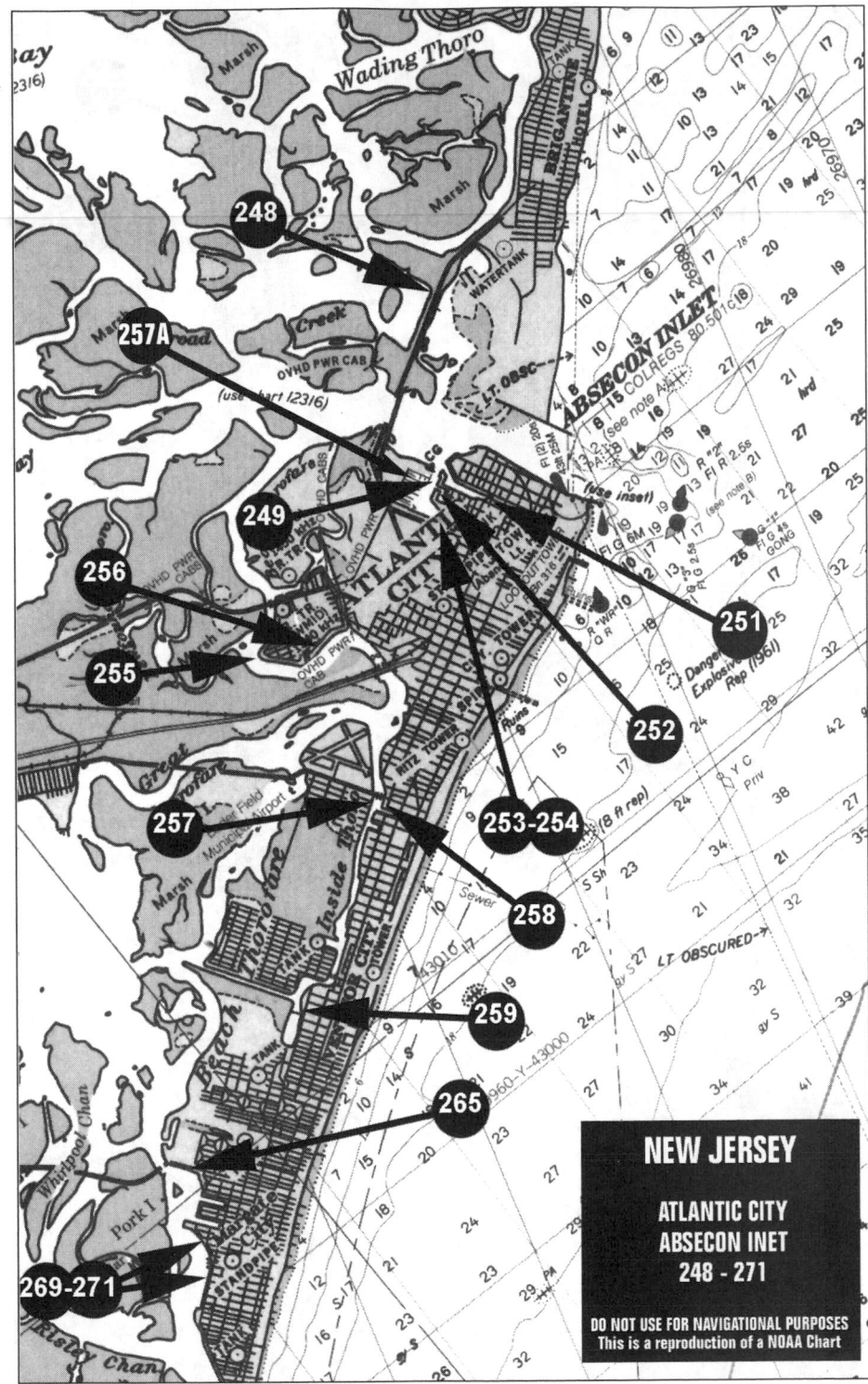

NEW JERSEY

ATLANTIC CITY
ABSECON INET
248 - 271

DO NOT USE FOR NAVIGATIONAL PURPOSES
This is a reproduction of a NOAA Chart

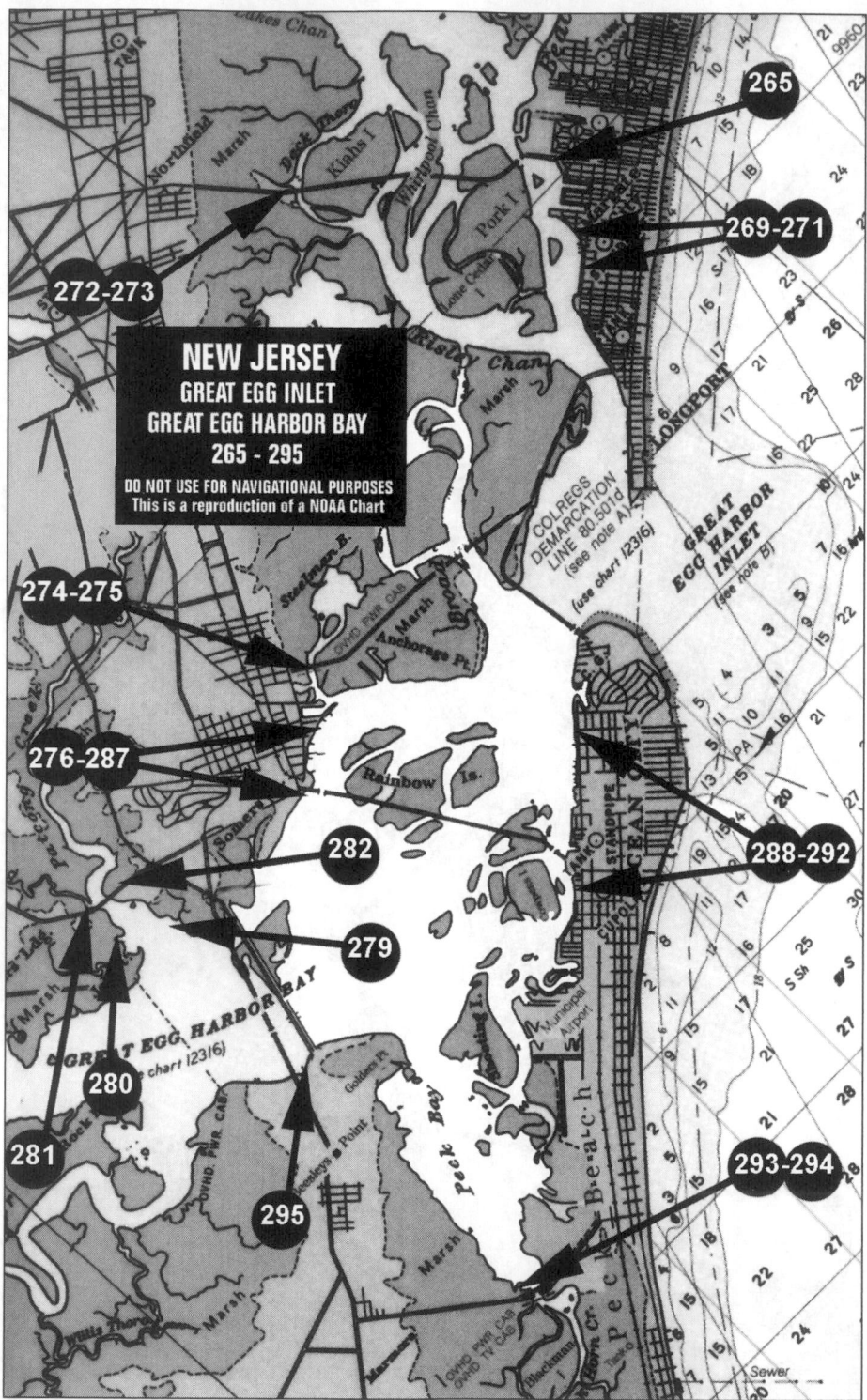

NEW JERSEY
GREAT EGG INLET
GREAT EGG HARBOR BAY
265 - 295

DO NOT USE FOR NAVIGATIONAL PURPOSES
This is a reproduction of a NOAA Chart

265

269-271

272-273

274-275

276-287

282

279

288-292

280

281

295

293-294

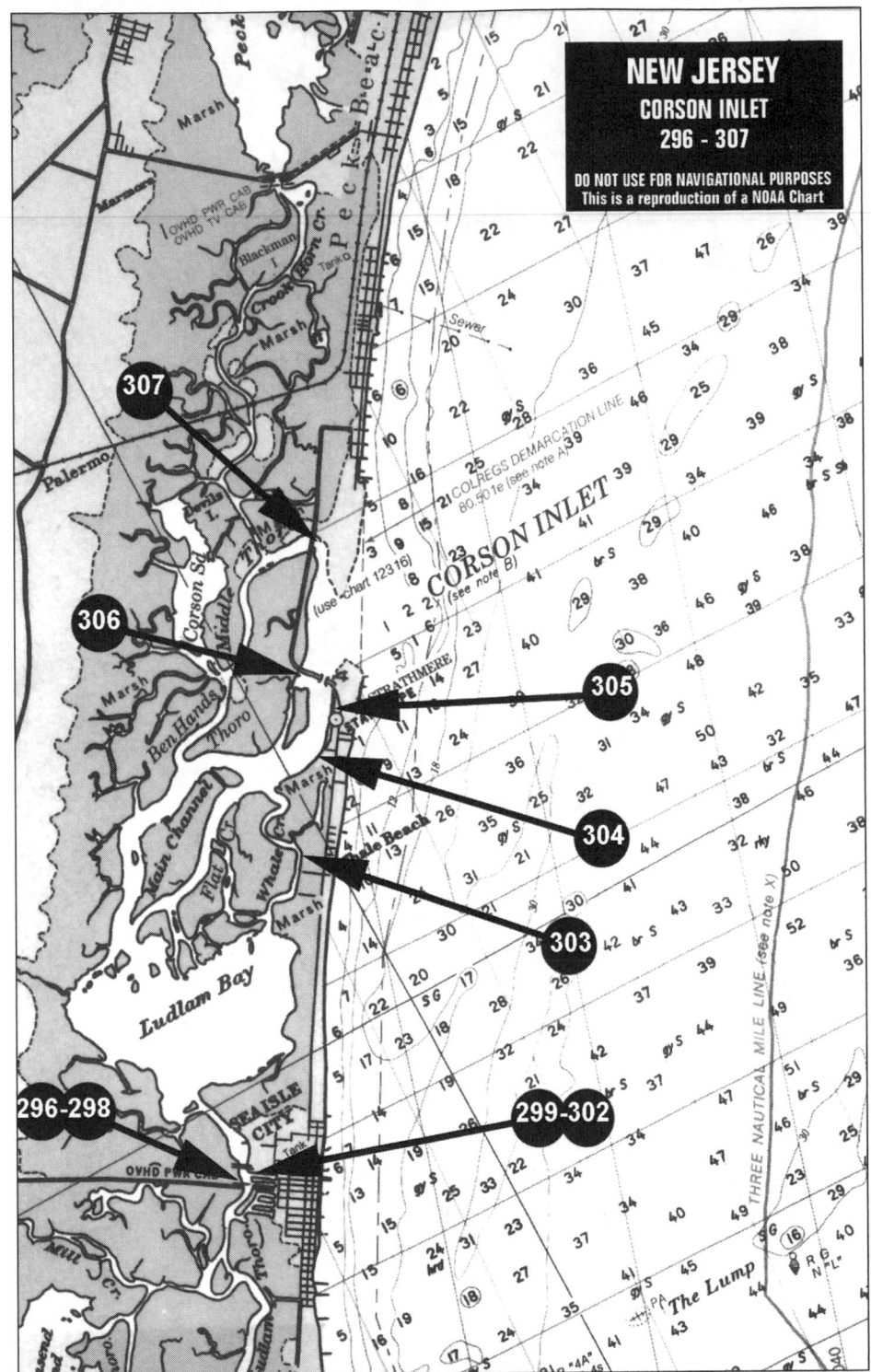

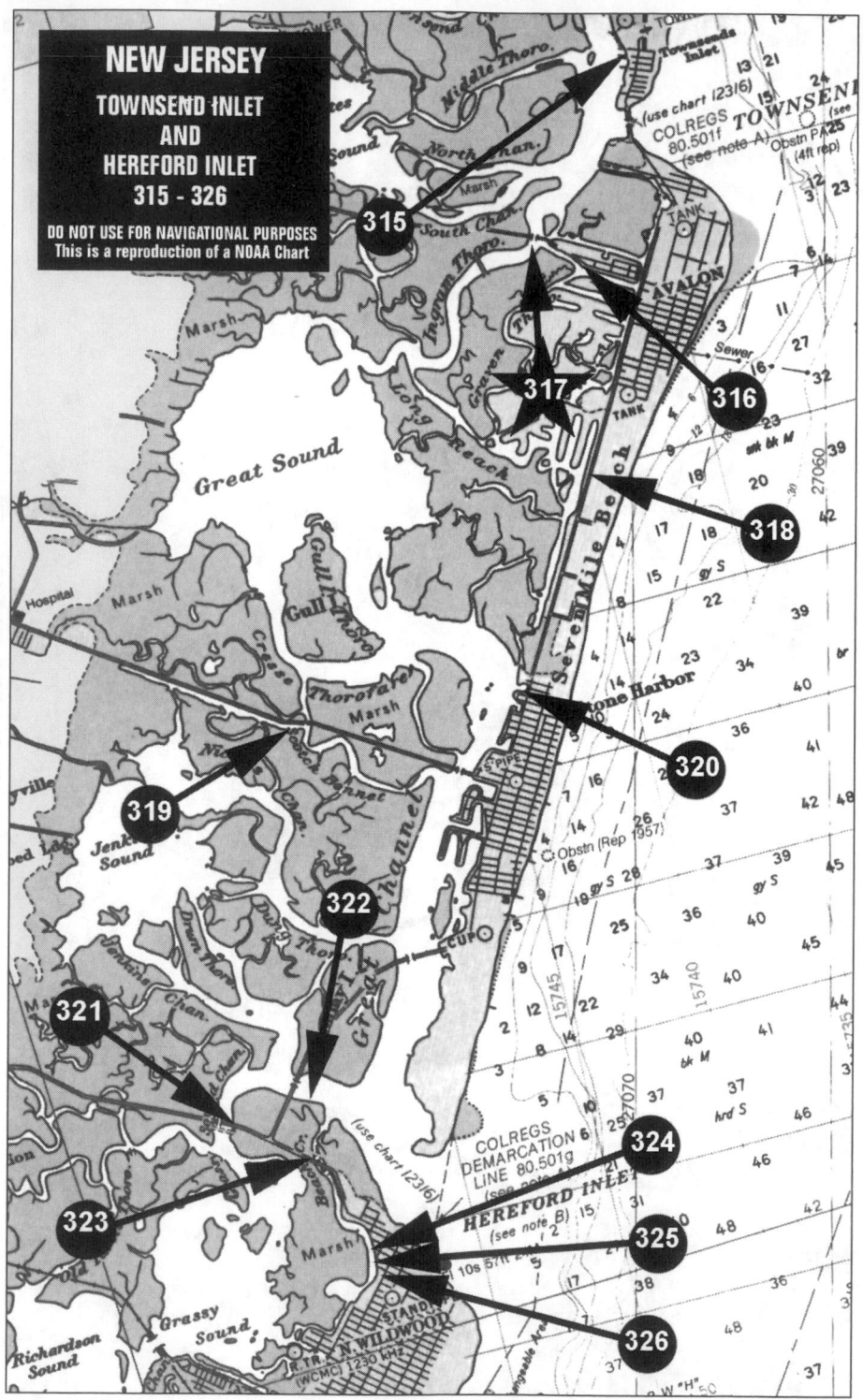

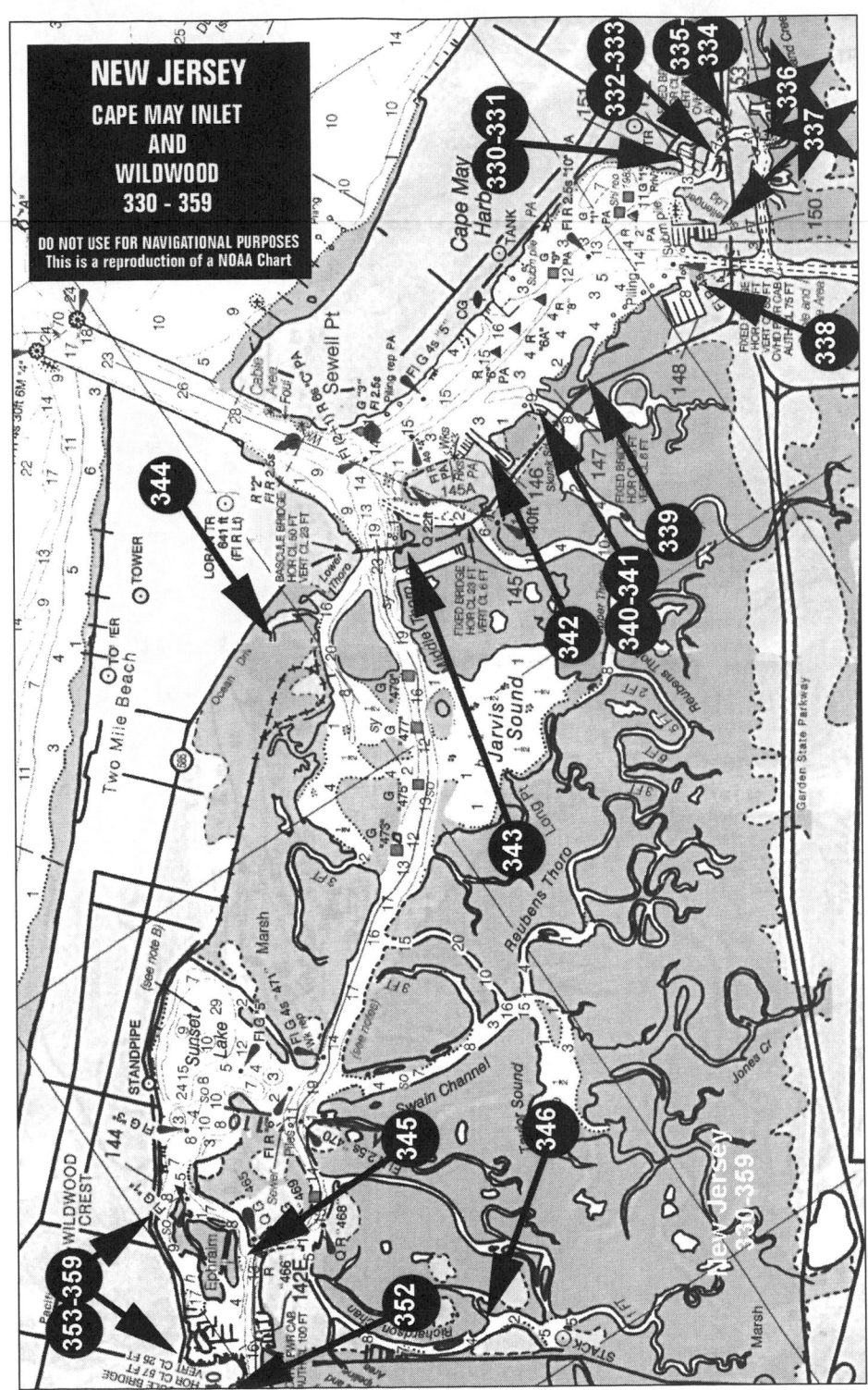

NEW JERSEY
CAPE MAY INLET
AND
WILDWOOD
330 - 359

DO NOT USE FOR NAVIGATIONAL PURPOSES
This is a reproduction of a NOAA Chart

315

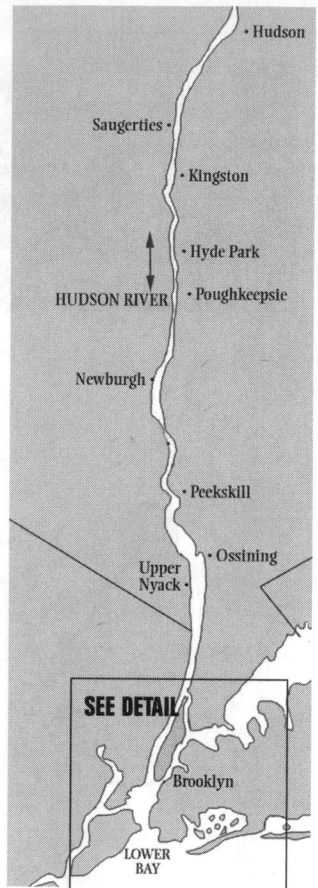

New York
West Chester
Hudson River
Manhattan

Map is not intended for navigational purposes.

USE NOAA CHARTS:

**12326 • 12327 • 12334 • 12335 • 12336 • 12339
12350 • 12364sc • 12343 • 12346 • 12401 • 12402**

THE FOLLOWING REGIONS ARE COVERED IN CHARTS IN THIS SECTION:

317

See page 666 for information about important security zones in New York waters.

Cruising New York Harbor, West Chester, and the Hudson River

CHART 12327. THE APPROACH TO NEW YORK HARBOR from seaward is generally along the south coast of Long Island or the east coast of New Jersey – the harbor is easily approached from any direction between east and south. During the approach, the south shore of Long Island will be seen to northward and the low sandy beaches of the New Jersey shore will be observed to westward. The Long Island shore is readily identified by sand hillocks and thickly settled beach communities, whereas the New Jersey shore is characterized by long stretches of sand and one summer resort settlement after another. The most prominent landmarks, which can be seen for a long distance at sea are: Fire Island Light, a tower at Jones Beach on the Long Island shore, the Highlands of Navesink, and the microwave tower at Atlantic Highlands. On the north end of New Jersey, Ambrose Light will be seen — it marks the entrance to Ambrose Channel which is the principal deepwater passage through the Lower Bay.

THE IMPORTANT CURRENTS affecting navigation in the approach to New York Harbor are those due to winds. The largest velocity likely to occur under storm conditions is about 1.5 knots. A sudden reversal in the direction of the wind produces a corresponding change in the current, either diminishing or augmenting the velocity. Sustained winds do not maintain the currents at the maximum velocity. The velocity is about 0.2 knots at Ambrose light — the largest velocity likely to occur is 2 knots.

 AMBROSE LIGHT is off the entrance to New York Harbor (40°27'00"N and 73°48'00"W) on red piles. A fog signal, a radiobeacon and a radar beacon are at the light. The light flashes white every 5 seconds; one horn blast every 15 seconds; height-75feet; range-18miles; racon "N." **AMBROSE CHANNEL,** the principal entrance to New York Harbor, extends from the sea to deep water in Lower Bay. Anchorage Channel, an extension of Ambrose Channel continues northward from the Battery. Hudson River Channel continues northward from the Battery for about 5 miles to West 59th Street, Manhattan. The projected depth for these channels is 45 feet.

FROM NEW JERSEY: SANDY HOOK CHANNEL has a projected depth of 35 feet, and provides a secondary route from the sea to deep water in Lower Bay. It connects with: Raritan Bay Channel to westward; Chapel Hill Channel to the north; and Terminal Channel to the south.

 CHARTS 12327,12401. SANDY HOOK, the southern entrance point to New York Harbor, is low and sandy. A Coast Guard station, a radar tower, and a radio tower are near the northern extremity of Sandy Hook. The towers and a large green standpipe to the southeast are the most prominent objects on the northern end of Sandy Hook. Southward of the standpipe are several houses and Sandy Hook Light — 88 feet

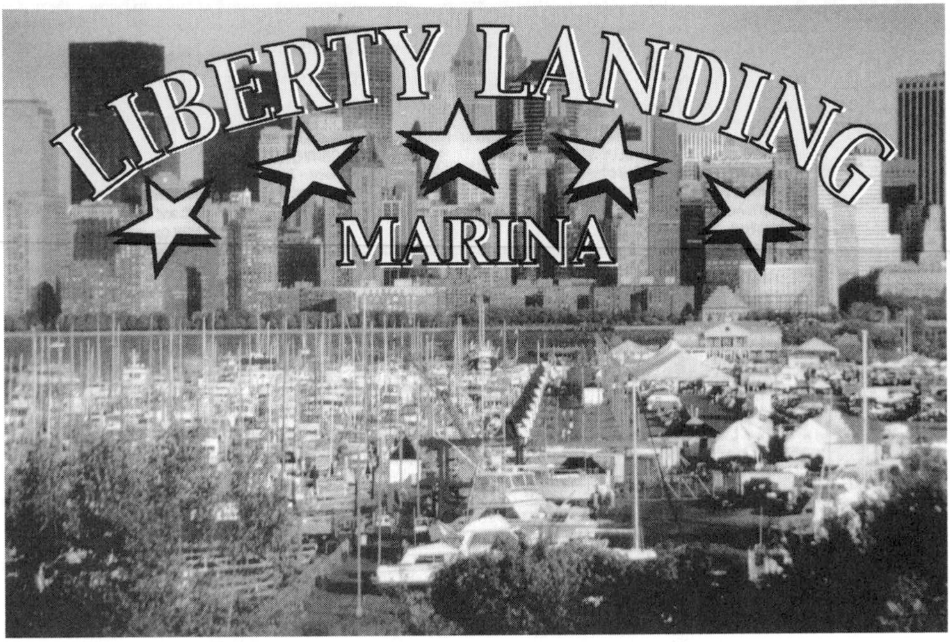

Easy Access from East River and Atlantic Ocean

24 HOUR AUTOMATED CREDIT CARD ACTIVATED HIGH SPEED PUMP AT OUR FUEL DOCK

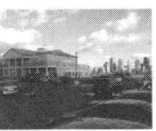

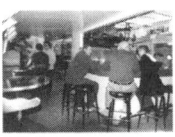

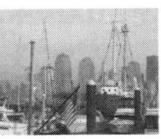

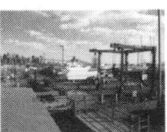

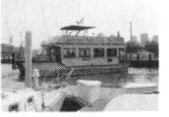

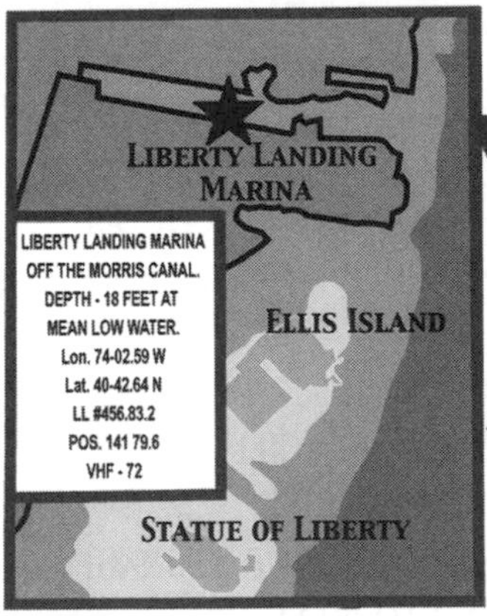

THE SMOOTHEST WATERS
IN NEW YORK HARBOR
NO FERRY WAKES
CONVENIENT ACCESS
TO NEW YORK CITY

CHART LOCATOR NO. 1

FULL SERVICE MARINA

- Extremely Quiet Harbor – No Wake
- 520 State-of-the-Art Floating Slips
- Marine Repair – Full Service
- Certified Mechanic on Duty
- 60 Ton Travelift
- Water Supply All Year 'Round
- Guest Showers and Laundry
- Winter Storage Wet & Dry
- Directly across the Hudson River from Manhattan's World Financial Center
- Water Taxi to NYC 7 Days a Week
- Off-Shore Sailing School
- Liberty Science Center
- Ellis Island

MARINE MAX - POWER BOATS **FREEDOM MARINE** - HP POWER BOATS **SANDY HOOK YACHT SALES** - SAILBOATS **D&R BOATS**

Liberty House Restaurant

Lightship Barge & Grill

Historic Lightship

Service Department

Water Taxi to NYC

80 Audrey Zapp Drive • Liberty State Park • Jersey City, NJ 07305 • 201-985-8000 • Fax 201-985-9866
www.libertylandingmarina.com Service Dept. 201-333-6755

above the water and shown from a white stone tower, 85 feet high. Established in 1764, this light is the oldest in continuous use in the United States. **Ed. Note:** See New Jersey section for details regarding Sandy Hook.

FROM LONG ISLAND'S SOUTH SHORE

CHART 12350, 12402. ROCKAWAY POINT, 17 miles westward of Jones Inlet , is the southwestern extremity of Long Island and the eastern entrance to New York Lower Bay. A breakwater, marked at its seaward end by a light, extends southward from the point. Rockaway Inlet forms a large deep entrance to Jamaica Bay.

ROCKAWAY INLET, the entrance to Jamaica Bay, is between Rockaway Point on the southeast side and Manhattan Beach and Barren Island on the north side. A shifting sandbar obstructs the inlet. A jetty, marked near the outer end by a light extends south from Rockaway Point. The entrance channel extends westward of the jetty and is marked by lighted and unlighted buoys. The channel has depths of 19 feet or more except for shoaling on the west side opposite the jetty light. A shoal with depths of less than 1 foot and marked by breakers is west of the entrance channel. An obstruction covered 20 feet is about 0.6 mile southwest of the jetty light.

SHEEPSHEAD BAY is to port as you enter Rockaway Inlet and is on the northern side of the eastern extremity of Coney Island and northward of Manhattan Beach. It is well protected and used by numerous pleasure and party fishing craft. The entrance channel is marked by buoys and has a depth of about 14 feet except for shoaling to 12 feet along the east edge of the channel north of Lighted Buoy 6.

CONEY ISLAND, on the northern side of the entrance to New York Harbor, is a large summer amusement resort. Numerous stacks, towers and amusement rides, including a red steel parachute tower 303 feet

NEW YORK

high are prominent on the island. Coney Island Light, 75 feet above the water, is shown from a white square skeleton tower on Norton Point the westernmost extremity of the island.

JAMAICA BAY is dead ahead as you enter Rockaway Inlet, on the south shore of Long Island. It is fifteen miles southeastward of The Battery, New York City. Numerous meadows, hassocks, and marshes characterize the bay. The north and east shores are bordered by marshlands which extend inland for a short distance. Several small tidal creeks enter the bay from the north. Channels and basins have been dredged to depths of 12 to 20 feet for use of craft operating in the bay. Rockaway Beach forms the south shore.

The bay is about 7 miles long and 3.5 miles wide, and covers an area of about 22.5 square miles. The greater portion of the bay is in Brooklyn and Queens, and a small section of the eastern extremity, consisting of parts of Motts Basin and Head of Bay, is in New York's Nassau County. Jamaica Bay is well protected from the Atlantic by barrier beaches.

MILL BASIN is northward of Barren Island on the west side of Jamaica Bay. **HOWARD BEACH,** about 2.5 miles eastward of Canarsie on the north side of Jamaica Bay, has several basins for boats. Beach Channel is on the north side of Rockaway Beach. A Federal project provides for a channel 18 feet deep from Rockaway Inlet to about 700 yards above Gill Hodges Memorial Bridge, thence 15 feet deep to the junction with Grass Hassock Channel. Cross Bay Memorial Bridge crossing Beach Channel at Rockaway Beach has a fixed span with a clearance of 52 feet. The railroad bridge, over Beach Channel 0.5 mile eastward, has a swing span with a clearance of 26 feet. **SOMMERVILLE BASIN**, about 1.2 miles eastward of the railroad bridge at Rockaway Beach, has depths of 27 to 40 feet inside. **MOTTS BASIN**, a tidal inlet in the eastern part of Jamaica Bay is entered through Negro Bar Channel and partially separates the communities of Inwood and Far Rockaway.

GRAVESEND BAY is a mile south of the Verrazano Narrows Bridge on the Brooklyn Shore and is a good harbor of refuge from all weather with the exception of storms and winds coming from the west.

NEW YORK HARBOR is the principal entrance by water to New York City and the surrounding Ports. The harbor is divided by the Narrows into Lower Bay and Upper Bay. The Battery, the southern tip of Manhattan, is at the junction of East River and Hudson River. The main channel from the sea to deepwater terminals in the Hudson River has a projected depth of 45 feet.

LIBERTY HOUSE RESTAURANT AT LIBERTY LANDING MAIRNA

CHART 12334. THE NARROWS, connecting the Lower Bay and Upper Bay of New York Harbor, has a clear width of over 0.6 mile at its narrowest point between Fort Wadsworth and Fort Hamilton. The Verrazano Narrows Bridge, a fixed suspension span, crosses The Narrows at these two points, linking Staten Island with Brooklyn. The bridge has a vertical clearance of 217 feet for a midchannel width of 2,000 feet. **Ed. Note:** Heading into the harbor, the entire panorama of Manhattan Island is always a photo-op no matter what the weather. To port, the Statue of Liberty (300 feet high) faces southeast from Liberty Island to welcome all who transit this waterway. Ferries run from The Battery in New York, and Liberty State Park in New Jersey, to both the Statue of Liberty and Ellis Island, just north of Liberty Island. Keep an eye out for other ferries crossing the harbor from both the New York and New Jersey shores.

Opposite **THE BATTERY**, and tucked in behind Lady Liberty anad Ellis Island is **Liberty Landing Marina** located on the southerly side of the **MORRIS CANAL** in **Liberty State Park, Jersey City**. Their well-protected, state-of-the-art, floating docks could possibly offer the smoothest, wake-free waters available in

New York's harbor. For sure, they have the most breathtaking view of Manhattan you'll ever see...looking more like a halogram than reality. From here you can take a water taxi or ferry to lower Manhattan, visit the Statue of Liberty, Ellis Island, and Liberty Science Center. The marina also offers the exquisite Liberty House waterfront sers up to 200 feet in length. Call for reservations on VHF 72 or 201-985-8000.

THE BATTERY is the crossroads for mariners entering New York's waterways. The **HUDSON RIVER ROUTE** runs north and the **LONG ISLAND SOUND TO NEW ENGLAND ROUTE** lies through the East River. Approach the East River between east side of Governor's Island, and Brooklyn, in Butter-milk Channel.

The Battery and Batter y Park, where the ferries an sightseeing boats are docked, are named from the 'battery' of 92 guns that were installed there by the British setting up a defense against the French, in 1693.

Anchorage for cruising boats is located behind Liberty and Ellis Islands, and just north of the West 79th Street Boat Basin. Avoid the temptaition to anchore at W. 79th Street and choose the moorings. The currents are fierce and the holding ground is poor. There is a dinghy dock with a landing charge. It has been reported that the moorings are in iffy shape, some dragging and others with damaged or missing pins in the mooring shackles.

FYI: **FLOTSAM** (to float) are things which have been swept overboard or are just found floating.

JETSAM (to throw out) are things thrown overboard to lighten the load during an emergency.

CHARTS 12335, 12339.

THE EAST RIVER is a 14-mile long tidal strait that connects Long Island Sound with New York Upper Bay and separates the western end of Long Island from the New York

Hell Gate HELP!
Time it right!
Leave the Battery two hours after low water to head for Hell Gate.

Mainland. The Sound entrance in between Throgs Neck and Willets Point, the Upper Bay entrance is between The Battery and Governors Island. Hell Gate, about halfway between Throgs Neck and The Battery is noted for its strong tidal currents. Harlem River extends northward from Hell Gate to the Hudson River. Both sides of the East River, from the Battery to Port Morris a distance of 9 miles present an almost continuous line of wharfs except where shoals or currents prevent access.

In the **EAST RIVER,** between the Brooklyn Bridge and Poorhouse Flats Range, shallow draft vessels customarily keep to the west (Manhattan side) of the channel whether northbound or southbound, reserving the east (Brooklyn side of the channel) for deep draft vessels. Vessels transiting the East River should be aware of this practice and anticipate northbound shallow draft vessels crossing from the east to west in the vicinity of Corlears Hook, and from west to east in the vicinity of Newtown Creek. **Ed. Note:** When transiting the East River keep a watchful eye from the bow for 'flotsam and jetsam.' Partially submerged debris can do extensive damage to your vessel. We've dodged everything from large logs and construction debris to a child's car safety-seat, a large piece of flotsam that appeared once again alongside our boat a week later, as we sailed out of Manhassett Bay!

Five miles above The Battery, Roosevelt Island, with its spectacular tramway, splits the East River in two. Take the western channel past the UN building, and passing under the Queensboro Bridge (131 feet vertical clearance).

CURRENTS IN THE EAST RIVER: The flood current sets eastward and the ebb sets westward. *Note well that this is the direct opposite of conditions in Long Island Sound* where the flood is generally westward and the ebb eastward. The velocity of current is 1.5 knots north of Governors Island, 3 Knots at Brooklyn Bridge, 4 knots in Hell Gate, 1.6 knots at Port Morris, and 0.7 knots at Throgs Neck. In Hell Gate, off Mill

Rock, the velocity is 3.4 Knots for the eastward current and 4.6 knots for the westward current. The direction and velocity of the currents are affected by strong winds, which may increase or diminish the periods of flood or ebb. The currents generally set with the channel but heavy swirls are found in Hell Gate.

CHART 12339. Hell Gate is the part of the East River between Wards Island and Roosevelt Island, 0.7 mile to the southwest. The crooked channel, the strong tidal currents, eddies and whirlpools, and the heavy traffic in Hell Gate require extra caution on the part of the navigator to avoid accident or collision. Set your VHF to Channel 13 listening for commercial traffic transiting Hell Gate. Vessels navigating Hell Gate on a rising tide sometimes find it necessary to pass starboard to starboard because of the strong currents between Negro Point and Hallets Point (green flashing light). This situation may arise when one of the vessels does not maneuver readily or is handling a tow. Northeastward of Negro Point and southwestward of Hallets Point the customary 'Port Passings' are made.

THE HARLEM RIVER joins the East River in **HELL GATE** between Wards Island and Manhattan Island and extends northward about 7 miles to connect with the Hudson River through Spuyten Duyvil Creek. The channel through Harlem River is narrow, tortuous, and navigable only for powered vessels needing less than 24 feet vertical clearance, and traffic is heavy. Vessels with heights too great (over 24 feet) to pass under the closed drawbridges should call NYC Department of Transportation two days in advance of your trip to request bridge openings. (Tel: 212-225-5368, then press "O" to speak to a real person)

Once at **Lawrence Point,** you are safely through Hell Gate and set to take the channel between **NORTH AND SOUTH BROTHER ISLANDS** to Long Island Sound. Follow only the buoy system going west-east to the Sound.

FLUSHING BAY is just east of Riker's island and it extends southeast between the town of College Point and LaGuardia Airport, 0.6 mile to the southwest. Marine facilities are located at College Point. **COLLEGE POINT** is on the Long Island side of the East River opposite Clason Point. College Point Reef covered 6 feet and marked by a light is 0.2 mile north- northeastward of the point. The town of College Point is south of the point and on the east side of the entrance to Flushing Bay.

ENTERING THE WATERS OF LONG ISLAND SOUND:

CHART 12336. THROGS NECK, on the northwest side of the entrance to the East River, is marked by a light, a stack, and a tall tank. Throgs Neck Light, 60 feet above the water, is shown from a skeleton tower with a black and white diamond shaped daymark on the outer end of the neck. The shoal ground which extends 0.1 mile southward and eastward from the light is marked by a lighted bell buoy. Throgs Neck

NEW YORK

Bridge marks the separation of the East River and Long Island Sound.

FORT SCHUYLER, on the outer end of Throgs Neck, is used as a base for the State University of New York Maritime Academy.

WESTCHESTER CREEK on the north side of the East River is entered through a dredged channel that leads northward through a shallow bight between Old Ferry Point and Clason Point, 0.7 mile to the westward, to the channel entrance.

WILLETS POINT, 0.7 mile southeastward across the entrance to East River from Throgs Neck is marked by Fort Totten, the granite walls of which are prominent.

WHITESTONE POINT, 2 miles westward of Willets Point, is a small bluff marked by light, a fog signal is sounded at the light. The town of Whitestone is between **LITTLE BAY** and Whitestone Point.

THE BRONX WHITESTONE BRIDGE is a suspension bridge that crosses the East River from Old Ferry Point on the Bronx side to a Long Island landing 0.4 miles southwestward of Whitestone Point.

EASTCHESTER BAY is narrow and over 1 mile in length. It is thickly settled and has a commercial appearance. A cove on the western side is a well-protected anchorage just inside **LOCUST POINT**. The cove is just southwestward of the point. Rocks that are bare at low water are located on the north side of the approach. The entrance has a depth of about 5 feet. Inside the cove depths range from 20 feet at the south end to about 4 feet at the north end.

CITY ISLAND HARBOR, 3 miles from Throgs Neck, is between Hart Island and City Island. It is well sheltered from easterly and westerly winds and is and important anchorage for cruising vessels in the western end of Long Island Sound. **Ed. Note:** A visit to City Island is like a step back in time in New York's history. While City Island is actually in the Bronx, it's really an enclave of seaside cottages, Victorian mansions, quaint shops, Italian and seafood restaurants — both a boater's and fishermen's haven. **Consolidated Yachts** (718-885-1900) is an excellent stopping point here, particularly if repairs are needed. We've swapped cruising stories with boaters from all parts of the country and Canada here while having service performed on our sailboat before entering Long Island Sound. They seem to have even the most obscure part in stock which ensures a quick and reliable fix. Just a short walk up the hill from Consolidated Yachts will take you to the main street of City Island with plenty of shopping and dining choices. The **North Minneford Yacht Club**, (718-885-2000) also on City Island, and right on the main street, welcomes transients up to 100 ft. with deep water floating docks, a sun deck and barbecue facilities. If you don't want to cook, head down the street a couple of blocks for fresh seafood and Maine lobsters at the Lobster Box Restaurant (718-885-1952) where you can dine with a lovely water view in upscale style.

NEW ROCHELLE HARBOR lies between the mainland and westward of Davenport Neck and Glenn Island. The main access of New Rochelle is through Echo Bay. Channels are well marked. The narrow dredged channel in the harbor has a controlling depth of 5.5 feet to within 100 yards of the dam. Anchoring is not recommended in the harbor because of its congestion. **Ed. Note: Castaways Yacht Club** (914-636-8444) is a full service marina, with gas and diesel fuel, tucked behind Davenport Neck. The marina offers tennis, swimming and a delightful waterfront restaurant.

THE HUDSON RIVER. Cruising the Hudson is an experience boaters talk about over and over long after the trip has ended. The scenery is magnificent, there's plenty of historic stops along the way, and many say it's better than cruising the Rhine in Europe! The 300 mile long Hudson has been designated one of the first "American Heritage Rivers" in the U.S. in 1998 which entitles it to a variety of federal programs and monies for tourism and environmental protection. The Hudson River's source – barely bigger than a few puddles – is in the Adirondack Mountains and it flows in a general southerly direction into New York's Upper Bay. Troy Lock and Dam, 134 miles above the Battery, permits vessels to pass

Consolidated
Yachts   Inc.

CHART LOCATOR NO. 27

★ THE HIGHEST QUALITY COMPLETE YACHT REPAIRS AND SERVICE
★ FULL CARPENTRY SHOP
★ MECHANICAL, ELECTRICAL AND CUSTOM METAL FABRICATIONS
★ IMRON / AWLGRIP AND FIBERGLASS REPAIRS / FABRICATIONS
★ FULL RIGGING SHOP
★ I / O SHOP AND MACHINE SHOP
★ 15 TON AND 60 TON TRAVILIFTS : CAN HANDLE TO 75FT X 20FT
★ VERY COMPETITIVE PRICES
★ SEASONAL AND TRANSIENT SLIPS
★ WINTER STORAGE INSIDE / OUTSIDE

Phone 718-885-1900   Fax 718-885-1904

40 YEARS OF EXPERIENCE IN THE MARINE INDUSTRY
157 Pilot Street, City Island New York 10464

from tidewater to the upper river and the New York State Barge Canal System. The river water is usually fresh as far south as Poughkeepsie, halfway from Troy Lock and Dam, to The Battery. New York City extends along the eastern bank of the Hudson River for a distance of about 14 miles above the Battery. For about 5 miles northward from the Battery, the Manhattan waterfront is an almost continuous line of wharfs and piers — some of which can accommodate the largest of transatlantic liners. On the opposite side of Hudson River from New York City are: Jersey City Hoboken, Weehawken, Guttenberg, Hudson Heights, Edgewater and Fort Lee, this entire stretch is lined with miles of piers. Vessels proceeding from New York to Albany anchor overnight in the vicinity of **KINGSTON**, 79 miles above the Battery and 47 miles below Albany, to await daylight hours for passing through the constricted part of the river. The Hudson averages about 0.6 mile in width along the 5-mile stretch above The Battery.

THE LOWER HUDSON RIVER has depths of 43 feet or more in midchannel, from deep water in Upper New York Bay — off Ellis Island — to the upper limit of New York City's major wharfs at 59th Street.

THE BRIDGES over the Hudson River, from New York to Albany, have either fixed or suspension spans. The limiting bridge clearance over the lower Hudson River is 139 feet (mhw) at the Tappan Zee Bridge. The middle Hudson River has a limiting bridge clearance of 137 feet (mhw) at the Mid Hudson Bridge at Poughkeepsie.

THE CURRENTS in the Hudson River are influenced by the same variables that affect the tides. The times of slack water and the velocities and durations of flood and ebb are subject to extensive changes. The times of strengths are less likely to be affected. The currents usually set fair with the channels except in the vicinities of bends and wharfs. Tidewaters extend to Troy, NY, and the mean tidal range varies from 3 to 5 feet. Mariners should pay close attention to tidal current tables here. Prevailing winds blow up and down the river, but near shore, the winds tend to sweep toward the banks.

MILEAGES shown in the following section (mile 0) are approximated nautical miles above The Battery. Mile 0.0 is a point at the mouth of the Hudson River - 40°42"10'N, 74°01"5'W.

    CHART 12346, 12343. THE TAPPAN ZEE BRIDGE (mile 23.5) crosses Tappan Zee from Nyack to Tarrytown. The fixed span over the main channel has a clearance of 139 feet (mhw). The 500 foot east and west spans, on either side of the main span, have clearances of 123 feet (mhw). Three auxiliary openings for small boats have clearances of 11 feet (mhw).

    CHART 12343. TARRYTOWN HARBOR, (mile 24E) just north of the bridge, is usually open to navigation throughout the year, but in severe winters ice floes from the upper river may temporarily block the channels. There is good provisioning here and walkable restaurants. **Ed. Note: The Tarrytown Marina** (914-631-1300) welcomes transients and offers all services. including gas and diesel, plus provisioning is an easy walk. Mariners will enjoy the marina's riverfront restaurant which offers alfresco dining. If you're stopping for the restaurant only, docking is free.

    CROTON POINT (mile 30E) juts out into the river on the eastern shore, and has a good anchorage for south to east winds. **Ed. Note:** If you prefer the security of a marina, head in to **Westerly Marina** (914-941-2203) in Croton Bay, which is full-service and welcomes transients.

    HAVERSTRAW BAY is the widest stretch of Hudson River and it is between Croton Point and Stony Point, 5 miles to the northward. The greatest width is about 2.5 miles. The extensive flats in the eastern half of the bay have depths of 5 to 9 feet. Seasonal lighted buoys and two lighted ranges mark the dredged channel through Haverstraw Bay.

On the western shore of the Hudson, is the town of **HAVERSTRAW** (mile 33W) between the cliffs of High Tor (820 ft. high) to the west and the Hudson. Look to **BOWLINE POINT** for the cement stacks and large red rectangular buildings of Indian Point Nuclear Power Plant.

Haverstraw Marina is ten miles north of the Tappan Zee Bridge. Head 260° off red buoy 26 to find the marina's 60 tree-lined waterfront acres. On the premises is the motor vessel Commander, built in 1917 and leased by the U.S. Navy in WWI to protect the Rockaway Air Station from German Zeppelins. Commander was awarded the Victory Medal for service.

STONY POINT (mile 35W) is marked at the outer end by a light. The north side has an excellent anchorage for cruisers in south to west winds. Good marina facilities are located here.

BEAR MOUNTAIN BRIDGE (mile 40.6) crosses the Hudson River from Bear Mountain to Anthony's Nose. The suspension span has a vertical clearance of 155 feet (mhw). This was the world's largest suspension bridge when it was built in 1924, and although it's a highway river crossing, it's also the Hudson River crossing for the Appalachian Mountain Hiking Trail.

WEST POINT (mile 45W) is the site of the U.S. Military Academy. The academy is easily recognized from the prominence of the buildings and the road leading up the hillside from the railroad station and wharfs on the riverbank. A special anchorage is at West Point. The northeastern extremity of West Point descends to Gees Point a rocky feature that is marked by a light with a fog signal. Another light marks the outer edge of a rocky shallow area along the west bank. **Ed. Note:** Call West Point Harbor master (845-938-3011 or VHF channel 16) for a berth at the Academy dock and an opportunity to visit the Academy itself. During the fall season, boaters often tie up for the Academy's home football games.

GARRISON, (mile 45E) across the river from West Point, is a charming small town stop and shop, plus it's a second choice berth for West Point visitors who have motorized dinghy power.

CHART 12347. North of the entrance to **WAPPINGER CREEK** (mile 58.5E) is **NEW HAMBURG** and **White's Hudson River Marina** offering fuel, service, and marine supplies.

KINGSTON is situated on the west side of the Hudson River, about 25 miles north of Poughkeepsie. It is partly on the lowlands adjacent to the north bank of Rondout Creek and partly on the elevated plateau to the north and westward of it. Rondout waterfront was a thriving port for over 300 years, bringing coal from the mountains of Pennsylvania. Today, the waterfront is home to the **Hudson River Maritime Museum** (founded in 1980) on Rondout Landing, **The Mathilda**, an 1898 steam tug, and **The Half Moon**, a replica of Henry Hudson's sailing ship. Exhibits illustrate the history of the Hudson River Region including the steamships that plied the Hudson for industrial and passenger needs.

RONDOUT CREEK, (mile 79W) is entered from the Hudson River at a dredged channel that leads between two long submerged jetties to Eddyville, about 3 miles above the channel entrance. The jetties are marked by lights at the outer ends and by daybeacons. The channel is partially marked by lights and buoys. The head of practical navigation is at the lock of the abandoned Delaware and

NEW YORK

Hudson Canal, 3.3 miles above the entrance. A fixed highway bridge, with a clearance to 56 feet (mhw) in the channel, crosses **RONDOUT CREEK,** about 1 mile above the entrance. A highway suspension bridge with a clearance of 86 feet (mhw) is about 0.1 mile above the fixed bridge and the fixed railroad bridge, with a clearance of 144 feet, is about 2 miles above the entrance. An overhead power cable with clearance of 75 feet crosses the creek about .45 mile above the Railroad Bridge. The channel hugs the north side of the creek with a controlling depth of 13 ft. (mlw). **Ed. Note: Rondout Yacht Basin** (914-331-7061) is west of the second fixed bridge on the creek's south shore. The marina welcomes yachts up to 140 ft. in this resort-style facility. Enjoy the pool, volleyball, horseshoes, and barbeques. Take a walk to Kingston's historic waterfront district, or a shuttle to Kingston proper. Mast stepping for the trip up-Hudson is available in this full service marina which also offers dive service, a canvas shop, fiberglass shop and mechanical services on site.

CATSKILL CREEK (mile 97.5W) is marked at the entrance by buoys. Catskill is about 1 mile above the mouth of the creek. A controlling depth of 6.5 feet is available to about 100 yards above the Highway Bridge, 0.9 mile above the mouth. The bridge, which remains in a closed position, has a bascule span with a clearance of 14 feet. **Ed. Note:** At the head of the creek watch for signs for **Riverview Marine Service**. The marina has complete repair services and is located for easy shoreside shopping and dining. Mast stepping services are available here for vessels heading north past Albany. Call ahead for services and reservations (518-943-5311).

CHART 12348. COXSACKIE. (mile 108W) North of Coxsackie is an anchorage between Coxsackie Island and the west bank of the river. Part of the anchorage is reserved for large shipping – small craft are advised to use the area on the east side of Houghtaling Island.

CASTLETON-ON-HUDSON. (mile 119E) Castleton Boat Club (518-732-7077; VHF 9,16) offers free do-it-yourself mast stepping and moorings to use while you wait your turn.

ALBANY. (mile 126W) Leave the pastoral beauty of the Hudson and enter the capital of New York with a tidal range of 4 to 5 feet. The Albany Yacht Club (518-445-9587; VHF 9, 16) welcomes all mariners.

TROY. (mile 132E) Troy Town Dock and Marina (518-272-5341; VHF 16) is 1/4 mile south of the Federal Lock and the last possible place for mast stepping. The marina accommodates vessels to 200 ft. and can supply you with river and canal charts, guides and permits.

SEE GREAT LAKES CHART CATALOG. THE NEW YORK STATE BARGE CANAL SYSTEM, comprising Erie Canal, Oswego Canal, Cayuga and Seneca Canal and Champlain Canal, is under the jurisdiction of the State of New York. Navigation on the State canals is free except for mooring, dockage,

storage or use of canal equipment of facilities for which a permit is required. Detailed data regarding movement through the New York State Barge Canal System may be obtained from the New York State Canal Corporation Office of Canals, (518) 436-2700. The Great Lakes-Hudson River Waterway Improvement is that part of the barge canals system including the Erie Canal from Waterford west to Three Rivers and thence the Oswego Canal to Lake Ontario. This section of the system, funded by the U.S. Government, and maintained by the The State of New York, has a projected depth of 14 feet at normal pool level between locks and 13 feet at normal pool level through all locks and guard gates. These channels have widths of 104 feet in earth cuts, 120 feet in rock cuts, and 200 feet in river and lake sections. ⚓

NEW YORK • HUDSON FACILITIES alphabetical index

New York West Chester Hudson River Manhattan

MARINA'S NAME & PHONE NUMBER

Chart Locater No.	Marina's Name & Phone	When Open	Monitors VHF Channel	Transient (Elec•Moor•Berths)	Hull•Engine repairs•Ramp	Winter Storage (Wet•Dry)	Lift Cap. (feet)	Lift Cap. (tons)	Boat Rental (Canoe•Row•Motor)	Boat Rental (Charter•House•Sail)	Restaurant•Lodging•Camping	Showers•Laundry	Pumpout•Toilets	Bait•Tackle•Water•Ice	Groceries•Hardware	Diesel•Gasoline
1 A	LIBERTY LANDING MARINA 201-985-8000	ALL	16	EB	HE	WD			C	C	RL	SL	T	WI	GH	GD
3 A	PORT IMPERIAL MARINA 201-902-8787	ALL YR.	88A	E B	HE	WD		35		CS	R C	S L	PT	IW BT	GH	GD
4 A	LINCOLN HARBOR Y.C. 201-319-5100	ALL YR.	9	E B	HE	WD						S	PT	IW BT	GH	D
5 A	NEWPORT MARINA 201-626-5550	ALL YR.	16 72	E B		W					RL	SL	PT	IW	GH	
6 A	LIBERTY HARBOR MARINA 201-451-1000	ALL YR	68	E B	HE	DW		60				SL	T	IW		GD
2	FOX ISLAND MARINA 914-937-3900	ALL YR.											T			
3	TIDE MILL YACHT BASIN 914-967-2995	MAY OCT	68	EB	HE	WD		35				S	T	W	H	GD
4	RYE MUNICIPAL MARINA 914-967-2011		9 16	EM B	ER	D							PT	W		
5	SHONGUT MARINE 914-967-3842	ALL YR.		B	HE	D		15					T	WB T	H	G
6	MAMARONECK YACHT CLUB 914-698-1130				HE			35					PT	IW	H	G
7	McMICHAEL YACHT YARD 914-698-4957	ALL YR.			HE	D		35					T			
8	DERECKTOR SHIPYARDS 914-698-5020	ALL YR.		EB	HE	D	100	99 +							H	GD
9	POST ROAD BOATYARD 914-698-0295	ALL YR.		EB	HE	D	70	50					S	PT	IW	GH	GD
10	MAMARONECK VILLAGE MARINA 914-698-3142	MAR NOV	9 16	MB	R						R		PT	W		
11	NICHOLS YACHT YARDS 914-698-6065	ALL YR.	9	EB	HE	D		35				RL	S	PT	IW	GH	
12	TOTAL MARINE LTD 914-698-2700	ALL YR.			HE	D		20						T	W		G
13	McMICHAEL RUSHMORE YARD 914-381-2100	ALL YR.			HE	D	20	35							W	
14	**CASTAWAYS YACHT CLUB 914-636-8444**	**ALL YR.**		**EB**	**HE**	**WD**		**35**				**R**	**SL**	**T**	**IW**		**GD**
16	IMPERIAL Y.C. 914-636-1122	ALL YR.	16	EB	HE	WD		70				R	SL		IW		GD
17	GLEN ISLAND PARK 914-632-9500				R											

New York
West Chester
Hudson River
Manhattan

Chart Locater Number	Marina's Name & Phone Number	When Open	Monitors VHF Channel	Transient: Electricity • Moorings • Berths	Hull repairs • Engine repairs • Ramp	Winter Storage: Wet • Dry	Railway Capacity in Tons	Lift Capacity in Feet	Boat Rental: Canoe • Row • Motor	Boat Rental: Charter • House • Sail	Restaurant • Lodging • Camping	Showers • Laundry	Bait • Tackle • Toilets	Pumpout • Water • Ice	Groceries • Hardware	Diesel fuel • Gasoline
18	WEST HARBOR YACHT 914-636-1524	ALL YR.		EB	HE	W D		25				S	T	IW		
19	WRIGHT ISLAND MARINA 914-235-8013	ALL YR.		EB M	HE	W D		50			R	SL	TP	IW		G D
20	SNUG COVE MARINA 914-939-7100	ALL YR.										S	T	IW		
21	NEW ROCHELLE MARINA 914-235-6930	ALL YR.	16	EM B	HE						RL	SL	T	W		G D
22	ECHO BAY MARINE 914-636-8334	ALL YR.		EB	HE	D		20						W		
23	POLYCHRON MARINA. 914-632-408	NOV			E	D					R		T	IW BT		
24	**NORTH MINNEFORD YACHT CLUB** **718-885-2000**	**ALL YR.**	**77**	**EB**	**HE**	**W D**		**40**			RL	SL		IW	GH	
24A	LOBSTER BOX RESTAURANT 718-885-1952		77	EB							R					
25	BARRONS BOATYARD 718-885-9802	ALL YR.	16	MB	HE	D		25			R	S	T	W		
26	FENTON MARINE 718-885-0844	ALL YR.			HE	D		40					T	W		
27	**CONSOLIDATED YACHTS** **718-885-1900**	**ALL YR.**	**11 68**	**EB**	**HE**	**D**				CS	R	S	T	IW	H	
28	KRETZER BOAT WORKS 718-885-2600	ALL YR.	23	EB	HE	W D	60	45				S	T	IW		G D
29	STELTER BOATS & MOTORS 718-885-1300	ALL YR.				D							T	W		
30	ROSENBERGERS BOAT LIVERY 718-885-1843								MR					IBT		
31	CITY ISLAND YACHT SALES 718-885-2300	ALL YR.		B	HE			30						I		G
32	CITY ISLAND LOBSTER HOUSE 718-885-1459										R		T	IW BT	GH	
33	JACAR CORP. 718-823-3847	AL YR.		EM B	HE	D		30					T	W		
34	PELBAMAR CORP. 718-822-8958	ALL YR.			HE	D	40	25				S	T	IW	GH	
35	EVERS MARINA 718-863-9111	ALL YR.			HE R	D		20					T	IW		
36	SHELTER COVE MARINA 718-822-3054	ALL YR.			HE R	D	30	15					T	IW BT	H	

CHART LOCATER NUMBER	MARINA'S NAME & PHONE NUMBER	WHEN OPEN	MONITORS VHF CHANNEL	TRANSIENT Electricity · Moorings · Berths	Hull repairs · Engine repairs	WINTER STORAGE · Ramp	RAILWAY CAPACITY: Wet · Dry	LIFT CAPACITY IN FEET	BOAT RENTAL: Canoe · Row · Motor	BOAT RENTAL: Charter · House · Sail	Restaurant · Lodging · Camping	Showers · Laundry	Pumpout · Toilets	Bait · Tackle · Water · Ice	Groceries · Hardware	Diesel fuel · Gasoline
37	LOCUST POINT MARINA 718-822-7974	ALL YR.			HE		D	35				S	T	IW	H	
38	BOAT HAVEN 718-824-4000	ALL YR.	69		HE		D	15					T		H	
39	METRO MARINE. 718-823-0300	ALL YR.			HE		D	10				S	T			
41	FRANK TIBORSKY MARINE 718-353-2653	ALL YR.			HE		D	12						BT	H	
42	COLLEGE POINT MARINA 718-428-1717	ALL YR.		EB	HE		W D	11					T	IW		
43	SKYLINE MARINA 718-961-7889	ALL YR.	72	EB	HE		W D	40						WT	GH	
44	WORLD'S FAIR MARINA 718-478-0480	ALL YR.	71	EB	HE		W D	50			R	S	T	IW	H	G D
45	NEW YORK SKYPORTS MARINA 212-686-4546	APR OCT		EB							R		T	W		G D
46	SOUTH STREET SEAPORT 212-669-9400	ALL YR.		B												
47	PORT IMPERIAL MARINA 201-902-8787	ALL YR.	88A	EB	HE		W D	35		CS	RL	SL	PT	IW	GH	G D
48	MARINE BASIN MARINA 718-372-5700	ALL YR.	68	EM B	HE	R	W D	30			R	S	PT	IW	H	G D
49	SURFSIDE MARINA 718-372-1322	ALL YR.					D	10								
50	PORT SHEEPSHEAD MARINA 718-332-4030				HE							S	T	W		
51	STELLA MARIS FISHING STATION 718-646-9754	ALL YR.											T	BT		
52	SHEEPSHEAD BAY PIERS									C						
53	PARKWAY FISHING CENTER 718-763-9265						D			C						
54	DEAUVILLE MARINA 718-634-5968						W									
55	BMW MARINE 718-743-2800	ALL YR.		EB	H			60			RL		T	I		
56	TAMAQUA BAR & MARINA 718-646-9212	ALL YR.								C	R		T			G D
57	BARREN ISLAND MARINA 718-338-4200	ALL YR.		EB	HE		D	35					T	IW	GH	G

New York West Chester Hudson River Manhattan

MARINA'S NAME & PHONE NUMBER

No.	Marina's Name & Phone Number	When Open	VHF	Transient Elec./Moorings/Berths	Hull/Engine Repairs	Winter Storage Wet/Dry	Railway/Ramp	Capacity (tons)	Boat Rental	Restaurant/Lodging	Showers/Laundry	Bait/Tackle	Pumpout/Toilets	Groceries/Water/Ice	Hardware	Diesel/Gas
58	SEA TRAVELERS MARINA 718-377-0216	ALL YR.			HE	D		20		RL	S		T	W		G
59	AIR QUEEN MARINE CO. 718-338-6803	ALL YR.			HE	D		8								
60	CORVETTE'S MARINA 718-252-6726				HE	W/D		12								
61	ALL SEASONS MARINE 718-253-5434	ALL YR.		EB	E	D								W	H	
63	VIKING MARINE 718-444-3506	ALL YR.			HE	D	R	50		R	S		T	IW	H	
64	BAY END DOCK CO. 718-444-7544	ALL YR.			HE	D		11					T		H	
65	MULLER BOAT WORKS 718-444-4343	ALL YR.			HE			99+								
66	DIMEGLIO'S BOATYARD 718-241-5011	ALL YR.	13	EM B	HE	W/D	R	50								
68	BUSTERS MARINE 718-945-4377	ALL YR.			HE	D									H	
69	CHANNEL MARINE SALES. 718-318-2000	APR NOV		EB	HE	D		10		R			T		H	
70	SMITTY'S FISHING STATION. 718-945-2642								R			BT				
72	CHANNEL FORTY MARINA. 718-641-2780	ALL YR.			HE			10							H	
81	**TARRYTOWN MARINA 914-631-1300**	**ALL YR.**		**EB**				**25**		**RL**	**SL**		**T**	**IW**		**GD**
82	NYACK LAUNCHING RAMP						R									
83	JULIUS PETERSEN 845-358-2100	ALL YR		EB	HE	D		60		R			T	I	H	G
84 (SEE AD)	WESTERLY MARINA 914-941-2203	ALL YR		EB	HE	D		35		R	S		T	IW	H	G
86	SAMALOT MARINE 845-429-0404	ALL YR.		EB	H	D		15	S		S		T	IW	H	
87	HAVERSTRAW MARINA 845-429-2001	ALL YR	9/16	EM B	HE	D	R	38.5	S	R	SL	BT	PT	IW	H	GD
88	MINISCEONGO Y. C. 845-786-8767	APR OCT		EB							S		T	IW		G
89	PENNYBRIDGE MARINE 845-786-5100	ALL YR.		ER									T	I	H	

CHART LOCATER NUMBER	MARINA'S NAME & PHONE NUMBER	WHEN OPEN	MONITORS VHF CHANNEL	TRANSIENT Electricity • Moorings • Berths	Hull/Engine repairs • Ramp	WINTER STORAGE: Wet • Dry	RAILWAY CAP. (TONS)	LIFT CAP. (FEET)	BOAT RENTAL Canoe • Row • Motor	BOAT RENTAL Charter • House • Sail	Restaurant • Lodging • Camping	Showers • Laundry	Pumpout • Toilets	Bait • Tackle • Water • Ice	Groceries • Hardware	Diesel fuel • Gasoline
90	BELLE HARBOR MARINA 845-786-5823	ALL YR.		EB	HE R	D		35				SL	T	IW	H	
91	WILLOW COVE MARINA SOUTH 845-786-5270	ALL YR.		EB	HE R	D		35				SL	PT	IW	H	
92	WILLOW COVE MARINA NORTH 845-429-0100	ALL YR.		EB	HE	D		35				S	PT	IW		
93	GEORGES ISLAND RAMP 845-737-7530	JUN OCT			R								T			
94	VIKING BOATYARD 845-739-5090	ALL YR.		EB	HE	D		60			R	S	T	IW	H	
95	KING MARINE 845-739-3413	ALL YR		EM B	HE	D		30				S	T	IW		
96	CHARLES POINT MARINA 845-736-7370	ALL YR.		EB	HE	D		25			R	S	PT	IW	H	G D
97	PEEKSKILL RAMP	ALL YR.			R											
99	NEWBURG DOCK	ALL YR.		B												
100	NEWBURG Y.C.	MAR NOV		EB							R	SL	T	IW		G D
101	CHELSEA RAMP	ALL YR.			R											
102	CHELSEA CARTHAGE MARINA 845-831-5777	APR OCT	9	EB	HE	D		30					T	IW		
103	**WHITES HUDSON RIVER MARINA** **845-297-8520**	ALL YR.		EB M	HE R	D		25			R	S	PT	IW	GH	G D
104	WEST SHORE MARINE 845-236-4486	ALL YR.	9 16	EB	HE R	D		25				S	T	IW	GH	G D
105	WARYAS PARK RAMP	ALL YR.			R											
106	MARINERS HARBOR 845-691-6011	ALL YR		EB	HE						R		T	I		G D
107	BASS ANCHOR MARINA 845-473-8283	ALL YR		EB	HE R	D		15			R	S	T	I		
108	GREAT HUDSON SAILING CTR 845-338-7313	ALL YR.							M	CS	R		T	B T		
109	HUDSON RIVER MARITIME MUSEUM 845-338-0071	MAY NOV									R	SL	T			
110	**RONDOUT YACHT BASIN** **845-331-7061**	APR NOV	9 16	EB	HE R	W D		45		C	C R	SL	PT	IW	GH	G D

New York
West Chester
Hudson River
Manhattan

Chart Locater Number	Marina's Name & Phone Number	When Open	Monitors VHF Channel	Transient: Electricity • Moorings • Berths	Hull repairs • Engine repairs • Ramp	Winter Storage: Wet • Dry	Railway Capacity in Tons	Lift Capacity in Feet	Boat Rental: Canoe • Row • Motor • Sail	Boat Rental: Charter • House	Restaurant • Lodging	Showers • Camping	Pumpout • Laundry	Bait • Tackle • Toilets	Groceries • Water • Ice	Diesel fuel • Gasoline • Hardware
111	RONDOUT REST. & MARINA 845-339-3917	ALL YR.		B							R					
112	CERTIFIED MARINE SERVICE 845-339-3060	FEB DEC	9 16	EB	HE R	D		30			R	S	T	IW	GH	G D
113	GOOSE ROOST MARINA 845-331-9100	APR OCT	9 16	EB	HE R	D					R	S		T	I	
114	LOUS BOAT BASIN 845-331-4670	APR DEC											T		H	G D
115	ULSTER MARINE CENTER 845-339-3943	ALL YR.		EB	HE	D					M			T		H
116	HIDEAWAY MARINA 845-331-4565	ALL YR.	9	EB	HE R	D		35		S			SL	T	IW BT	H
117	BRICKYARD REST 845-339-0093	ALL YR.		EB							R					

Find links to popular boating sites on
www.BoatersAlmanac.com

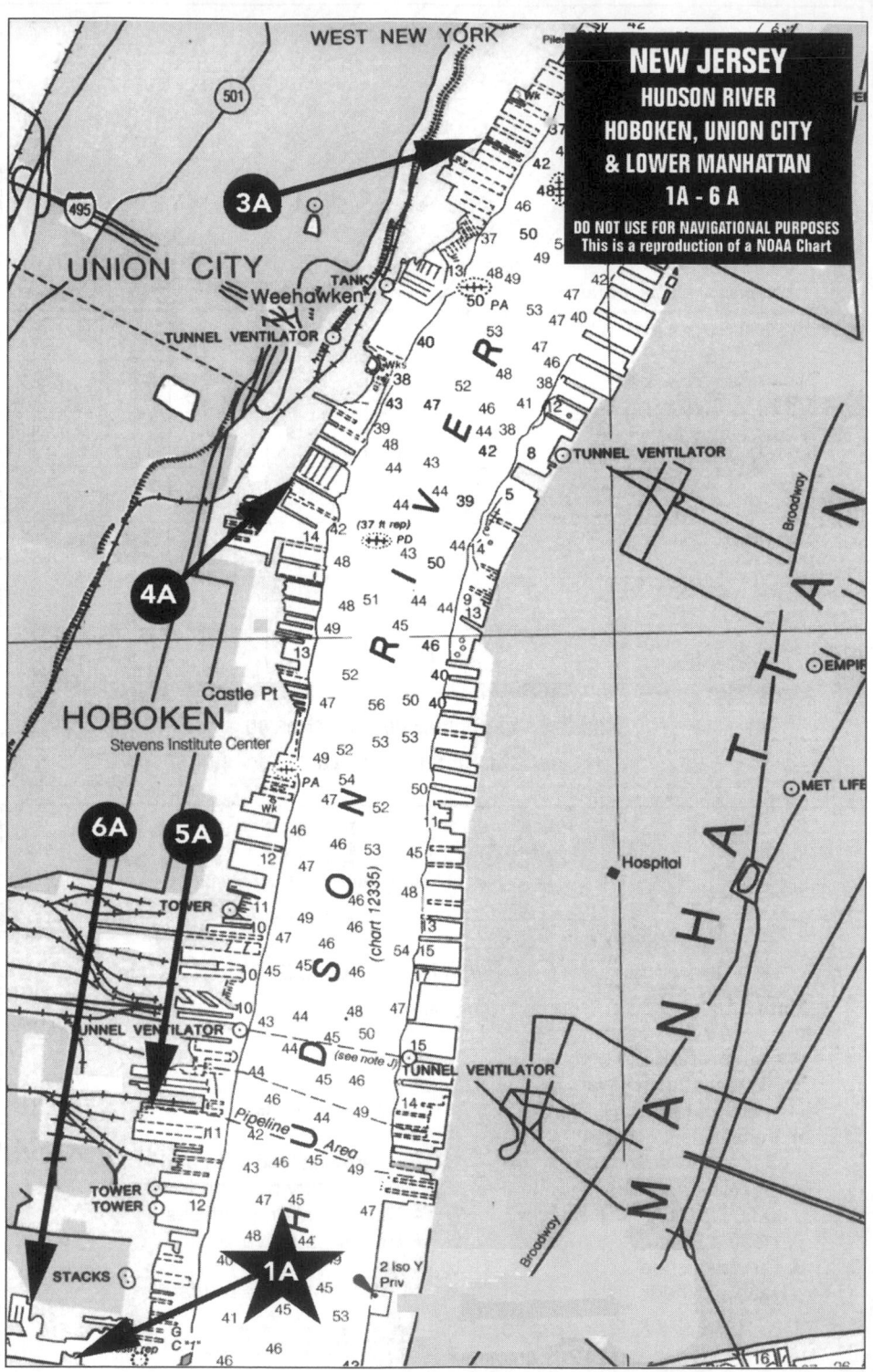

NEW JERSEY
HUDSON RIVER
HOBOKEN, UNION CITY
& LOWER MANHATTAN
1A - 6 A

DO NOT USE FOR NAVIGATIONAL PURPOSES
This is a reproduction of a NOAA Chart

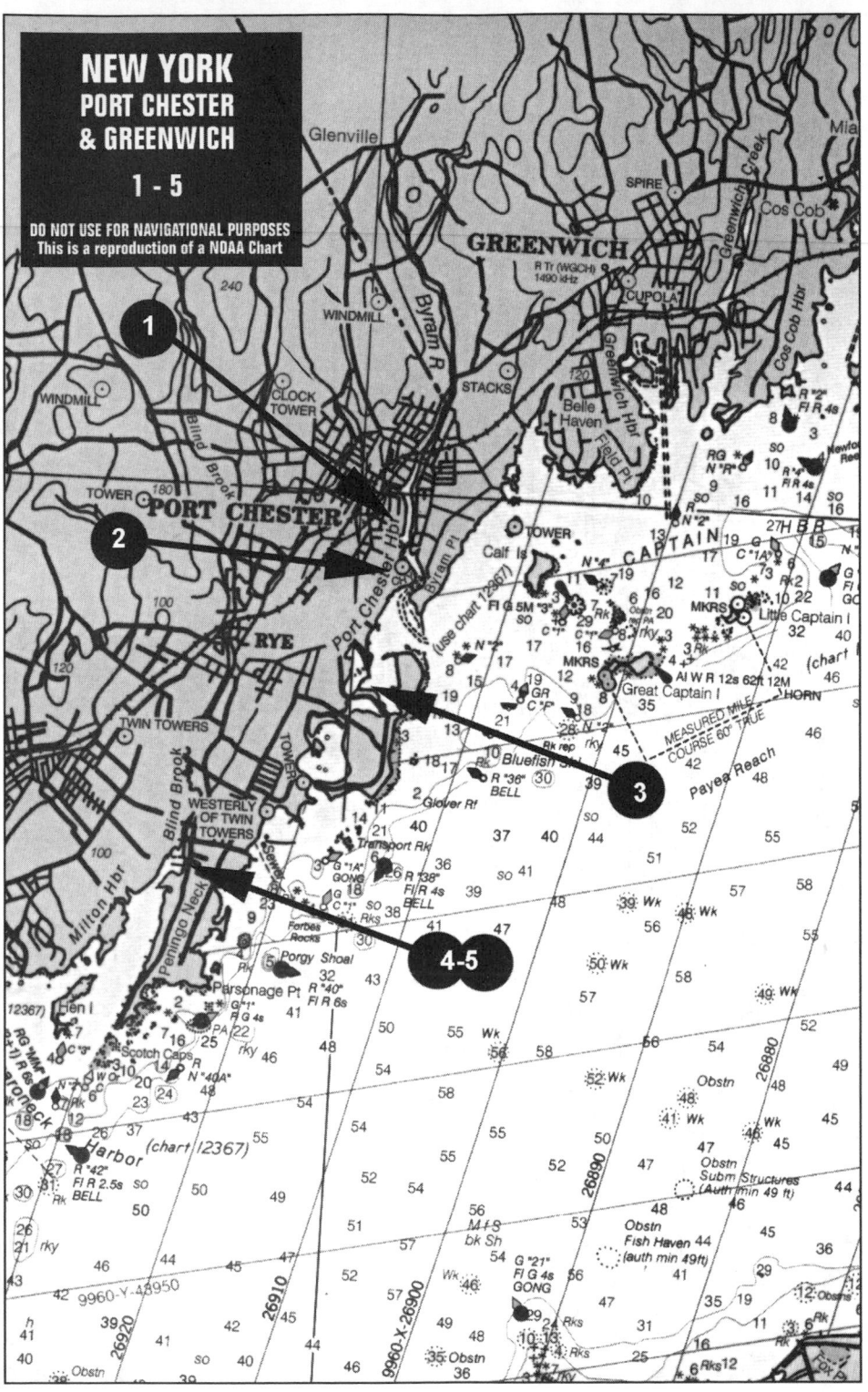

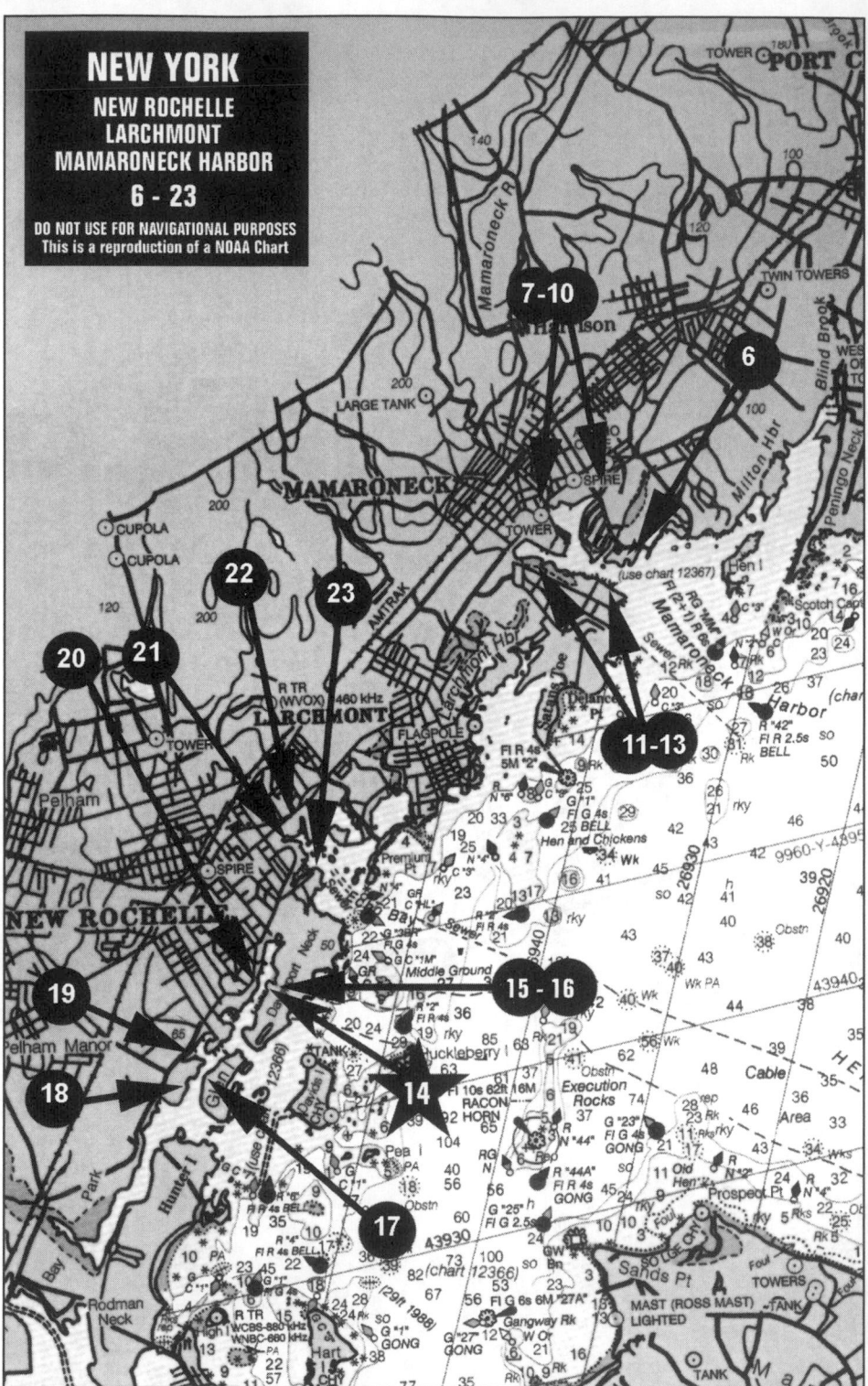

NEW YORK
NEW ROCHELLE
LARCHMONT
MAMARONECK HARBOR
6 - 23

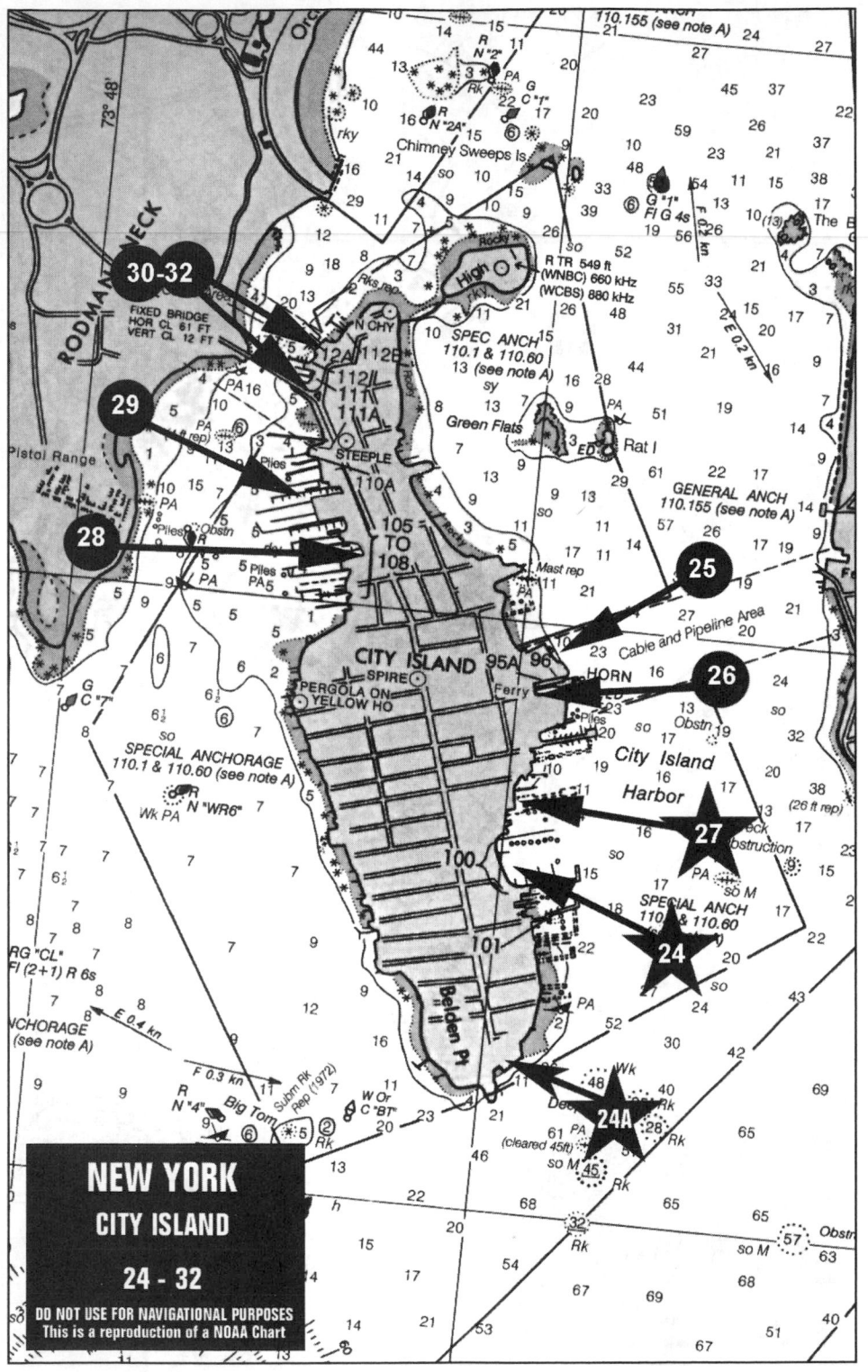

NEW YORK
CITY ISLAND
24 - 32
DO NOT USE FOR NAVIGATIONAL PURPOSES
This is a reproduction of a NOAA Chart

341

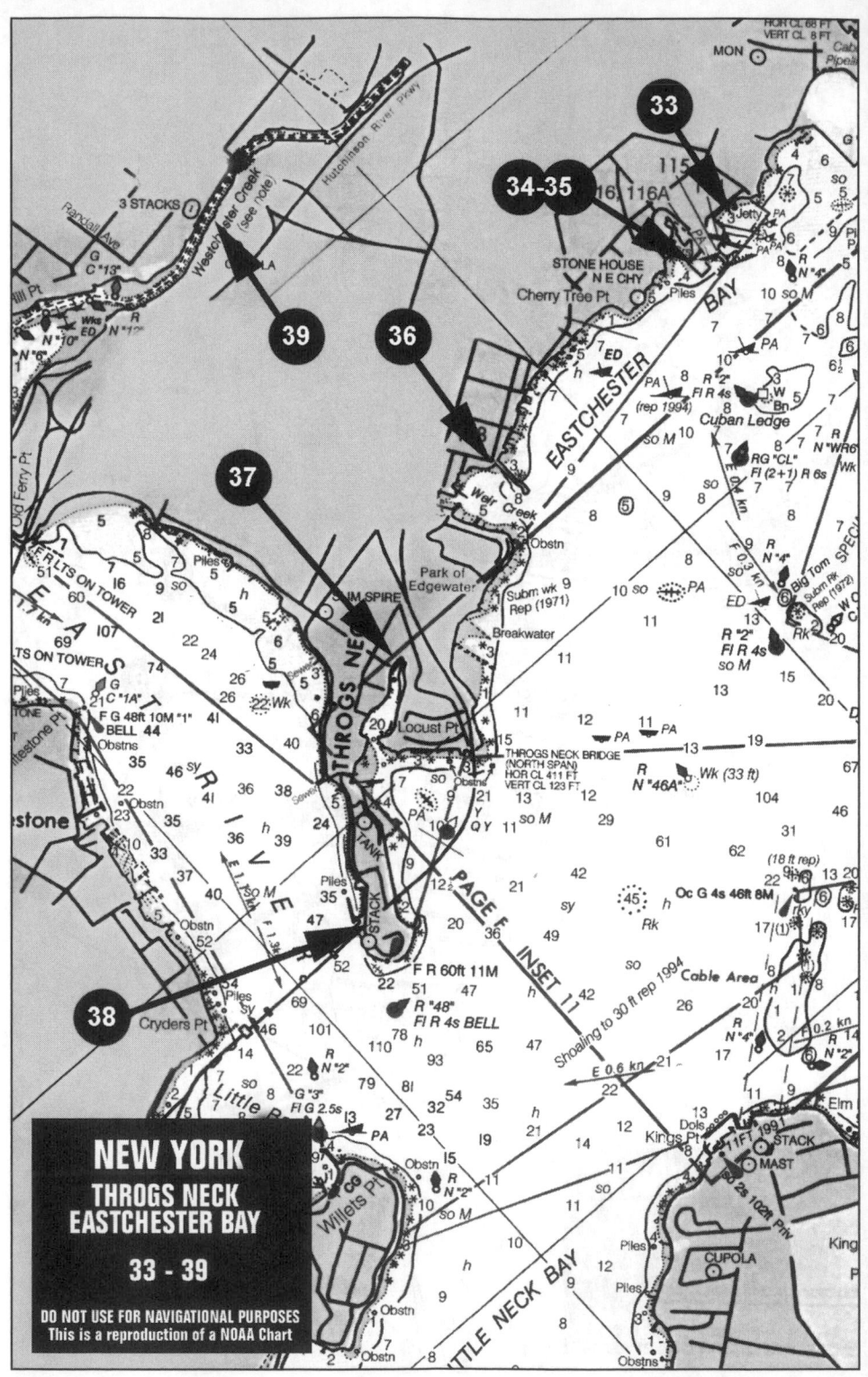

NEW YORK
THROGS NECK
EASTCHESTER BAY

33 - 39

DO NOT USE FOR NAVIGATIONAL PURPOSES
This is a reproduction of a NOAA Chart

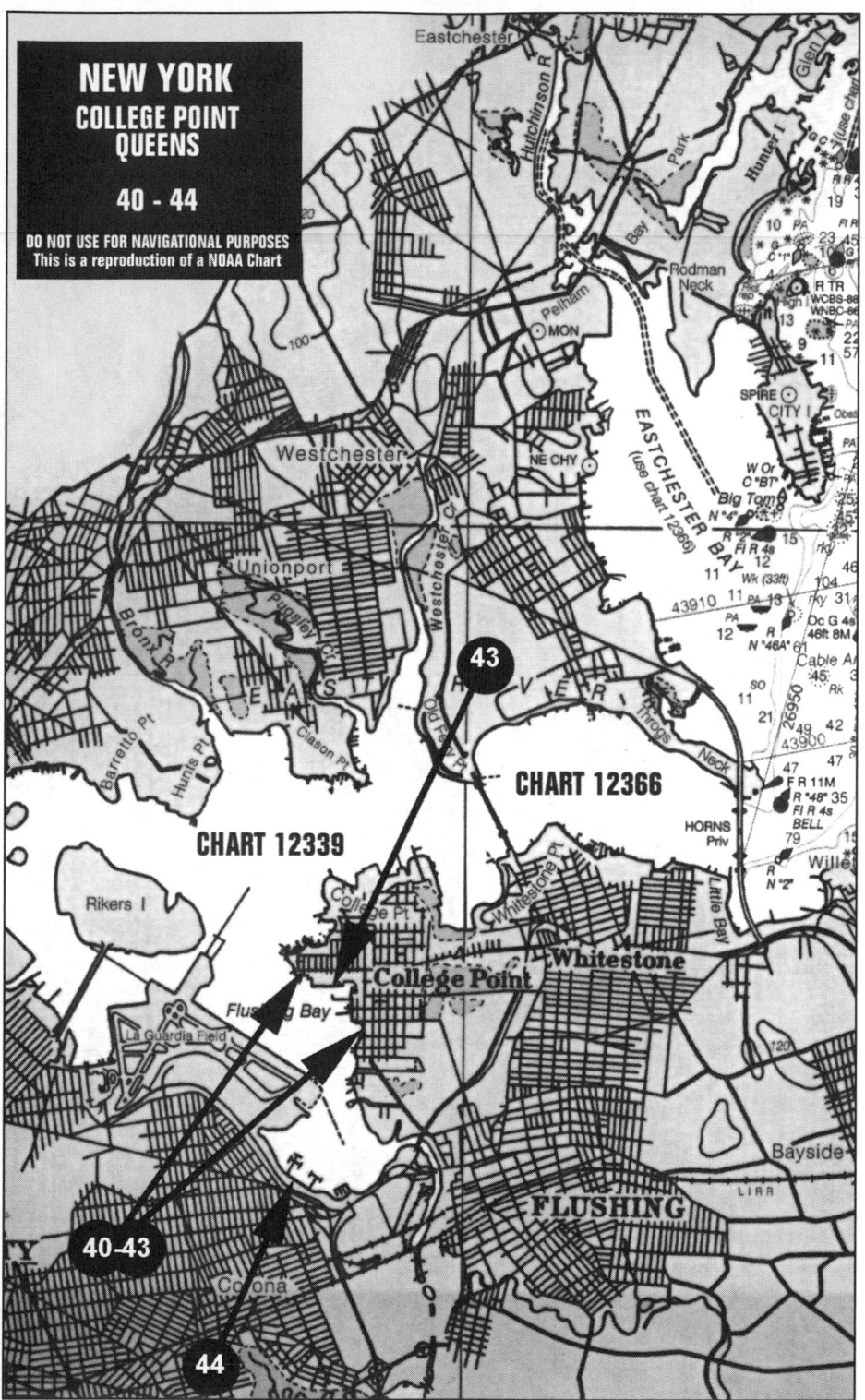

NEW YORK
COLLEGE POINT
QUEENS

40 - 44

DO NOT USE FOR NAVIGATIONAL PURPOSES
This is a reproduction of a NOAA Chart

CHART 12339

CHART 12366

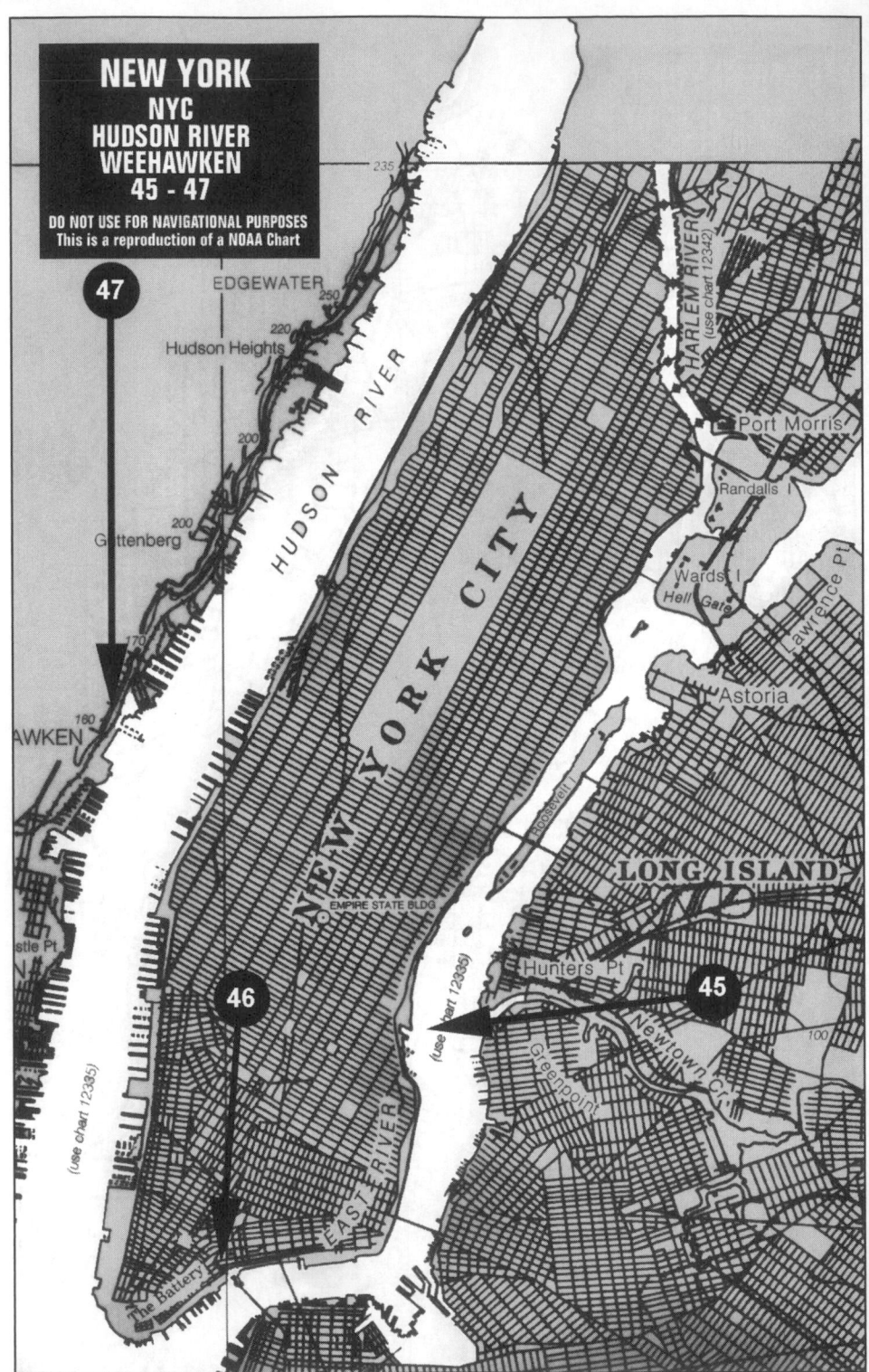

NEW YORK
NYC
HUDSON RIVER
WEEHAWKEN
45 - 47

DO NOT USE FOR NAVIGATIONAL PURPOSES
This is a reproduction of a NOAA Chart

47

EDGEWATER

235

250

220

Hudson Heights

200

HARLEM RIVER
(use chart 12342)

Port Morris

Randalls I

200

Guttenberg

200

HUDSON RIVER

Wards I

Hell Gate

Lawrence Pt

170

NEW YORK CITY

Astoria

180

AWKEN

Roosevelt I

LONG ISLAND

stle Pt

EMPIRE STATE BLDG

Hunters Pt

46

45

(use chart 12335)

(use chart 12335)

Newtown Cr.

100

Greenpoint

EAST RIVER

The Battery

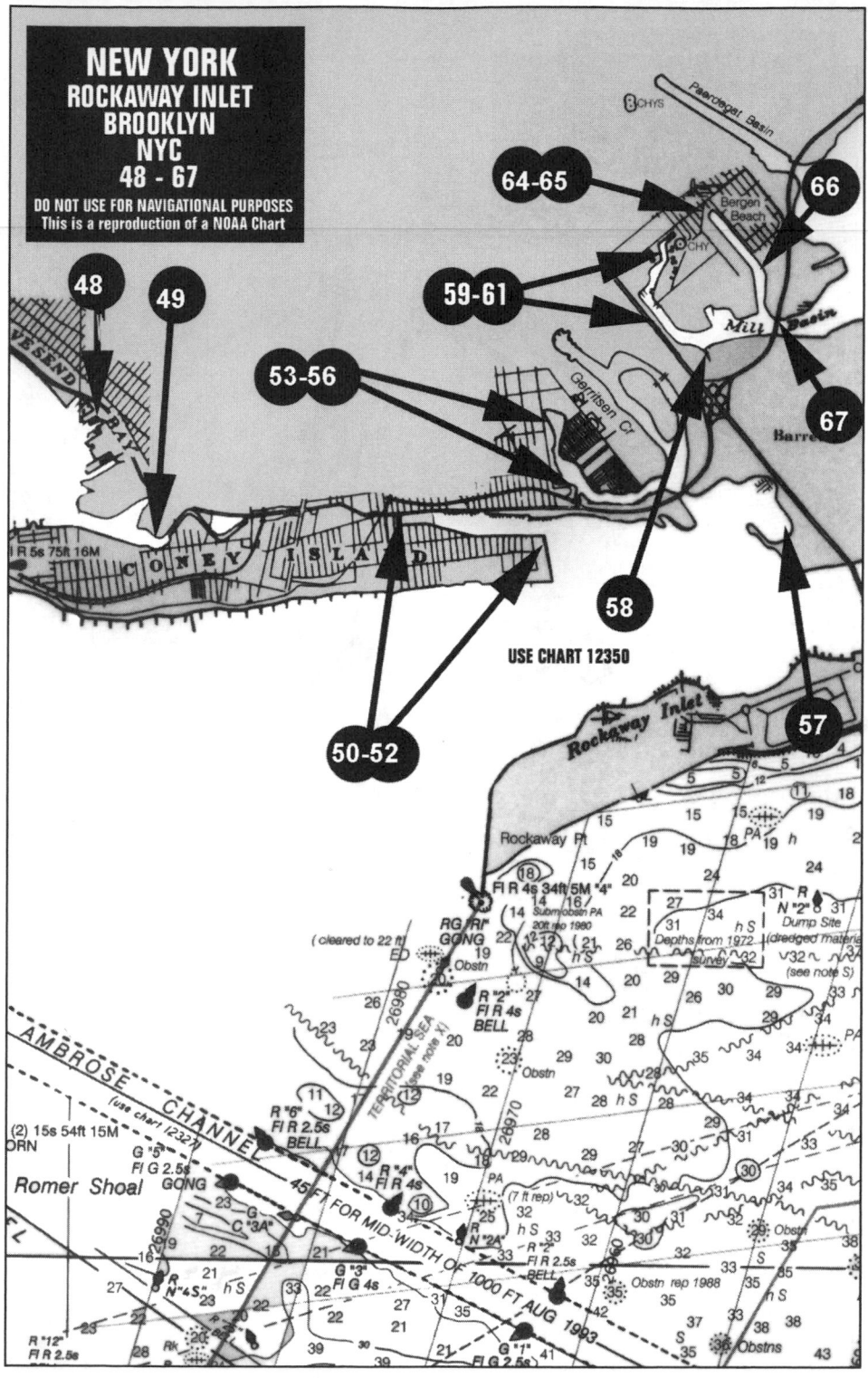

48

49

64-65

66

59-61

53-56

67

50-52

58

57

USE CHART 12350

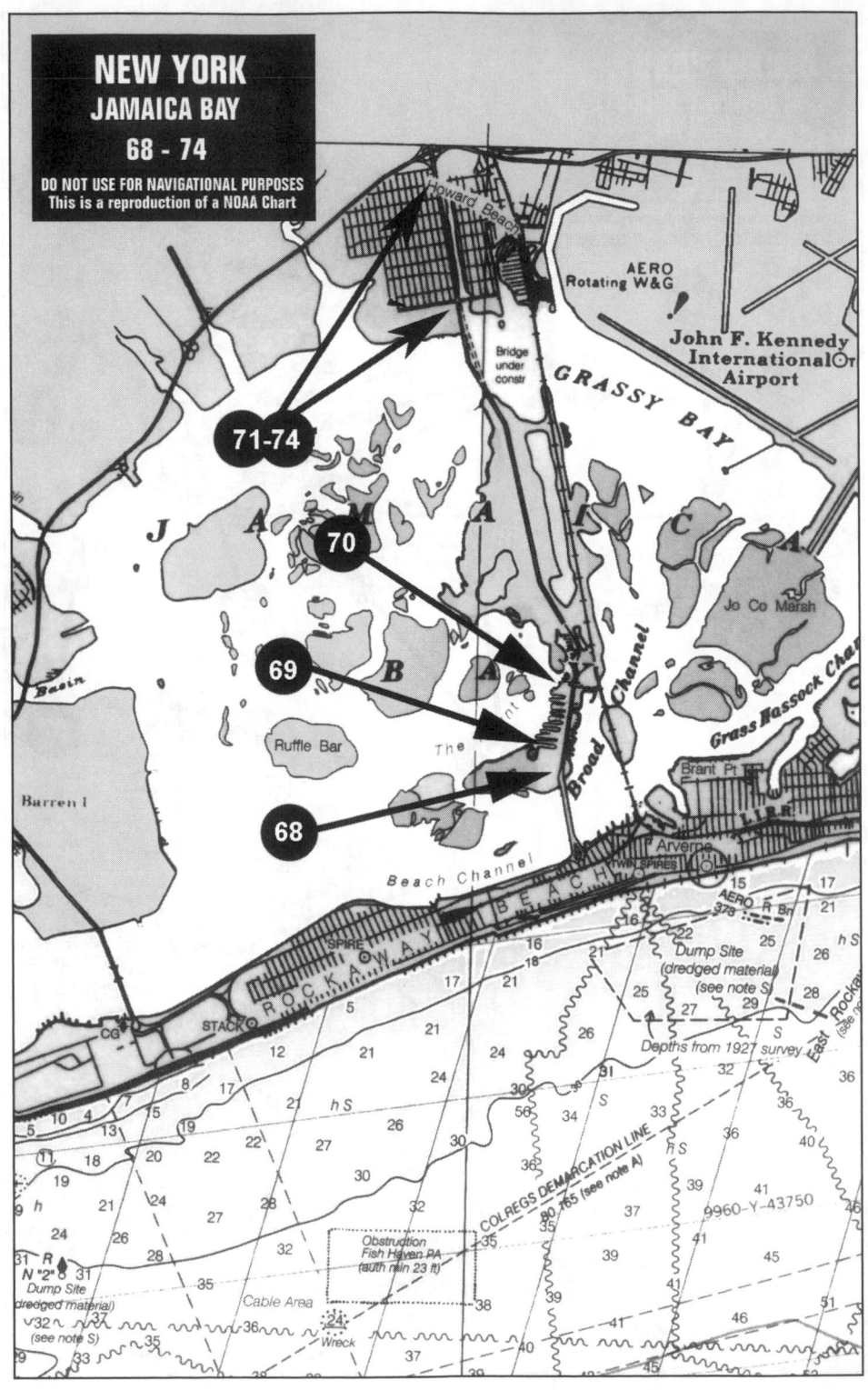

NEW YORK
JAMAICA BAY
68 - 74

DO NOT USE FOR NAVIGATIONAL PURPOSES
This is a reproduction of a NOAA Chart

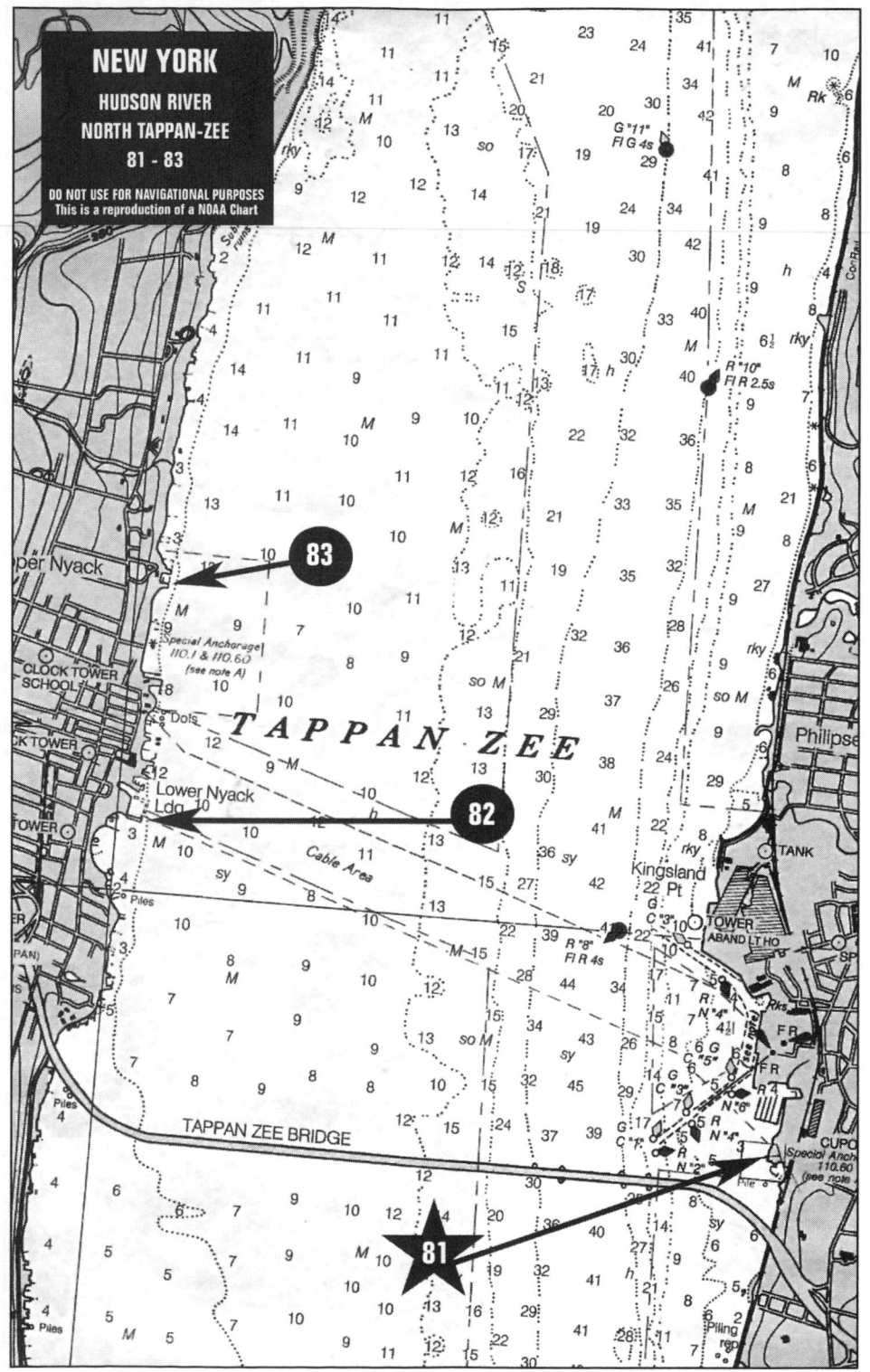

NEW YORK

HUDSON RIVER

NORTH TAPPAN-ZEE

81 - 83

DO NOT USE FOR NAVIGATIONAL PURPOSES
This is a reproduction of a NOAA Chart

83

82

81

per Nyack

CLOCK TOWER
SCHOOL

CK TOWER

TOWER

Special Anchorage
110.1 & 110.60
(see note A)

Dols

Lower Nyack
Ldg

Cable Area

Piles

T A P P A N   Z E E

Phillipse

Kingsland
22 Pt

TANK

TOWER
ABAND LT HO

G "11"
Fl G 4s

R "10"
Fl R 2.5s

R "8"
Fl R 4s

G "3"

G "5"

G "3"

TAPPAN ZEE BRIDGE

Piles

Piles

N "6"

N "4"

N "2"

FR

FR

Special Anch
110.60
(see note)

CUPO

Piling
rep

347

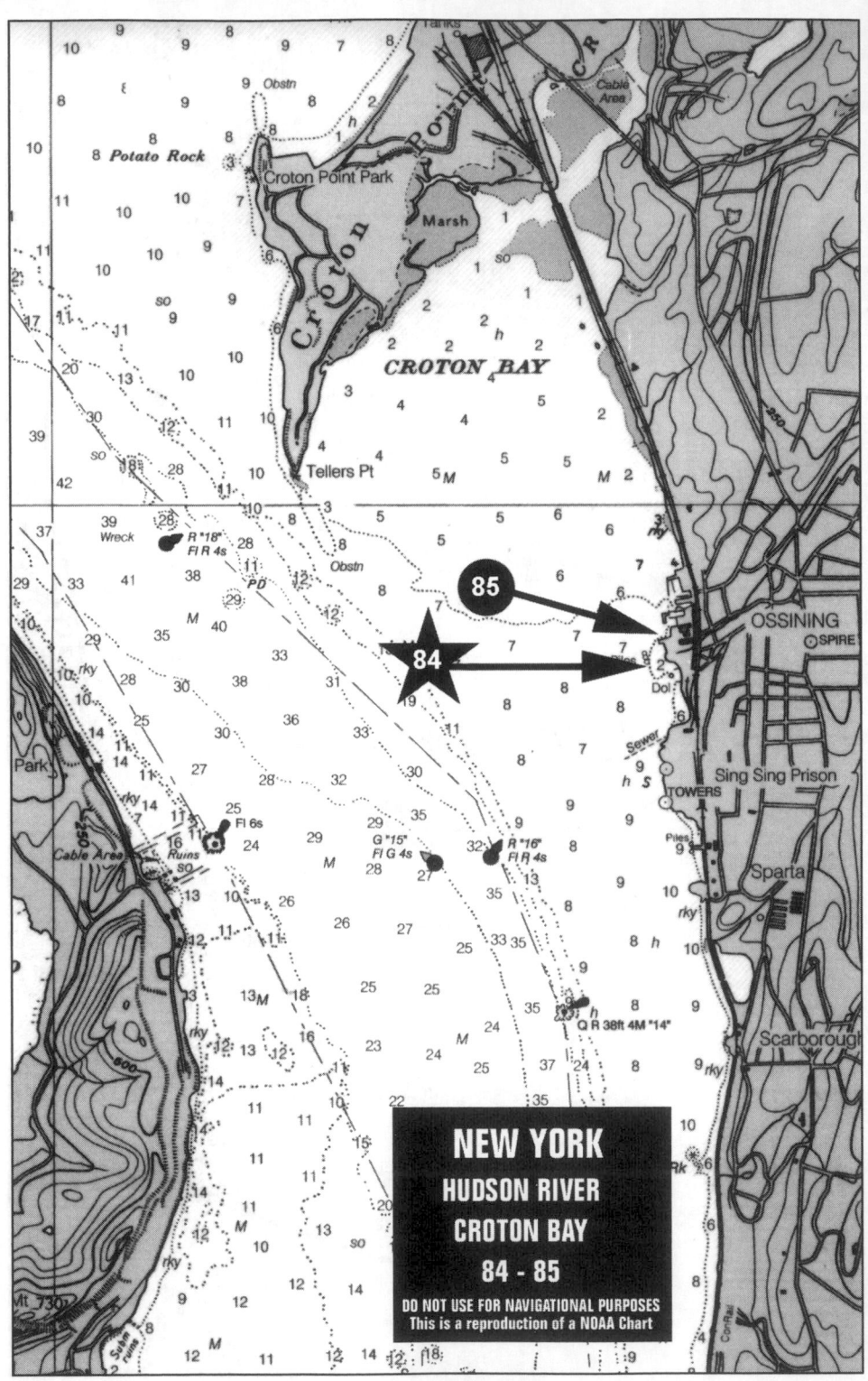

NEW YORK

HUDSON RIVER

CROTON BAY

84 - 85

DO NOT USE FOR NAVIGATIONAL PURPOSES
This is a reproduction of a NOAA Chart

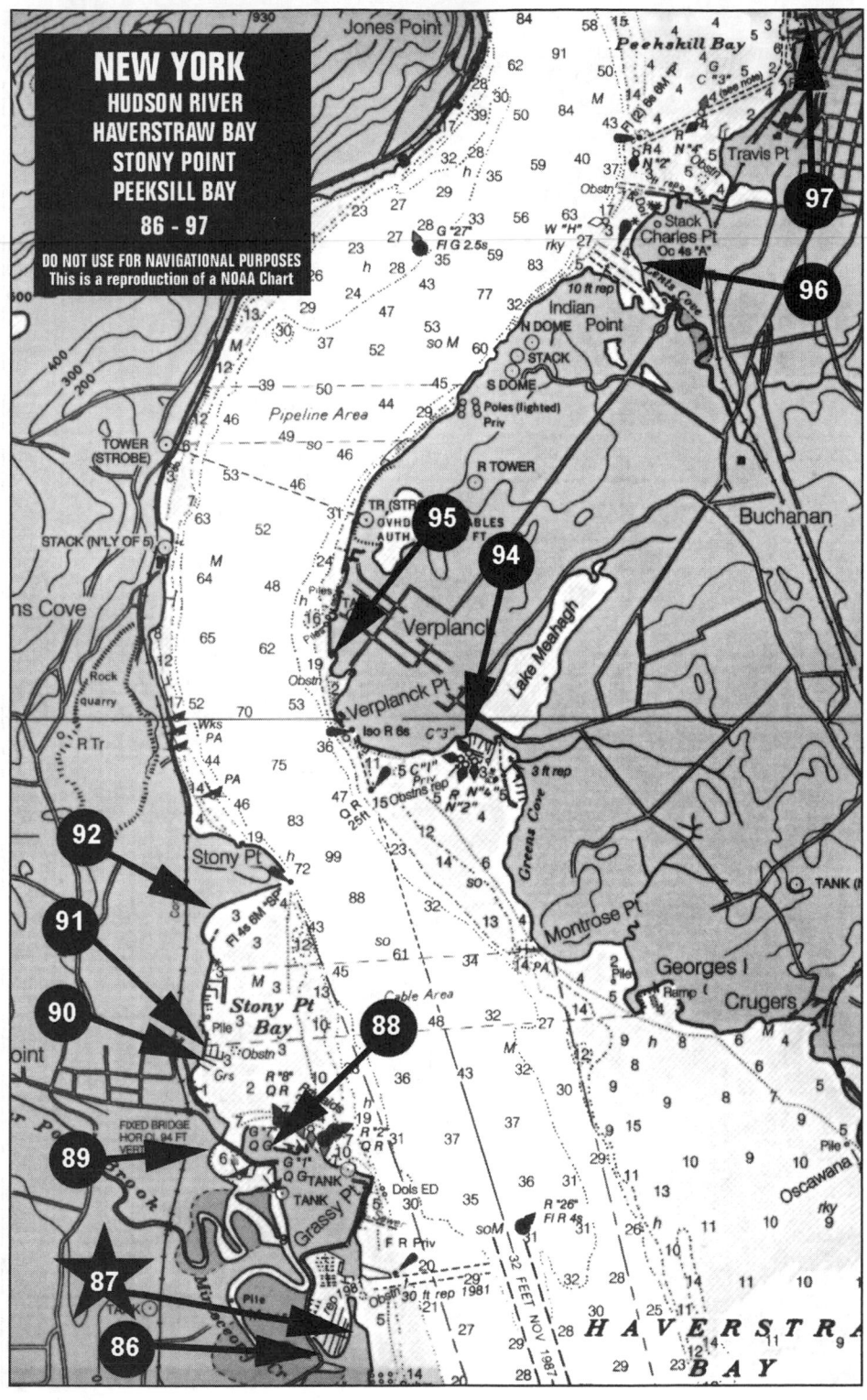

New York, Hudson River, Haverstraw Bay, Stony Point, Peekskill Bay

NEW YORK
HUDSON RIVER
HAVERSTRAW BAY
STONY POINT
PEEKSILL BAY
86 - 97

DO NOT USE FOR NAVIGATIONAL PURPOSES
This is a reproduction of a NOAA Chart

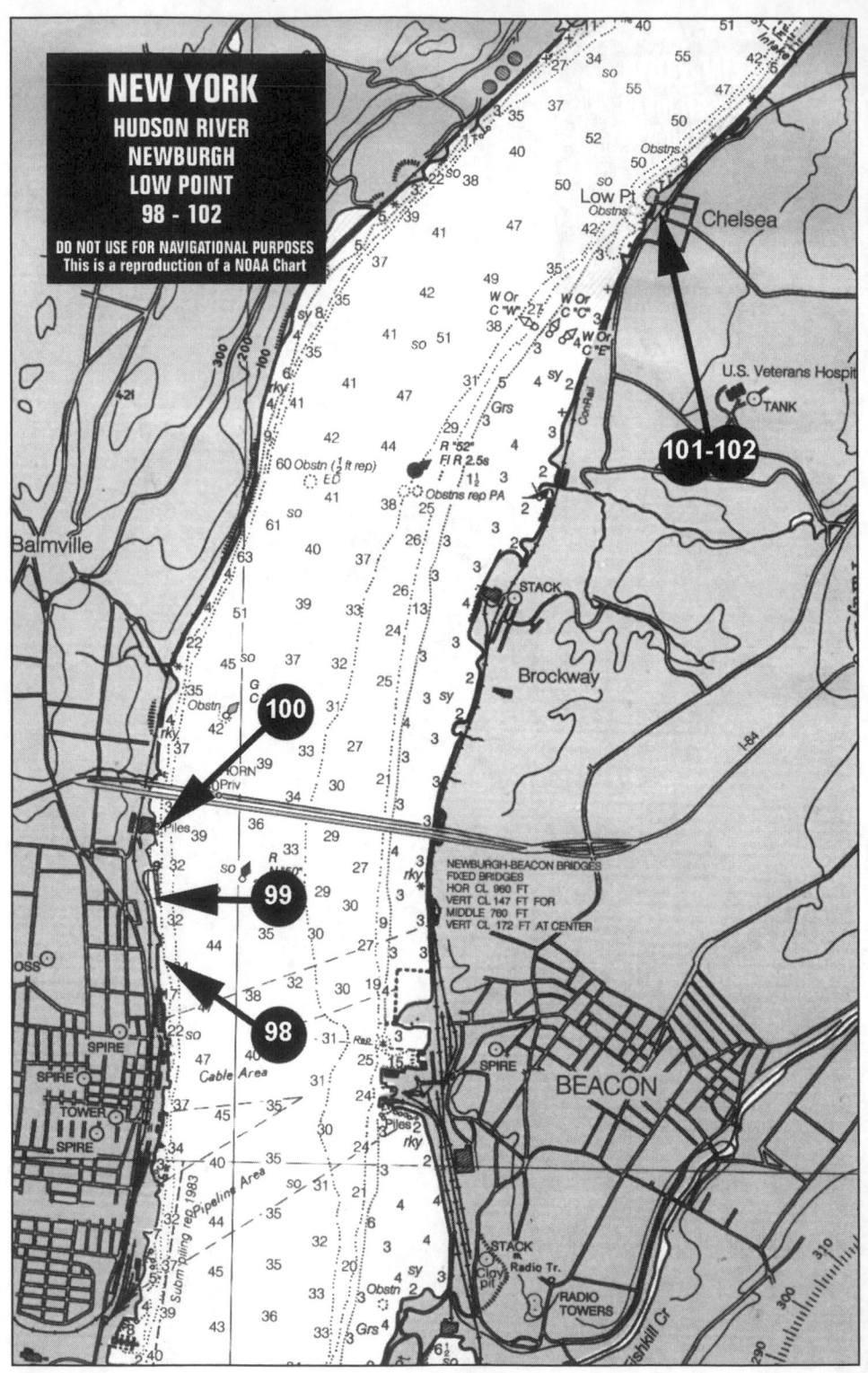

NEW YORK
HUDSON RIVER
NEWBURGH
LOW POINT
98 - 102

DO NOT USE FOR NAVIGATIONAL PURPOSES
This is a reproduction of a NOAA Chart

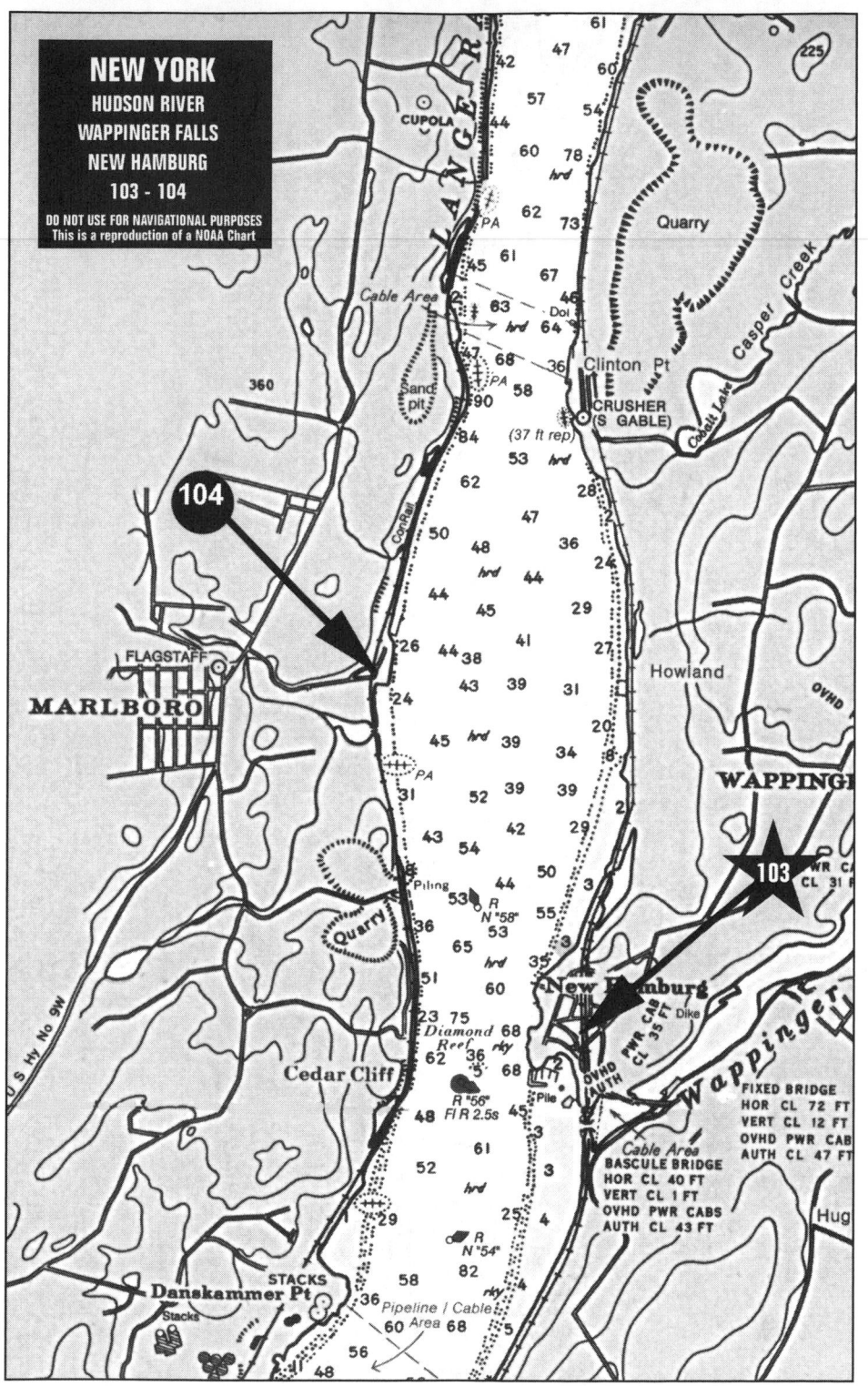

NEW YORK
HUDSON RIVER
WAPPINGER FALLS
NEW HAMBURG
103 - 104
DO NOT USE FOR NAVIGATIONAL PURPOSES
This is a reproduction of a NOAA Chart

CUPOLA

Quarry

Casper Creek

61
47
42
57
60 78
62 73
61
67
45
63
64
68
58
36
84
53
62
47
50
48
44
45
44
26 44 38
24
45 39
31
52 39
43
54
44
53
65
60
51
23 75
62
36
68
48
61
52
25
82

Cable Area

Sand pit

Clinton Pt
CRUSHER
(S GABLE)
Cobalt Lake

(37 ft rep)

28
24
29
27
20

Howland

WAPPINGER

WR CAB
CL 31 FT

104

FLAGSTAFF

MARLBORO

Quarry

Piling
R N "58"

Cedar Cliff

Diamond Reef
R "56"
Fl R 2.5s

R N "54"

STACKS
Danskammer Pt
Stacks

Pipeline / Cable Area

103

New Hamburg
Dike

OVHD PWR CAB
AUTH CL 35 FT

Wappinger

FIXED BRIDGE
HOR CL 72 FT
VERT CL 12 FT
OVHD PWR CAB
AUTH CL 47 FT

Cable Area
BASCULE BRIDGE
HOR CL 40 FT
VERT CL 1 FT
OVHD PWR CABS
AUTH CL 43 FT

Hug

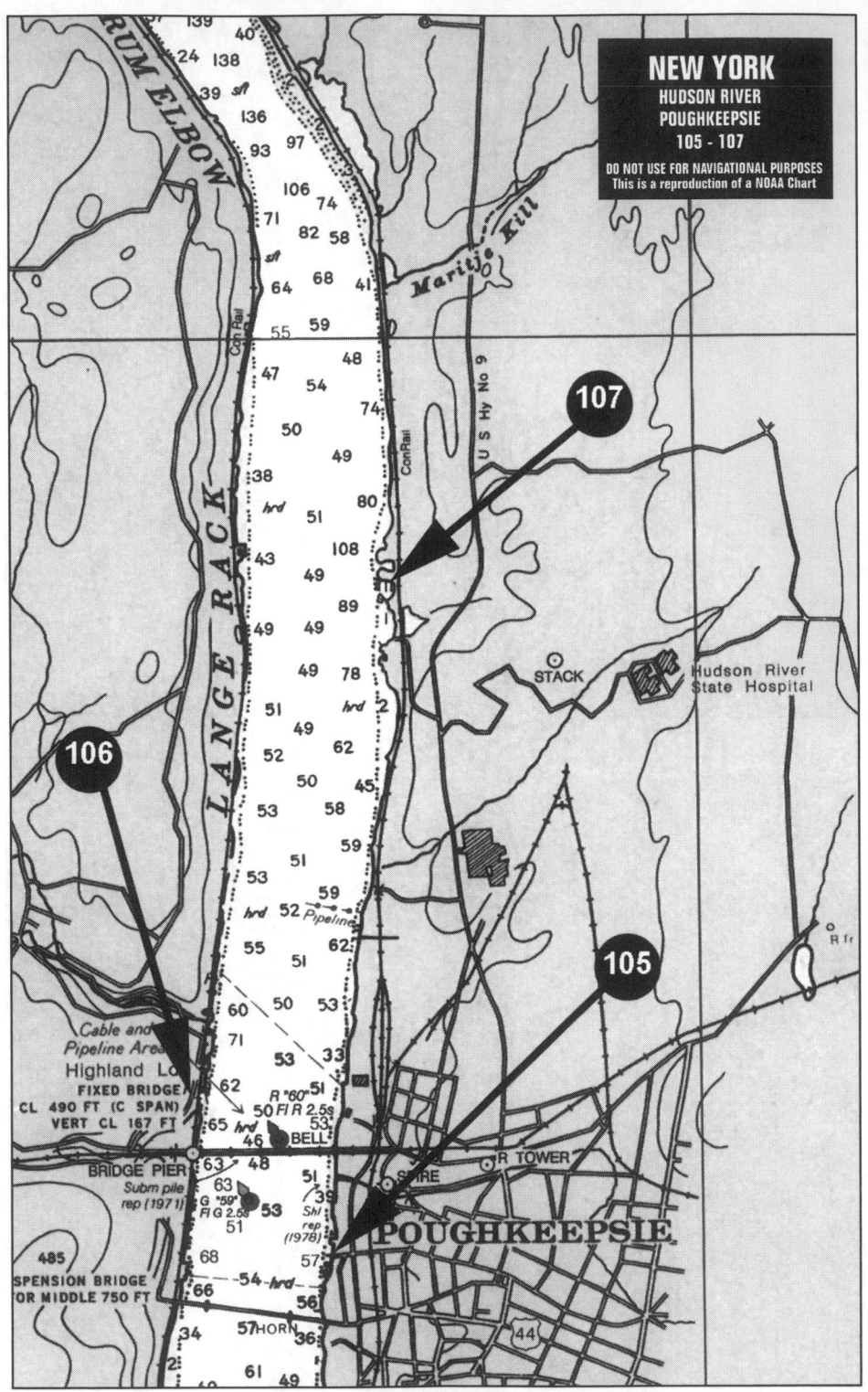

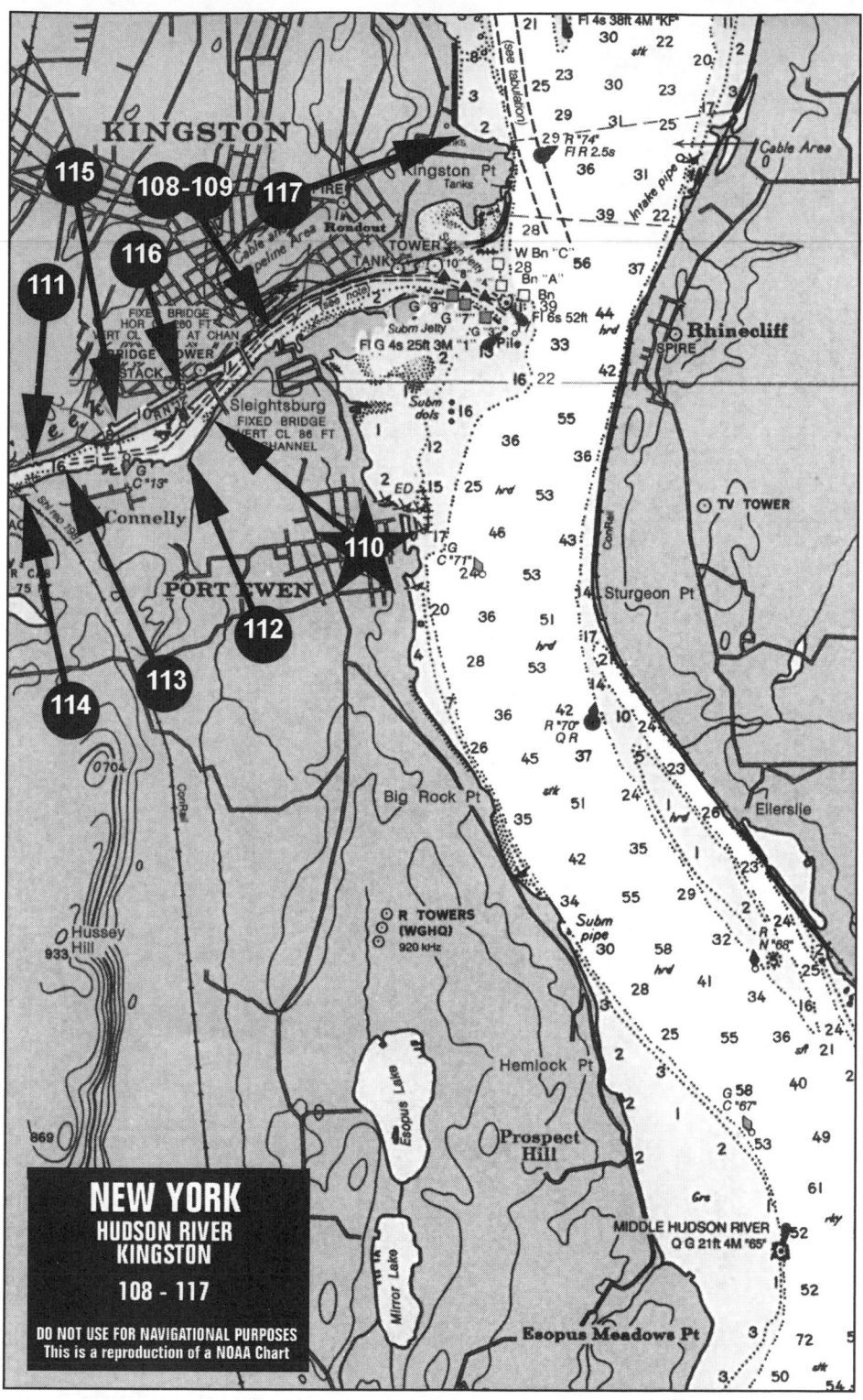

NEW YORK
HUDSON RIVER
KINGSTON

108 - 117

DO NOT USE FOR NAVIGATIONAL PURPOSES
This is a reproduction of a NOAA Chart

353

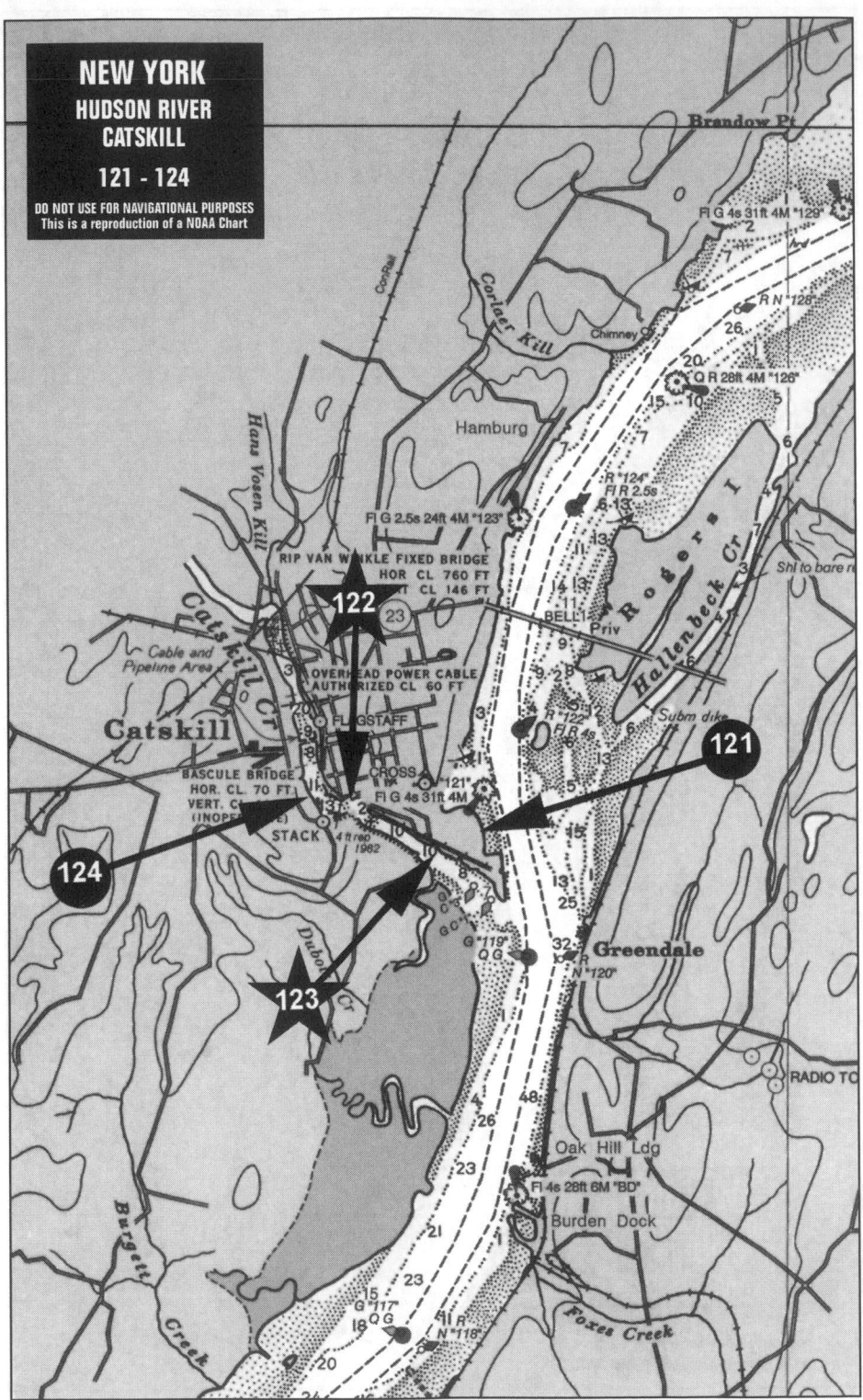

NEW YORK
HUDSON RIVER
CATSKILL
121 - 124

DO NOT USE FOR NAVIGATIONAL PURPOSES
This is a reproduction of a NOAA Chart

354

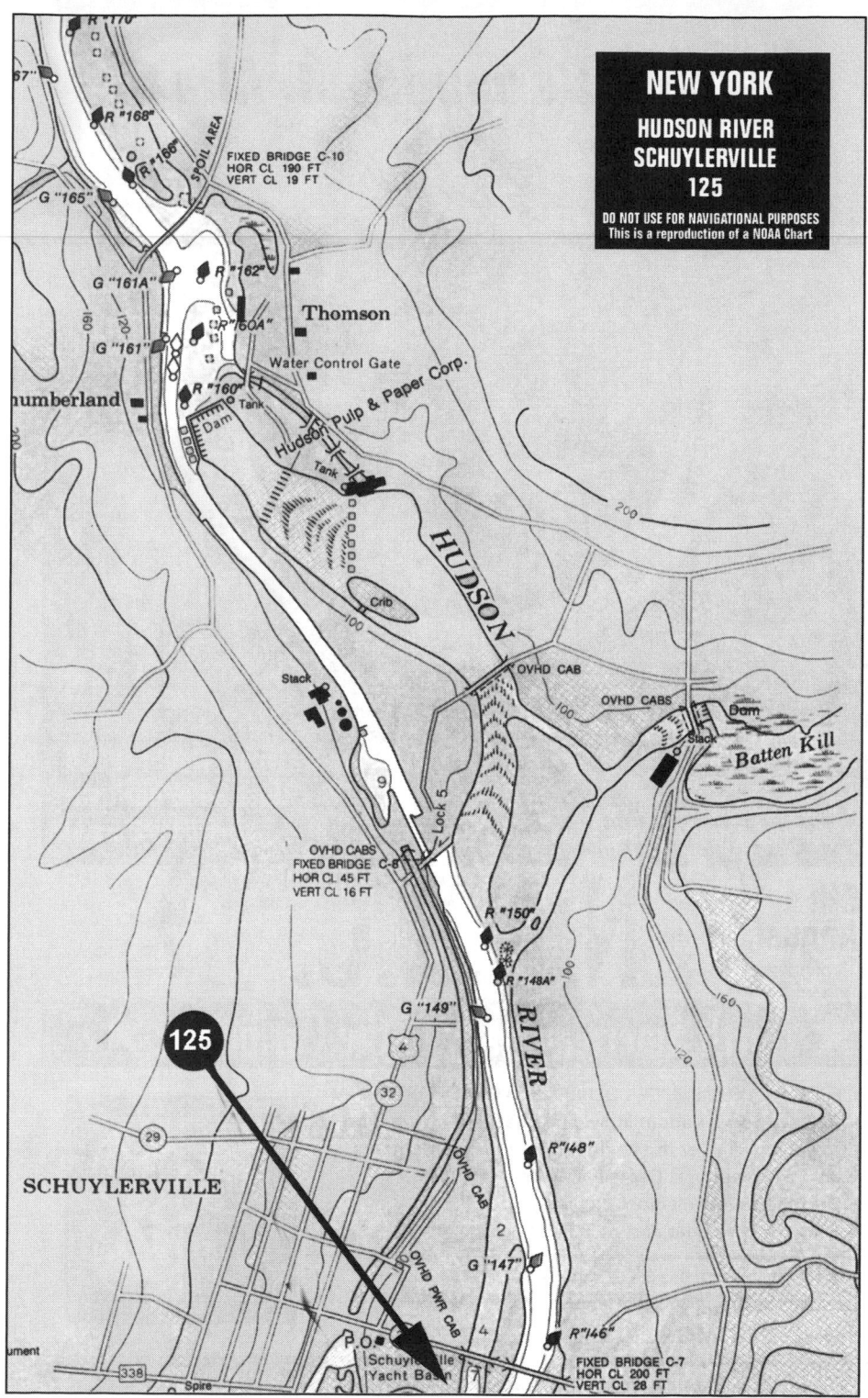

NEW YORK
HUDSON RIVER
SCHUYLERVILLE
125

DO NOT USE FOR NAVIGATIONAL PURPOSES
This is a reproduction of a NOAA Chart

355

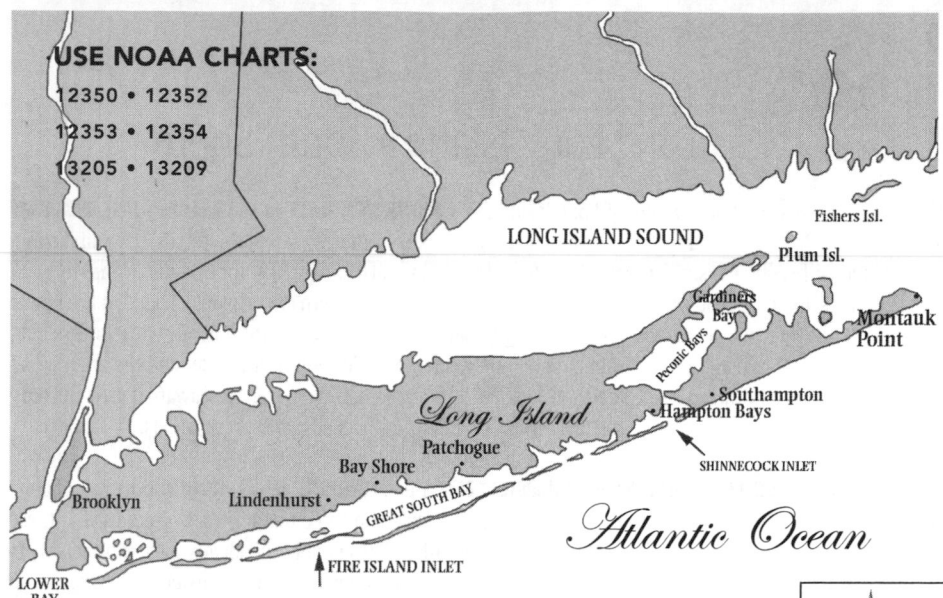

USE NOAA CHARTS:

12350 • 12352

12353 • 12354

13205 • 13209

LONG ISLAND SOUND

Fishers Isl.

Plum Isl.

Gardiners Bay

Montauk Point

Peconic Bays

Southampton

Hampton Bays

Long Island

Patchogue

Bay Shore

SHINNECOCK INLET

Brooklyn

Lindenhurst •

GREAT SOUTH BAY

Atlantic Ocean

↑ FIRE ISLAND INLET

LOWER BAY

Long Island's South Shore

Map is not intended for navigational purposes.

THE FOLLOWING REGIONS ARE COVERED IN CHARTS IN THIS SECTION:

www.BoatersAlmanac.com

Cruising Long Island's South Shore

This section covers the South Shore of Long Island from **SHINNECOCK INLET to and including EAST ROCKAWAY INLET**; several other inlets making into the beach along this part of the coast; and the canals, bays, and tributaries inside the beach. The south coast of Long Island has a general trend of 247° for 68 miles from Montauk Point to Fire Island Inlet, and then trends 263° for 36 miles to the western end of Coney Island in the Lower Bay on New York Harbor. It is a clear shore and may be safely approached as close as a mile with not less than 30 feet depth anywhere between Montauk Point and Rockaway Inlet. Fire Island Inlet and the inlets westward side the shore should be given a berth of a least 1.5 miles. When viewed from seaward it presents only a few prominent features, it is composed of a series of sand dunes backed by low dark woods.

SHINNECOCK, MORICHES, GREAT SOUTH BAY, and HEMPSTEAD BAYS are inside the beach along the south coast of Long Island and form an inside route for boats of about 3-foot draft. The three main inlets from the sea to these bays are Fire Island Inlet, Jones Inlet, and East Rockaway Inlet. These inlets and all auxiliary channels within the south coast of Long Island have numerous wrecks, obstructions, frequent and extensive changes, and although marked in many areas, local knowledge is advantageous. Two small inlets, Shinnecock Inlet and Moriches Inlet, which broke through in 1938 and 1931 respectively, are also used by small boats for entrance to these bays. Local knowledge is recommended.

LONG ISLAND INTRACOASTAL WATERWAY is a Federal project that provides for a 6-foot channel from **SHINNECOCK CANAL to GREAT SOUTH BAY**. The cuts provide an inland waterway along the south side of Long Island. This waterway, from the south end of Shinnecock Canal to a point in Great South Bay opposite Patchogue (a distance of about 29.2 miles) is subject to frequent shoaling. Mariners are advised to obtain local knowledge.

CHARTS 12352, 12353. SHINNECOCK CANAL, southwestward of Montauk Point, is about 1 mile long and connects Great Peconic Bay with Shinnecock Bay. The canal is owned and maintained by Suffolk County of New York. It is a partly dredged cut and is protected at the north entrance by two jetties; a light marks the east jetty. A lock about midway in the canal is 250 feet long, 41 feet wide, with a depth of 12 feet over the sills. Tide gates are parallel to and westward of the lock. The lock gates and tide gates are constructed so that tidal action open them to allow the current to set south through the canal and closes them to prevent water from Shinnecock Bay to flow back into Great Peconic Bay. The lock gates are tended 24 hours and are opened mechanically when the tidal current is flowing northward to allow the passage of boats. Red and green traffic lights are at each end of the lock. Vessels are allowed to enter the lock only on the green signal. The fixed bridges and overhead power cables across the canal have a least clearance of 22 feet. The maximum-recorded current is 4.3 knots, southerly, through the lock and tide gates at peak flow when the gates are open.

FYI: LONG ISLAND extends approximately 118 miles east-northeast from the mouth of the Hudson River. The island is 20 miles at its widest point and comprises 1,377 square miles. Surrounding the island are 23 lighthouses – five are on the South Shore.

SHINNECOCK INLET, 31 miles westward for Montauk Point along the south coast of Long Island, is the easternmost entrance from the Atlantic to Shinnecock Bay and the inland water route, also the south shore of Long Island. A lighted whistle buoy marks the approach to the inlet. Local knowledge is recommended.

SHINNECOCK LIGHT, 65 feet above the water is shown from a red skeleton tower on the west side of the inlet. A fog signal and radiobeacon are at the light. Private lights are on the jetties at the entrance to the inlet, and

TO FIND MARINA LOCATIONS - SEE THE TABLES AND LOCATOR CHARTS AT THE END OF THIS SECTION.

SOUTH SHORE

uncharted buoys mark the channel. The jetties extend about 120 yards beyond the lights marking them.

QUOQUE CANAL connects Shinnecock Bay with Quantuck Bay. A highway drawbridge with clearance of 15 feet closed, crosses the canal.

MORICHES BAY extends for about 8 miles from Quantuck Canal to Narrow Bay and provides an inside passage for small boats. The general depths in the bay range from 5 to 7 feet, but the southern part is shoal.

CHARTS 12326, 12353, 12352. FIRE ISLAND extends west from Moriches Inlet for about 28 miles along the south shore of Long Island to Fire Island Inlet. With the exception of the State Park occupying its westernmost 4.6 miles, all of Fire Island is part of the Fire Island National Seashore.

ORCHARD NECK CREEK, 1.7 miles west of Tuthill Point, is extensively used by local small craft as a mooring basin. A reported depth of about 3 feet is available to the head of navigation. A private seasonal lighted buoy marks the entrance. Yachtsmen use Areskonk Creek immediately westward of Orchard Neck Creek as a harbor. A privately dredged channel marked by private seasonal buoys leads to the head of the creek. Forge River at the northwest end of Moriches Bay about 0.5 miles westward of the common entrance to Senix and Mud Creeks is entered through a privately dredged channel that leads to the town dock and turning basin at Mastic.

The docks of a yacht club is on the northwest side of **BELLPORT BAY** at the town of Bellport. A seasonal passenger ferry operates between the yacht club and Bellport Beach on Fire Island. Swan River about 0.4 miles westward of Mud Creek is entered through a privately dredged channel that leads to the head of navigation about 1 mile above the mouth.

PATCHOGUE RIVER, on the north side of the Great South Bay 3.7 miles west of Bellport and 0.9 miles westward of Swan River, is entered through a dredged channel that leads from Great South Bay.

COREY CREEK, 0.6 miles westward of Patchogue River, is entered between two jetties each marked by a private seasonal light. **BROWN CREEK,** locally known as Browns River, is 3 miles westward of Patchogue. It is entered between two short jetties extending out to a depth of about 4 feet. The west jetty is marked at the south end by a light and the east jetty by a daybeacon.

The **CONNETQUOT RIVER,** locally known as 'Great River,' is 3 miles westward of Brown Creek and has a depth of 5 feet. A prominent mansion, once belonging to the Vanderbilts, with a tower (now part of a college campus) is on the north shore of the entrance. There is good anchorage and great dinghy exploring to be done. Favor the eastern shore when entering the area.

WATCH HILL, part of Fire Island National Seashore, is across Great South Bay from Patchogue. Private seasonal lighted buoys and a lighted range mark the channel. A passenger ferry operates between Watch Hill and Patchogue.

CHERRY GROVE is a summer resort across Great South Bay from the Connetquot River; it has a boat landing extending out to a depth of 5 feet. Seasonal ferry service is maintained with Sayville. Point 'O' Woods, Ocean

SOUTH SHORE

Beach, Fair Harbor and Saltaire are summer resorts on the Great South Bay westward of Cherry Grove. Sailor's Haven, across Great South Bay from Nicole Point, is part of the Fire Island National Seashore. A privately dredged and marked channel with a depth of about 4 feet leads from Great South Bay to a seasonally operated marina at which berthing, water, ice and some supplies are available.

FIRE ISLAND INLET, about 28 miles westward along the south coast of Long Island from Moriches Inlet, is the only direct entrance from the Atlantic To Great South Bay. The inlet is subject to frequent changes and has been moving westward for many years. Mariners are warned to beware of extreme tidal turbulence especially during times of tidal change and should seek local knowledge of the latest conditions before entering. Navigation of the inlet is difficult even with relatively calm seas, and for small craft it can be extremely dangerous. During heavy weather breakers usually obstruct the entrance.

FIRE ISLAND LIGHT, 167 feet above the water, is shown from a black and white horizontally banded tower about 14 miles east- northeastward of Democrat Point. Fire Island Coast Guard Station is about 2 miles west southwestward of the light. The Robert Moses Causeway Bridge over Fire Island Inlet, has a clearance of 65 feet at the 464-foot center span. The bridge is an excellent radar target at a range of more than 12 miles. The currents in Fire Island Inlet, after crossing the bar, have a velocity of about 2.4 knots at full strength and are influenced greatly by the force and direction of the wind.

From Fire Island Inlet the **STATE BOAT CHANNEL** leads westward through Great South Bay and South Oyster Bay to Zacks Bay at Jones Beach State Park, thence westward in Hempstead Bay through winding channels, well marked by lights buoys, and daybeacons to Reynolds Channel at Point Lookout, just west of Jones Inlet. Two buoys mark submerged obstructions on the south side of the entrance to the channel. The Robert Moses Causeway Bridge over the State Boat Channel, connecting oak Beach with Captree island has twin bascule spans with a clearance of 29 feet at the center.

HEMPSTEAD BAY is on the south side of Long Island inside the beach extending from the west end of Great South Bay to Far Rockaway. The bay has many sloughs that are subject to change in the vicinity of the inlets and where dredging is done to reclaim land. The town of Hempstead maintains navigational aids marking the main channels of the bay. Many shoal spots, some up to a foot or less, have been reported at several areas of the rivers and channels.

JONES BEACH STATE PARK on the south coast of Long Island comprises about 2500 acres and is under the jurisdiction of the Long Island State Park and Recreation Commission. A prominent red brick tower, 202 feet high, with a pyramid top is 3.5 miles eastward of Jones Inlet and marks the center of Central Mall. The tower, floodlighted at night, is visible 25 miles.

ZACHS BAY a dredged basin above Jones Beach State Park, has depths of 4 to 29 feet. The eastern part of Zachs Bay is used an anchorage; a swimming area marked by private buoys is in the western part of the bay.

JONES INLET, about 12 miles westward along the south coast of Long Island from Fire Island Inlet, is the principal entrance from the Atlantic to the inside passages and towns in Hempstead Bay. The inlet, which is used

mostly by pleasure craft and fishermen, should not be attempted without local knowledge because the channel and depths are constantly changing. A lighted whistle buoy marks the approach. A light is at the outer end and a radiobeacon is at the inner end of the jetty on the east side of the entrance to Jones Inlet. The tidal current in the inlet has a velocity of about 3 knots. The mean range of tide is 3.6 feet.

FREEPORT is a major boating center on the ocean side of Long Island appealing to sportfishing enthusiasts. The area is reached through **LONG CREEK**, and there are many marinas for transients starting from the entrance to Hudson Channel and the Woodcleft Canal. Recently the town has completed a major waterfront make-over and once again it has the feel of an old fashioned seafaring village bringing boaters to enjoy the services offered by dockside businesses. Freeport has several waterfront areas: Woodcleft Canal, Hudson Channel, and Freeport Creek.

SOUTH SHORE

FREEPORT CREEK leads northward from the Narrows. **HUDSON CHANNEL** extends northward to the piers at Freeport. **WOODCLEFT CANAL** is westward of Hudson Channel. Woodcleft Canal is the place to go for docking and dining. **Otto's Sea Grill** (516-378-9480) offers free dockage for hungry boaters, and caters to families, offering fresh seafood. The restaurant also has an outdoor clam bar so patrons can watch the comings and goings along the canal front. Also on the canal is **The Schooner Restaurant** (516-378-7575) offering dockage for diners and beautiful views of the waterfront.

HOG ISLAND CHANNEL, the main route to the towns of Oceanside and East Rockaway, joins Reynolds Channel southwestward of Island Park and leads westward of Island Park, then eastward of West, East and North Meadows. East Rockaway Channel privately marked and an alternate and shallower route to the towns, joins Hog Island Channel above Reynolds Channel. Oceanside and East Rockaway are along the east and west sides, respectively, of the northern part of East Rockaway Channel.

ATLANTIC BEACH is an oceanfront and bayside community on the east side of East Rockaway Inlet. Facilities for mooring are eastward and westward of the highway bridge.

EAST ROCKAWAY INLET, about 8 miles westward along the south coast of Long Island from Jones Inlet, is the westernmost entrance from the Atlantic to Hempstead Bay, and the inland water route along the south shore of Long Island. The inlet is subject to frequent changes, but is reported to be usually safer to navigate than Jones or Fire Island Inlets. The aids marking the inlet are periodically moved. Local knowledge is advised. ⚓

AUTHORIZED SERVICE CENTERS

Kydd's Marine Center

25 ALHAMBRA ROAD, MASSAPEQUA, NY 11758

CHART LOCATOR NO. 175

516-541-7747

Precision Marine

2936 ARROWHEAD PLACE, SEAFORD HARBOR, NY 11783

CHART LOCATOR NO. 186

516-785-3013

South Shore Boats - Surfside 3

P.O. BOX 1706, LIBRARY AVENUE, WESTHAMPTON BEACH, NY 11978

CHART LOCATOR NO. 26

631-388-2400

LONG ISLAND South FACILITIES alphabetical index

L.I. South Shore

MARINA'S NAME & PHONE NUMBER

Chart Locater Number	Marina's Name & Phone Number	When Open	Monitors VHF Channel	Transient: Electricity • Moorings • Berths	Hull repairs • Engine repairs • Ramp	Winter Storage: Wet • Dry	Railway Capacity in Feet	Lift Capacity in Tons	Boat Rental: Canoe • Row • Motor	Restaurant • Charter • Lodging • House • Camping • Sail	Showers • Laundry	Pumpout • Toilets	Bait • Tackle • Water • Ice	Groceries • Hardware	Diesel fuel • Gasoline
1	RIPTIDE RESTAURANT 631-728-7373	ALL YR		B						RL		T	I		
2	SHINNECOCK MARINA 631-852-8291	MAY SEP		EB						RL	S	PT	W		
3	MARINER'S COVE MARINE 631-728-0286	ALL YR.		EB	HE R	W D			C	RL	S	T	IW BT	H	
4	MODERN YACHTS 631-728-2266	ALL YR		EB	HE	D		40		RL	S	PT	IW	H	G D
5	SPELLMANS MARINE 631-728-9200	MAY SEP		EB	HE	D		25	M	RL	S	T	IW BT	HG	
6	HAMPTON HARBOR MARINA 631-728-8200	ALL YR.	16	EB	HE	D		30		R	S	PT	IW BT	H	G D
7	PELL'S DOCK 631-728-5100	APR OCT		EB	M					R	S	T	IW BT	GH	G D
8	OAKLAND'S MARINA 631-728-6900	ALL YR	68	EB	E				C	R	S	PT	IW BT	H	G D
9	SHINNECOCK Fishing Station 631-728-6116	APR NOV							RM	L			BT		
10	BAYVIEW HOUSE 631-728-3197	JUN SEP								RL	S	T	I		
11	TULLY'S HARBOR REST. 631-728-9111	MAR OCT		EB						RL					
12	OSCAR'S FISHING STATION 631-924-2224	MAR NOV								RL		T	IBT		
13	MOLNARS LANDING 631-728-1860	ALL YR	68		HE	D				R	S	T	IW BT		G
14	MILL RIVER BOAT WORKS 631-728-6768	ALL YR.		EB	HE R	D						T	W	H	
15	PONQUOGUE MARINA 631-728-2264	MAR DEC		EB	HE	W D	60	25			S	T	W	H	
16	BAYWATCH MOTEL & MARINA 631-728-4550	ALL YR.			R	D				L		T	I		
17	SPELLMAN'S MARINE INC. 631-728-1341	ALL YR.		EB	HE	D		25		L	S	T	IW	H	
18	HAMPTON Watercraft Marine 631-728-0922	ALL YR.			HE	W D		4	M			T		H	
19	FRANK'S LANDING 631-728-0619	ALL YR.			HE R	D						T	W	H	G
21	COLONIAL SHORES MARINA 631-728-0011	ALL YR.			R				RM	L	L		W	BT	

L.I. South Shore

MARINA'S NAME & PHONE NUMBER

Column legend (diagonal headers): MONITORS VHF CHANNEL · WHEN OPEN · TRANSIENT Electricity • Moorings • Berths · Hull repairs • Engine repairs • Ramp · WINTER STORAGE: Wet • Dry · RAILWAY CAPACITY IN FEET · LIFT CAPACITY IN TONS · BOAT RENTAL: Canoe • Row • Motor · BOAT RENTAL: Charter • House • Sail · Restaurant • Lodging • House • Camping · Showers • Laundry · Bait • Tackle · Pumpout • Toilets · Groceries • Water • Ice · Hardware · Diesel fuel • Gasoline

#	Marina Name & Phone	When Open	VHF	Transient	Repairs	Winter	Railway (ft)	Lift (tons)	Boat Rental C/R/M	Restaurant/Lodging	Showers/Laundry	Bait/Tackle	Pumpout/Toilets	Groceries	Hardware	Diesel/Gas
22	SWISS AIRE RESORT 631-728-6200	ALL YR								L						
23	TIANA BAY OWNERS INC 631-728-1488	APR NOV		EB						L	S	T		IW		
24	HAMPTON SHIPYARD 631-653-6777	ALL YR.		EB	HE	D	65	25		RL		T				
25	ALDRICH BOATYARD INC 631-653-5300	MAR NOV			HE	D		35								
26	**SOUTH SHORE BOATS 631-288-2400**	ALL YR.	79		HE	D		10				T		I WB	H	G
27	WESTHAMPTON MARINA 631-288-9496	APR OCT		EB	R						S	T				
28	BATH & TENNIS Y. C. 631-288-2500	MAY OCT		EB						RL	SL		PT	IW		
29	SOUTH HAMPTON TOWN RAMP				R											
30	EASTPORT MARINA 631-325-8900	ALL YR.		EB	HE	D		35			SL	T		IW BT	H	G
31	REMSENBURG MARINA LTD 631-325-1677	ALL YR.	68	EB	HE R	D		25	M		S		PT	IW BT	H	G D
32	BROOKHAVEN TOWN RAMP				R											
34	ABBOTT'S HARTS COVE MARINA 631-878-3700	ALL YR			HE	D		15				T		IW	H	G
35	WINDSWEPT MARINE 631-878-2100	ALL YR.		EB	HE R	D		7		R	S	T		IW BT	H	G
36	MORICHES BOAT & MOTOR 631-878-0023	ALL YR.			H			7				T				G
37	SILLY LILY FISHING STATION 631-878-0247	MAR NOV		B		W			MR	RM		T		IW BT		G
38	TADSEN'S FISHING STATION 631-878-1120	MAR NOV	13 / 9		R	D		5	RM	R		R		IW BT		G
39	CERULLO BROTHERS MARINA 631-878-1180	MAR NOV	9 / 68	EB	HE R	D		6	M	R		T		IW BT		G
40	DAVISON MARINA 631-878-9400	ALL YR.	68	EB	HE	D		10			S	T		W	H	G
42	AL GROVERS MARINA 631-874-2111	ALL YR.	68	EB	HE	D		10		RL	S	T		IW BT	H	G
43	F.J.M. MARINE SERVICE & 631-878-1235	ALL YR.				D		6						W		

L.I. South Shore

Chart Locater Number	Marina's Name & Phone Number	When Open	Monitors VHF Channel	Transient: Electricity • Moorings • Berths	Hull repairs • Engine repairs • Ramp	Winter Storage: Wet • Dry	Railway Capacity in Tons	Lift Capacity in Feet	Boat Rental: Canoe • Row • Motor	Boat Rental: Charter • House • Sail	Restaurant • Lodging • Camping	Showers • Laundry	Pumpout • Toilets	Bait • Tackle • Water • Ice	Groceries • Hardware	Diesel fuel • Gasoline
44	PENDZICK'S BOAT YARD 631-878-2244	ALL YR.			HE	D	35	20								
46	SENIX MARINA INC 631-874-2092	ALL YR.		B	HE R	D		15			R	S	T	IW	H	G D
47	CENTER Y. C. 631-874-2200	ALL YR.	68	EB	HE	W D		35			R	S	T	IW	H	G D
49	FORGE RIVER MARINA 631-395-3993			B	R								PT	W		
50	MASTIC BEACH Y. C. 631-281-9795										R		T	IW		
51	STIRIZ'S MARINA 631-399-0661	MAR NOV		EB	HE	D		18					T	IW BT	H	G
52	CAPT ANDY'S FISHING ST. 631-281-9897	ALL YR.		B						R	R		T	IW BT		
54	BEAVER DAM BOAT BASIN 631-286-0440	ALL YR.		B	E	W D		30								
55	BELLPORT VILLAGE DOCK				R								T			
56	PATCHOGUE SHORES 631-475-0790	ALL YR.		EB	HE	W D		25			R	S	PT	IW		
57	DOCKSIDE 500 INC 631-289-3800	ALL YR.		EB	HE	W D		30			R	S	T	IW	H	G
58	MORGAN Swan River MARINA 631-758-3524	ALL YR.		EB	HE R	W D					R	S	PT	IW	GH	
59	SANDSPIT MARINA 631-475-1592			B							R		T			
60	SUN-DEK MARINA 631-654-8826			EB	HE	W D					R	S	T	IW		G
61	PATCHOGUE RIVER MARINA 631-758-0257	ALL YR		EB	HE	D		25			R	S	TP	IW		
62	FRANK WEEKS YACHT YARD 631-475-1675	ALL YR.		EB	HE	W D		40					T	W	H	
63	LEEWARD COVE MARINA 631-758-2550	MAR JAN		EB	HE	W D		6				S	PT	IW		
64	THOMAS MARINE 631-289-0621	ALL YR.						10								
65	AMERICAN BOATWORKS INC 631-654-8939	ALL YR		B	H E	W D		40					T	W	H	
66	PIER 66 MARINA 631-654-3106	AL YR.		B	H E	D		25					S PT	IW		

L.I. South Shore

CHART LOCATER NUMBER	MARINA'S NAME & PHONE NUMBER	WHEN OPEN	MONITORS VHF CHANNEL	Transient Electricity • Moorings • Berths	Hull repairs • Engine repairs • Ramp	WINTER STORAGE: Wet • Dry	RAILWAY CAPACITY IN FEET	LIFT CAPACITY IN TONS	BOAT RENTAL: Charter • House • Motor	Restaurant • Lodging • Camping	Showers • Laundry	Pumpout • Toilets	Bait • Tackle • Water • Ice	Groceries • Hardware	Diesel fuel • Gasoline
67	SOUTH BAY BOAT REPAIR 631-758-0909	ALL YR.		EB	HE	W D	30			R		T	IW		
68	BROOKHAVEN TOWN DOCK			R											
69	BLUE POINT MARINE INC 631-363-2000	ALL YR.		EB	HE	D	30			R		T	IW BT	H	G D
70	COREY CREEK PARK											P			
71	DAVIS PARK 631-451-6100	MAY OCT		B						R	S	PT	IW	G	
72	WATCH HILL MARINA 631-597-6644	MAY OCT		EB						R	S	PT	IW	G	
74	TABAT MARINE 631-363-6065	ALL YR.		EB	HE R	D	15				S	T	I WT	GH	G
75	BAYPORT TOWN DOCK			R											
77	BAYPORT MARINE COMPANY 631-472-1844	ALL YR.			HE	D	25	C					W	H	
78	STEIN'S BOAT SALES INC 631-567-3313	ALL YR.	10	EB	ER	W D	15					T	I	H	
79	GREENE'S CREEK MARINA 631-549-5408	ALL YR.	16 11	EB	HE	W D	60	C			S	PT	BT WI	H	
80	BROWN'S RIVER MARINE INC 631-589-5550	ALL YR.			HE	D	65								
82	**WESTIN'S BOAT SHOP INC 631-589-1526**	**ALL YR.**	**10**	**EB**	**HE**	**D**	**12**					**T**	**W**	**H**	**D G**
83	LAND'S END MOTEL & MARINA 631-589-2040	ALL YR.	16 78	EB	HE R	WD	20			RL			IW	H	G D
85	BOATEL FIRE ISLAND PINES 631-597-6500	MAY SEP		EB						RL	S	T	IW	G	
88	WEST SAYVILLE BOAT BASIN 631-589-4141	ALL YR.		EB	HE R	W D	75	M	S	R	S	PT	IW BT	G H	G
89	SAILORS HAVEN 631-597-6183			B							S	PT		G	
90	SCHOONER INN 631-583-9561	JUN SEP	9					CR M	R			I	G		
92	VANDERBILT WHARF MARINA 631-567-1231	ALL YR.			HE	D	40	7		R			IW BT	G H	G
93	RIVERVIEW RESTAURANT 631-589-2694			B						R		T			

Chart Locater Number	Marina's Name & Phone Number	When Open	Monitors VHF Channel	Transient Electricity • Moorings • Berths	Hull repairs • Engine repairs • Ramp	Winter Storage: Wet • Dry	Railway Capacity in Tons	Lift Capacity in Feet	Boat Rental	Restaurant • Lodging • Camping	Showers • Laundry	Pumpout • Toilets	Bait • Tackle • Water • Ice	Groceries • Hardware	Diesel fuel • Gasoline
94	OAKDALE YACHT SERVICE 631-589-1087	ALL YR.		EB	HE	D		50			S	PT	I W		G D
95	NICOLL'S POINT MARINA 631-589-8282	ALL YR.				D		2				T	I WB	H	
96	SNAPPER INN 631-589-0248	ALL YR.								R					
97	SUFFOLK CO. EAST MARINA 631-854-4949			EB						R		PT	W		G
98	SUFFOLK COUNTY MARINA 631-854-4949									R			W		
99	HECKSCHER STATE PARK 631-581-2100	ALL YR.			R										
101	EAST ISLIP MARINA 631-224-5648				R							T	IW		
102	CHAMPLINS CREEK MARINA				R										
103	ARNOTT BOAT YARD 631-581-5808	ALL YR.			HE	D		25						H	
104	MARTIN'S MARINE 631-277-4558				E										
105	ISLIP TOWN DOCK				R										
108	COASTAL YACHTING MARINA 631-665-5144	ALL YR.		EB	HE	W D		30			S	T	W	H	D
109	SEABORN MARINA INC 631-665-0037	ALL YR.	16	EB		W D		75		RL		T	W	H	G D
110	POINT O' WOODS FERRY 631-665-1568														G D
111	SHORELINE MARINE 631-968-4600	ALL YR.			HE	D		35					WB T		G
112	BURNETT MARINE SERVICES 631-665-0293	ALL YR.			E	D		12				T		H	
113	FIRE ISLAND FERRIES INC 631-665-3600							60							
115	OUTBOARD MARINE SERVICE 631-665-3885	ALL YR.			HE	D		9				T		H	
116	BAY SHORE MARINA 631-224-5648	APR NOV			R						S	T	IW BT		G D
117	BURNETT BOATEL 631-665-9050	MAR DEC								R	S	T	IW BT	H	

CHART LOCATER NUMBER	MARINA'S NAME & PHONE NUMBER	WHEN OPEN	MONITORS VHF CHANNEL	TRANSIENT Electricity • Moorings • Berths	Hull repairs • Engine repairs • Ramp	WINTER STORAGE: Wet • Dry	RAILWAY CAPACITY IN FEET	LIFT CAPACITY IN TONS	BOAT RENTAL: Canoe • Row • Motor	BOAT RENTAL: Charter • House • Sail	Restaurant • Lodging • Camping	Showers • Laundry	Pumpout • Toilets	Bait • Tackle • Water • Ice	Groceries • Hardware	Diesel fuel • Gasoline
118	CAPT. BILL'S RESTAURANT 631-665-3677	ALL YR.		EB		W D					R		T			
120	ROBERT MOSES PARK 631-669-0449	ALL YR.											T	BT		
121	CAPTREE STATE PARK MARINA	ALL YR.									C		PT	IW BT		G D
123	SOUTHARD'S BOATYARD 631-669-2090	ALL YR.			H	D				S						
124	FROST BOATYARD 631-669-1645	ALL YR.			HE	D		25								
125	SUFFOLK MARINE CENTER 631-669-0907	ALL YR.			HE	W D		12						IW	H	D
127	BABYLON FISHING STATION 631-669-4503	MAR DEC							R M				T	IW BT		G D
128	DEGARMO'S BOATYARD 631-669-0789	ALL YR.		EB	HE	W D		25				S	T	IW	H	
129	OUTBOARD BARN 631-669-6060	ALL YR.			HE R	D	30						T	W		
130	BABYLON COVE MARINE 631-669-2822	ALL YR.			HE			15						W		
132	RAINBOW MARINE SERVICE 631-661-1218	ALL YR.		EB	HE	W D		10				S	T	W	H	
133	BABYLON MARINE INC 631-587-0333				HE	D		40					T	W	H	G
134	BERGEN POINT GAS DOCK 631-661-9234	ALL YR.												IW BT		G
135	BERGEN POINT YACHT BASIN 631-669-3990	ALL YR.			HE	W D		25						W	H	
136	SEA GULL MARINA & REST 631-669-9552			EB							R		T	IW BT		G
137	FRANK & DICK'S BAIT Station 631-587-8442	APR NOV											T	IBT		G D
138	VILLAGE OF LINDENHURST MARINA			EB												
139	RUTHERIG MARINE SERVICE 631-957-5885	ALL YR.			HE	D		15					T	W	H	
140	SURFSIDE 3 MARINA 631-957-5900	ALL YR.	68	EB	HE	W D		25			R	S	PT	IW BT	H G	G D
141	KARL TANK BOATYARD 631-957-5050	ALL YR.			HE	W D		15					T	W	H	

L.I. South Shore

MARINA'S NAME & PHONE NUMBER

Chart Locater No.	Marina's Name & Phone Number	When Open (Monitors VHF)	Transient (Elec/Moorings/Berths)	Hull/Engine Repairs (Ramp)	Winter Storage (Wet/Dry)	Railway Capacity (ft)	Lift Capacity (tons)	Boat Rental (Canoe/Row/Motor)	Charter/Lodging/House/Sail	Restaurant/Lodging/Camping	Showers/Laundry	Pumpout/Toilets	Bait/Tackle/Water/Ice	Groceries/Hardware	Diesel/Gasoline
142	HERBY'S BOATYARD 631-226-7920	ALL YR.		HE	W D		12						W		
143	STERLING MARINE CORP. 631-957-0038	ALL YR.		HE											
145	RPM MARINE 631-957-1901	ALL YR.	B	HE			16						B	H	
146	FIVE ONE NINE MARINA 631-842-1579	ALL YR.	EB	HE	W D		5					T	W	H	
147	LASALA BOATYARD 631-842-3222	ALL YR.	EB	HE	W D		10				S	T	W		G
148	HIDDEN HARBOR MARINE 631-842-0277	ALL YR.		HE	D		10				S	T	W		G
149	SEA-MAR MARINE 631-789-3311	ALL YR.		HE	D							T			
150	THE ANCHORAGE 631-957-7300	AL YR.		HE			70			R	S	PT	I WB	H	G D
151	GILGO BEACH BOAT BASIN 631-826-3339											S	T		
152	PAUL KETCHAM BOATYARD 631-264-5756				D		13								
153	BAYSIDE MARINE 631-598-1464	APR NOV		HE	D		5						W	H	G
155	AMITY HARBOR MARINE 631-842-1280	ALL YR.	E		D		9					T	W	H	G
156	SUMNER BOAT COMPANY 631-264-1830			H											
157	AMITYVILLE RAMP			R											
158	YACHT SERVICE 631-264-2267	ALL YR.		H	D		20					T	W	H	
161	CONSOLIDATED MARINE 516-264-0138			HE	D		12								
162	DELMARINE 516-598-2946	ALL YR.		HE	W D	46	20					T	W	H	
163	PEARL GREY MARINE 516-598-3938	ALL YR.		HE	D		20	RM		R		T	IW BT		G
164	COUNTY LINE MARINE 516-691-8436	ALL YR.		HE	D		15					T	W		
165	T. SMITH & SON MARINE 516-691-4384	ALL YR.		HE	D		20							H	

L.I. South Shore

Chart Locater Number	Marina's Name & Phone Number	When Open	Monitors VHF Channel	Transient: Electricity • Moorings • Berths	Hull repairs • Engine repairs • Railway	Winter Storage: Wet • Dry	Railway Capacity in Feet	Lift Capacity in Tons	Boat Rental: Canoe • Row • Motor	Boat Rental: Charter • House • Sail	Restaurant • Lodging • Camping	Showers • Laundry	Pumpout • Toilets	Bait • Tackle • Water • Ice	Groceries • Hardware	Diesel fuel • Gasoline
166	SEA JAY MARINE 516-691-1268	ALL YR.			HE	D										
167	ROVERY MARINE 516-264-0444	ALL YR.			HE	D	45	30								
169	BAY VILLAGE MARINA 516-691-4631		16		HE	D		12						W		
170	TOBAY BOAT BASIN 516-679-0720	MAY NOV										S	T	W		G
171	SEAFORD HARBOR Y. C. 516-785-8598				HE	D		7								
172	DICK & DORA'S RESTAURANT 516-798-0202										R					
173	ALHAMBRA MARINE REPAIR 516-799-5260	ALL YR.			HE R	D										
174	COCO'S BY THE BAY 516-798-9278										R					
175	KYDD'S MARINE CENTER 516-541-7747	ALL YR.		EB	HE	W D		6			R		T	W	H	
176	GUS' MARINE 516-541-1469	ALL YR.			E R	D	31						T	BT		G
177	TIDES ON THE BAY 516-798-9729										R		T	IW		
178	KREMER'S BOATYARD 516-221-8877	ALL YR.			HE	D	25	3					T	WB T	H	
179	OLD HARBOUR MARINA 516-785-0358	MAR NOV			HE R	W D				R M	R			IW BT		G
180	ATLANTIC VIEW MARINA 516-781-6004	ALL YR.			HE			3					T	W	H	
181	SEXTON'S Boathouse & Tavern 516-785-9769	ALL YR.											T	IW		
183	ANTHONY'S MARINA 516-785-5799				HE	D		10						W	H	G
184	ADVANCE MARINE Specialties 516-826-3377	ALL YR.		EB	HE	D		15					T			
185	FOUR CORNERS MARINA 516-785-1783				E	D		15								
186	**PRECISION MARINE 516-785-3013**	**ALL YR.**		**EB**	**HE**	**D**		**25**				S	PT	IW BT	GH	G
187	SEAFORD BOAT HAULERS 516-785-8517	ALL YR.			E	D	30	5					T	W		

CHART LOCATER NUMBER	MARINA'S NAME & PHONE NUMBER	WHEN OPEN	MONITORS VHF CHANNEL	TRANSIENT Electricity • Moorings • Berths	Hull repairs • Engine repairs • Ramp	WINTER STORAGE: Wet • Dry	RAILWAY CAPACITY IN TONS	LIFT CAPACITY IN FEET	BOAT RENTAL: Canoe • Row • Motor	BOAT RENTAL: Charter • House • Sail	Restaurant • Lodging • Camping	Showers • Laundry	Pumpout • Toilets	Bait • Tackle • Water • Ice	Groceries • Hardware	Diesel fuel • Gasoline
188	R&K MARINE 516-781-9352	ALL YR.		EB	HE	D		15								
189	TREASURE ISLAND MARINA 516-221-7156	ALL YR.		EB	HE R	W D		25				R	S PT	IW BT	H	
190	RITEWAY MARINE SERVICE 516-679-2628	ALL YR.	69	EB	HE	W D		35					T	IW	H	
191	NUWAVE MARINE 516-785-0128	ALL YR.	72	EB	HE	D		20					S T	IW	H	
192	VIKING MARINA 516-785-4883	ALL YR.			E	D		15					T	IW B	H	G
193	WANTAGH PARK 516-785-7811	APR NOV			R							R	S PT			
194	CLUBHOUSE MARINA 516-221-9818	MAR DEC		EB	HE	D		8				R	T	IW BT	H	G
195	MONTES MARINA 516-781-5891	MAR DEC			HE	D	30	2	CR M				T	W	H	
196	BAY MARINE 516-826-7881	ALL YR.			HE	D		20					T	W	H	
197	ISLAND MARINE 516-785-1768	ALL YR.			HE			10						IW		
198	OCEAN OUTBOARD 516-378-6400	ALL YR.		EB	E			30					T		H	
199	SUNRISE Y. C. 516-378-9481											S	T	W		
200	CHARLIE'S BOAT BASIN 516-868-7863	APR DEC			HE	D		12					T	IW BT	H	
201	BLUE WATER Y. C. 516-623-5757	APR NOV			HE	D		15				R		I		G
202	WHALENECK Marina & Lounge 516-378-8025	ALL YR.			HE	D		24				R	T	W		G
203	ED'S FISHING STATION 516-431-4193	MAY NOV			R						R M	R	T	IW BT		G
204	HEMPSTEAD MARINA EAST 516-897-4128	ALL YR.				W							S T	W		
205	SCOTTY'S MARINA 516-432-4665	MAR NOV			E	D						R	T	IW BT	GH	G D
206	POINT VIEW INN 516-431-2866	ALL YR.										R	T			
207	WEST END BOAT BASIN 516-785-1600				B							R	PT			

L.I. South Shore

MARINA'S NAME & PHONE NUMBER

Chart Locater Number	Marina's Name & Phone Number	When Open	Monitors VHF Channel	Hull repairs / Transient Electricity	Engine repairs / Moorings / Berths	Winter Storage: Wet • Dry	Railway Capacity in Tons	Lift Capacity in Feet	Boat Rental: Canoe • Row • Motor • Sail	Boat Rental: Charter • House	Restaurant • Lodging • Camping	Showers • Laundry	Pumpout • Toilets	Bait • Tackle • Water • Ice	Groceries • Hardware	Diesel fuel • Gasoline
208	HEMPSTEAD MARINA WEST 516-897-4127	ALL YR.		EB	R	W						S	T	W		
209	SALT AIR MARINA 516-379-4106	ALL YR.				D						S	T	W		
210	JOHNSON MARINE WORKS 516-379-3311	ALL YR.				D	33	12					T			
211	ROMEO'S MARINA 516-223-7102			EB	HE								T	W		
212	YACHTSMAN COVE 516-546-6026	ALL YR.			HE	D		60					T	W	H	G
213	FREEPORT MARINA 516-223-9084	ALL YR.		EB	E								T	W		
214	JONES INLET MARINE 516-623-8115	ALL YR.	16 68	EB	HE	D		40			RL	S	T	IW		
216	JIM'S MARINA 516-546-2762	ALL YR.			E			3					T			
217	JOHNNY'S DOCKSIDE RSTRNT 516-378-5544	ALL YR.									R					
218	HUDSON POINT MARINA 516-379-1871	ALL YR.			HE	D		12	M		R		T	IW BT	H	G D
219	W.D. MARINE INC 516-223-0229	ALL YR.			HE	D		12			RL		T	W		
220	B. TRUDY RESTAURANT 516-546-5555	ALL YR									R		T			
221	CHAMPION MARINE SERVICE 516-878-0100	ALL YR.		EB	HE	D		12								
222	MAKO MARINA 516-378-7331	ALL YR.	16	EB	HE	D	70	60			RL	S	T	WI BT	H	G D
223	TRAVELERS MARINE SERVICE 516-868-1193	ALL YR.			HE	W D	40	20								
225	HEMPSTEAD TOWN MARINA 516-378-3417	APR. NOV		EB	HE			25				S	T	W		
226	JOHN VIDAS MARINE SERVICE 516-378-6065	ALL YR.			HE	D		99 +					T		H	
227	FREEPORT BOATMEN ASSOC 516-378-4838	ALL YR.								C	R			IBT	H	
228	AL GROVER 516-379-7212	ALL YR.			HE R	D		3					T	W	H	G
229	OTTO'S SEA GRILL 516-378-9598	ALL YR.		B							R					

L.I. South Shore

CHART LOCATER NUMBER	MARINA'S NAME & PHONE NUMBER	WHEN OPEN	MONITORS VHF CHANNEL	TRANSIENT Electricity • Moorings • Berths	Hull repairs • Engine repairs • Ramp	WINTER STORAGE: Wet • Dry	RAILWAY CAPACITY IN FEET	LIFT CAPACITY IN TONS	BOAT RENTAL: Canoe • Row • Motor	BOAT RENTAL: Charter • House • Sail	Restaurant • Lodging • Camping	Showers • Laundry	Pumpout • Toilets	Bait • Tackle • Water • Ice	Groceries • Hardware	Diesel fuel • Gasoline
230	FRED CHALL MARINE PLUS 516-546-8960				HE			30								G
232	STATEN ISLAND BOAT SALES 516-623-6060	ALL YR			HE			35			R		T			
233	R.P.M. MARINE SERVICE 516-379-1175	ALL YR.		EB M	E						R			W	H	
234	SHELTER POINT MARINA 516-623-6599	ALL YR.			HE	D		10					T		H	
235	**THE SCHOONER RESTAURANT 516-378-7575**	**ALL YR.**		**B**							**R**					
236	WOODCLEFT Fishing Station 516-378-8748	MAR DEC	68								R		T	IBT		G D
237	FREEPORT BOAT RAMP				R											
238	FREEPORT BAY MARINA 516-623-0394	ALL YR.		EB	HE	D		60				S	T	W		
240	AL Grover's High & Dry Marina 516-546-8880	ALL YR.			HE	D		30					T	W		
241	DON'S YANKEE Clipper Motel	ALL YR.		EB							RL	S	T	I		
242	MORGAN'S MARINE 516-868-5021	ALL YR,			HE	D		15					T	W		
243	MILBURN CREEK RAMP				R											
244	BALDWIN YACHT BASIN 516-378-4334	ALL YR.			HE	D		3						W		
245	ANGLERS MARINE 516-546-1300	ALL YR.			HE			30					T	W		
246	HARBOR PERFORMANCE 516-867-7952	ALL YR.			HE	D		10						W		
247	BALDWIN HARBOR MARINE 516-223-1176	ALL YR.			HE	D	42	7						IW	H	
248	TONY'S MARINE SERVICE 516-623-7165	ALL YR.			E	D								W	H	
249	SEADOOR MARINA 516-378-2970	ALL YR.	68		HE	D							T	IW BT	H	G
250	THE MOORING 516-766-0080	ALL YR.			HE	D		3						W		
251	EMPIRE PT MARINA WEST 516-432-6648				HE	D		12						W		

L.I. South Shore
MARINA'S NAME & PHONE NUMBER

Chart Locater #	Marina's Name & Phone Number	When Open	Hull repairs • Engine repairs • Berths	Transient Electricity • Moorings • Ramp	Winter Storage: Wet • Dry	Railway Cap. (ft)	Lift Cap. (tons)	Boat Rental: Charter • House • Sail	Restaurant • Lodging • Camping	Showers • Laundry	Pumpout • Toilets	Bait • Tackle / Groceries • Water • Ice	Hardware	Diesel • Gasoline
252	K & K OUTBOARD 516-431-1868	ALL YR.	EB	HE	D		10		RL	S	T	IW BT	H	G
254	EMPIRE POINT MARINA 516-889-1067	ALL YR.	EB	HE			35				T	IW	H	G
255	K & K OUTBOARD 516-431-1865	ALL YR.		HE	D		10		RL	S	T	IW BT	H	G
257	J SPRATS ON THE WATER 516-432-2400		EB						R		T			
258	SACKEN'S BOATYARD 516-431-7533	ALL YR.	EB	HE		42	20				T	W	H	
259	HARRY ULTZEN BOAT YARD 516-431-2678			HE	D		20							
260	COYOTE GRILL 516-889-8009	ALL YR.							R		T			
261	PADDY MCGEE'S 516-431-8700	ALL YR.							R		T			
262	ANDY'S MARINE SERVICE 516-431-0768	MAR NOV		HE	D				R		T	IW BT		G
263	AERO MARINE 516-431-5061	ALL YR.		HE	D		4				T	W		
264	G&S MARINA WEST 516-678-7474	ALL YR.	EB	HE	D		10		RL	S	T	IW	H	
265	CLUB NAUTICO 516-889-5000	ALL YR.	EB	HE	D		17	C	R		T	IW BT	H	
266	O'REILLY'S COVE 516-766-9380	ALL YR.		H R	D						T	W		G
267	BAILEY'S MARINA 516-764-9682	ALL YR.		HE	D		3				T		H	
268	BAY PARK YACHT HARBOR 516-766-4112	ALL YR.		HE	D		35		R		T	IW	G	G D
269	CROW'S NEST MARINA 516-766-2020	ALL YR.	EB	HE	W D	35				S	T	IW		
270	PORT HOLE BAR & GRILL 516-766-9567	ALL YR.	B						R					
271	SKIP'S MARINA 516-536-4011			H	D		3							
272	BARNETT BOATYARD 516-763-1624	ALL YR.		HE	D		7							
273	DAKIS MARINE SERVICE 516-593-5377	MAR DEC			D		2		R		T			

L.I. South Shore

CHART LOCATER NUMBER	MARINA'S NAME & PHONE NUMBER	MONITORS VHF CHANNEL	WHEN OPEN	TRANSIENT Electricity • Moorings • Engine repairs • Berths	Hull repairs • Engine repairs • Berths	WINTER STORAGE • Ramp	RAILWAY CAPACITY IN FEET	BOAT RENTAL: Wet • Dry	LIFT CAPACITY IN TONS	BOAT RENTAL: Canoe • Row • Motor	Restaurant • Lodging • House • Sail / Camping	Showers • Laundry	Bait • Tackle • Water • Ice	Pumpout • Toilets	Groceries • Hardware	Diesel fuel • Gasoline
274	MILL RIVER MARINE 516-599-0548		ALL YR.			E						R				H
275	SALTAIRE DISC. MARINE 516-593-8331		ALL YR.			E	D		3				R				H
278	DAVISON'S BOAT YARD 516-593-8100		ALL YR.		EB	HE	W D		40				R	S	T	W	H
280	BAY PARK RAMP					R											
282	SOMMERVILLE MARINA 718-945-4500		ALL YR.		MB		D		35							W	
283	ARGO BOAT MANUFACTURER 718-527-9870		ALL YR.			E			5						T		H
284	EDDIE'S MARINE CORP 516-371-1640	68	ALL YR.		EM B	HE	W D		15						T		H

USING THE BAROMETER

Barometric Reading	Rising Needle	Falling Needle
29.8 and Below	Clear and Colder	Storm – Heavy Precipitation
30.0 and Below	Clearing within a few hours. Fair for several days.	Continuing Precipitation
30.10 and above	Fair for several days. Followed by precipitation within two days.	Precipitation likely in 12 to 24 hours
30.20 and above	Fair for several days Followed by precipitation	Slow rising temperatures Fair for 48 hours.

A stationary barometric reading
indicates continued fair weather with no significant temperature change.

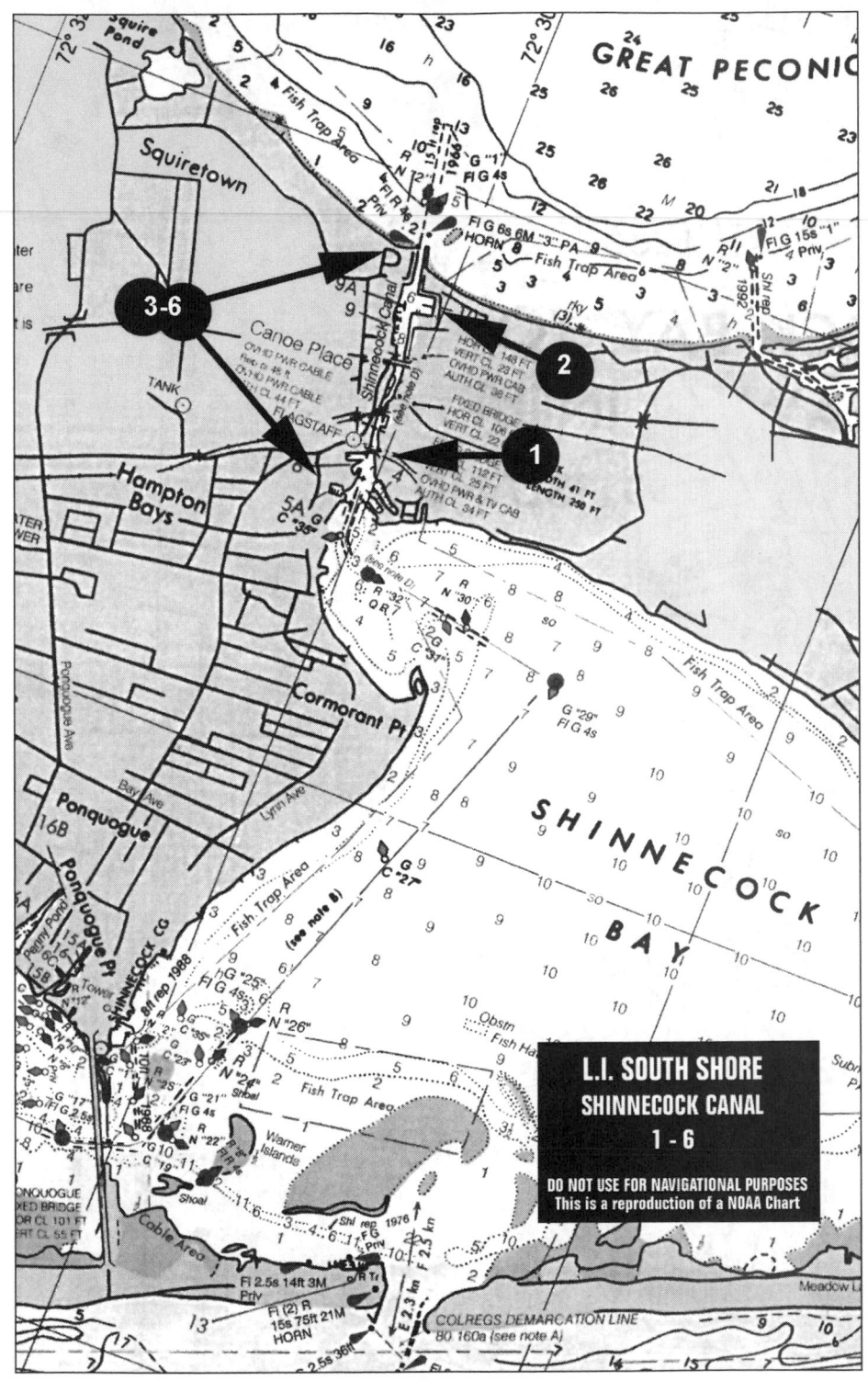

379

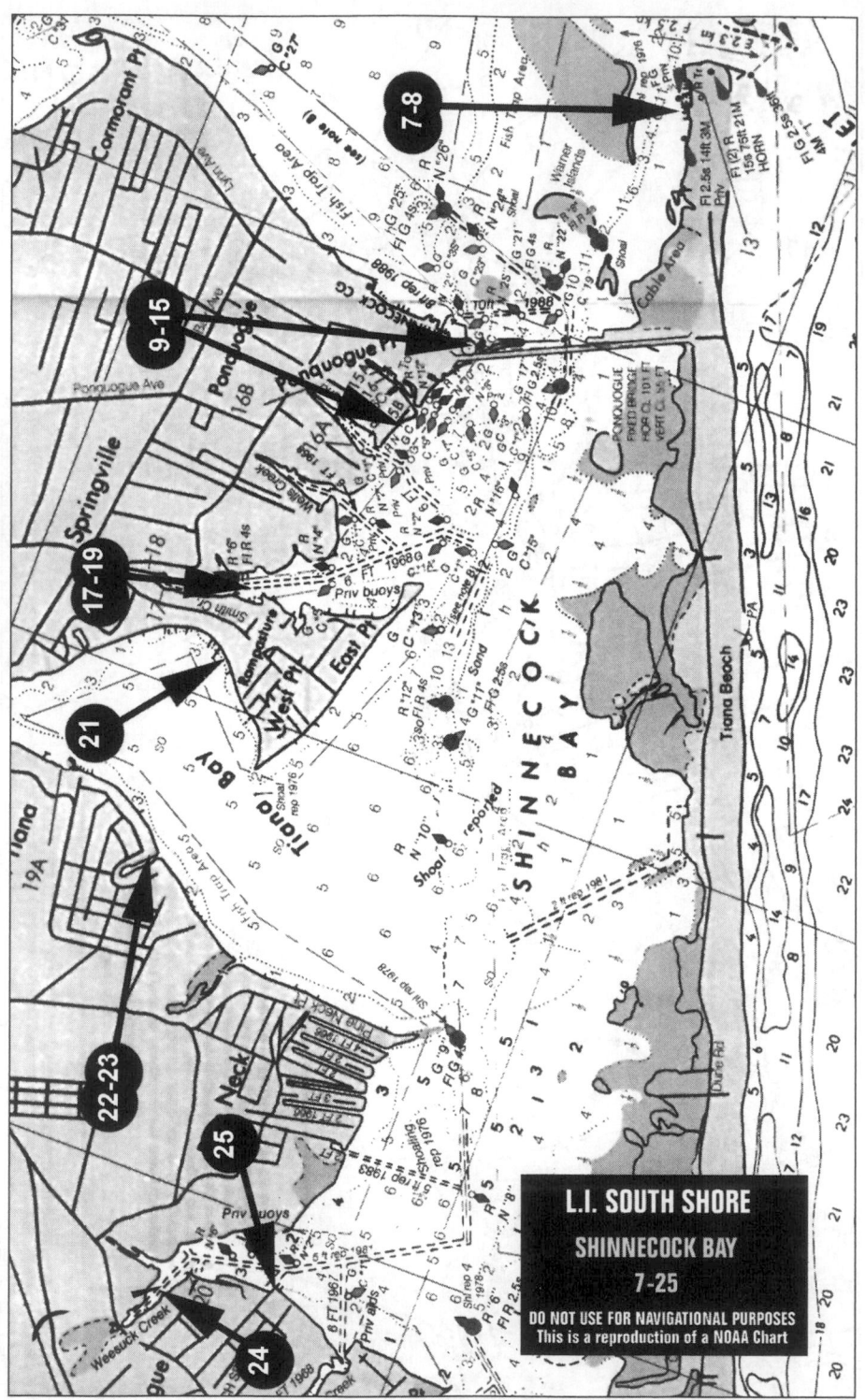

L.I. SOUTH SHORE

SHINNECOCK BAY

7-25

DO NOT USE FOR NAVIGATIONAL PURPOSES
This is a reproduction of a NOAA Chart

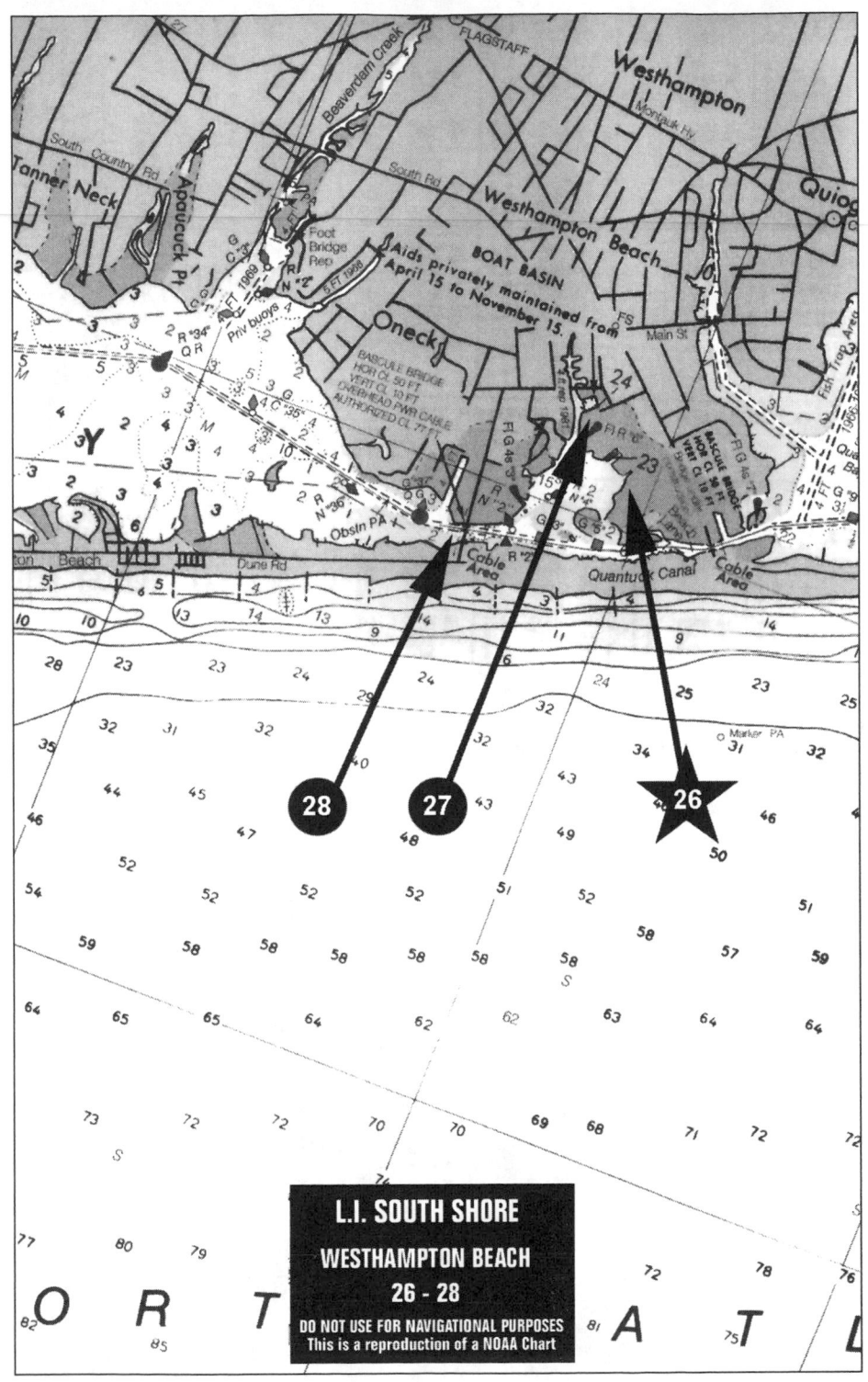

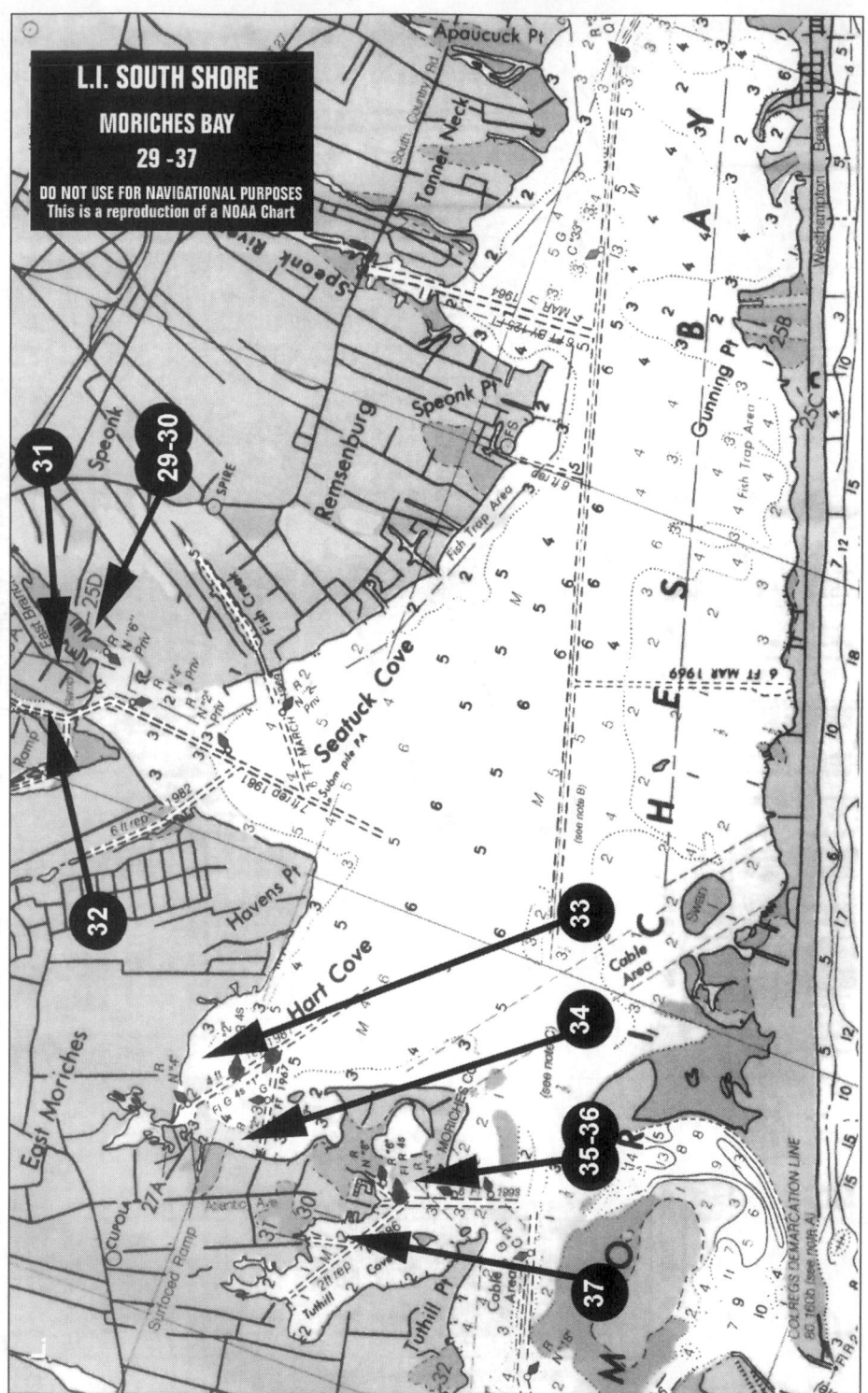

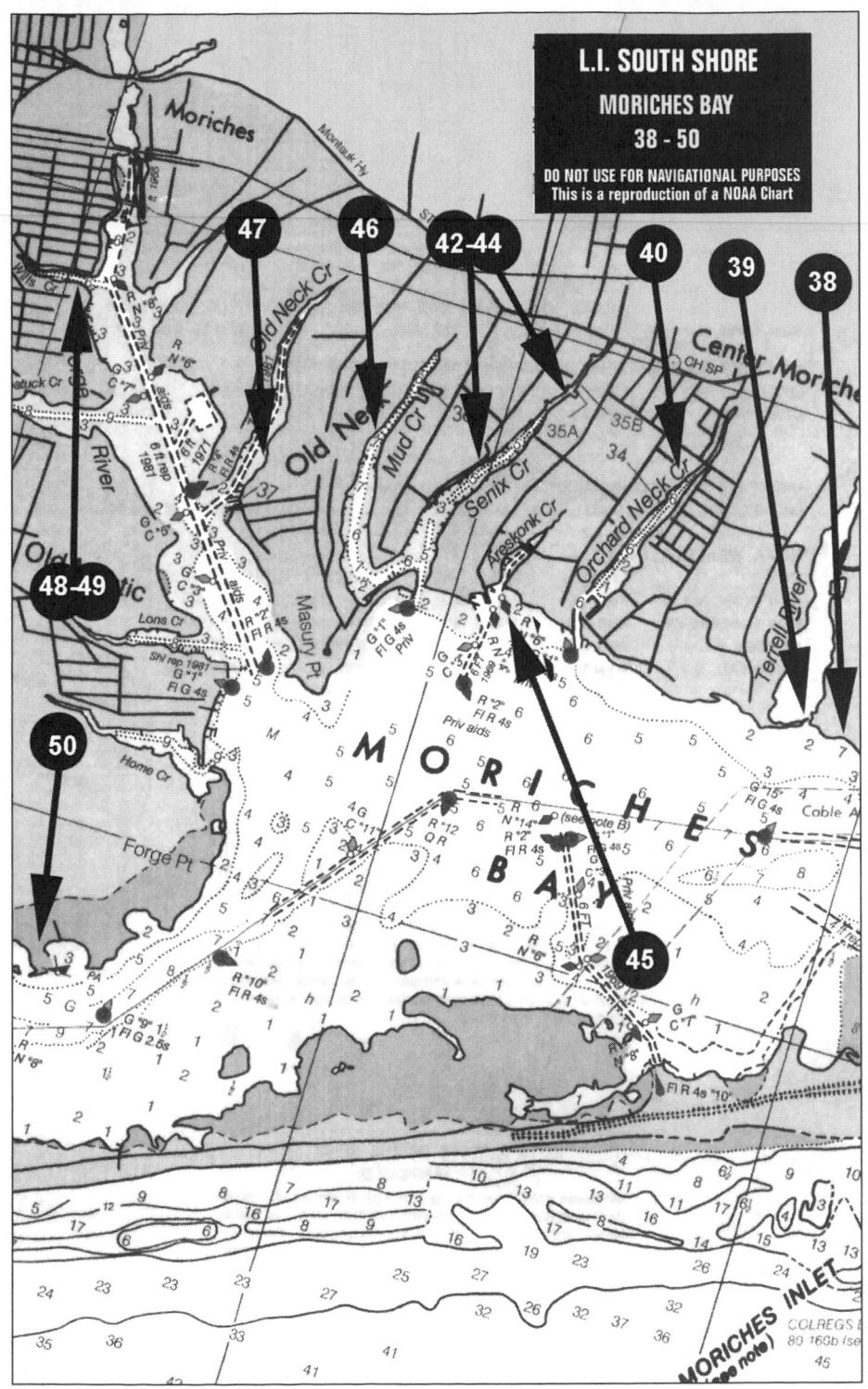

383

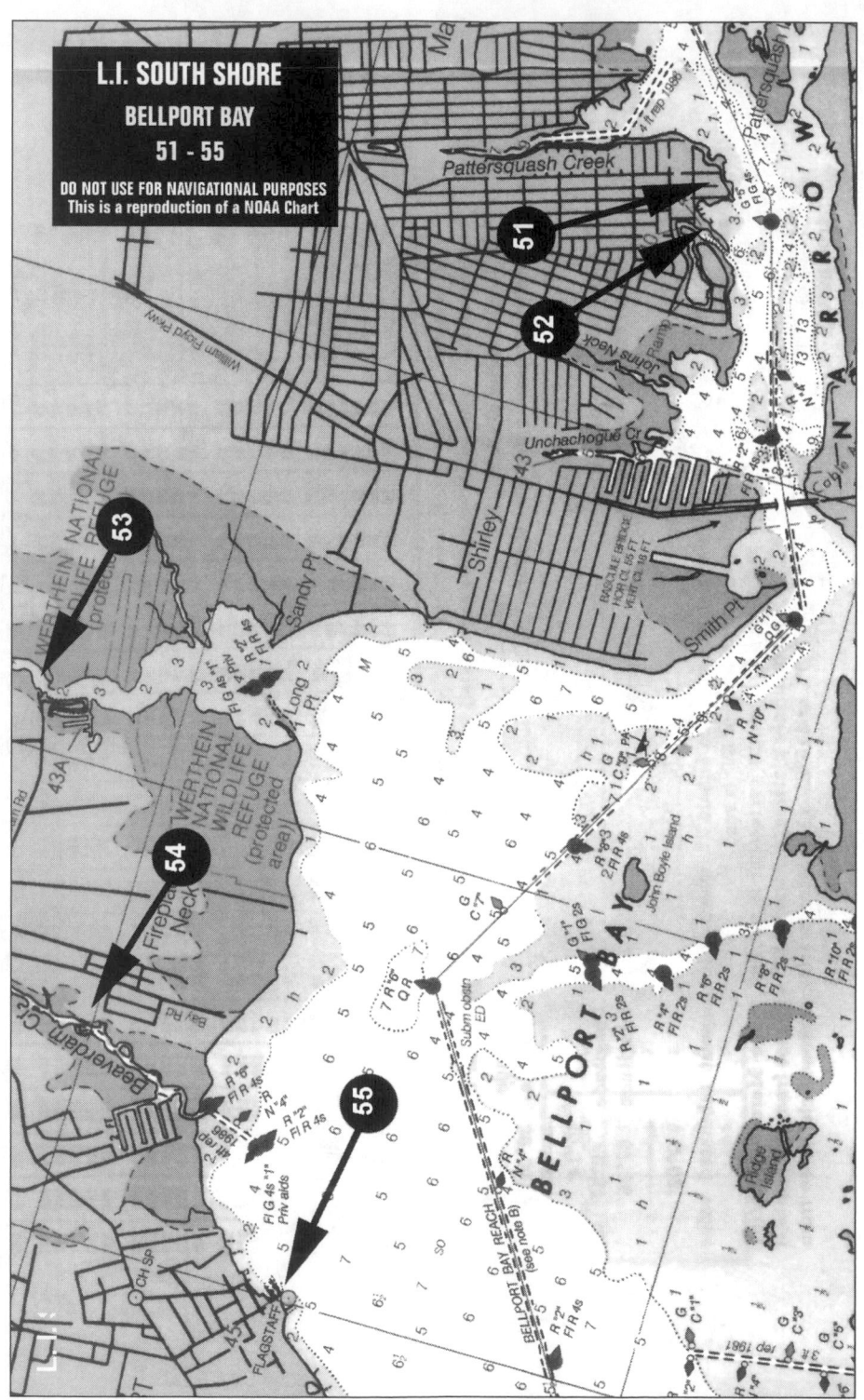

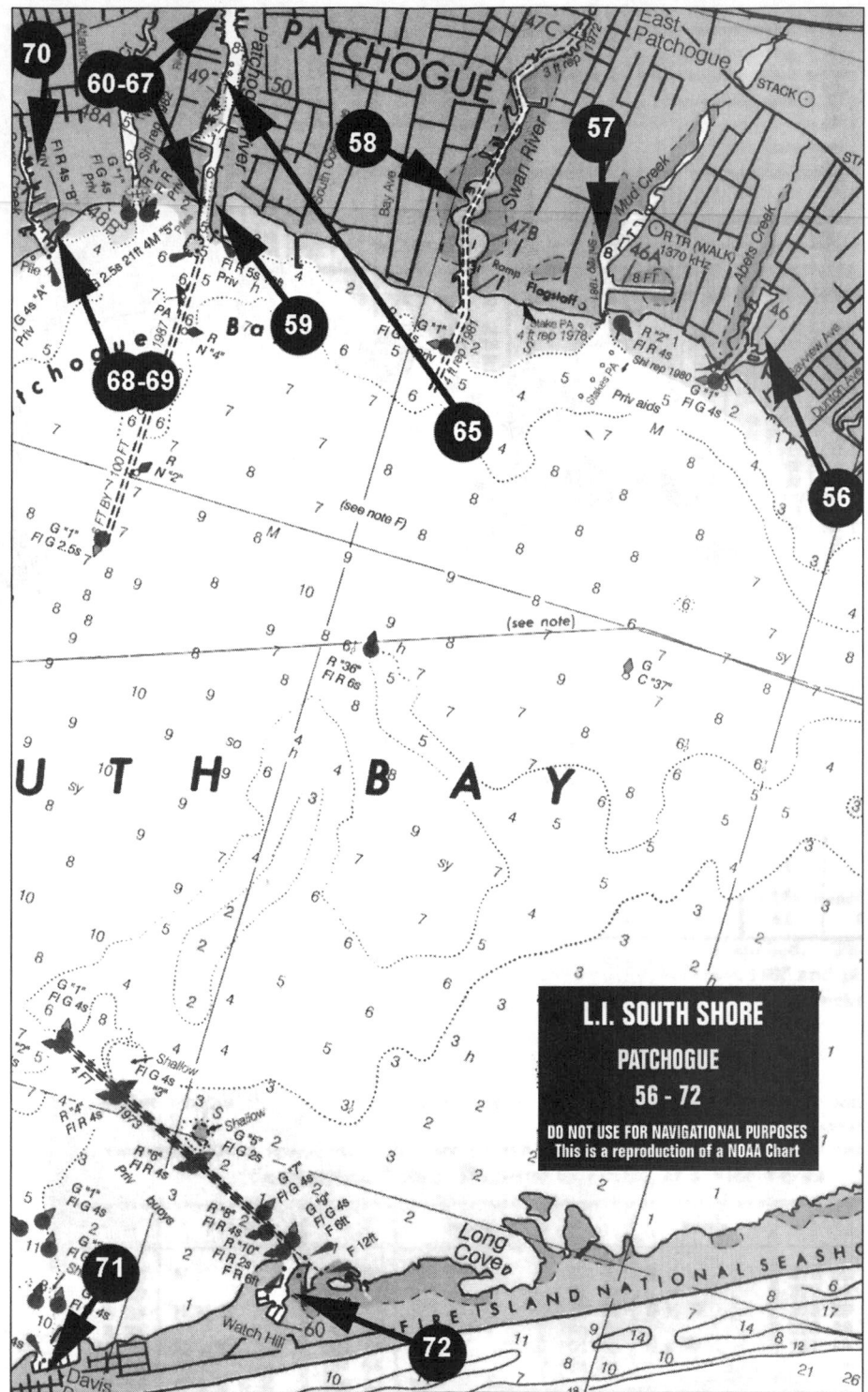

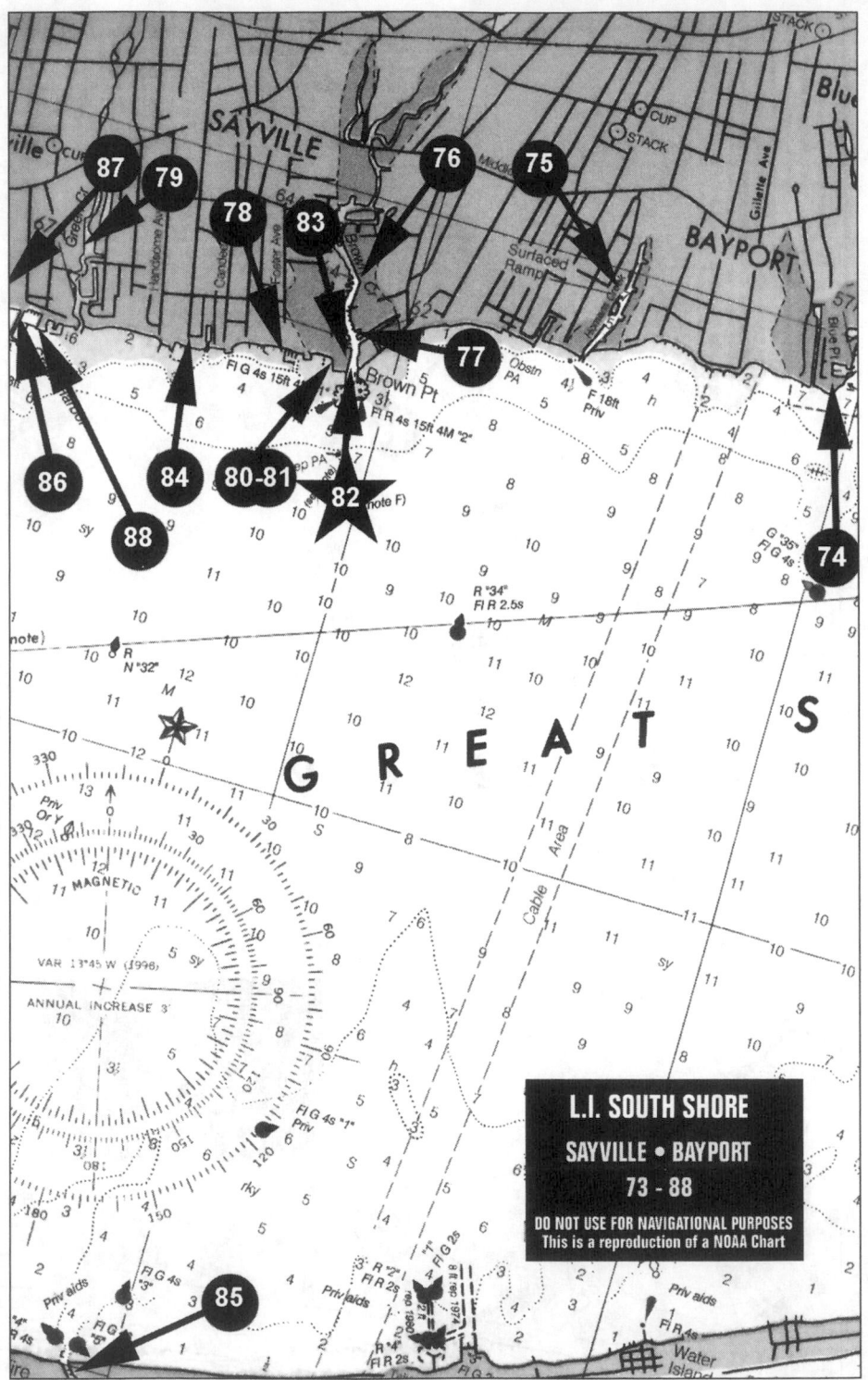

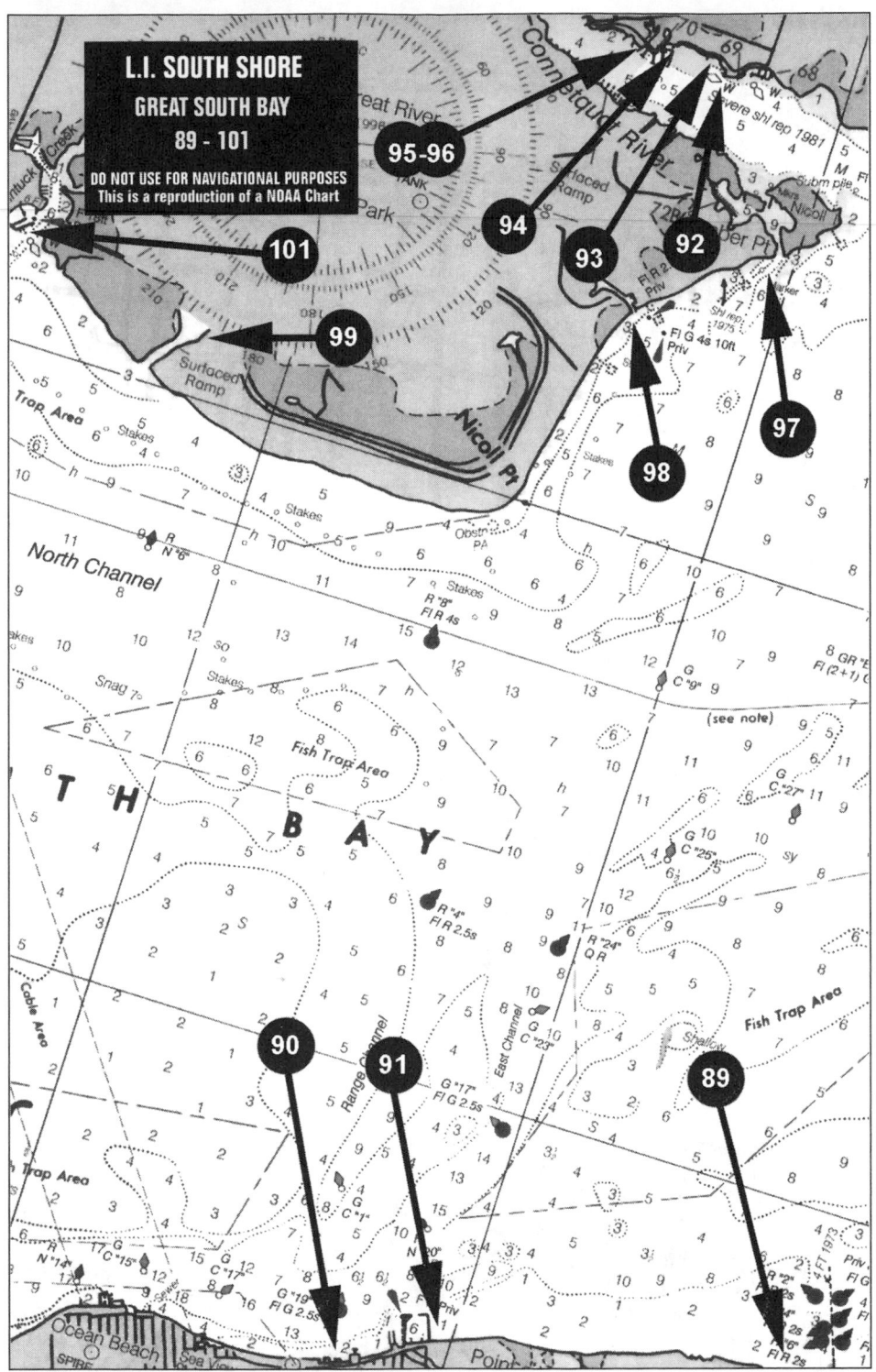

L.I. SOUTH SHORE
GREAT SOUTH BAY
89 - 101

DO NOT USE FOR NAVIGATIONAL PURPOSES
This is a reproduction of a NOAA Chart

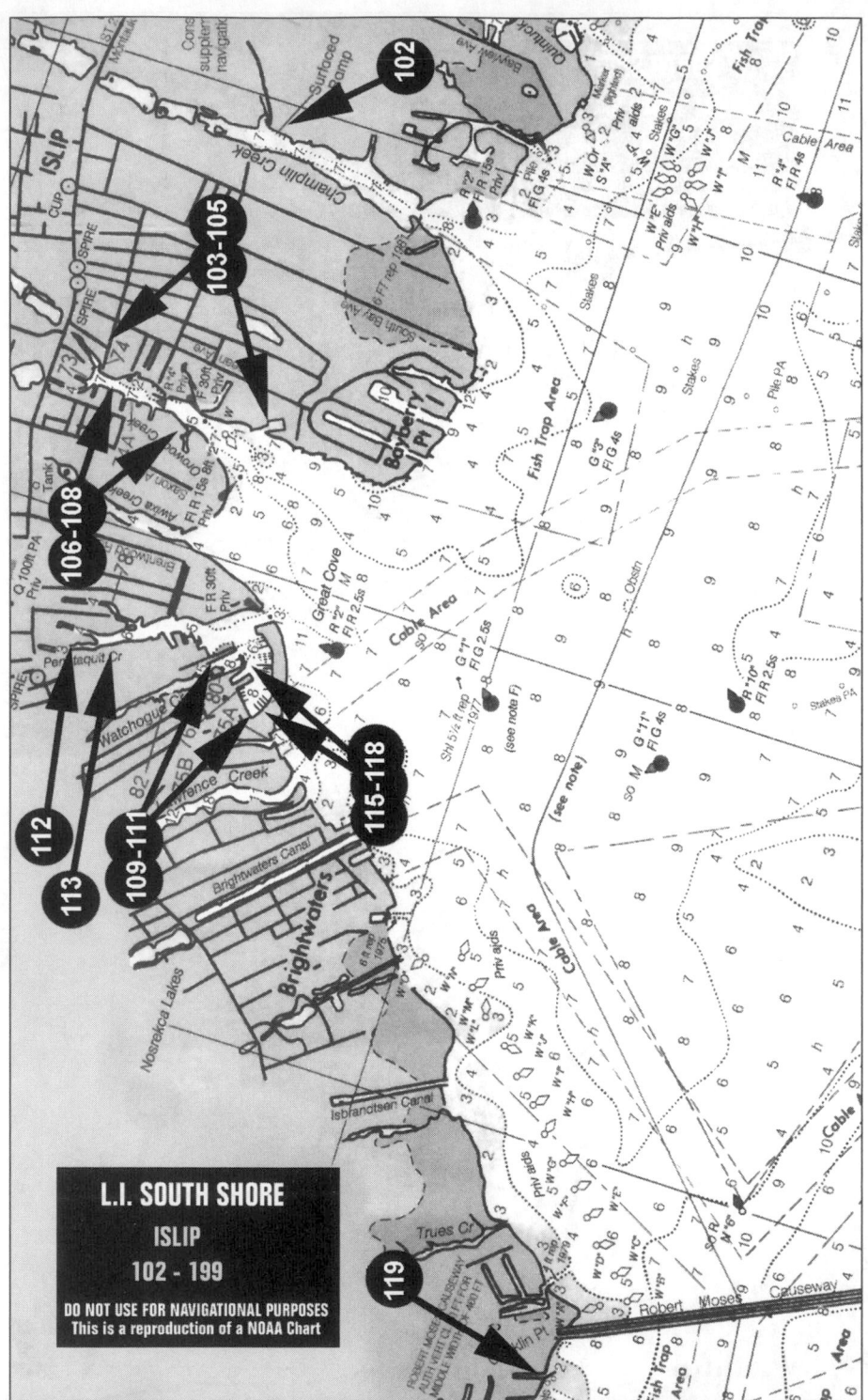

L.I. SOUTH SHORE

ISLIP

102 - 199

DO NOT USE FOR NAVIGATIONAL PURPOSES
This is a reproduction of a NOAA Chart

388

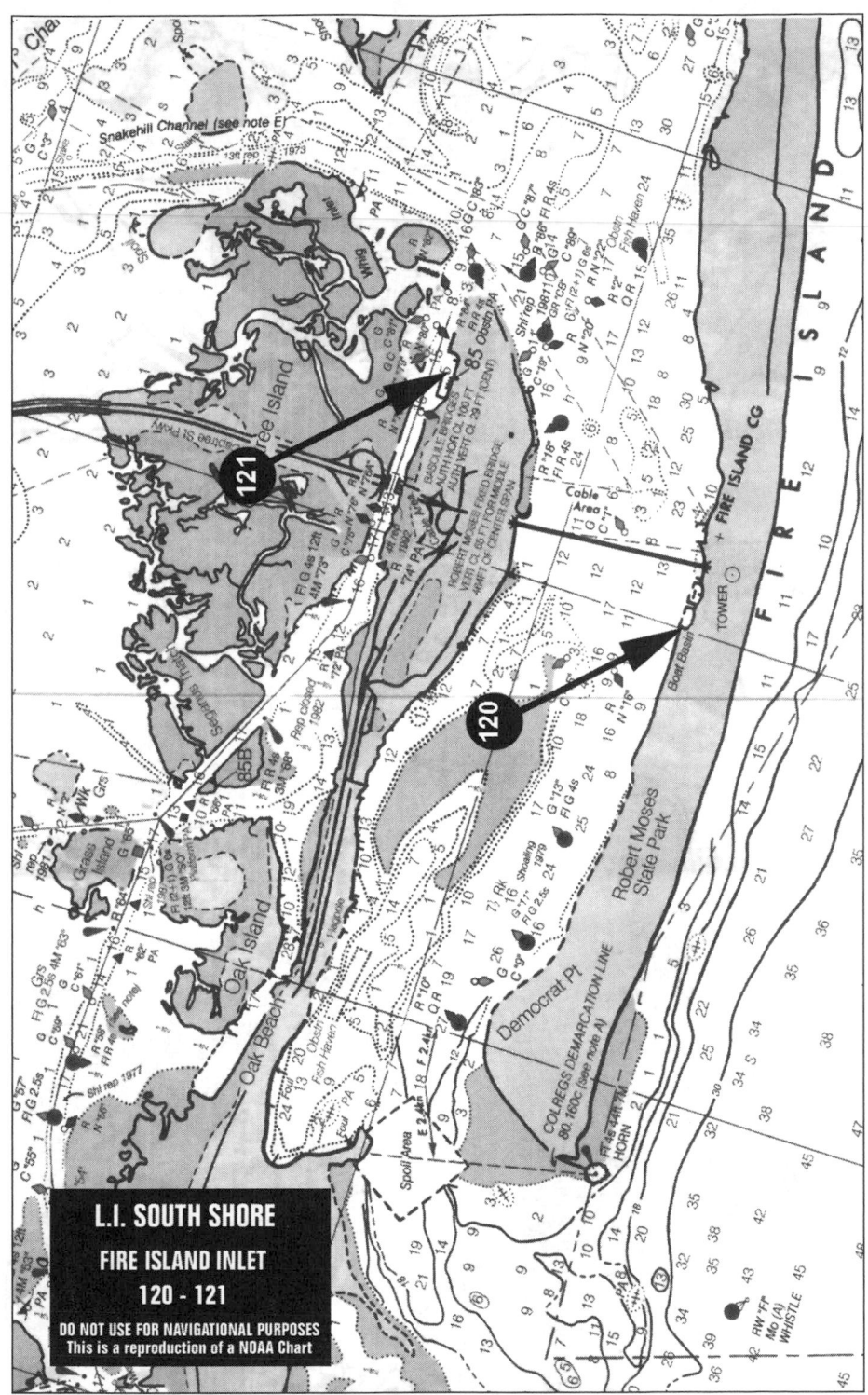

L.I. SOUTH SHORE

FIRE ISLAND INLET

120 - 121

DO NOT USE FOR NAVIGATIONAL PURPOSES
This is a reproduction of a NOAA Chart

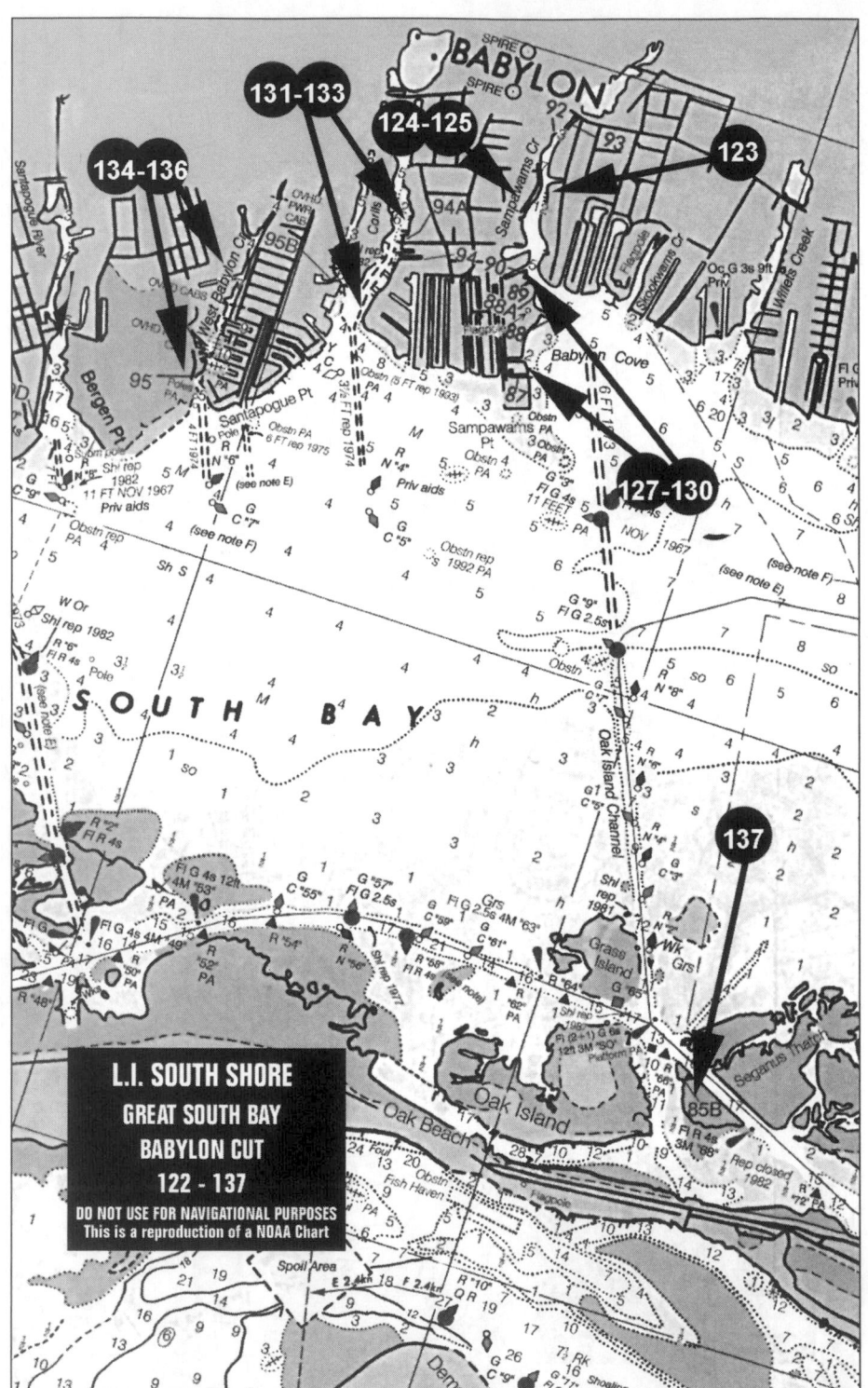

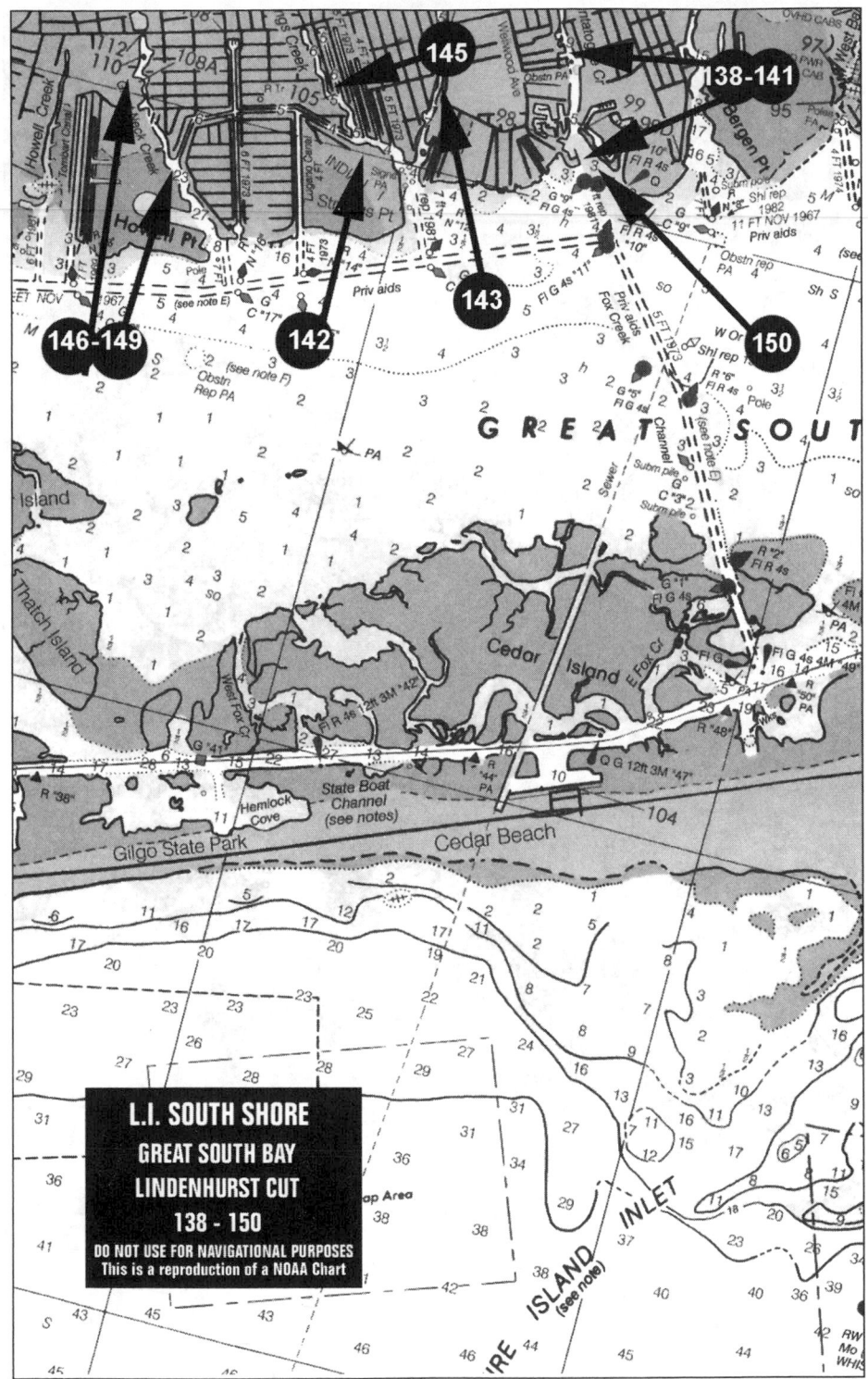

L.I. SOUTH SHORE
GREAT SOUTH BAY
LINDENHURST CUT
138 - 150
DO NOT USE FOR NAVIGATIONAL PURPOSES
This is a reproduction of a NOAA Chart

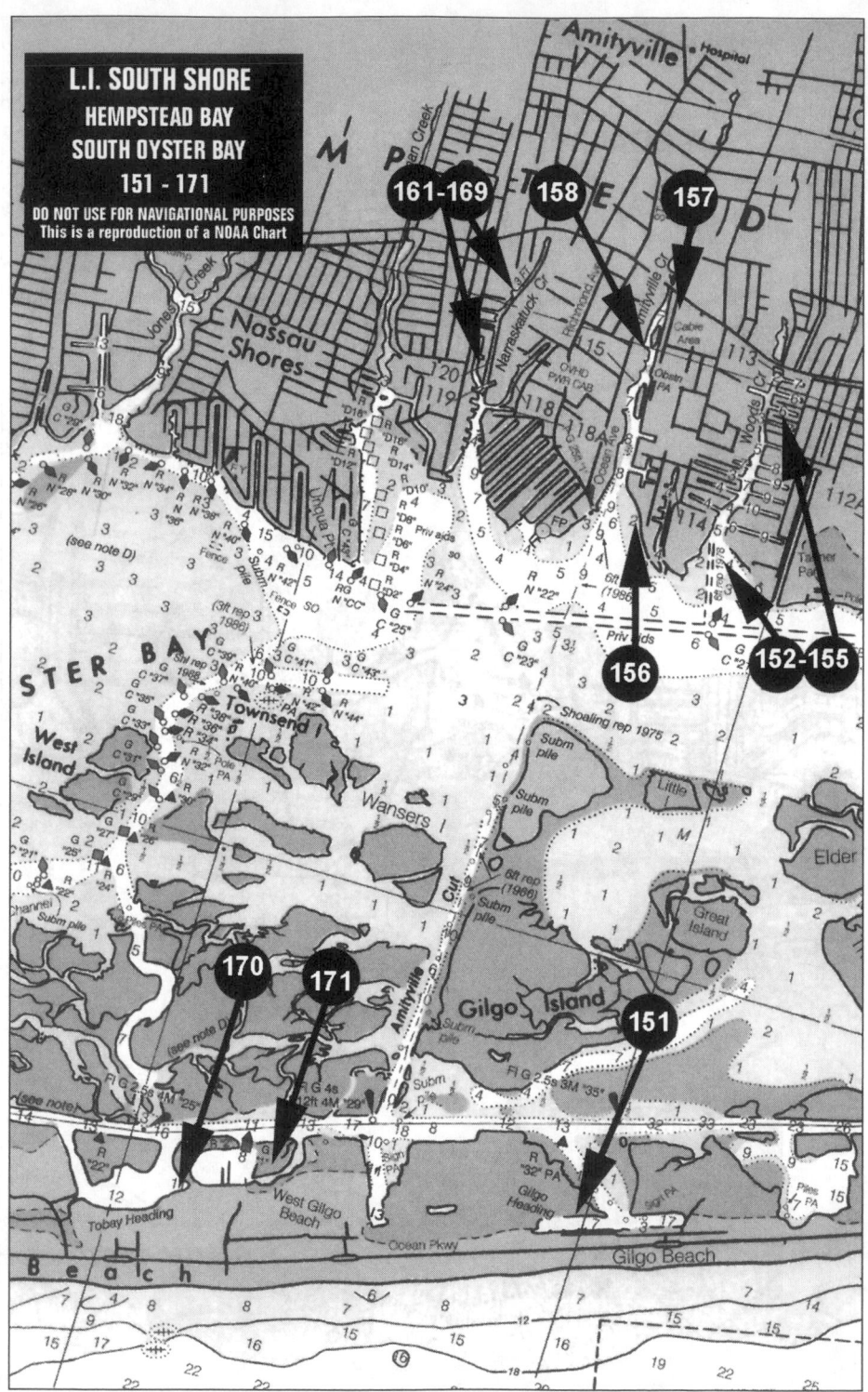

L.I. SOUTH SHORE
HEMPSTEAD BAY
SOUTH OYSTER BAY
151 - 171
DO NOT USE FOR NAVIGATIONAL PURPOSES
This is a reproduction of a NOAA Chart

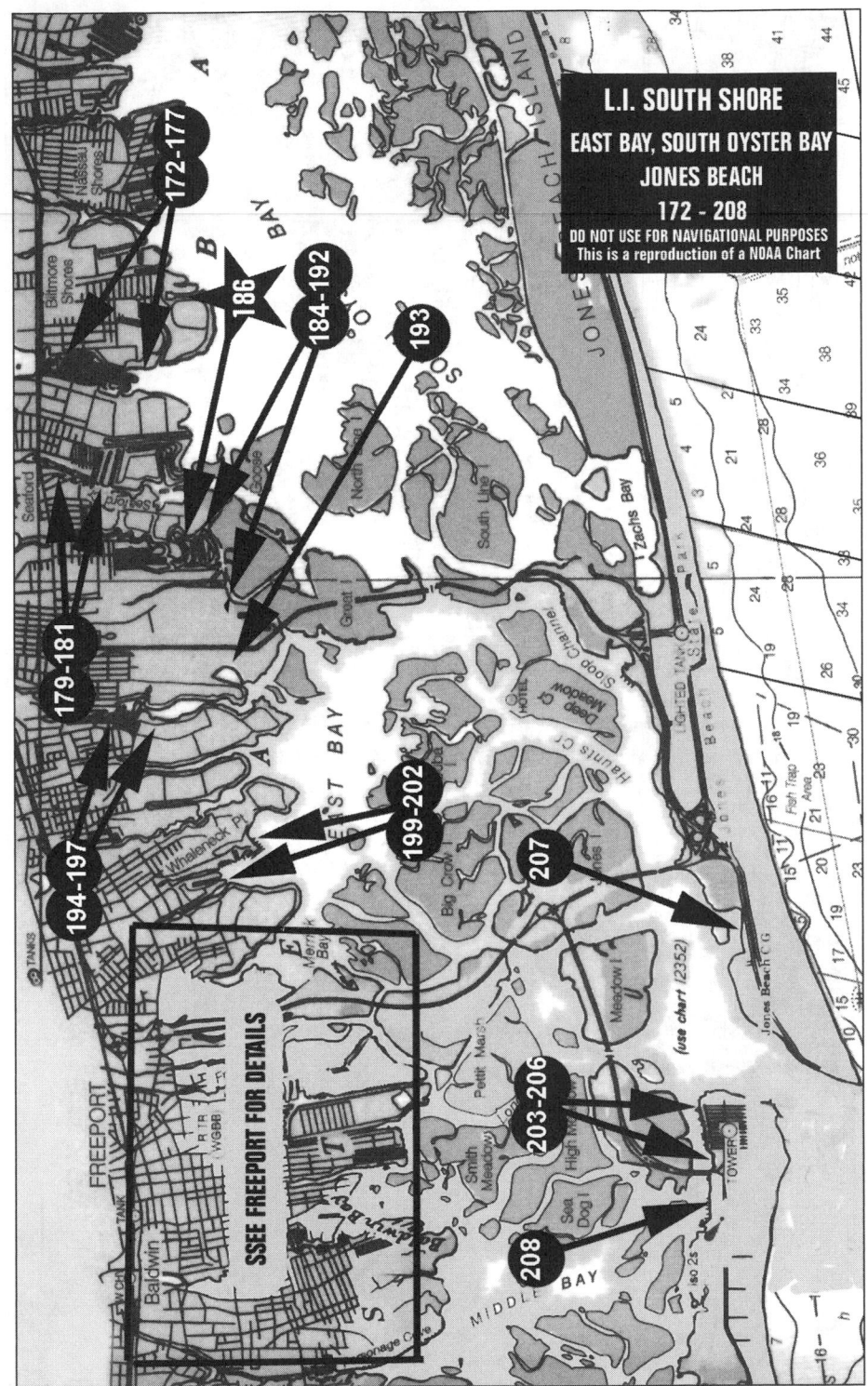

L.I. SOUTH SHORE
EAST BAY, SOUTH OYSTER BAY
JONES BEACH
172 - 208
DO NOT USE FOR NAVIGATIONAL PURPOSES
This is a reproduction of a NOAA Chart

SSEE FREEPORT FOR DETAILS

(use chart 12352)

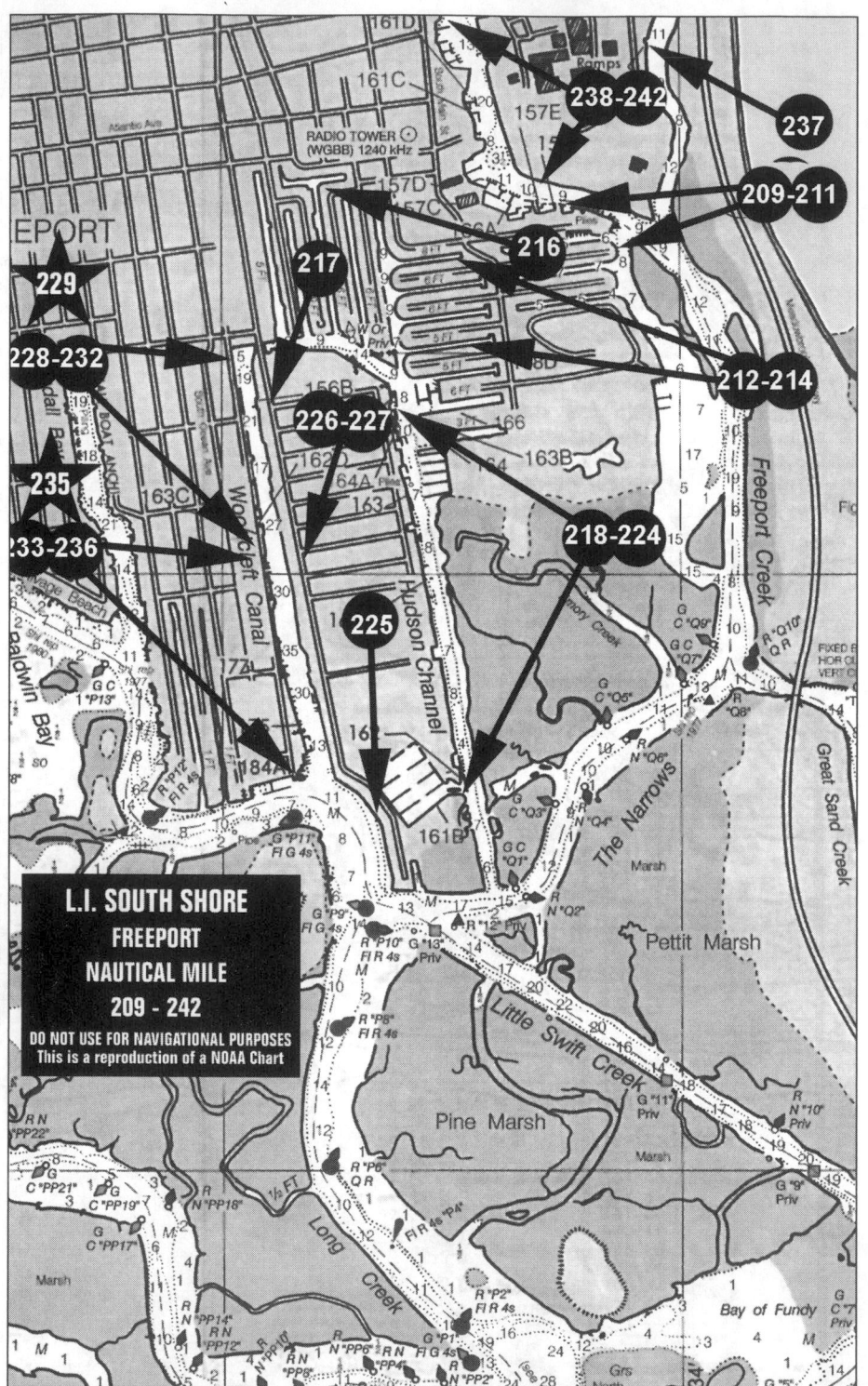

L.I. SOUTH SHORE
FREEPORT
NAUTICAL MILE
209 - 242

DO NOT USE FOR NAVIGATIONAL PURPOSES
This is a reproduction of a NOAA Chart

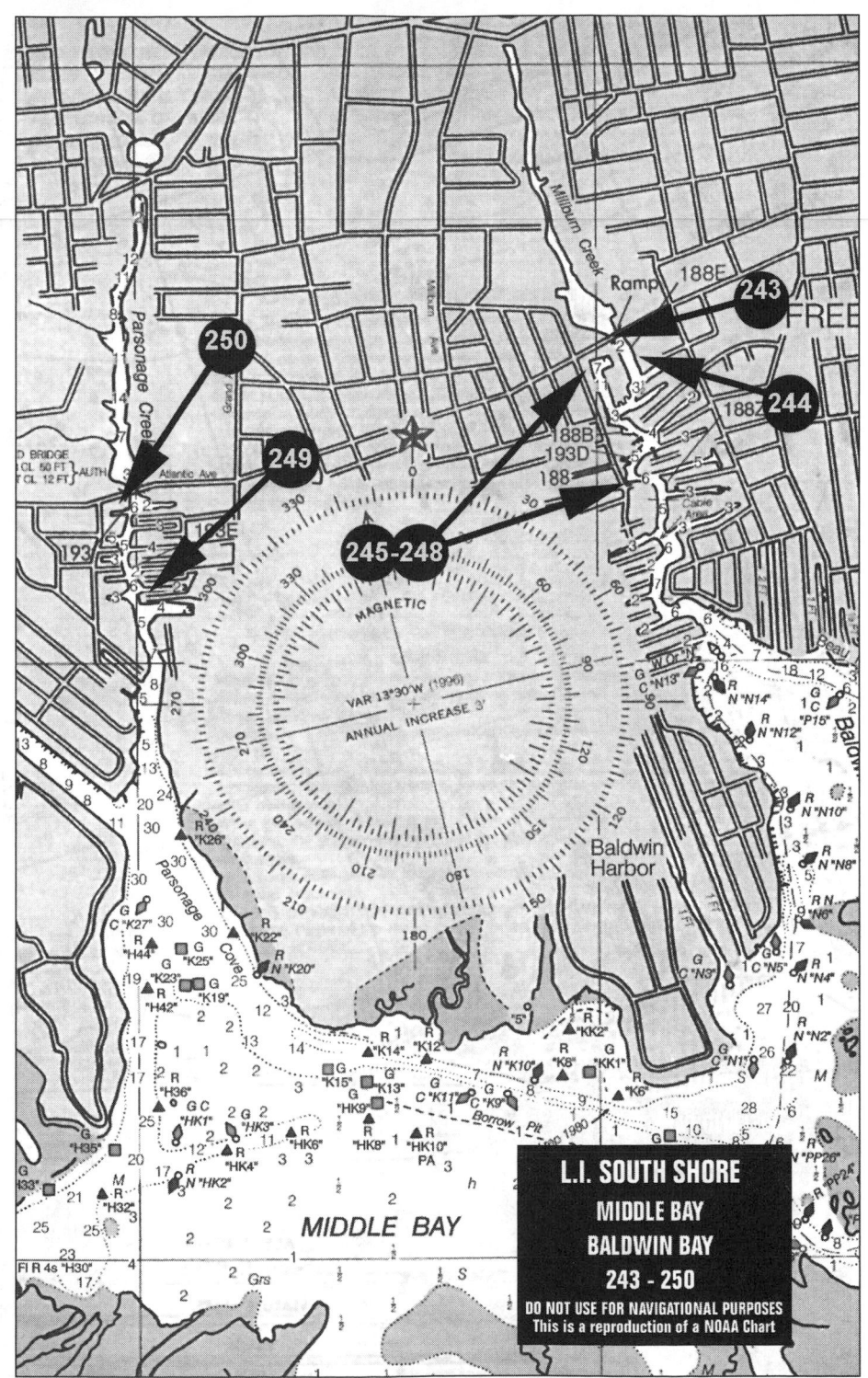

L.I. SOUTH SHORE
MIDDLE BAY
BALDWIN BAY
243 - 250
DO NOT USE FOR NAVIGATIONAL PURPOSES
This is a reproduction of a NOAA Chart

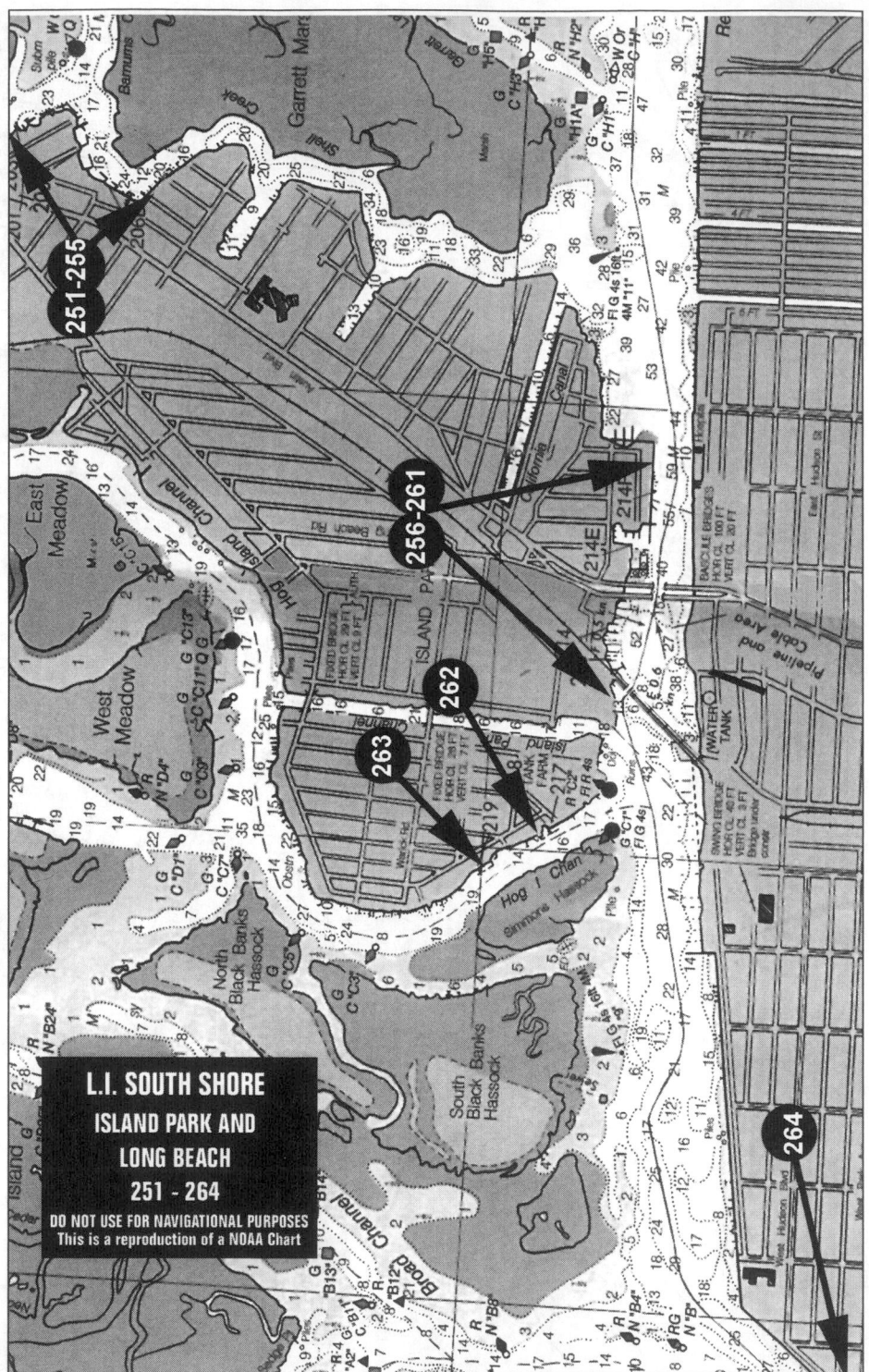

L.I. SOUTH SHORE
ISLAND PARK AND
LONG BEACH
251 - 264

DO NOT USE FOR NAVIGATIONAL PURPOSES
This is a reproduction of a NOAA Chart

396

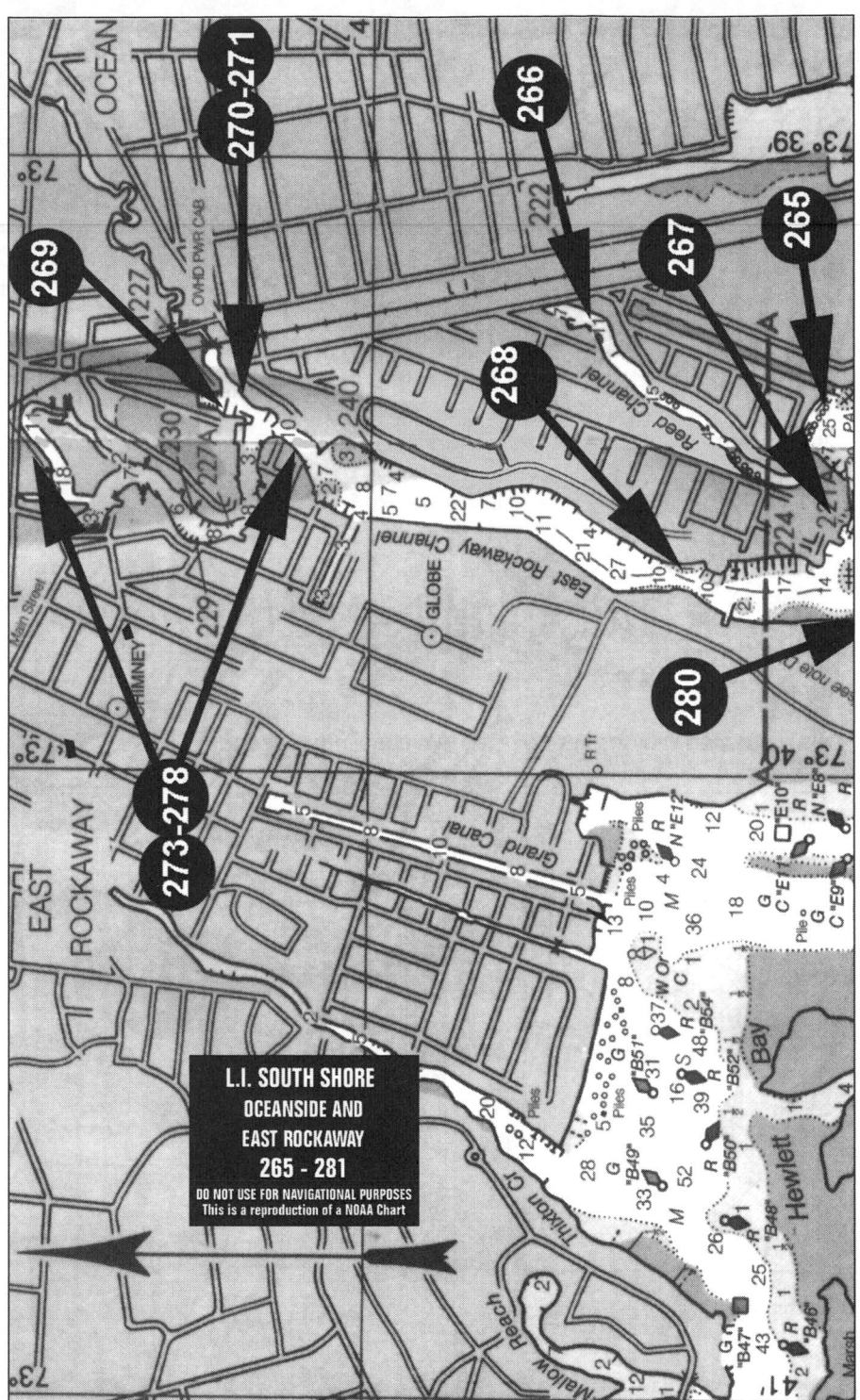

L.I. SOUTH SHORE
OCEANSIDE AND
EAST ROCKAWAY
265 - 281
DO NOT USE FOR NAVIGATIONAL PURPOSES
This is a reproduction of a NOAA Chart

397

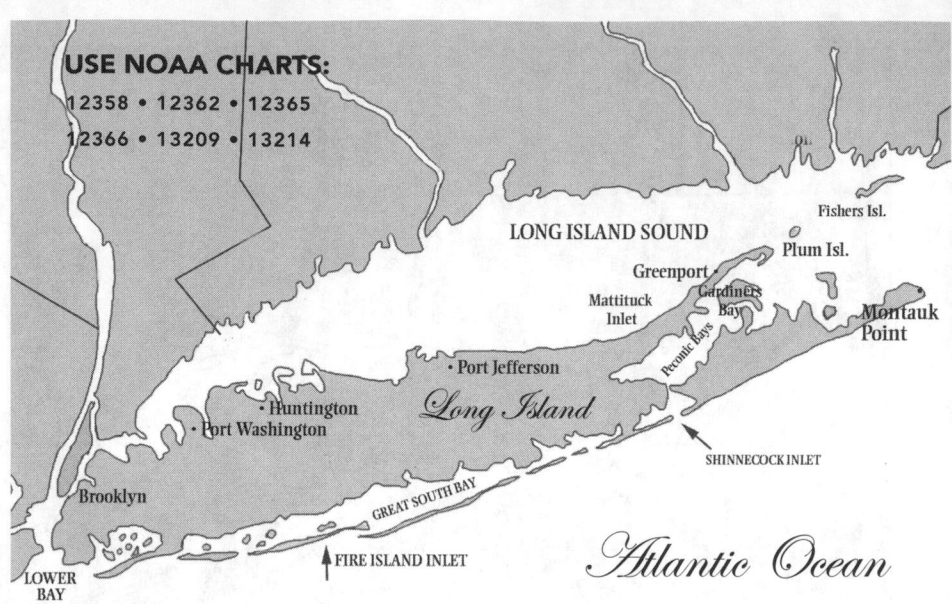

LONG ISLAND SOUND

Fishers Isl.

Plum Isl.

Greenport

Mattituck
Inlet

Gardiners
Bay

Montauk
Point

Peconic Bays

Port Jefferson

Long Island

Huntington
Port Washington

SHINNECOCK INLET

Brooklyn

GREAT SOUTH BAY

FIRE ISLAND INLET

Atlantic Ocean

LOWER
BAY

Long Island's North Shore

Map is not intended for navigational purposes.

THE FOLLOWING REGIONS ARE COVERED IN CHARTS IN THIS SECTION:

Cruising Long Island's North Shore

CHART 13214. FISHERS ISLAND SOUND extends between the mainland of Connecticut and Fishers Island, NY and forms one of the entrances into Long Island Sound that is used to some extent by light tows and other vessels up to a 14 foot draft. The sound has numerous shoals and lobster trap buoys and the entire area is exceedingly treacherous, characterized by boulder patches that rise abruptly form deep water. Vessels should follow the deeper channels between the shoals and proceed with caution if obliged to cross shoal areas. **NOTE:** In general, all shoal spots or abrupt changes of depth are indications of boulders and should be avoided as anchorage.

In **WATCH HILL PASSAGE** the tidal currents are strong and necessitate caution in navigating. Buoys may be towed under. The flood current sets nearly in the direction of the channel, but has a tendency to northward and the ebb a tendency to southward. In the main channel of **FISHERS ISLAND SOUND** the flood sets westward and the ebb eastward.

WEST HARBOR on the north side of Fishers Island southeastward of North Dumpling Light affords shelter form southerly winds. The channel leading into the harbor has a depth of about 12 feet. Hay Harbor at the West End of Fishers Island is used by small craft.

On the north side of Fishers Island Sound are **LITTLE NARRAGANSETT BAY** and **PAWCATUCK RIVER** leading to the town of **STONINGTON, CT,** and **MYSTIC HARBOR, CT,** leading to the towns of **NOANK and MYSTIC.**

LITTLE NARRAGANSETT BAY at the eastern end of Fishers Island Sound is entered at its extreme western end southward of Stonington Point. The channel, with dredged sections extends generally southeasterly across the bay into Pawcatuck River to **WESTERLY, RI.**

LONG ISLAND thrusts about 105 miles eastward from New York Bay to a point abreast of New London, CT. The island faces the New England coast across the Long Island Sound on the north. The long narrow outline of the island resembles that of a whale. In fact, from the late 1700s to the late 1800s, Long Island's Sag Harbor once boasted the second largest whaling fleet – next to New Bedford – on the eastern seaboard, followed by Greenport. The island's eastern end is split by Peconic Bay and the 35 and 25 mile peninsulas thus formed are the north and south flukes. On the north coast, bluffs rise to a height of 200 feet. South of these, extending well into the island midsection, run several chains of hills. The south shore is a barrier beach from about 30 miles west of the eastern extremity to the western end, which has been developed into a series of seaside resorts.

LONG ISLAND SOUND is a deep navigable waterway lying between the shores of Connecticut and New York and the northern coast of Long Island. In this region are boulders and broken ground, but little or no natural change in the shoals. As all broken ground is liable to be strewn with boulders, vessels should proceed with caution in the broken areas where the charted depths are not more than 6 to 8 feet greater than the draft. Dredged channels enter all of the more important places. Stakes usually mark the numerous oyster grounds in this region and they are dangerous to small craft as our numerous lobster buoys– keep a watchful eye. Mariners should proceed with caution especially at night.

EASTERN LONG ISLAND SOUND'S waters are well marked by navigational aids so that strangers should experience no difficulty in navigating them. Submarine operating areas are in the approaches to New London Harbor, Connecticut River, and off the northern shore of Long Island. As submarines may be operating submerged in these areas, vessels should proceed with caution.

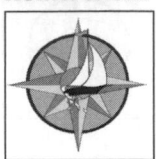

CHART 13209. MONTAUK POINT LIGHT, 168 feet above the water, is shown from a white octagonal, pyramidal tower with a brown band midway of its height and with a covered way to a gray dwelling. Surrounding **MONTAUK POINT** for about 4 miles is a shoal area that has been closely surveyed. The bottom is very broken and extra caution should be observed where the depths are less than 10 feet. In general the shoals are a series of long narrow ridges, in places, only a few yards wide, and their positions are indicated by the rips over them at the strength of the tidal currents.

Just inside **MONTAUK HARBOR,** in the northern part of Lake Montauk, is **STAR ISLAND,** which is connected to the mainland by a causeway. The channel is reported to have depths of 14 feet and the entrance is protected by lighted jetties. Local knowledge says to favor the western jetty, and also to allow for currents and off-channel rocks. A private light is shown from the eastern side of the island. Dead ahead–on the west side of the harbor–and next to the Coast Guard Station is **Star Island Yacht Club and Marina**, a resort marina with every possible amenity. Transient dockage is available for up to 140 ft. with side boarding. Stop awhile at Star Island Yacht Club and enjoy a swim in the boat-shaped pool, dancing under the stars on weekends, waterfront dining and an extensive ship's store before heading out to sea again. Fishing is a focus here and the ship's store even offers a tackle combination rod and reel set up for the kids.

THE NORTH SHORE OF LONG ISLAND from **ORIENT POINT** for about 11 miles to **HORTON POINT** on the south shore of Long Island Sound is generally bluff and rocky. The outlying dangers are Orient Shoal and the rocky Patch northward of Horton Point. **HORTON POINT LIGHT,** 103 feet above the water, is shown from a white square tower attached to a dwelling on the northwest part of the point. The former lighthouse tower is close by, southwestward of the present light. Several rocky shoals, including Orient Shoal with a depth of 7 feet, are offshore in the vicinity of Rocky Point —about 5 miles westward of Orient Point. A buoy marks the north end of Orient Shoal.

GARDINERS BAY is at the western end of Block Island Sound. The bay is an excellent anchorage easily entered day or night, and it's the approach to **SHELTER ISLAND SOUND** and the **PECONIC BAYS**. The principal entrance is northward of Gardiners Point. The entrance from Long Island Sound is through **PLUM GUT**. The principal guides for the entrance to Gardiners Bay from Block Island Sound are the lighted gong buoy north of Gardiners Point, Little Bull Light and Orient Point Light. The white church spires at Orient and Sag Harbor is prominent. When past the lighted gong buoy north of Gardiners Point, vessels can select the anchorage in Gardiners Bay, which affords the best lee in the prevailing winds. The principal danger in approaching Gardiners Bay from the northward are the broken ground between Constellation Rock and Plum Island, and the shoal off Gardiners Point. Once in the bay, Crow Shoal should be avoided. In general, the shoaling is rather abrupt. In nearing these dangers, a gradual approach of the shoals on the western side of the bay is advised.

Ed. Note: A WORD ABOUT PLUM GUT: seven currents come together here and you will be able to see evidence of it as you approach. Tide rips can run as fast as 10 knots.

PLUM ISLAND, 2 miles westward of Great Gull Island, is 2.5 miles long, hilly, and bare of trees except near the southwest end, and has several large buildings, a prominent tank and flagpole. Plum Island is marked on its western point by Plum Gut Light. The island is a Government reservation and is closed to the public.

SHELTER ISLAND SOUND and **PECONIC BAYS** extend westward from Gardiners Bay about 22 miles to **RIVERHEAD,** the head of navigation of **THE PECONIC RIVER.** Beware of fish traps and oyster stakes on many of the shoals.

CHART 12358. STIRLING BASIN, on the northeast side of Greenport, is a part of **GREENPORT HARBOR.** The reported controlling depth was 8 feet in the entrance channel with 10 to 12 feet in the mooring areas. The entrance channel is marked by private seasonal buoys.

CHART 12358. GREENPORT is the major port in the area for all mariners' facilities including an easy walk to the laundromat and grocery store. It is also the end of the line for a branch of the Long Island Railroad —an excellent spot for dropping off or picking up crew. The white church spires, near the northern end of town,

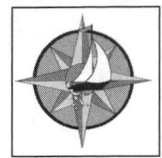

and a tank and TV/radio tower in the center of town are prominent landmarks for your approach. **GREENPORT HARBOR** is formed on the northeast by a 5 foot high breakwater which extends .02 mile southeastward of Youngs Point. The depths at the Greenport wharfs range from 7 to 21 feet.

Ed. Note: One of our favorite stops while cruising Eastern Long Island waters is the quaint seafaring village of Greenport. Walking about for shopping and provisioning, and even taking care of laundry, is easy. Set a course for **Claudio's Marina and Restaurant** to be docked in the heart of goings on in town. Here you can soak up good food and drink and the maritime history of this seaport. Find out that Greenport and whaling were like one word in the 1800s. One defined the other. Vessels from all over the world sailed into these waters for safe harbor and supplies. In 1854 the Portugese whaler, "Neva," arrived from the Azores bringing crew member Manuel Claudio to Greenport. In 1870 Manuel left the Neva and the arduous life of a whaler to open Claudio's Tavern which has been in the family ever since. The restaurant and bar are so steeped in America's nautical history that some say if you listen hard enough you can hear echoes of the men singing their sea chanties as they went in search of the leviathans of the deep.

SHELTER ISLAND. Just across from Greenport is **SHELTER ISLAND** and **DERING HARBOR.** This is the local mecca for sailing yachts. Dering Harbor is a pretty anchorage (there are also yacht club moorings) and is protected from winds from every direction but the the northwest. In entering the harbor, be sure to avoid shoaling off the northern end of Shelter Island Heights. From Shelter Island you can take a ferry to Greenport.

SMITH COVE a small bight on the **SOUTH SIDE OF SHELTER ISLAND** is a good anchorage for small craft in northerly weather. Depths range from 11 to 30 feet. A marina on the West Side of the cove can provide berths, gasoline, electricity and some marine supplies.

WEST NECK HARBOR AND WEST NECK BAY are shallow bodies of water on the **SOUTHWEST SIDE OF SHELTER**

ISLAND. The entrance is close eastward of the seaward end of a peninsula, marked by a private lighted buoy that separates the harbor from the sound, and the channel follows along the north side of this peninsula. Private buoys mark the channel.

Unspoiled by commercialism, **COECLES** (cockles) **HARBOR** on Shelter Island requires attention at the entrance, particularly in strong winds. The harbor is well marked with privately maintained tripods, beacons and buoys. Anchorage here is well-protected and mariners facilities are available. **RAM HEAD ISLAND** is connected to Coecles Island by a neck and is worth a visit.

FYI

In the late 1920s, Greenport became the mecca for the America's Cup and cup defenders, including the great "J" boat racing ships which were then outfitted by Greenport's S.T. Prestons... still open and working with nautical needs today.

SAG HARBOR, about 2.5 miles southwestward of the light on Cedar Point, is protected on the northeast by a breakwater marked at the outer end by a light. A spherical tank, a radio tower, and several flagpoles are prominent landmarks.

In entering **SAG HARBOR** do not round the breakwater too closely, as a depth of about 6 feet is found near its end. The deepest water is near the buoy. Anchor eastward or northeastward of the end of the former ferry wharf, locally known as Long Wharf. A 5-mph speed limit is enforced. The dredged channel into Sag Harbor has a controlling depth of about 8 feet, with 10 feet at midchannel through the entrance to the turning basin. **SAG HARBOR COVE** is about 8 feet deep. Private seasonal lights and buoys mark this channel and the cove. A 37-foot wide fixed bridge at the entrance has a vertical clearance of 20 feet MHW. Berths, electricity, gasoline, diesel fuel, storage, marine supplies, water ice, launching ramps, and complete engine hull rigging and sail repairs are available here.

GREAT PECONIC BAY, approximately 5 miles in diameter, is used mostly by local motorboats from **SHINNECOCK CANAL** and by cruising yachts. The bay is generally clear, but extensive shoals make off from the shores, except on its south side. The **SHINNECOCK CANAL** is the entrance to **GREAT PECONIC BAY** from the south.

LITTLE PECONIC BAY is nearly 5 miles long. The southerly shore of the bay is clear if given a berth of .4 mile, but shoals extend .6 mile at the south end of the bay. Local boats drawing 6 to 10 feet use **CUTCHOGUE HARBOR,** between Nassau Point and New Suffolk. On the east shore of the harbor, northwestward of Nassau Point, private interests have dredged three channels leading into the ponds.

A larger basin at the north end of **NEW SUFFOLK** locally known as **SCHOOL HOUSE CREEK** extends to the highway. A short rock jetty, covered at high water on the south protects the entrance channel. The depth to the boatyard at the head of the basin was reported to be 4 feet. **WICKHAM CREEK,** locally known as **BOATMEN'S HARBOR,** .7 mile north of New Suffolk, is entered through a privately dredged entrance channel with a reported controlling depth of 6 feet.

NASSAU POINT, the long neck on the northwest side of Little Peconic Bay, has high bluffs on the eastern side. A shoal with little depth over it extends .5 miles southward from Nassau Point and is marked by a lighted buoy.

BE AWARE OF ROBINS ISLAND ROCK, .8 mile westward of the south end of Robins Island. It is awash at low water. A buoy marks it, caution is recommended. The through channel in **NORTH RACE,** northward of Robins Island is marked and used only by light draft boats. **SOUTH RACE,** the channel southward of Robins Island, has a controlling depth of about 13 feet and is marked by buoys.

THE PECONIC RIVER empties into the western end of **FLANDERS BAY,** about 1.5 miles westward of South Jamesport. The river is entered through a dredged channel marked by private seasonal lights that lead from Flanders Bay to the head of navigation at Riverhead, about 2.4 miles above the channel entrance. **FLANDERS BAY** is the scene of considerable small boat activity.

SOUTH JAMESPORT is a village on **MIAMOGUE POINT,** 3.4 miles southwestward of **JAMES CREEK.** Local knowledge is necessary to avoid the shoals in this area, and strangers should take soundings frequently to keep in the best water. South Jamesport has railroad passenger and bus service.

TO FIND MARINA LOCATIONS - SEE THE TABLES AND LOCATOR CHARTS AT THE END OF THIS SECTION.

NORTH SHORE

A prominent sandy bluff known locally as Holmes Hill is just west of the entrance to **NORTH SEA HARBOR**. The Harbor is about 4 feet deep. The channel is marked by private seasonal buoys and by a private seasonal light at the entrance. This is an excellent harbor of refuge for small craft with drafts not exceeding 3.5 feet. The bottom is soft with good holding ground.

WOOLEY POND, 1-mile northeastward of North Sea Harbor, is entered through a dredged channel, which has a reported controlling depth of 6 feet. The channel is marked by private seasonal buoys and by private seasonal light on the north side of the entrance.

JESSUP NECK is a long narrow strip, partly high and wooded, separating **NOYACK BAY** from **LITTLE PECONIC BAY**. A shoal with depths of 5 to 7 feet extends 1.5 miles southwestward from Great Hog Neck on the northwest side at the entrance to Little Peconic Bay; a buoy marks this shoal.

NOYACK BAY is between North Haven Peninsula and Jessup Neck, and southward of the western end of Shelter Island. No dangers should be encountered if the shores are given a berth of .4 miles.

MILL CREEK in the southern part of Noyack Bay is entered through a privately dredged channel that leads to a basin. Private seasonal lights and buoys mark the channel. The reported controlling depths were 8 feet in the channel and 6 feet in the basin.

MATTITUCK INLET, 6.7 miles southwestward of Horton Point Light on the Sound, is entered between two short jetties. The inlet is marked by a long break in the bluffs, and numerous storage tanks inside the inlet are prominent. A light marks the outer end of the west jetty. A gong buoy about 1 mile north of the jetty light marks the entrance of the inlet. The side of the channel is sandy and although shoaling is liable to occur at the entrance, strangers can enter the inlet without great danger. The controlling depth was about 4 feet (6 feet at mid channel) from the entrance for about 1.8 miles to the turning basin at Mattituck with 7 feet available in the basin. Buoys and private markers mark the channel. The overhead power cables, about 1 mile above the entrance has a clearance of 78 feet.

Between **MATTITUCK INLET AND PORT JEFFERSON** the shore is fringed with rock shoals extending in places 1.5 miles offshore. Buoys mark the outer ends of the shoals.

CHART 12362. MOUNT SINAI HARBOR, 22.5 miles westward of Mattituck Inlet, is marked by a low break in the beach nearly 1 mile long. A buoy marks the approach to the harbor. Two jetties, the outer parts of which are awash at high water, protect the entrance. Extreme caution should be exercised when rounding them. A private light marks the outer end of the east jetty. A depth of about 8 feet was reported as available through the entrance. The northern part of the harbor has general depths eastward from the entrance to small craft facilities on the northern shore of the harbor.

PORT JEFFERSON HARBOR, on the north shore of Long Island, **EASTWARD OF OLD FIELD POINT,** is entered through a dredged channel that leads between two jetties to a docking area near the southwestern end of the harbor; the jetties are each marked by a light. A lighted whistle buoy about 1.1 miles northwest of the harbor entrance marks the approach. Three stacks on the west side near the head of the harbor are conspicuous landmarks. A 12-mph speed limit is enforced in the main entrance channel and a 5-mph speed limit is enforced at the head of the harbor in the vicinity of the mooring areas. Keep an eye out for the large passenger and car ferries heading to and fro across the Sound to Connecticut.

CHART 12362. PORT JEFFERSON Port Jefferson Harbor, on Long Island's north shore, is easily entered through a well marked channel that leads between two jetties to a docking area near the southwestern end of the harbor. The entry is marked by a lighted whistle buoy, approximately 1.1 miles northwest of the harbor entrance. Old Field Point, on the west side of the entrance is easily identified by two stacks clearly shown on the charts. There have been reports of shoaling close to shore at the entrance. Those without local knowledge should follow the channel through the entrance. The trip through will be a most enjoyable one. A 12-mph speed limit is strictly enforced in the main entrance channel and a 5-mph limit is enforced at the head of the harbor in the vicinity of the mooring areas. Keep an eye out for the large passenger and car ferries heading to and fro across the Sound to Connecticut. As you come southward, towards the head of the harbor to starboard you will pass a large municipal facility with three stacks. Danford's Inn and Marina (631-928-5200)is located on the east side of the ferry dock and offers first class accommodations for the traveling boater that enjoys life ashore. An overnight at Port Jefferson, in season, will afford you a great spectator's spot for sailing races and beautiful sunsets.

SETAUKET HARBOR on the western side of **PORT JEFFERSON HARBOR** has a narrow crooked channel. A reported depth of about 2.5 feet was available in the channel to the boatyard at Setauket. Private seasonal buoys mark the entrance from Port Jefferson. Setauket is a village on the south shore of Setauket Harbor about 1 mile above the entrance.

WESTERN LONG ISLAND SOUND is that portion of the deep navigable waterway between the shores of Connecticut and New York and the northern coast of Long Island westward of the line between Bridgeport and Old Field Point.

CHART 12365. NORTHPORT BASIN, about 10.5 miles westward of Old Field Point Light and 2.7 miles southeastward of Eaton's Neck Point, is a small privately maintained basin with general depths of 7 to 20 feet. The channel is marked by a private lighted buoy and unlighted buoys; submerged jetties extend northward from the east and west sides of the entrance.

EATON'S NECK is a prominent wooded headland with elevations of 100 feet or more and marked at its north end by a light and tower of Eaton's Neck Coast Guard Station. Note: white can buoys are for Coast Guard personnel only. Although a good harbor of refuge, overnighters will not enjoy the soundings of the fog signal.

EATON'S NECK LIGHT ,144 feet above the water, is shown from a 73-foot white stone tower. The fog signal is at the light.

HUNTINGTON BAY, just westward of Eaton's Neck, is the approach to **NORTHPORT BAY AND HARBOR, CENTERPORT HARBOR, HUNTINGTON HARBOR AND LLOYD HARBOR.** The bay protected against all but northerly winds is an excellent anchorage for large vessels.

NORTH SHORE

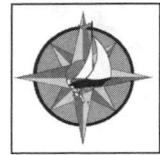

DUCK ISLAND HARBOR is a small, well-protected but shallow cove for light draft boats on the north side of Northport Bay westward of Duck Island Bluff.

NORTHPORT BAY, which opens off the southeast end of Huntington Bay, provides good anchorage in 20 to 50 feet in its western part, and in 8 to 11 feet in the eastern half. A lighted buoy marks the entrance to the bay, and the entrance channel, privately dredged to about 12 feet, is buoyed. An amber light, maintained at the public landing by the town of Northport, is a conspicuous mark at night for vessels making the wharfs at Northport. Anchorage is available at the Sand Hole near the power plant stacks. Make way slowly avoiding submerged rocks.

NORTHPORT HARBOR is at the southeastern end of Northport Bay and is entered by a dredged channel that leads along the waterfront of Northport and an anchorage basin west of the village. Private seasonal buoys mark the channel. **Bird Island,** a wildlife sanctuary in the southern part of the harbor, is a low grass covered, man-made island. Vessels should select anchorage according to draft in the harbor, the bottom is soft. Shelter is good with the exception of a nor'wester. The local pump-out boat can be contacted on VHF Channel 9.

Ed Note: The best bet in Northport Harbor is to take a mooring or an available slip at **Seymour's Boat Yard** for a visit to **Northport Village.** The village is within walking distance from Seymour's and is a charming seafaring town with Ship Captains' homes, lovely gardens to admire, and old-fashioned stores to bring on memories of days gone by. **Seymour's** staff offers a launch service to those boaters who choose moorings, plus fuel-up and ice. The marina is "pet-friendly" and kid-friendly too, with a playground and nearby park. Eight restaurants are in walking distance from their floating docks. The channel in to Seymour's is 7-8 feet MLW.

HUNTINGTON HARBOR, at the southwest end of Huntington Bay, is entered through a marked channel that leads to an anchorage off Huntington Town Dock, about 2 miles above the channel entrance. A depth of about 8 feet can be carried in the channel. Huntington Harbor Light, 42 feet above the water, and shown from a square concrete tower attached to a dwelling on a rectangular pier, is on the west side of the entrance to Huntington Harbor and on the south side of the entrance to **LLOYD HARBOR.** A fog signal is at the light. A light, and unlighted & lighted buoys, mark the channel. Some of the private buoys are seasonal. Huntington Harbor can become a sea of anchored and moored boats on summer weekends. The town is walkable and all manner of marine facilities are available.

LLOYD HARBOR extends westward from Huntington Bay nearly to Oyster Bay from which it is separated by a narrow strip of land. Vessels can anchor just inside the entrance, in depths of 7 to 11 feet. Buoys mark the entrance to the harbor. A speed limit of 5 mph is enforced in the harbor.

LLOYD NECK, between Huntington and Oyster Bays, is high and wooded, and has a high yellow bluff on its north side 0.8 miles eastward of Lloyd Point. Many patches of boulders having at least depths of 2 to 8 feet extend 0.2 to 0.5 miles offshore from East Fort Point to Lloyd Point. Small craft skirting this shore should keep well outside the line of buoys.

LLOYD POINT SAND HOLE is an anchorage for weekend partying. The Sand Hole was created out of the low-lying end of Lloyd Point. Look for masts of anchored sailboats. Enter carefully keeping an eye for submerged breakwater to starboard as well as shoals to port. Follow the dark deeper water and a local boater.

NORTH SHORE

TO FIND MARINA LOCATIONS - SEE THE TABLES AND LOCATOR CHARTS AT THE END OF THIS SECTION.

COLD SPRING HARBOR is one of the prettiest harbors on the Sound coupled with a charming seaside town that was once a whaling port and is home to a whaling museum worth visiting. The Cold Spring Harbor Light will guide you in through recently dredged channels.

OYSTER BAY, on the south side of Long Island Sound, is about 5 miles westward of Eaton's Neck Light. It lies between Lloyd Neck and Rocky Point, and is the approach to Cold Spring Harbor and Oyster Bay Harbor. The harbor is marked by Cold Spring Harbor Light, 37 feet above the water, and shown from a skeleton tower on a caisson with a red triangular daymark. The entrance and harbor are characterized by extensive shoals, boulder reefs, and broken ground making off from the shores. Vessels should proceed with caution if obliged to approach or cross shoal areas. The bay south of Cold Spring Harbor Light is a secured harbor with deep water.

OYSTER BAY HARBOR, a long crooked arm in the western side of Oyster Bay, has a channel with a depth over 30 feet leading into the area westward of Moses Point. Good anchorage is available southward of Moses Point. Vessels of less than 7 foot draft anchor in the bight between Cove Neck and wharf at Oyster Bay and also in West Harbor, the large bight on the northwest side of Centre Island. A speed limit of 5 mph is enforced in the harbor.

CHART 12366. GLEN COVE/HEMPSTEAD HARBOR, 4 miles wide at the entrance between Matinecock Point and Prospect Point, is free from dangers if the shores are given a berth of 0.3 miles. It is used by vessels seeking shelter in any but strong northerly winds and affords excellent anchorage with good holding ground. Vessels can anchor in any part of the harbor according to draft and direction of wind. A good anchorage for vessels is just inside a line from Mott Point to the breakwater at Glen Cove Landing. Small vessels can anchor behind the breakwater. Avoid anchoring in the pipeline area between Glenwood Landing and Bar Beach.

MANHASSET BAY between Barker Point and Hewlett Point affords excellent shelter for vessels of about 12 feet or less draft, and is frequented by a plethora of yachts — many of grand scale — in summer. The depths in the outer part of the bay range from 12 to 17 feet and 7 to 12 feet in the inner part inside Plum Point. The extreme south end of the bay is shallow with extensive mudflats. Depths of about 6 to 12 feet can be taken thorough a natural channel almost to the head of the bay. Extensive marine facilities are here and waterfront restaurants are plentiful.

PORT WASHINGTON, in Manhasset Bay, is a village with rail communication on the south side of a shoal bight about 1.2 miles southeastward of Plum Point. Depths of about 8 feet can be carried in the buoyed approach from the lighted buoy off Plum Point to the docks at Port Washington, and through the unmarked channel along the east side of the bight to its north end, northeastward of Tom Point.

HEWLETT POINT is on the west side of the entrance to Manhasset Bay. A boulder reef, mostly bare at low water (marked by a lighted buoy at its northern end)extends about 0.2 miles northward from the point. ⚓

#	Marina's Name & Phone Number	When Open	Monitors VHF Channel	Transient: Electricity•Moorings•Berths	Hull repairs•Engine repairs•Ramp	Winter Storage: Wet•Dry	Railway Capacity in Tons	Lift Capacity in Feet	Boat Rental: Canoe•Row•Motor	Boat Rental: Charter•House•Sail	Restaurant•Lodging•Camping	Showers•Laundry	Bait•Tackle•Pumpout•Toilets	Groceries•Water•Ice	Hardware	Diesel fuel•Gasoline
1	BAYSIDE MARINA 718-229-0097	ALL YR	9	MB		D					R			BI		
4	CAPRI MARINA INSPIRATION WHARF (516) 883-7800	ALL YR	9 72	EM B	H E	W D	60	30			R	SL	PT	IW	H	G D
5	NORTH HEMPSTEAD DOCK 516-767-4622												P			
6	GUY LAMOTTA BOATS 516-883-8411				H	D		35					T		H	
7	COASTLINE YACHT SALES 516-944-6000	ALL YR.	9 71	EB	HE	D		40								
9	MANHASSET BAY SHIPYARD 516-767-7447	ALL YR.			HE	D		30							H	
10	LOUIE'S SHORE RESTAURANT 516-883-4242	ALL YR.									R		T	IW	GH	
11	PORT WASHINGTON Y. C. 516-767-1614										R		PT	IB T		
12	TOM'S POINT MARINA 516-883-6630	ALL YR.	70		HE	D		20				SL	PT	W		
13	HAVEN MARINA 516-883-0937	ALL YR.		EB	HE	D		10	C	S		S	PT	W	H	
14	MANHASSET BAY MARINA 516-883-8411	ALL YR.	9	EB	HE	W D		80			R	SL	PT	IW	GH	G D
15	GULFWAY MARINE 516-767-0113				HE	D		25					T			
16	RANDAZZO YACHT MECHANICS 516-767-1666				E											
17	NORTH BAY MARINA 516-767-0110	ALL YR.		EB	HE	W D		10				S	PT	IW	H	
19	FEARON MARINE 516-767-0806	ALL YR.			H	D		25					T			
20	JOE WHITE MARINE 516-944-9200	ALL YR.			HE	D		20			R		T	W		
22	NORTH SHORE YACHT CLUB 516-883-9823											S	T	IW		
23	CAPRI MARINA 516-883-7800	ALL YR.	9 71	EM B	HE	W D		75			R	SL	PT	IW	GH	G D
25	BURTIS BOAT WORKS 516-676-4201	ALL YR.			HE	D		30				S	T	I WT	H	
26	TAPPEN BEACH AND MARINA 516-674-7100	JUN SEP		EB	R	W							PT	W		G D

#	Marina's Name & Phone Number	When Open	Monitors VHF Channel	Transient (Elec•Moorings•Berths)	Hull•Engine Repairs•Ramp	Winter Storage: Wet•Dry	Railway Cap. (ft)	Lift Cap. (tons)	Boat Rental: Canoe•Row•Motor	Boat Rental: Charter•House•Sail	Restaurant•Lodging•Camping	Showers•Laundry	Pumpout•Toilets	Bait•Tackle•Water•Ice	Groceries•Hardware	Diesel•Gasoline
27	BREWER YACHT YARD 516-671-5563	ALL YR.		EB	HE	W D		30					S	PT	IW	H	
28	GLEN COVE YACHT SERVICE 516-676-0777	ALL YR.		EB	HE	W D		60					S	PT	IW	H	G D
29	GLEN COVE MARINA INC 516-759-3129	ALL YR.	9	EB	HE	W D		35					S	T	IW		G D
32	MILL NECK BAY MARINE 516-671-5621	ALL YR.			HE	D		12						T	W	H	
33	BRIDGE MARINA 516-628-8688	ALL YR.		EM B	HE R	D						RL		T	IW BT	GH	
34	ROOSEVELT BOAT BASIN 516-922-5800				R									PT	W		G D
35	ROOSEVELT BEACH 516-922-5800													PT	W		G D
36	SAGAMORE Y.C. 516-922-0555												S	T	W		
37	JAKOBSON SHIPYARD 516-922-4500	ALL YR				D		99 +									
38	OYSTER BAY MARINE 516-922-6331	ALL YR	71	EM B		D		10			R			T	IW	H	G D
39	POWLES MARINA 631-367-7670	APR NOV		M	E	D					R	L		T	IW BT	GH	G D
40	WHALER'S COVE YACHT CLUB 631-367-9822	APR NOV		EB										T	IW		
41	LONG ISLAND YACHT SALES 631-549-4687	ALL YR			HE	D										H	
42	CONEYS MARINE 631-421-3366	MAR DEC	9	EM B	HE			30			R	S		T	IW	GH	D
43	DORNIC MARINE 631-385-0622	ALL YR.		MB	HE	W D		10						T			
44	WEST SHORE MARINA 631-427-3444	ALL YR.		EB	HE	W D		35			R	SL	PT	I W	GH		G
47	WILLIS MARINE CENTER INC 631-421-3400	ALL YR	9	EM B	HE	W D		35			R	S		T	IW	H	G D
48	KNUTSON MARINE STORES 631-673-4144				E											H	
49	KETEWOMOKE Y. C. 631-351-9762											R	S	T	IW	GH	
50	HUNTINGTON TOWN DOCK			B										P			

L.I. North Shore

MARINA'S NAME & PHONE NUMBER

Chart #	Marina Name & Phone	When Open	VHF	Transient (Elec/Moor/Berths)	Hull/Engine/Ramp	Winter Storage (Wet/Dry)	Railway Cap (ft)	Lift Cap (tons)	Boat Rental	Restaurant/Lodging	Showers/Laundry	Pumpout/Toilets	Bait/Tackle/Water/Ice	Groceries/Hardware	Diesel/Gasoline
51	CONEYS MARINE 631-421-3366	ALL YR.	9	MB	HE	W/D				R	S	T	IW	GH	
52	SPORT BOATS 631-421-3717	ALL YR.			HE			8				T		H	
53	KNUTSON'S MARINA INC 631-673-0700	ALL YR.		E B	HE	W/D		35		R	SL	T	IW	GH	G D
54	KNUTSON WEST 631-549-7842	ALL YR.	9	EM B	HE	W/D		35		R	SL	PT	W I	GH	
55	HUNTINGTON YACHT CLUB 631-351-8686									R	S	T	IW		G D
56	CENTERPORT BOATWORKS 631-757-8576	MAR NOV		EM B	E	D							IW		
58	BRITANNIA YACHTING 631-261-5600	ALL YR.	9	EB	HE	WD		55		R	L S	PT	BT IW	GH	G D
59	**SEYMOURS 631-261-6574**	**ALL YR.**	**68**	**EM B**	**HE**	**D**	**50**	**30**			**S**	**PT**	**IW**	**GH**	**G D**
60	NORTHPORT TOWN DOCK				R					RL	L	T	IW B	GH	
61	WOODBINE MARINA 631-421-1000											PT			
65	SMITHTOWN BAY Y.C. 631-862-9891									R	S	T	IW		
66	STONY BROOK BOAT WORKS 631-751-1230	ALL YR.		EB	HE	D		15				T			
69	WELLS SHIPYARD 631-751-2082	ALL YR.						20							
70	SETAUKET HARBOR MARINE 631-941-4640	AL YR.			HE R	D						T	IW		
71	THE BOAT PLACE 631-473-0612	ALL YR.			HE R	D		25					W	H	G
72	BASIL CARAFTIS & SONS 631-473-2288	APR NOV			HE	D			M	RL		T	IW BT	G	G D
73	PORT JEFFERSON MARINA 631-331-3567	MAY NOV		E B	R					RL		PT	IW	GH	G D
74	DANFORD'S MARINA AND INN 631-928-5200	APR. NOV		E B							S	PT	IW		G D
76	OLD MAN'S BOAT YARD 631-473-7330	ALL YR.			HE	D		25				P	W	H	
77	RALPH'S FISHING STATION 631-473-6655	ALL YR.	67	EM B	HE R	W/D		10	M	R		PT	IW BT	H	G D

L.I. North Shore

Chart Locater Number	Marina's Name & Phone Number	When Open	Monitors VHF Channel	Transient: Electricity • Moorings • Berths	Hull repairs • Engine repairs • Ramp	Winter Storage: Wet • Dry	Railway Capacity in Feet	Lift Capacity in Tons	Boat Rental: Canoe • Row • Motor	Boat Rental: Charter • House • Sail	Restaurant • Lodging • Camping	Showers • Laundry	Pumpout • Toilets	Bait • Tackle • Water • Ice	Groceries • Hardware	Diesel fuel • Gasoline
78	MOUNT SINAI Y. C. 631-473-2993	ALL YR.	9	EM B							R	S	T	IW		G D
79	MOUNT SINAI MARINA 631-928-0199	MAY NOV		EB	R								T	W		
80	MATTITUCK INLET STATION 631-298-9726	ALL YR.				D			M							
81	OLD MILL INN 631-298-8080	ALL YR.	13	EB							R		T	IW		
82	MATTITUCK INLET MARINA 631-298-4480	ALL YR.	68	EB	HE	D		80			R	S	T	W	H	G D
83	MATT-A-MAR MARINA 631-298-4739	ALL YR.	9 68	EB	HE	D		50	CR		R	S	T	IW	H	G D
84	MATTITUCK MARINA 631-298-8978	ALL YR.		B	R							S	T	W		
85	MATTITUCK VILLAGE MARINE 631-298-5800	ALL YR.			HE	D							T		H	
87	STRONG'S MARINE 631-298-4770	ALL YR.	68		HE R	D		20	M			S	PT	IW	H	G
88	CAPT. MARTY'S FISH STATION 631-734-6852	APR NOV			E				M					IB T		
90	NEW SUFFOLK SHIPYARD 631-734-6311	ALL YR.		EB	HE	D		15				S	T	W	H	G
91	CUTCHOGUE MARINA 631-734-6993	ALL YR.		EB	HE R	D						S	T	IW	H	G D
93	DAVE BOFILL MARINE 631-283-6739	ALL YR.			E								T		H	G
94	PECONIC MARINA 631-283-3767	ALL YR.			HE	D	30	30			R	S	T	W BT	H	G D
95	PECONIC RIVER YACHT BASIN 631-727-8386	ALL YR	9	EB		W D							PT	W		
96	LARRY'S LIGHTHOUSE 631-722-3400	ALL YR.		EB	HE	D		30			R	S	PT	IW	H	G D
98	DREAMER'S COVE MOTEL 631-722-3212	ALL YR.		B							L		T			
99	B & E MARINE 631-727-8619	ALL YR.			HE R	D										
100	GATEWAY MARINE 631-727-1028	ALL YR.		EB	HE R	D		15					PT	IW	H	G
101	GREAT PECONIC BAY MARINA 631-722-3565	ALL YR.		EB	HE	D		50				S	T	IW	H	G D

L.I. North Shore

CHART LOCATER NUMBER — MARINA'S NAME & PHONE NUMBER

Chart #	Marina's Name & Phone Number	When Open	Monitors VHF Channel	Transient: Electricity/Moorings/Berths	Hull/Engine Repairs/Ramp	Winter Storage: Wet/Dry	Railway Capacity (ft)	Lift Capacity (tons)	Boat Rental: Canoe/Row/Motor	Boat Rental: Charter/House/Sail	Restaurant/Lodging/Camping	Showers/Laundry	Bait/Tackle/Toilets	Pumpout	Groceries/Water/Ice	Diesel fuel/Gasoline	Hardware
102	EAST CREEK MARINA 631-722-4842	ALL YR.	7 68	EB	E	W						S	T		IW BT	G	H
104	ORIENT BY THE SEA MARINA 631-323-2424	MAY NOV	9	EB	R	W			C		R	S	T		IW	G D	
105	NARROW RIVER MARINA 631-323-2660			B	HE R	W D					C				W		
109	BREWER YACHT YARD 631-477-9594	ALL YR.		EB	HE	D		70			R	SL	T		IW		H
110	WHITE A.P. BAIT SHOP 631-477-0008	MAR NOV							C		R		T		IB		
111	STIRLING HARBOR MARINA 631-477-0828	ALL YR.	9	EB	HE R	W D		50			R	SL	T		IW	G D	
112	HANFF'S BOAT YARD 631-477-1550	ALL YR.			H	D	45	30					T				
113	TOWNSEND MANOR MARINA 631-477-2000	ALL YR	9	EB							RL	S	T		IW	G	
114	GREENPORT YACHT 631-477-2277	ALL YR.			HE	D	400	50				S	T				H
115	S.T. PRESTON & SON INC 631-477-1990	ALL YR.		B							R						H
116	CLAUDIO'S REST. & MARINA 631-477-0355	APR NOV	9	EB					C		R	S	T		IW	G D	
118	SOUTHOLD MARINE CENTER 631-765-3131	ALL YR.			HE	D							T				H
119	ALBERTSON MARINE 631-765-3232	ALL YR.	16	EB	HE	W D		45					T		W		H
120	PORT OF EGYPT 631-765-2445	YR.		EB	HE R	D	40	25	C		RL	SL		PT	IW BT	G D	H
121	BRICK COVE MARINA 631-477-0830	ALL YR.		EB	HE R	W D		30				S	T		W		H
122	MILL CREEK INN & MARINA 631-765-1010	ALL YR.		EB							R		T		IW		
123	GOLDSMITH'S BOAT SHOP 631-765-1600	ALL YR.	68	EB	HE R	D					R					G	H
124	DERING HARBOR MARINA 631-749-0045	ALL YR.	9	EM B								SL		PT	IW	G D	H
125	JACK'S MARINE & OUTBOARD 631-749-0114	ALL YR.		M	HE	D							T		BT	G	H
127	ISLAND BOATYARD 631-749-3333	ALL YR.	9	EB	HE	D						SL		PT	IW	G D	

L.I. North Shore

MARINA'S NAME & PHONE NUMBER

Chart Locater #	Marina's Name & Phone Number	When Open	Monitors VHF Channel	Transient (Electricity•Moorings•Berths)	Hull/Engine Repairs•Ramp	Winter Storage (Wet•Dry)	Railway Cap. (ft)	Lift Cap. (tons)	Boat Rental (Canoe•Row•Motor•Sail)	Boat Rental (Charter•House)	Restaurant•Lodging•Camping	Showers•Laundry	Pumpout•Toilets	Bait•Tackle•Water•Ice	Groceries•Hardware	Diesel fuel•Gasoline
128	SHELTER ISLAND MARINA 631-749-1030	MAY OCT		EM B	HE R							S	T	IW BT		
129	COECLES HARBOR MARINA 631-749-0700	ALL YR.	9	EM B	HE	D		30	S			SL	PT	IW	GH	G D
130	MILL CREEK MARINA 631-725-1351	MAR DEC		B	HE			25			R		T	IW	H	G
131	NOYAC MARINA 631-725-3333	APR OCT		MB	ER	D							T	IW BT		
132	WATERFRONT MARINA 631-725-3886	APR NOV	9	EB							RL	S	T	IW		
133	BARON'S COVE MARINA 631-725-3939	APR OCT	9	EB							R	SL	T	IW		G
134	SAG HARBOR DOCK 631-725-2368	APR OCT	16	MB	R											
135	SAG HARBOR Y. C. 631-725-0567	MAY SEP	9	EB							R	S	T	IW		G D
136	WHALERS MARINA 631-725-1605	MAY OCT	9	EB							R	SL	T	IW		
137	SHIP ASHORE MARINA 631-725-3755	ALL YR.			HE	D		30				S	T	W	H	G
138	EAST HAMPTON MARINA 631-324-4042	AL YR.	9		HE	D							T	W	H	G
141	EAST HAMPTON MARINA 631-324-5666	ALL YR.	9	EB	HE	D		15			R	S	PT	IW BT	H	G D
142	THREE MILE MARINA 631-324-5500	ALL YR.				D		15						W		
144	SHAGWONG MARINA 631-324-4830			EB		W					RL	SL	T	W		
145	HALSEY'S MARINA 631-324-9847	MAY OCT		EB		W						S	T	W		
146	MAIDSTONE HARBOR MARINA 631-324-2651	ALL YR.	9	EB		W					R	SL	T	IW		
147	GARDINER'S MARINA 631-324-9894	MAY OCT	9	B		W						S	T	IW		G D
148	THREE MILE HARBOR YARD 631-324-1320	ALL YR.		EB	HE	D		40			R			IW B	H	
153	CAPTAIN'S COVE MARINA 631-668-5995	MAR DEC		EB	HE			25		C	RL	S	T	IW BT	H	G D
154	SALIVAR RESTAURANT 631-668-2555	ALL YR.								C	R		T	I		

L.I.
North Shore

MARINA'S NAME & PHONE NUMBER

Chart #	Marina Name & Phone	When Open	Monitors VHF Channel	Transient (Elec/Moor/Berth)	Hull/Engine Repairs • Ramp	Winter Storage (Wet/Dry)	Railway Cap. (tons)	Lift Cap. (feet)	Boat Rental (Canoe/Row/Motor/Sail)	Boat Rental (Charter/House)	Restaurant/Lodging/Camping	Showers/Laundry	Pumpout/Toilets	Bait/Tackle/Water/Ice	Groceries/Hardware	Diesel/Gasoline
156	UIHLEIN'S MARINA 631-668-3799	MAR NOV		EB		D	25		M	C		S	T	IW BT	H	G
157	MONTAUK MARINE BASIN 631-668-5900	ALL YR.	9 19	EB	HE	D	70			C	RL	S	T	IW BT	H	G D
158	OFFSHORE SPORTS MARINA 631-668-2406	ALL YR.	9 19	EB	HE	D	50			C	R	SL	T	IW BT		G D
159	BLOCK ISLAND FERRY 631-668-5700									C						
160	THE LANDING 631-668-2165	APR OCT		B							R	SL	T	W		
161	TUMAS TACKLE 631-668-2707	APR NOV								C						
162	WESTLAKE FISHING LODGE 631-668-5600	MAR DEC	19	EB	ER					C	R	S	T	IW BT	H	
163	GOSMAN'S RESTAURANT 631-668-2447	APR NOV									R		T	I		
164	SNUG HARBOR MARINA 631-654-2139	MAR NOV	9	EB							RL	SL	T	IW		
165	INLET MARINA 631-668-3743	ALL YR.														D
166	STAR ISLAND YACHT CLUB 631-668-5052	ALL YR	9 16	EB	HE	D	75				RL	SL	T	IW BT	H	G D
167	GONE FISHING MARINA 631-668-3232	ALL YR.	19		HE R	D	25				RL	S	PT	IW BT	GH	G D
168	MONTAUK LAKE MARINA 631-668-5705	MAY OCT		EB							RL	SL	T	IW		G D
169	MONTAUK YACHT CLUB 631-668-3100	APR NOV	9 16 72	EB							RL	S	PT	IW		
170	ISLAND MOBIL & MARINA 631-788-7311	ALL YR.	9	B							R	S	T	IW		G D
171	FISHERS ISLAND MARINA 631-788-7245	MAY OCT	9	EB								SL	T	W		

Find links to popular boating sites on
www.BoatersAlmanac.com

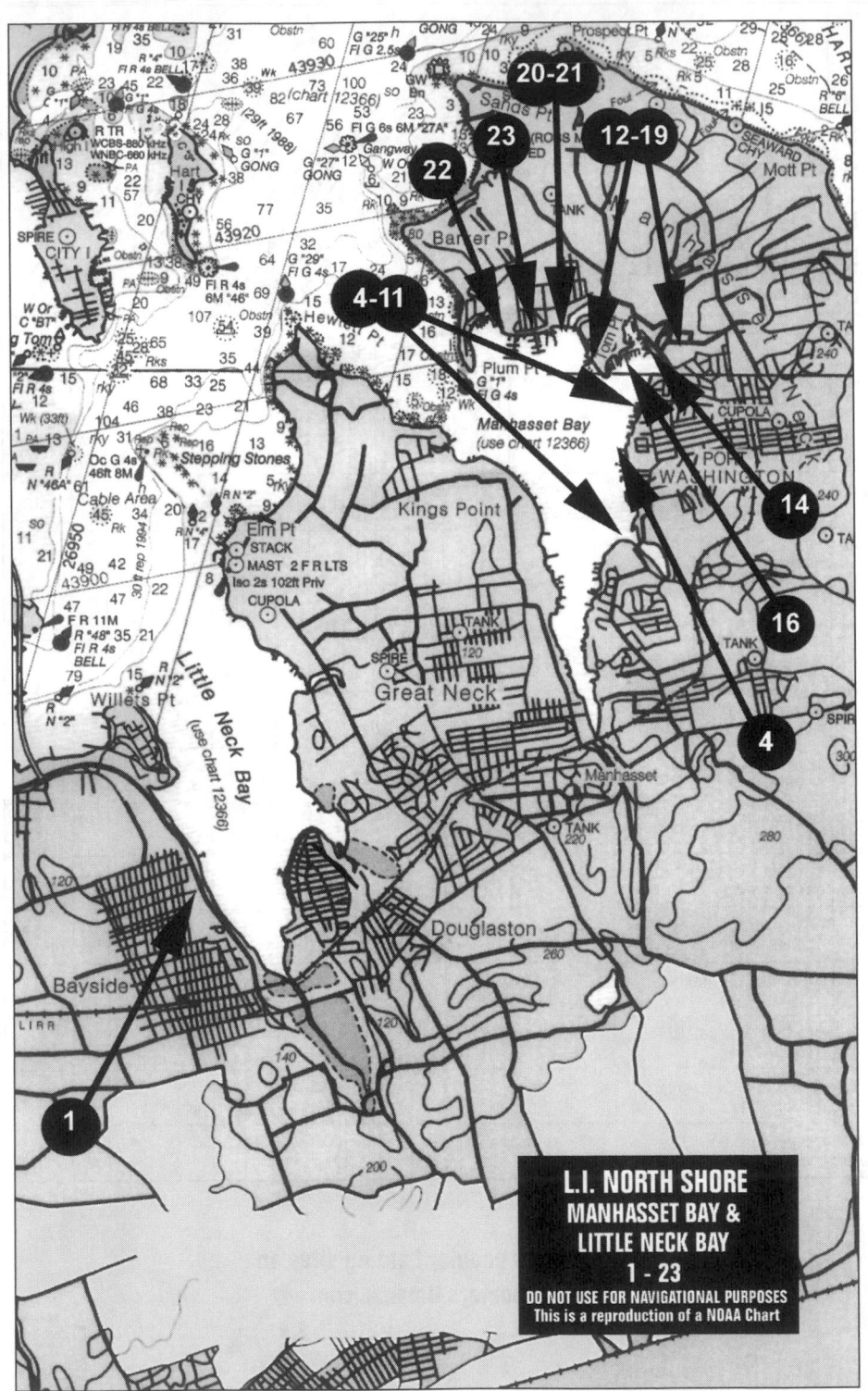

L.I. NORTH SHORE
MANHASSET BAY &
LITTLE NECK BAY
1 - 23
DO NOT USE FOR NAVIGATIONAL PURPOSES
This is a reproduction of a NOAA Chart

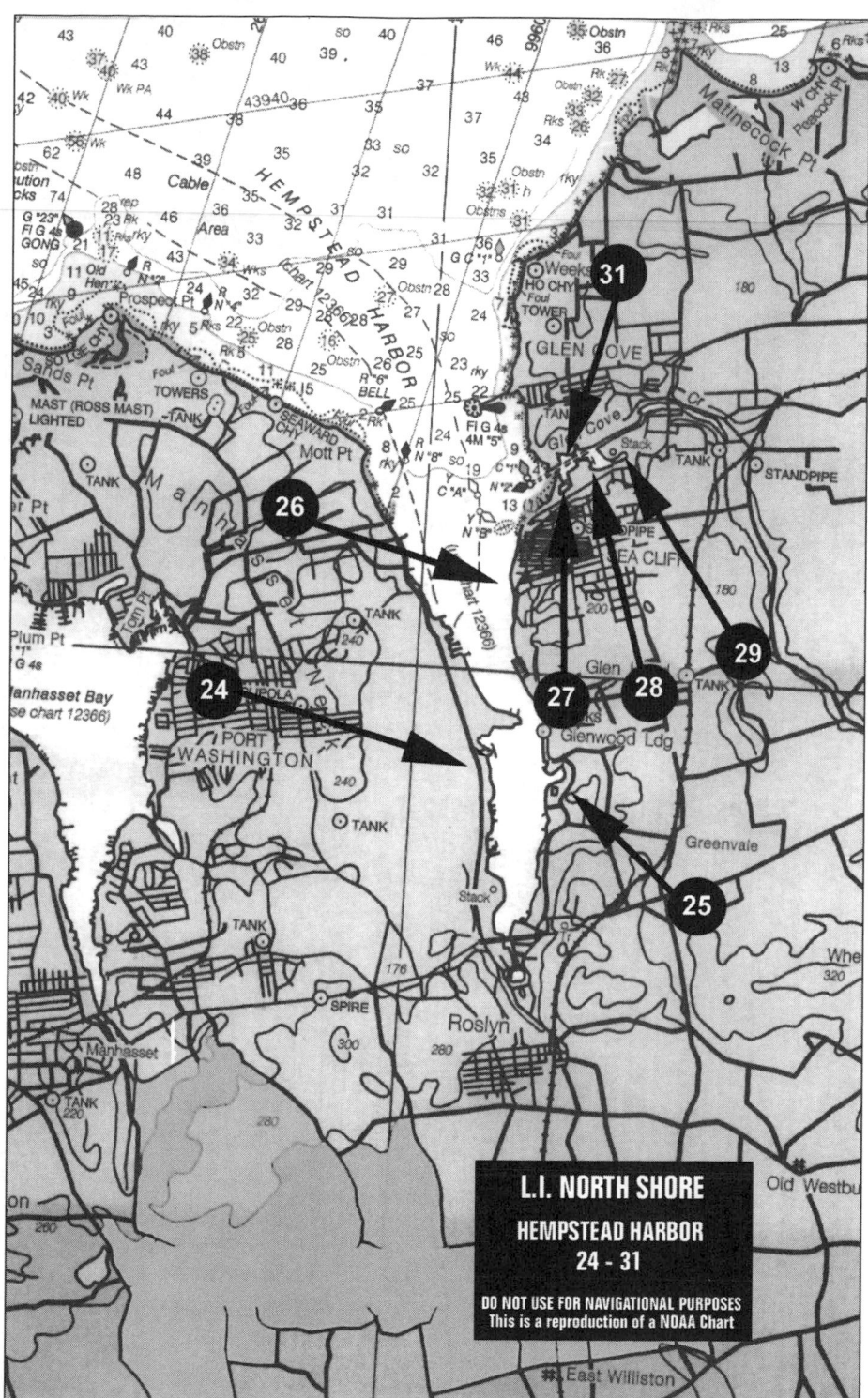

417

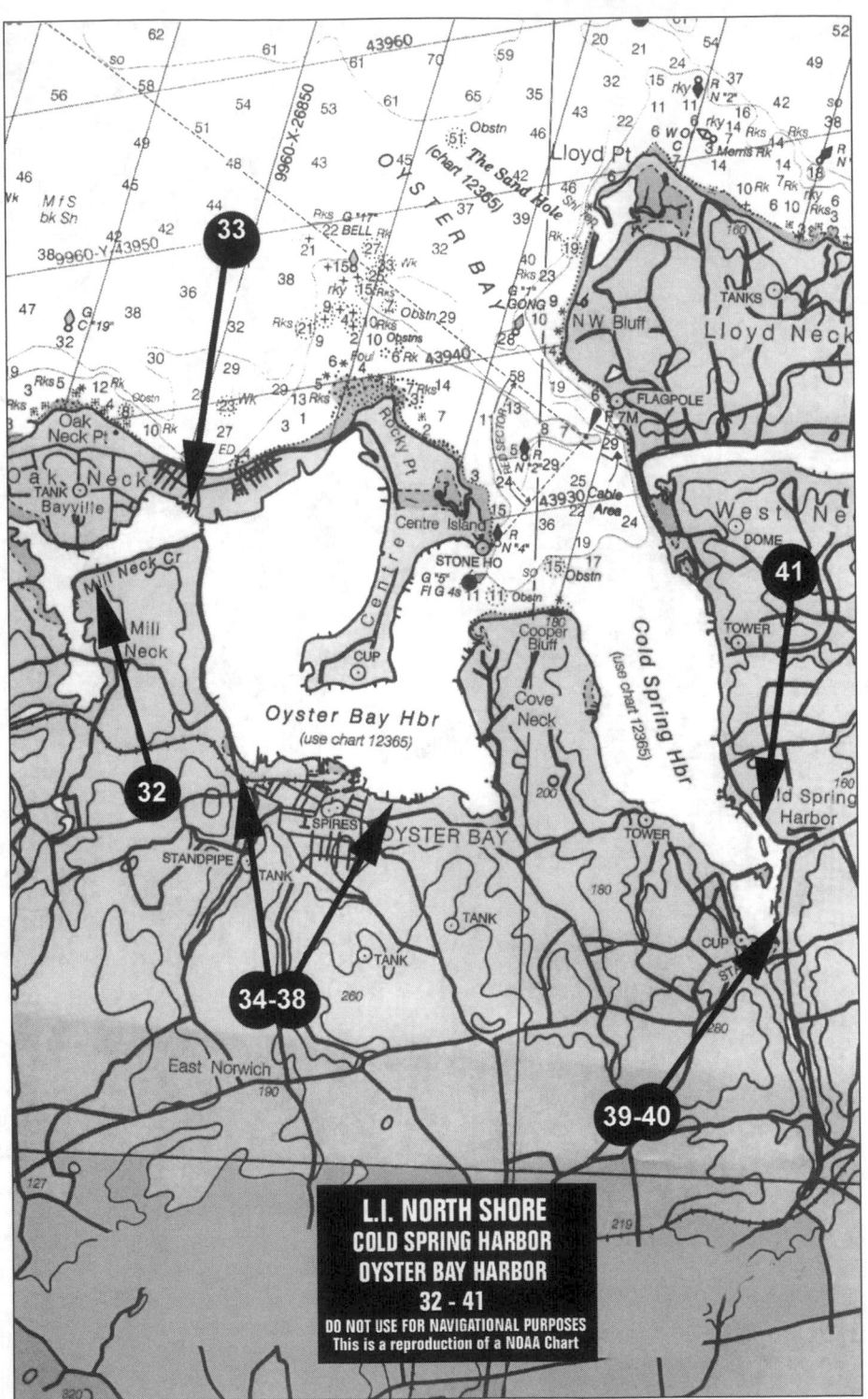

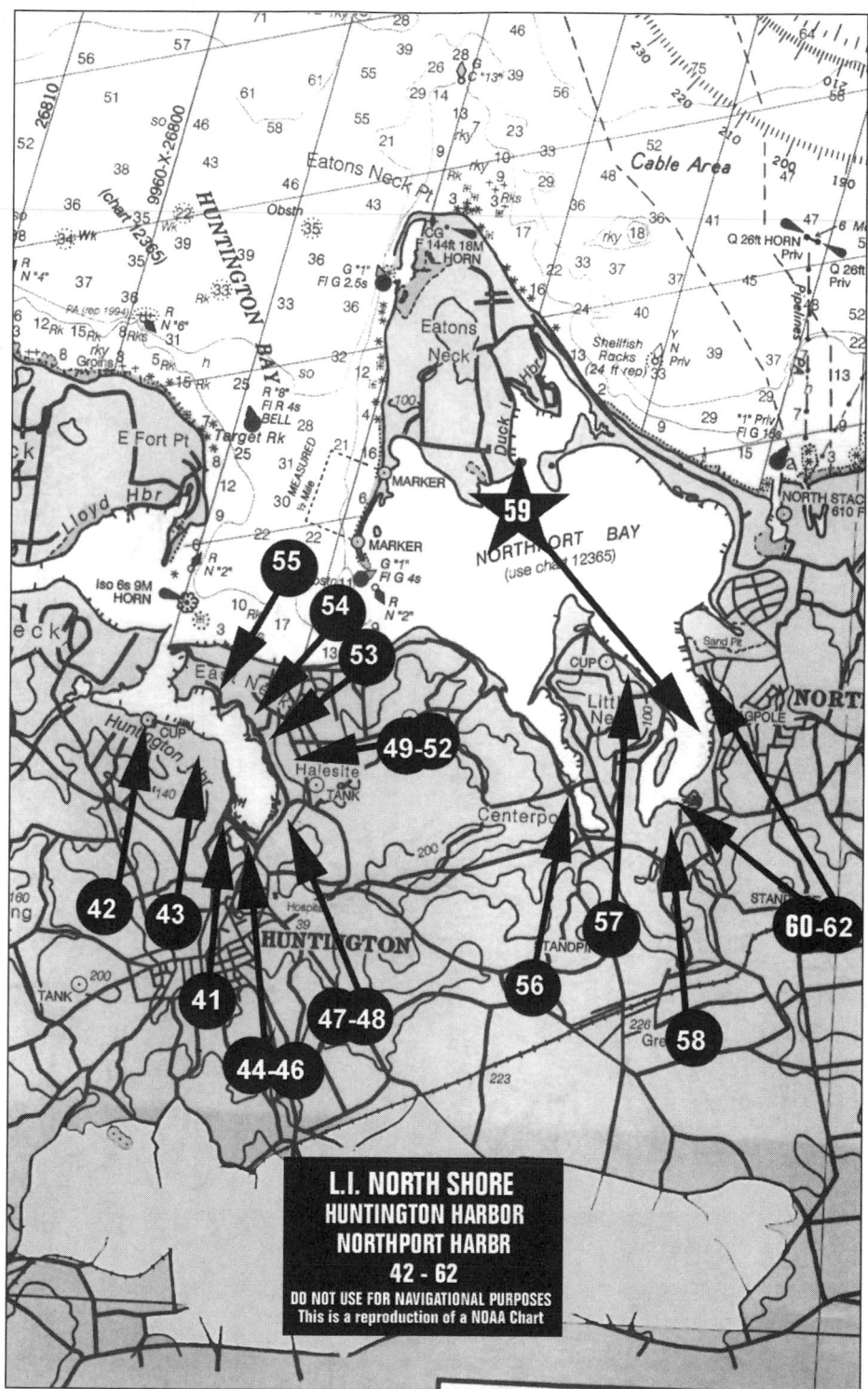

L.I. NORTH SHORE
HUNTINGTON HARBOR
NORTHPORT HARBR
42 - 62
DO NOT USE FOR NAVIGATIONAL PURPOSES
This is a reproduction of a NOAA Chart

419

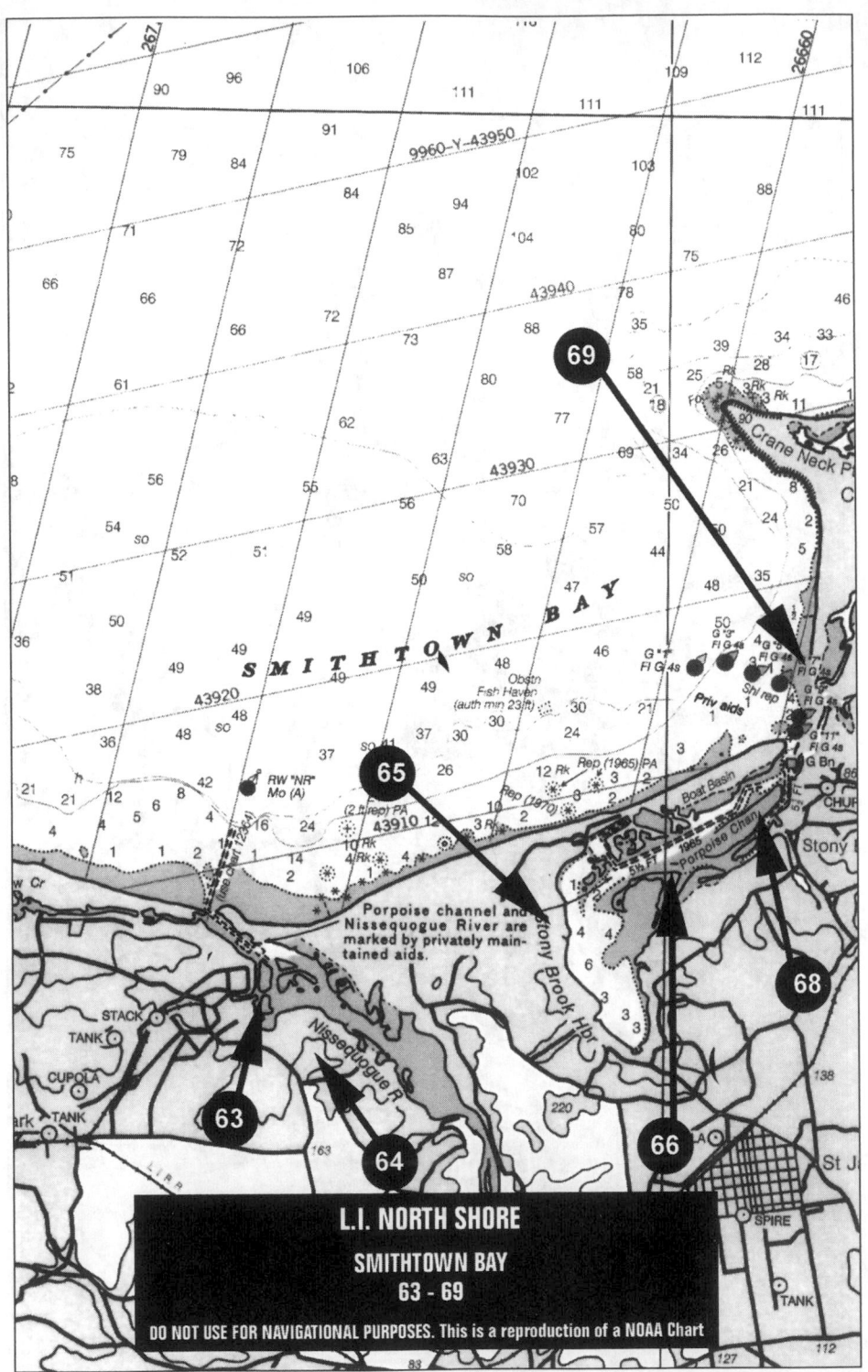

L.I. NORTH SHORE

SMITHTOWN BAY

63 - 69

DO NOT USE FOR NAVIGATIONAL PURPOSES. This is a reproduction of a NOAA Chart

Porpoise channel and Nissequogue River are marked by privately maintained aids.

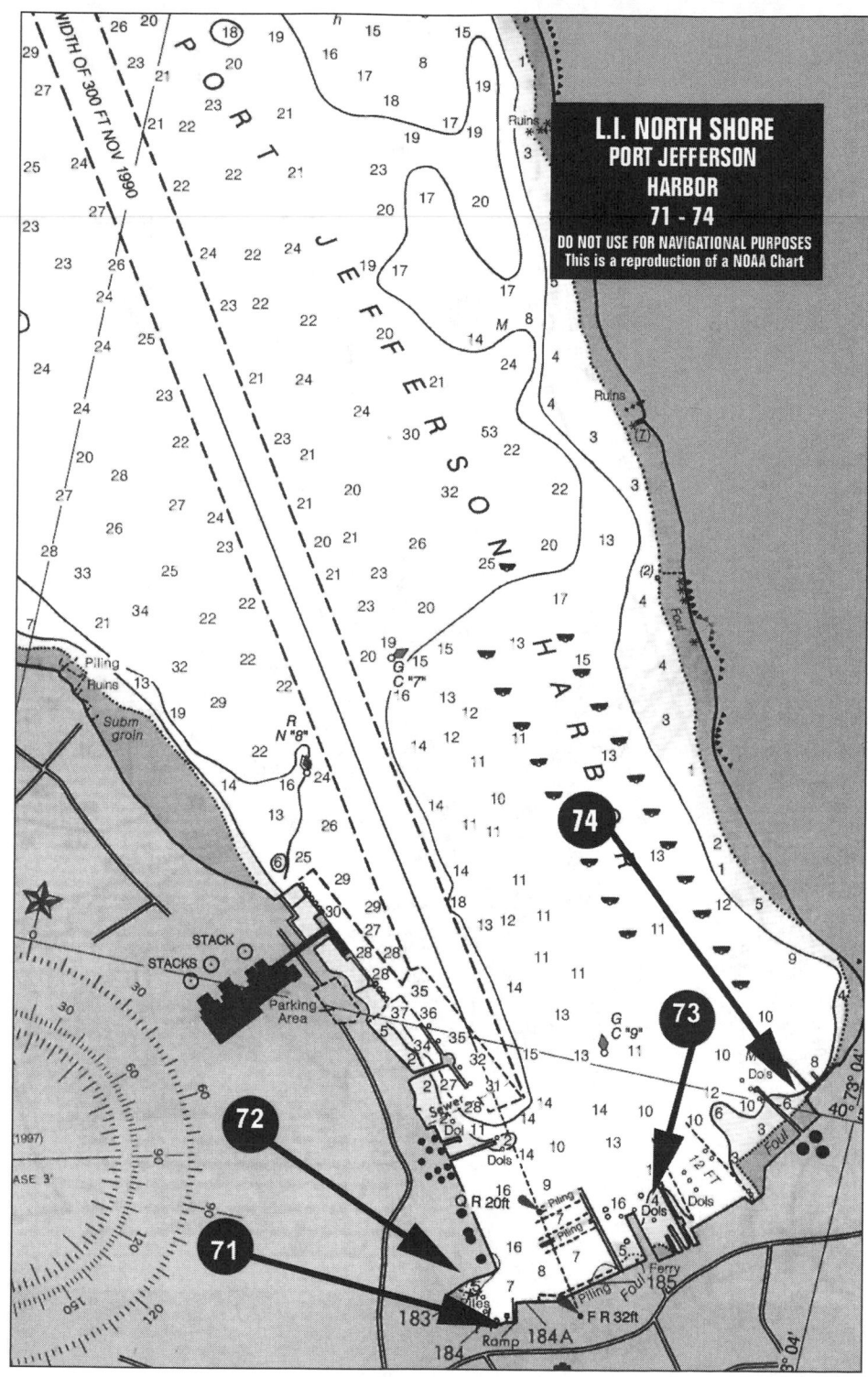

L.I. NORTH SHORE
PORT JEFFERSON
HARBOR
71 - 74
DO NOT USE FOR NAVIGATIONAL PURPOSES
This is a reproduction of a NOAA Chart

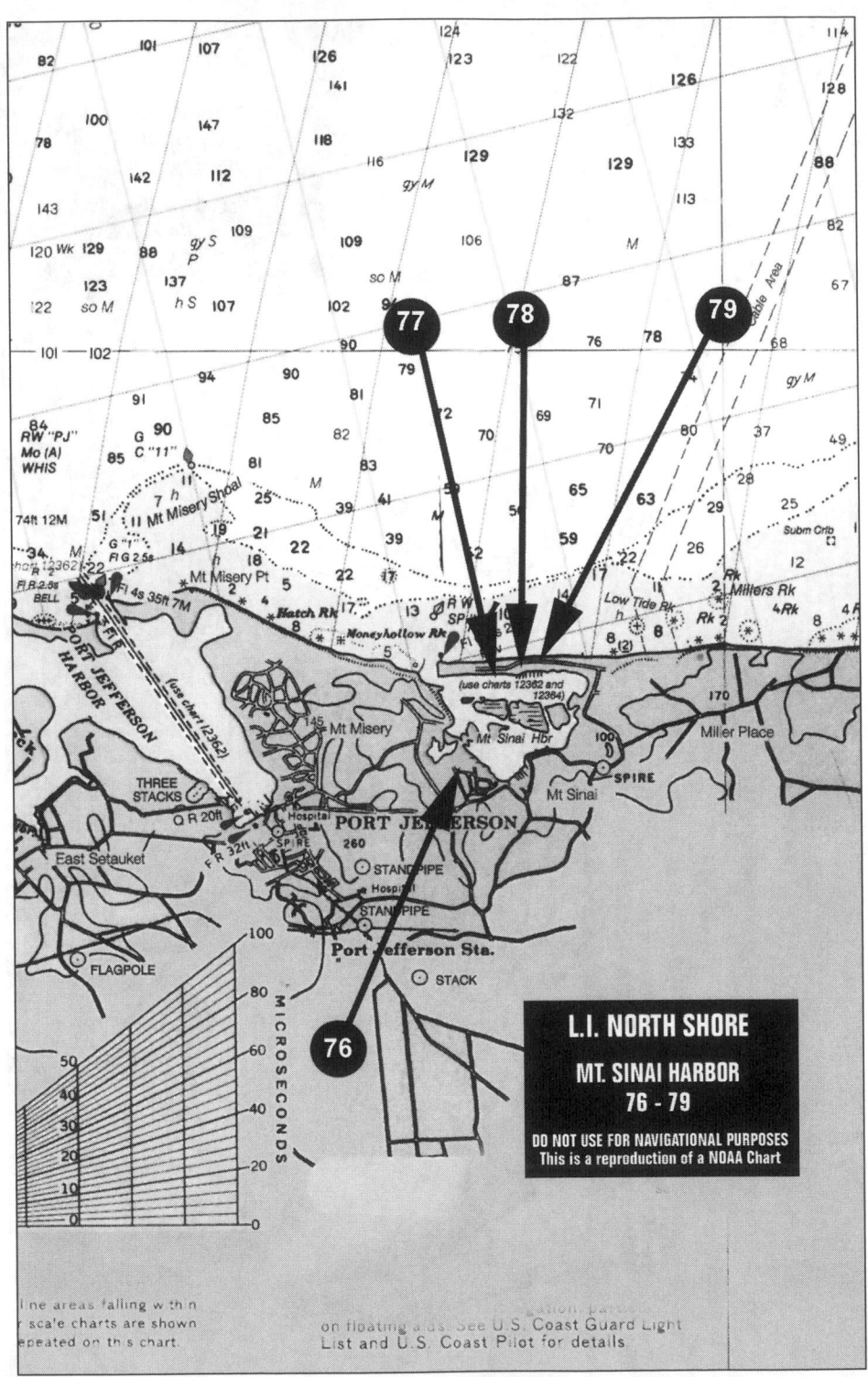

L.I. NORTH SHORE
MT. SINAI HARBOR
76 - 79

DO NOT USE FOR NAVIGATIONAL PURPOSES
This is a reproduction of a NOAA Chart

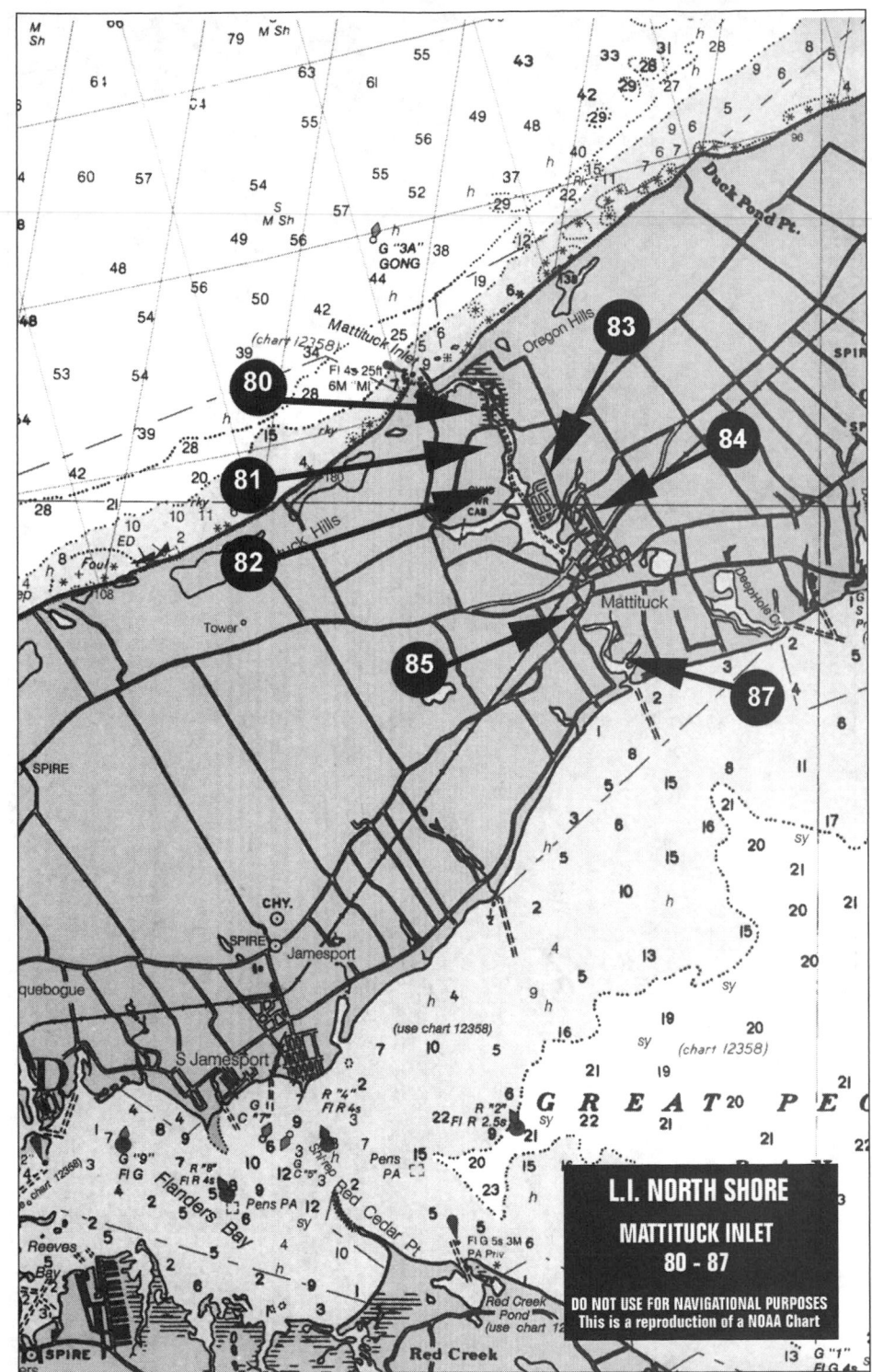

L.I. NORTH SHORE
MATTITUCK INLET
80 - 87

DO NOT USE FOR NAVIGATIONAL PURPOSES
This is a reproduction of a NOAA Chart

423

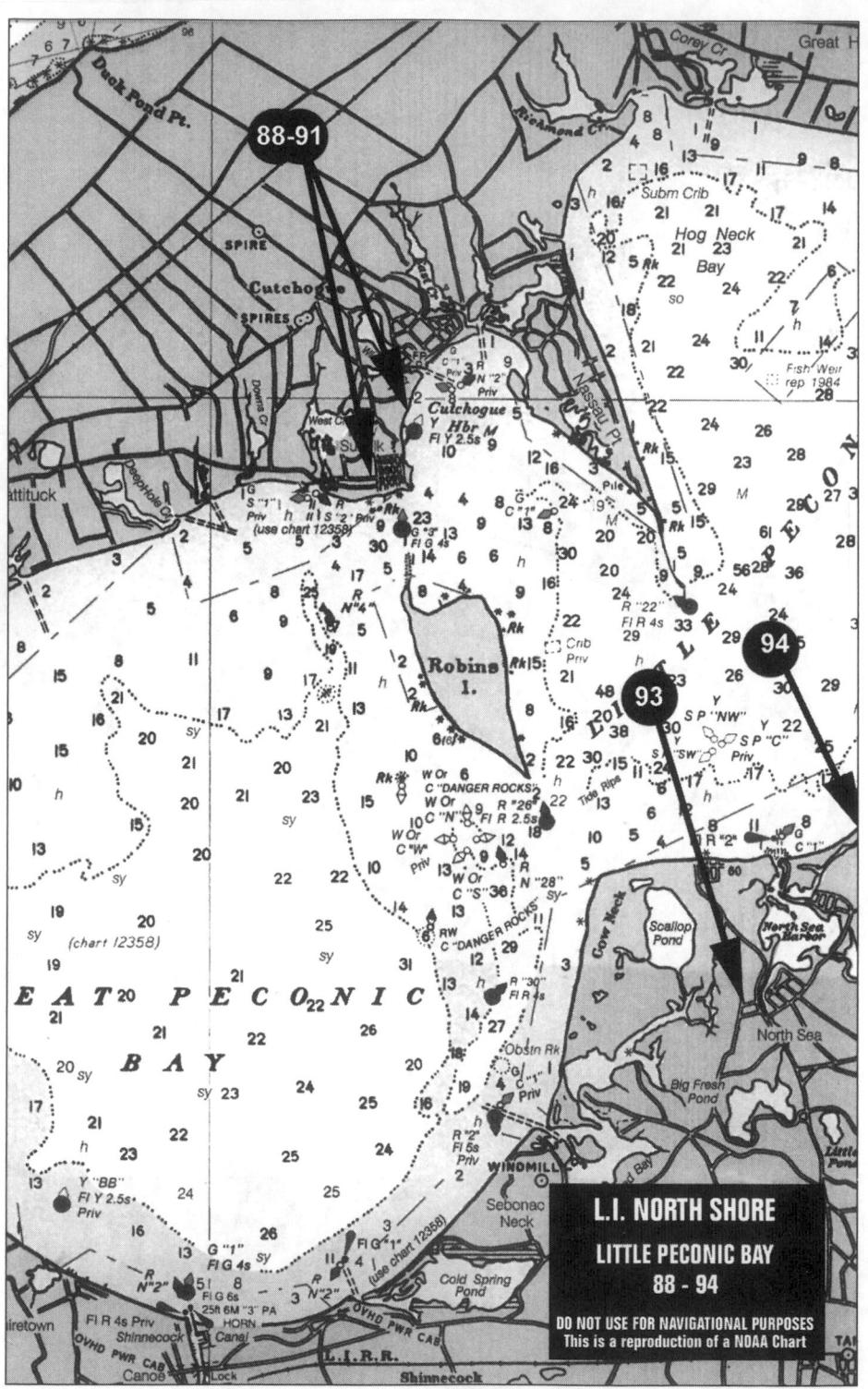

L.I. NORTH SHORE

LITTLE PECONIC BAY
88 - 94

DO NOT USE FOR NAVIGATIONAL PURPOSES
This is a reproduction of a NOAA Chart

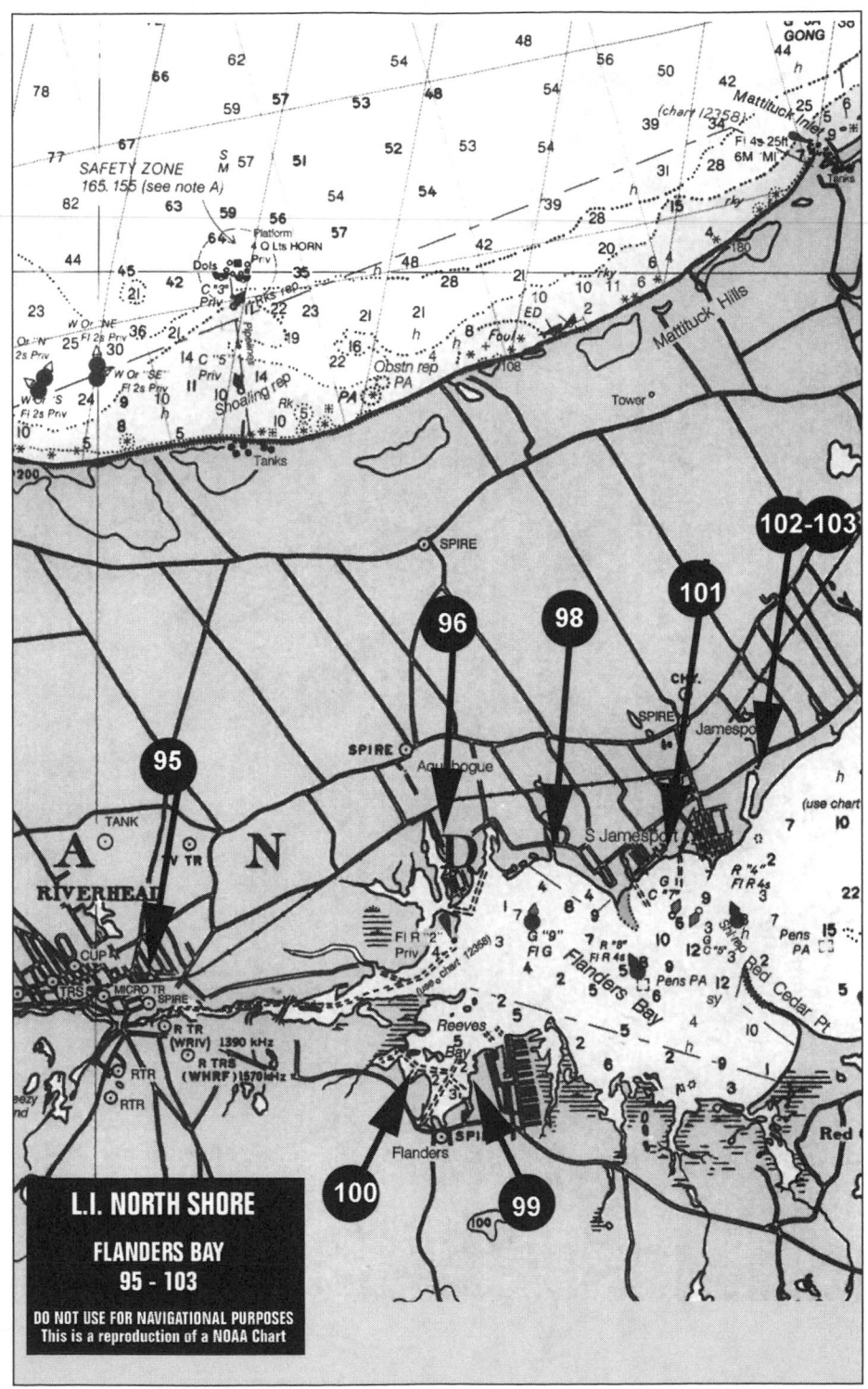

L.I. NORTH SHORE

FLANDERS BAY
95 - 103

DO NOT USE FOR NAVIGATIONAL PURPOSES
This is a reproduction of a NOAA Chart

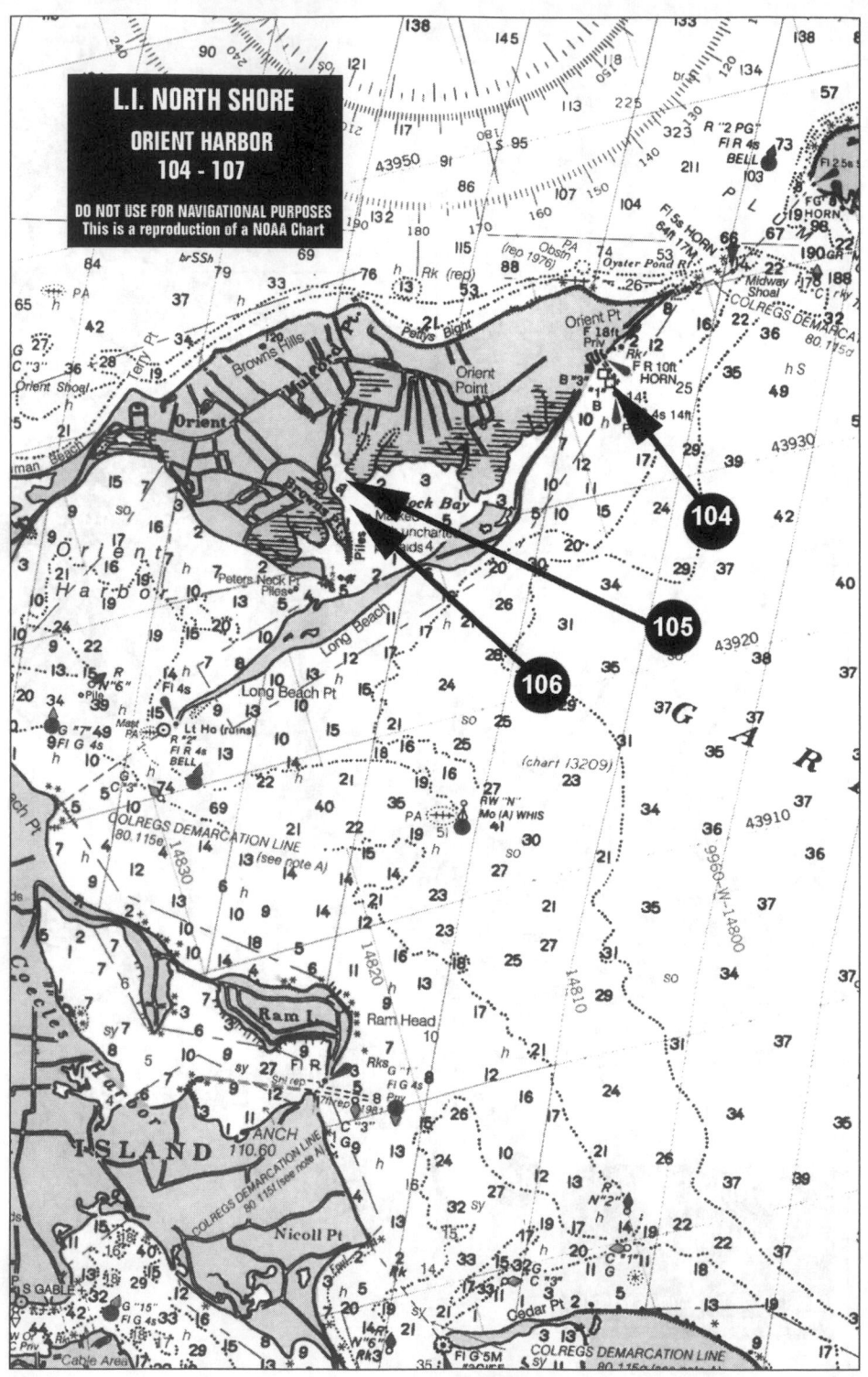

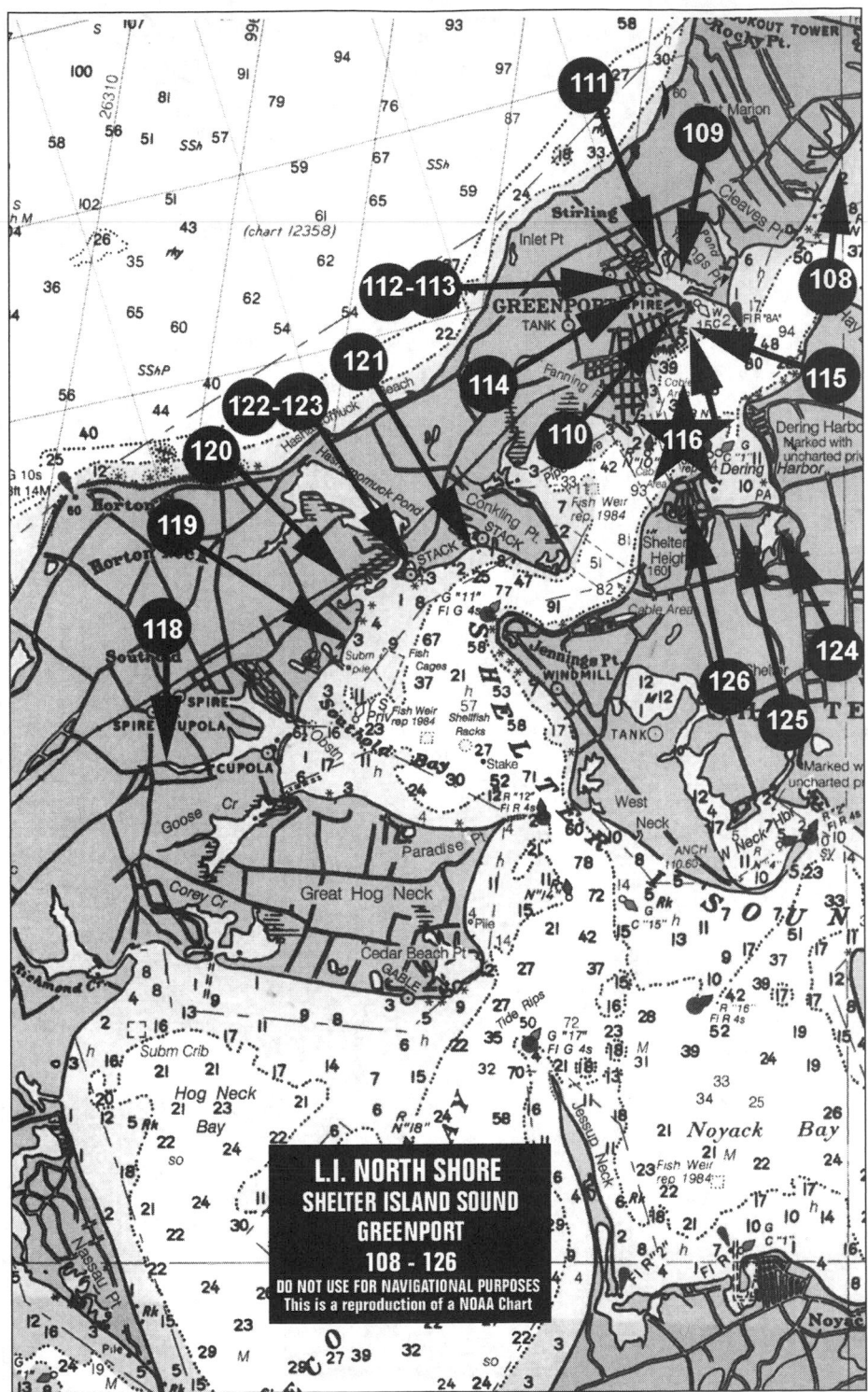

L.I. NORTH SHORE
SHELTER ISLAND SOUND
GREENPORT
108 - 126
DO NOT USE FOR NAVIGATIONAL PURPOSES
This is a reproduction of a NOAA Chart

427

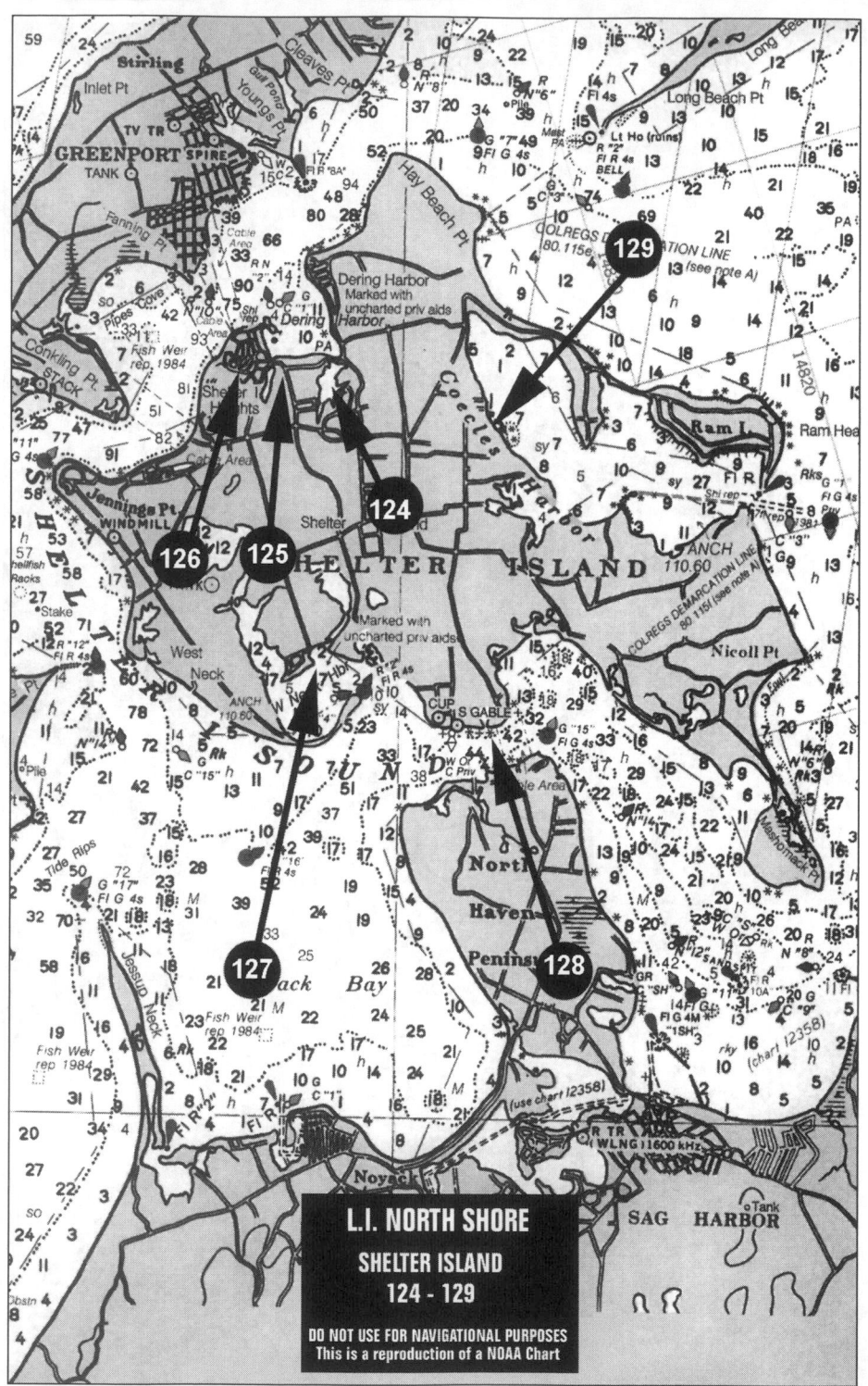

L.I. NORTH SHORE

SHELTER ISLAND
124 - 129

DO NOT USE FOR NAVIGATIONAL PURPOSES
This is a reproduction of a NOAA Chart

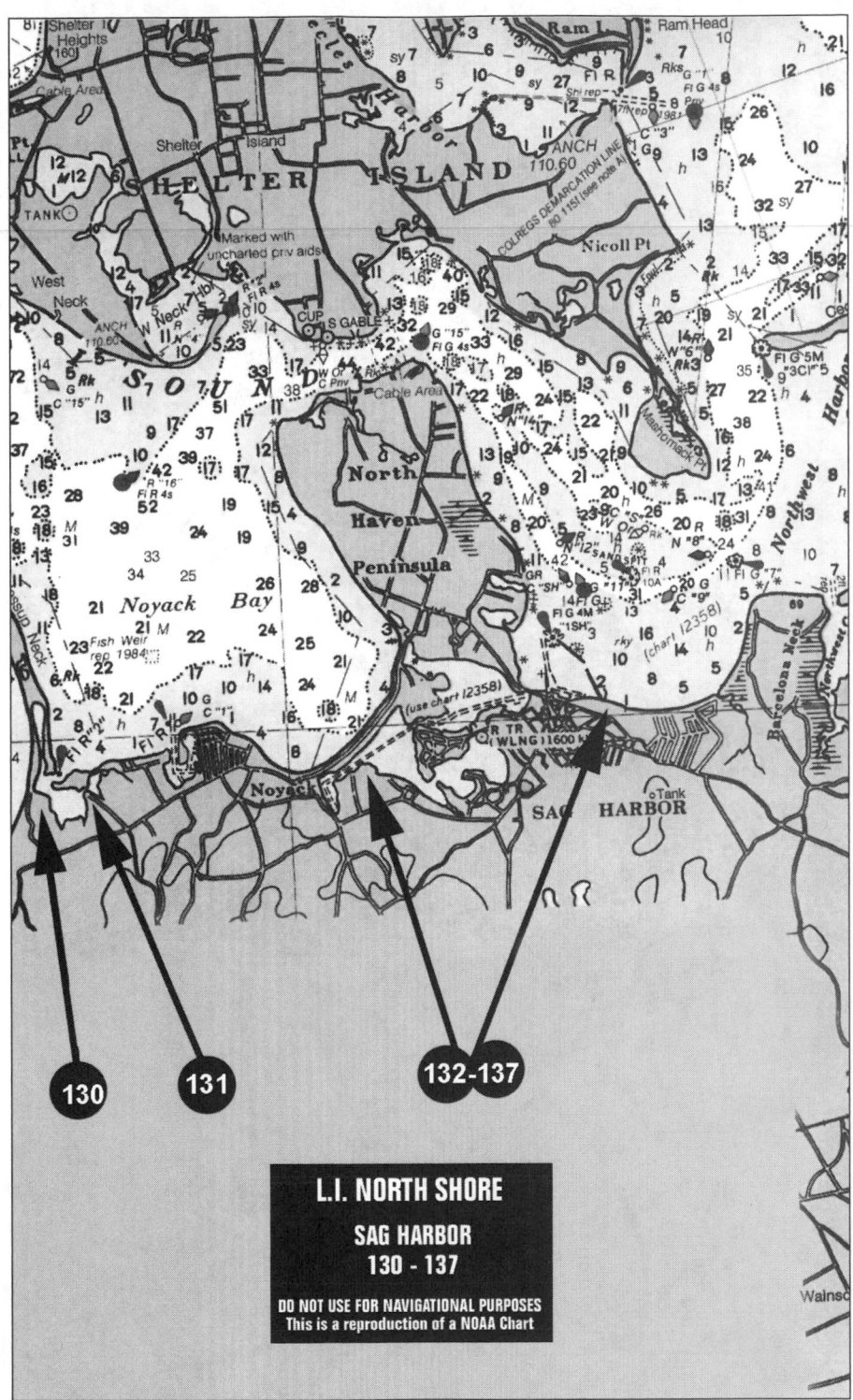

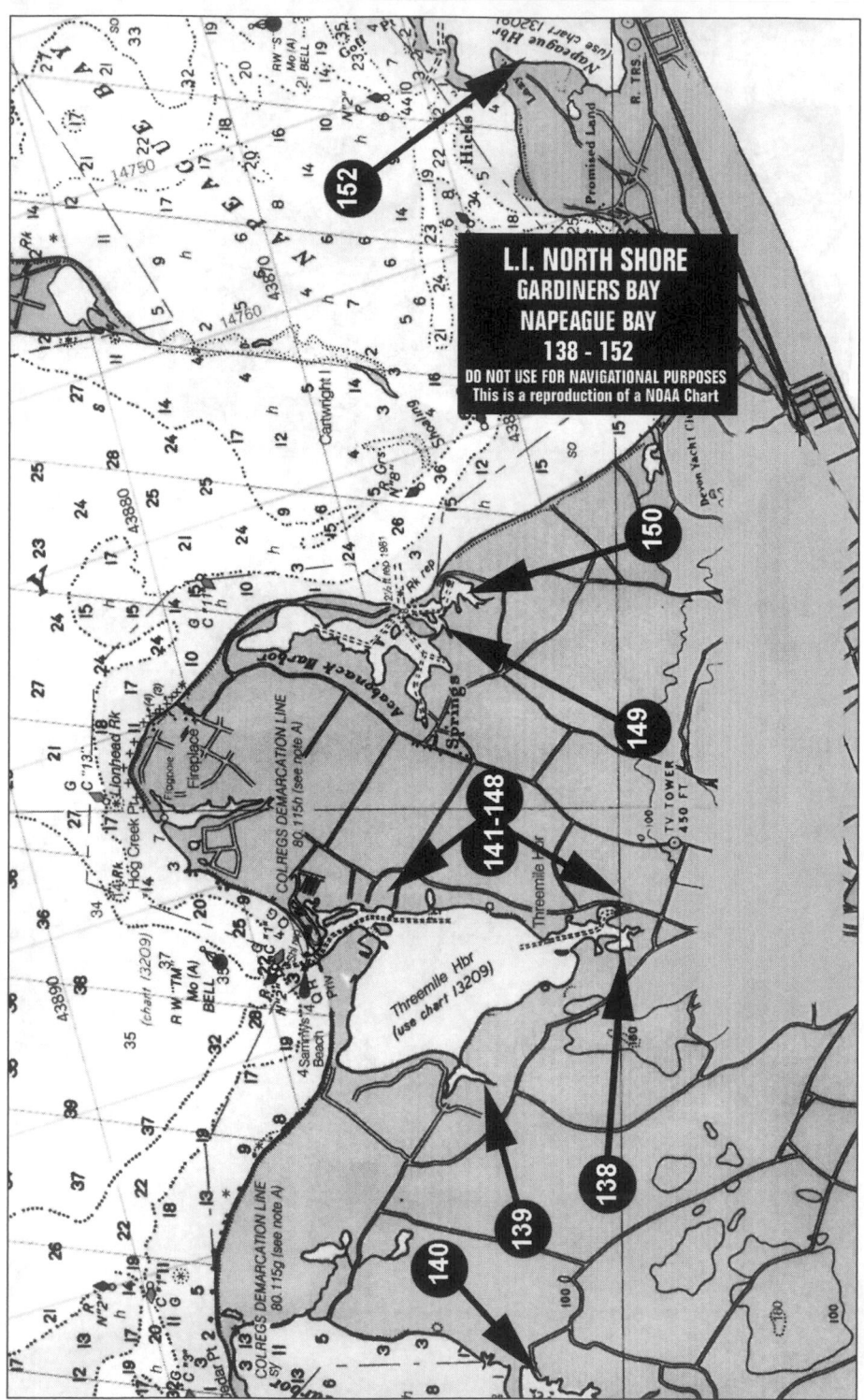

L.I. NORTH SHORE
GARDINERS BAY
NAPEAGUE BAY
138 - 152
DO NOT USE FOR NAVIGATIONAL PURPOSES
This is a reproduction of a NOAA Chart

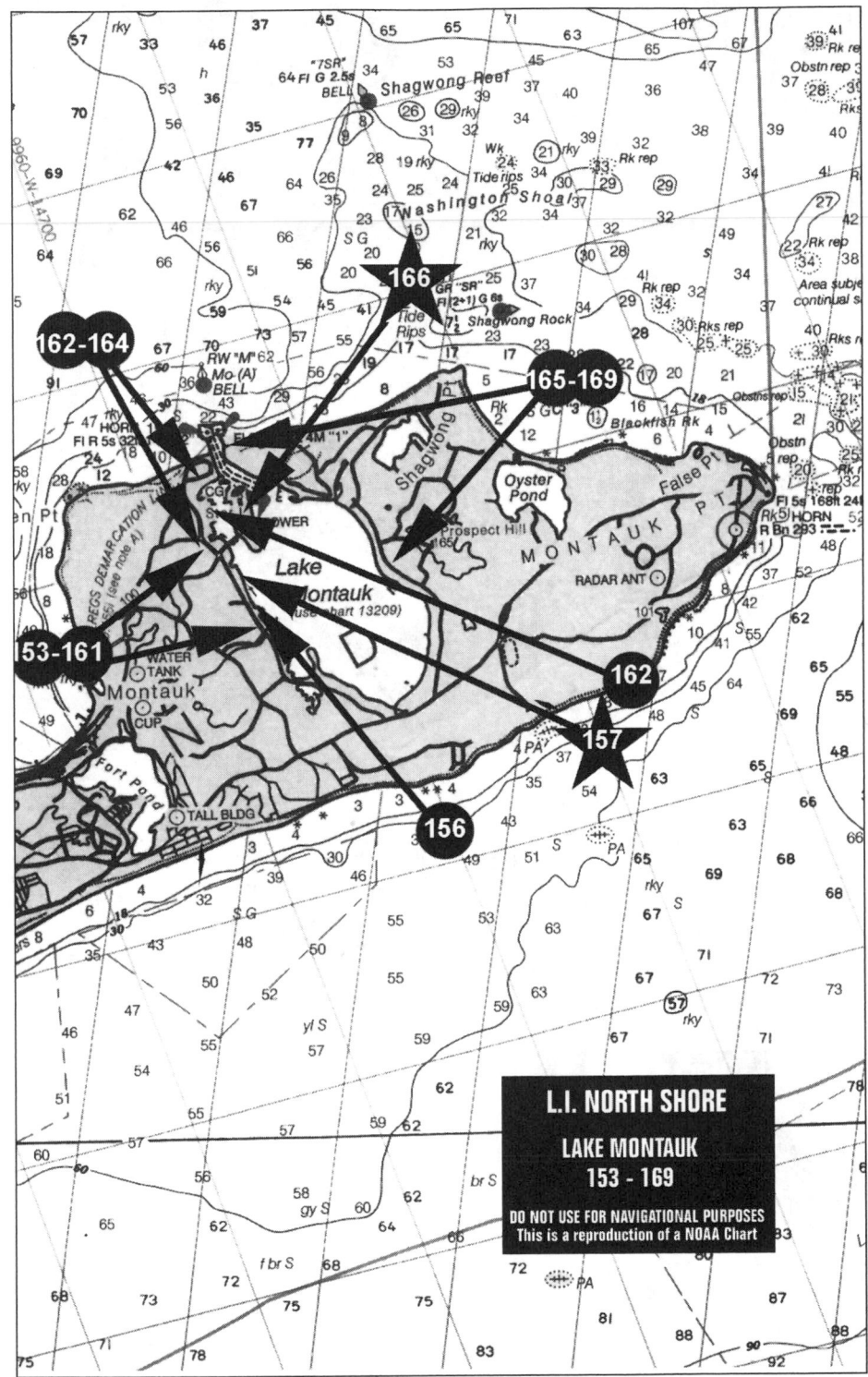

L.I. NORTH SHORE

LAKE MONTAUK

153 - 169

DO NOT USE FOR NAVIGATIONAL PURPOSES
This is a reproduction of a NOAA Chart

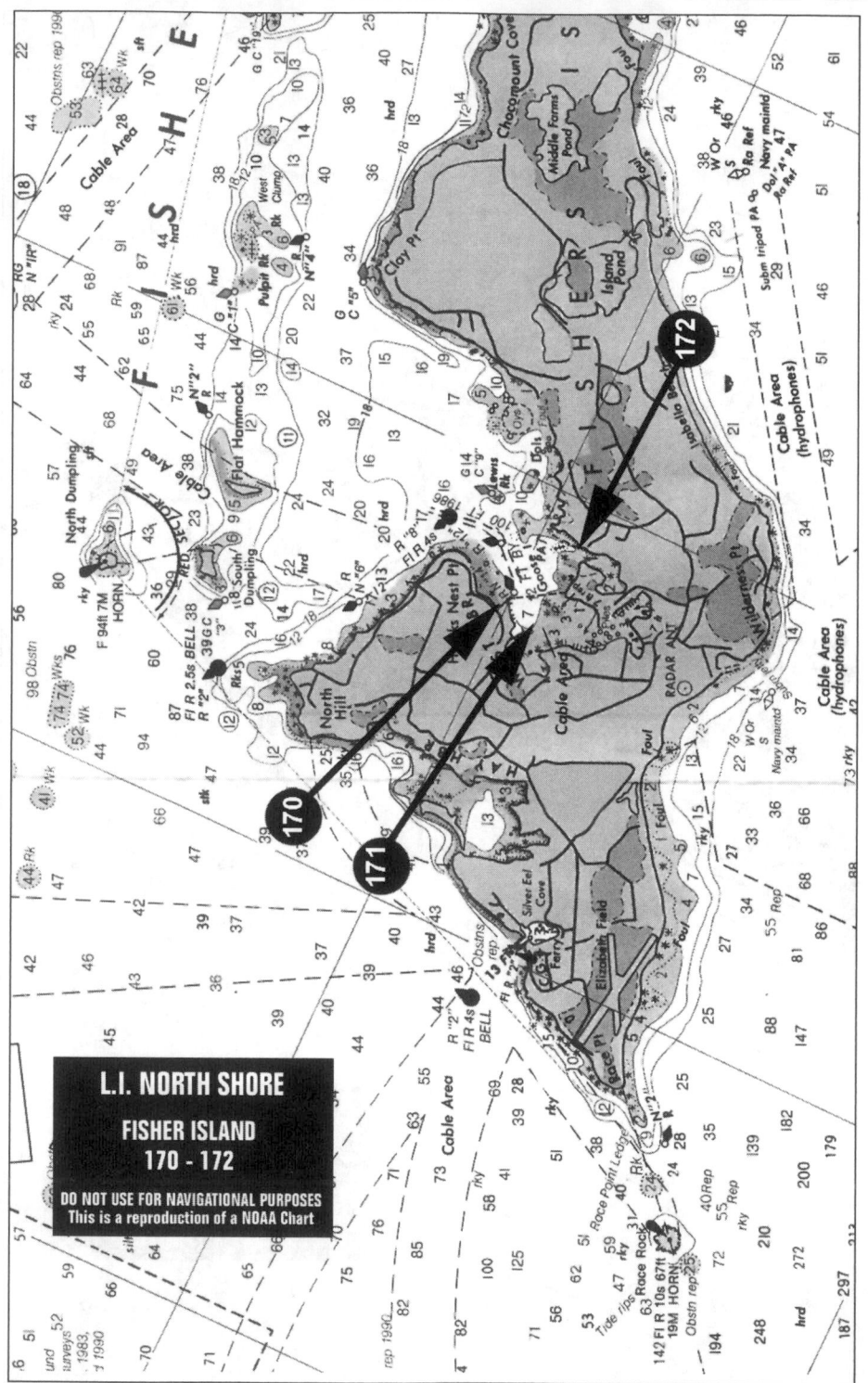

L.I. NORTH SHORE

FISHER ISLAND
170 - 172

DO NOT USE FOR NAVIGATIONAL PURPOSES
This is a reproduction of a NOAA Chart

432

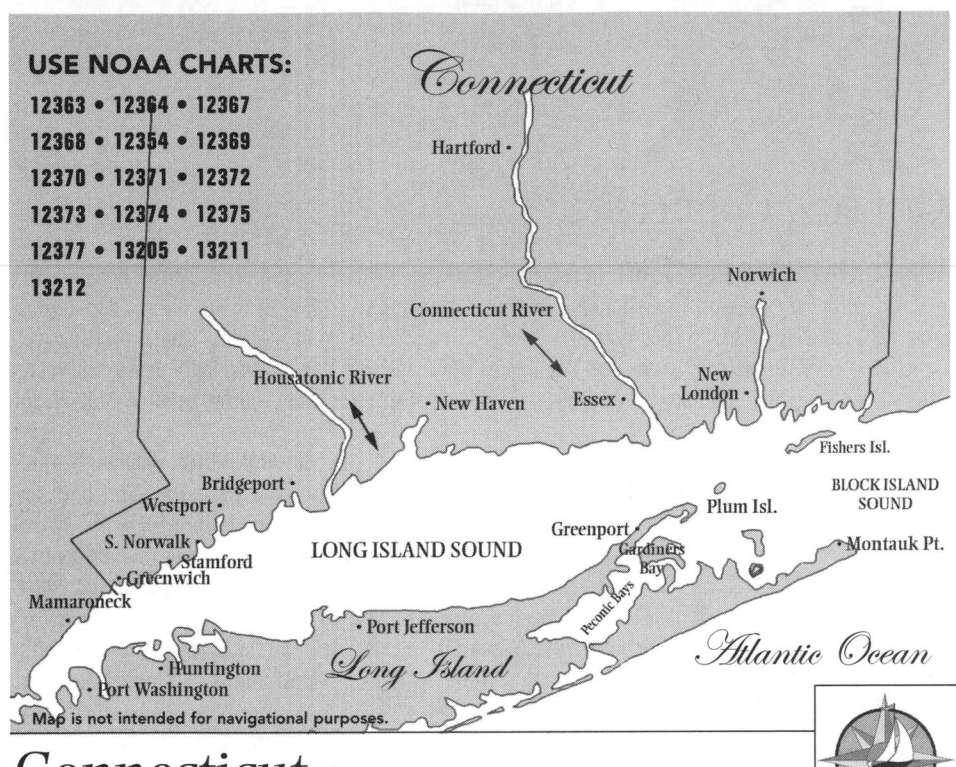

USE NOAA CHARTS:

12363 • 12364 • 12367

12368 • 12354 • 12369

12370 • 12371 • 12372

12373 • 12374 • 12375

12377 • 13205 • 13211

13212

Connecticut

Hartford •

Norwich •

Connecticut River

Housatonic River

• New Haven   Essex •

New London •

Fishers Isl.

Bridgeport •

Westport •

Plum Isl.

BLOCK ISLAND SOUND

S. Norwalk

Stamford

Greenwich

Greenport

Gardiners Bay

LONG ISLAND SOUND

• Montauk Pt.

Mamaroneck

Peconic Bays

• Port Jefferson

Long Island

Atlantic Ocean

Huntington

• Port Washington

Map is not intended for navigational purposes.

Connecticut

THE FOLLOWING REGIONS ARE COVERED IN CHARTS IN THIS SECTION:

Cruising Connecticut

THE CONNECTICUT COASTLINE is rockbound and rugged, with numerous sandy beaches and occasional salt meadows or marshlands. The surface is mildly rolling near the shore. The depression of small valleys along the shore has created a number of good harbors. The shoreline, well developed both commercially and residentially, is lined with seaside resorts, State parks, and recreational beaches. The boundary line between Connecticut and New York follows the Byram River for slightly over 1-mile.

CHART 13214. Connecticut's easternmost cruising port is beautiful **STONINGTON HARBOR,** 3 miles northwestward of **WATCH HILL POINT**. Breakwaters on each side protect the harbor and both are marked, at their seaward end, by a light. The controlling depth to the inner harbor is about 11 feet.

FYI

Stonington is the home port of Connecticut's only commercial fishing fleet.

Anchorage can be selected inside the west breakwater in depths of 15 to 18 feet, taking care to keep the south end of **WAMPHASSUC POINT,** bearing northward of 270°. Vessels drawing up to 8 feet can find anchorage in the inner harbor. A rock that bares at low water is about 50 yards southward of the fishing wharf and is marked by a private buoy.

STONINGTON HARBOR is approached from southeastward and westward. Vessels with local knowledge sometimes cross Noyes Shoal from southwestward but for transients, the southeastern approach is best, with fewer dangers, and navigational aids serve as excellent guides to avoid them. In daytime, with clear weather, no difficulty should be experienced in entering through any of the approaches. The town of Stonington is on the east side of the harbor. The wharfs have depths of 7 to 12 feet alongside. Following southerly weather, a surge is felt by vessels tied to the southern side of the seaward pier.

MYSTIC HARBOR, about 6 miles westward of Watch Hill Point, is the approach to the towns of **NOANK and MYSTIC.** A channel with two dredged sections leads from Fishers Island Sound through Mystic Harbor to the **MYSTIC SEAPORT MUSEUM WHARF.** Buoys and a light mark the channel. Special anchorages are in Mystic Harbor. To enter from eastward, lay a west-northwesterly course from south of the lighted bell buoy marking Napatree Point Ledge, for a little over 3 miles to about 400 yards south of the buoy marking the south end of Cormorant Reef. From here, steer a course of 261° toward the abandoned light tower on **MORGAN POINT**, in range with the north end of northern rocky islet off the north end of Ran Island, until **MASON POINT** is abeam. Then follow the buoyed channel. From westward, proceed cautiously from about 100 yards or more southward of the buoy southward of **GROTON LONG POINT**. Then continue on an easterly course for about 0.5 miles to **MYSTIC HARBOR CHANNEL BUOY 1**, steer a northerly course through the buoyed channel into Mystic Harbor rounding **NOANK LIGHT 5** (41°19'0"N, 71°59"30'W) at a distance of about 75 yards.

MYSTIC RIVER flows into **MYSTIC HARBOR** from northward just below Mystic. Transient craft visiting Mystic Seaport transit the river beyond the town's bascule bridge, sailing into the harbor that has inspired many a work of art. If you could sail into another century, this harbor might be your destination. **Ed. Note: Fort Rachel Marine** affords boaters a super location for walking about in the historic village of Mystic. Vessels up to 60 feet will enjoy their floating docks while crew will really appreciate 'five star' personal facilities in a well-protected harbor on the Mystic River. The folks at

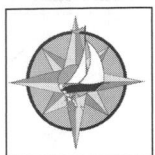

Fort Rachel are happy to see your well-behaved pets and sailboats are a specialty.

Navigating to Fort Rachel is easy with a short trip up the picturesque Mystic River, passing the town of Noank and the tidal wetlands of Six Penny Island, a haven for birdwatchers. The mouth of the Mystic River must be approached from the east or west since Ram Island is directly south of the channel entrance. The channel is clearly marked although buoys are frequently relocated by the USCG. One-half mile north of Mason's Island is a railroad bridge which is usually open to river traffic and only closes briefly when trains approach. The bridge tender is available on VHF 13 if needed. Fort Rachel Marina is located on the west bank of the river just north of the bridge.

NOANK is a town on the west side of the channel through Mystic Harbor. The mean range of the tide is about 2.3 feet.

CHART 13213, 13212. NEW LONDON LEDGE LIGHT, (58 feet above the water, 41°17"60'N, 72°04"80'W)is shown from a red brick building on a square white pier on the west side of New London Ledge. A fog signal is sounded at the station. Other prominent features in approaching New London Harbor are: **NEW LONDON HARBOR LIGHT,** (on the west side of the entrance channel, 41°19"ON, 72°05"40'W), and the monument at Fort Griswold. The microwave tower atop a building in downtown New London; the large sheds at the shipyard on the east side of the river opposite Fort Trumbull; and the highway bridge at New London are also prominent features.

NEW LONDON HARBOR, near the east end of Long Island Sound, at the mouth of the Thames River, is an important harbor of refuge. Vessels of deep draft can find anchorage here in any weather and all seasons. New London is a city on the west bank of the **THAMES RIVER** about 2.5 miles above the mouth. The town of **GROTON** on the east bank is connected to New London by a highway bridge and

a railroad bridge. The main harbor comprises the lower 3 miles of the Thames River from Long Island Sound to the bridges. It is approached through the main entrance channel extending from deep water in Long Island Sound to deep water in the upper harbor. Waterfront restaurants here have transient facilities and marine services are available. The new waterfront park (2000) has free, floating docks with a time limit plus city-owned moorings.

Ed. Note: Keep a watchful eye for: lobster buoys, the ferries coming and going from Fishers Island, Block Island, and Orient Point; and if you're lucky, you'll see the U.S. Coast Guard training ship, the barque "Eagle" heading home to the **U.S. Coast Guard Academy** under full sail.

CHART 12372. The city of **NORWICH**, at the head of navigation on the **THAMES RIVER**, has a relatively new luxury marina which is attracting mariners who have a penchant for the casino life. **Foxwoods Casino**, operated by the Mashantucket Indian tribe, is nearby. Before attempting to transit the Thames up to Norwich, check with the local Coast Guard (see USCG phone number pages) regarding restrictions in the proximity of the submarine base, due to the events of 9/11/01.

CHART 13211. NIANTIC BAY, 4.5 miles westward of New London Harbor, is a good anchorage sheltered from easterly northerly and westerly winds. It is a harbor of refuge in northerly gales and can be used by small vessels and tows. The general depth of the bay is about 19 feet; the water shoals gradually northward. The entrance is 1.5 miles wide, and the dangers are marked by buoys or show above water.

NIANTIC RIVER empties into the northeast end of Niantic bay and is entered through a dredged channel that leads form the bay, thence through a narrow passage at the entrance and thence to a point about 300 yards northward of the entrance to Smith Cove.

THE GRISWOLD INN, ESSEX

CHART 12375, 12377. The **CONNECTICUT RIVER** rises in the extreme northern part of New Hampshire, near the Canadian Border, and flows southerly between the States of Vermont and New Hampshire, across Massachusetts and Connecticut and through to Long Island Sound. The River is approximately 410 miles long and is one of the largest and most important rivers in New England. The head of commercial navigation is at Hartford –about 45 miles from the mouth. The river water is fresh at, and above, Deep River. Each year, after the spring freshets, shoals with least depths of 10 feet are found in places on bars in the upper river. Dredging to remove shoals begins as soon as the water subsides. Boaters need to be concerned with tidal currents – especially on the ebb – as far upriver as Middletown. The entire river is well marked but charts are still necessary. **Ed. Note:** Exploring the Connecticut River can be a whole planned vacation in itself. The river even has its own cruising guide, *A Complete Boating Guide to the Connecticut River,* published by the Connecticut River Watershed Council (Easthampton, MA).

OLD SAYBROOK is a village, with several marina facilities, on the west side of Connecticut River, about 1.4 miles northward of Saybrook Breakwater Light (41°14"80N, 72°20"60'W).

ESSEX is 6 miles upriver with several mariners' facilities. A stop in this seafaring town feels like walking right into a Norman Rockwell painting come alive. Strolling about takes visitors past charming clapboard New England homes with colorful pocket gardens, sparkling village shoppes,

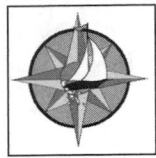

the **Connecticut River Museum**, and the legendary **Griswold Inn**–operating continuously since 1776. **Ed. Note:** The inn is noteworthy, not only for it's hearty fare, but also for its museum-quality collection of original Antonio Jacobsen marine paintings and Currier & Ives prints which illustrate the glory days of steamships. Look up to the inn's second floor windows and see what flag is is set for the day and then you'll know what the entertainment is for the evening in the lively bar at the Gris. It could be Sea Chanties or Dixieland or something else to tickle a sailor's fancy...you may even want to play the spoons or sing along! The cruise upriver against the currents may take a while but Essex is worth the trip. Relax and enjoy this special village seemingly untouched by time.

A little bit further up the Connecticut River, in **EAST HADDAM**, is the **Goodspeed Opera House** with transient slips available. Here you can enjoy a night of musical drama in this ornate refurbished Victorian theater.

CHART 12373. GUILFORD HARBOR, a bight 5.5 miles westward of Hammonasset Point, is used only by small craft. East River and Sluice Creek empty into Guilford Harbor from the northward. Rocks and foul ground obstruct the approach to the harbor. The outer most dangers are Half Acre Rock, about 0.8 mile southeastward of the entrance channel which shows at high water. Scattered rocks, some bare at low water and others with 7 to 16 feet over them, extend about a mile eastward from Half Acre Rock. The approach to Guilford Harbor, marked by buoys leads along the southeasterly side of Indian Reef thence westward of Half Acre Rock to a dredged channel about 0.5 mile northwestward of Half Acre Rock.

CHART 12373. THE THIMBLE ISLANDS, STONEY CREEK, are an unusual and picturesque anchorage with a collection of some 40 'islands.' Reminiscent of islands in Maine, the Thimbles are an experience. Looking at the charts, you'll find the best spot is between **HIGH ISLAND and POT ISLAND**. Be wary of nearby rocks and submerged cables. There is a tidal rise and fall of 6.5 feet so set your anchor accordingly so as to not swing into the rocks. From a distance it appears that the islands are too close together for easy passage but following the marked channels will get you to the right spot. A small passenger ferry has a scheduled route and will pick you up to go to the town of

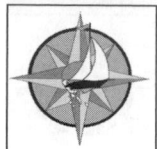

STONEY CREEK. Ed. Note: It is advisable not to use this anchorage if thunderstorms or high winds are predicted, but if it's good weather, don't miss the Thimbles. Enterprising island children may cruise by to collect your garbage for a donation.

BRANFORD RIVER, narrow and crooked, extends northeasterly for Branford Harbor. At low water bare shoals on each side define the channel above Branford Point. During the summer numerous stakes used as moorings mark both sides of the channel. With plenty of mariners' facilities, visitors can easily find a berth and walk about the charming village that was once the original home of Yale University.

CHART 12371. NEW HAVEN HARBOR, an important harbor of refuge, is about 68 miles from New York, 179 miles from Boston via the Cape Cod Canal, and 171 miles from Nantucket Shoals Lighted Horn Buoy N. It comprises all the tidewater northward of the breakwaters constructed across the mouth of the bay, including the navigational portions of the West, Mill and Quinnipiac Rivers. It is about 2 miles wide. New Haven, at the head of the harbor, is the third busiest commercial port in New England. The entrance is easy to navigate day or night or in weather. Follow all aids to navigation — buoy changes are frequent here. Strobe lights and range lights are on the West Haven shore. After entering the main channel to New Haven, head to port– about 3 miles above Southwest Ledge Light (41°14"10' N, 72°57"40' W, a white octagonal house on a cylindrical pier) and follow the West River to marina facilities. Sailboaters will want to stop at one of two marinas before the fixed bridge, which has a clearance of 23-ft. at high tide. Once under the bridge, you'll find **West Cove Marina** on your port side, a resort-style facility for powerboaters, with a heated swimming pool and a clubhouse for relaxing (203-933-3000). Restaurants, shopping and provisioning are an easy walk.

CHART 12370. MILFORD HARBOR, comprising the lower portion of **WEPAWAUG RIVER,** is entered at the mouth of the river between two jetties at the head of **THE GULF.** The westerly jetty extends southward from Burns Point, and the easterly jetty is marked by Milford Harbor Light 10 (41°12"60'N, 73°20"90'W). The harbor is used chiefly for recreational boating, and occasionally for the delivery of shellfish and fish. Milford is also home to a lab for the National Marine Fisheries Service, and a Connecticut Aquaculture Center. At the head of the harbor is a municipal marina for transients.

The **HOUSATONIC RIVER** rises in the Berkshire Hills of western Massachusetts and Connecticut, and empties into Long Island Sound about 10 miles southwestward of the New Haven Harbor entrance. The Housatonic is navigable, with mariners' facilities, to **SHELTON.** There is a bascule bridge with a closed clearance of 32-ft at **DEVON,** 2 miles north of **STRATFORD** on the east bank. The bridge tender is on VHF 13 but he won't be opening the bridge for anyone at rush hours. Next is a railroad bridge with a closed clearance of 19-ft. (call for opening (VHF 13 or (212) 340-2050). A fixed highway bridge, 3.7 miles above Stratford has a clearance of 85-ft. Continuing past Devon, this is a lovely cruise for shallow draft (less than 4-ft.) vessels.

CHART 12369. BRIDGEPORT HARBOR on the north side of Long Island Sound north-northwestward of Stratford Shoal Light and about 52 miles from New York, consists of two widely separated units. The main harbor and its branches serve the east and central portions of the city of **BRIDGEPORT** and **BLACK ROCK HARBOR** and its tributaries serve the western part. The large red and white horizontally banded stack of a power plant on Tongue Point is the most prominent landmark in this area. Other prominent landmarks include a group of stacks on Steel Point, the towers of a high voltage line and several church spires. **BRIDGEPORT HARBOR LIGHT,** 50 feet above the water, is shown from a black skeleton tower with a small white house on a black base on the west side of the entrance channel near the end of the west breakwater. Bridgeport itself is not a pretty destination but is useful in a

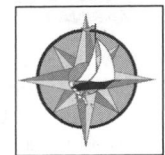

storm. Black Rock Harbor, west of Bridgeport, is well-marked and welcomes transient yachts.

CHARTS 12363, 12364, 12368. NORWALK RIVER empties through Norwalk Harbor into the north side of Long Island Sound, northward of the Norwalk Islands and about 40 miles east of New York. **NORWALK HARBOR and RIVER** are entered through a dredged channel that extends 3 miles northeasterly from Sheffield Island Harbor between Manresa Island on the west and White Rock, with numerous islets and foul ground on the east.

EAST NORWALK HARBOR, at the town of East Norwalk, is on the east side of the river about 2 miles above the main channel entrance. The harbor is entered through a dredged channel that leads westward of Fitch Point to the head and to North Anchorage Basin on the westerly side of the harbor.

SOUTH NORWALK is an important commercial and manufacturing city on the west side of Norwalk River about 3 miles above the channel entrance. The depths at the wharfs below the bridges range from 5 to 10 feet.

NORWALK, 1.3 miles above South Norwalk, is a city on both sides of the river, at the head of navigation. The wharfs have depths of about 7 feet alongside. The channel from South Norwalk to Norwalk is winding with extensive flats on both sides, and requires local knowledge to follow. There are excellent small craft facilities in **NORWALK COVE**.

CHART 12368. STAMFORD. The harbor has an easy entrance and the channel inside the breakwaters is well-marked. There is a light at the west breakwater is a 6-second green flasher. The Harbor Ledge Light marks the channel entrance and flashes every 4 seconds. Enter **WESTCOTT COVE** around Shippan Point, east of Stamford Harbor — the green flasher will be to your port. There is a well-marked channel but we advise entering at high tide. Deep draft boats should bypass this cove. Provisioning and restaurants are within walking distance. ⚓

CONNECTICUT FACILITIES alphabetical index

CONNECTICUT FACILITIES alphabetical index

Connecticut Yacht Clubs

The Yacht Clubs listed below offer reciprocity and courtesy dockage or moorings.
Only Yacht Clubs with space for 2 or more traveling Yacht Club members are listed.

BRANFORD
PINE ORCHARD YACHT &
COUNTRY CLUB
(203) 488-2575

BRIDGEPORT
BLACK ROCK YACHT CLUB
(203) 335-0587
EAST END YACHT CLUB
(203) 366-3330
FAYERWEATHER YACHT CLUB
(203) 576-6796
MIAMOGUE YACHT CLUB
(203) 334-9882
PEQUONNOCK YACHT CLUB
(203) 334-5708

CHESTER
MIDDLESEX YACHT CLUB
(203) 526-5634

EAST NORWALK
SHORE & COUNTRY CLUB
(203) 838-7507

ESSEX
ESSEX YACHT CLUB
(860) 767-8121

GREENWICH
BELLE HAVEN CLUB
(203) 861-5353

INDIAN HARBOR YACHT CLUB
(203) 869-2484
RIVER CLUB OF GREENWICH
(203) 661-0009

GROTON
SHENNESCOSSETT Y.C.
(203) 445-9854

MILFORD
MILFORD YACHT CLUB
(203) 877-5598

NEW FAIRFIELD
CANDLEWOOD YACHT CLUB
(203) 746-9303

NEW HAVEN
CITY POINT YACHT CLUB
(203) 789-9301
NEW HAVEN YACHT CLUB
(203) 469-9608
WAUCOMA YACHT CLUB
(203) 789-9530

NOANK
RAM ISLAND YACHT CLUB
(203) 536-9014
WEST COVE YACHT CLUB
(860) 536-4978

NORWALK
ISCHODA YACHT CLUB
(203) 853-8866

OLD GREENWICH
ROCKY POINT CLUB
(203) 637-2394

PORTLAND
HARTFORD YACHT CLUB
(203) 633-9669

ROWAYTON
WILSON COVE YACHT CLUB
(203) 853-0922

SOUTHPORT
PEQUOT YACHT CLUB
(203) 255-5740

STAMFORD
PONUS YACHT CLUB
(203) 323-7157

STRATFORD
HOUSATONIC BOAT CLUB
(203) 377-9195

WESTBROOK
DUCK ISLAND YACHT CLUB
(203) 399-9083

WESTPORT
MINUTEMAN YACHT CLUB
(203) 226-9279
SAUGATUCK HARBOR Y.C.
(203) 227-3607

Connecticut
MARINA'S NAME & PHONE NUMBER

Chart Locater Number	Marina's Name & Phone Number	When Open	Monitors VHF Channel	Transient: Electricity • Moorings • Berths	Hull repairs • Engine repairs • Ramp	Winter Storage: Wet • Dry	Railway Capacity in Feet	Lift Capacity in Tons	Boat Rental: Canoe • Row • Motor	Boat Rental: Charter • House • Sail	Restaurant • Lodging • Camping	Showers • Laundry	Pumpout • Toilets	Bait • Tackle • Water • Ice	Groceries • Hardware	Diesel fuel • Gasoline
1	RUDY'S TACKLE BARN 203-531-5928	MAR DEC		B										IW BT		
2	GREENWICH BAY MARINA 203-531-9255	ALL YR.			E	D		4						W		
3	J. CATALANO. & SONS INC. 203-531-9207	ALL YR.			HE	D		20					T	W	H	G
5	GRASS ISLAND BOAT BASIN 203-622-9782													IW		G D
6	GREENWICH HARBOR INN 203-661-9800	ALL YR.	9 78	EB							RL					
8	COS COB BOAT BASIN	APR NOV		R									P			
9	PALMER POINT MARINA 203-661-1243	ALL YR.	9		HE	W		35			R	S	T	IW	H	G D
10	MIANUS MARINE INC 203-869-2253	ALL YR.		E B	HE	W D		50						W		
11	RIVERSCAPE MARINA 203-661-0471	ALL YR.		EB	HE	w D		35				S	T	IW BT		
12	GREENWICH MARITIME CTR. 203-869-8690	ALL YR.			HE	D		25						W		
13	DRENCKHAHN BOAT BASIN 203-869-1892				HE	D		25						W	H	
14	O.M.A. 203-661-5217	ALL YR.	72	EB	HE	W D		30			R	SL	T	IW	H	
15	LONG MEADOW CREEK 203-637-0115	ALL YR.			HE	D		2							H	
17	STAMFORD LANDING MARINA 203-965-0065	ALL YR.	9	EB		W					R	SL	PT	IW		
18	HARBORS END MARINE 203-965-0888	ALL YR.	9	EB	HE	W D		20					T	I		
19	MAC DONALD YACHT 203-323-5431	ALL YR.													H	
20	ERIK'S BOATWORKS INC 203-359-3657	ALL YR.			H											
21	BREWERS Yacht Haven West 203-359-4500	ALL YR.	9 14	E B	HE	W D		60			R	SL	T	IW	GH	G D
22	HARBOR SQUARE MARINA 203-324-3331	ALL YR.	9	EB	HE	D W		50			R	S	PT	BT IW	G H	G D
24	SCHOONER COVE	ALL YR		B		W						S	PT	W		

Connecticut

MARINA'S NAME & PHONE NUMBER

Chart Locater Number	Marina's Name & Phone Number	When Open	Monitors VHF Channel	Transient (Elec•Moorings•Berths)	Hull•Engine repairs	Winter Storage (Wet•Dry)	Railway/Ramp	Lift Capacity (tons)	Boat Rental (Canoe•Row•Motor)	Boat Rental (Charter•House•Sail)	Restaurant•Lodging	Showers•Camping•Laundry	Bait•Tackle	Pumpout•Toilets	Water•Ice	Groceries•Hardware	Diesel•Gasoline
25	BREWERS YACHT HAVEN EAST 203-359-4500	ALL YR.	9	EB	HE	W		60			R	SL		T	IW	G H	G D
26	STAMFORD BOAT BASIN 203-327-8967						R							T			
27	WEST BEACH 203-977-4645						R										
28	PEAR TREE POINT BEACH 203-656-7325	ALL YR.					R										
29	THE BOATWORKS INC 203-866-9295	ALL YR.	68	EM B	HE	D		45						P T	WB	H	G D
30	THE BAIT SHOP INC 203-853-3811	ALL YR.	5 13		HE	W D								T	WB	H	
32	WHITE BRIDGE MARINA 203-838-9038	ALL YR.		EM B	HE	W D		45				RL		T	IW	H	
34	VILLAGE MARINE 203-866-1739	ALL YR.		E													
36	FIVE MILE RIVERWORKS 203-866-4226	ALL YR.	16	EB	HE	W D		35						T	W		
37	WILSON COVE MARINA 203-866-7020	ALL YR.			HE	W D		25					S	T	IW		
39	NORWEST MARINE 203-853-2822	ALL YR.	68	EM B	HE	D		30						T	IW	H	G D
40	TOTAL MARINE 203-853-0771	ALL YR.	16	E B	HE	D		35					S	T	W		
41	SONO SEAPORT SEAFOOD 203-854-9483										R			T	I		
42	REX MARINE CENTER 203-866-5555	ALL YR.		EB	HE	W D		30					S	PT	IW	H	
43	MAURICE MARINE 203-866-5169	MAR NOV	68 9		E	D		5			R			T	IW		
44	OYSTER BEND MARINA 203-854-6666	ALL YR.	9	EB									S	T	W		
45	VETERAN PARK RAMP 203-849-8823						R										
46	NORWALK DOCK 203-849-8823						B							P			
47	OVERTON'S OUTBOARD APR 203-838-2031	APR NOV			HE		R		5	M R	R	L		T	IW BT	G H	
48	BLOOM BROS MARINE 203-838-9273	ALL YR.	67	E B	E	D		5						T	W		G

Connecticut

Chart #	Marina's Name & Phone Number	When Open	Monitors VHF Channel	Transient (Electricity•Moorings•Berths)	Hull repairs•Engine repairs•Ramp	Winter Storage Wet•Dry	Railway Capacity in Feet	Lift Capacity in Tons	Boat Rental Canoe•Row•Motor	Boat Rental Charter•House•Sail	Restaurant•Lodging•Camping	Showers•Laundry	Pumpout•Toilets	Bait•Tackle•Water•Ice	Groceries•Hardware	Diesel fuel•Gasoline
49	NORWALK COVE MARINA 203-838-5899	ALL YR.	9	EB	HE	W D		99+			R	SL	PT	IW BT	GH	G D
50	SAUGATUCK HARBOR Y.C. 203-227-3607	ALL YR	71	EB		W						SL	T			
51	COASTWISE MARINE 203-226-0735	APR. DEC	9 16		HE	D		6					T	W	H	
52	NORTHROP YACHT 203-226-1915	ALL YR.	8	EM B	R HE	W D			C	C		RL	T	BT		G H
53	COMPO YACHT BASIN 203-227-9136	MAY NOV	9		R								T	IW		G
54	LONGSHORE MARINA 203-226-3688	MAY NOV			R								T	IW		G
55	SAUGATUCK RIVER RAMP				R											
56	SOUTH BENSON MARINA 203-256-3010	APR NOV			R								T	IW		
57	ASH CREEK RAMP 203-256-3010				R											
58	CEDAR MARINA 203-335-6262	ALL YR.		EB	H E	W D		15			R	SL	P T	IW		
59	FAYERWEATHER BOATYARD 203-334-4403	ALL YR.			HE	D	45	25					T			
60	CAPTAIN'S COVE MARINA 203-335-1433	ALL YR.	18	EB	HE	W D		85		CS	R	SL	T	IW	GH	G D
61	FAYERWEATHER Y. C. 203-576-6796	ALL YR.	14								R		T	I		G
62	BRIDGEPORT RAMP				R											
63	LOU'S BOAT BASIN 203-336-9809	MAR NOV	16			d					R			IW BT		G D
64	RIVERSIDE MARINE 203-335-7068	ALL YR.	9		E	D		30						IW	H	G
65	HITCHCOCK MARINE 203-334-2161	ALL YR.		EB	HE	W D		25			R	S	T	W		
66	KNAPP'S LANDING															G D
67	MILFORD HARBOR MARINA 203-877-1475	ALL YR.	68	EB	HE	W D		35			R	SL	PT	IW	HG	G D
68	MILFORD BOAT WORKS 203-877-1475	ALL YR.	68	EB	HE	D		35			R	SL	PT	IW	HG	GO D

Connecticut

MARINA'S NAME & PHONE NUMBER

#	Marina Name & Phone	When Open	VHF Ch.	Transient (Elec•Moor•Berth)	Repairs (Hull•Eng)	Ramp	Winter Storage (Wet•Dry)	Railway/Lift (ft)	Lift (tons)	Boat Rental (Canoe•Row•Motor)	Rest•Lodg•Camp	Showers•Laundry	Pumpout•Toilets	Bait•Tackle•Water•Ice	Groc•Hard	Fuel (D•G)
69	MILFORD RAMP 203-877-9990					R										
70	PORT MILFORD MARINA 203-877-7802	ALL YR		EB	HE		W D		35	R		SL	T	IW	GH	
71	DEVON-MILFORD PUBLIC RAMP					R										
72	FLAGSHIP MARINA 203-874-1783	ALL YR.		E			D	35	10			S	T	W		
73	SPENCER'S MARINA 203-874-4173			E			D		12			S	T	IW	H	G
74	BOND'S DOCK PARK					R										
75	BROWN'S MARINA 203-377-9303	ALL YR.	13 9	EB	H		W D		7	M			P T	IW BT	H	
76	STRATFORD TOWN DOCK 203-377-9114	MAR SEP				R										
77	STRATFORD MARINA 203-377-4477	ALL YR.	9	EB	HE	R	W D		35	R		SL	PT	IW	H	G D
78	THE MARINA AT THE DOCK 203-378-9300	ALL YR.	9	EB	HE		W D		50	C		SL	PT	I W	G	
80	FAIR HAVEN MARINA 203-777-0523	ALL YR.	9	EB					12				T	W	H	G
81	MARINE GENERAL 203-933-3208	ALL YR			HE	R									H	
82	SHINER'S COVE MARINA 203-933-3208	APR OCT	9		HE		W D		3					WB T		
82A	OYSTER POINT MARINA 203-624-5895	ALL YR.	9	E B M	HE		W D		8	R		SL	PT	BT WI	G	G D
83	**WEST COVE MARINA 203-933-3000**	**MAR NOV**							**35**			**SL**	**T**	**IW**		**G D**
84	NEW HAVEN MARINA 203-469-8230	APR NOV			HE				6				T	IW		
85	KELSEY'S MARINE RAILWAY 203-488-9567		13 16		HE	R	D	40	16						H	
87	C.T. MARINE 203-481-3067	ALL YR.					D		10							
88	GOODSELL POINT MARINA 203-488-5292	APR NOV		EB	HE		D		50				PT	W		
89	PIER 66 MARINA 203-488-5613	ALL YR.		EM B	HE		D		25			S	T	IW BT	H	G D

Connecticut

MARINA'S NAME & PHONE NUMBER

Chart Locater Number	Marina's Name & Phone Number	When Open	Monitors VHF Channel	Transient: Electricity • Moorings • Berths	Hull repairs • Engine repairs • Ramp	Winter Storage: Wet • Dry	Railway Capacity in Feet	Boat Rental: Canoe • Row • Motor • Sail	Lift Capacity in Tons	Boat Rental: Charter • House	Restaurant • Lodging • Camping	Showers • Laundry	Bait • Tackle • Pumpout • Toilets	Groceries • Water • Ice	Diesel fuel • Hardware • Gasoline
90	BRANFORD RIVER MARINE 203-488-8921	ALL YR.	9 11		HE	D			20						H
91	BRANFORD MARINE RAILWAY 203-488-9224	ALL YR.		B	HE R	D			5			S	T	W	
92	GUILFORD YACHT CLUB 203-458-3048		9 71	EB							R	S	PT	IW	
92A	BREWERS & JOHNSON'S 203-488-8329	ALL YR.	9	EM B	HE	W D			50			SL	PT	IW	H
93	GUILFORD BOAT YARDS 203-453-5031	ALL YR.			HE	D			15				T	W	H
94	GUILFORD TOWN MARINA 203-453-8092	APR NOV	9	EM B		D							T	W	
95	BEEBE MARINE 203-245-8665	ALL YR.			HE	D			8					W	H
96	BROWN'S BOAT YARD 203-453-6283	ALL YR.	9	EB		D			15				T	IW	H G
97	SEA MIST ISLAND CRUISE 203-488-8905	JUN SEP								C					
98	STONY CREEK MARINE 203-488-7061	ALL YR.		M	HE R	D					R		BT	IW	GH G
99	FREE SPIRIT MARINE WEST 860-669-3641	ALL YR.			HE	D			25			S	T	W	
100	FREE SPIRIT MARINE WEST 203-399-6462	ALL YR.		EB	HE	D			25			S	T	IW	H
102	PORT CLINTON MARINA 860-669-4563	APR NOV	9	EB	EH	W D			50			S	T	IW	H
103	INDIAN RIVER MARINA 860-453-9343	APR OCT			R	D							T		
104	GRAVES MARINA 860-669-6809					D									
105	HARBORSIDE MARINA 860-669-1705	ALL YR.			HE	W D			15			S	T	W	
106	CLINTON YACHT HAVEN 860-669-7254	ALL YR.		EB	HE	D						S	T	W	
107	HOLIDAY DOCK 860-669-2185	APR NOV		EB									T	IW BT	G
108	RIVERSIDE BASIN MARINA 860-669-1503	ALL YR.	9	EB	HE	W D			25			S	T	IW	H
109	CLINTON RAMP	ALL YR		EB	R						R		T		

Connecticut

Chart Locater Number	Marina's Name & Phone Number	When Open	Monitors VHF Channel	Transient Electricity • Moorings • Berths	Hull repairs • Engine repairs • Ramp	Winter Storage: Wet • Dry	Railway Capacity in Feet	Lift Capacity in Tons	Boat Rental: Canoe • Row • Motor	Boat Rental: Charter • House • Sail	Restaurant • Lodging • Camping	Showers • Laundry	Pumpout • Toilets	Bait • Tackle • Water • Ice	Groceries • Hardware	Diesel fuel • Gasoline
110	CEDAR ISLAND MARINA 860-669-8681	ALL YR	9	EB	HE	W/D		30			R	SL	P T	BT IW	H	G D
111	OLD HARBOR MARINA 860-669-8361	ALL YR		EB	E	D		15				S	T	IW	G	
112	WETMORE'S MARINA 860-399-9728	ALL YR			R							T	IW BT	H	G
113	PILOT'S POINT MARINA 860-399-5128	ALL YR.	9	EB	HE	W/D		75		CS	R	S	PT	IW	H	G D
114	DICK'S MARINA 860-399-6534	ALL YR.		EB	R							T	IW BT		
115	RITTS MARINE CENTER 860-399-8467	ALL YR		EB	HE	D		15				S	T	W	H	
116	PIER 76 MARINA 860-399-7122	ALL YR,	9	B	HE R	D					R		T	IW BT	H	
117	BILL'S SEAFOOD REST. 860-399-7224	ALL YR.									R					
118	PILOT'S POINT MARINA 860-399-7906	ALL YR.	9	EB	HE	D		30		S	R	SL	PT	W	H	G D
119	PILOT'S POINT MARINA EAST 860-399-6421	ALL YR.		EB	HE	W/D		25				S	T	W	H	
120	HARRY'S MARINE REPAIR 860-399-6165	ALL YR		EB	E	W/D		10				S	PT	W	H	G
121	HARBOR ONE MARINA 860-388-9208	MAY NOV	9	EB	E						RL	SL	T	I W	H	G D
122	DOCK AND DINE 860-388-4665	ALL YR									R					
123	SAYBROOK POINT MARINA 860-395-2000	ALL YR.	9	EB	E					C	RL	SL	PT	IW	H	G D
124	OLD SAYBROOK LAUNCHING				R											
125	BLACK HALL MARINA 860-434-9680	MAR NOV		B	HE R	D					CR		T	IW BT	H	
126	CONNECTICUT STATE RAMP				R											
127	ISLAND COVE MARINA 860-388-1275	APR NOV						5				S	T	W		
128	OFFSHORE EAST MARINA 860-388-4532	ALL YR.		EM B	H		40	20				S	T	IW	H	
129	FERRY POINT MARINA 860-388-3260	ALL YR.		EB	HE	D		25			RL	S	T	W	H	G D

Connecticut

Chart #	MARINA'S NAME & PHONE NUMBER	When Open	Monitors VHF	Transient Elec•Moorings•Berths	Hull•Engine Repairs	Winter Storage Wet•Dry	Railway•Ramp	Lift Cap. (Tons)	Rest•Lodging•Camping	Showers•Laundry	Pumpout•Toilets	Bait•Groc•Ice•Water	Hardware	Fuel (G•D)
130	PERSSON BOAT BUILDERS 860-388-2343	ALL YR.				D		1						
131	BALDWIN BRIDGE RAMP						R							
132	OAK LEAF MARINA 860-388-9817	ALL YR.	9	EB	HE	D	R	25	RL	SL	T	IW	H	G D
133	BETWEEN THE BRIDGES 860-388-1431	ALL YR.	9	EB	HE	D		65	R	SL	PT	IW	H	G D
134	RAGGED ROCK MARINA 860-388-1049	AL YR.		EB	H	W D		20	C RL	SL	P T	IW	H	
135	SAYBROOK MARINE 860-388-3614	ALL YR.		EB	HE	W D		12		S	T	IW	H	
136	OLD LYME TOWN LANDING 860-434-3660						R							
137	OLD LYME MARINA 860-434-1272	ALL YR.	9	EM B	HE	W D		25		S	T	W	H	
138	OLD LYME DOCK CO 860-434-2267	APR NOV	9	EM B	H				CS	SL	T	IW		G D
139	ESSEX ISLAND MARINA I 860-767-1267	APR NOV	9	EB	HE	W D		30	R	SL	T	IW	GH	G D
140	BREWERS Dauntless Shipyard 860-767-2483	ALL YR.	9	EB	HE	W D		35	R	SL	PT	IW	GH	
141	ESSEX BOAT WORKS INC 860-767-8276	ALL YR.	9	EM B	HE	W D		50			T		H	
142	**THE GRISWOLD INN 860-767-1776**								R L					
143	CONNECTICUT River Museum 860-767-8269	ALL YR		M							T			
144	THE CHANDLERY AT ESSEX 860-767-8267	ALL YR.	68	EM B	HE	W D	R		R	SL	T	IW	H	G D
145	DEEP RIVER MARINA 860-526-5560	ALL YR.		EM B	HE	D		15		S	PT	IW	H	G D
146	DEEP RIVER TOWN DOCK						R							
147	CHESTER MARINA 860-526-2227	ALL YR	16	EB	E	W D		25		S	PT	IW	H	
148	CASTLE MARINE 860-526-2735	ALL YR.		EB	HE	W D		30		S	T	IW	H	
149	HAYS HAVEN MARINA 860-526-9366	ALL YR.		EB		D		25		S	T	IW	H	G D

Connecticut

Chart Locater Number	Marina's Name & Phone Number	When Open	Monitors VHF Channel	Transient: Electricity • Moorings • Berths	Hull repairs • Engine repairs • Ramp	Winter Storage: Wet • Dry	Railway Capacity in Feet	Lift Capacity in Tons	Boat Rental: Canoe • Row • Motor	Boat Rental: Charter • Lodging • House • Sail	Restaurant • Lodging • Camping	Showers • Laundry	Pumpout • Toilets	Bait • Tackle • Water • Ice	Groceries • Hardware	Diesel fuel • Gasoline
150	CHRISHOLM MARINA 860-526-5147	MAR NOV		EB	HE	D		35				S	PT	IW	H	G D
151	HADDAM MEADOWS RAMP				R											
152	ANDREWS MARINA 860-345-2286	MAY NOV		EM B								S	T	IW	H	G
153	SALMON RIVER RAMP				R											
154	DAMAR / MIDWAY MARINA 860-345-4330	ALL YR.		EB	HE R	D		15		S	r	S	T	IW	H	
156	PORTLAND BOAT WORKS 860-342-1085	ALL YR.		EB	HE	D		35					T	W	H	G
157	YANKEE BOAT YARD 860-342-4735	ALL YR.	68	EM B	HE R	D		25			RL	S	PT	IW BT	H G	G D
158	PORTLAND RIVERSIDE MARINA 860-342-1911	ALL YR.		EM B	HE	D		40			C / RL	S	T	IW	H	
159	HARBOR PARK LANDING 860-344-3468										R		T			
160	PETZOLD'S MARINE 860-342-1196	ALL YR.		EB	HE	D		55					T	W	H	G
161	MIDDLESEX MARINE 860-342-2222	ALL YR.			HE R								T		H	
162	SEABOARD MARINA 860-657-3232	ALL YR.	68	EB	R HE	D		30	M	C	R	SL	PT	BT IW	H	G
164	RIVERSIDE PARK				R											
165	WETHERSFIELD COVE Y.C. 860-563-8780	APR OCT		M EB									T	W	H G	G
167	FOUR MILE RIVER MARINA 860-434-8971	APR OCT			R	D							T	W		G
168	SOUTH LYME MARINA 860-434-9295	ALL YR.			ER								S	T	W	H	G
169	PORT NIANTIC 860-739-2155	ALL YR.	10	EB	HE	D		35			RL	S	P T	IW	H	
170	HARBOR HILL MARINA 860-739-0331	APR NOV		EB	HE	D						S	T	IW		
171	BAYVIEW LANDING 860-739-6604	ALL YR.		EB				30			R	S	T	W		
172	EAST LYME TOWN				R											

Connecticut

Chart Locater Number	Marina's Name & Phone Number	When Open	Monitors VHF Channel	Transient: Electricity • Moorings • Berths	Hull repairs • Engine repairs • Ramp	Winter Storage: Wet • Dry	Railway Capacity in Feet	Lift Capacity in Tons	Boat Rental: Canoe • Row • Motor	Boat Rental: Charter • House • Sail	Restaurant • Lodging • Camping	Showers • Laundry	Pumpout • Toilets	Bait • Tackle • Water • Ice	Groceries • Hardware	Diesel fuel • Gasoline
173	BOATS INC 860-739-6251	ALL YR.	71	EB	HE R	D		3			R	S	T	IW BT	GH	G
174	BAYREUTHER BOATYARD 860-739-6264	ALL YR.	9	EM B	HE R	D		25			R	S	PT	IW	GH	G D
175	CONNECTICUT STATE RAMP				R								T			
176	MAGO POINT MARINA 860-444-1999	ALL YR	9	EB	ER	D			R		R	S	T	IW		G D
177	NIANTIC SPORTFISHING DOCK 860-447-3635									C	RL			IW		G D
178	CAPT JOHNS Sport Fishing Ctr 860-443-7259	ALL YR.	88A	EB						C				IW BT	H	G D
179	NIANTIC BAY MARINA INC 860-444-1999	ALL YR	9	EB	HE	D		7				S	T	BT IW	H	G
180	BLACK HAWK DOCK 860-739-9296	ALL YR.								C				I		
181	MIJOY DOCK 860-443-0663	APR NOV								C			T	I		
182	BURR'S YACHT HAVEN 860-443-8457	APR OCT	9	EM B	HE R	D		20			R	SL	T	IW BT	GH	G D
183	A.W. MARINA 860-443-6076	MAY SEP			E						R		T	W BT	H	
184	FERRY SLIP Y. C. 860-442-9038	ALL YR.		EB							R	SL	PT	IW		
185	FORT TRUMBULL MARINA 860-443-6020	ALL YR.				W D	40	5					T			
186	CROCKER'S BOAT YARD INC 860-443-6304	ALL YR.	9	EB	HE	W D		75			R	SL	PT	IW	GH	G D
187	STATE PIER RAMP				R											
188	NEW LONDON Municipal Pier 860-442-1777			B							R			IW		
189	KENNETH STREETER RAMP				R											
190	THAMES HARBOR INN 860-445-8111	ALL YR.		EB							RL	SL	T	IW		
192	HEL-CAT DOCK 860-535-2066									C				BT		
193	GROTON OIL & MARINA 860-445-5336	ALL YR.		E B									T	IW		G D

Connecticut
MARINA'S NAME & PHONE NUMBER

CHART LOCATER NUMBER	Marina's Name & Phone Number	WHEN OPEN	MONITORS VHF CHANNEL	TRANSIENT Electricity•Moorings•Berths	Hull•Engine Repairs / Ramp	WINTER STORAGE: Wet•Dry	RAILWAY CAPACITY IN FEET	LIFT CAPACITY IN TONS	BOAT RENTAL: Canoe•Row•Motor	BOAT RENTAL: Charter•House•Sail	Restaurant•Lodging•Camping	Showers•Laundry	Pumpout•Toilets	Bait•Tackle•Water•Ice	Groceries•Hardware	Diesel fuel•Gasoline
194	PALMER'S COVE MARINA 860-536-6207	ALL YR.	9	B	E R	D		20			R	S	T	IW		G
195	SPICER'S MARINA 860-536-4978	ALL YR.	68	EM B	HE R	W D		35			R	SL	PT	IW BT	GH	
196	BEEBE COVE MARINA 860-536-0221	ALL YR.			HR	D		8					T	W	H	
197	NOANK VILLAGE BOATYARD 860-536-1770	ALL YR.	16 68	EM B	HE	D		35		C	R	S	PT	IW	H	
198	FORD'S LOBSTERS 860-536-2842	ALL YR.	16 18	M										WB I	G H	G D
199	ABBOTTS Lobster in The Rough 860-536-7719	MAY SEP									RL		T			
200	STEAMBOAT WHARF COMPANY 860-536-8300	ALL YR			R					C	L					
201	NOANK SHIPYARD 860-536-9651	ALL YR.	9	EM B	HE	W D		35			R	SL	T	IW	GH	G D
202	GOLDEN ERA BOATS 860-536-1005	ALL YR.			H										H	
203	PINE ISLAND MARINAS 860-445-9729	ALL YR.	68	EM B	HE R	D		17		C	R	S	PT	IW BT	G H	
204	CONNECTICUT PUBLIC RAMP				R											
205	GROTON TOWN				R											
206	WILLOW POINT MARINA 860-536-9873				HE	D		4					T	IW		
207	**FORT RACHEL MARINE SERVICES 860-536-6647**	**ALL YR.**		**EB**	**HE**	**W D**		**30**				**S**	**PT**	**IW**		
208	MYSTIC HARBOR MARINE 860-433-5771	ALL YR.	9	EB		W							S	T	IW		
209	GROTON PUBLIC RAMP				R											
210	JOHN CARIJA & SON 860-536-9440	ALL YR.		EB	H	W							S	T	W		
211	MYSTIC DOWNTOWN MARINA 860-572-5942	ALL YR.		EB	HE	D		17			RL	S	T	W	H	
212	MYSTIC MARINE BASIN 860-536-4930	ALL YR.	68		HE	W D		20				SL	PT	IW	H	
213	MYSTIC SEAPORT MUSEUM & DOCKS 860-572-0711; 572-5391	ALL YR.	9 68	EB					R	SC	R	S	T	IW	GH	

Connecticut
MARINA'S NAME & PHONE NUMBER

Chart Locater No.	Marina's Name & Phone Number	When Open	Monitors VHF Channel	Transient (Electricity/Moorings/Berths)	Hull/Engine Repairs • Ramp	Winter Storage (Wet/Dry)	Railway Capacity in Feet	Lift Capacity in Tons	Boat Rental (Canoe/Row/Motor)	Boat Rental (Charter/House/Sail)	Restaurant/Lodging/Camping	Showers/Laundry	Pumpout/Toilets	Bait/Tackle/Water/Ice	Groceries/Hardware	Diesel fuel/Gasoline
214	MYSTIC COVE BOAT SALES 860-536-4945	ALL YR			HE									I	H	
215	GWENMOR MARINA 860-536-0281	ALL YR.	9		HE	D		30				S	PT	IW	H	
216	BREWER Yacht Yard at Mystic 860-536-2293	ALL YR.	9	EB	HE	W D		35			RL	SL	PT	IW	H	G D
217	SEAPORT MARINE INC 860-536-9681	ALL YR.		EB	HE	W D	100	60			R	S	T	W	G H	D
218	MYSTIC RIVER MARINA INC. 860-536-3123	ALL YR.	9	EB	HE	D		35			R	SL	PT	I	H	G D
219	MASON'S ISLAND MARINA 860-536-2608	ALL YR.		EM B		D		20		S		S	T	IW	GH	
220	BROWER'S COVE MARINA 860-536-8864	ALL YR.	9		HE R	D						S	T	IW		
221	SHAFFER'S BOAT LIVERY 860-536-8713	APR NOV	9	B	R	D			M		C			IW BT		G
222	SKIPPER'S HARBOR VIEW RESTAURANT 860-535-2720	MAR OCT		B							R					
223	DODSON BOAT YARD INC 860-535-1507	AL YR.	9 78	EM B	HE	D		35		C	R	SL	PT	I	H	G D
224	DON'S DOCK 860-535-0077	ALL YR.		MB	R	D			M	S	R		T	IW BT	H	G
225	CARDINAL COVE MARINA 860-535-0060	APR NOV			R	D			M				T	IW BT		
226	BARN ISLAND RAMP				R											
227	WEQUETEQUOCK COVE 860-599-5864	ALL YR.			ER	D			CR M		L		T	IW BT	H	G
228	WHEWELL'S MARINE 860-599-4322	ALL YR.		B	HE R	D		3			L	S	T	IW	H	
229	COVESIDE MARINA & MOTEL 860-535-2276	APR NOV		MB	ER	D		4			R L	S	T	IW BT	H	G D
230	PAWCATUCK RIVER DOCK 860-599-5680	AL YR				D		20								
231	CONNORS - O'BRIEN MARINA 860-599-5573	ALL YR			HE R	D							T		H	
232	STONINGTON-ON-THE-RIVER 860-599-8728			EB	R	D		15				SL	T	IW		
233	GREENHAVEN MARINA 860-599-1049	APR OCT		MB	R	D	40	5					T	IW		

454

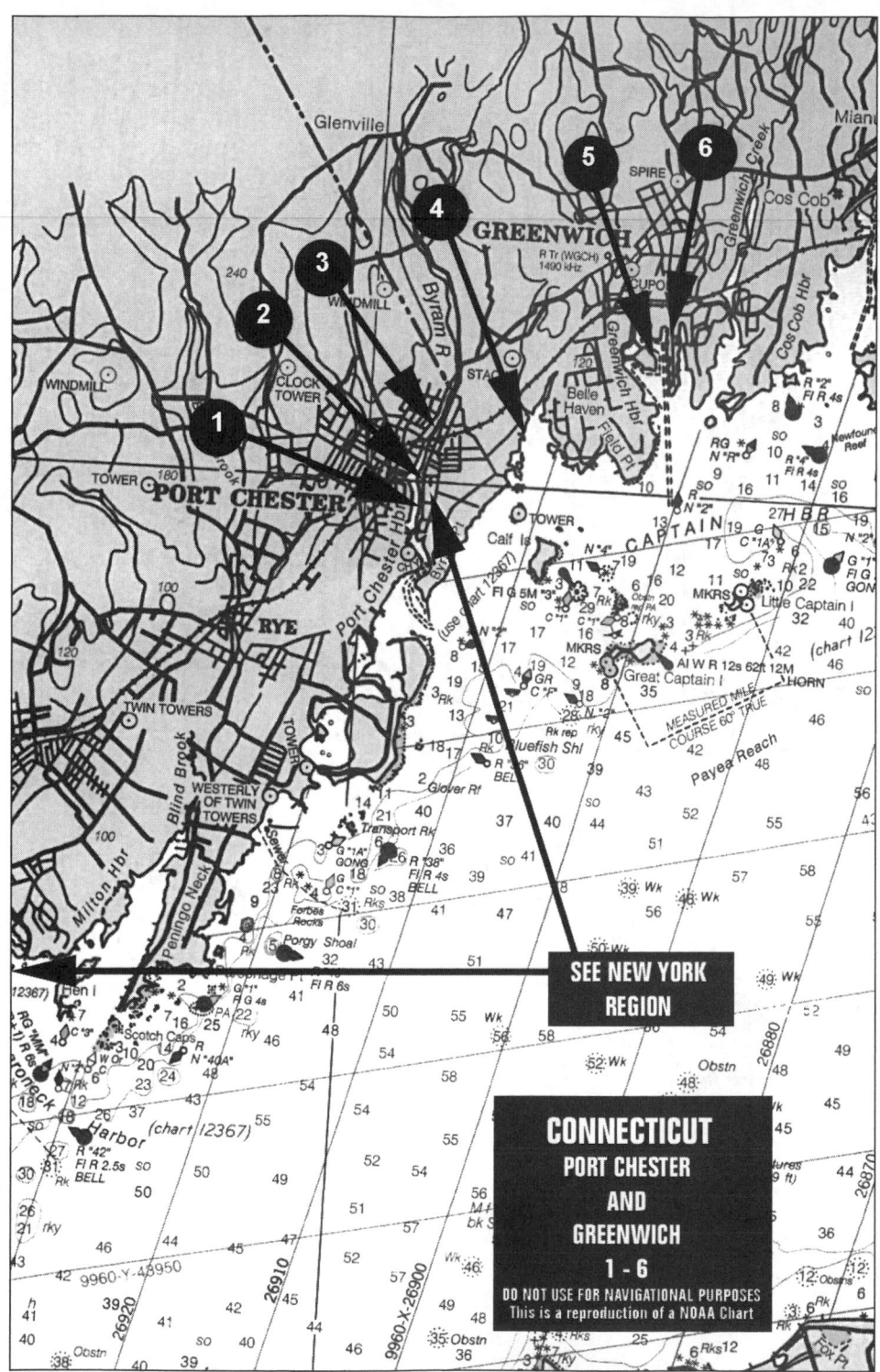

SEE NEW YORK
REGION

CONNECTICUT
PORT CHESTER
AND
GREENWICH
1 - 6
DO NOT USE FOR NAVIGATIONAL PURPOSES
This is a reproduction of a NOAA Chart

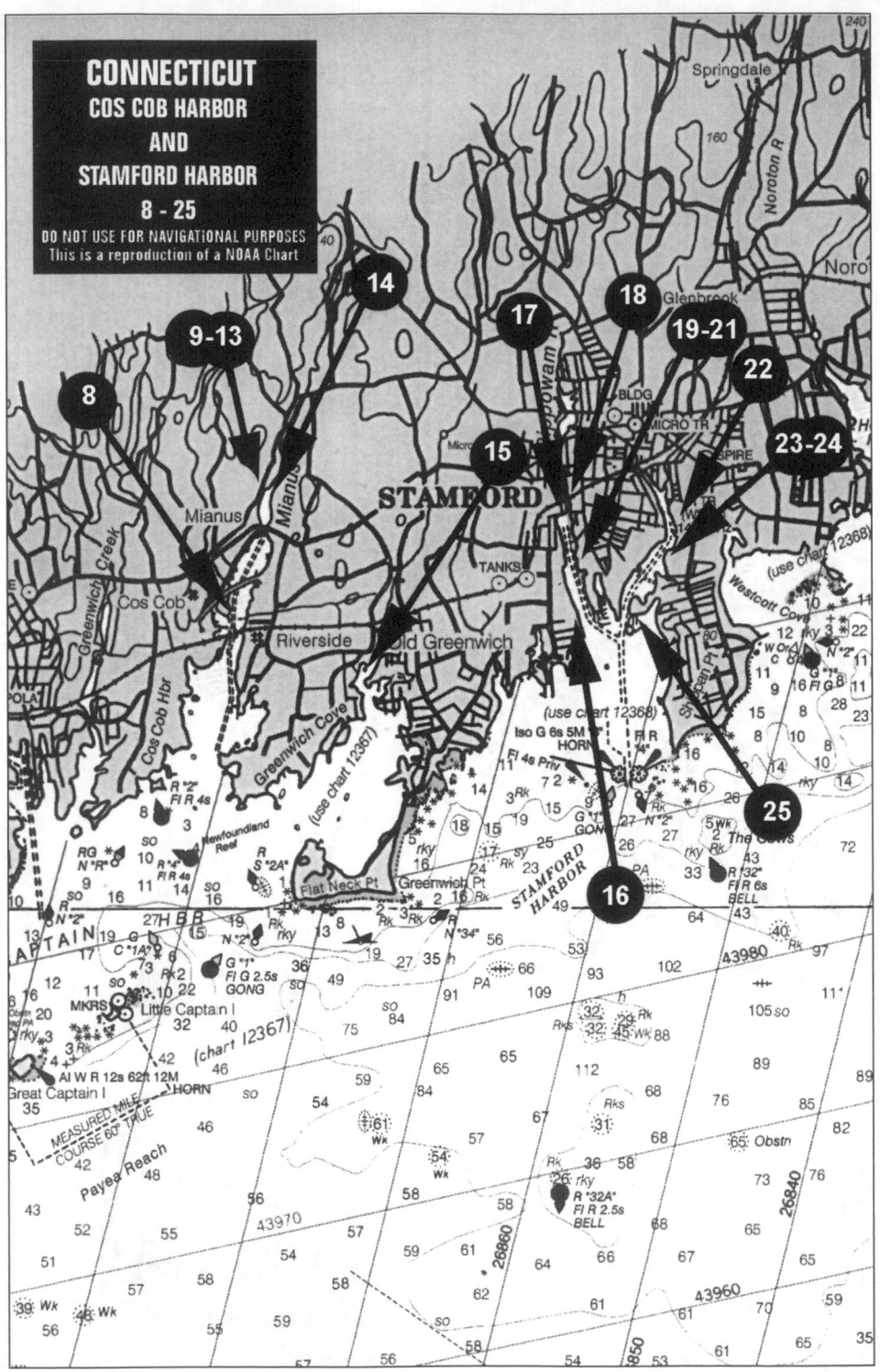

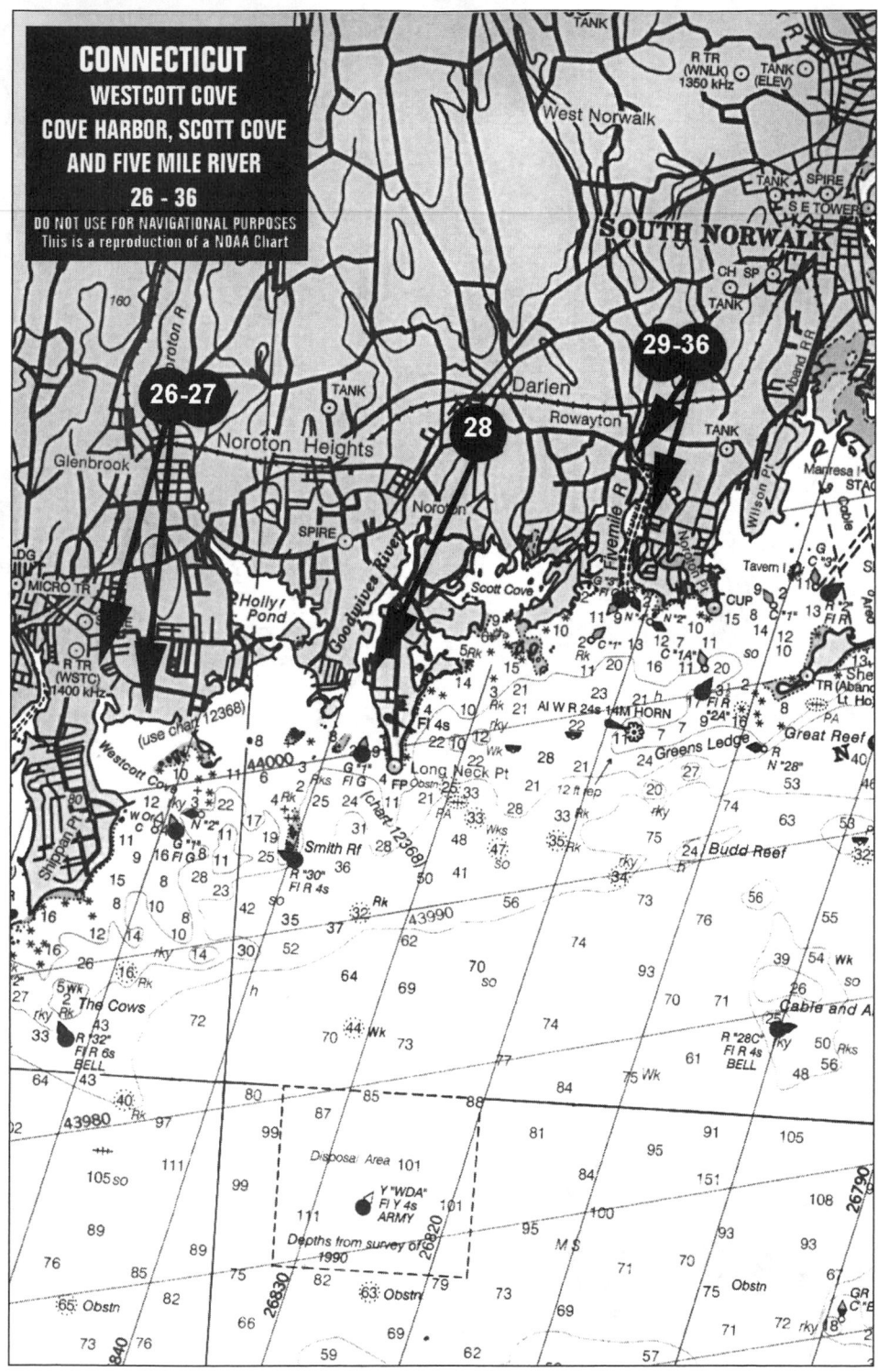

CONNECTICUT
WESTCOTT COVE
COVE HARBOR, SCOTT COVE
AND FIVE MILE RIVER
26 - 36
DO NOT USE FOR NAVIGATIONAL PURPOSES
This is a reproduction of a NOAA Chart

457

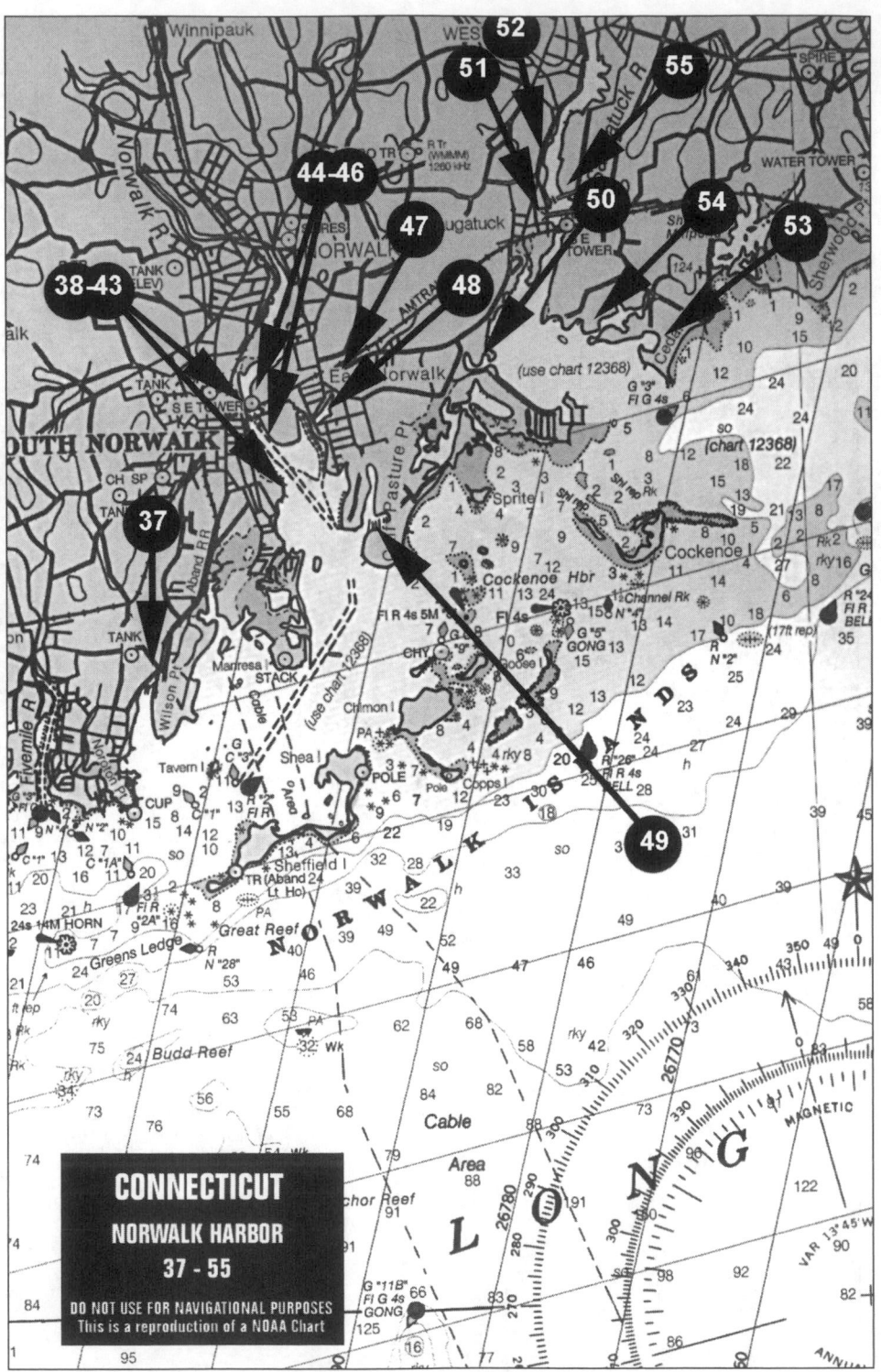

CONNECTICUT

NORWALK HARBOR

37 - 55

DO NOT USE FOR NAVIGATIONAL PURPOSES
This is a reproduction of a NOAA Chart

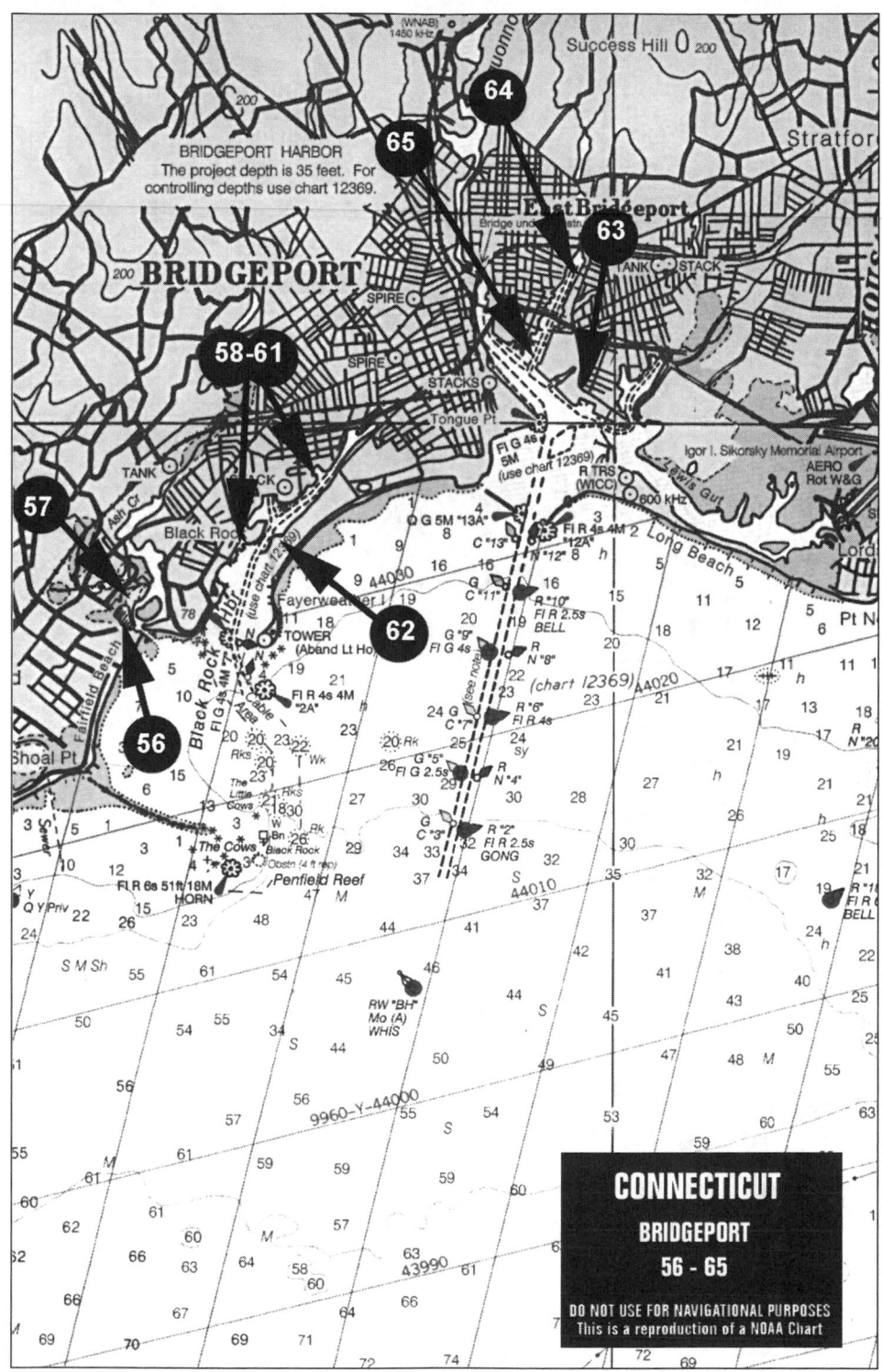

BRIDGEPORT HARBOR
The project depth is 35 feet. For
controlling depths use chart 12369.

BRIDGEPORT

East Bridgeport

Stratfor

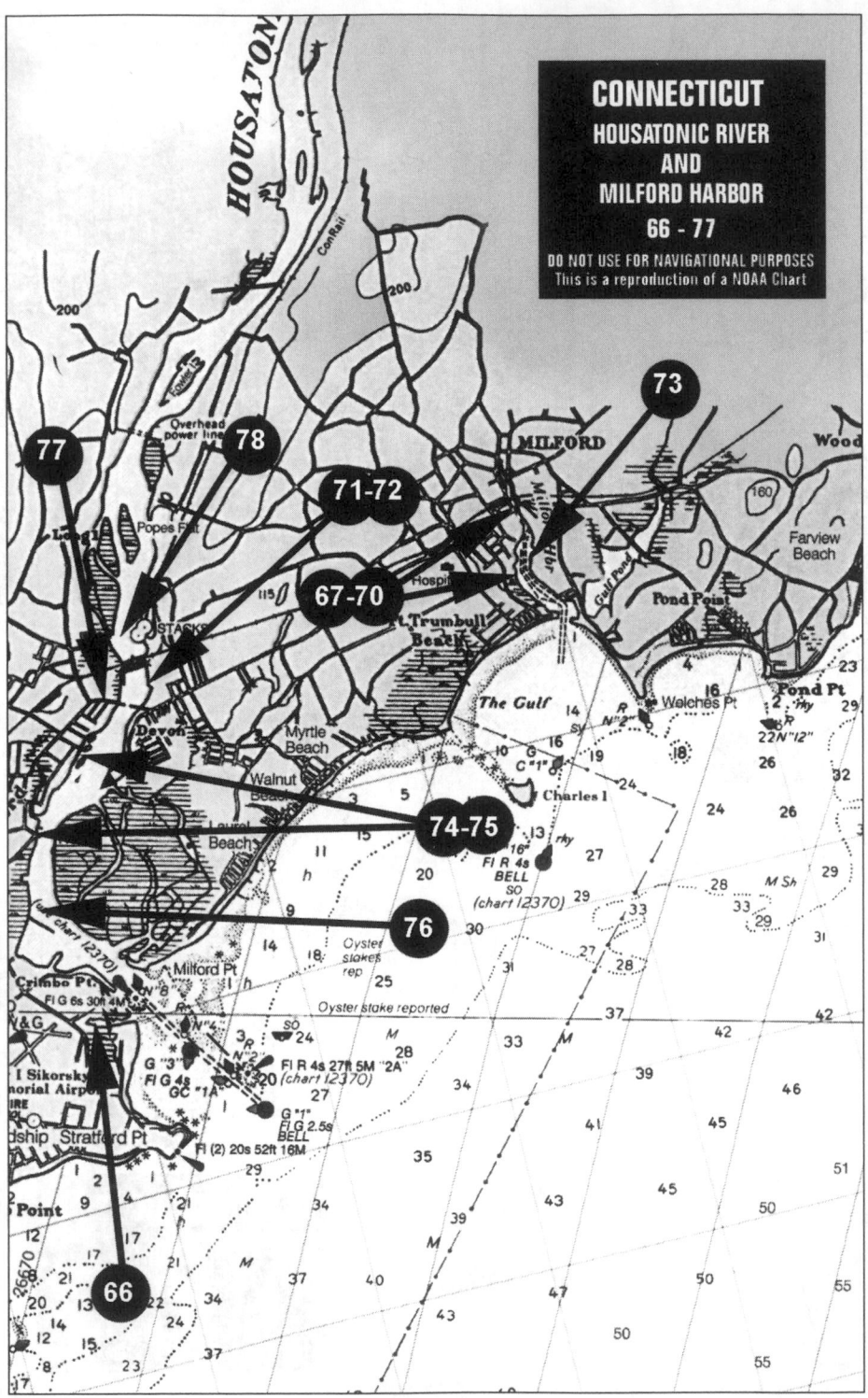

CONNECTICUT
HOUSATONIC RIVER
AND
MILFORD HARBOR
66 - 77

DO NOT USE FOR NAVIGATIONAL PURPOSES
This is a reproduction of a NOAA Chart

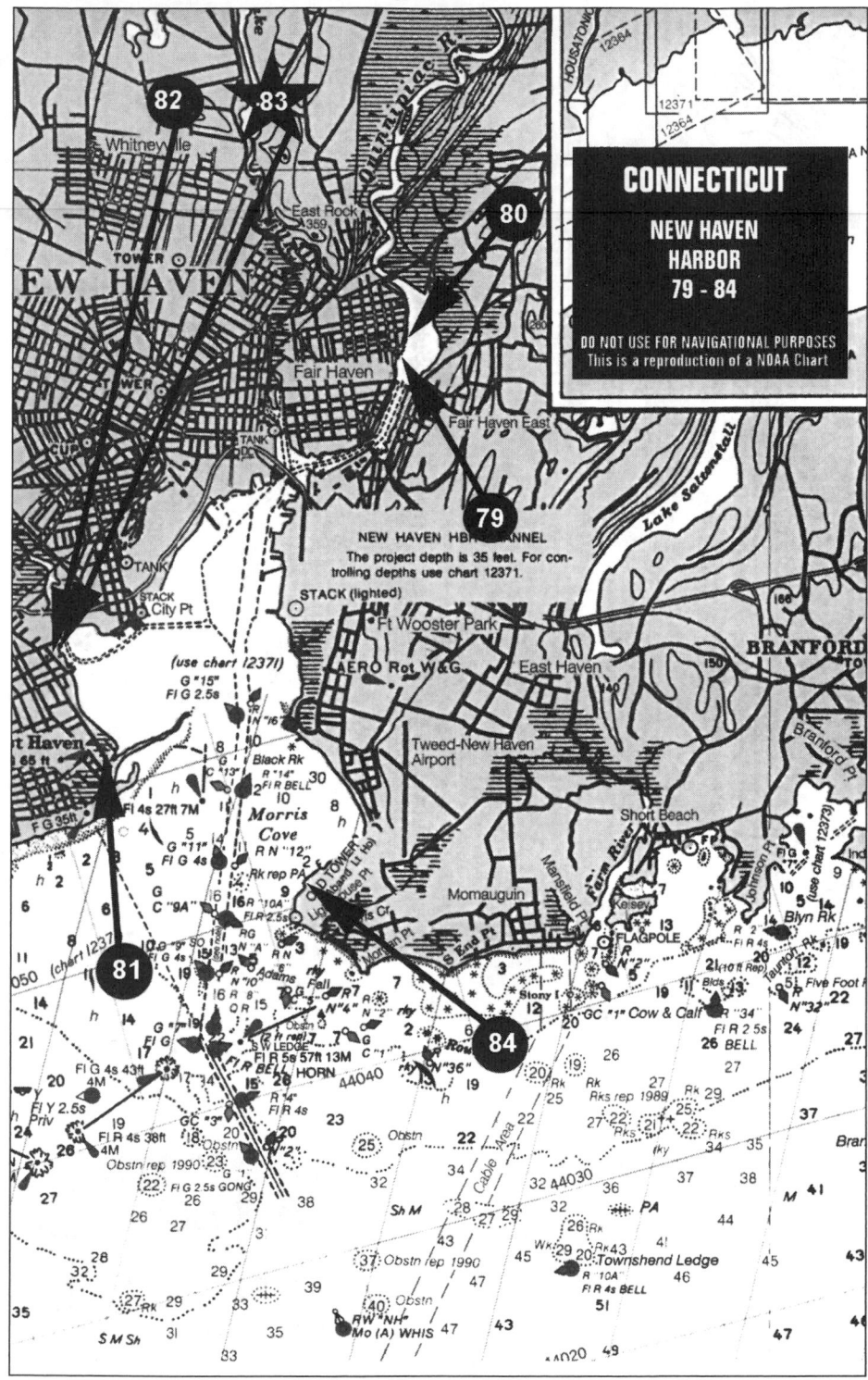

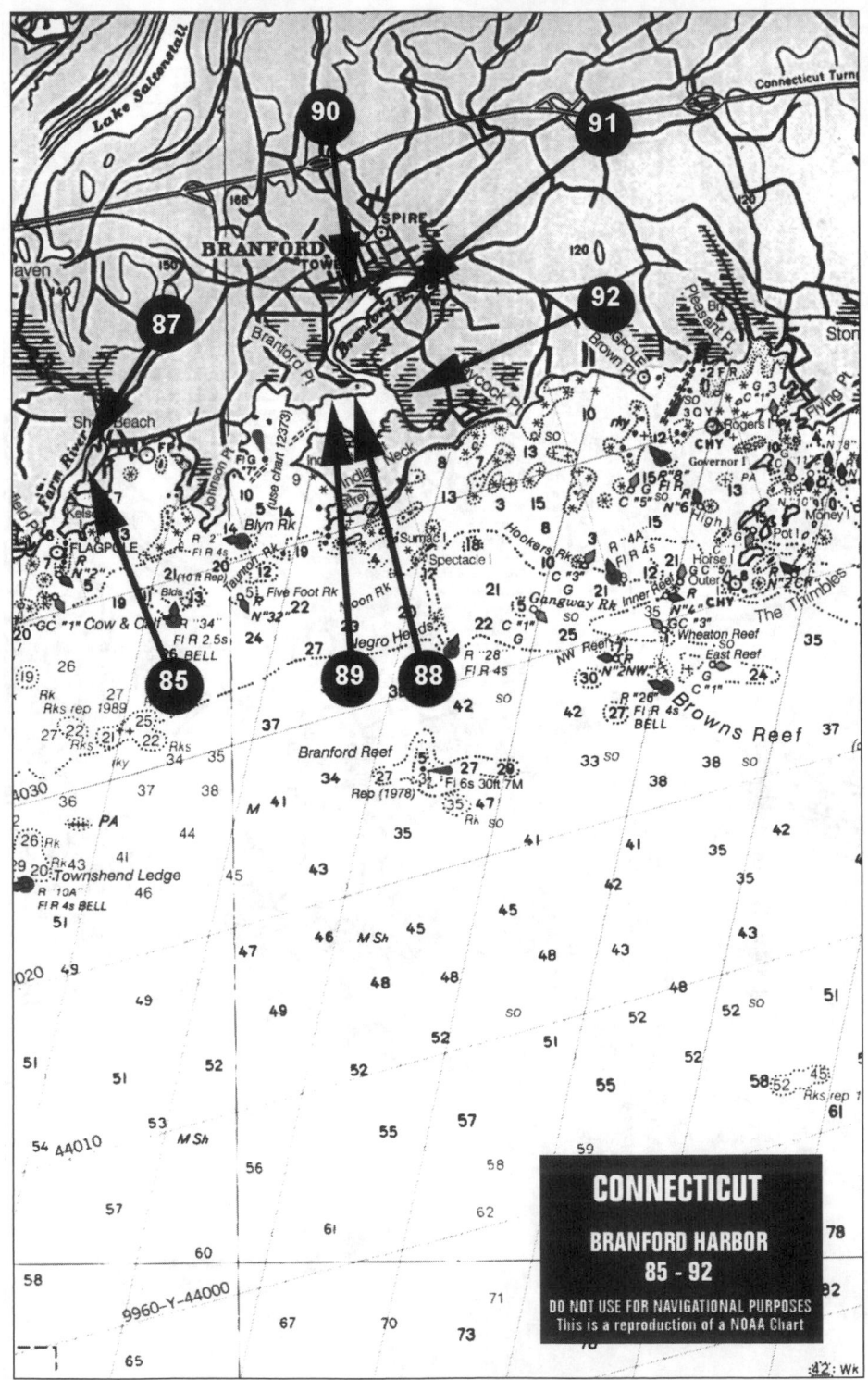

CONNECTICUT

BRANFORD HARBOR
85 - 92

DO NOT USE FOR NAVIGATIONAL PURPOSES
This is a reproduction of a NOAA Chart

462

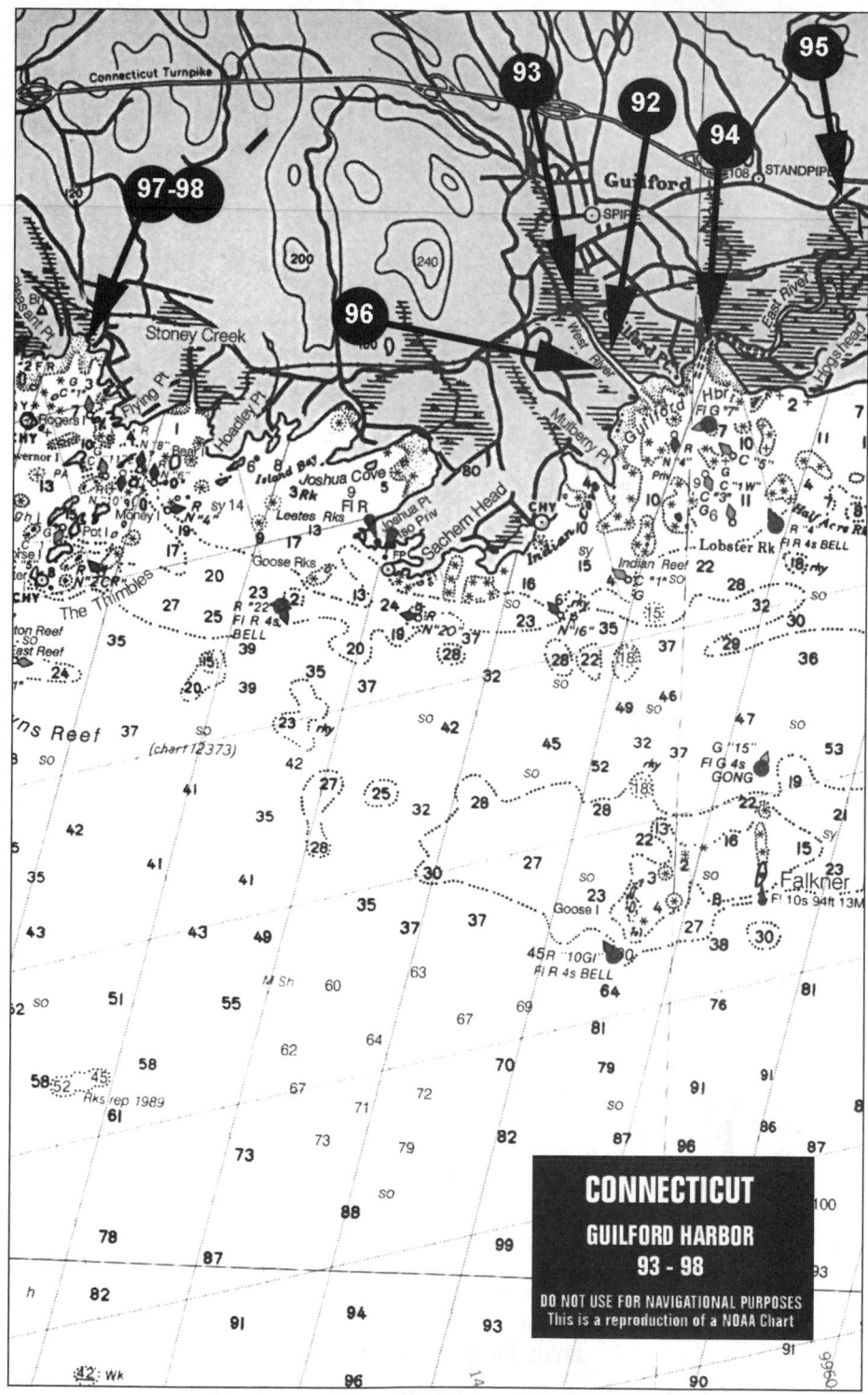

CONNECTICUT
GUILFORD HARBOR
93 - 98

DO NOT USE FOR NAVIGATIONAL PURPOSES
This is a reproduction of a NOAA Chart

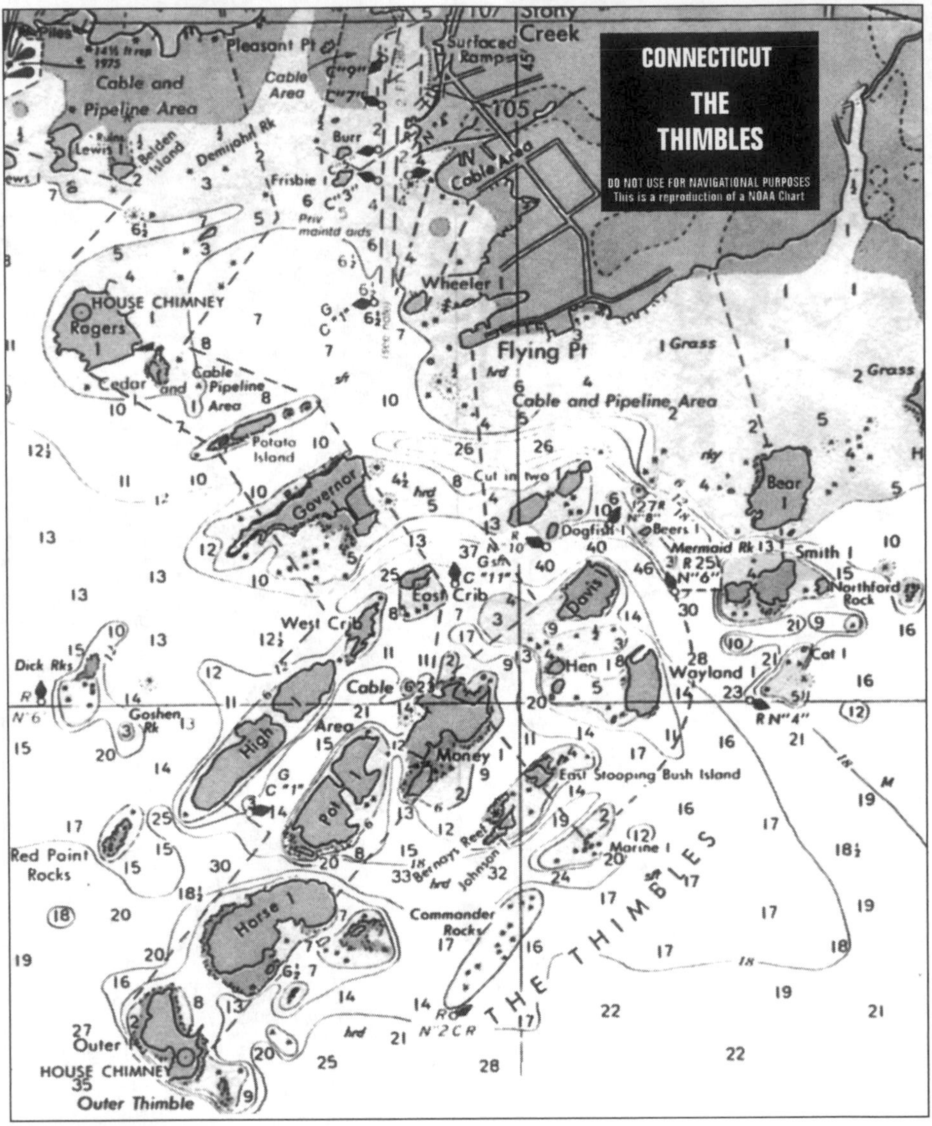

CONNECTICUT
THE THIMBLES
DO NOT USE FOR NAVIGATIONAL PURPOSES
This is a reproduction of a NOAA Chart
Stony Creek
Surfaced Ramp
Pleasant Pt
Cable and Pipeline Area
Cable Area
Lewis I
Belden Island
Demijohn Rk
Burr
Frisbie I
Priv maintd aids
Cable Area
Wheeler I
HOUSE CHIMNEY
Rogers I
Cedar
Cable and Pipeline Area
Flying Pt
Grass
Cable and Pipeline Area
Potato Island
Governor
Cut in two I
Dogfish I
Beers I
Mermaid Rk
Bear I
Smith I
Northford Rock
East Crib
West Crib
Davis
Hen I
Wayland I
Cat I
Dick Rks
Goshen Rk
Cable Area
High
Money I
Pot I
East Stooping Bush Island
Red Point Rocks
Bernays Reef
Johnson I
Marine I
Horse I
Commander Rocks
THE THIMBLES
Outer I
HOUSE CHIMNEY
Outer Thimble

WE'D LIKE TO HEAR FROM YOU!

The most valuable information a cruising boater can have is

LOCAL KNOWLEDGE.

We invite you to share your cruising experiences with our *Northeast Boaters Almanac* readers and website visitors. Tell us about your favorite destinations, the best way to navigate to an out of the way cove, great anchorages and hurricane holes, navigational hazards you've encountered, waterfront dining spots, boat cleaning tips, good things to cook aboard and more... and, if you find information we need to change for future editions... you can do it all on

www.BoatersAlmanac.com

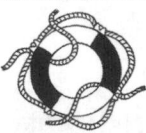

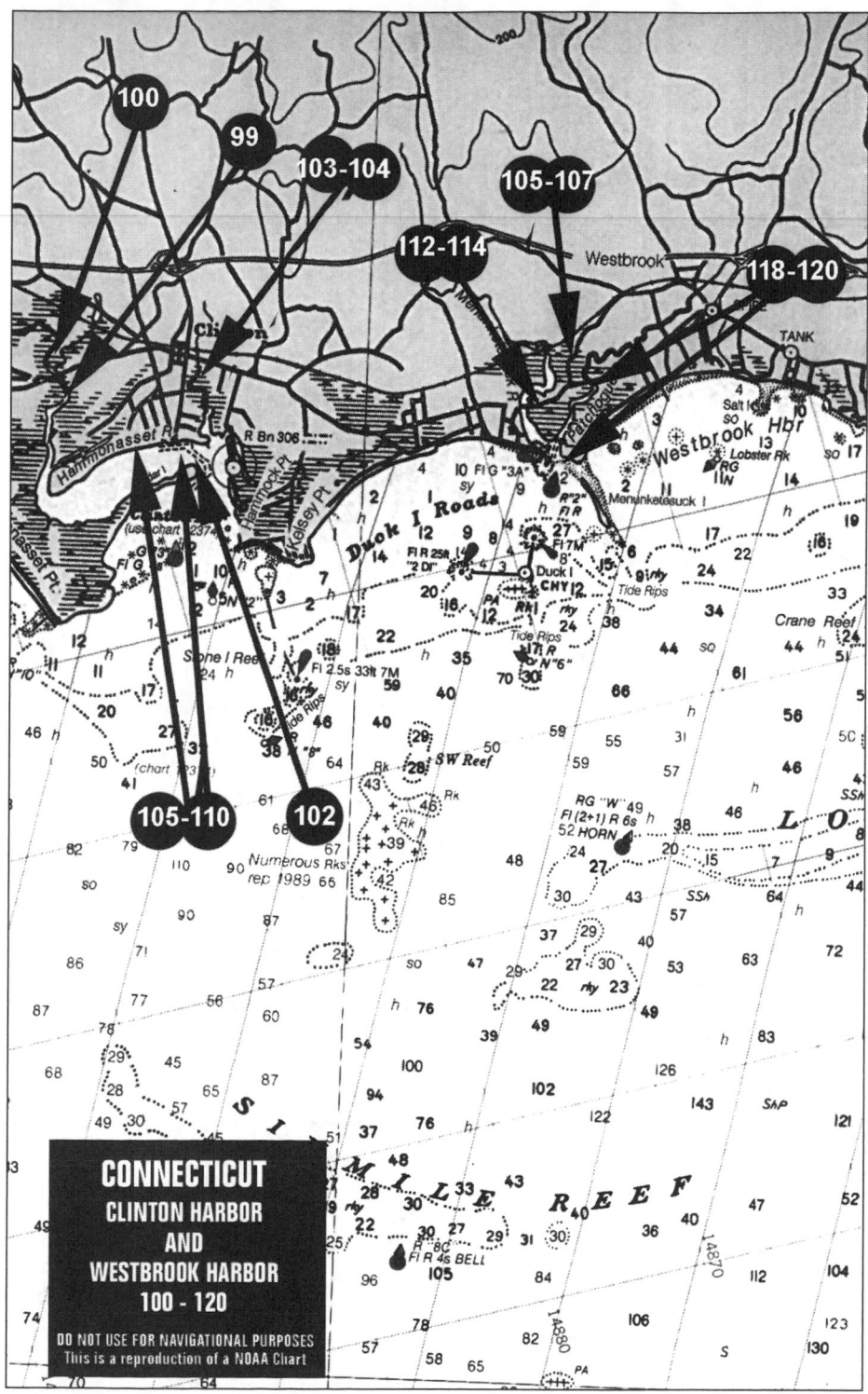

CONNECTICUT
CLINTON HARBOR
AND
WESTBROOK HARBOR
100 - 120

DO NOT USE FOR NAVIGATIONAL PURPOSES
This is a reproduction of a NOAA Chart

465

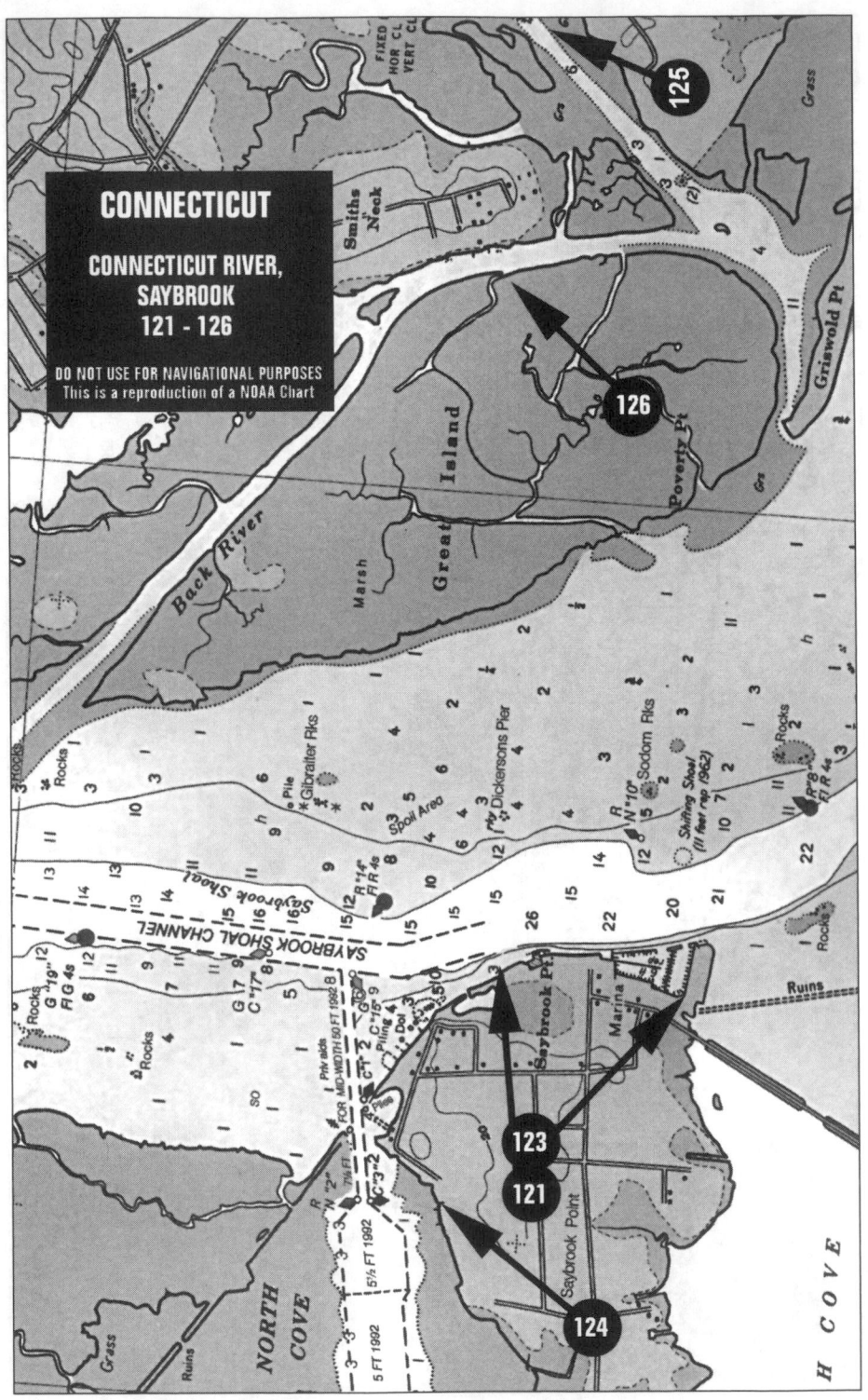

CONNECTICUT

CONNECTICUT RIVER,
SAYBROOK
121 - 126

DO NOT USE FOR NAVIGATIONAL PURPOSES
This is a reproduction of a NOAA Chart

466

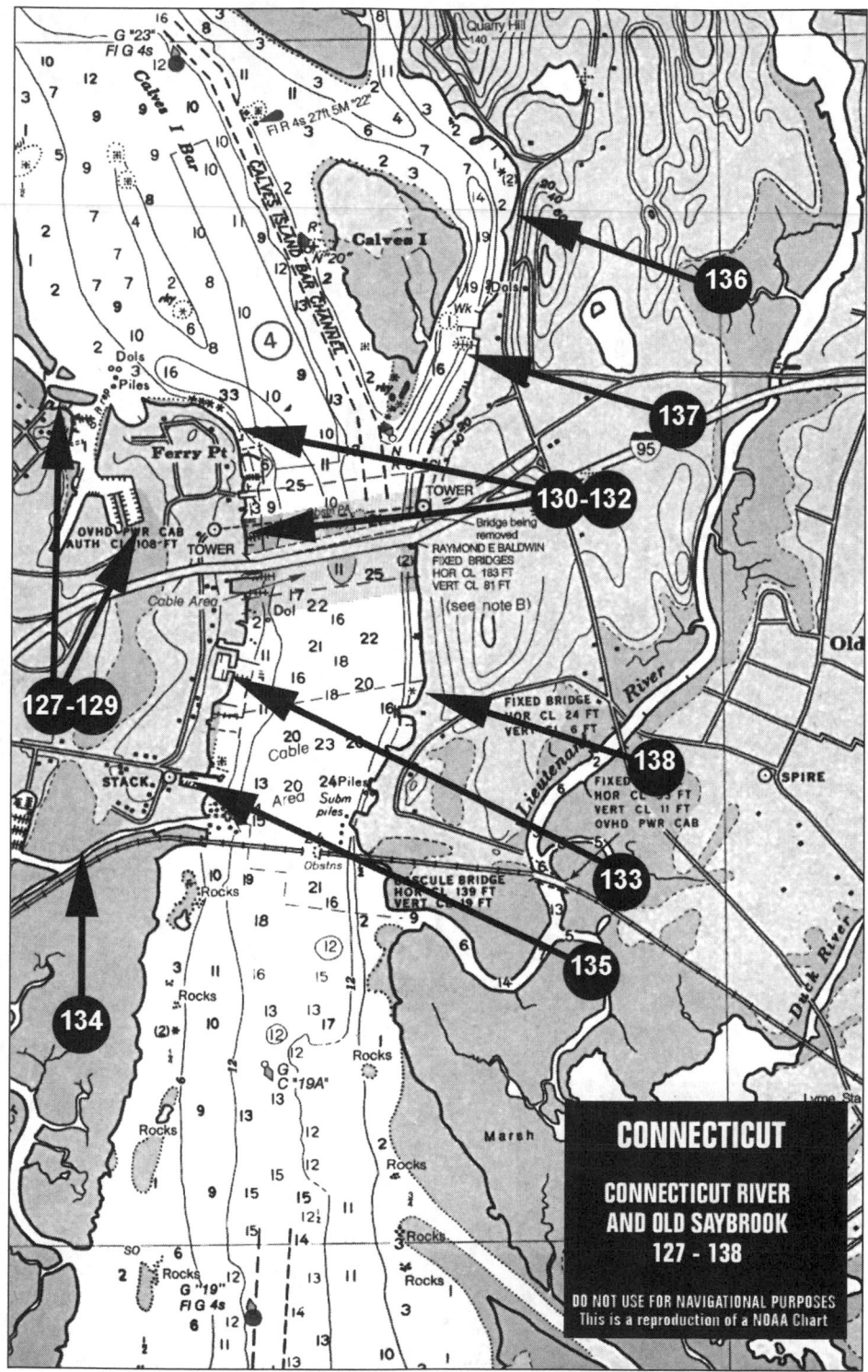

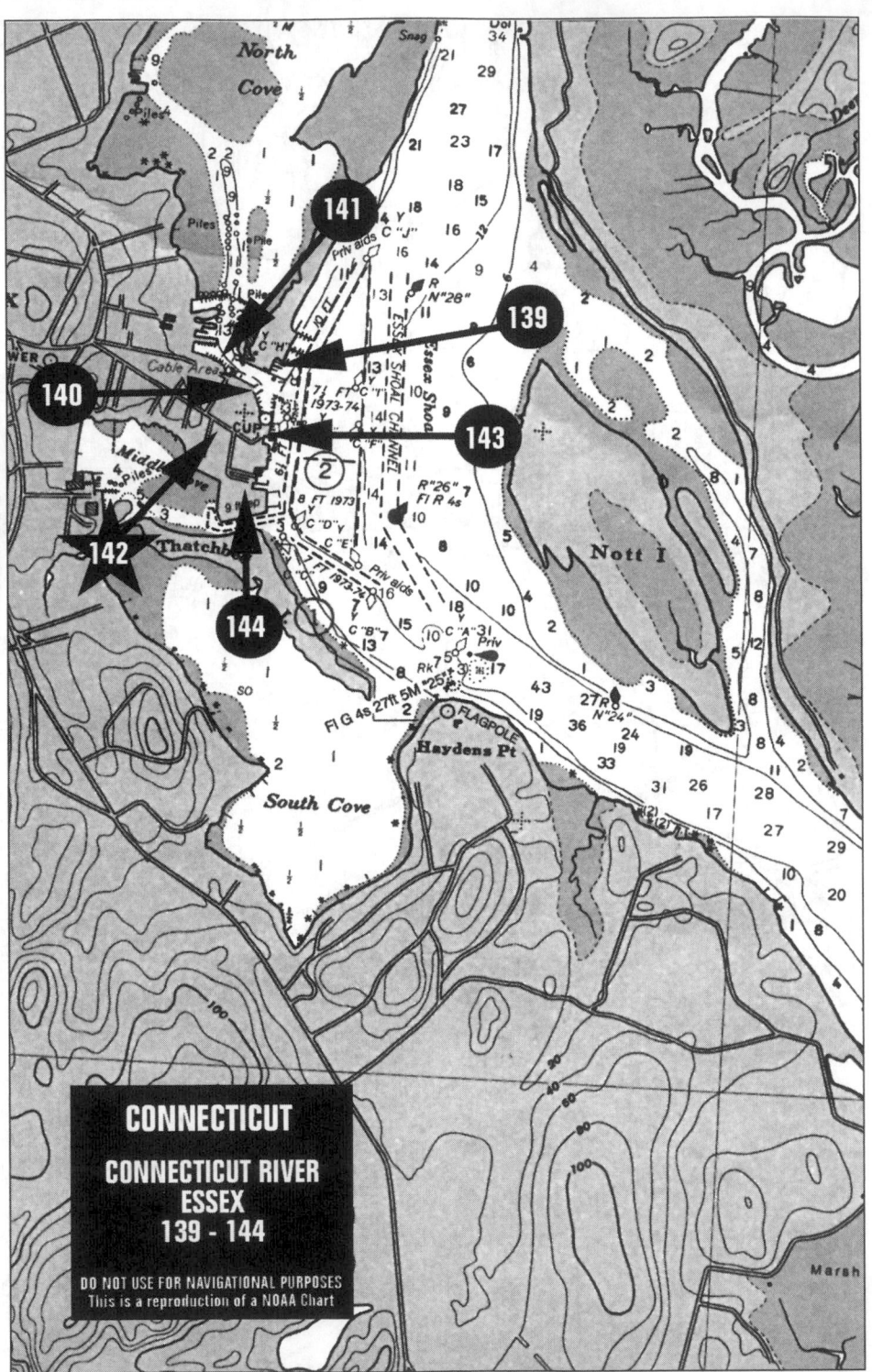

CONNECTICUT

CONNECTICUT RIVER
ESSEX
139 - 144

DO NOT USE FOR NAVIGATIONAL PURPOSES
This is a reproduction of a NOAA Chart

468

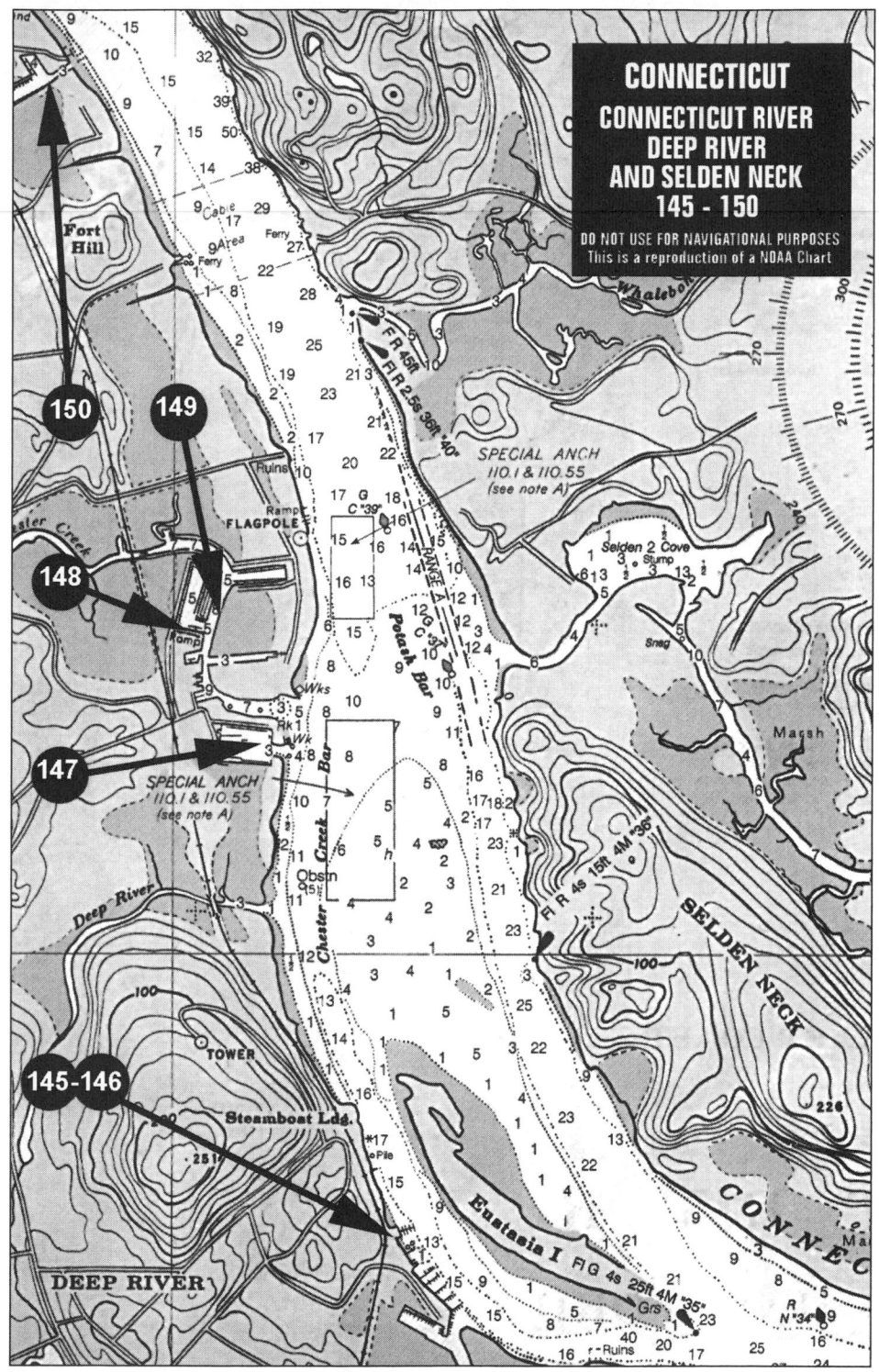

CONNECTICUT
CONNECTICUT RIVER
DEEP RIVER
AND SELDEN NECK
145 - 150

DO NOT USE FOR NAVIGATIONAL PURPOSES
This is a reproduction of a NOAA Chart

Fort Hill

150

149

148

147

145-146

Chester Creek

FLAGPOLE

Ramp

SPECIAL ANCH
110.1 & 110.55
(see note A)

SPECIAL ANCH
110.1 & 110.55
(see note A)

Deep River

TOWER

Steamboat Ldg.

DEEP RIVER

Potash Bar

Chester Creek Bar

Obstn

Whaleb

SPECIAL ANCH
110.1 & 110.55
(see note A)

Selden 2 Cove

Snag

Marsh

SELDEN NECK

C O N N E C

Eustasia I

F R 45ft

F R 2.5s 39ft "40"

RANGE

G C "39"

F R 4s 15ft 4M "36"

F R 4s 15ft 4M "36"

FI G 4s 25ft 4M "35"

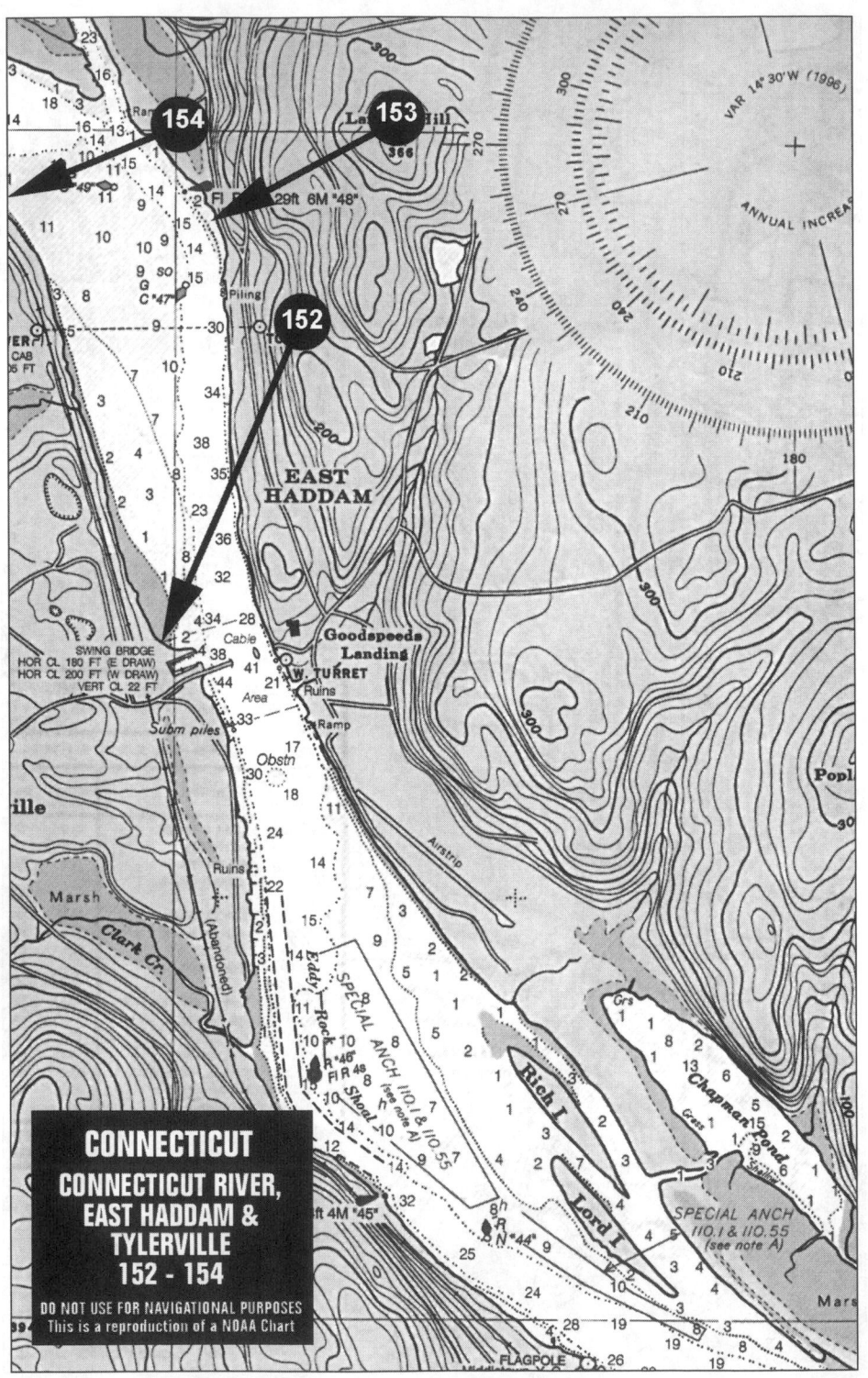

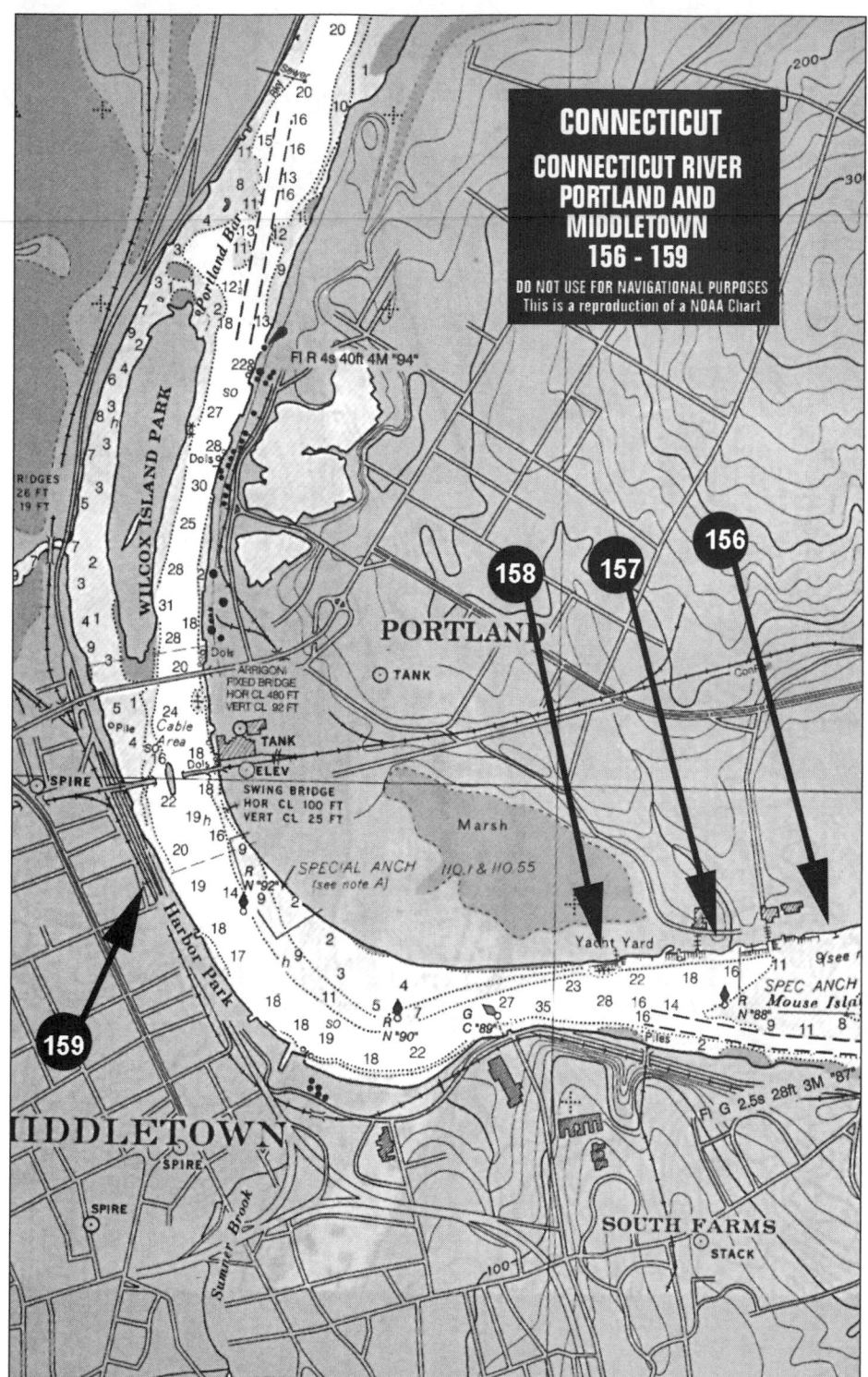

CONNECTICUT
CONNECTICUT RIVER
PORTLAND AND
MIDDLETOWN
156 - 159
DO NOT USE FOR NAVIGATIONAL PURPOSES
This is a reproduction of a NOAA Chart

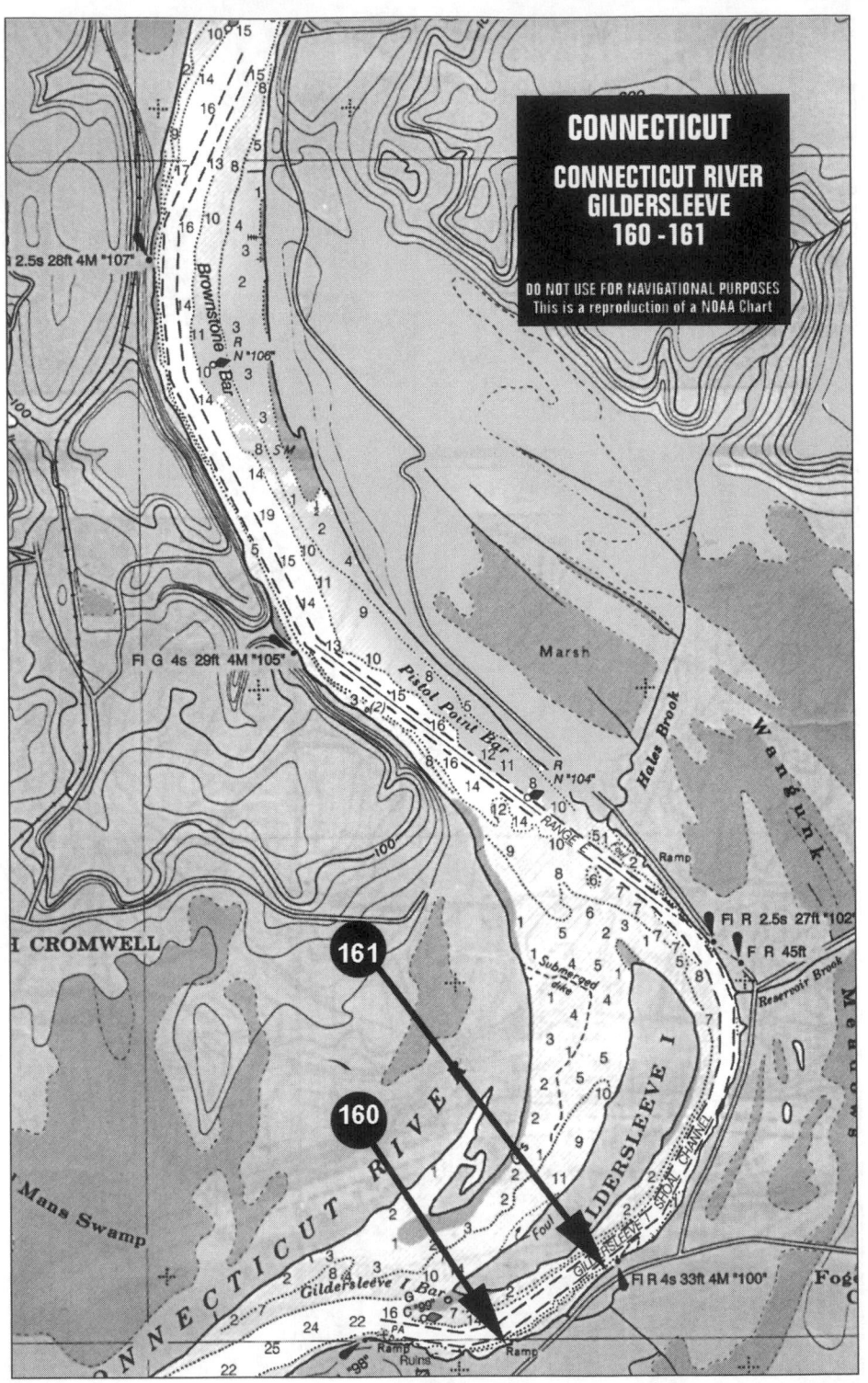

CONNECTICUT

CONNECTICUT RIVER
GILDERSLEEVE
160 - 161

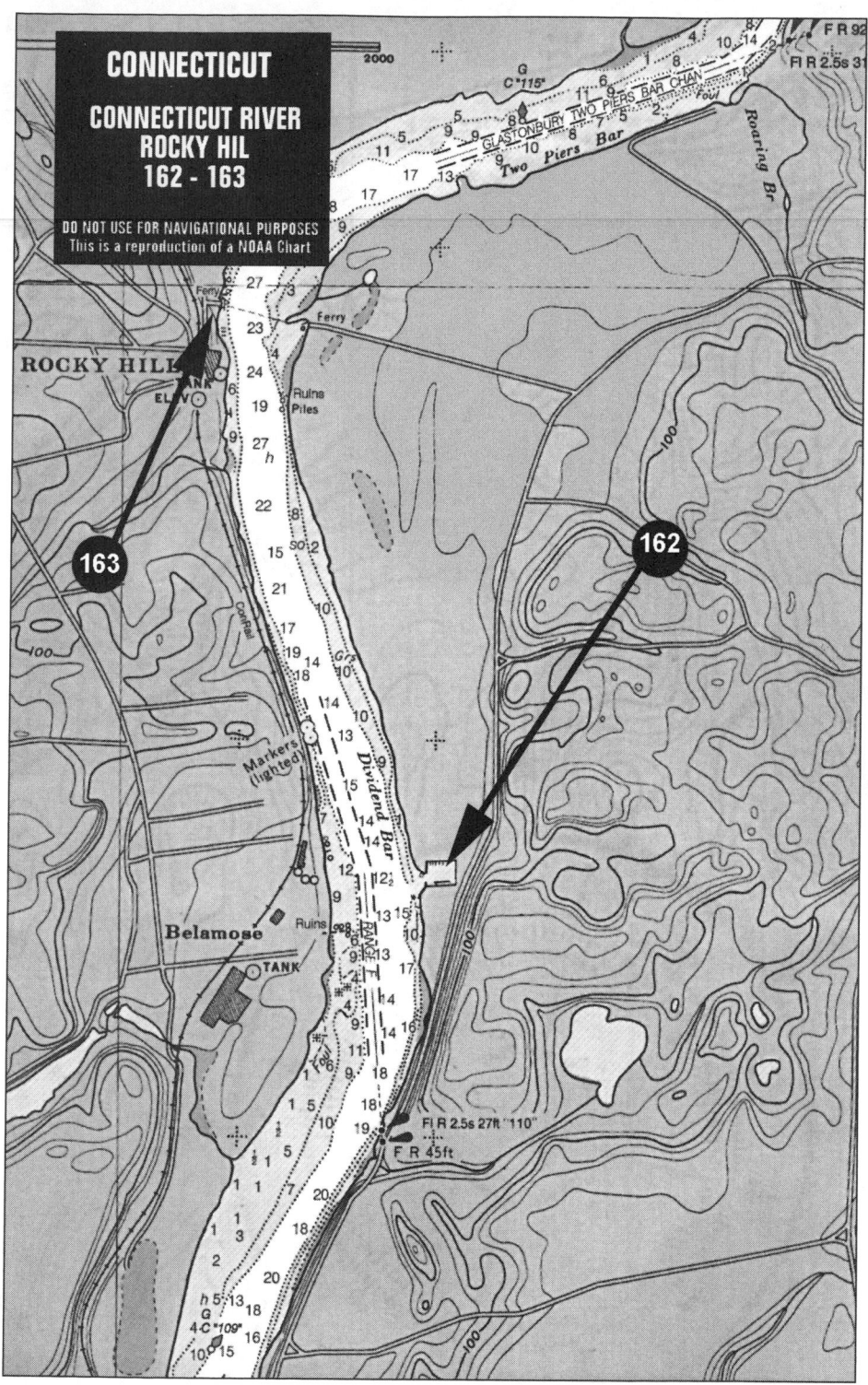

CONNECTICUT

**CONNECTICUT RIVER
ROCKY HIL
162 - 163**

DO NOT USE FOR NAVIGATIONAL PURPOSES
This is a reproduction of a NOAA Chart

ROCKY HILL

Belamose

163

162

473

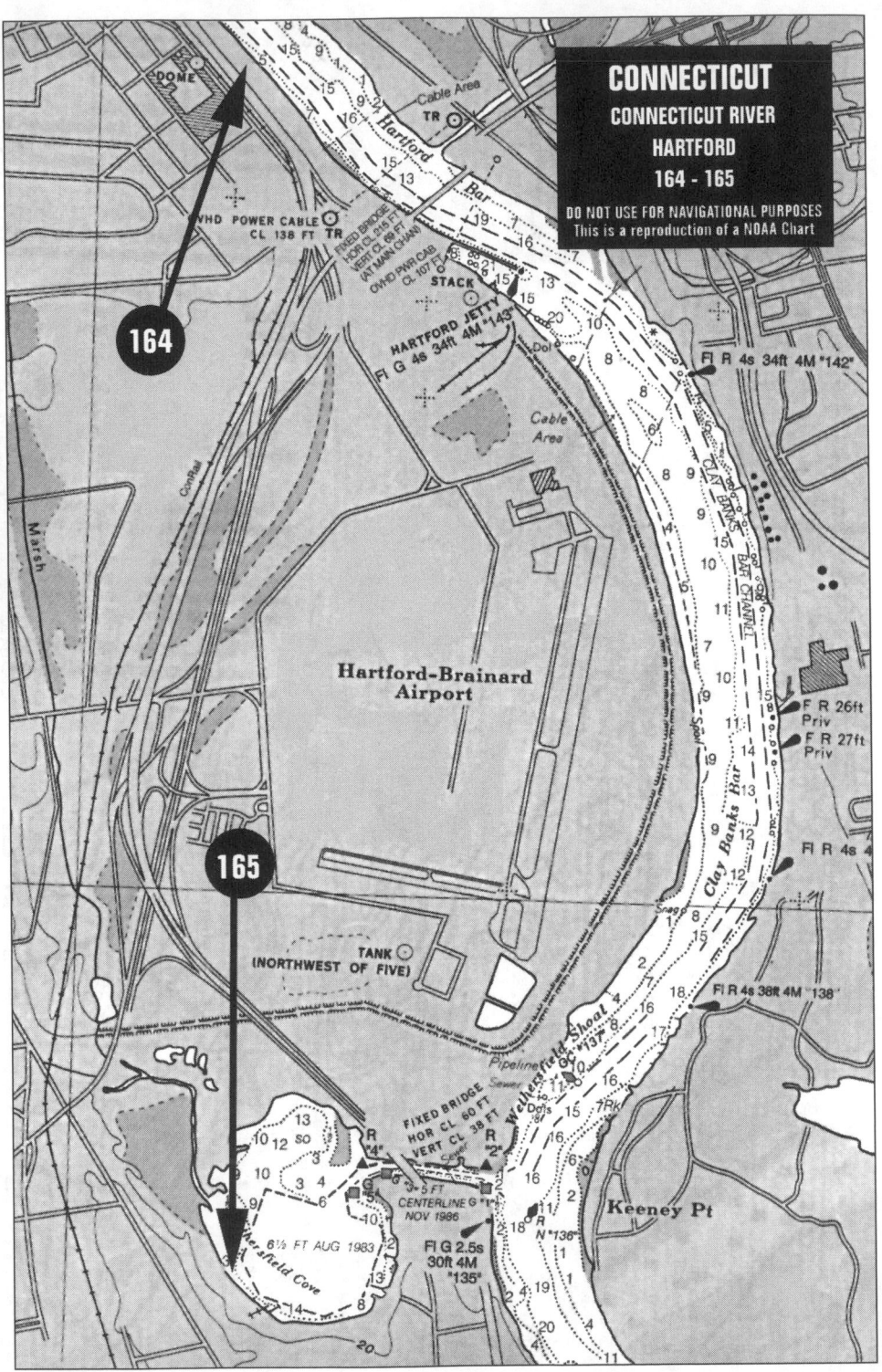

CONNECTICUT
CONNECTICUT RIVER
HARTFORD
164 - 165

DO NOT USE FOR NAVIGATIONAL PURPOSES
This is a reproduction of a NOAA Chart

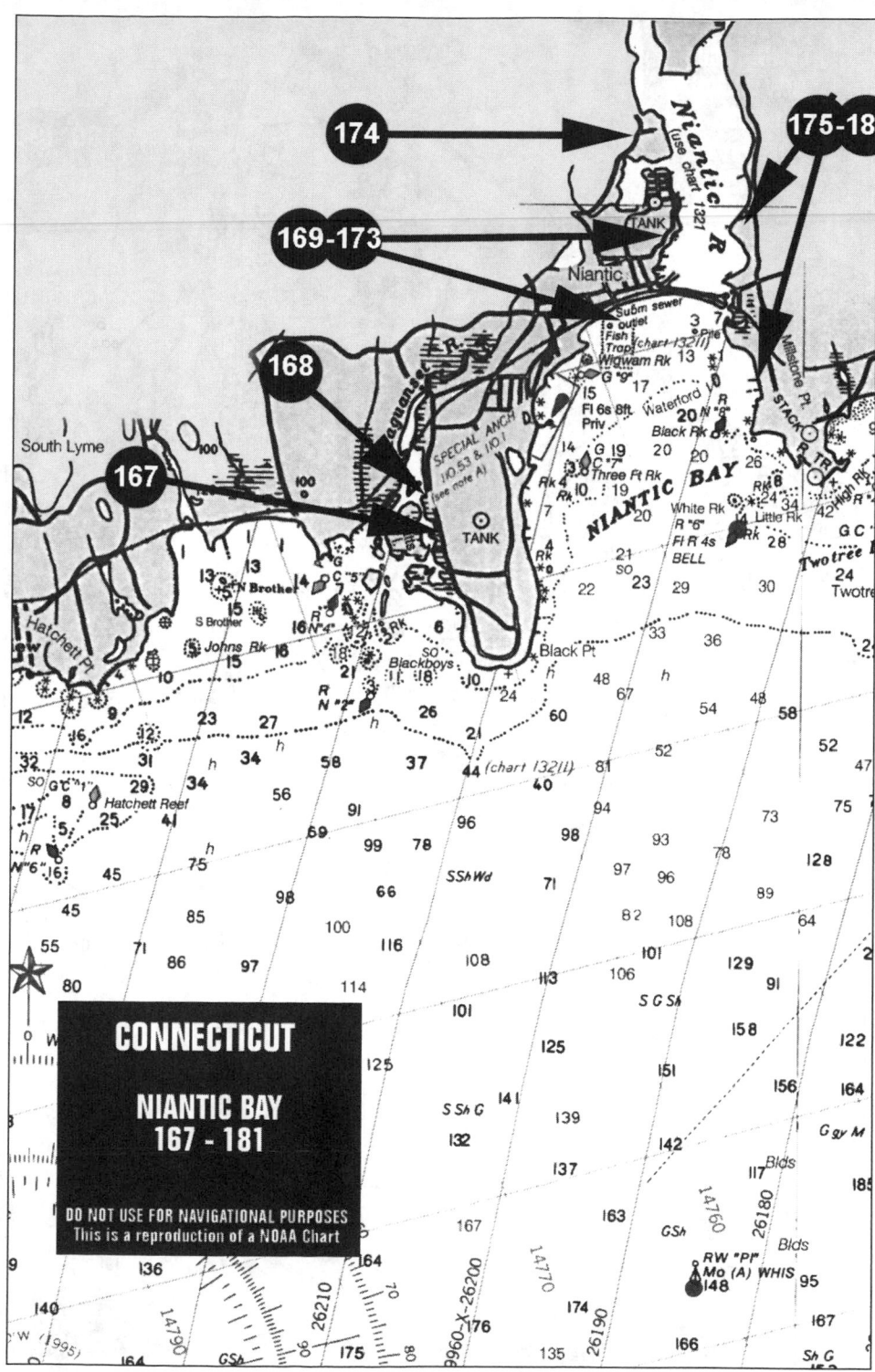

CONNECTICUT

NIANTIC BAY
167 - 181

DO NOT USE FOR NAVIGATIONAL PURPOSES
This is a reproduction of a NOAA Chart

475

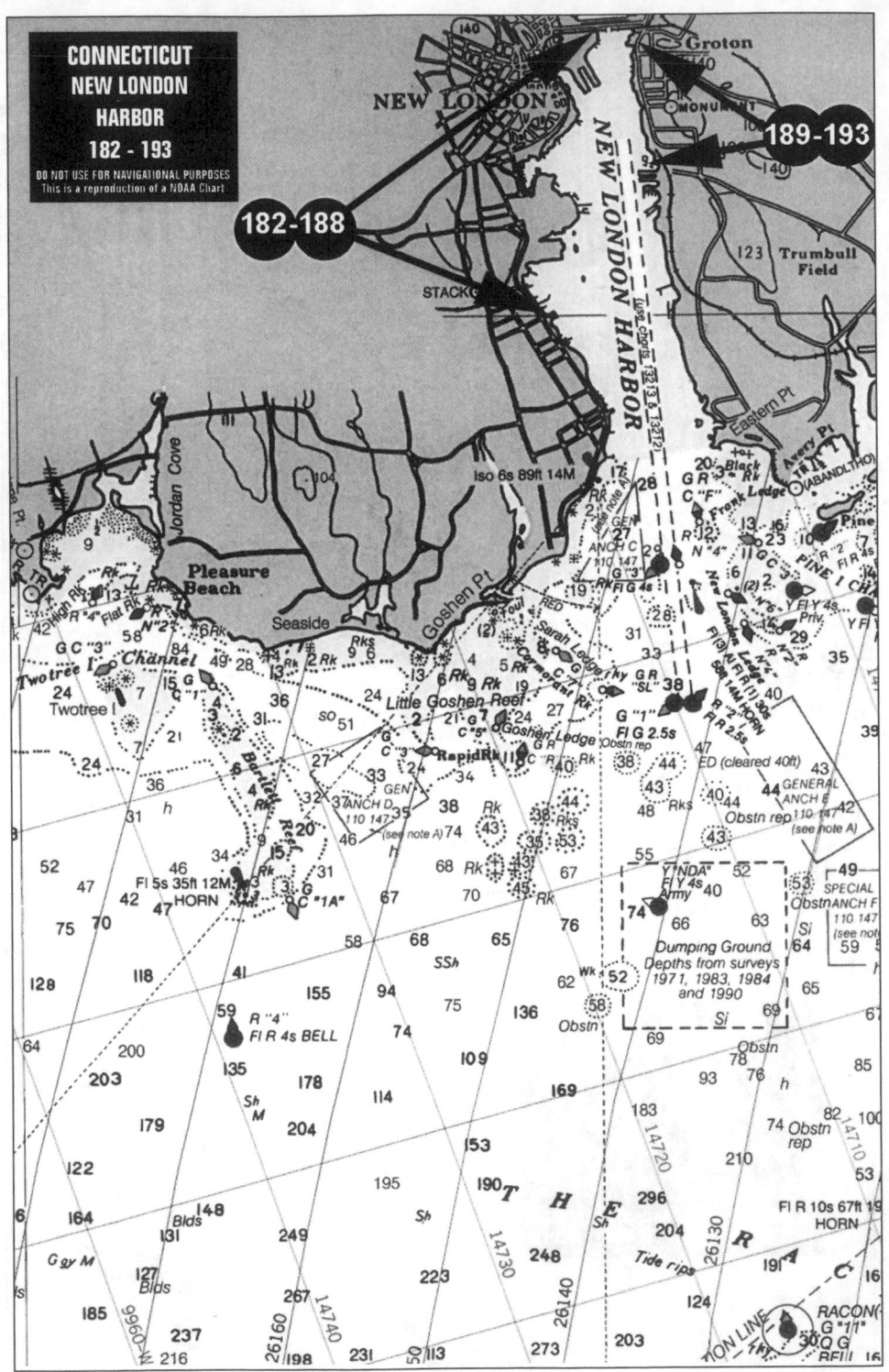

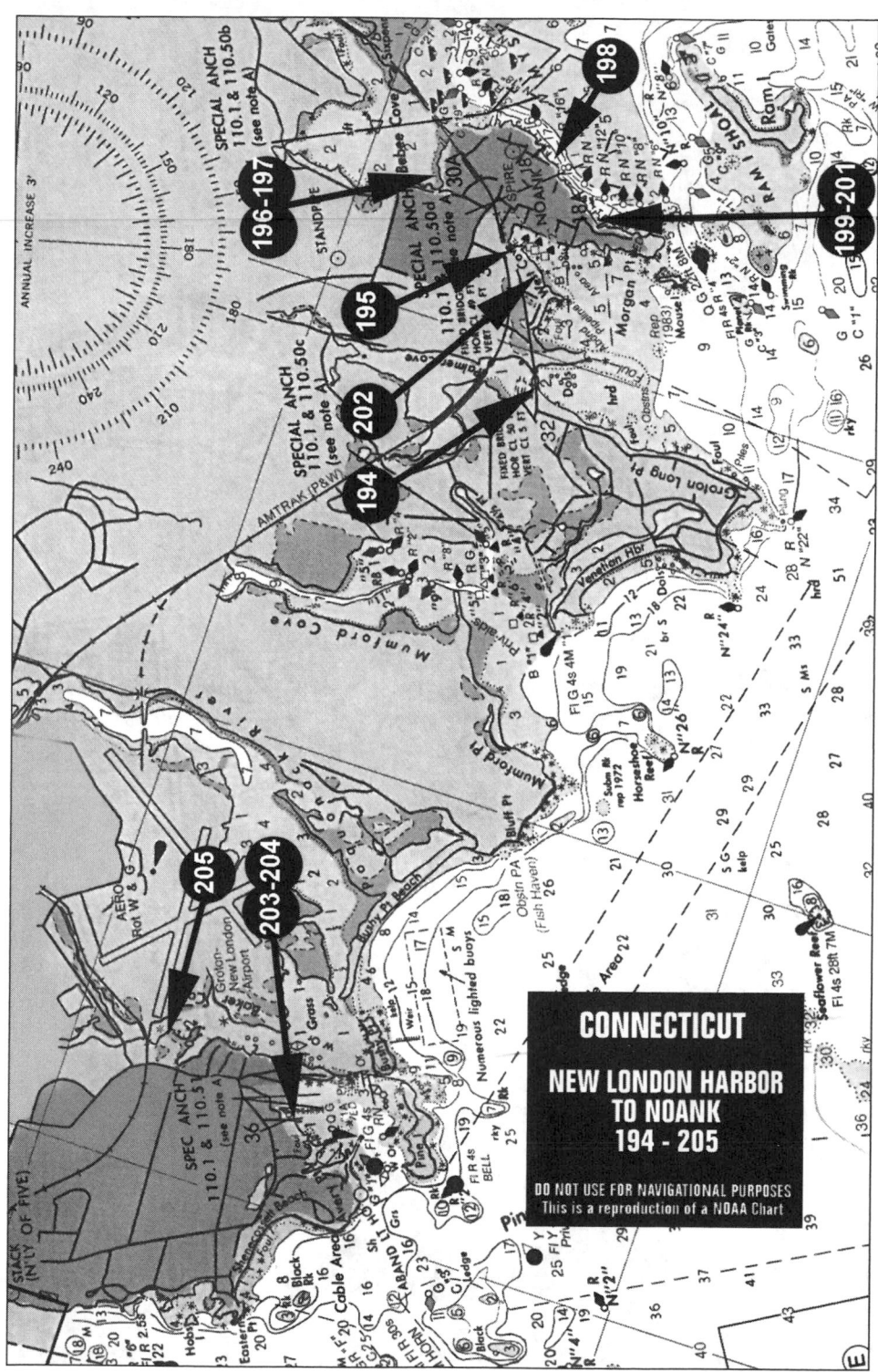

CONNECTICUT

NEW LONDON HARBOR
TO NOANK
194 - 205

DO NOT USE FOR NAVIGATIONAL PURPOSES
This is a reproduction of a NOAA Chart

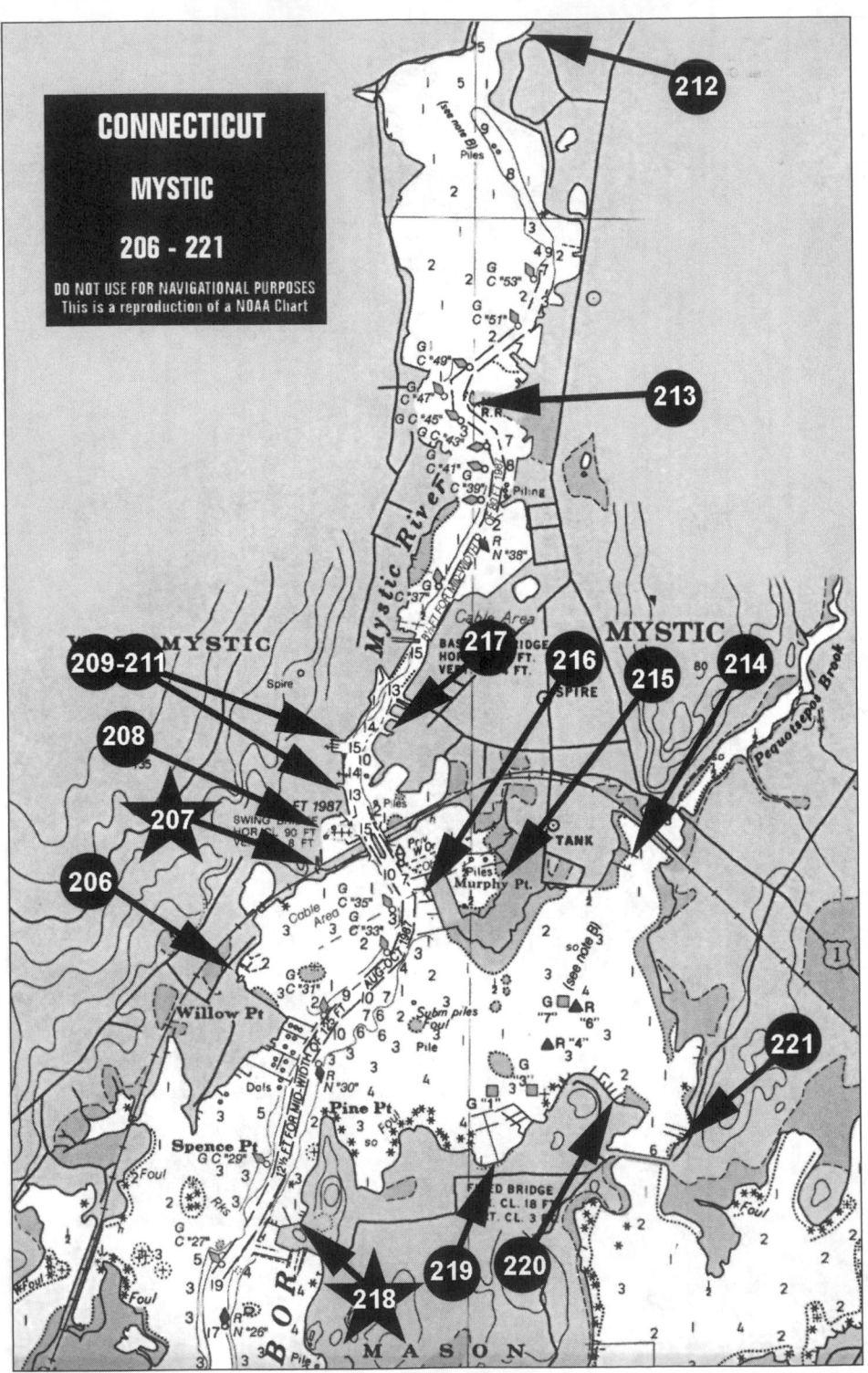

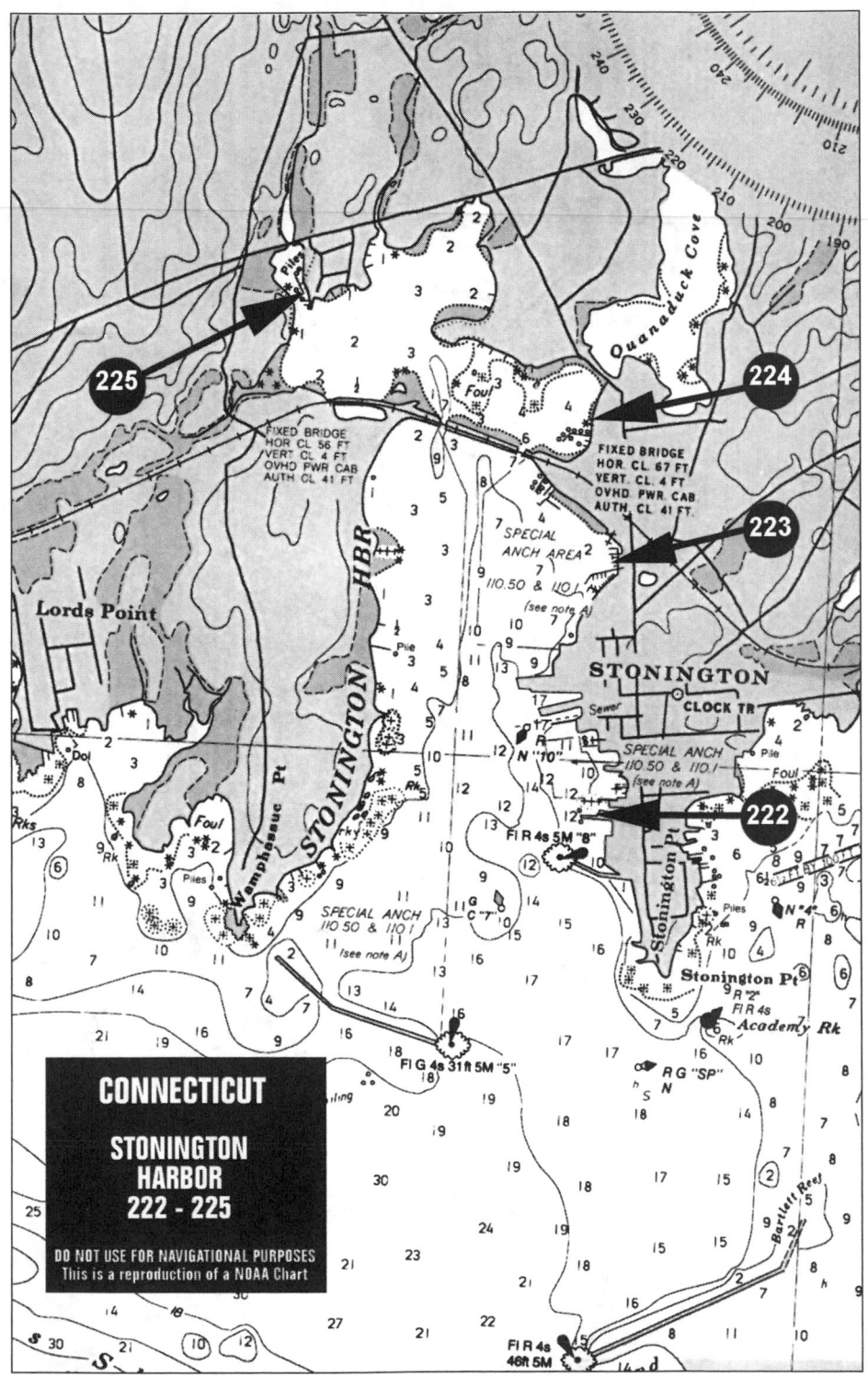

CONNECTICUT

STONINGTON HARBOR
222 - 225

DO NOT USE FOR NAVIGATIONAL PURPOSES
This is a reproduction of a NOAA Chart

479

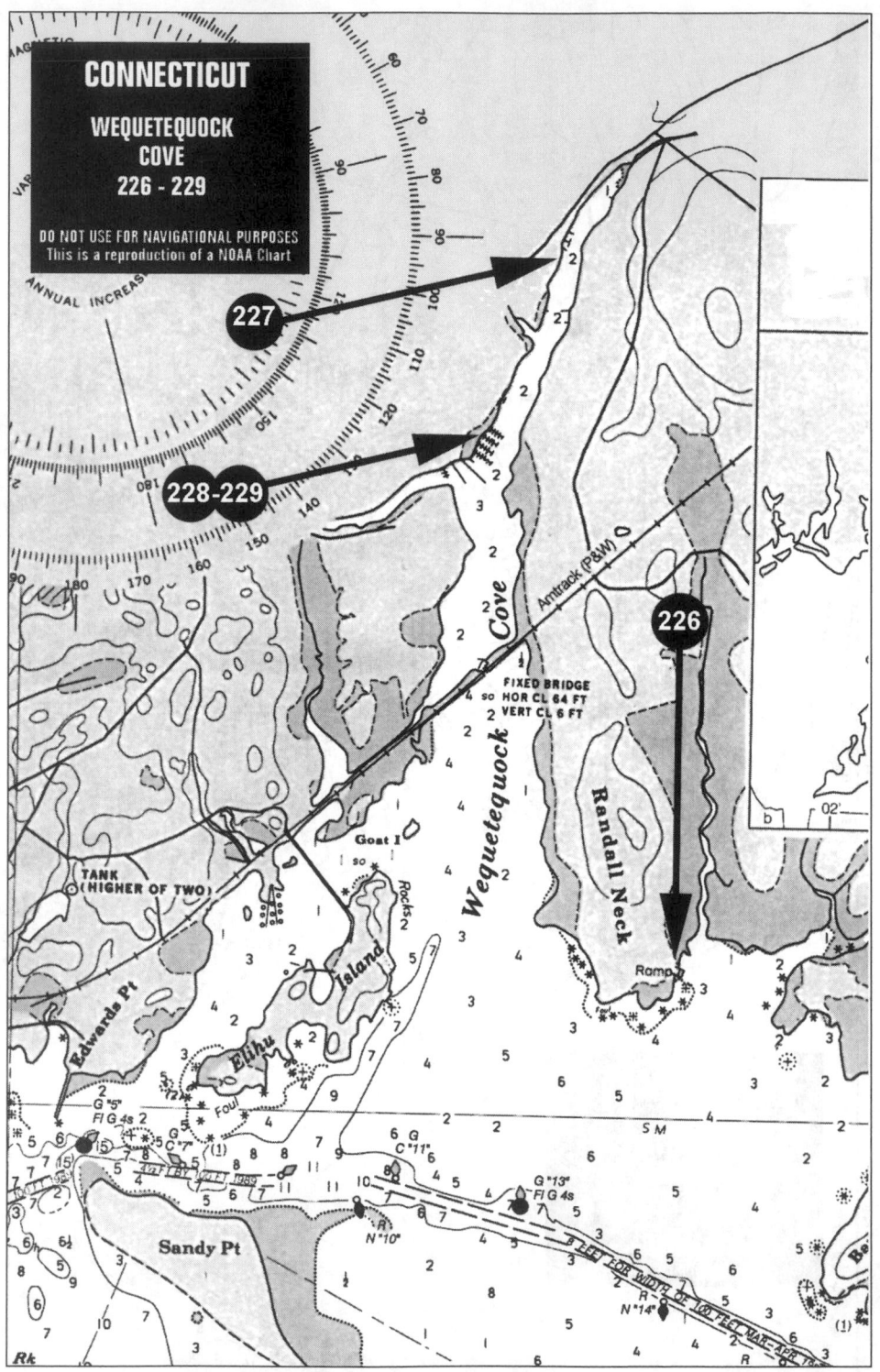

CONNECTICUT

WEQUETEQUOCK
COVE
226 - 229

DO NOT USE FOR NAVIGATIONAL PURPOSES
This is a reproduction of a NOAA Chart

227

228-229

226

FIXED BRIDGE
HOR CL 64 FT
VERT CL 6 FT

Amtrack (P&W)

Wequetequock Cove

Randall Neck

Ramp

Goat I

Rocks

Island

Elihu

Foul

TANK
(HIGHER OF TWO)

Edwards Pt

G "5"
Fl G 4s 2

G
C "7"

G
C "11"

G "13"
Fl G 4s

R
N "10"

Sandy Pt

SM

BLUE LINE FOR WIDTH OF 100 FEET MAR-APR 150

R
N "14"

Rk

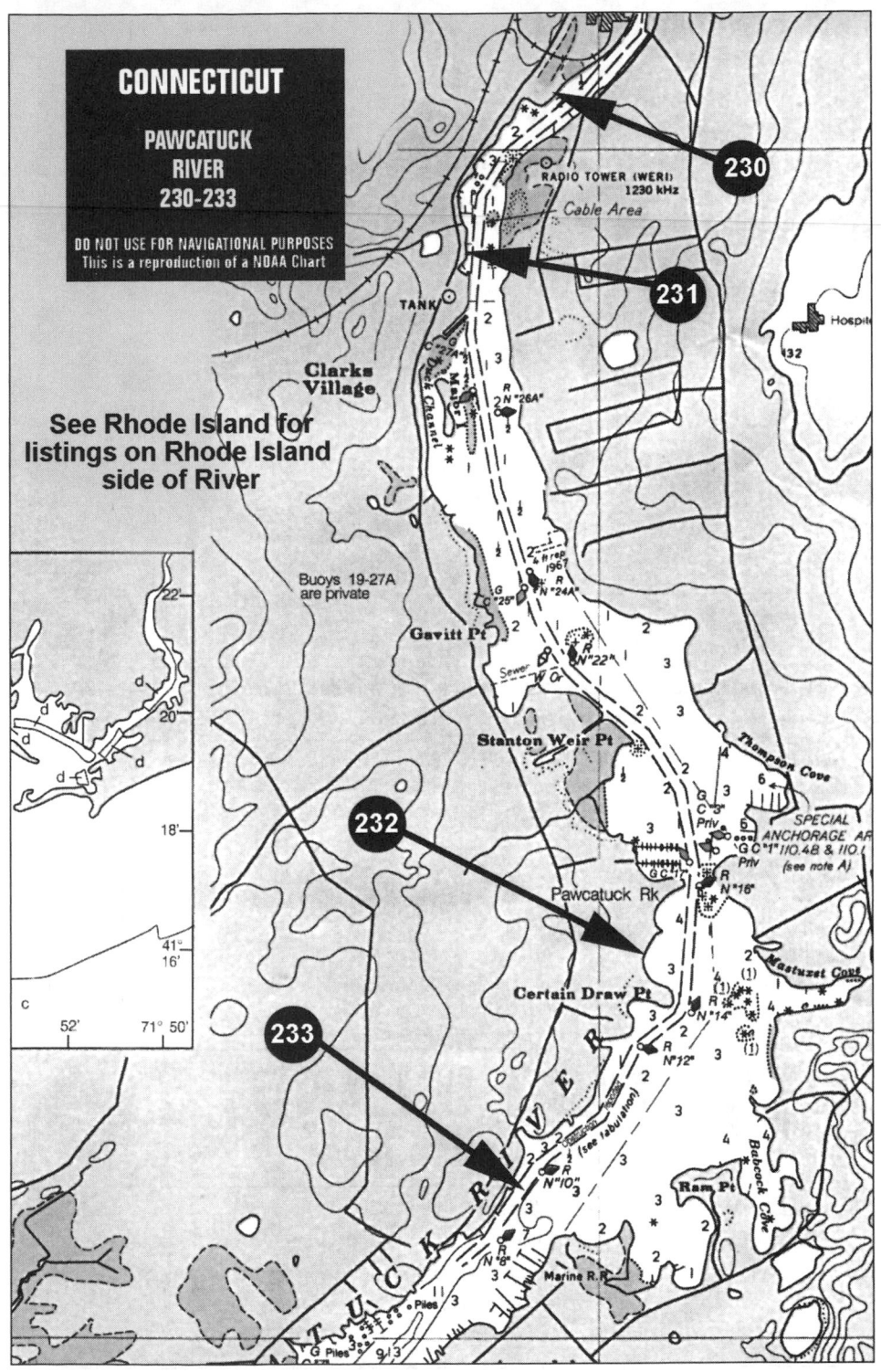

CONNECTICUT

PAWCATUCK
RIVER
230-233

DO NOT USE FOR NAVIGATIONAL PURPOSES
This is a reproduction of a NOAA Chart

**See Rhode Island for
listings on Rhode Island
side of River**

Buoys 19-27A
are private

**Clarks
Village**

TANK

RADIO TOWER (WERI)
1230 kHz
Cable Area

Hospital

Gavitt Pt

Stanton Weir Pt

Pawcatuck Rk

Certain Draw Pt

Thompson Cove

SPECIAL
ANCHORAGE AR
(see note A)
Priv

Ram Pt

Babcock Cove

Marine R.R.

481

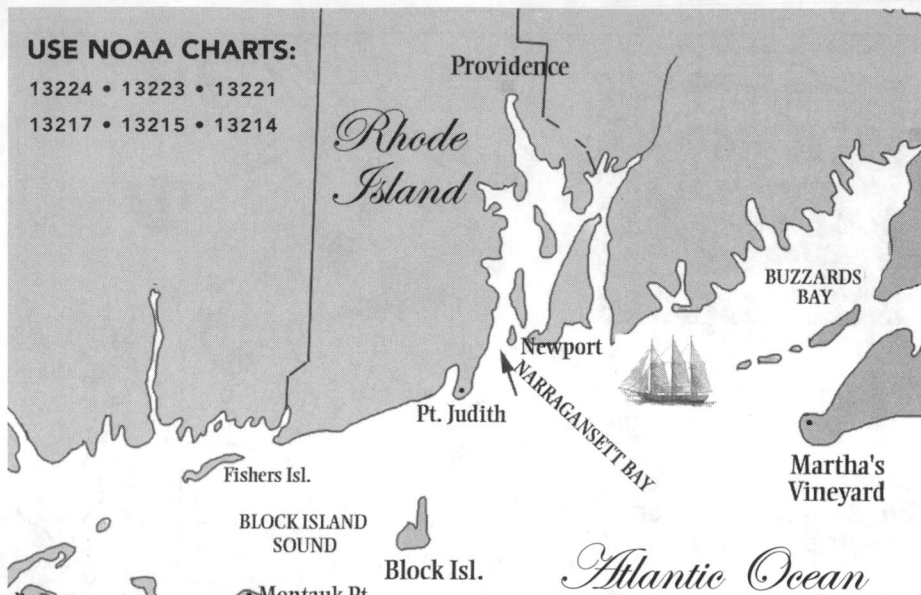

Map is not intended for navigational purposes.

Rhode Island

THE FOLLOWING REGIONS ARE COVERED IN CHARTS IN THIS SECTION:

Cruising Rhode Island

The boundary line between **Massachusetts and Rhode Island** strikes the coast just westward of Quicksand point. Among the islands in Narragansett Bay are Aquidneck Island, Conanicut, and Prudence. These rather large islands are gently sloping, undulating and covered with cultivated fields and orchards, and occasional groves of trees. Westerly from **Point Judith to Napatree Point** is a continuous line of beaches behind which are many salt ponds. The sea breaking through the outer sand barrier and then depositing sand to close the opening has formed these ponds. The shore near the water is low, grassy, and nearly level, but gradually rises with a series of gently curves to higher wooded lands some distance back.

CHARTS 13223, 13221. NARRAGANSETT BAY, opening into the north side of Rhode Island Sound, 17 miles westward of Buzzards Bay entrance, is the approach to the cities of Newport, Providence, Fall River, and Taunton, as well as numerous towns and villages. Rhode Island, the largest island in the bay forms the eastern shore of the bay proper. The entrance is between Brenton Point, the southwestern part of Rhode Island, on the east, and Point Judith Neck on the west. The bay is 18 miles long from the entrance to the mouth of Providence River. Navigation of the bay is easy, day or night, in clear weather as it is marked by navigational aids. The larger Conanicut Island, and Prudence Island and several smaller islands, divide the bay into two passages.

NEWPORT HARBOR on the western shore of Rhode Island and the eastern side of East Passage, 3.5 miles above Beavertail Light, is an important harbor of refuge. Its approach is well marked by navigational aids, and the harbor is of easy access both day and night. A state regulatory buoy in the entrance to the inner harbor marks a 5-mph no wake zone.

GOAT ISLAND, 0.6 mile long in a north-south direction, is a major pleasure-boating center and divides Newport Harbor into an outer and inner harbor. The outer harbor, on the western side of Goat Island, is northward of The Dumplings and southward of Gould Island. The inner harbor is on the eastern side of Goat Island, and extends along the western front of Newport. A depth of about 4 feet can be taken as far as Goat Island, about a mile above Sandy Point. A fixed railroad bridge, with a clearance of 6 feet, crosses the cove about 0.2 miles above Goat Island. **Ed. Note: Goat Island Marina** (401- 848-5511)is truly a vacation destination in itself. Attached to Newport by a causeway, the island is loaded with amenities: nature and fitness trails, a heated swimming pool, gourmet dining, a sailor's pub, tennis, a fitness center, laundry, provisioning, and for the women aboard...a beauty salon and an opportunity for a massage. What more can a mariner hope for after gruelling days at sea! Here at Goat Island, you can rent a car or hop the water taxi to enjoy Newport shopping and nightlife. Slips are available for vessels up to 160 ft. in length.

NEWPORT is one of the principal summer boating resorts on the Atlantic Coast and the former home of the America's Cup competition. A Naval Education and Training Center, from which several Navy ships operate, is here. General anchorages are in the outer and inner harbor and – except in emergencies – vessels must anchor in these areas. Newport is very walkable with dozens of fine restaurants, shops, ships' chandleries, and attractions. Visiting boaters will want to take time to tour the historic mansions, including The Breakers, "summer cottage" to the Vanderbilts. All manner of marine-related facilities are located around the harbor. The Newport Chamber of Commerce is conveniently located in the harbor and all the information you need for touring is available.

JAMESTOWN is a resort village on the east side of **CONANICUT ISLAND**, in a bight on the west side of East Passage. A standpipe in the southern part of the town and a hotel near the waterfront are prominent. The bight is a popular summer anchorage for local craft. **Ed. Note: Conanicut Marine** (401-423-1556) provides an ideal base for cruising Narragansett Bay, Block Island Sound and the Elizabeth Islands. It's a full service

RHODE ISLAND

TO FIND MARINA LOCATIONS - SEE THE TABLES AND LOCATOR CHARTS AT THE END OF THIS SECTION.

marina with excellent transient and repair facilities. Wooden boat lovers...they speak your language and understand your needs! Conanicut has a serious marine supply store with everything including engine parts, complete engines, marine supplies and sports clothing. The marina is within walking distance of village shopping, provisioning and spirits or take advantage of shuttle bus service to Providence Airport for crew changes. One half block west of the harbor is where most of the restaurants are located. If you choose a mooring, the marina has an all inclusive launch and alongside pumpout service. And if a trip to Newport is on your list, take the marina's passenger/bicycle ferry with stops at various points around Newport Harbor.

CHART 13224, 13221. HOG ISLAND, about 1 mile north of Arnold Point, lies in the entrance to **BRISTOL HARBOR,** dividing the waters into two channels. The island has a rolling wooded terrain. Shoal water surrounds the island extending as much as 0.4 mile southward and 0.8 mile northward the shoal area is marked by lights and buoys.

CHART 13224. PROVIDENCE RIVER, which empties into the head of Narragansett Bay between Nayatt Point and Conimicut Point, is the approach to the city of Providence, plus numerous towns and villages, and to Seekonk River. Providence is at the head of navigation of the Providence River, about 7 miles above the entrance at the junction of the Providence and Seekonk Rivers. The Port area includes both sides of the upper navigable channel of the river. The ports chief waterborne commerce is in petroleum products, cement, lumber, steel scrap metal, and automobiles.

BULLOCK COVE on the east side of Providence River 2 miles north of Conanicut Point is the scene of considerable pleasure boat activity. A dredged channel leads from the Providence River to a mooring basin on the east side of Bullock Point, then northward 0.5 mile to a mooring and turning basin. Buoys and daybeacons mark the entrance to the channel. **Bullock Cove Marine** (401-433-3010) offers a full service yard and specializes in both fiberglass and wooden boat restoration (up to 45 feet) and repairs.

WARWICK COVE, between Warwick Neck and Horse Neck, is in the northeastern part of **GREENWICH BAY.** A marked dredged channel leads from the bay to an anchorage basin at the head of the cove. Other anchorage basins in the cove are on the west side of the channel, 0.5 mile above the channel entrance, and on each side of the channel 0.7 mile above the channel entrance. A state regulatory buoy off Horse Neck marks a 5-mph speed limit.

CHART 13217, 13215. BLOCK ISLAND is a glacial formation like Long Island. A prominent feature of the island is the total lack of trees. The surface, when viewed from eastward, has a grassy undulating appearance and the hills show steep sandy faces. Near the shoreline the land is low but rapidly rises toward the center of the island to steep hills covered only with grass and dotted occasionally with houses. The island is approximately five miles long and and has an elevation of 211 feet, and it is often fog-bound during July and August. The island has three harbors: New Harbor, on the east side, is used primarily by commercial fishing vessels and the ferries bringing tourists from New London, and Point Judith. Old Harbor (**13217**), aka East Harbor, is best to avoid in a fog. There is a gas dock and the harbor is walking distance from provisioning. The Great Salt Pond (**CHART13217**) is the largest, protected harbor on the west side of the island filled with pleasure boaters.

BLOCK ISLAND SOUND is a deep navigable waterway forming the eastern approach to Long Island Sound, Fishers Island Sound, and Gardiners Bay from the Atlantic Ocean. Block Island Sound is a link for waterborne commerce between Cape Cod and Long Island Sound. It has two entrances from the Atlantic, and an eastern entrance from Rhode Island Sound–between Block Island and Point Judith–and a southern entrance between Block Island and Montauk Point. The Block Island Sound is also with Long Island Sound by the Race and other passages to the southwestward, and with Fishers Island Sound by several passages between rocky reefs from Watch Hill Point to East Point Fishers Island.

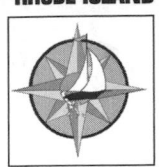

The north shoreline of Block Island Sound and Fishers Island Sound from Point Judith to New London is generally rocky and broken with short stretches of sandy beach. Many inlets and harbors, especially in the vicinity of Fishers Island afford harbors of refuge for vessels. Most of the rocks and shoals near the channels are marked with navigational aids. Block Island bound the southern part of Block Island Sound on the east, the eastern extremity of Long Island and Gardiners Island on the west. Plum Island and Fishers Island are at the western end of the sound. The deep water in the central part of Block Island Sound will accommodate vessels of the greatest draft.

POINT JUDITH LIGHT, 65 feet above the water, is shown from an octagonal tower 51 feet high, with the lower half white, upper half brown. The station has a fog signal and a radiobeacon. About 100 yards north of the light is Point Judith Coast Guard Station. A lighted whistle buoy is about 2.4 miles southward of the light. A prominent elevated water tank is about 3 miles northwest of the light.

The area around Point Judith including the approaches to Point Judith Harbor of Refuge is irregular with rocky bottom and indication of boulders. Caution is advised to avoid the shoal spots, even with a smooth sea, and to exercise extra care where the depths are not more than 6 feet greater than the draft. A main V-shaped breakwater and two shorearm breakwaters extending to the shore form Point Judith Harbor of Refuge on the west side of Point Judith. The harbor is of easy access for most vessels except with heavy southerly sea. The area within the V shaped breakwater affords protected anchorage for small craft. The breakwater should be given a berth of 200 yards to avoid broken and hard bottom; a rocky shoal area about 100 yards wide, paralleling the west side of the main breakwater northward from the angle should be avoided.

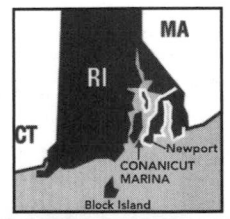

RHODE ISLAND

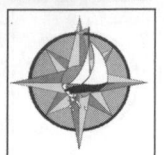

A good anchorage is on a line between Point Judith Harbor of Refuge East Entrance Light 3 and Point Judith Harbor of Refuge Light 2 midway between them is 22 to 30 feet. This position falls on the edge of the east west thoroughfare used by pleasure craft and fishing boats.

CHART 13214. WATCH HILL, about 17.5 miles west of Point Judith, is a high bare bluff on its easterly side with several large hotels and summerhouses. Watch Hill Light, 61 feet above the water, is shown from a square gray granite tower, 45 feet high, attached to a white building with a red roof, on Watch Hill Point. It is reported that the fog signal at the station is not easily heard eastward of the light, but from the southwest can be heard nearly to Montauk Point. A radiobeacon is 136 yards north northeast of the light. A lighted whistle buoy 2.5 miles southward of the light marks a passage through Block Island Sound. Watch Hill is a charming resort town with a public beach, inns, shops, gourmet dining and a restored carousel for younger crew members. **Watch Hill Docks** offers transient slips convenient to the village. Call for reservations (401-596-7807). ⚓

RHODE ISLAND FACILITIES alphabetical index

 # Rhode Island Yacht Clubs

The Yacht Clubs listed below offer reciprocity and courtesy dockage or moorings.
Only Yacht Clubs with space for 2 or more traveling Yacht Club members are listed.

BARRINGTON
BARRINGTON YACHT CLUB
(401) 245-1181

BRISTOL
BRISTOL YACHT CLUB
(401) 253-2922

CRANSTON
NARRAGANSETT YACHT CLUB
(401) 941-2000
RHODE ISLAND YACHT CLUB
(401) 941-0220

EAST GREENWICH
BLUE PARROT YACHT CLUB
(401) 884-2002
EAST GREENWICH Y.C.
(401) 884-7700

WEST BAY YACHT CLUB
(401)885-4414

JAMESTOWN
CONANICUT YACHT CLUB
(401) 423-1424
JAMESTOWN YACHT CLUB

NEWPORT
IDA LEWIS YACHT CLUB
(401) 846-1969
THE NEWPORT YACHT CLUB
(401) 846-9410

RIVERSIDE
NARRAGANSETT TERRACE
YACHT CLUB
(401) 433-4617

WAKEFIELD
POINT JUDITH YACHT CLUB
(401) 783-5603

WARWICK
GREENWICH COVE YACHT
CLUB
(401) 737-2446

WATCH HILL
WATCH HILL YACHT CLUB
(401)) 596-4986

WESTERLY
WESTERLY YACHT CLUB
(401) 596-7556

RHODE ISLAND

Chart Locater Number	Marina's Name & Phone Number	When Open	Monitors VHF Channel	Transient: Electricity•Moorings•Berths	Hull repairs•Engine repairs•Ramp	Winter Storage: Wet•Dry	Railway Capacity in Feet	Lift Capacity in Tons	Boat Rental: Canoe•Row•Motor	Boat Rental: Charter•House•Sail	Restaurant•Lodging•Camping	Showers•Laundry	Pumpout•Toilets	Bait•Tackle•Water•Ice	Groceries•Hardware	Diesel fuel•Gasoline
1	VIKING MARINA 401-596-7390	ALL YR.		EB	HE R	W D		25			RC	SL	T	IW BT	H	
2	PIER 65 MARINA 401-596-6350	ALL YR.		EB	HE	D		20				S	T	IW	H	
3	WESTERLY MARINA 401-596-1727	ALL YR.		E		D		20			R	S	T	W	H	
4	GRAY'S BOATYARD 401-348-8689	MAY NOV	9	B	HE R	D		30			R		T	IW B	GH	
5	COVEDGE BAIT & TACKLE 401-348-8888	MAR DEC		B	R								T	IB	H	
6	FRANK HALL BOATYARD 401-348-8005	ALL YR.	9		HE	D		20			R	S	T	IW	GH	
7	LOTTERYVILLE MARINA 401-348-8064	APR OCT		EM B	HE R	W D	40	10		H		S	T	IW BT	GH	
8	AVONDALE BOATYARD 401-348-8187	ALL YR.		EB	HE	D	60	35				S	PT	IW	H	G D
9	WATCH HILL BOATYARD 401-348-8148	ALL YR.	9	EM B	HE R	D		13			R	S	T	IW	GH	
10 SEE AD	WATCH HILL DOCKS 401-596-7807	MAY OCT	9	EB							RL			I	GH	
11	QUONOCHONTAUG								R				T			
12	THE SPORTSMANS COVE 401-322-7277	APR NOV							R		RL		T	IB	H	
13	OCEAN HOUSE MARINA 401-364-6040	ALL YR.	9	EB	HE R	D			CR W		RL		T	IW BT	H	G
14	CHARLESTOWN Breachway	APR OCT							R				T			
15	SHELTER COVE MARINE 401-364-0670								R M		R		T	IB		
16	SKIP'S DOCK 401-783-5031	MAY SEP											T	IB		
17	JIM'S DOCK 401-783-2050	APR OCT	65	EB		W				C	R	S	T	IW		
18	POINT JUDITH MARINA L. L. C. 401-789-7189	ALL YR.	9	EB	HE	W D		30		C	RL	S	T	IW	H	G D
19	SNUG HARBOR MARINA 401-783-7766	NOV NOV	9 65							C	RL		T	IW	GH	
21	KENPORT MARINA 401-783-2868	AL YR	65	EB	HE R	D				C	RL		T	IW BT	H	

RHODE ISLAND

Chart Locater Number	Marina's Name & Phone Number	When Open	Monitors VHF Channel	Transient: Electricity • Moorings • Berths	Hull repairs • Engine repairs • Ramp	Winter Storage: Wet • Dry	Railway Capacity in Feet	Lift Capacity in Tons	Boat Rental: Canoe • Row • Motor • Sail	Restaurant • Charter • Lodging • House • Camping	Showers • Laundry	Pumpout • Toilets	Bait • Tackle • Water • Ice	Groceries • Hardware	Diesel fuel • Gasoline
22	POINTVIEW MARINE 401-789-7660	ALL YR.	7	EB	HE	W D		35		C	S	T	IW	H	
23	GOOSEBERRY MARINA 401-789-5431	ALL YR		EB		W				C			W		
24	RAM POINT BOAT HAULING 401-783-4535	ALL YR.	9	EM B	HE	D					SL	PT	IW	H	G D
25	SILVER SPRING MARINE 401-783-0783	ALL YR.	7 9 69	EB	HE	D					S	T	IW	H	G
26	BILLINGTON COVE MARINA 401-783-1266	ALL YR.		EB	HE	D					S	T	IW	H	G
27	LONG COVE CAMPSITES & MARINA 401-783-4902	MAY OCT			HE R	D				C	S	T	IW BT	H	G
28	MARINA BAY DOCKING 401-789-4050			EB		W					R	S	T	IW		
29	SOUTH KINGSTON RAMP				R										
30	STONE COVE MARINA 401-783-8990	ALL YR.	71	EB	E	D					S	T	IW	H	G
31	GALILEE FUEL SERVICE 401-782-2410	ALL YR.	80											H	D
33	R.I. ENGINE CO 401-789-1021	ALL YR.	80		E			10				T		H	
34	POINT JUDITH Fishermen Co-op 401-782-1500	ALL YR.	80												
35	POINT JUDITH RAMP				R										
36	CHAMPLIN'S MARINA 401-466-2760	MAY OCT	68		HE								W	H	G D
37	BLOCK ISLAND BOAT BASIN 401-466-2631	MAY DEC	9	EB	ER						RL	S	PT	IW	GH	G D
38	A H EDWARDS Marine Repair 401-466-2655	APR NOV	68		E										
39	PAYNE'S NEW HARBOR DOCK 401-466-5572	MAY NOV		EB						MR	L	S	PT	IW BT	G H	G D
41	TWIN MAPLES 401-466-5547	JUN SEP									R			BT		
42	NEW SHOREHAM TOWN 401-466-3235	ALL YR.		EB							RL	S	T	W		
43	RHODE ISLAND STATE PIER 401-783-4711				R										

RHODE ISLAND

Chart Locater Number	Marina's Name & Phone Number	When Open	Monitors VHF Channel	Transient: Electricity • Moorings • Berths	Hull repairs • Engine repairs • Ramp	Winter Storage: Wet • Dry	Railway Capacity in Tons	Lift Capacity in Feet	Boat Rental: Canoe • Row • Motor	Boat Rental: Charter • House • Sail	Restaurant • Lodging • Camping	Showers • Laundry	Pumpout • Toilets	Bait • Tackle • Water • Ice	Groceries • Hardware	Diesel fuel • Gasoline
44	FORT GETTY RAMP			M							C		T			
46	DUTCH HARBOR BOATYARD 401-423-0630	ALL YR.	68	M	HE	D	50	35			R	S	PT	IW	H	G D
47	CONANICUT TOWN				R											
48 SEE AD	CONANICUT MARINA 401-423-1556	ALL YR.	71	EM B	HE			200			RL	S	PT	IW	H	G D
49	CLARK BOATYARD 401-423-1545	ALL YR.	71	M	HE	D	100	200						W		
50	JAMESTOWN BOATYARD 401-423-0600	ALL YR.	72	M	HE	D		50					T	W	H	
52	FORT WETHERILL RAMP				R									T		
53	WICKFORD SHIPYARD 401-294-3361	ALL YR.		EB	HE	D		60				SL	T	IW	H	G D
54	BREWER'S YACHT YARDS 401-884-7014	ALL YR.	9 10	EB	HE	W D		70			RL	S	PT	IW	H	G D
55	MILL COVE YACHT SALES 401-295-0504	ALL												I	H	
57	PUBLIC LAUNCHING				R											
58	JOHNSON'S BOATYARD 401-294-3700	ALL YR.			HE R	D							T	W	H	
59	WICKFORD TOWN				R											
60	PLEASANT STREET WHARF 401-294-2791	ALL YR.		EM B	HE	D		15				S	T	IW	H	G D
61	ALLEN HARBOR MARINA				R									T		
62	GODDARD MEMORIAL RAMP 401-884-2010	ALL YR.			R											
63	ANDERSON'S YARD	APR NOV				D										
64	EAST GREENWICH RAMP				R											
65	GREENWICH COVE MARINA 401-885-6611			EM B										W		
66	EAST GREENWICH MARINA 401-885-2911	ALL YR.		B		W					R					

RHODE ISLAND

MARINA'S NAME & PHONE NUMBER

Chart #	Marina's Name & Phone Number	When Open	Monitors VHF Channel	Transient (Electricity•Moorings•Berths)	Hull•Engine repairs•Ramp	Winter Storage Wet•Dry	Railway Capacity (ft)	Lift Capacity (tons)	Boat Rental Canoe•Row•Motor	Boat Rental Charter•House•Sail	Restaurant•Lodging•Camping	Showers•Laundry	Pumpout•Toilets	Bait•Tackle•Water•Ice	Groceries•Hardware	Diesel fuel•Gasoline
67	HARBOURSIDE Lobstermania 401-884-6363	ALL YR									R					
68	MILT'S MARINA 401-885-3700										R					
69	THE PONAUG MARINA 401-884-1976	ALL YR.	9		R	D		25			R			IW BT		
70	APPONAUG HARBOR MARINA 401-739-5005	ALL YR.		EB M	HE	W D		25			RL	SL	PT	IW BT		
71	GREENWICH BAY MARINAS 401-884-1810	ALL YR.	9	EB	HE	W D		35			R	SL	T	IW	H	
73	BREWER YACHT YARDS 401-884-0544	ALL YR.		EM B	HE	W D		35			R	S	T	IW	H	
74	PIER 36 MARINE CENTER 401-738-2194	ALL YR.		EB		D							T		H	
75	WARWICK COVE MARINA 401-737-2446	ALL YR.		EB		W D					RL	S	PT	IW BT	H	G
77	MARINE MACHINERY SERVICE 401-738-5133				HE			6								
78	ANGEL'S MARINA 401-737-9805	ALL YR.	9			D		20			R		T	IW		
79	BAYVIEW SHELLFISH CO 401-737-5040				R						R					
80	CARLSON'S MARINA 401-738-4278	ALL YR.	9	EB	HE	W D		25			R	S	T	IW	H	
81	WHARF MARINA 401-737-2233	ALL YR.		EB	HE R	W D		20			R		T	IW	H	
82	BAY MARINA 401-739-6435	ALL YR.			HE	D		25			R	S	PT	IW		
83	GREENWICH BAY MARINAS N. - YARD A & B 401-739-4278	ALL YR.		EB	E	W D		25			R	SL	PT	IW	H	G D
84	HARBOR LIGHT MARINA 401-737-6353	ALL YR.	14	EB	HE			60				S	T	W		
85	WINSTEAD'S MARINA 401-737-8723	ALL YR.										S	T	W		
86	BREEZY POINT DOCK 401-738-0357	ALL YR.			R											
87	GEORGE B. SALTER RAMP				R											
88	FRANK PETTIS BOATYARD 401-467-8982	ALL YR.		EB	HE	D		6					T	W	H	

RHODE ISLAND

MARINA'S NAME & PHONE NUMBER

Chart Locater Number	Marina's Name & Phone Number	When Open	Monitors VHF Channel	Transient Electricity • Moorings • Berths	Hull/Engine repairs • Ramp	Winter Storage Wet • Dry	Railway Capacity in Feet	Lift Capacity in Tons	Boat Rental Canoe•Row•Motor	Boat Rental Charter•House•Sail	Restaurant•Lodging•Camping	Showers•Laundry	Pumpout•Toilets	Bait•Tackle•Water•Ice	Groceries•Hardware	Diesel fuel•Gasoline
89	PAWTUXET COVE MARINA 401-941-2200	ALL YR.			HE / R	W/D		25					S	T	IW		
90	CRANSTON PUBLIC RAMP				R											
91	PORT EDGEWOOD LTD 401-941-2200	ALL YR.		EB	HE	W/D		30			R	S	T	IW		G
92	OLD HARBOR MARINA 401-751-7547	ALL YR.	9	EB	E	W					R	SL	T	IW	H	
93	OYSTER HOUSE MARINA 401-434-0400	ALL YR.		EB		W/D					R		T	W		
94	BOLD POINT PARK				R											
95	SABIN POINT PUBLIC RAMP				R											
96 SEE AD	BULLOCK COVE MARINE 401-433-3010	ALL YR.			HE	W/D		15					T	W	H	
97	HAINES STATE PARK RAMP				R											
98	COVE HAVEN MARINA 401-246-1600	ALL YR.	9	EB	HE	D		99+			R	S	T	IW	H	
99	LAVINS MARINA 401-246-1180	MAY NOV		EB	R	D						S	T	IW	H	G
100	POTTER'S GUEST MOORINGS 401-277-2632			M												
101	PRUDENCE ISLAND GUEST MOORINGS			M												
102	EAST PASSAGE Yachting Ctr 401-683-4000	ALL YR.	9	EB	HE	W/D		70		CS	R	SL	PT	IW	G	G/D
103	LITTLE HARBOR MARINE 401-683-7100	ALL YR.	9	EB	HE	D		99+			R	SL	PT	IW	H	D
105	BRISTOL TOWN DOCK			M												
106	BRISTOL TOWN RAMP				R											
107	THAMES STREET RAMP				R											
108	BRISTOL MARINE SVC CO. 401-253-2200	ALL YR.		EMB	HE	D		35				SL	T	W		
109	COLT STATE PARK RAMP 401-253-7482	ALL YR.			R											

RHODE ISLAND

MARINA'S NAME & PHONE NUMBER

Chart Locater Number	Marina's Name & Phone Number	When Open	Monitors VHF Channel	Transient: Electricity•Moorings•Berths	Hull repairs•Engine repairs•Ramp	Winter Storage: Wet•Dry	Railway Capacity in Feet	Lift Capacity in Tons	Boat Rental: Canoe•Row•Motor	Boat Rental: Charter•House•Sail	Restaurant•Lodging•Camping	Showers•Laundry	Pumpout•Toilets	Bait•Tackle•Water•Ice	Groceries•Hardware	Diesel fuel•Gasoline
110	BLOUNT MARINE CORP 401-245-8300	ALL YR.			HE		200	99+								
111	SPEED'S DIESEL SERVICE 401-245-3132	ALL YR.			HE	D		25							H	
112	WATER STREET YACHT SERV 401-247-1110	ALL YR.		EB	HE	D							T	W		
113	THE WHARF TAVERN 401-245-5043			B							R		T			
114	DYER BOATS ANCHORAGE 401-245-3300	ALL YR.			H										H	
115	GINALSKI'S BOATYARD 401-245-1940	ALL YR.			R	D		18						W	H	
116	STRIPER MARINA 401-245-6121	APR NOV		EM B		D	30	10				S	T	IW	H	G
117	STANLEY'S BOATYARD 401-245-5090	ALL YR.		EB M	HE	D		35			R	S	T	IW	H	
118	WALKER'S FARM RAMP				R											
120	FORT ADAMS STATE PARK 401-847-2400	ALL YR.			R								T			
121	SAIL NEWPORT 401-846-1983	APR OCT			R	D		3		S						
122	NEWPORT TOWN RAMP				R											
124	BROWN & HOWARD MARINA 401-846-5100	MAY OCT	9	EB		D		8						W		
125	NEWPORT ONSHORE MARINA 401-849-0480	MAY OCT	9	EB							L	SL	T	W		
126	NEWPORT MARINA 401-849-2293	APR OCT	9	B							RL	SL	T	IW		
128	NEWPORT YACHTING CTR. 401-847-9047	ALL YR.	9	EB		D		30			RL	SL	T	IW		G D
129	CHRISTIE'S RESTAURANT 401-847-5400	MAY OCT	9	EB							RL	S	T	IW		
129	BANNISTER'S WHARF 401-846-4500	MAY OCT	9	EB							RL	SL	T	IW		G D
130	OLD PORT MARINA 401-847-9109	ALL YR.	68	M	E				M	CS	RL			IW	H	
131	BOWEN'S WHARF 401-849-2243	ALL YR.									R					

RHODE ISLAND

CHART LOCATER NUMBER	MARINA'S NAME & PHONE NUMBER	WHEN OPEN	MONITORS VHF CHANNEL	Electricity / Hull / Engine / Moorings / Berths	WINTER STORAGE Wet • Dry	RAILWAY / Ramp	LIFT CAPACITY IN FEET	BOAT RENTAL Canoe • Row • Motor	BOAT RENTAL Charter • House • Sail	Restaurant • Lodging • Camping	Showers • Laundry	Pumpout • Toilets	Bait•Tackle / Groceries•Hardware / Water•Ice	Diesel • Gasoline
132	NEWPORT HARBOR MARINA 401-847-9000	MAY OCT	9	EB							RL	SL	T IW	
133	LONG WHARF CHARTERS 401-849-2210	ALL YR.	68 9	EM B	W				M	CS	RL	SL	T IW	
134	NEWPORT Y. C. 401-846-9410	ALL YR.	78	B							S		T IW	
135	NEWPORT HARBOR 401-848-6492		16	M										
137	AMERICAN SHIPYARD CORP 401-846-6000	ALL YR.			HE	D	70							
138 SEEAD	GOAT ISLAND MARINA SEE AD 401-849-5655	MAY OCT	9 16	EB	E						RL	SL	PT IW G	G D
139	NEWPORT PUBLIC RAMPS	ALL YR.			R									
142	STONEBRIDGE MARINA 401-683-1011	ALL YR.		EB	HE W						R		W	
143	PIRATE COVE MARINA 401-683-9818	ALL YR.	9	EM B	HE W D	40					R	S	PT IW H	G D
144	GULL COVE GROVE RAMP				R									
145	POINT BOATYARD 401-683-0433	ALL YR			H D	45 40							H	
146	BREWER'S SAKONNET MARINA 401-683-3551	ALL YR.	9	EB	HE R W D	35						S	PT IW H	G D
147	RIVERSIDE MARINE 401-625-5181	APR NOV			R	W							WB T H	
148	STANDISH BOATYARD 401-624-4075	ALL YR.	16	EM B	HE W D	55				CS	RL	SL	T IW H G	G D

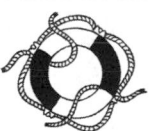

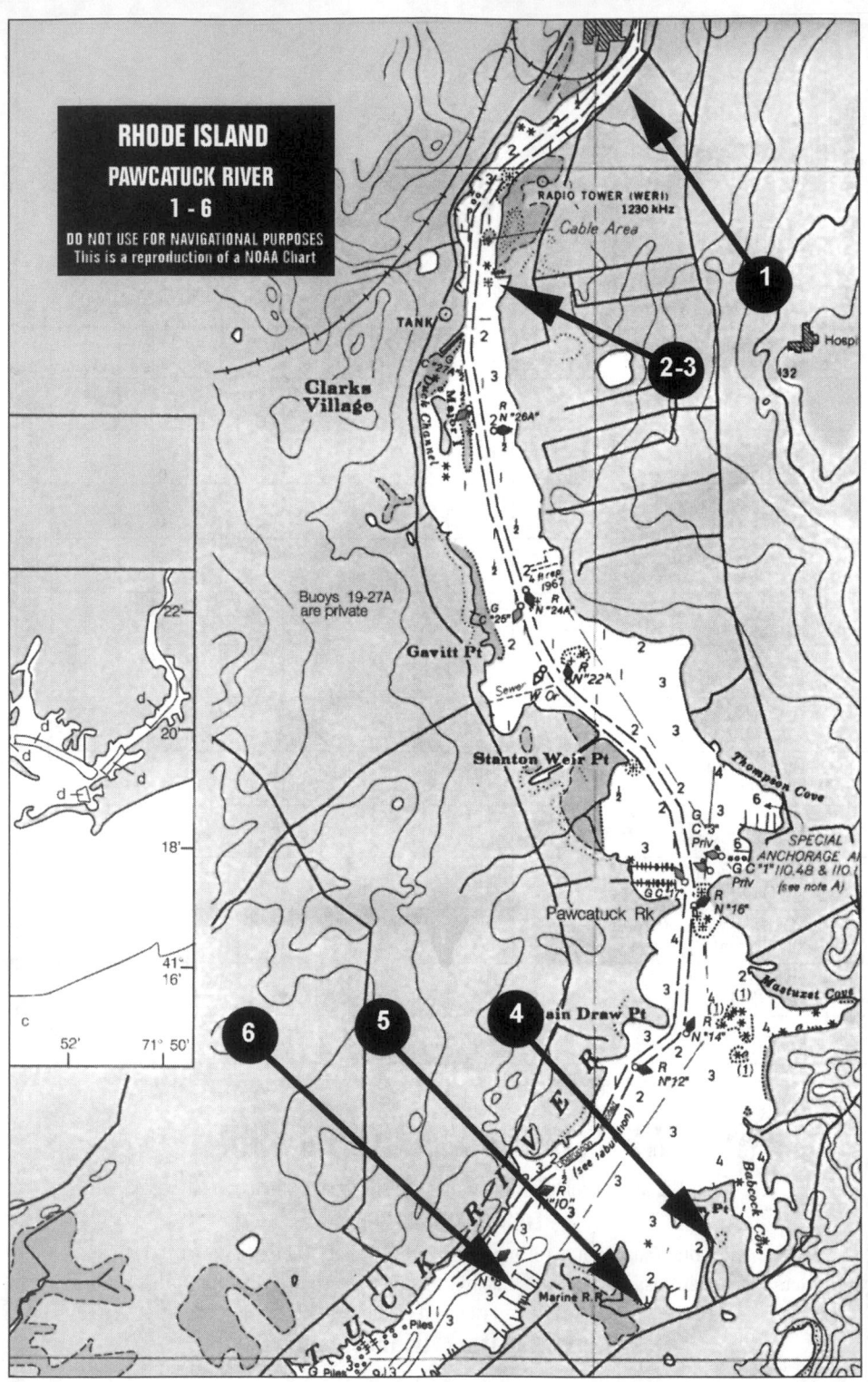

RHODE ISLAND
PAWCATUCK RIVER
1 - 6

DO NOT USE FOR NAVIGATIONAL PURPOSES
This is a reproduction of a NOAA Chart

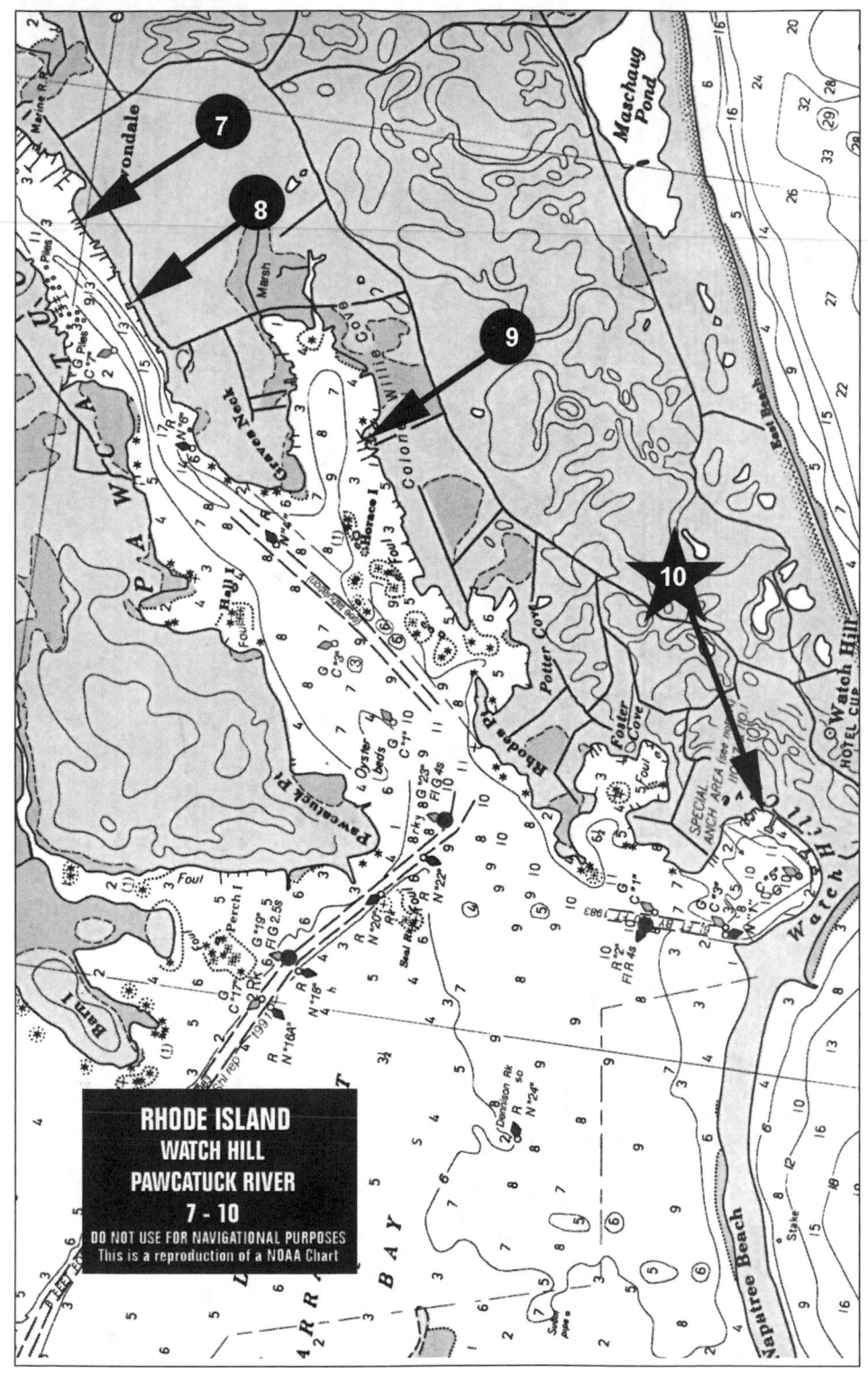

RHODE ISLAND
WATCH HILL
PAWCATUCK RIVER
7 - 10
DO NOT USE FOR NAVIGATIONAL PURPOSES
This is a reproduction of a NOAA Chart

497

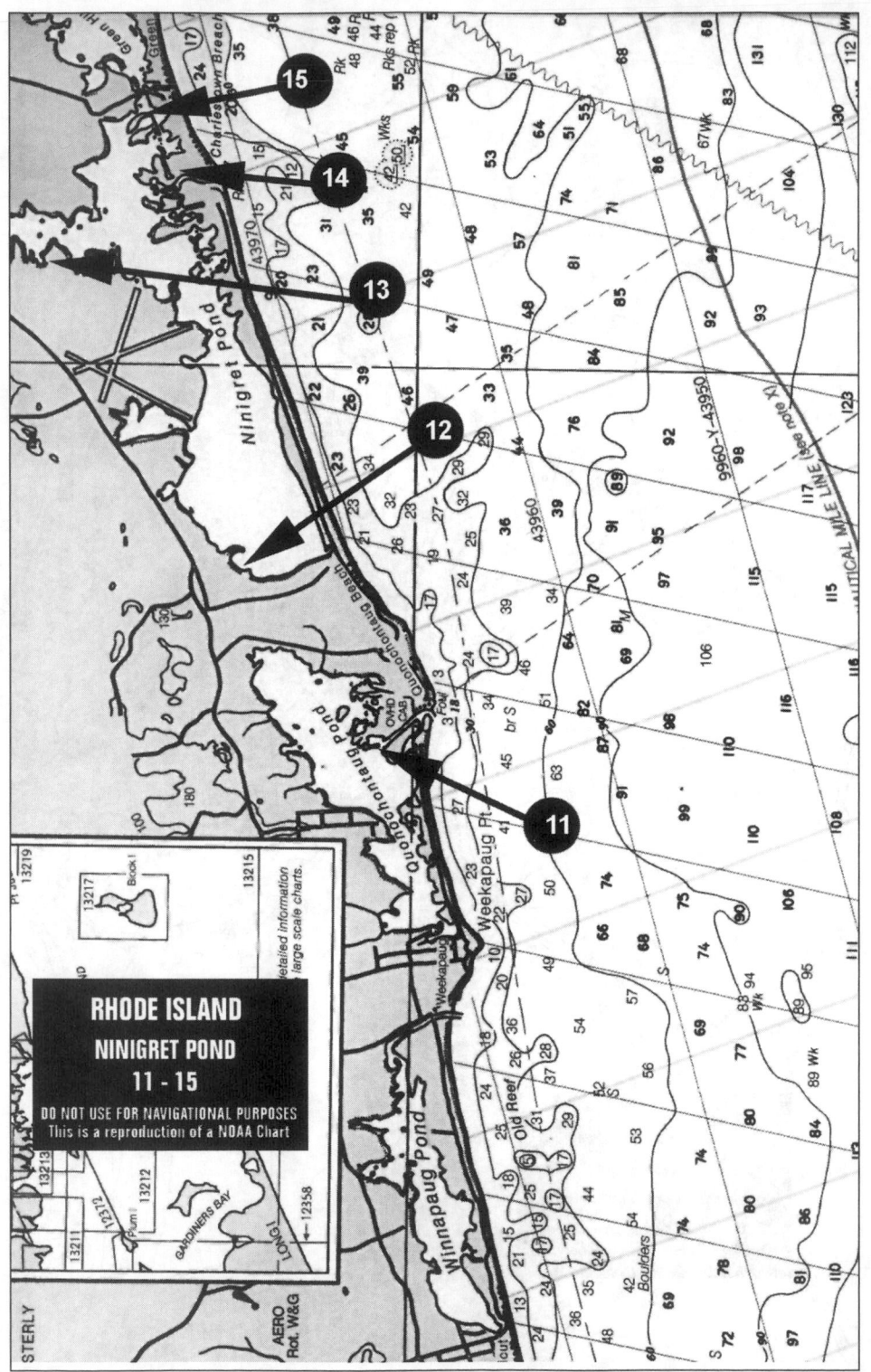

RHODE ISLAND
NINIGRET POND
11 - 15

DO NOT USE FOR NAVIGATIONAL PURPOSES
This is a reproduction of a NOAA Chart

498

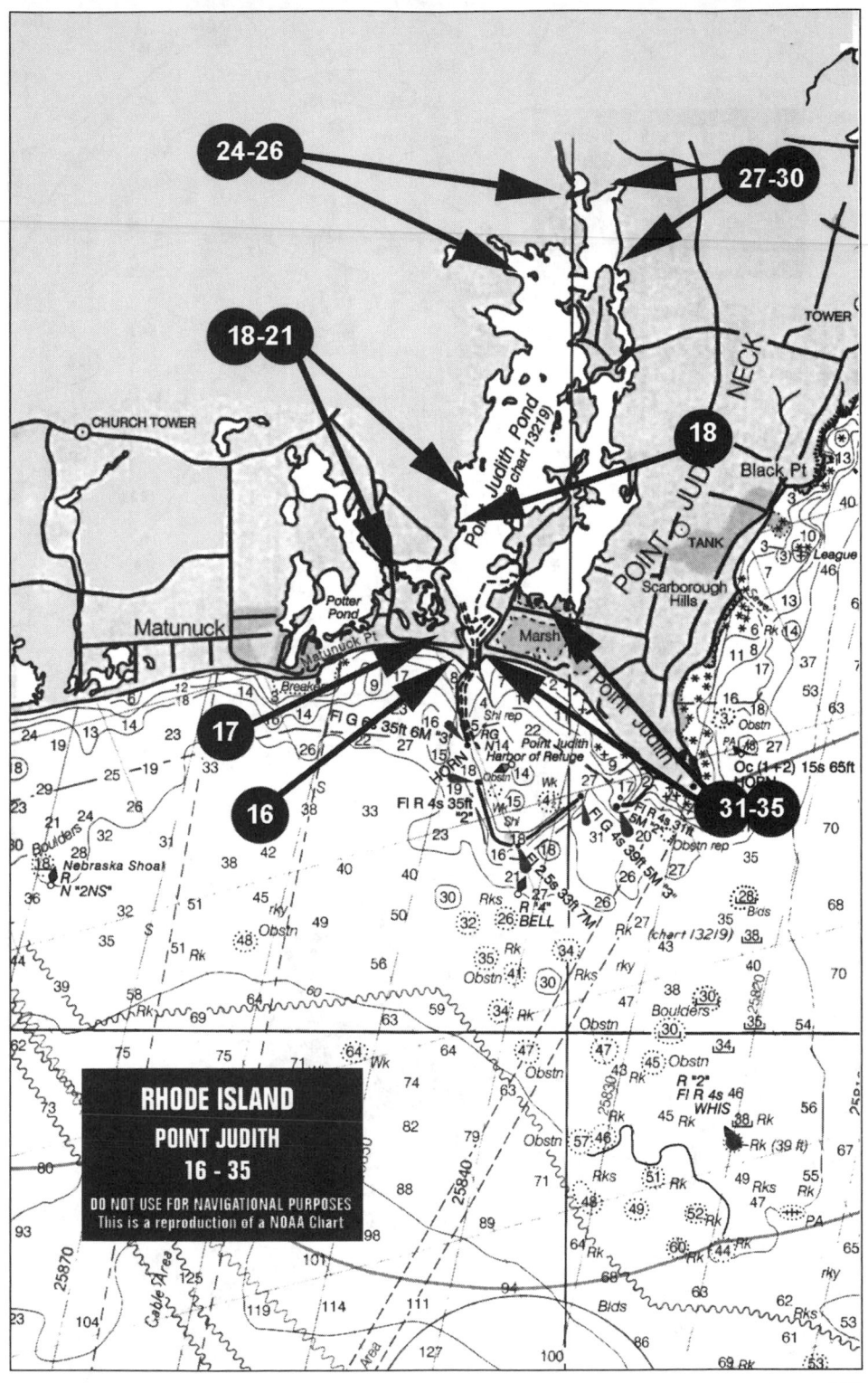

RHODE ISLAND
POINT JUDITH
16 - 35

DO NOT USE FOR NAVIGATIONAL PURPOSES
This is a reproduction of a NOAA Chart

499

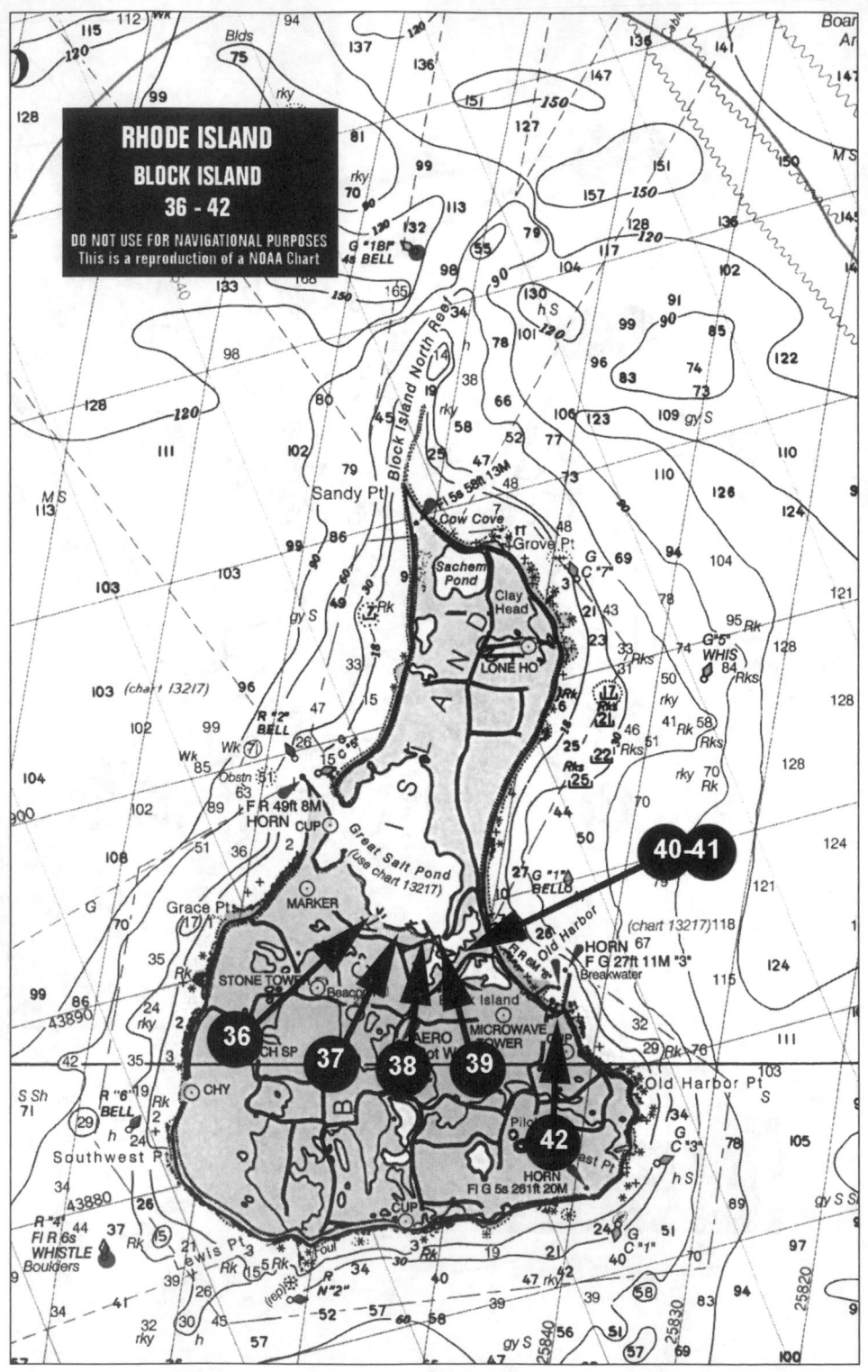

RHODE ISLAND
BLOCK ISLAND
36 - 42

DO NOT USE FOR NAVIGATIONAL PURPOSES
This is a reproduction of a NOAA Chart

500

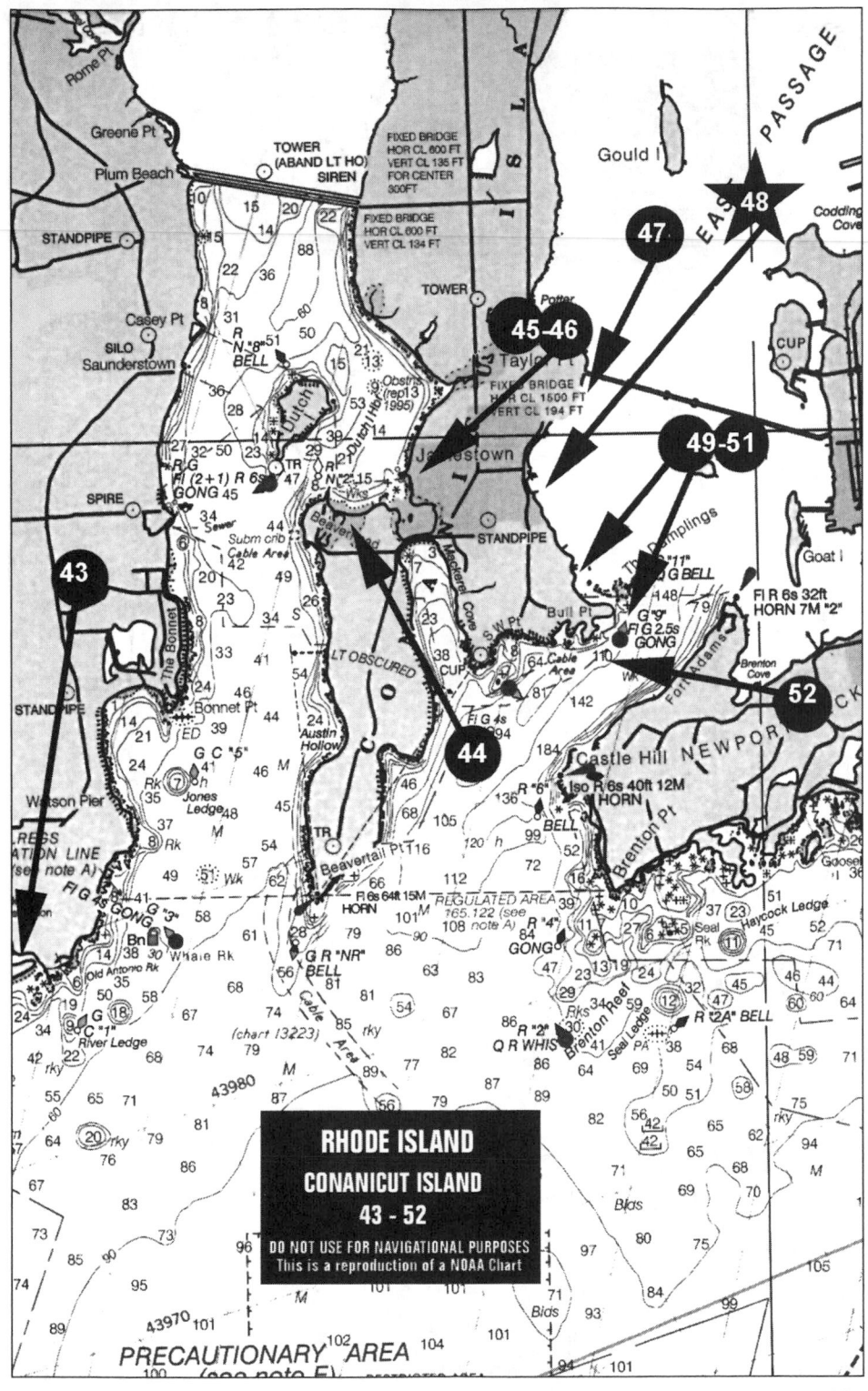

RHODE ISLAND
CONANICUT ISLAND
43 - 52
DO NOT USE FOR NAVIGATIONAL PURPOSES
This is a reproduction of a NOAA Chart

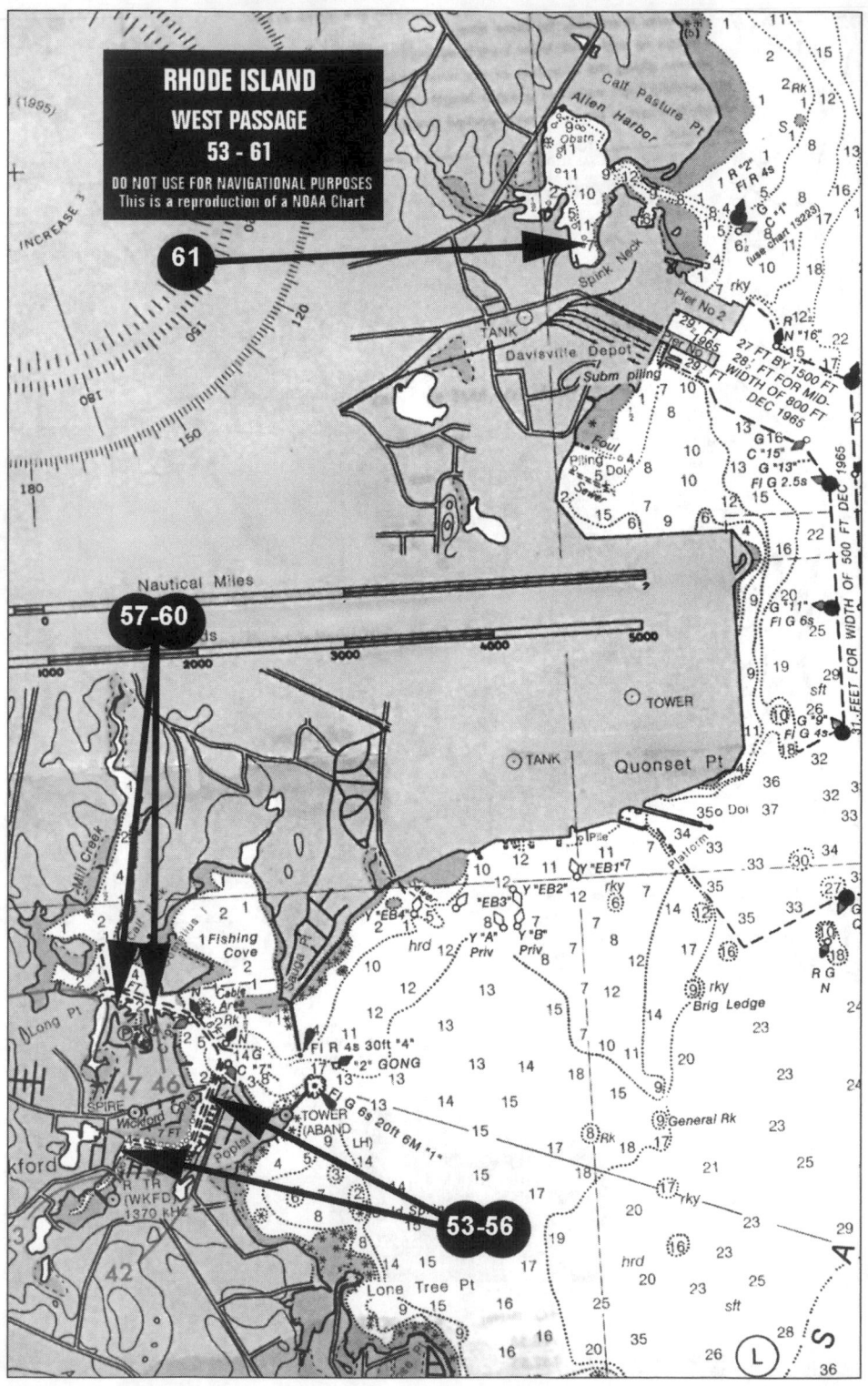

RHODE ISLAND
WEST PASSAGE
53 - 61

DO NOT USE FOR NAVIGATIONAL PURPOSES
This is a reproduction of a NOAA Chart

61

57-60

53-56

502

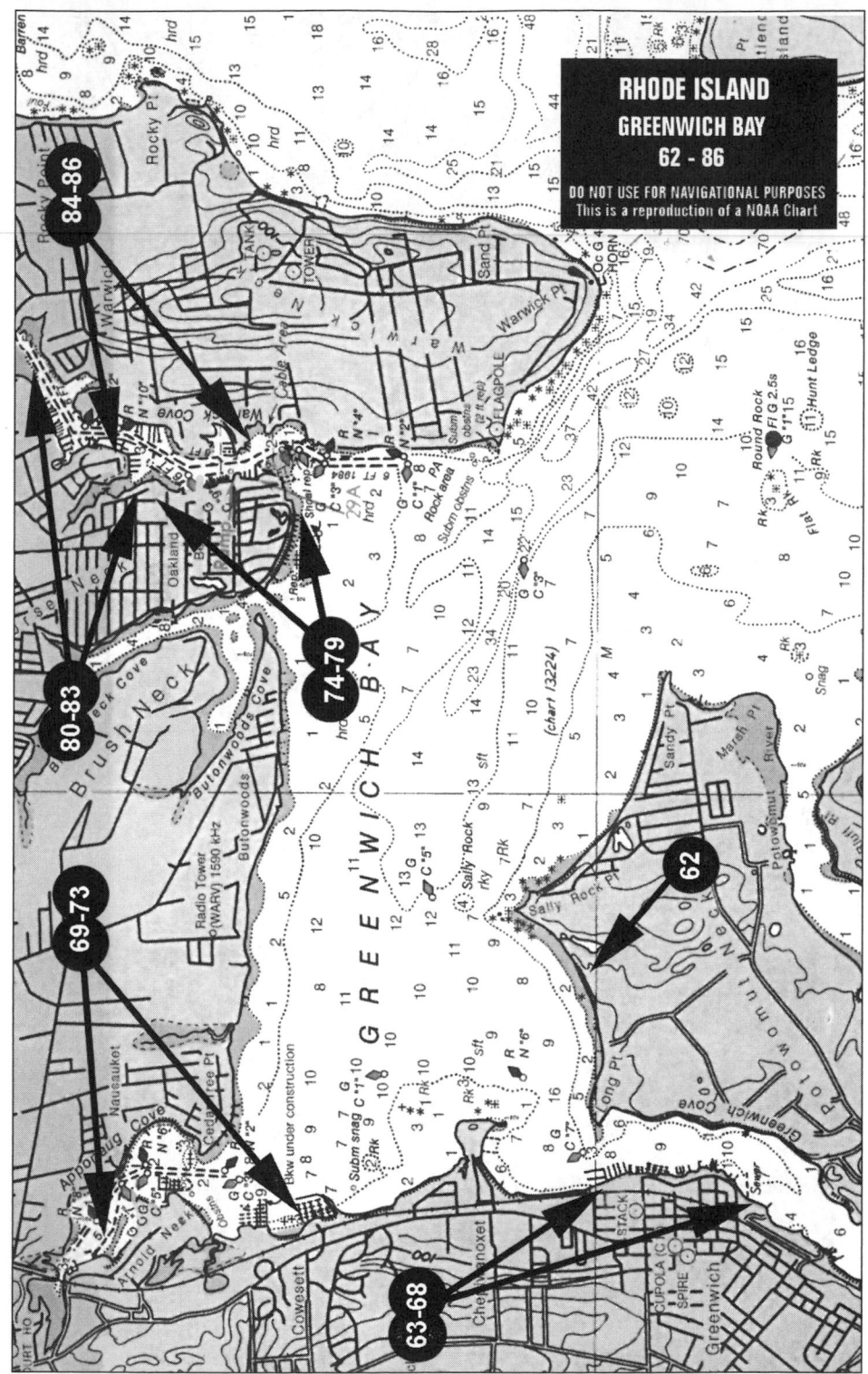

RHODE ISLAND
GREENWICH BAY
62 - 86

DO NOT USE FOR NAVIGATIONAL PURPOSES
This is a reproduction of a NOAA Chart

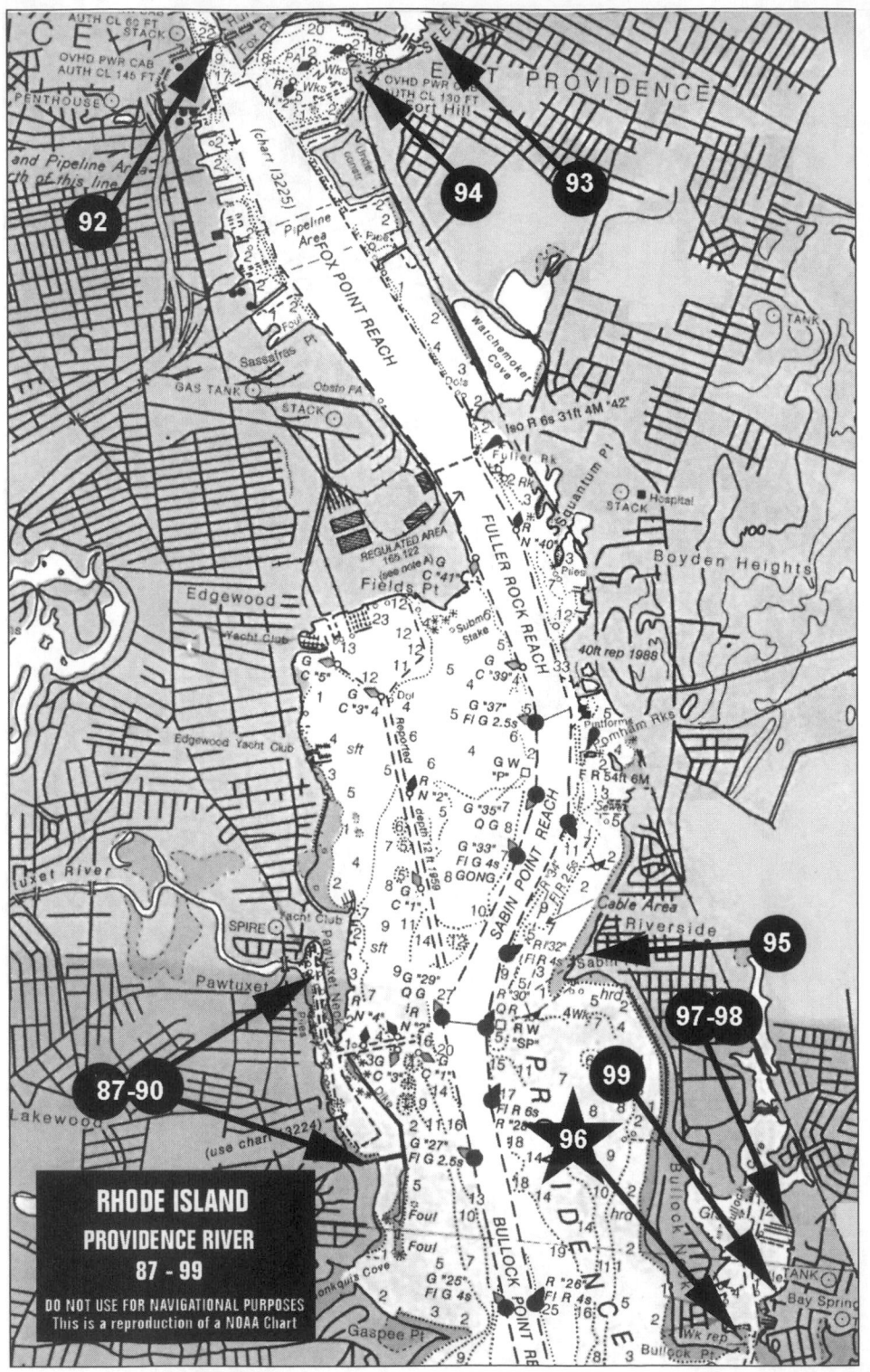

RHODE ISLAND
PROVIDENCE RIVER
87 - 99
DO NOT USE FOR NAVIGATIONAL PURPOSES
This is a reproduction of a NOAA Chart

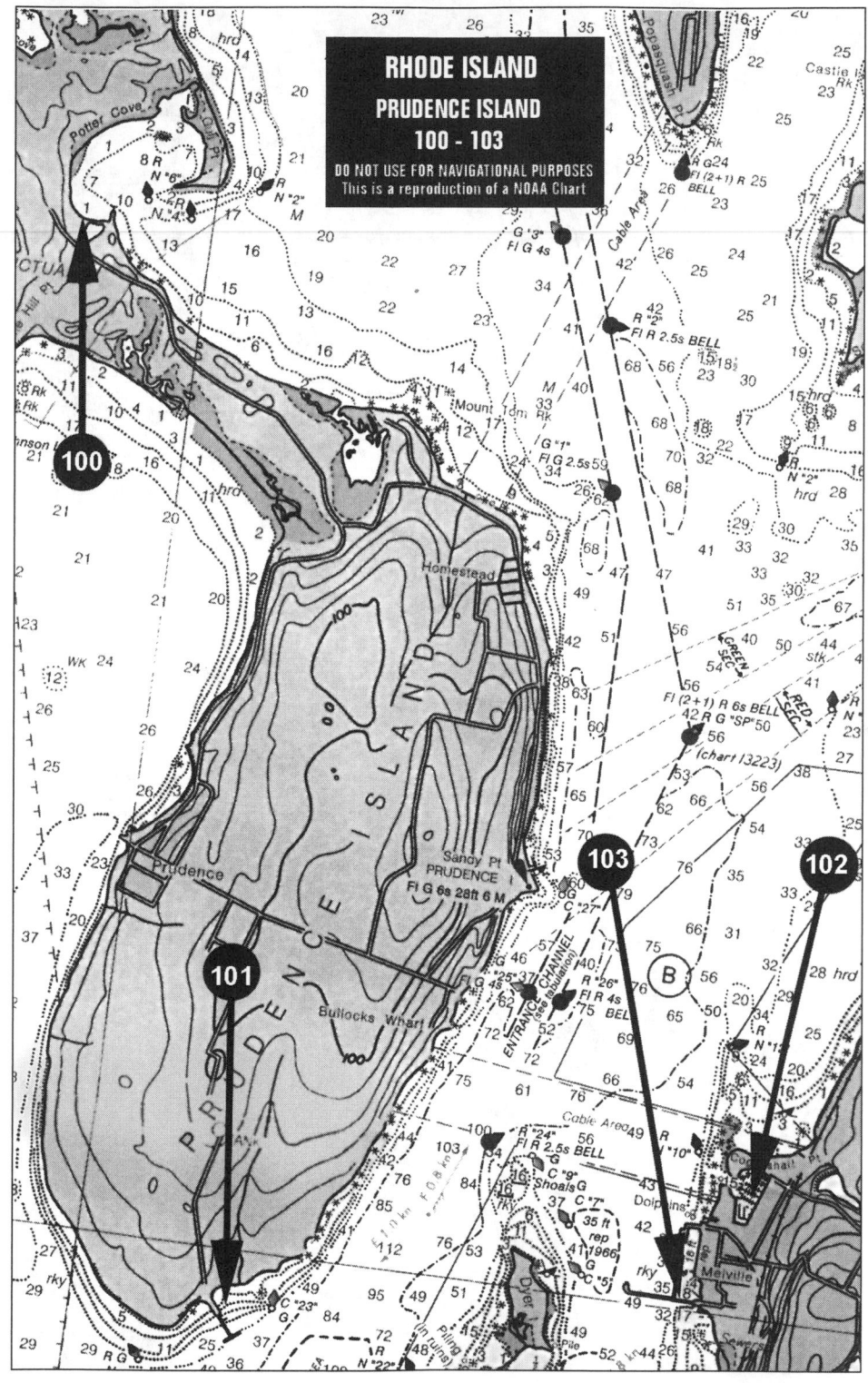

RHODE ISLAND

PRUDENCE ISLAND

100 - 103

DO NOT USE FOR NAVIGATIONAL PURPOSES
This is a reproduction of a NOAA Chart

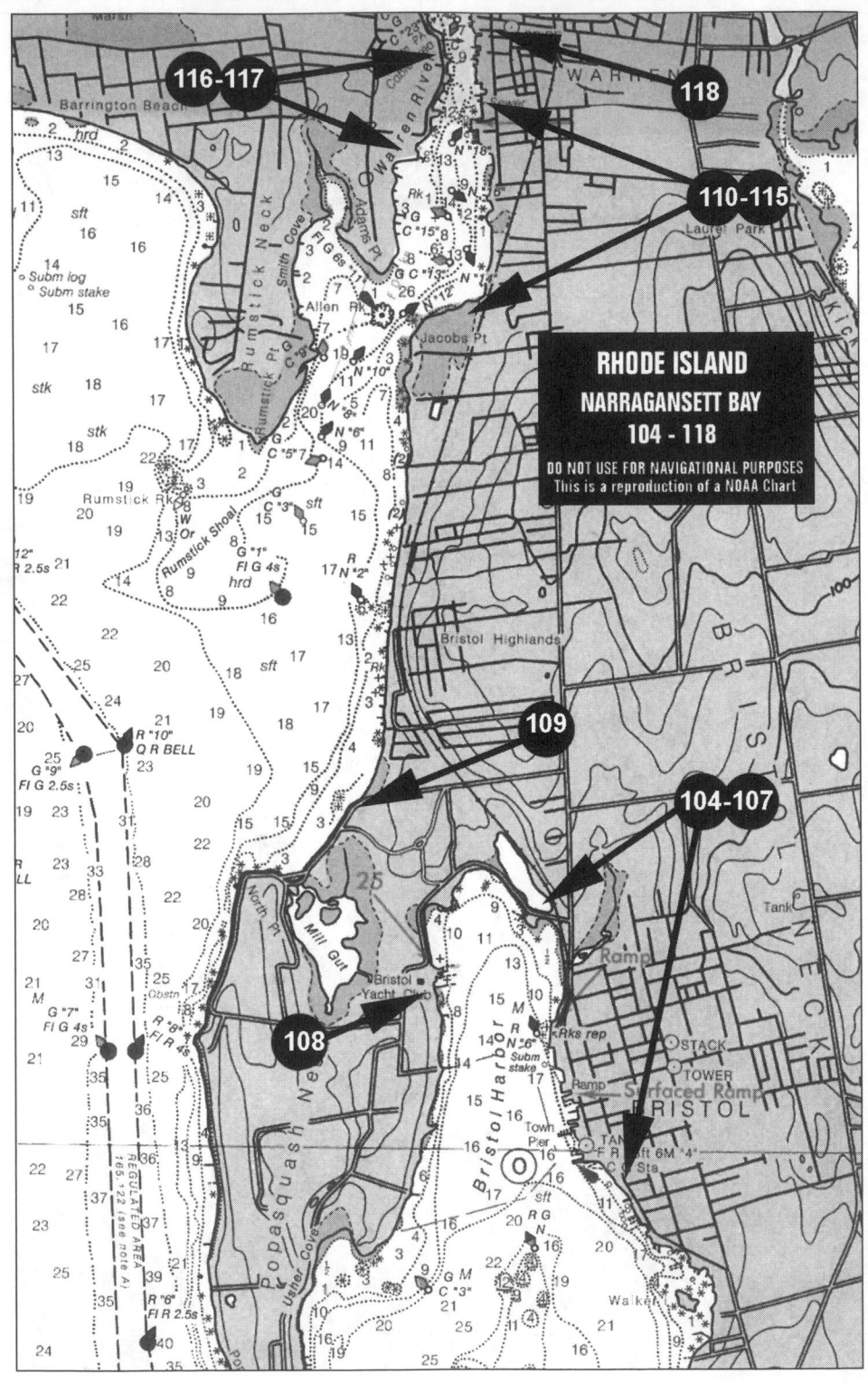

RHODE ISLAND
NARRAGANSETT BAY
104 - 118

DO NOT USE FOR NAVIGATIONAL PURPOSES
This is a reproduction of a NOAA Chart

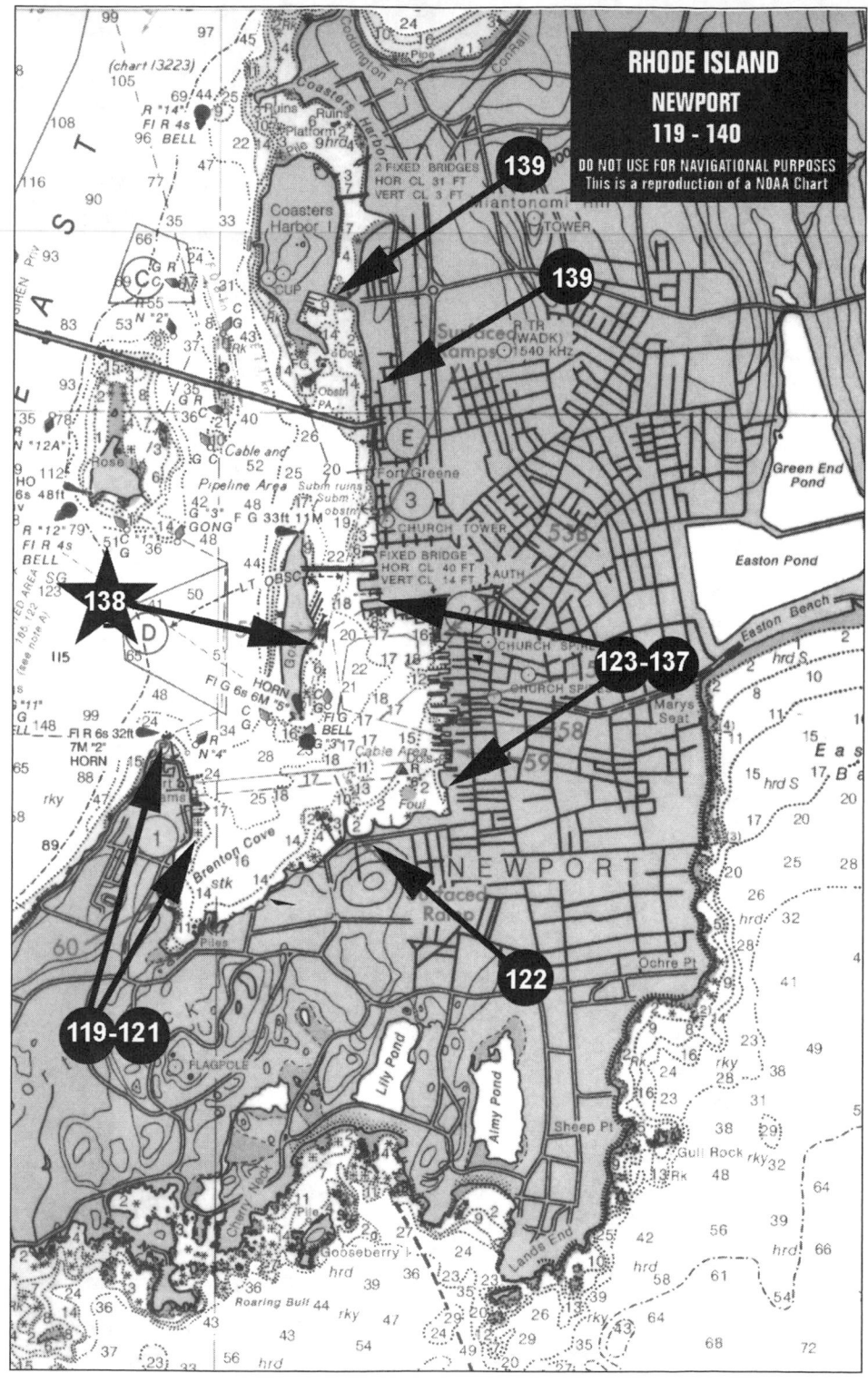

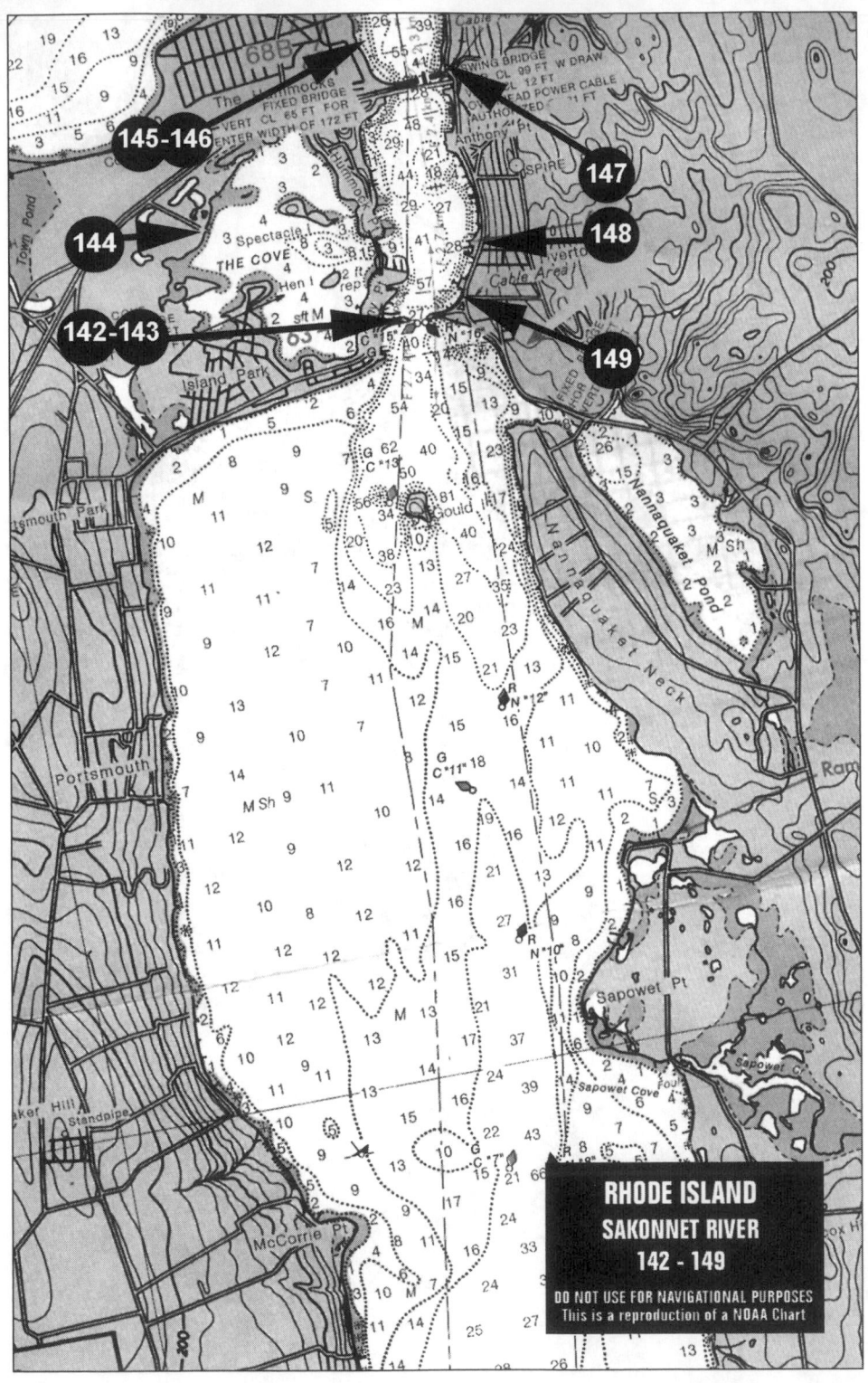

RHODE ISLAND
SAKONNET RIVER
142 - 149

DO NOT USE FOR NAVIGATIONAL PURPOSES
This is a reproduction of a NOAA Chart

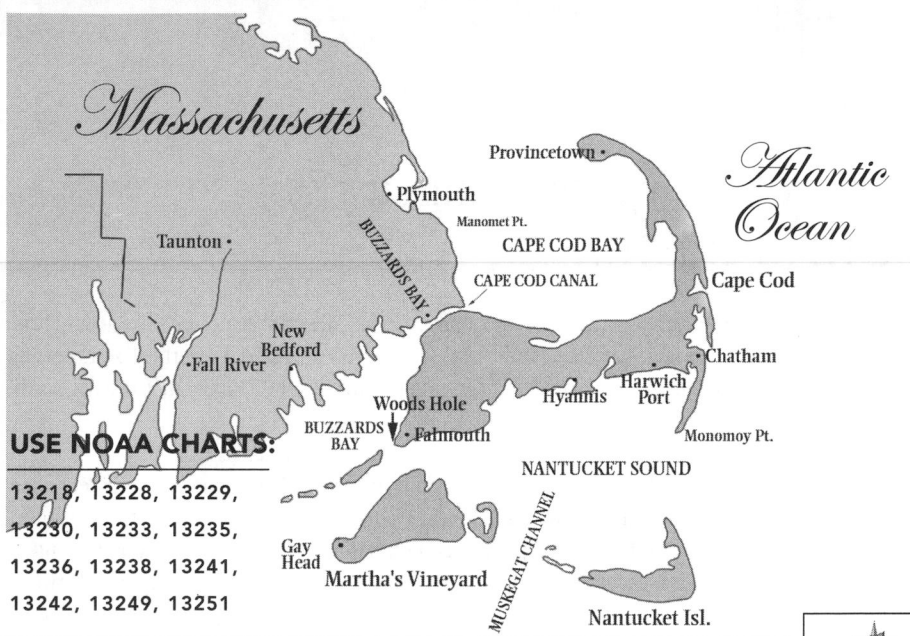

USE NOAA CHARTS:

13218, 13228, 13229,
13230, 13233, 13235,
13236, 13238, 13241,
13242, 13249, 13251

Massachusetts SOUTH OF BOSTON

Map is not intended for navigational purposes.

THE FOLLOWING REGIONS ARE COVERED IN CHARTS IN THIS SECTION:

Cruising Massachusetts:
SOUTH OF BOSTON

CAPE COD, a long peninsula jutting eastward from the mainland of Massachusetts, looks like an arm bent upward at the elbow. It was originally formed by the last great glacier but has been re-formed over the eons by seas and winds. It makes out from the mainland in an easterly direction for 31 miles then extends northward for over 20 miles.

This cape forms the southern and eastern shores of Cape Cod Bay, the northern shore of Nantucket Sound and the eastern shore of Buzzards Bay. The northern trend of Cape Cod, forming what is sometimes called the Hook of The Cape, is known as the Lower Cape. This section is well settled and composed almost entirely of sandy lands, with high bare sand dunes and low nearly level plains. The portion of Cape Cod between Chatham and Cape Cod Canal is known as the Upper Cape. This region is wooded and is well settled by numerous towns and villages.

The outer end of The Cape, as eastern New Englanders call it, is a barren region of sand dunes with long yellow beaches, while much of the remainder of the forearm is bleak grassy country. The surf and waves have cut the southern side of the delta like plain of Cape Cod along high bluffs. This section of the coast is covered with growth of pitch pine and scrub oak. Much of the outer shore of the lower cape is part of the Cape Cod National Seashore under the auspices of the U.S. Dept. of Interior.

CAPE COD BAY is between the peninsula of Cape Cod on the east and south, and the mainland of Massachusetts on the west. Between these limits the bay is about 20 miles in diameter with depths ranging from 10 to 32 fathoms, except close to the shore and in its southeasterly part. Race Point the northwesterly extremity of Cape Cod, is the eastern point; and Gurnet Point on the north side of the entrance to Plymouth Bay is the western point of the entrance to Cape Cod Bay. Within Cape Cod Bay are several harbors, including those of Plymouth on the western shore, Sandwich and Barnstable on the southern shore, and Wellfleet and Provincetown on the eastern shore. It is also the approach to Cape Cod Canal, which connects Cape Cod Bay with Buzzards Bay.

 CHART 13236. CAPE COD CANAL is a deep-draft sea level waterway that extends westward from Cape Cod Bay to the head of Buzzards Bay. The waterway has a project depth of 32 feet, and a least overhead clearance of 135 feet. A lighted 54' range marks the eastern entrance to the canal, lighted and unlighted buoys a light a fog signal, and a radiobeacon. A tall strobelighted stack and buildings of the power plant on the south bank of the canal about 0.75 miles above the eastern entrance is prominent. **CAPE COD CANAL** connects Buzzards Bay and Cape Cod Bay. The waterway is 15 miles long from Cleveland East Ledge Light to deep water in Cape Cod Bay. The canal shortens the distance between points north and south of Cape Cod by 50 to 150 miles and provides an inside passage to avoid Nantucket as a free waterway.

 CHART 13251. BARNSTABLE HARBOR 10 miles eastward of Cape Cod Canal entrance is the approach to the town of Barnstable and the village of Yarmouth Port. Mostly local fishing and charter fishing boats and pleasure boats use it. A seasonal lighted bell buoy, about 1.6 miles northward of Beach Point marks the approach.

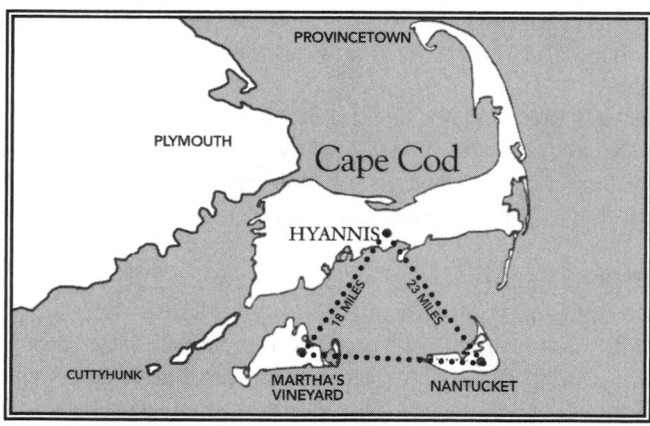

BOSTON SOUTH

From **RACE POINT,** the Cape Cod shore curves northeastward, eastward and then southeastward to the Highlands, a total distance of about 9 miles, and is composed of bare sand dunes of various heights. On the approach to the Highlands, the sand dunes are covered with brownish looking growth of grass and the land is higher. Much of this shoreline is also part of the Cape Cod National Seashore under the US Dept. of Interior.

The tidal current velocities between Race Point and Highland Light are very strong, but diminish to less than 1 knot between Highland Light and Chatham Light. Strengths of flood and ebb set northward and southward, respectively, along the coast. The time of current changes rapidly, the strength of flood or ebb occurring about 2 hours later off Nauset Beach Light than off Chatham Light.

CHART 13249. PROVINCETOWN HARBOR, formed by a turn in the northern end of the hook of Cape Cod, has a diameter of about 2 miles. It is one of the best harbors on the Atlantic Coast, having a sizable anchorage area in depths of 12 to 57 feet with excellent holding ground. Coasters and fishermen find protection here in gales from any direction. Historic Provincetown, on the northwestern side of the harbor, is the site of the first landing of the Mayflower in the New World. Supplies and hull & engine repair facilities are available here.

The approach and entrance to the harbor are free of dangers and are marked by three lights and by Pilgrim Monument, a slim stone structure 348 feet above the water: two standpipes are about 0.2 mile westward and a steel tank is 1.5 miles northeastward of the monument. A 2,500-foot stone breakwater is about 300 yards southeastward of the end of the town pier (MacMillan Wharf). The breakwater extends northeastward from a point in 42 02' 45" N., 70 10' 55"W., approximately parallel to the shoreline. The east and west ends of the breakwater are each marked by a light. Strangers should exercise caution when operating in the area. Numerous fishing vessels work out of Provincetown during the year. During the summer, floats are set out that are capable of mooring vessels up to 40 feet. Larger vessels must tie up on permanent piers. Anchorage inside the breakwater is reported to be fair to poor, mud bottom with much debris. All moorings and berthing in the harbor are under the control of the harbormaster, who has an office at the end of the town pier. The harbormaster monitors VHF 16, 24 hours. Provincetown Coast Guard Station is about 0.4 mile southwest of the town pier. The finger pier northeastward of the Coast Guard pier is in ruins. Mariners should exercise caution while navigating in the area.

CHART 13229. BASS RIVER 9.6 miles westward of Stage Harbor Light is entered between two jetties. A light is on the west jetty. A channel marked by private seasonal buoys goes to an anchorage basin in the lower part of the river. A 5 mph speed limit is enforced on the river.

HYANNIS HARBOR is protected by a break water and is used as a harbor of refuge by coasting vessels and pleasure craft of less than 14 foot draft. A light is on the end of the breakwater. The harbor is the approach to **Hyannis Port** on the west side of the harbor. The most prominent objects when approaching the harbor are the daybeacon, Great Rock, two red and white checkered standpipes, a light blue tank, the breakwater light, and the abandoned lighthouse tower on Point Grammon. **Ed. Note: Hyannis Marina** (508-790-4000 or VHF 9 or 72) is a luxury resort destination on Cape Cod for yachts of all sizes who want a great jumping off spot for cruising to Nantucket and Martha's Vineyard. Unlike many marinas, they provide dockside phone and TV at no charge. And they are savvy with the latest technologies – dockside wireless high speed internet service is available to cruisers

> **FYI.** **MONOMOY AND NANTUCKET SHOALS** are E. and S.E. of the eastern entrance to Nantucket Sound. Tidal Currents here are strong and baffling. Often occuring, thick foggy weather adds to the hazards. **GREAT ROUND SHOAL CHANNEL** is considered the dividing line between these two shoals. Transiting these waters should only be done with a GPS unless the weather is clear.

> **NANTUCKET SOUND HELP!**
> Avoid this area in a hard easterly during a flood tide. Watch out for Fish Traps.

TO FIND MARINA LOCATIONS - SEE THE TABLES AND LOCATOR CHARTS AT THE END OF THIS SECTION.

BOSTON SOUTH

who need to mind their business. Check out their website (www.hyannis marina.com) and tune into Hyannis Cam – a live view of the harbor so you can mentally be there with the click of a mouse. In fact you might just want to hang around and enjoy the pool, on-site great restaurants and the use of a courtesy car to go touring or shopping. The marina store offers discount parts, and there is a full repair service too.

The glacier also formed **NANTUCKET, MARTHA'S VINEYARD, THE ELIZABETH ISLANDS,** and numerous smaller islands. The plains of Martha's Vineyard and Nantucket are broad grassy heaths. The Elizabeth Islands are hilly and partly wooded, and generally the shores are low bluffs.

CHART 13241, 13241. NANTUCKET SOUND is between the south of Cape Cod on the north, Nantucket Island and part of Martha's Vineyard on the south, and joins Vineyard Sound on the west to provide an inside passage. Nantucket Sound has a length of about 23 miles. At the eastern entrance and within the sound are numerous shoals. Between these shoals are well-marked channels making the navigation of these waters comparatively easy for powered vessels and also sailing vessels with a fair wind. The shoals at the eastern entrance are subject to considerable shifting while those inside are somewhat stable. Boulders are along the shores. The channel through Nantucket Sound and Vineyard Sound has a controlling depth of about 30 feet and provides an inside passage for vessels of medium draft to avoid Nantucket Shoals. Principally coastwise vessels and pleasure craft use this route. The navigational aids are colored and numbered for passing through the sound from the eastward. In clear weather, the lights and buoys between Monomy and Nantucket Shoals render navigation of the two principal channels, Pollock Rip and Great Round Shoal, comparatively easy. Numerous fish traps are located in Nantucket Sound, particularly along the southern shore of Cape Cod. Private lights may mark these areas.

NANTUCKET ISLAND, on the southeast side of Nantucket Sound is about 13 miles long, hilly, partly wooded, and covered with vegetation that flourishes in sandy soil. The highest part of the island, about 100 feet high, is in the eastern part; the eastern and southern sides have steep sand bluffs. The northern shore is fringed with shoals for a distance of about 1-mile. For more than a century, the island was a principal part of the whaling industry. Nowadays tourism is the major industry.

Ed. Note: The town is famous for its charming shingled cottages surrounded by blooming colorful gardens, and stately mansions built by such notables as the Macys, the Coffins and the Starbucks. Smart boutiques fill the town. Bring home a highly collectible Nantucket-made basket. And, be sure to take time for a visit to the Whaling Museum. Also, remember to bring insect repellent as the island does have ticks.

NANTUCKET HARBOR is near the middle of the north shore of Nantucket Island. A shallow lagoon about 5 miles long extends northeastward from the harbor. The harbor is the approach to the town of Nantucket on the western shore. The principal industry is fishing. Year 'round passenger, vehicle, and cargo ferry service is maintained between Nantucket and the mainland, to either Woods Hole or Hyannis. A passenger ferry also operates from Falmouth and Oak Bluffs during the summer. Prominent from offshore are a radio tower about 1.2 miles east of Madaket Harbor; a standpipe about 1.5 miles west of Nantucket; a gilded cupola atop a church clock tower, and a church belfry about 500 yards northwestward of it; the spire of a large white church in the town; and the navigational lights at the entrance to Nantucket Harbor.

BOSTON SOUTH

NANTUCKET BOAT BASIN on the west side of Nantucket Harbor is entered about 0.4 mile south-southwestward of Brant Point Light. The basin is enclosed on the north and south sides by Straight Wharf and Commercial Wharf, respectively, and its entrances are protected by two long bulkheads on the east and southeast sides. Depths in the basin range from 3 to 10 feet. Excursion boats use the outer end of the north side of Straight Wharf. A private seasonal light is shown off the end of the wharf and is operated only when tour boats are approaching the wharf in fog. Gasoline, diesel fuel, and ice can be obtained on the south side of Commercial Wharf.

The Woods Hole, Martha's Vineyard and Nantucket Steamship Authority Wharf is about 0.1 mile northward of the boat basin. A private light is shown from the roof of a shed on the northeast end of the wharf and is operated only when authority vessels are approaching the wharf in fog. The submerged ruins of a pier, which uncover at low water, are between the boat basin and the steamship Authority Wharf. A buoy marks the ruins. Mariners are advised to exercise caution in this area.

CHART 13238. MARTHA'S VINEYARD AND CHAPPAQUIDDICK ISLAND have a combined length of 18 miles; Edgartown Harbor, Katama Bay and the narrow slough connecting them separate the two islands. The northern extremity of Martha's Vineyard is about 3 miles southeastward of the western end of Cape Cod. Approaching from the south, the principal landmarks are a standpipe at Edgartown, an aerolight near the center of the island, a church spire near Chilmark in the western part, a tall radar tower north of Chilmark, and Gay Head on the west side.

EDGARTOWN HARBOR has an easy entrance if you pay attention to the line of nuns leading a starboard path (away from rock outcroppings)from red bell '2.' Be aware of the sandbar between can '9' and Chappaquiddick. **Ed. Note: EDGARTOWN** is a very 'yachty' port of call. Celebrity spotting and yacht-watching are good sport here. Browsing in nautical themed shoppes and boutiques, and visiting trendy cafes and markets can easily fill a week of fun, along with wandering the tree-lined streets admiring the stately homes of another time. Whispers of sea-going tales of yore seem to float in the air and the ethereal spirits of bereaved sea wives surround many a Widows Walk. The ambience of this elegant port is a beacon for both artists and those who collect fine art. Connoisseurs of 19th century to contemporary fine maritime art and colectors of nautical antique artifacts can see important works in this genre at the **Edgartown Art Gallery** on South Summer Street, open everyday from 9 a.m. until 10 p.m.

OAK BLUFFS HARBOR, 4.8 miles northwestward of Edgartown Harbor Light, is a landlocked basin with two breakwaters protecting the entrance. A light is on the end of the north breakwater. Prominent is a church dome and a cupola in the village and the bluff north of the entrance. The channel has a reported controlling depth of 9 feet. Numerous submerged rocks, covered 10 to 15 feet, are in the harbor approach, in an area within 0.45 miles of shore bounded on the north by a line extending northeasterly from the breakwaters and on the south by Lone Rock. The chart is the best guide for approaching the harbor however; it is advised that mariners exercise extreme caution as uncharted rocks are likely to exist.

OAK BLUFFS WHARF, about 0.2 mile southward of the breakwater light, is reported to have a depth of 13 feet at the head. Several obstructions with lesser depths have been reported about 400 yards northeast of the wharf face. Private seasonal light and fog signals are operated from the seaward end of the wharf when ferry vessels are approaching the wharf in fog. There is seasonal ferry service from the wharf to **WOODS HOLE** and **NANTUCKET.** Seasonal ferry service is also maintained between **FALMOUTH** and **HYANNIS**. The ferries from Falmouth and Hyannis berth along the bulkhead on the east side of the harbor. Seasonal bus service connects most places on the island. There is air service from Martha's Vineyard Airport about 4.5 miles southwestward of the town.

TO FIND MARINA LOCATIONS - SEE THE TABLES AND LOCATOR CHARTS AT THE END OF THIS SECTION.

BOSTON SOUTH

VINEYARD SOUND AND BUZZARDS BAY are deep and easily navigated day or night. Vineyard Sound, together with Nantucket Sound, provides an inside route from New York to Boston which avoids Nantucket Shoals, Buzzards Bay, together with Cape Cod Canal and Cape Cod Bay provides the shortest deep draft route between New York and Boston.

VINEYARD SOUND is bounded on the north by the southwestern part of Cape Cod and the Elizabeth Islands and on the south by part of Martha's Vineyard, which presents a rugged and generally inaccessible shoreline. To the west, it joins Rhode Island Sound on a line between Cuttyhunk Island and Gay Head. To the east, it joins Nantucket Sound on a line between Nobska Point and West Chop and provides an inside passage clear of Nantucket Shoals. The navigational aids are colored and numbered for passing through the sound from the eastward. The channel throughout the sound is well marked and generally free of dangers.

EAST CHOP AND WEST CHOP are prominent points on the north side of Martha's Vineyard, and on the east and west side of the entrance to Vineyard Haven. Both points terminate in high wooded bluffs, which show prominently from the sounds. Each is marked by a light.

VINEYARD HAVEN HARBOR is a funnel shaped bight in the northern side of Martha's Vineyard between East Chop and West Chop about 1.4 miles long in a southwest direction and about 1.3 miles wide at the entrance. This is the most important harbor of refuge for boaters between Provincetown and Narragansett Bay. The depths range from 46 feet at the entrance to 15 feet near the head of the harbor. Although Vineyard Haven Harbor is exposed to northeasterly winds, vessels with good ground tackle can ride out most blows. The greatest danger encountered by vessels at anchor in a northeast gale is from vessels with poor ground tackle, which are likely to drift, foul others, and then go ashore.

The harbor is the approach to the village of Vineyard Haven. A detached breakwater, marked on its southeastern end by a light, is on the flats on the western side of the harbor near the head. A privately maintained fog signal is at the light on the flats of the harbor's western side. The fog signal and a private light, on the southeast corner of the ferry wharf at the head of the harbor, are activated when a ferry approaches the slip in a fog.

Vessels anchor according to draft, anywhere from the points at the entrance to the head of the harbor. Shallow draft vessels favor the western shore. Vessels entering the harbor with a head wind or light breeze, at the end of a favorable current through the sound, should continue on in the channel until the harbor is well opened before standing in for the anchorage. This helps clear the entrance.

Approaching from eastward, vessels will keep clear of Squash Meadow and East Chop Flats by keeping in the white sector of West Chop Light. Good anchorage is northeastward of the breakwater buoy in 20 to 23 feet and is usually filled to capacity during the summer. When anchoring in the harbor, care must be taken to avoid obstructing the approach to the ferry slip and the approach to the oil wharves on the southerly side of the harbor. The harbormaster has control of the anchoring of vessels in the inner harbor. He is usually found at the town dock on the west side of the harbor and can be contacted by radiotelephone on VHF Channel 16. A 4-mph speed limit is enforced inside the breakwater and within 150 feet of moored craft.

Ed. Note: It's worth hiring a cab or renting a car to take in as much of Martha's Vineyard as you can, and don't forget your camera.

FALMOUTH HARBOR, the open roadstead (*a place less enclosed than a harbor where ships may ride at anchor*) off the south shore of Cape Cod eastward of Nobske Point Light, affords an anchorage for vessels in 24 to 36 feet about 0.8 mile from shore. Smaller vessels can anchor closer to the shore in 15 to 18 feet. The bottom is generally sticky and good holding ground. The depths shoal gradually toward the shore.

BOSTON SOUTH

The anchorage affords a lee in northerly winds in southerly winds the sea is somewhat broken by L'Hommedieu Shoal and the shoals westward of it so that a vessel with good ground tackle can ride out a gale in comparative safety. Falmouth Harbor is frequently used by vessels with good ground tackle that prefer this anchorage to the anchorage in Vineyard Haven Harbor, which may be crowded in bad weather. Vessels approaching the anchorage are cautioned to stay clear of the two shoal areas with depths of 10 to 16 feet marked by buoys, which extend westward of L'Hommedieu Shoal. **FALMOUTH INNER HARBOR,** westward of Falmouth Heights, is a dredged basin about 0.7 mile long and less than 0.1 mile wide on the north side of Falmouth Harbor. A tall gray standpipe, about 1.5 miles westward of Falmouth, is one of the most prominent landmarks in this vicinity.

Ed. Note: Nestled neatly in **FALMOUTH HARBOR** is **MacDougalls' Marina** (508-548-3146) which has been servicing fine yachts and making cruising boaters happy for over 60 years. The marina is 30 NM from Nantucket, 14 NM from New Bedford, 17 NM from the Cape Cod Canal, and 5NM from Martha's Vineyard.

CHART 13230. ELIZABETH ISLANDS, including Nonamesset, Uncatena, Weepecket, Naushon, Pasque, Nashawena, Penikese and Cuttyhunk Islands, extend about 14 miles west-southwest from the southwest end of Cape Cod. The islands, forming part of the northern shore of Vineyard Sound, separate the sound from Buzzards Bay. They are hilly and partly wooded; the shores are in general low bluffs. Westward of Woods Hole are several buoyed channels between the islands, but Quicks Hole is the only one recommended for strangers.

CHART 13235, 13229. WOODS HOLE is that water area lying between the southwest tip of Cape Cod and Uncatena and Nonamesset Island. Woods Hole is also the approach to the town of Woods Hole on the northeastern shore of Great Harbor. The town is a busy commercial center and a transshipping point for passengers and freight to and from Nantucket and Martha's Vineyard. During the summer it is an active resort and frequently a port of call by yachts passing through to Vineyard Sound or Buzzards Bay. Woods Hole is the only anchorage providing shelter from all winds for vessels drawing more than 10 feet. In northerly and westerly winds, good anchorage may be had in Tarpaulin Cove. In southerly winds, shelter can be had in Menemsha Bight, although Vineyard Haven is generally used. Several general anchorages are in Vineyard Sound. **Ed. Note:** Choppy waters here are a result of the prevailing southwest winds and the comings and goings of ferries from New Bedford, Buzzard's Bay, and nearby islands.

HELP!

In approaching Woods Hole from Vineyard Sound westward, be wary of Great Ledge. See Chart.

CHART 13233, 13230, 13229. ROBINSON HOLE is a narrow buoyed passage from Vineyard Sound to Buzzards Bay between the western end of Naushon Island and the eastern end of Pasque Island. It has numerous rocks and ledges, and strong tidal currents. The buoys often tow under and strangers should never attempt the passage; it is used occasionally by local fishermen. It has been reported that currents sometimes reach a velocity of 5 knots in the passage. The velocity in the narrow part is around 3 knots. The flood sets southeastward and the ebb northwestward into Buzzards Bay.

The bight between Nashawena Island and Cuttyhunk Island, the western most of the Elizabeth Islands, forms **CUTTYHUNK HARBOR.** Northward of the harbor are Penikese and Gull Islands and several ledges, which shelter the harbor from winds from that direction. The harbor is exposed to winds from the northeastward. Weather bound cruising vessels and fishermen sometimes use the anchorage in the harbor. The harbor is the approach to the village of Cuttyhunk and to Cuttyhunk Pond. The latter is entered through a dredged cut in the eastern end of Cuttyhunk Island. Copicut Neck forms the northerly side of

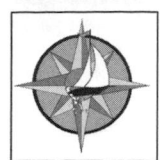

Cuttyhunk Pond.

CHART 13218, 13228, 13230, 13229. BUZZARDS BAY'S western shore is of moderate height, very gently sloping, cleared, and cultivated with occasional groves of trees. Several towns and the city of New Bedford are visible along the shores. Between Buzzard's and Narragansett Bay the coast is a mass of sand dunes with steep faces forming a line along the shore. Several headlands along this stretch of coast have fine sand beaches between them.

BUZZARDS BAY is the approach to **NEW BEDFORD,** many small towns and villages, and the entrance to Cape Cod Canal. The bay indents the south shore of Massachusetts, extending in a northeasterly direction from Rhode Island Sound. The bay is enclosed on the south side, and separated from Vineyard Sound by the Elizabeth Islands. The shores are irregular, rocky in character, and broken by many bays and rivers. Large boulders are common in places extending a considerable distance from shore, thus making close approach to shore dangerous. The bottom in the main part of the bay and approach is very broken with boulder reefs in places. Vessels should proceed with caution when crossing shoal areas in the tributaries of the bay where the depths are not more than about 6 feet greater than the draft. Caution must be also exercised in the vicinity of the wrecks shown on the chart. Deep water prevails as far as Wings Neck, above which the bay is full of shoals.

Buzzards Bay has six entrances but two of these are so narrow and dangerous as to exclude their use except by small craft with local knowledge. The four major entrances are the main channel, from westward, passing north of Cuttyhunk Island; Cape Cod Canal from the northeastward; and Quicks Holds and Woods Hole from the southward. The two hazardous entrances are Canapitsit Channel, between Cuttyhunk and Nashawena Islands, and Robinson Hole between Pasque and Naushon Islands.

The best guides for entering the bay from westward are **BUZZARDS BAY ENTRANCE LIGHT** (41°23'48"N., 71°02'01"W), **CUTTYHUNK LIGHT** (41°24'8"N., 70°57'0"W), and the lighted buoys in the entrance. Gay Head Light (41°20'9"N., 70°50'01"W) and Cuttyhunk Light are the guides for vessel approaching from the southward. Buzzard's Bay Entrance Light, 101 feet above the water, is shown from a tower on a red square superstructure on black piles about 4 miles from Cuttyhunk Light. The name 'Buzzards' is painted in white on the sides. A fog signal is at the light.

CHART 13230, 13229. WEST FALMOUTH HARBOR, 5 miles northward of Woods Hole, has depths of 1 to 6 feet and bares in places at low water. The entrance is protected by a breakwater extending about 700 feet southward of Little Island, the north point of the entrance and by a short jetty on the northwest end of Chappaquoit Point. A tower and the summer homes on Chappaquoit Point are prominent. The entrance

BOSTON SOUTH

is marked by a seasonal lighted bell buoy and an unlighted buoy on the south side and by an unlighted buoy on the north side; these buoys mark reefs that extend westward from both entrance points. Seasonal private buoys mark the channel in the harbor.

CHART 13236, ONSET BAY between Sias Point on the north and Hog Neck on the south is the approach to the village of Onset. A dredged marked channel leads westward from Cape Cod Canal along the southerly side of the bay to a turning basin off the village. Two anchorage areas, on each side of the channel are at the head of the channel.

CHART 13229, MATTAPOISETT HARBOR, about 3.5 miles southwest of Sippican Harbor and 5 miles northeastward of New Bedford Harbor, is the approach to the town of Mattapoisett. Numerous yachts use the harbor during the summer. Although exposed to southeasterly wind, the ledges at the entrance somewhat break the sea from the direction. A light on Ned Point marks the approach. A standpipe is in the town. Vessels anchor between Ned Point and the wharfs in 13 to 17 feet of water.

NEW BEDFORD HARBOR, a tidal estuary at the mouth of Acushnet River on the Northwestern side of Buzzards Bay, is the approach to the city of New Bedford and the town of Fairhaven. The harbor is about 166 miles from the Battery at New York via Long Island Sound and 83 miles for Boston via Cape Cod Canal. The harbor includes all the tidewater lying northerly of a line from Clarks Point at the southern extremity of New Bedford to Wilbur Point at the southern end of Fairhaven and extends to the head of navigation of Acushnet River at Acushnet. The outer harbor consists of the area south of the hurricane barrier at Palmer Island and the inner harbor consists of the area north of the barrier to a short distance above the New Bedford Fairhaven Bridge. New Bedford is a manufacturing city on the west side of Acushnet River. Fairhaven is on the east side of the river. Principal shipping includes receipt of general cargo and frozen fish. Commercial fishing craft operate from the ports.

APPONAGANSETT BAY about 2 miles southwestward of Clarks Point shelters numerous pleasure craft and a few fishermen in the summer, but the bay is insecure in southeasterly gales. Noquitt and Bayview are villages on the south side of the entrance and South Dartmouth is on the northerly shore. **PADANARAM BREAKWATER** is marked on the southern end by a light. Numerous ledges and rocks obstruct the approach to the bay, and strangers should enter only in daytime with clear weather. Inside the breakwater buoys mark the channel. Dartmouth Rock ,covered 4 feet is on the northeast side of the channel. Private seasonal anchorage buoys mark the area off South Dartmouth, which is usually very crowded in the summer. A highway bridge at the village has a swing span with a channel width of 31 feet and a clearance of 8 feet. Above the bridge, small craft anchor in a narrow channel near the eastern shore. The harbormaster controls anchoring and berthing in the harbor and can be contacted through the police department on VHF Channel 16. The speed limit in the harbor is 5 mph. ⚓

MASSACHUSETTS: South FACILITIES alphabetical index

WE'D LIKE TO HEAR FROM YOU!

The most valuable infomation a cruising boater can have is

LOCAL KNOWLEDGE.

We invite you to share your cruising experiences with our *Northeast Boaters Almanac* readers and website visitors. Tell us about your favorite destinations, the best way to navigate to an out of the way cove, great anchorages and hurricane holes, navigational hazards you've encountered, waterfront dining spots, boat cleaning tips, good things to cook aboard and more... and, if you find information we need to change for future editions... you can do it all on

www.BoatersAlmanac.com

Massachusetts
Boston-South
MARINA'S NAME & PHONE NUMBER

CHART LOCATER NUMBER	MARINA'S NAME & PHONE NUMBER	WHEN OPEN	MONITORS VHF CHANNEL	TRANSIENT Electricity•Moorings•Berths	Hull•Engine repairs	Ramp	WINTER STORAGE Wet•Dry	RAILWAY CAPACITY (FEET)	LIFT CAPACITY (TONS)	BOAT RENTAL Canoe•Row•Motor	BOAT RENTAL Charter•Sail	Restaurant•Lodging•House•Camping	Showers•Laundry	Pumpout•Toilets	Bait•Tackle	Groceries•Water•Ice	Hardware	Diesel fuel•Gasoline
1	SWANSEA MARINA 508-672-8633	ALL YR.					D		25						T	W	H	G
2	BORDEN LIGHT MARINA 508-678-7547	ALL YR.		EB	HE	R	W D						SL		T	IW		G D
4	FALL RIVER STATE PARK 508-675-5759	APR OCT	9	M														
5	FALL RIVER STATE RAMP					R												
6	LEONE'S ON THE WATERFRONT 508-679-8158	APR NOV	9	B	E	R						R	SL	T		I		
7	CAPT O'CONNELL CORP 508-672-6303	ALL YR.			HE	R	D		35						T	W	H	G
8	SOMERSET TOWN RAMP					R								T				
9	SOMERSET MARINE 508-678-0040	ALL YR.		EM B	HE		D		25			R	S		T	IW	H	G
10	SHAW'S BOATYARD 508-669-5714	ALL YR		EM B	HE		D		30			R				W	H	
11	DIGHTON TOWN BOAT					R												
12	TAUNTON Y. C. 508-669-6007			M									S		T	I		G
13	GOSNOLD	MAY OCT	9	EM B		R				C	RL		SL			I WT	G	G D
16	TRIPP F.L. & SONS 508-636-4058	ALL YR.	9	EM B	HE		W D	60	40			R	S	PT		IW	G	G D
17	MASSACHUSETTS RAMP					R												
18	MOBY DICK RESTAURANT 508-636-6500	APR DEC		EB								R						
19	LEES WHARF & LOBSTER 508-636-6161	ALL YR.														IB		
20	LEACH & SON 508-636-2411	MAY NOV				R	D								T		H	
21	WESTPORT TOWN DOCK 508-636-1105	ALL YR.	9	M														
22	SOUTH DARTMOUTH RAMP					R									T	BT		
23	CONCORDIA COMPANY 508-999-1381	ALL YR.	9	EB	HE		WD		30						T			

MARINA'S NAME & PHONE NUMBER

Column key (diagonal headers, left to right): CHART LOCATER NUMBER · MARINA'S NAME & PHONE NUMBER · WHEN OPEN · MONITORS VHF CHANNEL · TRANSIENT: Electricity • Moorings • Berths · Hull repairs • Engine repairs • Ramp · WINTER STORAGE: Wet • Dry · RAILWAY CAPACITY IN FEET · LIFT CAPACITY IN TONS · BOAT RENTAL: Canoe • Row • Motor · Restaurant • Charter • Lodging • House • Camping • Sail · Showers • Laundry · Pumpout • Toilets · Bait • Tackle • Water • Ice · Groceries • Hardware · Diesel fuel • Gasoline

#	Marina Name & Phone	When Open	Monitors VHF	Transient	Repairs/Ramp	Winter Storage	Railway (ft)	Lift (tons)	Restaurant/Lodging	Showers/Laundry	Pumpout/Toilets	Bait·Water·Ice	Groceries/Hardware	Diesel/Gas
24	NEW BEDFORD Y. C. 508-997-0762		68	M	R			2	R	S	T	IW		G D
25	DAVIS TRIPP 508-993-9232	ALL YR			HE	W D		35	RL		PT	IW	H	
26	MARSHALL MARINE CORP 508-994-0414	ALL YR			HE	W D		10						
27	MASSACHUSETTS RAMP				R									
29	GEAR LOCKER MARINA 508-994-3594	ALL YR.	16 79	EB		D			RL	S	T	IW	H	
30	BAYLINE MARINA 508-994-0891	MAY OCT			HE				RL			IW		
31	U.S.C.G. AUX. FLOTILLA													G
32	D.N.KELLEY & SONS 508-999-6266	ALL YR.	9	EB	HE		120	99 +						G D
33	FAIRHAVEN MARINA 508-997-2444	MAY NOV	69 73	EB	HE R	D		9		SL	PT	IW	H	
34	FAIRHAVEN TOWN RAMP				R									
35	SEAPORT MARINA 508-992-7985	ALL YR	9	EB					RL	S	PT	IW		
36	POPE'S ISLAND MARINE 508-993-1770	APR NOV	74	EB					RL	S	PT	IW		
37	FAIRHAVEN Shipyard & Marina 508-996-8591	ALL YR.	9	EM B	HE	W D	120	99 +		SL	T	IW	H	G D
38	MATTAPOISETT TOWN RAMP	ALL YR.			R						P			
38A	BROWNELL BOAT COMPANIES 508-758-3671	ALL YR.		EB	R									
39	MATTAPOISETT BOATYARD 508-758-3812	ALL YR.	9 68	M	HE	D		45		S	T	IW	H	G D
41	BLUE WATER YACHTS 508-758-2222	ALL YR.			HE R	D		3			T	IW	H	G D
42	ISLAND WHARF 508-748-3535				R									
43	BARDEN'S BOATYARD 508-748-0250	ALL YR.		M	E	D		30				IW	H	
44	BURR BROTHERS BOATS 508-748-0541	ALL YR.	68		HE R	D		30		SL	PT	IW	GH	G D

Massachusetts
Boston-South
MARINA'S NAME & PHONE NUMBER

CHART LOCATER NUMBER	Marina's Name & Phone Number	When Open	Monitors VHF Channel	Transient (Electricity•Moorings•Berths)	Hull repairs•Engine repairs•Ramp	Winter Storage (Wet•Dry)	Railway Capacity in Tons	Boat Rental (Canoe•Row•Motor)	Lift Capacity in Feet	Boat Rental (Charter•House•Sail)	Restaurant•Lodging•Camping	Showers•Laundry	Pumpout•Toilets	Bait•Tackle•Water•Ice	Groceries•Hardware	Diesel fuel•Gasoline
45	BEVERLY Y. C. 508-748-0540	ALL YR.	68	M								S				
46	WAREHAM BOATYARD 508-748-1472	ALL YR.	9		ER	D		M					T	W	H	G
47	ROSE POINT RAMP				R											
48	WARR'S MARINE 508-295-0022	ALL YR.	16		HE		45		3			S	PT	IW	H	G D
49	WAREHAM TOWN DOCK			M	HE R						RL		PT	W		
50	SWIFTS BEACH RAMP				R											
51	TEMPEST KNOB BOAT RAMP				R											
52	CAPE COD SHIP BUILDING CO. 508-295-3550	ALL YR.			H	D			15							
54	ONSET PIER 508-295-8160	MAY OCT	9 16	B							C		PT	I		
55	STONEBRIDGE MARINA 508-295-8003	ALL YR.	10 9	EB							RL	SL	PT	IW	G	G D
56	ONSET BAY MARINA 508-295-0338	ALL YR.	9	EM B	HE	D	70		65		RL	SL	PT	IW	GH	G D
57	MACO'S BAIT & TACKLE 508-759-9836	APR OCT	23 9	B	R			M					T	IW BT	G	G
58	BOURNE TOWN MARINA 508-759-2512	MAY OCT	9	EB	ER						R	SL	PT	IW BT	GH	G D
59	BUZZARDS BAY TOWN RAMP				R											
60	MARITIME ACADEMY 508-759-4431	ALL YR.	9 16													
61	CONTINENTAL MARINE. 508-759-5451	ALL YR.		EB	E	D					RL	S	PT	IW	H	G
62	CAPE MARINE 508-759-4455	ALL YR.			HE	D							T		H	
63	PERRY'S BOATYARD 508-759-3062	ALL YR.	8 9	M	HE	D							T	IW BT		
64	MONUMENT BEACH MARINA 508-759-3105	APR NOV		EM B	R						R	S	T	IW		G
66	BARLOW'S BOATYARD 508-563-3213	ALL YR.			HE	D	30							W		G

Massachusetts
Boston-South

Chart Locater Number	Marina's Name & Phone Number	When Open	Monitors VHF Channel	Transient: Electricity • Moorings • Berths	Hull repairs • Engine repairs • Ramp	Winter Storage: Wet • Dry	Railway Capacity in Tons	Boat Rental: Canoe • Row • Motor	Lift Capacity in Feet	Boat Rental: Charter • House • Sail	Restaurant • Lodging • Camping	Showers • Laundry	Pumpout • Toilets	Bait • Tackle • Water • Ice	Groceries • Hardware	Diesel fuel • Gasoline
67	BARLOWS LANDING 508-563-5100	ALL			R											
68	BOURNE TOWN RAMP				R											
69	PARKER'S BOATYARD 508-563-9366	ALL YR.	69	EM B	HE	D	20					S	T	IW	GH	G D
70	RED BROOK HARBOR RAMP				R											
71	KINGMAN MARIN 508-563-7136	ALL YR.	9	EM B	HE	W D	60				R	SL	T	IW		G D
72	WILD HARBOR				R											
73	MEGANSETT TOWN RAMP				R											
74	FIDDLER'S COVE MARINA 508-564-6327	ALL YR	9		HE	W D	45		15			SL	PT	IW	H	G D
76	WEST FALMOUTH RAMP 508-457-2550	ALL YR.			R											
77	QUISSETT Harbor Boatyard. 508-548-0506	ALL YR		M	R	D	40							IW	H	
78	PINKY'S MARINA 508-540-2310	ALL YR.		EB								S	T	W		
79	WOODS HOLE RAMP 508-548-7625				R											
81	EDGARTOWN RAMP				R											
82	HARBORSIDE INN & Boatyard 508-627-3421	APR OCT		B							RL		T	W		
83	MEMORIAL WHARF 508-627-4746	ALL YR.	9 74										P			
84	EDGARTOWN TOWN DOCKS 508-627-4746	MAY OCT	9 74	M												
85	MAD MAX MARINA 508-627-7400	MAY OCT	71							CS	RL			IW BT		
86	EDGARTOWN MARINE 508-627-4388	ALL YR.	9		HE	D	25				RL	S		IW	H	
87	OAK BLUFFS Harbor Marina 508-693-4355	ALL YR.	9 16 71	EM B	HE R						RL C	L	T	IW BT	GH	G D
89	DOCKSIDE MARINA 508-693-3392	MAY OCT		EB						C	RL			IW		G D

CHART LOCATER NUMBER	MARINA'S NAME & PHONE NUMBER	WHEN OPEN	MONITORS VHF CHANNEL	TRANSIENT Electricity • Moorings • Berths	Hull repairs • Engine repairs • Ramp	WINTER STORAGE: Wet • Dry	RAILWAY CAPACITY IN FEET	LIFT CAPACITY IN TONS	BOAT RENTAL: Canoe • Row • Motor	BOAT RENTAL: Charter • House • Sail	Restaurant • Lodging • Camping	Showers • Laundry	Pumpout • Toilets	Bait • Tackle • Water • Ice	Groceries • Hardware	Diesel fuel • Gasoline
90	COASTWISE WHARF CO. 508-693-3854	JUN SEP		EB							RL	SL	T	IW		
91	MACIEL MARINE LIMITED 508-693-4174	ALL YR.	9 16	EMB	HER	WD	50	70	M		RL	SL	PT	IW BT	G H	G
92	MARTHA'S VINEYARD Shipyard 508-693-0400	ALL YR.	9 16 73		HE	D	45	20					P	IW BT	H	G D
93	GANNON AND BENJAMIN 508-693-4658	ALL YR.	72	M	HE	D	60	40							H	
94	VINEYARD HAVEN MARINA 508-693-0720	ALL YR.	9	EMB	E			4			R	SL	T	IW	H	G D
95	VINEYARD HAVEN RAMP				R											
96	LAKE TASHMOO RAMP				R								P			
97	TASHMOO BOATYARD 508-693-9311	ALL YR			R	D								IW	H	
98	MENEMSHA TEXACORP. 508-645-2641	ALL YR	9							C				IW BT	H	G D
99	CHILMARK TOWN DOCK 508-645-2846	ALL YR.	9	EMB							R	S	T	W		
100	GAY HEAD RAMP				R											
101	MADAKET MARINE 508-228-9086	ALL YR.	9		HE	D		15							H	G D
102	HITHER CREEK RAMP				R											
103	NANTUCKET TOWN RAMP 508-228-6800				R											
104	ISLAND MARINE SERVICE 508-228-9095	ALL YR.	9		HE			20						I	H	G D
105	NANTUCKET TOWN PIER 508-228-7260	ALL YR.	9 14								RL	S	PT	I		
106	NANTUCKET MOORINGS 508-228-4472	MAY SEP	68	M												
107	NANTUCKET BOAT BASIN 508-228-1333		9	EB							RL	SL	PT	IW		G D
108	HARBOR LAUNCH 508-228-8565	MAY SEP	68		R											
109	DAVIS MARINE PARK 508-457-2550		9	EB									P	W		

Chart Locater Number	Marina's Name & Phone Number	When Open	Monitors VHF Channel	Transient: Electricity • Moorings • Berths	Hull repairs • Engine repairs • Ramp	Winter Storage: Wet • Dry	Railway Capacity in Feet	Lift Capacity in Tons	Boat Rental: Canoe • Row • Motor	Boat Rental: Charter • House • Sail	Restaurant • Lodging • Camping	Showers • Laundry	Pumpout • Toilets	Bait • Tackle • Water • Ice	Groceries • Hardware	Diesel fuel • Gasoline
110	FALMOUTH PIER 37 / 508-540-0123	ALL YR.	9		HE	D		6			RL		T	I		G
111	FALMOUTH HARBOR MARINA / 508-457-2550	MAY OCT	9 16	EB						C	RL	S	T	W		
112	BARBOUR MARINE SERVICE / 508-548-2222	MAR JAN		EB				6			RL			W	H	
113	FALMOUTH MARINE / 508-548-4600	ALL YR.	9	EM B	HE	W D	90	70				S	T	IW	GH	G D
114	HARBORSIDE MARINE / 508-548-0143	ALL YR.			HE	D							T	B	H	
115	WOODS HOLE BOAT / 508-548-2626	ALL YR.	78	B		W D					R		T	IW	G	D
117	REGATTA RESTAURANT / 508-548-5400	MAY SEP									R					
118	EAST MARINE / 508-540-3611	ALL YR.	9	EB		D		35			RL	S	T	W		G D
120	FALMOUTH HARBOR MARINE / 508-457-7000	ALL YR.	9		R						RL	SL	T	IW	G	
121	MACDOUGALLS' CAPE COD MARINE SERVICE / 508-548-3146	ALL YR.	9 16	EM B	HE	W D	100	50			RL	SL	PT	IW	H G	G D
123	GREAT POND TOWN LANDING / 508-548-5488				R											
124	WEST MARINE at Green Pond / 508-540-0877	MAR NOV		B	HE	D							T	IW BT		
125	GREEN POND MARINE / 508-548-2635	ALL YR.	9	B	R	D					R		T	IW BT	H	
126	DAVISVILLE TOWN LANDING / 508-548-1906			B	R											
127	EDWARD'S BOATYARD / 508-548-2216	ALL YR.	9 16	EB	HE R	W D	45					S	PT	I WT		G D
128	CHILD'S RIVER TOWN RAMP				R											
129	LITTLE RIVER BOATYARD / 508-548-3511	ALL YR.	9	EM B	HE R	D		10				S	T	IW	H	G
130	GREAT RIVER BOAT RAMP				R											
131	NEW SEABURY MARINA / 508-477-9197	MAY SEP	9		R											G
132	OCKWAY BAY RAMP				R											

Massachusetts
Boston-South

Chart Locater Number	Marina's Name & Phone Number	When Open	Monitors VHF Channel	Transient: Electricity • Moorings • Berths	Hull repairs • Engine repairs • Ramp	Winter Storage: Wet • Dry	Railway Capacity in Feet	Lift Capacity in Tons	Boat Rental: Canoe • Row • Motor	Boat Rental: Charter • Sail	Restaurant • Lodging • House • Camping	Showers • Laundry	Pumpout • Toilets	Bait • Tackle • Water • Ice	Groceries • Hardware	Diesel fuel • Gasoline
133	HALF-TIDE MARINA 508-477-2681	ALL YR.	9 16	MB	HE	D							T	IW	H	G
134	MASHPEE TOWN RAMP				R											
136	OYSTER HARBORS MARINE 508-428-2017	ALL YR.	79	EM B	HE	D		50				S	T	IW	H	G D
137	NAUTICUS MARINA 508-428-4537	MAY OCT	9 16	EB								S	T	IW		
138	CROSBY YACHT YARD 508-428-6958	ALL YR.	9 16	EM B	HE	D	55				R	S	T	IW	H	G D
139	OSTERVILLE TOWN RAMP				R											
140	PRE'S COVE MARINA 508-428-5885	ALL YR.	9 16 68	M	HE R	W D	30						T	W	H	
141	MARSTONS MILLS RAMP				R											
143	HYANNIS YACHT CLUB				R											
144	HYANNIS PORT YACHT CLUB				R											
147	JFK MEMORIAL PARK				R											
149	**HYANNIS MARINA 508-775-5662**	**ALL YR.**	**9 16**	**EB**	**HE R**	**D**		**35**			**R**	**SL**	**PT**	**IW**	**H**	**G D**
150	HYANNIS TOWN DOCKS				R											
151	TOWN RAMP				R											
153	SKIPPY'S PIER 1 508-398-9556	ALL YR.		EB	R	W D			C		RL	SL	T	IW		
154	BASS RIVER BEACH RAMP 508-398-2231	ALL YR.			R											
155	SHIP SHOPS 508-398-2256	ALL YR.	9 18 79	EB	HE R	W D		8					T	IW	H	G D
156	YARMOUTH TOWN DOCK												P			
157	YARMOUTH TOWN RAMP				R											
158	MAYFAIR BOATYARD & MARINA 508-398-3722	ALL YR.			HE	D		12					T	W		G

Massachusetts
Boston-South
MARINA'S NAME & PHONE NUMBER

Chart Locater Number	Marina's Name & Phone Number	When Open	Monitors VHF Channel	Transient: Electricity • Moorings • Berths	Hull repairs • Engine repairs • Ramp	Winter Storage: Wet • Dry	Railway Capacity in Tons	Boat Rental: Canoe • Row • Motor	Lift Capacity in Feet	Boat Rental: Charter • House • Sail	Restaurant • Lodging • Camping	Showers • Laundry	Pumpout • Toilets	Bait • Tackle • Water • Ice	Groceries • Hardware	Diesel fuel • Gasoline
159	DENNIS RAMP				R											
161	BASS RIVER MARINA 508-394-8341	ALL YR.	9	EB	E	D			15			S	T	IW	H	G
162	WEST DENNIS TOWN RAMP				R											
163	CAPE COD BOATS 508-394-9268	MAY OCT								S	RL					
164	WEST DENNIS TOWN RAMP				R											
165	WEST HARWICH RAMP				R											
166	HARWICH PORT LANDING 508-432-2562				R								T			
167	ALLEN HARBOR MARINE 508-432-0353	ALL YR.	9 68	EB	H R	D			15				T	IW	H	G D
170	HARWICH PORT LANDING 508-432-9867	ALL YR.									C		T			
171	HARWICH Port Boat Works 508-432-1322	ALL YR.	8	EB	H E	D	50							W	H	G D
172	THOMPSON'S CLAM BAR 508-432-3595	JUN SEP									RL					
173	SAQUATUCKET MARINA 508-432-2562	MAY NOV	9	EB	R							SL	T	IW		G D
174	CHATHAM TOWN LANDING				R											
175	OYSTER RIVER BOATYARD 508-945-0736	ALL YR.	9 16	B	HE R	D							T	W	H	G
176	CHATHAM YACHT BASIN 508-945-0728	ALL YR.		MB	HE R	D	40			MR			T	IW	H	G D
177	CHATHAM TOWN LANDING				R											
178	CHATHAM TOWN 508-945-9696				R								T			
179	STAGE HARBOR MARINE 508-945-1860	ALL YR.	9	EB M	HE R	W D			20				PT	IW BT	H	G D
180	CHATHAM TOWN RAMP				R											
181	MILL POND BOATYARD 508-945-1785	ALL YR.			H	D	50				L		T		H	

529

Massachusetts
Boston-South
MARINA'S NAME & PHONE NUMBER

Chart #	Marina's Name & Phone	When Open	Monitors VHF Channel	Transient: Electricity•Moorings•Berths	Hull•Engine Repairs•Ramp	Winter Storage: Wet•Dry	Railway Cap. (ft)	Lift Cap. (tons)	Boat Rental: Canoe•Row•Motor	Boat Rental: Charter•House•Sail	Restaurant•Lodging•Camping	Showers•Laundry	Pumpout•Toilets	Bait•Tackle	Groceries•Water•Ice	Hardware	Diesel•Gasoline
182	Harbor Marine OUTERMOST 508-945-2030	ALL YR.	9 16		HE	D		25						T	IW	H	G
183	CHATHAM FISH PIER 508-945-9566	ALL YR.								C	RL			T	I		G D
184	CHATHAM RAMP				R												
185	RYDERS COVE BOATYARD 508-945-1064	ALL YR.		EM B	HE	D								T	IW	H	G
186	CROW'S POND RAMP				R												
187	HARWICH TOWN RAMP 508-432-2562				R												
188	QUANSET RAMP				R												
189	SOUTH ORLEANS LANDING				R												
190	AREY'S POND BOATYARD 508-255-0994	ALL YR.	9		HE	D		3						T		H	
192	NAUSET MARINE 508-255-3045	ALL YR.	9 16	EB	HE	D		9			RL	S	PT	T	IW	H	G
193	POCHET TOWN LANDING				R												
194	PROVINCETOWN RAMP				R												
195	FLYER'S BOAT SHOP 508-487-0898	ALL YR.			HE		80	80	RM	S	RL			T	IB T	H	
197	PROVINCETOWN MARINA 508-487-0571	MAY OCT	9	EM B							RL	S		T	IW		G D
198	CAPE COD OIL CO 508-487-0205	MAY OCT															G D
199	MacMILLAN PIER 508-487-7030	ALL YR.	16 9							C	L						
200	PROVINCETOWN YACHT 508-487-9256										R						
202	EASTHAM TOWN DOCKS 508-255-0559				R												
203	ORLEANS TOWN DOCK 508-255-7337	MAY OCT	68	EB	R						C			T			G D
204	ORLEANS TOWN RAMP				R												

Massachusetts Boston-South

MARINA'S NAME & PHONE NUMBER

CHART LOCATER NUMBER	Marina's Name & Phone	When Open	Monitors VHF Channel	Transient (Elec·Moor·Berths)	Hull·Engine repairs·Ramp	Winter Storage (Wet·Dry)	Railway Capacity: Ramp	Boat Rental (Canoe·Row·Motor)	Lift Cap. (ft)	Lift Cap. (tons)	Boat Rental (Charter·House·Sail)	Restaurant·Lodging·Camping	Showers·Laundry	Pumpout·Toilets	Bait·Tackle·Water·Ice	Groceries·Hardware	Diesel·Gasoline
205	ORLEANS TOWN RAMP				R												
206	NAUSET MARINE 508-255-0777	ALL YR.	9 / 16		HE	D				7		RL		T	I	H	G
207	HEMENWAY LANDING				R												
208	WELLFLEET MARINA 508-349-0320	MAY-OCT	19 / 16	EMB	R						C	RL	S	T	IW		GD
209	WELLFLEET MARINE CORP 508-349-6578	MAY-OCT			HE	D		R			S	RL	S	T	WT	H	
211	NORTHSIDE MARINA 508-385-3936	ALL YR.	9	EB	HE	D				35	C		S	T	IW BT	H	GD
212	SESUIT HARBOR MARINA 508-394-8300	APR-NOV	9 9 / 16	EB	R						C						
213	BARNSTABLE MARINE SERV. 508-362-3811	ALL YR.			HE	D				20		R	S	T	IW BT	H	GD
214	MILLWAY MARINA 508-362-4904	ALL YR.		B	HE	D								T	I	H	G
215	BLISH POINT RAMP FACILITY	ALL YR.			R												
216	BARNSTABLE TOWN DOCKS			B													
217	MILLWAY RAMP				R												
218	MATTAKEESE WHARF 508-362-4511	MAY-OCT										R					
219	BARNSTABLE HARBOR RAMP				R												
220	SANDWICH MARINA 508-833-0808	ALL YR.	9 / 16	EB	R	D							S	T	IW BT	H	GD
222	TOWN WHARF ENTERPRISES 508-746-6193	ALL YR.	9 / 16												I		GD
223	BREWERS Plymouth Marine 508-746-4500	ALL YR.	9	EB	HE	D				60	CS	RL	S	T	IW	H	GD
224	PLYMOUTH TOWN WHARF 508-830-4182	ALL YR.	9 9 / 16		R						C	RL			IB T		
227	LEO F. DEMARSH RAMP				R												
228	PLYMOUTH BOATYARD 508-746-9547	ALL YR.			HE	D			75	99+				T			

Massachusetts
Boston-South
MARINA'S NAME & PHONE NUMBER

CHART LOCATER NUMBER	MARINA'S NAME & PHONE NUMBER	WHEN OPEN	MONITORS VHF CHANNEL	TRANSIENT Electricity • Moorings • Berths	Hull repairs • Engine repairs	Railway • Ramp	WINTER STORAGE: Wet • Dry	LIFT CAPACITY IN TONS	BOAT RENTAL: Canoe • Row • Motor • Sail	Restaurant • Charter • Lodging • House • Camping	Showers	Pumpout • Laundry • Toilets	Bait • Tackle • Water • Ice	Groceries • Water • Hardware	Diesel fuel • Gasoline
229	LANDING MARINE 781-585-6236	ALL YR.	9		HE	R	D	10						H	
230	KINGSTON TOWN LANDING 781-585-0519					R									
231	BAYSIDE MARINE CORP 781-934-0561	ALL YR.	8		HE		D	5		RL		PT	IW BT	H	G
232	DUXBURY TOWN PIER 781-934-2866		9 16	M		R									
233	LONG POINT MARINE 781-934-5302	ALL YR.	9 16		HE		D	30						H	
235	GREEN HARBOR MARINA 781-837-1181	ALL YR.	68	EB	HE		D	15		R	S	T	IW BT	H	G
236	GREEN HARBOR TOWN PIER 781-834-5541	ALL YR.	16	MB		R				C R					
237	TAYLOR MARINE 781-834-8567	ALL YR.		EB			D	5		R	S	T	IW	H	G D
238	SIMMS BROTHERS MARINE 781-659-1200	ALL YR.		EB	HE		D	30				T	IW		
239	MARSHFIELD TOWN RAMP 781-834-5541					R									
240	SOUTH SHORE STERN DRIVE 781-837-2687	ALL YR.		EM B	HE	R	D	25		RL		PT	IW BT	H	
241	NORTH River Marine Services 781-545-7811	ALL YR.					D								

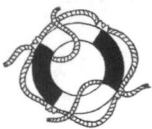

Massachusetts Yacht Clubs

The Yacht Clubs listed below offer reciprocity and courtesy dockage or moorings.
Only Yacht Clubs with space for 2 or more traveling Yacht Club members are listed.

BASS RIVER
BASS RIVER YACHT CLUB
(508) 398-970

BRAINTREE
BRAINTREE YACHT CLUB
(617) 843-9730
METROPOLITAN Y Y.C.
(617) 843-9882

CAMBRIDGE
CHARLES RIVER YACHT CLUB
(617) 354-8681

CATAUMET
RED BROOK HARBOR Y.C.
(508) 295-1016

CHATHAM
MONOMOY YACHT CLUB
(617) 945-3766

CHELSEA
CHELSEA Y.C. -9864
(617) 884

COHASSET
COHASSET YACHT CLUB
(617) 383-9633

DORCHESTER
SAVIN HILL YACHT CLUB
(617) 436-9633

DUXBURY
DUXBURY YACHT CLUB
(617) 943-2122

EAST BOSTON
ORIENT HEIGHTS Y.C.
(617) 561-111

GLOUCESTER
EASTERN POINT YACHT CLUB
(978) 283-3520

HARWICH PORT
ALLEN HARBOR YACHT CLUB
(508) 432-9774

HINGHAM
HINGHAM YACHT CLUB
(617) 749-9779

HULL
SPINNAKER ISLAND Y.C.
(617) 925-1800

HYANNIS
HYANNIS YACHT CLUB
(508) 778-6100

LYNN
LYNN YACHT CLUB
(617) 595-9825

MARBLEHEAD
BOSTON YACHT CLUB
(617) 631-3100
EASTERN YACHT CLUB
(617) 631-1400

MARION
BEVERLY YACHT CLUB
(617) 748-0540

MARSHFIELD
MARSHFIELD YACHT CLUB
(781) 834-9103

NORTH FALMOUTH
RED BROOK HARBOR Y.C.
(508) 295-1016

ORLEANS
ORLEANS YACHT CLUB
(508) 255-9091

PLYMOUTH
PLYMOUTH YACHT CLUB
(508) 7747-0473

SCITUATE
SCITUATE HARBOR Y.C.
(617) 545-0372

SOUTH BOSTON
SOUTH BOSTON YACHT CLUB
(617) 269-9628

SOUTH DARTMOUTH
NEW BEDFORD YACHT CLUB
(508) 997-0762

SOUTH YARMOUTH
BASS RIVER YACHT CLUB
(508) 398-9701

WESTPORT
WESTPORT YACHT CLUB
(508) 636-8885

WINTHROP
COTTAGE PARK YACHT CLUB
(617) 846-9362
WINTHROP YACHT CLUB
(617) 846-9774

WOLLASTON
SQUANTUM YACHT CLUB
(617) 328-9759

Find links to popular boating sites on
www.BoatersAlmanac.com

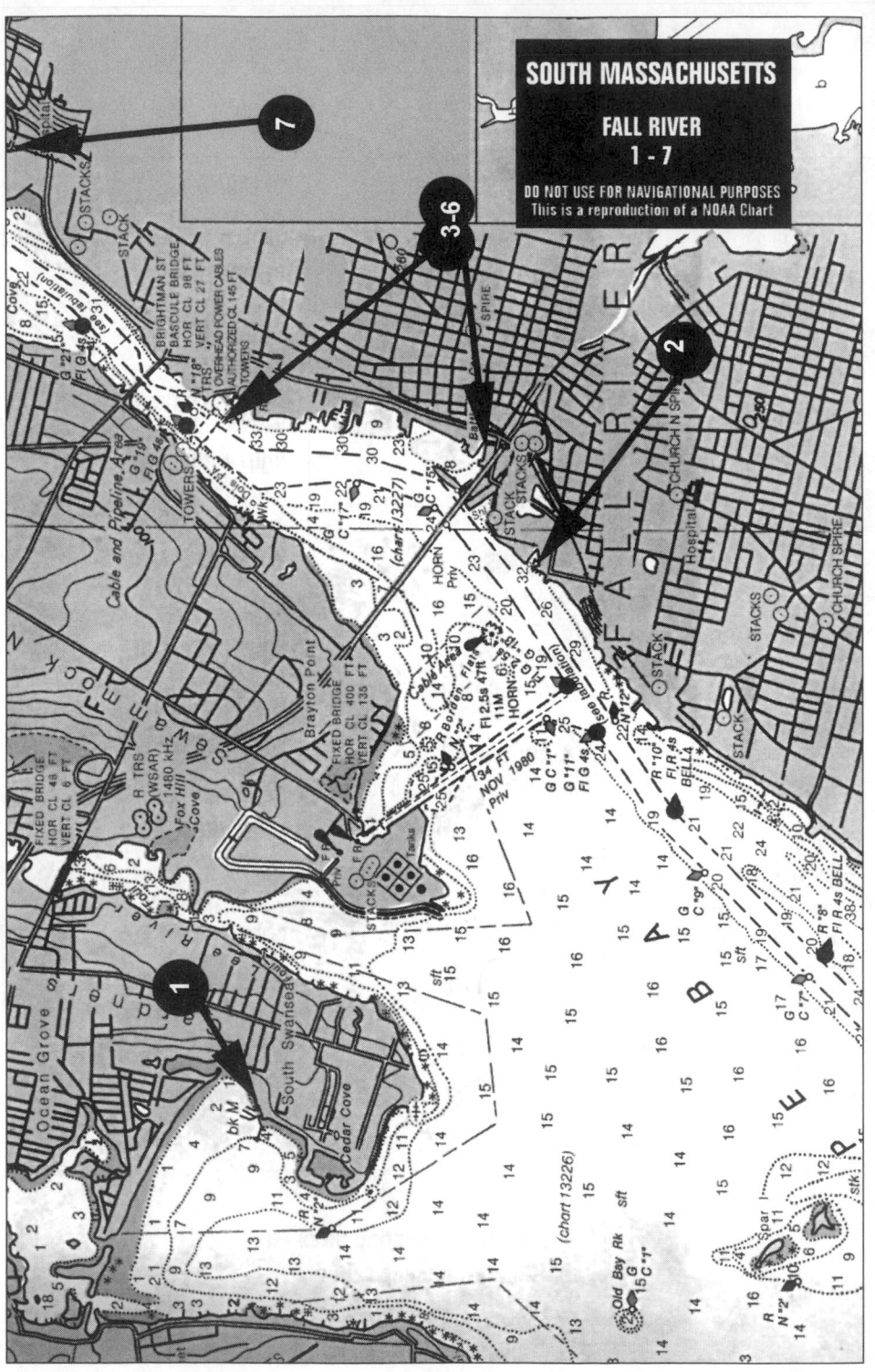

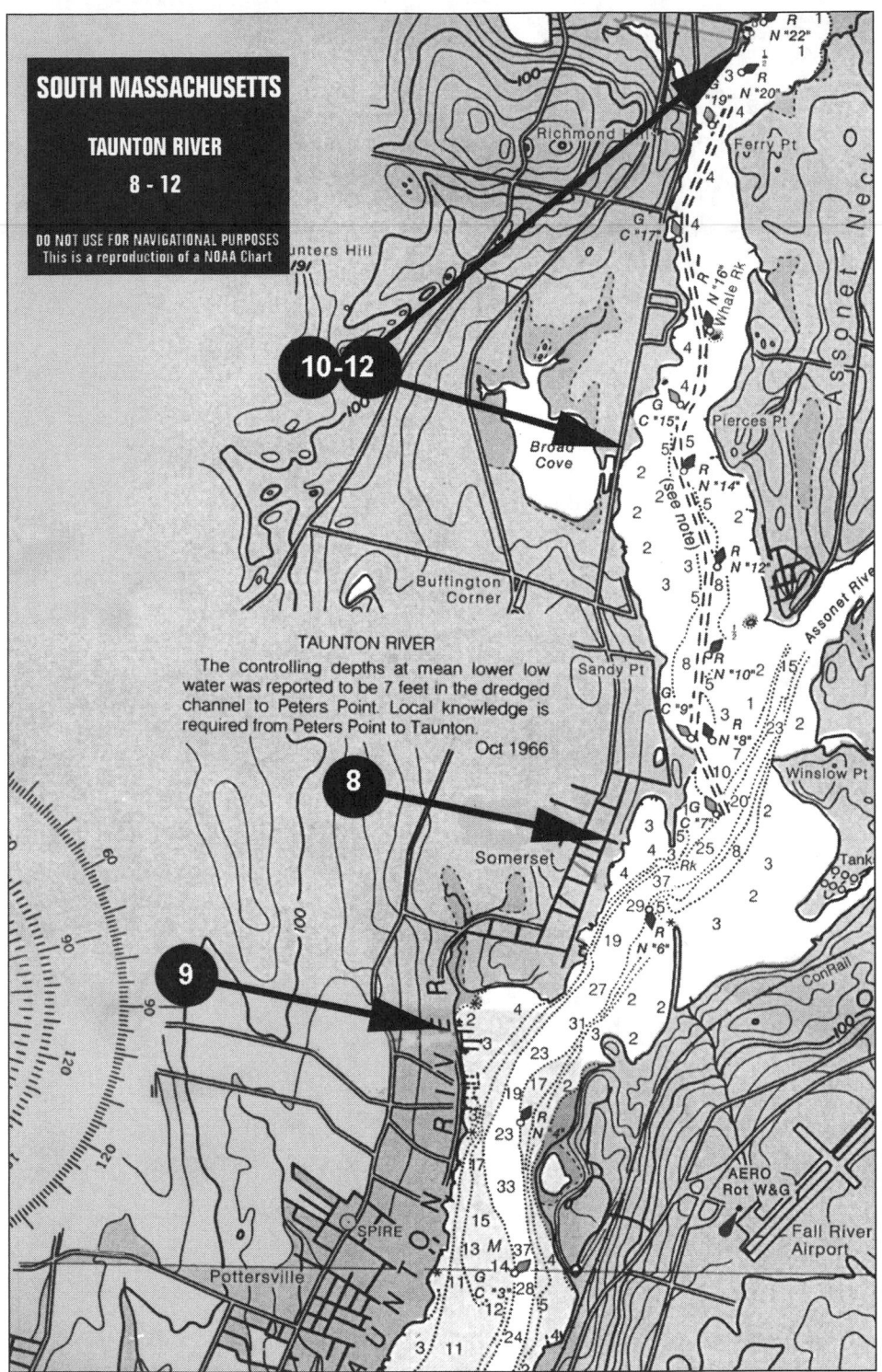

SOUTH MASSACHUSETTS

TAUNTON RIVER

8 - 12

DO NOT USE FOR NAVIGATIONAL PURPOSES
This is a reproduction of a NOAA Chart

TAUNTON RIVER
The controlling depths at mean lower low
water was reported to be 7 feet in the dredged
channel to Peters Point. Local knowledge is
required from Peters Point to Taunton.
Oct 1966

535

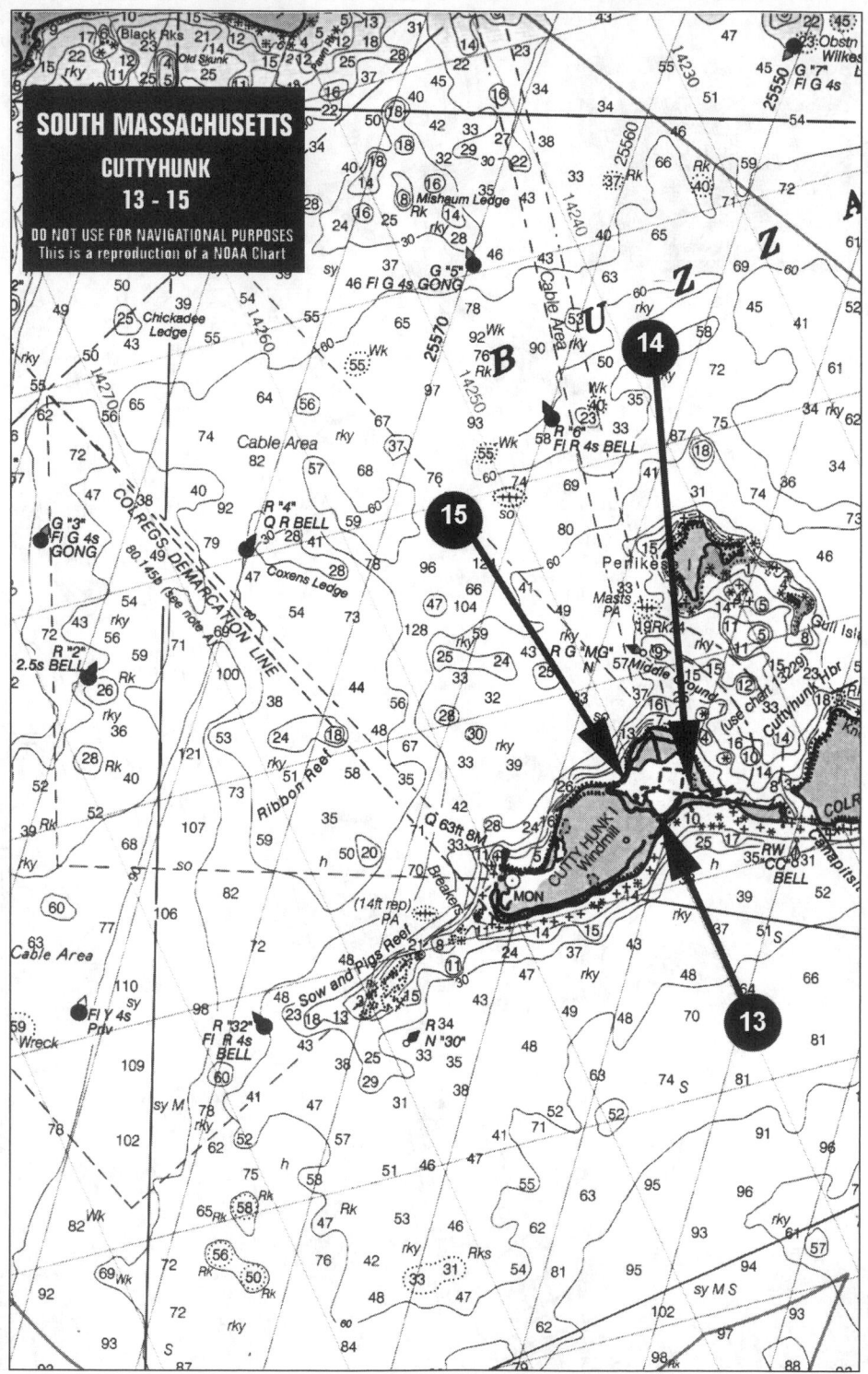

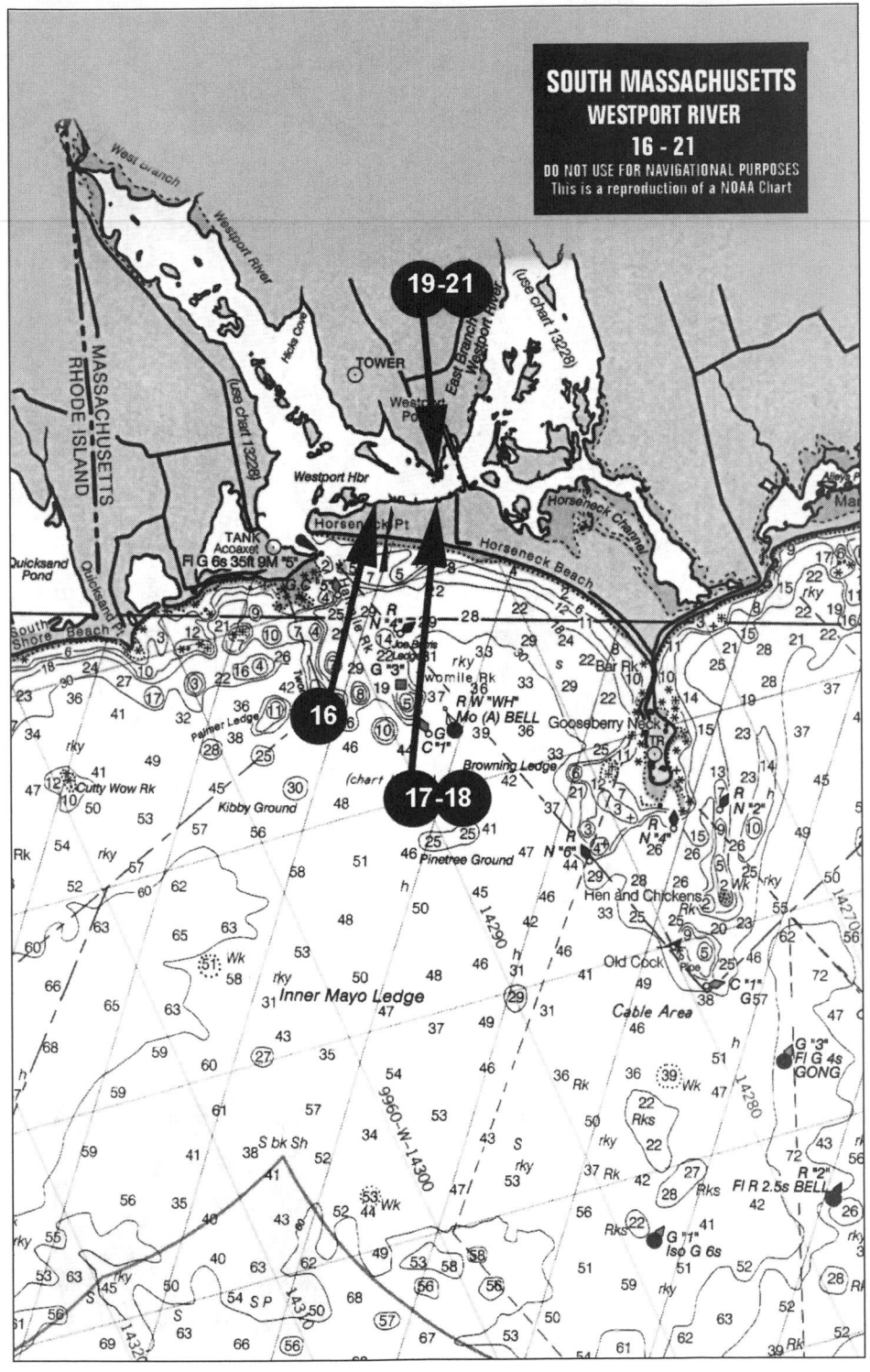

537

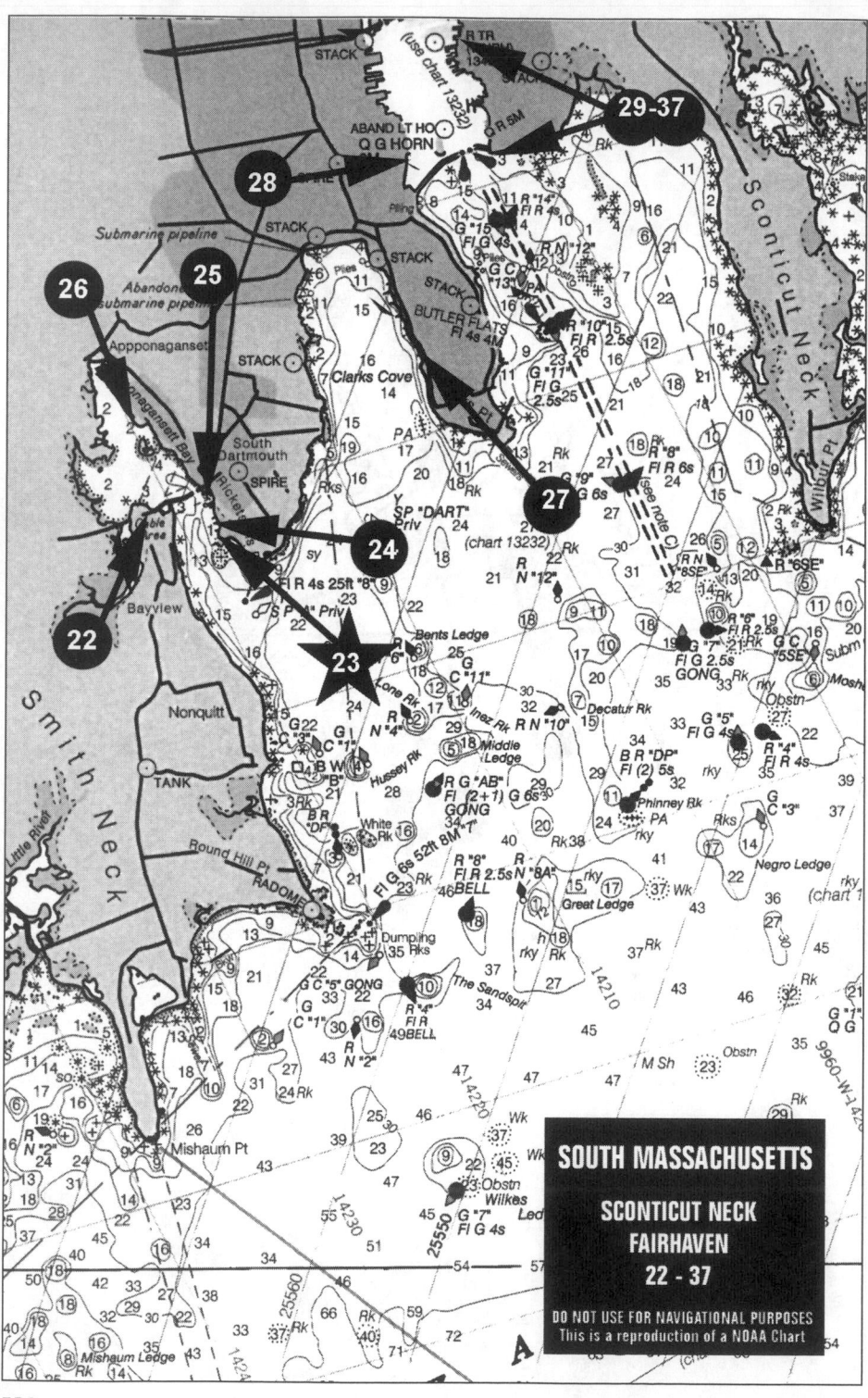

SOUTH MASSACHUSETTS

SCONTICUT NECK
FAIRHAVEN
22 - 37

DO NOT USE FOR NAVIGATIONAL PURPOSES
This is a reproduction of a NOAA Chart

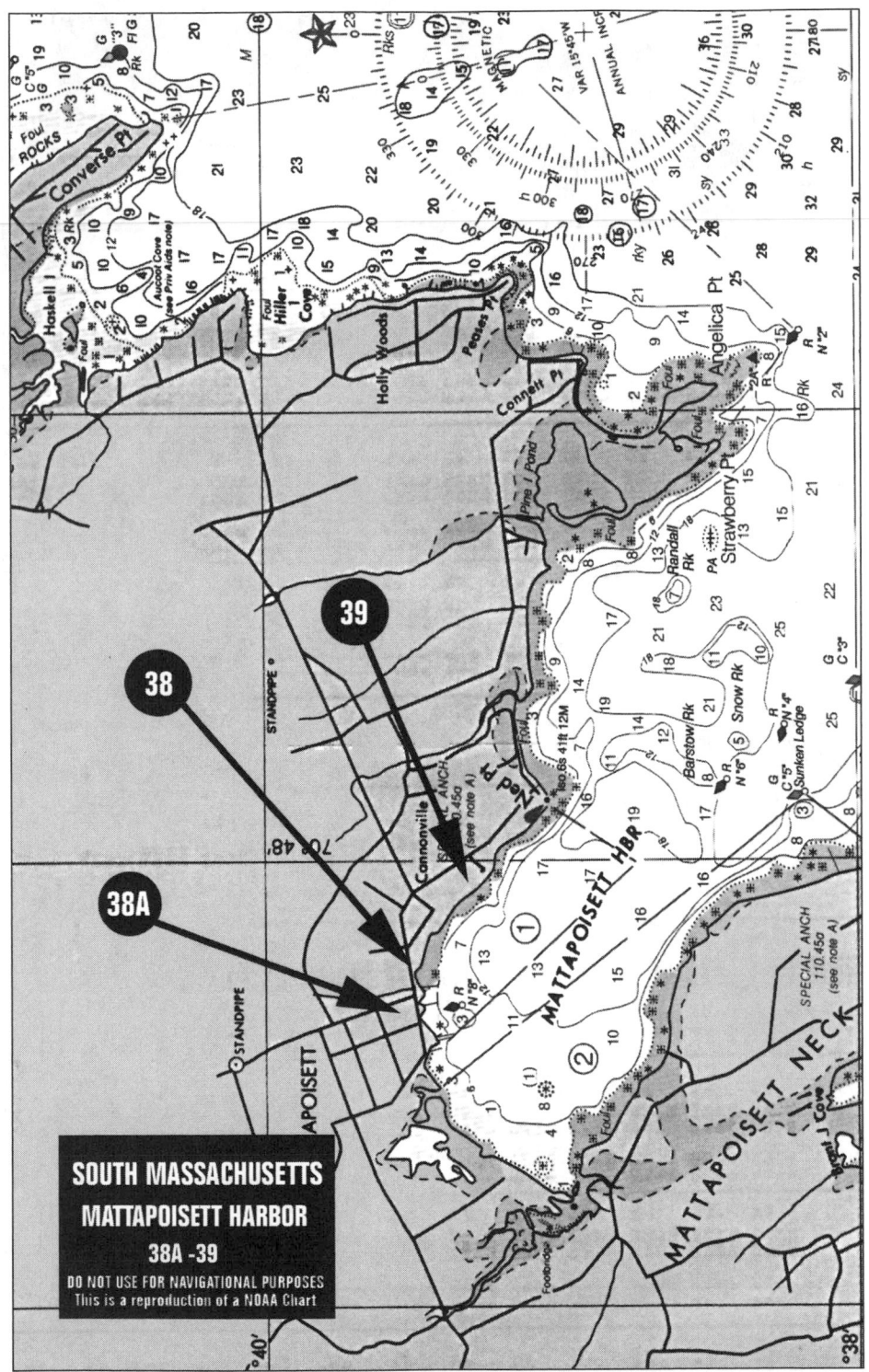

SOUTH MASSACHUSETTS
MATTAPOISETT HARBOR
38A -39
DO NOT USE FOR NAVIGATIONAL PURPOSES
This is a reproduction of a NOAA Chart

539

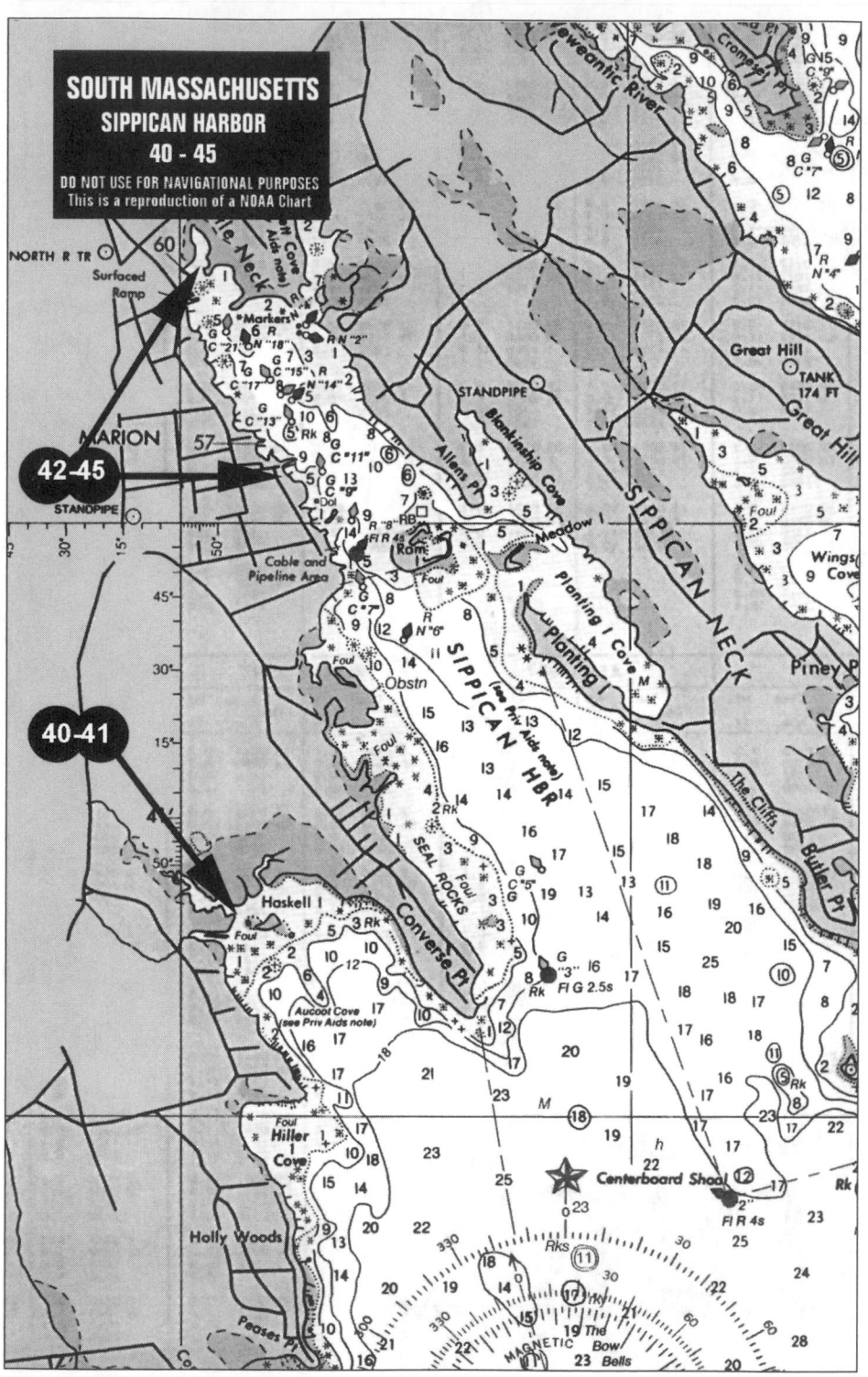

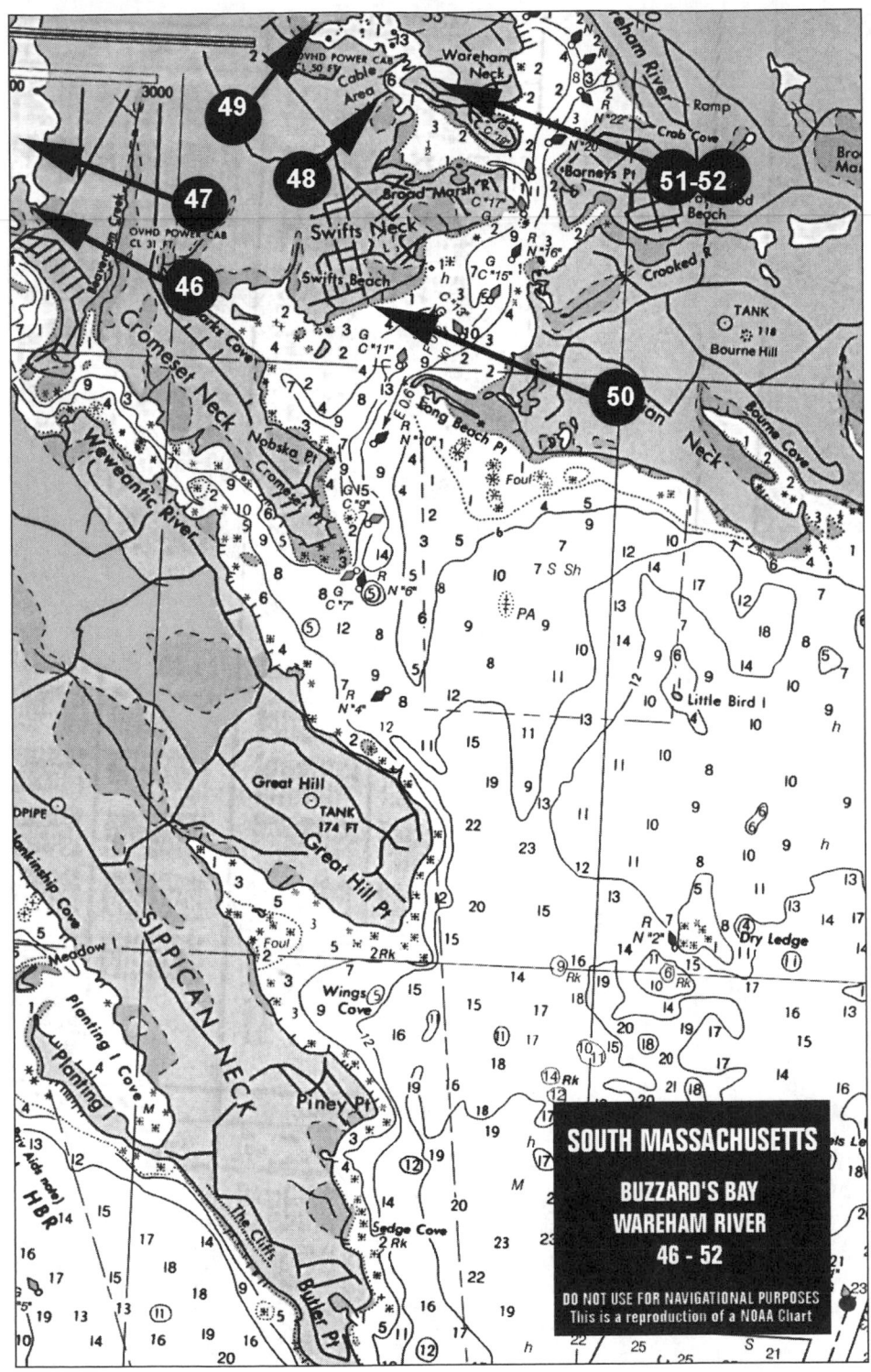

SOUTH MASSACHUSETTS

BUZZARD'S BAY
WAREHAM RIVER
46 - 52

DO NOT USE FOR NAVIGATIONAL PURPOSES
This is a reproduction of a NOAA Chart

541

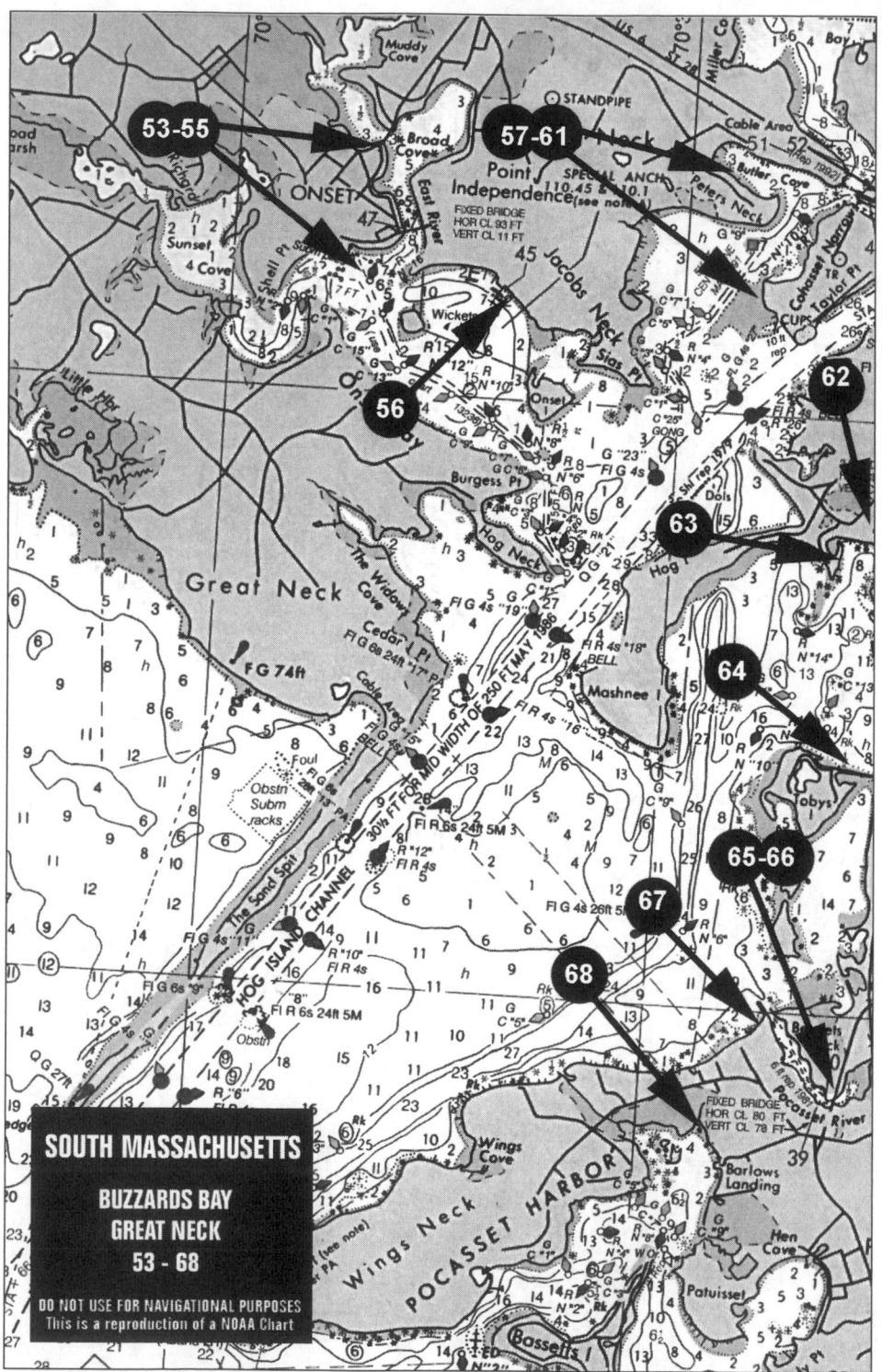

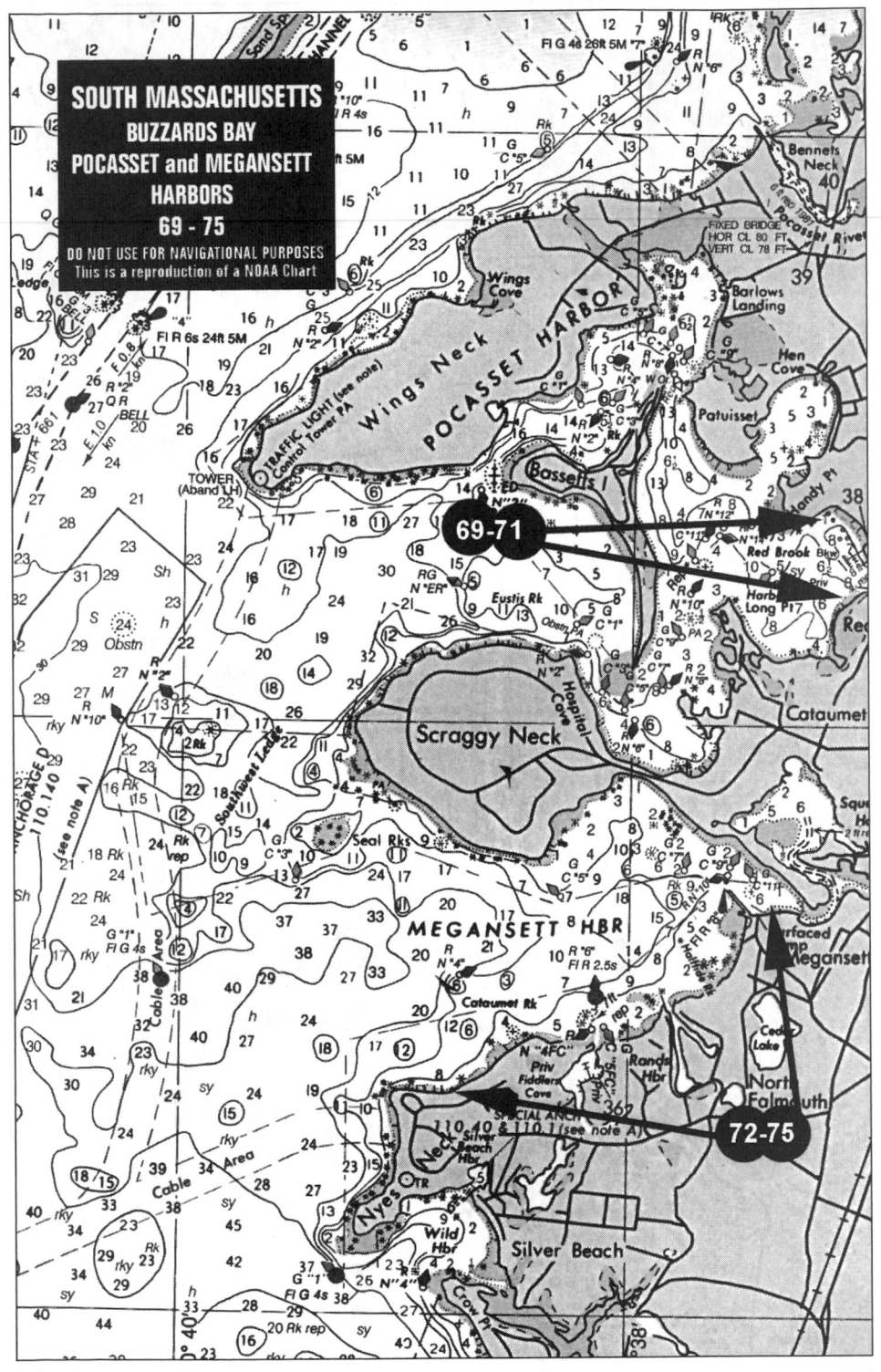

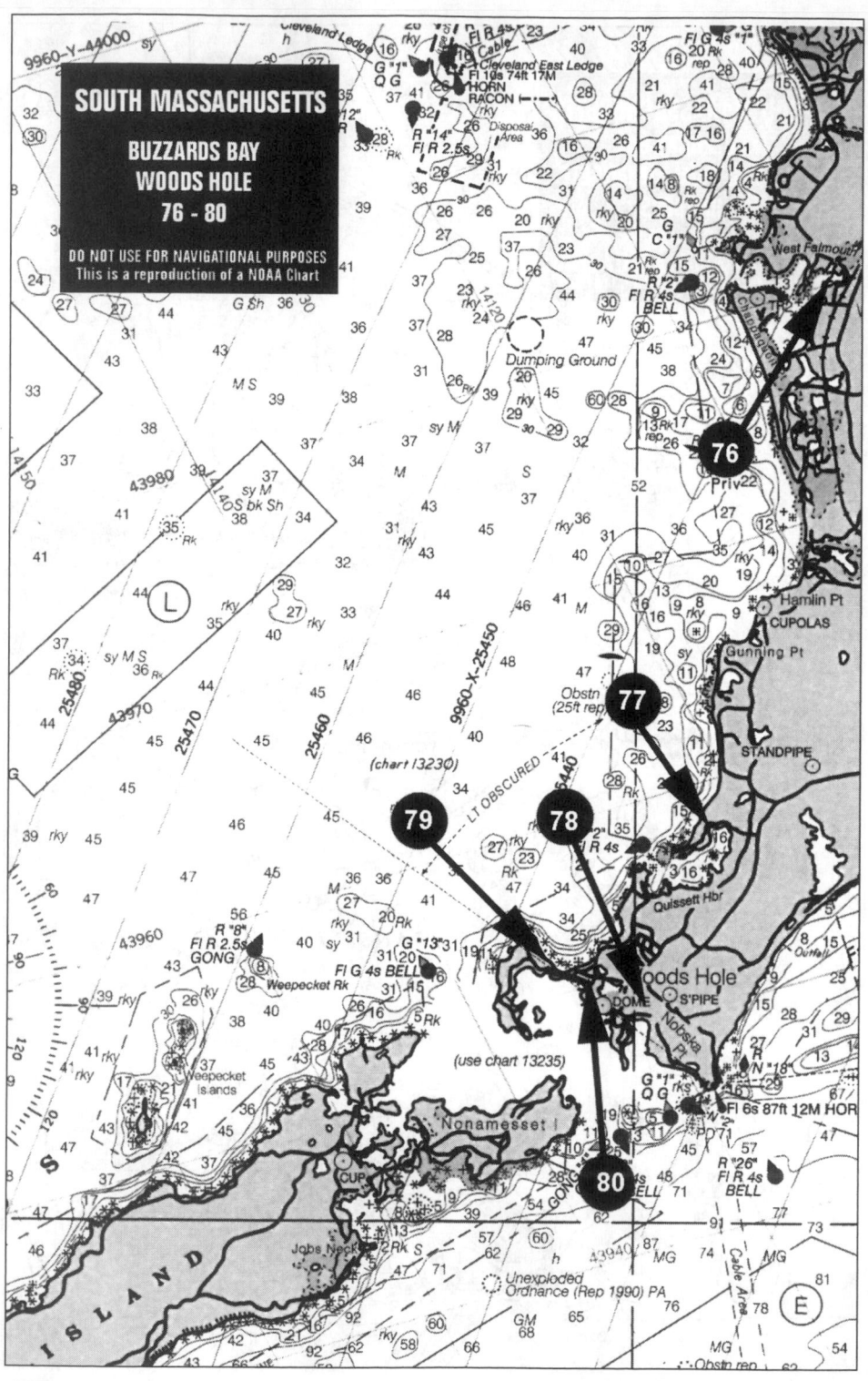

SOUTH MASSACHUSETTS

BUZZARDS BAY
WOODS HOLE
76 - 80

DO NOT USE FOR NAVIGATIONAL PURPOSES
This is a reproduction of a NOAA Chart

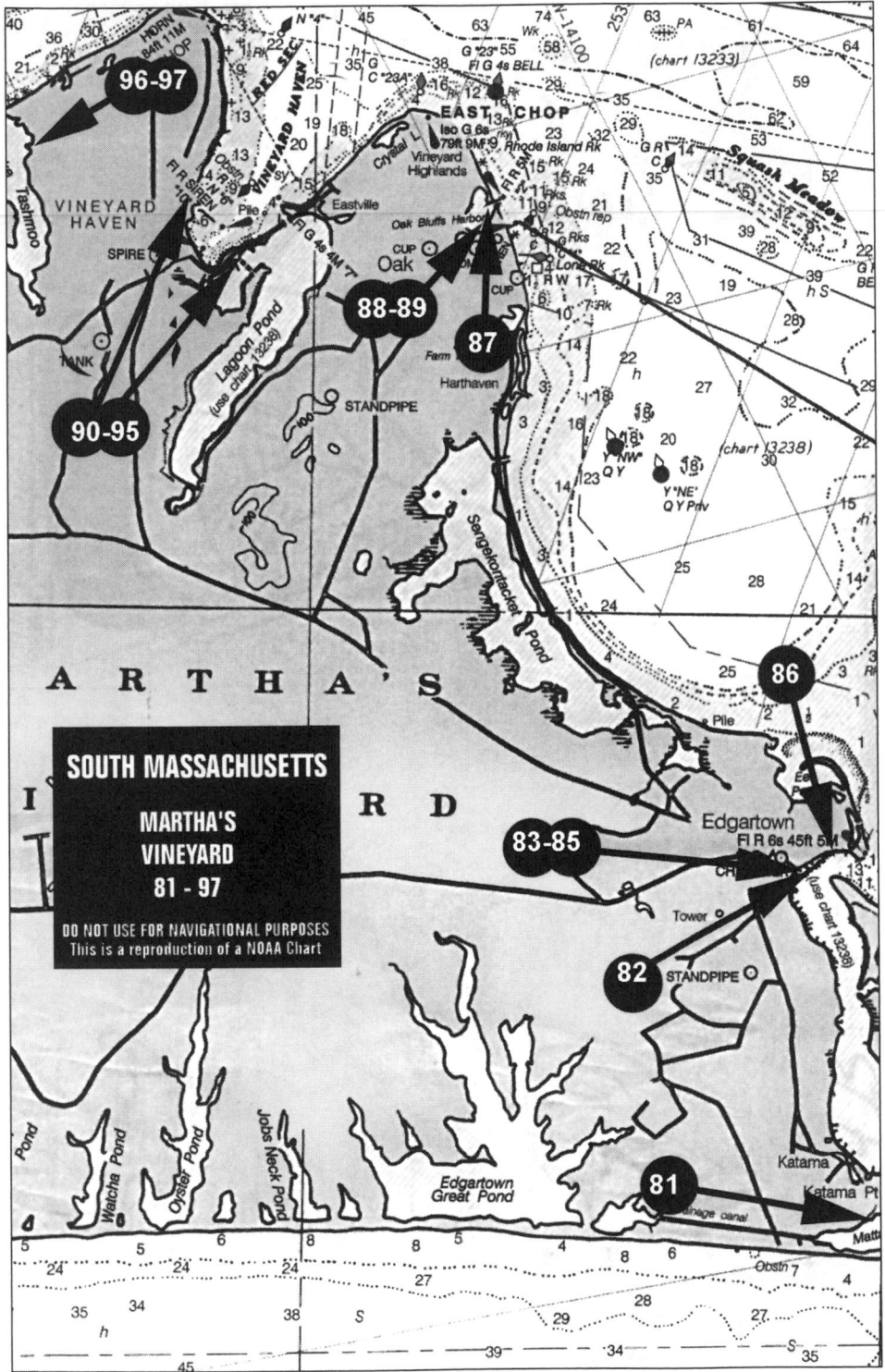

SOUTH MASSACHUSETTS

MARTHA'S
VINEYARD
81 - 97

DO NOT USE FOR NAVIGATIONAL PURPOSES
This is a reproduction of a NOAA Chart

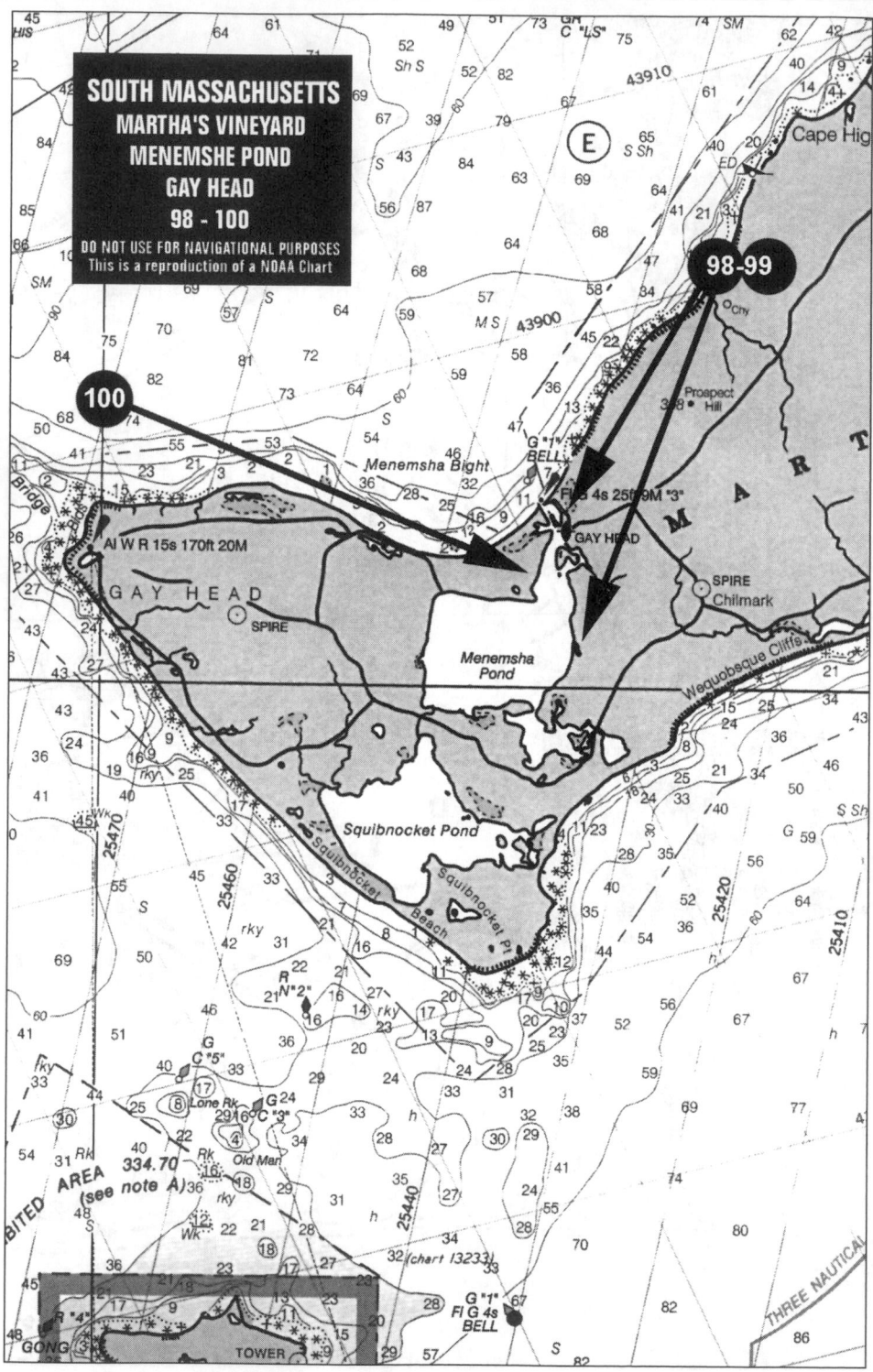

SOUTH MASSACHUSETTS
MARTHA'S VINEYARD
MENEMSHE POND
GAY HEAD
98 - 100

DO NOT USE FOR NAVIGATIONAL PURPOSES
This is a reproduction of a NOAA Chart

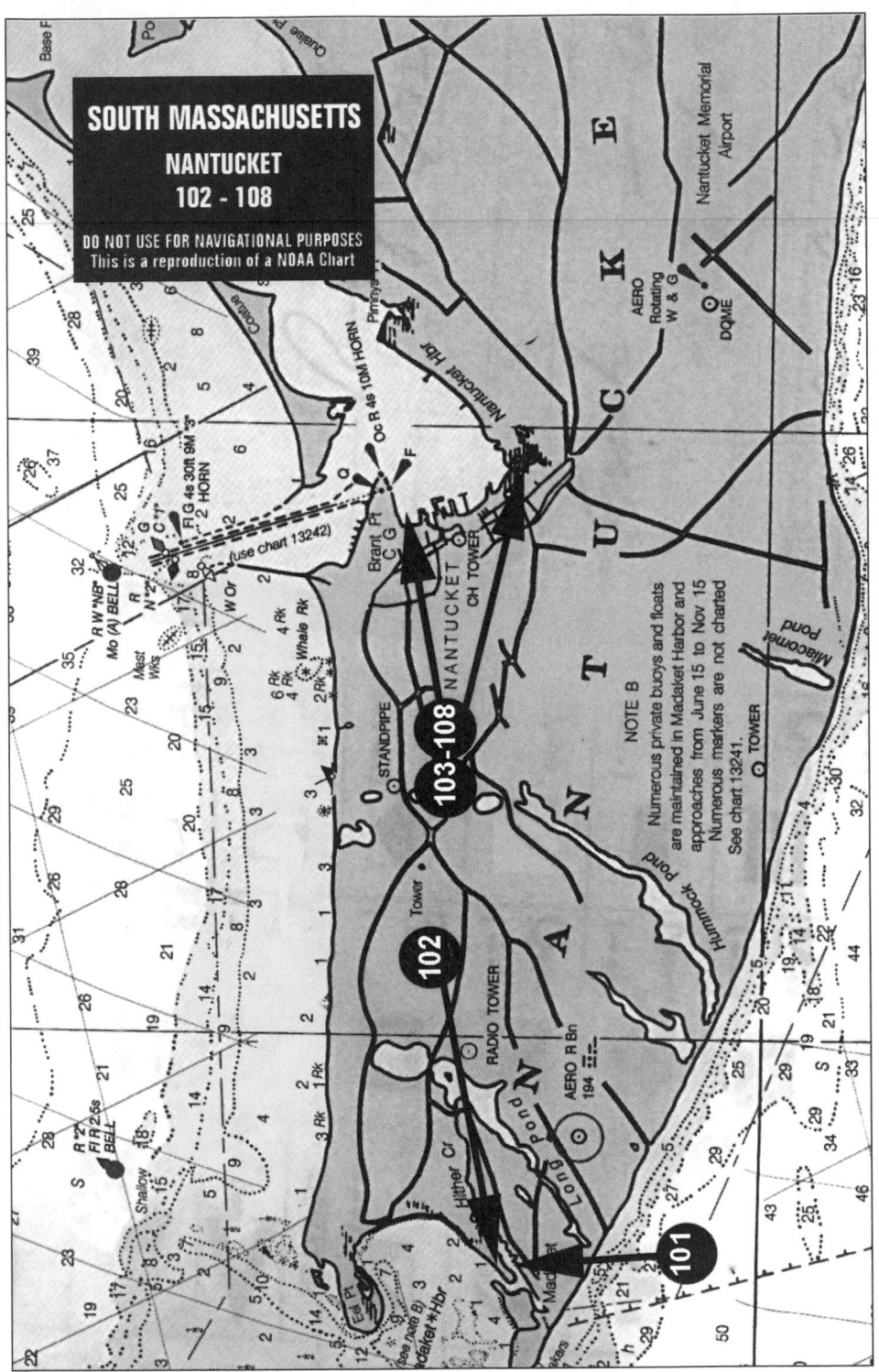

SOUTH MASSACHUSETTS

NANTUCKET

102 - 108

DO NOT USE FOR NAVIGATIONAL PURPOSES
This is a reproduction of a NOAA Chart

547

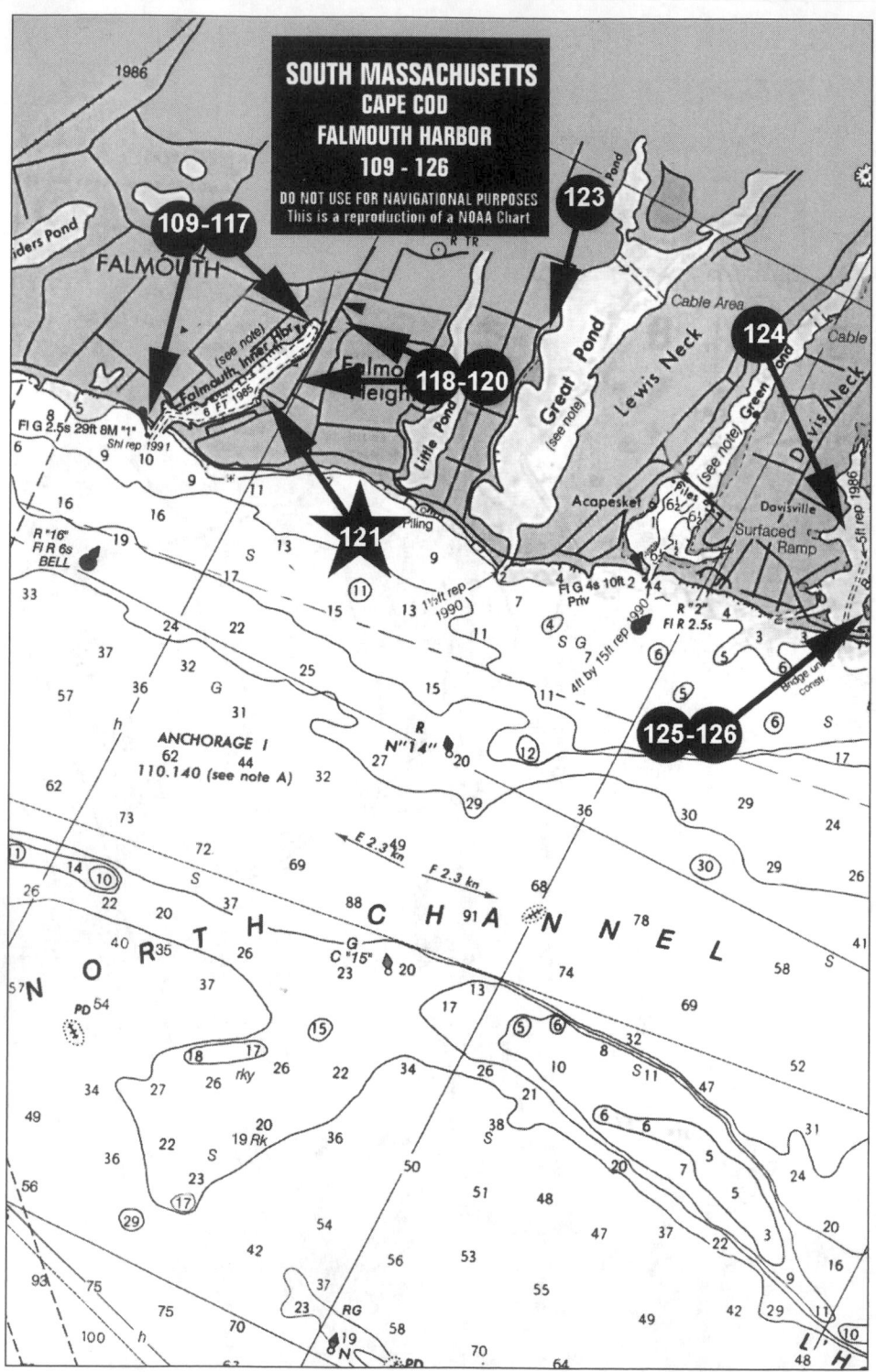

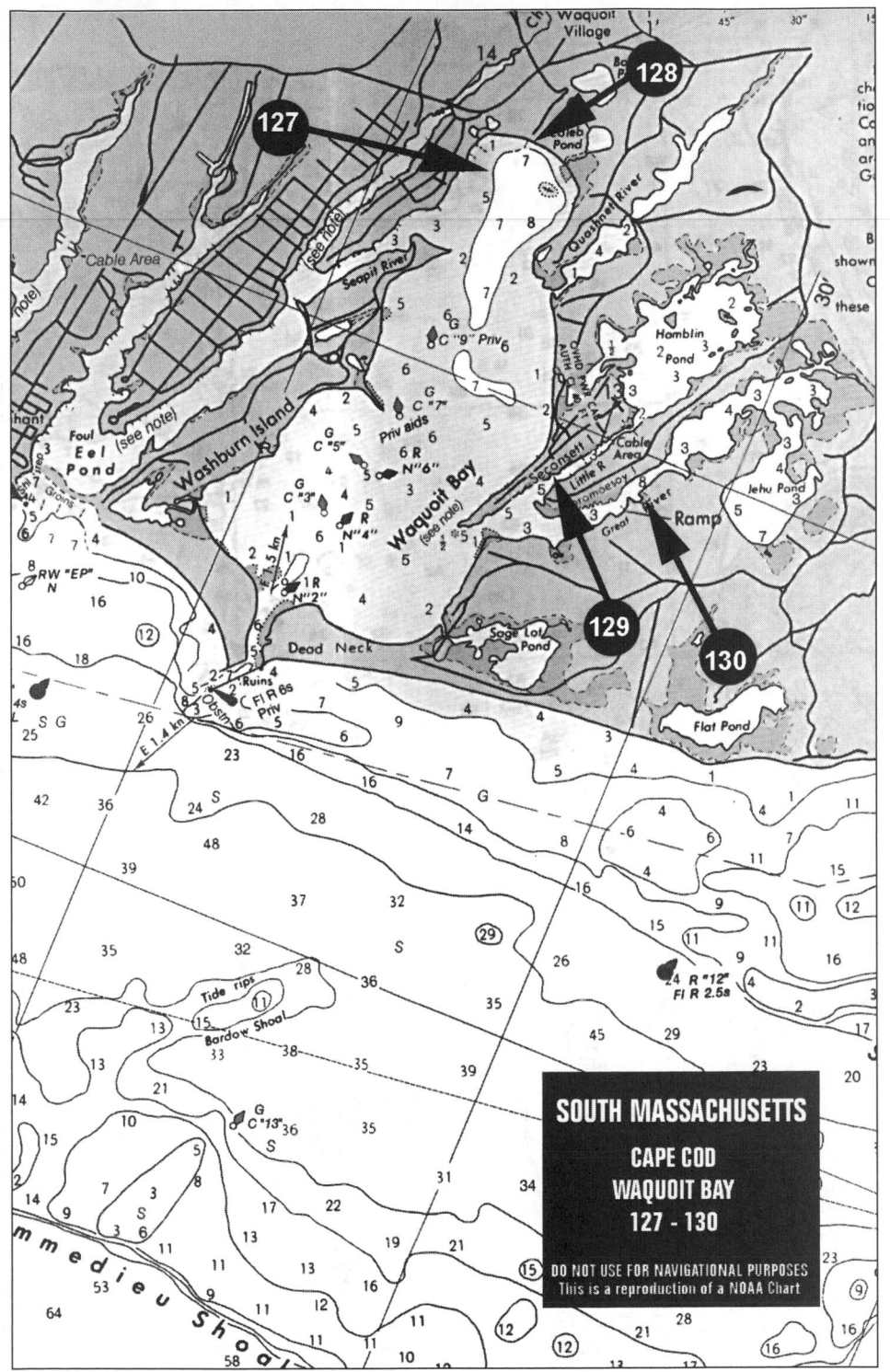

SOUTH MASSACHUSETTS
CAPE COD
WAQUOIT BAY
127 - 130

DO NOT USE FOR NAVIGATIONAL PURPOSES
This is a reproduction of a NOAA Chart

549

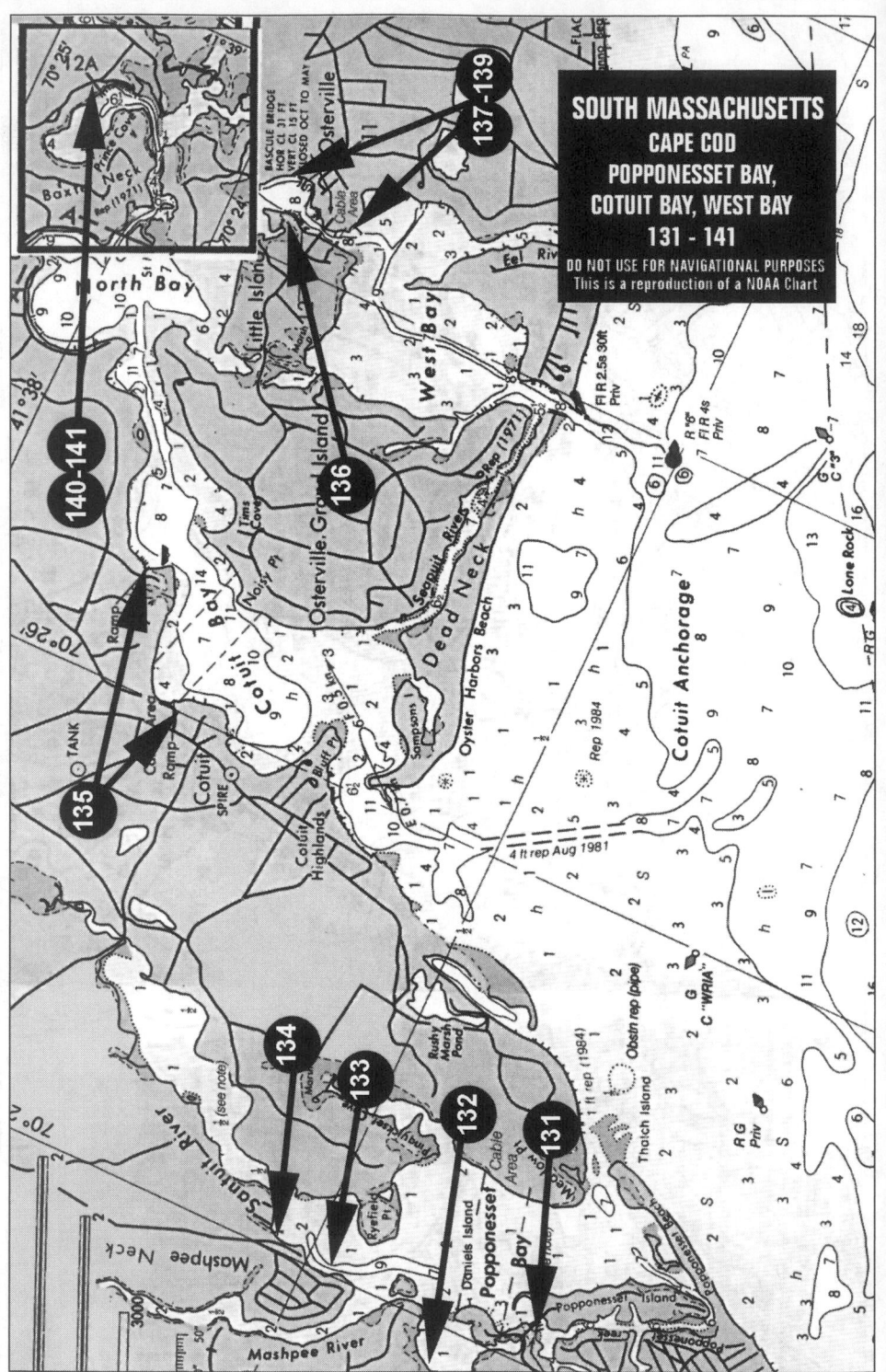

SOUTH MASSACHUSETTS
CAPE COD
POPPONESSET BAY,
COTUIT BAY, WEST BAY
131 - 141

DO NOT USE FOR NAVIGATIONAL PURPOSES
This is a reproduction of a NOAA Chart

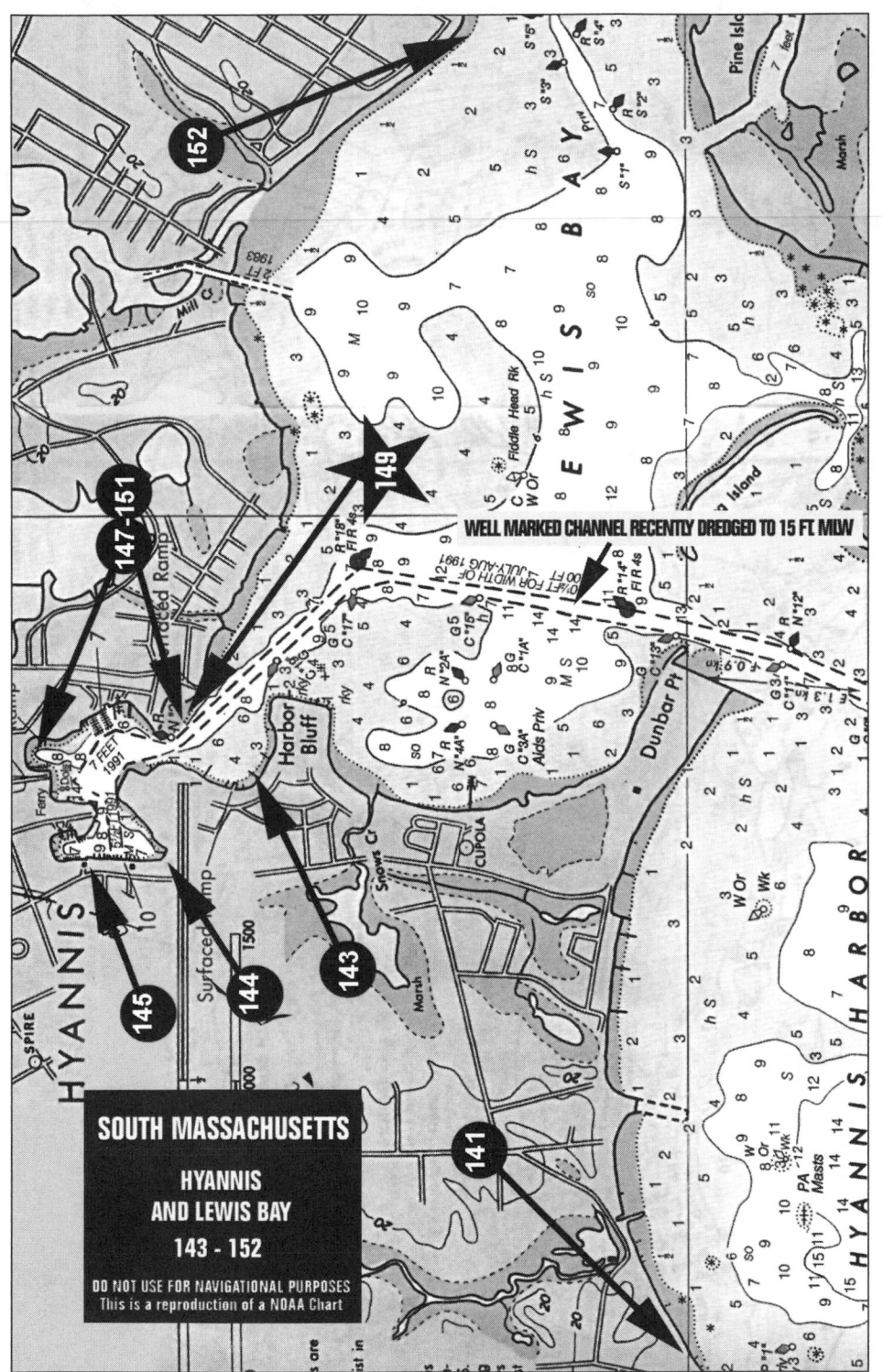

WELL MARKED CHANNEL RECENTLY DREDGED TO 15 FT MLW

SOUTH MASSACHUSETTS

HYANNIS
AND LEWIS BAY

143 - 152

DO NOT USE FOR NAVIGATIONAL PURPOSES
This is a reproduction of a NOAA Chart

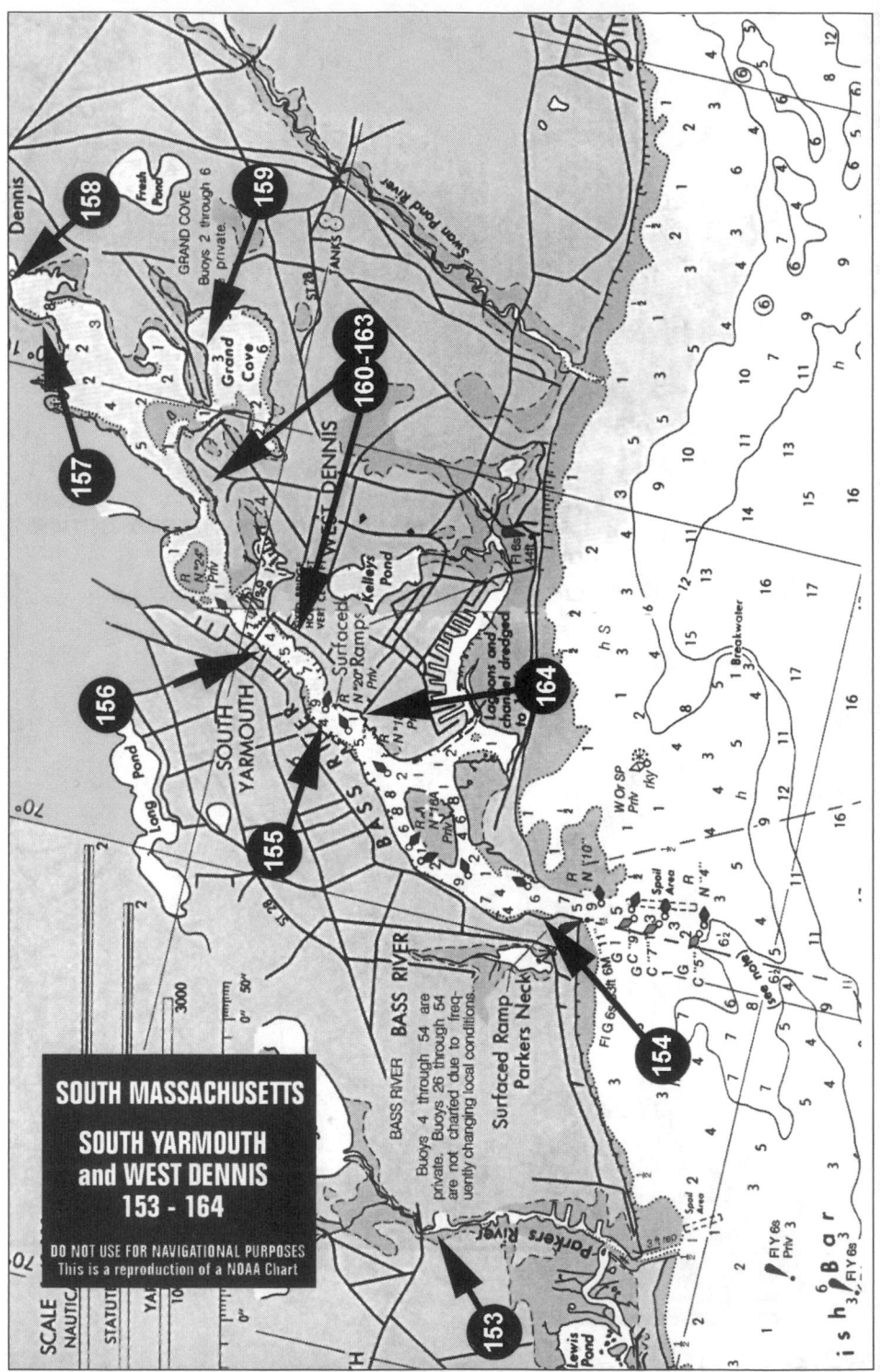

SOUTH MASSACHUSETTS

SOUTH YARMOUTH
and WEST DENNIS
153 - 164

DO NOT USE FOR NAVIGATIONAL PURPOSES
This is a reproduction of a NOAA Chart

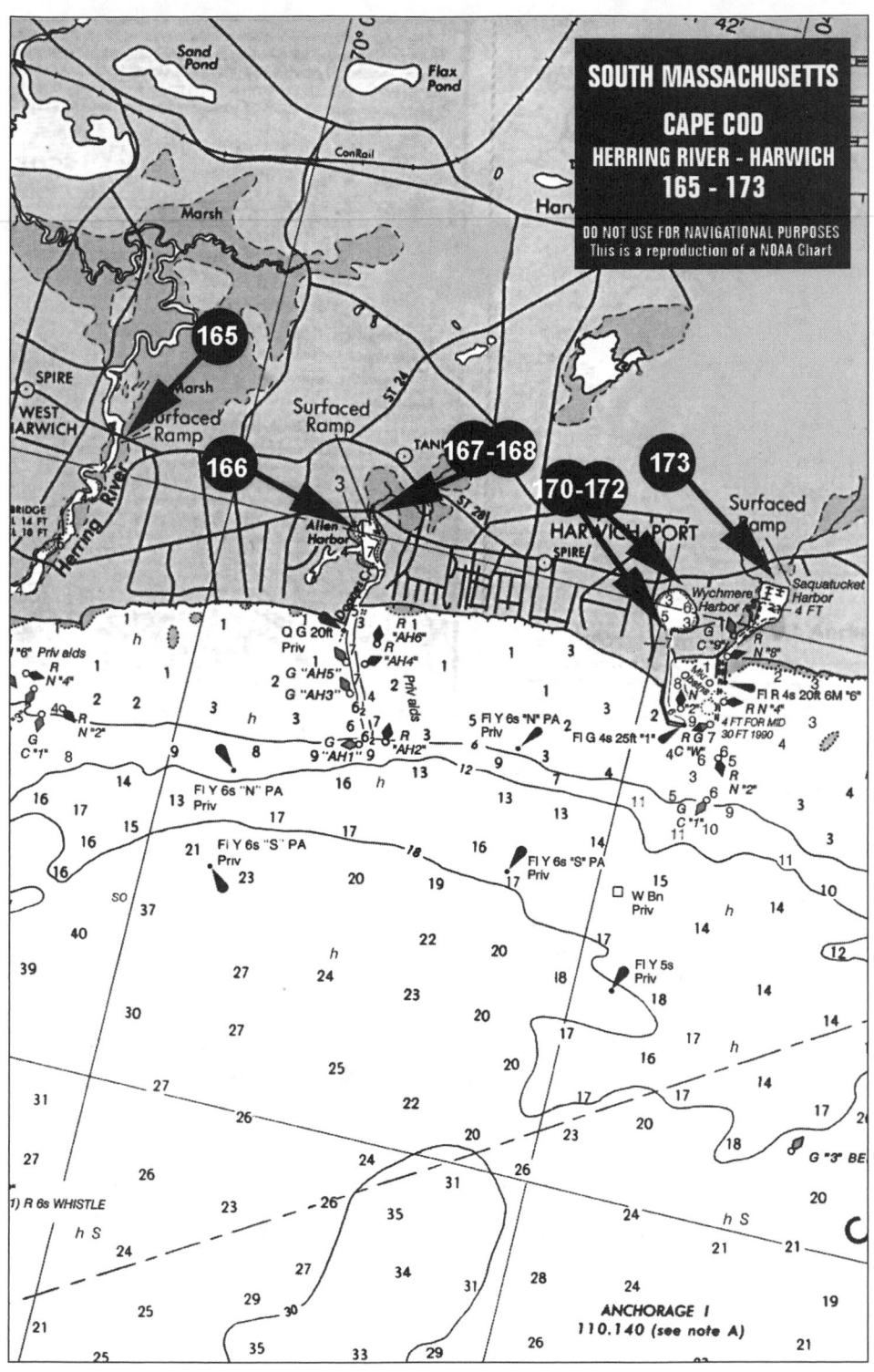

553

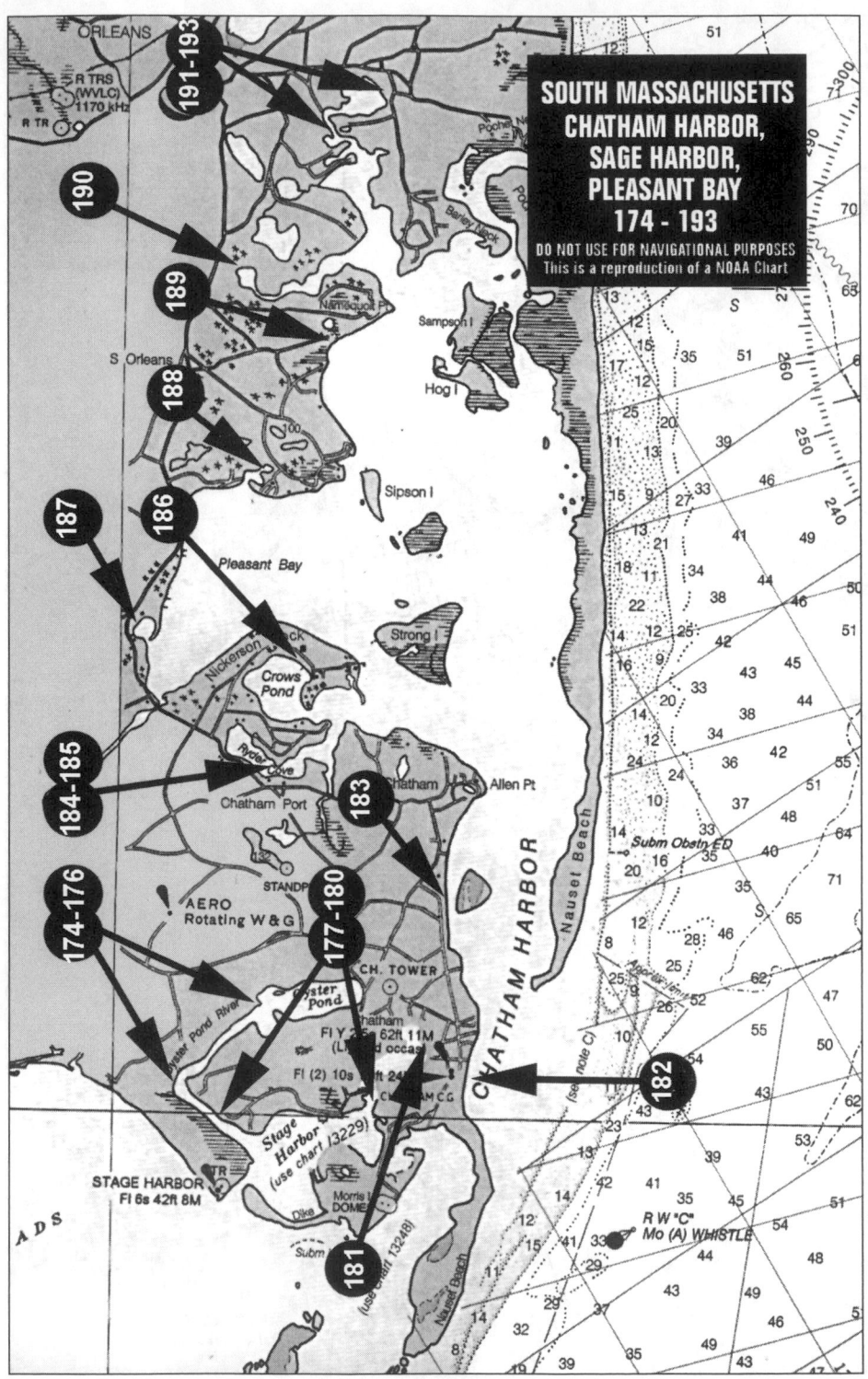

SOUTH MASSACHUSETTS
CHATHAM HARBOR,
SAGE HARBOR,
PLEASANT BAY
174 - 193
DO NOT USE FOR NAVIGATIONAL PURPOSES
This is a reproduction of a NOAA Chart

554

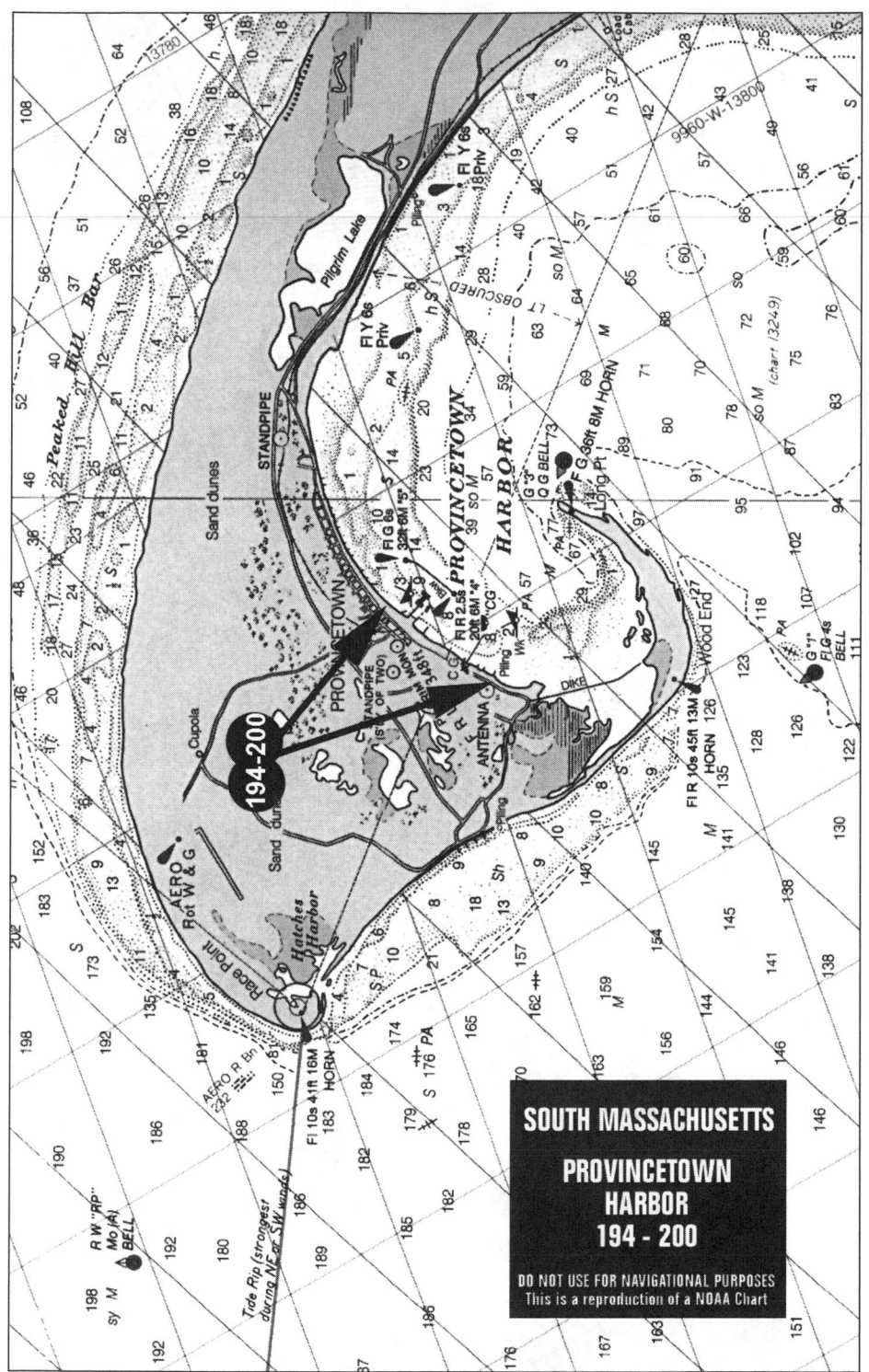

SOUTH MASSACHUSETTS

PROVINCETOWN HARBOR

194 - 200

DO NOT USE FOR NAVIGATIONAL PURPOSES
This is a reproduction of a NOAA Chart

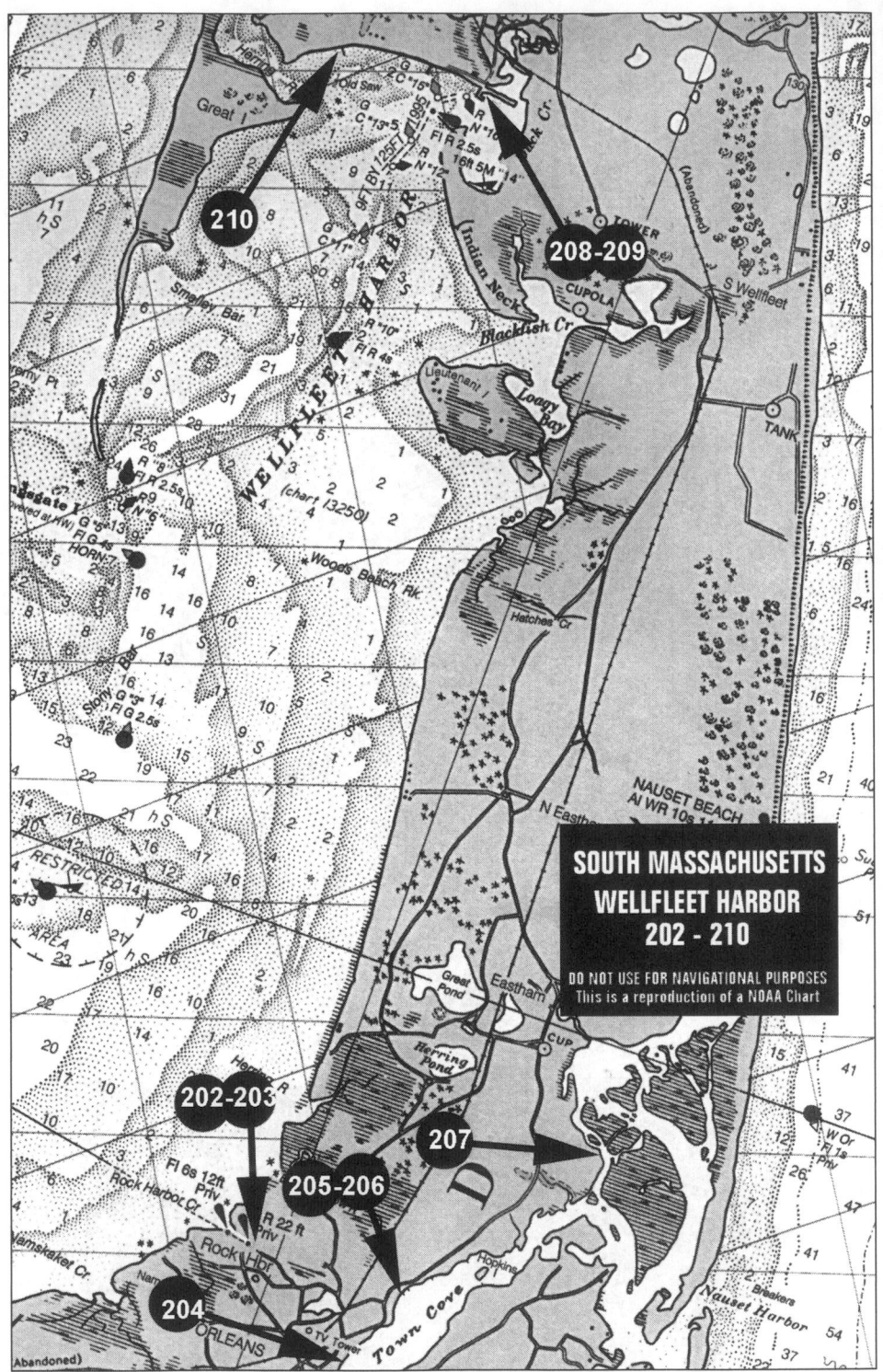

SOUTH MASSACHUSETTS
WELLFLEET HARBOR
202 - 210

DO NOT USE FOR NAVIGATIONAL PURPOSES
This is a reproduction of a NOAA Chart

210

208-209

202-203

207

205-206

204

556

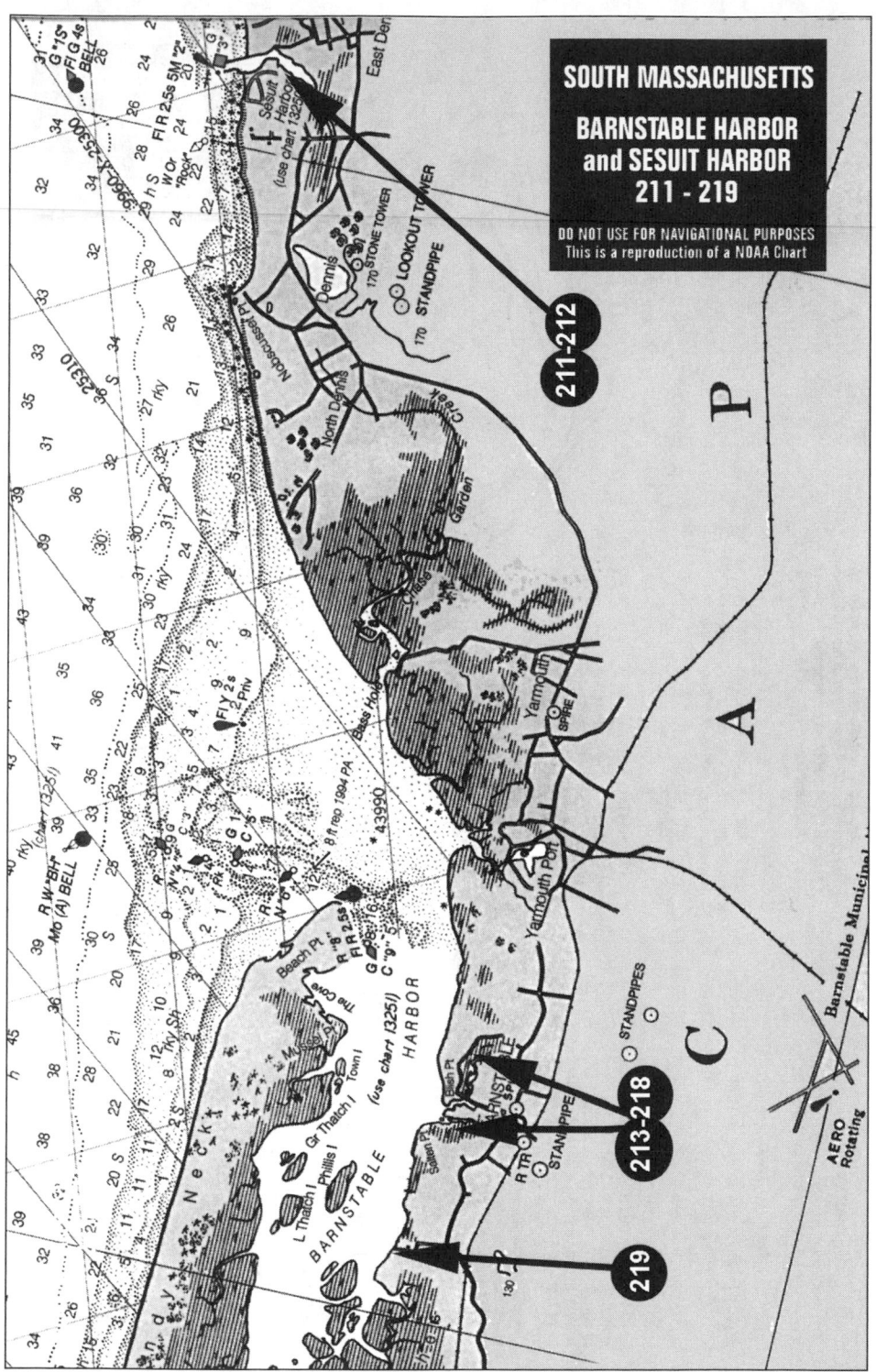

SOUTH MASSACHUSETTS

BARNSTABLE HARBOR
and SESUIT HARBOR
211 - 219

DO NOT USE FOR NAVIGATIONAL PURPOSES
This is a reproduction of a NOAA Chart

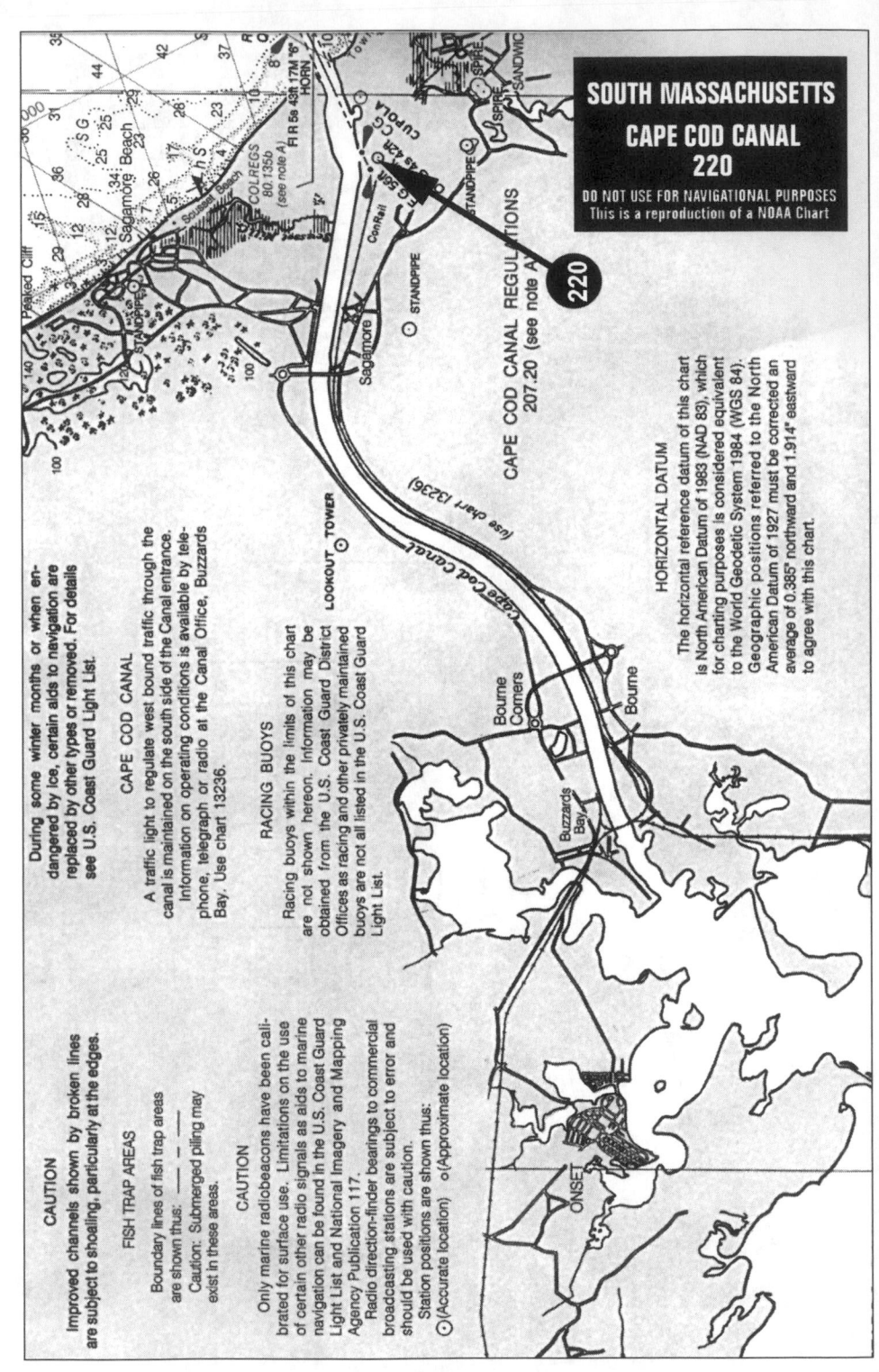

SOUTH MASSACHUSETTS
CAPE COD CANAL
220

DO NOT USE FOR NAVIGATIONAL PURPOSES
This is a reproduction of a NOAA Chart

CAUTION

Improved channels shown by broken lines are subject to shoaling, particularly at the edges.

FISH TRAP AREAS

Boundary lines of fish trap areas are shown thus: — — — —
Caution: Submerged piling may exist in these areas.

CAUTION

Only marine radiobeacons have been calibrated for surface use. Limitations on the use of certain other radio signals as aids to marine navigation can be found in the U.S. Coast Guard Light List and National Imagery and Mapping Agency Publication 117.

Radio direction-finder bearings to commercial broadcasting stations are subject to error and should be used with caution.

Station positions are shown thus:
⊙(Accurate location)   o(Approximate location)

During some winter months or when endangered by ice, certain aids to navigation are replaced by other types or removed. For details see U.S. Coast Guard Light List.

CAPE COD CANAL

A traffic light to regulate west bound traffic through the canal is maintained on the south side of the Canal entrance.

Information on operating conditions is available by telephone, telegraph or radio at the Canal Office, Buzzards Bay. Use chart 13236.

RACING BUOYS

Racing buoys within the limits of this chart are not shown hereon. Information may be obtained from the U.S. Coast Guard District Offices as racing and other privately maintained buoys are not all listed in the U.S. Coast Guard Light List.

CAPE COD CANAL REGULATIONS
207.20 (see note A)

HORIZONTAL DATUM

The horizontal reference datum of this chart is North American Datum of 1983 (NAD 83), which for charting purposes is considered equivalent to the World Geodetic System 1984 (WGS 84). Geographic positions referred to the North American Datum of 1927 must be corrected an average of 0.385" northward and 1.914" eastward to agree with this chart.

558

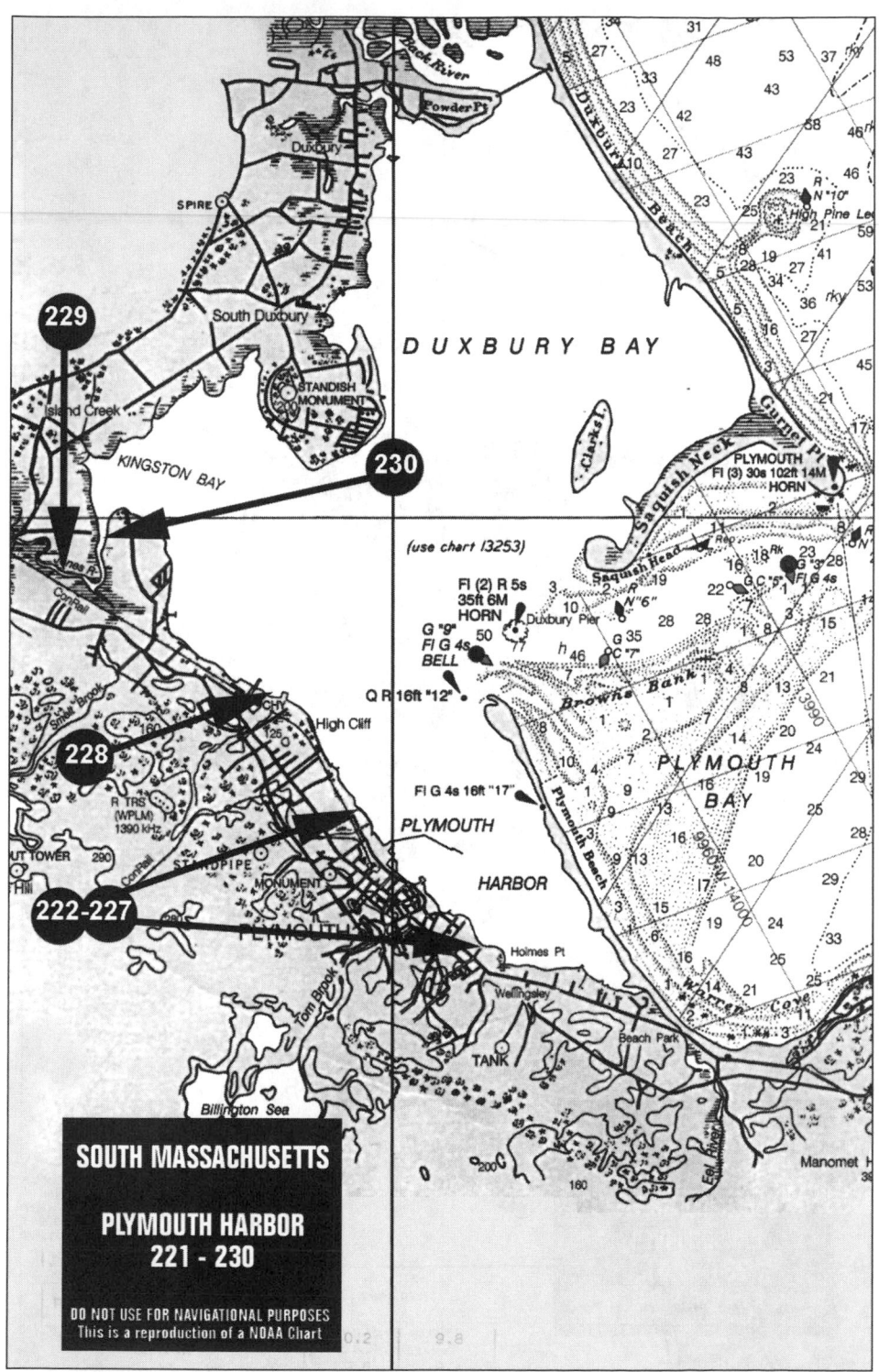

D U X B U R Y   B A Y

KINGSTON BAY

Island Creek

South Duxbury

SPIRE

Duxbury

Powder Pt

Back River

STANDISH MONUMENT

Clark I.

Saquish Neck

PLYMOUTH
Fl (3) 30s 102ft 14M
HORN

High Pine Le

Gurnet Pt

R
N "10"

Saquish Head

(use chart 13253)

Fl (2) R 5s
35ft 6M
HORN

Duxbury Pier

N "6"

G "9"
Fl G 4s
BELL

G 35
OC "7"

Q R 16ft "12"

Browns Bank

P L Y M O U T H

B A Y

Fl G 4s 16ft "17"

Plymouth Beach

PLYMOUTH

HARBOR

High Cliff

R TRS
(WPLM)
1390 kHz

UT TOWER

STANDPIPE

MONUMENT

PLYMOUTH

Tom Brook

Smelt Brook

Holmes Pt

Wellingsley

TANK

Beach Park

Warren Cove

Eel River

Manomet H

Billington Sea

229

230

228

222-227

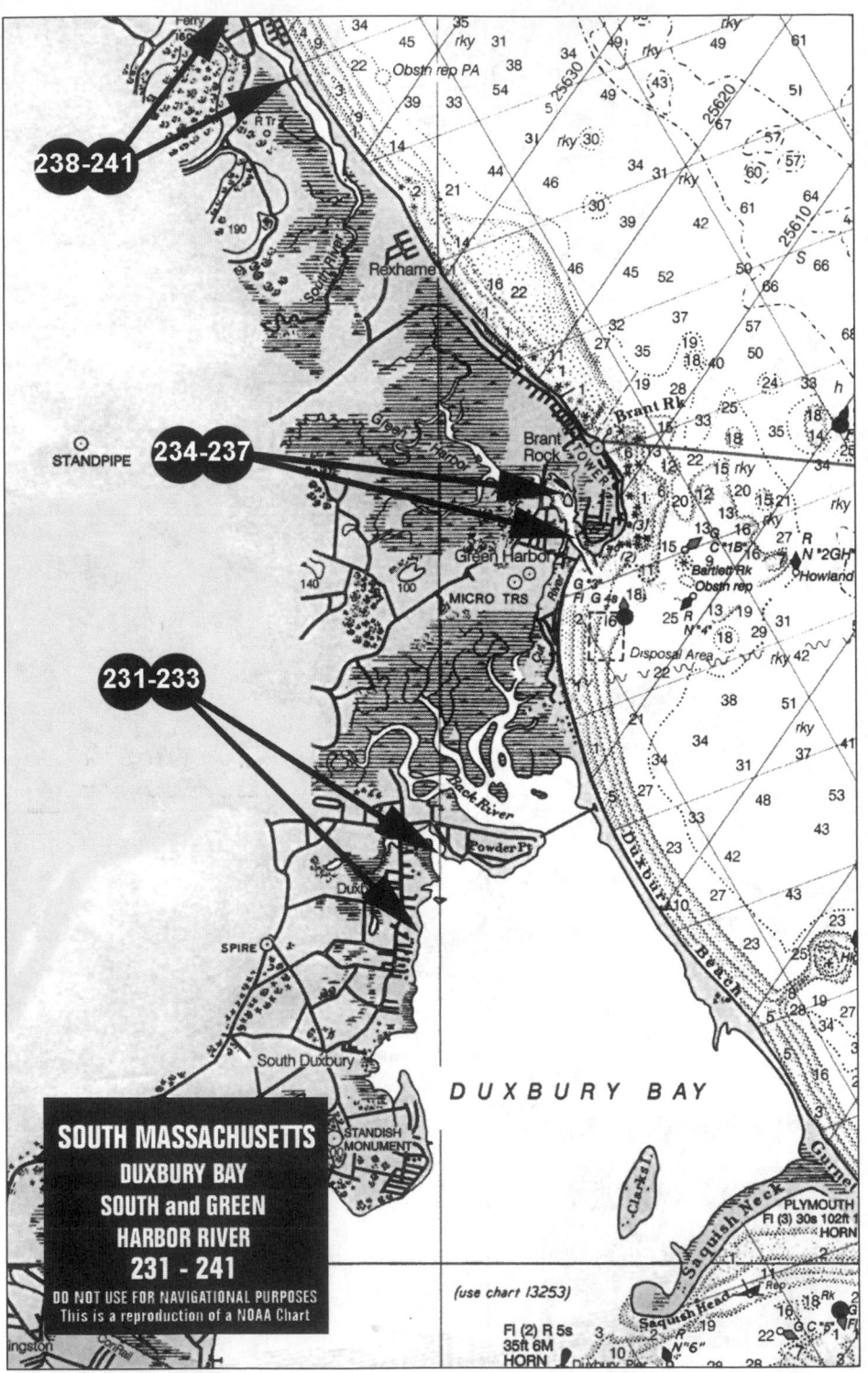

238-241

234-237

231-233

STANDPIPE

SOUTH MASSACHUSETTS
DUXBURY BAY
SOUTH and GREEN
HARBOR RIVER
231 - 241
DO NOT USE FOR NAVIGATIONAL PURPOSES
This is a reproduction of a NOAA Chart

DUXBURY BAY

(use chart 13253)

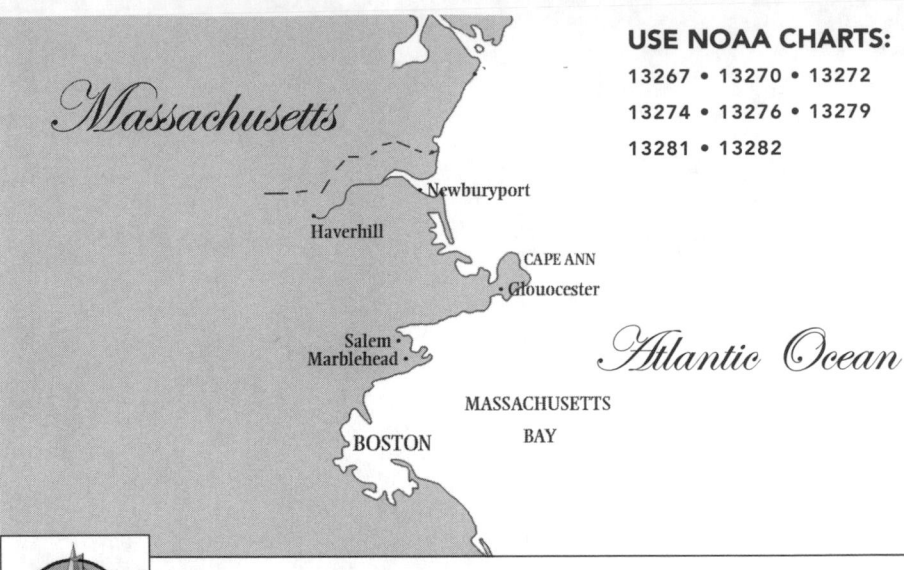

Massachusetts

Newburyport

Haverhill

CAPE ANN
Glouocester

Salem •
Marblehead •

Atlantic Ocean

MASSACHUSETTS
BAY

BOSTON

Massachusetts: BOSTON and NORTH

Map is not intended for navigational purposes.

THE FOLLOWING REGIONS ARE COVERED IN CHARTS IN THIS SECTION:

Cruising Massachusetts:
BOSTON and NORTH

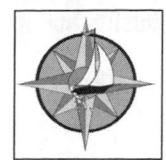

CHARTS 13282, 13274. The **MERRIMACK RIVER** is the largest river in the eastern part of Massachusetts and the approach to the cities of **NEWBURYPORT** and **HAVERHILL**, and the towns of Amesbury, Merrimacport, Groveland, and Bradford. Six-foot draft can travel at high water up to Haverhill and about 12-foot draft at high water to Newburyport. The river is seldom entered for refuge and has virtually no commercial traffic. The shifting bar at the entrance is dangerous to cross in heavy weather. The whole entrance breaks in easterly gales. A lighted fairway whistle buoy, about 1 mile off the jetties marks the approach. The channel leads through the bar between two jetties. The Coast Guard has installed a "rough bar advisory sign" — a white diamond shaped sign with international orange border and a a flashing white light which is activated when the seas here are deemed hazardous for small boats. Calling the Coast Guard (VHF 16 or 978-465-0731) for information before entering is advised.

The **Merri-Mar Yacht Basin**, in Newburyport (3 NM miles above the river entrance), caters to both sail and power from 25-ft. to 60 ft. in length for haul-out, and up to 100-ft in transient dockage. Owned and operated by the same family for 52 years, this professional, full-service marina is the perfect place to stop for any services needed — especially engine work — when headed up or down the coast. Visiting boaters will enjoy this historic seaport with its saltbox and Victorian houses, Federal mansions and colonial homes, the shipyards and a walking tour along the Merrimac River that takes you to the Custom House Maritime Museum highlighting the town as a major 19th C. shipbuilding and seaport. The folks at Merri-Mar will give you a lift to town or you can easily make it on foot.

PLUM ISLAND is an 11 mile long barrier island off the shore of Newburyport, with seaside homes, the Parker River Wildlife Refuge, home to over 800 species of birds, plants and animals, small shops and restaurants and miles of sandy beaches.

PLUM ISLAND SOUND the approach to several small rivers is frequented by many small craft. The Bar Channel at the entrance to the sound is subject to continual changes. The entrance is marked by a seasonal lighted bell buoy. The buoys on the bar are not charted because they are frequently shifted in position. The buoys marking the channels across the bar and through the sound and rivers inside are seasonal.

CHARTS 13282, 13279, 13274. **IPSWICH BAY** is the bight between the northern point of **CAPE ANN** and the south end of **PLUM ISLAND**. Between these points it is about 6 miles wide. The bay is the approach to Plum Island Sound and to the Essex and Annisquam Rivers. It has depths of 20 to 70 feet, except in its southern and southwestern sides where the shore should be given a berth of a little over 1-mile to avoid the shoals off the river entrances. Several rocks, covered 2 to 5 feet —that uncover 4 feet, are in the southern part of the bay. The most prominent landmark along this stretch of coast is The Castle, on Castle Hill.

CHARTS 13279, 13274. **ESSEX BAY and ESSEX RIVER** are about midway between Ipswich and Annisquam Harbor Lights. The entrance is through a shifting bar over which, with local knowledge, 5 feet can usually be carried. With onshore winds on an ebb tide, a heavy chop builds up and during heavy weather the bar is often impassable. Caution is always indicated especially for small craft. The river is navigable to the town of Essex, about 5 miles above the entrance. Local fishermen and numerous pleasure craft use the river. The entrance is marked by a seasonal lighted bell buoy, and the bay channel is marked from the bar to about 2 miles above the entrance by a daybeacon and seasonal buoys.

CHARTS 13281, 13279, 13274. **THE ANNISQUAM RIVER** and **BLYNMAN CANAL** form a thorofare leading from the eastern part of Ipswich Bay, northwest of Cape Ann to Gloucester harbor on the south side of the cape. Annisquam is a village and summer resort on the east side of Annisquam River just inside its north end. **LOBSTER COVE**, on the southeast side of the town, is the scene of a lot of small pleasure-boat activity during the summer. **CAPE ANN** is very rocky and broken, 235 feet high at Pool Hill, its highest point.

CHARTS 13267.MASSACHUSETTS BAY is the body of water lying westward of a line connecting Cape Ann Light (42°38"20'N, 70°34"50'W) on Thacher Island with Race Point Light on the northwestern extremity of Cape

BOSTON NORTH

Cod about 38 miles south- southeastward. It includes Boston Harbor and Cape Cod Bay. Between Cape Ann Light and Boston Harbor, 24 miles to the southwestward, the principal harbors are Gloucester, Beverly, Salem, Marblehead, and Lynn, all available to vessels of moderate draft. The coast is rocky and generally bold, with numerous detached islands, rocks, and sunken dangers.

CHARTS 13281, 13274. GLOUCESTER HARBOR is 5 miles southwestward of Emerson Point, the easternmost point of Cape Ann, 26 miles from Boston and 234 miles from New York. **Ed. Note: GLOUCESTER** is a seaport city of great historic interest — dating back to 1623 —which has gained notoriety again with the recent best-seller, "The Perfect Storm," by Sebastian Junger and the subsequent film. Gloucester is one of the most important fishing ports in the United States and an important harbor of refuge. Visiting mariners should take the harbor walk to visit the famous fisherman memorial to those lost at sea over the centuries. Numerous good restaurants line the harbor.

Gloucester has both an inner and outer harbor. The entrance to the outer harbor is marked by **EASTERN POINT LIGHT** (42°32"8'N, 70°39"9W - 57ft. high) on the harbor's eastern side. Gloucester inner harbor begins at a line between Black Rock Daybeacon 12 and Fort Point. The city has rail and bus connections for crew changes.

CHARTS 13274, 13279. MAGNOLIA HARBOR is a cove about 1.5 miles westward of the entrance to Gloucester Harbor and just north of Kettle Island. The summer resort of Magnolia is conspicuous on the eastern side. There is a public pier which has no facilities but can be a good stopping place for provisioning and marine supplies.

CHART 13276. BEVERLY HARBOR is north of Salem Neck, at the western end of Salem Sound, and is formed by the confluence of Danvers River, Bass River and North River. It forms the approach to the city of Beverly; a manufacturing and resort city on the north side of the harbor just inside the entrance. Special anchorages are on Monument Bar, north of Salem Neck, in Beverly Cove and in Mackerel Cove in the northern end of the Harbor.

CHART 13274. A cruise into **SALEM** is yet another voyage into maritime history with numerous maritime museums, architectural treasures (including Hawthorne's House of Seven Gables) , shops, restaurants, and, of course...witches. **SALEM HARBOR** is is about 1.5 miles long in a southwesterly direction. Approach the harbor from the northward through the dredged section of Salem Channel. Enter the channel between **BAKERS** and **MISERY ISLANDS**. This a a good harbor of refuge, particularly in autumn months. See our marina tables for plentiful Salem marine facilities.

CHART 13276. MARBLEHEAD HARBOR is well-protected from all points except the northeast. The renowned sailing center of **MARBLEHEAD** was once a commercial fishing village, but today it is more a layover port for serious cruising and racing yachts — many of which are members of the six yacht clubs on the harbor. You might want to take your dinghy on a "boatwatching" cruise. Eighteenth century buildings line the waterfront and shopping is a few blocks north and west of the waterfront.

CHART 13270, 13272. BOSTON HARBOR, the largest seaport in New England, includes all the tidewater lying within a line from the southern extremity of **DEER ISLAND** to **POINT ALLERTON**, about 4 miles to the southeastward. Numerous dangers lie in the approaches to the harbor. The northeastern approach is obstructed by islands and shoals which extend 4 miles from the entrance; between them are the dredged channels, which lead into the harbor. In the southeastern approach, broken ground extends as much as 3 miles from the shore. The approaches are marked by a number of powerful lights, and the principal dangers are buoyed. **TIDAL CURRENT CHARTS FOR BOSTON HARBOR** show the direction and velocity of the tidal current for each hour of the current at Deer Island Light. They present a comprehensive view of the tidal current movement for the harbor as a whole and also supply a means of readily determining, for any time, the direction and velocity of the current at various localities throughout the harbor. **CHELSEA RIVER** separates East Boston on the northeastern side of Boston Harbor from the city of Chelsea.

The city of Boston has friendly yacht clubs, protected marinas, anchorages, and boatyards and it welcomes cruising mariners for great sightseeing, shopping and eateries. Follow the buoyed courses and stay well off the islands due to rocks and ledges. Have an up-to-date chart on board because numerous buoys and

TO FIND MARINA LOCATIONS - SEE THE TABLES AND LOCATOR CHARTS AT THE END OF THIS SECTION.

BOSTON NORTH

channels could cause confusion on site without having planned your entrance in advance.

CHART 13270. HINGHAM BAY is that part of Boston Harbor southeastward of **PEDDOCKS ISLAND.** It is the approach to Weymouth Fore River, Weymouth Back River, Hingham Harbor and Weir River. Extensive shoals make out from the southerly shore and surround the islands in the bay. Hull Bay, the eastern part of the bay, also has many shoal areas. Special anchorages are in Hull Bay. The easterly entrance to Hingham Bay is through Hull Gut, but the entrance through West Gut, southward of Peddocks Island, is frequently used by vessels bound into Weymouth Fore or Weymouth Back Rivers.

CHART 13269 The entrance to **COHASSET** on Massachusetts Bay is marked by Minots Ledge Light (42°16.2'N., 70°45.5'W.) From here there are 3 approach channels. All channels are well marked. The Eastern Channel is narrower, but deeper, than the Gangway Channel. Newcomers to the area should use the Eastern Channel while locals prefer the Gangway Channel. No matter, all generally agree that the best time to make the passage is on a rising tide. This area is known for its rocks – maintain slow speeds and keep a close watch.

COHASSET HARBOR is a large, fairly shallow harbor, which lies to the southwest of Minots Ledge Light and about 6 miles southeast of Point Allerton. Anchorage is available in the outer harbor with reported depths of 6 to 10 feet. The town is on the west side of the inner harbor. The Harbormaster's office overlooks the town wharf and is just southwest of the entrance to Bailey Creek.

SCITUATE HARBOR, about 4 miles southeast of Cohasset Harbor, is easily entered between Cedar Point and First Cliff. There is an operating lighthouse at Cedar Point. The harbor is partially protected by breakwaters. The entrance is well marked and we recommend staying in the center of the channel as you enter. The reported depths are approximately 7 feet. Speed limits of 6 MPH within the harbor are strictly enforced, as is the "no-discharge" law. Anchoring is not allowed. However, there are many moorings available to transients. Also available are slip spaces. For mooring & slip space, launch service and advice contact "Cedar Point Launch" on VHF Channel 9 or call (781) 545-4154.

The town of Scituate is a delight to visit. There are convenient provisioning facilities, great restaurants, and you can even catch a refreshing shower for a mere two-bucks, payable at the Harbor Master's office located at the foot of the docks.

CHART 13267. NEW INLET, on the north side of **FOURTH CLIFF** and 2 miles southward of **SCITUATE HARBOR,** is the approach to **NORTH RIVER AND SOUTH RIVER.** The inlet had a reported depth of about 10 feet. It is marked by a fairway bell buoy off the entrance and by several channel buoys, but the channel is subject to change and is never entered except by small craft with local knowledge. Strangers should not attempt to cross the bar on the the ebb with an easterly wind or in heavy seas as waves break across the bar. The bar consists of boulders that are reported to be particularly numerous on the south side of the inlet. A strong current flows out of the inlet during the falling tide. ⚓

AUTHORIZED SERVICE CENTER

MASSACHUSETTS Boston & North FACILITIES alphabetical index

Massachusetts
North of Boston

CHART LOCATER NUMBER	MARINA'S NAME & PHONE NUMBER	WHEN OPEN	MONITORS VHF CHANNEL	TRANSIENT: Electricity • Moorings • Berths	Hull repairs • Engine repairs • Ramp	WINTER STORAGE: Wet • Dry	RAILWAY CAPACITY IN TONS	LIFT CAPACITY IN FEET	BOAT RENTAL: Canoe • Row • Motor	BOAT RENTAL: Charter • House • Sail	Restaurant • Lodging • Camping	Showers • Laundry	Pumpout • Toilets	Bait • Tackle • Water • Ice	Groceries • Hardware	Diesel fuel • Gasoline
1	KING'S LANDING MARINA, 781-659-7273				HE	D					C		T	I		
2	MARY'S BOAT LIVERY 781-837-2322	MAY OCT	9 16	M	R				R				T	IBT		
3	NORTH RIVER MARINE SERV. 781-545-7811	ALL YR.		EM B	HE R	D							T	IW BT	H	
5	DRIFTWAY RAMP				R											
6	JAMES LANDING MARINA 781-545-3000	ALL YR.		EB	HE	D		30				S	T	W	H	G D
7	YOUNG'S BOAT STORAGE 781-545-0440	ALL YR.			HE	D		15					T	I		
8	SCITUATE TOWN MARINA	MAY OCT	9	EB							RL	SL	PT	IW	H	
9	MILLWHARF PLAZA MARINA 781-545-3333	MAY OCT	9	EB							RL		T	IW BT		G D
10	SCITUATE TOWN PIER	ALL YR.	9								RL			W		
11	SCITUATE HARBOR MARINA 781-545-2165	MAY OCT		EB							RL			IW		
12	SCITUATE RAMP				R											
13	OLDE SALT HOUSE 781-383-1340	MAY OCT		B							R		T	IW	H	G D
14	MILL RIVER MARINE 617-383-1207	ALL YR.		EM B	HE	D	60	45					T			
15	COHASSET RAMP				R											
16	COHASSET HARBOR MARINA 781-383-1504	MAY OCT		MB		D										
17	NANTASKET MARINE 781-925-2300	ALL YR.			HE	D		10								
18	FIRST QUALITY MARINE 617-740-1456	ALL YR.			HE	D		15						W	H	
19	KEHOE'S SHIP'S CHANDLERY 781-749-9855	ALL YR.	9	M							R			I	H	
20	HINGHAM TOWN RAMP				R											
21	MARINE EXPERTS 781-749-6062	ALL YR.			HE	D									H	

Massachusetts
North of Boston

CHART LOCATER NUMBER	MARINA'S NAME & PHONE NUMBER	WHEN OPEN	MONITORS VHF CHANNEL	TRANSIENT Electricity • Moorings • Berths	Hull repairs • Engine repairs • Ramp	WINTER STORAGE: Wet • Dry	RAILWAY CAPACITY IN FEET	LIFT CAPACITY IN TONS	BOAT RENTAL: Canoe • Row • Motor	BOAT RENTAL: Charter • House • Sail	Restaurant • Lodging • Camping	Showers • Laundry	Pumpout • Toilets	Bait • Tackle • Water • Ice	Groceries • Hardware	Diesel fuel • Gasoline
22	HULL TOWN RAMP 781-925-3435				R											
23	BUMPKIN ISLAND										C		T			
24	SPINNAKER ISLAND Y. C. 781-925-1806	MAY OCT		EB								S	T	IW		
27	PEMBERTON PIER LANDING 781-925-3435				R											
28	PEDDOCK'S ISLAND 617-727-5359										C					
29	GRAPE ISLAND 617-740-1605	ALL YR.									C					
30	TERN HARBOR MARINA 781-337-1964	ALL YR.	9 16	EM B	HE R	W D		35				RL	SL	PT	IW	H	G D
31	HEWITTS COVE MARINA 781-749-6647	ALL YR.	9 16	EM B	HE	W D		35				RL	SL	PT	IW BT	GH	G D
32	LANDFALL MARINE CENTER 781-749-1255	ALL YR.			HE	D						R	SL	T	IW BT	GH	
33	NORTH WEYMOUTH RAMP 781-335-2000				R											
34	ROWE'S WHARF MARINA 617-439-3131	MAY OCT	9	EB							C	RL	SL	T	IW	G	
34	SCALISI MARINA 781-331-0446	ALL YR.			HE	D		25									
35	**MONAHANS MARINE 781-336-2746**	**ALL YR.**														**H**	
36	METROPOLITAN Y. C. 781-843-9882															G
37	BAY POINTE MARINA 617-471-1777	ALL YR.	9	EB	HE	W D		50			R	SL	PT	IW	H	G D
38	CAPTAIN'S COVE MARINA	ALL YR.										SL	PT	W		
39	ANCHOR MARINA 617-471-2666	ALL YR.		EM B	HE R	D							T	IW BT	H	
40	CLIPPER MARINA 617-479-1449	APR NOV			EB							S	PT	W		
41	BAYSWATER MARINE 617-471-8060				HE R	D										
42	HURLEY'S BOAT RENTAL 617-479-1239	APR OCT			ER				MR					I		

Massachusetts
North of Boston
MARINA'S NAME & PHONE NUMBER

Chart Locater Number	Marina's Name & Phone Number	When Open	Monitors VHF Channel	Transient: Electricity • Moorings • Berths	Hull repairs • Engine repairs • Ramp	Winter Storage: Wet • Dry	Railway Capacity in Feet	Lift Capacity in Tons	Boat Rental: Canoe • Row • Motor	Boat Rental: Charter • House • Sail	Restaurant • Lodging • Camping	Showers • Laundry	Pumpout • Toilets	Bait • Tackle • Water • Ice	Groceries • Hardware	Diesel fuel • Gasoline
43	HARVEY'S WHARF 617-773-3020				HE	D			MR					I		
44	MARINA BAY 617-847-1800		10	EB		D		35					PT	W		G D
45	VENEZIA MARINA 617-436-3120	APR NOV		EB							R		T	IW		
46	THOMAS MARINE 617-288-1000	ALL YR.	9 16 68	EB	HE			80					T	IW		G D
47	RAINBOW PARK				R											
52	BOSTON HARBOR POLICE 617-247-4721	ALL YR.	9 16													
53	PIER 7 617-742-7600	ALL YR.	9	B	H			10			R	SL	T	I WB		G D
55	BOSTON Water Boat Marina 617-523-1027	ALL YR.	9	EM B		W					RL	SL	T	IW		
57 SEE AD	BOSTON YACHT HAVEN 617-523-7352	ALL YR.		EB		W					R	SL	T	W		
58	BOSTON SAILING CENTER 617-227-4198								M	C						
59	LEWIS WHARF MARINA 617-227-4198	ALL YR.		EB		W								W		
60	CHARLESGATE Y. C. 781-933-2661													I		G
61	CHARLES RIVER RAMP				R											
62	CONSTITUTION MARINA 617-241-9640	ALL YR.	9 16 69	EM B	HE	W					R	SL	PT	IW	H	
64	COURAGEOUS SAILING CTR. 617-242-3821		68	B							R		T			
65	Shipyard Quarters Marina 617-242-2020	ALL YR.	9 16 71	EB							R	SL	PT	IW		
66	MYSTIC WELLINGTON RAMP 617-727-0537				R											
67	THE SCHRAFFT RAMP 617-242-2700	ALL YR.			R											
68	QUARTERDECK MARINE 617-569-5212	ALL YR.			HE	W D						SL	T	W		
69	BOSTON BOATYARD 617-561-1400	ALL YR.	9	EB		D		50				SL	T	IW		G D

Massachusetts
North of Boston
MARINA'S NAME & PHONE NUMBER

#	Marina & Phone	When Open	Monitors VHF Channel	Transient (Electricity•Moorings•Berths)	Hull/Engine Repairs	Ramp	Winter Storage (Wet•Dry)	Railway Cap. (ft)	Lift Cap. (tons)	Boat Rental	Restaurant•Lodging	Showers•Laundry	Pumpout•Toilets	Bait•Tackle•Water•Ice	Groceries•Hardware	Diesel•Gasoline
71	WINTHROP HARBOR RAMP	YR.				R										
72	CRYSTAL COVE MARINA	ALL YR.		EB	HE	R	W D		20		RL	SL	T	IW BT	GH	G
73	ZEOLI'S MARINE SERVICE 617-846-2800	ALL YR.		EB	HE	E	W D				R	SL	PT	IW	H	G
74	PLEASANT PARK Y. C. 617-846-9869							45						IW		G
77	NORTH SHORE MARINE 781-284-7657	ALL YR.				R					R		T	IW BT	H	G
78	NORTH SHORE BOAT WORKS 781-284-4220	ALL YR.			HE		D		40				T	W	H	
79	FOWLER MARINE 781-284-6249	ALL YR.		EB	HE		D		18		R		T	W		D
81	MARINE SALES 617-593-0643	ALL YR.	16	EB	HE	R	D		25		R		PT	IW BT	H	G
82	SAUGUS TOWN RAMP					R										
84	SEAPORT LANDING MARINA 617-592-5821	ALL YR.	9	EB			W					SL	PT	IW		G D
85	LYNN Y. C. 617-595-9825								25		R	S	T	IW BT	G	G D
86	LAUNCHING RAMP					R										
88	MARBLEHEAD RAMP					R										
89	HARBORMASTER 781-631-2386	ALL YR.	9 16													
90	MARBLEHEAD TRADING CO. 617-631-4650	ALL YR.			HE				15						H	
94	PHILIP T. CLARK LANDING	MAY NOV											T			
96	MARBLEHEAD TRADING CO 617-639-0029	ALL YR.			HE		D	75	99 +						H	
97	ROCKETT PARK													I		
98	WEST SHORE MARINE 781-639-1290		71	M							R					
99	FRED J. DION YACHT YARD 978-744-0844	ALL YR.	9	EM B	HE		D		50			S	T	W	GH	

Massachusetts North of Boston

MARINA'S NAME & PHONE NUMBER

Chart Locater Number	Marina's Name & Phone Number	When Open	Monitors VHF Channel	Transient (Electricity • Moorings • Berths)	Hull/Engine repairs • Ramp	Winter Storage: Wet • Dry	Railway Capacity (ft)	Lift Capacity (tons)	Boat Rental: Canoe • Row • Motor	Boat Rental: Charter • House • Sail	Restaurant • Lodging • Camping	Showers • Laundry	Pumpout • Toilets	Bait • Tackle • Water • Ice	Groceries • Hardware	Diesel fuel • Gasoline
100	PICKERING WHARF MARINA 978-744-2727	ALL YR.	9	EMB		W D					R	SL	T	IW		
102	HAWTHORNE COVE MARINA 978-740-9890	ALL YR	9	EMB	HE	D		35			RL	SL	PT	IW	GH	
103	WINTER ISLAND YACHT YARD 978-745-3797	ALL YR			HE	D	50	7						W	H	
104	WINTER ISLAND MARITIME 978-745-9430	ALL YR.	9		R	D					R	S	T	I		
105	Salem Willows Boat Livery 978-745-6996	MAY OCT							MR					IBT		
106	SALEM WILLOWS Y. C. 978-744-9684				R								T	IW		G
107	FRED'S BOAT SHOP					D	40	12								
108	KERNWOOD MARINA 978-744-0180	MAY OCT			R											
110	AMERICAN BOAT SALES 978-777-1993	ALL YR.			HE								T	IW BT	H	
111	POPE'S LANDING RAMP 508-774-9494	MAY OCT	12 16	M	R											
112	LANCTOT'S MARINA 508-774-0660	APR OCT			HE						R		T	I WB		
113	YANKEE ENGINE & MARINE 508-774-5887	AL YR.			HE R	D		50	M		R	S	T	IW BT	H	G
114	DANVERSPORT Y. C. 508-774-8620	ALL YR.				W D		50			R	SL	PT	IW		G
115	DESMOND YACHT YARD 978-927-1522	ALL YR.	13 78		HE	D		50			C		T		H	
116	BOWL-O-MAT RAMP				R											
117	BEVERLY HARBOR CENTER 978-921-6059	ALL YR.	9 16	B												
118	GLOVER WHARF MARINA 978-922-9661	ALL YR.		EB	E	D		50				SL	T	IW		
119	PORT MARINE 978-922-9595	ALL YR.	16	EB	HE	W D		35			RL	SL	T	IW BT	H	G D
120	TUCK POINT MARINA CORP 978-922-4631			EB		W						SL	T	W		
121	JUBILEE Y. C. 978-922-9611			M												

Massachusetts
North of Boston

#	Marina's Name & Phone Number	When Open	Monitors VHF	Transient (Elec•Moor•Berth)	Repairs (Hull•Eng•Ramp)	Winter Storage (Wet•Dry)	Railway Cap. (ft)	Lift Cap. (tons)	Boat Rental (Canoe•Row•Motor)	Boat Rental (Charter•House•Sail)	Restaurant•Lodging•Camping	Showers•Laundry	Pumpout•Toilets	Bait•Tackle•Water•Ice	Groceries•Hardware	Diesel•Gasoline
122	BEVERLY PUBLIC RAMP				R											
123	CROCKER'S BOATYARD 508-526-1971	ALL YR.			HE	W D		30					T	W	H	
124	MANCHESTER MARINE 508-526-7911	ALL YR	72	EM B	HE	D	70	30				S	T	IW	H	G D
125	MANCHESTER TOWN RAMP				R											
127	EASTERN POINT Y. C 978-283-3520		71	M							RL	S	T	I		
128	BICKFORD MARINA 978-283-0404	MAY OCT		EB		D		35			R	S	T	IW	H	
129	L.A. DAHLMER BOATS	ALL YR.					30	10								
130	THE STUDIO RESTAURANT 978-283-4123	APR OCT		B							R		T			
131	N. SHORE FISHING CLUB 978-283-9759	APR NOV		EB						C	R	L	T	IW		G D
132	BEACON MARINE BASIN 978-283-2380	ALL YR.		E	H	D	36	12					T	IW	H	G D
133	BROWN'S YACHT YARD 978-281-3200	ALL YR.		EM B	HE	D		35				S	T	IW	H	G D
135	DOCKSIDE BAR & GRILL 978-281-4554	APR OCT		B							R		T			
136	THREE LANTERNS SHIP SUPPLY 978-281-2080	ALL YR												BT	H	
137	ROSE'S YACHT YARD 978-281-1967				H	D	70									
138	GLOUCESTER HOUSE REST. 978-283-1812	ALL YR.									R					
140	GLOUCESTER MARINE 508-978-283-2775	ALL YR.			HE R	D	50	35			RL	SL	PT	IW BT	H	G D
141	CAPE ANN'S MARINA RESORT 978-283-2112	ALL YR.	10	EB	HE R	W D	100	60	C	C	RL	SL	T	IW BT	GH	G D
142	ATLANTIC YANKEE FLEET 978-283-0313	APR DEC								C	RL		T	IBT		
143	ENOS MARINE 978-281-1935	ALL YR.	9 / 16		HE										H	
144	DUNFUDGIN RAMP 978-281-9756				R											

Chart Locater Number	Marina's Name & Phone Number	When Open	Monitors VHF Channel	Transient: Electricity • Engine repairs • Moorings • Berths	Hull repairs / Railway / Ramp	Winter Storage: Wet • Dry	Railway Capacity in Feet	Lift Capacity in Tons	Boat Rental	Restaurant • Lodging • Camping	Showers • Laundry	Pumpout • Toilets	Bait • Tackle • Water • Ice	Groceries • Hardware	Diesel fuel • Gasoline
145	HERON WAY MARINA 978-283-4473	MAY OCT	9								SL	T	IW		
146	GLOUCESTER MARINA 978-283-2828	APR OCT		EB	HR	D		12			S	T	IW	GH	
147	MONTGOMERY BOATYARD 978-281-6524	ALL YR			HR	D		10							
148	WHEELER'S PT. BOATYARD 978-281-0303	ALL YR.	9		HE	D	50	10					W	H	
149	LONG WHARF RAMP				R										
150	LOBSTER COVE MARINA 978-283-3070	APR OCT	9	EMB	E				C	R	S	T	IW	G	GD
152	LANES COVE 978-281-3080				R										
154	GRANITE PIER 978-546-9334				R										
155	ROCKPORT HARBOR				M										
156	ESSEX RIVER MOTEL 978-768-6800	APR OCT								RL					
157	TOM SHEA'S RESTAURANT 978-768-6931									R					
158	PIKE MARINE 978-768-7161	ALL YR		EB	ER	D		12				T	IW	H	G
159	PERKINS MARINE 978-768-7145	APR OCT			HER	D	35	15		R		T	W		G
160	ESSEX TOWN RAMP residents only				R										
161	ESSEX MARINA 978-768-6833	MAY NOV			HER	D		10			SL	PT	IW BT		
163	IPSWICH TOWN WHARF 508-781-356-4321				R										
166	IPSWICH BAY Y. C. 781-356-2502										S	T	IW	G	
167	EAGLE HILL RAMP 781-356-4321 residents only				R										
168	PERLEY'S MARINA 978-948-2812	APR OCT			HER	D						T	IW	H	
170	PERT LOWELL CO 978-462-7409	ALL YR			H	D		5						H	

Massachusetts North of Boston

MARINA'S NAME & PHONE NUMBER

Chart Locater Number	Marina's Name & Phone Number	Transient / When Open	Monitors VHF Channel	Hull repairs • Electricity • Engine repairs • Moorings • Berths	Winter Storage: Wet • Dry • Ramp	Railway Capacity in Feet	Lift Capacity in Tons	Boat Rental: Canoe • Row • Motor	Boat Rental: Charter • House • Sail	Restaurant • Lodging • Camping	Showers • Laundry	Pumpout • Toilets	Bait • Tackle • Water • Ice	Groceries • Hardware	Diesel fuel • Gasoline
171															
172	RIVER FRONT MARINE 508-465-6090	ALL YR		EM B	HE	D	10					T	IW		G
173	NEWBURY RAMP			R											
174	CAPT. FISHING PARTY 508-465-7733	APR OCT	16 70 / 77	R					C	RL		T	IW BT	G	
175	NEWBURYPORT RAMP - residents only			R											
176	MACKENZIES MARINA 978-388-0902	APR NOV		EB							S	PT	IW		
177	NEWBURYPORT CITY MARINA											T			
178	HUDSON'S TACKLE & MARINE 978-462-1650	ALL YR.											IW BT	H	
179	HILTON AND STROUT 508-465-9885	ALL YR	19			D	75		C	R		PT	IW BT	H	G D
180	WINDWARD YACHT YARD 978-462-6500	ALL YR.	9 16	EM B	HE	D	75						W	H	
181	MICHAEL'S Harborside Rest. 978-462-7785	ALL YR.								R					
182	RIVER'S EDGE MARINA 508-465-5708	APR OCT		EM B						R	S	T	W		
183	CASHMAN PARK RAMP			R											
184	BOAT WORKS 978-465-1855	ALL YR.		EM B	HE	D	20				SL	T	IW	H	
185	FERRY LANDING MARINA 508-465-9110	MAY OCT		EB	ER	D	15				SL	T	IW	H	
186	**MERRI-MAR YACHT BASIN 978-465-3022**	**ALL YR.**	**10**	**EM B**	**ME R**	**D**	**35**			**RL**		**P**	**IW**	**GH**	
187	COVE MARINA 978-462-4998	MAY OCT	10	EB	HE	D					SL	PT	IW		
188	BRIDGE MARINA 462-462-2274	ALL YR.	9	EM BD		D	40		C	RL		T	IW BT	H	G D
189	DAWN MARINA 978-465-0307	APR OCT	9	EB	HE R	D	57	30			S	T	I WT	H	
191	SALISBURY BEACH 462-462-4481	ALL YR.		R							S	T			

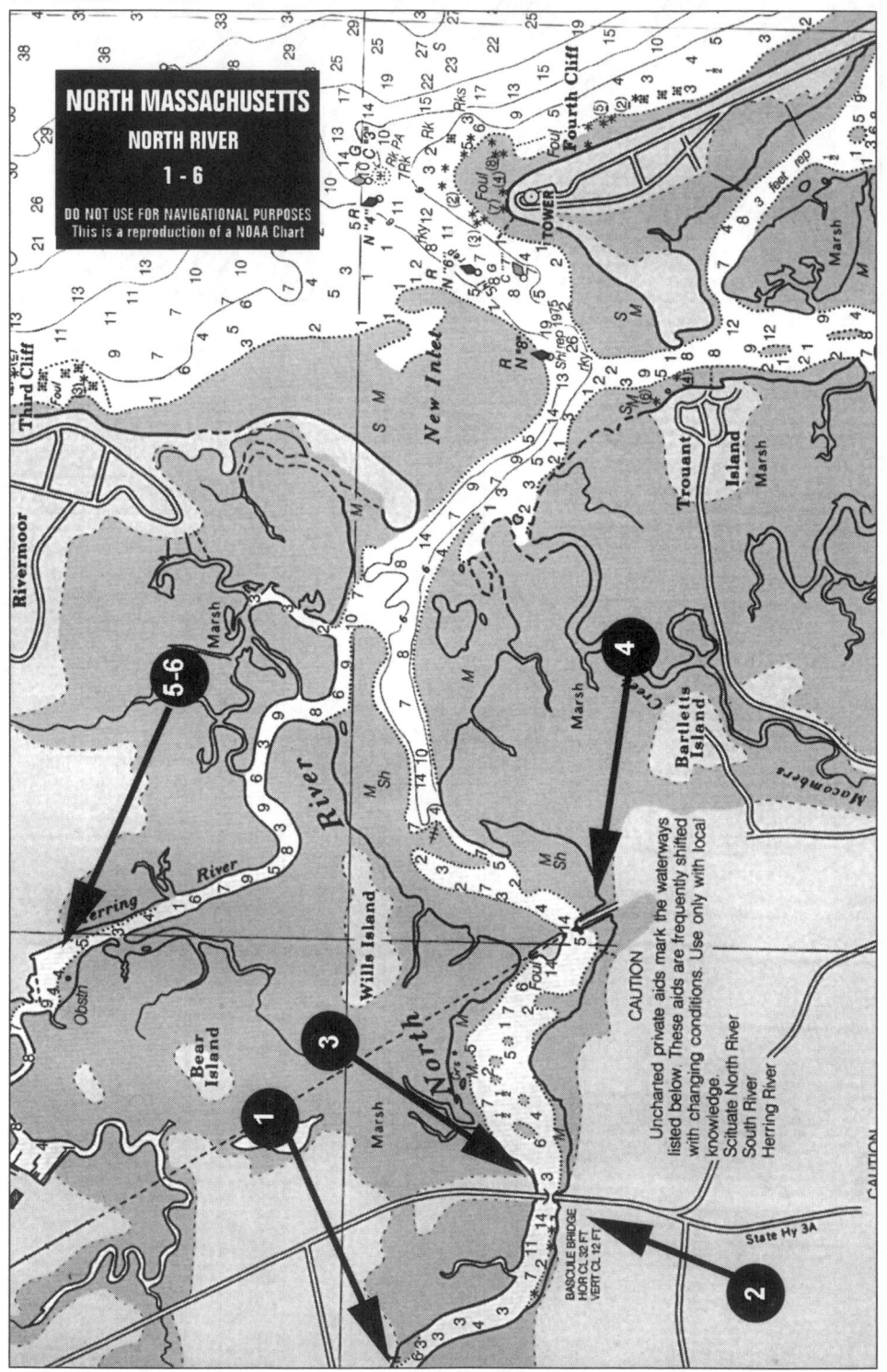

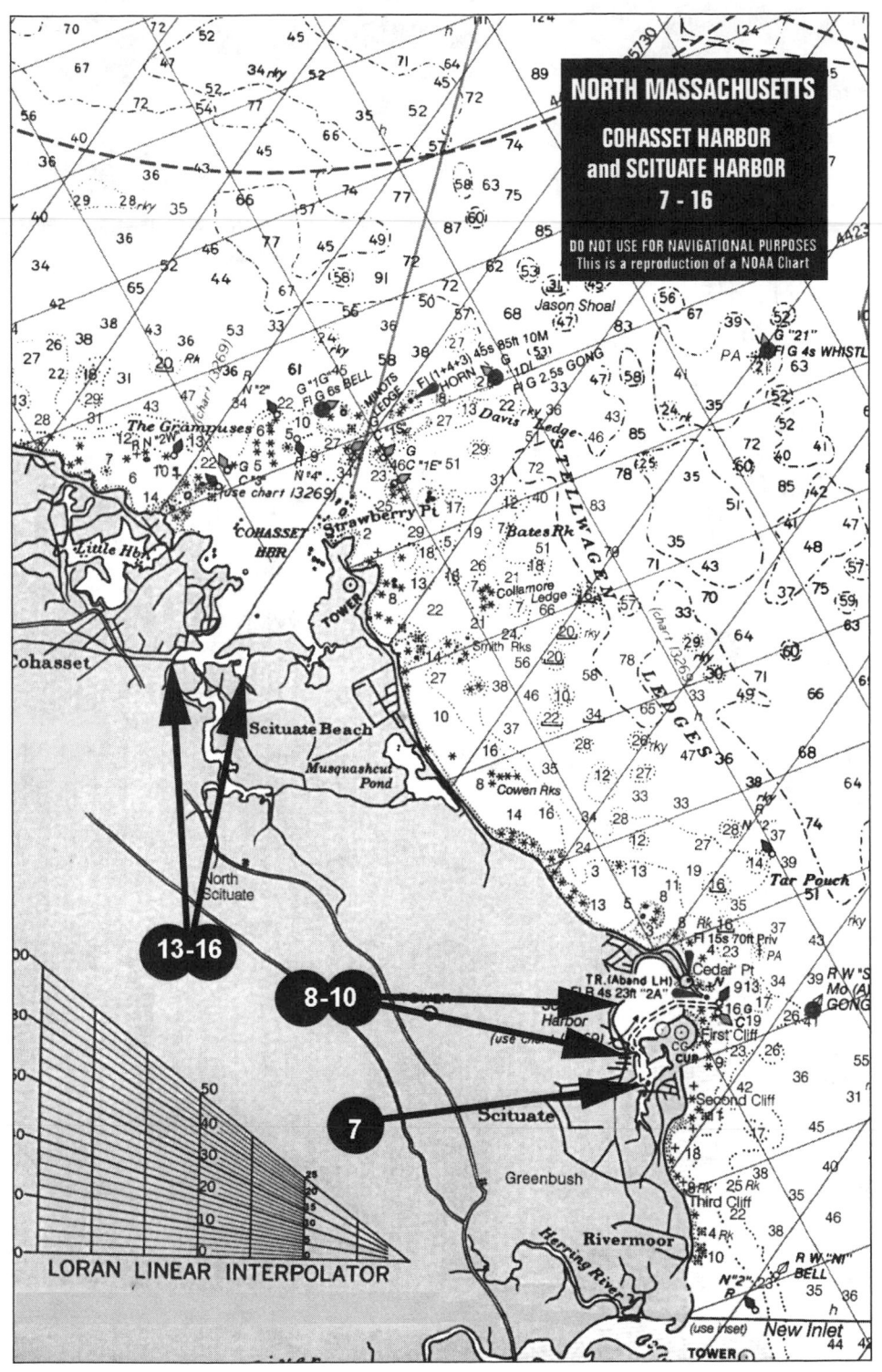

NORTH MASSACHUSETTS

**COHASSET HARBOR
and SCITUATE HARBOR
7 - 16**

LORAN LINEAR INTERPOLATOR

577

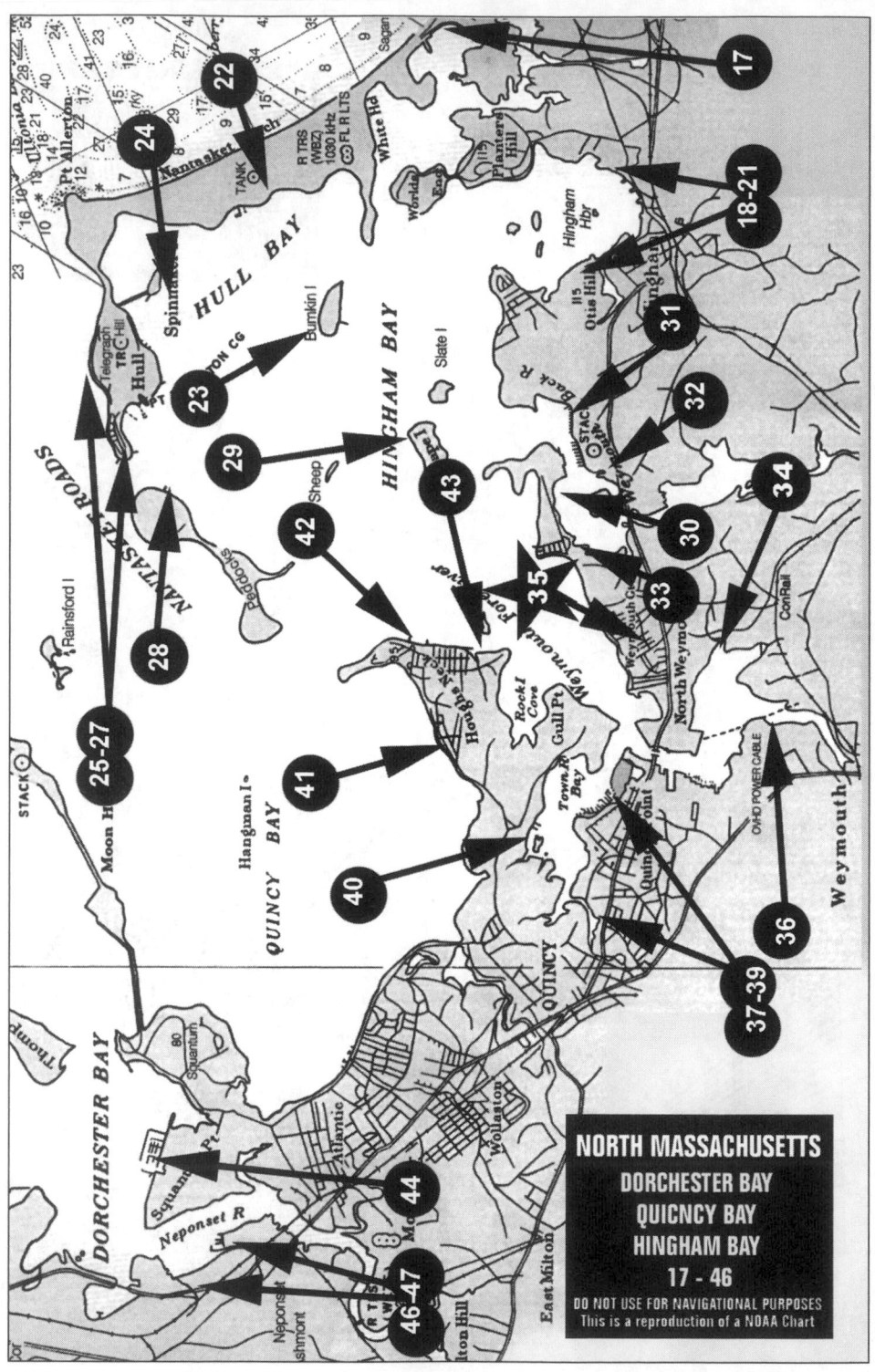

NORTH MASSACHUSETTS

DORCHESTER BAY

QUICNCY BAY

HINGHAM BAY

17 - 46

DO NOT USE FOR NAVIGATIONAL PURPOSES
This is a reproduction of a NOAA Chart

578

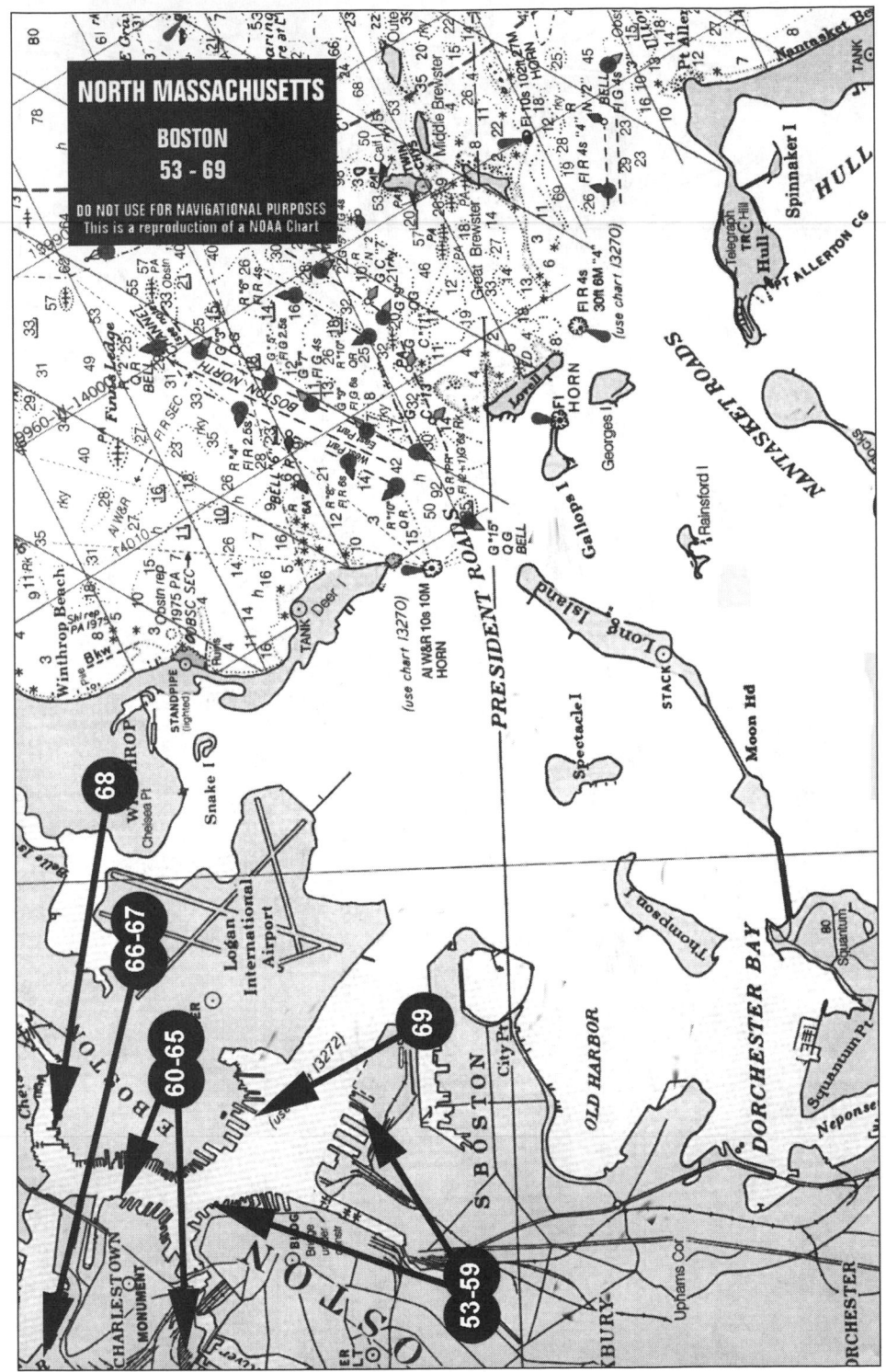

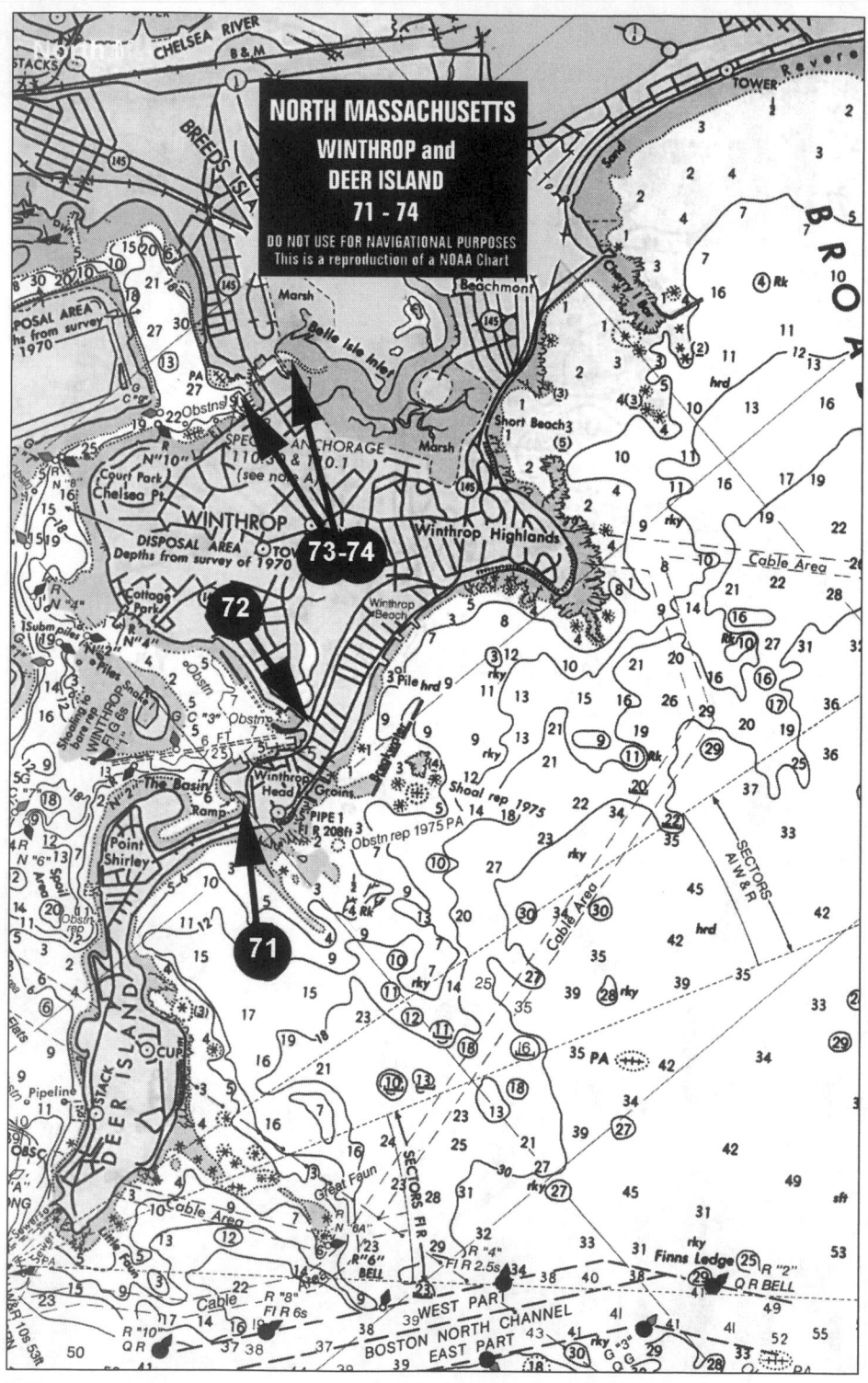

NORTH MASSACHUSETTS
WINTHROP and
DEER ISLAND
71 - 74

DO NOT USE FOR NAVIGATIONAL PURPOSES
This is a reproduction of a NOAA Chart

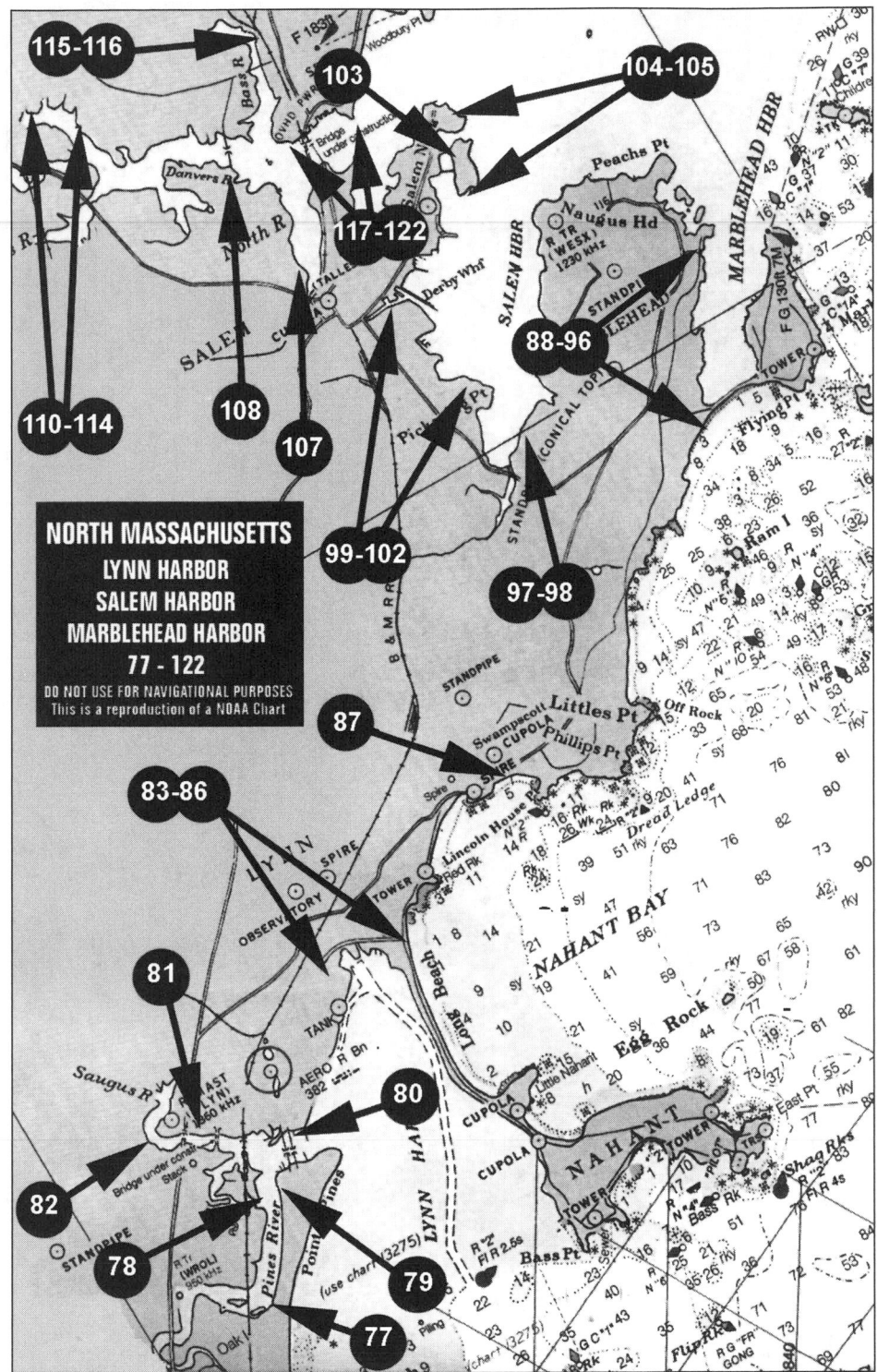

NORTH MASSACHUSETTS
LYNN HARBOR
SALEM HARBOR
MARBLEHEAD HARBOR
77 - 122
DO NOT USE FOR NAVIGATIONAL PURPOSES
This is a reproduction of a NOAA Chart

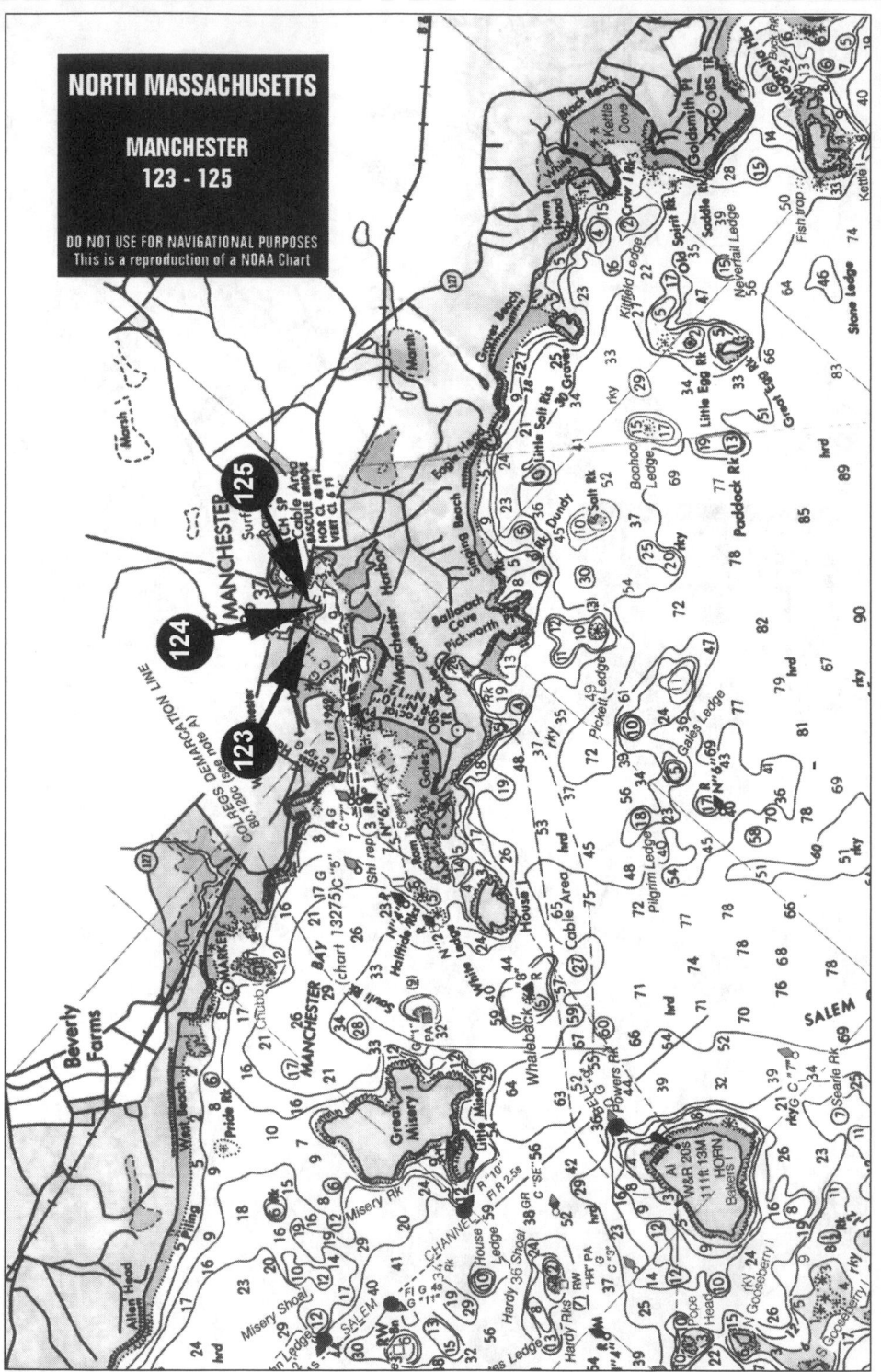

NORTH MASSACHUSETTS

MANCHESTER
123 - 125

125

124

123

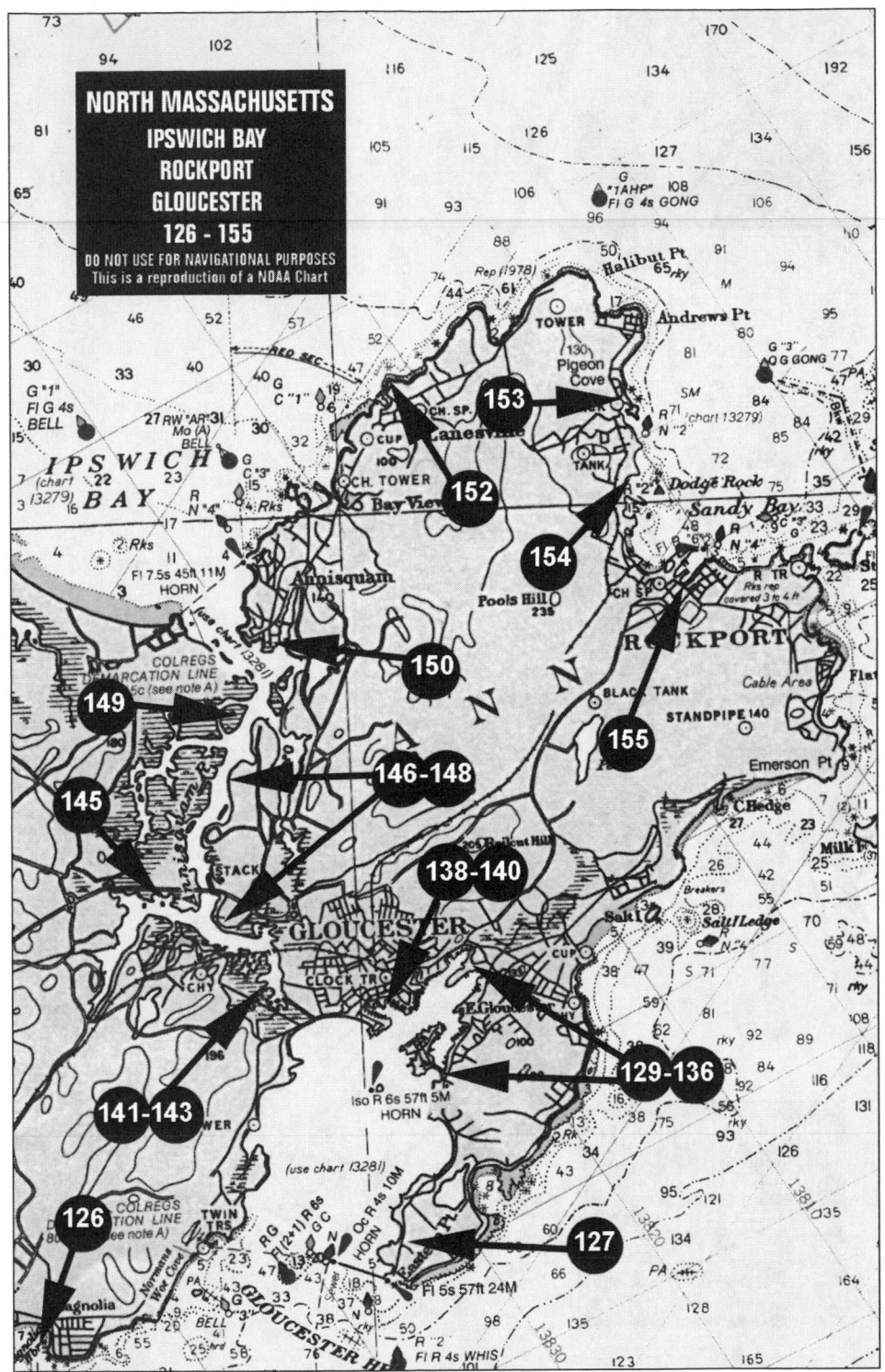

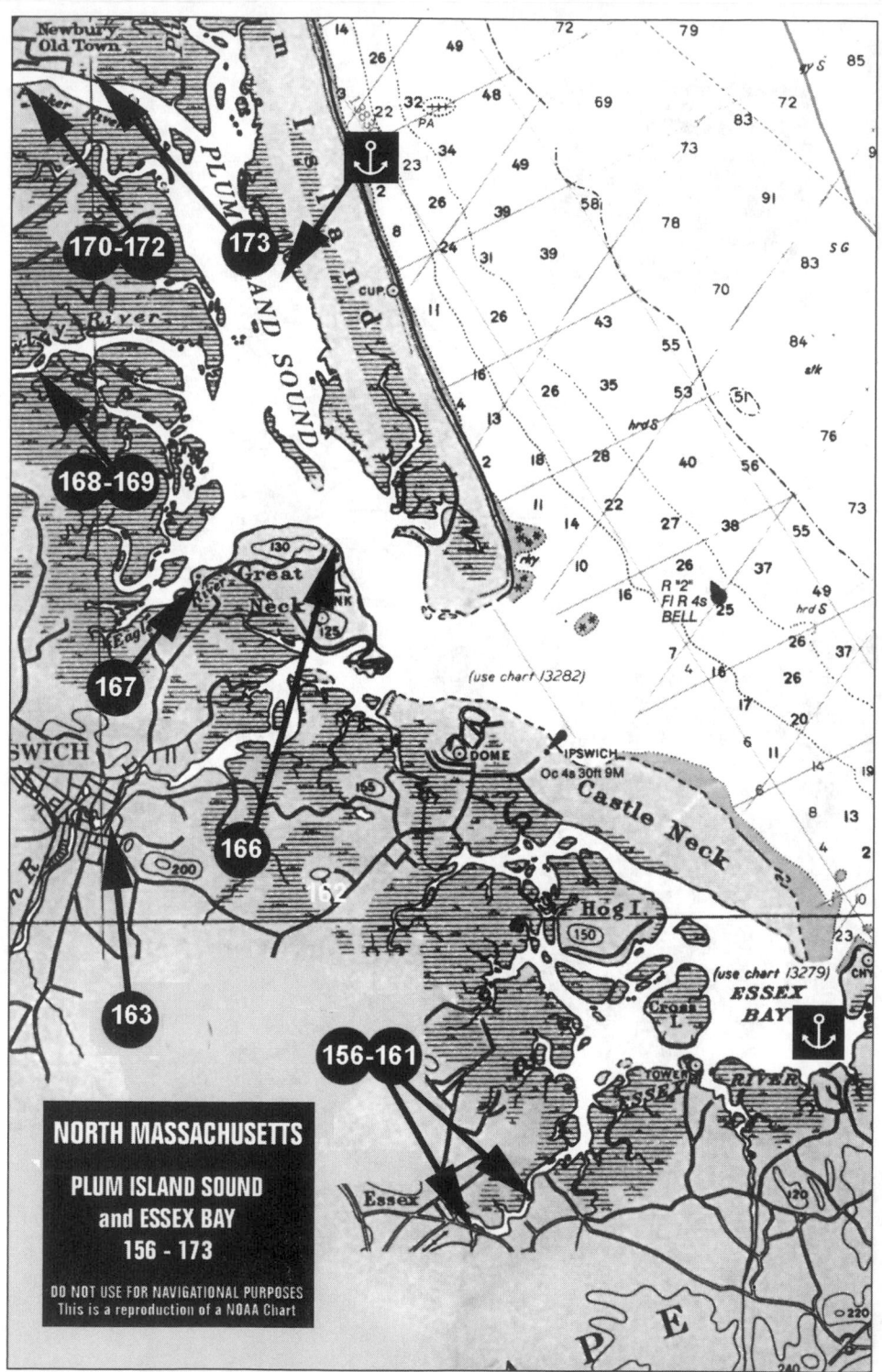

NORTH MASSACHUSETTS

PLUM ISLAND SOUND
and ESSEX BAY
156 - 173

DO NOT USE FOR NAVIGATIONAL PURPOSES
This is a reproduction of a NOAA Chart

584

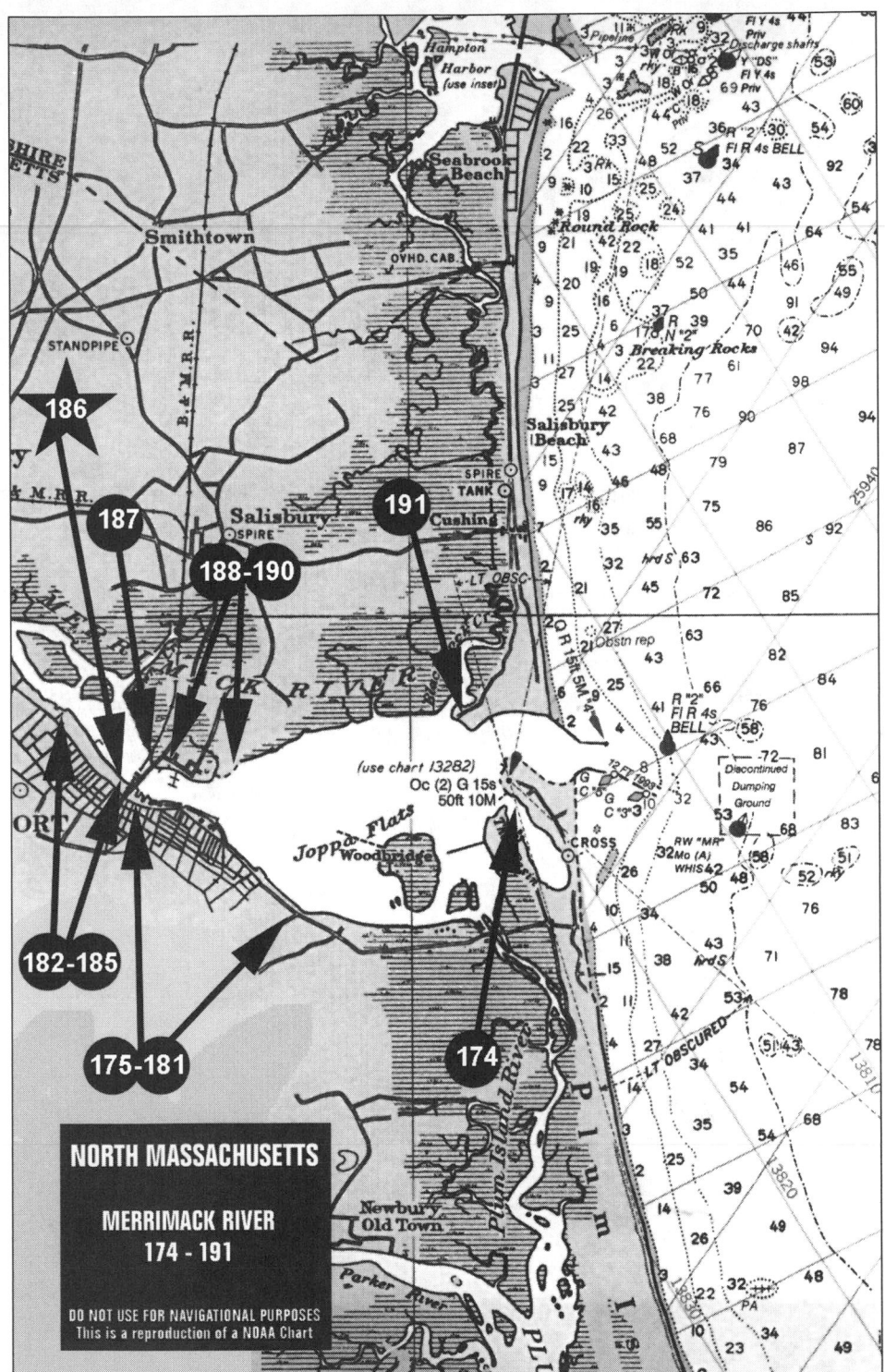

NORTH MASSACHUSETTS

MERRIMACK RIVER
174 - 191

DO NOT USE FOR NAVIGATIONAL PURPOSES
This is a reproduction of a NDAA Chart

Maine and New Hampshire

Map is not intended for navigational purposes.

USE NOAA CHARTS:

13283 • 13286 • 13288

13290 • 13292 • 13293

13295 • 13296 • 13298

13301 • 13302 • 13303

13305 • 13307 • 13308

13309 • 13312 • 13313

13315 • 13316 • 13318

13321 • 13323 • 13325

13327 • 13328

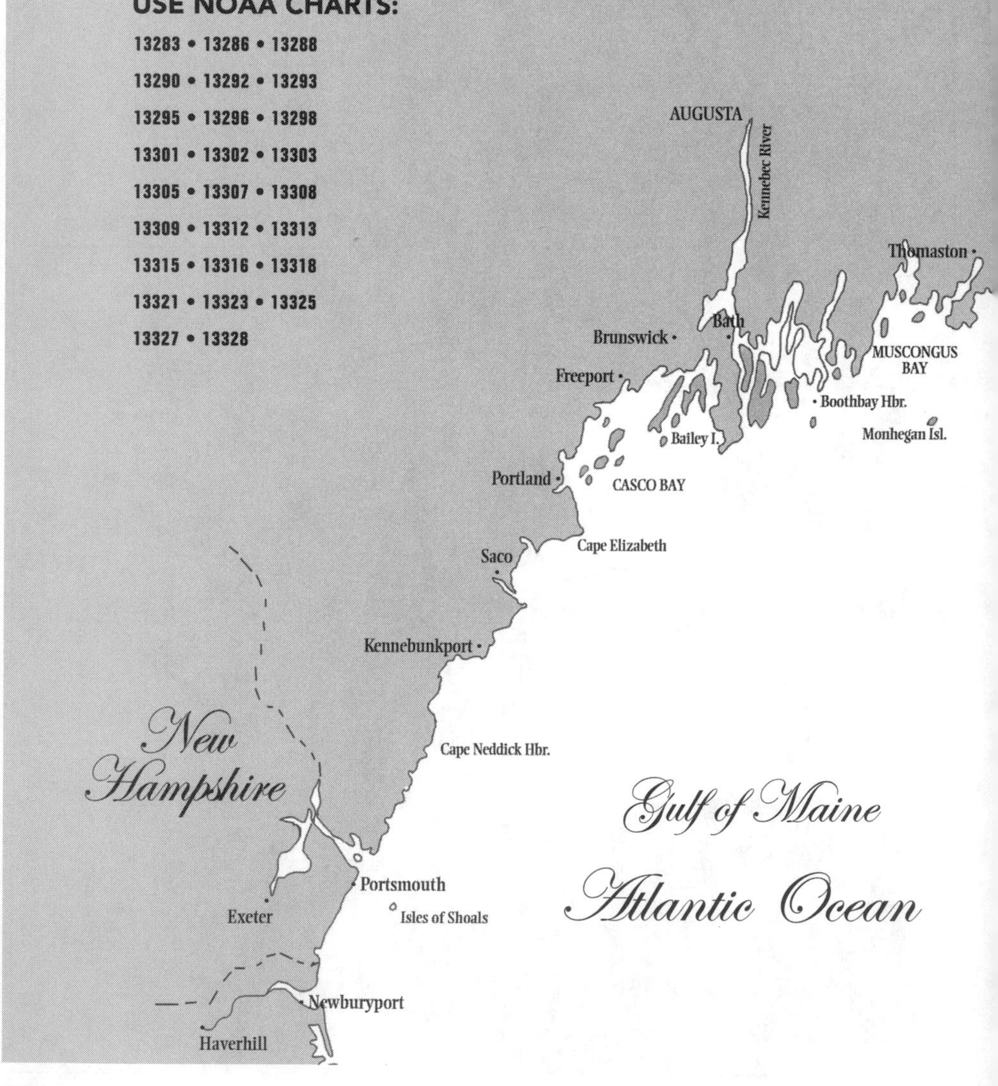

AUGUSTA

Kennebec River

Thomaston

Bath

Brunswick

MUSCONGUS BAY

Freeport

Boothbay Hbr.

Bailey I.

Monhegan Isl.

Portland

CASCO BAY

Saco

Cape Elizabeth

Kennebunkport

New Hampshire

Cape Neddick Hbr.

Gulf of Maine

Atlantic Ocean

Portsmouth

Exeter

Isles of Shoals

Newburyport

Haverhill

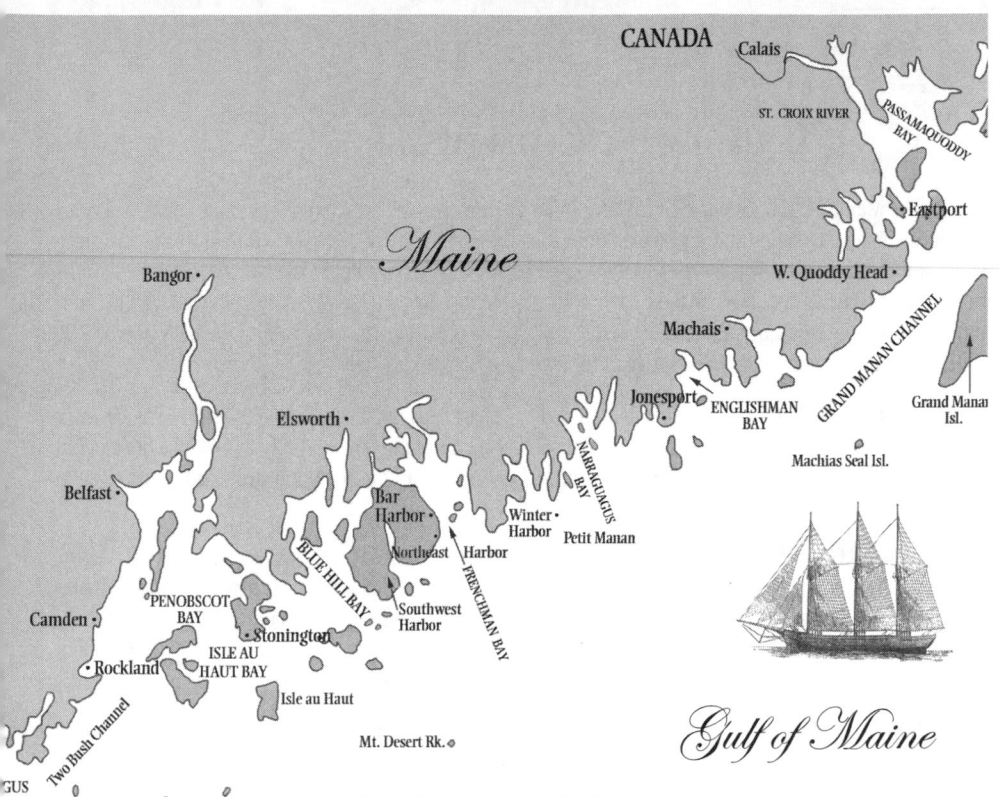

CANADA

Calais

ST. CROIX RIVER

PASSAMAQUODDY BAY

Maine

Bangor •

Eastport

W. Quoddy Head •

GRAND MANAN CHANNEL

Machais •

Grand Manan Isl.

Jonesport

ENGLISHMAN BAY

Elsworth •

NARRAGUAGUS BAY

Machias Seal Isl.

Belfast •

Bar Harbor •

Winter • Harbor   Petit Manan

Northeast   Harbor

BLUE HILL BAY

FRENCHMAN BAY

Camden •

PENOBSCOT BAY

Southwest Harbor

Stonington

Rockland

ISLE AU HAUT BAY

Isle au Haut

Two Bush Channel

GUS

Mt. Desert Rk.

Gulf of Maine

Martinicus Rk.

**THE FOLLOWING REGIONS ARE COVERED
IN CHARTS IN THIS SECTION:**

Cruising the Coast of Maine

Most of the Maine coast is irregular, rocky, and bold with numerous islands, bays, rivers, and coves. There are a variety of fishing villages and resort towns along the coast, which are popular with tourists during this area's short summer months. The more densely populated coasts of New Hampshire and Massachusetts have many sandy beaches and fewer islands, bays, and coves to discover -- which is what characterizes the fun of cruising in Maine. There are some 3,000 islands off Maine's coastline. As the crow flies, Maine's coast is 250 miles long but the actual running mileage of the coastline is approximately 3,500.

THE GULF OF MAINE is the great indentation of the coast between the Canadian Province of Nova Scotia on the northeast and Massachusetts on the southwest. It includes the Bay of Fundy and Massachusetts Bay as subsidiary features. Because of its fickle weather, frequent hazardous fogs, and strong tidal currents, this area provides a challenge to mariners.

THE PRUDENT MARINER will prepare well for a visit to this area. Bring at least two mooring lines no less than 100 feet in length -- a necessity due to extreme tidal drops. Anchor rode (calculate 6:1 at high tide) must also be long enough, and at least 18 feet of 3/8" anchor chain is recommended. Warm clothes are a must, and at least one wet suit and diving mask in case you snag one of the thousands of lobster buoys along the way. You might want to consider installing a prop cage for protection.

From **WEST QUODDY HEAD to PENOBSCOT BAY** the coast is mostly rocky and is indented by numerous large bays and excellent harbors. Among the many islands along this coast are passages that are frequently used, usually by vessels with less than 12 feet in draft, as they afford anchorage in head winds or thick weather. The many boulders, rocks, and ledges along, and off this coast require the closest attention of the navigator, as in many cases they rise abruptly from deep water and soundings do not generally indicate their proximity until it is too late to avoid them.

Between **PENOBSCOT BAY and CAPE ELIZABETH** the coast is rocky and broken by numerous bays and rivers — many are excellent harbors. In **MUSCONGUS and CASCO BAYS** good channels lead between the islands, affording inside passages that are used by the smaller class of vessels passing along the coast. Extreme caution should be exercised when approaching the bays, sounds, and rivers in this area due to the inset of the flood tidal currents. Particular caution is necessary for small craft crossing Penobscot Bay and the mouths of the Kennebec, Sheepscot, and New Meadows Rivers when the wind is contrary to the current because heavy tide rips are encountered. Great caution is also necessary when standing along this stretch of coast in thick weather due to the numerous dangers, which in some places lie nearly 10 miles offshore.

Between **CAPE ELIZABETH and PORTSMOUTH** there are fewer harbors and marked indentations. The shore is more thickly settled than farther eastward, and several of the beaches are popular summer resorts. The outlying dangers are well marked and fewer in number.

SOUTHWARD OF PORTSMOUTH the coast is low and mostly sandy, with a few outcropping ledges and outlying dangers, but the northern shore of Cape Ann is high and rocky.

Between **CAPE ANN and PLYMOUTH** the coast is rocky, mostly bold, and has numerous islands, dry rocks, boulders, and covered ledges near the shore, with deep channels between them. The shores of Cape Cod Bay are mostly sandy, with extensive sand shoals extending out well from the shore in many places. Boulders also occur in places in the Cape Cod Bay.

HELP!
Study the lobster buoys to judge current strength and direction.

CHARTS 13325, 13327, 13328: GRAND MANAN CHANNEL, between the coast of Maine and **GRAND MANAN ISLAND,** is an approach from westward to Quoddy

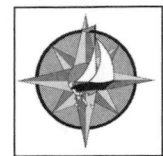

Narrows and Passamaquoddy Bay. It is the most direct passage for vessels bound up the Bay of Fundy from along the coast of Maine. The channel varies in width for 5.5 miles abreast of Campobello Island to 10 miles abreast of southwest Head, the southern point of Grand Manan Island. The western approach is marked by **MACHIAS SEAL ISLAND LIGHT** (82 feet tall, visible for 14 miles), which also marks most of the rocks and ledges that lie southwestward of Grand Manan Island. With the exception of the dangers between Machias Seal Island and Grand Manan Island, and the 33 ft. unmarked rocky patch known as Flowers Rock, (3.9 miles west-northwestward of Machias Seal Island) the channel is free and has a good depth of water. The tidal current's velocity is 2.5 knots and follows the general direction of the channel (Daily predictions are given in the Tidal Current Tables under Bay of Fundy Entrance.). Navigators should stay well off Machias Seal Island – shoals and tide rips are to its east and northeast. **Ed. Note:** Birdwatchers will want to take one of the tour boats from nearby harbors to this destination just to watch the puffins on parade. There is a quota set for the amount of people allowed on the island per day. Off West Quoddy Head, the currents run in and out of Quoddy Narrows, forming strong rips. Sailing vessels should not approach West Quoddy Head too closely with a light wind.

SOUTHWEST HEAD, the southern extremity of Grand Manan Island is a high cliff. Southwest Head Light 200 feet above the water is shown from a 30 foot white tower on the cliff. A fog signal and radiobeacon are at the light. It is the principal mark for Grand Manan Channel. A lighted whistle buoy is 0.7 mile south-south-westward of the light. Fogs often hang close in to the Maine coast between Manchias Bay and West Quoddy Head, extending about one-third the way across Grand Manan Channel.

From **MOOSE COVE to LITTLE RIVER,** a distance of about 6.5 miles, the coast has no features of importance. The several open, shallow coves include Bog Brook Cove, Holmes Cove, Black Point Cove and Long Point Cove. Just north of Little River are Almore Cove and Money Cove.

CHARTS 13312, 13318, 13322, 13323: The coast between **PETIT MANAN POINT and JERICHO BAY** is indented by **FRENCHMAN BAY, BLUE HILL BAY,** and numerous smaller bays and harbors. Mount Desert Island between Frenchman and Blue Hill Bays is mountainous and is the highest land feature on the coast of Maine. The summits are rounded, and several of them are nearly the same height, making it difficult to identify individual peaks at a distance.

CHART 13323. BAR HARBOR is a deep anchorage on the eastern side of Mount Desert island, 3.5 miles above Egg Rock Light, and an important summer resort and yachting center. Bar Harbor is also a town on the shore of the same name with a hospital, pharmacy, several banks, and good highway connections. During the summer many sightseeing cruises and fishing trips are scheduled daily for the vicinity of Frenchman Bay and Mount Desert Island. Keep an eye out for the CAT Ferry which runs from north of the harbor and makes daily trips to Yarmouth and Nova Scotia between 8a.m. and 4 p.m.

CHART 13318. ACADIA NATIONAL PARK comprises the greater part of the southern half of Mount Desert Island, particularly the mountainous areas and the lower half of Schoodic Peninsula on the eastern side of Frenchman Bay, including the scenic Schoodic Point and part of Isle au Haut. Schoodic Mountain, about 16 miles northward of Schoodic Point, is visible for a good distance off the coast.

CHART 13324. The bight between **PETIT MANAN BAR AND SCHOODIC PENINSULA** is the approach to **DYER BAY, GOULDSBORO BAY and PROSPECT HARBOR** . Local fishermen are the principal users of these waters. Vessels should use caution when crossing broken areas where the charted depth does not exceed the vessel draft by a considerable amount. The most important village is Prospect Harbor. Gouldsboro and Steuben can be reached by small craft at high water.

CHARTS 13305, 13315: Between **JERICHO BAY and PENOBSCOT BAY** are numerous islands. **DEER ISLE**, 10 miles westward of Mount Desert Island, is the largest. **EGGEMOGGIN REACH, DEER ISLAND THOROFARE, and MERCHANT ROW** are the three principal passages between the bays. Eggemoggin Reach, between Deer Isle and the mainland, connects Blue Hill Bay and the head of Jericho Bay with Penobscot Bay near its head. The reach is 11 miles long and has a width of about 0.4 miles at Byard Point. There are several villages along its shores.

MAINE

JERICHO BAY IS BETWEEN SWANS AND MARSHALL ISLANDS on the east, and Isle au Haut and Deer Isle and adjoining islands on the west. The inside routes from Casco Passage and York Narrows to Deer Island Thorofare and Merchant Row, and the passage north of Pond Island to Eggemoggin Reach, lead across the head of Jericho bay, this section of the bay is used by many craft. The part of the bay southward of these thoroughfares, has deep water but there are many ledges, rocks, and inlets. This area is used primarily by local fishermen and yacht owners. The dangers in the passages into Jericho Bay from the southward — eastward of Isle au Haut, in the channels between that island and Marshall Island — are for the most part not marked. This is the most direct way from the sea from that direction. There are however, a number of unmarked shoal spots, which must be avoided.

PENOBSCOT BAY, the largest and most important of the many indentations on the coast of Maine, is about 20 miles wide from Isle au Haut on the east to Whitehead Island on the west and 28 miles long from its entrance to the mouth of Penobscot River. A chain of large and small islands divides the bay into two parts, East Penobscot Bay and West Penobscot Bay. The southern part of East Penobscot Bay is Isle Au Haut Bay. Vinalhaven Island and North Haven Island are large islands dividing the southern part of the bay. Islesboro Island divides the bay near its head.

Numerous harbors indent the shores of Penobscot Bay, the most important being Rockland, Rockport, Camden, Belfast, and Searsport on the western shore; Castine and Stonington on the eastern shore; and Vinalhaven and North Haven in the center of the bay. The bay is the approach to Penobscot River, on which are several towns and the city of Bangor at the head of navigation. The bay ports collectively are among the leaders of the lobster industry in Maine.

The sea approaches to the bay are well marked by the lights on Monhegan Island and Matinicus Rock; the entrance is marked by **SADDLEBACK LEDGE LIGHT** on the east and by Whitehead and Two Bush Island Lights on the west side of the bay. The harbors are well lighted, and buoys or daybeacons marks the more important dangers. Deep-draft vessels use the bay throughout the year and recreational vessels are prevalent during the summer.

PENOBSCOT BAY, a region of rocks and ledges, requires extreme caution in navigating. After unusually high tides many logs are present in the bay, particularly from Belfast northward. These logs are dangerous to small craft. Penobscot Bay can be entered from eastward through Eggemoggin Reach, Deer Island Thorofare, or Merchant Row and from westward through Muscle Ridge Channel or Two Bush Channel.

There is no secure harbor for vessels at any of the islands southward off Penobscot Bay. However, small craft and local fishermen moor at Monhegan Island in Matinicus Harbor, which is the cove on the eastern side of Matinicus Island northward of Wheaton Island, and in Crehaven Harbor an indentation in the northwest part of Ragged Island. The waters of this area are well surveyed; deep passage exists between the islands, as shown on the chart. Because of the broken nature of the bottom, vessels, particularly deep-draft ones, should avoid all broken ground having depths less than 60 feet. Mostly local fishermen frequent these waters. The only settlements are on Monhegan, Matinicus, and Ragged Islands.

CHART 13305: EAST PENOBSCOT BAY is that part of Penobscot Bay located eastward of Vinalhaven, North Haven, and Islesboro Islands. The southern part of it, between Isle au Haut and Vinalhaven Island, is called Isle au Haut Bay.

There are many islands and numerous unmarked ledges in Isle au Haut Bay and East Penobscot Bay. The islands have numerous coves and small harbors, but few of these are available as anchorages, except for small craft, because of their shoal depths or obstructed entrances. The principal traffic through East Penobscot Bay moves in an east-west direction, with access through Eggemoggin

590

TO FIND MARINA LOCATIONS - SEE THE TABLES AND LOCATOR CHARTS AT THE END OF THIS SECTION.

MAINE

Reach, Deer Island Thorofare or Merchant Row from the eastward; or through Fox Islands Thorofare of the channels northward of North Haven Island, from the westward.

A seldom used clear channel, good for the deepest draft vessels, leads through **ISLE AU HAUT BAY** from Saddleback Ledge light to the head of East Penobscot Bay. The channel passes eastward of Eagle Island, marked by a light, and a gong buoy northeastward of the light; thence in a northwesterly direction through the islands, northward of Eagle Island, and northward passing close westward of Cape Rosier. The principal dangers in this channel are marked, with the exception of the areas near the shores. The principal thoroughfares east and west have also been swept.

SOUTHWEST HARBOR is on the western side of Deer Isle, about 4 miles north of Deer Island Thorofare Light. The harbor is about 0.3 mile wide at the entrance and 1 mile long.

LAWRYS NARROWS, between Leadbetter Island on the north and Lawrys and Cedar Islands on the south, is a part of the route between **CARVERS HARBOR and ROCKLAND**. The principal dangers are buoyed, except for a rock (covered 11 feet), reported in August 1979 to be 100 yards southwest of the southern end of Leadbetter Island. In February 1992 a submerged obstruction was reported at midchannel during periods of extreme low tides.

NORTH OF NORTH HAVEN ISLAND are numerous islands and reefs extending to Head of the Cape. The most westerly of the islands and reefs is Egg Rock, which is small and grass covered, and 2 miles north of Pulpit Harbor.

CHART 13307: OWLS HEAD BAY is between Sheep and Monroe Islands. The bay is a continuation of Muscle Ridge Channel northward of Fisherman Island Passage. The channel through Owls Head Bay is very narrow on the western side of Sheep Island between Sheep Island Bar and Hendrickson Point. Small vessels can anchor in the entrance to Owls Head Harbor, on the west side of the bay, between Dodge Point and the bar ledge, 0.2 mile southwestward, in depths of 9 to 24 feet. Anchorages in depths of about 6 feet can be found closer inshore. A lobster pound and wharf and a fish and lobster wharf is on the western shore with depth of 7 feet reported alongside.

CHARTS 13302, 13305, 13307: ROCKLAND HARBOR, one of the most important harbors in Penobscot Bay is on the west shore of West Penobscot Bay between Owls Head on the south and Jameson Point, 2.1 miles northwestward, on the north. The harbor offers anchorage for large vessels but is somewhat exposed to easterly winds. Northeasterly winds raise a heavy sea in the southwestern part of the harbor, but shelter may be found behind the breakwater.

ROCKLAND, a city on the western shore of the harbor has some trade in fish and petroleum products. State-run diesel-powered main, freight, automobile, and passenger ferries leave the Rockland Port Terminal in Lermond Cove several times daily for North Haven and Vinalhaven.

The most prominent objects in approaching **ROCKLAND HARBOR** are: the radio tower of station WRKD which is lighted at night; the aerolight at the Knox County Regional Airport; and the radio tower and signal mast at Rockland Coast Guard Station on Crockett Point.

MAINE

Several rocks and ledges are in the harbor. The visible ones are Shag Rock, on a cluster of bare rocks, 0.3 mile northwestward of Owls Head and marked by a daybeacon. Lowell Ledge, a cluster of rocks awash at low water on the south shore of the harbor opposite Jameson Point and Seal Ledge, which uncovers at about 5 feet, in the southwest end of the bay and marked by a daybeacon. A buoy marks Spears Rock, covered 5 feet about 300 yards northeastward of Lowell Ledge.

CAMDEN, a quaint walkable town on the western shore of Penobscot Bay, is the harbor of departure for many vessels in the windjammer fleet. From the eastern shore, follow East Penobscot Bay northward to the entrance of the Bagaduce River and **CASTINE**, home harbor to the "State of Maine," vessel to the Maine Maritime Academy. Entrance to the river is marked by Dice Head Light on the north shore. Although the river has strong tides, it's an easy and worthwhile trip. Head to Smith Cove or Hospital Island for anchoring as Castine's harbor has strong tidal currents.

CHARTS 13301, 13302: TENANTS HARBOR, 3 miles westward of Whitehead Light is an excellent anchorage frequently used as a harbor of refuge by small vessels and is of easy access. Southern Island on the southern side of the entrance is marked on its east side by an abandoned lighthouse, a white tower connected to a dwelling. A lighted bell buoy is east of the island. Northern Island is on the north side of the entrance. There are depths of 8 to 25 feet in the harbor.

The anchorage with most swinging room in Tenants Harbor is halfway from the western ends of Northern and Southern Islands to the stone pier on the north side. Small craft anchor more toward the head of the harbor. The bottom is mostly soft mud and good holding ground and shoals gradually westward. The north side of the harbor eastward of the stone pier is clear, while westward of it are spots with depths of 4 to 9 feet. The south side of the harbor, abreast the western entrance point of Long Cove, should be given a berth of 200 yards because of a ledge (covered 2 feet) making out into the harbor from the south shore. The harbor is open eastward and an easterly gale raises a choppy sea in the harbor, but vessels with good ground tackle can ride in safety. It is reported that a strong chop can also develop with a southwest wind and that craft of 6-foot draft or less can find calm anchorage in Long Cove on the north side of the harbor. The village of Tenants Harbor is on the northern shore near the head of the harbor.

MUSCONGUS, BOOTH, SHEEPSCOT, AND CASCO BAYS; MEDOMAK, DAMARISCOTTA, SHEEPSCOT, KENNEBEC, AND NEW MEADOWS RIVERS; and THE PORTS OF PORTLAND, BATH, BOOTHBAY HARBOR, and WISCASSET: These areas have many islands, rocks, and long peninsulas. Fixed highway bridges join many of the islands so as far as masted vessels are concerned, whole groups become additional peninsulas. In general, the outer islands and rocks rise from deep water and the lower parts of the rivers are deep.

CHARTS 13288, 13301: MUSCONGUS BAY between Georges Harbor on the east and Pemaquid Neck on the west forms the approach to Meduncook and Medomak Rivers and Muscongus Sound, the villages of Friendship, Round Pond, and Medomak, and the town of Waldoboro. The bay is frequented by small pleasure and fishing craft. Numerous islands and ledges and much foul ground obstruct it. Buoys mark many of the dangers.

Moser Ledge the outermost of the dangers, covered 15 feet and marked by a buoy lies about in the middle of the entrance to the bay, about on line between the north end of Monhegan Island and Pemaquid Point Light.

FRIENDSHIP HARBOR, about 1 mile long, with good anchorage in 21 to 28 feet, is used extensively by both fishermen and yachtsmen. The town of Friendship is on the north shore of Friendship Harbor. There are numerous wharves and piers with float landings on the north side of the harbor at Jameson Point; depths of 2 to 12 feet are reported alongside. Gasoline, diesel fuel and water are available at several of the landings, and marine supplies at some.

NEW HARBOR is on the western shore of **MUSCONGUS BAY** about 2.5 miles northeastward of

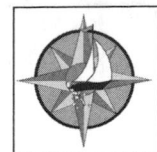

Pemaquid Point Light. A lighted bell buoy is off the entrance to the harbor. A church spire in the village of New Harbor at the head is prominent. The cove offers anchorage to small craft only and is open eastward. The channel is narrow between a shelving ledge extending northeastward from the south point at the entrance and a ledge just inside it, which extends halfway across from the north side and is marked at its end by a buoy. A 100-foot wide channel then leads northward of a day beacon between ledges to a dredged anchorage basin.

CHARTS 13288, 13293: JOHNS BAY (Johns River) is westward of **PEMAQUID NECK**. Its entrance is about 1.4 miles wide and the length of the bay is 2 miles to Johns Island which Pemaquid River empties into on the northeastern end. Johns River flows into the northwestern part. Depths in the bay are very irregular, and there are several ledges and rocks. A high square observatory tower on Rutherford Island and another tower 0.3 mile to the north are prominent. The bay has summer resorts on its shores and is used as an anchorage by fishermen and yachtsmen. The holding ground is poor except in a few spots near the head of the bay and in the coves. Port Clyde, eastward and Boothbay Harbor westward are preferable at all times.

CHARTS 13288, 13293, 13295, 13296, 13298: BOOTHBAY and LINEKIN BAY are between Linekin Neck and Fisherman Island on the east and Southport Island on the west. They form the approach to the town of **Boothbay Harbor** and many summer resorts which are frequented by a large number of fishing and pleasure craft in summer. Islands and rocks extend about 5 miles southward from the south end of Linekin Neck. The ground is very broken with rocks rising abruptly from deep water.

Ed. Note: Boothbay Harbor is deep and has easy access from all directions. In summer months it's also busier than a one-day-sale at Macy's. Shopping and chowing down on off-the-boat lobster, and soaking up local history (which some say dates back to the Vikings) are the to-dos in Boothbay. Mariners should plan well ahead and make a reservation at one of the many facilities in the harbor before arriving on the scene. If you want to be in the heart of village action, **The Tugboat Inn Marina** (207-633-4434 or VHF Channels 9 & 16) is the place to be with slips big enough for vessels up to 100 ft and moorings. The inn has a charming harbor-view restaurant and casual dining deck.

SHEEPSCOT RIVER is the approach to several small villages in the lower end and to the city of **WISCASSET** 14 miles above the entrance. The entrance is about 5 miles northeastward of Sequin Island, between The Cukolds and Griffith Head. The channel in Sheepscot River is deep and the principal dangers are marked. It is a region of rocks and ledges, many of them rising abruptly from deep water. The channel has a depth of over 30 feet to Wiscasset, it is navigable for small craft at high water for about 4

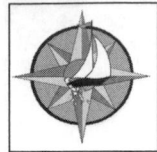

miles above Wiscasset, to the village of Sheepscot.

EBENECOOK HARBOR making into the northwest end of Southport Island is an excellent anchorage for vessels up to 20-foot draft. Its entrance about 1 mile above Hendricks Head on the eastern side of Sheepscot River leads between Dogfish Head on the south and the Green Islands on the north. It is the first large anchorage available for craft entering the river. The entrance is narrow.

The southern part of the harbor divides into three arms, the outer sections of which afford good, sheltered anchorage; the inner section to the heads is shoal and foul and should be avoided.

The mouth of the **KENNEBEC RIVER** is northward of Seguin Island and 20 miles eastward of the entrance of Portland Harbor. It is the approach to the cities of **BATH, AUGUSTA, RICHMOND, GARDINER** and smaller river towns. With the aid of the charts, small craft should have no trouble reaching Augusta, the head of navigation on the Kennebec River. There are two approaches to the entrance: the eastern (east of Seguin Island) which leads between Whaleback Rock and Pond Island, is the main channel. The entrance has strong tidal currents, and if the wind is opposed to the current, an ugly chop sea is encountered, which is at times dangerous for small craft.

Anchorage for pleasure craft is available on the western side of the channel off Parker Flats (about 4 miles above the entrance) in 20 to 36 feet of water. Above Parker Flats, vessels anchor wherever they find good holding ground and suitable depth – keeping out of the strength of the current.

CHART 13290: CASCO BAY is a very extensive area between Cape Small and Cape Elizabeth, a distance of 17.8 miles. Between the two capes, the bay extends up into the land an average distance of about 12 miles. There are 136 islands in Casco Bay, and many are fertile and under cultivation, but nearly all are inhabited.

In the eastern part of Casco Bay the best anchorage for strangers is in **NEW MEADOWS RIVER**. Local fishermen and boaters frequently use **SEBASCO and CUNDY HARBORS. POTTS HARBOR, HARPSWELL HARBOR and MACKEREL COVE** are good anchorages in the middle of the bay . Most of the dangers are marked, and waters are well charted. With the aid of the chart, no difficulty should be experienced in navigating Casco Bay in clear weather.

THE HARRASEEKET is a tidal river leading to **SOUTH FREEPORT**, a major yachting center with many facilities and good shoreside trips. The entrance to the Harraseeket is tricky and the currents are swift. Seek local knowledge especially at low tide. South Freeport is a well protected harbor at the north corner of Casco Bay.

CHART 13292: PORTLAND HARBOR , at the western end of Casco Bay, is the most important port on Maine's coast and is an active seaport for ocean-going vessels. Approaching Portland Harbor do be aware of commercial traffic such as inter-island ferries, commercial fishing vessels, cruise ships, and the high-speed "Scotia Prince," which runs at an amazingly fast clip. **Ed. Note:** The harbor-front area of the city (Old Port) has gone through a gentrification bringing back the charm and small storefronts of yesteryear, offering endless hours of browsing and munching up and down the narrow winding streets. Mariners lucky enough to grab a berth at DiMillo's Old Port Marina will be in a great spot to walk about. When in Portland, we never miss an opportunity to eat our fill of Oysters at J's Oyster Shack, adjacent to DiMillo's parking lot. Sit at the bar with the locals and the sweetest oysters you've ever tasted will just keep on coming.

CHART 13283: From Cape Elizabeth, the coast of Maine continues southwestward for about 37 miles to the Piscataqua River and the deepwater port of **PORTSMOUTH, NH.** The harbors along this part of Maine are few but they are welcoming to both fishing vessels and small pleasure craft. **Ed. Note:** Portsmouth has been an active seaport since the 17th century. The entrance is well-marked and water is deep. Be wary of the river currents as they can be downright wicked and time your transit at slack water.

As you enter Portsmouth's **LITTLE HARBOR** you'll see the majestic Wentworth Hotel on Castle Island.

This 1874 landmark has recently reopened after being closed for many years. Officially, it's now a Marriot. There is also snazzy resort marina nearby with slips to accommodate yachts up to 250 ft.

Extending south southwestward from **PORTSMOUTH HARBOR** is the 13 mile coast of New Hampshire. The Isles of Shoals are 6 miles southeast of the harbor. Southward and eastward from the New Hampshire line, the extreme northern part of the Massachusetts coast extends about 23 miles to Cape Ann Light. The Merrimack River approach to Newburyport, is about 3 miles south of the New Hampshire boundary.

CHART 13286: THE KENNEBUNK RIVER, about 2.5 miles southwestward of Goat Island Light, is the approach to the popular summer resort and yachting center of **KENNEBUNKPORT.**

CHART 13285: Above Portsmouth, the boundary between Maine and New Hampshire is the **PISCATAQUA RIVER** which forms the approach to Salmon Falls, and the Caoutchouc, Bellamy, Oyster, Lamprey, and Squamscott Rivers. It 's also the approach to the towns of Newington, Durham, Newmarket, and Exeter, and the city of Dover. **KITTERY** is a town worth visiting, on the north bank of the Piscataqua River opposite Portsmouth, where it seems the entire world goes for outlet shopping in the summer months.

THE PISCATAQUA RIVER is buoyed to a point about 2.5 miles above Dover Point and its western branch in Little Bay is marked for about 4.8 miles above Dover Point to a point in Great Bay, about 1 mile above Adams Point in Furber Strait. The channels in all the tributary rivers are narrow, crooked, shoal at the heads, and are unmarked. Local knowledge is necessary to navigate them. Some of the buoys are reported to tow under at times in strong currents, and in particular –Buoys 13 and 16 –which mark extensive shoals. Pay attention! This is the second fastest flowing river in the continental U.S.

The coast has a general southwesterly trend with no marked indentations from Portsmouth Harbor's entrance for 5 miles to Rye Ledge. It presents the appearance of a succession of sand beaches separated by ledges that extend out about 0.5 miles with occasional hotels and many summer homes in back of the high water line.

CHART 13283: The ISLES of SHOALS are about 6 miles offshore and about the same distance southeastward of Portsmouth harbor entrance. They consist of a group of nine main islands and a number of inlets, rocks, and ledges. They extend about 3 miles in a northeast- southwest direction and on a clear day can be seen for 10 miles. On a voyage of exploration northward from the Jamestown Colony in 1614, Captain John Smith drew a chart of the New England Coast and named these islands "Smith Isles." However the group had been known as the Isles of Shoals for some time before his arrival. Earlier, fishermen, mostly from England had found it profitable to sail there in early spring and return home in the fall with rich cargoes of fish –primarily cod –caught and cured at the isles. Five of the nine islands are in Maine (Duck, Appledore, Smuttynose, Malaga, and Cedar) and four are in New Hampshire (Star, Lunging, White, and Seaveys). These islands have been the subject of many a gory tale and numerous seafaring legends about piracy, buried treasure, and bloody battles, passed down through the years from one generation to another. ⚓

MAINE FACILITIES alphabetical index

NEW HAMPSHIRE FACILITIES
alphabetical index

New Hampshire

CHART LOCATER NUMBER	MARINA'S NAME & PHONE NUMBER	WHEN OPEN	MONITORS VHF CHANNEL	TRANSIENT Electricity • Moorings • Berths	Hull repairs • Engine repairs • Ramp	WINTER STORAGE: Wet • Dry	RAILWAY CAPACITY IN FEET	LIFT CAPACITY IN TONS	BOAT RENTAL: Canoe • Row • Motor	BOAT RENTAL: Charter • Lodging • House • Sail • Camping	Restaurant	Showers • Laundry • Toilets	Bait • Tackle • Water • Ice	Groceries • Hardware	Diesel fuel • Gasoline
2	EASTMAN'S FISHING PARTIES 603-474-3461	APR NOV	09 70							C		T	IBT	H	D
3	YANKEE FISHERMAN'S CO-OP 603-474-9850	ALL YR.	11 09									S T	I		G D
4	SMITH & GILMORE PIER 603-926-3503	APR NOV	09 70							R	C		T	BT IW		
5	HAMPTON RIVER MARINA 603-929-1422	ALL YR.		EB	R	D						S T	IW	G	G D
6	RYE HARBOR STATE MARINA 603-964-9008	APR OCT		M	R						C		T	BT IW		G D
8	B.G.S. BOATHOUSE MARINA 603-431-1074	MAR NOV		B	R								T	I		
9	WITCH'S COVE MARINA	ALL YR.	EB	HE	R	D		25				T	W	H	
10	WENTWORTH BY-THE-SEA MARINA 603-433-5050 SEE AD	ALL YR.	9 16 68 71	M EB	HE	W				R		SL PT	BT IW	GH	G D
11	PORTSMOUTH Y. C. 603-436-9877	MAY OCT	9	M	S							T	IW	G D	
13	PRESCOTT PARK DOCK 603-431-8748	APR OCT		EB	R							L T	W		
14	PIER II 603-436-0669	FEB DEC		B	R										
15	HARBOUR PLACE MARINA 603-436-0915	ALL YR.	13 16	EB	W								W		

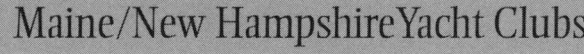

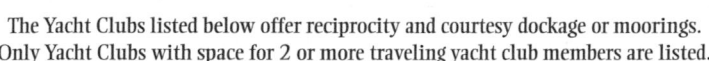

Maine/New Hampshire Yacht Clubs

The Yacht Clubs listed below offer reciprocity and courtesy dockage or moorings. Only Yacht Clubs with space for 2 or more traveling yacht club members are listed.

New Hampshire

NEW CASTLE
PORTSMOUTH YACHT CLUB
(603) 436-9877

Maine

BOOTHBAY
BURLEIGH HILL YACHT CLUB
(207) 633-6755

WEST BOOTHBAY HARBOR
BOOTHBAY HARBOR YC
(207) 633-5750

BRUNSWICK
MERE POINT YACHT CLUB
(207) 729-7284

CAMDEN
CAMDEN YACHT CLUB
(207) 236-3014

MARLBORO
MARLBORO YACHT CLUB
(207) 667-4742

ORR'S ISLAND
ORRS BAILEY YACHT CLUB
(207) 833-7374

PEAK'S ISLAND
PEAK'S ISLAND CRUISING
CLUB (207) 766-5090

Maine

MARINA'S NAME & PHONE NUMBER

CHART LOCATER NUMBER	MARINA'S NAME & PHONE NUMBER	WHEN OPEN	MONITORS VHF CHANNEL	TRANSIENT Electricity • Moorings • Berths	Hull repairs • Engine repairs • Ramp	WINTER STORAGE: Wet • Dry	RAILWAY CAPACITY IN FEET	LIFT CAPACITY IN TONS	BOAT RENTAL: Canoe • Row • Motor	BOAT RENTAL: Charter • House • Sail	Restaurant • Lodging • Camping	Showers • Laundry	Pumpout • Toilets	Bait • Tackle • Water • Ice	Groceries • Water • Hardware	Diesel fuel • Gasoline
1	BADGERS ISLAND MARINA 207-439-4456	ALL YR.	9	EB	HE	W		100				S	T	IW	H	
2	KITTERY LANDING 603-436-3611					W										
3	WARREN'S LOBSTER HOUSE 207-439-1630	ALL YR									R					
4	DION'S YACHT YARD 207-439-9582	ALL YR.	9 16 68	EM B	HE	W D	75	100			RL	SL	T	IW	G H	
5	PEPPERELL COVE Y. C.											S	T			
6	FRISBEE'S SUPERMARKET 207-439-0014	ALL YR.									R		T	I	G	G D
7	KITTERY TOWN WHARF 207-439-0912 RESIDENTS ONLY			M	R								T			
8	DONNELL'S 207-363-4308	ALL YR.	9		R									W		
9	YORK HARBOR TOWN DOCK		9	M												
10	YORK HARBOR MARINE SERV. 207-363-3602	ALL YR.	9	EB	HE	W D	80	100				SL		IW		D G
11	PORTSIDE LODGE 207-967-4050	APR OCT		EB							RL			I		
13	KENNEBUNKPORT MARINA 207-967-3411	ALL YR.	9 16	EB	R	D						SL	T	IW		
14	YACHTSMAN MARINA 207-967-2511	MAY OCT	9 16								L	SL	T	IW		G D
15	PERFORMANCE MARINE 207-967-5550	ALL YR.	9 68	EM B	HE	WD		13			C	S	T	IW	H	
16	MEETINGHOUSE EDDY RAMP				R											
17	RUMERY'S BOATYARD 207-282-0408	ALL YR.	16 68	B	HE	D		25				S	T			
19	RIVERSIDE ANCHORAGE 207-283-3727	JUN OCT			R											G
20	NORWOOD'S MARINA 207-282-7411	MAY OCT	9 72	MB		D						S				
21	CAMP ELLIS PIER 207-282-4072			M	R						C			W		D
22	PINE POINT HARBOR RAMP 207-883-5337	JUL AUG			R						C					

Maine

MARINA'S NAME & PHONE NUMBER

CHART LOCATER NUMBER	MARINA'S NAME & PHONE NUMBER	WHEN OPEN	MONITORS VHF CHANNEL	TRANSIENT (Electricity • Moorings • Berths)	Hull repairs • Engine repairs • Ramp	WINTER STORAGE: Wet • Dry	RAILWAY CAPACITY IN FEET	LIFT CAPACITY IN TONS	BOAT RENTAL (Canoe • Row • Motor) / Restaurant • Lodging • House • Sail	Showers • Laundry	Pumpout • Toilets	Bait • Tackle	Water • Ice	Groceries • Hardware	Diesel fuel • Gasoline
24	PINE POINT FISHERMAN CO OP 207-883-3588	MAR JAN									T		I		
25	HANDY BOAT SERV. 207-781-5110	ALL YR.	9		HE	D		35			PT		I	GH	G D
26	FALMOUTH RAMP				R										
29	SOUTH PORTLAND RAMP				R										
30	BREAKWATER MARINA 9207-799-1549	ALL YR.	9 16	EB						SL	T		IW		
31	SPRING POINT MARINA 207-767-3254	ALL YR.	9 79	EB	HE	W D		35	R	SL	PT	BT	IW	GH	G D
32	SOUTH PORT MARINE 207-799-8191	ALL YR.	9 78	EB	HE R	W		15	R	S	T		IW	GH	
33	PORTLAND YACHT SERV. 207-774-1067	ALL YR	.9	MB	HE R	D		50	C	S	T		W		
34	CHASE LEAVITT COMPANY 207-772-3751	ALL YR.	10 16	E										H	
35	GOWEN MARINE 207-773-1761	ALL YR.	9		HE	D		50			T		I	H	G D
36	DIMILLO'S MARINA 207-773-7632	ALL YR.	9	EB					R	SL	T		IW	GH	G D
37	EAST END BOAT RAMP 207-874-8300	MAY SEP			R										
38	STROUTS POINT WHARF CO. 207-865-3899	ALL YR	9	EM B	HE			25	CS	S	T		IW	H	G D
39	BREWER'S SO. FREEPORT MARINE 207-865-3181	ALL YR.	9	EB	HE	D		25		S	PT		IW		G D
40	WINSLOW MEMORIAL PARK	MAY SEP			R				C	S	T				
41	YARMOUTH TOWN LANDING				R						T				
42	YARMOUTH BOATYARD 207-846-9050	ALL YR	9	EB	HE R	D		14			T		W		
43	YANKEE MARINA & BOATYARD 207-846-4326	ALL YR.			HE	D		35		S	T		I	H	
44	ROYAL RIVER BOATYARD 207-846-9577	ALL YR.			HE	D		50		S	T		IW	H	G D
45	CHEBEAGUE ISLAND BOATYARD 207-846-4146	ALL YR.			HE	D	40	15						H	G D

Maine

MARINA'S NAME & PHONE NUMBER

CHART LOCATER NUMBER	MARINA'S NAME & PHONE NUMBER	WHEN OPEN	MONITORS VHF CHANNEL	TRANSIENT Electricity•Moorings•Berths	Hull repairs•Engine repairs•Ramp	WINTER STORAGE: Wet•Dry	RAILWAY CAPACITY IN FEET	LIFT CAPACITY IN TONS	BOAT RENTAL: Canoe•Row•Motor	BOAT RENTAL: Charter•House•Sail	Restaurant•Lodging•Camping	Showers•Laundry	Pumpout•Toilets	Bait•Tackle•Water•Ice	Groceries•Hardware	Diesel fuel•Gasoline
46	DOLPHIN MARINE SERV. 207-833-6000	ALL YR.	9	M	HE R	D		10					T	I	H	G D
48	MACKEREL COVE MARINA 207-833-6656		9 16										T	I WT		G D
49	COOK'S LOBSTER HOUSE 207-833-2818	ALL YR.		MB	R						R		T	I		G D
50	LOOKOUT POINT RAMP				R											
51	FINESTKIND BOATYARD 207-833-6885	ALL YR.			HE	D		15								
52	MAINE MARITIME MUSEUM 207-443-1316	ALL YR.	9 16	M									T			
53	GOOD CATCH MARINE 207-563-8496			E	EH						C		T			
54	BFC MARINE 207-443-3022	ALL YR.			HE R	D							T	T	H	G
55	BATH RAMP				R								T			
56	BATH LANDING	APR OCT											T	I		
57	NEW MEADOWS MARINA	ALL YR.		EB	E			8	M			S	T	W	H	G
58	NEW MEADOWS RAMP 207-443-6277				R											
59	WATER STREET RAMP				R											
60	GREAT ISLAND BOATYARD 207-729-1639	ALL YR.	9	EM B	HE R	D		22					T	IW	H	G D
61	QUAHOG LOBSTERMENS CO-OP 207-725-6222	APR DEC	8											I	H	G D
62	SEBASCO WHARF 207-389-2756	ALL YR.		EM B							R		T	IW	G	G
63	SEBASCO LODGE 207-389-1161	MAY OCT	9	M					CM	CS	RL	SL		WI		G
64	ALVIN BREWER'S BOATYARD 207-389-1388	MAY NOV			H	D		35							H	
66	SEAHORSE 207-389-2312	ALL YR.												B		G D
67	HOLBROOK'S LOBSTER WHARF 207-725-5697	ALL YR.	6 10											I	G	

Maine

MARINA'S NAME & PHONE NUMBER

Chart Locater Number	Marina's Name & Phone Number	When Open	Monitors VHF Channel	Transient: Electricity • Moorings • Berths	Hull repairs • Engine repairs	Ramp	Winter Storage: Wet • Dry	Railway Capacity in Feet	Lift Capacity in Tons	Boat Rental: Canoe • Row • Motor • Sail / Charter	Restaurant • Lodging • House • Camping	Showers • Laundry	Pumpout • Toilets	Bait • Tackle	Water • Ice	Groceries • Hardware	Diesel fuel • Gasoline
68	THE PIER 207-729-4810																G D
69	WATSON'S GENERAL STORE 207-725-7794	ALL YR.											T		I	GH	G D
70	HERMIT ISLAND CAMPING 207-443-2101	JUN–OCT										S	T	B	I	G	
71	PINEDEROSA CAMPGROUND 207-646-2492			M						C							
72	MIDCOAST LOBSTER 207-529-5622	MAR–DEC	5 9											B			G D
73	MUSCONGUS BAY LOBSTER CO 207-529-5528	MAY–NOV													I		G D
74	ROUND POND LOBSTER 207-529-5725	APR–DEC	5	M											I		D
75	ROUND POND RAMP					R											
76	PADEBCO CUSTOM BOATS 207-529-5106	ALL YR.		M	HE		D		20							H	
77	NEW HARBOR CO-OP 207-677-2791	ALL YR.	6								R		T				G D
78	GOSNOLD ARMS REST. 207-677-3727	MAY–NOV		MB						CR	RL						
79	SHAW'S LOBSTER WHARF 207-677-2200	MAY–OCT									R		T		I		G D
80	PEMAQUID FISHERMAN'S CO-OP 207-677-2801	ALL YR.	6						35				T	B		H	G D
81	KONITZKY BOAT WORKS 207-677-3726	ALL YR.		M	HE		D		30				T			H	
82	ROBINHOOD MARINE CTR. 207-371-2525	ALL YR.	9	EM B	HE		W D		35		R	SL	PT		IW	H	G D
83	GREY HAVENS INN 207-371-2616	JUN–OCT									RL						
84	FIVE ISLANDS TOWN DOCK												T		I		
85	SHEEPSCOT BAY BOAT CO. 207-371-2442	ALL YR.	9	EM B	HE		D		10	R							
86	RANDLETT'S GUY BOATYARD 207-633-4549	APR–OCT					D	25									
88	PRATT GENERAL MERCHANDISE 207-633-4929	JUL–SEP											T		I	G	G

MARINA'S NAME & PHONE NUMBER

Chart Locater Number	Marina's Name & Phone Number	When Open	Monitors VHF Channel	Transient: Electricity • Moorings • Berths	Hull repairs • Engine repairs • Ramp	Winter Storage: Wet • Dry	Railway Capacity in Feet	Lift Capacity in Tons	Boat Rental: Canoe • Row • Motor	Boat Rental: Charter • Row • House • Sail	Restaurant • Lodging • Camping	Showers • Laundry	Pumpout • Toilets	Bait • Tackle • Water • Ice	Groceries • Hardware	Diesel fuel • Gasoline
89	BOOTHBAY BOATYARD 207-633-2970	ALL YR.	9	EM B	HE	D		35				SL	T	IW	H	G D
90	NEWAGEN SEASIDE INN 207-633-5242	JUN SEP							R	S	RL					
91	OCEAN GATE MOTOR INN 207-633-3321	MAY NOV									RL		T	I		
92	WOTTON LOBSTER CO 207-633-6569															G D
93	FISHERMAN'S WHARF REST, 207-633-5090	MAY OCT									RL					
94	SAMPLES SHIPYARD 207-633-3171	ALL YR.	9	M	HE	D		50					T		H	
95	BOOTHBAY HARBOR LANDING		9 12 16										T			
96	BOOTHBAY HARBOR MARINA 207-633-6003	MAY OCT	9	MB		W			M	S	RL	SL	T	IW		
97	SHIP AHOY MOTEL 207-633-5222	MAY OCT									L			I		
98	ROBINSON'S WHARF 207-633-3033	JUN SEP	10								RL		T	I	H	
99	BLAKES BOATYARD 207-633-5040	ALL YR.	9 16	M	HE	D		6					T	IW	H	
101	SPRUCE POINT INN 207-633-4152	MAY OCT		MB							R					
103	ROCKTIDE INN 207-633-4455	JUN OCT									RL					
104	BROWN'S WHARF REST 207-633-5440	MAY OCT	9	EM B						C	RL			I		
106	CHANNEL MARINE SUPPLY 207-633-0709	APR OCT	9								RL		T	I	H	
107	CAPTAIN FISH'S MARINA 207-633-3244	MAY OCT	9 16	MB						C	RL					
108	BOOTHBAY LOBSTERMEN'S CO OP 207-633-4900	ALL YR.	10										T	I	H	G D
109	CAROUSEL MARINA 207-633-2922	MAY OCT	9	EM B	ER	D										G D
110 SEE AD	TUGBOAT INN RESTAURANT & MARINA 207-633-4434	ALL YR.	9 16	EM B		W				S	RL	SL	PT	IW	H	G
113	JONES J. ERVIN BOAT SHOP 207-633-2824	ALL YR			HE		45	20								

Maine

MARINA'S NAME & PHONE NUMBER

CHART LOCATER NUMBER	Marina's Name & Phone Number	When Open	Monitors VHF Channel	Transient Electricity • Moorings • Berths	Hull repairs • Engine repairs	Winter Storage: Wet • Dry	Railway Capacity (ft)	Lift Capacity (tons)	Boat Rental: Canoe • Row • Motor	Boat Rental: Charter • House • Sail	Restaurant • Lodging • Camping	Showers	Pumpout • Laundry	Bait • Tackle • Toilets	Groceries • Water • Ice	Groceries • Hardware	Diesel fuel • Gasoline
114	LOBSTERMAN'S WHARF 207-633-3443	APR OCT									RL			T	I		
115	BOOTHBAY MARINE 207-633-5501			M	H	D		30								H	
116	C & B MARINA 207-633-0773	ALL YR.	9 / 16	EM B	HE	D		25				R	S	L	T	IW	H	G D
117	OCEAN POINT INN 207-633-4200	MAY OCT									RL						
118	LUKE PAUL E. 207-633-4971	ALL YR			H	D	55	20								H	
119	SMUGGLERS COVE 207-633-2800	MAY OCT									RL			T	I		
120	LEEWARD VILLAGE 207-633-3681	MAY OCT		M							L						
121	LITTLE RIVER LOBSTER CO 207-633-2648	ALL YR.	6 / 10														G D
122	SPAR SHED MARINA 207-633-4389			MB													
123	MCFARLAND'S BOATYARD 207-644-8342	ALL YR			HE												
124	COVESIDE MARINA 207-644-8282	JUN SEP	9 / 68	EM B					R	CS	RL	S		T	IW		G D
126	SOUTH BRISTOL STORAGE 207-644-8181	ALL YR	16	EB M	HE	D		25			RL			T	IW	G H	G D
127	FARRIN'S LOBSTER POUND 207-644-8500	ALL YR.												B T	I	G	G D
129	S. BRISTOL FISHERMAN'S CO-OP 207-644-8224	ALL YR.	67												I	H	G D
130	EUGLEY'S WHARF 207-644-8301													T	I	H	G D
131	JOHN'S BAY BOAT COMPANY 207-644-8261	ALL YR.			HE		50	20						T			
132	PORT CLYDE GENERAL STORE 207-372-6543	ALL YR.	9	M							R	S		T	W	G H	G D
133	PORT CLYDE BOAT FACILITY								R								
134	PORT CLYDE CO-OP 207-372-8922	ALL YR.	8											B		H	G D
135	HALL'S DOCK 207-832-4830	ALL YR.															G D

Maine

MARINA'S NAME & PHONE NUMBER

Chart Locater Number	Marina's Name & Phone Number	When Open	Monitors VHF Channel	Transient: Electricity • Moorings • Berths	Hull repairs • Engine repairs • Ramp	Winter Storage: Wet • Dry	Railway Capacity in Feet	Lift Capacity in Tons	Boat Rental: Canoe • Row • Motor	Boat Rental: Charter • House • Sail	Restaurant • Lodging • Camping	Showers • Laundry	Pumpout • Toilets	Bait • Tackle • Water • Ice	Groceries • Hardware	Diesel fuel • Gasoline
137	COASTAL FISHERIES 207-832-5517	ALL YR.	73												H	G D
139	DUTCH NECK LANDING				R											
140	WALDOBORO TOWN LANDING				R											
141	BROAD COVE MARINE SERV. 207-529-5186	MAY OCT		MB	E								T	I	G	G D
142	MUSCONGUS MARINA				R											
143	SOUTH THOMASTON RAMP				R											
144	SPRUCE HEAD MARINE 207-594-7545	ALL YR.	16	EB	HE	D		20			RL		T		GH	
145	MERCHANT'S LANDING MOORINGS 207-594-7459	MAY SEP		M									T	IW		
146	SPRUCEHEAD FISHERMAN CO OP 207-594-7980	ALL YR.												B		G D
147	WILLIAM ATWOOD LOBSTERS CO 207-596-6691	ALL YR.												IB	G	
150	ARTS LOBSTER INC 207-372-6265	ALL YR.		M										I		G D
151	EAST WIND INN 207-372-6366	ALL YR									RL					
152	COD END WHARF 207-372-6782	MAY OCT	16								RL			I		G D
153	TENANTS HARBOR RAMP				R											
154	LYMAN MORSE BOAT BLD. 207-354-6904	ALL YR.			HE	D						S	T			
158	THOMASTON HARBOR	MAY NOV			R											
159	JEFF'S MARINE SERV. 207-354-8777	ALL YR.		EB	HE R	D		10	M		RL		T	W	H G	
160	ROCKPORT MARINE PARK 207-236-0676		9 16	M	R						C		T			
161	ROCKPORT MARINE 207-236-9651	ALL YR.		EMB	HE	D		35			R	S	T	IW		G D
162	WAYFARER MARINE CORP 207-236-4378	ALL YR.	9 16	EMB	HE	D	100	99+			RL	SL	PT	IW	HG	G D

Maine

Chart Locater Number	Marina's Name & Phone Number	When Open	Monitors VHF Channel	Hull repairs • Engine repairs	Transient: Electricity • Moorings • Berths	Winter Storage: Wet • Dry	Railway Capacity • Ramp	Lift Capacity in Feet	Lift Capacity in Tons	Boat Rental: Canoe • Row • Motor	Boat Rental: Charter • House • Sail	Restaurant • Lodging • Camping	Showers • Laundry	Pumpout • Toilets	Bait • Tackle • Water • Ice	Groceries • Hardware	Diesel fuel • Gasoline
163	HARBOR HEAD MARINA 207-236-3264	ALL YR.	9	HE	M	D						RL	SL	T	IW	H	
164	CAMDEN LANDING 207-236-7969		16									RL		T	I		
165	WILLEY WHARF 207-236-3256	APR OCT			EB							RL	S	T	IW		G D
167	A.L. CHARTER 207-273-3408		71		M						C						
169	REED'S WHARF 207-594-4604																G
170	OWL'S HEAD RAMP						R										
172	KNIGHT MARINE SERV 207-594-4068	ALL YR.	9 16	HE	EM B	W D			35			RL	SL	T	IW	G	G D
173	JOURNEY'S END MARINA 207-594-4444	APR OCT	9 16	HE	EB M	D			60		C	RL	S	PT	IW	GH	G D
174	ROCKLAND PUBLIC ACCESS						R										
175	ROCKLAND TOWN DOCK 207-594-0312				EM B		R					RL	SL	PT	IW		
179	CASTINE TOWN WHARF				MB												
180	EATON'S BOATYARD 207-326-8579	ALL YR.	9 16	HE	EM B								S	PT	IW		G D
181	DENNETT'S WHARF 207-329045	MAY OCT			M							R	S	T	I		
182	FOUR FLAGS SHIP CHANDLERY 207-326-8526	ALL YR														H	
184	STOCKTON RAMP 207-567-3404				M		R										
185	LOBSTER POUND 207-789-5550	MAY OCT			M							R		T	I		
186	LINCOLNVILLE RAMP						R										
188	PENDLETON YACHT YARD 207-734-6728	ALL YR.	9 10 16	HE	M	D		40	15							H	G D
189	ISLESBORO RAMP						R							T			
190	WARREN ISLAND STATE PARK 207-596-2253													T			

Maine

MARINA'S NAME & PHONE NUMBER

CHART LOCATER NUMBER	MARINA'S NAME & PHONE NUMBER	WHEN OPEN	MONITORS VHF CHANNEL	TRANSIENT Electricity•Moorings•Berths	Hull•Engine repairs•Ramp	WINTER STORAGE Wet•Dry	RAILWAY CAPACITY IN FEET	BOAT CAPACITY IN TONS	LIFT CAPACITY IN FEET	BOAT RENTAL Canoe•Row•Motor / Charter•House•Sail	Restaurant•Lodging•Camping	Showers•Laundry	Bait•Tackle	Pumpout•Toilets	Groceries•Water•Ice	Hardware	Diesel fuel•Gasoline
191	DARK HARBOR BOATYARD 207-734-2246	ALL YR.	9 16	M	HE	D	60	20				SL		T	IW	H	G D
192	BELFAST RAMP		9	M	R						R	S		T	I		G D
193	BELFAST BOATYARD 207-338-5098	ALL YR.		B	HE	D	40	20									
194	BELFAST HARBOR INN 207-338-2740	ALL YR									RL						
195	YOUNG'S LOBSTER POUND 207-338-1160	ALL YR.			R						RL			T	I		
196	SEARSPORT RAMP				R												
197	EAST BLUE HILL RAMP				R												
198	MORGAN BAY BOAT CO 207-374-2509	ALL YR.			HE	D		12								H	
199	RAYNES MARINE WORKS 207-374-2877	ALL YR.			HE R	D		12								H	
200	BLUE HILL TOWN LANDING				R												
201	FLYE POINT MARINE 207-359-4641	ALL YR.			H												
202	BRIDGES POINT BOATYARD 207-359-2713	ALL YR.				D										H	
204	ATLANTIC BOAT CO. 207-359-4658	ALL YR.			HE												
205	BROOKLIN BOATYARD 207-359-2236	ALL YR		M	HE	D	50	15								H	
206	BENJAMIN RIVER MARINE 207-359-2244	ALL YR.		M	HE	D	45	30								H	
207	JERICHO BAY BOATYARD 207-348-9923	ALL YR.		M	HE	D	100	30								H	
208	HEANSSLER LOBSTERS 207-348-2557	ALL YR.	28 88													H	G D
209	CONARY COVE LOBSTER CO 207-348-6185	ALL YR.											B			H	G D
210	EATON'S PIER 207-348-2489	MAY OCT		M	R						R						
211	BILLINGS MARINE SERV. 207-367-2328	ALL YR.	16	EM B	HE	D	150	400				SL		T	I	H	G D

Maine
MARINA'S NAME & PHONE NUMBER

#	Marina's Name & Phone Number	When Open	Monitors VHF Channel	Transient: Electricity•Moorings•Berths	Hull•Engine Repairs•Ramp	Winter Storage: Wet•Dry	Railway Cap. (tons)	Lift Cap. (feet)	Boat Rental: Canoe•Row•Motor	Boat Rental: Charter•Lodging•House•Sail	Restaurant•Lodging•House	Showers•Laundry•Camping	Bait•Tackle•Toilets	Groceries•Water•Ice	Pumpout•Hardware	Diesel fuel•Gasoline
214	BARTLETT'S MARKET 207-367-2386	ALL YR.												I		G
216	STONINGTON CO-OPS 207-367-2286	ALL YR.	68										T	IB	H	G D
219	EATON LOBSTER REST 207-348-2383	MAY SEP									R		T			
220	EGGEMOGGIN INN 207-348-2540	MAY OCT									L		T			
221	GOLDEN STAIRS 207-326-4369	MAY NOV			E								T		H	
223	BUCK'S HARBOR MARINE 207-326-8839	MAY OCT	9 16	M	E				R	C	RL	SL	T	I WT	GH	G D
224	ORCUTT'S HARBOR MARINE 207-326-4179	MAR DEC				D										
225	SEAL COVE BOATYARD 207-326-4422	ALL YR.			HE	D	50	30							H	
226	HOPKINS BOATYARD 207-863-2551	ALL YR.		M	HE	D	50	10							H	
227	FISHERMEN'S FRIEND 207-863-2140	ALL YR.	9										T	T	GH	
229	VINALHAVEN TOWN WHARF 207-863-2279				R											
230	VINALHAVEN FISHERMAN CO-OP 207-863-2263	ALL YR	6											B	H	G D
231	BROWN'S COAL REST. 207-867-4739	MAY SEP	9 16	MB							R					
232	J.O. BROWN & SON 207-867-4621	ALL YR.	9 16	MB	HE	D		15			R	SL	T	IW	GH	G D
233	THAYER'S Y-KNOT BOATYARD 207-867-4701	ALL YR	9	M	HE		40	20				S	T	W	H	
235	AIRPORT RAMP				R											
236	ABLE MARINE 207-667-6235	ALL YR.		M	HE	D		25					T		H	
237	LAMOINE STATE PARK 207-667-4778				R											
238	PRETTY MARSH TOWN DOCK 207-288-9959				R											
239	JOHN M. WILLIAMS CO 207-244-7854	ALL YR.		M	HE	D		30				S	T		H	

609

Chart Locater Number	Marina's Name & Phone Number	When Open	Monitors VHF Channel	Transient (Elec•Moor•Berths)	Hull/Engine Repairs•Ramp	Winter Storage (Wet•Dry)	Railway Capacity (ft)	Lift Capacity (tons)	Boat Rental (Canoe•Row•Motor)	Boat Rental (Charter•House•Sail)	Restaurant•Lodging•Camping	Showers•Laundry	Pumpout•Toilets	Bait•Tackle•Water•Ice	Groceries•Hardware	Diesel Fuel•Gasoline
240	BAR HARBOR BOATING CO 207-276-5838	ALL YR		M	HE	D	40	20					T	W		
241	HENRY R. ABEL YACHT YARD 207-276-5057	ALL YR.		MB	HE	D		50			R			I	H	
242	MT. DESERT YACHT YARD 207-276-5114	ALL YR.			HE	D		25								
243	BAR HARBOR BOATING CO 207-288-5797	ALL YR.			HE	D	44	20					T	I		G
244	ATLANTIC OAKS BY THE SEA 207-288-5801	ALL YR.									RL	L				
246	HOLIDAY INN SUN SPREE RESORT 207-288-9723	JUL AUG	9 16	E MB							RL	S	T	IW		
247	PARK ENTRANCE MOTEL 800-288-9703	MAY OCT		M	R						L			I		
248	BAR HARBOR TOWN WHARF 207-288-5571	ALL YR.	9 16	M	R						RL		PT	W		
249	HARBOR PLACE 207-288-3346	MAY OCT	9 16 80	EM B							RL	S	PT	I WT	H	G D
250	FISHERMAN'S LANDING 207-288-4632	JUN OCT		M							RL		T			G D
251	GOLDEN ANCHOR INN & PIER 207-288-5033	MAY OCT									RL		T			G D
252	SEAL COVE RAMP				R											
253	JAMES RICH BOATYARD 207-244-3208	ALL YR.			HE	D	46	20					T		H	
254	BASS HARBOR MARINE 207-244-5066	ALL YR.	9 16 71													
255	F.W. THURSTON COMPANY 207-244-3320	ALL YR									R				H	G D
257	LITTLE ISLAND MARINE 207-244-3466	ALL YR.	6		HE	D	40	10							H	
256	C.H. RICH COMPANY 207-244-3485	ALL YR.	88										T	I	H	G D
260	BASS HARBOR BOAT CORP 207-244-3514	ALL YR.			HE		65	20					T	I		
261	MANSET TOWN LANDING 207-244-7913				R											
262	THE HINCKLEY YACHT CO 207-244-5531	ALL YR.	9 16	M	HR	D		75				SL	T	I	H	D

CHART LOCATER NUMBER	MARINA'S NAME & PHONE NUMBER	WHEN OPEN	MONITORS VHF CHANNEL	TRANSIENT Electricty • Moorings • Berths	Hull repairs • Engine repairs • Ramp	WINTER STORAGE: Wet • Dry	RAILWAY CAPACITY IN FEET	LIFT CAPACITY IN TONS	BOAT RENTAL: Canoe • Row • Motor	BOAT RENTAL: Charter • House • Sail	Restaurant • Lodging • Camping	Showers • Laundry	Pumpout • Toilets	Bait • Tackle • Hardware	Groceries • Water • Ice	Diesel fuel • Gasoline
263	MANSET YACHT SERV. 207-244-4040	ALL YR.		M	HR	D		15					T		I	H
264	DOCKSIDE HOTEL 207-244-5221	MAY OCT									RL		T			
265	THE MOORINGS INN 207-244-5523	ALL YR	9	M							RL					
267	DOWNEAST DIESEL 207-244-5145	ALL YR.			E											
268	GREAT HARBOR MARINA 207-244-0117	ALL YR.	9	EM B		W					RL	SL	T		IW	
269	RALPH W. STANLEY 207-244-3795	ALL YR.			H	D	40	15								H
270	SO. WEST HARBOR RAMP 207-244-7913				R											
271	SOUTHWEST LOBSTER 207-244-9285	ALL YR.	6												G D
272	BEAL'S LOBSTER 207-244-3202	ALL YR.	16 88	M							RL		T		IW	
273	MORRIS YACHTS 207-244-5509	ALL YR.		MB	H	D		25		C	RL					
276	NORTHEAST HARBOR MARINA 207-276-5737	AL YR.	9 16 68	EM B							RL	S	PT		IW	
278	ASTICOU INN 207-276-3344	JUN SEP									RL					
280	MOUNT DESERT YACHT YARD 207-276-5114	ALL YR.			H	D		25			RL		T			
282	SEAL HARBOR MOORINGS 207-276-3980		9	M												
283	SEAL HARBOR TOWN WHARF 207-276-5823												T			
284	LITTLE CRANBERRY RAMP				R											
285	ISLEFORD DOCK REST.										R					
286	LITTLE CRANBERRY Y. C	ALL YR.		M												
287	CRANBERRY FISHERMAN CO-OP 207-244-5438	ALL YR.	72											B		G D
288	GREAT CRANBERRY RAMP				R											

Maine

MARINA'S NAME & PHONE NUMBER

CHART LOCATER NUMBER	MARINA'S NAME & PHONE NUMBER	WHEN OPEN	MONITORS VHF CHANNEL	Hull repairs • Engine repairs • Moorings • Berths	WINTER STORAGE: Wet • Dry • Ramp		RAILWAY CAPACITY IN FEET	LIFT CAPACITY IN TONS	BOAT RENTAL: Canoe • Row • Motor	BOAT RENTAL: Charter • House • Sail	Restaurant • Lodging • Camping	Showers • Laundry	Bait • Tackle • Pumpout • Toilets	Groceries • Water • Ice	Diesel fuel • Gasoline • Hardware
290	CRANBERRY ISLAND BOATYARD 207-244-7316	ALL YR		M	HE	D		20						H	
291	WEST COVE BOATYARD 207-422-3137	ALL YR			HE	D								H	
292	SORRENTO TOWN DOCK			M	R										
293	BUNKER'S BOATYARD 207-422-6841				H	D									
295	WINTER HARBOR CO-OP 207-963-5857	ALL YR.	13 11 12	M									B	H	G D
297	WINTER HARBOR MARINA 207-963-7449	ALL YR		M	HE	D		25			RL	S	T I	H	G D
298	SMITH'S DOCK	ALL YR.													G D
299	BEALS-JONESPORT CO-OP 207-497-2020	ALL YR											B	H	G D
300	JONESPORT SHIPYARD 207-497-2701	ALL YR.	6 16	M	H	D		20				SL	T	H	
301	JONESPORT RAMP				R										
302	LOOKS LIVE LOBSTER 207-497-5672	ALL YR.	77 78										B		G D
303	GOWER'S BOAT SHOP 207-497-2838	ALL YR			HE										
304	WILLIS BOATYARD 207-497-5630	JAN AUG			H		45								
305	B B S LOBSTER CO 207-255-8888	ALL YR.	6 7										B		G D
306	EAST ATLANTIC LOBSTER 207-255-8831	ALL YR.											B		G
307	PETTEGROW'S BOATYARD 207-255-8740	ALL YR.	6	M	HE	D	50	90						H	
308	LITTLE RIVER LOBSTER 207-259-7704	ALL YR		M										H	G D
309	LITTLE RIVER LODGE 207-259-4437	JUN SEP		M							RL	S			
310	LOOK'S WHARF 207-259-7712	APR JAN												H	D
311	MOOSE ISLAND MARINE 207-853-6058	ALL YR	9 16		E	D								H	

Maine

Chart Locater Number	Marina's Name & Phone Number	When Open	Monitors VHF Channel	Transient Electricity • Hull repairs • Engine repairs • Moorings • Berths	Winter Storage	Railway Capacity: Wet • Dry	Boat Rental: Canoe • Row • Motor	Lift Capacity in Feet	Restaurant • Charter • Lodging • House • Motor • Sail	Showers • Laundry • Camping	Pumpout • Toilets	Bait • Tackle • Water • Ice	Groceries • Hardware	Diesel fuel • Gasoline
312	EASTPORT MUNICIPAL PIER 207-853-2300	ALL YR.					R		RL					
313	NORTHEAST CHARTERS 207-853-4734	ALL YR.		B					C					
314	S.L. WADSWORTH & SON 207-853-4343	ALL YR.									T		H	
315	NORTHEAST MARINA & FUEL. 207-853-4295	ALL YR.	16 69	MB						S	T	IW	GH	G D
316	EASTPORT BOATYARD 207-853-6049	ALL YR.		M	HE	D		60					H	
317	REED TECHNOLOGY CTR. 207-853-2518	ALL YR.					R							
318	SEAVIEW CAMPROUNDS 207-853-4471			M			R		C	SL	T	I		
319	HARRIS POINT CABINS 207-853-4303	ALL YR.		M					L					
320	LUBEC BOAT RAMP						R							
321	COBSCOOK BAY PARK	MAY OCT					R			C				

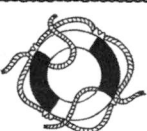

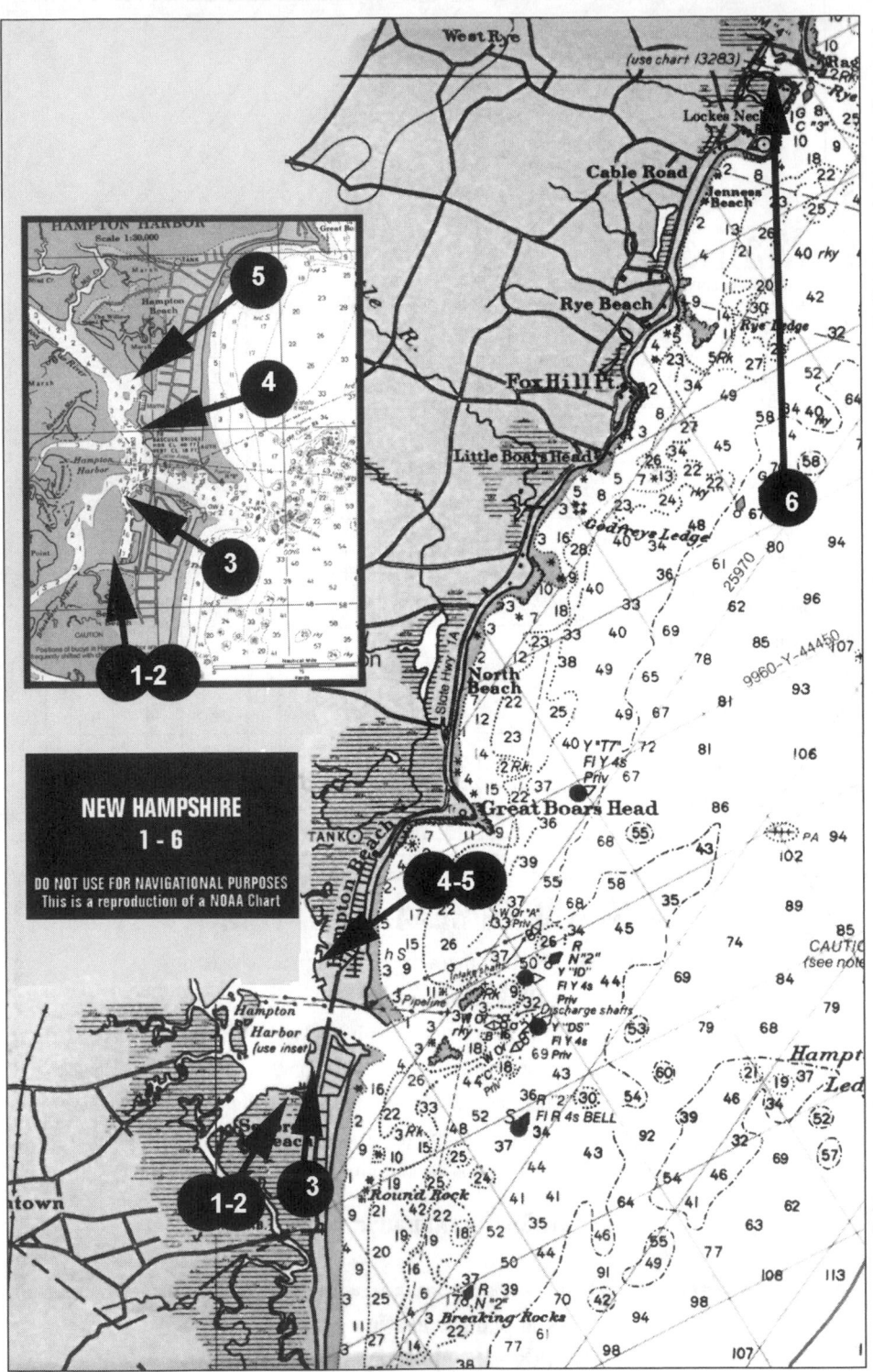

NEW HAMPSHIRE
1 - 6

DO NOT USE FOR NAVIGATIONAL PURPOSES
This is a reproduction of a NOAA Chart

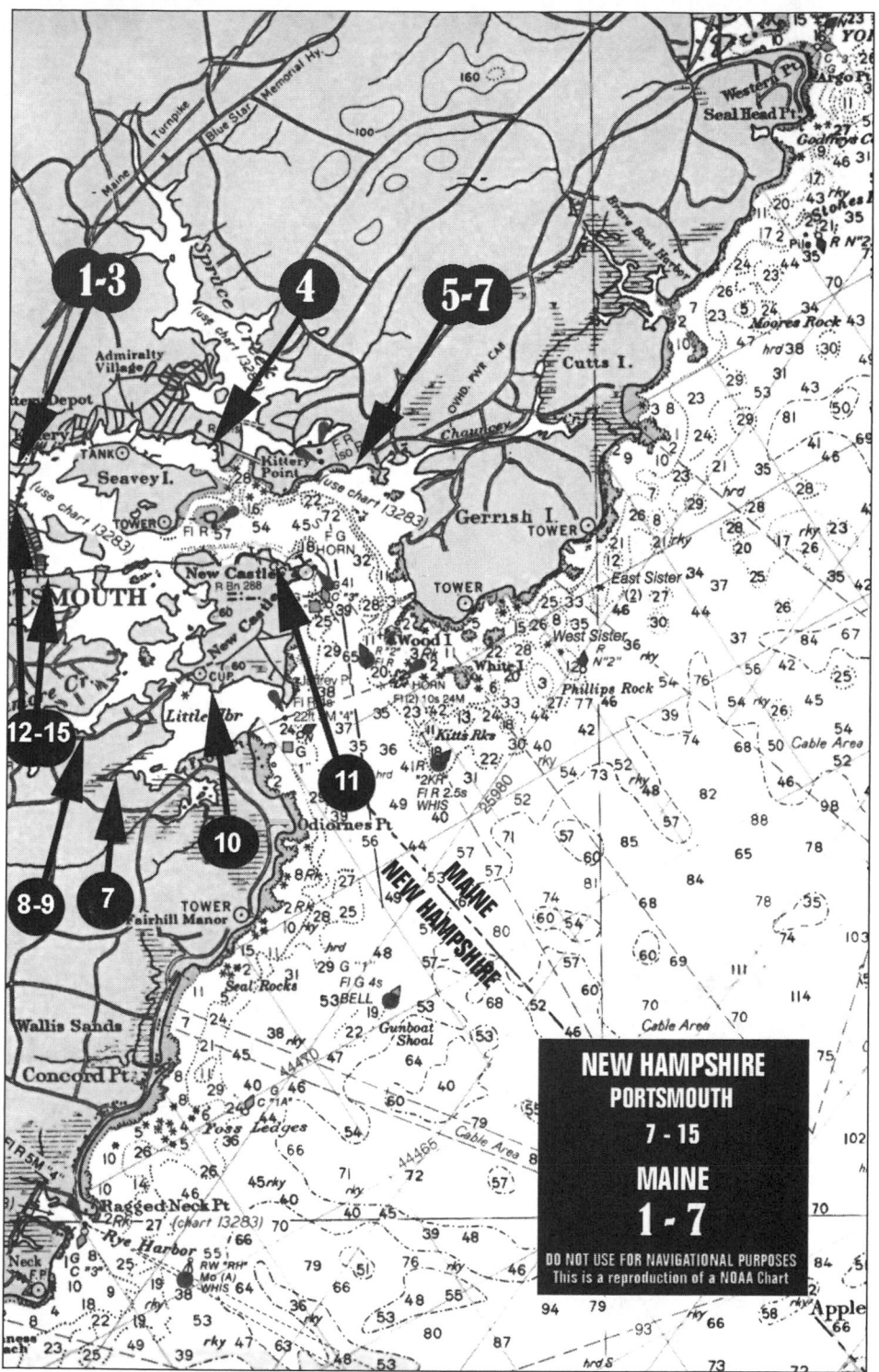

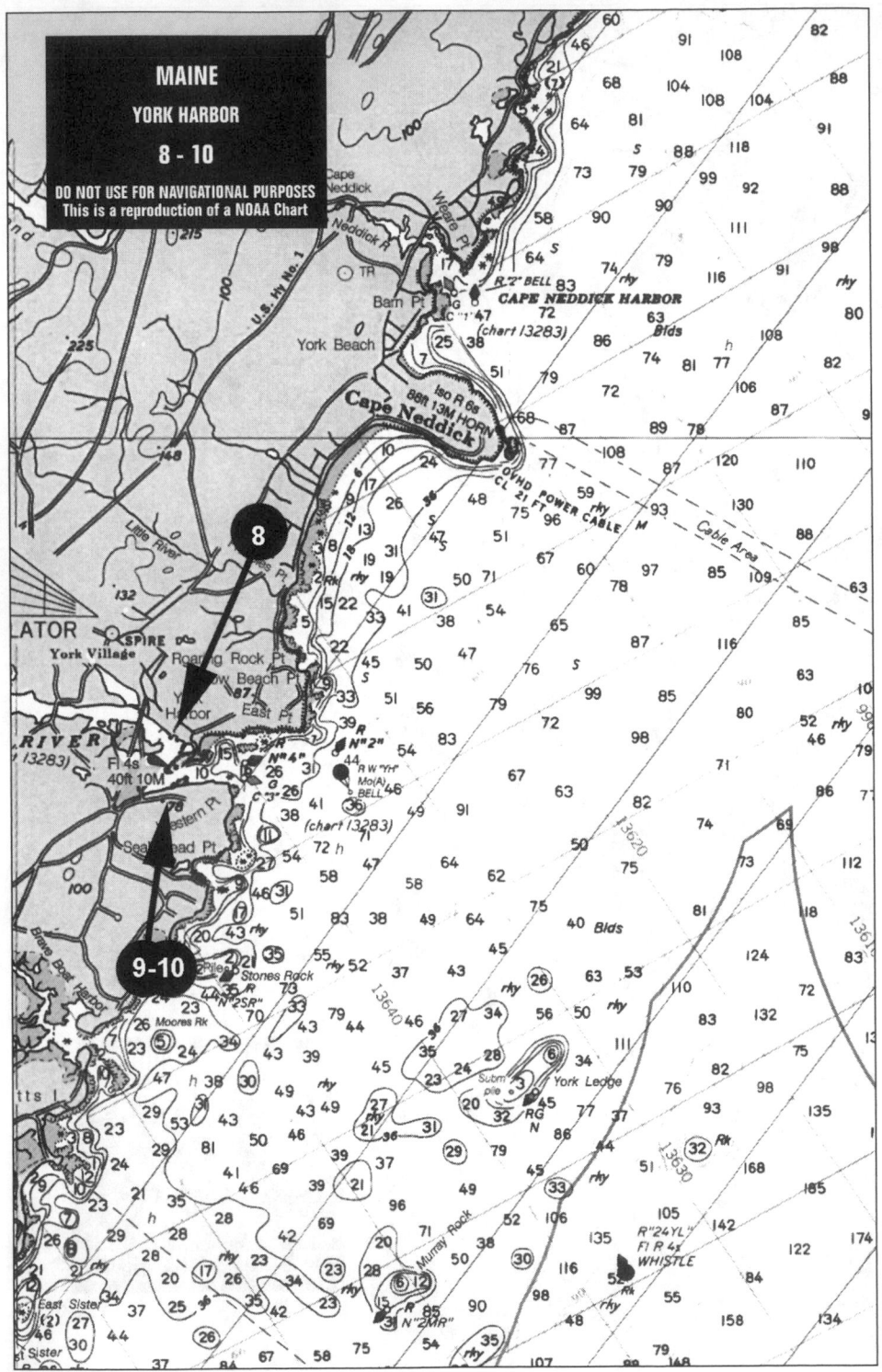

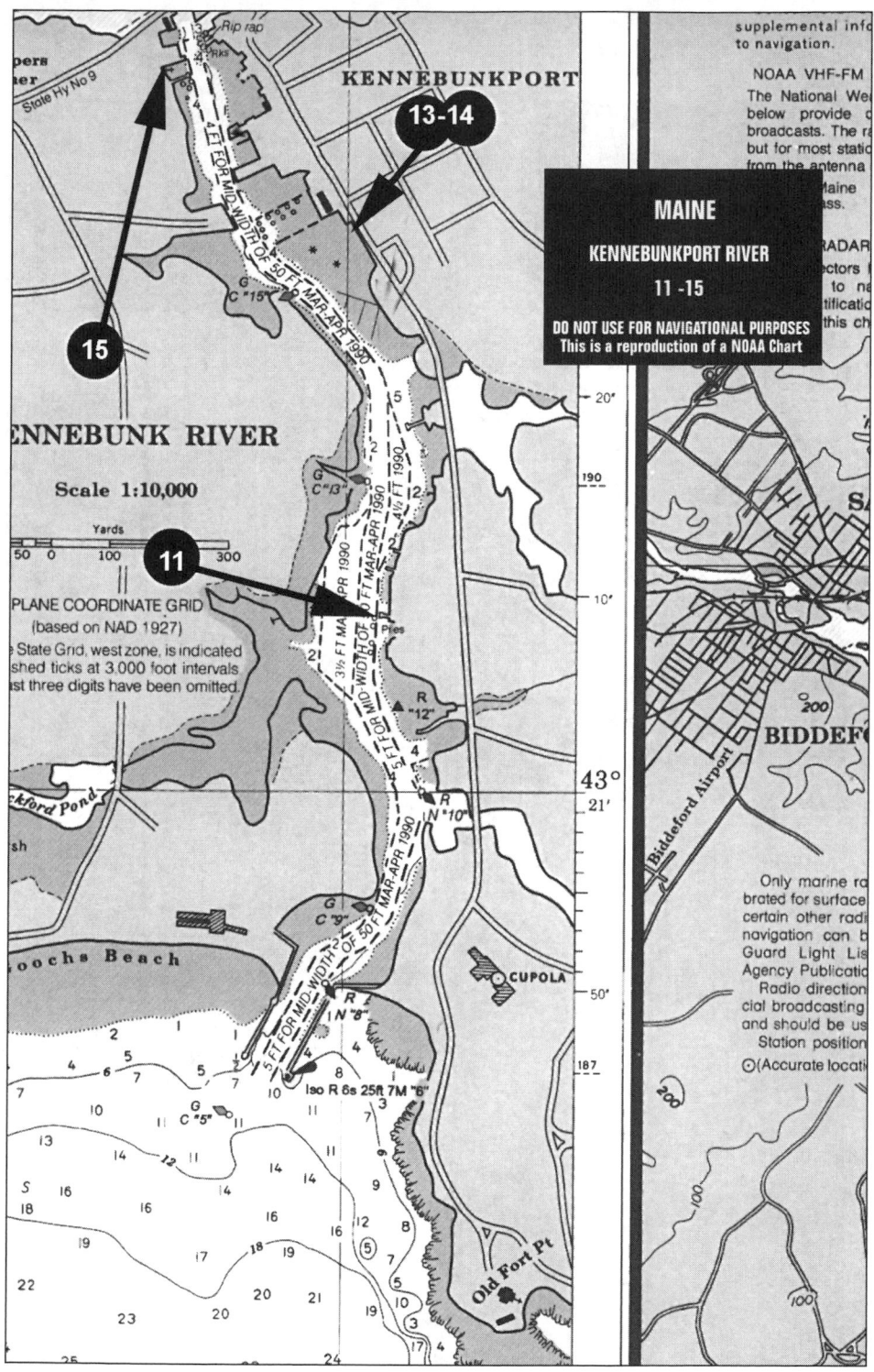

KENNEBUNKPORT

13-14

15

supplemental info
to navigation.

NOAA VHF-FM
The National We
below provide
broadcasts. The ra
but for most static
from the antenna
Maine
ass.

RADAR
ectors
to n
tificatio
this ch

KENNEBUNK RIVER

Scale 1:10,000

Yards
50   0   100   300

11

PLANE COORDINATE GRID
(based on NAD 1927)
State Grid, west zone, is indicated
shed ticks at 3,000 foot intervals.
st three digits have been omitted.

State Hy No 9

Rip rap

4 FT FOR MID WIDTH OF 50 FT MAR-APR 1990

G C "15"

G C "13"

1½ FT MAR-APR 1990

3½ FT MAR-APR 1990

5 FT FOR MID WIDTH OF

Piles

R "12"

R N "10"

G C "9"

CUPOLA

ochs Beach

R N "8"

G C "5"

Iso R 6s 25ft 7M "6"

Old Fort Pt

BIDDEF

SA

Biddeford Airport

200

Only marine ra
brated for surface
certain other radi
navigation can b
Guard Light Lis
Agency Publicatio
Radio direction
cial broadcasting
and should be us
Station position
⊙(Accurate locatio

617

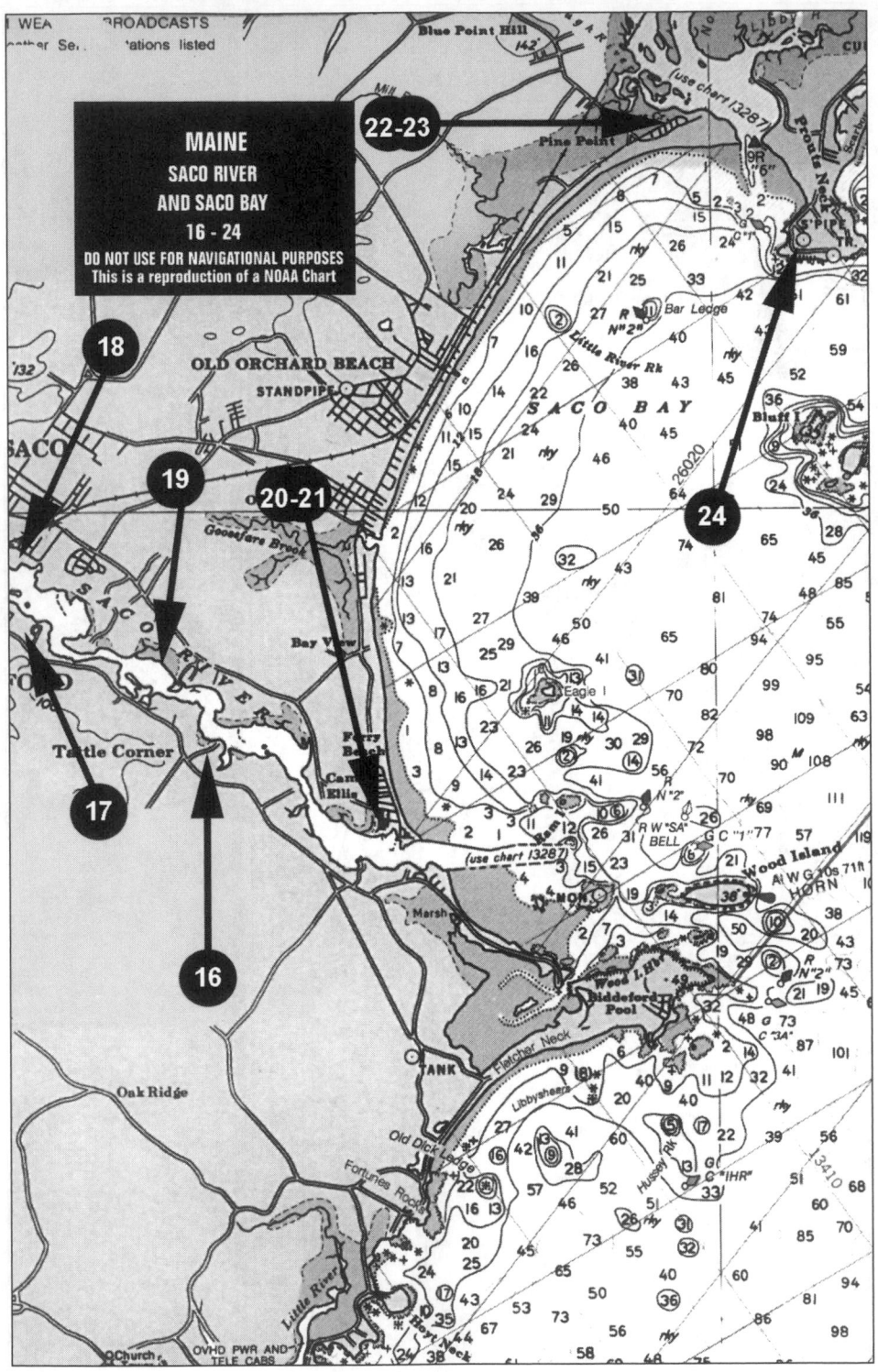

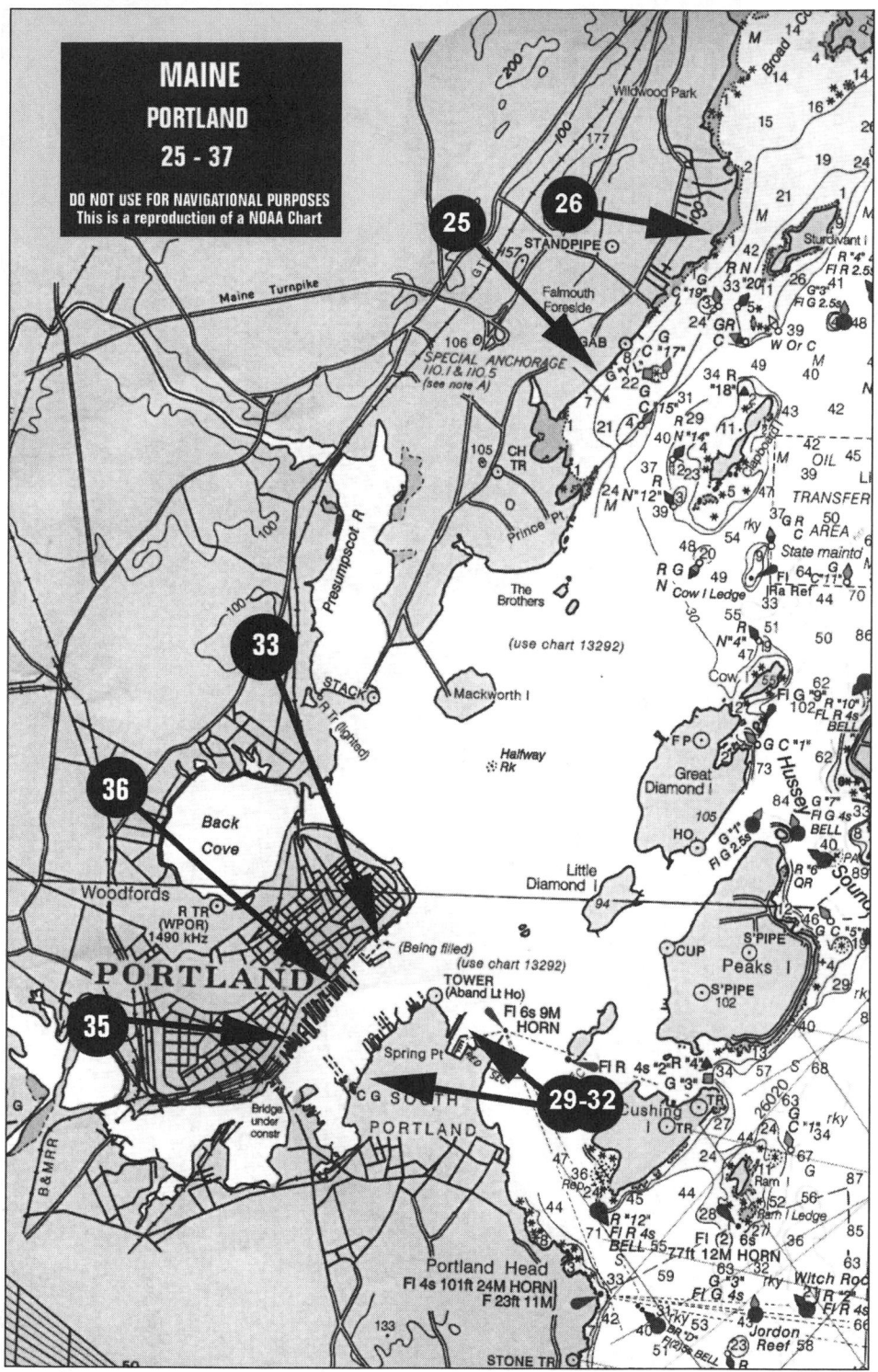

MAINE
PORTLAND
25 - 37

DO NOT USE FOR NAVIGATIONAL PURPOSES
This is a reproduction of a NOAA Chart

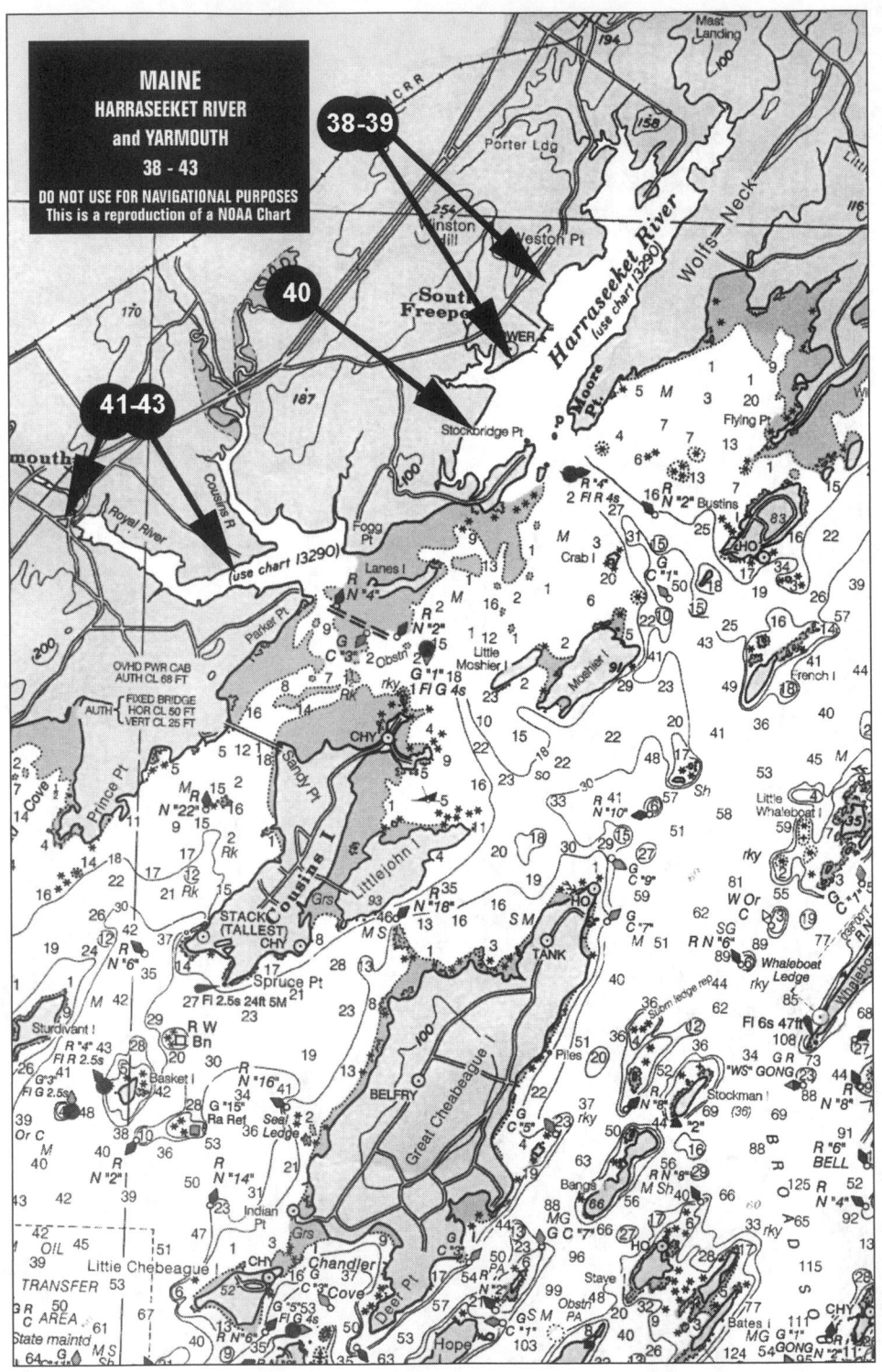

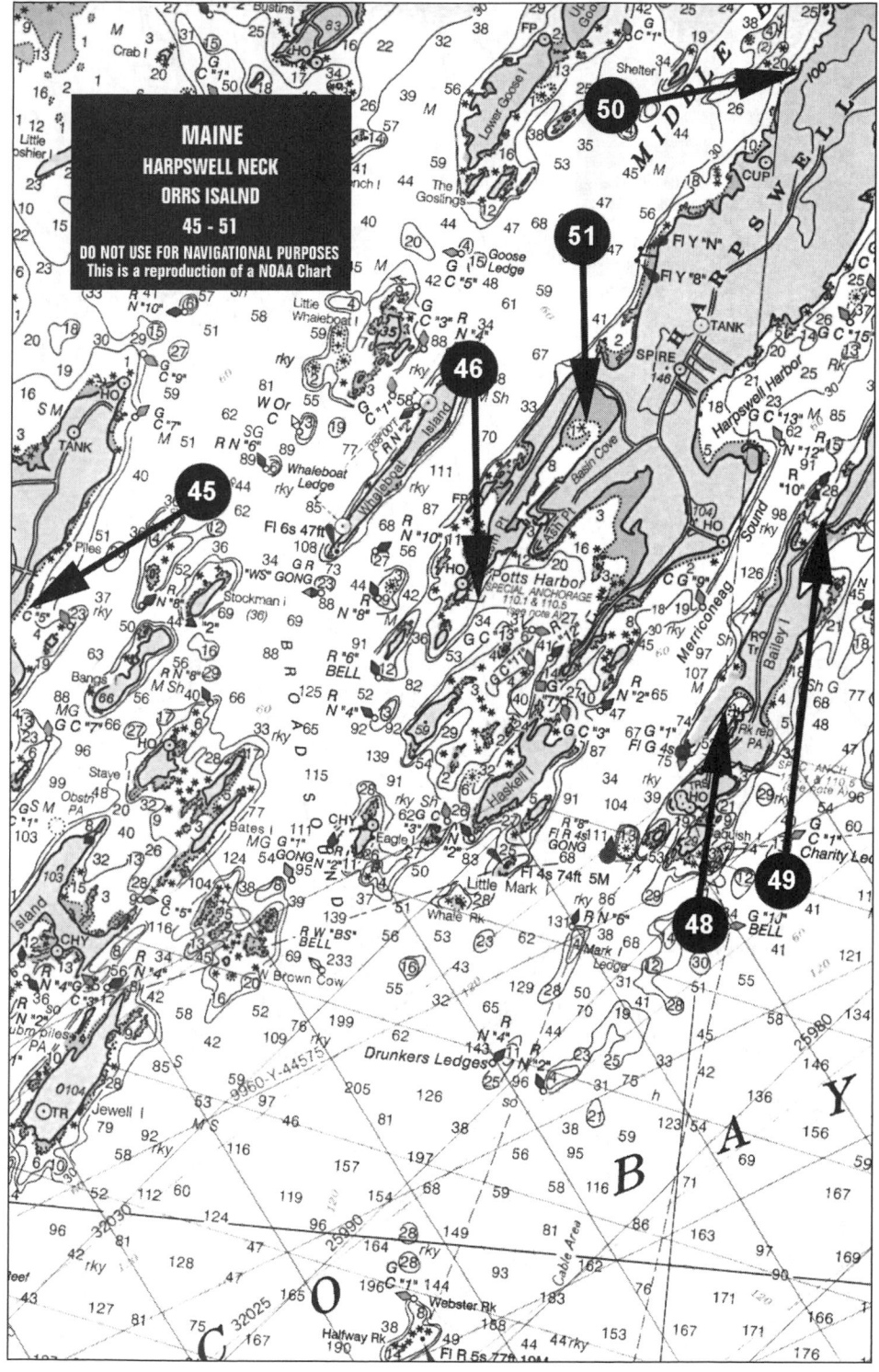

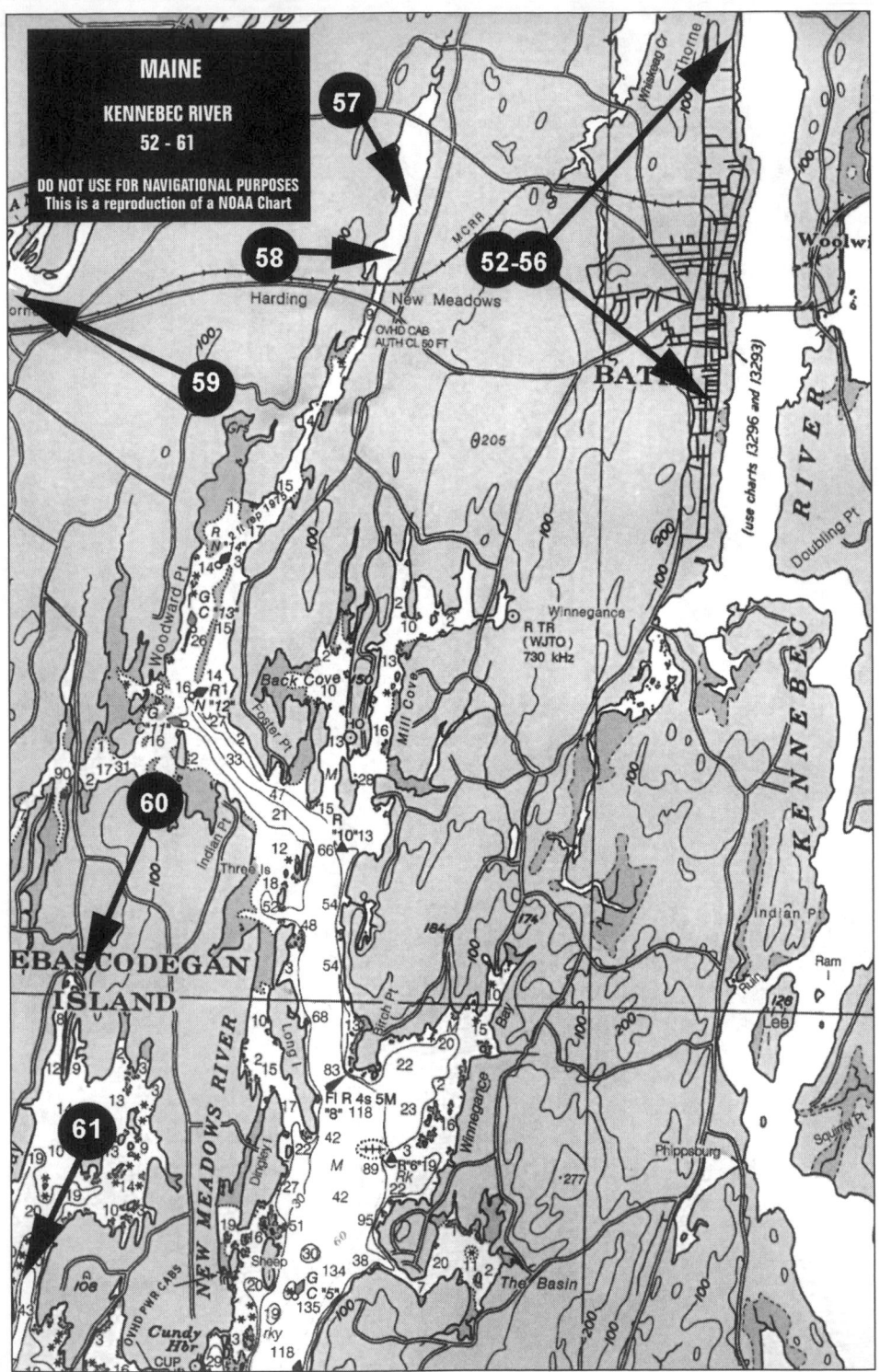

MAINE

KENNEBEC RIVER

52 - 61

DO NOT USE FOR NAVIGATIONAL PURPOSES
This is a reproduction of a NOAA Chart

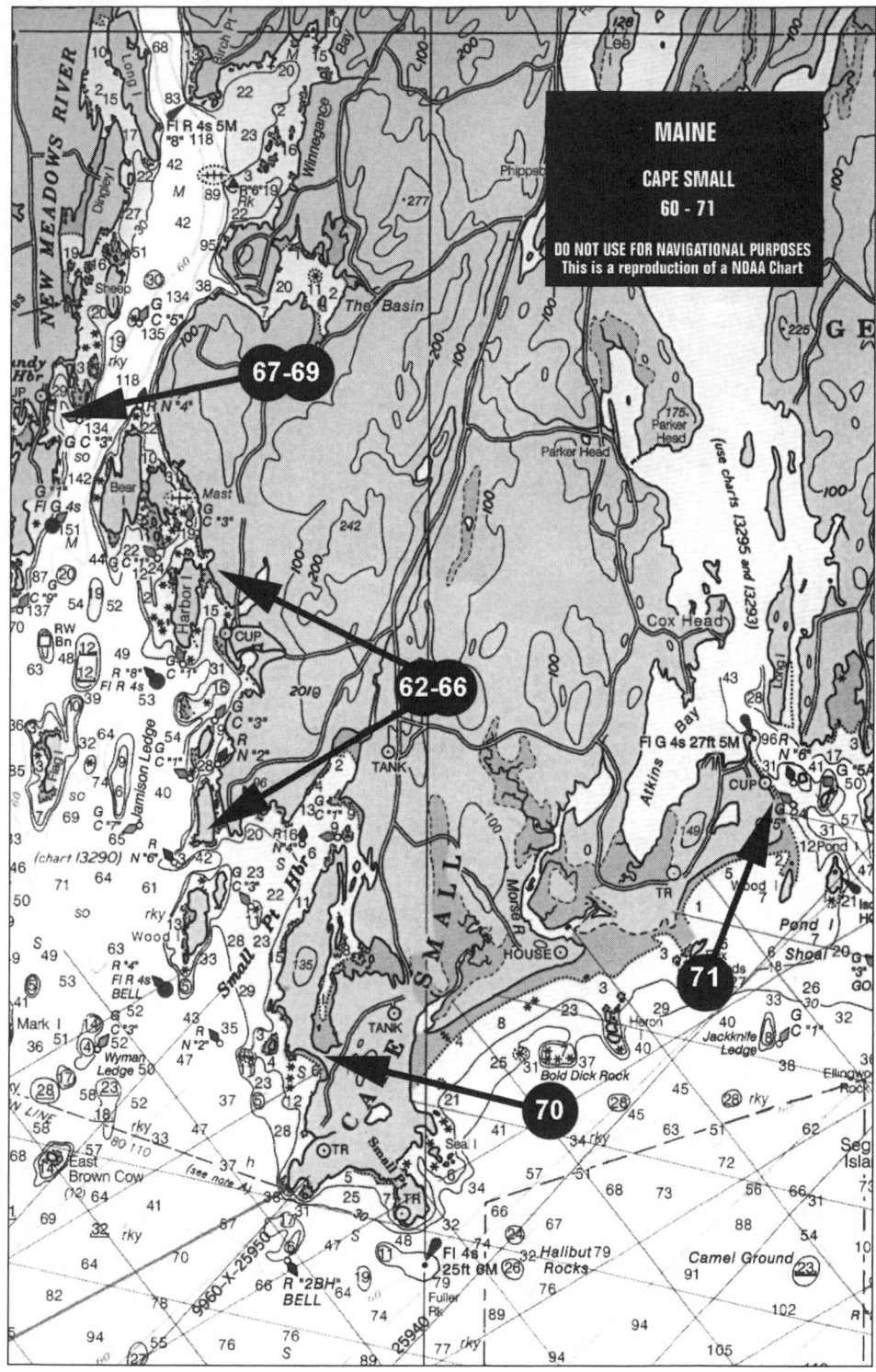

MAINE

CAPE SMALL
60 - 71

DO NOT USE FOR NAVIGATIONAL PURPOSES
This is a reproduction of a NOAA Chart

623

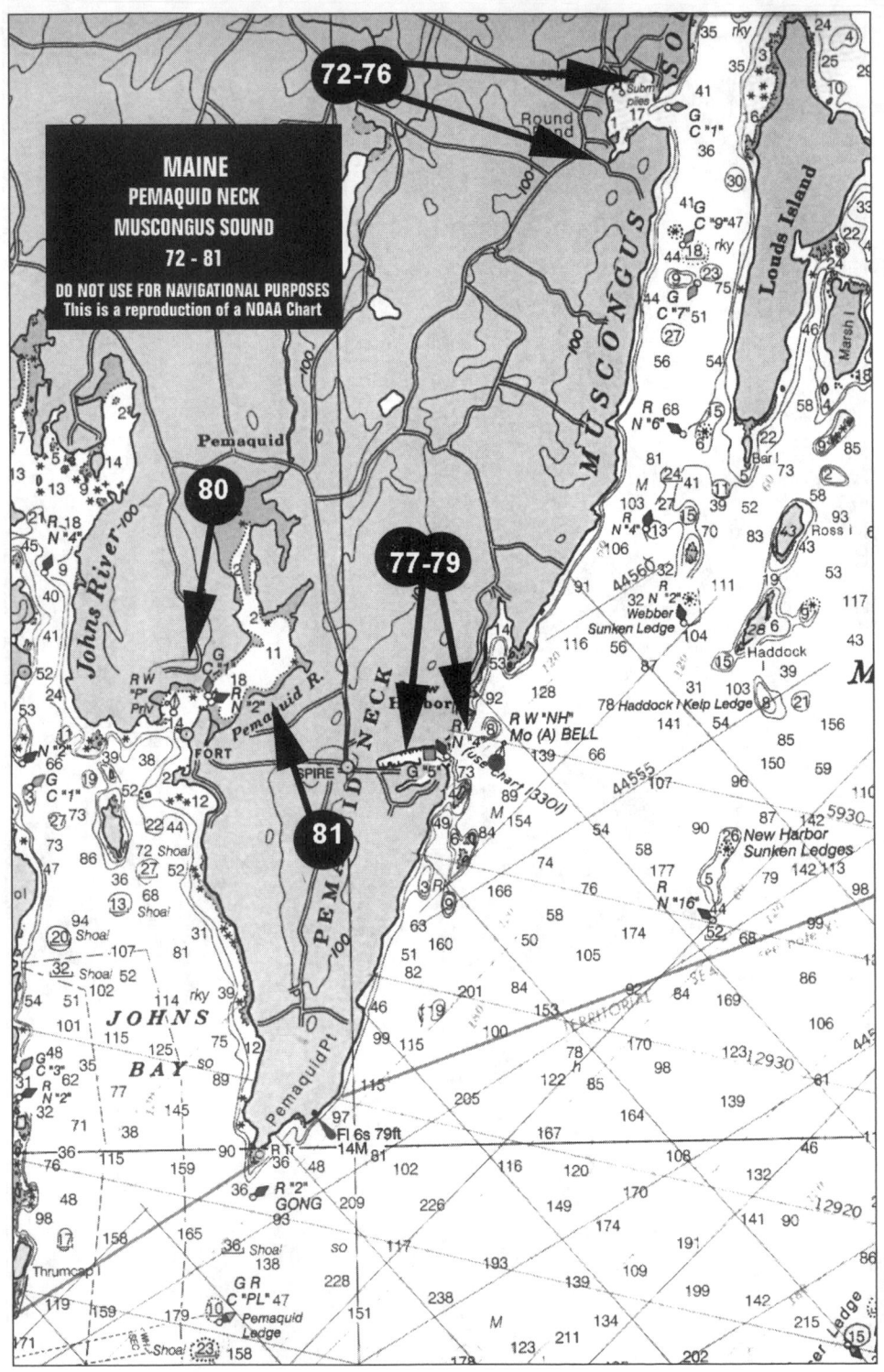

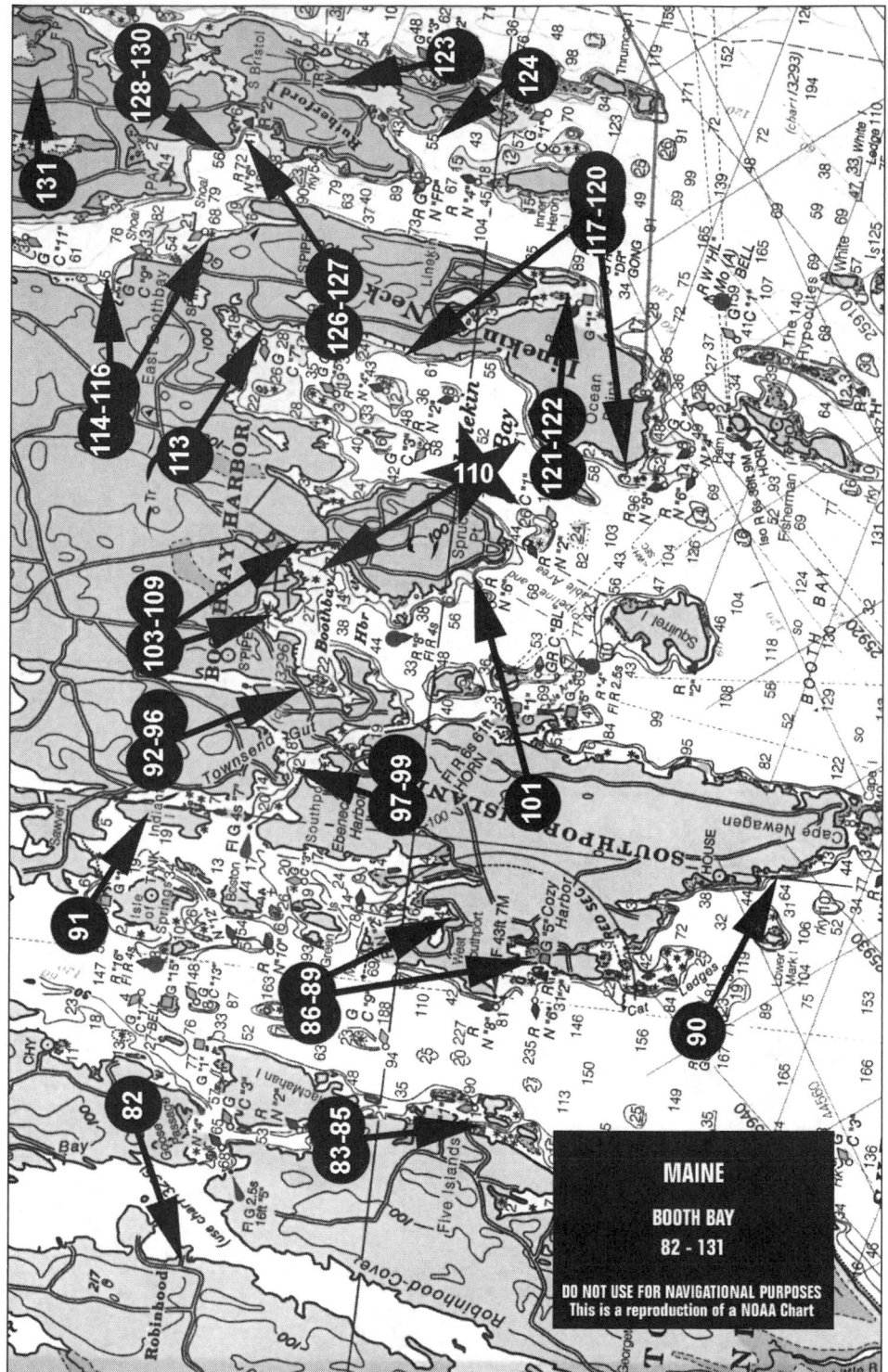

MAINE

BOOTH BAY

82 - 131

DO NOT USE FOR NAVIGATIONAL PURPOSES
This is a reproduction of a NOAA Chart

625

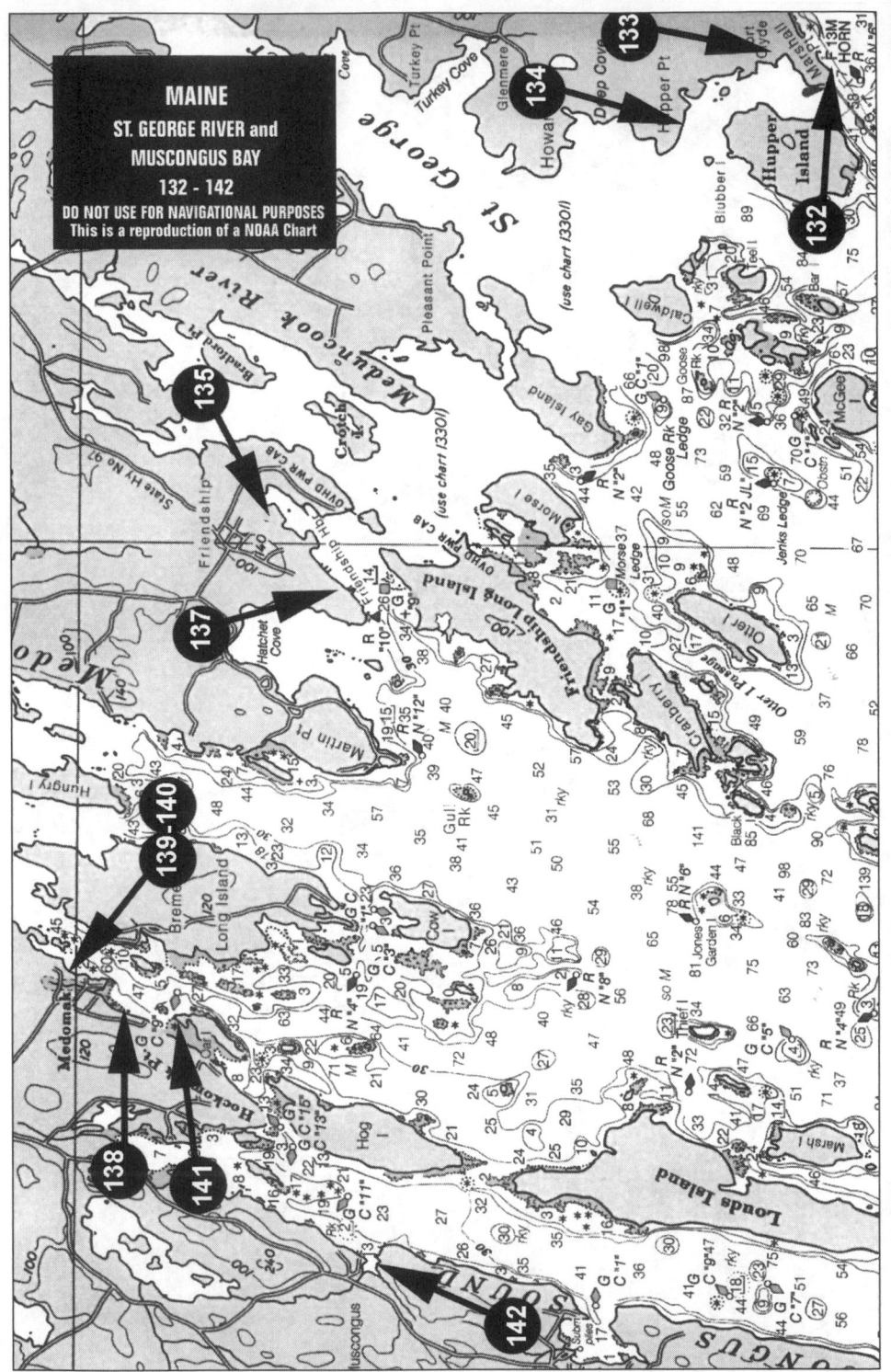

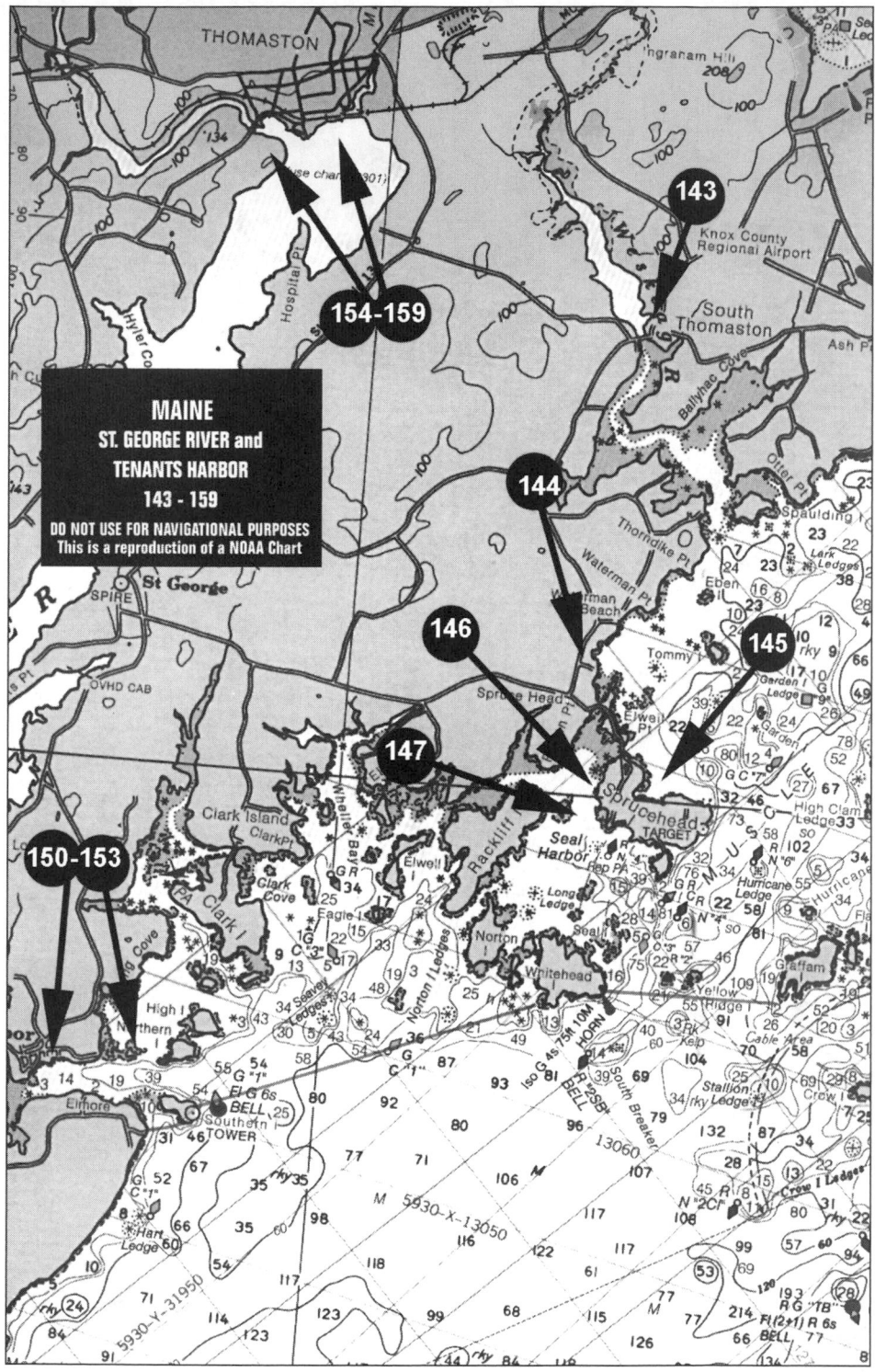

MAINE
ST. GEORGE RIVER and
TENANTS HARBOR
143 - 159

DO NOT USE FOR NAVIGATIONAL PURPOSES
This is a reproduction of a NOAA Chart

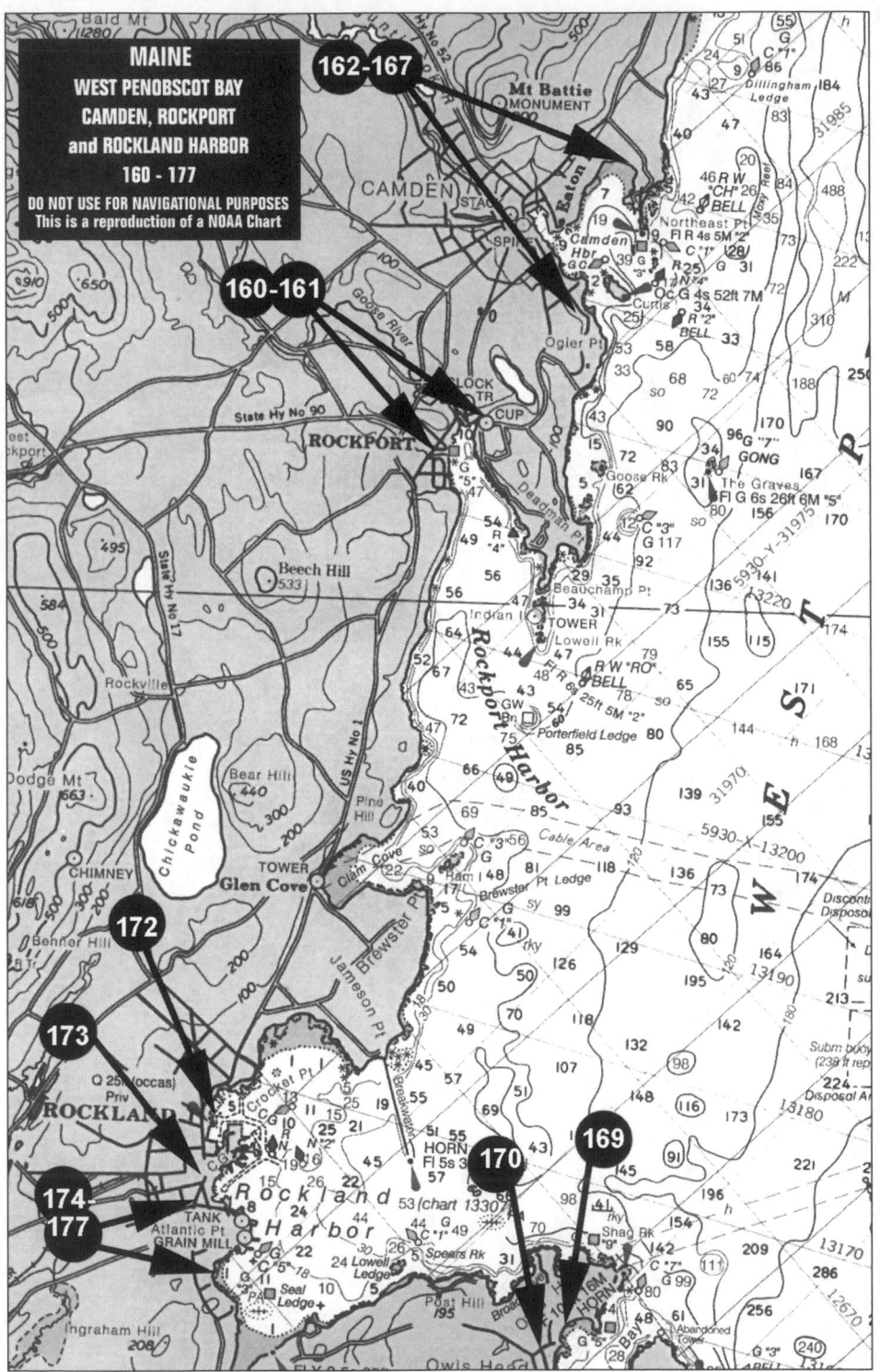

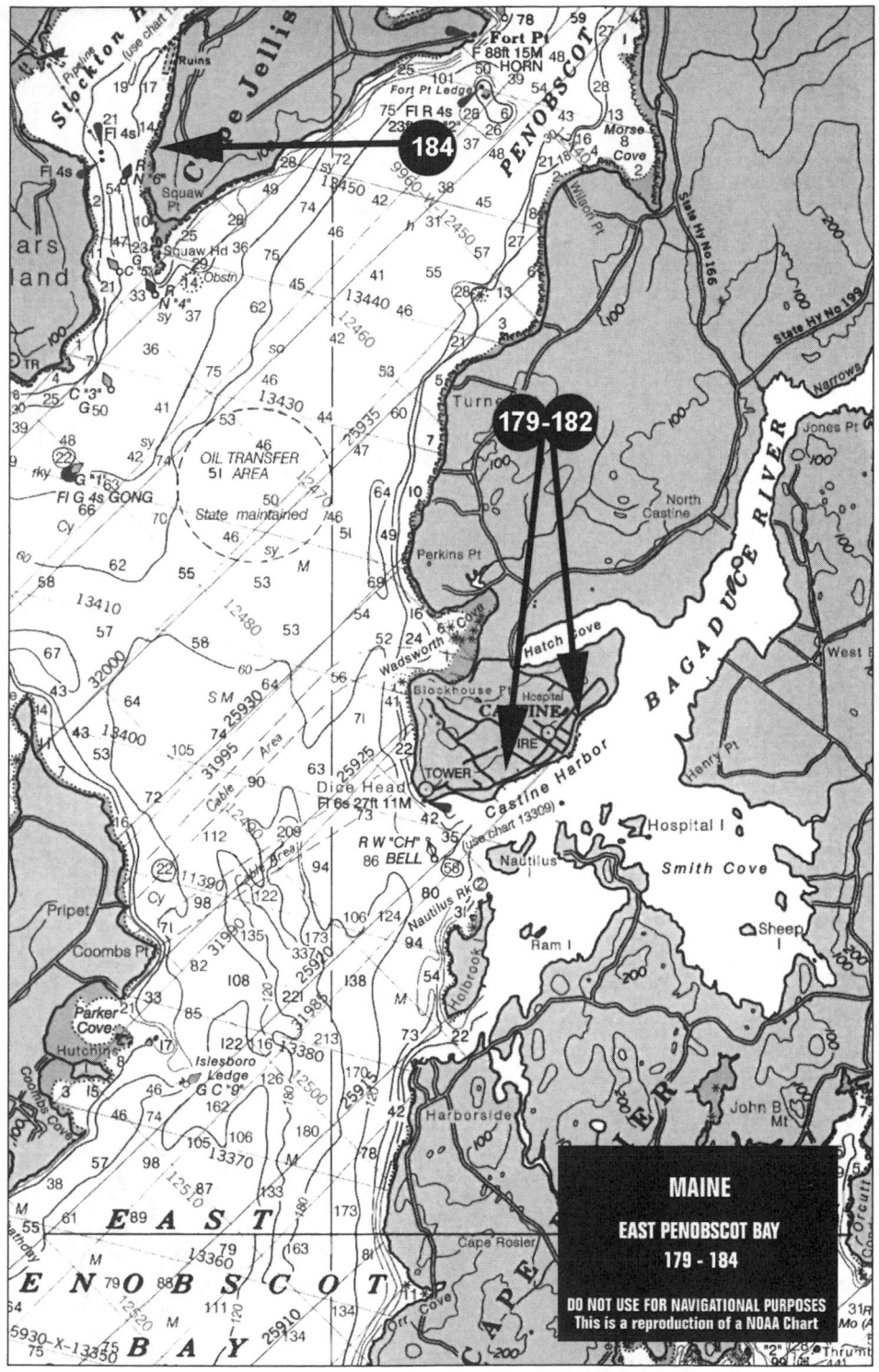

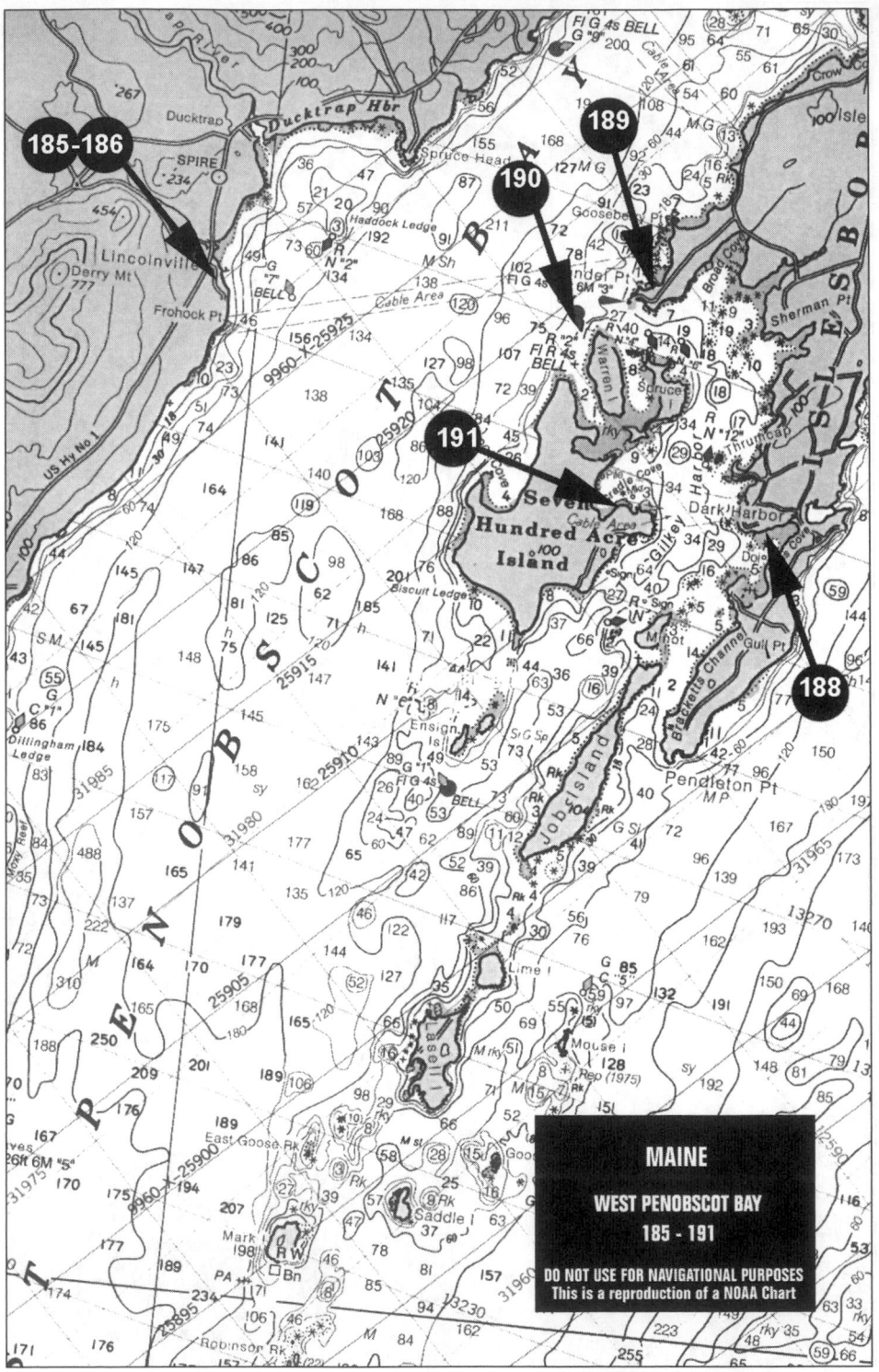

MAINE

WEST PENOBSCOT BAY

185 - 191

DO NOT USE FOR NAVIGATIONAL PURPOSES
This is a reproduction of a NOAA Chart

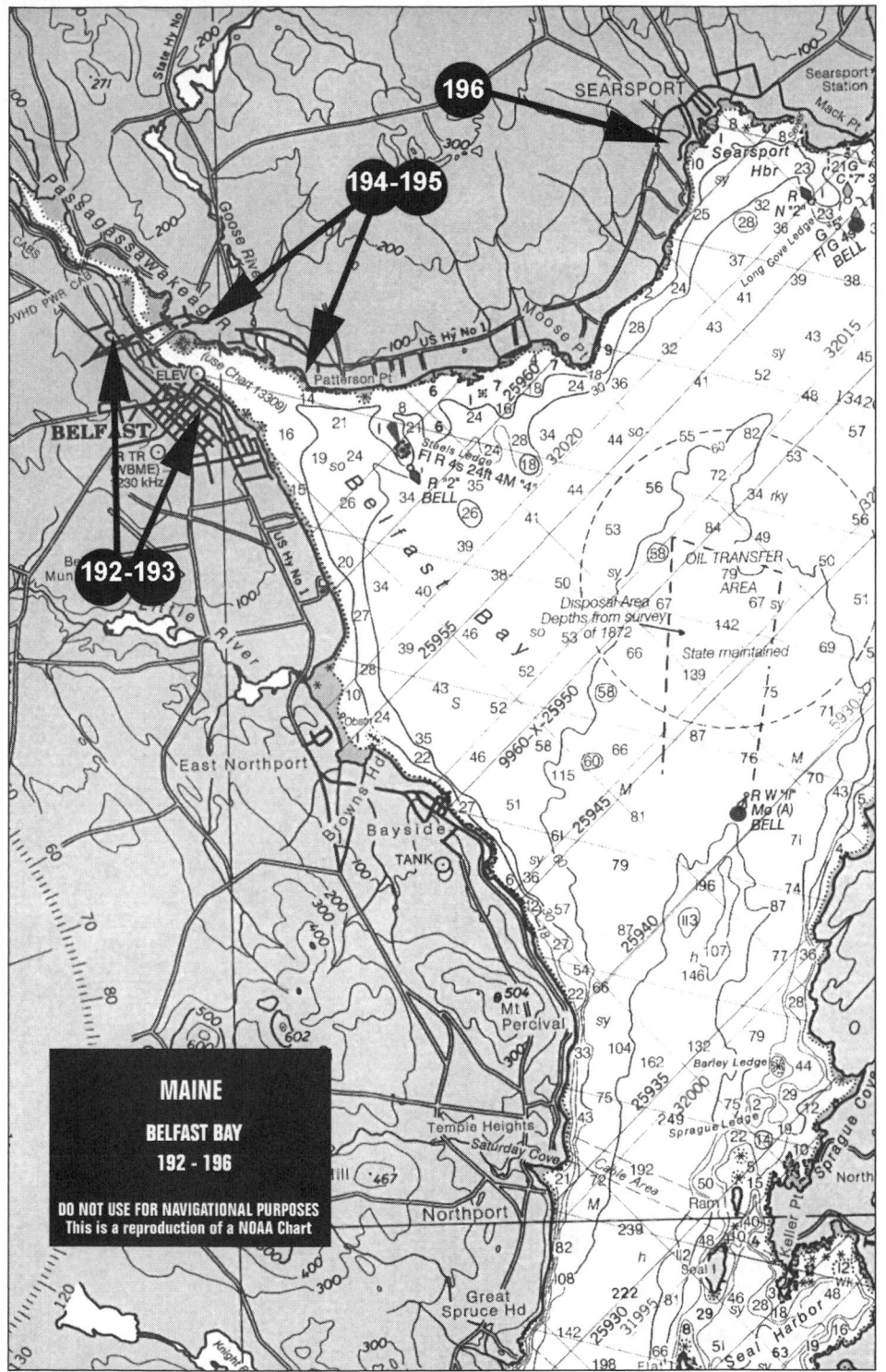

MAINE

BELFAST BAY

192 - 196

DO NOT USE FOR NAVIGATIONAL PURPOSES
This is a reproduction of a NOAA Chart

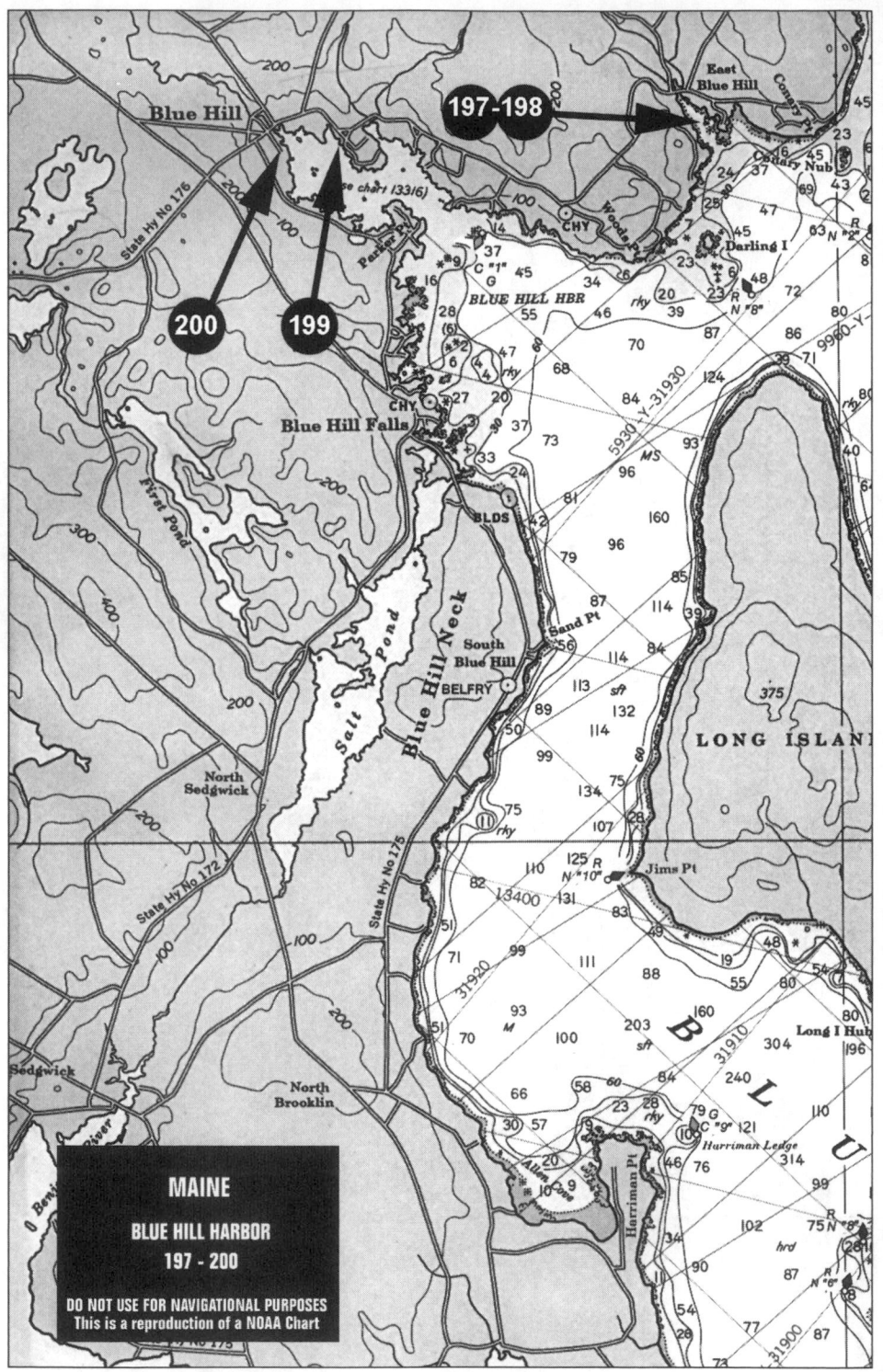

MAINE

BLUE HILL HARBOR
197 - 200

DO NOT USE FOR NAVIGATIONAL PURPOSES
This is a reproduction of a NOAA Chart

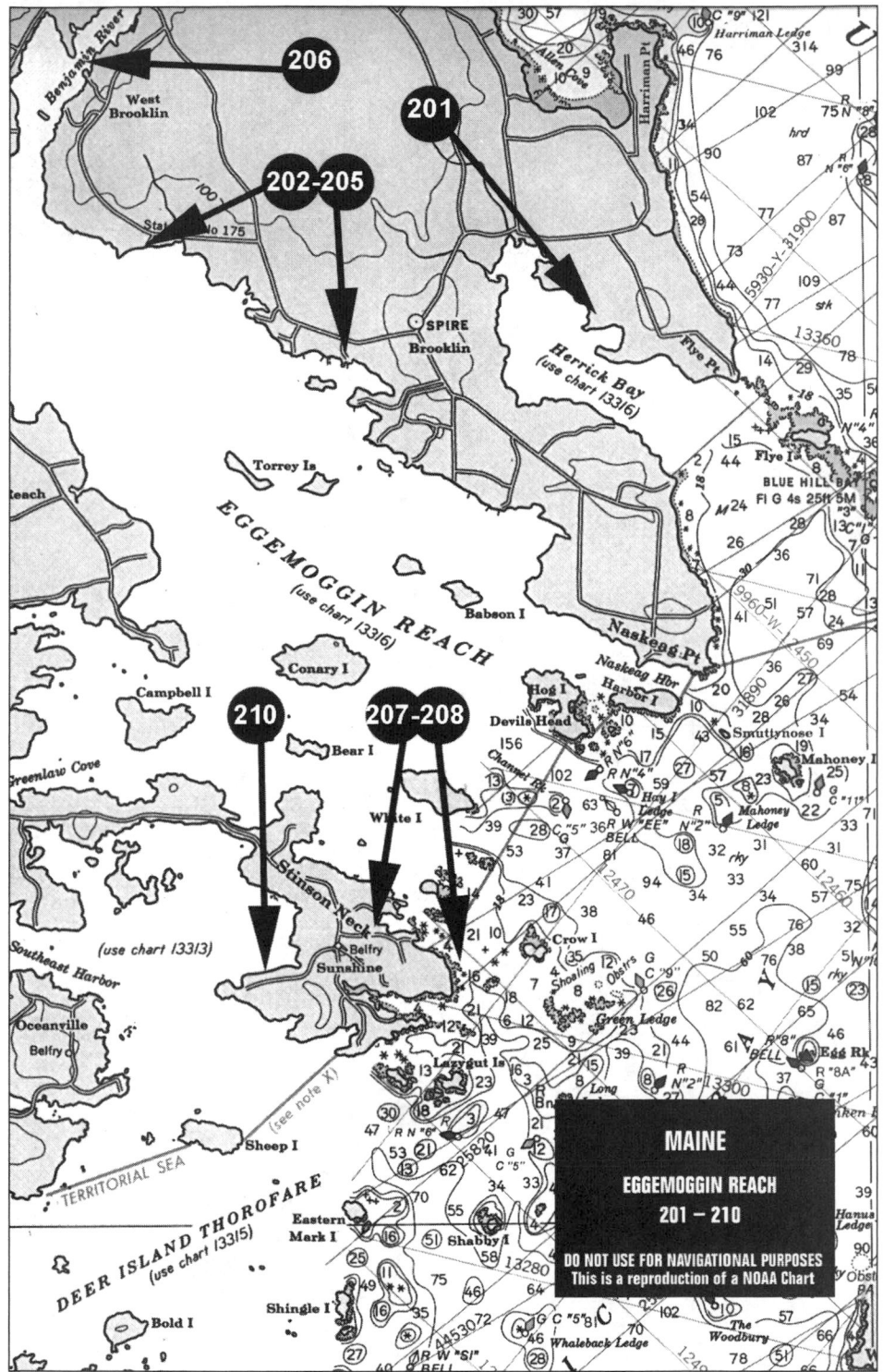

MAINE

EGGEMOGGIN REACH
201 – 210

DO NOT USE FOR NAVIGATIONAL PURPOSES
This is a reproduction of a NOAA Chart

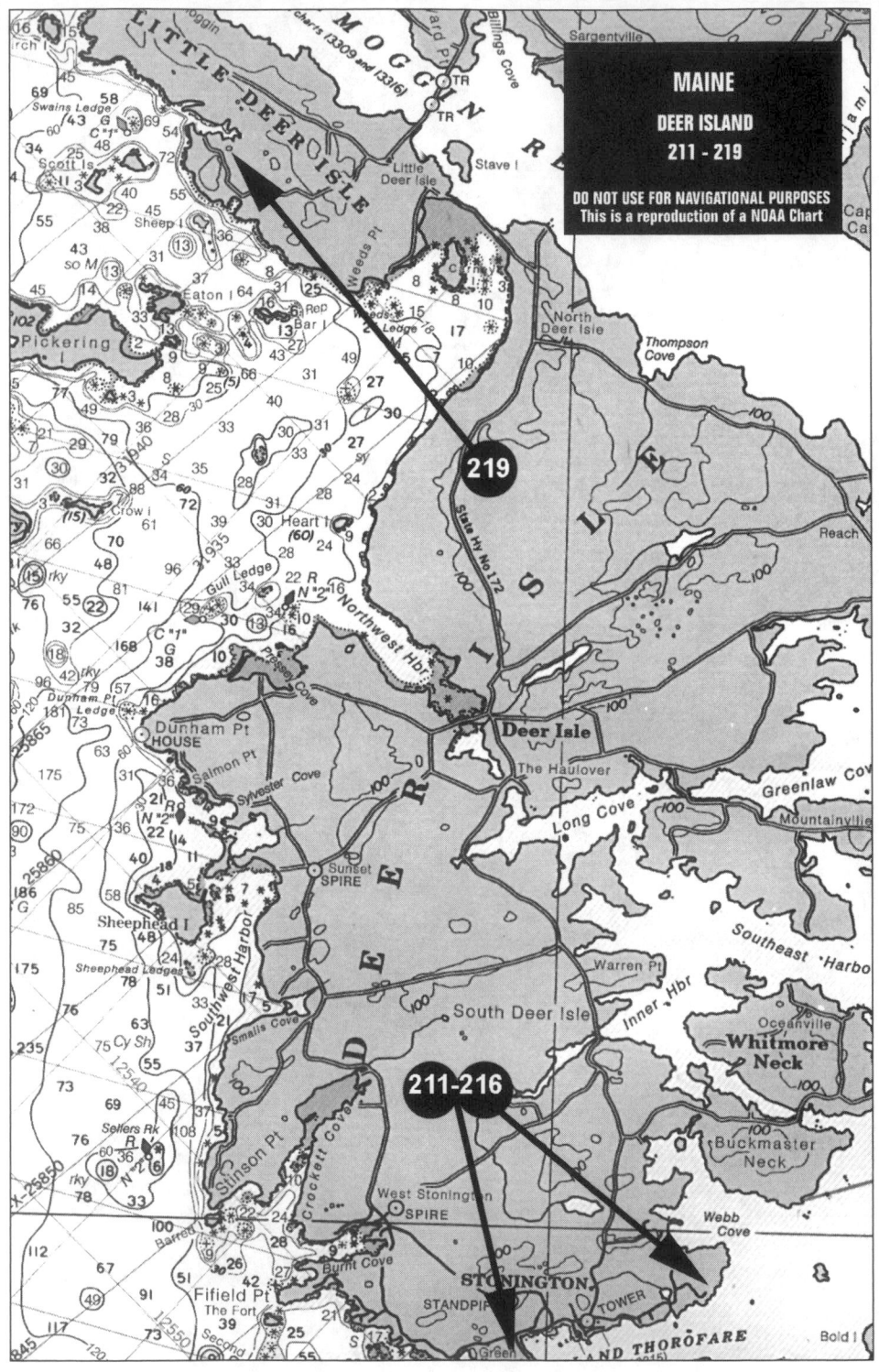

MAINE

DEER ISLAND

211 - 219

DO NOT USE FOR NAVIGATIONAL PURPOSES
This is a reproduction of a NOAA Chart

219

211-216

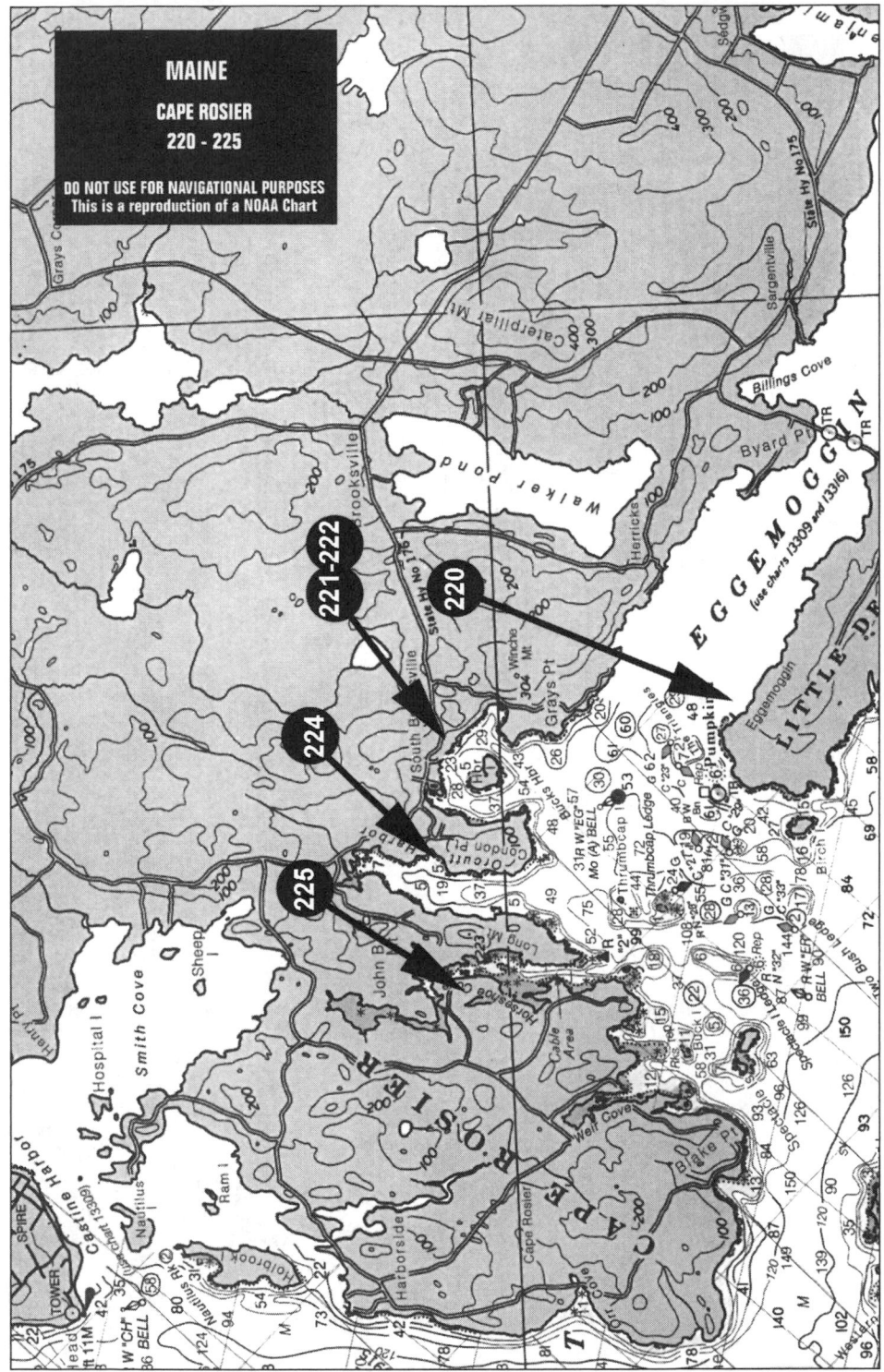

635

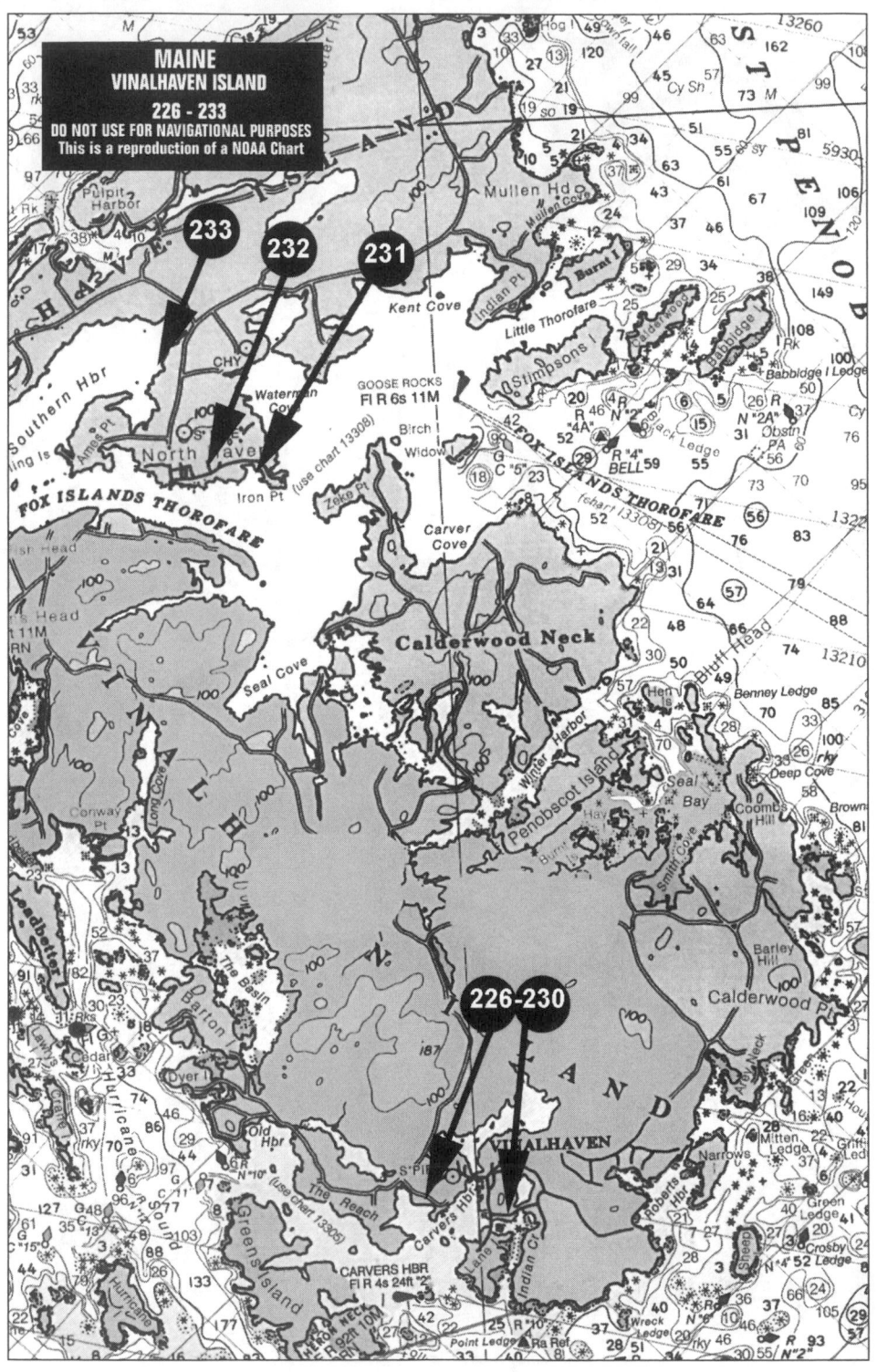

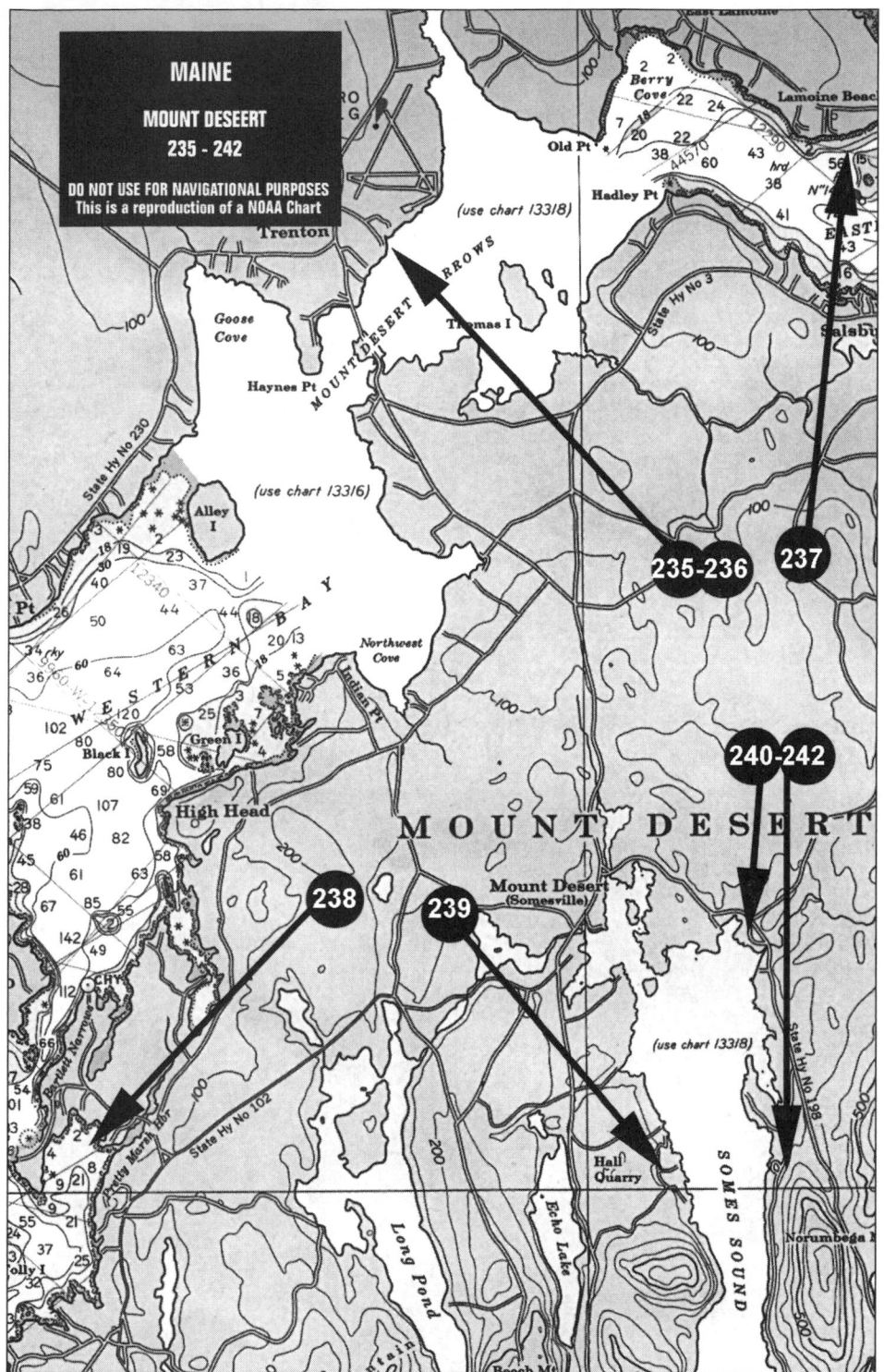

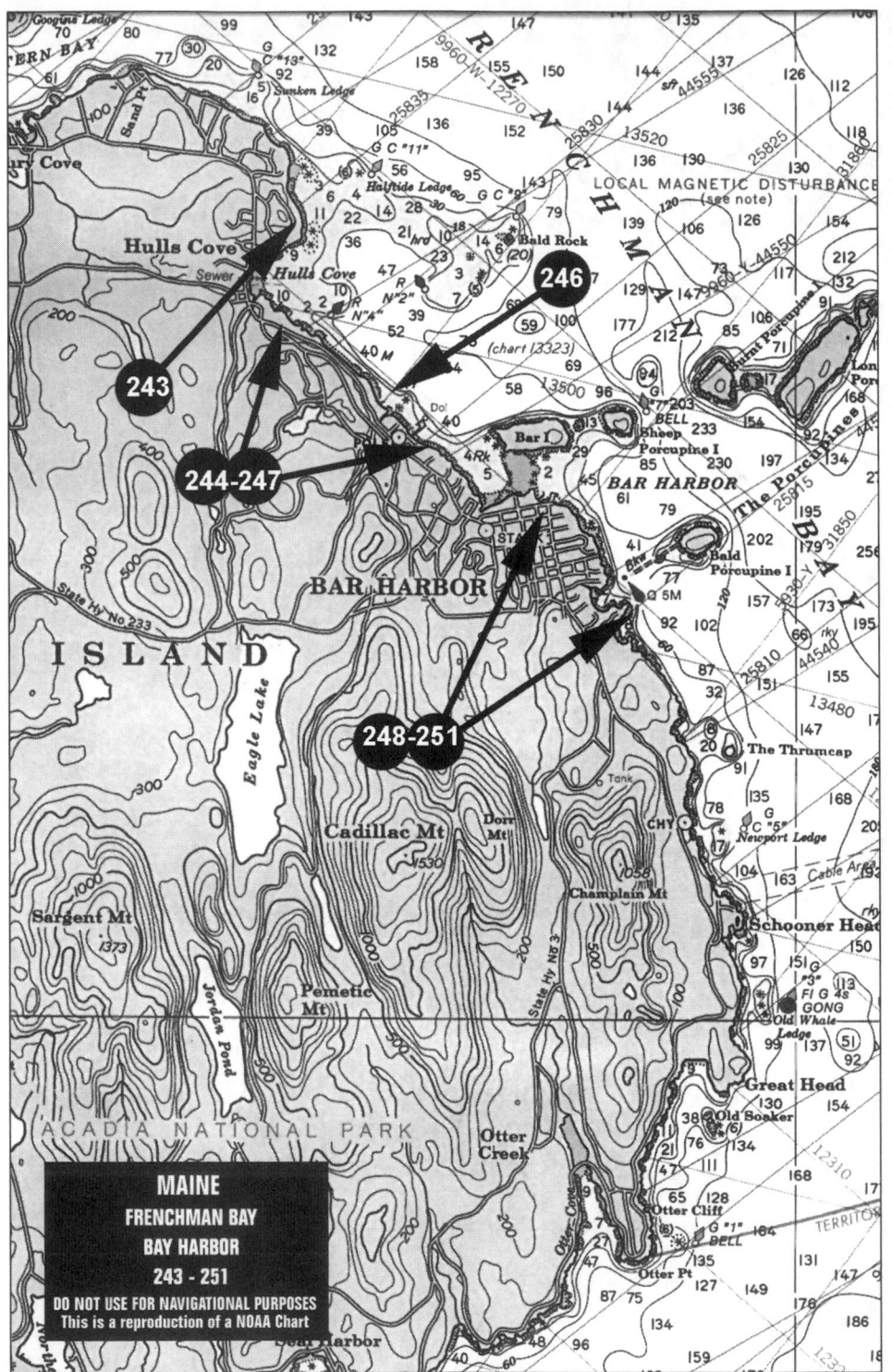

MAINE
FRENCHMAN BAY
BAY HARBOR
243 - 251
DO NOT USE FOR NAVIGATIONAL PURPOSES
This is a reproduction of a NOAA Chart

638

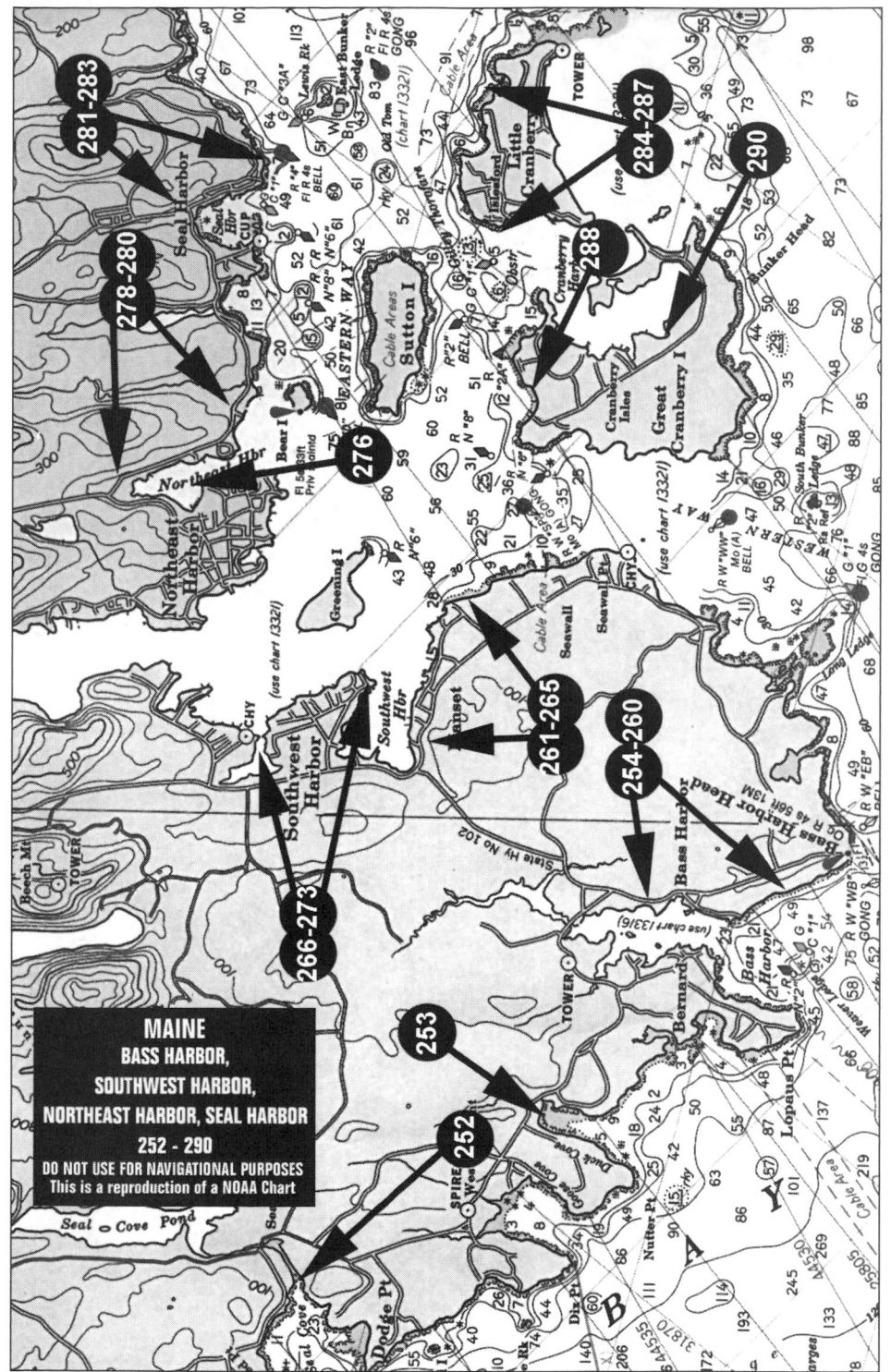

MAINE
BASS HARBOR,
SOUTHWEST HARBOR,
NORTHEAST HARBOR, SEAL HARBOR
252 - 290
DO NOT USE FOR NAVIGATIONAL PURPOSES
This is a reproduction of a NOAA Chart

639

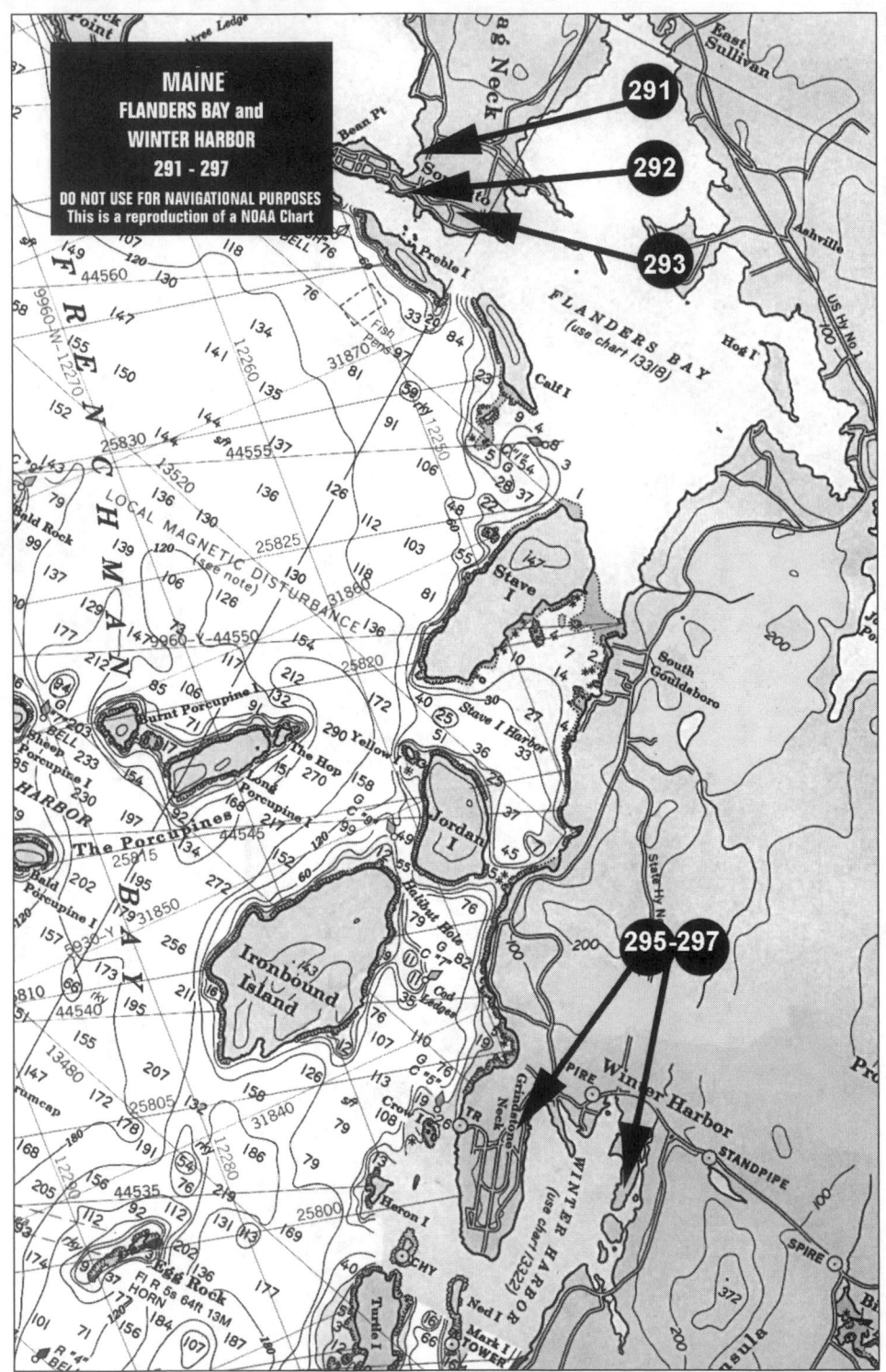

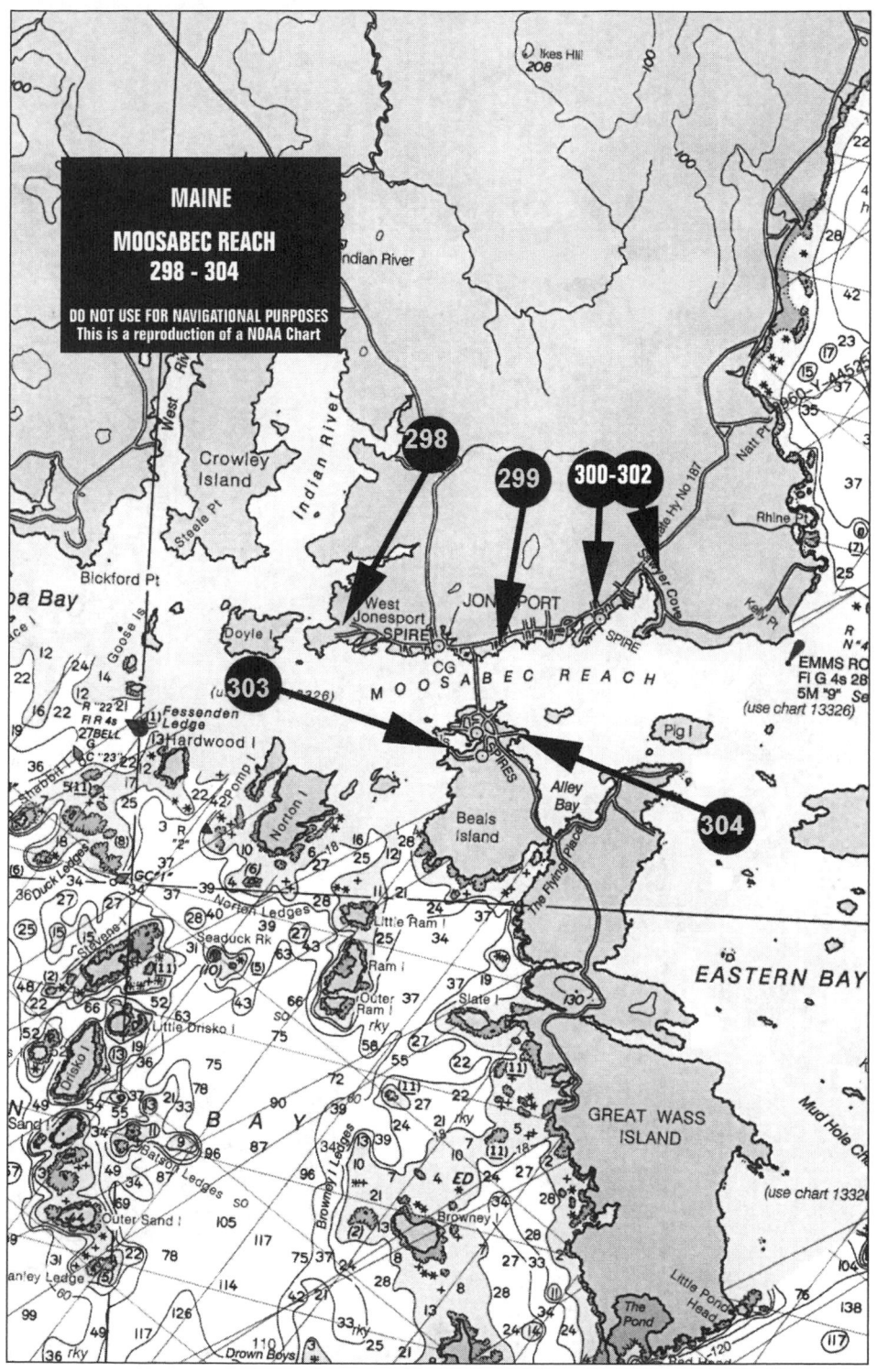

641

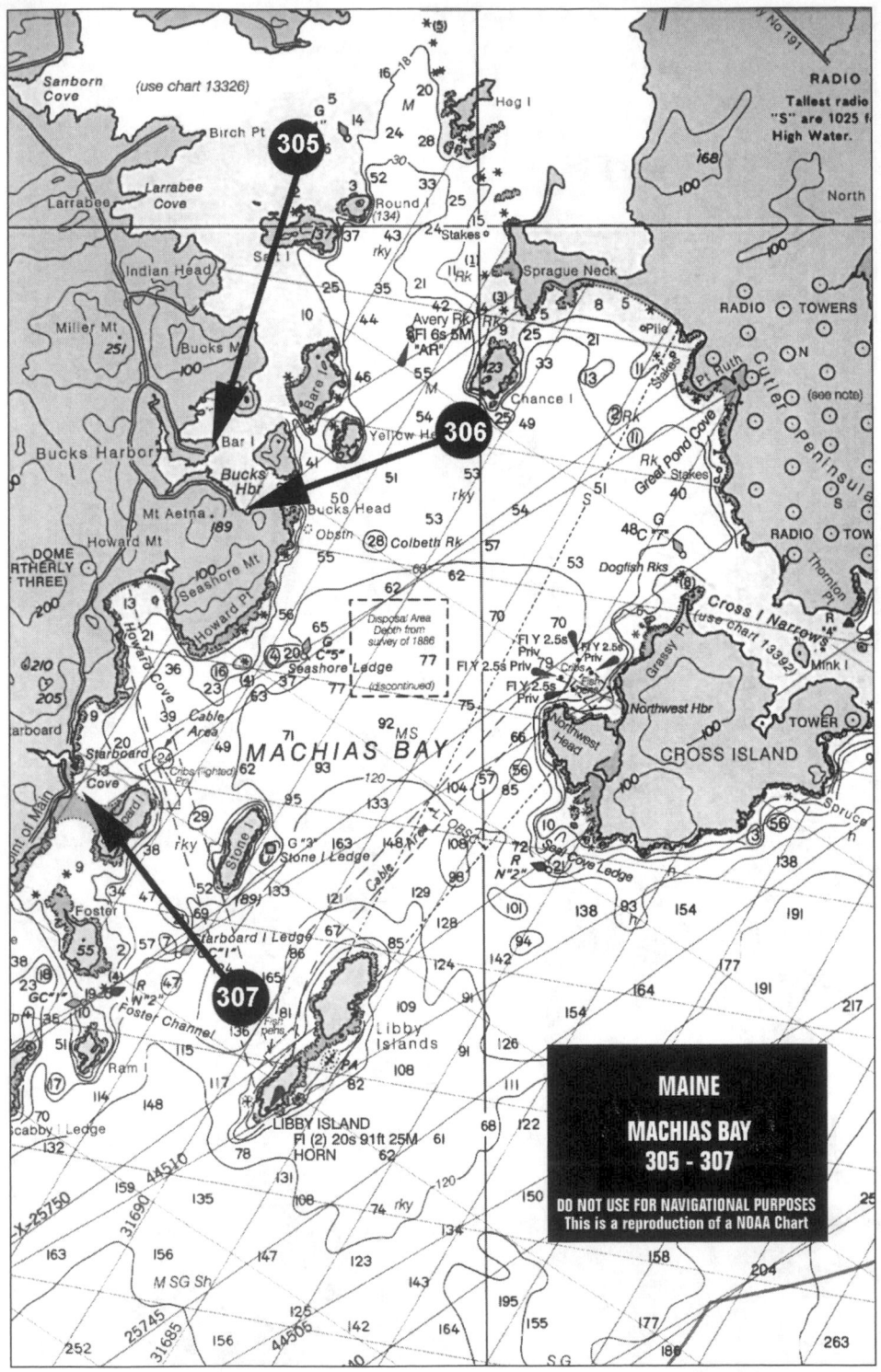

Sanborn
Cove

(use chart 13326)

*(5)

RADIO
Tallest radio
"S" are 1025 f
High Water.

Birch Pt

![305]

Larrabee
Cove

Larrabee

Indian Head

Round I
(134)

Sprague Neck

Stakes

RADIO ⊙ TOWERS

Miller Mt
251

Bucks Mt

Avery Rk
Fl 6s 5M
"AR"

⊙ N

(see note)

Bare I.

Yellow Hd

Chance I

![306]

Rk

RADIO ⊙ TOW

Bucks Harbor

Bar I

Bucks
Hbr

Rk Pond Cove

Stakes

Mt Aetna
189

Bucks Head

Obstn

Colbeth Rk

Dogfish Rks

Cross I Narrows
(use chart 13392)

Mink I

DOME
RTHERLY
THREE)

Seashore Mt

Howard Pt

Disposal Area
Depth from
survey of 1886

(discontinued)

Fl Y 2.5s
Priv

Fl Y 2.5s
Priv

Fl Y 2.5s Priv

RADIO ⊙ TOW

Howard Mt

Seashore Ledge

Fl Y 2.5s
Priv

Northwest Hbr

TOWER

Cable
Area

MACHIAS BAY

Northwest
Head

CROSS ISLAND

Starboard

Starboard I
Cove

Cribs (Lighted)

![307]

Stone I

Stone I Ledge

Cable

Foye Ledge

Foster I

Starboard I Ledge

Spruce
h

Foster Channel

Fish
pens

Libby
Islands

Ram I

MAINE

Libby Ledge

LIBBY ISLAND
Fl (2) 20s 91ft 25M
HORN

MACHIAS BAY
305 - 307

DO NOT USE FOR NAVIGATIONAL PURPOSES
This is a reproduction of a NOAA Chart

M SG Sh

S G

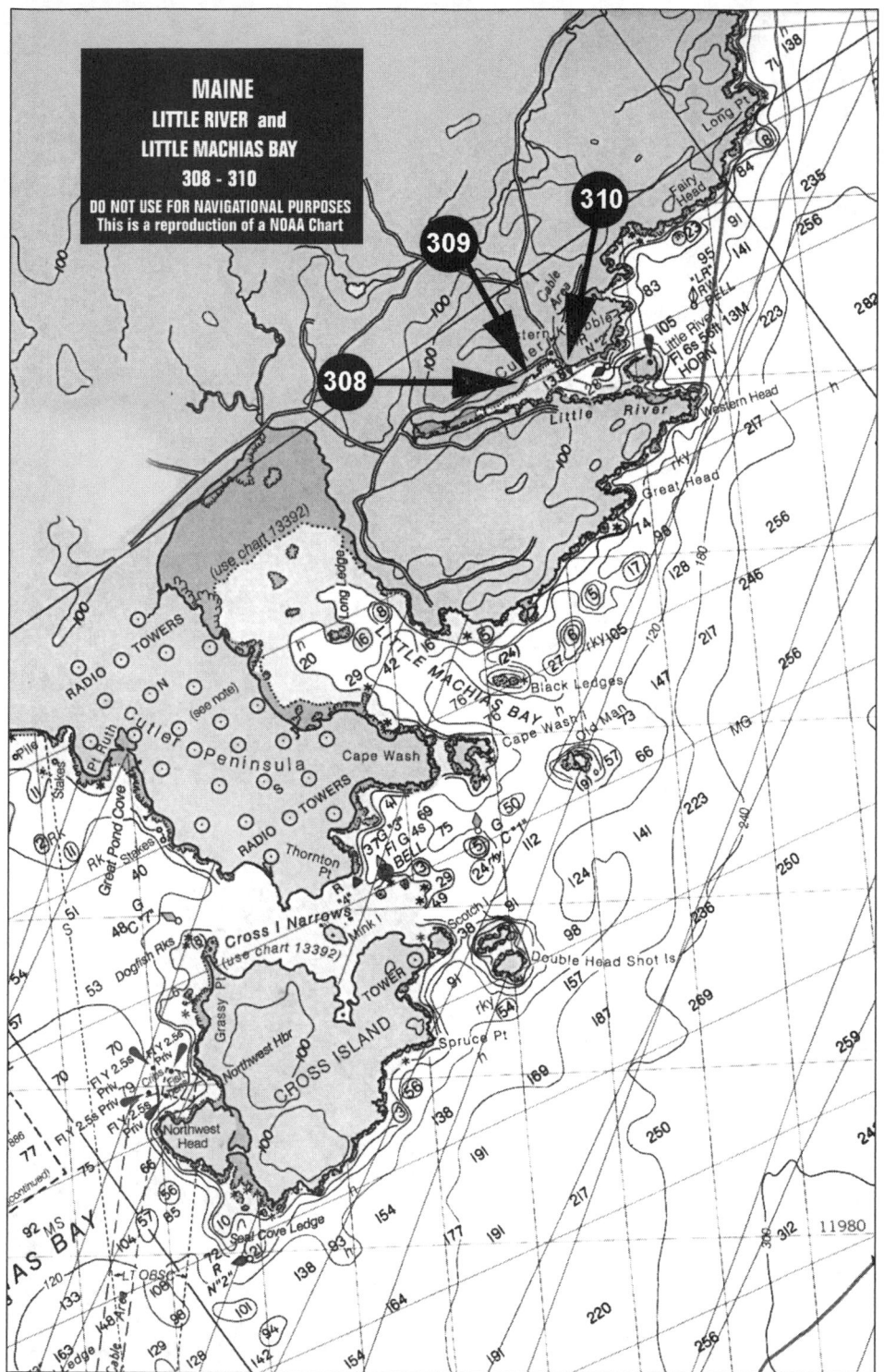

643

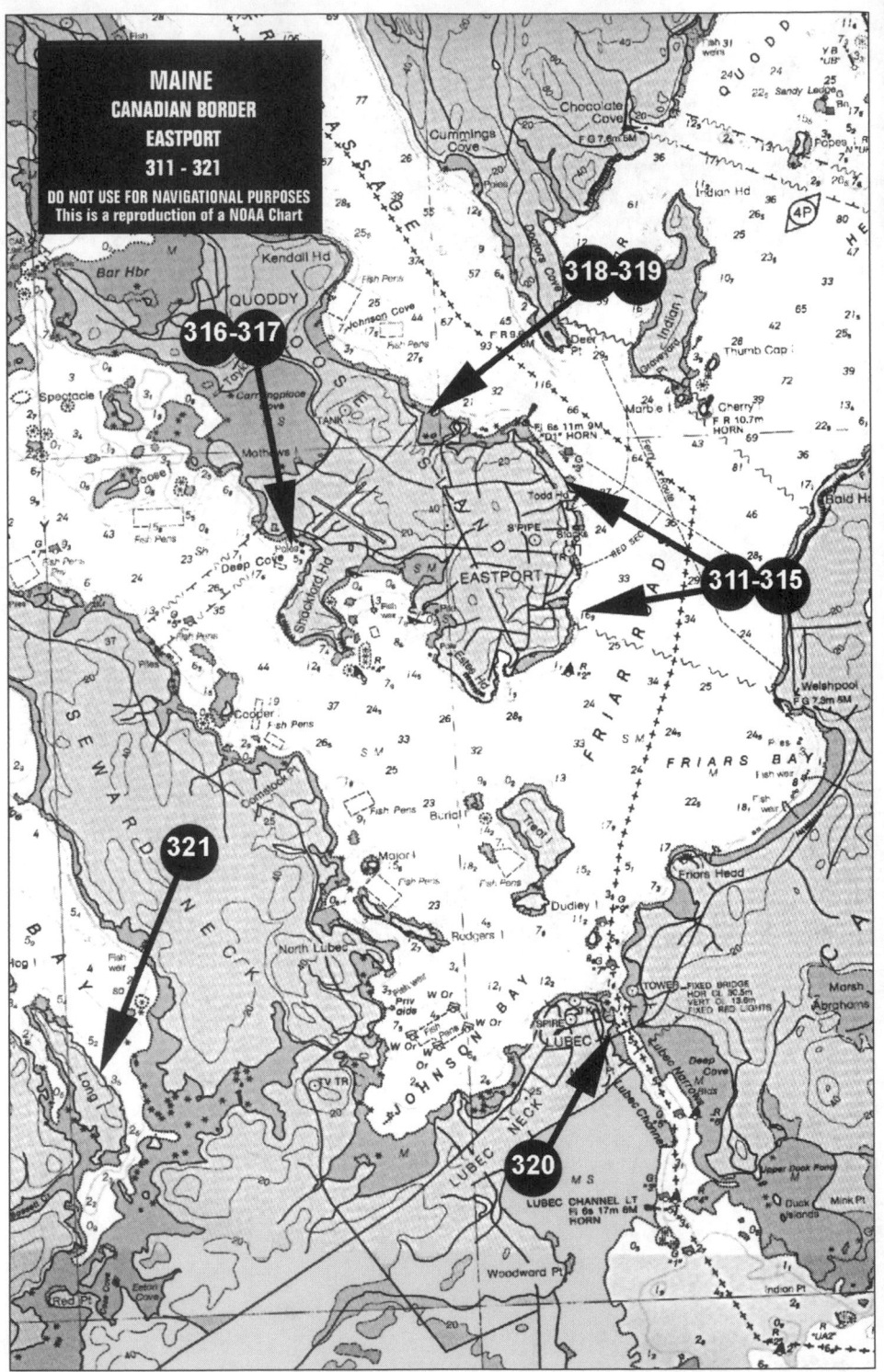

316-317

318-319

311-315

321

320

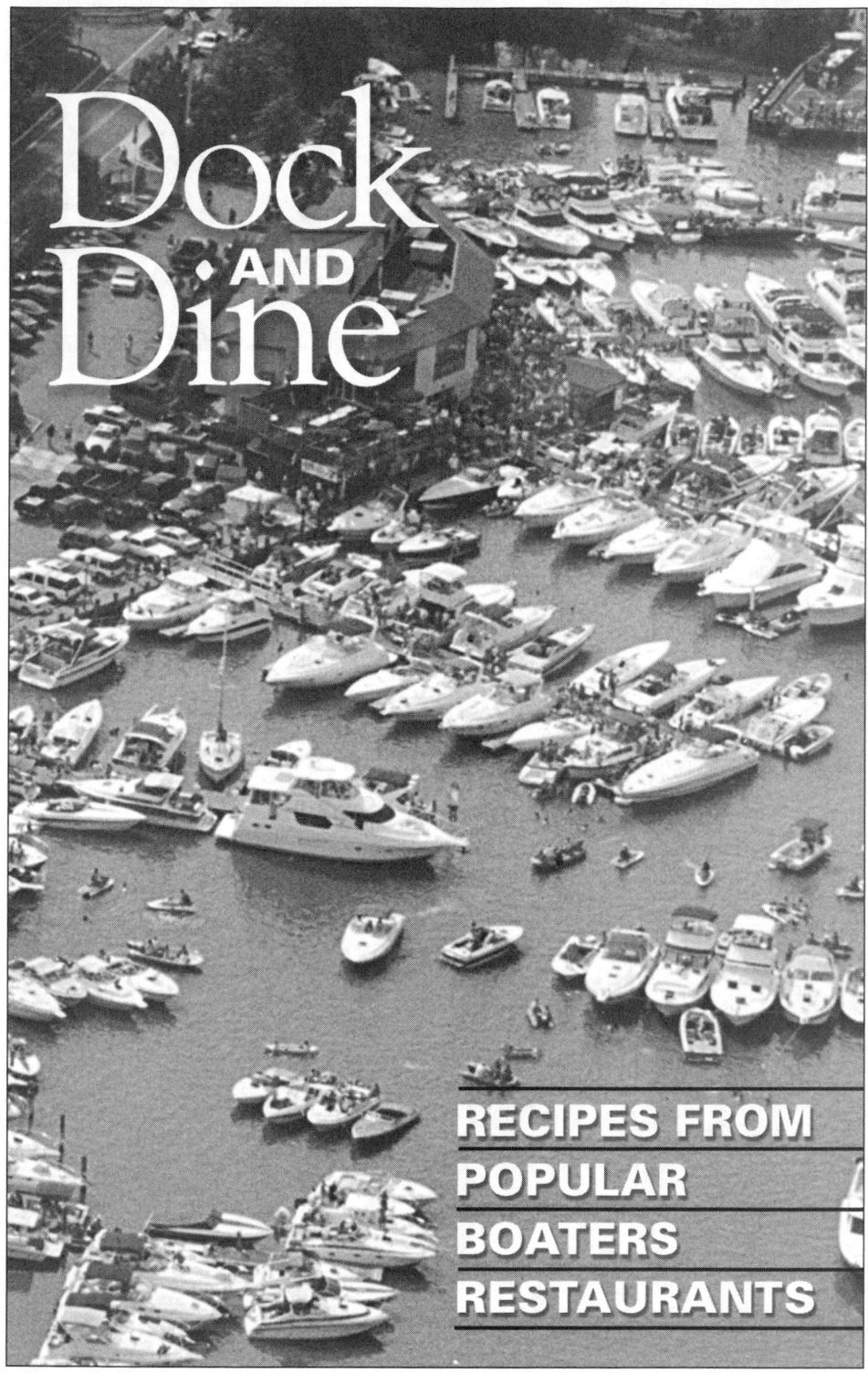

Dock AND Dine

RECIPES FROM
POPULAR
BOATERS
RESTAURANTS

IF THE DOCKS ARE FULL AT THE CHESAPEAKE INN ON THE C & D CANAL, A WATERTAXI WILL PICK YOU UP.

Signature Dishes from stops along the way

From the Chesapeake Bay all the way to Maine, there are hundreds of opportunities to Dock and Dine and do it well..

After a day on the water what could be better than pulling right up to a dockside restaurant that welcomes boaters with fresh seafood.

From chowing down on just-opened oysters in J's Oyster Shack in Portland, Maine to fresh-caught fish done to your specifications at Claudio's in Greenport, New York, there's no end of varied dining experiences available to boaters.

In Maine we want lobster. On the Chesapeake we want the Blue Crab and Rockfish. In New Jersey we eat Bluefish and clams. And so it goes.

Save cooking onboard for those times when you drop the hook. So many of the destinations featured in this boater's guide offer outstanding dining opportunities for visiting cruisers.

We've gathered recipes for signature dishes from some of our favorite stops along the coast. Try them at the restaurants in boating season, and try them at home to bring back summer memories.

IT'S EASY TO TIE UP AT CLAUDIO'S IN GREENPORT WHEN YOU'RE HUNGRY FOR SEAFARING FARE.

MAIN LOBSTER BISQUE
(2) 1 lb Maine lobsters
4 cups salted water

3/4 lb salted butter
1/2 cup flour
1 tbsp Paprika

32 oz. heavy cream
dash of salt
dash of cayenne pepper

In a 6 quart stock pot, bring to a boil the 4 cups of salted water. Add the lobsters and cook for 10 minutes. Remove lobsters and place in an ice bath to cool, saving the lobster broth. When lobsters have cooled, pick out the meat from the tails, knuckles and claws and set aside. Save the lobster bodies and shells. Combine the lobster bodies and shells, 1/4 lb. of the butter and the lobster broth. Boil until the liquid is reduced to 2 cups.

Using a thick bottomed 4 quart stock pot, melt 1/4 lb. butter. Add the flour and paprika and slowly cook on low heat for 5 minutes making a roux; stir continually with a wire whip. Add heavy cream slowly and continue to cook on low heat, stirring often. Strain lobster broth and add to the cream mixture. Slowly bring to a boil while stirring often. Turn off heat as soon as a boil is reached. Watch for scorching of cream mixture.

Cut lobster tail meat in half and remove the intestinal vein. Remove any inedible parts from the claw meat. Dice lobster meat; combine with the cream sherry and the final 1/4 lb. of butter and sauté for 3 minutes. Add this to the cream mixture and stir until smooth and silky. Add the dash of salt and cayenne pepper. Simmer for 3 minutes and serve in soup crocks. Garnish with chopped fresh parsley.

Note: Some people prefer a bisque that is pureed and creamy. Although this recipe has bits of lobster meat and is creamy, the lobster meat can be pureed in a food processor after it has been cooked with the sherry and before adding to the cream mixture. SERVES 8

Chef Michael Ham, Tugboat Inn & Restaurant

CRAB STUFFED SALMON FILLET ⚓ THE GRISWOLD INN, ESSEX, CT

4 –7oz salmon fillets (boneless)
8 oz lump crabmeat
1 bunch leeks
Butter
White wine
Salt and pepper

Slice each leek from top to bottom half way through to core. Rinse well under running cold water. Blanch leeks in boiling salted water for 2-3 minutes. Remove and rinse under cold water. Cut off whitest part of each leek. Separate green sheets of leeks and place face down on cutting board. Top each leek with one fillet of salmon. Cover each filet and place, stem facing down, onto buttered baking sheet or a sauté pan. Sprinkle with white wine; season with salt and pepper, and place into a 350 degree oven for 25-30 minutes.

SAUCE:
16 oz half & half
4 oz sundried tomato pesto
2 oz freshly chopped basil
8 oz of freshly sliced mushroom
Salt and pepper

Saute mushrooms in butter. In a separate sauté pan, reduce cream by one half. Add pesto, chopped basil and sliced mushrooms. Adjust seasoning. Place over fillets wrapped in leeks and serve.

SERVES 4

BAKED ROCKFISH WITH FENNEL
SCHAEFER'S CANAL HOUSE,
CHESAPEAKE CITY, MD

4 8oz Rockfish fillets
2 Fennel bulbs
1/4 cup extra virgin olive oil
Salt
Fresh ground black pepper

Cut off the tops of the fennel bulb and discard. Trim any bruised areas and then slice thinly, a one-third of an inch or so.

Put fennel, olive oil. Some salt and 1/2 cup of water into a sauté pan. Cover, turn on medium heat and allow to simmer down. If fennel is still hard after 25 minutes or so add more water. When done allow the fennel to turn golden brown in the olive oil.

Now add the Rock Fish, skin side down. Season with salt and the pepper from the mill. Spon some of the olive oil in the pan onto the fish. Bake at 350 degrees for 7 minutes. Turn filets over and finish cooking. When done. Plate the fish and top with the fennel.

SeaTow 800-4SEATOW
Tow Boat U.S. 800-888-4869
Vessel Assist 800-588-2227

POWERFUL

Phone Book

Yellow Pages

NOTABLE MARITIME ATTRACTIONS
INCLUDES MARINAS IN HIGH TOURISM AREAS

DELAWARE RIVER

FORT DELAWARE
Pea Patch Island, and Delaware City, DE
302-834-7941

INDEPENDENCE SEAPORT MUSEUM
Penn's Landing, Philadelphia, PA
215-925-5439

KALMAR NYCKEL SHIPYARD
& MUSEUM
Wilmington, DE
302-429-7447

THE RIVERFRONT COMPLEX
Wilmington, DE
302-984-2722 (River Taxi)

PHILADELPHIA MARINE CENTER
Penn's Landing, Philadelphia, PA
215-931-1000

PIER 3 AND 5
Penn's Landing, Philadelphia, PA
215-351-4101

CHESAPEAKE BAY

BALTIMORE MUSEUM OF INDUSTRY
Oystering Exhibits
Inner Harbor, Baltimore, MD
410-727-4808

BALTIMORE MARITIME MUSEUM
USS Torsk, Chesapeake Lightship
Inner Harbor, Baltimore, MD
410-396-3854

BRANNOCK MARITIME MUSEUM
Shipbuilding
Cambridge, MD
410-228-6938

C&D CANAL MUSEUM
Chesapeake City, MD
410-885-5621

CALVERT MARINE MUSEUM
Solomons, MD
410-326-2042

CHESAPEAKE BAY MARITIME
MUSEUM
St. Michaels, MD
410-745-2916

THE GANGPLANK MARINA
Coastal Properties Management, Inc.
Washington, DC
202-554-5500

HAVRE DE GRACE MARITIME
MUSEUM
Skipjack Martha Lewis
Havre de Grace, MD
410-939-4800

HM KRENTZ
Working Skipjack
Tilghman Island
410-745-6080

HORN POINT HARBOR MARINA
Coastal Properties Management, Inc.
Annapolis, MD
410-269-0933

MARYLAND SCIENCE CENTER
Inner Harbor, Baltimore, MD
410-685-2370

MEARS YACHT HAVEN
Coastal Properties Management, Inc
Oxford, MD
410-226-5450.

NATIONAL AQUARIUM
Inner Harbor, Baltimore, MD
410-576-3800

ORIOLE PARK AT CAMDEN YARDS
Inner Harbor, Baltimore, MD
410-685-9800

OXFORD BOATYARD
Coastal Properties Management, Inc.
Oxford, MD
410-226-5101

PINEY NARROWS YACHT HAVEN
Coastal Properties Management, Inc.
Chester, MD
410-643-6600

PORT DISCOVERY
Children's exhibits
Inner Harbor, Baltimore, MD
410-727-8120

SOLOMONS YACHTING CENTER
Coastal Properties Management, Inc.
Solomons, MD
410-326-2401

**ST. MICHAELS HARBOUR INN,
MARINA & SPA**
St. Michaels, MD
800-955-9001

UPPER BAY DECOY MUSEUM
North East, MD
410-287-5718

U.S. CONSTELLATION
Inner Harbor, Baltimore, MD
410-539-1797

U.S. NAVAL ACADEMY MUSEUM
Annapolis, MD
410-293-2108

NEW JERSEY

ATLANTIC CITY VISITORS BUREAU
888-AC-VISIT or 800-BOARDWK

BATTLESHIP NEW JERSEY
Camden, NJ 856-966-1652
www.battleshipnewjersey.org

BARNEGAT LIGHT STATE PARK
AND INTREPRETIVE CENTER
Barnegat Light, NJ
609-494-2016

CAPE MAY VISITORS BUREAU
Cape May, NJ
609-884-1341

GARDNERS HISTORIC BASIN
Atlan tic City, NJ
609-348-2880

NEW JERSEY MUSEUM OF BOATING
Classic Boats
Johnson Brothers Boat Works, Bldg. 12
Point Pleasant 07719
(732) 859-4767

NJ STATE AQUARUM
Camden, NJ 856-365-3300
www.njaquarium.org

TUCKERTON SEAPORT
Tuckerton 08087
(609) 296-8868

TWIN LIGHTS STATE HISTORIC SITE
Highlands, NJ
908-872-1814

NEW YORK & NEW YORK HARBOR

CITY ISLAND MUSEUM
America's Cup, Hell Gate Pilots exhibits
Bronx, NY
718-885-1616

ELLIS ISLAND
212-363-3206

INTREPID SEA-AIR-SPACE MUSEUM
USS Intrepid Aircraft Carrier
Pier 86, New York, NY
212-245-0072

LIBERTY LANDING MARINA
NY Harbor
Jersey City, NJ
201-985-8000

LONG ISLAND MARITIME MUSEUM
West Sayville, NJ
631-854-4974

SAG HARBOR WHALING MUSEUM
Sag Harbor, NY
631-725-0770

SOUTH STREET SEAPORT MUSEUM
See new exhibit: Harbor Voices 9.11
New York, NY
212-748-8600

CONNECTICUT

CONNECTICUT RIVER MUSEUM
Steamshipping, Essex, CT
203-767-8269

MYSTIC SEAPORT
MUSEUM & MARINA
Mystic 06355
860-572-0711

NOTABLE MARITIME ATTRACTIONS CONT.

PROJECT OCEANOLOGY
55 foot Enviroloab hands-on ocean
cruise with marine bioligists
Groton, CT
800-364-8472

SEA MIST THIMBLE ISLANDS CRUISE
www..seamistcruises.com
(203) 488-8905

SUBMARINE FORCE MUSEUM
USS Nautilus
Groton, CT
800-343-0079

U.S. COAST GUARD MUSEUM
U.S. Coast Guard Academy
New London, CT
203-444-8511

RHODE ISLAND
HERRESHOFF MARINE MUSEUM
Bristol, RI
401-253-5000

MUSEUM OF YACHTING
America's Cup
Fort Adamas State Park, Newport, RI
401-847-8320

NEWPORT CHAMBER OF COMMERCE
Mansion Tours
401-845-9120

THAMES & KOSMOS
Hands on Science exhibits
Long Wharf, Newport, RI
401-849-6966

MASSACHUSETTS
USS CONSTITUTION & MUSEUM
Charlestown Navy Shipyard
617-242-5670

CAPE ANN HISTORICAL MUSEUM
Fisheries & Area Maritime history
Gloucester, MA
978-283-0455

EXPEDITION WHYDAH
SeaLab and Learning Center.
Pirating, Provincetown, MA
508-487-7955

HMS BOUNTY
State Pier, Fall River, MA
508-675-6591

NEW BEDFORD WHALING MUSEUM
New Bedford, MA
508-997-0046

PEABODY ESSEX MUSEUM
Maritime History of New England.
SEE navigational instruments of
Nathaniel Bowditch. Largest museum in
MA. Salem, MA 800-745-4054

U.S. NAVAL SHIPBUILDING MUSEUM
Quincy, MA
617-479-7900

NEW HAMPSHIRE / MAINE
MAINE MARITIME MUSEUM
Bath, ME
(207) 443-1316

PORT OF PORTSMOUTH
MARITIME MUSEUM
USS Albacore
Portsmouth, NH
603-436-3680

BOAT DEALERS & BROKERAGE

CHESAPEAKE BAY

BELMONT BAY HARBOR
Woodbridge, VA
703-490-5088

BOAT DEALERS & BROKERAGE CONT.

**MARTIN ASSOCIATES
YACHT GROUP**
Chesapeake City, MD
877-922-4804, 302-545-5953

McDANIEL YACHT BASIN, INC
North East, MD
410-287-8121

SAILING ASSOCIATES, INC.
Georgetown, MD
410-275-8171

NEW JERSEY
UTSCH'S MARINA
1121 Route 109
Fisherman's Wharf
Cape May 08204
(609) 884-2051

NEW YORK
NORTH MINNEFORD YACHT CLUB
150 City Island Ave
City Island 10464
(718) 885-2000

NORTH PIER MARINA
549 Union Ave.
Saratoga Springs 12866
(518) 584-2628

**STAR ISLAND YACHT CLUB
& MARINA**
Star Island Road
Montauk 11954
(631) 668-5052
and
116 Woodcleft Ave.
Freeport 11520
(516) 623-6256

WESTERLY MARINA
Westerly Road
Ossining 10562
(914) 941-2203

CONNECTICUT

FORT RACHEL MARINE SERVICES
44 Water Street
Mystic 06355
(860) 536-6647

MYSTIC RIVER MARINA
Mason Island
Mystic 06355
(860) 536-3123

RHODE ISLAND
**HOB YACHT SALES
WATCH HILL DOCKS**
Bay Street
Watch Hill 02891
(401) 596-7807

MASSACHUSETTS
MERRI-MAR YACHT BASIN, INC.
364 Merrimac Street
Newburyport 01950
(978) 465-3022

MONAHAN'S MARINE
396 Washington Street
Weymouth 02188
(781) 335-2746

BOAT YARDS
CHESAPEAKE BAY
OXFORD BOATYARD
Coastal Properties Management, Inc.
Oxford, MD
410-226-5101

NEW JERSEY
UTSCH'S MARINA
1121 Route 109
Fisherman's Wharf
Cape May 08204
(609) 884-2051

NEW YORK
CONSOLIDATED YACHTS
157 Pilot Street
City Island 10464
(718) 885-1900

SEYMOURS BOAT YARD
63 Bayview Ave.
Northport 11768
(631) 261-6574

WESTIN'S BOAT SHOP
69 River Road
Sayville 11782
(631) 589-1526

BOAT YARDS CONT.

CONNECTICUT
FORT RACHEL MARINE SERVICE
44 Water Street
Mystic 06355
(860) 536-6647

RHODE ISLAND
BULLOCK COVE MARINE
254 Riverside Drive
Riverside 02915
(401) 433-3010

MASSACHUSETTS
BROWNELL BOAT & YARD
1 Park Street
Mattappoisett 02739
(508) 758-3671

MACDOUGALL'S
CAPE COD MARINE SERVICE, INC
145 Falmouth Heights Road.
Falmouth 02540
(508) 548-3146

MAINE
PORTLAND YACHT SERVICES
58 Fore Street
Portland 04101
(207) 774-1067

CANVAS SHOPS

NEW JERSEY
AVALON POINTE MARINA
701 Old Avalon Blvd.
Avalon 08202
(609) 967-4100

UTSCH'S MARINA
Fisherman's Wharf
Cape May 08204
(609) 884-2051

Visit our full service
Marina/Boatyard.
at the mouth of
Narragansett Bay
on Conanicut Island
in the village of
Jamestown,
Rhode Island.

401-423-1556
www.ConanicutMarina.com

NEW YORK
HAVERSTRAW MARINA
Beach Road
West Haverstraw 10993
(845) 429-2001

CONNECTICUT
FORT RACHEL MARINE SERVICE
44 Water Street
Mystic 06355
(860) 535-6647

MASSACHUSETTS
HYANNIS MARINA
1 Willow Street
Hyannis 02601
(508) 790-4000

MACDOUGALL'S
CAPE COD MARINE SERVICE, INC
145 Falmouth Heights Road.
Falmouth 02540
(508) 548-3146

ENGINE REPAIRS

SEE MARINA TABLES FOR EACH AREA

FIBERGLASS REPAIRS
AWLGRIP/VARNISH

CHESAPEAKE BAY
McDANIEL YACHT BASIN, INC
North East, MD
410-287-8121

OXFORD BOATYARD
Coastal Properties Management, Inc.
Oxford, MD
410-226-5101

SAILING ASSOCIATES, INC.
Georgetown, MD
410-275-8171

NEW JERSEY
AVALON POINTE MARINA
701 Old Avalon Blvd.
Avalon 08202
(609) 697-4100

FIBERGLASS REPAIRS AWLGRIP/VARNISH CONT.

NEW JERSEY CONTINUED

LOCKWOOD BOAT WORKS
1825 Hwy. 35, Morgan
South Amboy 08879
(732) 721-1605

UTSCH'S MARINA
1121 Route 109
Fisherman's Wharf
Cape May 08204
(609) 884-2051

NEW YORK

CONSOLIDATED YACHTS
157 Pilot Street
City Island 10464
(718) 885-1900

CONNECTICUT

FORT RACHEL MARINE SERVICE
44 Water Street
Mystic 06355
(860) 536-6647

RHODE ISLAND

BULLOCK COVE MARINE
254 Riverside Drive
Riverside 02915
(401) 433-3010

CONANICUT MARINA
One Ferry Wharf
Jamestown 02835
(401) 423-1556

MASSACHUSETTS

**MACDOUGALL'S
CAPE COD MARINE SERVICE, INC**
145 Falmouth Heights Road.
Falmouth 02540
(508) 548-3146

MERRI-MAR YACHT BASIN
364 Merrimac Street
Newburyport 01950
(978) 465-3022

NEW HAMPSHIRE

WENTWORTH BY THE SEA MARINA
Box 2079
New Castle 03854
(603) 433-5050

INSURANCE BROKERS

JACK MARTIN & ASSOCIATES, INC.
Yacht Insurance Specialists
www.jackmartin.com
Fax (410) 626-9966
326 First Street, Suite 27
Annapolis, MD 21403
(800) 497-8101

MARINAS

 = FULL SERVICE MARINA

= INTERNET CONNECTIONS

DELAWARE RIVER

PHILADELPHIA MARINE CENTER
Penn's Landing, Philadelphia, PA
215-931-1000

PIER 3 AND 5
Penn's Landing, Philadelphia, PA
215-351-4101

CHESAPEAKE BAY

BELMONT BAY HARBOR
Coastal Properties Management, Inc.
Woodbridge, VA
703-490.5088

BOWLEY'S MARINA
Coastal Properties Management, Inc.
Middle River, MD
410-335-3553

CHESAPEAKE INN AND MARINA
C&D Canal
Chesapeake City South, MD
410-885-2040

FORT WASHINGTON MARINA
Coastal Properties Management, Inc.
on the Potomac
Fort Washington, MD
301-292-7700

THE GANGPLANK MARINA
Coastal Properties Management, Inc.
on the Potomac, Washington, DC
202-554-5500

MARINAS CONT.

THE GRANARY
on the Sassafras
410-275-1603

 HACKS POINT MARINA
On the Bohemia River
Chesapeake City, MD
877-275-9151

HARBORVIEW MARINA
Coastal Properties Management, Inc.
Inner Harbor
Baltimore, MD
410-752-1122

HORN POINT HARBOR MARINA
Coastal Properties Management, Inc.
Annapolis, MD
410-269-0933

LANKFORD BAY MARINA, INC
Rock Hall, MD
410-778-1414.

LONG BAY POINTE MARINA
Coastal Properties Management, Inc.
Virginia Beach, VA
757-321-4550

McDANIEL YACHT BASIN, INC
on the North East River
North East, MD
410-287-8121

MEARS YACHT HAVEN
Coastal Properties Management, Inc
Oxford, MD
410-226-5450.

OXFORD BOATYARD
Coastal Properties Management, Inc
on the Tred Avon.
Oxford, MD, 410-226-5101

PINEY NARROWS YACHT HAVEN
Coastal Properties Management, Inc.
on the Chester River/Kent Narrows
Chester, MD
410-643-6600

SAILING ASSOCIATES, INC.
on the Sassafras River
Georgetown, MD
410-275-8171

**SCHAEFER'S CANAL HOUSE
RESTAURANT AND MARINA**
C&D Canal
Chesapeake City North
410-885-2200

SOLOMONS YACHTING CENTER
Coastal Properties Management, Inc.
Solomons, MD
410-326-2401

**ST. MICHAELS HARBOUR INN,
MARINA & SPA**
St. Michaels, MD
800-955-9001

TWO RIVERS MARINA
On the Bohemia River
Chesapeake City, MD
410-885-2257

NEW JERSEY

ATLANTIC HIGHLANDS MUNICIPAL HARBOR
Simon Lake Drive
Atlantic Highlands 07716
(732) 291-1670

AVALON POINTE MARINA, INC.
701 Old Avalon Blvd.
Avalon 08202
(609) 977-4100

LIBERTY LANDING MARINA
on NY Harbor
Jersey City, NJ
201-985-8000

PIER ONE MARINA, RESTAURANT & MOTEL
3430 State Hwy. 37
Toms River 08753
(732) 270-0914

UTSCH'S MARINA
1121 Route 109
Fisherman's Wharf
Cape May 08204
(609) 884-2051

NEW YORK

CASTAWAYS YACHT CLUB
425 Davenport Ave.
(914) 636-8444

CATSKILL MARINA
Foot of Greene Street
Catskill 12414
(518) 943-4170

CLAUDIO'S RESTAURANT & MARINA
Main Street
Greenport 11944
(631) 477-0627

CONSOLIDATED YACHTS, INC.
157 Pilot Street
City Island 10464
(718) 885-1900

HAVERSTRAW MARINA
600 Beach Road
West Haverstraw 10993
(845) 429-2001

MONTAUK MARINE BASIN
West Lake Drive
Montauk 11954
(631) 668-5900

NORTH MINNEFORD YACHT CLUB
150 City Island Ave.
City Island 10464
(718) 885-2000

RIVERVIEW MARINE SERVICES
103 Main Street
Catskill 12414
(518) 943-5311

RONDOUT YACHT BASIN
First Street
Connelly 12417
(845) 331-7061

SEYMOUR'S BOAT YARD
63 Bayview Ave.
Northport 11768
(631) 261-6574

SOUTH SHORE BOATS – SURFSIDE 3
Library Ave., PO Box 1706
Westhampton Beach 11978
(631) 288-2400

STAR ISLAND YACHT CLUB & MARINA
Box 2180
Montauk 11954
(631) 668-5052

TARRYTOWN MARINA
236 Main Street
Tarrytown 10591
(914) 631-1300

WESTERLY MARINA
Westerly Road
Ossining 10562
(914) 941-2203

WHITES HUDSON RIVER MARINA
15 Point Street
New Hamburg 12590
(845) 297-8520

MARINAS CONT.

CONNECTICUT

 **FORT RACHEL
MARINE SERVICE**
44 Water Street
Mystic 06355
(860) 536-6647

 MYSTIC RIVER MARINA
Mason Island
Mystic 06355
(860) 536-3123

WAUCOMA YACHT CLUB
279 Front Street
New Haven, 06512
(203) 789-9530

WEST COVE MARINA
13 Kimberly Ave.
West Haven 06516
(203) 933-3000

RHODE ISLAND

BULLOCK COVE
254 Riverside Drive
Riverside 02915
(401) 433-3010

CONANICUT MARINA
One Ferry Wharf
Jamestown 02835
(401) 423-1556

 GOAT ISLAND MARINA
Goat Island
Newport 02840
(401) 849-5655

WATCH HILL DOCKS
.   3 India Point Road
Watch Hill 02891
(401) 596-7807

MASSACHUSETTS

CASTAWAYS
YACHT CLUB & MARINA
308 Victory Road
North Quincy 02171
(617) 328-1800

CONCORDIA COMPANY
213 Elm Street – Box 203
South Dartmouth 02748
(508) 999-1381

 HYANNIS MARINA
1 Willow Street
Hyannis 02601
(508) 790-4000

 MACDOUGALLS
145 Falmouth Heights Road.
Falmouth 02540
(508) 548-3146

 MERRI-MAR YACHT BASIN
364 Merrimac Street
Newburyport 01950
(978) 465-3022

 MONAHAN'S MARINE
396 Washington Street
Weymouth 02188
(781) 335-2746

NEW HAMPSHIRE
WENTWORTH BY THE SEA MARINA
New Castle 03854
(603) 433-5050

MAINE

TUGBOAT INN & MARINA
80 Commercial Street
Boothbay Harbor 04538
(207) 633-4434

RENTALS (BIKES, CANOES, KAYAKS, BOATS)

CHESAPEAKE BAY

MEARS YACHT HAVEN
Coastal Properties Management, Inc
Oxford, MD
410-226-5450.

NEW YORK
RIVERVIEW MARINE SERVICES
103 Main Street
Catskill 12414
(518) 943-5311

REPAIRS

SEE MARINA TABLES FOR EACH AREA

RESTAURANTS FOR BOATERS

DELAWARE RIVER
PHILADELPHIA MARINE CENTER
Penn's Landing, Philadelphia, PA
215-931-1000

PIER 3 AND 5
Penn's Landing, Philadelphia, PA
215-351-4101

CHESAPEAKE BAY

CHESAPEAKE INN AND MARINA
C&D Canal
Chesapeake City South, MD
410-885-2040

FORT WASHINGTON MARINA
Coastal Properties Management, Inc.
on the Potomac
Fort Washington, MD
301-292-7700

THE GANGPLANK MARINA
Coastal Properties Management, Inc.
on the Potomac, Washington, DC
202-554-5500

THE GRANARY AND
SASSAFRASS GRILL
on the Sassafras
410-275-1603

HARBORVIEW MARINA
Coastal Properties Management, Inc.
Inner Harbor
Baltimore, MD
410-752-1122

KITTY KNIGHT HOUSE
AND THE ANCHORAGE B&B
on the Sassafras
410-648-5200

LONG BAY POINTE MARINA
Coastal Properties Management, Inc.
Virginia Beach, VA
757-321-4550

OXFORD BOATYARD
Coastal Properties Management, Inc
on the Tred Avon.
Oxford, MD, 410-226-5101

PINEY NARROWS YACHT HAVEN
Coastal Properties Management, Inc.
on the Chester River/Kent Narrows
Chester, MD
410-643-6600

SCHAEFER'S CANAL HOUSE
RESTAURANT AND MARINA
C&D Canal
Chesapeake City North
410-885-2200

NEW JERSEY
ATLANTIC HIGHLANDS
MUNICIPAL HARBOR
2 Simon Lake Drive
Atlantic Highlands 07716
(732) 291-1670

LOBSTER HOUSE
Fisherman's Wharf
Cape May
(609) 884-8296

PIER ONE MARINA,
MOTEL & RESTAURANT
3430 State Hwy. 37
Toms River 08753
(732) 270-0914

NEW YORK
CASTAWAYS YACHT CLUB
425 Davenport Ave.
New Rochelle 10805
(914) 636-8444

RESTAURANTS FOR BOATERS cont'd.

CLAUDIO'S RESTAURANT & MARINA
Main Street
Greenport 11944
(631) 477-0627

LOBSTER BOX
34 City Island Ave.
City Island 10464
(718) 885-1952

OTTO'S SEA GRILL
271 Woodcleft Ave.
Freeport 11520
(516) 378-9480

STAR ISLAND YACHT CLUB & MARINA
Box 2180
Montauk 11954
(631) 668-5052

TARRYTOWN MARINA
236 Main Street
Tarrytown 10591
(914) 631-1300

THE SCHOONER RESTAURANT
435 Woodcleft Ave.
Freeport 11520
(516) 378-7575

CONNECTICUT

MYSTIC RIVER MARINA
Mason Island
Mystic 06355
(860) 536-3123

THE GRISWOLD INN
36 Main Street
Essex 06426
(860) 767-1776

MASSACHUSETTS

CASTAWAYS YACHT CLUB & MARINA
308 Victory Road
North Quincy 02171
(617) 328-1800

HYANNIS MARINA
1 Willow Street
Hyannis 02601
(508) 790-4000

RHODE ISLAND

GOAT ISLAND MARINA
Goat Island 02840
401) 849-5655

NEW HAMPSHIRE

WENTWORTH BY THE SEA MARINA
Box 2079
New Castle 03854
(603) 433-5050

MAINE

THE TUGBOAT INN
80 Commercial Street,
Boothbay Harbor
(207) 633-4434

RIGGING

CHESAPEAKE BAY

SAILING ASSOCIATES, INC.
on the Sassafras River
Georgetown, MD
410-275-8171

NEW JERSEY

LOCKWOOD BOAT WORKS
1825 Hwy. 35, Morgan
South Amboy 08879
(732) 721-1605

UTSCH'S MARINA
1121 Route 109
Cape May 08204
(609) 884-2051

NEW YORK

CONSOLIDATED YACHTS
157 Pilot Street
City Island 10464
(718) 885-1900

RIVERVIEW MARINE SERVICE
103 Main Street
Catskill 12414
(518) 943-5311

RONDOUT YACHT BASIN
First Street
Connelly 12417
(845) 331-7061

WESTINS BOAT SHOP
69 River Road
Sayville (11782
631) 589-1526

CONNECTICUT
FORT RACHEL MARINE SERVICE
44 Water Street
Mystic 06355
(860) 536-6647

RHODE ISLAND
BULLOCK COVE MARINE
254 Riverside Drive
Riverside 02915
(401) 433-3010

CONANICUT MARINA
1 Ferry Wharf, Jamestown
(401) 423-1556

MASSACHUSETTS
MACDOUGALLS
145 Falmouth Heights Road.
Falmouth 02540
(508) 548-3146

SHIP STORES & SUPPLIES

DELAWARE RIVER
PHILADELPHIA MARINE CENTER
Penn's Landing, Philadelphia, PA
215-931-1000

CHESAPEAKE BAY
BELMONT BAY HARBOR
Coastal Properties Management, Inc.
Woodbridge, VA
703-490.5088

CHESAPEAKE INN AND MARINA
C&D Canal
Chesapeake City South, MD
410-885-2040

LANKFORD BAY MARINA, INC
Rock Hall, MD
410-778-1414

LONG BAY POINTE MARINA
Coastal Properties Management, Inc.
Virginia Beach, VA
757-321-4550

OXFORD BOATYARD
Coastal Properties Management, Inc
on the Tred Avon.
Oxford, MD, 410-226-5101

PINEY NARROWS YACHT HAVEN
Coastal Properties Management, Inc.
Chester, MD
410-643-6600

SOLOMONS YACHTING CENTER
Coastal Properties Management, Inc.
Solomons, MD
410-326-2401

NEW JERSEY
AVALON POINTE MARINA
701 Old Avalon Blvd.
Avalon 08202
(609) 967-4100

LOCKWOOD BOAT WORKS, INC.
1825 Hwy. 35, Morgan
South Amboy 08879
(732) 721-1605

UTSCH'S MARINA
Fisherman's Wharf
Cape May 08204
(609) 884-2051

SHIP STORES & SUPPLIES CONTD.

NEW YORK

BARGAIN BILGE
Patchogue
(631) 475-4650

RIVERVIEW MARINE SERVICES, INC.
Catskill
(518) 943-5311

RONDOUT YACHT BASIN
Connelly 12417
(845) 331-7061

**STAR ISLAND YACHT CLUB
& MARINA**
Montauk
(631) 668-5052
and.
Freeport 11520
(516) 623-6256

**WHITE'S HUDSON RIVER
MARINA**
New Hamburg 12590
((845) 297-8520

CONNECTICUT

MYSTIC RIVER MARINA
Mason Island
Mystic 06355
(860) 536-3123

RHODE ISLAND

CONANICUT MARINA
Jamestown 02835
(401) 423-1556

GOAT ISLAND MARINA
Goat Island
Newport 02840
(401) 849-5655

MASSACHUSETTS

HYANNIS MARINA
One Willow Street
Hyannis 02610
(508) 790-4000

MACDOUGALLS
145 Falmouth Heights Road.
Falmouth 02540
(508) 548-3146

SURVEYORS, MARINE

NEW YORK

LONG ISLAND MARINE SURVEYOR
P.O. Box 542
Sayville, 11742
(631) 589-6154

CONNECTICUT

FORT RACHEL MARINE SERVICE
44 Water Street
Mystic 06355
(860) 536-6647

WOODEN BOAT SPECIALISTS

CHESAPEAKE BAY
OXFORD BOATYARD
Coastal Properties Management, Inc
on the Tred Avon.
Oxford, MD, 410-226-5101

NEW JERSEY
LOCKWOOD BOAT WORKS, INC.
1825 Highway 35, Morgan,
South Amboy 08879
(732) 721-1605

**NEW JERSEY MUSEUM OF
BOATING**
Johnson Brothers Boat Works
Point Pleasant
(732) 859-4767

MASSACHUSETTS
MERRI-MAR YACHT BASIN
364 Merrimac Street
Newburyport 01950
(978) 465-3022

RHODE ISLAND
BULLOCK COVE MARINE
254 Riverside Drive
Riverside 02915
(401) 433-3010

CONANICUT MARINE
One Ferry Wharf
Jamestown 02835
(401) 423-1556

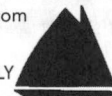

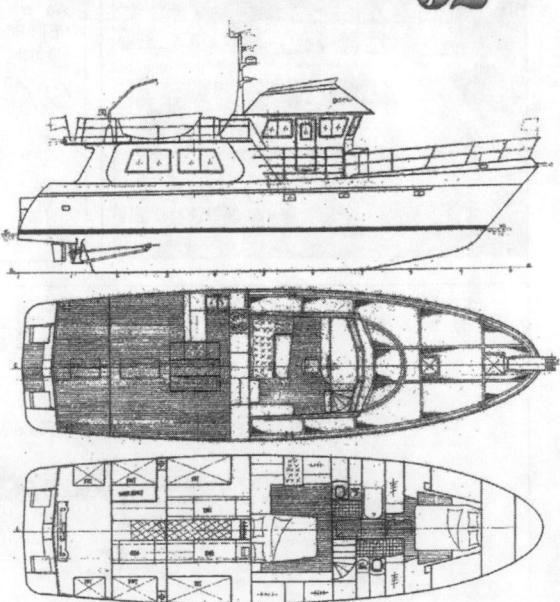

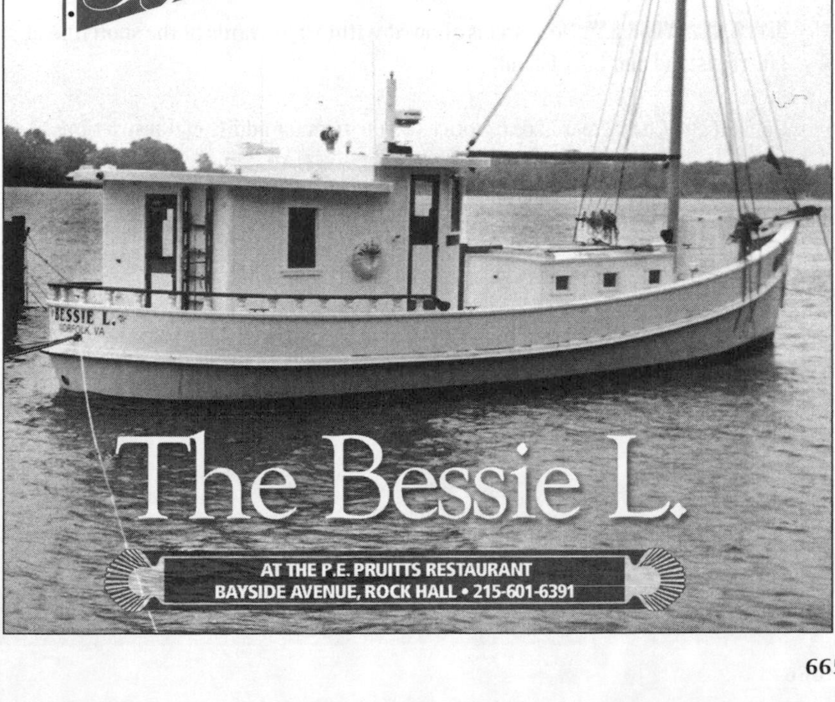

NEW YORK CITY AND SURROUNDING AREA
SECURITY ZONES

UNITED NATIONS: East River along the Manhattan shoreline from 125 yards offshore at the Queensboro Bridge to 175 yards offshore at E. 35th Street.

Piers 84-96: The area bound by the following points: the northeast corner of Pier 96 at the intersection of the seawall, to the approximate position of 40° 45'23.1" N , 073 59'59.0" W to the approximate position 40° 46'23.1" N, 074° 00'20.2" W , to the southeast corner of Pier 84 at the intersection of the seawall, then back along the shoreline to the point of origin at the northeast corner of Pier 96.

WITHIN 25 YARDS of all bridge piers, abutments, overhead power cables and tunnel ventilators in the greater New York area and along the Hudson River.

WITHIN 100 YARDS of all anchored or moored Coast Guard vessels.

HUDSON RIVER: Indian Point Nuclear Power Plant. Any vessel in the vicinity of Indian Point is subject to a random boarding by the Coast Guard. No vessel is permitted within a 300 yard radius of 41 16'12.4" N 073 57'16.2"W

UPPER NEW YORK BAY: No vessel is allowed within 150 yards of the shoreline of Liberty Island and Ellis Island.

Consult the Coast Guard Local Notice to Mariners for additional restrictions.

Ship's IMPORTANT PHONE Numbers

GPS wayPOINTS

WP NO	LATITUDE	LONGITUDE	IDENTIFICATION
	38°19.1"N	76°25.3"W	Drum Point Light 4
	38°40.0"N	76°23.5"W	Bloody Point Bar Light
	38°53.9"N	76°26.2"W	Thomas Point Shoal Light
	39°03.5"N	76°24.0"W	Baltimore Light
	39°33.9"N	75°33.3"W	Junction lighted bell CD (canal)
	39°18.3"N	75°22.6"W	Ship John Shoal
	38°58.0"N	74°58.8"W	Lighted Bell 8 Cape May Canal
	38°56.2"N	74°51.9"W	Jetty Light 5 Cape May Inlet
	39°21.0"N	74°23.7"W	Absecon Inlet Gong 1
	40°06.0"N	74°01.9"W	Manasquan Inlet Light 3
	40°30.8"N	73°48.0"W	Romer Shoal Light
	41°01.8"N	71°45.7"W	Montauk Whistle MP (S. Shore)
	40°49.5"N	73°46.5"W	Stepping Stones Light (L.I. North)
	40°52.7"N	73°44.3"W	Execution Rocks
	40°57.2"N	73°23.7"W	Eaton's Neck Light
	41°05.1"N	71°56.4"W	Montauk Harbor Entrance Bell M
	41°12.1"N	71°35.7"W	Great Salt Pond Bell R 2
	41°18.5"N	71°28.3"W	Point Judith Lighted Whistle 2
	41°25.9"N	71°21.8"W	Breton Point Lighted Whistle 2
	41°36.0"N	70°17.4"W	Hyannis Harbor Bell HH
	41°22.1"N	70°57.4"W	Vineyard Sound Entrance 32
	41°48.9"N	70°27.6"W	Cape Cod Canal Bell CC
	42°22.7"N	70°47.0"W	Boston Lighted Whistle B
	42°58.9"N	70°37.3"W	Isles of Shoals Bell IS
	43°31.6"N	70°05.5"W	Portland Lighted Horn P
	44°01.1"N	69°00.3"W	W. Penobscot Bay Ent. Gong PA
	44°49.4"N	66°56.7"W	W. Quoddy Head Bell WQ

WP NO	LATITUDE	LONGITUDE	IDENTIFICATION

END NOTES CONTINUED FROM PAGE 104

REFERENCE TO TABLE 2: CURRENT DIFFERENCE AND OTHER CONSTANTS

<36> Current tends to rotate clockwise. At times of "minimum before flood" there may be a weak current flowing northward while at times of "minimum before ebb" there may be a weak current flowing southeastward.

<37> For greater ebb only.

<39> For greater ebb. Lesser ebb is almost equal to greater ebb.

<40> Currents are materially affected by winds.

<41> Current is weak and variable. Current is somewhat rotary turning clockwise.

<42> Current is normally weak and variable, but winds may cause heavy swells.

<43> Minimum ebb is extremely weak, possibly flooding for a short period.

<44> Every other ebb phase exhibits a double ebb pattern. For single ebb phases use time differences and speed ratios of the first ebb.

<45> Ebb is weak and variable.

<46> Current is somewhat rotary, speed seldom exceeds 0.3 knot.

<47> Flood is weak and variable with speeds less than or equal to 0.2 knot. Minimums are indefinite.

<49> During period observed, the current flow was nearly continuous in a southwesterly direction with an average speed of about 0.4 knot.

<50> Observations during the spring showed an increase of about 0.4 knots in both the flood and ebb directions.

<51> Observations were made in the summer months when the freshwater discharge was at a minimum. Periods of heavier discharge will increase ebb current speeds and decrease flood current speeds.

<52> Observations were made in the spring during period of heavy freshwater discharge. Periods of lesser discharge will decrease ebb current speeds and increase flood current speeds.

<53> Observations at this location showed long periods of minimum currents and short durations of flood and ebb currents.

<54> Turbulence with hazardous current speeds of 6 to 7 knots have been reported near the bridges in the canal. Extreme caution should be exercised.

<55> The time of minimum before flood is indefinite.

<56> Maximum ebb time difference is for middle of phase. Speed near 0.7 knots throughout most of ebb phase. Speeds a short distance away may vary significantly.

<57> Maximum flood time difference is for middle of phase. Speed is very low throughout most of flood phase.

<58> It has been reported that under conditions of extreme river discharge, the currents can reach 7 or 8 knots. Caution should be exercised when docking and undocking vessels

<59> In the narrow part of Woods Hole Passage (Woods Hole, 0.1 mile SW of Devils Foots Island) the current velocity at times exceeds 4.5 knots. Velocities as high as 5.0 knots have been reported by the U. S. Coast Guard. Currents in Woods Hole Passage computed from the daily predictions at Cape Cod Canal in the Tidal Current Tables, Atlantic Coast should be used WITH CAUTION. actual velocities and directions shown on Tidal Current Charts, Narragansett Bay to Nantucket should be used only with EXTREME CAUTION. These differences result from dredging, filling, shoaling, and other modifications since the 1931 survey.

<60> Depths at the locations were previously averaged. The original data has been separated into it component depths.

<61> The time of minimum before ebb is indefinite.

<62> Short term observational data taken by United States Power Squadrons (USPS) as part of the NOS/USPS Tidal Current Predictions Quality Assurance Program has shown that predictions at this location are accurate.

<63> Short term observational data taken by United States Power Squadrons (USPS) as part of the NOS/USPS Tidal Current Predictions Quality Assurance Program have shown predictions at these locations to be inaccurate.

    - Observed speeds at "Little Creek" were approximately twice the predicted values.

    - Observations at "Newport News Channel, west end" showed both time and speed of the currents were altered by the Monitor-Merrimac Tunnel. Predictions should be used with caution.

    CAUTION—During the first 2 hours of flood in the channel north of Governers Island, the current in the Hudson River is still ebbing while during the first 1 1/2 hours of ebb in this channel, the current in the Hudson River is still flooding. At such times, special care must be taken by large ships in navigating this channel. ⚓